Managing Financial Institutions

An Asset / Liability Approach

FOURTH EDITION

MANAGING
FINANCIAL
INSTITUTIONS

An Asset / Liability Approach

FOURTH EDITION

MONA J. GARDNER
Illinois Wesleyan University

DIXIE L. MILLS
Illinois State University

ELIZABETH S. COOPERMAN
University of Colorado at Denver

THE DRYDEN PRESS

A Division of Harcourt College Publishers

Fort Worth   Philadelphia   San Diego   New York   Orlando   Austin   San Antonio

Toronto   Montreal   London   Sydney   Tokyo

Publisher	MIKE ROCHE
Executive Editor	MIKE REYNOLDS
Market Strategist	CHARLIE WATSON
Developmental Editor	TERRI HOUSE
Project Editor	COLBY ALEXANDER
Art Director	BURL SLOAN
Production Manager	EDDIE DAWSON

Cover Image and pp. 27, 28, 171, 172, 531, and 532: © Christy Bowe

ISBN: 0-03-022054-8
Library of Congress Catalog Card Number: 99-64778

Address for Domestic Orders
The Dryden Press, 6277 Sea Harbor Drive, Orlando, FL 32887-6777
800-782-4479

Address for International Orders
International Customer Service
The Dryden Press, 6277 Sea Harbor Drive, Orlando, FL 32887-6777
407-345-3800
(fax) 407-345-4060
(e-mail) hbintl@harcourtbrace.com

Address for Editorial Correspondence
The Dryden Press, 301 Commerce Street, Suite 3700, Fort Worth, TX 76102

Web Site Address
http://www.harcourtcollege.com
THE DRYDEN PRESS, DRYDEN, and the DP LOGO are registered trademarks of Harcourt, Inc.

Printed in the United States of America

9 0 1 2 3 4 5 6 7 8 043   9 8 7 6 5 4 3 2

The Dryden Press
Harcourt College Publishers

Dedication:

To our students—past, present, and future.

Gardner and Mills

To Bob, my muse.

Cooperman

THE DRYDEN PRESS SERIES IN FINANCE

Amling and Droms
Investment Fundamentals

Berry and Young
Managing Investments: A Case Approach

Besley and Brigham
Essentials of Managerial Finance
Twelfth Edition

Besley and Brigham
Principles of Finance

Boone, Kurtz, and Hearth
Planning Your Financial Future
Second Edition

Brigham and Houston
Fundamentals of Financial Management
Eighth Edition

Brigham, Gapenski, and Klein
2000 Cases in Financial Management:
Dryden Request

Brigham, Gapenski, and Ehrhardt
Financial Management: Theory and Practice
Ninth Edition

Conroy
Finance Interactive

Brigham, Gapenski, and Daves
Intermediate Financial Management
Sixth Edition

Brigham and Houston
Fundamentals of Financial Management: Concise Second Edition

Chance
An Introduction to Derivatives
Fourth Edition

Clark, Gerlach, and Olson
Restructuring Corporate America

Cooley
Advances in Business Financial Management: A Collection of Readings
Second Edition

Dickerson, Campsey, and Brigham
Introduction to Financial Management
Fourth Edition

Eaker, Fabozzi, and Grant
International Corporate Finance

Gardner, Mills, and Cooperman
Managing Financial Institutions: An Asset/Liability Approach
Fourth Edition

Gitman and Joehnk
Personal Financial Planning
Eighth Edition

Greenbaum and Thakor
Contemporary Financial Intermediation

Hall
Effective Use of a Financial Calculator

Harrington and Eades
Case Studies in Financial Decision Making
Third Edition

Hayes and Meerschwam
Financial Institutions: Contemporary Cases in the Financial Services Industry

Hearth and Zaima
Contemporary Investments: Security and Portfolio Analysis
Second Edition

Johnson
Issues and Readings in Managerial Finance
Fourth Edition

Kidwell, Peterson, and Blackwell
Financial Institutions, Markets, and Money
Seventh Edition

Koch and MacDonald
Bank Management
Fourth Edition

Leahigh
Pocket Guide to Finance

Maness and Zietlow
Short-Term Financial Management

Mayes and Shank
Financial Analysis with Lotus 1-2-3 for Windows

Mayes and Shank
Financial Analysis with Microsoft Excel

Mayo
Financial Institutions, Investments, and Management: An Introduction
Sixth Edition

Mayo
Investments: An Introduction
Sixth Edition

Osteryoung, Newman, and Davies
Small Firm Finance: An Entrepreneurial Analysis

Reilly and Brown
Investment Analysis and Portfolio Management
Fifth Edition

Reilly and Norton
Investments
Fifth Edition

Sandburg
Discovering Your Finance Career

Seitz and Ellison
Capital Budgeting and Long-Term Financing Decisions
Third Edition

Siegel and Siegel
Futures Markets

Smith and Spudeck
Interest Rates: Principles and Applications

Stickney and Brown
Financial Reporting and Statement Analysis: A Strategic Perspective
Fourth Edition

PREFACE

Previous editions of this book appearing in 1988, 1991, and 1994 were written during periods of dramatic change for the financial system in the U.S. Prior to the deregulatory period of the 1980s, regulatory policy and management practice for financial institutions for decades had been influenced by the Great Depression and World War II, events that most baby boomers, generation Xers, echo-boomers, and beyond never knew. With the deregulation of interest rates and volatility of financial markets during the 1980s, banks, as the dominant financial institution in the United States, faced a great challenge in managing interest rate risk. Hence, the previous editions' subtitle, "An Asset/Liability Management Approach," reflected the dependence of banks and other depository institutions on net interest income (interest revenues less interest expenses) for profits.

Over the later 1980s and 1990s, tremendous changes and challenges occurred for banks and other financial institutions. With increased competition from nonbank institutions and increased expenditures for new technology, larger banks realized that they could no longer depend solely on net interest income to cover rising operating expenses. Sources of noninterest revenue or fee income became increasingly important. Reflecting the reality of a very competitive marketplace, regulators began offering more liberal interpretations to product restrictions previously imposed under the Glass Stegall Act of 1933. Today approved, well-capitalized banks can engage in new types of nonbanking activities including operating their own mutual funds, selling annuities and some other insurance products, and engaging in security trading and underwriting activities through subsidiaries. Securitization—packaging and selling loans as securities to investors—has also become an important source of noninterest income, as well as many other off-balance sheet types of activities.

Other types of financial institutions have challenged banks' preeminence as the largest financial institution in the U.S. in the 1990s. Mutual funds have grown at an extremely fast rate, reflecting both the bull market of the 1990s and demographics favoring investing for retirement. As of January 1999, mutual funds achieved an asset size close to the more than $5.3 trillion held by U.S. commercial banks. Other formidable competitors to banks include federal and federally sponsored credit agencies, such as the Government National Mortgage Association and Federal National Mortgage Association; large finance companies, such as General Electric Capital Corporation; large securities firms, such as Merrill Lynch; mega-insurance companies, such as Prudential; large credit unions; and new online firms. This new edition reflects the rapid growth of these institutions. It also reflects the growing importance of noninterest revenue sources for banks, resulting in joint ventures between major banks and securities firms, mutual funds and, recently, insurance and other types of financial institutions as well.

The new edition also covers dramatic changes that are occurring. These include mega-mergers between giant financial institutions, such as the 1998 mergers between Travelers Group and Citicorp, Banc One and First Chicago, and Wells Fargo and U.S. Bancorp, which, as a 1998 *Business Week* article suggested, bring the prospect of the first trillion dollar bank in sight. This edition also discusses proposals for the Financial Modernization Act, which would allow mergers between securities firms, banks, and insurance companies for the first time in the U.S. since 1933. Important events that seriously affected financial markets and institutions in the 1990s are also discussed.

These include the international financial crises in East Asia and Brazil of the late 1990s, the growth of interstate branching following the Riegle Neal Act of 1994, and the emergence of the Euro in 1999. The new edition also covers other recent major events including the entrance of internet financial institutions and digital money, or e-cash. In addition, newer concepts including value at risk, economic value added, risk-adjusted return on capital, and M-square risk-adjusted performance measure are discussed, as well as recent financial innovations including credit derivatives, and catastrophic insurance futures.

We attempt to capture the major forces that are changing the financial landscape for financial institutions. However, with constant changes in financial markets and institutions, we continue to believe in our opening comment in the preface to the first edition, "Perhaps the only task more challenging than managing financial institutions today is writing for students who will manage them tomorrow."

Although much new information has been added, the new edition has been streamlined from 27 chapters to 22. Despite this streamlining, the text still strives to provide the depth that students need to have a comparative advantage as potential financial institution and nonfinancial institution managers. All chapters have been carefully updated to incorporate new research and political and economic events, as well as technological and financial innovations.

For a book this length, it would be impossible to list all the changes since the last edition. Among the most important, however, are

- ✦ Excellent Internet exercises at the end of each chapter by Ronnie Phillips at Colorado State University for students to gain Internet skills and become familiar with special resources available for financial institutions
- ✦ Recommended cases from the Darden School and Harvard Business School listed at the end of chapters to apply concepts from the text
- ✦ Coverage of the proposed Financial Modernization Act and Financial Conglomerates (Chapter 13)
- ✦ Updated chapters on nondepository institutions, including a detailed discussion of mutual funds and performance analysis for each institution (Chapters 10 to 13)
- ✦ Coverage of the advent of the Euro (Chapters 3A, 4, and 14)
- ✦ A new chapter on noninterest revenue management and associated risks, including a discussion of securitization, value at risk, and economic value added (Chapter 9)
- ✦ A detailed chapter on performance and risk analysis for depository institutions (Chapter 6)
- ✦ An updated chapter on capital regulation and management techniques including new thoughts on bank dividend policies and risk-adjusted return on capital (Chapter 8)
- ✦ A detailed discussion of consolidation trends, moral hazard issues, virtual banks and e-cash (Chapter 4)
- ✦ Coverage of new types of derivatives, including credit derivatives (Chapter 18)
- ✦ Consolidated chapters on different aspects of bank management, including an example of a loan officer report (Chapters 19 to 21)
- ✦ A new special chapter on international issues including international lending risk issues and an analysis of the international financial crises in 1997 to 1999 (Chapter 22)

✦ Updated problems for students to apply and improve their analytical skills
✦ Detailed performance analysis exercises

The early parts of the book continue to provide a theoretical framework that transcends the changes in the institutional environment that we now routinely expect. At the same time we hope to give students a sense of the dynamic nature of financial markets and institutions and the challenges faced by those who choose a career in institutions management. Also, as in other editions, latter portions of the book cover specific management problems in specific types of institutions. The book continues to be written for upper-level undergraduate and master's students, and all readers will benefit considerably from an introductory course in corporate finance. In many cases, introductory material in typical courses on money and banking or money and capital markets is useful, but not essential.

ORGANIZATION AND USE OF THE BOOK

The book is divided into five parts. The first part (Chapters 1 to 4) explores the domestic and international regulatory and market environment in which financial institutions operate. The second (Chapters 5 to 9) provides background and a performance analysis of depository institutions. Part three (Chapters 10 to 13) covers management and performance analysis for nondepository institutions including insurance companies, securities firms, mutual funds and pension funds, and finance companies and diversified financial firms. The final chapter discusses the proposed financial modernization act which would allow more diversified financial firms. Part four (Chapters 14 to 16) develops theories of interest rate determination, interest-rate risk, and exchange rate risk management. Part five (Chapters 17 to 22) discusses hedging to manage risk including using interest rate and foreign currency futures, index futures, swaps, swaptions, credit, and other derivatives, and investigates particular asset/liability management problems for depository institutions including liquidity and securities portfolio management, liability management, and lending. Chapter 22 is a special chapter on international lending and managing international risk, including a detailed synopsis of the global financial crisis of the late 1990s and what can be learned by financial institutions in reducing their future international risks from that crisis.

POSSIBLE COURSE OUTLINES

Faculty colleagues using previous editions of the book have found many ways to do so. At most schools, students have completed an introductory course in financial management and perhaps a course in money and banking or financial markets. Without the money and banking or markets prerequisite, instructors often place more emphasis on Chapters 1-4 and 14-16. Instructors also often supplement the text with cases or readings from the professional and academic literature (many cases and readings are suggested at the end of each chapter), and/or exercises, such as the Internet exercises provided at the end of each Chapter, or other spreadsheet exercises.

The book has an additional benefit in its proven flexibility, facilitating the use of a variety of alternative syllabi for instructors. A few suggested outlines adapted for the new edition include:

One-semester course for undergraduates

Management of Financial Institutions (comprehensive, all institutions)

- ✦ Chapters 1 to 4 , 14, and 15: Financial Markets, Interest Rates, and Exchange Rates review (2 to 3 weeks)
- ✦ Chapters 16 to 18: Interest Rate Risk Management—Duration, Futures, Other Derivatives (2 to 3 weeks)
- ✦ Chapters 5 to 9: Depository Institutions Management, Part I—Performance Analysis, Thrifts and Credit Unions, Capital Regulation, and Non-Interest Revenues (2 to 3 weeks)
- ✦ Chapters 10 to 13: Management and Performance Analysis: Nondepository Institutions (2 to 3 weeks)
- ✦ Chapters 19 to 22: Depository Institutions Management, Part II—Liquidity & Liability Management; Loan Management; International Issues (2 to 3 weeks)

Alternatively, move the discussion of financial markets and hedging (Chapters 14 to 18) to its chronological place in the text; or move this section along with international issues (Chapter 22) to the final three weeks of the course. Cases, Internet Exercises, and Spreadsheet Exercises can also be incorporated.

Management of Depository Institutions

- ✦ Chapters 1 to 4 , 14, and 15: Financial Markets, Interest Rates, and Exchange Rates review (2 to 3 weeks)
- ✦ Chapters 16 to 18: Interest Rate Risk Management—Duration, Futures; Other Derivatives (2 to 3 weeks)
- ✦ Chapters 5 to 9: Depository Institutions Management, Part I—Performance Analysis, Thrifts, Credit Unions, Capital Regulation, and Non-Interest Revenues (2 to 3 weeks)
- ✦ Chapters 19 to 22: Depository Institutions Management, Part II—Liquidity
- ✦ Liability Management; Loan Management; International Issues (2 to 3 weeks)

Incorporate cases on different depository institution issues or performance analysis on an institution of their choice to present to class; external speakers; bank simulation game; and/or spreadsheet exercises.

MBA or MS elective course

- ✦ Chapters 1 to 22 (entire book)
- ✦ Simulation and/or cases, research assignments; external speakers
- ✦ Journal articles and cases (suggested at end of chapters)

Two-Quarter Sequence for Undergraduates

First Quarter: Introduction to Financial Markets & Institutions

- ✦ Chapters 1 to 4, 14, and 15: Financial Markets, Interest Rates, and Exchange Rates
- ✦ Chapters 16 to 18: Interest Rate Risk Management—Duration, Futures, Other Derivatives
- ✦ Chapters 5, 7, 8, 9: Introductory Material on Financial Institutions

Second Quarter: Management of Financial Institutions
- ✦ Chapters 6, 10 to 13, and 19 to 22: Financial Institution Management Techniques
- ✦ Selected references from end of chapters, spreadsheet exercises, cases, or simulations

One-Quarter Course for Undergraduates: Introductory Course in Institutions

- ✦ Chapters 1 to 4, 14, and 15: Financial Markets, Institutions, and Interest Rates
- ✦ Chapters 5 to 9 and 19 to 22: Depository Institutions: Techniques for Asset/Liability Management
- ✦ Chapters 10 to 13: Management of Nondepositories

Omit some complex analytical material; if time permits, could add Chapters 16 and 17, Managing Interest Rate Risk.

SPECIAL FEATURES

We believe the book has several features that continue to distinguish it from others currently available. First, the book has a consistent framework of asset/liability management, emphasizing the necessity for financial institution managers to innovate and to react creatively to a constantly changing regulatory, technological, and global financial environment. Second, the book provides the depth that students need to have a competitive advantage in its historic overview of different types of financial institutions, including a discussion of Kane's regulatory dialectic that has occurred in the United States. The book also covers the history of recent events, including the global financial crisis of the late 1990s. As George Santayana, the Spanish-born American educator, philosopher, and poet, once said, "Those who forget the past are condemned to repeat it." Third, the book is thorough, providing students with the edge they need in a competitive financial environment. The thorough coverage of interest rates and tools for managing interest rate risk, for instance, provides a good foundation for appreciating the specific management problems that financial institutions face.

As in the previous editions, given the dynamic nature of the material, we put special effort into identifying issues for which significant change is possible in the next decade. Our approach is to outline clearly as many facets of these issues as possible, so that students understand the nature and history of current controversies. When change occurs, instructors should have a relatively smooth time incorporating the specific course of action taken by regulators or by Congress.

Users have told us that their students find the book interesting and well-organized. The opening quotations and vignettes, almost all of which have been completely revised with each edition, often inject a humorous or interesting note to catch students' attention. In addition, we have tried throughout to provide useful and interesting examples of the application of many management tools. Students should enjoy the new Internet exercises provided by Ronnie Phillips at the end of each chapter. In addition, case suggestions at the end of most chapters provide instructors with excellent cases to which students have responded favorably in previous financial institution management classes. We have also tried to attain a relatively challenging level for many of the end-of-chapter problems to help students develop analytical skills.

ANCILLARY MATERIALS

The *Instructor's Manual* is available in print and on the Internet with complete answers to end-of-chapter questions and problems. Students will no longer have to trot to the library to get feedback for questions and problems. A completely revised *Test Bank*, written by Ronnie Phillips at Colorado State University, is also available, as well as Lecture Presentation Software in PowerPoint, developed by Edward Waller and Yvette Bendeck at the University of Houston, Clear Lake.

ACKNOWLEDGMENTS

This edition has benefited immeasurably from the comments of the users of the first three editions and the reviewers of the revised manuscript. Although we know we have not succeeded in completely satisfying them in this edition, we have considered every suggestion seriously and carefully. We extend special appreciation to the following people:

Arthur T. Cox, University of Northern Iowa

David Durst, University of Akron

John W. Ellis, Colorado State University

Sylvia Hudgins, Old Dominion University

Richard Klein, Clemson University

Inayat U. Mangla, Western Michigan University

Ronnie Phillips, Colorado State University

Edward Waller, University of Houston, Clear Lake

Users or readers who provided complete or partial reviews of pervious editions and made suggestions that continue to shape the text in important ways include:

Sheldon Balbirer, University of North Carolina-Greensboro

Bruce Bagamery, Central Washington University

Elijah Brewer, III, Federal Reserve Bank of Chicago

Omer Carey, University of Alaska-Anchorage

M. Carry Collins, University of Tennessee

Tony Cherin, San Diego State University

Gary Dokes, San Diego State University

David Ely, San Diego State University

Harvey Faram, Northern Arizona University

Deborah Ford, University of Baltimore

James R. Gale, Michigan Technological University

Phil Glasgo, Xavier University

Erika Gilbert, Illinois State University

James Gilkeson, Central Florida University

George Hachey, Bentley College

John H. Hand, Auburn University

Muhamad Husan, Kent State University

Jack Hayden, Eastern Montana University

Muhammad Husan, Kent State University

Jerry Johnson, University of South Dakota

Keith Johnson, University of Connecticut

Han Bin Kang, Illinois State University

Dan Kaufman, Wright State University

Gary Koppenhaver, Iowa State University

William Kracaw, Pennsylvania State University

Rick LeCompte, Wichita State University

C. F. Lee, Rutgers University

John Lewis, Stephen F. Austin University

Pamela Lowry, Illinois Wesleyan University

Robert L. Mills, Jr., Western Southern Life Insurance

Jeff Moore, Texas Christian University

Theresa Morgan, Illinois State University

Louis Mougoue, Loyola University-New Orleans

Prasad Naisetty, Indian University

Joe Newman, Northern Illinois University

James Nielsen, Oregon State University

Carl Nielson, Wichita State University

Phillip R. Perry, State University of New York-Buffalo

Nanda Rangan, Southern Illinois University

Alan Reichert, Cleveland State University

John Rozycki, Pennsylvania State University

William Sartoris, Indiana University

William Scott, Illinois State University

Michael Seeborg, Illinois Wesleyan University

Alan Severns, University of Detroit

Todd M. Shank, University of Portland

John Simms, University of North Carolina-Greensboro

Mike Spivey, Clemson University

Roger Stover, Iowa State University

Maurice Tse, Michigan State University

Ronald Watson, Custodial Trust Company

Walter Woerheide, Rochester Institute of Technology

Harold Wolfe, University of Texas at Austin

Students who were particularly helpful in the development of various editions include Bala Balakumar, Rhonda Jenkins, Kristen McGavin Anthony (Allstate Insurance Company), Sergio Murer (Prudential Mortgage), Diane M. Hustad (Del E.

Webb Corporation), Thomas Smith (Continental Illinois National Bank), Kevin Stoelting (United Parcel Service), Michael J. Wright (Arthur Andersen and Company), Michelle Woodham and Lisa Wurm. Gardner and Mills appreciate the moral support they received from Robert Jefferson, Illinois State University, and from colleagues at Illinois State University and Illinois Wesleyan University. Cooperman appreciates the moral support she received from Robert Cooperman, whose cheer got her through the difficulties of this project; from dear family who also carried her through including Ann and Al Fox, Roz, Phil, Steven, and Michelle Lerner; Jeff and Lori Cooperman; Rae and Jerry Blumberg; Ann and Albert, Terrell, Albie, Caroline, and Lizzie Singleton; and Gail, Mike, Oakleigh and Roscoe Welply; and from friends extraordinaire including Eleanor Swanson and Bud Fogerty; Patty Moran and Charles Register; Sinan and Fatma Cebenoyan; Susan Baillet and Herman Asarnow; Liz and Dave Ingram and Liz's group; and from Rene Gash, Yash Gupta and other wonderful colleagues at the University of Colorado-Denver. Cooperman also thanks Virginia Berkeley, President of Colorado Business Bank in Denver (CBB) and other colleagues at CBB for taking her into the real world in her externship with the bank.

Finally, we thank the professional staff at the Dryden Press for this edition. We are particularly grateful to Terri House, Developmental Editor, and to Mike Reynolds, Executive Editor. We are also grateful for the patience and persistence of Colby Alexander, Project Editor; Eddie Dawson, Production Manager; and Burl Sloan, Art Director; and a special thanks also to the copyeditor, proofreader, and indexer. The book continues to benefit from the previous work of Liz Widdicombe, Ann Heath, Carla Houx, Betsy Webster, Dan Coran, Karen Vertovec, Karen Shaw, Jeanne Calabrese, Wendy Kemp, Judy Lary, Alan Wendt, and Karen Schenkenfelder, who held various editorial assignments for the first three editions. The inevitable errors, however regrettable, are our own.

Mona J. Gardner
Dixie L. Mills
Bloomington, Illinois

Elizabeth S. Cooperman
Denver, Colorado

May 1999

CONTENTS IN BRIEF

CHAPTER 1 Changing Times for Financial Institutions 1

Part I **The Environment of Asset/Liability Management 27**

CHAPTER 2 Asset/Liability Management 29

CHAPTER 3 Regulation, Technology and Financial Innovation 40

CHAPTER 4 Background 115

Part II **Overview and Performance Analysis of Depository Institutions 171**

CHAPTER 5 Overview of Financial Statements For Depository Institutions 173

CHAPTER 6 Depository Institution Performance and Risk Analysis 199

CHAPTER 7 Credit Unions and Savings Institutions 249

CHAPTER 8 Capital Regulations and Management 285

CHAPTER 9 Managing Noninterest Revenues and Associated Risks 320

Part III **Management Issues and Performance Analysis of Nondepository Institutions 355**

CHAPTER 10 Insurance Company Financial Management Issues 357

CHAPTER 11 Investment Banks, Retail Security Firms, and Venture Capitalists 396

CHAPTER 12 Mutual Fund and Pension Fund Management 441

CHAPTER 13 Managing Nonbanks 491

Part IV **Interest Rate and Foreign Exchange Environments 531**

CHAPTER 14 Interest Rates, Exchange Rates, and Inflation 534

CHAPTER 15 The Term Structure of Interest Rates 584

CHAPTER 16 Interest Rate Risk Measurement and Immunization Using Duration 621

CHAPTER 17 Interest Rate Risk Management 657

CHAPTER 18 Interest Risk Management 689

Part V Particular Asset/Liability Management Problems: Depository Institutions 729

CHAPTER 19 Asset Management 731

CHAPTER 20 Deposit and Liability Management 773

CHAPTER 21 Asset Management 817

CHAPTER 22 Global Financial Crises and International Management Issues 884

APPENDIX A Mathematical Tables 913

NAME INDEX 918

SUBJECT INDEX 925

CONTENTS

CHAPTER 1 Changing Times for Financial Institutions   1

What Do Financial Institutions Do?   3
Changing Times for Financial Institutions   3
Financial Versus Real Assets and Financial Versus Nonfinancial Firms   7
Financial Institutions: What Are They?   9
The Economic Functions of Financial Institutions   15
Why Intermediaries? Reduced Transactions and Information Costs   19
The Changing Role of Financial Institutions in the Technological Age   21
Societal Concerns with Change and Banking for the Unbanked   22
Summary   23

Part I   The Environment of Asset/Liability Management   27

CHAPTER 2 Asset/Liability Management: What and Why?   29

Managing the Spread   30
Managing the Burden   30
Asset/Liability Management Defined   31
Asset/Liability Management: Who Sets Objectives?   32
Managerial Objectives in Financial Institutions   34
A Balancing Act   36
Summary   36

CHAPTER 3 Regulation, Technology and Financial Innovation   40

Why Regulate?   41
*The Regulatory Dialect: A Conceptual Framework for Regulation, Innovation,
    and Reform   42*
Regulation of Depository Institutions   50
Regulation of Finance Companies   55
Regulation of Insurance Companies   56
Regulation of Pension Funds   58
Regulation of Investment Companies   59
Regulation of Securities Firms   60
Origins of Financial Innovation and Regulatory Reform in the 1980s   61
The Synthesis: DIDMCA and Garn–St. Germain   66
New Regulatory Stringency Under FIRREA and FDICIA   74
The Pendulum Swings Again: Further Deregulation in the 1990s   81
Globalization of Financial Markets   84
Renewed Emphasis on Business Ethics   84
Changes in the Regulatory Structure   85
Summary   86
Appendix 3A: The Federal Reserve System and International Policy Coordination   91

CHAPTER 4 Background: Consolidation Trends, Moral Hazard and Agency Issues,
Types of Ownership and Organizations   115

The Effect of Financial Leverage on Financial Institution Operations   117
The Effect of Equity Ownership on Manager/Owner Behavior   121
Organizational Forms: Financial Holding Companies   124
Growth of BHCs and the Regulatory Dialectic   124
Regulation of BHCs   131
Mutually Owned Institutions   143
Not-For-Profit Institutions   152
The Future: Virtual FIs and Smart Cards   154
Economies of Scale and Scope   157
Summary   160

Part II Overview and Performance Analysis of Depository
Institutions   171

CHAPTER 5 Overview of Financial Statements For Depository Institutions   173

Overview of Commercial Bank Financial Statements   174
FDIC-Insured Balance Sheets In 1996   177
Income Statements For FDIC-Insured Banks in 1996   182
Looking More Closely At Bank Profits   184
Using Income Relationships To Forecast Target NIMs   189
Summary   192
Appendix 5A: Overview of Off-Balance Sheet Items   195

CHAPTER 6 Depository Institution Performance and Risk Analysis   199

General Objectives and Guidelines   200
Performance Evaluation Illustrated   205
Further Analysis: First National Bank of Maryland   216
Summary   223
Appendix 6A: Sample Uniform Bank Performance Report   232

CHAPTER 7 Credit Unions and Savings Institutions   249

Savings Institutions: A Brief History and Recent Regulatory Changes   251
A Brief History of CUs   255
Comparison of Industry Structures: Banks, Thrifts, and CUs   260
Comparison of Assets and Liabilities: Banks, Thrifts, and CUs   263
Performance of Depositories: A Comparison   268
More on the Thrift Crisis of the 1980s   274
Are Depository Institution Failures Contagious?   278
Summary   280

CHAPTER 8 Capital Regulations and Management   285

Market Versus Book Value Definitions of Capital   286
Preferences by Different Agents for Capital and Its Uses   289
Balancing Shareholders' and Regulators' Interests   291
Calculating Risk-Based Assets and Risk-Based Off-Balance Sheet Assets   296
Definitions of Capital Adequacy   298
Beyond Regulatory Requirements   302
How Much Capital Should Be Returned to Shareholders?   309
Management of Capital: Dividend Policy   311
Summary   313

CHAPTER 9 Managing Noninterest Revenues and Associated Risks: Traditional and
Nontraditional Sources of Fee Income, Risk Management—Value at
Risk and Economic Value Added, Securitization, and Other
Off-Balance Sheet Items   320

Why Fee Income?   322
How Much Noninterest Revenues Do Banks Produce?   325
A Brief Overview of Traditional Fee-Based Services   325
Correspondent Banking   329
Corporate Cash Management and Management Consulting   331
*A Brief Overview of Newer Fee-Based Activities: Securities, Insurance Brokerage,
Mutual Funds, Real Estate, and Other Activities   333*
Banks' Entrance Into Nontraditional Fee-Generating Activities and Cultural Clashes   347
Fee Income From Off-Balance Sheet Activities   347
Loan Sales   348
Securitization   350
Summary   353

Part III Management Issues and Performance Analysis of
Nondepository Institutions 355

CHAPTER 10 Insurance Company Financial Management Issues 357

Overview of the Operations of Insurance Companies 358
Performance Evaluation of Life Insurance Companies 366
Performance Evaluation of P/L Companies 369
Social and Economic Forces Affecting Insurers 373
An Overview of Insurance Operations 378
U.S. Risk-Based Capital Requirements 380
Regulatory Monitoring for Solvency 381
Private Insurer Solvency Ratings 381
Types of Insurance Policies and the Determination of Premiums 381
Asset Management Considerations 386
Summary 387

CHAPTER 11 Investment Banks, Retail Security Firms, and Venture Capitalists:
Management and Ethical Issues 396

Structure of the Industry, Types of Firms, and Profit Cycles 398
Structure of the Industry and Its Cycles 398
Registering and Marketing the Traditional IPO 427
Summary 430

CHAPTER 12 Mutual Fund and Pension Fund Management 441

Overview of the Management Structure of Mutual Funds 443
Ownership Structure of Affiliates 444
Recent Diversification and Consolidation for Mutual Funds 446
Basic Groups of Investment Companies 448
Types of Mutual Funds 449
Mutual Fund Families 451
The Costs of Mutual Fund Ownership 453
Regulations for Mutual Funds and Regulatory Issues 457
Recent Regulatory Concerns 458
Measuring the Performance and Risk of Mutual Funds 459
Risk-Adjusted Performance Measures 464
Value at Risk 465
Sharpe Ratio 466
Modigliani or M-Square Measure 466
Morningstar Ratings 467
Pension Funds, Mutual Funds' Role, and the Retirement Market 468
Pension Plan Growth, ERISA, and Types of Employer Pension Plans 468
Management Issues in Defined Benefit Plans 473
What Is the Pension Contract Between All Stakeholders? 473
Should Pension Smoothing Activities Be Used? 479
Who Owns Pension Surplus Assets? 480
Recent Conversions of Pensions to New Cash-Balance Plans 482
Summary 483

CHAPTER 13 Managing Nonbanks: Finance Companies, Financial Service Firm
Conglomerates, and Merger Considerations 491

An Overview of Finance Companies 492
Types of Finance Companies 493
Structure of the Industry and Trends in the 1990s 496
Income, Expenses, and Profitability of Finance Companies 499
Regulations for Finance Companies 501
Performance Information and Measurement 502
An Overview of Diversified Financial Firms: What Are They? 504

Reasons for the Development of Financial Conglomerates 508
Trends in Financial Service Conglomerates 511
Some Firms Are Successful, Others Are Not: Examples 511
Managerial Implications of Diversified Financial Services Firms 518
Summary 522

Part IV   Interest Rate and Foreign Exchange Environments   531

CHAPTER 14   Interest Rates, Exchange Rates, and Inflation: Theories and
Forecasting   534

Overview of the Chapter 535
Why Theories Are Important to Managers 535
A Historical Look at Interest Rates 535
The General Level of Interest Rates 539
Loanable Funds Theory 540
Loanable Funds Theory and Interest Rate Forecasting 543
Expected Inflation and the Loanable Funds Theory 549
Further Evaluation of the Fisher Theory 551
Calculating Effective Annual Yields 556
Differences in Yields for Money Market Securities 560
Currency Exchange Rates 564
Brief Overview of the Process for Introducing the Euro 576
Summary 578

CHAPTER 15   The Term Structure of Interest Rates   584

The Term Structure Defined: A Closer Look 585
Identifying the Existing Term Structure 585
Unbiased (Pure) Expectations Theory 594
Criticisms of the Pure Expectations Theory 597
Empirical Tests of the Term Structure Theories 604
Application of Term Structure Theories to Financial Institutions Management 606
Interest Rate Forecasting 606
*Using Forward Rates Estimated from Yield Curves to Set Loan Credit Risk
  Premiums 610*
Managing the Securities Portfolio 611
Summary 612

CHAPTER 16   Interest Rate Risk Measurement and Immunization Using Duration   621

Interest Rate Risk Defined 622
The Price/Yield Connection 622
Putting Them Together 623
The Price/Yield Relationship Illustrated 623
The Two Sides of Interest Rate Risk 626
Bond Theories 627
Implications for Financial Institutions 629
Effects of Interest Rate Changes on Common Stock 630
Duration: An Idea Ahead of Its Time 631
Measuring Interest Rate Risk: The Relationship Between Duration and Price Changes 634
Estimating Percentage Price Changes 634
Estimating Interest Rate Elasticity 635
Applications of Duration to Asset/Liability Management 636
Portfolio Immunization 639
Financial Institutions and Immunization 643
Duration Gap: Measuring an Institution's Overall Interest Rate Risk 643
Example: Calculating a Bank's Duration Gap 644
Immunization and Its Cost 648
Summary 651

CHAPTER 17   Interest Rate Risk Management: Interest Rates and Foreign Currency Futures   657

Financial Institutions and Financial Futures   659
Futures Contracts   659
The Developing Global Marketplace   661
Interest Rate Futures   663
Futures Prices and Market Yields: An Illustration   665
Short Versus Long Hedges   666
Risk and the Financial Futures Markets   670
Choosing the Optimal Number of Contracts   673
Futures as a Supplement to Gap Management   675
Interest Rate Futures: Regulatory Restrictions and Financial Reporting   676
Foreign Currency Futures   678
Comparison of Forward and Futures Markets   680
Summary   683
Appendix 17A: A Duration-Based Futures Hedge   687

CHAPTER 18   Interest Risk Management: Index Futures, Options, Swaps, and Other Derivatives   689

Stock Index Futures   690
Theoretical Basis of Stock Index Futures   690
History and Characteristics of Stock Index Futures   691
Financial Institutions and Stock Index Futures   694
Program Trading: Index Arbitrage   697
Other Index Futures   700
Options on Financial Assets   700
Options and Financial Institutions   703
Hedging with Options   705
Options and Futures Hedging: A Comparison   709
Interest Rate Swaps   711
Motivations for Swaps   712
Swaps as a Hedging Tool   712
More Exotic Swaps   716
Swaps Versus Futures Hedging   717
Swap Options and Futures   717
Interest Rate Caps, Floors, and Collars   718
Other New Derivatives for Financial Institution Management   720
Summary   723

Part **V**   Particular Asset/Liability Management Problems: Depository Institutions   729

CHAPTER 19   Asset Management: Liquidity Reserves and the Securities Portfolio   731

Importance of Liquidity in Depository Institutions   732
Liquidity: The Risk/Return Trade-Off   733
Discretionary and Nondiscretionary Factors   740
Managing the Liquidity Position   743
The Securities Portfolio as a Source of Stored Liquidity   745
Securitization of Loans and Loan Sales as Liquidity Sources   746
Liquidity Risk of Other Financial Institutions   746
Depository Institution Investment Portfolio Management   748
The Typical Bank Investment Portfolio   753
Investments in Mutual Funds   759
Decline in Investments in Government Securities   760
Summary   761

CHAPTER 20 Deposit and Liability Management 773

Factors to Consider in Deposit and Liability Management 776
Brief History of Liability Management 782
History of Liability Management 784
Using Liabilities to Cover Reserve Deficiencies 784
Using Liabilities to Meet Loan Demand or Pursue Growth 787
Factors Influencing the Use of Liability Management 792
Noninterest Competition Among Depositories 793
Economic Efficiency of Noninterest Competition 793
Acquisition of Funds in a Deregulated Environment 797
Wholesale Versus Retail Funds 797
Mix of Fund Sources 799
Pricing 799
Disclosure Requirements: Truth in Savings 803
Pricing Strategies in Practice 804
Effect of Federal Deposit Insurance 805
Coverage Provided 807
Summary 808

CHAPTER 21 Asset Management: Commercial, Consumer, and Mortgage Lending 817

Trends in Types of Loans 818
Commercial Lending: Recent Trends 818
Unique Aspects of Bank Lending to Medium-Sized to Small Firms 819
Consumer Lending: Recent Trends 822
Who Makes Consumer and Home Mortgage Loans? 825
Functions of the Credit Process: The Credit Process as Protection Against Default Risk 826
The Role of the Credit Process in Business Development 827
Loan Committee Review 827
Bank Written Loan Policies 827
Compliance Policies 828
Credit Execution Policies 829
Lender Compensation Policies 829
Loan Request Procedures 830
Quantitative Credit Scoring Models 832
Commercial Lending: Financial Statement Analysis 835
Sample Loan Presentation 837
Establishing Loan Trends 839
Noninterest Terms and Conditions 840
Quoted Base Rates on Commercial Loans 843
Risk Premium on Loans 845
Other Terms: Collateral 845
Restrictive Covenants 846
Other Considerations 846
Term Loans 847
Commercial Real Estate Loans 847
Agricultural Loans 847
Consumer Loans 848
Special Considerations of Mortgage Loans 851
Small Business Loans 852
Types of Higher Risk Lending 853
Lending to Hedge Funds 854
Loan Monitoring and Review 854
Loan Monitoring, Regulation, and Financial Reporting 855
Other Lending Considerations 856
Lender Liability Including Environmental Liability 857
Community Reinvestment Act Revisions 858
Sales of Commercial Loans and Some Securitizations 859

Providing One-Stop Shopping for All Corporate Needs 859
Improvement in Credit Risk Management 860
Summary 860
Appendix 21A: Sample Loan Underwriting Guidelines 869
Appendix 21B: Fictional Sample Loan Presentation 873
Appendix 21C: Commercial Loan Pricing Formula 881

CHAPTER 22 Global Financial Crises and International Management Issues 884

Management of International Loans 893
Risk Analysis in International Lending 897
Understanding Surprises in Country and Currency Risk 898
A Recap of the Asian Financial Crisis and How It Spread 899
Warning Signs for the Asian Financial Crisis 902
Financial Institution Involvement in the Crises 905
Attempts to Try to Help Nations Avert Future Financial Crises 906
Cultural Management Issues 908
Summary 909

APPENDIX A Mathematical Tables 913

NAME INDEX 918

SUBJECT INDEX 925

"The $1,000,000,000,000 bank. Once it was unimaginable. But in eight days in April (1998), three eye-popping megamergers have brought the prospect of the first trillion-dollar bank within sight."

Quotation from *Business Week*, April 27, 1998, p. 32.

"As competition heats up in the financial-services industry, more banks are dropping the word 'bank' from their marketing and even their names."

Stephen E. Frank
"To More Bankers 'Bank' Is a Bad Word," *The Wall Street Journal*, November 15, 1997, p. B1.

"Mergers or not, laws or not, technology has changed banking forever."

Martin Mayer
Banking Analyst; quotation from *Barron's*, April 20 1998, p. 20.

1

CHANGING TIMES FOR
FINANCIAL INSTITUTIONS

As suggested by the opening quotations, managers of financial institutions are wrestling with dramatic changes today, as mergers between very large institutions of different types create mega-institutions that offer nontraditional products. Much of this change has happened— despite regulations that restrict change—as the result of the technological revolution. Martin Mayer in the Barron's *article cited in the opening quotes points out, "Technology has changed not only the preferred scale of financial services but also the nature of financial intermediation. Obviously, huge nation-spanning banks have been made possible by capacious data processing and cheap telecommunications. . . . Machinery has made it possible for bank executives to extend their span of effective control. Thanks to the accelerating capacity of the computer and the spread of electronic services on the credit card and ATM chassis, the addi-tion of another customer to the bank's books adds virtually no cost at all. Technology has given the banking industry economies of scale." Technology also allows new innovations to occur that make "gigantism really profitable" including the development of instruments that permit banks and other financial institutions to create, acquire, and trade mortgages and credit card receivables like securities. Immense data bases allow different types of financial institutions to enter each others' market areas and cross-sell products. With declining profits from traditional activities, particularly for banks, financial institutions have sought new ways of doing business, gaining synergies, and increasing fee income. As Martin Mayer points out, "Keeping banks, brokers, and insurers at arm's length from each other in their relations with customers they share merely increases costs." Technology also increases global competition, since information systems based*

1

on high-speed computers support sales of financial products to customers throughout the world.[1]

Despite the realities of a completely changed marketplace and the need for efficiency by financial institutions, regulations have not changed fast enough to meet these realities. In the United States, frustrated institutions and regulators, frustrated with slow change in recognized standards, have initiated changes by re-interpreting vague legal language, putting pressure on Congress for legal change. Large banks, in particular, have responded to increased competition in traditional lending markets by becoming diversified financial services firms. Fleet Financial Group, headquartered in Providence, Rhode Island with $83 billion in assets, is a prime example. Fleet makes traditional commercial, real estate, and consumer loans, but it also provides venture capital to start new companies, offers data-processing services, operates a discount brokerage unit, underwrites municipal bonds, and manages mutual funds. In 1997, Fleet made headlines when it acquired Quick and Reilly, a national discount brokerage firm and Advanta Corporation, a national credit card company. Like many other large banks, Fleet has actively acquired many out-of-state banks. The list includes Norstar Bank of New York in 1988, the distressed Bank of New England in 1991, and Shawmut National Corporation in 1985, and the U.S. operations of National Westminster Bank in 1995. Fleet has invested heavily in technology, opening a telephone service center in Rhode Island in 1997 and making a $40 million investment in marketing software.

During this transformation, Fleet encountered difficulties its founders could never have anticipated in 1791—the year George Washington gave his farewell address. Until the mid-1980s, laws prohibited regional, interstate bank mergers. National interstate branching did not become a reality for banks until June 1997. Ironically, to merge with Norstar Bancorp of New York in 1988, Fleet

had to divest its holdings in neighboring Connecticut, since a patchwork of state laws for regional branching existed at that time. To acquire Shawmut in 1995, Fleet had to increase its low-income lending to meet increasingly stringent Community Reinvestment Act regulations. Juggling the new product mix was not always easy. The stock market drop of 1987 adversely affected Fleet's discount brokerage unit. Fleet also ventured into Latin American lending and later faced almost $30 million in bad debts as a result. Commercial real estate losses in the late 1980s were heavy, and the firm tangled with regulators over its financial reporting practices. Despite being one of the largest banks in New England, Fleet suffered a weak stock price (13 times expected earnings versus an average of 19 times for other large banks). In 1997, this situation forced Fleet to face a difficult choice: to continue to buy other banks or to be bought amid increased industry consolidation associated with the advent of free interstate branching after June 1997. In 1999, Fleet became the eighth largest bank in the U.S. by merging with Bank Boston, providing both banks with a varied product line.[2]

Although not all financial institutions have adopted such aggressive strategies, all face similar challenges and opportunities. Some, like Fleet, are generally profitable operations; others, such as Bank of New England, have faltered or failed. Their success or failure is often traced to how well their managers understand the new financial environment and whether they respond by adopting financial management techniques. This book addresses financial management issues for financial institutions in the early 21st century.

This introductory chapter provides a macro view of the setting for financial institutions, discussing the changes that have occurred and are occurring for financial institutions, differences between financial institutions and nonfinancial institutions, the major types of financial institutions, and the economic services they provide.

✦ ✦ ✦

[1]Martin Mayer, "Apples Meet Oranges," *Barron's*, April 20, 1998, pp. 20, 22.

[2]Fleet/Norstar Financial Group, *Annual Report*, various years; John W. Milligan, "KKR, Member FDIC," *Institutional Investor*, June 1991, pp. 59–60; Ron Suskind, "Fleet/Norstar, Not Loved by All, Gets the Job Done," *The Wall Street Journal*, March 25, 1992, p. B4; Geoffrey Smith, "Fleet's Ship Comes In," *Business Week*, November 9, 1992, p. 104; Peter Truell, "Fleet Taking Another Fork in Road to Bank Expansion," *New York Times*, September 18, 1997, p. C4; Rose Kerber, "Fleet Financial Faces a Choice: Buy or Be Bought?" *The Wall Street Journal*, December 2, 1997, p. B4; and Rose Kerber, "Amid Banks' Merger Frenzy, Fleet Goes on the Prowl" *The Wall Street Journal*, May 4, 1998, p. B4. Leslie Miller, "Fleet-Bank Boston Merger May Presage New National Institution." *The Denver Post*, March 16, 1999, 5c.

WHAT DO FINANCIAL INSTITUTIONS DO?

Many observers think of financial institutions as "money specialists." Until recently, people paid little attention to the fact that financial institutions have their own financial management problems. Instead, the common belief was that financial institutions solve the financial management problems of others—not a surprising thought because most individuals initiate relationships with several financial institutions from early ages. A typical consumer might have:

- ✦ a checking account at a local bank
- ✦ a credit card issued by a bank headquartered in another state
- ✦ a home mortgage from an area savings and loan association
- ✦ an automobile loan from the credit union at work
- ✦ a life insurance policy from an insurer with offices in 50 states
- ✦ automobile and homeowner's insurance from a different firm
- ✦ savings for retirement entrusted to a mutual fund
- ✦ an account with the regional office of a national brokerage company

As Martin Mayer observes, "To an extent previously unknown in history, the American household is itself today a financial intermediary, owing big-time for mortgages and credit cards, owning big-time in mutual funds, stocks, certificates of deposit, insurance policies, asset-backed securities. Households are targets for the inventors of financial products, ways to borrow, ways to invest. Some of these inventors are bankers, some are brokers, some are insurers."[3] Times are changing for financial institutions. Financial institutions are changing, as well, with progressively more diversified financial institutions offering an expanding variety of services.

CHANGING TIMES FOR FINANCIAL INSTITUTIONS

A View From the 1930s

So many financial institutions operate today in the United States, and people have grown so accustomed to them, that their existence, functions, and continued operations are often taken for granted. This was not always the case. In the early 1930s, widespread concern about the safety and soundness of financial institutions provoked state and federal legislatures to enact laws to assure the public that financial institutions were sound and viable.

Laws limited the activities of most financial institutions for several decades, making their financial management not a terribly complex process. Managers engaged in specific, legally permissible activities, charging prices with legally mandated maximums, and incurring legally determined costs. Regulators set prices and costs that ensured that financial institutions could operate profitably, and relatively few failed.

A Different View From the 1970s and 1980s

As time passed and memories of the 1930s faded, the perceived need for regulation of financial institutions diminished. Also, as interest rates rose in the 1970s, depositors became dissatisfied with the low rates paid by financial institutions and with-

---

[3]Mayer, "Apples Meet Oranges," p. 22.

drew their funds in search of higher returns elsewhere. Many financial institutions could not respond because laws of the 1930s limited the rates they could offer.

Congress and government regulators reacted to these developments, and beginning in 1978, Congress loosened or removed many restrictions on financial institutions. This period of deregulation coincided with, and was encouraged by, rapid developments in technology and innovation in the products of financial institutions. Although virtually all financial institutions are still regulated, regulations are less restrictive than in previous decades.

During deregulation, the U.S. economy experienced significant changes, such as population migration toward the South and West and a decline in the fortunes of basic manufacturing, agricultural, and energy-related industries. These fundamental changes resulted in a movement of money from one region to another and from some industries to others. Because financial institutions are "money specialists," they were definitely affected. As a result of these combined forces, the complexity of managing a financial institution dramatically increased.

Increasingly volatile interest rates in the 1970s and 1980s created profitability problems for many financial institutions, particularly savings institutions. Technology expanded competition, as well, with direct financial markets allowing strong corporations to easily and cheaply sell securities directly to the public rather than borrow from banks. Widespread access to computers and increasingly sophisticated information technology allowed new financial innovations. An example is packaging mortgages for sale as securities (securitization of assets) by specialized financial institutions. Corporations also can obtain direct financing in global markets, since technology allows electronic transactions almost anywhere in the world. This flight of their best borrowers left banks with less creditworthy customers in the mid-sized to small business market. With lower profits as the result of increased competition, and overcapacity in their industries, banks and savings institutions increased loans to ever-riskier customers to make up for lost profits. Regional recessions in the late 1980s left many banks in failure. U.S. savings institutions experienced severe losses, as well, necessitating a massive government bailout. Hundreds of savings institutions were closed or merged in the late 1980s and early 1990s.[4] Management excess and abuse contributed to many failures, resulting in public outrage and demand for new approaches to regulation and supervision to protect customers and taxpayers from unacceptable risks.

A View of the 1990s

In response to widespread failures of banks and savings institutions in the 1980s, Congress imposed stringent new regulations for these institutions and recapitalized depository insurance funds in 1989 and again in 1991.

---

[4]For stories on the U.S. savings crisis in the late 1980s, see Frederic A. Miller, Teresa Carson, and Catherine Yang, "The Thrift Crisis: Now It's Bigger than Texas," *Business Week*, May 2, 1988, pp. 112–113; Paulette Thomas and Paul Duke, Jr., "Federal Rescue Efforts for Failed Thrifts Are a Crisis in Themselves," *The Wall Street Journal*, January 13, 1989, pp. A1, A10; and Denise Kalette, "Callers Want S&L Cheats Punished," *USA Today*, February 15, 1989, p. 1. For stories of the banking crisis in the northeastern United States in the early 1990s, see Bush and Morrall, 1989 (cited in full in the Selected References at the end of this chapter); Dean Foust et al. "How Deep Is the Hole?" *Business Week*, December 9, 1991, pp. 30–32; and Lawrence Ingrassia, "Banking Crisis in Rhode Island Nears Its Close," *The Wall Street Journal*, June 29, 1992, p. A2.

The 1990s clearly showed that changes in the economic and financial system would continue, requiring further adaptations in the regulatory environment as a result. The globalization of financial markets, reflected in unprecedented competition from Japanese and European financial institutions, forced Congress and U.S. regulators to recognize the need for international policy coordination. Later, in the mid-1990's, major crises for currencies in Japan, Indonesia, Thailand, and Korea confirmed this.

Thousands of mergers occurred, as financial institutions, particularly banks and savings institutions, took advantage of new technology that allowed greater economies of scale and cross-selling opportunities. Competition squeezed profits from traditional sources like lending and taking deposits for banks and savings institutions, creating the need for profits from other sources. Large banks merged with other types of financial institutions, as illustrated by Fleet. Interstate branching allowed after June of 1987 created the first coast-to-coast national banks with mergers, such as Nations Bank in North Carolina with Bank America in California.

Globalization and the development of a common currency in Europe brought opportunities for U.S. financial institutions to profit from providing advice as consultants, selling products to customers abroad, and international trading activities. Technology increased the use and trading of derivatives—futures, options, and swaps (financial contracts with payment streams based on the future price changes of underlying securities). These instruments now provide hedging benefits for financial institutions, but they also expand opportunities for risky speculation. A number of financial scandals and huge trading losses on derivatives rocked securities firms in the 1990s. For example, a single rogue trader, Nick Leeson, accumulated losses trading futures on the Japanese Nikkei stock market index totaling more than $1 billion in 1995. This resulted in the failure of Barings, a formerly prestigious British investment firm that had been in business for centuries.

In the 1990s, for the first time since the 1930s, regulators allowed mergers between large, creditworthy banks and securities firms. In 1998, a proposed merger between a huge bank, Citicorp, and a giant insurance/finance company, Travelers Group, challenged regulations that prevented banks and insurance firms from merging. Mergers between different types of financial institutions increased opportunities for synergies and new sources of noninterest revenues. However, they also increased risk-management problems for institutions. Cultural problems arose between conservative cultures of commercial banks and the more "gun-slinging" environment of securities firms. Risk and culture management have become important aspects of management practices for financial institutions. Managers have attempted to address these complex issues.

Looking Into the 21st Century

Financial institutions like Fleet also must determine whether they can afford to continue to operate independently or need to find merger partners. For instance, with changes allowing interstate branching for banks after June 1997, a dramatically declining number of independent banks now operate in single states. This change has created difficulties for smaller banks, which can only compete by finding distinct niches. Interstate branching also offers opportunities for small financial institutions to emphasize personalized service and gain customers who feel overlooked by very large institutions. With new technology, customers have come to expect new services, such as online cash management services, bill paying on the Internet, and other home banking services. Financial institutions have been pressured to invest in expensive new technology, increasing their fixed costs and increasing the incentive for mergers to spread costs over more customers.

Demographics have changed, favoring new savings and retirement products for aging Baby Boomers who desire higher returns than banks have typically offered depositors. Financial Institutions face challenges to hire increasingly well-qualified individuals who are flexible and ready and willing to cope with change and to serve diverse customers. With thousands of mergers and the creation of huge, diversified financial institutions, new management strategies for financial institutions must be developed.

New opportunities have also been created with the advent of a common currency for eleven European nations on January 1, 1999. National currencies for these countries will be abolished by July 1, 2002. The European countries involved will encompass more than 290 million inhabitants (more than the U.S. population). They will account for 19 percent of world trade and 19.4 percent of the world gross domestic product, similar to the U.S. percentage. U.S. investment banks such as Morgan Stanley, Goldman Sachs, and Merrill Lynch are shifting workers to Europe to create business opportunities within the new European Monetary Union (EMU), with its giant financial market. For example, the euro zone government bond market of $1.9 trillion is almost as big as the U.S. Treasury market and likely to diversify. Continental equity markets are likely to merge and grow, along with corporate bond markets. This growth increases opportunities for development of investment products. Europeans, with traditionally high savings rates, have found fewer investment opportunities than in the United States, limiting their abilities to invest in a wide variety of mutual funds or to take out home mortgages. Technology now helps financial service firms to offer products to such international customers.[5] Turmoil in Asia has created strong pressure for governments to initiate economic reforms, including opening up markets to foreign firms to support development of increasingly efficient and competitive financial markets. U.S. investment banks have opportunities to provide advice and help countries with reforms and financing needs.

Change Isn't Easy for Consumers, Either/A Problem of Ethics

Evidence suggests that the public may not be altogether comfortable with or accustomed to the new financial environment. Consumers have been very concerned about recent megamergers of financial institutions. For instance, a consumer group recently expressed concern about the Citicorp—Travelers Group merger, fearing misuse of personal data about customers and erosion of personal privacy. Large lawsuits in the 1990s targeted brokerage and insurance firms, claiming misrepresentation of products and unethical selling behavior.

A strong backlash by consumers and taxpayers occurred in reaction to the huge government bailout to resolve insolvencies at hundreds of federally insured savings institutions in the early 1990s. Few industries in financial difficulty reap the media attention accorded financial institutions, and indeed, few businesses seem as fragile. In 1997, the crisis of financial institutions in Thailand, Indonesia, South Korea, and

---

[5]"Special Report: The Euro," *Business Week*, April 27, 1998, pp. 90–108; and Terry Savage, "Euroland's Potential Awesome, but Pitfalls Abound," *Denver Post*, May 10, 1998, pp. 10–11

Japan contributed to serious economic problems for these countries. The Thai government, for instance, closed 56 of 58 ailing finance companies in December 1997. The causes of the financial crisis for these countries were similar to those of the U.S. thrift crisis, including excessive speculation and poor underwriting of risky commercial real estate loans by financial institutions. The Asian crisis led to a plunge in the value of regional currencies and a huge bailout program by the International Monetary Fund.[6] These events emphasize the importance of financial management in financial institutions as a topic of study.

It is appropriate to begin this study with some basic definitions. The next section discusses the difference between the financial assets that financial institutions handle and physical assets, such as plant and equipment. It also provides an overview of the differences between the balance sheets of financial versus nonfinancial firms.

FINANCIAL VERSUS REAL ASSETS AND FINANCIAL VERSUS NONFINANCIAL FIRMS

Financial institutions deal with financial assets, assets that promise future payments from financial contracts, such as securities and loans. These institutions also deliver services, relying on their reputations to attract customers for relationships often based on trust. Similarly, a nonfinancial business expects future benefits in the form of cash from sales of its tangible and service products, as well as from owning a recognizable trademark or slogan (like Nike's Just Do It) or a patent on a production process.

Because so many things are assets, it is convenient to divide them into two major subsets: **real assets** and **financial assets.** Real, tangible assets are those expected to provide benefits based on their fundamental qualities. A person's home transfers benefits commensurate with the quality of its construction, its location, and its size. A corporation's main computer provides benefits based on its speed, the size of its memory, the ease of its use, and the frequency with which it needs repair. A financial asset, in contrast, is a contract that offers a promise of payment in the future from the party that issued the contract.

Most business firms—steel makers, automobile manufacturers, restaurants, and department stores—acquire and use real assets in ways that make the value of future benefits received greater than the cost of obtaining them. Cash to acquire assets may come from lenders or creditors with legal expectations for repayment from the firm's use of real assets. Cash may also come from those who take an ownership (or equity) interest in the firm, hoping for (but with no legal promise of) shares in the excess of asset benefits over costs. Regardless of the sources of its funds, however, the firm has issued obligations that become the financial assets of others. Funds generated by issuing financial obligations are then used to acquire real assets.

Like other businesses, a financial institution acquires and uses assets so that the value of their benefits exceeds their costs. The key difference between financial institutions and other firms is that most of the assets financial institutions hold are financial assets. Financial institutions use funds from their own creditors and owners to acquire

---

[6]Seth Mydans, "56 Troubled Lenders Closed by Thailand," *New York Times*, December 9, 1997, p. C10; and Jathon Sapsford, "Seoul's Woes Pose Trade Threat to Japan," *The Wall Street Journal*, December 12, 1997, p. A13.

financial claims against others. They may lend funds to individuals, businesses, and governments, or they may purchase ownership shares in other businesses. The future benefits that financial institutions expect to receive thus depend on the performance of the parties whose financial liabilities they purchase. The main distinction between financial institutions and other firms is not so much in how they raise funds, because all businesses issue financial liabilities to do so, but in what they do with these funds.

To illustrate the difference between a nonfinancial and financial firm, see the respective assets on simplified balance sheets for a manufacturing firm and a bank:

Manny's Manufacturing Assets ($million)		The Manny Bank Assets ($million)	
Cash	$10	Cash	$20
Accounts receivable	350	Securities	724
Inventory	650	Loans	1,206
Net plant and equipment	1,000	Building/equipment	60
Total assets	$2,010	Total assets	$2,010

Notice that 50 percent of assets for Manny's Manufacturing are real, physical assets: inventory and net plant and equipment. In contrast, only 3 percent of a typical bank's assets are real, physical assets: its building and equipment. The manufacturing firm has higher operating leverage, with high fixed costs associated with its fixed assets. The bank has lower operating leverage, since it has a low percentage of fixed assets; it has a more labor-intensive operation. However, 92 percent of the bank's assets are financial assets, securities and loans, which are claims for future cash flows. Thus, the bank's profits depend on financial contracts promising future cash flows from other parties. A loan will provide future benefits only if the bank's customer continues to pay interest. The bank depends on the loan customer's performance to benefit from the financial asset.

This concept of financial assets implies that one party's financial asset is another party's **financial liability**—that is, the other party has an obligation (often a legal one) to provide future benefits to the owner of the financial asset. For instance, a customer with a savings account at the bank has a financial asset, which is a financial liability of the bank to pay interest on the balance in the savings account.

To illustrate this concept, look at the liabilities for Manny's Manufacturing and The Manny Bank. Their liabilities and equity accounts differ in important ways:

Manny's Manufacturing Firm Liabilities and Equity ($million)		The Manny Bank Liabilities and Equity ($million)	
Accounts payable	$ 10	Transaction deposits	$ 600
Notes payable	500	Savings deposits	800
Total current liabilities	510	Certificates of deposit	249
Long-term bonds	500	Total deposits	1,649
Total debt	1,010	Other borrowing	200
Common stock	200	Total debt	1,849
Retained earnings	800	Common stock	61
Total equity	1,000	Retained earnings	100
Total liabilities and equity	$2,010	Total equity	$ 161
		Total liabilities and assets	$2,010

The liabilities of the manufacturing firm, current and long-term debt, represent financial claims that are financial assets of suppliers for accounts payable, banks for notes payable, and investors for long-term bonds. Liabilities for the bank are deposit accounts and other borrowings. The Manny Bank has issued financial contracts for these deposits, promising to pay given interest payments. Unlike the liabilities of Manny's Manufacturing, which have definite maturities for repayment, the deposit liabilities at The Manny Bank can be withdrawn (repayment demanded on the spot) at any time. This creates liquidity problems for the bank that the manufacturer does not experience.

Notice that the manufacturing firm is financed with about 50 percent equity and 50 percent debt. The Manny Bank has much higher financial leverage with about 92 percent debt and 8 percent equity, typical proportions for financial institutions. Thus, the bank has much higher interest expenses than the manufacturing firm (i.e. higher financial leverage). By having such a low fraction of equity financing, financial institutions have greater risk of a fall in the value of their assets, wiping out the value of equity. For instance, if the Manny's Bank had loan losses of $161 milllion (about 13 percent loans), it would be technically bankrupt.

Banks and savings institutions can use higher financial leverage than other firms, because most of their deposits (liabilities) are federally insured. This protection gives depositors confidence in the banks' conditions and future repayment of liabilities, so they do not demand higher premiums for their funds. If a manufacturing firm had such a high debt ratio, it would experience a horrendous cost of funds, because lenders would demand a much higher risk premium for the bankruptcy risk they would incur. Also, since financial institutions have lower operating leverage, entailing lower fixed costs, they can afford higher financial leverage, which entails higher interest expenses. The Manny Bank, in essence, makes its profits from the spread between the interest rate it receives on its financial assets and the interest rate it pays on its financial liabilities. Manny's Manufacturing, in contrast, makes profits from the spread between the cost of producing and selling a physical product.

FINANCIAL INSTITUTIONS: WHAT ARE THEY?

Although all financial institutions have predominantly financial assets and low percentages of fixed assets, they specialize in varying types of financial assets and services. The major types are depository, finance, contractual, investment, and securities firms. The chapters to follow explore similarities and differences in detail. Table 1.1 introduces the specific institutions that are the focus of this textbook.

Depository Institutions

Depository institutions are financial institutions that take deposits and make loans. They control the largest proportion of financial assets. This category includes commercial banks, savings institutions (savings banks and savings and loan associations), and credit unions. Their primary financial liabilities are deposits.

In 1998, U.S. **commercial banks** held financial assets of over $5 trillion. They have long served the corporate community as a primary source of short-term and intermediate-term loans, and for years, regulatory restrictions made them the only de-

Table 1.1 ✦ PERCENTAGE DISTRIBUTION OF FINANCIAL ASSETS OF FINANCIAL INSTITUTIONS

An increasingly competitive financial environment is evident. The percentage of total financial assets held by commercial banks and life insurers has declined significantly over the past four decades. The total share held by thrift institutions (S&Ls and savings banks) peaked in 1980, then sharply fell. Investment companies (mutual and money market funds) share of financial assets has increased markedly since 1980.

	YEAR							
Institution	1950	1960	1970	1980	1985	1990	1996	1997
Commercial banks	56.88%	41.88%	40.38%	38.57%	35.26%	33.11%	37.33%	36.48%
Thrifts	13.23	18.22	19.70	20.65	18.88	13.47	8.84	7.90
Credit unions	0.34	1.02	1.40	1.80	1.99	2.15	2.73	2.60
Finance companies	3.13	4.49	5.00	5.27	5.75	7.73	5.55	5.25
Life insurers	21.55	19.44	15.67	12.08	11.79	13.54	15.67	15.15
Property/liability insurers	NA	4.89	3.89	4.54	4.27	5.08	4.65	4.39
Private pension funds	2.39	6.19	8.74	12.22	12.45	11.52	4.67	4.93
Investment companies	1.11	2.76	3.96	3.68	7.29	10.80	18.97	21.74
Securities firms	1.36	1.09	1.27	1.19	2.31	2.60	1.59	1.56
Total percent	100.0	100.0	100.0	100.0	100.0	100.0	100.0	100.0
Total assets (billions)	$296.94	$615.10	$1,281.73	$3,842.20	$6,752.60	$10,095.80	$10,555.30	$11,715.70

NA = Not available. Notes: Figures for commercial bank assets exclude bank personal trusts and estates managed (1997: $242.3 billion). The figure for finance companies in 1996 includes mortgage bank assets. Figures for investment company assets include money market securities, mutual funds, and REITs. Figures for private pension funds do not include state and government funds (1997: $718.8 billion). Government-sponsored enterprises, federally related mortgage pools, and asset-backed securities issuers are not included in total assets (1997: $3,593.9 billion).
Sources: "Flow of Funds," *Federal Reserve Bulletin,* 1964–1996; *Financial Assets & Liabilities,* April 1998; and U. S. League of Savings and Loans Fact Books.

positories allowed to offer checking accounts payable on demand. The Fleet Financial Group's activities discussed earlier indicate that such a description is hardly adequate in the current era. Banks are rapidly expanding their services and markets, and many offer diversified sets of products. They have recently encountered considerable competition in their traditional area of specialization—lending—as is apparent from the decline in banks' share of total financial institution assets from about 56.9 percent in 1950 to 36.5 percent in 1997. They have also lost deposits, as former depositors have turned to direct market investment securities and money market and mutual funds for higher yields.

In addition to competition from other financial institutions, banks and savings institutions face competition from government-sponsored enterprises dealing with mortgage financing, which held $3.6 trillion in assets at the end of 1997. Within the banking industry, increasingly aggressive competition has arisen in domestic and foreign markets. To compete in a global markets, a number of very large banks have merged in the U.S. and abroad to create megabanks.[7] As regulators have relaxed restrictions to match market realities, large banks have also acquired other types of fi-

[7]John Tagliabue, "Two of the Big 3 Swiss Banks to Join to Seek Global Heft," *New York Times,* December 9, 1997, p. C8.

nancial firms. With narrow profit margins and widespread overcapacity in the industry, banks underwent considerable restructuring and consolidation in the 1980s and 1990s. Between 1990 and 1996, for instance, approximately 2,500 bank mergers occurred in the United States.

Despite the decline in the banks' share of financial assets and the number of banks, their activities have expanded in other ways. Banks have packaged loans, selling them as securities to investors, provided conditional guarantees for firms, and served as dealers for instruments to hedge interest-rate risk. Consequently, off-balance-sheet activities of banks (activities that generate fee income not included as balance sheet assets) have expanded exponentially. These activities provide banks with fee income, reducing their reliance on traditional banking activities. Bank off-balance-sheet items at the end of 1997 totaled over $25 trillion.[8]

Thrift institutions include **savings and loan associations (S&Ls)** and **savings banks.** They traditionally rely on savings deposits as sources of funds, although they can now offer checkable deposits. S&Ls, the largest of the thrifts by total asset size, have expanded beyond their traditional role as suppliers of home mortgage loans since economic changes and congressional action gave them the power to do so. This expansion met with mixed success, and S&Ls faced greater asset restrictions in the 1990s, as discussed in more depth in a later chapter. Savings banks resemble S&Ls, but they have more diversified asset bases. Table 1.1 indicates that thrifts' share of total financial assets peaked in the 1970s and then began declining. Between 1980 and 1997, the size of the industry dramatically fell, with financial asset holdings falling from 20.65 percent in 1980 to only 7.9 percent in 1997. The number of thrifts dropped, as well, with hundreds of closures and mergers following the thrift crisis of the late 1980s. Many very large thrifts emerged from the crisis operating with nonthrift subsidiaries, much like large commercial banks. Small, profitable thrifts have developed local community banking niches. Analysts have observed alliances among small commercial banks and institutions traditionally classified as thrifts. These developments may eventually result in a new category of depositories emphasizing **community banking** and the disappearance of the thrift category.

Credit unions (CUs) are distinguished by offering their services only to members, who must share some "common bond" representing the basis for forming the union. Another important difference between CUs and other financial institutions is their status as not-for-profit organizations, which makes them exempt from taxation. Often they run on volunteer labor. Thus, their managerial objectives and resulting strategies may differ somewhat from those of other depositories. With banks raising their fees for consumer accounts to cover increasing costs and declining margins, many U.S. consumers have moved accounts to credit unions in the 1990s. On the other hand, with credit unions crediting deposits to the wrong accounts and committing other lapses, members of less professionally managed credit unions also have fled to the more capable banks. CUs are subject to a common bond requirement and cannot make commercial loans. In recent years, many large credit unions have aggressively stretched common bond boundaries, becoming more like banks by offering credit cards and other investment services. This extension and CUs' tax-exempt status are controversial among their competitors. As shown in Table 1.1, although

---

[8]See *Federal Reserve Bank of New York: Economic Policy Review* 1, No. 2 (July 1995) and *FDIC Statistics on Banking 1997.*

CUs' share of financial assets is relatively small, 2.60 percent in 1997, this share has grown dramatically from 1.80 percent in 1980.

Finance Companies

Similar to depositories in the financial assets that they hold are **finance companies,** which specialize in loans to businesses and consumers. Their financial liabilities are quite different from those of depositories, however. They acquire most of their funds by selling commercial paper and bonds and by borrowing from their rivals, commercial banks. Finance companies had a 5.25 percent share of financial institution assets in 1997. The 20 largest finance companies commanded a 70.9 percent share of total industry loans (called *receivables*). This dominance reflects the activities of some very large finance companies, often owned by manufacturing firms, such as General Motors Acceptance Corporation (GMAC). Finance companies have benefited from financing by increased securitization (packaging and selling loans as securities to investors). This practice gives finance companies increased liquidity (cash) to make new loans, removes previous loans from their balance sheets, and provides fee income for originating and continuing to service these loans.[9]

Contractual Intermediaries

A third category of institutions consists of **insurance companies** (both life insurers and property/liability insurers) and **pension funds,** which together are considered **contractual savings institutions,** because they operate under formal agreements with policyholders or pensioners who entrust their funds to these firms. The insurance industry has sold risk protection to the public for hundreds of years. Life insurers, because they make long-term commitments to customers, traditionally hold asset portfolios structured quite differently from those of property/liability insurers, which offer shorter-term policies such as automobile and home coverage. U.S. life insurers, like commercial banks and thrifts, underwent a period of restructuring and consolidation in the late 1980s and 1990s. A number of insurance firms, like many savings and loans and banks, took on risky investments in the 1980s and paid the price in the 1990s, with many failures. Massive layoffs accompanied restructuring of the firms, reducing costs to boost profitability. Until 1990, life insurers were the second-largest category of financial institutions in the United States. After 1990, however, investment companies moved into second place. As shown in Table 1.1, in 1997, life insurance companies held about a 15.15 percent share of financial institution assets, and property-casualty insurers held 4.93 percent.

   Pension funds generally are designed to collect funds from employers and sometimes employees and to repay those funds, along with investment returns, after employees have retired or become disabled. The most widely known retirement fund is the U.S. government's social security program, but the category includes many other public and private funds. Currently, the U.S. social security system runs a surplus, but the balance is projected to turn to a deficit in the next century, as the nation's largest demographic group, the Baby Boomers, begin and continue to retire. Congress has been devising plans to revise the current system,

---

[9]"Survey of Finance Companies, 1996," *Federal Reserve Bulletin,* July 1997, pp. 543–556.

but many Baby Boomers planning for retirement do not think they will be able to rely on social security funds, increasing their need for investments in private pension funds. Table 1.1 includes only the assets of private pension funds. The percentage of financial assets held in 1997 seems small at 4.93 percent. This figure is somewhat deceptive, however, since the pension fund assets managed by banks, investment companies, and insurance companies are excluded. Many pension plans have changed from being defined as benefit managed (by employers) to produce a given retirement benefit to defined contribution where money is given to employees for retirement that they must manage themselves by investing contributions in mutual funds of their choice. In 1997, private and government pension funds held over $1.35 trillion in financial assets.

Investment Companies

Investment companies include mutual funds, money market funds, and REITs (real estate investment trusts). In 1997, investment companies had the second largest share of financial assets for the institutions listed in Table 1.1, with 21.74 percent, rising from a mere 3.68 percent in 1980. Investment companies provide a means through which small savers can pool funds to invest in a variety of financial instruments. The resulting economies of scale offer investors the benefits of professional portfolio management, reduced transactions costs, and the reduced risk exposure within large, diversified portfolios. The best-known and largest type of investment companies are **mutual fund.** In the early 1980s, **money market mutual funds** dominated the industry. By providing easy access to funds and market rates of return, they achieved an enviable rate of growth. By the 1990s, the popularity of stock and bond funds increased, as well, despite rather pronounced swings in the financial markets. The lowest short-term interest rates in 50 years caused investors to flee money market funds in pursuit of higher returns. With the booming stock market in the mid- to late 1990s, equity funds and mixed funds—with both stock and bond investments—grew incredibly from $500 billion to $1.998 trillion from 1992 to 1996. Mutual funds had assets in 1998 of over $ 5 trillion.[10]

Securities Firms

Securities firms assist customers with purchasing and selling stocks, bonds, and other financial assets. The industry is often subdivided according to two major activities, investment banking and brokerage. **Investment bankers** assist in the creation and issuance of new securities, and **brokers** assist in transfers of ownership of previously issued securities. The second category includes both **full-service brokers** and **discount brokers.** Full-service brokers advise clients in addition to arranging securities purchases and sales; discount brokers execute trades but give no advice. Many securities firms engage in both investment banking and brokerage activities. After the October 1987 stock market crash, securities firms went through a major restructuring and consolidation phase. In 1997, a number of securities firms merged with other types of financial institutions. These deals include Salomon Brothers' merger with the Travelers Group, Alex Brown's merger with Banker's Trust, and Mont-

---

[10]Peter Fortune, "Mutual Funds, Part I: Reshaping the American Financial System," *New England Economic Review*, Federal Reserve Bank of Boston, July/August 1997, pp. 45–72, and *Mutual Fund Fact Book,* 1998.

gomery Securities' merger with NationsBank, among many others. With the relaxation of previous laws preventing commercial banks from engaging in securities activities, analysts predict a greater number of mergers between investment firms and banks in the next decade.

Balance Sheets Reveal Industry Differences

Differences in financial industry competitors are reflected in their asset and liability structures. Although comparisons are made in greater detail in later chapters, Figure 1.1 identifies major distinctions among three types of firms—commercial banks, life insurance companies, and mutual funds.

FIGURE 1.1 ◆ ASSETS AND LIABILITIES OF SELECTED FINANCIAL INSTITUTIONS

Commercial banks' asset portfolios are dominated by loans and their liabilities by deposits. In contrast, life insurers invest heavily in government and corporate securities, and their major liabilities are obligations to policyholders. Mutual funds also invest in corporate and government securities, but the major claims against them are from their own shareholders.

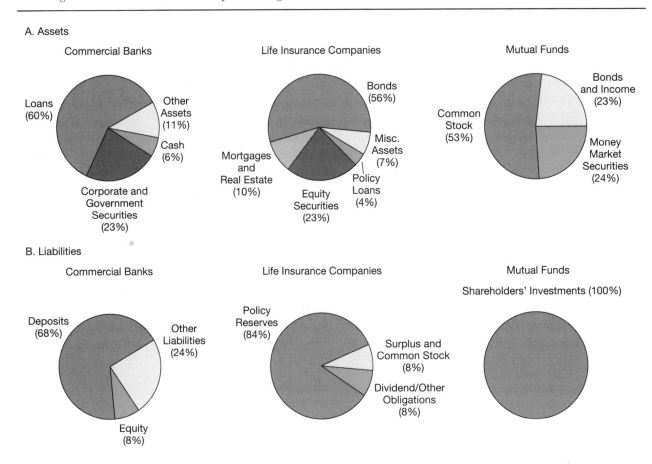

Source: Prepared by the authors with data from *Mutual Fund Fact Book,* 38th ed. (Washington, D.C.: Investment Company Institute, 1998); *Life Insurance Fact Book 1997* (Washington, D.C.: American Council of Life Insurance, 1998); *FDIC Statistics on Banking, Year-End 1997* (Washington, D.C.: Federal Deposit Insurance Corporation, 1997).

The upper panel shows the types of assets held by the three largest types of financial institutions: banks, investment companies (mutual funds), and life insurance companies as of year-end 1997. An average of 60 percent of commercial bank assets are loans to individuals and businesses and other financial institutions. Of the three institutions, banks alone hold a significant quantity of cash, averaging 6 percent of assets, since they need cash for federal reserve requirements and for depositor withdrawals. Insurance companies also make loans included in mortgages and real estate, but 56 percent of their assets are invested in corporate bonds and 23 percent in equity securities. In contrast, banks are not permitted to invest in equity securities and are permitted only limited investments in high-grade corporate bonds. The assets of the mutual fund industry at the end of 1997 included 53 percent in common stock, 23 percent in bond and other types of income-producing securities, and 24 percent in money market (short-term, liquid) securities.

Differences are also evident in the liability structures of the three types of institutions, shown in the lower panel of Figure 1.1. Deposits constitute a majority of the funds of commercial banks. In contrast, obligations to policyholders are the major liabilities of life insurers. Mutual funds are quite different, because they issue virtually no debt obligations and derive all their funds from shareholders' investments. The shareholders of banks and insurers (equity), in contrast, provide only small proportions of their funds. Commercial banks and life insurance companies have high financial leverage, with banks having an equity-to-assets ratio of about 8 percent and 8 percent for life insurance companies, at the end of 1997.

THE ECONOMIC FUNCTIONS OF FINANCIAL INSTITUTIONS

The previous section gave a brief overview of the major types of financial institutions. To understand why financial institutions exist and the economic services that they provide, it is important to understand the different ways in which funds are transferred within an economy between businesses, government, and households (economic entities) that need to borrow funds (borrowers) and those that have surplus funds to lend (investors).

In a very simple economy without financial institutions, transactions between different borrowers and lenders are difficult to arrange. Borrowers and savers incur significant search and information costs trying to find each other. Transactions between borrowers and savers may also be limited, because few financial contracts involve only two parties. Similarly, risks are great, since individual entities have little or no knowledge of each other and little ability to monitor each other's actions. Also, the transactions costs may be so high that small entities may be unwilling to supply funds. Investors also have little ability to diversify their risk, due to the high cost of many financial contracts. The lower panel of Figure 1.2 shows such direct transactions between lenders and borrowers.

Financial institutions help to reduce transactions, search, monitoring, and information costs. They provide risk management services and allow investors to diversify their risk and hold portfolios of financial assets by creating ways of indirect financing. Financial institutions also play important roles in an efficient payment system between entities and in managing pure risk (insurance).

The upper panel of Figure 1 shows the role of financial institutions as intermediaries between borrowers and lenders. This is explained in more detail in the following section.

Financial Institutions and the Transfer of Funds

The term **primary securities** refers to direct financial claims against individuals, governments, and nonfinancial firms.[11] A simple economy without any financial institutions would accommodate only direct financial claims or financial contracts. In effect, a borrower gives an investor a financial contract or direct financial claim or security that promises a stake in the borrower's company (i.e., shares of stock) or future payments returning the amount invested plus interest (i.e., a bond, or some other sort of IOU). These are examples of direct or primary securities.

As an economy develops, markets emerge for trading direct securities. Some function as auction markets, where trading is carried out in one physical location, as occurs on the New York Stock Exchange; others function as over-the-counter markets, where trading is carried out by distant contacts, perhaps over the phone and computer, as on the National Association of Security Dealers Automated Quotation (NASDAQ) system. Loans made directly with borrowers are another example of a primary or direct security, where a direct contract is made between a borrower and a bank or other individual lender. Table 1.2 provides examples of primary securities in the first column. The financial assets owned by banks, insurance companies, and mutual funds, such as loans, bonds, and common stock, are all direct securities, where the lenders give funds to the borrowers, and the lenders receive financial contracts guaranteeing repayment of funds plus interest or shares of ownership in the borrower companies. Again, this type of direct financing is shown in the lower panel of Figure 1.2. Investors lend funds in return for a direct or primary security.

Secondary securities, in contrast, are financial liabilities of financial institutions—that is, claims against financial institutions. In Table 1.2, financial institutions' liabilities—deposits, policyholder reserve obligations, and mutual fund shares—are secondary securities or claims against financial institutions. In effect, financial institutions created secondary securities that offer advantages over primary securities or direct financial claims. The top panel of Figure 1.2 shows this type of indirect financing.

Table 1.2 ✦ **EXAMPLES OF PRIMARY AND SECONDARY SECURITIES**

Primary Securities	Secondary Securities
Commercial loans	Savings deposits
Mortgage loans	Transaction deposits
Consumer loans	Certificates of deposit
Government bonds	Insurance policyholders reserves
Corporate bonds	Mutual fund shares
Corporate common stock	Pension fund reserves

---

[11]Unfortunately, like most fields, finance sometimes uses confusing terminology. Readers should carefully avoid confusing the use of the words *primary* and *secondary* in this discussion with their use in other contexts. For example, students who have previously studied corporate finance or investments may have encountered the terms *primary* and *secondary markets*; primary markets are those for originally issued securities, and secondary markets handle resales of securities. In the context of this chapter, *primary* and *secondary* distinguish between *issuers* of securities and not between changes in securities ownership.

FIGURE 1.2 ◆ INTERMEDIATION AND DIRECT FINANCIAL INVESTMENT

Direct financial investment occurs when lenders supply funds to ultimate borrowers, with the assistance of brokers or investment bankers. Indirect financial investment supplies funds to financial institutions, which issue secondary securities in return. Intermediation occurs when institutions transform secondary securities into primary securities through their own direct investments.

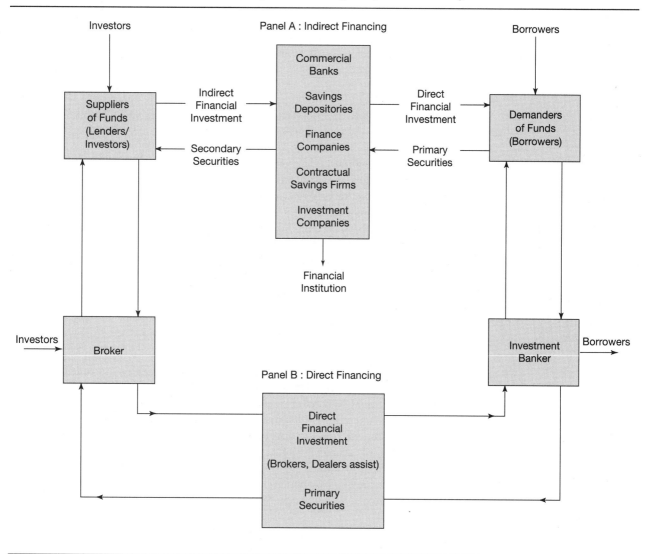

With indirect financing, an investor with excess funds purchases a secondary security, such as a life insurance policy or a savings account, allowing the financial institution to determine the ultimate recipient of the funds. For instance, a life insurer may invest the premium payments of its policyholders in corporate bonds, or a CU may invest the savings of some of its members in home-improvement loans to other members. The policyholder or the saver engages in **indirect financial investment,** receiving a claim on the financial institution, while the institution holds a direct claim on the corporation or the homeowner. The institution has thus transformed a secondary security into a primary security. This transformation is called **intermediation.**

Not all funds transfers involving financial institutions occur through intermediation. Sometimes an institution arranges or assists in the transfer of funds between parties without issuing its own financial liabilities in the process. When a financial institution acts in this limited capacity, it becomes a broker or a dealer. Dealers differ from brokers by actually owning and making a market for different types of securities. The role of brokers and dealers is illustrated in the lower portion of Figure 1.2. As noted earlier, securities brokers and investment bankers seldom issue secondary securities themselves but rather assist in transfers of funds from lenders to borrowers. Many financial institutions act as both intermediaries and brokers and dealers from time to time.

WHY INTERMEDIARIES? REDUCED TRANSACTIONS AND INFORMATION COSTS

In creating indirect investment possibilities through intermediation, and in acting as brokers and dealers, financial institutions provide important benefits that are unavailable with direct investment. Most of these benefits can be categorized as reductions in the costs of transactions, information, or both.[12] Because the return expected from a financial asset is reduced by the costs of acquiring the asset, an institution can create demand for its services if its costs are less than those incurred through direct financial investment. Conversely, institutions issuing financial liabilities want to minimize their transactions costs. Most costs reduced by intermediation or brokerage fall into five major categories. These categories or benefits of financial intermediation are discussed in greater deal in the following sections.

Search Costs

Financial institutions provide ways to identify entities with excess funds and those needing funds, eliminating the need for individual lenders and borrowers to find one another. Investment bankers of securities firms, for instance, maintain lists of institutional investors and other wealthy individual investors who would like to invest in new firms that can provide good returns on their money. In this sense, investment bankers facilitate direct financial investment. Banks attract deposits from small investors as secondary securities guaranteeing given interest rate returns; they transform these deposits into loans, helping corporations to gather funds indirectly from numerous small investors. In turn, borrowers know that banks reduce their search costs for funds.

Portfolio Selection Costs

Investors may wish to invest in financial assets in different dollar amounts, with different maturities, or with different risk levels from the financial liabilities borrowers wish to issue. Financial institutions issue secondary securities in forms attractive to lenders, and then repackage the funds they obtain in forms attractive to borrowers. Again, a good illustration is a bank, which gathers small deposits and packages them

---

[12]Parts of the following discussion are based on the analyses of Bentson and Smith, 1976; Diamond, 1984; Berlin, 1987; Williamson, 1987; Haubrich, 1989; Gorton and Pennacchi, 1990; O'Hara, 1990; and Seward, 1990.

into larger loans for individual borrowers. A mutual fund allows small investors to invest in a diversified portfolio, reducing the risk that they would incur if they held their savings only in one security. Mutual funds also provide diversification at much lower selection or transactions costs than the investors would incur if they picked and paid brokerage costs to create individual securities portfolios.

Monitoring Costs

When two parties agree to a transfer of funds, whether through direct or indirect investment, the arrangement is usually formalized by a **financial contract.** A typical contract specifies the terms of a funds transfer—for example, its maturity and the interest rate at which it will occur. The contract also outlines provisions to protect both borrower and lender, such as the lender's recourse in case the borrower absconds with the funds.

Finance theorists have noted that financial contracts are often characterized by **asymmetric information;** that is, the contracting parties are not equally and fully informed about each other. In particular, borrowers often know more about their own financial situations and their abilities to honor contracts than do lenders. Information asymmetry in turn gives rise to **monitoring costs**—ongoing expenses incurred by investors to gather information so they can intervene if borrowers' financial situations change.

Financial institutions provide economies of scale in monitoring by employing appraisers, financial analysts, and other specialists to investigate large numbers of claims on a full-time basis. For this reason, many lenders can reduce their monitoring costs by investing through financial intermediaries instead of purchasing primary securities. In recent years, some experts have concluded that the reduction of monitoring costs is the most important reason for the existence of financial intermediaries.

Risk Management Costs

Many investors want to hold varied financial assets to reduce the risk inherent in a single claim against a party who may fail to meet its obligations. The investor can avoid that risk by holding shares in a mutual fund, that is, in secondary securities of a financial institution that holds a diversified portfolio. Although the investor must still monitor the financial institution, its diversified portfolio reduces the probability that the institution will suffer serious setbacks, since all its investments probably will not simultaneously fail. Some secondary securities, such as bank deposits, offer low risk exposure, because they are insured against institutional failure.

Other specialized financial institutions also take on risk management services. Insurance companies pool premiums from thousands of individuals and businesses as secondary securities (policyholder reserves), which they invest in securities that provide income and capital gains to fund payouts to individuals and businesses in the event of property damage, theft, loss of life, or other contingencies. In this way, insurance companies reduce risk for individuals and businesses. By pooling premiums of large numbers of customers, insurance companies can provide risk management services at a much lower cost than if individuals and businesses had to save the funds themselves to meet such possible contingencies. As another example of risk management, banks provide letters of credit that guarantee payment by other parties. This activity facilitates trade transactions between different parties (such as importing and exporting), since the risk associated with the default of either party is eliminated.

Similarly, large investment banks and commercial banks provide instruments that can protect businesses and other financial institutions against interest rate and foreign exchange risk. The cash flows of these derivatives—swaps, forward contracts, caps and floors, as explained in a later chapter—are based on future price movements of underlying securities.

Maturity Intermediation and Liquidity

Often borrowers want to repay funds over long time horizons. An example is a business buying plant and equipment intended to generate returns for many years, from which the business will pay off debt incurred to purchase the assets. However, investors (particularly, small savers) may want or need their money back quickly and not be willing to lend funds for lengthy periods. Banks accept small amounts from numerous small investors as deposits (secondary securities) and transform them into longer-term loans (primary securities), in the process providing maturity intermediation services. Short-term funds are transferred into longer-term loans.

Depository institutions also provide liquidity to small investors, who can write checks or withdraw funds from deposit accounts at any time at little more than the cost of writing a check. If small investors had invested in long-term bonds, instead, when they needed liquidity, they would have to sell the bonds, incurring losses if rates had risen over the period, as well as brokerage fees. Financial institutions, particularly banks, are important in the flow of savings to productive investments by businesses, increasing the wealth of an economy. They also provide important support for an efficient payment system. Bank customers can write checks backed by the bank and do not have to carry around cash. Bank customers can also simply use a credit card or have funds electronically wired. These services increase the liquidity of the economy, leaving greater funds available for investment in productive assets.

Other specialized financial institutions including private pensions, mutual funds, and insurance companies, also carry out maturity intermediation services. They allow small investors to save for long-term goals, such as retirement, by investing savings in diversified portfolios. Financial institutions also provide long-term financial planning advice, reducing planning and search costs by investors. With demographic data indicating a rising average age for the U.S. population and those of many other countries as the result of the baby boom after World War II, this role has become increasingly important, generating an increasing share of revenues for financial institutions. Hence, mutual funds and other investment companies have boomed.

THE CHANGING ROLE OF FINANCIAL INSTITUTIONS IN THE TECHNOLOGICAL AGE

With the development of technology and the Internet, information has become more accessible to firms and individuals, reducing the role of financial intermediaries as monitors and information providers. For instance, technology allows large, creditworthy corporations to issue commercial paper and bonds around the world. As pointed out by Roy Smith in *Global Bankers:*

> Technology has made several things possible in international financial markets that would not have been otherwise: the ability to settle and deliver large numbers of transactions involving different instruments, currencies, and locations; the ability to keep track of more numerous and more complex trading

positions than anyone ever imagined only a few years ago . . . and the ability to transmit large volumes of market and competitive data internationally at comparatively low cost. (Smith, 1990, p. 6)

With technology, loans have been pooled and packaged into securities sold to investors. The remarkable boom in mortgage and credit card securities has transformed depository institutions and finance companies into more transaction-oriented institutions, reducing their monitoring (relationship-oriented) function. Technology also helps investors to find information about companies by accessing their Web pages. Internet services of discount brokers allow these securities firms to provide low-cost trading mechanisms, since they generally provide little or no investment advice, to support buying and selling securities. The role of financial intermediaries in having an information monopoly no longer exists. Firms with rich internal information sources such as AT&T and Sears have created their own credit cards using their immense collections of customer data. Later, these credit card divisions were sold to financial institutions. Software companies like Microsoft and Intuit are also developing new services that provide direct market access for financial transactions, such as bill paying, reducing the need for financial intermediaries for such transactions.[13]

Technology is reducing the role of financial intermediaries in the payments mechanism, as well. MasterCard, for instance, has invested millions in the development of an electronic (E-cash) system known as Mondex. The system's smart cards have tiny microchips embedded that store personalized electronic data that will allow consumers remote access to their funds at any time, anywhere. Hence, as pointed out by David Shaw, an investment banker, increasingly new technology implies greater change, and "The whole financial industry will likely be turned upside down, with shrinkage in some areas and perhaps some outright failures among those firms that are unable to use technology effectively."[14]

Other roles of financial institutions have taken on growing importance, however. With changing demographics and baby boomers approaching retirement, financial institutions' role in maturity intermediation has increased. Mutual funds have grown at a staggering rate as investors save for retirement. Financial institutions have taken advantage of technological advances to create information data bases that allow them to enhance financial planning services for customers and to develop new products to help customers save for retirement or meet other needs. Financial management needs for firms, such as working capital management, are also being offered by banks and securities firms through the benefits of technology. Banks and securities firms provide services that help businesses speed up cash collections and manage cash disbursements. They also provide automated clearinghouse (ACH) services that allow direct disbursement of payments to the accounts of employees within minutes, saving companies mailing and other accounting and transactions costs.

Financial institutions have entered new advisory roles, providing help and advice to small and medium-sized businesses for fee income. Many banks and securities firms advertise their services as small business partners. PC banking (allowing customers to initiate wire transfers of funds, move funds to different accounts, and

---

[13]Joshua Cooper Ramo, "The Big Bank Theory and What It Says about the Future of Money," *Time*, April 27, 1998, pp. 47–57. For an excellent case dealing with the entry of nonfinancial firms with informational advantages into the credit card industry, see Case 5, "Discover Card," in Crawford and Sihler, 1994.

[14]Ramo, "Big Bank Theory."

pay bills electronically) have gained popularity. Financial institutions have improved risk management services for business customers, as discussed in the previous discussion. The nature of financial institutions, the economic services they provide, and management techniques to meet new challenges and opportunities are constantly evolving. Technology provides opportunities for financial institutions to develop new, innovative products, and it also sharpens competition from the direct markets and nonfinancial firms.

New Risks with Technology

Expanding use of technology by financial institutions has increased the risks associated with technological failures. Technology can provide potential computer nightmares, such as the widely touted year 2000 problem, due to some computer systems' inability or recognize dates after 1999. Given the very technical nature of bank operations clearing millions of checks a day in which computers recognize a date, this problem is a significant one. This so-called "Y2K" problem is expected to cost Citicorp alone $600 million. Spreading use of electronic payment systems also brings a danger of illegal use, fraud, overdrafts, or other errors. Regulators now require banks to set up risk management systems for electronic fund transfers and disaster management plans in the event of technological breakdowns. Access to accounts through home banking services on the Internet also entails new opportunities for fraud and embezzlement.[15]

SOCIETAL CONCERNS WITH CHANGE AND BANKING FOR THE UNBANKED

In the midst of the dramatic changes for financial institutions and the bewildering array of new services for millions of customers, millions of poor citizens voice additional concerns. Those who cannot meet minimum bank balances or fee requirements are, in essence, unbanked. With banks growing in size, concern has increased that the unbanked will be ignored. Recent legislation has asked banks to provide services for the unbanked, with new policies for direct deposits of U.S. government checks. This system will save millions of dollars in government mailing costs and prevent thefts of checks, but it provides a significant, unreimbursed cost for financial institutions that must provide free banking services.

One type of financial institution that is often overlooked, pawnshops, have doubled since the mid-1980s, extending more than $9 billion in credit each year. Pawnshops cash checks for fees and offer cash loans for collateral at rates ranging from 24 percent to 240 percent. Pawnshops cater to poor customers not served by other financial institutions. Because of the great risk of default for these transactions, charges are very high to customers with little wealth; many who fail to repay their loans see their collateral sold.[16]

---

[15]"Are Mega Banks—Once Unimaginable, Now Inevitable—Better . . . for Customers, the Nation's Economy, or Even for Banks?" *Business Week*, April 27, 1998, pp. 32–37. For a discussion of the risk of electronic fund transfer overdrafts, see Koch (1995), pp. 465–466.

[16]Ramo, "Big Bank Theory." For a more detailed discussion of pawn shops, see John P. Caskey, *Fringe Banking: Check-Cashing Outlets, Pawnshops, and the Poor* New York: Russell Sage Foundation, 1994), pp. xiv, 165.

As part of banks' special charter to serve their communities, the Community Reinvestment Act requires them to provide some low-income financing. Regulators can reject merger and branch applications or require banks to increase low-income lending before applications will be approved. Banks have often argued that other types of financial institutions, such as finance companies and credit unions, should have similar requirements.

SUMMARY

Financial institutions are a unique set of business firms whose assets and liabilities, regulatory restrictions, and economic functions establish them as an important subject of study. Interest in techniques for financial management of these institutions has grown with the vast quantity of assets they control, changes introduced by deregulation in the 1970s and 1980s, and the challenges posed by globalization and the information technologies of the 1990s.

Firms classified as financial institutions hold portfolios primarily composed of financial assets, in contrast to the real asset holdings of nonfinancial firms. Institutions are designed to offer intermediary or brokerage services to assist savers in allocating their funds. The services provided by financial institutions reduce transactions and information costs, including search, portfolio selection, monitoring, risk management, and liquidity and maturity intermediation costs to investors. With dramatic changes in information technology, search, information, and monitoring costs have fallen, reducing the monopoly that financial institutions previously held in these areas. These changes have caused some disintermediation (reduction in the use of financial institutions) for these services and increased the number of direct market relationships between many borrowers and lenders. Other roles have increased, however, including risk management for corporate customers and maturity intermediation for consumers, especially through retirement and financial planning. The transaction role of financial institutions has increased with technology, allowing loans to be packaged and traded as securities. Information technology helps financial institutions to assess customer needs and develop and offer a wider array of financial services to satisfy these needs.

Plan of the Book

Part One of the book examines the environment of financial management of financial institutions. Topics include important concepts, regulations, and trends that a financial institution manager needs to recognize and cope with in the changing environment of the 21st century. Chapter 2 provides an overview of asset/liability management. Chapter 3 profiles the regulatory environment, with an appendix on the operations of the Federal Reserve System and international policy coordination. Chapter 4 provides background on consolidation trends, different types of ownership, moral hazard issues, and organization formats for U.S. financial institutions.

Part Two provides an understanding of the financial statements of depository institutions, which can be applied to other types of financial institutions, as well. This section of the book also presents trends and particular characteristics of the three different types of depository institutions. Capital requirements and management techniques are discussed, as well as noninterest management, which is gaining importance for depository institutions with declining profits from traditional lending activities. Chapter 5 presents an overview of bank financial statements and trends, followed by performance and risk analysis in Chapter 6. Chapter 7 discusses credit unions and thrifts, reviewing current issues that managers of these institutions face. Chapter 8 discusses capital regulations and management, and Chapter 9 covers management of noninterest revenue, and securitization risk management.

Part Three discusses other nondepository financial institutions and their trends and particular management problems. Chapter 10 examines insurance companies. Chapter 11 overviews the operations of investment banks and retail security firms and the particular ethical issues that they face. Chapter 12 discusses the management of mutual funds and pension funds, and Chapter 13 addresses finance companies, diversified financial firms, and merger considerations.

Part Four is concerned with the interest rate environment in which financial institutions operate. It deals with how interest rates are determined in the markets, how they affect the risks to which an institution is exposed, and how to manage those risks. This section of the book also discusses exchange rate risk. Chapter 14 discusses how rates are calculated and presents theories and forecasting techniques for interest rates and exchange rates. Chapter 15 presents theories of the term structure of interest rates and management applications. Chapter 16 describes different types of interest rate risk, overall measures of interest rate risk, and duration as an immunization technique.

Part Five presents techniques used to reduce or hedge interest rate risk using derivatives. It also covers new concepts for the overall risk management of financial institutions. Chapter 17 discusses the use of futures to hedge interest rate and exchange rate risk. Chapter 18 presents hedging techniques with index futures, options, swaps, and other derivatives.

Part Six presents special asset/liability management problems for depository institutions, including liquidity and securities portfolio management in Chapter 19; deposit and liability management in Chapter 20; commercial and international lending and consumer and mortgage lending in Chapter 21; and international issues in Chapter 22.

Discussion Questions

1. With what and how many financial institutions do you have relationships? What made you choose these particular financial institutions? Based on the changes mentioned for financial institutions from the 1930s to the 1990s, how have your relationships with institutions changed?

2. Find an article on the savings and loan crisis in 1988; the financial institution crisis in 1997 and 1998 in Japan, Indonesia, Korea, or Thailand; or another current crisis facing a financial institution. How does this incident highlight the increased globalization of financial markets and the importance of international policy coordination? How much did mismanagement by institutional managers contribute to the financial crisis? Do you think regulations could have prevented the crisis?

3. Explain why so many financial institution mergers occurred in the 1990s. Find an article on a recent merger, and report on the economic justifications cited. Why are consumers concerned about these mergers? Do you think a merger between different types of financial institutions, such as Citicorp and the Travelers Group, can work? Explain why or why not.

4. Give an example of a real physical asset and a financial asset that you use. How do they differ? What types of assets and liabilities do financial institutions have compared to most businesses? Why do nonfinancial companies have lower financial leverage than banks?

5. Give an example of different types of financial institutions including: depository institutions, finance companies, contractual intermediaries, investment companies, and securities firms. Discuss the types of assets and liabilities on the balance sheets of different institutions. Which institutions hold the most closely matched maturities of their assets and liabilities?

6. Why are insurance companies and pension funds called *contractual savings institutions?* Given the differences between the obligations of life insurers and pension funds and those of property/liability insurers, what types of investments would you expect each to hold? How do these institutions have a better maturity match of assets and liabilities than depository institutions?

7. What is the distinction between primary and secondary securities? If you want to own primary securities, what types of financial institutions should you contact? Contrast the concept of primary and secondary markets with that of primary and secondary securities.

8. How do services provided by securities firms differ from those offered by investment companies? Compare and contrast direct and indirect financial investment, and explain which industry is more closely associated with each type of investment.

9. Define *risk*. Why does owning financial assets involve risk? What types of risk do financial institutions face that nonfinancial firms do not?

10. Financial agreements typically require financial contracts characterized by information asymmetry. What is information asymmetry? How might an agreement such as an automobile or mortgage loan involve asymmetric information? How does asymmetric information affect the risk position of the investor (lender)?

11. Suppose you have a choice between buying corporate bonds or investing in a mutual fund. Explain how choosing the mutual fund would affect your liquidity and portfolio selection costs. Look in *The Wall Street Journal* for an advertisement for a mutual fund company. What advantages does the mutual fund stress in its advertisement?

12. Suppose you inherit $75,000. If you choose not to invest through a financial intermediary, how will your monitoring and risk management costs be affected? Provide an example of each type of cost. What financial institutions would you choose to help you invest your funds?

13. How might the same institution act sometimes as a broker and other times as an intermediary? Give an example of this distinction for a financial institution that you use. What is the difference between the two functions?

14. Discuss changes in the roles of financial institutions during the 1990s compared to the past. How much is the current revolution in information technology have to do with this? What future changes are likely to occur?

15. Discuss the societal concerns with banking for the unbanked. What does the Community Reinvestment Act require of banks? What are pawn shops, and why have they grown?

Selected References

Benston, George J., and Clifford W. Smith, Jr. "A Transactions Cost Approach to the Theory of Financial Intermediation." *Journal of Finance* 31 (May 1976): 215–231.

Berlin, Mitchell. "Bank Loans and Marketable Securities: How Do Financial Contracts Control Borrowing Firms?" *Business Review,* Federal Reserve Bank of Philadelphia, July/August 1987: 9–18.

Bush, Vanessa, and Katherine Morrall. "The Law: The Business Reviews a New Script." *Savings Institutions* 110 (October 1989): 30–35.

Crawford, Richard D., and William W. Sihler. *Financial Service Organizations: Cases in Strategic Management.* New York: HarperCollins, 1994.

Diamond, Douglas W. "Financial Intermediation and Delegated Monitoring." *Review of Economic Studies* 51 (July 1984): 393–414.

Gorton, Gary, and George Pennacchi. "Financial Intermediaries and Liquidity Creation." *Journal of Finance* 45 (March 1990): 49–71.

Haubrich, Joseph G. "Financial Intermediation: Delegated Monitoring and Long-Term Relationships." *Journal of Banking and Finance* 13 (March 1989): 9–20.

Koch, Timothy W. *Bank Management,* 3rd ed. Fort Worth: The Dryden Press, 1995.

O'Hara, Maureen. "Financial Contracts and International Lending." *Journal of Banking and Finance* 14 (1990): 11–31.

Smith, Roy C. *The Global Bankers.* New York: Truman Talley Books/Plume, 1990.

Williamson, Stephen D. "Recent Developments in Modeling Financial Intermediation." *Quarterly Review,* Federal Reserve Bank of Minneapolis (Summer 1987): 19–29.

Chapter 1 Internet Exercise

What Happened to My Bank?

The wave of bank mergers has led to some confusing name changes. Would you like to find out what happened to a local bank? The Board of Governors of the Federal Reserve System have made available a National Information Center (NIC) that provides comprehensive information on banks and other institutions for which the Federal Reserve has a supervisory, regulatory, or research interest, including both domestic and foreign banking organizations operating in the United States. The NIC summarizes historical information about the organizational structures of financial institutions and provides financial information for some of them for selected time periods.

To find out what happened to your bank, complete the following steps:

1. Go to: http://www.ffiec.gov/nic/default.HTM

2. Under Acquisition/Institution History, click on "What Happened to an Institution?"

3. Enter the institution's name and click "Submit." (If the institution is not found, select the option on the search page for a keyword in the name of the bank to be found "Anywhere in Name.")

You can look up a particular bank or all of the banks in your state that have been involved in merger activity.

Other useful sites for financial institution data:

Federal Financial Institutions Examination Council
http://www.ffiec.gov

Board of Governors of the Federal Reserve System
http://www.bog.frb.fed.us/

Office of the Comptroller of the Currency
http://www.occ.treas.gov/

Office of Thrift Supervision
http://www.ots.treas.gov

National Credit Union Association
http://www.ncua.gov/data/cudata.html

The Environment of Asset/Liability Management

I

■ ASSET/LIABILITY MANAGEMENT: WHAT AND WHY?

■ REGULATION, TECHNOLOGY, AND FINANCIAL INNOVATION
THE FEDERAL RESERVE SYSTEM AND INTERNATIONAL POLICY COORDINATION
BACKGROUND ISSUES

"Aggressive marketing, savvy use of technology, and cross-selling of financial services will be the key to making trillion-dollar banks work."

Hugh McColl, CEO of NationsBank
Quoted in *Business Week*, April 27, 1998, p. 34.

"The profitability of the bank—or the insurance company, or the securities house—is still determined in large part by its ability to make a gap of satisfactory size between the cost of its liabilities and the price of its assets. But that gap is now created by the exploitation of option mispricings, not by what we have always considered banking activities. And to play to that game requires great size."

Martin Mayer, Bank Analyst
Quoted in *Barron's*, April 20, 1998, p. 22.

2

ASSET/LIABILITY MANAGEMENT: WHAT AND WHY?

As noted in the beginning quotes, the operations of financial institutions have changed greatly, with technology and marketing playing much greater roles than in the past. In order to spread the cost of technology over progressively larger groups of customers, financial institutions have been merging at a rapid pace. Organizing and running a business whose primary function is reducing the transactions and information costs of others is itself a costly endeavor. By far the largest expenses of financial institutions are the interest costs resulting from their liabilities. They also face noninterest costs of intermediation and brokerage, such as the need to pay managers and other personnel and to maintain places of business. Like other firms, financial institutions can operate only if they can perform their functions as profitably as or more profitably than their competitors. Given the variety of financial institutions, single institutions often face substantial competition. Success therefore requires careful attention to the financial implications of intermediation and brokerage. With declining profits from traditional activities based on the spread between revenues from assets and the expenses from liabilities, financial institutions have entered new businesses to generate noninterest revenues.

Managing risk, or variability of earnings, is also a very important function. With high financial leverage, financial institutions are subject to high interest expenses that increase the volatility of their earnings. Hence, managing risk is crucial to an institution's viability. This short chapter provides a brief overview of the nature of financial institutions' profits and a discussion of conflicts in setting priorities between different agents, stockholders, regulators, managers, and customers. These conflicts are discussed in greater detail in Chapter 4.

◆　◆　◆

MANAGING THE SPREAD

Because financial institutions interact in the financial markets by issuing financial liabilities and purchasing financial assets, one critical element of their management is managing the **spread**, the dollar difference between the interest earned on assets and the interest cost of liabilities. This spread, expressed as a percentage of total assets, is called the **net interest margin (NIM):**[1]

$$\text{NIM} = \frac{\text{Interest on assets} - \text{Interest cost of liabilities}}{\text{Total assets}} \tag{1.1}$$

A high NIM value may allow the institution to offset the noninterest costs of the intermediation and brokerage services it provides. Most institutions charge fees for these services, but unless the fees are competitive, investors may find more economical options such as switching to other institutions or engaging in direct investment. When institutions experience negative spreads for extended periods, and interest costs actually exceed interest earned on assets, few can make up the difference with other sources of income, unless they have made strategic moves into other types of businesses that provide other sources of noninterest revenues. Hence, many institutions in this situation fail as a result.

Given the importance of the NIM, the profits of many financial institutions change with changes in relative rates of return on assets and liabilities. Many depository institutions, for instance, must cope with faster changes in the rates on their liabilities than on their assets, resulting in a fall in their NIMs and, hence, profits when rates rise, and corresponding rises in profits when rates fall, as they did in the early 1990s.

MANAGING THE BURDEN

Increasing competition and growing overcapacity for financial service firms dramatically reduced net interest margins in the 1980s and 1990s. To widen diminished margins, financial institutions focused on reducing other operating costs (noninterest expenses) and increasing fee income and other sources of revenue (noninterest revenues). The difference between noninterest expenses and noninterest revenues is commonly referred to as a financial institution's *burden*, often stated as a percentage of total assets. During the late 1980s and early 1990s, banks went through significant restructuring, making extensive efforts to change their structures to improve efficiency and profitability. Such an initiative can include massive layoffs to reduce costs, with potentially very painful results. Restructuring also often involves reorganizing operations to work more efficiently than before or replacing workers with technology that provides economies of scale.

$$\text{Burden (\%)} = \frac{\text{Noninterest expenses} - \text{Noninterest revenues}}{\text{Total assets}} \tag{1.2}$$

---

[1]Some sources, including banking industry publications, use earning assets in the denominator of the NIM equation. Earning assets are total assets minus those, such as buildings and equipment, on which no explicit return is generated. For simplicity, we use total assets in the denominator, since the majority of bank assets are earning assets. Definitions of financial ratios commonly vary among users.

Examples of mergers in similar markets followed by massive layoffs and cost-cutting efforts to reduce duplication are the merger between Chemical Bank and Manufacturers Hanover in 1991, and the later merger between Chemical Bank and Chase Manhattan in 1995. By getting rid of redundant branches and streamlining operations, banks attempt to lower operating expenses relative to assets, increasing overall operating efficiency. This streamlining can also be passed on to customers in terms of lower fees, since noninterest expenses that must be covered are reduced. Also, services may be carried on more efficiently, such as with the use of new technology.

Banks incur costs in the process, however. In particular, they must contend with negative public perceptions of massive layoffs and hundreds of employees losing their positions.

Financial services firms have also taken on new technology to boost operating efficiency and to develop new products as additional sources of noninterest revenue. Consequently, profits for financial services firms improved immensely in the 1990s, as they reduced their dependence on traditional net interest margins by generating noninterest revenues through product diversification. In the late 1990s, such reengineering, new sources of noninterest revenue, and a booming economy propelled bank profits to record levels. Many banks began rehiring, looking for technologically literate, flexible employees with excellent interpersonal skills to operate in the newly competitive, constantly changing environment and to handle many nontraditional products and services.

ASSET/LIABILITY MANAGEMENT DEFINED

As they manage the size of and institution's NIM, staff members must manage its risk. Both aspects of the NIM must be considered to achieve successful financial performance. **Asset/liability management** is the management of the net interest margin to ensure that its level and riskiness are compatible with the risk/return objectives of the institution.[2]

Asset/liability management is more than effective control of individual asset and liability categories. It is an integrated approach to financial management, requiring simultaneous decisions about the types and amounts of financial assets and liabilities the institution holds, that is, its asset/liability mix and volume. In addition, asset/liability management requires an understanding of a broad range of financial markets in which institutions operate. Among the most significant financial market issues are how interest rates are determined, why they change over time, and what impact those changes have on the NIM and the value of an institution's assets and liabilities. Asset/liability management entails understanding the noninterest revenue and expense implications of an institution's assets and liabilities, as well, along with efforts to limit the volatility of earnings.

---

[2]Some authors have defined asset/liability management as the attempt to *stabilize* net interest margin with no expected variation—that is, as the attempt to minimize risk. See O'Brian, Sollenberger, and Olson, 1982. As Deshmukh, Greenbaum, and Kanatas (1983) noted, however, such an objective is appropriate only for institutions choosing to perform brokerage, rather than intermediation, functions. The intermediation function, by definition, implies that the institution assumes some risk.

ASSET/LIABILITY MANAGEMENT: WHO SETS OBJECTIVES?

Because asset/liability management involves managing the institution's NIM in accordance with its objectives, managers require a clear understanding of those objectives and the responsibility for setting them. Identification of objectives is somewhat more complex for financial institutions than for other businesses. To understand this complexity, begin by considering a brief outline of theories on the setting of managerial objectives. These theories have arisen from the study of financial management of nonfinancial firms.

A Normative Approach

Observers often argue that owners should set objectives for nonfinancial firms operating in competitive product markets. Owners, unlike creditors, provide the initial funds to operate the business, so they are entitled to any benefits resulting from superior operations.

This **classical theory** directs managers to ignore their personal risk/return preferences in making the firm's investment decisions. Instead, they should concentrate on maximizing expected benefits to owners, consistent with the risk that owners are willing to bear. Managers who allow nonowner-determined objectives to influence their decisions will presumably be removed by unhappy owners. Also, financing decisions, such as whether or not to borrow, are regarded as much less important than decisions involving investments in real assets.

The classical theory of the firm focuses on how managers *should* act, and thus it is considered a **normative theory** of decision making.[3] This approach states a clear criterion for managerial decision making: If a decision provides net benefits to owners, it should be made; otherwise, it should not. The classical theory leaves no doubt that the institution's owners are the ones to set objectives for asset/liability management.

A Positive Approach

Positive theories of managerial behavior focus on explaining how decisions *are* made by business managers rather than on prescribing how they *should* be made. When owners also manage their firms, the way managers should behave with respect to owners matches the way they do behave. But if owners and managers are different people, managers' risk/return preferences may differ from those of owners. Under these circumstances, what do managers do? Positive theories of managerial objectives attempt to explain the behavior of managers arising from the separation of ownership and control.

Agency theory, a positive view of managerial decision making, suggests that managers are no different from other individuals: If left unmonitored, they will pursue their personal risk/return preferences. Thus, owners may incur costs in making sure that *their* preferences are recognized. Agency theory examines the relationships between nonowner-managers (**agents**) and owners (**principals**) and

---

[3]The classical theory of managerial objectives is developed in Fisher, 1930. Extensions of Fisher's work are provided in Hirschleifer, 1958 and in Hirschleifer, 1965.

the contracts arising as a result. (These agent/principal agreements are yet another form of financial contracting, leading to associated monitoring costs.) At one extreme, an agent/principal contract could be structured so that every action of the agent would be prescribed and closely monitored, leaving the manager no discretion. Such a contract would be very costly for the principal to enforce. At the other extreme, the owner could take a "hands off" approach, leaving all matters to the manager's judgment. Although monitoring costs would be nil under such a contract, the potential losses to owners could be considerable if managers exclusively pursued their own interests. Normally, therefore, terms of agent/principal contracts fall between these extremes. Any reductions in benefits to owners stemming from contracts governing the separation of ownership and control are known as **agency costs**.[4]

In practice, agency costs can take many different forms, such as legal expenses to draw up contracts that limit managers' salaries and expense accounts and the resources managers spend on annual reports convincing owners that decisions consider their wishes; both are examples of explicit monitoring costs. Agency costs arising from managers' unmonitored actions may be more difficult to measure. One example is the potential benefits lost when a manager lends to a friend's business at a rate lower than might be strictly justified by the risk of the loan.

A firm may incur a special type of agency cost when managers are not closely monitored; this **managerial expense preference** is the tendency for some managers to enhance the benefits they receive from their institutions by hiring larger staffs than necessary, furnishing offices lavishly, or enjoying large travel and expense accounts.[5] Financial institutions face even greater chances than nonfinancial firms for potential abuse by managers and other employees in the form of fraud and embezzlement. All types of agency costs reduce owners' welfare and would not be incurred if owners managed their companies. Examples of expense preference behavior are widespread. In particular, managers of a number of savings and loans in the 1980s made purchases that approached looting their institutions. David Paul, the CEO of Centrust Savings in Miami, Florida, for instance, bought expensive, rare art worth $29 million with bank funds, also spending $1.4 million for a corporate jet, $7 million for a yacht, $43,000 for limousines, while paying himself $15 million a year in salary and bonuses.

Many experts argue that the agency relationship is so important today that a discussion of managerial objectives is realistic only if it includes agent/principal contracts. Thus, attention must focus on ways to minimize agency costs. Under this positive theory, managers make decisions according to criteria based on whether they receive net benefits from the proposed actions. If they do, they will undertake the actions; otherwise, they will not. Owners must therefore structure contracts that align managers' rewards with their own to keep their costs lower than the costs they would incur by letting managers operate unchecked. Agency theory implies that managers set asset/liability objectives and that owners protect their interests by setting appropriate constraints.

---

[4]Formal development of agency theory is attributed to Jensen and Meckling, 1976. Jensen and Meckling, however, were not the first to recognize potential inadequacies in the classical theory of firm behavior when owners and managers are different people.

[5]The theory of managerial expense preference was developed by Williamson, 1963.

MANAGERIAL OBJECTIVES IN FINANCIAL INSTITUTIONS

Although the classical theory has been applied to managerial decision making in financial institutions, one can argue that it is inadequate on both theoretical and empirical grounds.[6]

Customer Needs Affect Objectives

Because financial institutions provide liquidity to customers when issuing secondary securities such as demand deposits, the problems of financial institutions differ from those of nonfinancial firms, which face no need to honor financial liabilities on demand. Therefore, the need to provide customers with the benefits of intermediation must be considered in establishing managerial objectives for financial institutions. In addition, asset and liability decisions must be made simultaneously in financial institutions, but the classical theory of nonfinancial firms does not assume joint consideration of investment and financing decisions.[7]

Ownership Structure Affects Objectives

The ownership structures of many financial institutions also differ from those of nonfinancial firms. Instead of being owned by stockholders (people who have risked funds to start a business and who are entitled to residual profits that the firm generates), many financial institutions are mutually owned. The **mutual form of organization** is particularly prevalent among insurance companies, savings banks, and S&Ls, although many have converted in recent years to stockholder-owned organizations.

The implications of mutual ownership are explored in detail in a later chapter, but for now it is enough to recognize that so-called *owners* of mutual institutions are not owners in the classical sense, because they are not entitled to personal claims on residual profits. Therefore, the classical theory—based on the idea that those who risk funds are entitled to establish the objectives of the enterprise—may not be directly relevant to mutual organizations.

Some Evidence from Research

Empirical evidence for stockholder-owned institutions suggests that unmonitored managers *do* act to maximize their own rather than owners' welfare, whether or not they *should* do so.[8] Thus, agency costs arise. Researchers have noted, however, that built-in "brakes" on management behavior in stockholder-owned firms may help to reduce these costs. These limitations arise both from potential monitoring actions by current stockholders themselves and from the discipline imposed on managers by external financial market participants. For example, contracts may specify that managers will be compensated in part through stock options, thus ensuring at least partial compatibility between their interests and those of current owners. Further, stockholders exercise voting control, so they can oust managers for overly self-interested

---

[6]An example is Towey, 1974.
[7]See Sealey, 1983.
[8]See Edwards, 1977; Hannan and Mavinga, 1980; Gorton and Rosen, 1995.

decisions. Finally, stockholder-owned firms operate within a **market for corporate control;** outsiders who believe that an institution is not well-served by current management may bid for the firm's stock and hire new managers to control the assets.[9]

Experts have noted that mutual firms lack some of these mechanisms to reduce agency costs, however. For example, no market for corporate control influences actions of a mutual firm, nor can managers' compensation contracts be structured to include stock options. Thus, some researchers have argued that managers' tendencies to pursue their own goals are even stronger in mutually owned firms than in stockholder-owned firms. Recent empirical evidence on this question gives mixed results.[10]

Regulation Affects Objectives

Furthermore, even if owners were to manage their own financial institutions, they would experience agency relationships. These situations would arise from another agent/principal relationship between financial institutions and government representatives. This agency relationship is quite strong for some financial firms, such as commercial banks, which for many years have been expected to assist in carrying out the federal government's fiscal and monetary policies.

Virtually all financial institutions encounter agency relationships with government, because most are involved in carrying out public policies such as the distribution of credit to disadvantaged borrowers. Also, because governments provide insurance for many financial institutions, they regularly employ examiners to monitor activities and ensure that managerial decisions do not unduly strain government insurance funds. In some instances, government agencies may actually remove managers from their positions for improper performance of their roles.[11] Although the S&L crisis of the 1980s revealed inadequacies in the financial contracts between regulators and some thrift managers, the agent/principal relationship between regulators and managers will continue. For example, some observers argued in the early 1990s that bank managers were too sensitive to the views of regulators when they denied some loan applications that might have been approved in earlier periods. Critics accused banks of creating a credit crunch, worsening the effects of a weakened economy. Under such scrutiny, the managers of any financial institution probably will not, or cannot, pursue asset/liability management solely for the benefit of their institutions' owners.

---

[9]See Mester, 1989. Empirical research on large banks and thrifts suggests that rising management compensation corresponds to increased firm performance, and that managers' risk-taking behavior is related to the value of their holdings of the firm's stock, subject to the regulatory environment. See Cole and Mehran, 1991; Joskow and Rose, 1994; Hubbard and Palia, 1994; Yan, 1996; Mullins, 1991; Saunders, Strock, and Travlos, 1990; Allen and Cebenoyan, 1991; Cebenoyan et al., 1995; and Brewer and Saidenberg, 1996. Cebenoyan, et al., 1999 find lower risk taking for thrifts with higher institutional investor (outside) ownership as well.

[10]See Mester, 1993; Cebenoyan et al., 1993; Akella and Greenbaum, 1988; and Verbrugge and Jahera, 1981. Esty, 1997; Cordell, MacDonald, and Wohar, 1993; and Cole and Eisenbeis, 1996 also find greater evidence of risk-taking for stockholder-owned versus mutual thrifts in the 1980s. Early research is reviewed in Woerheide, 1984.

[11]For instance, regulators removed Charles Knapp as CEO of Financial Corporation of America, a giant California thrift, during its crisis in 1984, replacing him with their own selection, William Popejoy.

A BALANCING ACT

How, then, are asset/liability management objectives set? The perspective in this book reflects a model recognizing that owners, regulators, and managers themselves all influence managerial behavior. The model was developed specifically for banking firms, but its insight holds for other financial institutions, as well. As the author expresses it:

> The banking firm is a complex organization. As a financial intermediary, it performs both a brokerage and a risk transformation function. As a business, it must yield a return to its owners. As a regulated enterprise, it must operate within the bounds specified by the supervisory agencies.[12]

In most institutions, an individual manager or a management team is responsible for balancing the risk/return preferences of all parties. Most managers may personally wish to maximize the NIM because their salaries and expense accounts come from funds remaining after interest obligations are paid. However, they also recognize that institutions must provide liquidity to customers, a requirement that may prohibit a risky plan to maximize spread. Owners whose risk/return preferences differ from those of managers may further restrict managers' actions by imposing constraints such as salary or expense limitations or by structuring incentive plans, such as stock options, that reward managers for minimizing noninterest costs.

Finally, public policy expressed in government regulation also influences managers, and ultimate NIM targets differ from those that would result in the absence of an institution/government relationship. Thus, from a manager's point of view, the objective of asset/liability management is to maximize the institution's NIM, subject to the constraints imposed by owners, regulators, and the intermediation function. These constraints result in the pursuit of a NIM target and a risk level that differs from the specific preferences of any single individual or group but that considers the priorities of all parties.

SUMMARY

As in any other business, successful management of a financial institution depends on earning a return on assets that exceeds the cost to the firm of acquiring those assets, including financing costs. Because financial assets dominate the balance sheets of financial institutions, the difference between returns and costs can be measured by the NIM, the focus of asset/liability management. Targets for the size of an institution's NIM also consider its riskiness, or potential variability. The chapters to follow examine techniques for managing the NIM to ensure that its level and riskiness are compatible with the institution's risk/return objectives.

Financial institutions also need to manage their burdens, the difference between noninterest expenses and noninterest revenues. New sources of noninterest revenues are essential to cover operating (noninterest) expenses, which have risen in recent times as banks have made significant investments in technology. New sources of noninterest revenue are particularly important, as traditional earnings from NIMs have fallen with increased competition among financial institutions and from the direct financial markets. Nonoperating expenses also require careful management.

Institutions need asset/liability objectives that respond to the risk/return preferences of four important audiences: owners, regulators, customers, and managers themselves. In recent years, agency theory has provided useful insights into the costs associated with managing complex organiza-

---

[12]For a discussion of the origin of the agency relationship between governments and commercial banks, see Shull, 1984.

tions such as intermediaries and the financial contracts arising as a result. Proper management of a financial institution requires simultaneous decisions about asset choices and sources of funds while balancing the frequently disparate needs and preferences of those four groups.

Discussion Questions

1. What is a financial institution's net interest margin? The spread? What is the role of the NIM in asset/liability management?
2. What is a financial institution's net burden, and why has it gained importance in recent years?
3. What is the classical theory of firm behavior? Is it a normative or positive theory? How does the separation of ownership and management complicate this theory of the firm?
4. Explain the role of monitoring costs in the agent/principal view of the firm. Give an example of a monitoring cost in a large commercial bank. What is the trade-off between monitoring costs incurred by owners and the degree of discretion allowed to managers?
5. Give an example of an agency cost owners incur through lax monitoring of managers. What can owners do to reduce agency costs?
6. What is managerial expense preference behavior? How does this form of behavior affect agency costs? Give an example of such behavior that you may have experienced as an employee.
7. Find an article on a poorly performing financial firm and one with good performance. What factors lead to the difference in performance? Is expense preference behavior involved?
8. Explain how the stockholder form of ownership may allow owners, even in a large firm, to exert control over managerial behavior without incurring high agency costs. Are any similar controls available for mutual firms?
9. In addition to owners, what important groups influence the asset/liability management objectives pursued by financial institutions? Give an example of a situation in which the objectives of regulators and those of owners might conflict. How do managers set asset/liability objectives?
10. Find an article about a recent controversial bank merger. Were layoffs expected to follow after the merger? What types of reactions did community groups have? How do the interests of community groups conflict with those of bank stockholders and managers?

Selected References

Akella, Srinivas R., and Stuart I. Greenbaum. "Savings and Loan Ownership Structure and Expense-Preference." *Journal of Banking and Finance* 12 (September 1988): 419–437.

Allen, Linda, and A. Sinan Cebenoyan. "Bank Acquisitions and Ownership Structure: Theory and Evidence." *Journal of Banking and Finance* 15 (1991): 425–448.

Brewer, Elijah, and Mark R. Saidenberg. "Franchise Value, Ownership Structure, and Risk at Savings Institutions." Working paper, 1996, Federal Reserve Bank of New York.

Cebenoyan, A. Sinan, Elizabeth S. Cooperman, Charles A. Register, and Sylvia C. Hudgins. "The Relative Efficiency of Stock versus Mutual S&Ls: A Stochastic Cost Frontier Approach." *Journal of Financial Services Research* (1993): 151–170.

Cebenoyan, A. Sinan, Elizabeth S. Cooperman, and Charles A. Register. "Deregulation, Regulation, Equity Ownership, and S&L Risk-Taking. *Financial Management*, Autumn 1995: 63–76.

Cebenoyan, A. Sinan, Elizabeth S. Cooperman, and Charles A. Register. "Ownership Structure, Charter Value and Risk-Taking Behavior for Thrifts." *Financial Management* (Spring 1999), forthcoming.

Cole, Rebel A., and Robert A. Eisenbeis. "The Role of Principal—Agent Conflicts in the 1980s Thrift Crisis." Federal Reserve Board, Finance and Economics Discussion Series, Division of Research and Statistics Division of Monetary Affairs, working paper 95–27, 1996.

Cole, Rebel A., and Hamid Mehran. "Executive Compensation and Corporate Performance: Evidence from Thrift Institutions." *Proceedings of a Conference on Bank Structure and Competition.* Chicago: Federal Reserve Bank of Chicago, 1991: 227–247.

Cordell, L. R., G. D. MacDonald, and M. E. Wohar. "Corporate Ownership and the Thrift Crisis." Research Report No. 93-01, Office of Thrift Supervision Research Report, January 1993.

Day, Kathleen. *S&L Hell: The People and the Politics behind the $ 1 Trillion Savings and Loan Scandal.* New York: W. W. Norton, 1993.

Deshmukh, Sudhakar D., Stuart I. Greenbaum, and George Kanatas. "Interest Rate Uncertainty and the Financial Intermediary's Choice of Exposure." *Journal of Finance* 38 (March 1983): 141–147.

Edwards, Franklin R. "Managerial Objectives in Regulated Industries: Expense-Preference Behavior in Banking." *Journal of Political Economy* 85 (February 1977): 147–162.

Esty, Benjamin C. "A Case Study of Organization Form and Risk Shifting in the Savings & Loan Industry." *Journal of Financial Economics* (April 1997), 57–76.

Fisher, Irving. *The Theory of Interest.* New York: Macmillan, 1930.

Gorton, Gary, and Richard Rosen. "Corporate Control, Portfolio Choice, and the Decline of Banking," *Journal of Finance* 50 (December 1995): 1377–1420.

Gup, Benton E. *Bank Fraud: Exposing the Hidden Threat to Financial Institutions.* Rolling Meadows, Ill.: Bankers Publishing, 1990.

Hannan, Timothy H., and Ferdinand Mavinga. "Expense Preference and Managerial Control: The Case of the Banking Firm." *The Bell Journal of Economics* 11 (Autumn 1980): 671–682.

Hirschleifer, Jack. "On the Theory of Optimal Investment Decision." *Journal of Political Economy* 67 (August 1958): 329–352.

———. "Investment Decision under Uncertainty: Choice Theoretic Approaches." *Quarterly Journal of Economics* 79 (November 1965): 509–536.

Hubbard, R. Glenn, and Darius Palia. "Executive Pay and Performance Evidence from the U.S. Banking Industry." National Bureau of Economic Research, Working paper, No. 4704, April 1994.

Jensen, Michael C., and William H. Meckling. "Theory of the Firm: Managerial Behavior, Agency Costs, and Ownership Structure." *Journal of Financial Economics* 3 (1976): 305–360.

Joskow, Paul L., and Nancy L. Rose. "CEO Pay and Firm Performance: Dynamics, Asymmetries, and Alternative Performance Measures." National Bureau of Economic Research, Working paper No. 4976, December 1994.

Mester, Loretta J. "Owners versus Managers: Who Controls the Bank?" *Business Review,* Federal Reserve Bank of Philadelphia (May/June 1989): 13–22.

———. "Efficiency in the Savings and Loan Industry." *Journal of Banking and Finance* 17 (April 1993).

Mullins, Helena M. "The Management Reward Structure and Risk-Taking Behavior of U.S. Commercial Banks." *Proceedings of a Conference on Bank Structure and Competition.* Chicago: Federal Reserve Bank of Chicago, 1991: 248–272.

O'Brian, J. A., Harold M. Sollenberger, and Ronald Olson. *Asset/Liability Management: A Model for Credit Unions.* Richmond, Va.: Robert F. Dame, 1982.

Saunders, Anthony, Elizabeth Strock, and Nicholas G. Travlos. "Ownership Structure, Deregulation, and Bank Risk Taking." *Journal of Finance* 45 (June 1990): 643–654.

Sealey, C. W. "Valuation, Capital Structure, and Shareholder Unanimity for Depository Financial Intermediaries." *Journal of Finance* 38 (June 1983): 857–871.

Shull, Bernard. "The Separation of Banking and Commerce: An Historical Perspective." *Proceedings of a Conference on Bank Structure and Competition.* Chicago: Federal Reserve Bank of Chicago, 1984: 63–78.

Towey, Richard E. "Money Creation and the Theory of the Banking Firm." *Journal of Finance* 29 (March 1974): 57–72.

Verbrugge, James A., and John S. Jahera, Jr. "Expense-Preference Behavior in the Savings and Loan Industry." *Journal of Money, Credit, and Banking* 13 (November 1981): 465–476.

Williamson, Oliver. "Managerial Discretion and Business Behavior." *American Economic Review* 53 (December 1963): 1032–1067.

Woerheide, Walter J. *The Savings and Loan Industry: Current Problems and Possible Solutions.* Westport, Conn.: Quorum Books, 1984.

Yan, Ying. "The Effects of the FDICIA on Bank CEO Pay, Performance, and Their Relationship." Federal Reserve Bank of Cleveland, Working paper, March 1996.

Chapter 2 Internet Exercise

Where can I find current interest rate data for the U.S. economy?

Through the Federal Reserve Economic Data (FRED) data base, the Federal Reserve Bank of St. Louis provides consumers, economists, and financial institutions around the world with historical U.S. economic and financial data, including daily U.S. interest rates, monetary and business indicators, exchange rates, and regional economic data for Arkansas, Illinois, Indiana, Kentucky, Mississippi, Missouri, and Tennessee.

To find current interest rate data:

1. Go to: http://www.stls.frb.org/fred/
2. Under "Data Base Categories", click on "Monthly Interest Rates."

All data is available in ASCII files, or you can download versions for Lotus 1-2-3 and Excel. You can also subscribe to the FRED mailing list by entering your e-mail address as instructed at the site.

Other useful sites for financial institutions data:

Economic Data and Links
http://www.csufresno.edu/Economics/econ_EDL.htm

Graphs and Charts of U.S. Financial Data from the St. Louis Fed as Graphic Image Format (gif) and Adobe Portable Document Format (PDF) files
http://www.stls.frb.org/publ/usfd/

> *"Given the significant changes and integration of the world's financial markets and of market participants, I believe that significant revisions in this country's banking laws are now required."*

Susan M. Phillips
Former Member, Federal Reserve Board
Dean, School of Business and Public Management
George Washington University, Washington, D.C.
Quoted in *New York Times*, May 5, 1998, p. C2.

> *"Going and calling on $50 million banks and trying to get them to join us was a lot more fun than reading books on investment banks."*

William T. Boardman, Senior Vice President, Banc One
Quoted in *The Wall Street Journal*, March 10, 1998, pp. A1, A10.

> *"The Transformation of the U.S. Banking Industry: What a Long, Strange Trip It's Been"*

Title from Allen N. Berger, Anil K. Kashyap, and Joseph M. Scalise,
Brookings Papers on Economic Activity 2 (1995).

3

REGULATION, TECHNOLOGY, AND FINANCIAL INNOVATION

As the chapter opening quotations suggest, banks and other financial institutions have undergone a significant transformation over the last two decades. In the United States, much of the change has resulted from liberalization of bank regulations in the 1980s and a movement by both regulators and financial institutions to reinterpret regulations to meet market realities in the 1990s. For instance, in December 1997, Zions Bancorporation won approval from federal regulators to underwrite municipal revenue bonds under a system pioneered earlier in that year by the Office of the Comptroller of the Currency. This system allows national banks to establish or expand operating subsidiaries to market new products. The ruling for Zion opened the door for small and mid-sized banks to underwrite municipal revenue bonds and market other types of security and insurance services. Earlier in 1997, the Federal Reserve (the Fed) expanded the percentage of revenues that bank holding company subsidiaries engaging in securities and other nonbank related activities (known as Section 20 subsidiaries) to 25 percent of revenues. In the 1990s and the 1980s, the Fed also liberalized the types of activities it permitted subsidiaries of large bank holding companies under its jurisdiction, including investment banking and mutual fund activities.

In April 1998, a proposed merger of a giant insurance company with security and finance subsidiaries, Travelers Group, with Citicorp, a bank holding company, challenged provisions of the Glass–Stegall Act of 1933. This act had prevented banks and insurance companies from operating together for the previous 64 years. This action by Sanford Weill of Travelers Group and John Reed of Citicorp forced Congress to consider *enacting a financial modernization bill to eliminate these restrictions. Throughout the 1990s, Congress had been debating but failing to pass such a bill. Although the bill prompted by the Travelers–Citicorp merger passed the House of Representatives by a margin of one vote in May 1998, obstacles awaited in the Senate, as well as a threatened presidential veto, delaying consideration the bill until 1999. One of the biggest obstacles is the decision about which federal agency would regulate combined bank-insurance -securities firms. Many community activists criticized the proposed act for placing too much financial power in the hands of a few financial institutions.*

The Riegle–Neal Interstate Banking and Branching Act of 1994 allows banks to branch across the United States. This additional source of regulatory transformation has provided an impetus for consolidation in the banking industry. Previously, banks could operate across state lines only by organizing separate, expensive subsidiaries, and only where reciprocal state agreements allowed them to do so. Under the 1994 act, as of June 1997, banks in the U.S. could branch nationwide for the first time in 70 years.

In international finance, December 1997 brought a sweeping accord among members of the World Trade Organization to deregulate the global financial services industry. Under this pact, over 90 nations opened their banking, insurance, and securities industries to foreign competition. A study by Andersen Consulting suggests that competition encouraged by this action will promote innovative and efficient management increasing returns to stockholders of financial services firms in these countries.[1]

Although these trends point to a period of accelerating deregulation for many financial services firms over the last decade, financial institutions in general, and depository institutions in particular, are among the most closely regulated U.S. businesses, and the same pattern prevails in other countries. Over the years, regulations have limited the way they raise funds, the costs they can incur in doing so, their asset choices, their product and geographical diversification, and more. Initial justifications for these regulations emphasized protection for the safety and soundness of the economic system. With the entry of nonregulated competitors into depository institution markets, the costs that many regulations imposed created difficulties for regulated depository institutions trying to compete. Consequently, depository institutions found loopholes to circumvent regulations. Subsequent modifications to regulations reflect an evolutionary process that has responded to innovations in the financial markets and realities of the marketplace. Gradually, after considerable pressure, regulations have slowly switched to improve efficiency for financial institutions in their operations.

The pages that follow explore the traditional regulatory structure and recent developments. A discussion like this one is never complete, because more changes are always on the horizon, and many proposals were pending as this book was written. The possibility of continued change means that managers can never take a given set of regulations for granted, and they must anticipate frustrating efforts to develop strategies in a fluid environment. Successful financial managers need to understand not only existing regulations but also the regulatory process.

✦ ✦ ✦

WHY REGULATE?

Governments regulate financial institutions for several reasons, including ensuring stability in the financial marketplace by maintaining safety and soundness, protecting consumers, preventing fraud and misrepresentation in sales of financial products, promoting efficiency in the operations of financial institutions and markets, provid-

---

[1]"New Door Opens for Banks to Enter Securities Markets," *New York Times*, December 12, 1997, p. C2. Subsidiaries for securities underwriting must maintain separate records, have different names from those of the parent banks, maintain adequate capital levels, and comply with federal rules governing broker-dealers. See also Edmund L. Andrews, "Accord Is Reached to Lower Barriers in Global Finance," *New York Times*, December 13, 1997, p. A1; and Brian A. Johnson, "Financial Accord Will Benefit a Superbreed of Firms." *The Wall Street Journal*, December 16, 1997, p. A22.

ing efficiency and liquidity in the payments system, and promoting social policies, such as enhancing the welfare of underprivileged groups.

Many of the U.S. regulations to promote stability were passed in the 1930s following the Great Depression, during which thousands of banks failed. Depository institutions have been particularly closely regulated, since they play such an important role in maintaining the liquidity of the payment system. With the development of money market and mutual funds with check-writing privileges, electronic fund transfers, Internet bill-paying services, and credit cards offered by nonbank firms, other nonregulated institutions have taken on an important role, as well, but without such heavy regulation. With their comparatively heavy and costly regulatory burden, depository institutions have had difficulty competing. Over time, many regulations have become very costly and inefficient problems, particularly for depository institutions. Recognizing this fact, both depository institutions and regulators have devised loopholes to keep up with changes and the reality of the marketplace. Many of these loopholes have created suboptimal situations, however. Eventually, Congress eliminates or changes regulations to match economic reality. Currently, for instance, Congress is considering a bill dealing with burdensome banking regulations. This dialectic is discussed, along with regulations and how they have changed, in the following sections.

THE REGULATORY DIALECTIC: A CONCEPTUAL FRAMEWORK FOR REGULATION, INNOVATION, AND REFORM

A simple list of regulations and regulatory agencies governing U.S. financial institutions cannot capture the impact of the restrictions on managerial decisions. The complex relationship between regulators and regulated institutions is best described as an interactive exchange. Only through an exploration of the interaction can historical developments and potential changes be viewed in proper perspective.

The word **dialectic** refers to changes occurring through a process of action and reaction by opposing forces. In his classic presentation, the philosopher Hegel described the dialectic process as: (1) an initial set of arguments or rules (the **thesis**); (2) a conflicting set of arguments or responses (the **antithesis**); and (3) a change or modification (the **synthesis**) resulting from an exchange or interaction between the opposing forces. The idea that regulation of financial institutions is a dialectic—a series of cyclical interactions between opposing political and economic forces—was introduced by Professor Edward Kane in the late 1970s.[2] Kane's model of a **regulatory dialectic** has since been widely adopted as an insightful characterization of regulatory developments that are continuing today.

Thesis: Financial Institution Regulations

Relationships between financial institutions and government regulators precede even the National Currency and Banking Acts of 1863 and 1864, but the Federal Reserve Act of 1913 set the stage for comprehensive regulation of the U.S. banking system. Table 3.1 provides a chronological summary of major federal legislation af-

---

[2]The concept of the regulatory dialectic was introduced in Kane, 1977 and further developed in readings from 1981, 1986, 1989a, and 1996. (Selected references are listed in full at the end of this chapter.)

Table 3.1 ✦ MAJOR FINANCIAL LEGISLATION IN THE UNITED STATES

Year	Law	Key Provisions
I. Legislation before 1930 Setting up Bank Regulators and Branching Restrictions		
1863	National Currency Act	Established the Office of the Comptroller of the Currency (OCC)
		Set limits on the asset choices of banks
		Issued national bank notes
		Established system of reserve requirements
1864	National Banking Act	Authorized granting federal bank charters
		Originated the dual system of banking
1913	Federal Reserve Act	Established the system of Federal Reserve banks with several duties:
		Serve as lenders of last resort
		Promote elastic money supply
		Maintain a nationwide payment system
		Tighten bank supervision
1919	Edge Act	Permitted subsidiaries of banks to conduct international banking outside their home territories
1927	**McFadden–Pepper Act**	Gave states authority over branching laws
		Prohibited interstate branching without the state agreement
II. Legislation in the 1930s for Safety and Soundness and Regulating Thrifts after the Depression		
1932	**FHLB Act**	Established the Federal Home Loan Bank System as a lender of last resort to S&Ls
1933	Home Owners' Loan Act	Authorized granting federal charters for S&Ls
		Established the Federal Home Loan Bank Board
1934	National Housing Act	Established the Federal Savings and Loan Insurance Corporation
1934	National Credit Union Act	Established the Federal Credit Union Regulator (later renamed the National Credit Union Administration)
1933	**Glass–Steagall Act**	Regulation Q set interest rate ceilings on deposits
	(Banking Act of 1933)	Limited banking activities to banks
		Established the Federal Deposit Insurance Corporation
1935	Banking Act of 1935	Elaborated the autonomy and power of the Federal Reserve Board
		Gave the OCC discretion in granting national bank charters
1933	**Securities Act of 1933**	Mandated registration of new securities–issues
		Required disclosure of truthful financial information on issuers
1934	**Securities Exchange Act**	Established the Securities and Exchange Commission
III. Legislation in the 1940s for Securities Firms and Insurance Companies		
1940	**Investment Company Act**	Required disclosure of financial statements and investments held
		Mandated articulation of objectives by investment companies
		Determined shareholders' rights
1940	Investment Advisers Act	Required individuals or firms selling investment advice to register with the Securities and Exchange Commission
1945	**McCarran-Ferguson Act**	Established the right of the federal government to regulate insurance companies if states fail to do so adequately
		Exempted insurers from certain antitrust laws

Table 3.1 ✦ MAJOR FINANCIAL LEGISLATION IN THE UNITED STATES (CONTINUED)

Year	Law	Key Provisions

IV. Legislation in the 1950s to 1970s Patching up Regulatory Loopholes

1956	**Bank Holding Company Act**	Gave the Federal Reserve control over multibank holding companies
	Douglas Amendment to the Act	Prohibited MBHCs[a] from acquiring out-of-state banks
		Identified factors in evaluating BHC acquisitions
1959	Spence Act	Forbade S&Ls from having multiple S&L holding companies
1966	Interest Rate Adjustment Act	Extended Regulation Q to thrifts
1968	S&L Holding Company Act	Allowed unitary holding companies meeting the IRS "thriftness test" to engage through non-FSLIC subsidiaries in any activity
1966	Interest Rate Adjustment Act	Extended Regulation Q to thrifts
1970	Amendments to National Credit Union Act	Established the National Credit Union Share Insurance Fund
1970	**Amendments to the BHC Act**	Gave the Fed authority over single-bank holding companies
		Limited acquisitions to businesses "closely related" to banking

V. Legislation in late 1960s and 1970s, Primarily for Consumer Protection

1968	Consumer Credit Protection Act	Required disclosure of lending terms to consumers
1970	Securities Investor Protection Act	Established the securities investor protection corporation to promote investor confidence in the securities industry
1974	Equal Credit Opportunity Act	Prohibited discrimination in granting of credit
1974	**Employee Retirement Income Security Act (ERISA)**	Assigned fiduciary responsibility for pension fund managers
		Set standards for vesting of benefits and full funding of pension funds
		Established the Pension Benefit Guaranty Corporation
1975	Securities Acts Amendments	Mandated the development of a national securities market
1977	Community Reinvestment Act	Required depository institutions to consider the needs of all economic groups in their communities in granting credit

VI. Legislation in the Late 1970s and Early 1980s Regulating Foreign Banks/Deregulation

1978	International Banking Act	Imposed requirements for insurance premiums and branching restrictions on foreign banks operating in the United States
1980	**Depository Institution Deregulation and Monetary Control Act of 1980**	Phased out Regulation Q by 1986
		Revised reserve requirements for depository institutions
		Extended federal insurance to $100,000 account balances
		Expanded asset powers for thrifts
		Preempted state usury ceilings
1982	**Garn–St. Germain Depository Act**	Gave emergency powers of regulators for failed thrifts
		Authorized net worth certificates to provide capital to thrifts
		Broadened asset/liability powers for thrifts
		Allowed MMDAs[b]

VII. Legislation in Late 1980s and 1990s for Regulatory Stringency and Geographic Deregulation

1987	**Competitive Equality Banking Act**	Declared a moratorium on nonbanks and nonbank activities
		Recapitalized the FSLIC
		Stated the full faith and credit of federal insurance
		Allowed forbearance in closure of weak institutions
		Extended net worth certificates
		Expedited check clearing by depositories

Table 3.1   ✦   Major Financial Legislation in the United States (continued)

Year	Law	Key Provisions
1989	**Financial Institutions Reform, Recovery, and Enforcement Act**	Improved supervision/regulation of thrifts
		Established a new insurance fund; FDIC-SAIF, for thrifts
		Created the Resolution Trust Corporation
		Permitted BHCs to acquire healthy thrifts
		Stiffened penalties for fraud
		Imposed product restrictions for thrifts
1991	**Federal Deposit Insurance Corporation Improvement Act**	Mandated specific examination schedules, tripwire, and prompt corrective action system
		Recapitalized the FDIC, Set risk-based insurance premiums
		Increased penalties for manager/director fraud
		Imposed the same limits on activities of state-chartered banks as for national banks
		Encouraged institutional involvement in communities
		Called for a review of regulator's minimum capital requirements
		Strengthened the Fed's authority over foreign banks in the United States
1992	OTS Policy Change	Allowed interstate branching for federally chartered thrifts
1994	**Riegle–Neal Interstate Banking and Branching Efficiency Act**	Allowed interstate branching as of June 1, 1994, requiring states to opt in or out as of that date

ᵃMBHC = multiple bank holding companies.

ᵇMMDA = money market deposit account.

fecting financial institutions. This list may look intimidating, but thinking of regulations in terms of a dialectic helps with remembering key legislation highlighted in the table.

Legislators and government agencies usually articulate justifications for regulations when they are introduced, but experts believe that unannounced motivations often influence the regulators' decisions. Although financial institution regulations have eventually served other purposes, from the 1930s to 1980, their stated intent was to maintain stability in the nation's financial system.

The 1930s: Safety and Soundness   The core of modern financial regulation was drafted in the aftermath of the financial crisis of the 1930s. Laws and regulations centered on prohibiting excessive competition among financial institutions, which legislators viewed as a source of unacceptable risk. With the failure of thousands of banks and unemployment affecting millions of people during the Depression, lawmakers blamed abusive practices of banks and their securities arms for the economic problems, in effect making a scapegoat of banks. Hearings highlighted tales of banks foisting bad investments on the public, lending on overly easy terms to securities affiliates, and purchasing poorly performing stocks for trust funds underwritten by securities affiliates. Some critics argue that securities abuses contributed minimally to bank failures, while others argue that legislation at this time restored confidence in banks and securities firms. The **Banking Act of 1933**, widely known as the **Glass–Steagall (G–S) Act**, attempted to restore confidence by:[3]

1. Establishing ceilings on deposit rates that banks could charge (in Regulation Q) and prohibiting payment of interest on demand deposit accounts by businesses. This act prevented banks from competing on deposit rates, discouraging them from taking on risky assets with high returns to cover these rate obligations.

2. Forcing banks to divest securities, investment banking, and insurance activities, allowing banks to engage only in banking-related services to avoid conflicts of interest and using bank funds to foster speculation. Such product restrictions on banks are frequently referred to as Glass Stegall restrictions.

3. Reinforcing geographic restrictions of the McFadden Act of 1927, forbidding banks from branching across state lines, and making banks subject to state branching laws. The intent of the McFadden Act was to prevent formation of undesirably large and powerful banks.

4. Establishing the Federal Deposit Insurance Corporation (FDIC) to insure the balances of deposit accounts up to a specified limit. The FDIC was created to instill confidence in the banking system after massive bank failures and deposit runs in the 1930s.

Savings and loans (S&Ls) received geographic, product, and rate restrictions along with deposit insurance protection under the **Federal Home Loan Act** of 1932, the **National Housing Act** of 1934, and the Interest Rate Adjustment Act of 1966. Credit Unions came under increasing regulation under the **National Credit Union Act** of 1924, and later amendments in 1970 established a deposit insurance fund. Through these regulations, depository institutions were more strictly regulated than other financial institutions, a difference justified by their importance to the U.S. economy and its payment system.

Regulations restricting nondepository institutions were already in place in the 1930s, and additional ones were added in the following decades. Of particular importance were the **Securities Act of 1933** and the **Securities Exchange Act** of 1934, placing federal restrictions on brokers and investment bankers. These laws were followed by the **Investment Company Act** of 1940, bringing the practices of investment companies under federal control. For other finance firms, such as insurers and finance companies, regulations were and still are concentrated at the state level. Table 3.1 includes these and other federal acts mentioned later in the chapter; they constitute the thesis in the regulatory dialectic.

The 1960s to the 1980s: Other Intentions?   In the years after the Great Depression, the economic environment changed but regulations did not. Limitations continued to inhibit formation of new financial institutions, entry of existing institutions into distant markets, and development of new products, to name a few activities. Kane has argued that the implicit thrust of regulations eventually sought to limit

---

[3]In fact, Congress passed two Glass–Steagall acts. The first in 1932 specified a bookkeeping provision allowing the Treasury to balance its account. The Banking Act of 1933, commonly known as the *Glass–Steagall Act*, contains a provision creating a wall between the banking and securities businesses. However, the act also provided groundwork that allowed the Federal Reserve to let banks into the securities business in a limited way. See Michael Schroeder, "It's Alive: Why Glass–Steagall, Reviled for Decades, Just Won't Go Away." *The Wall Street Journal*, April 10, 1998, pp. A1, A6.

competition, *not* for safety reasons, but to benefit selected market participants, such as small or weak institutions, that would suffer in a fiercely competitive environment. Restrictions of chartering, product creation, and interstate branching illustrate such intentions to keep other institutions outside the markets of some depository institutions. Exit restrictions, such as refusal to allow troubled depository institutions to fail, are other examples. Kane has more recently suggested that regulators and legislators may delay revelations of serious and costly problems in the institutions they regulate to hide defects in existing regulations. In this way, they reduce their own embarrassment and may avoid removal from office.

The Late 1980s and Early 1990s: Backlash and a Move toward Efficiency   In the early 1990s, new legislation again emphasized safety and soundness, as discussed later in the chapter, as a backlash against failures by hundreds of banks and savings institutions in the late 1980s. However, other legislation liberalized and removed many of the previous restrictions of the Banking Act of 1933, shifting regulatory emphasis toward the efficiency of the banking system and market realities. These changes came about through the antithesis (reaction) and synthesis (resolution) phases of the regulatory dialectic, discussed in the following sections.

Antithesis: Regulatory Avoidance and Other Reactions to Regulation

The relationship between regulators and regulated institutions has been described as a cat-and-mouse game. According to Kane, operating rules that benefit a protected class provide a strong incentive for other regulated institutions to find loopholes. The desire to compete may eventually make regulatory avoidance an end in itself that consumes institutions' energy and resources rather than simply a means to achieving competitive freedom. One of management's goals becomes circumvention of restrictions in an effort to capture a portion of a market otherwise denied. Regulators look unfavorably on this "avoidance" behavior, and if institutions are too successful in circumventing the rules, regulations will be revised to remove loopholes. The revisions inspire further avoidance efforts, and the cycle begins anew.

Financial Innovation   Regulatory avoidance often extends beyond psychological warfare between regulated institutions and regulators. Regulated firms incur costs—often called **regulatory taxes** by economists. Some regulations place operating restrictions that prevent firms from conducting business in a profit-maximizing fashion. Managers' logical desire to reduce these taxes creates fertile ground for the birth of **financial innovations**—new financial products and processes that improve the economic efficiency of financial transactions, either by serving customers' needs in new, unregulated ways or by lowering costs.

The process of financial innovation has been studied extensively in recent years.[4] Many of the financial products and asset/liability management tools discussed in later chapters (such as negotiable certificates of deposit, zero-coupon securities, securitization of loans, and financial futures) were introduced as financial

---

[4]Thought-provoking discussions of financial innovation are found in Flood, 1992; Finnerty, 1988; Miller, 1986; Van Horne, 1985; and Silber, 1983. The Miller article is the source for the definition of a "successful, significant" innovation.

innovations and have since become permanent parts of the landscape, even after the regulations motivating their origins have disappeared. Experts term these products and techniques "successful, significant" innovations; both institutions and customers have found uses for them that were unintended at the time of their introductions. Other innovations arise in a climate of regulatory avoidance and wither after only short periods with temporary and limited economic significance. Whether successful or not, financial innovations add to the challenges that both regulators and managers face.

The Antithesis Illustrated   Many examples illustrate the cat-and-mouse game of financial innovation to avoid regulation. In 1863, the National Currency Act attempted to create a national currency for the Union during the Civil War by allowing only federally chartered banks to issue bank notes. Rather than eliminating state-chartered banks, however, it resulted in the creation of check-writing accounts by those banks, which continue to operate alongside federally chartered banks today creating a dual regulatory system.

Another good example comes from institutions' activities to avoid restrictions on sources of funds and interest rates paid on deposits. In the 1960s, large commercial banks developed new kinds of deposits and tapped foreign markets to avoid **Regulation Q ceilings** on domestic deposit interest rates. Small institutions found a loophole by offering gifts, such as silverware or toasters, to supplement low interest payments. As regulators observed the success that institutions achieved by raising funds through these unconventional methods, they changed regulations to again limit institutions' ability to compete. Large banks responded to each regulatory adjustment by introducing a substitute sufficiently different to avoid the new rules. In playing this game, regulator and regulated institution alike expended considerable resources, but the activity spawned several successful financial innovations that are widely used today, such as Eurodollar deposits and negotiable certificates of deposit (CDs). Other regulations resulted in more expensive, suboptimal avoidance mechanisms, such as the creation of bank holding companies that established expensive subsidiaries instead of branches to circumvent state branching restrictions. This organizational form is discussed in greater detail in chapter 4.[5]

A regulatory synthesis (resolution) replaced Reg Q in 1980 when the **Depository Institutions Deregulation and Monetary Control Act (DIDMCA)** phased out deposit rate ceilings by 1986. Figure 3.1 illustrates the regulatory dialectic resulting in the gradual elimination of Regulation Q. A similar synthesis eliminated interstate branching restrictions with the Riegle–Neal Interstate Banking and Branching Efficiency Act (IBBEA) of 1994. Both DIDMCA and IBBEA will be discussed later in more detail.

Further Catalysts for Financial Innovation: Technology and Economic Conditions
Additional incentives drive the antithesis of the regulatory dialectic. As institutions search for financial innovations that do not violate existing regulations, changes in technology and the economy enhance opportunities for institutions to innovate and cause customers to demand new products. For example, along with the effects of regulated institutions, catalysts for change included the computer revolution and in-

---

[5]Summary discussions of the economic costs of avoidance behavior are available in the Federal Reserve Bank of Chicago's discussion of The Depository Institutions Deregulation and Monetary Control Act of 1980, and in Gilbert, 1986.

Figure 3.1✦ DIAGRAM OF THE REGULATORY DIALECTIC

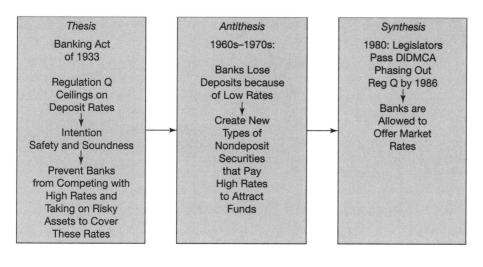

creased volatility in inflation and interest rates.[6] Globalization of financial markets also helped financial institutions to find avoidance mechanisms abroad where Glass–Steagall was not in effect. These developments are also discussed later, along with the antithesis (reaction) in the 1980s that resulted in DIDMCA. a synthesis (resolution).

Synthesis: Origins of Financial Innovation and Regulatory Change

Regulation of financial institutions is a dynamic process. Forces for change arise in part from the objectives of managers and owners of regulated institutions, but market forces also drive change. After a period of delay and analysis, regulations are adjusted. As long as any regulatory restrictions remain—and they certainly will—the dialectic continues. Synthesis in the regulatory dialectic is only a temporary equilibrium, because legal revisions immediately provoke new avoidance behavior. One cycle's synthesis is the next cycle's thesis.

Since 1978, regulatory changes have been introduced rapidly in the United States. Between 1978 and 1980, depository regulators took tentative actions consisting of incremental changes in deposit regulations. By the end of 1982, however, Congress had lightened or eliminated Regulation Q and many product restrictions for banks and thrifts. Those changes, in turn, affected the competitive positions of other financial institutions, as depositories expanded product lines and market areas. The reactions of financial institutions to new laws and continuing problems led to further synthesis embodied in additional laws passed in the late 1980s and 1990s. Six laws culminating this period of regulatory synthesis are:

1. DIDMCA of 1980, mentioned earlier
2. Garn–St. Germain Depository Institutions Act of 1982 (G–St. G)

---

[6]The role of technology in the regulatory dialectic was initially identified by Kane; more elaborate discussion appeared in subsequent studies. See Broaddus, 1985; Van Horne, 1985; and Finnerty, 1988.

3. Competitive Equality Banking Act of 1987 (CEBA)
4. Financial Institutions Reform, Recovery, and Enforcement Act of 1989 (FIRREA)
5. Federal Deposit Insurance Corporation Improvement Act of 1991 (FDICIA)
6. Riegle–Neal Interstate Banking and Branching Efficiency Act of 1994 (IBBEA), mentioned earlier

These and remaining regulations from a prior era are today's thesis. Before these laws can be appreciated, it is necessary to review the regulatory structure under which financial institutions have traditionally operated. The following discussion provides an overview of decision areas addressed by financial institution regulators. A more detailed treatment of specific regulations is reserved for subsequent chapters, including the proposed Financial Modernization Act of 1999 that would eliminate product restrictions under the G–5 Act in Chapter 13.

REGULATION OF DEPOSITORY INSTITUTIONS

Regulations for depository institutions affect almost every aspect of their operations. The complexity of the regulatory process extends beyond the quantity of regulations. The rules are numerous, and so are the regulators.

Who Are The Regulators?

The federal regulatory structure is so complex that one institution may be answerable to four or five different agencies.

Commercial Banks Banks may operate under charters granted at the federal or state level. Those in the first group are **national banks**, and those in the second are **state banks**. Many regulations for national banks are made and enforced by the **Office of the Comptroller of the Currency (OCC)**.

The comptroller's office was created in the **National Currency Act of 1863** and given additional powers in the **National Banking Act of 1864**. Together, these laws established standards a bank had to meet before receiving a national charter. They also promoted the development of a uniform, nationwide currency by authorizing only by banks with federal charters to issue national bank notes as mentioned before. Although public confidence in the notes encouraged many state-chartered banks to switch to federal charters, other state banks remained viable by popularizing checking accounts and encouraging customers to accept checks as an alternative to currency for the payment of bills. The current **dual banking system**, in which both state and federal governments issue bank charters, is traced to this period.

The **Federal Reserve System (the Fed)** supervises federally chartered institutions, which must be members of the system; state-chartered banks may voluntarily choose Fed membership. The Fed was created by the **Federal Reserve Act of 1913** to ensure the benefits of both a flexible payments system and a lender of last resort for troubled banks. The Fed's role in setting monetary policy and providing leadership in the international financial markets is so important that Appendix 3A at the end of the chapter discusses it in detail.

State-chartered banks also must comply with the regulations of banking authorities in the state. All banks are eligible to purchase deposit insurance from the **Bank Insurance Fund (BIF)** of the **Federal Deposit Insurance Corporation**

(FDIC); the FDIC was created by the Glass–Steagall Act in 1933. Fed member banks must be insured by the FDIC. If a bank purchases insurance, it must comply with rules set by the FDIC.

Because the three major federal banking regulators—the Comptroller, the Fed, and the FDIC—arose at different times to serve different purposes, they are independent of one another. They are not always legally required to coordinate their actions, and conflicts and even competition arise among them, adding an additional dimension to the regulatory dialectic.

Thrifts   Like commercial banks, thrifts may operate under either state or federal charters. In 1989, one of the major acts to be discussed in a later section of this chapter, FIRREA, mandated a major restructuring of the federal regulatory and insurance functions for the thrift industry, the most notable of which was the abolition of the **Federal Home Loan Bank Board (FHLBB)** and the **Federal Savings and Loan Insurance Corporation (FSLIC)**. These agencies, created in the **Federal Home Loan Bank Act of 1932** and the **National Housing Act of 1934**, had comprised the federal chartering, regulatory, and insurance authority for thrifts for more than 50 years. The Federal Home Loan Bank still exists as a lending organization providing liquidity for thrifts.

FIRREA replaced them with an even more complex supervisory structure. The regulatory authority for federally chartered thrifts now rests with the **Office of Thrift Supervision (OTS)**, which was established within the Treasury department but operates independently of the Secretary of the Treasury. Federal deposit insurance for thrifts is now provided by a newly created **Savings Association Insurance Fund (SAIF)**, a subsidiary of the FDIC. The Federal Reserve Board continues to set reserve requirements on deposits held by thrift institutions.

A number of proposals for modernizing the U.S. financial system have suggested eliminating of the thrift category altogether. For example, a legislative proposal from the Treasury department recommended in 1997 that thrifts be required to convert to bank charters, merging the OTS and OCC at the end of a 2-year conversion period. An alternative approach within this proposal would leave the current thrift system intact, but the prohibition against combining functions of the OTS and OCC would be lifted, and BIF and SAIF would be merged.[7]

Credit Unions   Credit Unions (CUs) also operate under a dual chartering system. The major federal credit union regulator is the **National Credit Union Administration (NCUA)**. CUs may purchase deposit insurance from state funds or from the **National Credit Union Share Insurance Fund (NCUSIF)**, established in 1970 amendments to the National Credit Union Act. Reserve requirements on deposits are enforced by the Federal Reserve Board.

What Is Regulated?

Table 3.2 provides a summary, prepared by the Federal Reserve Bank of New York, of regulated management areas and the agencies responsible for monitoring institutions' behavior in each area. That compilation provides convincing evidence of ex-

---

[7]See "Financial Restructuring: Highlights of Treasury's 1997 Legislative Proposal on Financial Modernization," *Banking Policy Report*, June 16, 1997, pp. 7–9.

Table 3.2 ✦ DEPOSITORY INSTITUTIONS AND THEIR REGULATORS

The regulatory structure for depository institutions is based on a dual banking system, in which both state and federal governments issue charters. A single institution may be supervised by state officials and by several federal regulators, depending on the activities in which it is engaged.

		Chartering and Licensing	Branching	Mergers and Acquisitions[a]
A.	National banks	OCC	OCC	Fed and OCC
B.	State member banks	State	Fed/State	Fed/State
C.	Insured state nonmember	State	FDIC/State	FDIC/State
D.	Noninsured state banks	State	State	State
E.	Savings banks			
	Federal	OTS	OTS	FDIC/OTS
	State	State	FDIC/State	FDIC/State
F.	Savings and Loans			
	Federal	OTS	OTS	FDIC/OTS
	State	State	FDIC	
G.	Credit unions			
	Federal	NCUAB	None	NCUA Board
	State	State	State	State/NCUA Board

[a]For mergers and acquisitions, regulators' involvement varies depending on characteristics of merged or acquired firms.

Source: Adapted from Federal Reserve Bank of New York, "Depository Institutions and Their Regulators," 1988; updated by the authors.

tensive restrictions within a complex structure. For example, the table identifies 12 categories of control ranging from initial entry into an industry (chartering and licensing) to customer relationships (consumer protection).[8]

Table 3.2 identifies the agencies with which a single institution interacts. Consider, for example, a state-chartered S&L, in Row F of the table. Four state or federal authorities (the OTS, the state, the Fed, the FHLB, and the FDIC) either set the rules for its operations, enforce the rules, or do both. For instance, a state savings institution gets its charter from a state agency, but both state authorities and the OTS control its ability to branch or acquire other institutions. Its regional Federal Home Loan (FHL) Bank serves as a source of liquidity and provides funds for housing finance under terms established by FIRREA. Both the state and the OTS may conduct periodic examinations of the institution's financial condition and operations. The Federal Reserve Board determines the S&L's reserve requirements on deposits, and these deposits may be insured by the FDIC (through its SAIF division) or by a nonfederal insurance fund. If insured by SAIF, the thrift is subject to additional regulations that the FDIC may choose to impose at any time to preserve the insurance fund's financial health.

Examination Process The previous example highlights a major function of depository institution regulators: examining the financial condition and operations of

---

[8]Discussion of the details of these regulations is reserved for later chapters on individual management activities.

Reserve Requirements	Access to the Discount Window	Deposit Insurance	Supervision/ Examination	CONSUMER PROTECTION	
				Rulemaking	Enforcement
Fed	Fed	FDIC (BIF)	OCC	Fed	OCC
Fed	Fed	FDIC (BIF)	Fed/State	Fed/State	Fed/State
Fed	Fed	FDIC (BIF)	FDIC/State	Fed/State	FDIC/State
Fed	Fed	None/State	State	Fed/State	State/FTC
Fed	Fed	FDIC (SAIF)	OTS/FDIC	Fed/OTS	OTS
		FDIC (BIF)/State	FDIC/State	Fed/OTS/State	FDIC/OTS/State
Fed	Fed/FHLB	FDIC (SAIF)	OTS/FDIC	Fed/OTS	OTS
		or State	FDIC/State	Fed/OTS/State	FDIC/OTS/State
Fed	Fed/CLF	NCUSIF	NCUA Board	Fed/State	NCUA Board
		or State	State		State

the firms they supervise. At the federal level, the **Federal Financial Institutions Examination Council (FFIEC)** coordinates procedures for assuring compliance with a variety of regulations. The FFIEC consists of representatives from the Board of Governors of the Fed, the FDIC, the OTS, the NCUA, and the Comptroller of the Currency. It controls requirements for financial reporting and disclosures that institutions must make to regulators, negotiates sharing of information between state and federal agencies, and even provides training programs for examiners of the member agencies.

Examinations performed by the regulators consist of on-site visits by agency personnel, who audit the policies and procedures used to grant loans, purchase and sell securities, process deposits, manage cash, and keep financial records. Typically, from one to four examiners remain at an institution for a month or more. The frequency of examinations varies with the existing condition of a depository.

The FDICIA of 1991 increased the examination frequency for many financial institutions. All insured institutions with assets of $100 million or more must be examined at least once annually by federal bank regulators. Smaller institutions that are adequately capitalized and have superior examination ratings must be examined at least every 18 months. Troubled or inadequately capitalized firms are subject to more frequent examinations. Frequent on-site examinations are intended to identify emerging problems for sound institutions and to help solve lingering problems of troubled firms.

Since 1993, regulators have used a set of so-called **tripwires** to identify unsafe or unsound banking practices. These tripwires establish minimum standards for virtually every area under management's influence or control. Four federal regulatory agencies—the Fed, the FDIC, the Comptroller of the Currency, and the NCUA—use a uniform rating system known by the acronym, **CAMELS**. This system assigns 1 to 5 (best to worst) ratings to the institution's Capital, Assets, Management, Earnings, Liquidity, and Sensitivity to market risks, including its interest rate, price, and foreign exchange exposure. The CAMEL system has been in effect since 1978; however, the last component, **S**, or **sensitivity to market risk**, was added in 1997.

CAMELS factors are viewed together, so the acceptability of one factor depends on the quality of the others. For instance, the acceptability of a bank's capital ratio may depend on the quality of its assets and its interest rate risk. Judgments of capital adequacy are based not only on meeting capital requirements, but also on the composition of the bank's assets and liabilities as well as off-balance-sheet items. Judgments of asset quality are based on the risk of the bank's assets and their classification as good, substandard, doubtful, or losses. To evaluate management ability, examiners consider not only the quality of bank's management, but the quality of its board of directors, as well. Evaluations of earnings are based on the earnings trends and levels relative to those of the institution's peers. Liquidity scores reflect credit conditions, volatility of deposits, loan commitments and other contingent claims, liquid assets, and ability to borrow funds quickly in case of need. For market rate risk, banks must demonstrate what will happen to earnings with changes in interest rates and other factors affecting market exposure. The CAMELS system was revised in 1996 to give banks separate ratings for each of the five categories, as well. The new system is based on regulators' perception that banks need all the help they can get in a current global competitive environment, which entails greater perils, as well as opportunities, than ever before. Regulators have also added a risk management element to each of the CAMELS components.[9]

CAMELS ratings are not publicly available to protect banks from potential deposit runs. However, a number of private agencies, such as Sheshunoff in Austin, Texas, provide similar ratings, leaving out the management and market risk components. These agencies also sell software that allows banks/thrifts to perform computer simulations to estimate market risks. Methods to estimate market risk exposure are discussed later in the text.

The OTS has a separate, very similar system known as **MACRO**. Its composite ratings provide one basis for determining how often examiners arrive and even whether regulators can restrict institutions from activities available to safer depositories. Other examiners, such as state regulators, may operate on different schedules.

Does This Regulatory Structure Make Sense?

Few disagree that regulatory agencies duplicate the efforts of others. In 1974, Arthur Burns, then chairman of the Board of Governors of the Federal Reserve, called the bank regulatory system "a jurisdictional tangle that boggles the mind." Beginning with the Hoover Commission in 1949, considerable resources have been devoted to analyzing the system and recommending reforms. Some studies have advocated consolidating supervisory power in a single agency, whereas others have warned against giving any single organization too much power, arguing that competition between regulators provides cross checks that promote safety. The Bush Task Force on

---

[9]"CAMEL Is Evolving into CAMELS," *Banking Policy Report*, November 4, 1996, p. 3.

Deregulation of Financial Services recommended to Congress in 1984 that the agencies be reorganized along functional lines, giving one agency the authority over federal deposit insurance, another authority over examination and supervision, and so forth. As with earlier reports, however, Congress delayed action on the proposals.

In the late 1990s, regulators themselves became more liberal in their interpretation of product restrictions under Glass–Steagall. In 1997, a number of different types of financial services firms merged, including banks with investment banking firms and insurance companies with securities firms. Consolidation of different types of financial firms worried lawmakers, since the current regulatory structure is designed to analyze separate activities of securities firms, insurance firms, and banks. A number of financial modernization bills were proposed in 1997 dealing with these issues, but compromise evaded congressional committees at the end of the year. Interestingly, major opponents of reorganization included some regulated institutions, which enjoyed the protection of existing agencies, as Kane's dialectic predicts.[10]

REGULATION OF FINANCE COMPANIES

In contrast to depositories, the sources and uses of funds of finance companies are not heavily regulated at the federal level. These institutions raise funds in the debt markets rather than from deposits and do not have to meet federal reserve requirements or other asset restrictions. Some experts believe that finance companies' recent success in competition against commercial banks is the result of technological and financial innovations, such as securitization, that have aided them in raising funds.[11]

Licensing Restrictions

Finance companies must seek permission from state authorities to open new offices. They enjoy more freedom than banks or thrifts to expand across state lines, however, because no federal restriction limits their interstate operations. Most states evaluate requests to open new offices by applying the **"convenience and advantage" rule**, which holds that expansion should occur only if the community will benefit. As a result, individual states or communities may limit competition.[12]

Consumer Protection Legislation

Finance companies face other regulations, as well. An extensive body of consumer protection legislation has accumulated since 1968 and affects the managerial decisions of finance companies and other consumer lenders. In the finance company industry, the Federal Trade Commission monitors compliance with consumer protection laws such as the **Consumer Credit Protection (Truth-in-Lending) Act of 1968** and **Equal Credit Opportunity Act of 1974**.

---

[10]Joseph B. Treaster, "Financial Services Consolidate, but Regulation Is Still Fragmented," *New York Times*, January 2, 1998, pp. D1, D5. For earlier discussions of these issues, see Johnson, 1984 and Gilbert, 1984.

[11]Gorton and Pennacchi, 1992.

[12]Although the absence of a federal chartering agency removes one layer of regulation, it also means that a firm lacks any recourse if it is denied a state charter. The competitive effect of this and other state restrictions is explored more fully in Selden 1981.

Federal regulations have focused on equality in the availability of credit and on the completeness, accuracy, and uniformity of information disclosed to potential borrowers. State regulations concentrate on the rates of interest that finance companies charge. In recent years, attention has focused on state **usury ceilings**, which are legal limitations on lending rates. When market interest rates rise significantly above the usury ceilings, as they did in the early 1980s, lenders experience severe problems, and the amount of available credit is restricted.

Once again validating the spirit of Kane's regulatory dialectic, state regulations were modified in the 1980s in moves necessitated by market conditions and by federal regulatory actions. For example, in 1980, federal law removed usury ceilings from residential mortgage loans unless states overrode the action by 1983; most states did not. Many states increased or removed usury ceilings on personal loans after market interest rates rose to historic highs in 1980 and 1981.

REGULATION OF INSURANCE COMPANIES

Life insurers and property/liability insurers operate within a regulatory system that falls somewhere in between those of depository institutions and finance companies. The **McCarran–Ferguson Act of 1945** gave the federal government the right to regulate insurance companies.[13] Congress agreed, however, that the federal government would not exercise the right to impose regulations if states adequately established and enforced standards for the industry. Although, the legal basis for federal regulation of insurers continues, for all practical purposes, insurers operate under the oversight of state agencies. Some critics complain that state insurance commissions are often too tied to the industry, often being ex-insurance executives whose oversight too often becoming overlooking. Commissioners of insurance in each state wield considerable power individually and exert influence collectively through the **National Association of Insurance Commissioners (NAIC)**. NAIC has no legal power but substantial political clout. States also organize life insurance guaranty funds to guard against problems due to failure of insurers. In effect, solvent insurance companies in the state contribute to compensate the policyholders of the failed insurer in that state.

Recent increases in the cost of property/liability insurance have renewed calls for federal regulation of that industry or, at a minimum, for tighter regulation at the state level. The McCarran–Ferguson Act recognized that insurers often pool data on the frequency and causes of their customers' accidents, natural disasters, fires, and so forth to establish statistical data bases that help them price insurance policies. Yet federal antitrust laws prohibit data sharing by competitors in most industries on the grounds that it can lead to collusion and price fixing. Thus, McCarran–Ferguson specifically exempts insurers from federal antitrust laws, unless

---

[13]Before 1945, the insurance regulatory structure was based on the ruling of the Supreme Court in *Paul* v. *Virginia* [75 U.S. 168, 8 Wall 168, 19 L ED 357 (1869)]. Under this ruling, insurance was not deemed to be interstate commerce and was therefore not subject to federal regulation. Thus, no federal regulatory structure existed before the McCarran–Ferguson Act was passed. More details on the McCarran–Ferguson Act can be found in "Open Season on an Old Law," *Journal of American Insurance* 63 (First Quarter 1987): 8–12.

firms can be shown to be engaged in "boycott, coercion, or intimidation" as a result of data sharing.

State regulators are supposed to ensure that these prohibited activities do not occur, but in the late 1980s, some critics complained of lax oversight of the insurance industry. By November 1988, charges of unfair pricing in the property/liability segment of the industry were widespread in some states. In California, voters decided that they paid too much for automobile insurance and passed **Proposition 103**. This referendum mandated a substantial reduction in the prices of some insurance policies issued in that state.

The success of Proposition 103 encouraged other consumer advocates to challenge the antitrust exemptions of McCarran–Ferguson and to advocate the law's repeal, substituting instead direct federal regulation of the industry. Responding to criticisms of laxity and inadequate expertise among state regulators and hoping to avert federal regulation of the industry, the NAIC developed an accrediting system for state insurance regulators. The system did not, however, quiet congressional critics of the industry. These developments are discussed in greater detail in a later chapter.

Licensing and Solvency Requirements

Regulatory structure aside, the scope and focus of regulations for insurers resemble those for depository institutions in many ways. For example, strict standards designed to protect the solvency of insurers are applied in granting company licenses. After entry is granted, annual financial statements are closely scrutinized, and insurers are subject to frequent examinations. Finally, analogous to deposit insurance agencies, insolvency guarantee funds are established in all states to protect policyholders in case insurers go bankrupt.

Rate Regulation

Insurance regulators devote considerable time to overseeing rate. Generally, regulators agree that rates charged by insurers, when combined with income from investments, must be sufficient to cover the firms' potential liabilities. At the same time, insurers must not charge excessive or unfairly discriminatory rates. Although insurers must differentiate between high-risk and low-risk customers and set charges according to risk, regulations attempt to prevent rate discrimination not justified by differing levels of risk. The approach that state legislators and commissioners of insurance take toward achieving ideal rates differs from state to state and varies according to the category of insurer.

Generally, regulators do not directly control the policy premiums that life insurers may charge, but most states impose standards designed to guarantee sufficient reserves to cover future claims. Thus, the regulations establish floors for policy rates, because insurers must set rates high enough to generate the required reserves. For property/liability insurers, state regulations deal more extensively with policy rates. Most states require property/liability insurers to obtain the approval of regulators before increasing policy rates.[14]

---

[14]For an exhaustive review of the effect of rate regulations on property/liability firms, see Harrington, 1984.

Product Regulation

Just as depository institutions have operated under asset and deposit restrictions for many years, insurers must comply with limitations on the types of policies they can offer. In many states, insurers must seek the approval of the insurance commissioners before they can sell new products. The close scrutiny is intended to protect customers against unfair policy provisions and to protect the insurance firms from commitments that may undermine financial stability.

Asset Structure

Insurers' investments are also regulated. State insurance codes specify permissible categories and quality grades of assets. Many states restrict the percentage of firms' total assets that may be invested in specific types of securities, such as common stock. Despite these restrictions, however, the industry attracted attention in the early 1990s, when several large insurers with extensive junk bond and commercial real estate holdings failed, leaving policyholders stranded. Since that time some state regulation passed stronger product restrictions. These events strengthened congressional interest in federal regulation of insurers.

REGULATION OF PENSION FUNDS

Pension funds operate under contractual savings agreements that obligate them to pay retirement benefits to workers. The pension plans of private corporations are subject to the **Employee Retirement Income Security Act**, passed by Congress in 1974 and more commonly known as **ERISA**.

Investment Management

ERISA covers almost all areas of pension fund management. Two provisions set standards for **vested benefits** to plan participants and for funding a plan so that assets equal accrued liabilities. Vested benefits are those to which employees are entitled even if they leave their firms before retirement. ERISA requires early vesting of benefits and ensures that most employees are 100 percent vested after 15 years of service.

ERISA also sets standards for employer contributions in relation to a fund's investment income and benefit liabilities. Generally, ERISA attempts to ensure that an employer works toward maintaining pension assets equal to the fund's obligations. Pension fund managers have **fiduciary responsibility** for investments of assets. Fiduciary responsibility is the obligation to act in the best interests of clients under a "prudent man" rule, (i.e., acting as a prudent person would behave in managing his/her own investments). Fund managers are required to act solely in the interests of the fund's beneficiaries.

Pension Insurance

Another ERISA provision, also designed to protect the financial interests of fund members, established an insurance fund to guarantee that benefits are paid to eligible members even if a pension plan defaults on its obligations. This insurance is provided by a federal agency called the **Pension Benefit Guaranty Corporation (PBGC)** and funded by assessments on employers according to the numbers of employees their fund's cover and the risk of the funds' assets. To ensure the continuing financial stability of pension funds, the law imposes requirements for extensive and frequent reporting and disclosure. As explained later in the text, federal pension insurance has been plagued by many of the same difficulties as federal deposit insurance, evoking considerable concern among regulators and retirees, whose future incomes may be in jeopardy.

REGULATION OF INVESTMENT COMPANIES

Investment companies act as portfolio managers for those to whom they sell ownership shares. Because investment company shares are sold publicly and because many of their assets are publicly traded, investment companies must comply with federal securities laws. The obligations of fund managers to shareholders are also defined by federal and state laws.

Federal Securities Laws

The issuance of ownership shares by investment companies and the frequency and accuracy of their financial reports are monitored by the **Securities and Exchange Commission (SEC)**, under authority granted by the Securities Act of 1933 and the Securities Exchange Act of 1934. Many provisions affecting investment companies also apply to other firms that issue securities for sale to the public. Some provisions address investment companies specifically, however, to ensure regular and truthful disclosures to current and potential shareholders.

The Securities Act of 1933 focused on new security issues, requiring firms to provide full and accurate information about their financial positions and about new securities they offered. The Securities Exchange Act of 1934 established the SEC as the chief regulator of the securities markets and required regular disclosure of financial information by firms with publicly traded securities.

Securities laws are rooted in the belief that access to information is the best guarantor of the public interest. Depository institution legislation, in contrast, has produced elaborate regulatory systems for gathering information, much of it unavailable to the public. The securities and investment company industries operate within strong systems of self-regulation monitored by trade organizations, whereas depository trade organizations resemble political action groups, seeking to preserve existing laws or to promote new legislation.

Regulations on Sources and Uses of Funds

The Investment Company Act of 1940 and subsequent amendments, and the **Investment Advisers Act** of the same year, are the foundations for specific regulations governing investment companies. These laws identify the responsibilities of investment advisers and fund managers. For example, they can make only limited use of financial leverage. Also, mutual fund managers must obtain shareholder approval of changes in investment objectives, so shareholders are guaranteed at least some control over their risk exposure and return potential.

The Investment Company Act also imposed diversification requirements to protect shareholders against the risk of total loss. An investment company may invest no more than 5 percent of its assets in securities issued by any one firm, and it may hold no more than 10 percent of the outstanding voting shares of a company. These restrictions apply to 75 percent of an investment company's portfolio; the remaining 25 percent is exempted from such restrictions to encourage investment in small businesses.

Another influence on managers is the exemption of investment company income from federal taxes if it distributes at least 90 percent of net capital gain income and 97 percent of dividend and interest income to shareholders. Taxes on such gains are paid only by individual shareholders, and no taxes are assessed on fund income, an approach to taxation known as the **conduit theory**. Finally, the federal regulatory and tax codes are supplemented by state codes placing additional responsibilities on fund managers.

In contrast to savings at depository institutions, pension funds, or insurance firms, people entrust funds to investment companies without any guarantee of recovery in case of fund failure. Regulation seeks instead to ensure availability of truthful information. If investors choose the wrong investment companies, however, no federal or state insurance will mitigate their losses.

REGULATION OF SECURITIES FIRMS

Like investment companies, securities firms are subject to SEC scrutiny under the Securities Exchange Act and its amendments. The act established maximum levels of indebtedness for securities dealers and gave the Fed the authority to set **margin requirements** governing the proportions of loans by securities firms to customers for securities purchases and the proportions customers must pay in cash. In addition, securities firms are prohibited from using inside information about firms to profit at the expense of the public. Firms selling investment advice to clients are subject to the Investment Advisers Act of 1940, which seeks to prevent fraudulent practices. The scope of a firm's operations determines additional constraints to which it is subject. For example, members of the New York Stock Exchange must conform to the self-regulating rules of the exchange. The **National Association of Securities Dealers (NASD)** is a self-regulating body that sets standards for all brokers and dealers interacting with the public.

The industry operates under congressional objectives for a national securities market articulated in the **Securities Acts Amendments of 1975**. This legislation directed the SEC to promote a fully competitive trading system under which investors nationwide have equal and instantaneous access to information. The policy sought to eliminate historic practices concentrating trades in a few locations, such as New York City. Despite progress toward this goal, it has not yet been fully achieved.

Before 1970, the daily volume of transactions processed by securities firms remained relatively small, and manual processing could accommodate all facets of each transaction, including the physical transfers of securities between buyers and sellers. As in other financial industries, however, investment activity quickened as memories of the Great Depression faded. In 1968 and 1969, several securities firms failed under the burden, and customers' securities were discovered missing. To promote public confidence in the industry, Congress passed the **Securities Investor Protection Act** in 1970, mandating the creation of the **Securities Investor Protection Corporation (SIPC)**. The SIPC is an industry-funded organization providing reimbursement to customers of securities firms if they lose securities or cash balances due to failure of affiliated firms. The SIPC, however, does not insure against market losses. Although initiated by Congress, the SIPC's promises to investors are not guaranteed by the federal government, and it has no legal regulatory powers. Instead, it is a visible symbol of the industry's obligation to self-regulation.

Whether securities firms will continue to enjoy the relative freedom that many depository institutions seek is an important question. The last half of the 1980s brought many assaults on the industry's image for integrity. Between 1985 and 1991, several major scandals, led by disclosures discrediting junk bond king Michael Milken, rocked the industry. Charges focused on the practice of **insider trading**— transactions in which corporate managers, directors, or their securities advisors illegally profit from private information affecting the value of a firm's securities. Some observers blamed self-interested computerized trading by securities firms for the stock market crash of October 1987. In 1991, Salomon Brothers, a major securities firm, admitted to manipulating activities in the Treasury securities market for its own benefit.

Incidents such as these evoked cries for stepped up government regulation. Congress responded to some of the criticisms with the passage of the **Insider Trading and Securities Fraud Enforcement Act of 1988**, more commonly known as the **Insider Trading Act**. The legislation established deterrents to the practice by strengthening penalties for violators and requiring firms to develop formal policies to prevent abuses. The act also increased federal agencies' ability to enforce regulations. The Salomon Brothers scandal resulted in rule changes in the Treasury securities market.

Despite the recognized need to increase scrutiny of securities activities, global market forces have increased competition from foreign firms and caused many experts to warn against shackling the industry with additional, costly regulatory taxes. Furthermore, as discussed earlier, technological change cannot be regulated away, and attempts to prevent securities firms from using today's computerized trading strategies are likely to lead only to different, unregulated strategies tomorrow.

Origins of Financial Innovation and Regulatory Reform in the 1980s

The discussion of the regulatory dialectic introduced forces that promote regulatory reform, including financial market changes and regulatory avoidance behavior. No example of the confluence of these forces and the regulatory response is clearer than events leading to two of the most important pieces of financial legislation of the 1980s, DIDMCA and G–St. G.

By 1980, the need for reforms was a widely recognized fact. Several government commissions had studied the problems of financial institutions and recommended revisions in the regulatory structure. Congress, however, had failed to respond with substantive changes.[15] Banks and thrifts faced many problems, discussed next, included inflation and historically high interest rates, declining Fed membership, falling profit margins, and antiquated regulations given new technology, and competition from nonbank financial institutions.

---

[15]See West, 1982 and Shull, 1981.

Problems Requiring Regulatory Attention

Economic Conditions Rising Rates and Interest Rate Ceilings   As 1980 approached, inflation and interest rates were reaching historically high levels. Great uncertainty about future interest rates reflected expectations of inflation and fears that changes in the Fed's monetary policy would increase rate volatility.

When financial market participants feel unusual uncertainty about future economic conditions, they respond by demanding investments that reduce their risk exposure. A rigid regulatory structure prevents financial institutions from responding to customer demands rapidly; in some cases, it prevents any response at all. Regulatory restrictions may also prevent managers of financial institutions from making investment decisions necessary to protect the stability and levels of their institutional incomes.

With high inflation and volatile interest rates, investors in the late 1970s were uncertain about future inflation and interest rates. Consequently, they demanded interest rates high enough to cover interest rate risk (the risk of holding an investment earning a lower-than-market rate) and loss of future purchasing power due to expected inflation. Regulation Q placed a ceiling on rates that depository institutions could offer, however. Hence, depositors withdrew their funds from banks and thrifts and invested them in the direct financial markets, acquiring money market securities such as Treasury bills that offered market rates of return. This phenomenon is known as **disintermediation**. Since money market securities require large minimum amounts, often $10,000 or more, small savers needing liquidity had few alternatives. However, brokerage firms developed cash management accounts and **money market mutual funds (MMMFs)**, allowing small savers to invest in low-risk portfolios of money market securities and receive limited check-writing privileges. This innovation cost depositories an even greater volume of deposits from **cross-intermediation**, the transfer of funds from one financial intermediary to another. Large depository institutions found loopholes by developing nondeposit securities that could offer market rates.

With rising interest rates, some financial institutions needed to increase their flexibility to protect against interest rate risk, but regulations prevented them from adjusting asset portfolios quickly in response to market conditions. For example, profits in the thrift industry suffered because S&Ls could comply with regulations only by investing in long-term, fixed-rate mortgages. Only a few states allowed adjustable-rate loans in the late 1970s. Consequently, while interest expenses rose along with rates, interest revenues on fixed-rate assets did not, resulting in declining net interest margins. Thrifts needed to boost interest revenues from assets to cover their rising interest expenses, but the law left them little ability to diversify. Profits declined at an alarming rate, leaving many thrifts technically insolvent with market values of assets less than the market values of liabilities.[16] With the problems that S&Ls faced, recognition grew that interest rate ceilings and product restrictions had a destabilizing effect on the economy, provoking an intense reevaluation of regulations intended to prevent competition among depositories. Observers no longer accepted that regulations promoted institutional safety; the possibility arose that regulations might actually raise the in-

---

[16]See White, 1991; Kane, 1989b; Barth, 1991; and Brock, 1980 for good summaries of the plight of thrift institutions.

terest rate risk of depository institutions, resulting in severe losses and failures, particular for S&Ls in the early 1980s.

As early as 1973, regulators began several patchwork attempts to revise regulations that had contributed to disintermediation and cross-intermediation. New types of deposit accounts were permitted, each designed to allow small savers to earn market rates of interest or to earn modest returns on checking account balances. However, these innovations failed to stem the tide of deposit withdrawals, which soared to unprecedented levels in 1979, raising interest expenses for financial institutions. Furthermore, legal challenges questioned the right of federal regulators to introduce deposit innovations without explicit congressional action, and eventually a Court of Appeals ruling established a January 1, 1980, deadline for eliminating the innovations unless Congress acted.[17]

Insurers also had problems. Consumers no longer demanded traditional insurance products. Many states limited insurers' holdings of high-yielding assets, such as common stock, that would enable them to offer high-yielding insurance products. Property/liability insurers suffered, because inflation increased their claims expenses more rapidly than they could increase income. These pressures added to the call for regulatory changes, as well as financial innovations, in the insurance industry.

Nonbank Competition   At this time, depository institutions saw their competitors grow in number. Investment companies, insurance firms, securities brokerages, and even diversified firms such as Sears Roebuck introduced financial products that encroached on territory previously controlled by depositories. They, in turn, grew more vocal in their demands for regulatory reform, arguing that they labored under restrictions not faced by competitors. For example, while Merrill Lynch and Sears were free to offer services nationwide, many depositories could not even open branches in adjoining counties, let alone neighboring states. Even though competitors could offer wide varieties of products, regulations limited services offered by depositories. Protests called for a "level playing field," a set of rules allowing all to compete on an equal footing.

Declining Fed Membership   Mounting regulatory avoidance in the late 1970s added to the need for reform legislation by 1980. Before then, only commercial banks that were members of the Fed were required to keep nonearning reserves at regional Federal Reserve banks. Reserve deposits are intended to provide an institution with sufficient liquid funds to meet customers' deposit withdrawals and to assist the Fed in controlling lending. Nonmember banks, thrifts, and CUs were not subject to the same kinds of reserve requirements. As interest rates rose, the oppor-

---

[17]In 1973, federal regulators permitted banks and thrifts to offer "Wild Card" certificates— 4-year, $1,000-minimum certificates of deposit (CDs) with no rate ceilings. The experiment lasted only 4 months, because commercial banks immediately offered rates above those thrifts that could offer, since they were locked into fixed-rate mortgages. In 1972, the negotiable order of withdrawal (NOW) account was introduced by savings banks in Massachusetts. NOW accounts quickly proved to be popular in New England, but Congress was reluctant to allow them nationwide and passed a law in 1976 restricting the innovation to banks and thrifts in New England, New York, and New Jersey. In 1978, federal regulators also introduced a money market certificate (MMC), a 6-month, $10,000-minimum CD with a rate ceiling tied to the 6-month T-bill rate with a $\frac{1}{4}$ percentage advantage given to thrifts and credit unions over commercial banks.

tunity cost of nonearning reserves a more and more burdensome requirement for member banks.

To the dismay of Fed officials, increasing numbers of banks resigned Fed membership, and most newly organized banks chose to obtain state charters to avoid the Fed's reserve requirements. The Fed argued that as the proportion of deposits held by member banks declined, so did the effectiveness of reserve requirements as a tool of monetary policy. Fed officials pressured Congress to introduce a more equitable system.

Technological Innovation   The technological revolution enhanced opportunities for institutions to innovate and violate current regulations. Table 3.3 identifies several "successful, significant" innovations that have emerged over the past four decades, many of which will be discussed in detail later in the book. The table places these innovations in context with key technological developments and important contemporary economic/political events. Scholars studying the process of financial innovation see no coincidence in the timing of a wave of innovation over the past two decades. Financial economist and Nobel Laureate Merton Miller argues that before the middle to late 1960s, the country was preoccupied with more pressing concerns; global warfare and economic depression threatened the nation's survival, dominating the thoughts of managers and regulators alike. But as the nation recovered from these traumas, regulatory taxes imposed during an earlier era began to gain importance. The new period of relative prosperity and security coincided with the rise to prominence of tools that are now standard in the financial markets—video screens, calculators, and computers. Thus, the antithesis is driven by economic and technological changes, as well as by the attitudes of regulators and the regulated institutions.

Computer technology has affected many aspects of business systems and personal habits. During the 1970s, developments provided new capabilities to analyze large quantities of information quickly and efficiently and to transmit it rapidly, raising the expectations of customers at financial institutions. Demand grew rapidly for customer services such as cash management and electronic banking.

However, legal limitations on depository institutions often slowed their response to demands by customers for the new products. For example, installation of electronic banking equipment at grocery stores and shopping centers was initially challenged on grounds that the change would make such facilities the equivalent of branch banks. In states with limited-branching laws, electronic banking was delayed. Similarly, Reg Q interfered with the introduction of cash management services by depository institutions, while securities firms were free to pioneer these programs.

Also, computers supported efficient analysis of large quantities of data and revolutionized the availability of information. Electronic fund transfers, or movement of funds by electronic messages rather than by paper check or other traditional methods, were increasing. As a result, financial institutions could expand their service offerings and speed up their responses to market conditions; they made increasingly forceful demands for authority to diversify services.

In the face of advancing technology, regulations began to seem like antiquated relics. As information systems enabled some participants in the financial markets, such as securities firms, to respond almost instantaneously to changes in interest rates or other market conditions, restrictive regulations on others, such as depositories, appeared to produce anticompetitive effects. Said Henry Wallich, member of the Board of Governors of the Federal Reserve, "Deregulation has been driven by

Table 3.3   ✦   Timing and Context of Selected Financial Innovations

Regulatory avoidance is often manifest in financial innovations devised by the regulated. In turn, financial innovations are encouraged by technological and economic change, as seen from the increase in the number of financial innovations in the past 20 years.

Decade	Financial Innovation	Technological Innovation	Economic/Political Environment
1930s			Stock market crash
			Bank holiday, Great Depression
Major Laws and Policies: Thesis of Dialectic Instituted			World War II begins
1940s			World War II ends
			Fed controls interest rates
			Baby Boom
1950s		Television	Fed/Treasury "Accord:" Controls lifted on rates
			Cold war/ Korean war
1960s	Eurodollar deposits	Mainframe computers	Vietnam war escalates
	Bank credit cards		
	Fed funds market		
	Negotiable CDs		
1970s	Financial futures	Handheld financial	Gold standard abandoned:
	Automated teller machines	calculators	exchange rates float
	Money market mutual funds		Vietnam war ends
	Adjustable rate mortgages		Oil embargo
	Negotiable order of withdrawal		Double-digit inflation
	(NOW) accounts		Change in Federal Reserve
	Discount brokerage accounts		System's open market policies
	Options, junk bonds		
1980s	Interest rate swaps	Microcomputers	Double-digit inflation ends
	Zero-coupon bonds	Fax machines	Stock market crash
	24-hour securities trading		Collapse of commercial real estate market
	Program trading		
	Universal/variable life insurance		
	Off-balance sheet guarantees		
	Securitization		
1990s	Global futures trading	Internet	Corporate downsizing
	Bank mutual funds/annuities	Low-cost computers	Early 1990s: low interest rates (recession)
	Home banking and Internet	Increasing accessibility	Bilateral free-trade agreements and NAFTA
	security trading	of technology	International accord: deregulation of financial
	Mergers among diverse		services firms
	financial firms		Tax law changes (new types of IRAs)
			Demographics: aging Baby Boomers
			and demand for retirement products

technological innovation. Anti-competitive practices have had to be abandoned, on pain of being circumvented; bureaucratic resistance had to yield to the pressures of the market."[18]

---

[18]Henry C. Wallich, "A Broad View of Deregulation," unpublished paper presented at the Conference on Pacific Basin Financial Reform, Federal Reserve Bank of San Francisco, San Francisco, California, December 1984, p. 3.

Changing Views on Regulation: Does It Really Promote Safety?

A final catalyst for change acted in a more subtle way. As memories of the financial crisis of the 1930s faded, some researchers believe, regulators may have modified their views on the rationale for regulation.[19] For example, many increasingly recognized that interest rate ceilings had a destabilizing effect on the economy, and the insight provoked reevaluation of regulations intended to prevent competition among depositories. Furthermore, people recognized that forcing specialization on institutions such as S&Ls did not ensure their stability or solvency. The deterioration of the financial position of the thrift industry was one more incentive for an examination of the philosophy that had traditionally guided regulators. Many no longer agreed that regulations promoted institutional safety; they considered the possibility that regulations might actually increase risk for financial institutions.

THE SYNTHESIS: DIDMCA AND GARN–ST. GERMAIN

DIDMCA

These factors led Congress to enact landmark legislation, including the Depository Institutions Deregulation and Monetary Control Act (DIDMCA) in March 1980, and later the Garn–St. Germain (G–St. G) Depository Institutions Act in October 1982. The detailed provisions of these acts are summarized, respectively, in Tables 3.4 and 3.5.

   DIDMCA incorporated two major components, as its name revealed: (1) deregulation of depository institutions and (2) improved monetary control. The deregulation provisions encouraged competition among depositories while improving financial services for small savers. The monetary control provisions improved the effectiveness of the Fed's responses to changing economic conditions and equalized the monetary policy burden among depositories. The provisions of DIDMCA accomplished several goals.

1. Phase out Reg Q Deposit Rate Ceilings, and Introduce New Sources of Funds
Rate ceilings were phased out over a 6-year period. The only restriction remaining on deposit accounts was that no interest could be paid on business demand deposits. Banks and thrifts could offer interest-bearing transaction accounts called negotiable order of withdrawal (NOW) accounts; credit unions called their accounts *share drafts*.

2. Raise Deposit Insurance Coverage from $40,000 to $100,000 per Account Holder per Institution   This provision was intended to boost confidence in depositories and stem deposit disintermediation. Since DIDMCA, many observers have criticized raising the limit as a most serious legislative error by encouraging depository institutions to take greater risks.

3. Allow New Uses of Funds for Thrifts   New investment opportunities for thrifts included commercial paper, investment company shares, education loans,

---

[19]References to the changing regulatory philosophy are found in Cargill and Garcia, 1985; West, 1982; and Carron, 1982.

Table 3.4   ✦   **PROVISIONS OF THE DEPOSITORY INSTITUTIONS DEREGULATION AND MONETARY CONTROL ACT OF 1980**

DIDMCA brought about the most sweeping changes in financial regulation since the 1930s. Its main effects were to deregulate deposit accounts, to extend the same reserve requirements to all depositories, to broaden the asset choices of thrifts, and to increase deposit insurance coverage.

Title I: Monetary Control Act of 1980

Phased in reserve requirements on transactions accounts at all depository institutions; authorized the Fed to impose supplemental interest-bearing reserve requirements if necessary; extended discount window borrowing privileges and other Fed services to any depository institution issuing transactions accounts or nonpersonal time deposits; mandated the development of a fee structure for Fed services

Title II: Depository Institutions Deregulation Act of 1980

Provided for the orderly phase-out and ultimate elimination of interest rate ceilings on deposit accounts

Title III: Consumer Checking Account Equity Act of 1980

Authorized interest-bearing transactions accounts at all depositories; increased federal deposit insurance coverage from $40,000 to $100,000 per account

Title IV: Expanded Powers for Thrifts

Allowed federally chartered S&Ls to invest in consumer and other loans, commercial paper, corporate bonds, and mutual funds; authorized federal thrifts to issue credit cards; increased powers for savings banks, including demand deposit accounts to commercial loan customers

Title V: Preemption of State Interest Rate Ceilings

Eliminated state usury ceilings on residential mortgage loans; tied ceilings rates on business and agricultural loans of $25,000 or more to the Fed discount rate; gave states until April 1, 1983, to reinstate usury ceilings on these loan categories; overrode state laws imposing ceilings on deposit interest rates

Title VI: Truth-in-Lending Simplification

Revised the Truth-in-Lending Act to help creditors comply with disclosure requirements; gave consumers additional rights in case of false disclosure

Title VII: Amendments to the National Banking Laws

Miscellaneous provisions on national banks and bank holding companies

Title VIII: Financial Regulation Simplification Act of 1980

Required regulators to limit regulations to those "for which a need has been established" and to minimize compliance costs

Title IX: Foreign Control of U.S. Financial Institutions

Imposed a moratorium until July 1, 1980, on foreign takeovers of U.S. financial institutions

and to a limited extent consumer loans. Congress intended the law to allow thrifts to improve their balance between asset and liability maturities. It also allowed thrifts to offer credit card and trust services to strengthen their competitive positions. Savings banks gained the opportunity to make limited percentages of commercial loans and to accept demand deposits in conjunction with corporate loan relationships.

4. Remove State Usury Ceilings   Congress preempted state usury ceilings on certain categories of loans so that thrifts and CUs could align the rates they charged with their cost of funds.

5. Establish Universal Reserve Requirements for All Depository Institutions

The monetary control portion of DIDMCA extended reserve requirements to

Table 3.5 ✦ Provisions of the Garn–St Germain Depository Institutions Act of 1982

Passage of G–St. G was hastened by an earnings crisis in the thrift industry. The law provided for interstate acquisitions and other measures to aid regulators of failing institutions. It further deregulated thrifts' asset portfolios and expanded the types of accounts depositories could offer.

Title I: The Deposit Insurance Flexibility Act

Gave the FDIC, FSLIC, and NCUSIF expanded options to handle failing institutions; established a priority system for emergency acquisitions of insolvent depositories, permitting interstate, interindustry acquisitions as a last resort

Title II: The Net Worth Certificate Act

Permitted the FSLIC and FDIC to issue net worth certificates to provide capital assistance to qualifying S&Ls and savings banks

Title III: The Thrift Institution Restructuring Act

Broadened investment powers for federally chartered thrifts, allowing commercial loans up to 10 percent of total assets by 1984; increased the permissible percentage of consumer loans from 20 percent to 30 percent of total assets; authorized the creation of an account directly competitive with MMMFs (later named the MMDA) for all depositories; overrode state laws preventing the enforcement of due-on-sale clauses in mortgages; permitted S&Ls to offer demand deposits to commercial loan customers; increased chartering flexibility for thrifts

Title IV: Provisions Relating to National and Member Banks

Increased the amount that could be loaned to a single borrower; exempted small institutions from reserve requirements

Title V: Credit Union Amendments

Streamlined the regulatory process for federal CUs; expanded CUs' real estate lending powers; increased their authority to invest in government securities

Title VI: Amendment to the Bank Holding Company Act

Prohibited BHCs from selling or underwriting insurance

Title VII: Miscellaneous

Authorized the issuance of NOW accounts and share drafts to state and local governments

Title VIII: The Alternative Mortgage Transaction Act of 1982

Permitted state-chartered institutions to offer the same types of adjustable-rate mortgages authorized for federally chartered institutions, unless overridden by new state laws within 3 years

---

all depositories offering transaction accounts to arrest the decline in Fed membership. To improve the Fed's ability to monitor the economy, Congress authorized the Federal Reserve Board to require regular reports on assets and liabilities.[20] The incentive for banks to resign from the Fed then disappeared, because electing nonmembership no longer offered an escape from the burden of reserve requirements.

---

[20]In practice, severe problems arose in fulfilling the requirement to monitor the assets and liabilities of almost 40,000 U.S. depository institutions. Recognition of these data collection and analysis problems led to an exemption from required reserves for the first $2 million in transaction deposits. In effect, the ruling entirely exempted a large number of small depositories, especially CUs, and Congress permanently enacted it in G–St. G. The amount of reservable liabilities subject to the 0 percent requirement is adjusted annually using a formula stipulated by Congress. Normally, marginal reserve requirements range from 3 percent to a maximum of 10 percent. A provision allows the Fed to impose a supplemental requirement of up to 4 percent under specified conditions, but the Fed is required to pay interest on those supplemental reserves.

After DIDMCA: Continuing Need for Reform

Despite DIDMCA, thrifts' profitability continued to decline at an alarming rate. In 1981, the FHLBB authorized thrifts to offer **adjustable-rate mortgages**, hoping the industry could then earn interest revenues above interest expenses. Since previous fixed-rate mortgages dominated thrift portfolios, this measure was too little too late, and mounting operating losses led to predictions of massive failures. Since depositories still could not offer rates as high as those of money market funds, disintermediation continued. Regulators also found that geographic constraints limited their responses to troubled institutions. The FSLIC had begun to increase its reliance on forced mergers for failing thrifts with stronger institutions, thus avoiding immediate payments to insured depositors; the difficulty of finding merger partners located near large, troubled institutions forced consideration of interstate mergers.[21]

Garn–St. Germain

To address continuing problems and rescue thrifts, Congress passed the Garn–St. Germain Act, which became law in October 1982. G–St. G provided for additional deregulatory steps.

1. Additional Sources of Funds: Insured Money Market Deposit Accounts (MMDAs)   Banks and thrifts could compete with money market funds armed with the advantage of deposit insurance. NOW accounts could also be offered to new groups of customers, although not to businesses, and S&Ls could offer demand deposits to corporate borrowers.

2. Additional Asset Powers for Thrifts   Federally chartered S&Ls could make commercial loans up to 10 percent of total assets by 1984, and they could invest increased percentages of their assets in consumer loans (from 20 percent to 30 percent of total assets). Also, they gained opportunities to invest in securities issued by state and local governments. Thrifts received relief from remaining limitations on adjustable-rate mortgages and abilities to enforce due-on-sale provisions in mortgage loan contracts.[22]

3. Flexibility in Changing Charter and Ownership Form   Thrifts were permitted to convert from state to federal charters and vice versa, to switch between S&L and savings bank charters, and to switch forms of ownership. This provision eased the process through which thrifts could convert from mutual ownership to stock

---

[21]The material in this section draws on a discussion in Chapter 5 of Cargill and Garcia, 1985. The extent of the financial crisis in the S&L industry is documented in Carron, 1982. Carron's predictions of high failure rates in the industry were widely quoted.

[22]Several summaries of the act's provisions are available. See *Capsule*, Federal Reserve Bank of New York, Special Issue No. 27, January 1983; Garcia et al., 1983; and Cargill and Garcia 1985. A due-on-sale clause requires the borrower to repay the mortgage loan in its entirety if the home is sold before the loan has been completely repaid. Without the clause, the new owner may be able to assume the remaining balance of the mortgage loan without renegotiating the interest rate. S&Ls argued that they needed to enforce due-on-sale clauses to escape old loans made at low interest rates.

ownership, helping them to raise capital. Savings banks also gained the advantage of choosing FDIC or FSLIC insurance and somewhat fewer product restrictions than S&Ls. Some state charters also imposed more liberal product restrictions on them.

4. Emergency Powers for Regulators   G–St. G gave the FDIC and the FSLIC broad powers to assist troubled banks and thrifts. The assistance could take the form of loans to or deposits in financially troubled institutions or assumptions or purchases of some of their assets and liabilities.

Net Worth Certificates The deposit insurers were temporarily authorized to issue a new form of support known as a *net worth certificate*. Although essentially a bookkeeping transaction, net worth certificates were intended to prevent insolvency and outright failure. The accounting rules devised by regulators in conjunction with net worth certificates conflicted with generally accepted accounting principles prescribed by the Financial Accounting Standards Board and gave rise to major controversies that plagued the financial system into the 1990s, discussed in more detail in Chapter 7.

Arranging Emergency Acquisitions The FDIC, FSLIC, and federal CU regulators were authorized to arrange interstate and interindustry mergers if suitable partners for an ailing institution could not be found within the state and/or industry.[23] Regulators were first required to look for merger partners among firms in the same industry in the same state. If a suitable partner could not be found, an out-of-state institution could be sought. If intraindustry efforts failed, regulators were to seek an acquiring firm within the same state. They could allow an interstate, interindustry merger as the last resort. These emergency powers could be applied to deal with failing S&Ls institutions of any size, but they could apply only to faltering commercial or savings banks with assets of more than $500 million.

The Dialectic Continues: in the 1980s

Like DIDMCA, G–St. G left important questions either partially or completely unanswered, and few doubted that the cat-and-mouse game between regulators and institutions would continue. Many points of controversy continued to separate institutions from regulators and other institutions, including pressure to remove geographic and product restrictions for depository institutions, the accelerating thrift crisis, and bank failures.

Pressure to Remove Geographic Restrictions   Although G–St. G allowed failing S&Ls to be merged across state lines, depository institutions could not cross state lines unless states allowed this under the McFadden Act. Congress failed to act on pressures to allow interstate banking, but some state legislatures invited out-of-state banks to enter their borders. Other states approved reciprocal laws, under formal legal authority granted by the Supreme Court in 1986, allowing out-of-state banks to enter if their home states allowed reciprocal opportunities. In some areas, such as New England, the Southeast, and the Midwest, groups of states formed regional

---

[23]Actually, more than one emergency takeover had been arranged and approved before G–St. G was passed. The first allowed interstate acquisitions of S&Ls in California, New York, and Florida. The most controversial decision, however, allowed an interindustry acquisition in which Citicorp acquired Fidelity Federal S&L of California in mid-1982.

reciprocal compacts allowing interstate banking among participating states. Some states set national triggers allowing reciprocal agreements with all states after certain periods of time.

Depositories and nondepositories alike created a new loophole for geographic and product expansion by establishing **limited service banks**, often called **nonbank banks**. Many of these institutions were created when out-of-state entities took over failing banks or thrifts and divested transaction deposits or commercial loans. The change removed the legal status of banks, allowing the institutions to engage in nonbank activities or cross state lines. Although the Fed opposed nonbank banks, the courts allowed them. Non banks are discussed in more detail in Chapter 4.

Pressure to Remove Product Restrictions   Product deregulation for banks moved more quickly at the state level. By 1987, several states allowed banks they chartered to sell and even underwrite insurance and own insurance companies. In some states, state-chartered banks, thrifts, and CUs could engage in brokerage activities. In the early 1980s, national banks entered the securities business by acquiring discount brokerage houses. In 1986, the Fed authorized banks to engage in full-service brokerage activities for institutional customers. In 1987, it permitted bank holding companies to underwrite selected debt securities under limited conditions, as well.

For S&Ls, state-chartered one savings and loan holding companies (OSLHCs) could set up service corporation subsidiaries, allowing them diversify even more widely, particularly in states with liberal regulatory attitudes, such as Texas and California.[24] They could invest in areas unrelated to banking, from acquiring food chains to holding stock in corporations to making direct real estate investments that were forbidden to other depository institutions. Ironically, as depositories escaped one set of regulations by gaining new markets in the securities industry, the SEC attempted to expand its authority over depositories.

The Continuing Thrift Crisis: Round Two

By 1987, hundreds of thrifts were technically insolvent when evaluated under generally accepted accounting practices (GAAP), but they continued operating, propped up by net worth certificates and other regulatory gimmicks allowed by DIDMCA's new regulatory accounting practices (RAP) provisions. The General Accounting Office (GAO) declared that the FSLIC was technically insolvent, with insufficient reserves to protect insured S&L depositors. As early as 1985, the FSLIC could not afford to close or arrange mergers for a number of very large thrifts, placing them instead in a consignment program, in which other thrifts or hand-picked executives took over their management. Many technically insolvent thrifts, which Kane called **zombie S&Ls**, attempted to gamble their way back to solvency in the mid-1980s by taking on great risks including overly rapid growth. This growth was funded by attracting large deposits insured up to $100,000 **(jumbo deposits)**, often sold by brokers **(brokered)** from depositors across the country. As mentioned earlier in the chapter, in liberally regulated states, such as California and Texas, allowed state-chartered thrifts to take on very risky investments forbidden to other S&Ls. Some thrift managers made bad—even fraudu-

---

[24]See Cebenoyan et al., 1998; Benston, 1985; and Brumbaugh, 1988.

lent—investment decisions that drove their institutions into insolvency as loans soured in the late 1980s.

These types of activities depleted privately insured savings funds. Private funds in Ohio and Maryland failed in 1985, and many depositors waited several years before receiving their deposits. Kane pointed out that the poor handling of these crises provided a wake-up call to the public concerning the poor condition of the FSLIC, resulting in a general loss of public confidence and a silent stream of deposit withdrawals from thrifts. The average rates that thrifts paid to keep deposits rose relative to bank rates at this time, particularly in states suffering economic distress, and thrifts suffered net deposit withdrawals.[25]

By 1987, about 15 percent of the industry had suffered overwhelming losses, straining the FSLIC's resources and creating a national crisis. The banking industry was not immune to the problems. In particular, the banking sector suffered severe strains in the middle to late 1980s. Many institutions failed and others reported record losses on commercial real estate and other risky loans. Most serious were the effects of economic problems in Texas, which led to the failure or near-failure of almost all the largest banks in that state, including First Republic and M Corp.

The Competitive Equality Banking Act of 1987 (CEBA)

CEBA, enacted in August 1987, placed a moratorium on nonbank activities, recapitalized the FSLIC, extended the net worth certificate program for 5 years, and made permanent provisions for the G–St. G emergency acquisition powers. It also placed the "full faith" of the U.S. government behind deposit insurance funds to stem deposit withdrawals from healthy thrifts. The provisions of CEBA are summarized in Table 3.6.

1. Recapitalization and Reorganization of the FSLIC   This measure was intended to rebuild confidence and slow deposit withdrawals.

2. Moratorium on Regulatory Loopholes   Limitations included a prohibition against bank regulators approving nonbank banks and additional securities, real estate, or insurance activities. The restriction applied to state regulators, as well.

3 Limited Relief from Closure for Insolvent Institutions   Some institutions could remain open in economically troubled areas. The rest of CEBA includes some rather specific consumer-oriented provisions such as expediting check clearing by thrifts and requiring depository institutions to cash government checks for customers, among others.

Beyond CEBA: The Stock Market Crash of 1987 and the Continuing Thrift Crisis

As many had foreseen, the thrift crisis continued unabated after CEBA, and problems even escalated. In October 1987, the nation's attention was temporarily diverted by a stock market crash, when the value of major stock indexes fell more than

---

[25]See Kane, 1989b; Cooperman, Lee, and Wolfe, 1992, review the Ohio S&L crisis.

Table 3.6 ✦ PROVISIONS OF THE COMPETITIVE EQUALITY BANKING ACT OF 1987

CEBA was a short-run fix for several issues facing the financial system. It authorized additional funds to assist the FSLIC with the continuing thrift crisis, but the problem was much larger than the law recognized. CEBA also prohibited the spread of nonbank banks and temporarily postponed action on further expansion of banking powers.

Title I: Financial Institutions Competitive Equality Act

Expanded the definition of *bank* to include any institution insured by the FDIC (which did not apply to 168 nonbank banks in existence on March 5, 1987); permitted nonbank banks to acquire failing savings institutions; clarified regulations applying to thrift holding companies

Title II: Moratorium on Certain Nonbanking Activities

Prohibited federal bank regulators from approving new securities, real estate, or insurance activities until March 1, 1988, beginning retroactively on March 5, 1987; brought state-chartered banks that were not members of the Fed under G–St. G with regard to affiliations with securities firms; limited the securities activities of thrifts until March 1, 1988, unless those activities were in place before March 5, 1987

Title III: FSLIC Recapitalization Act

Authorized the FHL Bank system to borrow up to $10.825 billion, collateralized by zero-coupon Treasury securities, to assist the FSLIC; permitted assessment of FSLIC institutions to service the authorized debt; phased out the special assessment of FSLIC-insured institutions in effect since 1985; specified circumstances under which "exit fees" could be charged to institutions departing the FSLIC; established an FSLIC oversight committee

Title IV: Thrift Industry Recovery Act

Required regulators to forbear in closing troubled savings institutions during the period in which FSLIC recapitalization occurred, provided an institution's problem could be attributed to economic conditions; required uniform, generally accepted accounting standards for commercial banks and savings institutions by 1993

Title V: Financial Institutions Emergency Acquisitions Act

Extended the net worth certificate program for 5 years; made G–St. G emergency acquisition powers permanent; equalized emergency acquisition rules for commercial banks and savings institutions

Title VI: Expedited Funds Availability Act

By September 1, 1990, required depositories to make funds from local deposits available to customers within 1 business day

Title VII: Credit Union Amendments

Provided the NCUA with additional powers to tighten regulation of CUs

Title VIII: Loan Loss Amortization

Instituted special provisions for banks in agricultural areas, permitting them to write off selected loan losses over an extended period

Title IX: Full Faith and Credit of Federally Insured Depository Institutions

Reaffirmed the Congress's intent to provide federal insurance for all qualifying depositors up to the legal limit

Title X: Government Checks

Required depository institutions to cash government checks for customers

Title XI: Interests to Certain Depositors

Ordered the FDIC to pay a specific rate of interest to depositors of a New York bank it had previously closed

Title XII: Miscellaneous Provisions

Mandated a study of junk bonds; required lenders to designate and disclose a cap on adjustable-rate loans

20 percent in a single day. All eyes turned toward the securities industry, and several commissions studied potential reform of the affected markets, continuing their work into 1988. To no one's surprise, the March 1, 1988, moratorium on additional banking powers under CEBA expired without more legislation. The stock market began rebounding to its level before the crash.

In an effort to assist domestic banks in competition with large foreign banks, the Fed began to approve further securities activities. By 1989, these powers included underwriting small amounts of corporate bonds, an activity prohibited since 1933. The Fed set up strict rules on so-called **firewalls** between commercial banks and their securities units, however, designed to prevent potential difficulties in securities operations from threatening the deposit insurance funds.[26] Several states also moved to give resident banks additional securities, insurance, and even real estate investment powers. An FDIC study in late 1988 found, in fact, that 22 states permitted real estate development by banks, five allowed insurance underwriting, and eight sanctioned securities underwriting.[27]

New Regulatory Stringency Under FIRREA and FDICIA

By December 1988, the FSLIC had fallen into such a desperate situation that the FHLBB was accused of virtually giving away thrifts to wealthy investors, who stood to make millions on the deals. The regulators launched a massive new program to find buyers for troubled thrifts, requiring that the acquirers inject cash into the institutions in exchange for long-term government assistance and substantial tax breaks.[28] In February 1989, President George Bush announced a plan to rescue the FSLIC and to eliminate loopholes that had permitted the abuses in the thrift industry. He immediately directed the FDIC, which had substantially more resources than the FSLIC (although clearly not enough to solve the problem), to close or to merge as many insolvent thrifts as possible. Other parts of the plan required congressional action, leading to delays of several months. Meanwhile, thrift industry losses mounted at a rate exceeding $10 million per day. By the summer of 1989, the FDIC had taken over more than 200 thrifts. The cost of resolving the crisis was pegged as high as $285 billion at that time, almost triple the highest estimate from 2 years earlier and almost 30 times the amount that Congress had authorized to help the FSLIC under CEBA.[29]

---

[26]Rules for bank firewalls included prohibitions on sharing of facilities, staff, or marketing. See Paul Duke, Jr., "Fed Moves to Allow Banks to Underwrite Corporate Debt; Equity Powers Withheld," *The Wall Street Journal*, January 19, 1989. Alan Greenspan, chairman of the Federal Reserve Board, asked for a repeal of remaining Glass–Steagall provisions at this time, with the support of President George Bush. The chairman of the SEC also offered support as long as the SEC was given jurisdiction over the securities activities of banks. See Robert E. Taylor, "Fed Moves to Require Bank Units to Seek Its Approval for Any Outside Businesses," *The Wall Street Journal*, November 22, 1988.

[27]An FDIC study in late 1988 found, in fact, that 22 states permitted real estate development by banks, five allowed insurance undewriting, and eight sanctioned securities and underwriting activities.

[28]See "Are Big S&L Rescues Giveaways to Buyers? Questions Are Growing," *The Wall Street Journal*, December 30, 1988. Also informative is Jill Abramson, "S&L Mess Isn't All Bad, at Least for Lawyers Who Were Regulators," *The Wall Street Journal*, January 31, 1989, pp. A1, A16.

[29]Paulette Thomas, "GAO Puts Cost of S&L Rescue at $285 Billion," *The Wall Street Journal*, May 22, 1989, p. A5. For more details, see "Bank Structure Conference Proceeding on FDICIA," Federal Reserve Bank of Chicago, May 7, 1992.

FIRREA: Thrift Bailout Legislation

On August 9, 1989, Congress enacted the **Financial Institutions Reform, Recovery, and Enforcement Act (FIRREA)**, introducing policies of regulatory stringency in reaction to the thrift crisis. The provisions of FIRREA are summarized in Table 3.7. FIRREA tightened supervision and regulatory standards for thrifts, mak-

---

Table 3.7   ◆   PROVISIONS OF THE FINANCIAL INSTITUTIONS REFORM, RECOVERY, AND ENFORCEMENT ACT OF 1989

FIRREA was passed in response to the financial crisis of the FSLIC. The law abolished existing federal thrift regulators, created a new supervisory structure, and transferred thrift deposit insurance to the FDIC. The law was viewed as a punitive strike at the thrift industry and a shortsighted attempt that failed to address more fundamental questions.

Title I: Purposes

Summarized Congressional intentions to strengthen the thrift industry through improved supervision and stricter regulatory standards, to place the FDIC on sound financial footing, and to promote a safe and stable system of affordable housing finance

Title II: Federal Deposit Insurance Corporation

Designated the FDIC (with its BIF and SAIF divisions) as the sole federal deposit insurer for banks and thrifts; restricted thrifts' junk bond and real estate investments; gave FDIC increased authority over state-chartered thrifts

Title III: Savings Associations

Created the OTS under the Treasury department as the principal thrift regulator; required thrift institutions to adhere to capital standards "no less stringent" than those of national banks; increased enforcement powers of FDIC and OTS over insolvent or *potentially* insolvent institutions; mandated uniform accounting rules for banks and thrifts; increased the percentage of mortgage assets thrifts must hold to avoid stricter regulations

Title IV: Transfer of Functions, Personnel, and Property

Abolished the FSLIC and FHLBB and transferred their regulatory functions to other agencies

Title V: Financing for Thrift Resolution

Created the Resolution Trust Corporation, the Resolution Funding Corporation, and the Oversight Board to dispose of insolvent thrifts

Title VI: Thrift Acquisition Enhancement Provisions

Permitted BHCs to acquire healthy thrifts

Title VII: Federal Home Loan Bank System Reforms

Created the Federal Housing Finance Board to oversee the 12 district FHL banks; required the FHL banks to promote affordable housing and community investment programs; removed all thrift supervisory authority from the FHL banks

Title VIII: Bank Conservation Act Amendments

Clarified procedures related to bank conservatorships

Title IX: Regulatory Enforcement Authority

Stiffened penalties for depository institution managers and directors who commit fraudulent acts

Title X: Studies of Federal Deposit Insurance, Banking Services, and the Safety and Soundness of Government-Sponsored Enterprises

Mandated studies on federal deposit insurance, cost and availability of retail banking services, and capital adequacy of government-sponsored organizations

Title XI: Real Estate Appraisal Reform Amendments

Required regulators to develop and enforce minimum standards for property appraisals

Title XII: Miscellaneous Provisions

Addressed community reinvestment, CUs, consumer protection, and other matters

Title XIII: Participation by State Housing Finance Authorities and Nonprofit Entities

Permitted state agencies to buy mortgage-related assets from the Resolution Trust Corporation or FDIC

Title XIV: Tax Provisions

Lowered tax benefits to acquirers of failed or failing thrifts

ing them equivalent to those for banks. Also, the act imposed new restrictions on the types of assets that thrifts could hold, turning back the "regulatory clock" to a time preceding DIDMCA. Congress's intent clearly was to punish the thrift industry and the FHLBB for the insolvency of the FSLIC. At the same time, legislators chose to ignore their own role in ducking the crisis throughout the mid-1980s and failed to address what many view as the root cause of depository institutions' difficulties: a generous deposit-insurance system not tied to the risk of insured institutions.

FIRREA included a number of basic provisions.

1. Replacement of the FHLBB and FSLIC by the OTS and FDIC-SAIF The Office of Thrift Supervision (OTS) was created to regulate thrifts, and the FDIC was divided into SAIF, the Savings Association Insurance Fund, and BIF, the Bank Insurance Fund. The 12 district FHL banks were put under a new bureaucracy, the Federal Housing Finance Board (FHFB), to provide loans to thrifts in their regions to develop and administer programs for affordable housing and community-oriented lending.[30]

2. Resolution Funding Corporation (REFCORP) and Resolution Trust Corporation (RTC) REFCORP, an "off-budget" agency, was set up to sell bonds to raise cash for covering obligations previously incurred by the FSLIC to avoid increasing the federal deficit. Cash raised by REFCORP was transferred to the **Resolution Trust Corporation (RTC)**, a new agency charged with the enormous task of managing the disposition of insolvent thrifts, including salvaging or liquidating assets of nearly 250 insolvent thrifts that the FDIC had acquired since 1989, plus any subsequent insolvencies. The act arranged for repayment of REFCORP's debt through a combination of Treasury borrowing (thus, taxpayer financing) and contributions from healthy members of the thrift industry. Complicating the regulatory scene was the Oversight Board, a committee consisting largely of cabinet members and regulators, that formulated the overall strategy of the RTC and REFCORP. The FDIC was made the "exclusive manager" of the RTC's day-to-day operations, and the FDIC chairman was also given the title of chairman of the RTC. Later in 1991, a separate chief executive officer for the RTC was named and the board was expanded to seven members. At the time FIRREA was passed, lawmakers acknowledged that the disposition cost was to be about $160 billion or higher. Also, many observers doubted that the solvent portion of the industry could shoulder the financial burden of its

---

[30]FIRREA created a complex new regulatory structure. The editors of *The Wall Street Journal* noted, "We doubt that we can add much to what any rational person would think of the . . . flowchart" ("Uncle Sam's House Sale," *The Wall Street Journal*, February 23, 1990, p. A10). The Office of Thrift Supervision was created within the Treasury department, joining the OCC, to regulate, supervise, and examine thrifts, including savings institution holding companies and savings institutions. The OTS also assumed extensive authority over the FHL bank system, reducing the influence of that system's regulators. Deposit insurance for savings institutions shifted to the SAIF, part of the FDIC, eliminating the FHLBB and FSLIC altogether. The OCC, Fed, OTS, and FHFB all maintained supervisory relations with the RTC oversight board; further, the FDIC, OTS, and RTC Oversight Board exercises oversight powers over the RTC, making a very complicated structure. For a diagram of the structure, see "Current Issues in the Financial Services Industry," Ernst and Young, October 1989, p. 24; and "The S&L Maze," *The Wall Street Journal*, February 23, 1990, p. A10.

failed counterparts, suggesting that the law might actually produce more failures than would have occurred without its passage.

3. Reimposition of Product Restrictions   FIRREA required thrifts to divest junk bond investments, and it reduced the permissible percentage of real estate mortgages and investments in service corporations that they could hold. State-chartered thrifts were prohibited from engaging in activities barred to federally chartered thrifts. The act revised the **qualified thrift lender test (QTL)**, which set standards for giving regulatory and tax advantages to thrifts and not banks. To pass, thrifts had to have 70 percent (later reduced under FDICIA to 65 percent) of their adjusted assets in mortgage related products, reducing their ability to diversify holdings.[31]

4. New Capital Requirements for Thrifts   **Capital requirements** equivalent to those for banks were phased in, along with uniform accounting rules. Regulators were given the power to halt risky practices in thrift institutions before the activities completely depleted the institutions' capital, and penalties for managers and directors who committed fraud increased. Thrifts that could not meet new capital requirements were mandated to be closed or merged with other institutions. These capital requirements are discussed in detail in Chapter 8.

5. Interindustry, Interstate Mergers of Healthy Thrifts   Another provision of FIRREA overrode state laws, assaulting regulatory duality, to reduce obstacles to mergers between institutions. Commercial banks reacted positively to this provision, which allowed them to acquire healthy thrifts across state lines. Banks could enter states from which they had previously been barred by converting acquired healthy thrifts to operate under bank charters. With capital at a premium at the time, this change allowed acquisitions of healthy thrifts, which could continue to operate as subsidiaries of bank or nonbank holding companies.

Deja Vu All over Again

FIRREA had failed to address comprehensively the systemic flaws in federal deposit insurance. Therefore, few experts were surprised that the newly restructured FDIC almost immediately encountered problems ominously reminiscent of those that had

---

[31]The FHLB's QTL test ratio divides QTL assets (home mortgages, mortgage-backed securities, and other narrowly defined, housing-related assets) by portfolio assets (total assets less the sum of fixed assets, goodwill, and other intangible assets, liquid assets, and cash greater than 10 percent of total assets). Prior to FIRREA, the QTL minimum required mortgage-related assets equal to 60 percent of portfolio assets using a more comprehensive definition (see Cole and McKenzie, 1994). FIRREA added more stringent product regulations. Thrifts had to dispose of junk bonds by 1994, and commercial real estate loans were restricted to four times a thrift's capital. Direct real estate investments could be made only through a separately capitalized subsidiary, and real estate loans had to meet loan-to-value limits. State S&Ls were required to abide by the same restrictions as federal thrifts, including a maximum of 3 percent of assets in service companies (see Cole and McKenzie, 1994; Cebenoyan, Cooperman, Register, and Hudgins, 1998). The IRS QTL test uses a more comprehensive definition of thrift assets. Thrifts failing this QTL test face IRS demands to recapture bad debt reserves. Legislation proposed in 1997 would eliminate this recapture, which has been the major impediment facing many thrifts contemplating conversion to bank charters.

earlier threatened the FSLIC. Some also raised concerns about the effect of FIR-REA on the future profitability of healthy thrifts.[32] Also overhanging the financial system were questions of commercial bank powers, international competition, and reform of the regulatory structure. FIRREA reversed some previous deregulation, further overlapped regulatory authority, and ignored important causes of institutions' antithetical behavior. Within the regulatory dialectic, it was perhaps as far from synthesis as any law could have been.

A recession beginning in the summer of 1990 accelerated banks' losses from already shaky commercial real estate loans. Drowning in a sea of bad loans and pressured by regulators applying progressively more stringent policies in reaction to the huge S&L bailout, some institutions tightened credit standards, resulting in widely publicized fears of a **"credit crunch"** that would withhold funds from even creditworthy borrowers. Although many experts were skeptical that a crunch really existed, plummeting consumer confidence dried up loan demand by "good" borrowers in virtually every region.

In this uncertain environment, nearly 300 commercial banks failed in 1990 and 1991, and the cost of handling the failures eroded BIF's available funds from $15 billion to almost nothing. With a host of new bank closures predicted through 1993, forecasters estimated that BIF would soon be insolvent without new sources of cash.[33] Meanwhile, the RTC surprised no one when it determined by the fall of 1990 that the funding initially provided in FIRREA was far less than it would need to dispose of the assets of the many failed and failing S&Ls for which it was responsible. RTC officials sought additional borrowing authority, as public outrage at the bailout continued to grow. Further, considerable partisan bickering between a Republican administration and a Democratic Congress, both seeking to avoid blame, delayed action for many months. In April 1990, the General Accounting Office stated that the cost of the bailout could exceed an incredible $500 billion. By the fall of 1991, The RTC clearly needed additional funding to continue efforts to "clean up" the thrift industry.

FDICIA: FDIC Bailout Legislation

The funding crises at BIF and the RTC served as catalysts for the next step in the regulatory dialectic, signed by President Bush on December 19, 1991. To assure that assistance reached the FDIC before it formally was declared insolvent, both legislators and administration officials were forced to abandon efforts to address the controversial issues of expanding bank powers and streamlining the regulatory structure. FIRREA had clearly shown Congress's ire at thrift regulators and especially at thrift managers. Although the act provided borrowing authority for the FDIC, in FDICIA, Congress revealed its extreme displeasure with bank regulators by imposing unprecedented limits on their judgment in evaluating institutions' safety and soundness. Some experts, such as Professor Kane (who had long charged regulators with **"regulatory malpractice"**) welcomed many of FDICIA's provisions, while others believed it prescribed actions for regulators in too much detail. Several of the rules it

---

[32]Robert M. Garsson, "2d Thrift Bill Takes Shape, But Congress Is Reluctant," *American Banker*, January 22, 1990, pp. 1–17; Robert M. Garsson, "Bailout to Cost $325 Billion, GAO Reports," *American Banker*, April 9, 1990, p. 2.

[33]At first, FDIC officials announced they would use their authority under FIRREA to raise insurance premiums high enough to cover anticipated needs, but experts noted that such a drastic increase might drive marginal institutions into failure.

mandated, described only briefly in the following paragraphs and in Table 3.8, were laid out in truly microscopic detail in the text of the law. The approach contrasted with much previous financial legislation, in which Congress left the determination of most policy details to regulatory agencies.[34] The major provisions of FDICIA deal with safety and soundness and regulatory improvement.

1. Recapitalization of the FDIC   The authority of the FDIC to borrow from the U.S. Treasury was increased to $30 billion to be repaid over the 15 years after passage of the bill. The agency was also permitted to borrow additional funds from the

---

Table 3.8   ✦   PROVISIONS OF THE FEDERAL DEPOSIT INSURANCE CORPORATION IMPROVEMENT ACT OF 1991

FDICIA was passed amidst growing concern about the financial condition of the FDIC and the problems left unattended in FIR-REA. The new law imposed risk-adjusted deposit insurance premiums and detailed rules of conduct on both regulators and depositories to prevent any reoccurrence of the crises of the 1980s.

Title I: Safety and Soundness
Increased the borrowing authority of the FDIC; established minimum level for the FDIC's reserves; mandated specific examination schedules for depositories and created tripwire system for detecting problem institutions; strengthened financial reporting rules for insured firms, including use of generally accepted accounting principles, market valuation of assets and liabilities, and complete analysis of contingent obligations; required regulators to take prompt corrective action against unsound firms; insisted that regulators resolve institution failures in the least costly manner

Title II: Regulatory Improvement [Foreign Banks and Consumer Protection]
Strengthened the Fed's authority over expansion or termination of foreign banking operations in the United States; required foreign banks accepting small deposits in the United States to obtain federal deposit insurance; reduced deposit insurance premiums to institutions offering low-cost checking accounts to consumers; encouraged institutions' involvement in "distressed" communities; imposed uniform disclosure of deposit account rates and fee schedules

Title III: Regulatory Improvement [Deposit Insurance]
Limited institutions' ability to take excessive risks in attracting new deposits; mandated risk-based federal deposit insurance premiums, effective no later than January 1, 1994; unless federal regulators approve, restricted the activities of state-chartered banks to those permitted to federally chartered banks; required periodic review of regulators' minimum capital standards

Title IV: Miscellaneous Provisions
Revised technical policies relating to interbank funds transfers, rights to financial privacy, the QTL test for thrifts, discount window borrowing, and real estate appraisal

Title V: Depository Institution Conversions
Changed rules under which merged institutions obtain federal deposit insurance

---

[34]Details of FDICIA are contained in Public Law 102-242, 102nd Cong. (December 19, 1991), "Federal Deposit Insurance Corporation Improvement Act of 1991." Further discussion can be found in "Summary of Federal Legislation," *Banking Legislation and Policy* 10, Federal Reserve Bank of Philadelphia (October–December 1991), pp. 1–4; Muckenfuss et al., 1992; Kenneth H. Bacon, "The New Banking Law Toughens Regulation, Some Say Too Much," *The Wall Street Journal*, November 29, 1991; Alan Greenspan, "Putting FDICIA in Perspective," paper presented at the Conference on Bank Structure and Competition, Federal Reserve Bank of Chicago, May 7, 1992. Updated information on regulatory revisions and the implementation of FDICIA provisions may be found in "Recent Developments Affecting Financial Institutions," a regular feature of the *FDIC Banking Review*.

Federal Financing Bank, an established source of working capital for federal agencies, according to a formula based on the FDIC's assets. BIF could also charge whatever premiums or assessments it needed to repay its loans. Congress mandated that the agency's reserves must be rebuilt over the next 15 years to a level equal to 1.25 percent of insured deposits.

2. Universal Examination Schedule   The law required exams for all depositories every 12 or 18 months, depending on their size and condition. It also created a tripwire system that examiners must use to determine their ratings of particular management areas. Except for the very smallest, all insured institutions were required to undergo annual independent audits, with publicly available results. The law also required depositories to use generally accepted accounting principles, unless regulators specified even more conservative reporting methods. Congress also required regulators to develop new accounting standards in several controversial areas, including disclosure of the market values of on-balance-sheet and off-balance-sheet assets and liabilities, discussed in greater detail at several points later in the book.

3. Prompt Corrective Action (PCA) by Regulators   FDICIA also required regulators to classify institutions by combining their CAMEL or MACRO ratings and their capital-to-assets ratios. The prompt corrective action provision mandated that regulators must close troubled institutions with very low CAMEL ratings and/or severe undercapitalization. Any depository that does not meet minimum capital requirements must provide regulators with a plan to bring its net worth up to standards. Regulators also must impose a variety of operating restrictions on such institutions. The law limited access by these institutions to loans from the Fed to stay afloat, discussed in more detail in Chapter 8. Regulators were required to choose the least costly methods for resolving depository institution failures, and a controversial provision mandated closures even of large insolvent banks that had been considered "too big to fail." Still, at the urging of regulators, Congress permitted exceptions to the new rule if regulators and the president agreed that uninsured depositors must be protected in a given situation to prevent the failure of other institutions (the **"systemic risk" exception**).

4. Increased Supervision of Foreign Banks Operating in the United States   The FDICIA also included reactions to the 1991 scandal surrounding the Bank of Credit and Commerce International (BCCI), in which thousands of small depositors worldwide lost nearly $20 billion as the result of fraud and mismanagement. The law increased the Fed's authority to approve or deny proposals for entrance and expansion of foreign banks and to terminate their operations. Foreign banks that are not subject to comprehensive examination and supervision by home country regulators may not operate in the United States. Newly opening foreign banks were required to accept deposits of $100,000 or less were to obtain federal deposit insurance.[35]

---

[35]The worldwide regulatory nightmares created by the BCCI scandal are discussed in David Lascelles et al., *Behind Closed Doors* (London: Financial Times, 1991); and "Statements to Congress by J. Virgin Mattingly, Jr., William Taylor, and E. Gerald Corrigan," *Federal Reserve Bulletin* 78 (November 1991): 902–920.

5. Directives to Reduce Risk to the Deposit Insurance System   Insured institutions were prohibited from paying excessive interest rates or engaging in risky and aggressive efforts to attract new deposits, practices that many believe contributed to the thrift debacle. Also, in a major departure from historical practice, Congress required regulators to develop a system of risk-based deposit insurance. This system, which became effective January 1994, will be discussed later in the text.

6. Product Extensions and Restrictions   The FDICIA increased the percentage of consumer loans to assets for thrifts to 35 percent. The QTL test was reduced to 65 percent holdings of mortgage-related assets, and the definition of mortgage-related assets was broadened. Banks' hard-won permission to underwrite insurance in several states was rolled back, however, with selected exceptions.

A few provisions were included for consumer protection. Under a **truth in savings** provision, depository institutions must inform borrowers of their credit costs on a comparable basis to facilitate "shopping" for credit. The law provided special benefits to institutions that offer inexpensive deposit accounts for low-income customers and encouraged lending to households and businesses in communities experiencing economic distress.

The Impossible Dream: A Law in Pursuit of the Last Loophole

Thus, the regulatory pendulum had swung back toward regulatory stringency and away from the deregulation of the 1980s. Many of the most sweeping provisions of the FDICIA were not effective until months or even years after its passage. As early as 1993, writers for *American Banker* had already dubbed FDICIA the "red tape act." They noted that bankers had changed their legislative priorities from securing new powers to rolling back the regulatory taxes FDICIA imposed. Students of the regulatory dialectic understand that, no matter how many existing doors may be closed by one law, financial and technological innovations are busy opening others. Legislation to remove Glass–Steagall was proposed throughout the 1990s, but public acceptance remained limited until recently given the abuses from the savings and loan and banking crises of the late 1980s.

THE PENDULUM SWINGS AGAIN: FURTHER DEREGULATION IN THE 1990S

OTS, Interstate Branching, and the Riegle–Neal Interstate Banking and Branching Efficiency Act

No matter how much legislation has been passed since 1980, the pressure for additional changes remains. As mentioned earlier in the chapter, regulators themselves interpreted Glass–Steagall more liberally in the late 1990s than they had in earlier years, allowing subsidiaries of BHCs to expand their nonbank activities. Similarly, pressures for geographic diversification in the early 1990s led the Office of Thrift Supervision in 1992 to announce a policy, supported by the White House, to allow interstate branching for federally chartered thrifts. Since the National Housing Act gave federal thrift regulators responsibility for the branching laws of federally insured thrifts, the OTS found legal support for this policy, following court challenges, and it became effective on May 11, 1992.

Large, regional banks, such as NationsBank, lobbied hard for permission to develop national branching networks. In 1994, passage of the **Riegle–Neal Interstate Banking and Branching Efficiency Act (IBBEA)** permitted subsidiaries of bank holding companies to engage immediately in interstate banking. It also permitted interstate branching for all banks beginning June 1, 1997, unless states opted out of the legislation by that time. By 1997, only two states, Montana and Texas, had opted out, although their prohibitions were scheduled for reconsideration after several years. For the first time since 1927, banks were free to establish branches across state lines. Previously, even under regional interstate pacts, BHCs were forced to establish expensive, separate subsidiaries in individual states with separate officers and directors. Table 3.9 shows the major provisions of IBBEA, including certain restrictions on concentration of a state's total deposits in an out-of-state bank. The law also requires an out-of-state bank to meet Community Reinvestment Act standards, as discussed in Chapter 4.[36]

Table 3.9 ✦ MAJOR PROVISIONS OF THE RIEGLE–NEAL INTERSTATE BANKING AND BRANCHING EFFICIENCY ACT OF 1994

IBBEA brought about interstate branching for the first time in 70 years.

Title I: Interstate Banking and Branching

1. Permits adequately capitalized and managed BHCs to acquire banks in any state 1 year after enactment. They could consolidate their affiliated interstate banks into branch offices via merger as early as June 1, 1997, except in states that outlawed interstate branching by that time. Individual states could opt in prior to this time.
2. Banks headquartered in states opting out of the legislation could not engage in interstate mergers.
3. Regulatory agencies of states opting into the legislation could set up cooperative agreements to supervise multistate depository institutions
4. Preserved state laws that required an acquired company to be in existence for 5 years or less.
5. Prohibited the Fed from approving an interstate acquisition if the BHC could control more than 10 percent of the insured deposits in the United States or 30 percent of those in the home state of the acquired bank.
7. Allowed states to establish their own caps on the percentages of deposits in the home states of acquired banks.
8. Required acquiring banks and branch offices to meet state community reinvestment laws. Branch offices taking deposits across state lines must create adequate volumes of loans (equal to half or more of the statewide average loan/deposit ratio) to support local communities. Written evaluations of an interstate bank's overall CRA performance in each state where it has branches must be prepared for state agencies.
9. Allowed federally insured banks to branch *de novo* into a state where they have no offices, if permitted by state law. States can tax branches as if they were full-service banks.
10. Subjected foreign-based banks to the same branching rules and subject to the same CRA reviews.
11. Subjected national banks to state laws in the areas of community support, consumer protection, fair lending, and interstate branching.
12. Required federal banking agencies to consult with community organizations before closing branch offices owned by interstate BHCs if the branches are located in low- or moderate-income areas.

Sources: J. Mark Leggett, Richard M. Whiting, and Julie L. Williams, editors, *Interstate Banking under the Riegle–Neal Interstate Banking and Branching Efficiency Act of 1994* (Englewood Cliffs, NJ: Prentice-Hall Law & Business, 1994). See also Peter S. Rose. "The 1994 Interstate Banking Law and Its Implications for the Structure of U.S. Banking," in *Banking across State Lines: Public and Private Consequences* (Westport, Conn.: Quorum Books, 1997), Chapter 3.

---

[36]See Brumbaugh, 1988 and Cebenoyan, Cooperman, Register, and Bauer, 1997.

Continuing Regulatory Concerns

With each new law passed, the pressure for additional changes will remain. While regulated institutions push for freedom to compete, regulators and lawmakers still express concerns about safety and soundness and about overlapping regulatory authority. Depository institutions are often concerned about the high costs of their regulatory burdens compared to those of other financial institutions that offer similar products. Regulators also sometimes recognize the possibility that their regulations may actually increase rather than decrease risk.

Measuring Risk

Risk-based deposit insurance and risk-based capital requirements, both products of recent legislation, require regulators to reduce complex sets of financial characteristics to small numbers of categories into which they can slot institutions. Sharp disagreements continue between regulators themselves on the most appropriate techniques for quantifying risk. These debates will continue in the first decade of the 21st century.

Securitization   Many intermediaries have abandoned buy-and-hold management strategies, in which they collect funds from customers to fund investments in financial assets that they hold until maturity. Instead, institutions seek flexibility to sell financial assets to other investors, should operating needs or economic conditions dictate a change in strategy. Although some financial assets, such as stocks, bonds, and mortgages, trade in well-developed resale markets, similar markets have developed only very recently for others, such as consumer and commercial loans. With the tremendous growth in securitization, pooling and packaging homogeneous types of loans into securities for sale to investors, financial institutions have dramatically improved their liquidity. To change their structures, they can simply sell assets that would otherwise be held to maturity. As these markets emerge, institutions that purchase these asset-backed securities are exposed to new kinds of risks. Securitization is explored in a later chapter.

Impact of Technology   The risks to which institutions are exposed change as technology changes. Traditional examinations of the safety and soundness of financial institutions focus on balance sheets and income statements, as well as on subjective assessments of management quality. Technology enables institutions to enter and leave financial markets virtually instantaneously, assuming risks on a given day that may never appear on a balance sheet or arise in an examiner's conversation with a manager. The pace and sophistication of technological change now challenge managers' and regulators' abilities to understand, much less control, the level of risk to which institutions are exposed. Some experts believe that measuring and controlling the risks posed by technology are the most difficult problems facing regulators of financial institutions today.

Banking, insurance sales, and security trading over the Internet also raise many security concerns for regulators. In August 1997, the OCC granted preliminary approval of its first virtual national bank charter to Houston, Texas-based CompuBank, which planned to offer deposit products and electronic bill payment over the telephone or through customers' personal computers. The OTS granted thrift charters to electronic thrifts, as well, including Security First Network and Atlanta Internet Bank. In 1997, the OTS also gave the green light to Principal Mutual Life Insurance Company to create a chartered thrift institution operating in cyberspace. This activity opens up new security concerns for managers of financial institutions and regulators.[37]

Contingent Liabilities   Besides instantaneous risks posed by technology, institutions are exposed to ongoing risks not reported in accounting records. For example, some institutions regularly offer advance commitments to lend or to pay the debts of customers who go into default. These **contingent liabilities**, sometimes called **off—balance-sheet items** because they have not traditionally appeared in financial statements, may or may not require cash outflows from the institution. Under pre-FDICIA accounting rules, these items were not reported as obligations on the balance sheet. Because some institutions carry billions of dollars in contingent liabilities, the arrangements inspired growing concern for regulators. A first step toward controlling them was taken in the late 1980s with the **Basle Accord**, which calls for explicit consideration of off—balance-sheet items in the determination of required capital. The Basle Accord emerged from a major effort by regulators from 12 western nations to coordinate their policies. The agreement established capital requirements based on the risk of individual institutions, as discussed in detail later in this book. FDICIA went further by requiring regulators and accountants to develop specific methods for reporting contingent liabilities. The law stopped short, however, of setting limits on their use. Other complexities remain to be addressed, as discussed in later chapters.

GLOBALIZATION OF FINANCIAL MARKETS

At several points, this chapter has mentioned increasing international competition among financial institutions. U.S. institutions now operate around the world, as do foreign firms. Managers must understand exchange rate fluctuations, interest rate differentials among countries, international supervisory agencies, and varying cultural attitudes toward banking and financial management that they may encounter in the course of routine business. These and other facets of the global financial markets are discussed throughout the text. Regulators, too, must consider the effect of new policies abroad as well as at home. The importance of international policy coordination is so great, in fact, that it is addressed in more detail in Appendix 3A.

RENEWED EMPHASIS ON BUSINESS ETHICS

The public did not ignore headlines reporting scandal and greed in financial institutions during the late 1980s. Even the seemingly invincible—including Michael Milken, until 1988 a kingpin at Drexel Burnham Lambert (a prominent securities firm), and Jim

---

[37]For more discussion of these points, see Goodman, 1986; Corrigan, 1986; and "OCC Says OK to First National Bank Charter." *Banking Policy Report* 16, no. 18 (September 16, 1997), p. 6. "OTS Says New Thrift Can Operate in Cyberspace," *Banking Policy Report* 16, no. 24 (December 15, 1997), p. 6. In 1997, 10 insurance companies operated thrift subsidiaries, allowed under the Savings and Loan Holding Company Act of 1968, which allows unitary S&L holding companies meeting an IRS thriftiness test to engage in almost any activity.

Wright, speaker of the House of Representatives until the summer of 1989—were brought down by charges of unethical financial dealings. Scores of less well-known thrift, insurance, and securities industry personnel were accused of fraud. It is interesting to note that a decade later, after being released from prison, Milken is paying his debt to society by doing community service activities. He has also built an education industry empire by investing in companies that provide technology software training for children. Many others have been indicted, including former Secretary of Defense Clark Clifford in 1992 in connection with the BCCI international banking scandal. These examples by no means exhaust the list of managers, regulators, and politicians whose behavior has been called into question since 1985. Numerous securities firms have been sued for providing misleading advice to customers on security products. Few doubt that new standards of conduct and integrity will be expected of future managers, and policies and procedures of institutions and regulators will, in turn, be affected.

CHANGES IN THE REGULATORY STRUCTURE

As suggested in earlier sections, another factor driving the need for regulatory reform is the substantial economic burden of maintaining the current complex, duplicative supervisory structure. In a 1992 study, the Federal Financial Institutions Examination Council estimated an average cost to the banking and thrift industries of complying with pre-FDICIA regulation between $7.5 billion and $17.0 billion per year. Because FDICIA increased regulatory taxes as much as any financial legislation in recent years, this cost can only inflate as all of the act's provisions take effect. In the coming decade, Congress will have to consider whether institutions make their best use of their resources in paying such costs, or whether opportunities regulators can and should support more productive resource allocation.[38] The question "Are banks special types of financial institutions?" is often posed. If the consensus answer is yes, then a structure that treats banks differently from other institutions will continue. If the answer is no, a more integrated regulatory structure is likely to emerge.

Events have also led to calls for regulatory reform in deposit insurance, and in the insurance, pension fund, and securities industries. With an increasingly global and deregulated market environment, the stage is set for another chapter of the regulatory dialectic, as old rules meet new forms of regulatory avoidance, financial and technological innovations, and economic change. In turn, a new antithesis will arise, and a new synthesis will follow, as financial institutions move into the 21st century.

Political factors also affect regulatory changes. Continuing debate calls for a financial modernization bill that allows U.S. securities firms, banks, and insurance companies to combine as discussed in Chapter 13, but political obstacles remain in place. Different groups of banks and insurance companies often see particular bills helping other groups of companies more than themselves. Thus, threatened institutions have often joined with consumer groups, who fear consolidation of power through mergers of large institutions, to prevent passage of such a bill. Some also express concern over the structure of federal deposit insurance and regulatory controls need to cope with combinations of different types of financial institutions and to control risks for bank-brokerage-insurance firms. These concerns are discussed in greater detail in Chapter 4.

---

[38]Kenneth H. Bacon, "Rules Cost Banks, Thrifts $7.5 to $17 Billion Annually, Panel Says," *The Wall Street Journal*, December 16, 1992, p. A2.

SUMMARY

Financial institutions have historically operated under tight regulation, although specific rules evolve as part of the regulatory dialectic. According to this concept, regulators articulate a set of regulations and the rationale for them (thesis); regulated firms respond by attempting to avoid regulations (antithesis); eventually, a new set of regulations emerges (synthesis) as a result of these actions. In the course of the dialectic, financial innovation and technical and economic change powerfully influence the outcome. The dialectic has been especially evident in recent years.

Depository institutions have received the most attention from regulators. Over the years, a dual regulatory structure with state and federal oversight has emerged. Despite repeated expressions of concern about overlapping authority, Congress has not yet enacted any proposals to simplify the bureaucracy. Nondepository institutions are also regulated, but to a lesser extent. Most regulations governing finance companies are established at the state level and are less complex than those for depositories. Insurance companies are also governed by state regulators, which impose substantial regulation. Pension funds, investment companies, and securities firms are regulated by major federal statutes and by state laws. Depository institutions often feel that they struggle under an overly heavy regulatory burden.

Two of the most important regulatory reforms in the early 1980s were DIDMCA and G–St. G. These laws removed some restrictions on depositories' asset choices and on their sources of funds; they also increased similarity in the regulation of banks, thrifts, and credit unions. Regulators also received additional flexibility to handle failing institutions.

Almost immediately, however, forces for additional change were at work, spurred by the crisis in the thrift industry. In 1987, CEBA was passed, but it proved to be "too little, too late" to rescue the ailing FSLIC and served only to postpone more drastic action until 1989. FIRREA, passed in 1989, was a punitive law that did little to solve the systemic problems of deposit insurance and failed to address the question of appropriate bank powers. In 1991, FDICIA attempted to reform the deposit insurance system, reigned in risk-taking behavior of depository institution managers, and required regulators to step up their aggressiveness in enforcing restrictions. Congress once again avoided important decisions on bank powers and regulatory restructuring. In 1997, banks experienced major changes in their geographic reach with the implementation of interstate branching under IBBEA, which allowed them to establish interstate branches for the first time in 70 years.

Current issues include continued diversification of depository institutions' operations; better ways of measuring and controlling the risks taken by financial institutions, including the impact of securitization and contingent liabilities; reform of the regulatory structure; regulation of institutions with international operations; and renewed emphasis on ethical behavior. Technology has offered financial institutions new opportunities, but also new nonbank competitors. Only one thing is certain: Change is an inevitable constant.

Discussion Questions

1. Explain in your own words the meaning of the term *regulatory dialectic*. Describe the three stages of the dialectic, and provide a historical example of each. Using current publications, identify a recent regulatory decision and explain the reaction of financial institutions to it. Why do financial institutions seek to avoid regulations? How does the regulatory burden of banks compare to those of other institutions?

2. How is the process of financial innovation linked to regulation and the regulatory dialectic? How are developments in the economic/political/technological environment related to innovation? Based on emerging technology, economic conditions, and forecasts for the next decade, do you predict numerous or few financial innovations? Explain. Look on the Internet for a particular bank, insurance company, or securities firm. Does the institution maintain a Web page and offer services over the Internet?

3. The 1980s brought significant progress to ease the regulatory burden of financial institutions. Give an example of a regulatory restriction that hindered depository institutions' responses to changes in economic or technological developments in the 1980s. Discuss the rationale for revising regulations, many of which had their origins in the post-Depression years.

4. Explain how DIDMCA and G–St. G changed asset and liability management for depository institutions. How did this change reduce the risk of depository institutions? How did it increase the risk?

5. Explain the events and conditions that led to the creation of the Garn–St. Germain Act and CEBA. How did the deterioration in the financial condition of the thrift industry and the FSLIC contribute to rapid congressional action? Briefly summarize the powers they gave to regulators to assist troubled institutions. In retrospect, were these provisions appropriate courses of action? Why or why not?

6. Do you agree with Professor Kane's opinion that the goals and objectives of legislators and financial institution regula-

tors changed in the 1960s and 1970s from safety and soundness to limiting competition? Why or why not? How would you characterize the intent of legislators and regulators as demonstrated in FIRREA and FDICIA?

7. Some observers viewed the CEBA provisions on nonbank banks and nonbanking activities of commercial banks as a reversal of the trend toward deregulation. Briefly explain these points of the legislation. Do you believe they conflicted with the direction set in DIDMCA and Garn–St. Germain? Why or why not? How may they have contributed to the regulatory dialectic?

8. What is the QTL test, as revised by FIRREA (and again by FDICIA)? How does this requirement affect a thrift's ability to diversify its portfolio? How could thrifts be negatively affected by this provision? In your opinion, what was FIRREA's wisest provision? Why?

9. What developments, beginning almost immediately after FIRREA, prompted the passage of FDICIA? Do you believe that FDICIA was an adequate response? Why or why not? Explain FDICIA's prompt corrective action (PCA) provision? Why did Congress see a need for such a measure? Some provisions in FDICIA were intended to solve permanently the financial problems of the deposit insurance system. What measures did Congress enact for this purpose? Do you believe different policies should be applied to large versus small institutions that are failing? Why?

10. Choose two of the areas of continuing regulatory concern discussed in the last part of the chapter. Which one of these issues do you think will precipitate the next major congressional action? Using current publications, find a reference to or discussion of these issues by a legislator, a regulator, or practitioner.

11. What explanations can you offer for the long-standing tradition of concentrating insurance regulation at the state rather than at the federal level? Do you believe other industries, such as banks, pension funds, or investment companies, could be effectively regulated only by the states?

12. Explain the impact of the McCarran–Ferguson Act on insurance pricing and the application of antitrust legislation to insurers. How did California's Proposition 103 present a challenge to the spirit of the McCarran–Ferguson law?

13. Briefly discuss the safeguards for employees included in the Employee Retirement Income Security Act (ERISA). What is the role of the Pension Benefit Guaranty Corporation (PBGC)?

14. Provide several examples of the types of regulations imposed on investment companies to control the risk exposure of shareholders.

15. In the 1970s and 1980s, Congress created regulatory safeguards to supplement the self-regulation already in place in the securities industry. What motivated these laws, and how did they restrict the activities of securities firms? What is insider trading, and what was its importance in the 1980s?

16. In the late 1980s and early 1990s, two prominent securities firms—Drexel Burnham Lambert and Salomon Brothers—were involved in financial scandals. Find a newspaper or journal article analyzing a recent example of unethical behavior within a financial institution. Do you anticipate a need for further legislation affecting the securities industry? Why?

17. What are CAMELS and MACRO ratings? How are they used in evaluating depository institutions? Explain how FDICIA's tripwires strengthen examiners' authority.

18. Regulations are the rules under which financial institutions may operate, while supervision determines enforcement of those rules. Do you attribute the deposit insurance crisis primarily to shortcomings in regulations or supervision? How much did a mismatch in asset/liability maturities contribute to the crisis? Explain.

19. Define the following terms:

- ✦ dual banking system
- ✦ regulatory avoidance
- ✦ usury ceilings
- ✦ vested benefits
- ✦ conduit theory of taxation
- ✦ disintermediation
- ✦ cross-intermediation
- ✦ electronic fund transfer
- ✦ level playing field
- ✦ securitization
- ✦ firewall
- ✦ Federal Financial Institutions Examination Council (FFIEC)
- ✦ regulatory taxes
- ✦ Basle accord
- ✦ tripwire
- ✦ contingent liability

Selected References

Barth, James R. *The Great Savings and Loan Debacle*. Washington D.C.: American Enterprise Institute, 1991.

Benston, George J. *On Analysis of the Causes of Savings and Loan Association Failures*. Salomon Brothers Center for the Study of Financial Institutions Monograph Series (1985–4/5), Graduate School of Business, New York University.

Berger, Allen N., Anil K. Kashyap, and Joseph M. Scalise. "The Transformation of the U.S. Banking Industry:

What a Long, Strange Trip It's Been." *Brookings Papers on Economic Activity* 2 (1995): 55–218.

Broaddus, Alfred. "Financial Innovation in the United States—Background, Current Status, and Prospects." *Economic Review*, Federal Reserve Bank of Richmond 71 (January/February 1985): 2–22.

Brock, Bronwyn. "Regulatory Changes Bring New Challenges to S&Ls, Other Depository Institutions." *Voice*, Federal Reserve Bank of Dallas (September 1980): 5–9.

Brumbaugh, R. Dan, Jr. *Thrifts under Siege.* Cambridge, Mass.: Ballinger, 1988.

Cargill, Thomas F., and Gillian Garcia. *Financial Reform in the 1980s.* Stanford, Calif.: Hoover Institution Press, 1985.

Carron, Andrew S. *The Plight of the Thrift Institutions.* Washington, D.C.: Brookings Institution, 1982.

Cebenoyan, A. Sinan, Elizabeth S. Cooperman, Charles A. Register, and Sylvia C. Hudgins. "Cost Inefficiency and the Holding of Nontraditional Assets by Solvent Stock Thrifts." *Journal of Real Estate Economics*, 26 (November 1998) 695–718.

Cebenoyan, A. Sinan, Elizabeth S. Cooperman, Charles A. Register, and Daniel L. Bauer. "Interstate Savings and Loans in the 1990s: A Performance and Risk Appraisal." *Working Paper,* University of Colorado at Denver, September, 1997.

Cole, Rebel A., and Joseph A. McKenzie. "Thrift Asset-Class Returns and the Efficient Diversification of Thrift Institution Portfolios." *Journal of Real Estate Economics* 22 (1994): 95–116.

Cooperman, Elizabeth S., Winson B. Lee, and Glenn A. Wolfe. "The Ohio Savings and Loan Crisis and Contagion for Retail CDs." *Journal of Finance* 3 (July 1992): 919–941.

Finnerty, John D. "Financial Engineering in Corporate Finance: An Overview." *Financial Management* 17 (Winter 1988): 14–33.

Flood, Mark D. "Two Faces of Financial Innovations." *Review*, Federal Reserve Bank of St. Louis 74 (September/October 1992): 3–17.

Garcia, Gillian, et al. "The Garn–St. Germain Depository Institutions Act of 1982," *Economic Perspectives*, Federal Reserve Bank of Chicago 7 (March/April 1983): 2–31.

Gilbert, Gary G. "An Analysis of the Bush Task Group Recommendations for Regulatory Reform." *Issues in Bank Regulation* 7 (Spring 1984): 11–16.

Gilbert, R. Alton. "Requiem for Regulation Q: What It Did and Why It Passed Away." *Review*, Federal Reserve Bank of St. Louis 68 (February 1986): 22–37.

———. "Implications of Annual Examinations for the Bank Insurance Fund." *Economic Review*, 75 Federal Reserve Bank of St. Louis (January/February 1993): 35–52.

Goodman, Laurie S. "The Interface between Technology and Regulation in Banking." In *Technology and the Regulation of Financial Markets*, ed. by Anthony Saunders and Lawrence J. White. Lexington, Mass.: D. C. Heath, 1986, pp. 181–186.

Gorton, Gary, and George Pennacchi. "Nonbanks and the Future of Banking." *Proceedings of a Conference on Bank Structure and Competition.* Chicago: Federal Reserve Bank of Chicago, 1992.

Greenspan, Alan. "An Overview of Financial Restructuring." In *The Financial Services Industry in the Year 2000.* Chicago: Federal Reserve Bank of Chicago, 1988, pp. 3–9.

Harrington, Scott. "The Impact of Rate Regulation on Prices and Underwriting Results in the Property-Liability Insurance Industry: A Survey." *Journal of Risk and Insurance* 51 (December 1984): 577–623.

Johnson, Verle B. "Reorganization?" *Weekly Letter*, Federal Reserve Bank of San Francisco, March 2, 1984.

Kane, Edward J. "Good Intentions and Unintended Evil: The Case against Selective Credit Allocation." *Journal of Money, Credit, and Banking* 9 (February 1977): 55–69.

———. "Accelerating Inflation, Technological Innovation, and the Decreasing Effectiveness of Banking Regulation." *Journal of Finance* 36 (May 1981): 355–367.

———. "Technology and the Regulation of Financial Markets." In *Technology and the Regulation of Financial Markets*, ed. by Anthony Saunders and Lawrence J. White. Lexington, Mass.: D. C. Heath, 1986, pp. 187–193.

———. "Changing Incentives Facing Financial-Services Regulators." *Journal of Financial Services Research* 2 (1989a): 265–274.

———. *The S&L Insurance Mess: How Did It Happen?* Washington, D.C.: Urban Institute Press, 1989b.

———. "De Jure Interstate Banking: Why Only Now?" *Journal of Money, Credit, and Banking* 28 (May 1996): 141–161.

Miller, Merton H. "Financial Innovation: The Last Twenty Years and the Next." *Journal of Financial and Quantitative Analysis* 21 (December 1986): 459–471.

Myers, Forest, and Catharine Lemieux. "Three Decades of Banking." *Annual Banking Studies* (Federal Reserve Bank of Kansas City) (1991): 1–27.

Neuberger, Jonathon. "FIRREA and Deposit Insurance Reform." *Weekly Letter*, Federal Reserve Bank of San Francisco, December 1, 1989.

O'Keefe, John. "The Scheduling and Reliability of Bank Examinations: The Effect of FDICIA." Working paper, Division of Research and Statistics, Federal Deposit Insurance Corporation, 1996.

Rhoades, Stephen A., and Donald T. Savage. "Controlling Nationwide Concentration under Interstate Banking." *Issues in Bank Regulation* 9 (Autumn 1985): 34–40.

Selden, Richard T. "Consumer-Oriented Intermediaries." In *Financial Institutions and Markets*, 2nd ed., ed. by Murray E. Polakoff and Thomas A. Durkin. Boston: Houghton Mifflin, 1981, pp. 207–212.

Shull, Bernard. "Economic Efficiency, Public Regulation, and Financial Reform: Depository Institutions." In *Financial Institutions and Markets*, 2nd ed., ed. by Murray E. Polakoff and Thomas A. Durkin. Boston: Houghton Mifflin, 1981, pp. 671–702.

Silber, William. "The Process of Financial Innovation." *American Economic Review* 73 (May 1983): 89–95.

Spong, Kenneth. *Banking Regulation: Its Purposes, Implementation, and Effects*, 3rd ed. Kansas City: Federal Reserve Bank of Kansas City, 1990.

Van Horne, James C. "Of Financial Innovations and Excesses." *Journal of Finance* 40 (July 1985): 621–631.

West, Robert Craig. "The Depository Institutions Deregulation Act of 1980: A Historical Perspective." *Economic Review*, Federal Reserve Bank of Kansas City 67 (February 1982): 3–13.

White, Lawrence J. *The S&L Debacle.* New York: Oxford University Press, 1991.

Chapter 3 Internet Exercise

How do I find information on individual banks?

The Federal Deposit Insurance Corporation (FDIC) maintains an Institution Directory that provides a great deal of information about institutions covered by federal deposit insurance. This class includes virtually all U.S. financial institutions. Given the maze of banking regulatory agencies, confusion can sometimes cloud questions about the primary federal regulators for individual banks.

To find out the primary regulator, or the bank charter class, for a particular institution:

1. Go to the FDIC Institution Directory at http://192.147.69.50/id/

2. In the right-hand frame, "Find an Institution," enter the name of your bank in the space provided.

3. Select the appropriate state, and then click "Find."

4. The directory will return the certificate number of the institution along with its name, location, class, and total assets for the most recent call report period. The classes of institutions are:

   N = commercial bank, national charter, and Fed member: Supervised by the Office of the Comptroller of the Currency

   SM = commercial bank, state charter, and Fed member: Supervised by the Federal Reserve Board (FRB)

NM = commercial bank, state charter, and not Fed member: Supervised by the FDIC

SB = savings bank, state charter: Supervised by the FDIC

SA = savings association, state or federal charter: Supervised by the Office of Thrift Supervision

OI = insured U.S. branch of a foreign chartered institution:

5. Click on the institution number and you will see the latest balance sheet summary. You can then compare your institution with others or look up data for different time periods.

Other useful sites for financial institutions data:

U.S. Senate Committee on Banking, Housing, and Urban Affairs
http://www.senate.gov/~banking/

U.S. House Committee on Banking and Financial Institutions
http://www.house.gov/banking/

FDIC List of Major Banking Laws since 1864
http://www.fdic.gov/publish/banklaws.html

Appendix

THE FEDERAL RESERVE SYSTEM AND INTERNATIONAL POLICY COORDINATION

"For years, the secrecy surrounding the [Federal Reserve's] meetings has only served to give rise to a rumor-and-leak industry that benefits certain market players over others."

Congressman Henry Gonzales (1992)

"America's financial markets are in many respects the wonder of the world for their efficiency and dynamism. But they are also constrained by numerous obsolete regulatory policies, and their very dynamism makes them a tempting target for new political impositions. The stakes for the U.S. economy are considerable."

Charles W. Calomiris, Paul M. Montrone Professor of Finance and Economics,

Columbia University Graduate School of Business (1997)

Quote from his book, *The Postmodern Bank Safety Net: Lessons from Developed and Developing Economies* (Washington, D.C.: American Enterprise Institute, 1997).

Fed officials are routine targets for public criticism like that in the quote from Representative Gonzales alleging that they favor certain segments of society or political interest groups over others. Similarly, the quote by Charles Calomiris praises but at the same time questions many of the regulations in U.S. markets, including many imposed by the Fed. Professional "Fed watchers" attempt to divine the future direction of interest rates—and thus the best management strategies for financial institutions—from even the most seemingly inconsequential remarks by the chairman.

Why does such an august institution play such a controversial yet influential role? This appendix answers that question by exploring the Fed's actions beyond the supervisory and regulatory functions discussed in Chapter 3. In particular, the appendix focuses on the Fed's role as a lender of last resort, guardian of the nation's payments system, architect of monetary policy, and major participant in the international regulatory scene. Rapid technological and economic changes in the last decade have raised the Fed's profile in the financial environment, and its importance will undoubtedly increase as globalization of financial markets progresses.[1]

WHY THE FED?

Although the nation's has entered its third century, the Fed only recently celebrated the 75th anniversary of its creation by a law signed by President Woodrow Wilson on December 23, 1913. For most of the country's history, it operated without such an organization.[2] Yet few financial institution managers envision a future without the Fed. Clearly, the financial system before 1913 suffered from inadequacies that the Fed has addressed with success, if not to everyone's complete satisfaction. Even economists at the St. Louis, Minneapolis, Cleveland, and Richmond Federal Reserve banks continue to question assumptions of defects in the system prior to the Fed, however, and whether it has made the right policy choices. The Fed's important economic role is regularly subjected to scrutiny.

A Brief History of the Days before the Fed

Historians identify the most important recurring and inter-related financial problems plaguing the nation before the Fed as (1) an unsatisfactory currency, (2) a deficient payments system for transferring funds from one party to another, and (3) periodic panics that led to widespread bank failures.[3] Resolving each of these problems was an important objective to the framers of the Federal Reserve Act.

The Money Supply Problem   As noted in the Chapter 3 text, the National Currency Act of 1863 and the National Banking Act of 1864 attempted to solve problems created by lack of a uniform currency by authorizing the formation of federally chartered banks that could issue national bank notes. To encourage public confidence and promote their acceptance as legal tender for transactions, national bank notes had to be collateralized by U.S. government securities. In the decades to follow, the U.S. Treasury also issued a fixed quantity of paper money backed by gold and silver reserves.

Although this system clearly improved confidence in paper money, promoted growth in the number and size of financial transactions, and encouraged interstate commerce, problems remained. The number of Treasury notes outstanding was tied directly to gold and silver reserves, and the number of national bank notes was tied to the volume of Treasury securities outstanding. These conditions made for an *inelastic* currency, the volume of which could not change spontaneously as the economy changed.

The Payments Problem   The Fed was designed to resolve additional difficulties related to a lack of confidence in the nation's payments system. Transactions depend on people's confidence that money used they exchange has value and that they can rely on financial institutions to transfer funds efficiently, honestly, and reasonably quickly between parties. Without a strong authority to enforce minimum performance levels, some banks did not keep enough reserves to cover customers' withdrawals, and others failed to provide effective, fairly priced methods of clearing checks.

The "Panic" Problem   Variability of economic cycles was compounded by unsettling questions about the value of currency, its quantity, and the reliability of funds transfers, leading to periodic financial panics. At these times, banks failed when they were unable to meet demands for withdrawals. The failures of some banks created drains on others, causing them to fail, as well.

The Bank of England helped to prevent this problem in its homeland by acting as a **lender of last resort**—a central bank that could and would supply liquidity to other banks in emergencies. Because Americans distrusted centralized authority and resisted emulating Great Britain, however, no such institution operated in the United States. Thus, the banking system went through periods of severe contraction. A particularly drastic panic in 1907 caused political leaders to conclude that opposition to a central bank was no longer in the nation's best interests. They took 6 years more, however, to devise the political solutions necessary to create the Federal Reserve System.

Organization of the Federal Reserve System

The law authorizing the Fed was an artful compromise. Advocates of a strong central bank wanted an institution with sweeping authority to supervise the money supply and the payments system; others feared that such a bank would support large institutions located in urban areas and ignore the needs of small, rural ones. The cornerstone of this compromise was the creation of not one but 12 Federal Reserve banks overseeing more than 20 additional branches located throughout the nation, as indicated in Figure 3A.1. Private-sector banks choosing to become members of the Fed contributed funds to begin district banks' operations. All national banks were required to be members, but state-chartered institutions could voluntarily join. A seven-member Board of Governors, located in Washington, D.C., was charged with coordinating the activities of the district banks. Board members were required to represent diverse geographic regions.

In the early days, the regional banks had considerably more authority than they have today. They could set the rates at which they would lend to banks in their districts (the **discount rate**) without consultation with the board; now, board approval is required. The district banks were also originally envisioned as the primary sources of influence on the nation's money supply. Events subsequently demonstrated defects in this approach, and today monetary policy is centralized in a single committee dominated by the seven Federal Reserve Board members. As a result, the district banks and their branches play a less important policy role than originally envisioned (although

Figure 3A.1   ✦   FEDERAL RESERVE BANKS AND BRANCHES

The dispersion of district banks and branches around the country reflects a political compromise by the Fed's organizers, who recognized the need for a central banking system but feared concentration of financial power. The numbers and corresponding letters assigned to a district appear on Federal Reserve notes issued in that district.

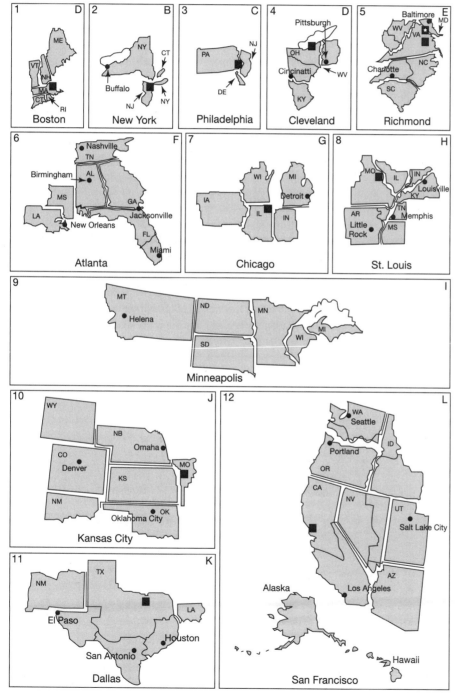

Source: *Federal Reserve Bulletin*, July 1993, p. A79.

they actively assist in funds transfers). The Fed has gradually moved away from the original intent that it be the world's only *de*centralized central bank.

THE FED AS A FINANCIAL INSTITUTION

The Fed is a critical policy-making entity and a regulator of others, but it is also a financial institution. It holds primarily financial assets, on which it earns interest revenues. An examination of a recent consolidated balance sheet from the Fed, shown in Table 3A.1, is a useful way to understand its primary functions today and their relative importance to financial institution management.

Assets of the Federal Reserve System

Clearly the Fed's largest asset is its holdings in U.S. Treasury and federal agency securities. Almost as an af-

terthought, the Federal Reserve Act gave the Fed the power to own and trade these assets. The inclusion of that power is fortuitous indeed, because the trading of government securities—called **open market operations**—is the single most important tool in the Fed's monetary policy activities, as discussed in more detail in subsequent sections.

Other asset accounts are much less significant on the balance sheet, arising as the Fed carries out important responsibilities. For example, the Fed occasionally buys and sells gold, often to assist the Treasury in international transactions. The Federal Reserve Banks do not physically store precious metals, so the "gold certificates and coin" account represents the Fed's claim on bullion stored in federal depositories, such as that at the U.S. Army installation at Fort Knox, Kentucky. The "loans to depository institutions" account symbolizes another major Fed activity—its role as lender of last resort.

Table 3A.1   ◆   TYPICAL BALANCE SHEET OF THE FEDERAL RESERVE SYSTEM ($ BILLION)

The Fed's balance sheet reflects its important responsibilities. Particularly notable are its securities portfolio, the vehicle through which it conducts open market operations; Federal Reserve notes, which serve as the nation's currency; and deposits of depository institutions, which are the reserves of the nation's banking system.

			PERCENTAGE OF TOTAL
Assets			
Gold certificates and coin		$ 21.605	6.12%
Loans to depository institutions	$ 0.218		
Federal agency securities	6.598		
Treasury securities	281.831		
Total loans and securities		288.647	81.75
Items in process of collection		8.285	2.35
Other assets		34.524	9.78%
Total assets		$353.061	100.00%
Liabilities and Net Worth			
Federal reserve notes		$287.906	81.55%
Deposits of depository institutions	29.413		
Other deposits	20.371		
Total deposits		49.784	14.10
Other liabilities		10.068	2.85
Capital		5.303	1.50
Total liabilities and capital		$353.061	100.00%

Source: Prepared by the authors with data from the Board of Governors of the Federal Reserve System, *78th Annual Report* (Washington, D.C. Board of Governors of the Federal Reserve System, 1991), pp. 244–245.

As noted, the Fed is also responsible for promoting an effective and efficient payments system. The "items in the process of collection" account is the dollar amount of uncleared checks in process at the time the balance sheet was prepared. Although the volume on any one day is a relatively small proportion of Fed assets, as shown in Table 3A.1, a staggering volume of fund transfers pass through the Federal Reserve banks annually— running well into the trillions of dollars. The "other assets" account primarily represents physical facilities.

Liabilities and Capital of the Federal Reserve System

The largest liabilities of the Fed by far are Federal Reserve notes in circulation—the paper money Americans exchange daily in millions of transactions. The 1913 Federal Reserve Act called for replacing national bank notes with Federal Reserve notes. Originally, the Fed's notes had to be backed partially by gold and partially by other assets (not including government securities), a system that retained limitations on the total volume of currency that could be issued. Gradually, the asset categories allowed as backing for Federal Reserve notes were broadened. Today, the Fed recognizes many forms of money besides currency and is not bound by a particular formula in determining the amount of its notes outstanding as a proportion of total media of exchange. Each district bank issues paper money. (Figure 3A.1 shows the letter of the alphabet that appears on currency issued in a district.) Worn notes must be retired from circulation frequently, and currency production costs are among the Fed's largest expenses.

The account "deposits of depository institutions" reflects two of the Fed's main functions—regulator and architect of monetary policy. As mentioned in the Chapter 3 text, the Depository Institutions Deregulation and Monetary Control Act of 1980 (DIDMCA) authorized the Fed to establish universal reserve requirements for all depositories. These reserves appear as deposits of depository institutions on the Fed's balance sheet and serve both as assurances of sufficient liquidity for individual institutions to meet normal operating needs and also as targets for the Fed's monetary policy activities. Reserves are discussed in more detail later in the appendix.

"Other liabilities" comprise a collection of relatively small Fed obligations, including accounts payable that arise in the normal course of business. The "capital" account represents the contributions of member institutions, on which they earn a flat 6 percent dividend, plus a relatively small accumulated surplus. As a financial institution, the Fed has been quite profitable in recent years. In 1991, for example, it earned a net income of over $21 billion. After paying a 6 percent dividend to member banks and retaining a small sum, the Fed turned over more than $20 billion to the Treasury. It considered this payment to the Treasury as a form of interest on its outstanding Federal Reserve notes.[4]

THE FED AS GUARDIAN OF THE PAYMENTS SYSTEM

Even in the 1990s, centuries-old methods of fund transfers persist; most Americans use both currency and checks to execute transactions. They never wonder whether a dollar bill received in Denver will be the equivalent of 100 cents in Boston the next day, nor do they worry about whether a utility company's bank will accept a check written on a local bank account at face value (assuming the account contains enough funds to honor the check). This confidence was not always so widespread, and the Fed has been instrumental in eliminating skepticism, and even panic, about predictable functioning of the payments system.

The Federal Reserve Act charged the Fed with improving the check-clearing process, especially between distant points. As a first step, member banks were required to clear checks drawn on other banks at face value, a practice by no means universal before 1913. Among other major improvements was the development in 1918 of **Fedwire**, through which member banks could transfer funds among themselves by telegraph, free of charge. Today, many types of electronic fund transfers occur, and the Fed led the way in their development, although checks and wire transfers (no longer free) are still common payment tools. In 1991, for example, the Fed cleared almost 19 billion paper checks, handled more than 66 million wire transfers, and electronically processed more than 1 billion commercial transfers.

Privately owned and operated fund transfer systems operate alongside the Fed's system, providing interesting (and not altogether friendly) competition among regulators and regulated institutions. Prior to 1980, the Fed had a monopoly role in the payments system, which many economists criticized. DIDMCA allowed private institutions to compete with the Fed by offering clearing services. Also, acknowledging banks' allegations of unfair competition, the Fed announced in 1990 that it would begin to reduce—but certainly not eliminate—its involvement in fund transfers and to allow the private sector to earn more of the rewards (while bearing more risk). Today, the Fed is rapidly losing its monopoly in the payments system, and many economists expect improved competitiveness and cost efficiency as a result.[5]

Daylight Overdrafts

Current banking practices give rise to **daylight overdrafts**, which some experts believe pose a growing risk to the payments system. Daylight overdrafts arise when depository institutions overdraw their reserve deposit accounts at the Fed while making transfers through Fedwire during the course of a business day. Although the Fed has yet to lose money as a result, the volume of overdrafts is so large (averaging $112 billion daily in 1987) that the Fed now requires institutions to set internal policy limits on their overdrafts. Since 1991, it has required collateral for certain types of overdrafts. The Fed limits the dollar volume of overdrafts it will process for institutions, especially those under financial stress. In April 1994, the Fed began charging institutions when daylight overdrafts occur in their reserve and clearing accounts.[6]

Privately owned payments systems, such as Clearing House Interbank Payments System (**CHIPS**) in New York City, are also exposed to losses from members' daylight overdrafts. CHIPS members, about 130 important domestic and foreign banks, routinely exchange large volumes of funds and securities among themselves. Although the Fed would absorb a loss should a bank fail while overdrawn in its clearing balances, CHIPS members would have to bear the losses themselves in case of the failure of an overdrawn CHIPS user. To limit this risk, the Fed requires that institutions include both CHIPS and Fedwire transactions in establishing their policy limits on daylight overdrafts.

THE FED AS LENDER OF LAST RESORT

The Fed's first test as a lender of last resort came more than 15 years after its founding, when the 1929 stock market crash and the Great Depression resulted in a series of bank failures. Many borrowers defaulted on bank loans, and depositors responded to the economic uncertainty by attempting to withdraw their deposits in cash. To obtain cash to meet depositors' demands, banks were forced to dump large quantities of their government securities holdings into the financial markets at "fire sale" prices, further weakening their financial positions. Despite its mandate to support member banks needing cash, the Fed was slow to react to the crisis. Economic historians, although not in complete agreement, attribute the Fed's disappointing performance to inadequate tools, a lack of understanding of the economic system's needs, or both.[7] By 1933, nearly 9,000 banks had failed, almost half those in existence in 1929.

As noted in Chapter 3, experts now view much Depression-era legislation as outmoded and even based on erroneous interpretations of the events of the time. At least one legislative response to the Depression, however, established procedures that remain the foundation of some of the Fed's current activities. The Banking Act of 1935 made permanent several changes in Fed procedures that had been introduced as temporary measures in 1932 and 1933. Notably, the act widened the Fed's latitude in deciding what collateral to accept from banks wishing to borrow at the discount window (not a physical location but merely a set of procedures through which financial institutions can borrow from the Fed). The policies governing the Fed's discount window lending are stipulated in Regulation A. In general, the Fed can lend only on very safe collateral, such as Treasury securities provided by banks, but at times of great distress, this policy allows other types of collateral.

The Fed's actions in recent financial market crises have been almost universally praised. For example, in the aftermath of the 1987 stock market crash, the Fed received high marks for its responsiveness. By standing ready to buy unlimited quantities of government securities from banks that needed cash, and by clearly and frequently communicating its intention to do so, the Fed maintained liquidity in the financial system, and not one bank failure was attributed to the crash. Subsequent analysis has led experts to conclude that the Fed successfully balanced its monetary policy objectives with its actions as lender of last resort.

However, some economists see moral hazard problems in the Fed's role as lender of last resort. Very large banks, knowing that the Fed waits to bail them out, may take on risks that they would otherwise avoid. As Charles Calomiris notes, "Thus, many [economists] came to view the safety net—previously lauded as a risk reducer—as the single most important destabilizing influence in the financial system." Economists have also expressed concern over the types of institutions that are allowed to borrow from the Fed.[8]

Whom Should a Lender of Last Resort Protect?

Today, questions surrounding the role of a lender of last resort are receiving renewed attention, primarily because of the thrift crisis and the failure of several large banks in the 1980s. Classical resort theory on the matter holds that the lender of last resort should (1) protect the *aggregate* money supply, not the safety of individual institutions; (2) lend only to well-managed institutions with temporary cash needs; (3) allow poorly managed institutions to fail; (4) require good collateral for all loans; and (5) announce these conditions well in advance of a crisis so that market participants know what to expect.[9] The Fed departed from these principles in 1974 in responding to Franklin National Bank, a large New York institution whose impending failure the Fed attempted to "manage" to avoid hurting other large banks. This limited action fortunately averted the collapse of other large banks, and Franklin National was merged with a large European bank shortly thereafter without losses to the Fed. Similar lending by the Fed helped to avert a banking crisis in the collapse of Continental Illinois National Bank 10 years later.

Observers note, however, that the Fed and other regulators have kept hundreds of failing thrift institutions afloat since the early 1980s, departing drastically from the principles of safe lending. Concern escalated in April 1989, when the Fed lent $70 million to a bankrupt but still operating thrift institution that had *no* collateral, because its parent company had previously transferred all its good assets to other subsidiaries before declaring bankruptcy. With no apparent prospects for repayment, the Fed faced continuing withdrawals by the thrift's customers as their confidence deteriorated. During the same period, the Fed agreed to make similar loans to at least eight other thrifts. Most experts criticize discount window lending under these conditions as outside the intent of lender-of-last-resort legislation. In the Federal Deposit Insurance Corporation Improvement Act (FDICIA), Congress attempted to curtail such practices by prohibiting the Fed from extending discount window loans to institutions in poor financial condition with no prospects of recovery. In the 1990s, conditions improved for banks and savings institutions, so this provision of FDICIA has not been stringently tested. Calomiris and others wonder whether loans will be withheld when political motives push regulators toward extending them.[10]

THE FED AS ARCHITECT OF MONETARY POLICY

Perhaps the Fed's single most important responsibility, and the one for which it most often receives criticism, is the conduct of monetary policy. **Monetary policy** encompasses the Fed's attempts to influence both the money supply and the level of interest rates. This section of the appendix identifies the goals of monetary policy, the primary methods by which the Fed attempts to achieve those goals, and the main effects of monetary policy on financial institution management.

Goals of Monetary Policy

Controlling the money supply is not an end in itself. Instead, most economists see a relationship between money and other important economic variables such as interest rates (and through them the supply and demand for credit), inflation, employment, national income, and currency exchange rates. Thus, the ultimate goal of monetary policy is to promote a healthy economy with low inflation, satisfactory growth in output, full employment, and an acceptable balance of trade. The importance of particular goals may change, as when Congress mandated special emphasis on jobs in the Full Employment and Balanced Growth Act of 1978. This act required the Fed to report to Congress semiannually on the impact of its policies on the unemployment rate and other economic measures. Also the goals of monetary policy sometimes conflict; for example, a booming economy with a low jobless rate may lead to inflation and high interest rates. Nonetheless, the goals listed earlier are generally accepted.

First Things First: What Is Money?

Successful monetary policy cannot be conducted unless the Fed can define and measure money. Economists agree that "money" as an abstract concept is something accepted as a medium of exchange that holds its value. In a modern financial system, this definition can apply to a wide variety of financial instruments. For example, currency and balances in checking accounts, money market accounts, and even savings accounts can all pay for transactions. Recognizing this range, the Fed has defined several categories of money (called the **monetary aggregates**) as targets of its monetary policy operations. Recent definitions of main categories are summarized in Table 3A.2. The most fundamental type of money, the

Table 3A.2 ✦ COMPONENTS OF THE MONETARY BASE
AND MONETARY AGGREGATES

In today's sophisticated financial markets, many assets qualify as money, because they have lasting value and can be used to make transactions. The narrowest definition is the monetary base, but several broader monetary aggregates also exist. Deciding which definition is best for monetary policy purposes is a difficult choice.

Monetary Base
   Currency in circulation (Federal Reserve notes, coins, U.S. Treasury certificates)
   Reserve deposits of financial institutions
Aggregate Measures of the Money Supply
   M 1
      Cash held by the public
      Traveler's checks of nonbank issuers
      Demand deposits at commercial banks
      Negotiable order of withdrawal (NOW) and Super NOW accounts
      Automatic transfer service accounts
      Credit union share draft accounts
      Demand deposits as thrift institutions
   M 2
      M 1 plus
         Overnight repurchase agreements
         Overnight Eurodollars
         Money market deposit accounts (MMDAs)
         Most money market fund balances
         Savings and small time deposits at depository institutions
   L
      M 3 plus
         Liquid assets held by U.S. residents (such as Treasury bills, bankers' acceptances, commercial paper, U.S. savings bonds)

Source: Federal Reserve Bulletin 79 (July 1993): A4.

monetary base, consists of currency and reserves of depository institutions held within the Fed. Closely related is the narrowest monetary aggregate, M1, which adds checking account balances to the monetary base. M2 adds balances in other relatively liquid, interest-bearing accounts, and M3 and L are yet broader measures.[11]

Economists also attempt to measure **money multipliers**, or relationships between the monetary base and the monetary aggregates, determined by the complex interactions of reserve requirements and public and institutional preferences for holding money. Recent research indicates, for example, that the multiplier between the monetary base and M2 during the period 1980 to 1988 ranged between 10 and 12; that is, for every $1 change in the monetary base, a $10 to $12 change in M2 would have been expected.[12] Unfortunately for the smooth con-

duct of monetary policy, money multipliers change as a result of economic changes and financial and technical innovations, magnifying the uncertainty of the policy-making process.

Policy makers must make a difficult decision about which measure of money to target to achieve ultimate monetary policy goals. A desirable target should be clearly related to important economic variables *and* an effect the Fed can influence directly without undesirable economic side effects. Economists debate the question vigorously without achieving consensus. For example, many experts believe that M2 currently shows the most stable relationship with ultimate policy variables, although that relationship is far from certain.[13] However, the monetary base is the most easily controlled measure of money, and its changes should, through the multiplier effect, result in changes in M2. Some argue, however, that manipulation of the monetary base could have undesirable effects on interest rates. Deregulation, increasing globalization, and shocks to the economic system—such as the stock market crash of 1987 and the 1989 culmination of the crisis in the thrift industry—further confuse the relationship between measures of money and monetary policy goals, fueling a continuing debate over appropriate targets.

Innovations continue to change the nature of money, such as new home-finance software that lets consumers pay bills directly on bank Web sites, electronic cash services, and systems to send money in coded E-mail messages instead of checks. Such constant change further complicates efforts to define and control money.

Money or Interest Rate Targets?

In another important issue for monetary policy, some economists argue that the Fed can achieve ultimate economic goals most effectively not by focusing directly on money, however defined, but rather by establishing interest rate targets and managing the monetary aggregates to achieve the desired rates. According to this belief, interest rates at desirable levels will lead to acceptable levels of economic growth, inflation, employment, and trade. In this view, the level of any particular monetary aggregate is important only insofar as it increases or decreases interest rates beyond target levels.[14]

In recent years, the Fed itself has seemed to vacillate over the choice between monetary aggregates and interest rates as its true policy targets. Although public statements by Fed officials consistently have stressed monetary aggregates, Fed watchers universally believe that during the 1970s, monetary policy was really directed at maintaining interest rate levels by controlling the **federal funds rate**, the interest rate that depository institutions charge on the excess reserves they lend to one another. In October 1979, however, with inflation rising precipitously, the Fed took an abrupt turn toward focusing on monetary aggregates regardless of the effect on interest rates. In October 1983, the Fed switched back to target both monetary aggregates and interest rates. Statements in the early 1990s by Fed Chairman Greenspan suggest that interest rates are once again the primary monetary policy target.

The perception of Fed ambivalence about the best targets arises from the political as well as economic pressures that influence its monetary policy. For example, many politicians, including presidents, focus on interest rates as highly visible symbols of the economy's perfor-

mance. Thus, a monetary policy that targets monetary aggregates exclusively is unlikely to please prominent politicians if it leads, for example, to high mortgage rates. Similarly, inflation disturbs politicians, so a policy that targets interest rates but leads to inflationary monetary growth will also fail to win friends. Although the Fed is nominally independent of politics, the members of the board are appointed by the president, and the Fed chairman must report regularly to Congress. Thus, many expert Fed watchers believe that the political climate influences monetary policy as much as does economic theory. Further complicating monetary policy is the Fed's regulatory role. Some observers believe the Fed may delay or forgo certain monetary policy actions if these actions would adversely affect institutions it regulates.[15]

Tools of Monetary Policy

Regardless of the economic and political difficulties, Fed officials must reach decisions about monetary policy; then they must put policy directives in motion. The current structure for implementing monetary policy has its roots in post-Depression legislation. The Banking Act of 1935 made a permanent fixture of the **Federal Open Market Committee (FOMC)**, although similar groups had operated since the early 1920s. The FOMC is the body through which all important monetary policy decisions are made. It consists of the seven members of the Board of Governors along with the presidents of five district Federal Reserve banks.[16] Besides deciding the appropriate targets of monetary policy activities, since the 1970s the FOMC has identified specific quantitative objectives, such as the rate of growth in the monetary aggregates. Finally, it considers how to apply its major policy tools—buying and selling government securities in the financial markets (open market operations).

In addition to open market operations, the Fed can pursue its desired monetary policy by changing reserve requirements for depository institutions and changing the discount rate. Although some disagree, most experts believe that these tools are relatively insignificant in monetary policy (even though they are important for other reasons).[17] Increasing or decreasing the amount of required reserves would instantaneously affect the money supply, but perhaps at the cost of a quite drastic expansion or contraction. Thus, changes in reserve requirements are seldom used to influence the money supply. A recent exception was the Fed's 1992 decision to lower, from 12 to 10 percent, the maximum proportion of selected deposits institutions must hold as reserves.

The Fed could also attempt to increase (or decrease) the level of reserves available to the banking system by lowering (or raising) the discount rate. Such a policy would influence the level of borrowing by depository institutions, as occurred many times during the recession of the early 1990s. Yet the Fed cannot force institutions to borrow, nor, as lender of last resort, can it easily refuse qualifying loan applications even if they conflict with monetary policy objectives. Thus, the subsequent discussion focuses exclusively on open market operations.

How Open Market Operations Influence the Money Supply and Interest Rates The effect of open market operations was discovered accidentally in the early days of the Fed, as individual district banks purchased and sold government securities to increase their incomes. These activities immediately affected the monetary base. When district banks accepted payment for the securities they sold, reserve accounts of purchasers were debited, decreasing total reserves in the banking system and the money supply; when the Fed purchased securities, the payments effectively injected reserves into the system, raising the money supply. A simplified example

illustrates these effects in Figure 3A.2. When the Fed sells securities to a commercial bank, as shown in Panel A of Figure 3A.2, the bank pays, and its reserves—and thus the monetary base and monetary aggregates—decrease. The decline in the money supply causes an increase in interest rates. When the Fed purchases securities in open market operations (Panel B), the opposite occurs: Bank reserves and the money supply grow, while interest rates decline.

Officials soon recognized that they should manage sales and purchases of government securities by Federal Reserve banks to avoid unplanned contractions or expansions of the monetary base and, thus, other monetary aggregates. Eventually, the authority to manage open market purchases and sales was vested in the FOMC, which implements the entire system's plans through a trading desk at the Federal Reserve Bank of New York. In between FOMC meetings, members of the board staff and at least one member of the FOMC talk daily with representatives of the trading desk.[18]

The FOMC meets several times a year to review progress toward annual targets and to provide short-run direction to the trading desk. To avoid undue interfer-

---

Figure 3A.2 ✦ EFFECTS OF OPEN MARKET OPERATIONS ON BANK RESERVES

A sale of securities by the Fed decreases the level of reserves and thus the monetary base. A Fed purchase of securities has the opposite effect.

A. Open Market Sale of Securities to a Commercial Bank:

Fed		BANK A	
– Securities Sold	– Reserve Deposits of Bank A	– Reserves on Deposit at Fed	
		+ Securities Purchased from Fed	

B. Open Market Purchase of Securities from a Commercial Bank:

Fed		BANK A	
+ Securities Purchased	+ Reserve Deposits of Bank A	+ Reserves on Deposit at Fed	
		– Securities Sold to Fed	

ence from politicians and overreaction from the financial markets, the FOMC doesn't immediately release minutes of its meetings. This delay does not stop Fed watchers from speculating about changes in monetary policy and from attempting to divine the "true" motivations for the current activities of the New York trading desk.

Monetary Policy: A Summary

Theoretical relationships among monetary policy goals, targets, and tools are summarized in Figure 3A.3, which was designed by economists at the Federal Reserve Bank of Dallas. The three policy tools are shown on the left. Actions resulting from the tools are directed at some type of target, that either the monetary base or a broader monetary aggregate, as the figure illustrates. The figure

assumes that monetary policy focuses on a measure of money, but the Fed may substitute an interest rate target. Finally, the supply of money resulting from these activities interacts with the demand for money, ideally in a way that supports ultimate policy goals. Unfortunately, straight path in theory becomes a winding road in practice, and along the way, the Fed sometimes catches financial institutions managers by surprise, as illustrated in the next section.

Monetary Policy and Asset/Liability Management

To understand how monetary policy affects financial institutions, recall that asset/liability management involves managing the spread (the difference between interest

---

Figure 3A.3 ◆ RELATIONSHIPS AMONG MONETARY POLICY GOALS, TOOLS, AND TARGETS

The path from tools of monetary policy through intermediate monetary or interest rate targets to ultimate policy goals seems direct in theory, but it is difficult to find in practice.

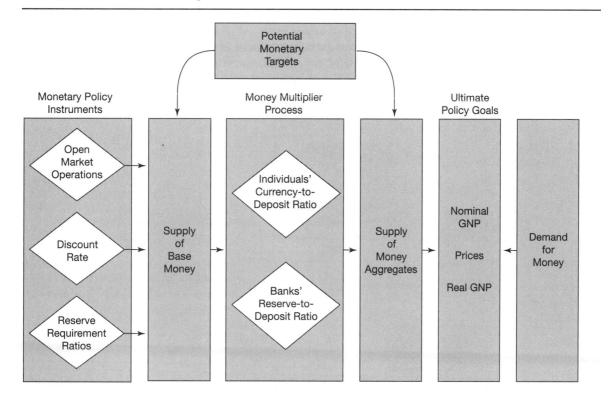

Source: Adapted from W. Michael Cox and Harvey Rosenblum, "Money and Inflation in a Deregulated Financial Environment: An Overview," *Economic Review*, Federal Reserve Bank of Dallas (May 1989): 2.

earned on assets and the interest cost of liabilities) as well as the associated risk (variability). Thus, anything that affects the level and variability of interest rates has a direct effect on asset/liability management.

Figure 3A.4 diagrams the process by which monetary policy actions affect a large financial institution's asset/liability policies. Specific lending, investment, and liability management policies are established only after reviewing the institution's current and projected financial position (balance sheet analysis) and forecasting interest rates (based on a forecast of monetary policy decisions). Unexpected changes in monetary policy, or a monetary policy that produces unexpected changes in interest rates, can be hazardous to a financial institution's health.

The Classic Example: October 1979 The effect of monetary policy on financial institutions shows up clearly in the Fed's change in October 1979 from a policy that concentrated primarily on interest rates to one that attempted to control inflation, regardless of the effect on interest rates. Under the policy in effect before October, the Fed had specified a relatively narrow range for the federal funds rate, then directed the trading desk to buy and sell securities in the financial markets to keep the rate within the target range. In September 1979, for example, the target range for the federal funds rate was $\frac{111}{4}$ to $\frac{113}{4}$ percent.[19] Relatively low interest rate volatility accompanied rates that were to seem rather modest, although they were climbing at the time of the change.

By October, the FOMC saw undesirably rapid monetary growth under the existing policy, resulting in unacceptable inflation. The trading desk was instructed to focus on targets for the monetary aggregates, reducing limits on control of the federal funds rate. Although targets for the funds rate remained in effect, they were much wider than those under the previous policy. For example, by December 1980, the FOMC's federal funds rate target range was between 15 and 20 percent.

Figure 3A.5 traces the trend in selected short-term interest rates before and after October 1979. Many financial institution managers reacted with astonishment to the level and volatility of rates after the monetary policy change. Eventually, banks' best customers had to pay interest rates of $\frac{211}{2}$ percent if they wanted loans, and mortgage rates also reached historic highs. Business ac-

---

Figure 3A.4 ✦ EFFECTS OF MONETARY POLICY ON ASSET/LIABILITY MANAGEMENT

Monetary policy affects a financial institution's asset/liability management through the interest rate forecasts that managers use to plan loan, investment, and liability management activities.

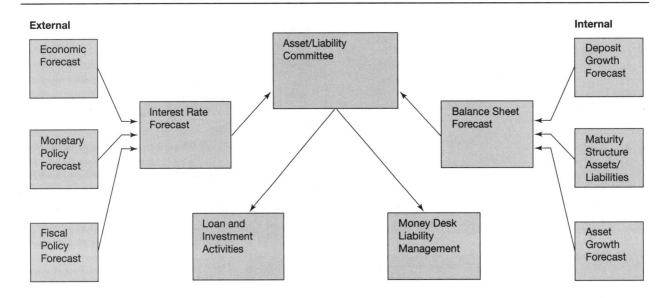

Source: Paul Meek, *U.S. Monetary Policy and Financial Markets* (New York: Federal Reserve Bank of New York, 1982), p. 42.

Figure 3A.5   ✦   SHORT-TERM INTEREST RATES BEFORE AND AFTER A CHANGE IN MONETARY POLICY

Before October 1979, the Fed's monetary policy targeted interest rates, but for several years afterward, monetary policy focused on the monetary aggregates, allowing freer movement in interest rates. Dramatic change in the level and volatility of interest rates greatly increasing financial institution managers' concern for interest rate risk management.

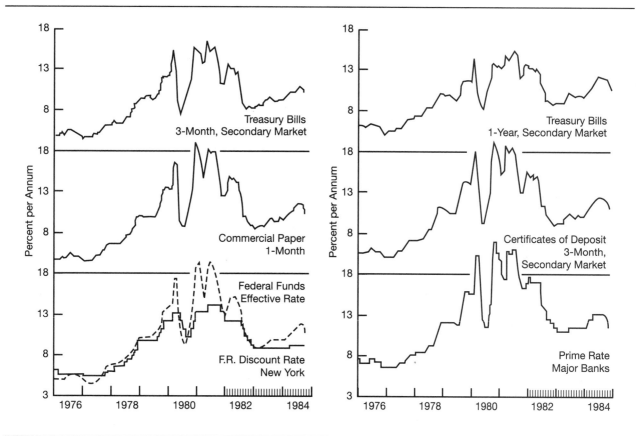

Source: Board of Governors of the Federal Reserve System, *Federal Reserve Chart Book*, November 1984, p. 72.

tivity virtually ground to a halt, resulting in an economic recession. But inflation was licked, and the Fed Chairman Paul Volcker declined to apologize.

The 1979 change sparked an unprecedented wave of attention to interest rate risk management tools—attention that persists today and is the basis for much of the rest of this book. Financial institution managers are well-advised to continue their concern with risk management; recent research shows that potential risk-reduction benefits available to depositories (and especially to thrifts) after the passage of DIDMCA in 1980 were more than offset by the increase in interest rate volatility from the Fed's 1979 monetary policy change.[20] The policy change also sparked an unprecedented wave of "Fed-bashing"

that persisted for several years. One cartoon, widely circulated in late 1981, showed the Federal Reserve Board in medical attire, operating on a patient (the U.S. economy) and using high interest rates as the surgical tool. The caption read, "Congratulations, Doctor! It was a good operation on inflation . . . too bad the patient died."

Fortunately, reports of the patient's death were premature, and by 1982, Fed watchers had noted narrowing in the FOMC's target ranges for the federal funds rate. For example, in December 1988, the FOMC announced a target range between 7 percent and 11 percent, but results showed much small actual variations in the rate. Financial institutions managers have learned, however, that they can never again afford to ignore monetary policy effects.

THE FED AND INTERNATIONAL POLICY COORDINATION

The Fed is not a strictly domestic institution; its actions affect, and are affected by, the larger world. This international dimension further complicates the Fed's attempts to conduct monetary policy and to regulate financial institutions operating in the United States.

The Gold Standard

International responsibilities are not new for the Fed. From its inception, it was charged with managing U.S. adherence to the **gold standard**. For decades before the formation of the Fed, the United States and several other countries had agreed to honor gold as the definitive standard of value and to maintain a fixed exchange rate between their currencies based on the price of gold. After 1913, the Fed's mandate required it to tie the expansion of the U.S. monetary base to the nation's supply of gold. As the world's supply of gold changed and as this country's share of that supply fluctuated, the U.S. money supply also changed, without regard for the effects on domestic economic conditions. Some economic historians, in fact, cite overriding loyalty to the gold standard to explain the Fed's failure to provide sufficient reserves to illiquid U.S. banks between 1929 and 1933.

Events of the Great Depression clearly showed that the gold standard was no longer workable, although fixed exchange rates between dollars and other currencies, based in part on gold reserves, continued from 1945 to 1971. In 1971, President Richard M. Nixon set in motion the transition to a "floating" system of exchange rates unrelated to gold in any way.[21] That transition did not, however, end the Fed's international responsibilities in the exchange markets. More and more, in fact, the Fed is required to coordinate its policies with those of central banks around the world.[22]

International Coordination and Monetary Policy

Any discussion of monetary policy leads inevitably to a discussion of the Fed in the international financial markets. Recall that one goal of monetary policy is to promote a satisfactory trade balance between the United States and other nations. To accomplish this goal, the Fed must be concerned about rates of exchange between U.S. dollars and the currencies of other countries. How does monetary policy affect exchange rates?

A full discussion of exchange rate determination is deferred until a later chapter, but basic principles are useful at this point. Under a floating exchange rate system, familiar supply–demand relationships apply in the currency markets. Increased demand for U.S. dollars (which results from high U.S. interest rates compared with those in other countries) pushes up the value of the dollar as investors seek to take advantage of high returns on dollar-denominated financial assets. When the value of the dollar rises, goods that U.S. firms hope to export become more expensive for purchasers in Japan, Germany, and other countries. Thus, U.S. exports may drop, causing an unfavorable change in the trade balance between the United States and other nations. The imbalance in trade may worsen if the Fed takes monetary policy actions that cause interest rates to increase even more for different reasons—say, because of concern about inflation at home.

G-5 and G-7 Agreements   Conflicts between these two *domestic* goals—keeping inflation down and promoting a favorable export climate—are not the only ones the Fed faces as it takes monetary policy actions. In 1985, the United States and four other major industrialized nations—called the *Group of Five* (G-5)—agreed to coordinate efforts to keep the U.S. dollar within a specified trading range relative to the currencies of other countries; in 1987, the Group of Five was expanded to the **Group of Seven (G-7)**.[23] The actual range, a closely guarded secret by the G-7 governments, represents perceptions of the best collective interests of the nations. Experts believe that policy makers set a very flexible target rather than a narrow one.

To carry out the agreement, central banks in the G-7 nations buy or sell dollars in the exchange markets whenever its value threatens to break outside the range. When open market purchases and sales of dollars fail to reverse what the group considers an undesirable trend, the non-U.S. G-7 central banks sometimes attempt to increase or decrease interest rates in their own countries to counteract differentials between U.S. and non-U.S. interest rates. If the Fed decides to change its monetary policy approach for reasons unrelated to the G-7 agreement, that change can conflict with simultaneous actions of the other central banks, frustrating the process of policy coordination. Fed watchers continually monitor the Fed to determine whether it resolves any conflict between domestic and international objectives in favor of one or the other. Although the process of international policy coordination has not continued long enough to draw firm conclusions, many observers believe the Fed has favored domestic policy needs. The same statement seems to be true of central bankers in the other G-7 nations.[24]

International Coordination of Financial Institution Regulation

Other reasons besides intertwining domestic monetary policy with foreign exchange activity require the Fed to consider international issues. Technological and financial innovations that have spurred regulatory revisions in the United States influence international regulatory reform, as well.

Increasing Globalization   As Fed Chairman Alan Greenspan noted, in recent years technology has permitted many products to be downsized, greatly reducing the cost of shipping between countries. Increased international trade means increased demands on institutions to facilitate financing. Recent advances in technology also permit rapid transmission of financial information, bringing the financial markets of many countries closer to one another. The world's financial markets are becoming increasingly integrated, with increased communication and competition among financial institutions throughout the world.[25]

When financial institutions interact internationally, the pressure for domestic regulatory adjustments increases. If U.S. officials establish restrictive rules, the regulatory dialectic suggests an immediate incentive for markets to move to countries with more accommodating rules, initiating a chain of responses by regulators. One possible result is a reciprocal agreement giving foreign banks in the United States powers that U.S. banks are seeking abroad. Then, to avoid the perception that foreign banks in the United States have special privileges prohibited to domestic banks, domestic rules may change. Similarly, U.S. markets cannot flourish if some domestic institutions, such as securities firms, are permitted to engage in international transactions that give them advantages over their domestically chartered competitors, such as commercial banks. Hence, rules governing domestic institutions' relationships with one another may also change. In recent years, the proper regulatory response to international events has inspired extensive debate.

Regulatory Responses to Globalization   As early as 1919, the **Edge Act** recognized the need for competitive equality among domestic and foreign banks, permitting U.S. banks to establish operations outside their home territories to conduct international banking. At that time, branching by out-of-state commercial banks was restricted in most states, so the Edge Act represented an early loosening of regulations in the face of competitive pressures. Edge corporations also have been permitted to invest in a greater variety of assets than banks conducting business solely within the United States; they are, however, subject to some domestic banking regulations, such as reserve and minimum capital requirements. In 1991, the Fed amended its rules to permit Edge corporations to provide domestic banking services to foreign persons and governments.

Additional steps toward uniform banking regulations in the United States resulted from the **International Banking Act of 1978**, which required any foreign bank operating in the United States to purchase deposit insurance and to choose a home state and operate under its branching laws. Because most states continued to prohibit interstate branching at that time, Congress intended not to loosen restrictions on domestic banks but to tighten them on foreign banks. One main exception to that intent subsequently returned to haunt the Congress a decade later: The International Banking Act exempted 15 large foreign banks from Glass–Steagall prohibitions against the underwriting corporate debt and equities. Thus, by the late 1980s, domestic commercial banks and securities firms were losing business to the 15 foreign banks that could provide both types of financial services.[26]

The restrictions imposed on foreign banks were not popular in those banks' countries of origin. In response to criticism of the International Banking Act, the Fed in 1981 authorized domestic and foreign banks to establish **international banking facilities (IBFs)** to conduct business solely with international customers. Unlike Edge corporations, IBFs are not subject to reserve requirements, nor does deposit insurance protect their account balances. The Fed made IBFs relatively inexpensive to establish. They need not be separate physical facilities; rather, separate bookkeeping entities meet Fed requirement, making IBFs very popular innovations.[27]

In the wake of the scandal over the Bank of Credit and Commerce International (BCCI), Congress included in FDICIA the **Foreign Bank Supervision Enhancement Act (FBSEA)**, directing the Fed to tighten regulations on foreign banks operating in the United States. FBSEA requires Fed approval of the establishment of all new branches or agencies of foreign banks. Also, in determining whether foreign banks can enter the United States, the Fed must evaluate home country supervisors' procedures for monitoring and controlling the institutions' *worldwide* operations, including relationships between banks and nonbank affiliates. (The term used for this worldwide scrutiny is **comprehensive consolidated supervision**.) The extent to which the home country supervisor enforces safety and soundness regulations on all the bank's activities is also an important consideration.

A further restriction imposed by the FBSEA mandates that all banks accepting domestic retail deposits under $100,000 purchase deposit insurance. Finally, the Fed analyzes secrecy laws from the home countries of foreign financial institutions. Such secrecy laws might prohibit these institutions from providing the Fed with complete financial information. If Fed officials believe that foreign laws interfere substantially with adequate disclosure in the United States, regulators may deny entry to a foreign institution. Effects of FBSEA soon appeared. Between its passage in late 1991 and April 1993,

the Fed approved only three applications from foreign banks to open U.S. offices.[28]

Continuing Pressure for Policy Coordination in the 1990s These laws and regulations, although intended to equalize treatment of commercial banks in the United States, do not consider the impact of other countries' laws and regulations on U.S. institutions. Pressure is increasing for uniform treatment, regardless of country. U.S. institutions linked to those in other countries through global markets have found foreign regulators less restrictive than U.S. regulators for several years. Most impose fewer balance sheet constraints on commercial banks and acted to deregulate deposit interest rates long before the 1986 demise of Regulation Q, as mandated by DIDMCA.[29]

Table 3A.3 summarizes major regulatory differences between the United States and other Group of Ten (G-10) nations in the 1990s.[30] Countries identified in the

---

Table 3A.3 ✦ COMPARISON OF BANK REGULATIONS IN THE G-10 COUNTRIES

Although few G-10 nations give securities firms access to discount window and payments system privileges, U.S. regulators impose more restrictions on commercial banks engaging in securities activities than do regulators in other nations. U.S. institutions are subject to regulation by a variety of agencies, whereas other countries limit the number of banking and securities regulators to one or two.

Country	Form of Bank/Securities Integration			Number of Banking and Securities Regulators	Access to Central Bank Lending		Access to Central Bank Payments System	
	Within Bank	Thin Firewalls	Thick Firewalls		Depositories	Depositories and Securities Firms	Depositories	Depositories and Securities Firms
Universal system								
France	x			One	x		x	
Germany	x			One	x		x	
Italy	x			One	x		x	
The Netherlands	x			One	x		x	
Switzerland	x			One	x		x	
Blended system								
Belgium		x		One	x		x	
Canada		x		Two		x	x	
Japan		x[a]		Two		x		x
Sweden		x		One	x		x	
United Kingdom		x		Two	x		x	
United States			x	Multiple		x	x	

[a]Banks permitted to invest in, and bank subsidiaries permitted to underwrite, equity securities; equity brokerage prohibited to banks and bank subsidiaries.

Sources: Adapted from Cumming and Sweet, 1987–1988; Robert H. Dugger et al., "EC 1992: The Financial Competitiveness Implications," paper presented at the 26th Annual Conference on Bank Structure and Competition, Chicago, May 1990; and Frankel and Morgan, 1992.

table as having "universal" regulatory systems permit banks to provide virtually all types of financial services and products, including securities and insurance. Those with "blended" systems permit some diversification by banks but maintain some separation (that is, require firewalls of varying thicknesses) between traditional commercial banking activities and other operations. Recall from Chapter 3 that firewalls are regulatory limitations on combinations of banking and nonbanking activities within the same organization. Regulators intend such limitations to keep financial crises arising in nonbanking activities from spreading to banking and thus imposing costs on the deposit insurance system. Note that the United States is more restrictive than most other G-10 nations and requires institutions to report to more regulators. Only Japan allows securities firms both discount window and payments system privileges. However, like the United States, Japan has been more adamant than other G-10 nations about separating the banking and securities businesses. Although financial regulations in Japan have been liberalized in the 1990s, they are still less progressive than those in other developed economies.

Financial crises among so-called **less developed countries (LDCs)**—such as many in Latin and Central America, Africa, and parts of Asia—have added to the pressure for international policy coordination. Many large financial institutions in the United States, Europe, and Japan lent billions to LDCs during the 1980s, loans that began to look very risky as domestic financial conditions in many of the borrowing countries deteriorated. Government officials in the G-7 nations recognized the need to work together to avert collapses of major banks as a result of defaults by LDCs and simultaneously to buy time for the LDCs' governments to emerge from their financial crises with strengthened economies. Financial crises have occurred in 1997 in relatively developed countries, as well, including Japan, Korea, Thailand, and Indonesia, necessitating loans from other countries and the IMF. The IMF imposed conditions for granting loans, including closing down insolvent financial institutions, improving financial disclosure for financial institutions, and freeing market competition.[31]

Policy Coordination with the European Community

Perhaps the strongest impetus for U.S. regulators to participate in international policy coordination has come from the decision by the 12 member countries of the **European Community (EC)** to remove all internal barriers among themselves to trade, travel, and employment after December 31, 1992.

The EC's Second Banking Directive of 1989 outlined uniform regulations for financial institutions. Member countries agreed on permissible banking powers, including securities but not insurance activities, and established the principle that an institution, once it is authorized by its home country to operate as a bank, may operate as a bank anywhere in the EC without formal approval from other host governments. The rules also include a **national treatment** policy, under which a financial institution from a non-EC country will be granted full competitive powers within the EC as long as EC banks are allowed to operate in the other country on an equal footing with that nation's domestic institutions. Hence, countries need not establish identical regulations; as long as EC banks are not at a competitive disadvantage when operating in another country, its banks will not be at a disadvantage in European markets. Finally, a proposal called for a pan-European central bank (initially nicknamed the **Eurofed**) with authority over the central banks of EC nations. As the early name suggests, EC officials carefully studied the U.S. Fed when developing the proposal for the **European Central Bank (ECB)**.

Perhaps the most dramatic financial development accompanying European integration in 1992 was the decision by EC nations to consider abandoning separate currencies and forming a **European Monetary Union (EMU)** with a common currency, the **European Currency Unit (ECU or Euro)**. This agreement, known as the **Maastricht Accord** (for the city in the Netherlands in which it was signed), originally called for the ECU to become operational no later than 1999. In May 1998, the European Union officially scheduled the launch of the new European currency, the Euro, on January 1, 1999. Exchange rates were set for the currencies of the 11 nations scheduled to join the monetary union, including Austria, Belgium, Finland, France, Germany, Ireland, Italy, Luxembourg, Netherlands, Portugal, and Spain. Greece is expected to join by 2001. Britain, Sweden, and Denmark have opted out at this time. By July 1, 2002, Euro notes and coins will be in circulation, and the national currencies of the 11 participating nations will be fully abolished. Monetary policy governing the ECU is the responsibility of the European Central Bank.

In another development in May 1998, the European Union summit struggled with a bitter controversy between France and its partners over which candidate would be appointed to head the ECB. In a compromise, Wim Duisenberg, the Dutch candidate, was appointed to an 8-year term as the chairman of the ECB with an agreement that he would step down voluntarily to permit Jean-Claude Trichet, the French candidate, to take the post in 2002. Each of the 11 countries will also have an independent central bank, governors of which participate in ECB decision making. This system is analogous to relationships within the Fed between Federal Reserve banks and the Board of Governors. This process was facilitated by the operation since 1986 of an ECU-denominated bond market within the EC. Compromises have emerged from a difficult process, as illustrated by the problems with selecting a chairperson of the ECB. In some EC countries, voters showed initial resistance to eliminating individual currencies. Additional challenges come from the timing of converting existing debt into debt denominated in Euros. For instance, France announced that as of January 1, 1999, all outstanding public debt, all bond and stock markets, and all futures markets a well as interbank and foreign exchange transactions will be denominated in Euros. Germany, in contrast, opted for a more graduate transition under pressure from large banks and institutional investors.[32]

The economic unification of Europe has stepped up international competition for U.S. financial institutions. However, it has also provided new opportunities for U.S. and other international financial firms to offer products and provide financial advice in Europe. U.S. investment banks have actively advised prospective partners in mergers and acquisitions. European financial institutions, spurred by the anticipated 1992 agreement, moved quickly to restructure. By the end of 1988, nearly 400 banks and other financial firms in Europe had merged to position themselves for expansion, and the merger wave continued well in the 1990s. In 1997, U.S. investment banks Morgan Stanley Dean Witter & Co.; Goldman, Sachs & Co.; and J. P. Morgan and Co., were three of the five top merger and acquisition advisers, handling 57 percent of the deals in Europe in that year.

With the launch of the Euro, numerous other mergers and acquisitions are expected in Europe. New products have emerged, and joint marketing agreements have affected current product lines, since European financial institutions can commercialize their products in the same currency throughout the continent. Some experts estimate that the cost of financial services for Europeans may decline by as much as 10 percent due to increased competition. Observers expect success for large, prominent financial institutions with cash-management systems that can handle economic needs of corporate customers in EC nations; likely winners include ABN Amro Holding NV of the Netherlands, Societé Generale of France, HSBC Holdings PLC of Britain, and Deutsche Bank AG of Germany. Giant U.S. banks such as Citicorp, strengthened by its planned merger with Travelers Group, and Chase Manhattan already have established large European retail operations.[33]

Fed officials, greatly concerned about the viability of U.S. institutions in foreign markets, began in 1987 to encourage international regulatory cooperation. Although the Fed has supported the removal of Glass–Steagall prohibitions against mixing commercial and investment banking in the U.S. market, it seeks to limit the risks to the deposit insurance system from potential losses if depositories based in other countries engage in securities activities. The Fed was influential in the Basle Agreement in 1987, under which commercial banks' minimum capital requirements are uniform in the G-10 nations. These regulations are covered in greater detail in a later chapter.

Other differences may be more difficult to reconcile. For example, most foreign governments do not offer deposit insurance. Although some economists see no real need for it, most observers agree that the U.S. system will probably continue. Still other experts warn of the danger of relying on international policy coordination and regulation as a substitute for market-determined solutions to economic problems. Thus, the Fed's challenge is to promote competitive equality with other countries while maintaining free markets and preserving the unique features of the U.S. system. Regulation and economic policy in the international arena are certain to play a major role in the regulatory dialectic of the future.

SUMMARY

Although many regulators oversee financial institutions, the Fed exerts the most pervasive influence. As the central bank of the United States, the Fed is charged with issuing currency, maintaining an efficient payments system, serving as a lender of last resort to institutions with liquidity problems, and developing and executing monetary policy that promotes the nation's economic well-being. The Fed must also coordinate its regulatory and monetary activities with those of central banks around the world. As might be expected, given the evolution and globalization in financial markets, each of these tasks has become increasingly complex in recent years.

In administering the payments system, the Fed finds that more and more funds are transferred by electronic means, and the daylight overdrafts of large banks pose new risks. Increasing numbers of depositories have borrowed from the Fed's discount window, raising questions about its proper role as a lender of last resort. Yet monetary policy poses perhaps the stiffest challenges for the Fed. Monetary policy decisions are made by members of the FOMC, who meet periodically to plan the Fed's purchases and sales of government securities. Unfortunately for the FOMC, innovations have introduced new difficulties in defining "money," and tenuous relationships link different measures of money and desirable economic outcomes. The growth of electronic and Internet-transmitted payments is changing the nature of money. The Fed and its critics debate whether the money supply ought to be targeted directly or whether interest rates are the appropriate targets for monetary policy. Through their effects on interest rates, monetary policy decisions have a substantial impact on financial institutions' asset/liability management decisions.

An issue of growing importance is the Fed's need to coordinate monetary policy and regulatory initiatives with those of central banks in other countries. Recent currency exchange agreements between the United States and other G-7 nations have affected the value of the U.S. dollar and the way in which monetary policy is conducted and interpreted. With the birth of the Euro on January 1, 1999, the new European Central Bank will also have considerable power. The degree to which U.S. regulations are more or less restrictive than those abroad determines the competitiveness of U.S. institutions and markets. Although central banks have made strides toward greater policy coordination since the late 1980s, the U.S. financial system continues to be less integrated than those of other major powers. This fact is sure to influence the Fed's behavior, and thus the management of financial institutions, in the 21st century.

Discussion Questions

1. The Federal Reserve System was created by Congress in 1913 to solve several persistent economic problems, two of which were inadequate control over the money supply and uncertainties in the payments system. Explain briefly the nature of these problems, and describe how the powers of the Fed were designed to solve them.

2. The Fed is sometimes called a *decentralized* central bank. Explain how this term describes the structure of the Fed.

What political and economic forces provided the motivation for this structure? Has the balance of power shifted toward or away from the Board of Governors since the system was created? Explain.

3. What is a Federal Reserve note? Do you have any? To what extent is the quantity of Federal Reserve notes issued today tied to the amount of gold or other assets held by the Fed? Does the current system reflect an elastic or an inelastic currency? Why?

4. Suppose you were hired by the Fed as a consultant to evaluate the safety and stability of the payments system. How would you describe the characteristics of an ideal system? What are daylight overdrafts, and what risks to the payments system do they present? What incentives and disincentives motivate institutions to use daylight overdrafts?

5. An important activity of the Federal Reserve is serving as the lender of last resort for member banks. What is the meaning of this term, and how does this Fed power contribute to the stability of the banking system? Ideally, under what circumstances should the Fed lend money to an institution experiencing liquidity difficulties? In your opinion, was the Fed's support of problem thrifts in the late 1980s consistent with the theoretical objectives of a lender of last resort? Why or why not?

6. One of the Fed's important functions is to implement monetary policy. What principles guide the long-term objectives of monetary policy? Is the Fed always free to set its own targets for the level of economic activity and growth? Provide an example to support your answer.

7. The discount window and the discount rate are important tools for implementation of monetary policy and the Fed's role as lender of last resort. Explain how the discount window functions. How may management of the discount rate create conflicts between monetary policy goals and obligations as lender of last resort?

8. Should the Fed be required to publish verbatim transcripts of its deliberations on open market operations? If so, what are the benefits? If not, what are the potential dangers of such public disclosure?

9. Economists have never agreed on a single definition of money. Develop your own general definition of money and its purpose. What monetary aggregate best matches your definition? Is the monetary base a better match for your definition? Why or why not?

10. Suppose that you must develop a procedure for controlling the money supply. Your salary and benefits depend on your success in keeping money within a target range. Would you prefer to use as your definition the monetary base or M2? Why? Now suppose instead that your future depends on your success in controlling inflation and the rate of growth in GNP. Under these circumstances, which definition of money would you choose to watch most closely, and why?

11. The FOMC has just voted unanimously to sell $100 million in government securities to dealers, who in turn will sell them to First National Bank. Explain how this transaction

will affect (1) the total assets of First National Bank, (2) the assets and liabilities of the Fed, and (3) the monetary base. What is the role of money multipliers in determining the potential effect on M2?

12. In addition to open market operations, the Fed has two other monetary policy tools. Describe these tools, and explain why some experts view them as less effective than the work of the FOMC. How does the Fed's obligation to protect the safety and soundness of the financial system complicate the use of these second and third monetary policy tools?

13. In October 1979, the Fed made an important change in monetary policy procedures by switching its focus from the money supply to interest rates as the principal policy target. Explain the subsequent effects on interest rates and the rate of inflation. What has been the lasting effect on financial management techniques in financial institutions? Why?

14. Survey current periodicals and newspapers for a recent report on the Fed's monetary policy decisions. What is the author's evaluation of the effectiveness of recent Fed decisions? What policy tools are mentioned? In the author's opinion, what intermediate target (i.e., money supply or interest rates) currently guides Fed policy decisions? How have innovations such as securitization, electronic banking, and cyberbanking affected the Fed's control of the money supply?

15. For several decades prior to 1971, the rate of exchange between the currencies of many countries was related to the value of gold. Is the floating system introduced in 1971 related in any way to gold? If not, what factors influence currency exchange rates? How do the activities of the G-7 countries reduce variability in exchange rates?

16. Explain the term *globalization*. Describe at least two recent developments contributing to globalization. Provide an example that indicates how globalization has increased the need for international coordination of the regulations under which financial institutions operate.

17. The Edge Act and later legislation included provisions that contributed to a balance of power between domestic and international institutions. Compare and contrast Edge corporations and international banking facilities, and explain how they promote international banking activities.

18. How did international banks operating in the United States react to the restrictive provisions imposed on them by the International Banking Act of 1978? Evaluate these developments in the context of the regulatory dialectic. What was the Fed's response?

19. Explain the impact of a unified single European market on sales of financial services in Europe. Why does a single European market pressure U.S. regulators to modify longstanding laws and policies?

20. Do you believe U.S. regulators should change policies to conform with international standards? What are the benefits to U.S. financial institutions and the overall financial system from such policy coordination? Can you think of any circumstances under which major changes in the regulation of capital, deposit insurance, or the scope of banking activities, for example, might pose new risks for the U.S. economy? If so, how can regulators respond to those risks in light of increasing pressure from globalization?

Selected References

Abken, Peter A. "Globalization of Stock, Futures, and Options Markets." *Economic Review*, Federal Reserve Bank of Atlanta 76 (July/August 1991): 1–22.

Adamantopoulous, Constantinos G. "A Single Market for Financial Services in 1992." *Journal of Business and Society* 2 (Spring 1989): 49–59.

Aharony, Joseph, Anthony Saunders, and Itzhak Swary. "The Effects of DIDMCA on Bank Stockholders' Returns and Risk." *Journal of Banking and Finance* 12 (September 1988): 317–331.

Baer, Herb L., and Douglas D. Evanoff. "Payments System Risk in Financial Markets that Never Sleep." *Economic Perspectives*, Federal Reserve Bank of Chicago 14 (November/December 1990): 2–15.

Belton, Terrence M., et al. "Daylight Overdrafts and Payments System Risk." *Federal Reserve Bulletin* 73 (November 1987): 839–852.

Bennett, Thomas, and Craig S. Hakkio. "Europe 1992: Implications for U.S. Firms." *Economic Review*, Federal Reserve Bank of Kansas City 74 (April 1989): 3–17.

Board of Governors of the Federal Reserve System. *78th Annual Report*. Washington, D.C.: Federal Reserve System, 1991.

Bohne, Edward G. "Is There Consistency in Monetary Policy?" *Business Review*, Federal Reserve Bank of Philadelphia (July/August 1987): 3–8.

Bordo, Michael D. "The Lender of Last Resort: Alternative Views and Historical Experience." *Economic Review*, Federal Reserve Bank of Richmond 76 (January/February 1990): 18–29.

Boucher, Janice L. "Europe 1992: A Closer Look." *Economic Review*, Federal Reserve Bank of Atlanta 76 (July/August 1991): 23–38.

Cargill, Thomas. *Central Bank Independence and Regulatory Responsibilities: The Bank of Japan and the Federal Reserve.* New York: Salomon Brothers Center for the Study of Financial Institutions, 1989.

Carlson, John B. "The Indicator P-Star: Just What Does It Indicate?" *Economic Commentary*, Federal Reserve Bank of Cleveland (September 15, 1989).

Carré, Hervé, and Karen Johnson. "Progress toward a European Monetary Union." *Federal Reserve Bulletin* 77 (October 1991): 769–783.

Chriszt, Michael J. "European Monetary Union: How Close Is It?" *Economic Review*, Federal Reserve Bank of Atlanta 76 (September/October 1991): 21–27.

Chrystal, K. Alec. "International Banking Facilities." *Review*, Federal Reserve Bank of St. Louis 66 (April 1984): 5–11.

Corrigan, E. Gerald. "Challenges Facing the International Community of Bank Supervisors." *Quarterly Review*, Federal Reserve Bank of New York 17 (Autumn 1992): 1–9.

Cox, W. Michael, and Harvey Rosenblum. "Money and Inflation in a Deregulated Financial Environment: An Overview." *Economic Review*, Federal Reserve Bank of Dallas (May 1989): 1–19.

Crabbe, Leland. "The International Gold Standard and U.S. Monetary Policy from World War I to the New Deal." *Federal Reserve Bulletin* 75 (June 1989): 423–440.

Cumming, Christine M., and Lawrence M. Sweet. "Financial Structure of the G-10 Countries: How Does the United States Compare?" *Quarterly Review*, Federal Reserve Bank of New York 12 (Winter 1987–1988): 14–25.

Espinosa, Marco, and Chong K. Yip. "International Policy Coordination: Can We Have Our Cake and Eat It Too?" *Economic Review*, Federal Reserve Bank of Atlanta 78 (May/June 1993): 1–12.

Feldberg, Chester B. "Competitive Equality and Supervisory Convenience." *Economic Perspectives*, Federal Reserve Bank of Chicago 14 (May/June 1990): 30–32.

Frankel, Allen B., and Paul B. Morgan. "Deregulation and Competition in Japanese Banking." *Federal Reserve Bulletin* 78 (August 1992): 579–593.

Friedman, Milton, and Anna J. Schwartz. *A Monetary History of the United States, 1867–1960.* Princeton, N.J.: Princeton University Press, 1963.

Garfinkel, Michelle R. "The FOMC in 1988: Uncertainty's Effects on Monetary Policy." *Review*, Federal Reserve Bank of St. Louis 71 (March/April 1989): 16–33.

Germany, J. David, and John E. Morton. "Financial Innovation and Deregulation in Foreign Industrial Countries." *Federal Reserve Bulletin* 71 (October 1985): 743–753.

Gilbert, R. Alton. "Operating Procedures for Conducting Monetary Policy." *Review*, Federal Reserve Bank of St. Louis 67 (February 1985): 13–21.

————. "Payments System Risk: What Is It and What Will Happen if We Try to Reduce It?" *Review*, Federal Reserve Bank of St. Louis 71 (January/February 1989): 3–17.

Hayes, Alfred E. "The International Monetary System—Retrospect and Prospect." *Quarterly Review*, Federal Reserve Bank of New York, special 75th anniversary issue (1989): 29–34.

Houpt, James V. "International Trends for U.S. Banks and Banking Markets." *Federal Reserve Bulletin* 74 (May 1988): 289–290.

Humphrey, Thomas M. "Lender of Last Resort: The Concept in History." *Economic Review*, Federal Reserve Bank of Richmond 75 (March/April 1989): 8–16.

————. "Precursors of the P-Star Model." *Economic Review*, Federal Reserve Bank of Richmond 75 (July/August 1989): 3–9.

Juncker, George R., and Bruce J. Summers. "A Primer on the Settlement of Payments in the United States." *Federal Reserve Bulletin* 77 (November 1991): 847–858.

Kane, Edward J. "Selecting Monetary Targets in a Changing Financial Environment." In *Monetary Policy Issues in the 1980s* Kansas City: Federal Reserve Bank of Kansas City, 1982: 181–206.

Kasman, Bruce. "A Comparison of Monetary Policy Operating Procedures in Six Industrial Countries." *Quarterly Review*, Federal Reserve Bank of New York 17 (Summer 1992): 5–24.

Key, Sidney J. "Mutual Recognition: Integration of the Financial Sector in the European Community." *Federal Reserve Bulletin* 75 (September 1989): 591–609.

Kindleberger, Charles P. *Manias, Panics, and Crashes: A History of Financial Crises*, rev. ed. New York: Basic Books, 1989.

Meek, Paul. *U.S. Monetary Policy and Financial Markets.* New York: Federal Reserve Bank of New York, 1982.

Meulendyke, Ann-Marie. "A Review of Federal Reserve Policy Targets and Operating Guides in Recent Decades." *Quar-

terly Review, Federal Reserve Bank of New York 13 (Autumn 1988): 6–17.

————. "Reserve Requirements and the Discount Window in Recent Decades." *Quarterly Review*, Federal Reserve Bank of New York 17 (Autumn 1992): 25–43.

Misback, Ann E. "The Foreign Bank Supervision Enhancement Act of 1991." *Federal Reserve Bulletin* 79 (January 1993): 1–10.

Motley, Brian, and Herbert Runyon. "Interest Rates and the Fed." *Weekly Letter*, Federal Reserve Bank of San Francisco (February 20, 1981).

Osborne, Dale K. "What Is Money Today?" *Economic Review*, Federal Reserve Bank of Dallas (January 1985): 1–15.

Parthemos, James. "The Origins of the Fed." *Cross Sections*, Federal Reserve Bank of Richmond 5 (Fall 1988): 9–11.

————. "The Federal Reserve Act of 1913 in the Stream of U.S. Monetary History." *Economic Review*, Federal Reserve Bank of Richmond 74 (July/August 1988): 19–28.

Pavel, Christine, and John N. McElravey. "Globalization in the Financial Services Industry." *Economic Perspectives*, Federal Reserve Bank of Chicago 14 (May/June 1990): 3–18.

Roberds, William. "What Hath the Fed Wrought? Interest Rate Smoothing in Theory and Practice." *Economic Review*, Federal Reserve Bank of Atlanta 77 (January/February 1992): 12–24.

Robinson, Kenneth J. "Banking Difficulties and Discount Window Operations: Is Monetary Policy Affected?" *Financial Industry Studies*, Federal Reserve Bank of Dallas (August 1992): 15–23.

Schwartz, Anna J. "The Misuse of the Fed's Discount Window." *Review*, Federal Reserve Bank of St. Louis 74 (September/October 1992): 58–69.

Sellon, Gordon H., Jr. "The Instruments of Monetary Policy." *Economic Review*, Federal Reserve Bank of Kansas City (May 1984): 3–20.

————. "Restructuring the Financial System: Summary of the Bank's 1987 Symposium." *Economic Review*, Federal Reserve Bank of Kansas City 73 (January 1988): 17–28.

Smith, Stephen D., and Larry D. Wall. "Financial Panics, Bank Failures, and the Role of Regulatory Policy." *Economic Review*, Federal Reserve Bank of Atlanta 77 (January/February 1992): 1–11.

Spong, Kenneth. *Banking Regulation: Its Purposes, Implementation, and Effects*, 3rd ed. Kansas City: Federal Reserve Bank of Kansas City, 1990.

Sproul, Allan. "Reflections of a Central Banker." *Quarterly Review*, Federal Reserve Bank of New York, special 75th anniversary issue (1989): 21–28.

Stevens, E. J. "Comparing Central Banks' Rulebooks." *Economic Review*, Federal Reserve Bank of Cleveland 28 (Third Quarter 1992): 2–15.

Summers, Bruce J. "Clearing and Payments Systems: The Role of the Central Bank." *Federal Reserve Bulletin* 77 (February 1991): 81–91.

Todd, Walker F. "Lessons of the Past and Prospects for the Future in Lender of Last Resort Theory." In *Proceedings of a Conference on Bank Structure and Competition*. Chicago: Federal Reserve Bank of Chicago, 1988: 533–560.

Wallich, Henry C. "The Role of Operating Guides in U.S. Monetary Policy." *Federal Reserve Bulletin* 65 (September 1979): 679–691.

Walter, John R. "Monetary Aggregates: A User's Guide." *Economic Review*, Federal Reserve Bank of Richmond 75 (January/February 1989): 20–28.

Weatherstone, Dennis. "A U.S. Perspective on Europe 1992." In *New York's Financial Markets: The Challenges of Globalization*. Ed. by Thierry Noyelle. Boulder, Colo.: Westview Press, 1989: 115–118.

Weiner, Stuart E. "The Changing Role of Reserve Requirements in Monetary Policy." *Economic Review*, Federal Reserve Bank of Kansas City 77 (Fourth Quarter 1992): 45–63.

Wenninger, John, and John Partlan. "Small Time Deposits and the Recent Weakness in M2." *Quarterly Review*, Federal Reserve Bank of New York 17 (Spring 1992): 21–35.

Wheelock, David C. "The Fed's Failure to Act as Lender of Last Resort during the Great Depression, 1929–1933." In *Proceedings of a Conference on Bank Structure and Competition*. Chicago: Federal Reserve Bank of Chicago, 1989: 154–176.

White, Betsy Buttrill. "Foreign Banking in the United States: A Regulatory and Supervisory Perspective." *Quarterly Review*, Federal Reserve Bank of New York 7 (Summer 1982): 48–58.

Wormuth, Diana. "Europe Gets Ready for a New Era." *Best's Review* (Property/Casualty Edition) 90 (November 1989): 22–28.

Notes

[1] Alan Murray and Tom Herman, "Why the Fed's Efforts to Forestall Inflation Have Thus Far Failed," *The Wall Street Journal*, March 29, 1989, pp. A1, A8; and Claudia Cummins, "House Panel Scrutinizing Minutes of Fed's District Bank Meetings," *American Banker*, November 3, 1992, p. 2; and Bart Fraust, "Fed's Secrecy Comes under More Scrutiny," *American Banker*, July 26, 1993, pp. 1, 16.

[2] Forerunners of the Fed included the First and Second National Banks of the United States; the charter for the latter expired in 1836. Although intended to perform functions similar to those of the Bank of England, which many credited for financial stability in Great Britain, these two institutions were widely distrusted by many Americans, who feared concentration of financial power in a central bank.

[3] This discussion draws on the views of James Parthemos, as expressed in "The Origins of the Fed" (1988) and "The Federal Reserve Act of 1913" (1988); it also reflects the influence of Spong, 1990 and Kindleberger, 1989. (References are listed in full at the end of the appendix.)

[4] See Board of Governors, 1991, pp. 256–261.

[5] See Board of Governors, 1991, pp. 227–229; and Jeanne Iida, "Fed Planning to Privatize Funds–Transfer Operations," *American Banker*, May 3, 1990, pp. 1, 3.

[6] For further discussion of payments system risks, see Gilbert, 1989; Belton et al., 1987; Summers, 1991; Juncker and Summers, 1991; Baer and Evanoff, 1990; and *Fed Wire*, Federal Reserve Bank of Chicago (February 1993).

[7] See, for example, Friedman and Schwartz, 1963; Todd, 1988; Wheelock, 1989; and Bordo, 1990.

[8] See Charles W. Calomiris, *The Postmodern Bank Safety Net: Lessons from Developed and Developing Countries* (Washington, D.C.: American Enterprise Institute, 1997), p. 8. Also see Robinson, 1992; and Alan Murray, "Fed's New Chairman Wins a Lot of Praise on Handling the Crash," *The Wall Street Journal*, November 25, 1987, pp. 1, 7. The Fed was also praised for its handling of a crisis in the commercial paper market in 1970. For an account of its actions, see Evelyn Hurley, "The Commercial Paper Market," *Federal Reserve Bulletin* 63 (June 1977): 525–536. For a discussion of the Fed's role as lender of last resort and systemic risk issues, see George G. Kaufman, *Research in Financial Services, Banking, Financial Markets, and Systemic Risk*, Vol. 7 (Greenwich, CT: JAI Press, 1995).

[9] A history of lender-of-last-resort theory is found in Humphrey, March/April 1989.

[10] Paulette Thomas, "Fed, Fulfilling Pledge, Advances Funds to Lincoln S&L as Lender of Last Resort," *The Wall Street Journal*, April 25, 1989, p. A2; Smith and Wall, 1992; and Schwartz, 1992.

[11] Definitions of money have received intense scrutiny in recent years. See, for example, Walter, 1989; Osborne, 1985; and Wenninger and Partlan, 1992.

[12] See Cox and Rosenblum, 1989. Derivation and complete analysis of money multipliers are not within the scope of this text. A representative discussion is found in Frederic S. Mishkin, *The Economics of Money, Banking, and Financial Markets* (Glenview, Ill.: Scott, Foresman, 1989).

[13] Recently, for example, **P-star (P°)**, a predictor of the relationship between the current level of M2 and future inflation, has become a widely watched indicator of the success of monetary policy in controlling inflation. For more details, see Humphrey, July/August 1989 and Carlson, 1989.

[14] These arguments are summarized in Motley and Runyon, 1981; Bohne, 1987; and Roberds, 1992.

[15] See Cargill, 1989 and Kane, 1982.

[16] The early history of open market operations is described in Sproul, 1989. Other accounts of monetary policy before the 1970s can be found in Wallich, 1979 and Crabbe, 1989. In recent years, the district presidents have become more outspoken and influential members of the FOMC. See Alan Murray, "Fed Banks' Presidents Hold Private Positions But Major Public Role," *The Wall Street Journal*, August 1, 1991, pp. A1, A7.

[17] For arguments in defense of reserve requirements and the discount rate as effective tools of monetary policy, see Meulendyke, 1992; Weiner, 1992; and Sellon, 1984.

[18] Detailed discussions of the process that translates policy targets into open market actions are found in Meek, 1982; Gilbert, 1985; Meulendyke, 1988; and Garfinkel, 1989.

[19] FOMC targets are reported in minutes of committee meetings and appear in press reports and several Fed publications.

[20] See Aharony, Saunders, and Swary, 1988.

[21] See Crabbe, 1989; for more information on exchange rates from World War II to the 1970s, see Hayes, 1989.

[22] Kasman, 1992 finds similarities in monetary policy procedures of central banks in six countries. Stevens, 1992 compares rules and regulations in four countries.

[23] The G-7 nations are the United States, Canada, France, Great Britain, Italy, Japan, and Germany. Canada and Italy were not included in the Group of Five.

[24] See, for example, Alan Murray and Walter S. Mossberg, "Raising Discount Rate, Fed Puts Inflation War ahead of Dollar Policy," *The Wall Street Journal*, August 10, 1988, pp. 1, 8; Alan Murray and Michael R. Sesit, "As Dollar Marches On, Central Banks Prepare Big New Intervention," *The Wall Street Journal*, May 19, 1989, pp. A1–A2; David Wessel and Terence Roth, "As Central Banks Go Their Own Ways, Global Tensions Rise," *The Wall Street Journal*, August 3, 1992, pp. A1, A9; Clay Chandler, "Japan's Central Banker Begins to Win Praise for Saving Its 'Soul,'" *The Wall Street Journal*, June 15, 1993, pp. A1, A5; and Michael Sesit, Glenn Whitney, and Terence Roth, "German Stance on Rates Sends ERM to Brink," *The Wall Street Journal*, July 30, 1993, pp. C1, C13.

[25]See Espinosa and Yip, 1993; Pavel and McElravey, 1990; "A Survey of World Banking," *The Economist*, May 2, 1992; Spong, 1990; Abken, 1991; and Corrigan, 1992.

[26]Deirdre Fanning, "Set Us Free," *Forbes*, February 23, 1987, pp. 94–96.

[27]See White, 1982; Chrystal, 1984; Houpt, 1988; and Board of Governors, 1991, p. 211.

[28]See Misback, 1993; and James R. Kraus, "Foreign Banks Face Hurdles," *American Banker*, April 19, 1993, p. 2A.

[29]See Germany and Morton, 1985; Sellon, 1988; Cumming and Sweet, 1987–1988; and Frankel and Morgan, 1992.

[30]Readers may be surprised to learn that the Group of Ten includes 11 countries and one territory: the G-7 nations (United States, Canada, France, Great Britain, Japan, Germany, and Italy) plus Belgium, the Netherlands, Sweden, Switzerland, and the Grand Duchy of Luxembourg.

[31]For a discussion of Japan's financial crisis in 1998, see Brian Bremner, "Japan's Real Crisis: Until Its Hidden-Debt Mess Is Cleared Up, No Recovery Is Possible," *Business Week*, May 18, 1998, pp. 137–142.

[32]Carl W. Walsh, "EMU and the ECB," *Weekly Letter*, Federal Reserve Bank of San Francisco, June 5, 1992; Chriszt, 1991; and Carré and Johnson, 1991. Also see, "EMU Is Born Amid Battle over Central Bank," *The Wall Street Journal*, May 4, 1998, pp. A17–A18; and Paul Mentre, "The Case for the Euro," in *A Single European Currency?* ed. by Jeffrey Gedmin (Washington D.C.: American Enterprise Institute, 1997), pp. 22–28.

[33]See Jeffrey Gedmin, ed., *A Single European Currency?* (Washington D.C.: American Enterprise Institute, 1997); and Nicholas Bray, "Economic Climate Looks Good for Launch of New Currency," *The Wall Street Journal*, May 4, 1998, pp. A17–A18; Christopher Rhoads, "Euro Expected to Spur European Bank Shakeout," *The Wall Street Journal*, May 4, 1998, p. A17. For more information on the EC 1992 agreement, see "Survey of World Banking"; Boucher, 1991; Feldberg 1990; Weatherstone, 1989; Wormuth, 1989; Bennett and Hakkio, 1989; Adamantopoulous, 1989; and Key, 1989.

4

BACKGROUND: CONSOLIDATION TRENDS, MORAL HAZARD AND AGENCY ISSUES, TYPES OF OWNERSHIP AND ORGANIZATIONS

Financial service firms experienced a merger wave in the 1990s that linked very different types of institutions; banks merged with investment banks, securities firms, mutual funds, savings institutions, and finance companies. A merger was proposed in 1998 between a commercial bank and an insurance company, which would violate Glass–Steagall. As Arnold Danielson, a prominent bank consultant, states in the first opening quote, this consolidation wave creates a new set of competitive realities for the financial services industry. Many middle-sized financial institutions face "increased risk of falling behind in achieving economies of scale unless [they] too, find a like-sized partner."[1]

With the creation of giant, diverse financial service firms, many observers, such as Anthony Saunders and Ingo Walter in the second opening quote, argue that the current organizational structure required for financial service companies with banking and diverse nonbanking activities is out of date. They point out that the economic and global market realities that financial institutions face are changing at a much faster rate than are U.S. regulations.

The history of Travelers Group epitomizes the consolidation of the nation's financial service industry and the changing market realities of U.S. financial institutions. The company emerged when Wall Street veteran Sanford I. Weill purchased a troubled consumer loan

---

[1]See Rick Brooks, "First Union to Pursue 'Merger of Equals,' Shifting Its Focus from Smaller Targets," *The Wall Street Journal*, June 15, 1998, p. A8; and Arnold G. Danielson, "Bankers' Choice: Adapt to the New Direction or Wait for Last Dance," *Banking Policy Report* 16 (April 21, 1997), pp. 5–10.

company, Commercial Credit (CC), in 1986 and a diversified financial company, Primerica, in 1988. Primerica—originally the finance division of American Can—had transformed itself into a financial service conglomerate in the 1980s by acquiring insurance, mutual fund, and mortgage banking firms, as well as a major retail investment banking firm, Smith Barney. In 1992, Primerica became Travelers Group after the purchase of Travelers Insurance Company. Travelers shocked Wall Street by becoming a major player in the investment banking industry when it acquired Salomon Brothers (now Salomon–Smith Barney) in 1997. In 1998, Sandy Weill shocked regulators, as well, by proposing a merger with Citicorp, a major New York commercial bank. This daring proposal, illegal under the Glass–Steagall Act, forced the U.S. House of Representatives to reconsider a financial modernization bill allowing such an affiliation. Although the bill scraped by in the House by a single vote in May 1998, the need for Senate approval and a possible presidential veto clouded its prospects. If the bill fails, Travelers will have to divest much of its insurance operations within a few years to complete the merger with Citicorp. In June 1988, Travelers expanded its international presence by spending $1.6 billion to buy a 25 percent stake in Nikko Securities Company, the largest investment by a U.S. company in a Japanese financial institution. Merrill Lynch and other securities firms entered similar joint ventures as part of strategic investment banking partnerships in Asia.[2]

The Riegle–Neal Interstate Banking and Branching Act of 1994 (IBBEA) encouraged interstate acquisitions. In the 1990s, bank mergers averaged over 400 a year, totaling about 2,900 mergers during 1990 to 1996. Between 1983 and 1998, the number of U.S. banks and savings institutions fell 21 percent, even while employment at banks rose 3.1 percent to 1.93 million jobs, and assets grew 32 percent to $6.1 trillion. In the past two decades, over one-third of independent banking organizations have disappeared.[3] The year 1998 also marked the creation of the first coast-to-coast bank in the United States with the merger proposed between NationsBank and Bank America, combining $570 billion in assets. Merger proposals between super-regional banks, Banc One Corp. and First Chicago NBD Corp. (total assets of $240 billion), and Wells Fargo and Norwest (total assets of about $191 billion) created other giant banks, with mergers between other large banks likely to follow.

Although the consolidation trend is heralded by many analysts as a way to improve efficiency in the U.S. financial system, it has also been criticized. Consumer groups express concerns over concentration of financial power in the hands of too few financial institutions. Economists also question the effect of consolidation on the financial health of the banking industry. Little doubt remains about the importance of geographic and product expansion on the operations and organization of financial service firms in the 21st century, though. How will gigantic financial service firms be organized and managed in the future? What will be the effect of megabanks entering risky activities on the federal programs that oversee bank safety?

As the trends discussed here suggest, the operations of financial service firms are in constant flux. As they become larger and more diverse, their organizational structures become very important determinants of their success. Depository institutions also encounter unique agency problems because of their combined high financial leverage and federal deposit insurance obligations. These special characteristics may encour-

---

[2]For a brief history of Travelers Group, see Joseph B. Treaster, "Financial Services Consolidate, but Regulation Is Still Fragmented," *New York Times*, January 2, 1998, pp. D1, D5. For a case history of Primerica, see "Case 12: Primerica Corporation: Evaluating Exit Strategies," in Crawford and Sihler, 1994, p. 12.1. Also see, Stephen E. Frank, "Brokers, Insurers Queue Up for Thrift Charters," *The Wall Street Journal*, September 24, 1997, p. C1; Patrick McGeehan and Bill Spindle, "Travelers to Acquire 25% Stake in Nikko," *The Wall Street Journal*, June 1, 1998, p. A3; Michael Schroeder, "House Approves Landmark Banking Bill," *The Wall Street Journal*, May 14, 1998, p. A2; and Marcy Gordon, "House Votes to Lift Banking Barriers," *Denver Post*, May 14, 1998, p. 4A. See Nolle, 1995, for a summary of consolidation in the banking industry.

[3]See Banerjee and Cooperman, 1998; Rose, 1997; and Berger, Kashyap, and Scalise, 1995. For a study of the history and future prospects of bank industry consolidation, see Noelle, 1995. Also see Joseph A. Giannone, "Banks', Thrifts' Tanks Dwindle, but Employment Increases 3.1%," *Denver Post*, June 16, 1998, p. 5C; and Steven Lipin and Anita Raghavan, "One-Two Punch," *The Wall Street Journal*, April 13, 1998, pp. A1, A14.

age stockholders to expand risk at the expense of debtholders and deposit insurers, creating moral hazard problems. With depository institutions entering new product areas in the 1990s, regulators have been particularly concerned over the development of control mechanisms to limit the risk to federal deposit insurance funds. This chapter presents background on these problems, the evolution of organizational forms used by U.S. financial service firms, and recent trends in these forms.

Before beginning that discussion, however, the chapter elaborates on special characteristics of financial firms that create unique agency problems. The following sections discuss the nature of bank equity and the effect of high financial leverage on the operations of financial institutions.

✦ ✦ ✦

The Effect of Financial Leverage on Financial Institution Operations

Equity Is Ownership

Webster's *Tenth New Collegiate Dictionary* defines *equity* as "a risk interest or ownership right in property." Individuals with equity in a business may be sole owners, as in a proprietorship, with full personal liability for any debt obligations of the business; they may share ownership and legal liability with others, as in a partnership; they may have ownership interest but no personal responsibility for the firm's debt obligations (limited liability), as in a corporation.

The "ownership right" part of Webster's definition means that those with equity in a business are entitled to all **residuals**, or profits remaining after the debt of the organization is serviced. Residual profits may be paid to owners in the form of cash dividends or retained in the business to support future operations. In either case, under current tax laws, they are subject to corporate and personal income taxes. Even if earnings are retained, each owner holds claim to a proportionate amount and may realize cash by selling shares to new owners.

The "risk interest" part of Webster's definition means that a business may generate no residuals at all, as the owners of Braniff Airlines found when the firm went bankrupt in 1982, 1989, and again in 1992. However, residuals may be larger than ever imagined, as long-term owners of Travelers Group and Microsoft have learned. Because such potential variability is risk, holders of equity are subject to considerable risk. Yet their willingness to invest allows the very existence of a business. Not surprisingly, then, much of finance theory is devoted to understanding and improving the risk/expected return relationship for equity holders of nonfinancial firms. Financial firms have different types of equity ownership, as discussed in this section.

Privately Owned Firms   Some financial institutions are privately owned as closely held companies owned by individuals or a few owners who make initial investments. For instance, some small community banks are privately owned by families or a few investors. Under a proprietorship or partnership, the bank's earnings are taxed as private income of the investors. Most privately held small, community banks are Subchapter S corporations, a form of organization that allows limited liability, subject to a number of restrictions, with tax treatment of income at the owners' personal tax rates.

Stock-Owned Firms   Financial institutions frequently are incorporated, which allows shareholders limited liability, a protection that helps institutions to raise funds by selling new shares or tapping the commercial paper and bond markets. The primary disadvantage of the corporate form of ownership is double taxation of earnings, once when recognized by the corporation and again when paid as dividends to owners. Stockholder buy shares in a firm at a given par value (such as $1 a share) plus a surplus market value. Stockholders' equity interests, however, also include shares in a company's retained earnings or undivided profits, amounts not paid out as dividends but reinvested in the firm. Thus, equity for shareholder firms includes the common stock accounts as well as retained earnings, often called *undivided profits* for financial institutions. However, financial institutions as a group are unusual among other firms, because many are not organized as stock-owned firms. FIs can be mutually owned or nonprofit entities.

Mutual Firms: Not All Ownership Is Equity   Many financial institutions are mutually organized, including many savings and loan associations (S&Ls), savings banks, and insurance companies. Depositors of mutual S&Ls or policyholders of mutual insurance companies are the "owners" of the mutual financial institutions. Their initial deposits or premium payments provide the funds for the institutions to begin operations. Profits earned from investing these funds are returned to owner—customers as interest on deposits or refunds on past premiums. Unlike shareholder-owned businesses, in which an owner may sell shares to realize capital gains, however, profits not distributed to owner-members of a mutual are available for use only by the institution itself. Net income that is retained is subject to corporate taxes in the year earned, but profits distributed to policyholders or depositors of mutual firms are taxable as personal income.

Not-for-Profit Organizations   Other financial institutions, such as credit unions (CUs), are organized as **not-for-profits**. Not-for-profit organizations provide goods and services at below-market or no cost to specific groups of beneficiaries. The organizations either distribute income they earn in excess of expenses to the beneficiary groups in the form of increased services or reduced costs, such as reduced loan interest rates or increased deposit rates. They may also provide refunds for previous payments or retain the income to provide a cushion against potential losses. No one holds any claim to residuals. Because not-for-profit organizations are presumed to serve charitable purposes, they do not pay taxes, even if they retain excess income. In recent years, independent banking groups have challenged CUs' exemption from taxes, arguing that many credit unions that have expanded rapidly operate similarly to community banks.[4]

Concept and Measurement of Equity or Net Worth

Although financial institutions differ because of the presence or absence of equity ownership interests, all have one thing in common: Each institution must focus attention on its equity (for stock owned firms) or net worth (for mutual firms), the dif-

---

[4]Federal CUs are not the only financial institutions that owe no institutional taxes on earnings. The earnings of investment companies and pension funds receive similar treatment. Because investment companies and pension funds lack the charitable objectives of CUs, however, they are not considered not-for-profit institutions, even though they receive similar tax treatment.

ference between the market values of its assets and liabilities. In this text, that difference is referred to generically as *equity*. Equity is the cushion between bankruptcy and continued existence in either case.

Formally stated, equity is defined as the amount by which the value of total assets can decline before it will be exceeded by the total value of liabilities:

$$\text{Value of Equity} = \text{Value of assets} - \text{Value of liabilities} \qquad (4.1)$$

This definition simply restates the basic balance sheet identity for an organization:

$$\text{Value of assets} = \text{Value of liabilities} + \text{Value of equity}^5 \qquad (4.2)$$

Equity, often called **equity capital**, performs several functions. For a firm to continue to operate, its assets must be greater than its liabilities, and increasing equity financing reduces the likelihood of bankruptcy. This protection is particularly important for financial institutions, whose businesses are based on public trust. Equity capital builds confidence in creditors, such as bank depositors, and provides protection against losses to federal deposit insurance funds. To protect deposit insurance funds and the safety of the banking system, regulators impose minimum equity-to-asset requirements. Equity capital provides long-term funds for investment and asset growth, as well. These functions are covered in greater detail in Chapter 8 on Capital Management.

Book Value versus Market Value Measures of Equity   Ideally, according to its definition in Equation 4.2, equity should be calculated as the amount by which *the market value of assets* exceeds the *market value of liabilities*. From a practical standpoint, book (historical) values have been traditionally used for financial institutions, with the exception of securities firms. However, the Federal Accounting Standards Board (FASB) has moved rapidly toward market-value accounting. For instance, as of January 2000, all firms, including financial institutions, must report the market values of derivatives (financial contracts used to reduce—or hedge— risk through links to the values of underlying assets or defined indexes). Depository institutions must also report market values for securities not expected to be held to maturity and for other real estate owned (OREO). As discussed in Chapter 3, under the new CAMELS system, regulators also require periodic estimates of changes in the market value of a bank's equity with a fall or rise in interest rates of up to 2 percent.

Although FASB has moved toward market-value accounting (MVA), financial institutions base figures for equity primarily on book value (historical) accounting from their financial statements. Proponents of MVA point out that the current book-value accounting system reduces public confidence in the financial system by inaccurately portraying the economic health of financial firms. Opponents of MVA argue that such a system would create great volatility in equity values for financial institutions, making otherwise healthy institutions appear to be "troubled" when temporary changes in interest rates change the market values of financial assets and liabilities. Since FIs have small equity holdings, the market value of equity can easily be

---

[5]Since *equity* is the commonly used term for net work or capital in finance, it is used here in the sense of the definition already stated. For some purposes, especially to meet regulatory requirements, preferred stock is considered part of an institution's equity or net worth. Details on the measurement of equity by regulators are considered in Chapter 8.

depleted with changes in the market values of assets and liabilities. High financial leverage exerts a magnifying effect.[6]

Equity and the Effect of Financial Leverage on Financial Institutions

In contrast to a nonfinancial firm, which might be financed with 40 percent debt and 60 percent equity, financial institutions are generally financed with high amounts of debt, often 90 percent or more, and correspondingly low amounts of equity. High **financial leverage**, financing with borrowed funds instead of equity, affects the level and variability of returns to shareholders. Financial leverage magnifies return on equity (ROE) to stockholders, since stockholders own a relatively small equity stake.

$$\text{Return on stockholder's equity (ROE)} = \text{Net income/Equity} \tag{4.3}$$

The Dupont relation (developed by the Dupont Corporation) represents the magnification effect of financial leverage as an equity multiplier (EM) for a given ROA:

$$\text{Return on equity} = \text{Return on Assets} \times \text{Equity Multiplier} \tag{4.4}$$

Substituting calculations for these terms:

$$\text{Net income/Equity} = \text{Net income/Assets} \times \text{Assets/Equity}$$

An increase in EM (Assets/Equity) reflects rising financial leverage and an increasing ROE. Note that the EM is just the reciprocal of the firm's equity–capital ratio (equity/assets). A fall in the equity–capital ratio is the same as a rise in the equity multiplier.

For example, suppose a financial institution has a ROA of 1.5 percent. This value may seem quite small, but it is good for many financial institutions. If the financial institution has a 10 percent equity–capital ratio (i.e., 10 percent equity and 90 percent debt financing), its equity multiplier is:

$$\text{EM} = 1/(\text{Equity/Assets}) = 1/0.10 = 10$$

Inserting this value in Equation 4.4 gives the firm's ROE:

$$\begin{aligned} \text{ROE} &= \text{ROA} \times \text{EM} \\ &= 1.5\% \times 10 = 15\% \end{aligned} \tag{4.5}$$

High financial leverage allows the financial institution to make a very decent ROE despite a low ROA. Holding other factors constant, for any positive ROA, an increase in the equity multiplier (that is, a reduction in the equity–capital ratio increases the ROE. The equity multiplier magnifies a negative ROA, as well; with ROA equal to −1.5 percent, an EM equal to 10 results in a large negative ROE of −15 percent. An equity multiplier of 5 results in a less devastating ROE of −7.5 percent.

This analysis implicitly assumes that a rise in EM does not significantly reduce ROA. The equity multiplier may increase to the point, however, where a burdensome interest expense significantly reduces ROA. In such a case, the joint effects of a fall in ROA and a rise in EM would need to be evaluated.

---

[6]See Thomas Mondaschean, "Market Value Accounting for Commercial Banks," in *Readings on Financial Institutions and Markets*, 1994–1995 edition, ed. by Peter S. Rose (Burr Ridge, Ill.: Richard D. Irwin, 1995), pp. 86–101.

Application: Calculating a Target ROA   A firm can use the Dupont relationship to determine the ROA that it must achieve to reach a target ROE for a given EM. Suppose an insurance company desires a ROE of 18 percent, and it has an equity capital ratio of 8 percent (implying an equity multiplier of 12.5). The Dupont equation gives the ROA needed to reach the target ROE:

$$ROA = ROE/EM$$
$$= 18\%/12.5 = 1.44\% \qquad (4.6)$$

Specific equity–capital ratios and regulatory requirements usually guide financial institutions' asset/liability management decisions. With a higher EM, a lower ROA will be needed. For instance, what would the target ROA have to be if the bank only had a 6 percent equity to asset ratio? Daily decisions concerning asset and liability management contribute to achieving a given ROE target. The high financial leverage of financial institutions has significant implications for agency conflicts between debtholders, stockholders, and regulators, as the following sections discuss.

THE EFFECT OF EQUITY OWNERSHIP ON MANAGER/OWNER BEHAVIOR

Conflicts Between Stockholders and Debtholders

High financial leverage allows stockholders of successful FIs to make exorbitant returns on small equity stakes. They experience low downside risk, since limited liability ensures that the maximum they can lose only their small equity investments. Thus, stockholders of highly leveraged FIs have strong incentives to favor risky projects with high potential payoffs. In contrast, debtholders prefer less risky projects to ensure repayment of the funds that they lent to the firm. This difference in preferences is likely to create agency conflicts. Debtholders may resolve such conflicts by demanding high interest rates on investments in risky firms as compensation for comparably high default risk. They may also demand protective covenants, such as limits on debt ratios. These measures may dampen the enthusiasm of stockholders for excessive risk-taking.[7]

Moral Hazard Problem of Deposit Insurance: Does Deposit Insurance Create Greater Depository Institution Risk?

However, if debtholders are, in fact, insured depositors, they have few incentives to impose such market discipline. Insured depositors are unlikely to monitor their

---

[7]Esty (1997) studied the effect of limited liability on risk-taking behavior by highly leveraged firms, finding evidence that risk taking is negatively correlated with the severity of liability. He examined national and state banks subject to different degrees of stockholder liability during 1863 to 1935, including double liability for national banks and single, limited, or unlimited liability for state banks. For a more detailed discussion of agency conflicts between stockholders and debtholders, see Jensen and Meckling, 1976, and John and John, 1993. Galai and Masulis, 1976, point out that stockholders in effect have a call option on the residual value of the firm, the difference between the market values of assets and liabilities. By taking on risky assets, stockholders can maximize the potential residual value of the firm that will be distributed to them. Bondholders demand covenants and high interest rates as penalties to prevent stockholders from taking on excessive risk.

financial institutions or to set terms for rates or covenants, since their claims are already protected. In effect, equity holders of insured depository institutions receive as a subsidy, a risk-free cost of funds regardless of how risky their assets are. This subsidy, the difference between the cost of funds for a risky firm and a risk-free firm, increases in value as a firm takes on progressively greater risk, providing an additional incentive for a risk preference.

This moral hazard problem is often blamed for depository institutions taking on greater risk and for the failures of many banks, as well as the savings and loan crisis in the late 1980s. In particular, S&Ls with negative net worth that regulators allowed to continue to operate in the 1980s presented moral hazard problems. Owners of such technically insolvent thrifts had no equity investment left to lose and every incentive to take on risky assets and gamble their way back to solvency.[8]

Regulators as a Risk-Reducing Force?   Although debtholders of government-insured financial institutions may no longer moderate a financial institution's risk, regulators may serve this function. They may take the place of debtholders by monitoring insured institutions and providing constraints and interference—such as restrictions on growth, threats of closure, and loss of charter value (an institution's right to engage in banking activities and receive deposit insurance). Buser, Chen, and Kane (1981) and Marcus (1984) point out that stockholders of banks with high charter values (the value of being allowed to operate and offer products that other firms are not allowed to offer) have strong incentives not to take excessive risk to avoid regulatory interference and closure. During periods of regulatory laxity, overcapacity, and competition from nonbank firms, however, the charter values of banks fall, reducing the effectiveness of the threat of regulatory closure and loss of charter value as a deterrent for excessive risk-taking behavior. Thus, many financial economists blame the poor performance and increased risk of banks in the 1980s on an increase in competition and reduction in charter values for banks during that time period.[9]

Proposals to Reduce Deposit Insurance and Moral Hazard Problems of Insured FIs   Regulators are particularly concerned that new megabanks that incorporate banking with securities and other activities may become so important to the economy that the U.S. government will have to provide some bailout assistance if such firms experience difficulties. Some bank analysts argue that deposit insurance should be eliminated altogether or that a narrowly defined banking entity be delineated that is financed with insured deposits, while other nonbank affiliates are separated. Others argue for regulations requiring banks to be financed with at least 10 percent uninsured debt to impose market discipline. Monitoring by uninsured debtholders would then create a market-based early warning system for banks having problems. Also, uninsured debtholders would impose market-based sanctions to prevent excessive bank risk-taking. Such an experiment is taking place in Argentina, which suffered three waves of expensive banking collapses in the 1980s. Argentina abolished deposit insurance in 1992 and developed a public data base to publicize the characteristics of bank borrowers and the risks that they

---

[8]See Kane, 1989, and Barth, 1991.
[9]See Buser, Chen, and Kane, 1981; Merton, 1977; Marcus, 1984; Keeley and Bennett, 1989; and De Young, Hughes, and Moon, 1998.

pose for individual banks. Beginning in 1996, banks were also required to finance at least 2 percent of their total deposits in the form of subordinated, uninsured debt to encourage market monitoring. Time will determine the effectiveness of this experiment.[10]

Does Managerial Stock Ownership Increase or Reduce FI Risk?

Managers of FIs may limit risk to protect their jobs and reputations. This effect may be particularly powerful if managers have sufficient ownership to prevent their ouster, but insufficient ownership to be aligned with external stockholders. At lower levels of ownership, managers may become entrenched acting in their own interests to take on levels of risk that may be below levels that maximize stockholders' wealth. However, as managers become large stockholders in a firm, their interests may approach those of external stockholders favoring greater risk. Based on this argument, some critics claim that the abolishment of thrift stockholder concentration laws encouraged risk-taking by manager-owned thrifts in the 1980s.[11]

Alternatively, managers with significant ownership positions as well as their employment status at stake may manage prudently for the good of the firm. Many financial institutions, including Banc One and Travelers Group, mandate that executives purchase significant ownership stakes in the firms, sometimes at least five times their annual salaries based on this premise. Similarly, stock option plans and bonuses based on an institution's stock price performance are popular compensation alternatives. Whether mandatory ownership or compensation based on stock prices improve the performance of firms is a hot topic.[12] Bank regulators also express concern about the relationships between ownership, compensation, performance, and risk. State bank regulators, for instance, often mandate minimum stock ownership positions by bank directors. FDICIA included a mandate to study these issues and gave regulators the power to limit the compensation of executives of significantly under-capitalized depository institutions.

The Evidence on FI Ownership, Compensation, and Risk-Taking   Researchers examining the link between financial institution ownership and risk generally find evidence of greater risk-taking behavior for manager-owned banks and thrifts in the 1980s, a period of low charter values and regulatory laxity, consistent with suggestions of moral hazard. Yet one major study by Gorton and Rosen (1995) finds lower risk and superior performance for well-capitalized manager-owned banks during 1984 to 1990. Studies of banks and thrifts in the 1990s, a period of regulatory stringency, find either no link or a reduction in risk with rising managerial stock ownership. In 1994 and 1995, a period of expansion and, hence high rewards for risk-taking, one study finds hints of greater risk by manager-owned thrifts, consistent with manager/stockholder alignments and stockholder preferences for risk. Researchers do not generally find a link between bank risk and compensation.

---

[10]See Calomiris, 1997; Litan, 1987; and Whalen 1997.

[11]See Amihud and Lev, 1981; Barth, 1991; Strunk, 1991.

[12]See Adam Bryant, "Stock Requirements for Execs Can Be Cushy," *New York Times*, February 8, 1998, p. 26; and Helen K. Snider, "CEO Pay and Firm Performance: Theory vs. Practice," *Financial Markets, Institutions, and Instruments* 3, no. 5, pp. 60–75.

They do find a strong, positive relation between stock price performance and CEO compensation levels.[13]

Having established the dimensions of the moral hazard problems of stock-owned firms, the next few sections will discuss the major organizational form for stock financial institutions in the United States: the financial holding company and, in particular, bank holding companies.

ORGANIZATIONAL FORMS: FINANCIAL HOLDING COMPANIES

Shareholder-owned institutions also can take advantage of another organizational arrangement called the **holding company**. Holding companies are businesses formed to acquire the stock of other companies to control their operations. They make up the dominant proportion of U.S. financial organizations. Holding companies can be quite complex structures, with many subsidiary holding companies as well. Bank holding companies (BHCs) are subject to special regulatory treatment and are discussed first, with other forms reviewed in the following sections.

GROWTH OF BHCs AND THE REGULATORY DIALECTIC

In the past several decades, commercial banks have increasingly turned to the BHC form of organization, in which a single holding company owns a controlling interest in the stock of one or several banks called **subsidiaries**. The stock of the BHC is owned by shareholders. BHCs are also permitted to own nonbank subsidiaries, provided that they obtain regulatory approval.

A bank holding company (BHC) form is required for banks that engage in permissible nonbank activities under the Glass–Steagall Act. Ironically, however, BHCs became popular initially as an innovation to avoid regulations, as part of the antithesis of the regulatory dialectic discussed in Chapter 3. Basically, BHCs provided loopholes to circumvent regulatory geographic and product restrictions, as well as capital requirements. With banks entering new product areas, the number of U.S. BHCs grew rapidly in the 1970s to early 1990s, with as many as 400 approved in a single year, and an annual growth rate of about 9 percent. With hundreds of mergers later in the 1990s, the numbers fell. At the end of 1998, about 8,900 bank and thrift holding companies existed, down from 11,230 in 1992. BHCs control more than 93 percent of the assets in insured commercial banks operating in the United States.[14] The motivations for forming different types of BHCs are discussed in this section, along with trends in geographic and product restrictions for depository institution holding companies.

---

[13]For surveys of studies on the relations between managerial ownership and risk-taking behavior, see Cebenoyan, Cooperman, and Register, 1995 and 1998. Also, see Chen, Steiner, and Whyte, 1998; Brewer and Saidenberg, 1996; Saunders, Strock, and Travlos, 1990; Mullins, 1991; John and John, 1993; Gorton and Rosen, 1995; and Esty, 1993. For studies examining the effect of compensation on bank performance and risk, see John and John, 1993; Barro and Barro, 1990; Ezzell and Miles, 1995; Houston and James, 1995; Hubbard and Palia, 1995; Yan, 1996. Hermalin and Wallace, 1997, provides a study of savings and loans.

[14]See Giannone, "Ranks Dwindle"; and Board of Governors, 1991, pp. 208, 271.

BHCs as a Loophole for Equity Capital Regulations

One motivation for forming a BHC organization is its ability to raise capital, ironically, since investors are more willing to invest in a corporation that provides them limited liability. The BHC form has also provided a loophole for banks to get around capital requirements. Regulators establish minimum capital standards, including equity–capital ratios, for commercial banks. These standards affect the possible rates of expansion by individual banks, because for every dollar by which assets and deposits increase, equity must also increase. For example, if a bank's equity capital must equal at least 8 percent of total assets, then 8 cents of every dollar increase in assets must be financed by retaining earnings or selling new stock, even though management might prefer to finance expansion solely by increasing deposits. Although BHCs are also subject to minimum capital standards, equity capital from their nonbank affiliates is currently included in the calculation of overall capital. Therefore, affiliation with a BHC whose nonbank subsidiaries have relatively high capital ratios can assist a bank in expansion without jeopardizing its position with regulators.

Figure 4.1   ✦   **DOWNSTREAMING: BHC LEVERAGE AS A SOURCE OF BANK EQUITY CAPITAL**

The holding company structure allows a parent organization to borrow money and then downstream the borrowed funds as new equity in a subsidiary bank.

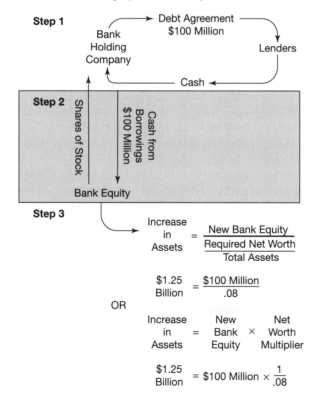

The potential assistance provided by holding company affiliation is illustrated in Figure 4.1. If a commercial bank is owned by a holding company, the BHC may borrow money under its own name, then invest the borrowed funds as equity capital in the bank, a practice known as **downstreaming**. As long as the BHC maintains its own required capital ratio, funds borrowed by the holding company may be used to meet the bank's capital needs in an expansion. In Step 1 of the figure, a BHC borrows an additional $100 million. In Step 2, the BHC downstreams those funds as equity capital to a subsidiary bank with an 8 percent required ratio for equity to total assets. In the third step, the bank uses the funds, as well as $1.15 billion in additional deposits, to finance a $1.25 billion increase in assets ($100 million divided by 0.08) while still meeting regulatory capital standards.

This so-called **double leverage** substantially reduces the amount of equity capital required for the holding company to control a large dollar volume of bank assets. Also, the level and riskiness of expected ROE are greatly affected by the extent to which financial institutions are leveraged. There are two major types of bank holding companies: multibank holding companies and one bank holding companies, which are discussed in the following sections.

Multibank Holding Companies and Geographic Diversification

A multibank bank holding company (MBHC) consists of a holding company with a number of different banks as subsidiaries, as shown in the upper panel of Figure 4.2. Banks formed MBHCs initially to circumvent state branching restrictions under the McFadden Act. Unit banking states, for instance, did not allow banks to branch within their jurisdictions. By creating a holding company with several affiliate banks operating in different parts of a state, an MBHC could create de facto subsidiary branches. MBHCs could circumvent interstate branching restrictions, as well, by establishing separate interstate bank subsidiaries.

Within the regulatory dialectic, regulators closed the loophole that MBHCs opened for interstate banking. Under Section 3(d) the BHC Act of 1956, known as the Douglas Amendment, MBHCs were prohibited from acquiring banks in other states unless state laws in which they would acquire the banks allowed it. Seven interstate MBHCs were **"grandfathered,"** allowed to keep their previous interstate acquisitions. Although a few states passed laws restricting MBHCs, many allowed these companies to continue de facto intrastate branching through subsidiaries.[15] Hence, MBHCs predominate in states that previously were unit banking states, such as Illinois, Colorado, and Texas. The list also includes many midwestern states with large agricultural interests that feared overly powerful banks. Since affiliates of MBHCs had to maintain separate officers and directors for each state or intrastate affiliate—which branches did not—MBHC subsidiaries were an expensive form of de facto branching. As a consequence, BHCs in unit banking states had much higher costs than banks operating in states allowing statewide branching. With the elimination of unit banking in all states by

---

[15]See Goldberg and Hanweck, 1988. Other exceptions to restrictions on interstate branching have included a provision allowing foreign banks to keep their existing interstate networks under the International Banking Act of 1978. Regulators have also permitted interstate acquisitions of failing banks where no feasible alternatives existed.

Figure 4.2 ✦ STRUCTURE OF BANK HOLDING COMPANIES

Note: Large banks combine numerous holding companies. Citicorp includes both multibank and one-bank holding companies. *The Directory of Corporate Affiliates* (found in the reference sections of most libraries) provides detailed listings.

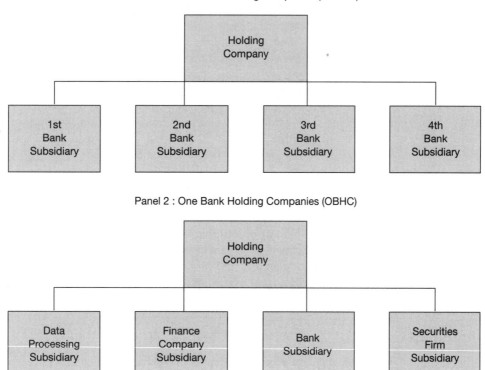

Panel 1: Multibank Holding Companies (MBHCs)

Panel 2 : One Bank Holding Companies (OBHC)

1992, only a couple of states continue to limit the areas within which banks may branch.[16] Interstate branching became a reality for most banks under the Riegle–Neal Interstate Banking and Branching Efficiency Act of 1994 (IBBEA) beginning in 1997, and branching became the dominate form of geographic expansion.

[16]The last unit banking state to remove its branching restrictions was Colorado in 1992. Almost all states now permit statewide branching. As of 1994, only Georgia, Iowa, and Kentucky retained some intrastate branching restrictions. In Kentucky, MBHC affiliates could merge and become branches. See Kidwell, Peterson, and Blackwell, 1997, p. 397. Also, see Kenneth Spong, *Banking Regulation: Its Purposes, Implementation and Effects*, 4th ed. (Kansas City: Federal Reserve Bank of Kansas City, Division of Bank Supervision and Structure, 1994). The effects of liberalized branching laws on statewide and local banking markets are discussed in Amel and Jacowski, 1989.

Non Banks as an Alternative Loophole for Geographic and Product Expansion

MBHCs such as Citicorp, as well as other firms including industrial companies, circumvented geographic and product-based restrictions by acquiring banks in other states and divesting them of commercial loans, creating units called **nonbanks** or **consumer banks**. Until the Competitive Equality in Banking Act (CEBA) of 1987 patched up this loophole by redefining a bank as any institution insured by the FDIC, MBHCs and other holding companies were able to circumvent regulations by placing themselves technically outside the definition of a bank, i.e., taking deposits and making commercial loans. By 1987, over 50 grandfathered consumer banks continued to operate.[17] BHCs could also circumvent geographic restrictions by operating loan production offices (LPOs) to negotiate loans with no funds dispensed in other states and out-of-state Edge corporations to pursue international business. Meanwhile, in the 1980s, many states made regional, reciprocal agreements that allowed MBHC to maintain interstate affiliates.

MBHCs' Role in Regional Interstate Pacts Regional interstate banking pacts arose in the 1980s, and a Supreme Court ruling in 1996 confirmed their legality. These pacts granted reciprocal privileges between banks in different states. Most pacts required that out-of-state banks maintain separate affiliates in each state, i.e., set up MBHC structures. Pacts in many regions prevented giant New York banks from entering for a number of years, helping regional banks to build strength. Many of these large, regional MBHCs rapidly made acquisitions and became known as **superregionals**. The list includes Banc One, Fleet, US Bancorp, Norwest, and NationsBank, among others. Some MBHCs followed a centralized strategy, like that of NationsBank, in which the holding company in North Carolina directs all operations. Others, like Banc One, followed a decentralized strategy allowing acquired banks to operate as independent subsidiaries under the umbrella of an overall holding company support system called an "uncommon partnership." Banc One adopted a new centralized system in 1997 to gain economies in operations.[18]

The New National Bank Model under IBBEA

With IBBEA of 1994, interstate branching became a reality, and MBHCs with interstate operations could convert costly subsidiaries into interstate branches. MBHCs could also make acquisitions across the country. For instance, Nations-

---

[17]In the early 1990s, several large industrial and nonbank corporations (such as Sears Roebuck, Merrill Lynch, AT&T, and General Motors) created another loophole by purchasing industrial loan companies in Utah, which had been allowed to apply for federal deposit insurance after the failure of the state's private insurance fund. At this time, prior to the change in definition of a bank, they were not subject to G–S or branching law restrictions. See Tim Carrington, "Freeze on New Consumer Banks Renewed, but Comptroller Prods Congress to Act," *The Wall Street Journal*, May 10, 1984; Stephen Wermiel and Monica Langley, "Top Court Clears Limited-Service Banks and Deals Major Blow to Power of Fed," *The Wall Street Journal*, January 23, 1986, p. 4; and Peter Pae, "Corporate Giants Buy Tiny Thrifts in Utah in Bid to Start Banks," *The Wall Street Journal*, November 17, 1992, A1, A4.

[18]Matt Murray, "After Long Overhaul, Banc One Now Faces Pressures to Perform," *The Wall Street Journal*, March 16, 1998, pp. A1, A10.

Table 4.1   ✦   BANKING ORGANIZATIONS WITH SECTION 20 SUBSIDIARIES[a]

Some 39 bank holding companies have formed Section 20 securities over the last 9 years in order to conduct some "ineligible" securities activities denied to banks for direct participation. Here is a list of those institutions and the year their applications were approved by the Federal Reserve Board:

ABN Amro Bank N.V. (1990)[b]
Banco Santander, S.A. (1995)[b]
Banc One Corporation (1990)
BankAmerica Corporation (1992)[b]
Bankers Trust New York Corporation (1987)[b]
Bank of Montreal (1988)[b]
Bank of Nova Scotia (1990)[b]
Bank South Corporation (1993)
Barclays Bank PLC (1990)[c]
Barnett Banks (1989)
Canadian Imperial Bank of Commerce (1990)[b]
Chase Manhattan Corporation (1987)[b]
Chemical Banking Corporation (1987)[b]
Citicorp (1987)[b]
Dai-Ichi Kangyo Bank, Ltd. (1991)
Dauphin Deposit Corporation (1991)[b]
Deutsche Bank AG (1992)[b]
First of America Corporation (1994)[c]
First Chicago NBD Corporation (1988)[c]
First Union Corporation (1989)[b]
Fleet Financial Group (1988)
HSBC Holdings PLC (1996)[b]
Huntington Bancshares, Inc. (1992)
J. P. Morgan and Co., Inc. (1987)[b]
KeyCorp (1996)
Long-Term Credit Bank of Japan, Ltd. (1990)
Mellon Bank Corporation (1995)
National City Corporation (1994)[b]
NationsBank Corporation (1989)[b]
Norwest Corporation (1989)
PNC Financial Corp (1987)
Republic New York Corporation (1994)[b]
Royal Bank of Canada (1990)[b]
Sanwa Bank, Ltd. (1990)
SouthTrust Corporation (1989)
SunTrust Banks, Inc. (1994)
Swiss Bank Corporation (1994)[b]
Synovus Financial Corporation (1991)
Toronto-Dominion Bank (1990)[b]

[a]As of February 21, 1996.

[b]Including corporate debt and equity securities powers.

[c]Including corporate debt securities powers.

Source: Michael J. Conover, "Section 20 Subsidiary May Still Be Viable Option for Some Banks," *Banking Policy Report* (May 20, 1996), p. 19.

raised from 10 percent to 25 percent). Previously, a firm had to maintain "stringent firewalls" separating the activities of other affiliates from those of bank units. Hence, under the spirit of corporate separateness, employees of different affiliates could not work together, and marketing and other endeavors of a nonbank affiliate had to be kept separate from those of the bank. These rules favored large banks entering securities activities, since small banks had trouble justifying the cost of such a separate affiliate. In 1987, the Fed allowed member banks to underwrite, distribute, and trade certain securities through Section 20 holding company affiliates, including municipal revenue bonds, commercial paper, and mortgage-backed securities. Privileges were extended to include corporate bonds in 1989 and corporate equity in 1990. The securities affiliate had to be a separate and adequately capitalized entity, and no more than 10 percent of the affiliate's revenues could come from securities activities, extended to 25 percent in 1997.

A number of large U.S. banks have built Section 20 subsidiaries to play major roles in securities markets. For instance, J. P. Morgan and Citicorp ranked among the top 15 underwriters of U.S., domestically issued securities in 1994. In February 1996, about 39 U.S. BHCs had Section 20 subsidiaries, as shown in Table 4.1. Under the Federal Reserve's Regulation K, BHCs may also maintain affiliates associated "with the transaction of banking or other financial operations abroad" —including overseas securities activities. Large banks in major cities are major players in these markets, including Bank of Boston, Bank of New York, Bank America Corporation, Chase, Citicorp, J. P. Morgan, and Republic New York Corporation.[26]

Relaxation of Product and Affiliate Regulations

Expanded Brokerage and Mutual Fund Activities for BHCs   As in their treatment of underwriting activities, regulators became much more lenient over time in their interpretation of activities allowable for subsidiaries of BHCs. Along with underwriting new issues, affiliates gained authority to engage in other types of investment activities. In the early 1980s, banks entered the discount brokerage business, with BankAmerica's acquisition of Charles Schwab in 1981 as the first venture. In the early 1980s, Security Pacific National Bank also formed a joint venture with the Fidelity Group to sponsor mutual funds; Fidelity also began clearing security trades and carrying brokerage accounts for the bank's customers. The OCC also allowed Security Pacific to acquire and run subsidiaries to provide discount brokerage and back-office brokerage services for other banks. Other banks followed suit and began offering low-cost brokerage services through BHC affiliates.

In 1983, the OCC allowed BHCs to begin providing investment advice through security subsidiaries. In several rulings between 1986 and 1988, the Fed permitted BHC affiliates to offer investment advice to retail and institutional investors, as well, and to broker **nonproprietary** mutual funds (those managed and marketed by separate companies, such as Fidelity) and **private-label funds** (those managed by separate companies, but marketed exclusively by the banks). In 1992, banks were allowed to broker and have their affiliates manage **proprietary** funds (those managed by the affiliates and brokered to investors exclusively by the banks). In promoting funds,

---

[26]The material in this section comes predominantly from Benston and Kaufman, 1997; and Benston, 1991.

banks must inform customers of the risks the funds entail and their lack of deposit insurance. As pointed out by Kaufman (1995), by 1992 over 90 percent of banks offered mutual funds, accounting for more than one-third of mutual fund sales, most of them trading shares in money market funds. In 1994, Mellon Bank in Pittsburgh bought Dreyfus, one of the largest sponsors of money market and mutual funds. By 1995, banks captured 14 percent of total mutual fund assets, and many have converted their trust activities to proprietary mutual funds. Banks can also participate in joint ventures, such as leasing lobby space to companies that offer real estate brokerage, insurance, and other services still prohibited for banks.[27]

Reduction in Firewalls Separating Bank and Nonbank BHC Subsidiaries

The Fed's Eight Operating Standards   In 1997, the Fed passed eight operating standards, shown in Table 4.2, that smoothed the process for BHCs to conduct securities business through Section 20 subsidiaries, replacing **firewalls** created about 10 years before to insulate investment banking activities from traditional deposit-taking functions. Previously, firewalls had created practical limitations on how banks conducted securities activities, such as prohibitions on relations between employees, officers, and directors of the separate units and limits on information transfers between the Section 20 subsidiaries and any other affiliates. These restrictions created obstacles for many BHCs that wanted to establish Section 20 subsidiaries. The Fed argued that the new rules would allow Section 20 affiliates "to operate more readily in conjunction with an affiliated bank, thereby maximizing synergies, enhancing services, and possibly reducing costs." Other Fed rules protect against affiliates compromising the safety of a BHC.[28]

Fed Streamlining of Procedures for Nonbank Acquisitions   Recently the Fed also adopted comprehensive revisions to Regulation Y that have streamlined the application and notice process for both bank and nonbank acquisitions for well-capitalized and well-managed banks. The Fed liberalized the types of activities it permitted for subsidiaries of BHCs, and it allowed acquisitions of investment banking and security

---

[27]The information in this section comes from Benston and Kaufman, 1997; Kaufman, 1995; and Gallo, Richardson, and Apilado, 1996. See the last source for an evaluation of the performance of bank-sponsored equity mutual funds.

[28]See "Fed Starts Off New Year by Proposing to Eliminate More Section 20 Firewalls," *Banking Policy Report* 16, no. 2 (January 20, 1997), pp. 1, 12; and "Fed Votes to Replace Section 20 Firewalls with New Standards," *Bank Policy Report* 16 (September 1, 1997), pp. 6, 7. The Fed repealed mandates for 28 firewalls in place since the late 1980s that had insulted extraordinary investment banking activities from deposit banking. Remaining firewalls were incorporated into a statement of operating standards designed to ensure safety and soundness and to avoid conflicts of interest. The Fed pointed out that many of these firewalls duplicated or overlapped restrictions of the Federal Reserve Act's Section 23B, which requires interaffiliate transactions on arm's-length terms, prohibiting any representation that a bank is responsible for a Section 20 affiliate's obligations, and prohibiting a bank from purchasing certain products from a Section 20 affiliate. Some remaining restrictions continue to prevent significant conflicts of interest or other concerns not addressed by this section.

Table 4.2 ✦ FED'S EIGHT NEW SECTION 20 STANDARDS

1. Capital	• A bank holding company that operates a Section 20 must be "well-capitalized" or risk reimposition of credit enhancement and funding restrictions. • Relief from the existing firewalls is conditioned on a bank holding company maintaining the capital of its subsidiary banks at "well-capitalized" levels; in the extreme, the Fed could require a bank holding company to divest of a Section 20 company, if a subsidiary bank fell below "well-capitalized" and the holding company didn't recapitalize it. • In the interest of national treatment, foreign banks applying for and operating Section 20 subsidiaries must maintain capital at "levels well above" the Basle minimums. • A new requirement compels Section 20 subsidiaries to notify the Fed whenever they are required to notify the SEC of any failure to maintain capital above "early warning" levels.	• Eliminates: —requirement that capital invested in the Section 20 subsidiary be deducted from consolidated capital. —implied policy that Section 20 subsidiaries need capital of 2 × the SEC "haircut."
2. Internal controls	• Banks, thrifts, branches, and agencies must establish written policies and procedures, including appropriate limits on exposures, governing their participation in transactions originated by their affiliated Section 20 subsidiaries. • Banks, thrifts, branches, and agencies must conduct and document their own independent credit analysis for any Section 20-linked transaction.	
3. Interlocks	• The majority of directors, officers, employees of a bank and its affiliated Section 20 subsidiary cannot be the same. • The CEO of a bank (or, in the case of a foreign bank, the manager of a branch or agency) may not be the CEO of an affiliated Section 20 subsidiary.	Retains the status quo
4. Customer dislosure	• A customer must receive a disclosure statement describing the difference between a Section 20 unit and its bank affiliates, and pointing out that the bank could be a lender to an issuer. • No bank may express an opinion on the value or advisability of purchase or sale of an ineligible security offered by its Section 20 affiliate, subject to the "knowledge requirement" set forth in SEC Rule 10-b-10 and NASD Rule 2250.	• Eliminates the requirement that disclosures be provided to institutional customers.
5. Credit for clearing purposes	• Intraday extensions of credit to a Section 20 subsidiary by an affiliated bank, thrift, branch, or agency must be on market terms, per the requirements of Section 23B and limited to the quantitative limitations in Section 23A.	• Does not require that banks collateralize intraday extensions of credit, as had initially been proposed by the Fed.
6. Funding of securities purchases from a Section 20 affiliate	• Prohibits a bank, thrift, branch, or agency from extending credit to a customer secured by or for the purpose of buying an ineligible security during a 30-day underwriting period unless: —The extension of credit is made under the terms of a pre-existing line of credit, not established in anticipation of the underwriting. —The bank, thrift, branch, or agency is clearing for the Section 20 unit.	• Eliminates the following restrictions: —prohibition of a bank, as trustee or fiduciary, from acquiring an ineligible security during a 60-day underwriting period.

Table 4.2 ✦ Fed's Eight New Section 20 Standards (continued)

	—prohibition of a bank or any of its subsidiaries from purchasing as principal any ineligible security during a 60-day underwriting period (though investment limitations and Section 23B requirements remain that such purchases have board of director approval—or, the case of a foreign bank, in lieu of majority approval, the approval of a majority of the senior executive officers of the bank located out of the United States.
7. Reporting requirements	• Requires that the Fed be furnished with quarterly FOCUS reports (and "early warning" capital notices required by the SEC as noted above).
8. Foreign banks	• Extends the requirements of Sections 23A and 23B to extension of credit to and purchases from an affiliated Section 20 by a branch or agency. • Prohibits a branch or agency from advertising or suggesting they are in any way responsible for the obligation of a Section 20 affiliate.

This table provides a summary rather than a thorough, legal review of the changes and their effects.

Source: "Fed Votes to Replace Section 20 Firewalls with New Standards," *Banking Policy Report* 16, no. 17 (September 1, 1997), pp. 6, 7.

firm subsidiaries, such as Bankers Trust's acquisition of Alex Brown; BankAmerica's acquisition of Robertston, Stephens and Company; NationsBank's acquisition of Montgomery Securities; and Mellon Bank's acquisition of Dreyfus Funds, among many others.[29]

The OCC's OP-SUB or Part 5 Rule   In 1997, the OCC set up its **Part 5 rule**, also known as the **Op-Sub (operating subsidiary) rule**, allowing national banks to apply to conduct new activities through subsidiaries rather than forming cumbersome holding companies. This system was a response to criticism by many banking organizations that security activities could be more efficiently conducted by an operating

---

[29]See "Fed Trumps Section 20 Move with Proposed Overhaul of Reg Y," *Banking Policy Report* 15 (September 16, 1996). Craig M. Wasserman, "Fed's New Reg Y Tests Conventional Approaches on Holding Company Deals," *Banking Policy Report* 16 (April 7, 1997), pp. 1, 15. A key benefit of the streamlined approach is the potential for approval of a bank acquisition in as few as 50 days following the announcement of a transaction and approval of "qualifying nonbank acquisitions" in as few as 12 business days for well-managed and well-capitalized BHCs. A candidate for this accelerated approval process must have a satisfactory rating under the Community Reinvestment Act, one of the top two CAMELS ratings, and growth no greater than 35 percent during the previous year. Applicable transactions must also satisfy regulatory market concentration limits.

subsidiary of a national bank than by a Section 20 subsidiary under a holding company regulated by the Fed. New procedures allow national banks to approach the OCC about any activity "that is part of or incidental to the business of banking" —even if it cannot be conducted directly by national banks, with case-by-case review of applications. For instance, in December 1997, Zions Bancorporation won approval from the OCC under the new system to underwrite municipal revenue bonds through an operating affiliate. NationsBank also filed two applications in 1997 to engage in limited real estate development activities and real estate leasing. Conflicts between regulators became apparent when the Fed issued a statement that it was fundamentally opposed to the use of Op-Subs for banks to enter new product areas, arguing that the OCC should not allow these to engage in activities not permitted for direct involvement by national banks.[30]

Greater Insurance Type Activities for BHCs   Banks have been allowed to expand their involvement in insurance-type activities, too. Banks can enter joint ventures with insurance companies to sell insurance to bank customers, gaining fee income as agents. A handful of banks have served as agents selling health insurance for small businesses. Legal reserve life insurance, amounting to about $42.9 billion in 1995, has been issued by state-chartered savings banks where allowed in Connecticut, Massachusetts, and New York. In 1995, the Supreme Court ruled in favor of the legality of national banks selling annuities in *NationsBank* v. *Variable Annuity Life Ins. Co*. In 1997, the OCC supported a proposal by First Union Corporation to conduct insurance agency activities (acting as a broker versus underwriting insurance) through subsidiaries of its affiliate national banks. Courts also have upheld the rights of national banks and most state-chartered banks to allow subsidiaries to sell insurance in small towns of less than 5,000. The proposed financial modernization bill would allow BHCs to have insurance company affiliates.[31]

Current Considerations Debated under the Proposed Financial Modernization Bill   As mentioned earlier, the Fed and OCC have liberalized the activities of bank affiliates. The Financial Modernization Bill approved in the House in 1998 and awaiting consideration in the Senate pits the Fed's model for structuring and regulating nonbank affiliates against that of the OCC. The House-passed proposal calls

---

[30]See "Lawmakers Squirm As OCC Considers Zions' Op-Sub Plan," *Banking Policy Report* Vol. 17 (May 5, 1998), p. 4. For a summary of the OCC's new system, see "New Door Opens for Banks to Enter Securities Markets," *New York Times*, December 12, 1997, p. C2. Also see, Melanie L. Fein, "OCC's Op-Sub Rule Could Spark Changes in Banking Structure," *Banking Policy Report* 16 (January 6, 1997), pp. 1, 19; "Op-Sub Debate Heats Up As Fed Circulates Plan to Curb Their Activities," *Banking Policy Report* 16 (July 21, 1997), pp. 2–3; Robert D. Hershey, Jr., "U.S. to Ease Banks' Way in Selling Stocks and Insurance," *New York Times*, November 21, 1996, p. C1. Under the OCC's Part 5 rule, subsidiaries for security underwriting must maintain separate records, have different names from the parent banks, maintain adequate capital levels, and comply with federal rules governing broker-dealers.

[31]See *Life Insurance Fact Book* (City: Washington DC: American Council of Life Insurance). Also see, Joseph B. Treaster. "Keybank to Sell Health Coverage to Businesses," *New York Times*, October 17, 1997, p. C1. Also see, "Leach Says Congress Can Resolve Differences in Banking Legislation," *Banking Policy Report* 16, no. 19 (October 6, 1997), pp. 4–7; and "Warning to Banks on Insurance Sales: Seller Must Beware," *Banking Policy Report* 16, no. 17 (September 1, 1997), pp. 18–22.

for nonbank activities in BHC subsidiaries overseen by the Fed. However, an alternative proposal from the Treasury department would let national banks diversify through their own operating subsidiaries, overseen by the OCC under the Treasury department's auspices. That department is concerned that under the current bill, banks would gravitate away from the national banking system, and that the elected administration would lose its influence on bank policy. Politics are clearly involved in determining what organizational structures will emerge.

Lobbying groups in the banking, securities, and insurance industries also have advanced slightly different proposals from the current legislation. Over the past two decades, Congress has tried and failed nine times to repeal G–S. If the bill is not considered at the end of the 1999 session of Congress, a new version may be presented as a starting point the following year.[32]

Risks Associated with Relaxed Product Restrictions   The previous sections have described a relaxation of regulations requiring corporate separateness between banks and their affiliates. As opposed to corporate separateness, the Fed has followed a **source of strength doctrine** that requires the holding company to be a source of financial and managerial support to its subsidiary bank(s). Rather than promoting separation by firewalls, the source of strength policy implies a close relationship between the parent and the subsidiary. Congress took a similar approach in FDICIA when it required holding companies to guarantee plans to restore capital in undercapitalized subsidiary banks. Thus, debate continues about the optimal relationship between holding companies and subsidiary banks.[33]

Whether corporate separateness is synonymous with economic and financial separateness is another debatable question. Connections between holding company affiliates may be subtle and even undetectable by outsiders. Suppose, for example, that BHC management diverts resources that could just as easily be used in a bank subsidiary to a troubled holding company affiliate. An affiliate may provide services to a bank at a higher price than would be charged in the open market. Public confidence in a bank may diminish in response to a failure of an affiliated or nonbank. Even though Federal Reserve Board regulations limit the activities of BHC subsidiaries

---

[32]See Michael Schroeder, "House Approves Landmark Banking Bill," *The Wall Street Journal*, May 14, 1998, p. A2; Michael Schroeder, "Greenspan, Rubin to Push for Financial Reforms," *The Wall Street Journal*, June 18, 1998, p. A26; Leslie Wayne, "Signs of Shift in Senate Stance on Bank Law," *New York Times*, June 5, 1998, p. C1; Mary Gordon, "House Votes to Life Barriers," *Denver Post*, May 14, 1998, p. 4A; and "Op-Sub Debate Heats Up as Regulators Consider Merits of H.R. 10," *Banking Policy Report* (June 15, 1998), pp. 5–10. The major provisions of HR-10, the House-passed modernization bill, include: (1) a provision that nonbank affiliates would be supervised by the Fed, with the SEC and state insurance agencies overseeing the products of any affiliate; (2) a provision requiring public disclosure of fees and commissions on financial products; (3) a mandate to the Treasury department to conduct a study on the possible application of Community Reinvestment Act rules to security and insurance activities; and (4) a provision that banks cannot have industrial company affiliates, but securities and insurance firms can keep such affiliates for 10 years as long as they generate no more than 15 percent of the firms' revenues.

[33]See Mester (1992) for a review of source of strength arguments. Further discussion is found in Gilbert, 1988 and 1991; Keeton, 1990; Greenspan, 1990; Keeley and Bennett, 1989; Corrigan, 1987; and Keehn, 1989.

and transactions between affiliates of the same BHC, regulations may not address the potential problem of a bank run in response to failure of an affiliated subsidiary. As discussed earlier, regulators may be obligated to assist the entire corporation as part of the federal safety net, because problems at a nonbank affiliate may threaten a banking unit. For the purpose of credit ratings, holding companies are often viewed as one entity, even if two firms are legally separate companies.[34]

In addition to concerns about protecting the federal safety net with the relaxation of G–S, regulators have been concerned about consumer protection issues. For instance, in May 1998, Arthur Levitt, Jr., chairman of the Securities and Exchange Commission, announced that NationsBank had agreed to pay almost $7 million to settle charges of misleading elderly customers on the risks of two bond funds sold in 1993 and 1994 under a joint venture with Morgan Stanley–Dean Witter. When bond funds fell in value as interest rates rose, a class-action suit was taken against Nations-Bank, which refurbished funds with $20 million for declines and changed procedures that had mislead customers.[35]

Universal Banking and Organizational Forms in Other Countries

In different countries, universal banking activities (banking, underwriting, brokerage, insurance, and other activities) are carried out by banks using different types of organizational forms. As noted by Saunders and Walter (1994), the German model of universal banking allows a choice between conducting activities within a bank or through separate affiliates, with the exception of certain activities such as insurance, which require separately capitalized insurance subsidiaries of parent banks. German banks are also allowed to place members on the supervisory boards of industrial corporations and to own equity in industrial companies, practices disallowed in the United States. In the United Kingdom, a relatively broad range of financial activities can be carried out by separate affiliates of a bank. In the United States, as noted earlier, a holding company structure with separately capitalized subsidiaries is required.[36]

---

[34]See Wall, 1984; Liang and Savage, 1990; Pozdena, 1988; Whalen, 1981–1982; Eisenbeis, 1983; Chase and Mingo, 1975; Cornyn and Talley, 1983; and Frieder and Apilado, 1982. Research generally finds centralized BHCs operating as single units versus as separate units. Surveys of MBHCs indicate that the budgeting, capital management, and portfolio management policies of their bank subsidiaries were highly centralized and that the degree of centralization has increased over time. Subsidiary banks affiliated with nonbank subsidiaries appear to shift to relatively risky loans, reduced liquidity, and falling capital ratios. A Fed study finds that nonbank BHC affiliates have riskier assets but operate more profitably than banking affiliates. The results suggest that parent companies would provide capital assistance to subsidiaries in financial difficulty. See Whalen, 1997; Boyd, Graham, and Hewitt, 1993; Liang and Savage, 1990; Rosen, Lloyd-Davies, Kwast, and Humphrey, 1989; Cornyn and Talley, 1983; Cornyn, Hanweck, Rhoades, and Rose, 1986; Benston, 1991; Hunter and Timme, 1989; Brewer, 1988; Eisenbeis, Harris, and Lakonishok, 1984; and Wall, 1986a and b and 1987 for reviews of arguments and research on the effect of greater product diversification for BHCs.

[35]See Leslie Eaton, "Risks Are Cited in Bank-Broker Combinations," *New York Times*, May 5, 1998, p. C1; and "Are Mega Banks—Once Unimaginable, Now Inevitable—Better," *Business Week*, April 1998, pp. 32–37.

[36]See Saunders and Walter (1994) and Swary and Topf (1992) for detailed information on universal banking in other countries.

Holding Companies for Nonbank Financial Institutions

The previous discussion has focused on BHCs. Other types of financial institutions, including finance companies and insurance companies, are also affiliated with holding companies that operate under fewer restrictions than BHCs. For example, no federal requirements mandate that subsidiaries of insurance holding companies must engage in activities "closely related" to the insurance business. As a consequence, stockholder-owned insurers are partially or fully owned by firms in retailing and other industries; Sears, Roebuck and Company's former Allstate Insurance subsidiary is a good example. Many finance companies are part of holding company organizations diversified well beyond financial services, such as General Electric Financial Services, Inc., the finance subsidiary of GE.

Investment Banking Organizations   Investment banking firms were typically partnerships in the past. To compete and raise capital in the last two decades, many have converted to corporate holding companies. With accelerating mergers of investment banking firms with large, well-capitalized banks, many remaining industry competitors realized that they could be significant players only if they could raise significant capital. For instance, in 1998 Goldman, Sachs, a venerable investment banking partnership founded in 1869, announced that it would sell stock to the public. Publicly traded firms improve opportunities for capital formation and growth, and it makes investment banking firms targets for acquisitions by other firms. Consequently, numerous mergers have occurred between investment banking firms and brokerage firms, such as the merger between Dean Witter and Morgan Stanley in 1997. Other mergers have combined BHCs and investment banking firms, such as Bankers Trust with Alex Brown in 1997.

One Savings and Loan Holding Companies   The one savings and loan holding company (OSLHC) is an extremely popular organizational form for S&Ls. Under the SLHC Act of 1968, Congress allowed OSLHCs to engage in almost any type of activity, as long as they held primarily home-mortgage related assets. Interestingly, this act allows nonfinancial firms to own thrifts, permitting Ford Motor Company, Southwest Gas, and Household International Finance Company to own networks of thrifts in the 1980s.[37]

FIRREA placed new restrictions on OSLHCs. They must notify the Office of Thrift Supervision (OTS) and the FDIC of intended acquisitions or planned new activities in current subsidiaries. If regulators conclude that new activities or acquisitions could endanger an institution's stability or the safety of the deposit insurance system, permission can be denied. Furthermore, thrift holding companies whose portfolios fail to meet FIRREA's qualified thrift lender (QTL) test can subsequently be brought under more stringent BHC regulations.

In 1997, about 40 to 50 diversified SLHCs engaged to some degree in activities impermissible to BHCs, including insurance underwriting, real estate development, and general manufacturing. The list includes American Mutual Life Insurance Co.; B.A.T. Industries, PLC; Hawaiian Electric Industries, Inc.; Prudential Insurance Company; and United Services Automobile Association (USAA). At times, Congress has expressed concerned over the potential threat of diverse activities on the

---

[37]See Brumbaugh (1988) for a history of OSLHCs.

risk of federal deposit insurance funds. A recent failed legislative proposal would have eliminated the thrift charter and forced OSLHCs to become BHCs with activities limited to those approved for that form. In 1997, a number of insurance and finance companies, including Travelers, applied for thrift charters. GE Capital Corporation, for instance, sought to convert its state-chartered credit card bank to a federal S&L to allow it a wider variety of banking services, including a proposal to preempt various state laws that applied to its Ohio-based bank. In 1997, the OTS approved the application of an Iowa-based insurance company to start a cyberspace thrift.[38] Under the 1999 Financial Modernization Act proposal, new diversified OSLHCs would not be permitted.

Franchising and Chain Banks

Another alternative to a holding company structure is the franchise agreement, under which an independent financial institution leases the right to use the name and marketing programs of a larger umbrella organization. The initial application of franchising to financial institutions is attributed to First Interstate Bancorp, one of the interstate banking organizations grandfathered under BHC legislation, which leased its name and promotional strategies to independent banks around the country beginning in 1982. A franchised bank would not be a member of a bank holding company, but would use its name. Franchisees enter such relationships to obtain the benefits of association with BHCs, such as wide ranging marketing and other managerial talents, while still retaining operational independence. Thrifts, such as First Nationwide, also have participated in franchising by offering management support systems. Later, with the name changed to U.S. Banking Alliance, the thrift extended network membership opportunities to community banks.[39]

Chain banking is an arrangement that allows several banks to operate under one umbrella organization. Chain banking occurs when one investor owns 5 percent of the voting stock in one or more individual banks *and* holds a managerial post in each bank or when an individual or group owns at least 10 percent of the voting shares of two or more banks. In a few instances, chain-banking organizations have been formed by individuals with common ownership shares in two or more one-bank holding companies.

Because of the relatively informal structure of chain banking, it allows a single investor or group to control a substantial amount of banking assets, while the banks remain independent units and are not subject to multiple reporting requirements or other regulations that govern BHCs.[40]

---

[38]See Ira L. Tannenbaum, "House Legislation Attacks Diversified Savings and Loan Holding Companies," *Banking Policy Report*, 14 (November 6, 1995), pp. 2–4; "GE Unit Seeks Shift to Federal S&L," *New York Times*, December 25, 1997, p. C6; and Stephen E. Frank, "Brokers, Insurers Queue Up for Thrift Chartes," *The Wall Street Journal*, September 24, 1997, p. C1; and "OTS Says New Thrift Can Operate in Cyberspace," *Banking Policy Report* 16 (December 15, 1997), p. 6.

[39]See Eickhoff (1985) and Carner (1986–1987).

[40]For more information on chain banks, see Federal Reserve Bank of Kansas City, 1983, pp. 9–11; and Cyrnak, 1986.

MUTUALLY OWNED INSTITUTIONS

Unlike stockholder-owned institutions, mutually organized firms, such as thrifts and insurers, are "owned" by their customers. Depositors, policyholders, or borrowers become owners when they initiate business relationships with the institutions.

Distribution of Mutual Institutions

Table 4.3 provides information on the number of shareholder-owned versus mutually owned thrifts and life insurance companies. For reasons explored later, the number of stock companies has been increasing in recent years. Nonetheless, a comparably large percentage of S&Ls, savings banks, and property/liability insurers (for which data are not shown in the table), are mutually owned, although this percentage has been declining in recent years. At the end of 1996, about 55 percent of savings institutions were mutual companies. Most life insurers are organized as stockholder-owned corporations, and these firms control the majority of insurance assets, about 64 percent at the end of 1996. The largest and oldest firms in the industry, however, are mutually organized. The opposite is true for savings institutions. About 55 percent are mutual companies, but the largest are shareholder-owned. At the end of 1996, stock firms held about 75 percent of savings institution assets.

Origin and Characteristics of Mutual Ownership

The primary rationale for the mutual form of organization presumes that it ensures operation of an institution for the benefit of its customers, who have supplied most of its funds and depend on it for service and security. In the United States, this rationale dates to the early 1800s, when consumer-oriented financial institutions first

---

Table 4.3   ✦   OWNERSHIP FORM IN THE THRIFT AND LIFE INSURANCE INDUSTRIES

About 55 percent of thrifts are mutually owned, although most large firms are stockholder-owned. Mutual ownership limited the industry's ability to attract new external capital. The opposite prevails in the life insurance industry, where the largest firms and oldest firms are mutuals, but most firms have stock charters. Many large firms are considering going public or becoming mutual holding companies.

Federally Insured Savings Institutions	Number	Percentage	Percentage of Assets Controlled
Mutual	970	54.7	25.0
Stock	801	45.2	75.0
Total	1,771	100.0	100.0
Life Insurance Companies			
Mutual	91	5.4	36.1
Stock	1,604	94.6	63.9
Total	1,695	100.0	100.0

The percentages of assets controlled for savings institutions are approximate figures.

Sources: Thomson Savings Directory, 1997 (Skokie, Ill.: Thomson Financial Publishers, 1996); and Life Insurance Fact Book, 1996 (Washington, D.C.: American Council of Life Insurance, 1997).

appeared. Instead of focusing exclusively on profits, managers of mutual institutions supposedly make decisions that emphasize their customers' needs.[41]

Owners' Rights   Ownership rights in a mutual organization are considerably different from those in a stockholder-owned firm. Both give owners the right to elect boards of directors to monitor management's performance. But potential control over management is stronger in a stockholder-owned firm for a number of reasons. First, ownership rights in a mutual institution cannot be sold to another party (in legal language, they are nonnegotiable), leaving little chance that anyone can obtain enough influence to control the outcome of elections. Furthermore, some thrift institutions ask owners to sign away their rights to vote when they open accounts or take out loans, in effect giving managers a permanent proxy. Some observers of thrifts have stated, in fact, that a mutual organization often results in a "self-perpetuating" board.

For another difference in management control, although owners of a mutually organized company theoretically have a pro rata claim on the institution's retained earnings, they have no way to exercise that claim. Because they hold no negotiable ownership shares, they can earn no capital gains. An owner who cancels a policy or closes a deposit account also cancels the right to this pro rata share. Finally, mutually owned institutions are not legally required to disclose as much detail about their financial condition as are stockholder-owned firms. Thus, depositors or policyholders may lack access to information about the safety and soundness of these institutions.

Performance of Mutually Organized Firms   As a result of these differences, some argue that managers have more latitude in mutual organizations than in stockholder-owned firms. The benefits or drawbacks of this latitude depend on its effect on institutional performance relative to the performance of similar stockholder-owned institutions. Much of the research evidence on this point has been accumulated for S&Ls. Some scholars have hypothesized that stock associations should be more cost-efficient and more profitable than equivalent mutually owned institutions, because managers should perform better fearing removal by shareholders for excessive costs and inferior profits. Managers of mutuals may have more opportunities for expense preference type of behavior, as discussed in Chapter 1; however, they may have incentives to limit risk to protect their jobs than stockholder-owned firms have. Tests of these hypotheses have yielded mixed results. Generally, researchers conclude that stock associations are riskier and more aggressive because they grow at faster rates, but they are not necessarily more efficient or more profitable than their mutual counterparts.

In the 1980s, an unprofitable time for the thrift industry as a whole, events demonstrated the importance of one key difference between mutuals and stocks—their ability to raise capital. When they experience negative profits or negative and reduced retained earnings, mutual associations have no way to replenish lost net worth. If losses persist, mutual thrift institutions may be forced into positions of negative net worth, eventually leading to failure. Similar profitability difficulties, as well as tax considerations, have troubled mutually owned insurance companies. More and

---

[41]See Blyn, 1981, pp. 40–41; and Smith and Stutzer, 1990.

more, the thrift and insurance industries have turned to **conversion** as a way to raise external capital by transferring ownership of an institution from customers to shareholders.[42]

Conversion for Thrifts

In the 1980s, more than 500 thrifts converted from mutual to stock ownership, a rapid rate compared with the past. The pace continued in the 1990s, as thrifts struggled to meet increasingly stringent capital requirements imposed by FIRREA and FDICIA.[43] Stock conversions also simplify mergers, a fact related to extensive consolidation in the industry. Requirements for conversion are strictly defined by the OTS and are intended to promote conversions while limiting the possibility that only a few individuals can benefit at the expense of others. The process involves preparation of a conversion plan by management with the approval of directors, regulators, and most owner-depositors. Stock sold in a conversion is first offered to eligible depositors, none of whom may purchase more than 5 percent of the issued shares. Depositors not interested in the stock may not sell their rights to those who are. Legislation passed under the Small Business Jobs Protection Act in 1996 (discussed in greater detail in Chapter 7) eliminates tax impediments for stock thrift-to-bank conversions, making mutual-to-stock conversions for thrifts more attractive than before for mutual thrifts that might wish to be acquired.[44]

Research finds that thrifts increase their risk after conversions. Converted thrifts also appear to grow faster than they did as mutual institutions. For instance, a recent study by Schrand and Unal (1998) found that 571 thrifts converting during 1983 to 1988 increased their credit risk following the conversions, consistent with increased opportunities and incentives for risk taking. Hence, conversion increases some institutions' access to capital but does not ensure that managers will make good investment decisions. Another study found that the proportion of stock owned by managers

---

[42]Conversions to stock ownership have not only helped thrifts to raise capital by issuing stock but also allowed acquisitions of thrifts that could not meet capital requirements by other banks or thrifts.

[43]From 1945 to 1955, when few restrictions limited conversion, only 30 thrifts converted. From 1955 to 1974, conversions were prohibited altogether. After 1974, few conversions occurred until 1980. See Dunham, 1985; and Simons, 1992. For a review of conversions in the 1980s, see Cordell, MacDonald, and Wohar, 1993. In the 1980s, regulations for conversions incorporated an antitakeover rule in which any beneficial ownership position could control no more than 10 percent of any class of equity security for 3 years following conversion. Regulations also limit the amount of stock that can be offered during this period to 5 percent for any person or identified group and to 15 to 25 percent for all officers and directors (see Cebenoyan et al., 1995).

[44]See Ira L. Tannenbaum, "Bad Debt Legislation Clears Way for Thrifts Converting to Banks," *Banking Policy Report* 15 (August 19, 1996), pp. 1, 15. Also see FHLBB, "Conversions from Mutual to Stock Form and Acquisitions of Control of Insured Institutions," 12 CFR parts 543, 546, 552, 562, 563, 563b, and 574, October 17, 1986; and U.S. League of Savings Institutions, "Conversions from Mutual to Stock Form and Acquisitions of Control of Insured Institutions," *Special Management Bulletin*, August 28, 1987.

of a converted institution greatly influences whether they engage in expense-preference behavior. As managers acquire increasingly large blocks of stock, they become progressively more likely to favor on-the-job perquisites for themselves, and behave in ways progressively more similar to managers in mutual thrifts. When managers of converted thrifts own relatively little stock, nonmanager-owners can exert strong control on the institutions' expenses. Studies also show that stock S&Ls took on greater risk than mutual S&Ls in the 1980s, resulting in higher resolution costs for stock versus mutual thrifts.[45]

After some controversy over pricing of initial public offerings (IPOs) for converting thrifts in some states and possible abuses by officers at the expense of depositors, regulators tightened restrictions to prevent abuses. Still, recent studies find very high average returns to investors who buy shares in thrift IPOs on the offering dates. Pettigrew, Page, Jahera, and Barth (1998), for instance, find an average 1-day, risk-adjusted return of 27 percent for mutual-to-stock conversions. This figure represents a difference of 15.65 percent for first-day offerings in other IPOs. Some researchers suggest that these offerings may be underpriced, while other point out that high initial returns compensate investors for great risk.[46]

Conversion to "Demutualize" Insurers

The insurance industry, too, has faced profitability problems recently because changing consumer preferences, increasing litigation of claims, inflation, and changing interest rates have required large cash outflows. Like their thrift counterparts, mutual insurers have faced pressures from reduced net worth caused by low or negative earnings. Consequently, many have considered conversion as a survival strategy. Several property/liability insurers have converted since 1984, and in that year the first application in 80 years for conversion of a mutual life insurer was filed with the Maine insurance commission by Union Mutual Life. Earlier conversions were fueled by the Tax Reform Act of 1984, which lowered the amount of tax-deductible "dividends" that mutual insurers can pay to policyholder-owners, removing a provision

---

[45]Discussions of mutual vesus stock S&L performance can be found in Simpson and Kohers, 1979; Woerheide, 1984, pp. 29–31; "Well-Run Mutuals Deserve the Needed Latitude to Succeed," *Savings Institutions* 112 (May 1991): 14–15; Marsalis 1987; Carter and Stover 1990; Akella and Greenbaum, 1988; Fields, 1988; Mester, 1993; Cebenoyan et al., 1993. Studies by Cordell, MacDonald, and Wohar (1993) and Esty (1996) find evidence of greater risk-taking behavior for stock S&Ls that for mutual institutions and that newly converted stock thrifts increased risk after their conversion in the 1980s. Schrand and Unal (1998) find that newly converted thrifts take on increased credit risk but hedge interest rate risk. Also, see Unal and Vojislav (1993) and Hasan and Carhill (1997) for reviews of the performance of newly converted thrifts. Barth, Bartholomew, and Bradley (1990) and Cole and Eisenbeis (1996) find evidence of higher thrift resolution costs for stock versus mutual S&Ls, as well. See Burns, Jordan, and Verbrugge, 1988; LeCompte et al., 1994; and Jahera, Barth, and Page, 1997 for studies of the stock market performance of converted thrifts.

[46]See Cagle and Porter, 1994; Burns, Jordan, and Verbrugge, 1988; LeCompte et al., 1994; Barth, Page, and Jahera 1997 for studies on thrift IPOs. Also for summaries of studies of the performance of initial public offerings, see Roger G. Ibbotson, Jody L. Sindelar, and Jay R. Ritter, "Initial Public Offerings," *Journal of Applied Corporate Finance* 1 (Summer 1988), pp. 37–45; and Roger G. Ibbotson, Jody L. Sindelar, and Jay R. Ritter, "Initial Public Offerings," *Journal of Applied Corporate Finance* Vol. 7 (Spring 1994).

that previously had been a major reason for the popularity of the mutual form of organization.[47] In the 1990s, a number of large life insurance firms converted from mutual to stock ownership, as well, to gain access to capital markets and to increase their flexibility for purchasing other businesses and for pursuing growth opportunities around the world. Especially noteworthy are the 1992 conversion by Equitable Life Assurance Society, the fourth largest firm in the industry, the 1997 conversion of Canada Mutual Life, one of Canada's largest life insurers, and the 1998 conversion of Prudential Insurance Company, the biggest seller of life insurance. To allow Prudential to convert, New Jersey had to pass a special law in 1998 to ensure fair compensation for its policyholders as owners. Prudential plans to complete the conversion in 2 years through a complex process of determining how to fairly allocate the shares to eligible policyholders. For the conversion to be allowed, at least three-fourths of its 23-member board must vote for the demutualization plan, as well as two-thirds of at least 1 million shareholders. The state insurance commissioner also must hold a public hearing on the plan, giving policyholders at least 45 days' notice. A key issue is how Prudential will allocate its estimated $20 billion in accumulated profits to the company's 11 million policyholders. Thus, demutualization is not an easy process.[48]

Because regulation of insurers rests largely with state rather than federal agencies, no uniform procedure governs their conversions analogous to the policies governing thrifts. Many companies also feel that a stock-based structure with managerial stock ownership will improve the efficiency of the organization.

Critics of recent conversions suggest, however, that managers and some policyholders may gain more from conversion than others. They conclude that state officials should, therefore, closely scrutinize conversion plans. Consumer groups have argued that managers receiving stock options may benefit at the expense of policyholders. Hence, for instance, Prudential must disclose any arrangements for executive stock options included in its conversion plan. Others argue that life insurance conversions are likely to be motivated by needs to improve economic efficiency and provide additional capital for expansion rather than by one group's desire to increase its wealth at the expense of others. Francis de Regnacourt, an analyst at Moody's Investors Service has made such an argument in a recent *Wall Street Journal* article about Canada Mutual Life's conversion: "People are realizing at a time when consolidation is a major factor, that by not having stock as currency, you're potentially locking yourself out of the largest deals and maybe even some of the best ones."[49] The decisions of Equitable and Prudential were clearly spurred by the need to raise

---

[47]Dan Baum, "Union Mutual's Plan to Be Stock Owned Leads to Suits against Some Agents and a Proxy Fight," *The Wall Street Journal*, February 26, 1985; Laura Meadows, "Minuet in Maine," *Forbes*, November 18, 1985, p. 208; Murray, 1985; and Jeffrey H. Birnbaum, "Tax Battle between Stocks and Mutual Insurers," *The Wall Street Journal*, April 25, 1989, p. A30.

[48]Susan Pullian, "Equitable Life to Convert to Stock-Owned Company," *The Wall Street Journal*, December 12, 1990, p. A3; and Greg Steinmetz, "Equitable Sets Offering Price below Target," *The Wall Street Journal*, July 15, 1992, p. A4; Leslie Scism, "Prudential to Move to Stock Ownership," *The Wall Street Journal*, February 13, 1998, pp. A3, A5; and "Prudential Clears a Hurdle in Its Move to a Public Company," *The Wall Street Journal*, June 23, 1998, p. B13.

[49]"Canada's Mutual Life Plans to Issue Stock, Seek U.S. Purchases," *The Wall Street Journal*, December 9, 1997, p. C26.

additional capital to compete with other large companies, such as Travelers. Some experts have predicted that the number of insurers will decline as a result of the heightened need for capital in a more competitive environment.

Observers also note that international insurance firms—particularly those in the European Community—are increasingly interested in the U.S. markets, as evidenced by Group AXA's investment in Equitable. Such international firms create a strong market for the shares of converted mutuals. A number of large European firms have U.S. insurance firms as subsidiaries. For example, Zurich Insurance Company became the largest property-casualty firm in the world in 1997 by taking over B.A.T. Industries PLC, which includes Farmers Group, the fifth-largest U.S. property-casualty insurer. In Europe, bidding wars have erupted over insurance companies such as Assurances Generales de France, the target of both Italy's Assicurazioni Generali SpA and Germany's Allianz AG in December 1997. European insurers are using mergers to increase revenues, cut overhead costs, and raise profits for investors. With the birth of the Euro, additional mergers are expected in Europe as companies try to reach critical mass in an increasingly competitive market. The European Monetary Union will also simplify mergers by eliminating worries about foreign exchange effects.[50]

Holding Companies for Mutual Insurance Companies

In the 1990s, many large mutual insurers pushed state legislatures to adopt laws permitting a hybrid structure known as a *mutual holding company* that would allow them to raise capital by setting up as affiliates of separate, publicly owned companies. Recently, observers have noted that the mutual holding company provides a way to retain the mutual form of organization while giving stock-option incentives to management, thus reducing agency costs. Among companies pushing such proposals are large, venerable mutuals in New York including Mutual Life Insurance Company of New York (MONY), Metropolitan Life, and New York Life. New York Life pushed for such a law in New York, which failed to pass in 1998. Consumer activists criticize New York's proposed new laws for providing inadequate compensation to policyholders for the accumulated surplus that they give up when part of their company, the new affiliate, goes public. Under most previous state laws, when a mutual company sells stock, it must first divide up most accumulated profits or surplus among policyholders as compensation for giving up their ownership. Under recent laws, adopted in about 20 states and pending in Washington, D.C. and Massachusetts, however an insurer can issue stock without any payment to policyholders by setting up a series of holding companies, with policyholders remaining as the majority owners of the company. Under this new system, policyholders receive no compensation, but are permitted to buy a limited amount of stock at a preferential price. Future profits are not reserved exclusively to policyholders, but a portion are regularly distributed as dividends to be shared

---

[50]Heimann, 1984; McNamara and Rhee, 1992; "AXA Feels Equitable," *The Economist*, May 30, 1992, pp. 78–79; Russ Banham, "Tough Times, Tough Choices," *Insurance Review*, September 1992, pp. 24–27; Greg Steinmetz and Margaret Studer, "Zurich to Expand in U.S. with B.A.T. Deal," *The Wall Street Journal*, October 14, 1997, p. A19; Charles Fleming, "Allianz and Generali Reach Agreement on Carving Up Assets of Insurer AGF," *The Wall Street Journal*, December 22, 1997; and Ted Hampton, "Switch to Euro Opens Doors for Insurers," *Denver Post*, May 9, 1998, p. 2C.

with new stockholders. Consumer activists in New York contended when such a law was proposed for their state that policyholders would be deprived of a small fortune at the expense of executives who could initially own only 5 percent of shares, eventually rising to 18 percent. Conversions can involve quite substantial amounts of money, such as the $12 billion surplus of Metropolitan Life and the $6 billion surplus for New York Life in 1997. In response to consumer criticism, in June 1998, the New York legislature decided not to act on the bill that would have permitted mutual holding companies there.[51]

Holding Companies for Mutual Thrifts

CEBA ushered in a similar new organizational form for mutually owned thrift institutions, which have gained the ability to form holding companies. In the unusual procedure, a mutual thrift first transfers assets, insured liabilities, and capital to a newly formed, stockholder-owned savings bank subsidiary. Common stock in the new subsidiary bank can be sold to the public to raise additional capital. The mutual institution (now the parent holding company with the same management and board as before) can retain operating control over the new bank simply by continuing to hold at least 51 percent of the shares. The parent company can also invest in other stockholder-owned thrifts. The first successful market test of the provision was conducted by Peoples Bank in Bridgeport, Connecticut, which formed a mutual holding company in 1989, attracting $55 million in new equity capital in the process.[52]

Mutual funds, one of the most popular FIs in the 1990s, have organizational structures similar to those of discuss mutual insurers and thrifts, as the following section discusses.

Organizations for Mutual Funds

Mutual funds manage almost 95 percent of professionally managed financial assets. The funds' assets are owned, in turn, by the investors who buy fund shares. However, almost all mutual funds are externally managed, with their operations conducted by investment companies and other affiliated organizations. Figure 4.3 depicts a typical mutual fund complex, including its principal service providers. A board of directors elected by shareholders governs fund activities. At least 40 percent of the fund's board of directors must be independent of its investment adviser

---

[51]"Mutual Insurers Lose Bid as New York Lets Holding-Firm Bill Die," *New York Times*, June 19, 1998, p. A6. See also, Leslie Scism, "Mutual-Life Insurers Going Public," *The Wall Street Journal*, December 9, 1997, p. C1; Joseph B. Treaster, "Insurers' Plan to Sell Stock Riles Consumer Advocates," *New York Times*, October 9, 1997, p. C2; "Canada's Mutual Life,"; Leslie Scism, "MONY Plans Switch to Stock Ownership," *The Wall Street Journal*, September 9, 1997, p. B1.

[52]"The Competitive Equality Banking Act of 1987," *Special Management Bulletin*, U.S. League of Savings Institutions, October 16, 1987; Resa W. King, "The Shape of Thrifts to Come?" *Business Week*, September 18, 1989, p. 102; "Mutual Holding Companies May Be a Growing Trend," *Savings Institutions* 110 (December 1989): 6–7; Tom Parliment, "To Raise Capital, Consider a Mutual Holding Company," *Savings Institutions* 112 (May 1991), pp. 52–53; Phillip Britt, "Mutual Holding Companies Unlock Needed Capital," *Savings Institutions* (January 1992), p. 9; and Brian Nixon, "Going Full Stock or Mutual Stock," *Savings and Community Banker* 2 (February 1993), pp. 22–26.

Figure 4.3 ◆ THE ORGANIZATION AND OPERATION OF A MUTUAL FUND

The *Board of Directors* oversees management of the fund's business affairs. *Shareholders* elect the directors and vote on any change in the fund's investment objectives or policies. The *Investment Adviser* selects portfolio investments consistent with objectives and policies in the mutual fund's prospectus and promotes the best possible overall execution of portfolio orders. The *Principal Underwriter* distributes shares. The *Transfer Agent* conducts record-keeping and related functions. The *Administrator* oversees the performance of other companies that provide services to the fund and ensures that its operations comply with federal requirements. The *Custodian*, usually a qualified bank, protects the mutual fund's portfolio securities.

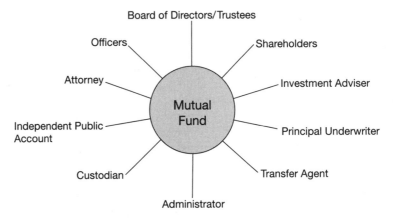

Source: Mutual Fund Fact Book, 37th ed. (Washington D.C.: Investment Company Institute, 1997), pp. 32–34.

or principal underwriter under a provision of the Investment Company Act of 1970. Investment adviser affiliates manage funds and receive annual fees based on percentages of average net assets they control. They also often provide administrative and accounting services, or an unaffiliated party does this work. Mutual funds usually distribute their shares through separate organizations designated as principal underwriters. The principal underwriters are regulated as brokers and dealers to continuously offer new shares to the public. Mutual funds are required by law to protect portfolio securities by placing them with custodians, usually qualified banks. Finally, transfer agents help mutual funds to conduct record-keeping and related functions and maintain customer service.[53]

Although mutual funds are owned by investors, the affiliated firms that run their operations can be mutually owned by shareholders, privately held, publicly owned, or subsidiaries of other companies. For instance, the holding company for Kansas Southern Railroad owns a number of prominent funds, including American Century. Mellon Bank owns Dreyfus Funds, and Zurich Insurance, a Swiss Company, owns Scudder. The management company of Vanguard, one of the largest U.S. funds, is unusual since the shareholders of the funds it manages also own it. Its investor-shareholders do not receive dividends on the management company's performance, but they do reap benefits from low expenses.

---

[53]See *Mutual Fund Fact Book*, 37th ed. (Washington, D.C.: Investment Company Institute, 1997).

In contrast, Fidelity Investment Company, which manages $681.7 billion in assets, is closely held by the family of Edward C. "Ned" Johnson, III, its chairman and chief executive officer. Unlike many other financial institution managers, Mr. Johnson believes that public shareholders' emphasis on short-term profits would undermine his philosophy of investing for long-term growth. Desiring to remain independent, Fidelity has turned down purchase offers by Travelers and other companies. Fidelity went through a radical restructuring of its ownership in 1995 giving its top 50 executives and mutual fund managers a 51 percent voting stake and reducing the Johnson's family's voting stock to 24.5 percent held by Ned Johnson's daughter, a senior vice president who also runs mutual funds. This restructuring prevented the need to go public to raise money to pay estate taxes in the event of the CEO's death.

Figure 4.4 shows the diverse group of operating units for Fidelity Investments. Operating units manage and distribute Fidelity mutual funds and perform retail and institutional brokerage services as well as 401(k) and trust company services. The company also includes real estate and systems units, a life insurance unit, and a capital investments unit, which itself owns a Boston Coach car service, community newspaper company, and the World Trade Center in Boston. This diversity of assets highlights the role of mutual funds as jacks of all trade, offering wide varieties of financial services including those previously mentioned for Fidelity, plus discount brokerage, automated bill paying, insurance, annuities, debit

Figure 4.4 ✦ OPERATING COMPANIES OF FIDELITY INVESTMENTS

This example illustrates the diversity of operating companies associated with mutual funds.

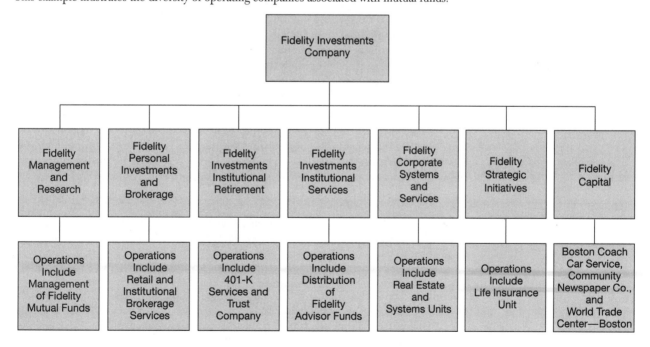

Source: James S. Hirsch and Robert McGough, "Fidelity Denies Rumors of Intention to Sell Firm," *The Wall Street Journal*, June 12, 1998, pp. C1, C26.

cards for automated teller machines, check-writing services against fund balances, and even for some Internet-based investing and home banking services.[54]

Service Corporations: The Holding Company Alternative

Alternative structures besides holding companies permit thrift mutuals (and stock institutions, too, if they so desire) to diversify outside their traditional functions of accepting deposits and making mortgage loans. Since the 1950s, S&Ls with federal charters have been permitted to form **service corporations (SCs)** to conduct diversified lines of business. An SC is formed when one or more associations purchase the stock of a new organization. The associations, as residual owners of the SC, are entitled to all profits from its operations. The amount invested in SCs is limited to 3 percent of a thrift's total assets. Although laws vary from state to state, similar arrangements allow mutual insurance companies to form SC subsidiaries by using some of their assets to purchase stock in affiliated stockholder-owned organizations.

Typically, investment in SCs has remained below 2 percent of the S&L industry's assets. SC activities include real estate development and property management, insurance agency and brokerage services, appraisal services, data processing services, and consumer lending. In the 1980s, controversy surrounded SCs affiliated with state-chartered thrifts in liberally regulated states. These service companies were allowed to invest in almost any activity, and many took great risks. Under FIRREA, state-chartered thrifts are subject to the same investment restrictions as federally chartered thrifts. Little long-term evidence is available on the effect of SCs on institutional profitability.[55]

NOT-FOR-PROFIT INSTITUTIONS

Another main organizational structure in financial institutions is the not-for-profit form. Credit Unions (CUs) are currently the only major financial group with this structure. CUs resemble mutually owned institutions with two major exceptions: Membership in a CU is restricted by law to a group with a common bond, and federal CUs need not pay taxes on profits retained to increase their net worth.

The **common bond** requirement for membership in a CU—usually a tie formed as a result of occupational, religious, or social affiliations—is related to the cooperative motivation that theoretically underlies the formation of mutual financial institutions. Because federal CUs are exempt from taxation based on the purported strength of this cooperation, the common bond requirement is intended to ensure

---

[54]See James S. Hirsch and Robert McGough, "Fidelity Denies Rumors of Intention to Sell Firm," *The Wall Street Journal*, June 12, 1998, pp. C1, C26; Vanessa O'Connell, "It's a Broker! It's a Banker! It's a Mutual-Fund Group!" *The Wall Street Journal*, February 19, 1998, pp. C1, C27; and Jonathan Clements, "Money Machine," *The Wall Street Journal*, July 16, 1990, pp. A1, A5.

[55]Pat Allen, "Service Corporations Fight for Earnings," *Savings Institutions* 108 (May 1987): 42–49; "Service Corporations Are Ideal Diversification Tool," *Savings Institutions* 104 (October 1983): 52–55; and Harold B. Olin, "Service Corporations Help the Business Diversify," *Savings Institutions* 105 (April 1984): 120–127. See Brumbaugh (1988) for a detailed discussion of thrift-affiliated service companies in the 1980s.

realization of the spirit of colleague helping colleague. In practice, the interpretation of the phrase *common bond* has been expanded over the years, resulting in quite a liberal interpretation. For example, AT&T Family Federal Credit Union includes members from 150 unrelated companies; only 35 percent of its 112,000 members are employees of AT&T and its affiliates. In response to a lawsuit by community banking groups, the Supreme Court ruled in 1998 that credit union regulators had overstepped their bounds by allowing CUs to extend their common bonds. However, within a few months, Congress responded to intense lobbying by CUs and consumer groups and passed legislation in April 1998 that would allow CUs to accept outside members as long as they come from companies or groups with fewer than 3,000 people. CUs could also apply for exceptions to accept even larger groups. The Senate confirmed a similar bill in July of 1998.[56]

CU members are "owners" of the organization. In fact, their savings are called *shares*, although these shares resemble deposits more than stock, because they are eligible for federal deposit insurance coverage. As in mutuals, members cannot sell shares to profit from capital gains. Also like mutuals, CUs must maintain sufficient net worth (called *reserves*) by retaining earnings to withstand potential declines in asset values; they have no other source of equity-like capital. Nevertheless, their tax exemption may enable federal CUs to charge lower loan rates, yet achieve the same additions to net worth, as comparably sized S&Ls or savings banks. CUs will be discussed in greater detail in chapter 7.

Service Organizations and Corporate Credit Unions

Federal CUs can form for-profit **credit union service organizations (CUSOs)**. As with thrift service corporations, investments in CUSOs are limited, although the restriction is expressed as a percentage of a CU's net worth, not of its assets. A CUSO enables a CU to earn income from sources that would be prohibited without the separate unit, such as insurance, brokerage, and financial planning services. The small sizes of most CUs have prevented them from using CUSOs up to this point, although managers in large CUs found them to be an attractive diversification vehicle in the 1980s.

Credit Unions also cooperatively own **corporate credit unions (CCUs)** to provide correspondent services for member institutions. Such services include leasing, financial management, mortgage corporation services, credit and debit cards, ATM networks, and mutual insurance agencies. Corporate and central credit unions (of which CCUs are also members) also provide liquidity services to manage severe cash flow swings, along with investment services.[57]

---

[56]See Walker, 1997; and Phillip C. Meyer, "High Court Decision Is Awaited on Credit Union 'Common Bond,'" *Banking Policy Report* 16 (October 20, 1997), pp. 1, 12; "House Votes to Let Credit Unions Expand Their Memberships," *New York Times*, April 2, 1998, p. C5. Also see Moody and Fite, 1971, Chapter 10; Pearce, 1984, p. 18; and Phil Gasteyer, "New Challenges Threaten Credit Union Advantages," *Savings Institutions* 112 (November 1991), p. 17.

[57]"CUSOs Open New Service Areas," *Credit Union Magazine* 50 (November 1984): 8–14; and "Leagues and Regulators Take a Hard Look," *Credit Union Magazine* 50 (December 1984): 42–45.

THE FUTURE: VIRTUAL FIS AND SMART CARDS

Virtual FIs

In the technological age of the late 20th and dawning 21st centuries, new forms of virtual financial institutions are emerging. In August 1997, the OCC granted its first national charter for such an institution to CompuBank based in Houston, Texas. This cyberbank will serve a payments system function, making no loans, and holding only government securities as assets. In 1997, the OTS granted electronic thrift charters to Security First Network, an Atlanta-based Internet bank, and to a cyberthrift unit of Principal Mutual Life Insurance Company. In 1998, Lindner Funds, a St. Louis fund group with $3.2 billion in assets, began offering Internet-based investing and home-banking services. A large number of firms offer on-line stock brokerage services. For instance, Charles Schwab's on-line discount brokerage service averages 100,000 trades a day. Also, thousands of financial institutions maintain home pages or offer services on the Internet, allowing investors to apply for loans, do home banking and bill paying, order electronic funds transfers, and perform other banking activities at any hour of the day. Virtual services allow FIs to develop nationwide relationships. Deposits can be gathered electronically or by mail. Information systems can be set up so individualized products can be created and relayed for particular virtual customers to meet their future needs.[58]

Home banking services are not new functions. In 1981, Chemical, Citibank, Wachovia, Banc One, and Security Pacific among others tried and failed to get customers into home banking, generally through interactions using TV sets. A decade later, however, home banking revived with the dramatic growth in the use of home personal computers and new financial programs, such as Quicken from Intuit and Microsoft Money, along with electronic bill payment services, such as Check Free and National Payments Clearinghouse. Alliances by large banks, such as Citibank, NationsBank, and Bank of America with Intuit and Microsoft provide an interface between home computers and banks' electronic payments projects. Now numerous banks offer home banking and cash management services via personal computers.[59]

One of the first virtual banks, First Direct in Leeds, England, appeared as a subsidiary of Midland Bank in 1989. Its development was a reaction to profitability problems that Midland Bank faced with its largely unprofitable 2,000 branch system. Midland Bank used its franchise value to create a phone-only bank that would run at a much lower cost than its branching system while providing 24 hour, seven day-a-week banking services, including making loans and paying bills for customers. By operating in Great Britain, with an electronic funds transfer system better developed

---

[58]See O'Connell, "Broker! Banker!"; Vanessa O'Connell, "Branchless Banks Are Attracting Savers," *The Wall Street Journal*, November 14, 1996, p. C1; Saul Hansell, "On-Line Banking Doesn't Always Cover the Basics," *New York Times*, November 10, 1997, p. C12; David Bank, "Uneasy Banks Must Make a Deposit on On-Line Future," *The Wall Street Journal*, p. B4; Arthur M. Louis, "Online Brokers Rush for Speed," *New York Times*, p. B1; Saul Hansell, "500,000 Clients, No Branches," *New York Times*, September 3, 1995, pp. B1, B10; Michael Dresser, "Banking on the Internet," *Baltimore Sun*, September 4, 1995, pp. 8C–9C. Also see McCoy et al., 1994 for a discussion of the use of MIS systems for BHCs.

[59]See Mayer, 1997.

than that in the United States, First Direct attracted customers with less compelling reasons to deposit paper checks than U.S. bank customers had. First Direct became one of the fastest growing banks in Britain, capturing 2 percent of that country's banking population within 2 years and opening up about 10,000 new accounts each month, the equivalent of two or three new branches.

In the United States, several large banks opened similar direct banks as subsidiaries, such as Chase/Chemical Direct. Other virtual banks include consumer banks that were "grandfathered" under CEBA in 1987, such as First Deposit National Bank in New Hampshire, owned by Providian Insurance Company in Louisville, Kentucky. First Deposit markets consumer loans, money market deposit accounts, and certificates of deposit to both retail and institutional customers, as well as cross-selling insurance-based products, over the phone and on the Internet. In 1994, First Direct had a phenomenal ROE of 57.67 percent, with an extraordinary ROA for a bank of 6.32 percent. Other branchless banks include TeleBank Financial Corp. of Arlington, Virginia, and credit card banks, such as MBNA Corp. in Wilmington, Delaware.[60]

In June 1998, Citibank U.K. teamed with a British Internet provider, Virgin Group PLC, to offer all of its bank-account customers free, unlimited Internet access. With this access, customers can do all their banking on-line at Citibank's Web site, including transferring funds between accounts, paying bills, printing out statements, and updating personal finance software. Since Citibank U.K. has no branches, saving infrastructure costs, it also can pay a higher interest rate to Internet customers than other British banks pay. One problem with electronic financial institutions is the need to replace authorized, hand-written signatures for on-line transactions. Early in 1998, Zion's Bank won approval from U.S. regulators to offer an electronic authentication system known as *digital signature authentication (DSA)* for electronic mail. DSA assures that e-mail signatures are actually inscribed by the appropriate people, similar to a notary public.[61]

A Cashless Future? Smart Cards and E-Cash

Smart Cards   In a number of countries, consumers complete transactions and perform other functions using **smart cards**, credit-card sized devices containing tiny computer chips that can store information for a variety of purposes. Recently, U.S. FIs in the banking and credit card industries have been experimenting with these cards to cut costs and improve customer service. Conventional magnetic strips are replaced with ones that can not only give access to automated teller machines (ATMs), but can also be "**loaded**" with **digital cash** that serves as legal tender for trades with merchants who have compatible decoder terminals. Such cards are in wide use in Europe, helping with tasks like keeping medical records in Germany and Finland, paying highway tolls in Italy, and paying for parking meters, telephone calls, transit rides, newspapers, groceries, and other goods in Belgium and France, where smart cards were pioneered. In Belgium, each bank customer carries a debit card to pay for

---

[60]See Kimberley A. Strassel, "Citibank U.K. to Introduce Web Banking," *The Wall Street Journal*, June 5, 1998, p. B9.

[61]See Mayer, 1997; and Philip S. Corwin, "The Virtual Dotted Line: Understanding Digital Signatures," *Banking Policy Report* 16, no. 4 (February 17, 1997), pp. 1, 11.

purchases and to pay bills through ATMs. By the summer of 1996, 7,000 banks associated with the European affiliate of Master Card, Europay, began using a "clip" card that can be replenished with cash value from an ATM or home computer.[62]

U.S. banks have begun experimenting with smart cards. For instance, Chase Manhattan is doing a test of MasterCard International's Mondex system on the upper west side of Manhattan. The banking industry hopes that smart cards will help to cut costs. Central approval of a debit or credit transaction is no longer needed, since all authorization information and even the money itself for a transaction would be included on a smart card's chip. The estimated cost of a single smart-card transaction would average less than a penny. In contrast, the 25-cent average cost for a credit card transaction must cover a long-distance computer network accessing a large centralized data base to approve each transaction. To prevent fraud, Visa International's smart card system incorporates a central data base, which receives reports from merchant terminals each day. However, Mondex refuses to implement such a system, contending that it would contradict the purpose of a smart card, which allows customers to use the money on the card just like cash. Concerns about security for smart cards remain. Recently, a 25-year-old expert at Cryptography Research broke the code of several smart cards by drawing mathematical inferences from fluctuating electric power consumption in the chips. This code breaking success sent a warning to Mondex and other smart card pioneers that better security safeguards need to be implemented.[63]

E-Cash   Direct electronic transfers of funds have gained widely expanded use in the 1990s. For instance, direct deposits of salaries through automated clearing house (ACH) systems have become commonplace in the United States. Similarly, in Germany, over 1 million people pay their bills through Telekom On-Line, which allows customers to transfer funds directly from their bank cards to the bank accounts of the firms whose bills they are paying. U.S. government payments are now relayed through direct deposits, unless recipients can prove hardship, and banks have been mandated to provide accounts for the unbanked.[64]

In 1995, a Financial Services Technology Consortium of large banks organized and established a technique to make purchases through the Internet. By means of a credit card slot for a PC, the system generates an electronic check sent via e-mail to a merchant and collected as an ACH item. The first demonstration of this technique included purchasing a Teddy bear for Vice President Al Gore. First Virtual also developed a way to buy merchandise without leaving the Internet through recognition of VISA, MasterCard, and Discover credit cards. David Chaum of Amsterdam created DigiCash, which relies on doubly encrypted credit information as an alternative currency allowing customers to buy products on the Internet from vendors that accept this form of electronic currency. The first commercial use of DigiCash occurred in November 1995, when Mark Twain Bancshares in Missouri advertised an Internet account called "The Mint" to issue "Digibucks." Anyone with a real account at Mark Twain could transfer funds to a DigiCash account to pay for purchases on an Internet site. If the merchant also had an account at Mark Twain, the transaction could be

---

[62]See Mayer, 1997; Peter Wayner, "Code Break Cracks Smart Cards' Digital Safe," *New York Times*, pp. C1, C2.

[63]See Mayer, 1997.

[64]Ibid.

completed through a transfer between accounts upon delivery of the product to the customer. As pointed out by Martin Mayer (1997) in an excellent book entitled, *The Bankers, the Next Generation*, electronic money or e-cash represents a very feasible alternative for the future. Credits may be issued not only by banks, but also by technology firms, creating a dual monetary system. For instance, Microsoft could offer accounts in whatever currency Bill Gates might wish to create.

With financial institution mergers becoming commonplace, the final section discusses possible benefits for these firms through economies of scale and scope. The balance of the chapter discusses research in this area.

ECONOMIES OF SCALE AND SCOPE

As noted earlier, managers must be able to evaluate alternative organizational structures not only because of their relative regulatory advantages and disadvantages but also because answers to questions about firm structure (and its close relative, firm size) may affect financial performance. Are banks that grow by branching more or less efficient than small unit banks? Are MBHCs that combine bank and nonbank subsidiaries more or less efficient than banks and nonbanks operating as entirely separate entities? Can a thrift with $15 billion in assets provide loans at lower cost than a thrift with only $500 million in assets? These and similar questions part of an extensive body of research on financial institutions—studies of economies of scale and scope.

Economies of Scale and Scope Illustrated

Economies of scale occur when the average cost of producing a good or service declines as the amount produced increases. Economies of scope occur when the cost of producing two or more products jointly is less than the cost of separately producing an equivalent quantity of each product. Economies of scale and scope are by no means mutually exclusive, and Table 4.4 provides a numerical illustration of each.

Suppose that Bank A decides to make only commercial loans. It purchases a computer and hires two loan officers, thus incurring fixed costs. Bank A will also have variable costs, such as interest paid on funds that it will lend; these costs increase as the size of the loan portfolio increases. Bank A may be able to make 400 commercial loans at a lower average cost than if it made only 100 loans, because the computer's cost and the loan officers' salaries would be spread over a greater number of loans. If Bank B across the street made only consumer loans, it might also find, for the same reasons, that the average cost of 200 loans would be lower than the average cost of only 100. Each bank recognizes economies of scale, as illustrated at the top of Table 4.4.

It is important to recognize, however, that economies of scale might occur only for selected ranges of loan volumes. For example, even if the average cost of making 200 consumer loans were lower than the average cost of 100, the average cost of 300 loans might not continue to fall. Perhaps a new computer or another loan officer would be needed, increasing the average cost per loan; an increase in volume could actually cause *dis*economies of scale, as shown in the table when Bank B makes more than 200 consumer loans.

Suppose further that if either bank makes both commercial and consumer loans, the *total* cost is lower than if each institution continues to make only one type of loan. If the same computer and loan officers could handle both operations, the bank could enjoy economies of scope, and a diversified bank would be more efficient than a single-product institution. This situation is illustrated at the bottom of Table 4.4. Again, economies of scope might not span all levels of lending. In the example, a diversified bank would spend more to make 400 commercial and 400 consumer loans ($396,000) than two single-product banks would spend to make 400 specialized loans each ($156,000 and $220,000 equaling $376,000). The table also shows that some lending combinations reduce costs through joint production. For example, one bank would spend less to make 200 commercial *and* 200 consumer loans ($196,000) than two banks would spend to make 200 loans of only one type ($100,000 and $100,000, or $200,000).

Table 4.4 ✦ ECONOMIES OF SCALE AND SCOPE

Both Banks A and B are subject to economies of scale, because at certain levels of lending, the average cost per loan declines. Bank B is subject to diseconomies of scale, as well; if it makes more than 200 loans, the average loan cost rises. At certain levels of output, economies of scope are also present. A bank spends less to make both commercial and consumer loans than separately to make an equivalent amount of each type.

A. Bank A (Commercial Loans Only)			B. Bank B (Consumer Loans Only)		
No. of Loans	Total Cost	Average Cost	No. of Loans	Total Cost	Average Cost
0	$ 12,000		0	$ 12,000	
100	60,000	$600	100	52,000	$520
200	100,000	500	200	100,000	500
300	132,000	440	300	156,000	520
400	156,000	390	400	220,000	550
	Economies of scale at all levels			Economies of scale at some, but not all, levels	

C. Both Commercial and Consumer Loans

No. of Loans (Commercial)	No. of Loans (Consumer)	Total Cost if Made Jointly	Total Cost if Made Separately
100	100	$102,000	$112,000
	200	152,000	160,000
	300	210,000	216,000
	400	276,000	280,000
200	100	144,000	152,000
	200	196,000	200,000
	300	256,000	256,000
	400	324,000	320,000
300	100	178,000	184,000
	200	232,000	232,000
	300	294,000	288,000
	400	364,000	352,000
400	100	204,000	208,000
	200	260,000	256,000
	300	324,000	312,000
	400	396,000	376,000
Economies of scope for some combinations of commercial and consumer lending, but not for all.			

Source: Adapted from Mester, 1987, pp. 20–21.

Economies of Scale and Scope in the "Real World"

For decades, researchers have attempted to identify economies of scale and scope for depositories. Although controversy remains about the proper way to measure their output (for example, are deposits inputs or outputs of a bank?), this research has provided valuable insights. The findings provide guidance not only for managers concerned with the advisability of changing firm size, structure, or both, but also for regulators attempting to tackle many of the thorny issues discussed in this and other chapters. Recent studies suggest that costs should not be viewed separately from revenues. They have reached this conclusion after closely evaluating bank profit functions, which encompass the relationships between inputs that entail costs and outputs that produce revenues.[65]

Bigger Is Sometimes—but Not Always—Better As Berger et al. (1993) note in a survey of financial institution efficiency, prior studies generally suggest a U-shaped average cost curve for financial institutions. The flat center makes medium-sized firms a little more scale efficient than very large or very small firms. Studies differ, however, in the location of the most scale-efficient point, that is, the bottom of the average cost *U*. Early studies, most targeting banks with under $1 billion of assets, find average costs to be minimized between $75 million and $300 million. However, studies targeting banks with over $1 billion in assets generally find the minimum average cost range between $2 billion and $10 billion in assets. Studies for life insurance companies, securities firms, thrifts, and foreign banks offer similarly mixed results, some indicating economies of scale or scope, while others finding none. Although the results are mixed, they generally suggest that if managers use resources efficiently and if the marketplace rewards firms for doing so, the financial system is unlikely to be dominated by a few large institutions. Studies also indicate weaknesses in regulations that keep institutions relatively small, such as limitations on branching, because they may prevent customers from enjoying potential scale economies.

Berger et al. (1993) point out that the mixed results also suggest that the functional forms of these studies may not effectively evaluate the technologies of both large and small banks in a single model. The studies may also leave out some important dimension. More recent studies concentrate on estimating scale as well as scope efficiencies from a profit function that takes into account both revenue and cost effects. A recent study by Akhavein, Berger, and Humphrey (1997) examines the effect of megamergers on efficiency using a bank profit function. It finds that merged banks experienced a statistically significant 16 percentage point average increase in profit efficiency rank relative to other large banks. Most of the improvements result from increasing revenues by shifting to higher-yielding assets. Improvements result from combinations of comparably inefficient banks prior to merging that begin with substantial capacity for improvement. The results of this study and other recent studies using profit functions suggest that large banks may receive revenue and not just cost benefits from recent consolidations and gains in size.

---

[65]Excellent summaries of this literature and of the methodological questions facing researchers are found in Berger, Hunter, and Timme, 1993; Berger and Humphrey, 1992; Clar, 1988; Mester, 1987; Benston, Hanweck, and Humphrey, 1982; Evanoff and Israelevich, 1991; Humphrey, 1990; Berger and Humphrey, 1997; Saunders, 1997; Akhavein, Berger, and Humphrey, 1997; and Berger and Mester, 1997.

What about Diversification?   Research has encountered more difficulty generalizing about economies of scope. Even though this line of research is newer than the literature on economies of scale, most studies were conducted before significant product deregulation for depositories. Thus, research is needed that examines possible complimentary benefits between banking and nonbanking services, not just between different combinations of banking products.

Available studies suggest possibilities for economies of scope for some combinations of banking products but not for others. Results for U. S. and foreign banks have been generally mixed with an equal number of studies finding no economies of scope. Studies for thrifts, insurance firms, and securities firms generally find no economies of scope among outputs. However, studies also find no diseconomies of scope, implying but not stating with certainty that diversified firms can introduce benefits without creating dangers in the financial system. The lack of wide-ranging economies of scope suggests that financial firms may not suffer disadvantages by specializing in limited ranges of products when competing with more diversified counterparts. Given pressures for continued product deregulation in the banking, insurance, and securities industries, many experts consider economies of scope to be among the most researchable issues in financial institutions management in the next decade. Studies examining benefits versus risks of entering new activities are also important. A recent study conducted by the Bank for International Settlements (BIS) shows that the benefits outweigh the risks of allowing banks to enter the securities business.[66]

SUMMARY

This chapter reviews background information on recent trends for financial institutions (FIs) including widespread mergers between different types of FIs, the emergence of nationwide interstate banks in the United States, and the creation of megainstitutions. The special characteristic of high financial leverage for FIs is introduced with consideration of its effect on FI profitability along with agency problems. Financial institutions implement many different types of organizational forms that are important for their operations, including mutuals (owned in effect by customers), not-for-profit firms, privately owned firms, and stock firms. Stock firms are also often organized as holding companies.

The holding company form of ownership is important for FIs, particularly commercial banks. Bank holding companies (BHCs) have become increasingly popular because they provide access to capital, potential for diversification and geographic expansion, and the benefits of financial leverage, The Federal Reserve Board monitors BHCs. As of 1997, BHCs have been allowed to expand nationally through interstate branches. With increasingly liberal interpretations of Glass–Steagall by the

---

[66]See Mester, 1990; Mester, 1987; and LeCompte and Smith, 1990. A number of studies have investigated whether thrifts or dedicated mortgage lenders that specialize outperform more diversified thrifts or banks. In general, the studies find that specialized mortgage lenders perform as well as other firms. However, recent studies find that movement into other types of assets has a positive effect on firm efficiency or market returns, particularly for thrifts that are fixed-rate lenders with little diversification. See Eisenbeis and Kwast, 1991; Cebenoyan, Cooperman, Register, and Hudgins, 1997; Brewer, Jackson, and Mondschean, 1996; and Cole and McKenzie, 1994. For a summary of the study, see "Washington Outlook: Study Supports Commercial Banks to Engage in Securities Activities." *Banking Policy Report* Vol. 17, (August 3, 1998), p. 2.

Fed, BHCs have also gained opportunities to expand security-type activities using special Section 20 subsidiaries, as long as revenues from security activities are no greater than 25 percent of those of the affiliate. The OCC also now allows national banks to carry on new types of nonbank activities on a case-by-case basis through operating subsidiaries. Financial modernization proposals give BHCs the ability to engage in insurance and securities activities through affiliates. These proposals pit the OCC and Fed against each other to determine whether securities and insurance activities should be carried out under separate affiliates of a BHC (regulated by the Fed) or under operating subsidiaries of a national bank itself (regulated by the OCC). With the politics involved, it is difficult to tell when a modernization bill will be passed and what it will look like.

Controversy continues, however, about the effect of BHCs on the safety and soundness of institutions. Regulators have recently relaxed form requirements for firewalls between bank and nonbank subsidiaries. The potential for economies of scale and scope in MBHCs also continues to be a topic of great concern. Meanwhile, new forms of electronic FIs have emerged on the Internet. New forms of digital cash, known as *smart cards*, are also emerging in the United States after wide acceptance in many European countries. The nature of money is changing dramatically, as well, with the development of E-cash systems for payments on the Internet. Direct deposit and payment systems and wider use of home banking are reducing costs and moving the nation closer to a "cashless" form of financial intermediation that may be widespread in the future.

Discussion Questions

1. Summarize opposing views concerning the recent consolidation of the financial services industry and creation of megainstitutions such as Travelers. Why are consumer groups concerned about this activity? What benefits may be achieved? How many independent banks are left in your state? What would be some advantages of national banking in the United States?

2. What is the effect of high financial leverage on the risk and return of a financial institution? Holding the ROA constant, what happens to ROE when a FI's equity–asset ratio falls? What is the equity multiplier?

3. What are the alternative preferences of stockholders, debtholders, and managers of highly leveraged financial institutions for risk-taking behavior? How do debtholders protect their interests?

4. How does deposit insurance create a moral hazard problem for highly leveraged financial institutions? How do regulators act as a risk-reducing force? What proposals have been made to reduce moral hazard problems of insured FIs?

5. What are the opposing arguments for the effect of managerial stock ownership on financial institution risk? Do you think that managers with mandatory stock ownership or compensation tied to the firm's stock price will work harder for external stockholders? What evidence has been found on the relations between FI ownership, compensation, and risk-taking behavior by FIs?

6. What are the advantages of a bank holding company (BHC)? How have BHCs served in the past as loopholes to avoid equity capital regulations, geographic restrictions, and product restrictions? How were nonbanks used as a loophole?

7. What are superregional banks? What is the new national bank model under IBBEA? What community protections are given under IBBEA? How can banks benefit from geographic diversification?

8. How are BHCs currently regulated? What is the idea behind corporate separateness? What are Section 20 subsidiaries, and how have product restrictions been relaxed in the 1980s and 1990s? What types of entry have BHCs made into brokerage, investment banking, insurance, and mutual fund activities?

9. How have the Fed and OCC relaxed product restrictions for BHCs and national banks respectively in the 1990s? On what aspect of financial modernization bill proposals do the Fed and OCC disagree?

10. What risks to the federal safety net are associated with relaxed product restrictions? Give a possible example of what could happen to a banking firm if its securities subsidiary got into trouble. What is the Fed's source of strength doctrine? How does this position differ from the doctrine of corporate separateness? What type of organizational structures support universal banking in other countries, such as Germany?

11. What is a one savings and loan holding company? What advantages does such a firm have over BHCs? What are franchising and chain banks? What are service corporations?

12. How do mutual firms differ from stock firms in their ownership relationships and preferences for risk-taking? Why have so many mutual financial institutions, including mutual thrift and insurance companies, converted to stock ownership in recent years? What is a mutual holding company? Why have they become controversial in recent years?

13. How do credit unions as not-for-profit organizations differ from other firms? Why have extensions of their common bond requirement sparked controversy? What did the Supreme Court decide about this question in 1998? What did Congress do in turn?

14. Define virtual financial institutions, smart cards, and E-cash. What dramatic changes are occurring for financial institutions in the computer age? What costs do FIs incur?

What benefits do they gain? Give some examples of recent innovations. Do you think a new electronic monetary system will evolve? Why or why not? Can you find a local financial institution with a presence on the Internet? What kind of information does the source present?

15. What are economies of scale and economies of scope? In general, what have researchers found concerning economies of scale and scope for financial institutions? What have studies found about advantages/disadvantages of diversification for depository institutions?

Problems

1. Suppose the Paine Gaine Securities Firm has a ROA of 2 percent, with an equity to asset ratio of 10 percent. What are its equity multiplier and ROE? If the firm raises its equity–asset ratio to 20 percent, what are its new equity multiplier and ROE? When the firm raises its equity–asset ratio to 20 percent, if a drop in interest expense raises its ROA to 2.3 percent, what is its new ROE?

2. If the EuphoriaSavings Bank in Brooklyn, New York, run by the Lerner-Fox families desires a ROE of 15 percent, and has a ROA of 1 percent, what equity–assets ratio (and equity multiplier) must it have? What debt-to-asset ratio does this imply?

3. The very ambitious Register-Cebenoyan Finance Company hopes to have a ROE of 25 percent next year. If the firm's debt-to-assets ratio is 85 percent, what ROA does it have to earn to reach this target?

4. The Dave Cather Insurance Company is preparing a financial plan based on the following data: Target ROE 15 percent, marginal tax rate (t) 35 percent, total assets $700 million, total liabilities $640 million.
    a. What is the current equity multiplier?
    b. What ROA must the firm earn to reach its target ROE?
    c. What before-tax ROA must the firm earn to reach its target ROA?
    d. What before-tax income must the firm earn to reach its target before-tax ROA?

5. The board of directors of the Ski-Bob Bank in Crested Butte, Colorado, has requested a presentation on the relationship between financial leverage and ROE. The bank has assets of $2 billion and an equity multiplier of 10. Net income in the coming year is expected to be between 1.2 percent and 2.0 percent of total assets.
    a. Based on the current equity multiplier, what is the expected range for ROE?
    b. The new chief financial officer (CFO), Bobby Dew, hopes to persuade the directors to operate aggressively and increase the equity multiplier to 12. If this result happens, interest expense will rise, because the level of borrowed funds will increase. The estimated range of ROA changes to a low of 0.5 percent to a high of 1.9 percent, depending on whether the economy goes into a recession or remains in an expansion. What will be the resulting range for ROE? Based on these estimates, what recommendations should the directors follow?

6. The Singleton Savings Bank (SSB) in Colorado Springs, Colorado, has total assets of $500 million and a equity–assets ratio of 10 percent. The Dave Murphy Bank (DMB), a competitor bank of equal size, has an equity–assets ratio of 8 percent. SSB estimates a range of ROA from 0.75 percent to 2.0 percent. DMB estimates a range of ROA from 0.5 percent to 1.75 percent, because of a projected rise in interest expenses. What will be the resulting ROE range for each bank? Which shareholders will be better off in a downturn? In an expansion?

7. A BHC subsidiary of the Grow Glow Holding Company has set ambitious growth targets. The bank currently has a minimum capital requirement of 8 percent and wants to expand total assets by $300 million.
    a. If the bank takes advantage of double leverage, how much must the BHC borrow and downstream to the bank to provide capital support for the expansion plan?
    b. Suppose a change in the bank's asset portfolio causes regulators to lower the allowed net worth multiplier to 11. By how much will the bank be able to expand total assets if the BHC borrows $95 million and invests the proceeds in new bank equity?

8. The Mountain KingNational Bank reports the following functional cost data for its commercial and industrial (C&I) and commercial real estate loan portfolios:

Number of Loans	Total Cost
Commercial Loans	
50	$ 75,000
150	200,000
300	350,000
500	500,000

Commercial Real Estate Loans

50	$ 90,000
150	240,000
300	515,000
500	900,000

Combined Costs

Number of Commercial Loans	Number of Commercial Real Estate Loans	Total Cost
50	50	$150,000
	150	325,000
150	50	280,000
	150	435,000

a. Does the bank realize economies of scale at higher volumes of C&I loans? Of commercial real estate loans? Explain.

b. Does the bank benefit from economies of scope by having both types of loans in its portfolio? Why or why not?

a. Does the bank realize economies of scale at higher volumes of C&I loans? Of commercial real estate loans? Explain.

b. Does the bank benefit from economies of scope by having both types of loans in its portfolio? Why or why not?

Selected References

Akella, Srinivas R., and Stuart I. Greenbaum. "Savings and Loan Ownership Structure and Expense-Preference." *Journal of Banking and Finance* 12 (September 1988): 419–437.

Akhavein, Jalal D., Allen N. Berger, and David B. Humphrey. "The Effects of Megamergers on Efficiency and Prices: Evidence from a Bank Profit Function." *Review of Industrial Organization* 12, no. 1 (February 1997): 95–139.

Amel, Dean F., and Michael J. Jacowski. "Trends in Banking Structure since the Mid-1970s." *Federal Reserve Bulletin* 75 (March 1989): 120–133.

Amihud, Y., and B. Lev. "Risk Reduction as a Managerial Motive for Conglomerate Mergers." *Bell Journal of Economics* 12 (1981): 605–617.

Banerjee, Ajeyo, and Elizabeth S. Cooperman. "Returns to Targets and Acquirers: Evidence for Bank Mergers in the 90's." Working paper, University of Colorado at Denver, 1998.

Barro, Jason R., and Robert J. Barro. "Pay, Performance, and Turnover of Bank CEOs." *Journal of Labor Economics* 8 (1990): 448–481.

Barth, James R., Philip E. Bartholomew, and Michael G. Bradley. "Determinants of Thrift Institution Resolution Costs." *Journal of Finance* 45 (July 1990): 731–754.

Barth, James R. *The Great Savings and Loan Debacle*. Washington, D.C.: American Enterprise Institute, 1991.

Barth, James R., Daniel E. Page, and John S. Jahera, Jr. "Abnormal Returns of Thrift Versus Non-Thrift IPOs." Working paper, Auburn University, 1997.

Benston, George J. "Analyzing the Case against Commercial Firms Owning Banks." *Banking Policy Report* 10 August 5, 1991: 4.

Benston, George J., Gerald A. Hanweck, and David B. Humphrey. "Scale Economies in Banking: A Restructuring and Reassessment." *Journal of Money, Credit, and Banking* 14 (November 1982): 435–456.

Benston, George J., and George G. Kaufman. "Commercial Banking and Securities Activities: A Survey of the Risks and Returns." In *The Financial Services Revolution: Understanding the Changing Roles of Banks, Mutual Funds, and Insurance Companies*. Edited by Clifford E. Kirsch. Burr Ridge, Ill.: Irwin Professional, 1997, pp. 3–28.

Berger, Allen N., and David B. Humphrey. "Competition, Efficiency, and the Future of the Banking Industry." *Proceedings of the Conference on Bank Structure and Competition*. Chicago: Federal Reserve Bank of Chicago, 1992.

Berger, Allen N., and David B. Humphrey. "Efficiency of Financial Institutions: International Survey and Directions for Future Research." *European Journal of Operational Research* 98 (April 16, 1997): 175–212.

Berger, Allen N., William C. Hunter, and Stephen G. Timme. "The Efficiency of Financial Institutions: A Review and Preview of Research Past, Present, and Future." *Journal of Banking and Finance* 17 (April 1993): 219–574.

Berger, Allen N., Anil K. Kashyap, and Joseph M. Scalise. "The Transformation of the U.S. Banking Industry: What a Long, Strange Trip It's Been." *Brookings Papers on Economic Activity* 2 (1995): 55–218.

Berger, Allen N., and Loretta J. Mester. "Inside the Black Box: What Explains Differences in the Efficiencies of Financial Institutions?" *Journal of Banking and Finance* 21, no. 7 (July 1997): 895–947.

Blyn, Martin R. "The Evolution of the U.S. Money and Capital Markets and Financial Intermediaries." In *Financial Institutions and Markets*, 2d ed. Edited by Murray E. Polakoff and Thomas A. Durkin. Boston: Houghton Mifflin, 1981, pp. 31–45.

Board of Governors of the Federal Reserve System. *Annual Report, 1991.* (Washington, D.C.: Board of Governors of the Federal Reserve System, 1991).

Boyd, John H., Stanley L. Graham, and R. Shawn Hewitt. "Bank Holding Company Mergers with Nonbank Financial Firms: Effects on the Risk of Failure." *Journal of Banking and Finance* 17 (1993): 43–64.

Brewer, Elijah. "A Note on the Relationship between Bank Holding Company Risk and Nonbank Activity." Staff memorandum 88-5. Federal Reserve Bank of Chicago, 1988.

Brewer, Elijah, William E. Jackson, and Thomas H. Mondschean. "Risk, Regulation, and S&L Diversification into Nontraditional Assets." *Journal of Banking and Finance* 20 (May 1996): 723–744.

Brewer, E., and M. R. Saidenberg. "Franchise Value, Ownership Structure and Risk at Savings Institutions." Working paper, Federal Reserve Bank of New York, 1996.

Brown, Donald M. "Bank Holding Company Performance Studies and the Public Interest: Normative Uses for Positive Analysis?" *Review*, Federal Reserve Bank of St. Louis 65 (March 1983): 26–34.

Brumbaugh, R. Dan. *Thrifts under Siege: Restoring Order to American Banking.* Cambridge, Mass.: Ballinger, 1988.

Burns, Richard M., Bradford D. Jordan, and James A. Verbrugge. "Returns to Initial Shareholders in Savings Institution Conversions: Evidence and Regulatory Implications." *Journal of Financial Research* 2, no. 2 (1988): 125–136.

Buser, Stephen A., Andrew H. Chen, and Edward J. Kane. "Federal Deposit Insurance, Regulatory Policy and Optimal Bank Capital," *Journal of Finance* 36 (March 1981), 51–60.

Cagle, Julie and Gary E. Porter. "The Influence of Conversions on FPO Underpricing of Savings Institutions." Working Paper, Xavier University, December 1994.

Calomiris, Charles W. *The Postmodern Bank Safety Net: Lessons from Developed and Developing Economies.* Washington, D.C.: American Enterprise Institute, 1997.

Carner, William J. "An Analysis of Franchising in Retail Banking." *Journal of Retail Banking* 8 (Winter 1986–1987): 57–66.

Carter, Richard B., and Roger D. Stover. "The Effects of Mutual to Stock Conversions of Thrift Institutions on Managerial Behavior." *Journal of Financial Services Research* 4 (1990): 127–144.

Cebenoyan, A. Sinan, Elizabeth S. Cooperman, and Charles A. Register. "Firm Efficiency and the Regulatory Closure of S&Ls: An Empirical Investigation." *Review of Economics and Statistics* 3 (August 1993): 540–545.

Cebenoyan, A. Sinan, Elizabeth S. Cooperman, and Charles A. Register. "Deregulation, Reregulation, Equity Ownership, and S&L Risk-Taking." *Financial Management* 24 (Autumn 1995): 63–76.

Cebenoyan, A. Sinan, Elizabeth S. Cooperman, and Charles A. Register. "Charter Value, Ownership Structure, and Risk-Taking Behavior for Thrifts." *Financial Management*, forthcoming 1999.

Cebenoyan, A. Sinan, Elizabeth S. Cooperman, Charles A. Register, and Daniel L. Bauer. "Risk Effects of Geographical Diversification through Interstate Branching by Savings and Loans." Working paper, University of Colorado at Denver, 1997.

Cebenoyan, A. Sinan, Elizabeth S. Cooperman, Charles A. Register, and Daniel L. Bauer. "Interstate Savings and Loans in the 1990s: A Performance and Risk Appraisal." Working paper, University of Colorado at Denver, 1998.

Cebenoyan, A. Sinan, Elizabeth A. Cooperman, Charles A. Register, and Sylvia C. Hudgins. "The Relative Efficiency of Stock versus Mutual S&Ls: A Stochastic Cost Frontier Approach." *Journal of Financial Services Research* 7 (June 1993): 151–170.

Cebenoyan, A. Sinan, Elizabeth S. Cooperman, Charles A. Register, and Sylvia C. Hudgins. "Cost Inefficiency and the Holding of Nontraditional Assets by Solvent Stock Thrifts," *Real Estate Economics*, Vol. 26 (November 1998), 695–718.

Chase, Samuel B., Jr., and John J. Mingo. "The Regulation of Bank Holding Companies." *Journal of Finance* 30 (May 1975): 281–292.

Chen, Carl R., Thomas L. Steiner, and Ann Marie Whyte. "Risk-Taking Behavior and Management Ownership in Depository Institutions." *Journal of Financial Research* 21 (Spring 1998): 1–16.

Clair, Robert T., and Paula K. Tucker. "Interstate Banking and the Federal Reserve: A Historical Perspective." *Economic Review*, Federal Reserve Bank of Dallas (November 1989): 1–20.

Clark, Jeffrey A. "Economies of Scale and Scope at Depository Financial Institutions: A Review of the Literature." *Economic Review*, Federal Reserve Bank of Kansas City 73 (September/October 1988): 16–33.

Cole, Rebel A., and Robert A. Eisenbeis. "The Role of Principal-Agent Conflicts in the 1980s Thrift Crisis." *Journal of American Real Estate Economics* 24(1996).

Cole, Rebel A., and Joseph A. McKenzie, "Thrift Asset-Class Returns and the Efficient Diversification of Thrift Institution Portfolios." *Journal of the American Real Estate and Urban Economics Association* 22 (1994): 95–116.

Cordell, Lawrence R., Gregor D. MacDonald, and Mark E. Wohar. "Corporate Ownership and the Thrift Crisis." *Journal of Law and Economics* 36 (1993): 719–756.

Cornyn, Anthony G., and Samuel H. Talley. "Activity Deregulation and Bank Soundness." *Proceedings of a Conference on Bank Structure and Competition*. Chicago: Federal Reserve Bank of Chicago, 1983: 28–31.

Cornyn, Anthony, Gerald Hanweck, Stephen Rhoades, and John Rose. "An Analysis of the Concept of Corporate Separateness in BHC Regulation from an Economic Perspective." *Proceedings of a Conference on Bank Structure and Competition*. Chicago: Federal Reserve Bank of Chicago, 1986: 174–212.

Corrigan, E. Gerald. "A Framework for Reform of the Financial System." *Quarterly Review*, Federal Reserve Bank of New York 12 (Summer 1987): 1–8.

Crawford, Richard D., and William W. Sihler. *Financial Service Organizations: Cases in Strategic Management*. New York: HarperCollins, 1994.

Cyrnak, Anthony W. "Chain Banks and Competition: The Effectiveness of Federal Reserve Policy since 1977." *Economic Review*, Federal Reserve Bank of San Francisco (Spring 1986): 5–15.

Demirguc-Kunt, Asli. "Deposit Institution Failures: A Review of the Empirical Literature." *Economic Review*, Federal Reserve Bank of Cleveland 4 (1989): 2–16.

DeYoung, Robert, Iftekhar Hasan, and Bruce Kirchhoff. "Out-of-State Entry and the Cost Efficiency of Local Commercial Banks." *Journal of Economics and Business*, forthcoming 1998.

DeYoung, Robert, Joseph P. Hughes, and Choon-Geol Moon. "Regulatory Distress Costs and Risk-Taking at U.S. Commercial Banks." OCC working paper 98–1, January 1998.

DiClemente, John J. "What Is a Bank?" *Economic Perspectives*, Federal Reserve Bank of Chicago 7 (January/February 1983): 20–31.

Dunham, Constance. "Mutual-to-Stock Conversion by Thrifts: Implications for Soundness." *New England Economic Review*, Federal Reserve Bank of Boston (January/February 1985): 31–45.

Eickhoff, Gerald. "Going Interstate by Franchises or Networks." *Economic Review*, Federal Reserve Bank of Atlanta 70 (January 1985): 32–35.

Eisenbeis, Robert. "How Should Bank Holding Companies Be Regulated?" *Economic Review*, Federal Reserve Bank of Atlanta 68 (January 1983): 43–47.

Eisenbeis, Robert A., Robert S. Harris, and Josef Lakonishok. "Benefits of Bank Diversification: The Evidence from Shareholder Returns." *Journal of Finance* 39 (July 1984): 881–892.

Eisenbeis, Robert A., and Myron L. Kwast, "Are Real Estate Specializing Depositories Viable? Evidence from Commercial Banks." *Journal of Financial Services Research* 5 (1991): 5–24.

Esty, Benjamin C. "Ownership Concentration and Risk-Taking in the S&L Industry." Working paper, Harvard Business School, 1993.

Esty, Benjamin C. "A Case Study of Organizational Form and Risk Shifting in the Savings and Loan Industry." *Journal of Financial Economics*, (April 1997), 57–76.

Esty, Benjamin C. "The Impact of Contingent Liability on Commercial Bank Risk Taking." *Journal of Financial Economics*,(February 1998), 189–218.

Evanoff, Douglas D., and Philip R. Israelevich. "Productive Efficiency in Banking." *Economic Perspectives*, Federal Reserve Bank of Chicago 15 (July/August 1991): 11–32.

Ezzell, John R., and James A. Miles. "Bank CEO Pay-Performance Relations and the Effects of Deregulation." *Journal of Business* 63 (April 1995): 231–256.

Federal Reserve Bank of Kansas City. "Report on Chain Banking Organizations in Kansas, Nebraska, and Oklahoma." *Banking Studies* 1 (1983).

Fields, Joseph A. "Expense Preference Behavior in Mutual Life Insurers." *Journal of Financial Services Research* 1 (January 1988): 113–129.

Frieder, Larry A., and Vincent P. Apilado. "Bank Holding Company Research: Classification, Synthesis, and New Directions." *Journal of Bank Research* 13 (Summer 1982): 80–95.

Galai, D., and R. W. Masulis. "The Option Pricing Model and the Risk Factor of Stock." *Journal of Financial Economics* (January/March 1976): 53–81.

Gallo, John G., Gary M. Richardson, and Vincent P. Apilado. "The Performance of Bank-Sponsored Equity Mutual Funds: Implications for Bank Profitability." *Journal of Banking and Finance*, forthcoming.

Gilbert, R. Alton. "A Comparison of Proposals to Restructure the U.S. Financial System." *Review*, Federal Reserve Bank of St. Louis 70 (July/August 1988): 58–73.

——— "Do Bank Holding Companies Act as "Sources of Strength" for Their Bank Subsidiaries?" *Review*, Federal Reserve Bank of St. Louis 73 (January/February 1991): 3–18.

Goldberg, Lawrence G., and Gerald A. Hanweck. "What We Can Expect from Interstate Banking." *Journal of Banking and Finance* 12 (March 1988): 51–67.

Goldberg, Lawrence G., Gerald A. Hanweck, and John O'Keefe. "Prospects for Interstate Banking." Working paper, University of Miami, 1997.

Gorton, Gary and Richard Rosen. "Corporate Control, Portfolio Choice, and the Decline of Banking." *Journal of Finance* 50 (December 1995): 1377–1420.

Greenspan, Alan. "Subsidies and Powers in Commercial Banking." *Proceedings of the Conference on Bank Structure and Competition*. Chicago: Federal Reserve Bank of Chicago, 1990: 1–8.

Hasan, Iftekhar, and Mike Carhill. "Mutual to Stock Conversions, Information Cost, and Thrift Performance." *The Financial Review* 32 (August 1997): 545–568.

Heimann, John. "Market-Driven Deregulation of Financial Services." *Economic Review*, Federal Reserve Bank of Atlanta 69 (December 1984): 36–41.

Hempel, George H., Donald G. Simonson, and Alan B. Coleman. *Bank Management: Text and Cases*, 4th ed. New York: John Wiley & Sons, 1994.

Hermalin, Benjamin E., and Nancy E. Wallace. "Firm Performance and Executive Compensation in the Savings and Loan Industry." Working paper, University of California at Berkeley, 1997.

Houston, Joel F., and Christopher James. "CEO Compensation and Bank Risk: Is Compensation in Banking Structured to Promote Risk Taking." *Journal of Monetary Economics* 36 (November 1995): 405–431.

Hubbard, R. Glenn, and Darius Palia. "Executive Pay and Performance: Evidence from the U.S. Banking Industry." *Journal of Financial Economics* 39 (1995): 105–130.

Hughes, Joseph P., William Lang, Loretta J. Mester, and Choon-Geol Moon. "Efficient Banking under Interstate Branching." *Journal of Money, Credit, and Banking* (November 1996, Part 2): 1045–1071.

Humphrey, David B. "Why Do Estimates of Bank Scale Economies Differ?" *Economic Review*, Federal Reserve Bank of Richmond 76 (September/October 1990): 38–50.

Hunter, William C., and Stephen G. Timme. "Does Multiproduct Production in Large Banks Reduce Costs?" *Economic Review*, Federal Reserve Bank of Atlanta 74 (May/June 1989): 2–9.

Jensen, M. C., and W. H. Meckling. "Theory of the Firm: Managerial Behavior, Agency Costs, and Ownership Structure." *Journal of Financial Economics* 3 (1976): 305–360.

John, Teresa A., and Kose John. "Top-Management Compensation and Capital Structure." *Journal of Finance* (July 1993): 949–972.

Kane, Edward J. *The S&L Insurance Mess: How Did It Happen?* Washington, D.C.: Urban Institute Press, 1989.

Kaufman, George G. *The U.S. Financial System: Money, Markets, and Institutions*, 6th ed. Englewood Cliffs, NJ: Prentice-Hall, 1995.

Keehn, Silas. *Banking on the Balance: Powers and the Safety Net*. Chicago: Federal Reserve Bank of Chicago, 1989.

Keeley, Michael C., and Barbara A. Bennett. "Corporate Separateness." *Weekly Letter*, Federal Reserve Bank of San Francisco, June 3, 1989.

Keeton, William R. "Bank Holding Companies, Cross-Bank Guarantees, and Source of Strength." *Economic Review*, Federal Reserve Bank of Kansas City (May/June 1990): 54–67.

Kidwell, David S., Richard L. Peterson, and David W. Blackwell. *Financial Institutions, Markets, and Money*, 6th ed. Fort Worth, Tex.: Dryden Press, 1997.

Laderman, Elizabeth S., and Randall J. Pozdena. "Interstate Banking and Competition: Evidence from the Behavior of Stock Returns." *Economic Review*, Federal Reserve Bank of San Francisco (Spring 1991): 32–47.

LeCompte, Richard L. B., and Stephen D. Smith. "Changes in the Cost of Intermediation: The Case of Savings and Loans." *Journal of Finance* 45 (1990): 1337–1346.

LeCompte, Richard L. B., Atul Gupta, and K. Misra. "On the Gain to Acquiring Capital Stock S&Ls in Merger Conversions: A Comment." *Journal of Banking and Finance* 8 (1994): 595–599.

Liang, J. Nellie, and Donald T. Savage. "The Nonbank Activities of Bank Holding Companies." *Federal Reserve Bulletin* 76 (May 1990): 280–292.

Litan, Robert E. *What Should Banks Do?* Washington, D.C.: Brookings Institution, 1987.

Marcus, A. J. "Deregulation and Bank Financial Policy." *Journal of Banking and Finance* 8 (1984): 557–565.

Masulis, Ronald W. "Changes in Ownership Structure: Conversions of Mutual Savings and Loans to Stock Charter." *Journal of Financial Economics* 18 (March 1987): 29–59.

Mayer, Martin. *The Bankers: The Next Generation.* New York: Truman Talley Books/Plume, 1997.

McCoy, John, Larry A. Frieder, Robert B. Hedges, Jr. *Bottomline Banking: Meeting the Challenges for Survival and Success.* Chicago: Probus, 1994.

McNamara, Michael J., and S. Ghon Rhee. "Ownership Structure and Performance: The Demutualization of Life Insurers." *Journal of Risk and Insurance* 59 (June 1992): 221–238.

Mengle, David L. "The Case for Interstate Branch Banking." *Economic Review*, Federal Reserve Bank of Richmond 76 (November/December 1990): 3–17.

Merton, R. C. "Analytic Derivation of the Cost of Deposit Insurance and Loan Guarantees." *Journal of Banking and Finance* 1 (1977): 3–11.

Mester, Loretta J. "Efficient Production of Financial Services: Scale and Scope Economies." *Business Review*, Federal Reserve Bank of Philadelphia (January/February 1987): 15–25

———. "A Multiproduct Cost Study of Savings and Loans." *Journal of Finance* 47 (1987): 423–445.

———. "The Costs of Traditional and Nontraditional Banking." *Proceedings of the Conference on Bank Structure and Competition*. Chicago: Federal Reserve Bank of Chicago, 1990: 170–174.

———. "Banking and Commerce: A Dangerous Liaison?" *Business Review*, Federal Reserve Bank of Philadelphia (May/June 1992): 17—29.

———. "Efficiency in the Savings and Loan Industry." *Journal of Banking and Finance* 17 (April 1993): 267–286.

Moody, J. Carroll, and Gilbert C. Fite. *The Credit Union Movement.* Lincoln: University of Nebraska Press, 1971.

Mullins, Helen M. "The Management Reward Structure and Risk-Taking Behavior of U.S. Commercial Banks." *Proceedings of the 27th Annual Conference on Bank Structure and Competition*, Chicago Federal Reserve Bank, May 1991: 248–272.

Murray, Gregory E. "Demutualization of Insurance Companies—Advantages and Disadvantages." *Journal of the American Society of Chartered Life Underwriters* 39 (January 1985): 52–54.

Nolle, Daniel E. "Banking Industry Consolidation: Past Changes and Implications for the Future." OCC working paper 95–1, April 1995.

Pettigrew, Gene R., Daniel E. Page, John S. Jahera, Jr., and James R. Barth. "Thrift Conversions and Windfall Profits: An Empirical Examination." *Journal of Real Estate Finance and Economics*, forthcoming 1998.

Pearce, Douglas K. "Recent Developments in the Credit Union Industry." *Economic Review*, Federal Reserve Bank of Kansas City 69 (June 1984): 3–19.

Pozdena, Randall Johnston. "Banks Affiliated with Bank Holding Companies: A New Look at Their Performance." *Economic Review*, Federal Reserve Bank of San Francisco (Fall 1988): 29–40.

Reising, Joseph J. "The Wealth Effects of Interstate Branching." Working paper, Texas A&M University. *Journal of Banking and Finance*, forthcoming.

Rose, Peter S. *Banking across State Lines: Public and Private Consequences.* Westport, Conn.: Quorum Books, 1997.

Rose, Peter S. "The Diversification and Cost Effects of Interstate Banking." *The Financial Review* 31 (May 1996): 431–451.

Rosen, Richard J., Peter R. Lloyd-Davies, Myron L. Kwast, and David B. Humphrey. "New Banking Powers: A Portfolio Analysis of Bank Investment in Real Estate." *Journal of Banking and Finance* 13 (1989): 355–366.

Saunders, Anthony, Elizabeth Strock, and Nicholas G. Travlos. "Ownership Structure, Deregulation, and Bank Risk Taking." *Journal of Finance* 45 (June 1990): 643–654.

Saunders, Anthony. *Financial Institutions Management: A Modern Perspective,* 2nd ed. Burr Ridge, Ill.: Irwin, 1997.

Saunders, Anthony, and Ingo Walter. *Universal Banking in the United States: What Could We Gain? What Could We Lose?* New York: Oxford University Press, 1994.

Schrand, Catherine, and Haluk Unal. "Hedging and Coordinated Risk Management: Evidence from Thrift Conversions." *Journal of Finance* 53 (June 1998): 979–1013.

Shull, Bernard. "Economic Efficiency, Public Regulation, and Financial Reform: Depository Institutions." In *Financial Institutions and Markets,* 2nd ed. Edited by Murray E. Polakoff and Thomas A. Durkin. Boston: Houghton Mifflin, 1981, pp. 671–702.

Simons, Katerina. "Mutual-to-Stock Conversions by New England Savings Banks: Where Has All the Money Gone?" *New England Economic Review,* Federal Reserve Bank of Boston (March/April 1992): 45–53.

Simpson, Gary W., and Theodor Kohers. "The Effects of Organizational Form on Performance in the Savings and Loan Industry." *Financial Review* 14 (Fall 1979): 1–14.

Smith, Bruce D., and Michael J. Stutzer. "Adverse Selection, Aggregate Uncertainty, and the Role for Mutual Insurance Contracts." *Journal of Business* 63 (1990): 493–510.

Strunk, N. "The Savings and Loan Story." In *The Risk of Economic Crisis.* Edited by M. Feldstein. Chicago: University of Chicago Press, 1991.

Swary, Itzhak, and Barry Topf. *Global Financial Deregulation: Commercial Banking at the Crossroads.* Cambridge, Mass.: Blackwell, 1992.

Unal, Haluk, and Maksimovic Vojislav. "Issue Size Choice and "Underpricing" in Thrift Mutual-To-Stock Conversions." Journal of Finance 48 (1993), 1659–1692.

Walker, David A. *Credit Union Insurance and Regulation.* Washington, D.C.: Center for Business-Government Relations, Georgetown University, 1997.

Wall, Larry D. "Insulating Banks from Non-Bank Affiliates." *Economic Review,* Federal Reserve Bank of Atlanta 69 (September 1984): 18–27.

————. "Nonbank Activities and Risk." *Economic Review,* Federal Reserve Bank of Atlanta 71 (October 1986a): 19—34.

————. "Risk and BHC Nonbank Activities." *Economic Review,* Federal Reserve Bank of Atlanta 71 (November 1986b): 10–15.

————. "Has Bank Holding Companies" Diversification Affected Their Risk of Failure? *Journal of Economics and Business* 39 (1987): 313–326.

Whalen, Gary. "Operational Policies of Multibank Holding Companies." *Economic Review,* Federal Reserve Bank of Cleveland (Winter 1981–1982): 20–31.

————. "The Competitive Implications of Safety Net-Related Subsidies." OCC working paper 97–9, May 1997.

————. "Bank Organizational Form and Risks of Expanded Activities." OCC working paper 97–1, January 1997.

Whitehead, David D. "Interstate Banking: Probability or Reality?" *Economic Review,* Federal Reserve Bank of Atlanta 70 (March 1985): 6–19.

Woerheide, Walter J. *The Savings and Loan Industry.* Westport, Conn.: Quorum Books, 1984.

Yan, Ying. "The Effects of the FDICIA on Bank CEO Pay, Performance, and Their Relationship." Federal Reserve Bank of Cleveland working paper, 1996.

Chapter 4 Internet Exercise

Organizational structures

Banks and credit unions have different organizational structures as discussed in the text. Banks are either privately held or owned by stockholders. Credit unions are typically a mutual organization.

To compare the return on assets for banks vs. credit unions, compare the following:

1. Go to the National Credit Union Association data base at: http://www.ncua.gov/data/cudata.html

2. Enter the name of a credit union, or search by state or city to find the name of a credit union.

3. When you have found the credit union, click on its charter number, and then you will be able to select data to view. To find the return on average assets, select the Financial Report Ratios ("FPR Ratios"). Note the values for the credit union.

4. To find comparable bank data, go to the FDIC Institution Directory at: http://192.147.69.50/id/ In the right hand frame, "Find an Institution," enter the name of a bank in the space provided, select the appropriate state, and then click "find." The directory will return the certificate number of the institution, name, location, class, and total assets for the most recent call report period. Click on the certificate number and you will then see a summary balance sheet for the bank.

5. In the top frame, select "Performance and Condition Ratios" and click on "Run Report." Scroll down until you see the category "Return on Assets." Are the ROA's similar to the credit union? What explains the differences?

Will Internet payments replace cash? For a demonstration of paying with electronic cash go to: http://www.digicash.com/ecash/demo/ Simply follow the instructions (indicated by the arrow) and you will be guided through some typical transactions:

- Buy a CD from an online CD shop
- Buy a software upgrade over the World Wide Web
- Send an ecash payment by e-mail to another ecash user
- Receive an e-cash payment from another user

Other useful sites for financial institution data:

Thomas Legislative Information on the Internet
http://thomas.loc.gov/

Compubank: The First Virtual Nationally Chartered U.S. Bank
http://www.compubank.com/

Many banks have established Web sites. For a list of the top 100 banks with Web sites, go to:
http://www.onlinebankingreport.com/top100banks2.html

Overview and
Performance
Analysis of
Depository
Institutions

II

▣ OVERVIEW OF FINANCIAL STATEMENTS FOR DEPOSITORY INSTITUTIONS

▣ DEPOSITORY INSTITUTION PERFORMANCE AND RISK ANALYSIS

▣ CREDIT UNIONS AND SAVINGS INSTITUTIONS

▣ CAPITAL REGULATIONS AND MANAGEMENT

▣ NONINTEREST REVENUE MANAGEMENT

"A depositor in an S&L has almost no knowledge of the particular loans the institution is making. Are they local or national, secured or not? Little of this is visible to the participant."

Stephen A. Ross
Professor, Yale School of Organization and Management, Quote from *The Journal of Finance* 44 (July 1989), p. 541.

"By the time financial statements are sent to the shareholders, they are a stewardship document, not the relevant current information about the company."

J. Michael Cook
Chairman, Deloitte and Touche (1991)

5

OVERVIEW OF FINANCIAL STATEMENTS FOR DEPOSITORY INSTITUTIONS

As the first quote suggests, information asymmetries may separate investors and managers, particularly for financial institutions, given the confidential nature of lending. Investors often lack information to evaluate the full implications of managers' decisions. Even executives may not be privy to the decisions of some managers.

A case in point is the recent accounting problems of Cendant, formed in December 1997 through the merger of HFS Inc. with CUC International Inc. Cendant has insurance, publishing, and discount membership club interests, and it franchises well-known brands, including Century 21 real estate, Ramada and Howard Johnson hotels, and Avis rental cars. In April 1998, auditors disclosed accounting fraud in Cendant's books. Managers of CUC had booked close to $500 million in fake revenue between 1995 and 1997; the correc-

tion eliminated 67 percent of CUC's 1997 income. Investors distressed when Cendant's share price fell by more than 50 percent pressured Walter Forbes, Cendant's chairman, to resign. He told the press, "I had absolutely no knowledge of the accounting irregularity." Similarly, previous auditors of CUC had not reported managers' deceptions.[1]

Since financial firms buy, sell, and invest in money, they are more subject to fraud than other firms. Their accounting also requires more complex procedures. As Michael Cook, chairman of a major accounting firm, suggests, financial statements reflect historic, not current operations.

In addition, since almost all of a financial institution's assets are financial products, the value of those assets and, therefore, the value of equity, changes with market conditions. Hence, the use of book value versus

---

[1]See Emily Nelson, "Cendant Shares Rise 8% as Investors Are Relieved by Forbes's Resignation," *The Wall Street Journal*, July 30, 1998, p. A4; Emily Nelson and Joann S. Lublin, "Cendant Chairman Walter Forbes Quits in Board Stalemate," *The Wall Street Journal*, July 29, 1998, pp. A3–A6; and "Cendant's CEO Outlines Plans for a Comeback," *The Wall Street Journal*, July 31, 1998.

market value accounting obscures valuable information. In 1992, Sun Trust Bank of Atlanta, for instance, reported a book value for its stock holdings in Coca Cola as $110,000, while the current market value of the bank's Coke stock was actually over $1 billion. Similarly, in 1992 Roosevelt Financial Group of St. Louis, a believer in market-value accounting, voluntarily reported a 9 percent drop in the market value of the company's equity to unhappy investors, who otherwise would have been unaware of this drop.[2]

Financial statements may fail to reveal all an investor needs to know about a financial institution, but they do provide clues about how well the institution has been doing, as well as signaling risks and trends. Because financial reports are influenced by the accounting rules that managers are permitted to use, experienced observers carefully look at many dimensions and sources of information before drawing conclusions. Superior analysts know too that small as well as large management decisions influence the relative performance of a bank, thrift, or credit union. They consider multiple sources of income, expense, and risk in conducting a financial analysis.

Financial statements of financial institutions differ in important ways from those of nonfinancial firms. To understand these differences, this chapter presents details for depository institutions which have the most complex financial statement, focusing on commercial banks, the dominant depository institution. Chapter 6 presents techniques of financial analysis for depository institutions. Chapter 7 discusses credit unions and thrifts in expanded detail, followed by overviews of capital and noninterest revenue management in Chapters 8 and 9.

✦ ✦ ✦

OVERVIEW OF COMMERCIAL BANK FINANCIAL STATEMENTS

Commercial banks facilitate the flow of funds in an economy by accepting funds from depositors and providing them to borrowers. In effect, banks buy funds from depositors at low, insured rates and sell funds at higher rates to borrowers. Traditional bank profits come from interest revenues on loans and securities less interest expenses paid on deposits and other borrowings. As discussed in Chapter 2, a bank's net interest margin (NIM) is a measure of the profitability of its traditional lending activities.

Figure 5.1 shows the four major classes of bank assets as a percentage of total assets: loans, securities, cash and due, and other assets. Loans clearly dominate bank assets (58 percent in 1997) generating the majority of interest revenues, followed by securities (28 percent of assets). During recessions when loan demand falls, the security portfolio grows, providing countercyclical income. Securities are also a source of stored liquidity.

Cash and due (17 percent of assets) includes **vault cash**, deposits held at Federal Reserve banks and other financial institutions, and cash in the process of collection (CIPC). Vault cash covers deposit withdrawals. However, deposits at Federal Reserve banks form the largest portion of a bank's reserve requirements. Small banks often hold deposits at other financial institutions (compensating balances) as payments for check-clearing, advisory, and other services provided by these **correspondent banks**. CIPC includes checks written against other finan-

---

[2]Ford S. Worthy, "The Battle of the Bean Counters," *Fortune*, June 1, 1992, pp. 117–126.

Figure 5.1   ✦   ASSETS AND LIABILITIES FOR AN AVERAGE FDIC-INSURED BANK

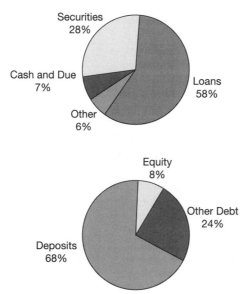

Source: FDIC Statistics on Banking, 1997.

cial institutions but not yet cleared. Since cash and due funds do not earn interest, banks try to minimize these holdings within safe limits on liquidity. Banks have low operating leverage, with a very small percentage of fixed assets. Other assets in 1997 averaged 6 percent of banks' assets. In Figure 5.1, the category other assets includes bank premises and equipment, other real estate owned, other interest receivable, prepaid expenses, and intangible assets.

The lower panel of Figure 5.1 shows sources of bank financing: deposits, other borrowings, and equity. Banks have high financial leverage (92 percent debt financing) with deposits the major financing source (68 percent of assets in 1997). Equity financing during the same year was only 8 percent.

Trends In Balance Sheet Composition: 1950 to 1996

The composition of bank balance sheets has changed remarkably over time. Figure 5.2 shows differences in bank assets and liabilities from 1950 to 1996. In 1950, banks had very conservative balance sheets with only 32 percent of assets invested in loans and the majority held as cash and securities. Financing was cheap, since deposits financed over 90 percent of bank assets. By 1996, deposit financing had fallen to a low of 70 percent of assets. Banks lost deposits to the direct financial markets and to other financial institutions, especially money market funds and other mutual funds. Consequently, banks had to rely on more expensive, nondeposit funds, increasing their interest expenses. To compensate for the rise in interest expenses, banks increased interest revenues by more aggressive asset use. Banks increased their per-

Figure 5.2 ✦ Trends in Bank Assets and Liabilities: 1950 to 1996

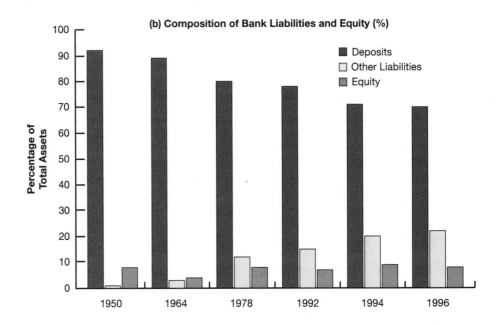

Source: *Federal Reserve Bulletin*, various issues.

centage of loans from 48 percent in 1964 to about 60 percent in 1996. As FDICIA raised profits and capital requirements in 1991, the average bank equity to asset ratio rose in the 1990s.

Banks' balance sheets show several items that may seem unfamiliar, as discussed in the next section.

FDIC-Insured Bank Balance Sheets

Table 5.1 summarizes the balance sheets for FDIC-insured commercial banks using 1996 figures. Note that the most liquid items (those with the shortest maturities) appear first, followed progressively by less liquid assets and liabilities that pay progressively higher interest rates. Also, note that the percentage of different assets held varies for institutions of different sizes. The largest category of banks—those with over $1 billion in assets—have greater access to the financial markets than others, so they can hold smaller percentages of securities than smaller banks and still meet future liquidity needs. However, large banks hold high percentages of cash and due to meet their comparatively high reserve requirements that result from their large volumes of deposits.

Bank Assets

A bank holds a large portion of its investment portfolio in short-term securities that it can easily sell with little or no loss of value to meet future deposit withdrawals and loan demands. **Fed funds sold and repurchase agreements** (repos) are such very liquid, short-term securities with maturities ranging from overnight to a year. Fed funds are excess reserves with the Fed that are traded at market rates between financial institutions. **Fed funds sold** are assets of the lending bank, and **Fed funds purchased** are liabilities of the borrowing bank. The Fed funds rate is a key indicator of liquidity in bank markets. A high rate indicates scarce liquidity. Repos are short-term sales of Treasury bills or other liquid securities that are repurchased at a higher price on a negotiated maturity date. Large banks tend to be net Fed funds purchasers and repo borrowers, while small banks tend to be net Fed funds sellers.

Assets held in trading accounts are securities, primarily Treasury or municipal securities, that are traded by large banks (those with greater than $1 billion in assets). Large banks often serve as government security dealers and/or municipal security underwriters, bearing any market risk for these issues. They make profits by selling securities for higher prices than they pay for the assets. Trading securities must appear on a bank's balance sheet at market value, with any market value losses or gains reflected in income.

Investment securities of banks provide additional income, as well as longer-term storage for liquidity than the assets listed above them offer. Regulators require banks to hold securities with low default risk. They can hold unlimited amounts of U.S. Treasury and federal agency securities, including mortgage-backed securities issued by government agencies. They also can hold unlimited amounts of general obligation municipal securities (those guaranteed by the general funds of the issuers) as well as limited amounts of investment grade (BBB/Baa ratings or better) corporate bonds and municipal revenue bonds (those guaranteed by the revenues for the projects they finance).

To reduce their interest rate risk, banks generally prefer to avoid securities with maturities greater than 10 years. Banks cannot own stock except shares they acquire as loan collateral or stock they hold in Federal Reserve banks. If a bank has uninsured government deposits as a liability, these **"pledged" deposits** must be held in low-risk securities; the funds cannot be invested in loans. Banks must classify investment securities as **"held to maturity"** (held at book values) or **"available for sale"** (held at market values).

Table 5.1 ◆ Assets and Liabilities of FDIC-Insured Commercial Banks, December 31, 1996
($ Millions)

	Total Commercial Banks	Percentage of Total Assets	Banks with Assets of Less than $100 Million	Percentage of Total Assets	Banks with Assets of $100 Million to $1 Billion	Percentage of Total Assets	Banks with Assets of $1 Billion or More	Percentage of Total Assets
Assets								
Cash and due	$ 335,998	7.3%	$ 14,906	5.3%	$ 37,474	5.3%	$ 283,619	7.9%
Investment securities	800,827	17.5	83,091	29.7	191,858	26.9	528,878	14.8
Fed funds sold and repurchase agreements	164,076	3.6	13,240	4.8	25,423	3.6	125,234	3.5
Assets held in trading accounts	240,978	5.3	71	0.0	295	0.0	240,612	6.7
Gross loans	2,811,016	61.4	160,132	57.2	435,768	61.1	2,215,116	61.8
Allowance for loan losses	53,621	1.2	2,403	0.9	6,759	0.9	44,459	1.2
Net loans and leases	2,757,395	60.2	157,728	56.3	429,010	60.1	2,170,658	60.6
Bank premises and fixed assets	64,605	1.4	4,948	1.8	12,490	1.8	47,167	1.3
Other real estate owned	5,439	0.1	461	0.2	1,079	0.2	3,899	0.1
Intangible assets	44,681	1.0	566	0.2	3,137	0.4	40,979	1.1
All other assets	164,344	3.6	4,963	1.8	12,577	1.8	146,804	4.1
Total assets	**$4,578,343**	**100.0%**	**$280,153**	**100.0%**	**$713,341**	**100.0%**	**$3,584,849**	**100.0%**
Total Liabilities, Limited-Life Preferred Stock, and Equity Capital								
Total deposits	$3,197,234	69.8%	$242,694	86.6%	$593,572	83.2%	$2,360,968	65.9%
Fed funds purchased and repurchase agreements	317,928	6.9	2,709	1.0	25,465	3.6	289,755	8.1
Trading and other liabilities	172,372	3.8	148	0.1	950	0.1	171,275	4.8
Other borrowed money	338,284	7.4	2,447	0.9	17,389	2.4	318,448	8.9
Subordinated notes and debentures	51,177	1.1	18	0.0	389	0.1	50,770	1.4
All other liabilities	126,051	2.8	2,557	0.9	8,250	1.2	115,245	3.2
Total liabilities	**$4,203,047**	**91.8%**	**$250,573**	**89.4%**	**$646,014**	**90.6%**	**$3,306,460**	**92.2%**
Perpetual preferred stock	2,011	0.0	61	0.0	366	0.1	1,583	0.0
Common stock	35,099	0.8	4,053	1.4	7,605	1.1	23,441	0.7
Surplus	167,664	3.7	10,728	3.8	25,146	3.5	131,789	3.7
Undivided profits	171,633	3.7	14,737	5.3	34,209	4.8	122,687	3.4
Total equity capital	**$ 374,183**	**8.2%**	**$ 29,580**	**10.6%**	**$ 67,327**	**9.4%**	**$ 278,388**	**7.8%**
Total liabilities and equity	**$4,578,343**	**100.0%**	**$280,153**	**100.0%**	**$713,341**	**100.0%**	**$3,584,849**	**100.0%**

Loans appear on the balance sheet as **Gross loans and leases**, which reports the book value of loans and leases the bank has made. Following this category, **Allowance for loan losses** records an offsetting account to cover expected loan losses. **Net loans and Leases** then reports gross loans less this allowance. Bank managers expense a subjectively determined amount for expected loan losses, called **provision for loan losses**, each year. This amount is added to the cumulative allowance for loan losses account as a reserve against future loan losses. Similarly, any actual net loan charge-offs (losses less recoveries) are subtracted from the allowance for loan losses account.[3] These accounts report on a variety of different types of loans, as discussed in the following paragraphs.

Different Types of Loans   In 1997, according to *Sheshunoff Bank Quarterly 1997* (Sheshunoff Information Services, Austin, Texas), bank loan portfolios consisted of: 22.6 percent commercial loans, 18.7 percent consumer loans, 46.8 percent real estate loans, 2.5 percent agricultural loans, 2.1 percent loans to other depository institutions, and 7.3 percent all other loans. Thus, banks are very diversified lenders. **Commercial loans** generally have intermediate-term maturities ranging from a few months to 5 or more years. Banks often join with other banks to make large loans, since the maximum that any institution can lend to any one borrower is limited to 15 percent of its equity capital or 25 percent if the loan is collateralized by risk-free securities. **Consumer loans** include loans to individuals for various purposes including home improvements, car purchases, educational expenses, and credit card charges. They generally are short-term loans ranging from a few months to 3 years. To cover proportionally high administrative costs for these small loans and their high potential bad debt losses, rates charged on consumer loans, particularly credit card loans, are often higher than those on other loans.

Real Estate loans are secured by real property and generally have long-term maturities. Although real estate collateral limits default risk, the long maturities of real estate loans creates a problem with interest rate risk. Real estate loans also expose lenders to **market value risk**, the possibility of loss due to a fall in the market value of a fixed-rate loan if interest rates rise. Fixed-rate real estate loans also have **reinvestment risk**. If interest rates fall below a certain threshold, such as 2 percent below the fixed loan rate, borrowers are likely to **prepay** them by refinancing at the

---

[3]Although bank managers subjectively determine the provision for loan losses for accounting purposes, regulators may ask for larger provisions. Tax laws determine the maximum amount of reserves that can be deducted from taxable income, which can differ from that reported for accounting purposes. Since 1997, the IRS has required banks larger than $500 million in assets to employ a direct charge-off method based on their actual net losses as incurred during a current reporting period. Prior to 1997, large banks could opt for a more flexible method of calculating reserves based on their average ratios of net charge-offs to total loans for the previous 6 years. (Now, only banks with less than $500 million in assets or with problem loans equal to 75 percent or more of their capital can employ this method.) As discussed by Koch (1995, Chapter 23), banks often took the maximum provision for loan loss (PLL) for tax purposes and a lower provision for accounting purposes. This practice gave them excess tax savings equal to the excess of PLL on tax documents over that on accounting statements times their marginal tax rates. This excess represented the residual amount of retained earnings that would appear on tax documents if the two PLLs had been the same and was allocated to a special deferred tax reserve account.

low current rates; banks must then reinvest these prepayments at much lower rates than they earned on the original loans.

Banks can reduce interest rate risk by selling loans to other long-term lenders, such as pension funds or insurance companies, or by pooling and packaging mortgage loans and selling them as securities to investors (securitization). With securitization, banks receive fee income for originating and servicing the loans. Variable rate loans also reduce a bank's interest rate risk, passing this risk on to the borrower. However, variable rate loans increase default risk, since borrowers may have difficulty making interest payments that rise during times of high rates.

On the balance sheet, **Other loans** include a variety of credit-granting activities, such as loans of nonFed funds to other financial institutions; loans to brokers, dealers, and individuals for securities purchases; loans to not-for-profit organizations; agricultural loans; loans to governments; and loans not clearly falling into any of the other major categories.

Other assets include bank premises and fixed assets, other real estate owned, intangible assets, and other items that are not significant enough to merit their own categories. **Bank premises and equipment** encompasses the depreciated value of bank buildings and equipment. **Other real estate owned** (OREO) includes property taken as collateral for unpaid loans, listed at market value. Problem banks carry large OREO accounts. Intangible assets include goodwill associated with bank mergers and acquisitions.

Bank Liabilities, Stock, and Equity Capital

As shown in Table 5.1, deposits make up the majority of bank financing. Small banks relied on 87 percent deposit financing in 1996, compared with only 67 percent for the largest banks.

Deposits span many different types, with these percentages reported in the *Federal Reserve Bulletin* in 1997:

+ Transaction deposits 22%
+ Nontransaction deposits 67%
+ Large time deposits 11%

Deposits are eligible for federal deposit insurance up to $100,000 per account. These types are described below.

Transaction deposits are deposit accounts with check-writing privileges. Regulations prohibit payment of interest on demand deposits for businesses. Certain checking accounts for individuals, **negotiable order of withdrawal (NOW) accounts**, pay interest at rates set by individual banks. Banks often require minimum balances before paying interest or impose service charges. They may also limit the number of checks that can be written each month. **Money market accounts (MMDAs)** also allow limited check-writing privileges (often no more than six checks or automatic transfers per month) but pay higher interest rates than NOW accounts. Restrictions on the number of checks written exempts banks from reserve requirements on these accounts, while they must hold reserves on NOW accounts.[4]

---

[4]Reserve requirements for net transaction deposits, as reported in the *Federal Reserve Bulletin* in 1999 were 3 percent of deposits for net transaction accounts up to $46.5 million and 10 percent of deposits for larger net transaction accounts.

Nontransaction deposits include **passbook savings accounts** and **time deposits**. Passbook savings accounts offer no check-writing capabilities, but a customer can withdraw funds by presenting a passbook to a teller. Since passbooks bring inconveniences and often earn lower rates than other accounts, they have lost some popularity in recent decades. Time deposits are often called **certificates of deposit (CDs)** and set fixed maturity dates. They often impose prepayment penalties equal to stated numbers of interest payments for early withdrawals. Relatively small CDs (those for less than $100,000) are often called **retail CDs**, while larger time deposits are called **jumbo CDs**. Negotiable jumbo CDs of large, well-known banks typically hold balances of about $1 million and trade in a well-established secondary market. Securities firms often broker jumbo CDs for large banks, allowing their customers to buy securities with high rates, called **brokered CDs**. Deposit insurance covers the balances of NOW accounts, MMDAs, savings and retail CDs. These accounts are often called **core deposits**, since they tend to be stable and less interest-rate sensitive than others.

Banks also hold uninsured deposits and other borrowings, often called **purchased funds, volatile liabilities**, or **hot funds**. The list includes jumbo CDs, uninsured CDs greater than $100,000, and other types of borrowing that are very sensitive to interest rate changes. These volatile liabilities may leave a bank at any time if higher rates are offered elsewhere or bad news appears.

Below deposits, the liabilities section of a bank's balance sheet lists **Fed funds purchased (FFP) and repos**. These short-term sources of financing are popular among large banks, often trading in amounts of $1 million or more. Large banks engage in more active liability management than smaller institutions, issuing short-term securities for short-term liquidity needs. **Other borrowed money** includes **commercial paper**, which matures in 270 days, and other short-term securities issued by large, well-known banks. By issuing these securities, banks avoid the lengthy SEC registration process. This category also includes **Eurodollar CDs**, which are large dollar deposits held in foreign subsidiaries of U.S. banks. Also, **bankers acceptances** are short-term securities that represent firm IOUs to a bank as payments for foreign trade; they can be sold at a discount prior to maturity.

The balance sheet category **Subordinated notes and debentures** includes all notes and bonds issued with maturities greater than 1 year that give claims subordinated to those of depositors. Subordinated debentures and perpetual preferred stock represent rather long-term capital for a bank. Since their claims are subordinated to those of deposits, regulators allow them to be included as secondary capital for regulatory capital requirements (as discussed in more detail in Chapter 8). **Other liabilities** include taxes and dividends payable, acceptances, and trade credit outstanding, among other miscellaneous items that do not fit in other categories.

Stockholder's equity, which is quite small relative to debt for a bank, includes **Common stock** reported at par value, Surplus (the amount paid over a legal par value), and **Undivided profits**. Undivided profits, somewhat similar to retained earnings of a nonfinancial corporation, are earnings retained in excess of the common stock surplus account. Equity accounts also often include **Other equity or contingency reserves**. This amount reflects reserves against losses on securities or other contingencies. Small banks have higher equity–capital ratios than large banks.

Table 5.1 reports more than $4.5 trillion in total assets for all FDIC-insured banks in 1996, but this figure underestimates bank activities. Banks engaged in numerous other off-balance-sheet activities with associated assets totaling over $23 trillion in 1996. This off-balance-sheet activity provides significant noninterest revenues, primarily in the form of fee income, particularly for large banks. These activities are discussed in greater detail in Appendix 5A. The asset items just reviewed on the balance sheet generate interest revenues, and the liability items generate interest expenses, as discussed in the following overview of bank income statements.

INCOME STATEMENTS FOR FDIC-INSURED BANKS

Table 5.2 shows a detailed income statement for insured banks using 1996 as an example. It is divided into three size categories: the typical bank income statement reports interest revenues and interest expenses together near the top, followed by net interest income, provision for loan losses, and noninterest revenue and expenses.

Revenues

A bank's income statement gives details for different types of revenues it generates from individual types of assets described on the balance sheet. Typically, a bank income statement reports any interest revenues for municipal securities that are not subject to federal taxes after dividing by $(1 - t)$, to present **tax equivalent revenues**. Large banks generate greater proportions of noninterest revenue than smaller banks. In 1996, noninterest revenue for banks greater than $1 billion was over 25.0 percent of total revenues compared to only 12.5 percent for those in the smallest category. Fees, service charges, and income from trust or fiduciary operations are the primary sources of noninterest revenues. Trading account gains and fees and income related to foreign exchange come from gains that banks realize by operating trading accounts, making markets for securities and foreign exchange trading and services.

Expenses

In past years, interest expenses dominated banks' expenses. In 1996, noninterest expense was 39.55 percent of revenues, and interest expense was 36.92 percent. Banks' major interest expense is interest paid on deposits, followed by other borrowed money and Fed funds purchased and repos. The largest noninterest expense relative to revenues is Other noninterest expense. This amount includes utilities and deposit insurance premiums along with other operating expenses. Salaries and employee benefits are the next largest expense. Occupancy expenses follow, including rent and depreciation of premises and machinery. Banks have tried to improve their efficiency in the past decade to reduce large noninterest expenses.

Net Income

This income statement shows both amounts and percentages of total revenues, making it a common size statement. The percentage next to net income at the bottom of the statement is the average bank **net profit margin** (NPM), calculated as net income divided by revenues. Pretax net operating income is often used to calculate an operating NPM or ROA that accurately reflects a bank's ordinary operations before one-time gains and losses on securities and extraordinary items. In 1996, the average bank's **operating NPM** was 19.54 percent, with similar figures for the three size classes of banks.

Table 5.2 ◆ REPORT OF INCOME FOR ALL INSURED COMMERCIAL BANKS, DECEMBER 31, 1996 ($ MILLIONS)

	Total Commercial Banks	Percentage of Total Revenues	Banks with Assets of Less than $100 Million	Percentage of Total Revenues	Banks with Assets of $100 Million to $1 Billion	Percentage of Total Revenues	Banks with Assets of $1 Billion or More	Percentage of Total Revenues
Total revenues	**$406,363**	**100.0%**	**$23,448**	**100.0%**	**$61,841**	**100.0%**	**$321,074**	**100.0%**
Total interest revenues	**312,791**	**76.97%**	**20,526**	**87.54%**	**52,045**	**84.16%**	**240,200**	**74.81%**
Loans and lease financing	239,131	58.85	14,709	62.73	38,947	62.98	185,474	57.77
Balances at depository institutions	5,363	1.32	128	0.55	220	0.36	5,015	1.56
Investment securities	50,710	12.48	4,974	21.21	11,567	18.70	34,168	10.64
Assets held in trading accounts	8,534	2.10	3	0.01	13	0.02	8,533	2.66
Fed funds sold and repos	9,053	2.23	711	3.03	1,296	2.10	7,045	2.19
Interest expenses	**150,011**	**36.92%**	**9,038**	**38.54%**	**22,687**	**36.69%**	**118,285**	**36.84%**
Deposits	107,401	26.43	8,777	37.43	20,551	33.23	78,074	24.32
Fed funds purchased and repos	16,762	4.12	123	0.52	1,188	1.92	15,451	4.81
Other borrowed money	22,170	5.46	134	0.57	914	1.48	22,122	6.89
Mortgage indebtedness	134	0.03	3	0.01	11	0.02	121	0.04
Subordinated notes and debentures	3,543	0.87	2	0.01	24	0.04	3,517	1.10
Net interest income	**162,780**	**40.06%**	**11,488**	**48.99%**	**29,357**	**47.47%**	**121,935**	**37.98%**
Provisions for loan losses	**16,244**	**4.00%**	**551**	**2.35%**	**2,015**	**3.26%**	**13,678**	**4.26%**
Total noninterest revenues	**93,572**	**23.03%**	**2,922**	**12.46%**	**9,796**	**15.84%**	**80,854**	**25.18%**
Fiduciary activities	13,654	3.36	217	0.93	1,421	2.30	12,016	3.74
Service charges on deposit accounts	16,934	4.17	1,234	5.26	2,778	4.49	12,923	4.02
Foreign exchange and related income	2,682	0.66	1	0.00	20	0.03	2,661	0.83
Trading account gains and fees	−2,644	−0.65	0	0.00	−13	−0.02	−2,630	−0.82
All other noninterest income	55,437	13.64	1,471	6.27	5,550	8.97	48,416	15.08
Total noninterest expense	**160,697**	**39.55%**	**9,294**	**39.64%**	**24,300**	**39.29%**	**127,103**	**39.59%**
Salaries and employee benefits	67,046	16.50	4,681	19.96	11,273	18.23	51,092	15.91
Premises and equipment	20,729	5.10	1,229	5.24	3,270	5.29	16,230	5.05
All other noninterest expense	72,922	17.95	3,384	14.43	9,757	15.78	59,781	18.62
Pretax net operating income	79,411	19.54	4,565	19.47	12,839	20.76	62,008	19.31
Gains (losses) on securities	1,114	0.27	15	0.06	79	0.13	1,020	0.32
Applicable Income tax	28,227	6.95	1,427	6.09	4,187	6.77	22,055	6.87
Income before extraordinary items	52,299	12.87	3,153	13.45	8,731	14.12	40,415	12.59
Extraordinary items, net	91	0.02	2	0.01	10	0.02	79	0.02
Net income	**$ 52,390**	**12.89%**	**$ 3,154**	**13.45%**	**$ 8,741**	**14.13%**	**$ 40,494**	**12.61%**

Source: FDIC Statistics on Banking, 1966.

Gains (Losses) on Securities and Net Extraordinary Items Security gains (or losses) come about when a bank sells securities from its investment portfolio at a higher or lower price than its book values for those assets. Losses and gains on security sales are taxed as ordinary income for banks. Extraordinary items are losses or gains on one-time items, such as a bank selling and leasing back its buildings or expenses for settling a lawsuit. Since these items do not recur, they are placed at the bottom of the income statement, although they can represent significant amounts. The average commercial bank had a NPM after these items and taxes of 12.89 percent in 1996.

LOOKING MORE CLOSELY AT BANK PROFITS

Based on the balance sheets and income statements reviewed above, the sources of a bank's net income (NI) excluding extraordinary items and security gains/losses equals:

$$NI = [NII - PLL - \text{Burden}] (1 - t) \tag{5.1}$$

where NII = Net interest income = Interest revenues − Interest expenses; PLL = Provision for loan losses; Burden = Noninterest expenses − Noninterest revenues; t = a bank's marginal tax rate.

Stating these items as a fraction of assets gives operating ROA becomes:

$$ROA = [NIM \text{ - } PLL\% - Burden\%] (1 - t) \tag{5.2}$$

Equation 5.2 shows that a bank's profits depend on how well it manages its NIM, provision for loan losses, and noninterest expenses and revenues (burden). These components and their trends in the 1990s are discussed individually in the following sections.

Trends in NIM

Table 5.3 shows the trends in NIM, Burden, and ROA from 1992 to 1997. NIMs appear to be fairly stable over this time period, despite fairly volatile interest rates. In 1992 to 1993, interest rates fell, and in 1994 and 1995, rates rose. As discussed in Chapter 2, NIM equals interest revenue (IR) less interest expense (IE), both divided by total assets:

$$NIM = \frac{\text{Interest revenues}}{\text{Assets}} - \frac{\text{Interest expenses}}{\text{Assets}} \tag{5.3}$$

Thus, NIM is a function of changes in IR (in effect, the average rate paid on assets) and changes in IE (the approximate cost of funds). Figure 5.3 graphs trends in IR, IE, and NPM in the 1990s. NIM is stable (the curve is flat), because IR and IE changed by similar amounts. For instance when rates fell during 1992 to 1993, IR fell 0.74 percent, and IE fell 0.67 percent. The fall in NIM by 0.07 percent or 7 basis points (1 basis point = 0.01%) resulted because of the 7 basis point larger fall of IR than IE. Similarly, between 1994 and 1995, NIM fell only 7 basis points, because IR rose 7 basis points less than IE. In 1996, IR rose 4 basis points and IE fell 6 basis points, resulting in a 10 basis point rise in NIM.

Table 5.3   ✦   TRENDS IN NET INTEREST MARGIN, BURDEN, AND ROA: 1992 TO 1997

Commercial banks had fairly stable NIMs, with small declines from 1994 to 1997. Provision for loans losses percentages fell by half, and the net burden also fell, resulting in a higher ROA in 1996 than before.

	Percentage of Average Assets					
	1992	1993	1994	1995	1996	1997
Interest income (tax adjusted)	7.74%	7.00%	6.85%	7.52%	7.56%	7.57%
Interest expense	−3.67	−3.00	−2.93	−3.67	−3.61	−3.67
Net interest margin (NIM)	**4.07**	**4.00**	**3.92**	**3.85**	**3.95**	**3.90**
Provision for loan losses (PLL)	**−0.77**	**−0.47**	**−0.28**	**−0.30**	**−0.38**	**−0.42**
NIM after PLL	3.31	3.53	3.64	3.55	3.57	3.48
Noninterest expense	−3.85	−3.88	−3.73	−3.62	−3.78	−3.70
Noninterest income	1.89	2.04	1.93	1.96	2.16	2.24
Burden	**−1.96**	**−1.84**	**−1.80**	**−1.66**	**−1.62**	**−1.46**
ROA before taxes and adjustments[a]	1.35	1.69	1.84	1.89	1.95	2.02
ROA after taxes and adjustments	**0.93**	**1.14**	**1.17**	**1.19**	**1.24**	**1.30**

[a]Adjustments include security gains/losses and any gains/losses on extraordinary items.
Source: Sheshunoff Bank Quarterly, 1993 and 1997 issues, Sheshunoff Information Services, Inc., Austin, Texas.

Figure 5.3   ✦   TRENDS IN INTEREST REVENUE, INTEREST EXPENSE, AND NIM: 1992 TO 1997

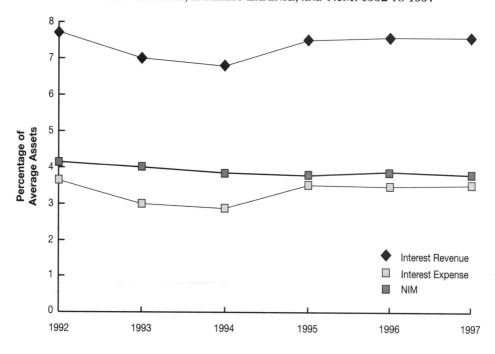

Relative changes in IR and IE depend on the composition or mix of a bank's assets and liabilities, as well as on how much a bank's assets and liabilities change in value due to changes in interest rates. If a bank holds matched fixed-rate assets and liabilities, IR and IE will change very little. However, if its assets or liabilities are repricable (rate-sensitive) in different amounts over a given time period, its NIM will change with a change in rates. Repricable (rate-sensitive) assets include short-term and maturing securities and loans along with variable rate loans. Repricable (rate-sensitive) liabilities include short-term deposits and other maturing liabilities. The relationship between repricable assets and liabilities for any given time period is called a bank's *repricing* or *funding gap*:

$$\text{Repricing gap} = \text{Repricable assets} - \text{Repricable liabilities} \qquad (5.4)$$

A larger gap indicates increasing interest rate risk to a bank through volatility of its NIM caused by interest rates change.

To illustrate the effect of a bank's funding gap on its net interest income (NII), suppose you are a stockholder in Bank Negative, which has the following simple balance sheet:

Bank Negative Balance Sheet ($ million)

Assets		Liabilities and Equity	
10-year fixed-rate loans		1-year deposits	$ 80 (9% rate)
(10% rate)	$100	Equity	$ 20
		Total claims	$100

Bank Negative has fixed-rate assets of $100 million financed with $80 million of 1-year deposits and $20 million in equity. Thus, for a 1-year period, Bank Negative has a repricing gap (repricable assets less repricable liabilities) of: $0 − $80 million = −$80 million. As a stockholder, you calculate the bank's expected net interest income (NII), consisting of interest revenues less interest expenses, as:

$$NII = (\text{Loans} \times \text{Loan rate}) - (\text{Liabilities} \times \text{Liability rate})$$

$$NII = (\$100 \times .10) - (\$80 \times 0.09) = \$2.8 \text{ million}$$

If short-term interest rates rise 1 percent, however, you may be disappointed next year when the interest rate on deposits rises to 10 percent, resulting in a lower NII of:

$$NII = (\$100 \times 0.10) - (\$80 \times 0.10) = \$ 2 \text{ million}$$

Interest expense rose by $0.8 million, while fixed interest revenue stayed the same. The expected change in NII with a change in rates can be calculated using the bank's repricing gap as:

$$\text{Expected change in } NII = \text{Repricing gap} \times \text{Change in rates} \qquad (5.5)$$

$$\text{Change } NII = -\$80 \text{ million} \times (0.01) = -\$0.8 \text{ million}$$

Alternatively, if short-term rates fall by 100 basis points (1 percent), you will be a happy stockholder. The deposit rate will fall to 8 percent, reducing interest expense by $0.8 million, while interest revenue remains the same. Therefore, NII will rise by $0.8 million.

Banks can also experience positive repricing gaps. For example, consider the situation of Bank Positive:

Bank Positive Balance Sheet ($ million)

Assets		Liabilities and Equity	
1-year consumer loans (rate 10%)	$100	10-year long-term deposits (Rate 9%)	$ 80
		Equity	20
		Total claims	$100

Bank Positive has a 1-year positive repricing gap of $100 million − $0 = $100 million. It uses long-term deposits to finance short-term consumer loans. With such rate-sensitive assets, if rates rise 100 basis points or 1 percent, interest revenues will rise, but interest expenses will not. The change in NII for Bank Positive will be:

$$\text{Change in } NII = \text{Gap} \times \text{Change rate} = \$100 \text{ million} \times 0.01 = \$1 \text{ million}.$$

On the other hand, if rates fall 100 basis points (1 percent), interest revenues will fall by $1 million, while interest expense will stay the same, and NII will fall instead by $1 million.

A bank's repricing gap determines whether NII will remain stable, fall, or rise when interest rates rise. Bank Positive and Bank Negative illustrate exaggerated cases, since real banks mix rate-sensitive assets and rate-sensitive liabilities. Yet, the same principles hold. A negative repricing gap puts a bank at risk if interest rates rise. A positive repricing gap puts a bank at risk if interest rates fall. A larger gap corresponds to larger risk of an unhappy fall in net interest income if rates move in the unfortunate direction. However, if rates move in the favorable direction, such banks will experience rising net interest income. As the gap approaches zero, the bank gains an increasingly stable NIM. The stable NIMs for banks in the 1990s shown in Table 5.3 suggest that on average banks had small funding gaps.

Effect on ROA of Provision for Loan Losses and Burden

Provision for loan losses (PLL) is the expense a bank recognizes to cover expected loan losses. Table 5.3 shows PLL as a percentage of average bank assets (PLL%) in 1996. This percentage appears very small, but since a bank earns only a very small return on assets, PLL is a very important component of profits. In 1992, a period when many U.S. banks suffered large losses, the PLL% was 0.77 percent. As the economy improved, the PLL% fell significantly in 1993 to 0.47 percent and in 1994 to 0.28 percent. The decline in PLL is a major reason for the rise in bank ROA in 1993 and 1994. PLL is affected by a bank's loan mix. A rising percentage of loans in a bank's assets and increasingly risky types of loans should produce a rising PLL. Sometimes, however, banks do not set aside sufficient reserves for future loan losses, given their risk profiles.

Management of burden has become increasingly important for banks as competition has eroded their NIMs. Recall that a bank's burden equals its noninterest expense (NIE) less noninterest revenues (NIR). NIE includes salaries and employee benefits, costs for premises and equipment, and other noninterest costs. NIR includes income from trust activities, service charges, and other fee income. As shown in Table 5.3, the burden percentage for banks fell about 17 percent between 1992 and 1996, from 1.96 percent to 1.62 percent. Although the percentage of noninterest expense in assets (NIE%) fell only 0.07 percent (7 basis points), the percentage of noninterest revenue in assets (NIR%) rose by 0.27 percent (27 basis points), resulting in a 0.34 percent (34 basis point) decline in banks' burden percentage. With declining NIMs and rising noninterest expenses, banks have attempted to find new sources of noninterest revenues. Figure 5.4 graphs the trends in the NIR percentage, NIE percentage, and burden percentage from 1992 to 1997. The figure shows that the plunge in the average bank burden over time resulted from a fall in noninterest expense from 1992 to 1995 coupled with a rise in noninterest revenues in 1996 and 1997.

Asset and liability mix affect a bank's burden, as well as its NIM. For instance, commercial loan customers often provide noninterest revenue by paying fees for other services such as working capital management services or other personal banking services. On the other hand, cheap transaction deposits generate higher noninterest administrative expenses than other types of deposits that involve fewer transactions.

The Net Effect on Trends in ROA Putting these components together, bank ROAs rose in the 1990s, as shown in Table 5.3. NIMs remained fairly stable during that time, although NIM dropped a total of 17 basis points between 1992 and 1997. Provision for loan losses to assets fell 35 basis points. The net effect was a rise in NIM after PLL by 17 basis points in 1997. Noninterest expense fell 15 basis points as a percentage of assets, and noninterest revenue rose 35 basis points, reducing bur-

Figure 5.4 ✦ TRENDS IN NONINTEREST REVENUE, NONINTEREST EXPENSE, AND BURDEN: 1992 TO 1997

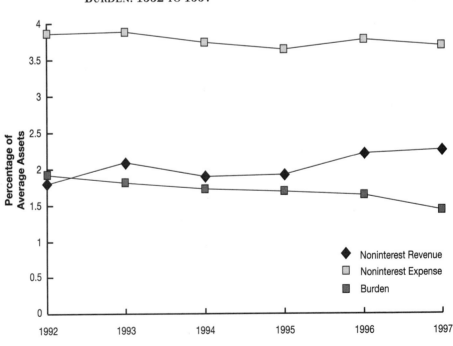

den as a percentage of assets by 50 basis points by 1997. Consequently, operating ROA rose dramatically by 67 basis points to 2.02 percent in 1997, almost 50 percent higher than in 1992. With securities gains/losses, extraordinary items, and taxes, the net ROA was 1.3 percent in 1997, about 40 percent higher than in 1992.

USING INCOME RELATIONSHIPS TO FORECAST TARGET NIMS

Forecasting NIM Based on a Target ROA

The income statement relationships in Equation 5.2 can help managers to find the NIM a bank must achieve to meet a target ROA. The process begins with the ROA equation:

$$ROA = (NIM - PLL - \text{Burden}) \times (1 - t)$$

Solving for NIM, the equation becomes:

$$NIM = \frac{ROA}{(1 - t)} + PLL\% + \text{Burden}\% \qquad (5.6)$$

Suppose you are a manager for Bank Star National Bank, which has set a target for ROA of 1.24 percent. The company has a marginal tax rate of 30 percent, a PLL percentage of 0.30 percent, and a burden percentage of 1.5 percent. What NIM must the company achieve to make its target ROA? Using Equation 5.6, Bank Star's target NIM is:

$$NIM = \frac{1.24\%}{(1 - 0.3)} + 0.30\% + 1.5\% = 3.57\%$$

What ratio of interest revenue to assets would Bank Star have to average to reach this NIM goal, if its interest expenses amount to 3.61 percent of assets? To answer the question, solve Equation 5.3 ($NIM = IR\% - IE\%$), for the interest revenue percentage:

$$IR\% = NIM + IE\% = 3.57\% + 3.61\% = 7.18\%$$

Bank Star would have to earn an average of 7.18 percent on its assets to meet its NIM goal.

Forecasting NIM Based on a Forecast of ROE

This analysis can be extended to find goals that will produce a desired target ROE using the relationship from Chapter 4:

$$ROA = \frac{ROE}{EM} = \frac{ROE}{(\text{Assets/Equity})}$$

This equation implies that:

$$ROA = ROE \times (\text{Equity/Assets})$$

Substituting this expression into Equation 5.5 gives:

$$NIM = \left[\frac{ROE}{(1 - t)} \times \text{Equity/Assets} \right] + PLL\% + \text{Burden}\%$$

Equation 5.7 indicates that a bank's target NIM is also a function of its financial leverage. An increase in the equity–asset ratio (that is, a decline in financial leverage), would require an offsetting rise in NIM to achieve the goal.

To demonstrate this principle, suppose Bank Star has set a target ROE of 18 percent. Assume also that the bank's equity capital ratio is 8 percent, the burden percentage is 1 percent, the expected PLL% is 0 percent, and the marginal tax rate is 34 percent. What target NIM does Bank Star need to achieve?

$$\text{Target } NIM = \frac{(18\% \times 0.08)}{(1 - 0.34)} + 0\% + 1\% = 3.18\%$$

The minimum NIM necessary to achieve the target ROE is 3.18 percent. However, if the desired equity–capital ratio falls to 6 percent, a much lower target NIM will allow the bank to generate the same 18 percent ROE:

$$\text{Target } NIM = \frac{(18\% \times 0.06)}{(1 - 0.34)} + 0\% + 1\% = 2.64\%$$

This difference demonstrates that financial leverage is an important component in daily bank decisions to determine the NIM needed to achieve a target return for bank stockholders. The effect of financial leverage on bank profitability can be more closely examined by looking at the relationship between ROA, the equity multiplier, and ROE over time.

Trends in ROA, EM, and ROE Over Time

Table 5.4 shows trends in ROA, EM, and ROE from 1990 to 1997. From 1990 to 1993, the U.S. economy suffered a severe recession. Bank ROAs were low then, but ROEs stayed in the low but respectable range because of high equity multipliers.

Table 5.4 ✦ TRENDS IN PROFITABILITY (ROA, EM, AND ROE) FOR U.S. BANKS, 1990–1997

Commercial bank ROEs improved over the 1990s as ROAs improved, despite a decline in financial leverage, as indicated by the fall in equity multipliers (EM), i.e., the rise in equity to asset ratios over time.

All Banks	Return on Assets	Equity Multiplier	Return on Equity
1990	0.49%	15.59	7.64%
1991	0.54	14.91	8.05
1992	0.93	14.23	13.24
1993	1.14	12.77	14.56
1994	1.17	12.50	14.63
1995	1.19	12.37	14.72
1996	1.24	12.06	14.95
1997	1.30	11.89	15.46

Source: Sheshunoff Bank Quarterly, 1993 and 1997 issues. Sheshunoff Information Services, Inc., Austin, Texas.

For instance, a low 0.49 percent ROA times a high equity multiplier of 15.59 resulted in a ROE of 7.64 percent in 1990.

FDICIA raised capital requirements in 1991, and the EM fell for banks after 1992. However, an economic expansion brought increasing ROAs. In 1997, the EM was only 11.89, but the ROA of 1.30 percent resulted in a ROE of 15.46 percent, 102 percent higher than in 1990.

Trends in NPM and AU Over Time

The reason for the rise in bank ROAs in the late 1990s can be examined more closely by looking at their net profit margins (NPMs), which measure cost management, and asset utilization (AU) ratios, which measure revenue management. The well-known Dupont system for ratio analysis multiplies NPM by AU to get ROA:

$$ROA = NPM \times AU \qquad (5.8)$$

$$\frac{\text{Net Income}}{\text{Assets}} = \frac{Net\ Income}{Revenues} \times \frac{Revenues}{Assets}$$

Table 5.5 shows trends in NPM and AU for U.S. banks from 1990 to 1997. Low ROAs in 1990 and 1991 can be explained by very low net profit margins. Asset utilization ratios fell slightly after 1991, but NPMs improved immensely, increasing from 4.94 percent in 1991 to 13.35 percent in 1997. This change dramatically improved ROA, which rose 145 percent from 0.51 percent in 1991 to 1.25 percent in 1997.

Thus, a combination of cost management measured by NPM, revenue management reflected by AU, and financial leverage demonstrated by EM affect a bank's ROE. Figure 5.5 illustrates this relationship by graphing trends in NPM, AU, EM, and ROE for U.S. banks from 1992 to 1997. This figure shows that the rise in the average bank ROE is the result of a rising NPM, despite a falling average EM and a flat AU ratio. Chapter 6 will demonstrate a more detailed method for bank performance and risk analysis.

Table 5.5   ✦   TRENDS IN ROA (NPM AND AU) FOR U.S. BANKS, 1990–1997

Commercial bank ROAs improved over the later 1990s as NPMs improved, despite a slight decline in asset utilization (AU).

All Banks	Net Profit Margin	Asset Utilization	Return on Assets
1990	4.39%	.1117	0.49%
1991	4.94	.1093	0.54
1992	9.65	.0984	0.95
1993	13.38	.0852	1.14
1994	13.32	.0878	1.17
1995	12.64	.0941	1.19
1996	12.86	.0964	1.24
1997	13.35	.0974	1.30

Source: Figures calculated by authors from reports published in William B. English and William R. Nelson, "Profits and Balance Sheet Developments at U.S. Commercial Banks in 1997," *Federal Reserve Bulletin* (June 1998): 391–419.

Figure 5.5 ✦ TRENDS IN NPM, AU, EM, AND ROE, 1992 TO 1997

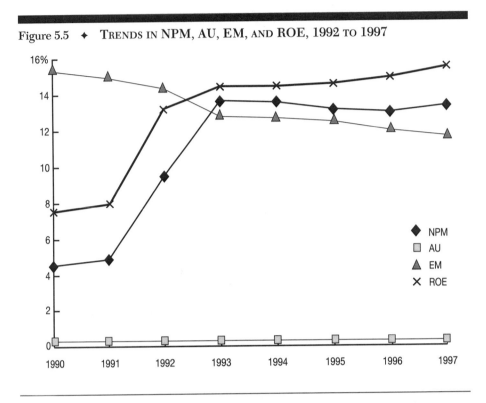

SUMMARY

This chapter provides an overview of the financial statements for depository institutions, focusing particularly on commercial banks. Traditional bank profits come from buying funds from depositors at low rates and selling them at higher rates to borrowers as loans. Traditional analysis evaluates bank profitability based on the net interest margin (NIM), interest revenue less interest expense as a percentage of total assets. Every bank also must cover its burden, equal to noninterest expenses less noninterest revenues. Noninterest revenues have gained importance for banks as traditional NIMs have fallen. Banks also must cover the expense of expected loan losses, captured by the provision for loan loss expense that bank managers take each year.

Banks' NIMs are a function of the repricing gap, equal to repricable assets less repricable liabilities on their balance sheets. A bank with a negative gap has more repricable liabilities than repricable assets. Hence, if interest rates rise, the bank's interest expense will rise more than its interest revenue, reducing NIM. However, a bank with such a negative gap will have a rise in its NIM, as interest expenses will fall more than interest revenues, if interest rates fall. If a bank has a positive gap, it holds more repricable assets than repricable liabilities, and it will benefit from a rising NIM if interest rates rise, but it will suffer from a falling NIM if interest rates fall.

The return on assets (ROA) for a bank is a function of both its cost management, reflected by its net profit margin (NPM), and its revenue management, captured by its asset utilization (AU) ratio. In the 1990s, increasing NPMs along with fairly stable AUs resulted in rising ROAs. The return on equity (ROE) for a bank is a function of its ROA and its financial leverage. Banks have relatively low ROAs, but they can generate acceptable ROEs because of their high financial leverage (low equity–capital ratios).

Discussion Questions

1. What are the major sources of revenues and expenses for banks? What are a bank's major assets and liabilities? How have bank assets and liabilities changed from the 1950s to the 1990s? Why did these changes occur?

2. What are Fed funds purchased and Fed funds sold? What are repos? If the Fed funds rate is high, what does this condition imply about banks' need for short-term funds?

3. Discuss how provision for loan losses on a bank's income statement is related to a bank's allowance for loan losses on its balance sheet. How is the allowance for loan losses adjusted each year?

4. What types of loans do banks typically hold on their balance sheets? Why do real estate loans expose banks to more interest rate risk than other loans?

5. What types of deposits does a bank accept? What are the differences between NOW accounts, business checking accounts, MMDAs, retail CDs, jumbo CDs, and negotiable CDs? What is the difference between core deposits and volatile liabilities?

6. Looking at Table 5.1, how do very small banks and very large banks differ in their assets and liabilities? Why do large banks rely less on deposit financing? Why do they hold fewer securities?

7. What is a bank's repricing gap? If Bank Mountain King has a positive gap, what will happen to its NIM if interest rates rise? What if rates fall? If the Big Wave Bank has a negative gap, what will happen to its NIM if rates rise and fall?

8. Using Table 5.3, discuss precisely why the average bank ROA rose between 1992 and 1993, a period of falling rates, and precisely why ROA rose between 1993 and 1994, a period of rising rates?

9. How do a bank's NPM, AU, and EM interact to affect its ROE? What do each of these figures indicate about a bank's management? Why did bank ROEs improve in the late 1990s?

10. Why did banks' equity multipliers (EMs) fall in the 1990s? What effect does an EM fall have on ROE?

Problems

1. The Texas Independence Bank has the following balance sheet:

Assets

Fixed rate loans (9.5% 30 yrs.)	$50 mil.	Rate 9.5%
Total Assets	**$50 mil.**	

Liabilities and Equity

Demand deposits	$12 mil.	Rate 0.0%
Fed funds purchased	30 mil.	Rate 7.0%
Equity	8 mil.	
Total Claims	**$50 mil.**	

a. What is the bank's 1-year funding gap? What risk does the bank have? What is the bank's expected net interest income?

b. Using the bank's funding gap, determine the expected change in net interest income if rates rise 1 percent and if rates fall 1 percent.

2. First Caroline Bank and Trust Company has this year-end financial data for the most recent period: ROA 0.99 percent, ROE 12.57 percent, net income $11,798,000.

a. Calculate the bank's equity multiplier and equity to assets ratio.

b. Calculate the bank's total assets and equity.

c. Suppose that the bank increases total liabilities by $10 million and reduces equity by the same amount. Given a higher interest expense, suppose Net Income goes down by 35 million, what will be the new ROE? What do these changes reveal about the impact of financial leverage?

3. The board of directors of The First National Bank of Sydney Elizabeth have approved these target rates of return for shareholders:

✦ Target ROE: 16 percent
✦ Target EM: 12
✦ Tax Rate (t): 35 percent
✦ Total assets: $850 million
✦ Interest expense: $80 million
✦ Net noninterest expense: $11.5 million
✦ Provision for loan losses: $1 million

a. What should be the bank's target NIM for the planning period?

b. What target interest revenues must First National earn to meet its financial goals?

c. Suppose interest expenses rise 10 percent above target, what return on equity will the bank actually earn?

4. Albie Singleton, a management trainee at Bank Sussman is to examine the institution's ROE under the following conditions: NIM, 4.2 percent; EM, 11; Marginal tax rate, 35 percent; Total assets, $1,750 million; Burden, $40 million; Provision for loan loss, $0

   a. What will be the bank's ROE?

   b. If the bank's board of directors decide to increase the net worth multiplier to 12 and hold other factors constant, what will be the expected ROE?

5. Terrell Savings Bank is preparing a financial plan based on the following data: Target ROE, 15 percent; Tax rate (t), 35%; Total assets, $700 million; Total liabilities, $640 million.

   a. What is the bank's current equity multiplier?

   b. Given this EM, what before-tax income must the bank earn to reach its target ROE?

   c. What is the bank's NIM, assuming that net noninterest expense is 1.1 percent of total assets?

6. The board of directors of the Oakleigh-Elizabeth Regional Bank has requested a presentation on the relationship between financial leverage and return on net worth. The bank has assets of $2 billion and an equity multiplier of 10. Net income in the coming year is expected to be between 1.2 percent and 2.0 percent of total assets.

   a. At the bank's current capital level, what is the expected range for ROE?

   b. The new chief financial officer (CFO) hopes to persuade the directors to operate aggressively by increasing the equity multiplier to 12. If they do, interest expense will rise because of the increased reliance on borrowed funds. The estimated range of ROA changes range from a low of 0.5 percent to a high of 1.9 percent. What will be the resulting range for ROE?

   c. Based on these estimates, what recommendation should the directors follow?

7. Roscoe-Antony Savings, a small regional bank, has total assets of $500 million and an equity multiplier of 10. A competitor of equal size has 8 percent equity to assets. Both managers are estimating returns, and both forecast interest revenues ranging from 7 percent to 13 percent of total assets. Interest costs for both firms are expected to average 9 percent of total liabilities. Both banks have a burden to assets ratio of 1.5% and PLL to assets ratio of .40%, and a marginal tax rate of 30%.

   a. Calculate the potential range of net income and ROE for each bank.

   b. Graph the relationship between IR/TA and ROE for each bank.

   c. Which shareholders would be better off in an economic downturn? Which owners would benefit in a strong economy?

   d. If shareholders placed a high probability on earning interest revenues equal to 13 percent of total assets, which capitalization plan should they prefer?

Selected References

Hempel, George H., Donald G. Simonson, and Alan B. Coleman. *Bank Management: Text and Cases*, 4th ed. New York: John Wiley & Sons, 1994.

Koch, Timothy W. *Bank Management*, 3rd ed. Fort Worth, Tex.: Dryden Press, 1995.

Sinkey, Joseph F., Jr. *Commercial Bank Financial Management*, 5th ed. Englewood Cliffs, NJ: Prentice-Hall, 1998.

Appendix 5A

OVERVIEW OF OFF-BALANCE-SHEET ITEMS

Table 5A.1 summarizes off-balance-sheet items for all banks in 1996. At the end of that year, gross total off-balance-sheet activity was over $23 trillion.[5] Off-balance-sheet items are often activities that create potential or contingent liabilities in the future. These items include contingent loan commitments, such as unused loan commitments, letters of credit, securities borrowed and lent, participation in acceptances, securities committed to be purchased or sold, nonrecourse mortgage sales, futures contracts (financial, foreign exchange, and others), interest rate swap agreements, and option contracts.

Because of the tremendous growth in off-balance-sheet items, FDICIA required regulators and managers to focus attention on these emerging areas and mandated new financial reporting methods. Regulators have been especially concerned with contingent liabilities and other instruments that might increase the riskiness of an institution and in turn threaten deposit insurance funds. Some off-balance-sheet contracts, however, such as interest rate contracts and foreign exchange contracts, actually help banks to hedge risk and produce revenues to offset potential losses for on-balance-sheet items. Off-balance-sheet items also generate noninterest (fee) revenues reducing the risk of lower profits for banks if traditional revenues fall. Each of the major off-balance sheet-items listed is briefly described in the following paragraphs. Chapter 9 discusses the fee income generated from securitizations and other off-balance sheet items.

Letters of Credit Commercial letters of credit are often used in international trade when lenders agree to provide financing for customers to purchase specific goods. Upon documentation of the completion of a transaction between the customer and a third party, the bank fully expects to advance funds. A standby letter of credit is a similar instrument with an important difference. Rather than making a definite commitment to finance a transaction, the bank states its obligation to pay a third party *only if the bank's customer defaults*. Standby letters are used not only in commercial transactions but also to enhance the marketability of municipal bonds or to guarantee performance on construction contracts. They act as insurance for risk-averse third parties. Ideally, banks provide this insurance only for the obligations of customers with little likelihood of nonperformance. The bank charges a fee for the commitment and, most importantly, assumes that standby letters will expire unused. Because they require no advance commitment of funds, standby letters are not included as liabilities on issuing banks' balance sheets, but they are considered contingent liabilities. The volume of commitments made with standby letters of credit more than quadruped in the 1980s to $300 billion, falling somewhat to $242 billion in 1996. Banks with $1 billion or more in assets issued 97 percent of these letters.

Loan Commitments This category of off-balance-sheet liabilities includes bank commitments for revolving lines of credit, credit lines backing the commercial paper of large corporations, and note issuance facilities, in which banks agree to buy short-term notes if a borrower is unable to sell them elsewhere. In the late 1980s, loan commitments at insured commercial banks were almost ten times the estimated volume of standby letters of credit. In 1996, loan commitments were over $2.5 trillion or about 11 percent of off-balance-sheet items for all banks, but they accounted for more than 91 percent of the off-balance-sheet items for banks under $1 billion in assets. Like standby letters, loan commitments are often activated only if borrowers' financial situations deteriorate. Ideally, they should be considered by external analysts in assessing an institution's total risk, particularly its liquidity risk. Unused loan commitments often serve as

---

[5]See the primary source for this information, the *Economic Policy Review* Federal Reserve Bank of New York (July 1995): 22–42. Also, for informative articles and more detailed information, see the other sources cited in Appendix 5A's Selected References.

Table 5A.1 ✦ Off-Balance-Sheet Items, FDIC Insured Commercial Banks, December 31, 1996 ($Millions)

	Total Commercial Banks	Percentage of Total Assets	Banks with Assets of Less than $100 Million	Percentage of Total Assets	Banks with Assets of $100 Million to $1 Billion	Percentage of Total Assets	Banks with Assets of $1 Billion or More	Percentage of Total Assets
Unused loan committments	$ 2,528,683	10.7%	$52,917	96.0%	$246,765	90.9%	$ 2,229,002	9.5%
Letters of credit	241,885	1.0	1,015	1.8	7,018	2.6	233,852	1.0
Securities borrowed	25,501	0.1	63	0.1	1,096	0.4	24,342	0.1
Securities lent	207,961	0.9	78	0.1	1,083	0.4	206,801	0.9
Mortgatges transferred with recourse (sold or unsold)								
Outstanding principal balance	11,337	0.0	18	0.0	903	0.3	10,417	0.0
Amount of recourse exposure	8,139	0.0	12	0.0	418	0.2	7,710	0.0
When-issued securities								
Gross commitments to purchase	14,103	0.1	35	0.1	184	0.1	13,885	0.1
Gross commitments to sell	14,509	0.1	42	0.1	323	0.1	14,144	0.1
Interest rate contracts								
Notational value interest rate swaps	7,069,382	29.8	76	0.1	7,114	2.6	7,062,192	30.2
Futures and forward contracts	3,201,160	13.5	274	0.5	779	0.3	3,200,107	13.7
Written option contracts	1,588,559	6.7	200	0.4	281	0.1	1,588,078	6.8
Purchased option contracts	1,567,626	6.6	354	0.6	2,330	0.9	1,564,942	6.7
Foreign exchange contracts	6,503,923	27.4	1	0.0	2,497	0.9	6,501,426	27.8
Contracts on other commodities and equity	733,268	3.1	0	0.0	348	0.1	732,920	3.1
All other off-balance-sheet items	15,504	0.1	9	0.0	65	0.0	15,428	0.1
Gross total OBS activity	$23,731,540	100.0%	$55,094	100.0%	$271,485	100.0%	$23,405,246	100.0%

one measure of a bank's liquidity risk. A high proportion of unused loan commitments indicates high potential liquidity needs, if borrowers call on these commitments.

Mortgages Transferred with Recourse This category includes securities transferred or sold to another institution for which the bank is still liable for losses.

When-Issued Securities This class of off-balance-sheet items are associated with banks' security dealer and underwriting activities. They reflect commitments to purchase or sell securities in the future.

Interest Rate Contracts These contracts associated predominantly with hedging activities intended to reduce interest rate risk. Although generally banks and thrifts are allowed to engage in financial futures transactions only for hedging purposes, hedges are accompanied by exposure to basis risk, the risk that prices on contracts used to hedge a position on the bank's balance sheet will not move with the prices of the balance-sheet items. Such a mismatch could result in an imperfect hedge and losses. It is difficult to assess a depository's involvement in hedging by looking at published statements. Ordinarily, an analyst must consult regulatory sources to get specific information, although institutions must now provide more information on their annual reports than they once gave. However, they still often give only aggregated information.

Foreign Exchange Contracts These contracts set terms for future exchanges of foreign currency. Many large banks deal in forward contracts for foreign currencies, agreeing with customers to buy or sell foreign currencies in the future at currently agreed rates. Contracts on other commodities and equity are similarly futures or forward contracts dealing with purchases or sales of commodities or stock in the future at currently agreed prices. All other off-balance-sheet items are items that are not large enough to fit in their own separate category.

Discussion Questions

1. Why is the examination of off-balance-sheet (OBS) items important for a bank financial analyst? Why are OBS items termed *contingent commitments*? What contingencies affect them?
2. What are unused loan commitments? How do they reflect the future liquidity needs of banks?
3. What is a standby letter of credit?
4. What are interest rate contracts and foreign exchange contracts?
5. Although bank regulators are greatly concerned about the risk of off-balance-sheet (OBS) items, in what ways do some of these items reduce a bank's risk?

Selected References For Off-Balance Sheet Activities

Andrews, Suzanna, and Henny Sender. "Off-Balance Sheet Risk: Where Is It Leading the Banks?" *Institutional Investor* 20 (January 1986): 75–84.

Bennett, Barbara. "Off-Balance Sheet Risk in Banking: The Case of Standby Letters of Credit." *Economic Review* Federal Reserve Bank of San Francisco (Winter 1986): 19–29.

Benveniste, Lawrence M., and Allen N. Berger. "An Empirical Analysis of Standby Letters of Credit." In *Proceedings of a Conference on Bank Structure and Competition*. Chicago: Federal Reserve Bank of Chicago, 1996: 387–412.

Chessen, James. "Off-Balance Sheet Activity: A Growing Concern? In *Proceedings of a Conference on Bank Structure and Competition*. Chicago: Federal Reserve Bank of Chicago, 1986.

James, Christopher. "Off-Balance Sheet Banking." *Economic Review*, Federal Reserve Bank of San Francisco (Fall 1987): 5–19.

Koppenhaver, Gary D. "Standby Letters of Credit." *Economic Perspectives*, Federal Reserve Bank of Chicago 11 (July/August 1987): 28–38.

Saunders, Anthony. *Financial Institutions Management: A Modern Perspective*, 2nd ed. Burr Ridge, IL: Irwin, 1997.

Chapter 5 Internet Exercise

Financial Statements for Depository Institutions

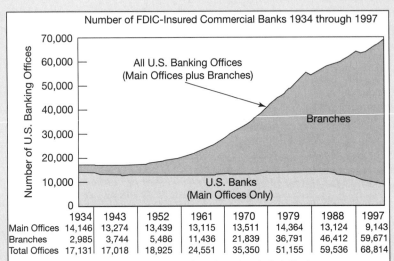

Number of FDIC-Insured Commercial Banks 1934 through 1997

	1934	1943	1952	1961	1970	1979	1988	1997
Main Offices	14,146	13,274	13,439	13,115	13,511	14,364	13,124	9,143
Branches	2,985	3,744	5,486	11,436	21,839	36,791	46,412	59,671
Total Offices	17,131	17,018	18,925	24,551	35,350	51,155	59,536	68,814

Beginning in 1982, remote service facilities (ATMs) were not included in the court of total branches. (At the end of 1981, there were approximately 3,000 such facilities.)
Includes U.S. Territories and Possessions.

The FDIC Statistics on Banking provide a useful overview of aggregate bank data, including balance sheets, income statements, deposits, and so on. The tables and charts in this chapter can be updated via the FDIC home page on the WWW.

1. First, to find this information, go the FDIC home page at: http://www.fdic.gov.

2. Click on "Bank Data" and then, under "Industry Information," click on "Statistics on Banking." http://www.fdic.gov/databank/sob/

3. To update the information in Table 5.1: Assets and Liabilities of Insured Commercial Banks, click on "Section C: FDIC-Insured Commercial Banks." Select the reporting period you desire, and then select the report type: "Balance Sheet, Current Quarter." This information can be retrieved as an HTML Document (.HTML), Lotus 1-2-3 v2.3 Data File (.WK1), or Lotus 1-2-3 v.2.3 Format File (.FMT).

From the "Statistics on Banking" page, you can also update the information in Table 5.2: Report of Income for All Insured Commercial Banks, click on "Section C: FDIC-Insured Commercial Banks." Select the reporting period you desire, and then select the report type: "Income Statement, Current Quar-

ter." This information can be retrieved as an HTML Document (.HTML), Lotus 1-2-3 v2.3 Data File (.WK1), or Lotus 1-2-3 v.2.3 Format File (.FMT).

Historical trends on number, assets, income, and deposits of FDIC-insured commercial banks and trust companies can be found from the "Statistics on Banking" page http://fdic.gov/databank/sob/ by clicking on "Section A: Highlights and Trends" At left is the chart of the number of FDIC-insured commercial banks from 1934 to 1997.

The FDIC also provides information on five-year trends in banking balance sheet, income and expenses, and performance ratios. From the FDIC home page, http:www.fdic.gov/index.html.

Click on "Bank Data" and under "Industry Information" click on "Quarterly Banking Profile." The page that then appears will let you select which QBP product you wish: the Quarterly Banking Profile with summary information on trends, a graph book, and state tables. If you choose "Graph Report" you will be able to retrieve the graphical information on five year trends in net income, net interest margins, non-interest income, capital ratios, loan quality, and other useful summary information.

Other useful sites for financial institution data:

Deloitte and Touche
http://www.icsdeloitte.com/

The Federal Reserve Bank of Cleveland's *Economic Trends* publication provides useful charts on Banking Conditions: cost of funding and yield on earning assets, net interest margin by asset size, percent of loans outstanding, and growth in bank assets. A sample issue can be found at: http://www.clev.frb.org/research/Aug98et/bnkcnd.pdf

"Today one must manage through the period of transition with the highest standard of performance always as a guide."

John B. McCoy, Larry A. Frieder, and Robert B. Hedges, Jr.
Bottomline Banking: Meeting the Challenges for Survival & Success (Chicago: Probus, 1994), p. 7.

"For consolidating banks, bigger is better only if it brings greater efficiency."

Joseph B. Cahill
"Doubts Grow over Banc One's Skill with Cost Scalpel," *The Wall Street Journal*, August 3, 1998, p. B6.

6

DEPOSITORY INSTITUTION PERFORMANCE AND RISK ANALYSIS

To manage a bank effectively, a manager needs to set goals and then benchmark performance to these goals. Often goals are set based on a bank's aspirations to perform as well as high-performance competitors. As the second quote suggests, meeting efficiency goals is particularly important for banks to reap benefits from consolidation. For instance, Banc One Corp. recently promised to deliver savings with its proposed merger with Chicago NBD Corp. If it fails to deliver on this promise, analysts fear that Banc One could become a takeover target itself. Earlier, Banc One promised efficiency savings of $345 million by merging the back-office systems of already acquired concerns. However, the change produced cost savings of only $268 million, and additional costs for improvements, like insulating the bank's computer systems against year 2000 problems, outstripped cost estimates by 70 percent. Wall Street punished Banc One's stock for expenses above expectations. The company's share price plunged 15 percent over a 10-day period after a disappointing earnings announcement on July 21, 1998. Banc One also scored poorly on industry efficiency ratings published by Keefe, Bruyette, and Wood, Inc., ranking only seventh of the ten largest banks, with an efficiency ratio (operating expenses to net revenues) of 62 percent versus 53 percent for the top-ranked bank, First Chicago NBD.[1] In 1999, Banc One's efficiency, earnings, and stock price improved.

Because depository institution managers face a critical need to interpret financial statements quickly as they look for bank weaknesses and risks, this chapter focuses on methods for efficiently evaluating a depository institution's performance. The chapter also presents ratios peculiar to depository institutions that help with analysis of different aspects of performance and risk.

✦ ✦ ✦

---

[1] Joseph B. Cahill, "Doubts Grow Over Banc One's Skill with Cost Scalpel," *The Wall Street Journal*, August 3, 1998, p. B6.

GENERAL OBJECTIVES AND GUIDELINES

The objectives of performance evaluation and the information used in such an analysis vary depending on the evaluator's perspective. For example, examiners for bank, thrift, and CU regulators are concerned about an institution's ability to serve the public without placing the deposit insurance system at unnecessary risk. They have developed special data collection and evaluation procedures (introduced in Chapter 3), which serve as indexes of performance based on criteria important to their concerns. Regulators may focus on potential loan losses and capital adequacy ratios, while investors may be more concerned about after-tax profitability, and depositors may look for solid liquidity.

Many stakeholders with different motivations evaluate the performance of depository institutions; however, all attempt to evaluate accounting and other data to assess the financial condition of an institution at a point in time to determine how well it has been managed. Results of such an analysis form a basis for projecting the institution's future performance. A thorough performance analysis may assist managers in diagnosing areas of greatest strength and weakness and in formulating plans for improvement of asset/liability decisions.

Performance: More than Profitability

It is often helpful to analyze depository institution managers based on different aspects of their activities, including liquidity management, investment management, loan portfolio management, capital management, and overall interest rate sensitivity management. These decision areas affect an institution's risk and return. Analysis of each area helps to explain the bottom line results, as a later section of the chapter explains.

A Profit by any Other Name May Not Smell as Sweet

Differences in regulatory and accounting standards for reporting financial data leave some discretion to managers of depository institutions in reporting performance. For instance, accounting for tax purposes must follow somewhat different guidelines than regulatory accounting, and both differ from generally accepted accounting principles (GAAP). Off-balance-sheet items, mentioned in Appendix 5A, have a significant effect on bank performance and potential risks. Further, a single "snapshot" of one year's performance can portray a deceiving picture. For example, Financial Corporation of America (FCA), at one time the nation's largest thrift holding company, earned an amazing 82 percent ROE in 1983. Only a year later, its CEO was forced to resign, and Wall Street pundits referred to FCA as "Financial Corpse of America."[2] Heed the moral to the story: One or two reported performance indicators seldom provide a complete picture of an institution's financial position.

---

[2]Jennifer Bingham Hull, "Financial Corp. of America's Auditor Questions Its Future as a Going Concern," *The Wall Street Journal*, January 2, 1985, p. 2; and Teresa Carson, "FCA Still Has to Live Up to Its Stock Price," *Business Week*, March 10, 1986, p. 34.

Common Size Statements and Trend Analysis

Besides calculating financial ratios, an analyst can glean useful information by expressing balance sheet accounts as percentages of total assets and income statement items as percentages of total revenues. The resulting common-size statements allow comparisons among firms through which managers and external analysts can identify performance areas that are out of line with those of competitors.

In addition, evaluators always find useful input in the patterns of financial ratios over time. Usually called **trend analysis**, this technique reveals long-term patterns in financial measures, indicating whether a firm's performance is improving or deteriorating in different categories.[3]

Interpreting the Numbers

Performance evaluation is more complicated than simply calculating ratios and common-size statements. The hard part of performance analysis is interpreting the numbers. One calculation, viewed in isolation, means little. It gives informative results only when compared either with a standard for the industry or industry subgroup or with the firm's recent past performance.

Sources of Industry Information   To perform a careful performance analysis, an analyst needs information on trends and/or comparative benchmarks for similar-size peers. The Federal Financial Institutions Examination Council provides detailed Uniform Bank Performance Reports based on individual bank call reports along with peer comparisons for similar-size banks. Appendix 6A shows a complete sample UBPR report for NationsBank's subsidiary operating in Maryland in 1994. Near the end, the UBPR report shows average state reports for banks operating in the same state, so analysts can judge whether peer comparison differences are due to regional effects. Such a report currently costs about $45 and can be obtained by writing to:

UBPR

Department 4320

Chicago, Illinois 60673

or calling the FDIC Disclosure Group, 1-800-945-2186. SWS Associates, LLC, a private company, also provides these reports for $55 each, adding a detailed execu-

---

[3]Financial institutions operating in international markets and engaging in transactions denominated in currencies other than the U.S. dollar must abide by Financial Accounting Standards Board (FASB) Statement No. 52, "Foreign Currency Translation," which lays out procedures for isolating the effects of gains and losses resulting solely from changes in exchange rates. FASB No. 52 requires reporting of currency translation gains or losses by foreign subsidiaries, not as increases or decreases in an institution's current income, but rather in a separate section within the capital accounts. In contrast, for inventories of currency traded for the convenience of customers, gains and losses are reported as direct increases or decreases in income for the period in which they occur, since these activities contribute to the institution's ongoing risk exposure.

tive report with a discount for multiple copies (2 through 5 for $20 each, 6 to 10 for $16 each, and 11 or over for $12 each):

SWS Associates, LLC

P.O. Box 3265

Brentwood, TN 37024

(615) 832-4990

e-mail: swsdata@aol.com

Other private companies provide quarterly and annual bank data, ratings, and/or other information, including Sheshunoff & Company of Austin, Texas; Veribanc, Inc. of Woburn, Massachusetts; SNL Securities of Charlottesville, Virginia; and IDC of Rockville, Maryland. Libraries often have copies of annual directories produced by these sources. Bank Compustat (Standard and Poor's of Denver, Colorado) and Sheshunoff also offer personal computer CDs with detailed quarterly and annual data for large bank holding companies, banks, savings and loans, and credit unions. University libraries may have these resources.

Other sources of aggregate information for all banks are a regular report by the FDIC's Division of Research and Statistics, *Annual Statistics on Banking*, which provides income and balance sheet statements and other information for all FDIC-insured banks and savings institutions. This report can be obtained from:

FDIC

Public Information Center, Rm. 100

801 17th Street, N.W.

Washington, DC 20434-0001

(202) 416-6940

The Federal Reserve also publishes annual summaries of performance information on commercial banks and bank holding companies in editions of its *Federal Reserve Bulletin*. The Economic Research Division of the Credit Union National Association (CUNA) regularly publishes summaries of CU data, entitled *Credit Union Annual Report* and available from CUNA in Madison, Wisconsin.[4]

Beware Nonstandard Ratio Definitions   Before choosing among many possible ratio or common-size calculations, an analyst is well-advised to select the industry standards to use for the comparison. The publishers of aggregate performance data

---

[4]Also see the FDIC Web page, an excellent reference that provides tools for comparing/contrasting a bank or S&L's performance against that of another or a peer group. The Federal Reserve Bank of Chicago also offers this kind of information on its Web page. The Web site for the Board of Governors of the Federal Reserve System is at http://www.bog.frb.fed.us. Copies of the *Federal Reserve Bulletin* can be found in libraries, or a subscription costs $25 a year, available from Publications Services, Mail Stop 127, Board of Governors of the Federal Reserve System, Washington, DC 20551, (202) 452-3244 or 3245. The U.S. Bureau of the Census also publishes time series data, including performance ratios on all types of depository institutions, in its annual *Statistical Abstract of the United States*. Sources of aggregate performance data on thrifts are on the Office of Thrift Supervision (OTS), the district Federal Home Loan Banks (FHLBs), and the Saving and Community Bankers of America.

often use different definitions for particular ratios. Unless ratios are calculated in the same way as industry comparison data, analysis will yield suspect conclusions.

Caveat for Peer Group Comparison   UBPRs and other private data sources compare banks against similar-size peers. These comparison firms are often from different states than the bank being analyzed, so peculiarities such as regional economic conditions and differences in state banking regulations may bias such a comparison. For instance, most banks in states that previously required unit banking are part of multibank holding companies (MBHCs), while those in states that allowed free branching emphasize historically less expensive branches versus subsidiaries. MBHCs allowed firms to circumvent branching laws, but only at the cost of much more expensive branching facilities. Consequently, comparisons often showed banks in unit banking states as less efficient than others in branching states, although this inefficiency was uncontrollable at the time.

Similarly, banks operating in states suffering regional recessions compared to national averages generally show inferior performance, often primarily the results of uncontrollable regional conditions. To determine what portion of this poor performance is due to regional economic problems, analysts should try to compare banks to similar-size banks within their own states. UBPRs provide general ratios for state bank averages that can help to determine how well banks operated under similar economic conditions.

Defined peer groups of banks also represent wide ranges of institutions. For instance, a peer group for banks with between $3 billion and $10 billion in assets spans a wide range of banks. If a bank is on the high or low end of the size spectrum, the comparison may be somewhat biased. Annual reports for BHCs also aggregate data for all bank subsidiaries, so ratios reflect the operations of the lead bank versus the operations of many smaller subsidiaries.

Categories of Performance Evaluation

Ratios should be categorized according to the area of performance with which they are most closely connected. Many ratio measures can help with every area of a performance evaluation. Each can contribute something, but too many may cause confusion. Consequently, analysts use many other ratios in addition to those described in this chapter. Rather than memorizing ratios, an analyst should think conceptually about what different ratios indicate. For instance, loan loss ratios can take many different forms, but they all reveal basic information about a bank's current and expected credit risk. Although one may interpret varying measures in ways similar to the ratios discussed in this chapter, data availability, sources of industry data, or special purposes for the analysis may cause an analyst to choose one measure over another.

Overview of a Performance Analysis for a Depository Institution

Figure 6.1 outlines the major criteria for analyzing a bank's profitability. As noted in Chapters 4 and 5, Dupont analysis suggests evaluating return on equity (ROE) as a function of a bank's ROA and its financial leverage. ROA is a function of cost management, indicated by a bank's net profit margin (NPM) and its revenue management or asset utilization (AU) ratio. Asset utilization can be analyzed by looking at the ratios of interest revenue to assets and noninterest revenue to assets. The NPM

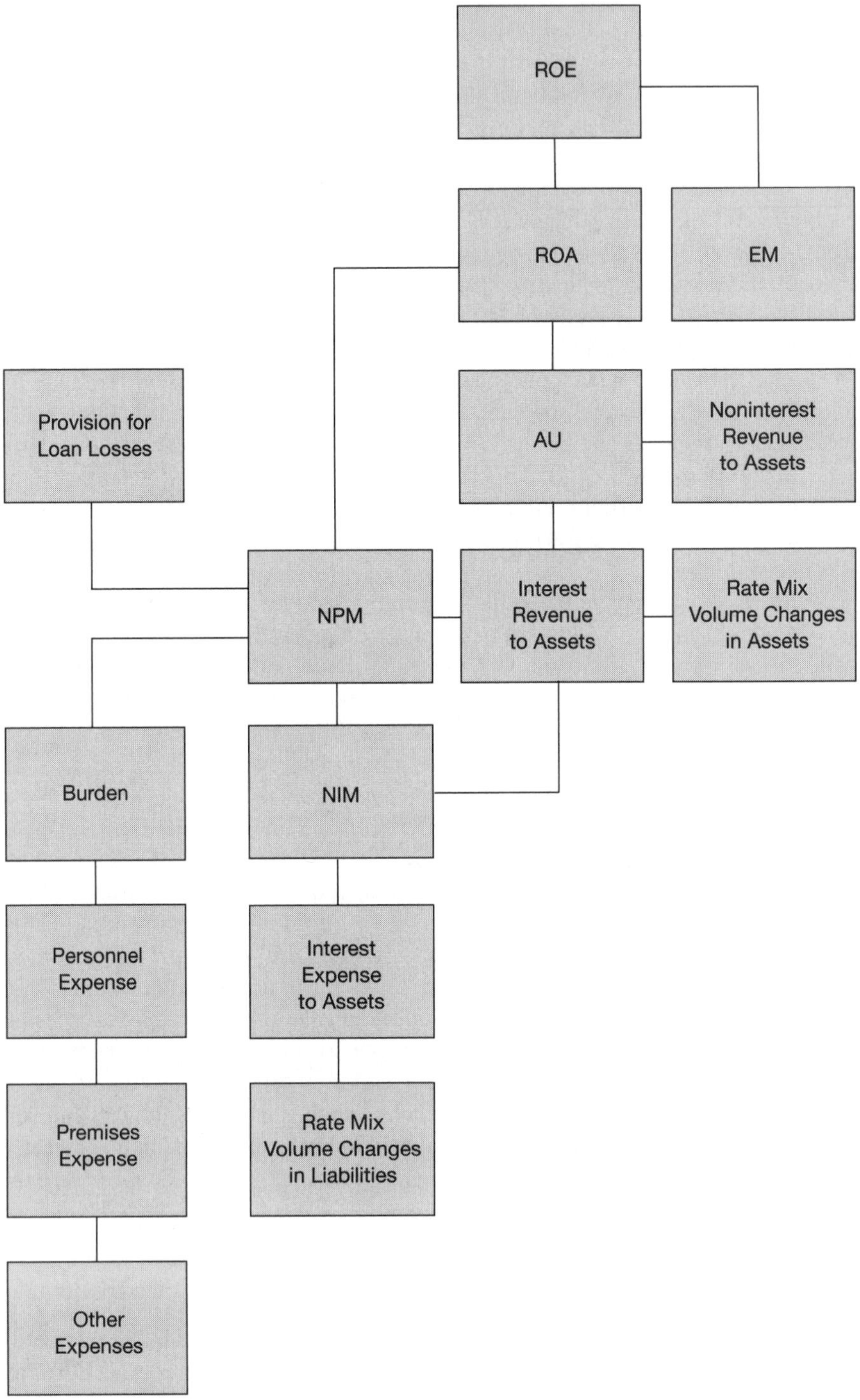

Figure 6.1   ◆   DUPONT ANALYSIS FOR DEPOSITORY INSTITUTIONS

can be analyzed in more detail by looking at the NIM, burden, PLL, and any security gains or losses or extraordinary items. NIM, as the traditional source of a bank's profitability, can be analyzed more thoroughly by analyzing relative changes in interest revenue to assets (IR) and interest expense to assets (IE). Changes in these measures are determined by changes in the bank's mix of assets and liabilities and the rates it earns and pays on individual assets and liabilities. Burden can be analyzed more thoroughly by considering different types of operating expenses and sources of noninterest revenues.

PERFORMANCE EVALUATION ILLUSTRATED

The best way to learn about a performance analysis is to do one. To illustrate a framework for calculating and interpreting financial ratios and other performance data, this section presents the financial statements and common-size statements for Wells Fargo Bank for March 1997 and March 1998.

Wells Fargo, a large, western bank headquartered in San Francisco, agreed to a $31.4 billion merger agreement with Norwest Bank of Minneapolis, Minnesota in June 1998. Wells Fargo began a unique branching scheme, putting 922 mini-branches in supermarkets by 1990. However, the bank had profitability problems in recent years. After winning a hostile takeover battle for First Interstate Bancorp in 1996, Wells Fargo struggled to integrate its own culture of a traditional, very centralized commercial lending bank with that of First Interstate, a retail bank specializing in consumer lending. Wells Fargo eliminated 12,000 jobs, creating major defections and morale problems among surviving employees. It also lost many customers who were upset about poor service during a painful integration.[5]

Table 6.1 presents the balance sheets for 1997 and 1998 for Wells Fargo Bank taken from its UBPR. Besides raw data, the table shows common-size percentages along with percentage changes, which are helpful to assess changes in the company's asset and liability mix over time. Table 6.2 presents Wells Fargo's income statements for 1997 and 1998, along with common-size percentages. Table 6.3 provides a profitability and NIM analysis of Wells Fargo in 1997 and 1998, compared to similar-size peer banks and other large California banks. Table 6.4 provides risk ratios examining different aspects of the bank's management of risks for loans, liquidity, interest rate sensitivity, capital, and operations.

Analysis of Common Size Statements

The raw and common-size balance sheets for Wells Fargo in Table 6.1 provide useful information about changes in the bank's mix of assets and liabilities between 1997 and 1998. By looking at the changes in assets, an analyst can evaluate the aggressiveness of Wells Fargo's asset mix by determining whether it has moved toward comparatively high-yield assets, such as loans, or toward liquid assets, such as cash, interest-bearing deposits, or short-term securities. Changes in asset mix may represent responses to changes in yields for different types of securities. For instance, if rates go up on one type of asset and down on another, banks may move investments from

---

[5]See Matt Murray, "Norwest, Wells Fargo Agree to a Merger," *The Wall Street Journal*, June 9, 1998, pp. A2, A6; and Cahill, "Doubts Grow."

Table 6.1 ✦ WELLS FARGO BANK NATIONAL ASSOCIATION BALANCE SHEET, MARCH 31, 1997 AND 1998 ($000)

	1998	Percentage of Assets	1997	Percentage of Assets	Percentage Change
Assets					
Cash due from banks	$ 7,972,230	9.14%	$ 6,966,399	7.61%	14.44%
Interest bearing balances	22,614	0.03	17,914	0.02	26.24
U.S. Treasury and agency securities	5,166,508	5.92	7,989,883	8.73	−35.34
Municipal securities	205,065	0.24	10,697	0.01	18.17
Foreign debt securities	137,290	0.16	135,865	0.15	1.01
Other securities	2,598,110	2.98	3,593,467	3.93	−27.70
Fed funds sold and reverse repos	**110,754**	**0.13**	**724,812**	**0.79**	**−84.72**
Trading account assets	737,172	0.85	219,561	0.24	235.75
Total investments	**8,977,513**	**10.30**	**12,692,199**	**13.86**	**29.27**
Real estate loans	26,834,390	30.77	28,206,023	30.81	−4.86
Commercial loans	19,797,153	22.70	18,213,269	19.89	8.70
Installment and credit card	6,445,455	7.39	7,159,949	7.82	−9.98
Agricultural loans	1,398,404	1.60	1,252,300	1.37	11.67
Other loans	5,430,990	6.23	4,642,863	5.07	16.98
Total loans	**59,906,392**	**68.70**	**59,474,404**	**64.96**	**0.73**
Less allowance for loan losses	1,320,119	1.51	1,389,104	1.52	−4.97
Net loans	**58,586,273**	**67.18**	**58,085,300**	**63.44**	**0.86**
Premises and equipment	1,828,134	2.10	2,010,547	2.20	−9.07
Other real estate owned	344,681	0.40	410,089	0.45	−15.95
Other assets	9,493,423	10.89	11,388,514	12.44	−16.64
Total premises, OREO, and other assets	**11,666,238**	**13.39**	**13,809,150**	**15.09**	**−15.52**
Total assets	**$87,202,254**	**100.00**	**$91,553,048**	**100.00**	**−4.75**
Average assets during quarter	87,380,369		95,660,221		
Liabilities and Net Worth					
Demand deposits	$22,658,454	25.98%	$22,851,196	24.96%	0.85%
NOW accounts	2,190,033	2.51	2,094,253	2.29	4.57
Money market deposit accounts	16,667,102	19.11	17,654,600	19.28	−5.59
Other savings accounts	11,518,279	13.21	13,186,984	14.40	−12.65
Time deposits under $100,000	10,842,139	12.43	11,349,257	12.40	−4.47
Time core deposits	**63,876,007**	**73.25**	**67,136,290**	**73.33**	**−4.86**
Time deposits of $100,000 or more	3,718,465	4.26	3,224,259	3.52	15.33
Deposits in foreign offices	582,652	0.67	1,137,241	1.24	−48.77
Total deposits	**68,177,124**	**78.18**	**71,497,790**	**78.09**	**−4.64**
Fed funds purchased and repos	2,591,623	2.97	2,103,159	2.30	23.23
Other borrowings					
Maturity < 1 year	36,921	0.04	30,503	0.03	21.04
Maturity > 1 year	181,133	0.21	539,550	0.59	−66.43
Acceptances and other liabilities	1,889,927	2.17	2,731,445	2.98	−30.80
Subordinated notes and debentures	1,366,000	1.57	996,000	1.09	37.15
Total nondeposit debt	**6,065,604**	**6.96**	**6,400,657**	**6.99**	**−5.24**
Total debt	74,242,728	85.14	77,898,447	85.09	−4.69
Equity capital	**12,959,526**	**14.86**	**13,654,601**	**14.92**	**−5.09**
(includes perpetual preferred stock)					
Total liabilities and capital	**$87,202,254**	**100.00**	**$91,553,048**	**100.00**	**−4.75**
Memo: Available for Sale Securities	8,106,973		11,729,912		

the low-yielding asset into a higher-yielding asset. Similarly, a bank may make changes in deposit mix to take advantage of falling rates for a particular type of liability. As an example, banks with large percentages of demand deposits and insured core deposits have low interest expenses. In effect, a bank's net interest margin (NIM) is determined by the respective rates, mix, and volume (size) of its assets and liabilities. To see how a bank's asset mix changes, percentage changes in balance-sheet items over time are also often calculated.

Changes in Volume and Asset and Liability Mix for Wells Fargo   The final column of Table 6.1 shows the percentage changes in balance sheet items for Wells Fargo between 1997 and 1998. Wells Fargo's total assets shrunk between 1997 and 1998 by 4.75 percent, predominantly due to reductions in investments and other assets. Investments fell 29.27 percent, while net loans rose slightly by 0.86 percent. Other assets, including premises and equipment, OREO, and other assets, fell 15.5 percent.

The figures for percentages of assets next to the raw dollar figures on the balance sheet allow comparison of mix changes. Wells Fargo changed its asset mix in 1998. Cash and due, trading securities, and municipal securities rose as a percentage of assets, while U.S. Treasury and agency securities and other securities fell. In contrast to a decline in the percentage of investments held, the percentage of net loans rose from 63.44 percent in 1997 to 67.18 percent in 1998. The loan mix changed slightly with a small rise in the percentage of commercial and other loans held. Real estate and consumer loans fell by a slight fraction, while agriculture loans rose by a slight fraction.

On the liability side, the 4.75 percent shrinkage in assets was accompanied by a decline in equity capital and deposits. Wells Fargo's equity capital declined by 5.09 percent; total deposits declined by 4.64 percent; and nondeposit borrowing declined by 5.52 percent. The mix of liabilities and equity that financed those assets stayed relatively constant as percentages of total assets. Other savings accounts declined by a small fraction, and time deposits of $100,000 or more rose by a small fraction.

With the shrinkage in the bank's asset and investment portfolio, interest revenues would be expected to fall in 1998. However, the changes in asset mix toward loans would have a positive effect on interest revenues. Wells Fargo also appears to have a favorable liability mix, with a large percentage of core deposit financing and a large percentage of noninterest paying demand deposits.

Changes in Income and Expenses for Wells Fargo   Table 6.2 reveals the effect on interest revenues and expenses of the changes in volume (the asset size of the bank) as well as changes in the asset and liability mix and rates earned. Interest revenue fell by 4.7 percent in 1998, a decline of about $72.2 million. About $57.5 million of the decline was due to lower investment revenue, associated with the shrinkage of the bank's investment portfolio by over 29 percent. Interest revenue from loans also fell by about $17.8 million. In contrast, interest expenses rose $14.7 million, or 3.2 percent, in 1998. The net effect of the lower interest revenue and higher interest expense was a fall in net interest income by over $86.9 million.

Fortunately, the bank's burden fell, with noninterest income rising $74.0 million or 14 percent, and noninterest expense falling $24.8 million or 2.4 percent. In 1997, Wells Fargo had a negative provision for loan losses (PLL), but in 1998, PLL rose to over $113.0 million. In 1997, Wells Fargo showed a gain on the sales of securities, but, in 1998, there was no gain. Consequently, despite a drop in burden of $.09 million, the net effect of a fall in interest revenues, a rise in interest ex-

Table 6.2 ✦ WELLS FARGO BANK QUARTERLY INCOME STATEMENTS, MARCH 31, 1997 AND 1998 ($000)

	1998	Percentage of Revenue	1997	Percentage of Revenue	Percentage Change
Interest Revenues					
Interest on Loans and Leases (TE)	**$1,310,346**	**63.72%**	**$1,328,100**	**64.64%**	**−1.34%**
Investment interest income (TE)	136,299	6.63	193,788	9.43	−29.67
Interest on due from banks	120	0.01	109	0.01	10.09
Interest on FFS and repos	6,002	0.29	11,976	0.58	−50.00
Trading account income	13,592	0.66	4,626	0.23	193.00
Total interest income (TE)	**1,466,360**	**71.31**	**1,538,599**	**74.89**	**−4.70**
Interest Expenses					
Interest on deposits in foreign offices	12,520	0.61	23,770	1.16	−47.33
Interest on time deposit over $100,000	48,887	2.38	41,247	2.01	18.52
Interest on all other deposits	329,379	16.02	341,839	16.64	−3.65
Interest on Fed funds purchases and repos	55,125	2.68	30,201	1.47	82.53
Interest borrowed money	4,857	0.24	5,061	0.25	−4.03
Interest on subordinated notes and debentures	25,634	1.25	19,557	0.95	31.07
Total interest expense	**476,402**	**23.17**	**461,675**	**22.47**	**3.18**
Net interest income (TE)	**989,958**	**48.14**	**1,076,924**	**52.42**	**−8.08**
Noninterest income (TE)	**589,934**	**28.69**	**515,882**	**25.11**	**14.35**
Noninterest expense	**995,123**	**48.39**	**1,019,938**	**49.64**	**−2.43**
Provision for loan and lease losses	**113,529**	**5.52**	**−2,742**	**−0.13**	**41.40**
Pretax operating income (TE)	**471,240**	**22.92**	**575,610**	**28.02**	**−18.13**
Realized gains on securities held to maturity					
Realized gains available for sale securities	17	0.00	3,574	0.17	
Pretax net operating income (TE)	471,257	22.92	575,610	28.02	
Applicable income taxes	219,120	10.66	267,595	13.02	
Net operating income	252,137	12.26	311,589	15.17	
Net extraordinary items	0		0		
Net income for quarter	**$ 252,137**	**12.26**	**$ 311,589**	**15.17**	**−19.08**
Profitability Ratios					
Net income to revenues (NPM)	12.26%		15.17%		
Annualized asset utilization	0.094		0.086		
Return on assets (ROA)	1.15		1.30		
Common equity to assets	(EM = 14.14)		(EM = 14.60)		
Return on equity (ROE)	16.27		18.98		
Cash dividends declared	$ 517,553		$ 515,992		
Dividend to net income (Dividend payout)	205.27%		165.60%		
Retained earnings	$−265,416		$−204,403		
Memo: **Total revenue**	**$2,056,294**		**$2,054,481**		

penses, and a rise in provision for loan losses was a 19 percent fall in net income, a drop of $59.45 million.

Expressing net income as a percentage of total revenues, Wells Fargo's net profit margin fell from 15.17 percent in 1997 to 12.26 percent in 1998. However, since the bank shrunk, its asset utilization (AU) based on average assets actually rose from 0.086 to 0.094. (Note that quarterly statements for asset utilization ratios must be multiplied by 4 to get the annual AU.) The net effect of the rise in AU and fall in NPM in 1998 was a decline in ROA of 15 basis points, from 1.30 percent in 1997 to 1.15 percent in 1998. With the average equity multiplier falling slightly from about 14.60 in 1997 to 14.14 in 1998, Wells Fargo's ROE (ROA × EM) fell from about 19.00 percent in 1997 to 16.27 percent in 1998.

Profitability and NIM Analysis for Wells Fargo and Peer Banks   UBPRs also report income statement items as percentages of average assets. This analysis helps to determine why ROA changed. For Wells Fargo, this information is presented at the top of Table 6.3. Information for peer banks and similar-size California banks is also provided. Calculating ratios with average assets as the denominator reduces a bias that might be introduced by using total assets figures, which could include end of year window dressing.[6]

Trend Profitability Analysis for Wells Fargo   Before comparing Wells Fargo with peer banks, trends in its own profitability relative to assets can be analyzed. As shown at the top of Table 6.3, the bank's declining size helped to raise Wells Fargo's interest income to assets (IR) ration by 0.28 percent. Interest expense to assets (IE) rose 0.25 percent, resulting in a 0.03 percent higher NIM in 1998 than in 1997. Wells Fargo's burden to assets fell 0.24 percent, with a rise in noninterest revenue to assets, despite a smaller rise in noninterest expense to assets. The ratio of provision for loan loss to assets (PLL), however, rose 0.53 percent. Since the rise in PLL was larger than the slight fall in the NIM and the fall in the burden, the operating ROA fell by 0.26 percent.

Trend NIM Analysis for Wells Fargo   The reason for the rise in IR and IE can be examined more closely by looking at changes in yields earned on assets and rates paid on liabilities, along with the change in Wells Fargo's asset and liability mix. The average yield on loans and leases fell from 8.80 percent in 1997 to 8.62 percent in 1998. The average yield on investment securities, in contrast, rose from 6.34 percent in 1997 to 6.47 percent in 1998. Also, the average tax-equivalent yield on municipal securities, which Wells Fargo had emphasized in its investments, went up dramatically from 5.91 percent in 1997 to 9.08 percent in 1998. With this movement into comparatively high-yielding assets in 1998, IR rose despite the fall in the average loan rate. Wells Fargo's mix of liabilities as a percentage of assets changed very little, but the average rate it paid on liabilities rose, resulting in the increase in IE in 1998. The bank's NIM remained stable, due to similar rises in IR and IE.

Peer Comparison of Profitability Ratios for Wells Fargo   Despite lower interest income to assets than the peer banks, Wells Fargo had a much lower IE, resulting in a higher NIM in both 1997 and 1998. However, California peers had both a higher IR and a lower IE, giving them a higher NIM than both the peers and Wells Fargo in 1998. Well Fargo's burden was not as low as the peers because of its higher ratio of noninterest expense to assets. Other California banks, however, had a higher burden because of very low noninterest revenue to assets. Wells Fargo's PLL was higher than both the peers and other California banks in 1998. Wells Fargo had a similar operating ROA to the peers because of its higher NIM despite a higher burden and PLL. Because Wells Fargo experienced a lower burden than the California

---

[6]Average assets are calculated by summing assets at the beginning of the year and the end, then dividing by 2.

Table 6.3 ✦ Peer Comparison for Profitability and NIM Analysis for Wells Fargo Bank, March 31, 1997 and 1998

Profitability Analysis Percentage of Average	1998	Peers	California Banks with Assets over $100 Million	1997	Peers
Interest income to assets (TE)	6.71%	7.23%	7.90%	6.43%	7.20%
Less interest expense	2.18	3.52	2.88	1.93	3.37
Net interest margin	**4.53**	**3.71**	**5.02**	**4.50**	**3.83**
Plus noninterest income to assets	2.70	2.20	1.02	2.16	2.02
Less noninterest expense to assets	4.56	3.43	4.19	4.26	3.46
Burden	**1.86**	**1.23**	**3.17**	**2.10**	**1.44**
Less provision for loan losses	**0.52**	**0.30**	**0.18**	**−0.01**	**0.27**
(ROA pretax operating income [TE])	**2.15**	**2.18**	**1.67**	**2.41**	**2.12**
Realized gains/losses securities	0.00	0.02	0.00	0.01	0.01
Adjusted net income after extraordinary items	1.54	1.46	1.35	1.36	1.41
ROA (net income to average assets)	**1.15**	**1.38**	**1.16**	**1.30**	**1.35**
Cash dividend to net income	**205.27**	**41.80**	**8.73**	**165.60**	**43.41**
Tier one equity to asset ratio	7.07	7.19	8.66	6.85	7.14
ROE (ROA/Equity to Assets)	**16.27**	**19.19**	**13.40**	**18.98**	**18.91**
Percentage of earning assets to average assets	**77.91**	**88.94**	**91.54**	**75.99**	**88.36**
Percentage of net loans and leases to average assets	67.10	65.40	59.57	62.33	65.67
Percentage of securities	9.83	13.88		12.81	12.75
Percentage of noninterest cash and due from banks	8.72	4.84		9.45	5.40
Percentage of premises, fixed assets and capital leases	2.09	1.18		2.16	1.26
Percentage of demand deposits	25.28	12.28		25.50	13.94
Percentage of core deposits	72.04	52.69		72.69	53.00
Yield on loans and leases (TE)	**8.62**	**8.43**		**8.80**	**8.48**
Total loans in domestic offices	8.60	8.42		8.78	8.47
Real estate loans	8.68	8.23		9.26	8.27
Commercial and industrial loans	9.33	8.04		9.35	8.10
Consumer loans	9.11	9.89		9.23	10.01
Agricultural loans	8.60	8.95		8.58	8.52
Loans in foreign offices	6.86	7.01		6.35	6.73
Yield on investment securities (TE)	**6.47**	**6.61**		**6.34**	**6.60**
U.S. Treasuries and Agencies	6.43	6.48		6.28	6.45
Municipal securities (TE)	9.08	8.19		5.91	8.70
Other debt securities	6.62	6.75		6.57	6.54
Interest-bearing bank balances	2.37	5.54		2.10	5.29
Federal funds sold and repos	5.61	5.54		2.74	5.31
Average rate on liabilities	**3.68**	**4.58**		**3.38**	**4.47**
All interest-bearing deposits	3.41	4.24		3.26	4.09
Transaction accounts	1.42	1.89		1.06	1.81
Money market deposit accounts	3.25	3.08		3.11	3.05
Other savings deposits	1.67	2.41		1.65	2.22
Time deposits over $100,000	5.20	5.43		5.12	5.28
All other time deposits	5.06	5.34		4.92	5.23
Foreign office deposits	5.35	5.35		5.19	5.17
Fed funds purchased and repos	5.41	5.30		3.77	5.14
Other borrowed money	3.72	5.54		3.63	5.58
Subordinated notes and debentures	8.10	6.86		8.27	7.02

peers despite a lower NIM, it had a higher operating ROA. After security gains and extraordinary items, the ROAs for Wells Fargo and the California banks were almost the same, but Wells Fargo had a higher ROE—16.27 percent versus 13.40 percent for the California banks—because of its higher equity multiplier (i.e., lower equity to assets ratio). Wells Fargo had a much higher dividend payout than comparable institutions in both years.

NIM Comparison with Peers and Wells Fargo   The bottom portion of Table 6.3 shows differences in asset and liability mixes and in yields earned on assets and rates paid on liabilities. These differences allow a closer examination of Wells Fargo's NIM.

Wells Fargo's lower IR relative to the peer banks is related to its lower percentage of earning assets (77.9 percent versus 88.9 percent for the peers and 91.54 percent for other California banks). Although Wells Fargo held a larger percentage of loans, it also had much larger percentages of cash and due and premises and fixed assets, as well as a smaller percentage of securities. With the exception of consumer and agricultural loans and loans in foreign offices, Wells Fargo earned higher loan rates, generating a higher average yield on its loans. Its average yield on investment securities was about 14 basis points lower than that of the peers.

Wells Fargo's lower IE resulted from a much lower average rate paid on liabilities than the peers. With the exception of MMDAs, Fed funds purchased in 1998, and subordinated debentures, all of Wells Fargo's rates were lower than those of comparable institutions. Wells Fargo had a much more favorable liability mix, as well, with a much larger percentage of demand deposits and cheaper core deposits than the peers.

Summary of Performance Analysis for Wells Fargo   In summary, Wells Fargo Bank's operating ROA fell because a rise in PLL reduced the bank's NPM in 1998. Wells Fargo's AU rose as it expanded the percentage of loans and earning assets it held, and its burden fell as the result of a rise in noninterest revenues to assets. Wells Fargo had an ROA similar to that of California banks, but lower than that of other peer banks. This was because it had a higher PLL and higher noninterest expenses to assets, despite a higher NIM.

The following sections illustrate analysis of Wells Fargo's risks associated with operating efficiency and with liquidity, loan, and interest rate risk and capital management.

Liquidity Management

As a depository institution functions as an intermediary, it takes on certain risks, removing these risks from savers. This activity encourages saving and, hence, increases the funds available to borrowers for productive uses within an economy. Thus, many risks are inherent to banking.

One function of banking is providing liquidity to depositors. Since funds can be withdrawn at any time, banks face liquidity risk. To manage this risk, they can hold short-term assets to meet liquidity needs or use liability management techniques, borrowing short-term funds as needed. The cost of holding short-term assets is lower interest income, while the cost of borrowing short-term funds is a possible rise in interest rates, increasing the bank's cost of funds. Such borrowing, or so called *purchased funds*, are also very interest-sensitive, and deposits may leave the bank at any time or not be renewed if any bad news about the bank appears.

Hence, to measure the liquidity risk of a depository institution, analysis must consider the composition of both assets and liabilities. Table 6.4 shows some commonly used measures of liquidity. As a bank becomes progressively more loaned up, that is its net loans amount to a higher proportion of total assets or deposits, its liquidity diminishes, since it cannot quickly sell or securitize loans to change its position. Also, as loans make up a rising percentage of a bank's assets, securities make up a falling percentage.

Since cash and due is generally held to meet reserve requirements, it is not often treated as a liquidity measure. However, the ratio of short-term securities (those with 1 year or shorter maturities) to assets is frequently used as a measure of short-term liquidity available on the asset side. On the liability side, the type of deposits a bank holds also determine expected future liquidity needs. Core deposits are stable liabilities. As a bank's ratio of core deposits to assets rises, its liquidity risk diminishes, since it faces a smaller threat from unexpected future withdrawals. The opposite is true of noncore deposits to assets, since these balances are interest-sensitive and may leave at any time. Frequently, the ratio of short-term securities to noncore (or purchased fund) liabilities is also used as relative measure of liquidity, with a rising ratio indicating greater liquidity. Finally, off-balance-sheet items affect a bank's future liquidity needs. For instance, unused loan commitments are likely to be drawn down in the future, so the percentage of loan commitments is a measure of these future needs.

Liquidity Risk Assessment for Wells Fargo   Examining the liquidity measures in Table 6.4, Wells Fargo seems to have been less loaned up relative to deposits than peer banks, with a similar ratio for net loans to assets. Wells Fargo had a lower percentage of short-term securities to assets, suggesting greater liquidity risk on the asset side. However, on the liability side, Wells Fargo had much lower liquidity risk, with a larger percentage of core (stable) deposits and hence a low percentage of noncore (volatile) deposits for funding. The relationship between liquidity on the asset side and that on the liability side is captured by the short-term assets to volatile liabilities ratio. This ratio is much larger for Wells Fargo than for comparable institutions, suggesting lower overall liquidity risk. Its percentage of outstanding loan commitments is only slightly larger than that of the peers.

Loan Management and Credit Risk

Credit risk assessment and monitoring is one of the most important functions of management for banks as financial intermediaries. Banks take on the credit risk that savers would otherwise experience, a necessary risk inherent in banking. Similarly, increasingly risky loans should pay progressively higher loan rates to compensate for this risk. If a bank has a loan portfolio composed of risky loans, but it earns lower rates than its peers, the bank is not properly pricing its loans.

Some types of loans have more credit risk than others by their nature. For instance, commercial real estate loans are more risky than home mortgage loans. Often, commercial real estate loans depend for repayment on revenues projected after shopping malls or apartment buildings have been built. If the economy goes into recession, projections of low vacancy rates may lose meaning, and borrowers' revenue streams may dry up, threatening loan repayment. Consumer loans also often expose banks to higher bad debt losses on average than other types of loans. Differences in net losses by types of loans for Wells Fargo and its peers appear in Table

Table 6.4   ✦   RISK MEASURES FOR WELLS FARGO BANK, MARCH 31, 1997 AND 1998

Liquidity Risk	1998	Peers	1997	Peers
Net loans and leases to assets	67.18%	65.50%	63.44%	65.57%
Net loans and leases to deposits	85.93	93.65	81.24	92.28
Core deposits to total assets	73.25	52.22	73.33	52.41
Noncore deposits to total assets	9.00	34.87	7.72	33.40
Short-term securities to assets	1.28	4.92	1.79	6.42
Short-term securities to volatile liabilities	129.82	67.49	110.00	75.99
Percentage of outstanding loan committments	45.04	41.71	42.27	41.57
Credit Risk				
Net loss to average total loans	0.50	0.41	0.56	0.40
Noncurrent loans to gross loans	0.91	0.79	1.23	0.88
Earnings coverage to net loss	7.59	9.28	6.78	9.91
Loan loss provision to average assets	0.52	0.30	−0.01	0.27
Loan loss allowance to total loans	2.20	1.63	2.34	1.80
Loan loss allowance to net losses	4.31	4.32	4.13	4.92
Loan loss allowance to nonaccrual loans	2.99	3.29	2.36	3.49
Net Losses by Type of Loans				
Real estate loans	−0.07	0.03	−0.08	0.02
Commercial and industrial loans	0.92	0.20	0.88	0.14
Consumer loans	2.05	1.85	1.73	1.71
Agricultural loans	0.14	−0.01	0.10	−0.03
Lease financing	0.82	0.13	0.87	0.09
All other loans and leases	0.27	0.04	1.26	0.02
Interest Rate Risk				
Loans and securities over 3 years to assets	17.09	25.78	NA	NA
Liabilities over 3 years to assets	0.73	2.01	NA	NA
Net 3-year position	16.36	23.25	NA	NA
Loans and securities over 1 year	26.72	37.86	NA	NA
Liabilities over 1 year	3.03	8.02	NA	NA
Net over 1-year position	23.69	29.23	NA	NA
Mortgage loans and pass-through to assets	11.44	16.22	NA	NA
Total loans and securities over 15 years	2.34	4.15	NA	NA
Total loans and securities 5–15 years	9.07	8.96	NA	NA
Capital Risk				
Equity capital to assets	7.07	7.19	6.85	7.14
Cash dividends to net income	205.27	41.80	165.60	43.41
Growth rate equity capital	−5.09	26.33	230.93	18.14
Equity growth less asset growth	−0.34	3.54	139.45	0.34
Operational Risk				
Efficiency ratio[a]	62.99	NA	65.40	NA
Total overhead expense to assets	4.56	3.43	4.26	3.46
Average personnel expense per employee ($000)	$50.79	$48.62	$48.50	$46.84
Personnel expense to assets	1.85	1.47	1.81	1.47
Occupancy expense to assets	0.82	0.42	0.75	0.44

[a]Noninterest expense/(Net interest income—Noninterest income)

6.4. Consumer loans had the highest net loss rate. However, Wells Fargo had a low percentage (7.39 percent) of consumer loans.

Other UBPR ratios deal with past, current, and pending losses. Net losses or charge-offs are dollar losses written off for loans that are uncollectable, less recoveries of charge-offs that are repaid. Nonperforming loans are loans currently experiencing some repayment problems. Nonaccrual (noncurrent) loans are those currently not paying interest. Past-due loans are loans for which borrowers have not made interest and principal payments 90 days after due dates. Ratios of these items to total loans or average assets are frequently used to measure current and past loan losses. Loss provision to average assets is a proxy for expected losses in the future. Loan loss allowance relative to losses or nonaccrual loans gives information on how adequately a bank's reserves protect it against future losses. Earnings coverage to net loss provides a measure of the bank's ability to cover its loan losses from current earnings.

Credit Risk Assessment for Wells Fargo   Table 6.4 shows that Wells Fargo had slightly higher percentages of net losses and noncurrent loans than peer banks had. It also had a higher percentage of loans than its peers. Hence, it appears to have experienced slightly higher credit risk. Wells Fargo appears to have been reserving more than its peers, as well, with a higher provision for loan losses and loan allowance relative to losses. UBPR data provides details on loan mix that amounts to additional indications of credit risk. Although not shown here, Wells Fargo's UBPR indicates that most of its real estate loans are low-risk home mortgages versus higher-risk commercial real estate loans.

Interest Rate Risk Management

Chapter 5 discussed interest rate risk by detailing a depository institution's repricing gap. Analysts apply other, more comprehensive measures of this risk, as well, such as a bank's duration gap, discussed later in Chapter 16. A bank's repricing gap as a percentage of assets is a frequently used interest rate risk indicator for a given time period. This measure indicates reinvestment or repricing risk for a bank, which suggests the likelihood that a bank's NIM will change with a change in market interest rates. Other measures include a bank's market value risk, the threat that the market value of assets will falling more than the market value of liabilities with a rise in interest rates, reducing the market value of equity.

Table 6.4 shows interest rate risk measures reported in recent UBPRs. Early UBPRs reported repricing gaps, as discussed in Chapter 5. New UBPRs give measures of potential market value risk by reporting the percentage of relatively long-term assets less the percentage of long-term loans. Table 6.4 separately reports these differences for assets and liabilities with maturities longer than 1 year and longer than 3 years. Increasing positions suggest that the maturities of assets are lengthening relative to liabilities. Hence, a rise in rates seems likely to bring a larger the fall in assets than in liabilities, and therefore a fall in the market value of the bank's equity, which amounts to greater interest rate risk. Similarly, the table gives the percentage of long-term assets. The percentage of mortgage loans and pass-through securities is used as a measure of potential reinvestment risk due to prepayment for the banks holding these securities if falling rates create favorable conditions.

Interest Rate Risk Assessment for Wells Fargo   Wells Fargo had a slightly lower net position of long-term assets less long-term liabilities for both the 1-year and 3-year categories, suggesting slightly lower interest rate risk, than the peers. Similarly, Wells Fargo held fewer securities with maturities over 15 years and about the same percentage of securities in the 5-to-15-year range. Wells Fargo had a lower percentage of mortgage loans and pass-through securities to assets, as well. The stability of Wells Fargo's NIM from 1997 to 1998 also suggests lower interest rate risk.

Capital Management

Depository institutions by their nature have high financial leverage. Higher returns on equity are generated in this way, but higher financial leverage also implies greater insolvency risk. Capital risk ratios include equity capital to assets, the growth rate of equity relative to the growth rate in assets, and the bank's dividend payout ratio, among others. If a bank's equity growth rate is less than the growth rate in assets, its equity is gradually being eroded. Similarly, if high dividend payouts are made, the bank is retaining less earnings for equity. The larger the other types of risks that a bank has, the higher its capital ratio should be.

Capital Risk Assessment for Wells Fargo   As shown in Table 6.4, Wells Fargo had a similar ratio of equity capital to assets to the peer banks, and its equity to assets ratio rose slightly in 1998. Recently, however, its equity growth has fallen short of the growth in assets. This trend indicates a possible future deterioration in capital. Also, Wells Fargo has been paying out enormous dividends relative to net income, relying on raising external capital for its equity growth.

Operating Efficiency

Banks incur significant operating expenses for functions like clearing and processing millions of checks each day and administering loans. These operating divisions are often called the heart of a bank. A bank's burden is a measure of the effectiveness of its expense control relative to its productivity in producing noninterest revenues.

Table 6.4 shows several operating risk ratios. One of the most popular is a bank's efficiency ratio, equal to total noninterest expenses divided by the sum of net interest income plus noninterest income. This ratio represents the fraction of cost that operating expenses represent for each dollar of revenue the bank produces, often listed as a percentage. The efficiency ratios of the largest ten banks for the second quarter of 1998, as reported by Keefe Bruyette & Woods, Inc., are:[7]

Bank	Ratio
First Chicago NBD	53%
First Union	56
NationsBank	57
Fleet Financial Group	57
Chase Manhattan	58
BankAmerica	59
Banc One	62
Citicorp	66
J. P. Morgan	72
Bankers Trust	82

[7]As reported in Cahill, "Doubts Grow," see footnote 1.

McCoy, Frieder, and Hedges (1994) analyzed 50 large regional and money-center banks and found that the most efficient of them had mean efficiency ratios of 55 percent in 1998 and 59 percent in 1992. The highest-cost banks had means of 69 percent in 1988 and 66 percent in 1992, with greater improvement in efficiency ratios for the least-efficient banks. Banks have been particularly concerned about improving their efficiency ratios and improving measurement of efficiency over the last decade.[8]

Operating Efficiency for Wells Fargo   In 1998, Wells Fargo had an efficiency ratio of 62.9 percent, showing improvement from the 65.4 percent ratio in 1997. However, all other operating efficiency ratios rose from 1997 to 1998. Wells Fargo's overhead expense to assets, occupancy expense to assets, personnel expense per employee, and personnel expense to assets all were higher than its peers' ratios, indicating lower operating efficiency for Wells Fargo.

Volatility of Earnings

Another measure of a depository institution's risk is the volatility of its NIM, ROA, and ROE, as defined by their standard deviations over time. Since UBPRs encompass only the previous 3 years, these measures could not be calculated for Wells Fargo without going back to earlier reports. In 1997 and 1998, the bank had a stable NIM and a fairly stable ROA. However, it is difficult to access overall volatility in returns for just 2 years.

Summary of Risk Analysis for Wells Fargo

In summary, Wells Fargo appears to have experienced similar liquidity and interest rate risk to its peers. Wells Fargo had larger net losses on loans, suggesting higher credit risk, and it appeared to be making higher provisions for future loan losses. Equity to asset ratios were similar to those of peers, suggesting similar capital risk. However, dividend payout ratios in excess earnings suggest a disturbing trend. Operating efficiency is lower for Wells Fargo than for its peers, as measured by higher expenses for both occupancy and personnel.

FURTHER ANALYSIS: FIRST NATIONAL BANK OF MARYLAND

To consolidate the expertise you gained in analyzing Wells Fargo's performance, try another analysis of the First National Bank of Maryland. This large, commercial bank in Baltimore, Maryland, held about $7 billion in assets in 1994. It is a subsidiary of a large bank holding company, Allied Irish Banks, Ltd. of Dublin, Ireland. Its peer group includes banks with assets of $3 billion to $10 billion.

Table 6.5 provides common size statements and balance sheets for First National Bank of Maryland, along with average yields earned on assets and rates paid on liabilities. Table 6.6 analyzes profitability as a percentage of average assets and offers additional detail on the types of loans and deposits that First National holes, along with its noninterest expenses. Table 6.7 provides risk measures. Try a profitability and risk

---

[8]John B. McCoy, Larry A. Frieder, and Robert B. Hedges, Jr., *Bottomline Banking: Meeting the Challenges for Survival & Success* (Chicago: Probus, 1994).

Table 6.5 ✦ Summary Performance Ratio Measures Example for First National Bank of Maryland, September 30, 1993 and 1994

Overall Profitability Ratios	1994	Peers	1993	Peers
Return on equity (net income to equity)	**15.25%**	**17.26%**	**18.80%**	**17.32%**
Return on assets (net income to assets)	**1.02%**	**1.30%**	**1.13%**	**1.28%**
Equity multiplier (assets to equity)	14.95	13.28	16.64	13.53
Common Size Income Statement to Assets				
Interest revenue (tax equivalent)	6.21%	6.61%	6.47%	6.76%
Interest expense	2.34	2.57	2.30	2.49
Net interest margin (NIM)	**3.87**	**4.04**	**4.17**	**4.27**
Noninterest revenue	1.96	1.62	1.80	1.66
Noninterest expense	4.34	3.67	4.05	3.79
Types of noninterest expenses				
Personnel expense	2.44	1.46	2.23	1.49
Occupancy expense	0.74	0.44	0.69	0.46
Other operating expense	1.17	1.66	1.13	1.74
Burden	**2.38**	**2.05**	**2.25**	**2.13**
Provision for loan losses	**0.04**	**0.17**	**0.24**	**0.37**
Net income before gains and taxes	1.45	1.82	1.68	1.77
Gains/losses on securities	0.21	0.00	0.36	0.02
Net income after taxes	**1.02**	**1.30**	**1.13**	**1.28**
Common Size Balance Sheet to Assets				
Assets				
Deposits at other banks	0.08	0.12	0.10	0.35
Fed funds sold and repos	5.83	2.56	3.43	2.85
Securities	**31.49**	**20.07**	**34.38**	**22.57**
Gross loans and leases	53.24	61.51	51.88	60.46
Allowance for loan and lease losses	1.57	1.30	1.67	1.48
Net loans and leases	**51.67**	**61.08**	**50.21**	**59.98**
Total loans and leases (as a percentage of gross loans and leases)				
Real estate loans	48.31	43.70	46.03	42.82
Commercial loans	28.14	20.70	30.10	22.37
Consumer loans	6.57	23.27	8.05	22.52
Other loans	16.98	12.23	15.82	12.29
Liabilities				
Demand deposits	22.96	14.94	23.51	15.09
Total deposits	79.35	74.17	79.32	77.14
Core deposits	69.28	66.09	71.31	68.92
Volatile liabilities	20.55	23.35	20.65	21.54
Average Yields Earned on Different Types of Assets				
Average yield on securities	**6.18**	**5.74**	**7.28**	**6.29**
Average yield on loans and leases	**7.44**	**8.05**	**7.55**	**8.19**
Average yield on real estate loans	7.58	7.88	7.78	7.98
Average yield on commercial loans	8.08	7.50	7.48	7.09
Average yield on consumer loans	7.85	9.26	8.93	9.95
Average Rates Paid on Different Types of Liabilities				
Average rate on interest-bearing deposits	**3.23**	**3.23**	**4.31**	**3.59**
Average rate on large uninsured CDs	4.56	4.05	3.56	3.87
Average rate on other borrowed funds	6.59	3.88	4.35	3.14
Average rate on all interest-bearing liabilities	**3.47**	**3.39**	**3.45**	**3.24**

analysis, including a trend and peer comparison. Once you've done this analysis, read further and see how your analysis compares with the one presented here.

Performance Comparison to Peers

Using the analysis sequence shown in Figure 6.1, begin by comparing ROE, ROA, and EM. Table 6.6 gives an ROE for First National Bank of 15.25 percent versus 17.26 percent for peer banks. Its ROE was lower despite a higher equity multiplier of 14.95 versus 13.28 for the peers. Hence, the lower ROA (1.02 percent versus 1.30 percent for the peers) was responsible for the lower ROE.

This finding calls for further analysis of ROA. UBPRs do not report net profit margin and asset utilization, but they do provide common size income statements and balance sheets. This data allows inference of the cost and revenue management performance compared to its peers. The first points of comparison will be NIM, PLL, and burden.

The bank's NIM was 3.87 percent versus 4.04 percent for the peers. The 17 basis point deficiency resulted from First National's 40 basis point shortfall in interest revenue to assets (IR) compared to the peers, offset somewhat by interest expense to assets (IE), which was 23 basis points lower than that of the peers. The PLL for First National was only 0.04 percent versus 0.17 percent for the peers. Noninterest income to assets was 34 basis points higher for First National (1.96 percent versus 1.62 percent). Noninterest expense to assets, however, was 67 basis points higher (4.34 percent versus 3.67 percent). First National also had security gains of 0.21 percent of assets compared to none for the peers. Hence, First National Bank's lower ROA is the result of a lower NIM resulting from lower interest revenues to assets, together with a much higher ratio of noninterest expenses to assets.

Analyzing asset utilization, First National's lower interest revenue to assets was related to its lower percentage of net loans and leases (55.7 percent vs. 62.0 percent for the peers). First National had a larger percentage of securities (31 percent versus about 20 percent for the peers). Its loan mix was predominantly made up of commercial and real estate loans, while the peers held a larger percentage of consumer loans. First National's loan portfolio yielded a lower average rate: 7.44 percent versus the 8.05 percent average loan yield for the peers. The combination of a less aggressive loan mix, fewer loans and more securities, and lower average rates on loans resulted in First National's lower interest revenue to assets and lower NIM.

One caveat deserves attention. Maryland was undergoing a recession during this period, which inhibited loan demand. First National's less aggressive loan mix may be related to differences in economic conditions relative to those faced by other banks around the country of similar size.

First National's lower interest expense can be explained by a more favorable liability mix than its peers, with a larger percentage of demand deposits (22.96 percent versus 14.94 percent), larger percentage of inexpensive core deposits (69 percent versus 66 percent), and fewer volatile liabilities (20.55 percent versus 23.35 percent). Its average rate on deposits of 3.23 percent was the same as its peers, but its average rate on all interest-bearing liabilities was slightly higher: 3.47 percent versus 3.39 percent.

Closer analysis of noninterest expense to assets requires another look at the common size income statement. First National had a much higher personnel expense to average assets than its peers (2.44 percent versus 1.46 percent). Its occupancy expense to average assets is also higher (0.74 percent versus 0.44 percent).

Table 6.6 ✦ PROFITABILITY ANALYSIS: MIX AND RATE DATA FOR FIRST NATIONAL BANK OF MARYLAND, SEPTEMBER 30, 1992–1994 FINANCIAL RATIOS AND COMMON SIZE FINANCIAL STATEMENTS

Profitability Ratios	1994	Peers	1993	Peers	1992	Peers
Return on equity	**15.25%**	**17.26%**	**18.80%**	**17.32%**	**18.06%**	**17.92%**
Return on assets	1.02	1.30	1.13	1.28	1.10	1.31
Equity multiplier	14.95	13.28	16.64	13.53	16.42	13.68
Percentage of Average Assets						
Interest income (TE)	6.21%	6.61%	6.47%	6.76%	6.40%	6.69%
Interest expense	2.34	2.57	2.30	2.49	2.28	2.46
Net interest margin	**3.87**	**4.04**	**4.17**	**4.27**	**4.12**	**4.23**
Noninterest income	1.96	1.62	1.80	1.66	1.83	1.70
Noninterest expense	4.34	3.67	4.05	3.79	4.08	3.81
Burden	**2.38**	**2.05**	**2.25**	**2.13**	**2.25**	**2.11**
Provision for loan losses	**0.04**	**0.17**	**0.24**	**0.37**	**0.20**	**0.34**
Pretax operating ROA	1.45	1.82	1.68	1.77	1.67	1.90
Gains/losses on securities	0.21	0.00	0.36	0.02	0.27	0.02
Taxes	0.64	0.52	0.91	0.51	0.84	0.49
Return on assets	**1.02**	**1.30**	**1.13**	**1.28**	**1.10**	**1.31**
Asset Classes as a Percentage of Average Assets						
Interest-bearing bank balances	0.08	0.12	0.10	0.35	0.08	0.35
Fed funds sold and resales	5.83	2.56	3.43	2.85	3.37	2.93
Securities	**31.49**	**20.07**	**34.38**	**22.57**	**34.66**	**23.12**
Loans and leases	53.24	61.51	51.88	60.46	51.81	59.80
Allowance for loan losses	1.57	1.30	1.67	1.48	1.65	1.44
Net loans and leases	**51.67**	**61.08**	**50.21**	**59.98**	**50.17**	**59.30**
Summary loan composition as a Percentage of gross loans and leases						
Real estate loans	48.31	43.70	46.03	42.82	46.53	42.89
Commercial loans	28.14	20.70	30.10	22.37	29.77	22.29
Consumer loans	6.57	23.37	8.05	22.52	7.85	22.41
Other loans	16.98	12.23	15.82	12.29	15.85	12.41
Average yield on loans and leases	**7.44**	**8.05**	**7.55**	**8.19**	**7.51**	**8.17**
Real estate loans	7.58	7.88	7.78	7.98	7.76	8.02
Commercial loans	8.08	7.50	7.48	7.09	7.55	7.07
Consumer loans	7.85	9.26	8.93	9.95	8.61	9.90
Average yield on securities	**6.18**	**5.74**	**7.28**	**6.29**	**7.34**	**6.14**
Summary Liability Composition as a Percentage of Average Assets						
Demand deposits	**22.96**	**14.94**	**23.51**	**15.09**	**23.77**	**15.36**
Total core deposits	**69.28**	**66.09**	**71.31**	**68.92**	**71.33**	**68.52**
Total deposits	79.35	74.17	79.32	77.14	79.65	76.69
Volatile liabilities	**20.55**	**23.35**	**20.65**	**21.54**	**20.53**	**21.91**
Average rate on interest-bearing deposit	**3.23**	**3.23**	**4.31**	**3.59**	**4.50**	**3.58**
Average rate on large CDs	4.56	4.05	3.56	3.87	3.80	3.82
Average rate on other borrowed funds	6.59	3.88	4.35	3.14	4.03	3.10
Average rate on all interest-bearing funds	**3.47**	**3.39**	**3.45**	**3.24**	**3.44**	**3.21**
Types of Noninterest Expenses as Percentage of Assets						
Personnel expense	**2.44**	**1.46**	**2.23**	**1.49**	**2.22**	**1.48**
Occupancy expense	0.74	0.44	0.69	0.46	0.70	0.45
Other operating expense	1.17	1.66	1.13	1.74	1.16	1.75
Total overhead expense	**4.34**	**3.67**	**4.05**	**3.79**	**4.08**	**3.81**

The net effect is a much higher noninterest expense to assets of 4.34 percent versus 3.67 percent.

In summary, First National's ROA fell short of the average for its peers because of: (1) lower asset utilization (weak interest revenues to assets because of a less aggressive asset mix and lower yields earned on assets), and (2) lower operating efficiency (high personnel expenses and occupancy expenses relative to average assets). First National had advantages over peers by maintaining a more favorable deposit mix and higher noninterest revenues to assets. First National's less favorable asset mix may be related to a recession in Maryland at the time.

Review of Trends

Table 6.6 also suggests trends for First National Bank of Maryland between 1993 and 1994. ROA fell 12 basis points during that time. The income statement indicates that rates fell in 1994, resulting in falling interest income and interest expense to assets. The bank's NIM fell from 4.16 percent to 3.87 percent, 29 basis points, because interest revenues to assets fell 25 basis points, while interest expense to assets rose 4 basis points. Noninterest revenue to assets rose 16 basis points, but noninterest expense to assets rose more, 29 basis points, resulting in a rise in the bank's burden of 13 basis points. Its provision for loan losses fell 20 basis points. The net effect of the rise in noninterest expense, fall in NIM, rise in noninterest revenue, and fall in the provision in loan losses was a 12 basis point fall in ROA.

Again, trends in noninterest expenses indicate problems with cost management which reduced profits. The decline in interest revenues to assets over time also indicates an asset utilization problem. First National's percentage of net loans to assets rose slightly in 1994, and its mix changed, as well, with a 2 percent rise in real estate loans, a 2 percent fall in commercial loans, and a slight fall in consumer loans. With the exception of the rate on commercial loans, the average yield earned on loans fell, resulting in the decline in interest revenues. Since interest revenues fell more than interest expenses to assets with this drop in rates, First National Bank may have had a positive funding gap (more rate-sensitive assets than rate-sensitive liabilities).

Caveats for Analysis of First National Bank of Maryland

As noted in the preceding analysis, a simple look at comparisons between a bank and its peers may miss important aspects, such as differences in the economic environment facing a bank and those of its peers. Also, the analyst needs to be aware of the current interest rate environment. Although First National Bank of Maryland maintained a positive funding gap, placing it at comparatively high risk if interest rates continued to fall, its risk would decline if interest rates were to rise.

Comparisons should refer to banks of similar size, since large and small banks have different types of operations. However, peer comparison can employ wide size categories. For instance, First National of Maryland, with $7 billion in assets, is here compared to banks ranging from $3 billion to $10 billion, which can differ in many important ways. Although regulations across states are now more homogeneous than before interstate branching became the norm, at the time of this analysis, Maryland allowed only limited branching, which could affect First National's operating expenses relative to banks in free branching states. Also, a bank's emphasis on consumer lending, commercial lending, or diversified lending can affect its operations relative to peers.

Risk Comparison

Risk ratios for First National Bank are presented in Table 6.7.

Credit Risk   First National had lower credit risk than its peers, indicated by a lower percentage of net loans and leases to assets and a lower loan loss provision to average assets. Its loan loss allowance to total loans, nonaccrual loans, and net losses are much higher than those of its peers, indicating that it is reserving well for future loan losses. Its earnings coverage to net losses is also higher, with a lower ratio of net losses to loans. First National also has a smaller growth rate in loans than its peers.

Reviewing trends, loan loss allowances appear to have been rising, noncurrent loans were falling, and earnings coverage was rising from 1993. First National's percentage of loans rose slightly, and loan growth increased in 1994.

Interest Rate Risk   Table 6.7 reports interest rate risk measures only for 1994. First National had a positive funding gap as a percentage of average assets of about 11 percent for both 3-month and 12-month periods, compared to about a −6 percent funding gap to assets for these periods for the peer banks. Thus, First National is exposed to more interest rate risk if rates fall than the peer banks. As noted in the performance analysis, interest revenues fell more than interest expenses, resulting in a lower NIM, for this reason. First National appears to have been positioning itself to benefit if rates started to rise in 1995.

Liquidity Risk   First National had a lower percentage of loans, a larger percentage of securities, and fewer volatile liabilities (20.54 percent versus 24.72 percent) than its peers, indicating lower liquidity risk.

Its ratio of temporary securities less volatile liabilities to assets was lower than that of its peers (−8.01 percent versus −13.58 percent), indicating less liquidity risk on both the asset and liability side. First National had a larger contingent liquidity exposure, however, indicated by a larger percentage of unused loan commitments and a larger percentage of standby letters of credit relative to assets than its peers. Trends indicate a rise in temporary securities. Otherwise, ratios are pretty much the same in both years relative to peers.

Capital Risk   First National Bank had a lower equity to assets (Tier 1) ratio than its peers (6.69 percent versus 7.53 percent). However, it also had a lower dividend payout ratio (27 percent versus 42 percent). First National's risk-based capital ratios were all above the regulatory minimums but lower than those of peers. Tier 1 to risk-based assets was 8.32 percent versus 10.66 percent for the peers, and total Tier 1 and Tier 2 capital to risk-based assets was 10.55 percent versus 12.51 percent. Trends indicate an improvement in capital ratios and a higher growth rate in equity capital in 1994.

Overall Analysis Summary

First National had lower liquidity and credit risk than the peers, but it showed somewhat more capital and interest rate risk. Its capital ratios, however, were well above regulatory minimums, and its interest rate risk did not appear to be an inordinate threat. Also, risk ratios had been improving over time.

Table 6.7 ✦ SUMMARY OF RISK MEASURES FOR FIRST NATIONAL BANK OF MARYLAND, SEPTEMBER 30, 1993 AND 1994

Credit Risk Measures	1994	Peers	1993	Peers
Net loans and leases to assets	51.67%	61.08%	50.21%	59.98%
Loan loss provision to average total loans and leases	0.08	0.27	0.52	0.61
Loan loss allowance to total loans and leases	2.73	2.09	3.11	2.50
Loan loss allowance to nonaccrual loans	2.88	3.14	1.53	2.07
Loan loss allowance to net losses	35.17	7.31	10.42	5.13
Noncurrent loans and leases to gross loans and leases	1.02	1.02	2.15	1.82
Earnings coverage to net losses	30.20	13.52	11.25	7.49
Net loss to average loans and leases	0.08	0.27	0.31	0.53
Growth rate in net loans and leases	11.34	13.56	3.23	7.01
Liquidity Ratios				
Net loans and leases to assets	51.67	61.08	50.21	59.98
Net loans and leases to total deposits	69.54	85.08	63.00	80.53
Securities with maturities less than 1 year to total assets	12.53	10.57	5.04	11.61
Volatile liabilities to assets	20.54	24.72	19.99	22.82
Core deposits to assets	69.14	64.36	71.79	67.48
(Securities with maturities less than 1 year volatile liabilities) to assets	−8.01	−13.58	−14.95	−10.31
Unused loan and lease commitments to assets	33.64	27.39	30.17	23.87
Standby letters of credit to assets	5.55	1.84	5.16	2.07
Interest Rate Risk				
(Rate earned on sensitive assets − rate paid on sensitive liabilities) to assets				
Within 3 months	11.27	−6.00	NA	NA
Within 1 year	11.19	−5.62	NA	NA
Rate earned on sensitive assets to rate paid on sensitive liabilities				
Within 3 months	1.36	0.854	NA	NA
Within 1 year	1.298	0.90	NA	NA
Capital Risk				
Equity (Tier 1 capital) average assets	6.69	7.53	6.01	7.39
Cash dividends to net income	27.04	42.42	38.46	36.44
Tier 1 capital to risk-weighted assets	8.32	10.66	8.10	10.60
Tier 1 and Tier 2 capital to risk-weighed assets	10.55	12.51	10.52	12.65
Growth rate in Tier 1 equity capital	8.12	9.37	6.19	14.65
Growth rate in assets	0.03	9.22	7.91	7.81
Equity growth less asset growth rate	8.09	0.86	−1.72	6.04
Operating Efficiency Measures				
Average personnel expense per employee ($000)	$50.09	$36.47	$43.45	$35.41
Assets per employee ($ million)	$ 2.1	$ 2.66	$ 2.04	$ 2.55
Total overhead expense to assets	4.34%	3.67%	4.05%	3.79%
Personnel expense to average assets	2.44%	1.46%	2.23%	1.49%
Occupancy expense to average assets	0.74%	0.44%	0.69%	0.46%

Given the economic situation at the time in Maryland, First National appeared to have low asset utilization but also low credit risk. Banks often face temptations to take on risky loans during such periods to make up for lower loan demand by their best customers. First National resisted this temptation. First National's chief problem appeared to be its high operating risk, caused by poor efficiency relative to peers. Otherwise, the bank appeared to be a profitable enterprise with a relatively low overall risk profile.

SUMMARY

Financial performance evaluation for a depository institution is a multifaceted procedure involving ratio analysis, common size financial statements, trend analysis, and consideration of additional data not always found in published financial reports. Analysts look behind the reported numbers, because financial statements are prepared using accounting rules that may disguise important developments. Relationships among different financial ratios and between financial and nonfinancial data must also be considered.

Integrated models, such as the Dupont analysis model presented in Figure 6.1, help observers to analyze and determine exactly why a bank's performance has improved or deteriorated in comparison to peers or its own past record. Return on equity is decomposed as a function of a bank's cost management (as measured by its net profit margin), its revenue management (as measured by its asset utilization), and its financial leverage (as measured by its equity multiplier). Further analysis of net profit margin can pinpoint cost problems by focusing on net interest margin, burden, and provision for loan losses as a percentage of total assets or revenues. A bank's net Interest Margin can be examined more closely by reviewing its asset mix and the yields it earns on assets, both determinants of interest revenue to assets, and its liability mix and rates paid, which determine its interest expense to assets.

Trend analysis shows whether the depository's performance has changed over time, a judgment as important as knowing the current position of the institution. Analysts should also look at off-balance-sheet items that may affect projections of future performance.

This chapter focused on commercial banks. However, the financial analysis methods discussed apply also to thrifts (savings and loans and savings banks) and to credit unions (CUs). Thrifts and CUs will be discussed in greater detail in Chapter 7.

Questions

1. Using the Dupont analysis method laid out in Figure 6.1, explain what indicators an analyst considers to evaluate a bank's profitability.
2. Explain how rate, mix, and volume of assets and liabilities affect a bank's NIM.
3. Explain different types of risks for a bank and how they can be analyzed. Why is trend analysis especially important in evaluation of credit risk ratios?
4. Why has enhancing operating efficiency gained importance in recent years? What does a bank's efficiency ratio tell an analyst? How much does the efficiency ratio of a high-performance bank differ from that of a poor performer?

Problems

1. Do a financial analysis for NationsBank compared to its peers in 1994, given the information in Table 6.8. Why was NationsBank's ROA higher than the average of its peers in 1994? Be sure to do a detailed analysis, as shown in Figure 6.1, and give a thorough explanation why it had a higher NIM.
2. Do a risk analysis for NationsBank compared to its peers in 1994, including analysis of credit risk, interest rate risk, liquidity risk, capital risk, and operating risk using the information in Table 6.9.
3. Using Tables 6.8 and 6.9, do a trend profitability and credit analysis for the period 1993 to 1994. Why did NationsBank's ROA and NIM rise in 1994? Give a very precise analysis following Figure 6.1.
4. Do the same analysis as for Colorado National Bank as you completed for NationsBank, based on data shown in Tables 6.10 and 6.11.
5. Do the same analysis for Provident Bank of Maryland, based on data in Tables 6.12 and 6.13.
6. Look at the UBPR in Appendix 6A. What additional useful information does it provide? Based on this report, what additional information would you add to the analysis of NationsBank that you did not mention in your work on Problems 1 through 3?

Table 6.8 ✦ FINANCIAL ANALYSIS FOR NATIONS BANK, SEPTEMBER 30, 1993 AND 1994

Overall Profitability Ratios	1994	Peers	1993	Peers
Return on equity (net income to equity)	16.29%	16.41%	5.56%	17.32%
Return on assets (net income to assets)	1.43	1.14	1.13	1.28
Equity multiplier (assets to equity)	11.39	14.39	16.64	13.53
Common Size Income Statement to Assets				
Interest revenue (tax equivalent)	6.34%	6.25%	5.33%	6.76%
Interest expense	2.28	2.47	2.21	2.49
Net interest margin (NIM)	**4.06**	**3.78**	**3.12**	**4.27**
Noninterest revenue	1.65	1.87	1.05	1.66
Noninterest expense	3.91	3.72	3.41	3.79
Types of noninterest expenses				
Personnel expense	1.50	1.59	1.05	1.49
Occupancy expense	0.51	0.50	0.39	0.46
Other operating expense	1.89	1.59	1.97	1.74
Burden	**2.26**	**1.85**	**2.36**	**2.13**
Provision for loan losses	**−0.71**	**0.15**	**0.21**	**0.37**
Net income before gains and taxes	2.51	1.79	0.55	1.86
Gains/losses on securities	0.00	0.00	0.01	0.02
Net income after taxes	**1.43**	**1.14**	**0.34**	**1.28**
Common Size Balance Sheet to Assets				
Assets				
Deposits at other banks	0.00	1.56	0.00	0.35
Fed funds sold and repos	8.95	3.61	19.27	2.85
Securities	**27.06**	**18.19**	**30.44**	**22.57**
Gross loans and leases	55.22	59.76	42.53	60.46
Allowance for loan and lease losses	3.38	1.37	2.09	1.48
Net loans and leases	**51.84**	**58.39**	**40.44**	**58.98**
Total loans and leases (as a percentage of gross loans and leases)				
Real estate loans	46.20	34.34	57.86	42.82
Commercial loans	18.80	27.49	16.10	22.37
Consumer loans	23.74	21.87	25.23	22.52
Other loans	11.26	16.30	0.81	12.29
Liabilities				
Demand deposits	18.44	15.36	16.85	15.09
Total deposits	68.80	68.54	79.21	77.14
Core deposits	64.20	55.20	75.29	68.92
Volatile liabilities	20.47	31.45	16.69	21.54
Average Yields Earned on Different Types of Assets				
Average yield on securities	4.92	5.96	5.24	6.29
Average yield on loans and leases	8.29	7.68	8.12	8.19
Average yield on real estate loans	7.92	7.74	7.79	7.98
Average yield on commercial loans	9.19	7.38	8.68	7.09
Average yield on consumer loans	11.63	9.26	9.46	9.95
Average Rates Paid on Different Types of Liabilities				
Average rate on interest-bearing deposits	2.77	3.02	3.04	3.25
Average rate on large, uninsured CDs	3.11	3.75	3.18	3.87
Average rate on other borrowed funds	3.79	4.05	2.15	3.14
Average rate on all interest-bearing liabilities	3.18	3.29	2.98	3.24

Table 6.9 ✦ RISK MEASURES FOR NATIONS BANK, SEPTEMBER 30, 1993 AND 1994

Credit Risk Measures	1994	Peers	1993	Peers
Net loans and leases to assets	52.06%	59.22%	38.75%	59.98%
Loan loss provision to average total loans and leases	−1.27	0.25	0.52	0.61
Loan loss allowance to total loans and leases	5.65	2.30	5.30	2.50
Loan loss allowance to nonaccrual loans	2.69	2.49	1.31	2.07
Loan loss allowance to net losses	181.08	8.50	19.75	5.13
Noncurrent loans and leases to gross loans and leases	2.42	1.26	4.13	1.82
Earnings coverage to net losses	100.77	13.70	7.22	7.49
Net loss to average loans and leases	0.03	0.31	0.26	0.53
Growth rate in net loans and leases	518.81	9.91	−18.34	7.01
Liquidity Ratios				
Net loans and leases to assets	52.06	59.22	38.75	59.98
Net loans and leases to total deposits	74.42	86.49	49.09	80.53
Securities with maturities less than 1 year to total assets	15.63	14.04	31.23	11.61
Volatile liabilities to assets	20.35	32.13	17.11	22.82
Core deposits to assets	64.88	53.78	75.62	67.48
(Securities with maturities less than 1 year volatile liabilities) to assets	−4.72	−16.94	14.12	−10.31
Unused loan and lease commitments to assets	20.01	38.11	17.22	23.87
Standby letters of credit to assets	3.67	5.37	3.82	2.07
Interest Rate Risk				
(Rate-sensitive assets − rate-sensitive liabilities) to assets				
Within 3 months	5.22	5.84	NA	NA
Within 1 year	6.64	8.79	NA	NA
Rate-sensitive assets to rate-sensitive liabilities				
Within 3 months	1.14	1.16	NA	NA
Within 1 year	1.15	1.18	NA	NA
Capital Risk				
Equity (Tier 1 capital) average assets	8.78	6.95	6.12	7.39
Cash dividends to net income	157.60	57.49	0.00	36.44
Tier 1 capital to risk-weighted assets	NA	NA	NA	NA
Tier 1 and Tier 2 capital to risk-weighed assets	NA	NA	NA	NA
Growth rate in Tier 1 equity capital	501.31	10.37	4.03	14.91
Growth rate in assets	360.58	10.10	−2.04	7.81
Equity growth less asset growth rate	140.73	0.37	6.07	7.10
Operating Efficiency Measures				
Average personnel expense per employee ($000)	$40.32	$43.59	$38.09	$35.41
Assets per employee ($ million)	$ 2.7	$ 3.05	$ 3.38	$ 2.55
Total overhead expense to assets	3.91	3.72	3.41	3.79
Personnel expense to average assets	1.50	1.59	1.05	1.49
Occupancy expense to average assets	0.51	0.50	0.39	0.46

Table 6.10 ✦ FINANCIAL ANALYSIS FOR COLORADO NATIONAL BANK, MARCH 1993 AND 1994

Overall Profitability Ratios	1994	Peers	1993	Peers
Return on equity (net income to equity)	**14.11%**	**17.51%**	**23.16%**	**15.70%**
Return on assets (net income to assets)	**1.18**	**1.29**	**1.79**	**1.19**
Equity multiplier (assets to equity)	11.96	13.57	12.94	13.19
Common Size Income Statement to Assets				
Interest revenue (tax equivalent)	6.07	6.30	7.49	6.98
Interest expense	2.20	2.30	2.03	2.66
Net interest margin (NIM)	**3.87**	**4.00**	**5.46**	**4.32**
Noninterest revenue	2.32	1.60	5.78	1.32
Noninterest expense	4.25	3.60	7.67	3.70
Types of noninterest expenses				
Personnel expense	1.30	1.44	3.44	1.44
Occupancy expense	0.34	0.44	1.14	0.45
Other operating expense	2.60	1.62	3.09	1.67
Burden	**1.93**	**2.00**	**1.89**	**2.38**
Provision for loan losses	**0.13**	**0.18**	**0.47**	**0.30**
Net income before gains and taxes	1.81	1.82	3.10	1.64
Gains/losses on securities	0.00	0.01	0.02	0.01
Net income after taxes and adjustments	**1.18**	**1.29**	**1.79**	**1.19**
Common Size Balance Sheet to Assets				
Assets				
Deposits at other banks	0.00	0.16	0.54	0.09
Fed funds sold and repos	10.22	2.74	8.98	3.03
Securities	**20.01**	**21.99**	**24.39**	**27.79**
Gross loans and leases	59.98	54.57	54.57	59.65
Allowance for loan and lease losses	1.31	1.36	1.97	1.23
Net loans and leases	**58.67**	**53.21**	**52.60**	**58.42**
Total loans and leases (as a percentage of gross loans and leases)				
Real estate loans	42.80	43.00	31.14	49.05
Commercial loans	22.18	21.32	18.37	19.89
Consumer loans	29.07	23.08	41.80	20.45
Other loans	5.95	12.60	8.69	10.60
Liabilities				
Demand deposits	19.66	15.52	27.44	13.76
Total deposits	85.46	75.14	82.34	83.66
Core deposits	82.16	67.38	75.76	76.18
Volatile liabilities	5.78	22.22	14.77	14.99
Average Yields Earned on Different Types of Assets				
Average yield on securities	5.42	5.59	6.50	6.61
Average yield on loans and leases	7.69	7.72	10.23	8.33
Average yield on real estate loans	7.60	7.58	6.89	8.28
Average yield on commercial loans	7.38	6.91	5.59	7.20
Average yield on consumer loans	9.12	9.24	14.18	10.13
Average Rates Paid on Different Types of Liabilities				
Average rate on interest-bearing deposits	3.09	2.99	3.28	3.45
Average rate on large, uninsured CDs	4.63	3.62	4.09	3.83
Average rate on other borrowed funds	4.35	3.05	5.90	3.14
Average rate on all interest-bearing liabilities	3.09	3.04	3.21	3.44

Table 6.11 ✦ RISK ANALYSIS FOR COLORADO NATIONAL BANK, SEPTEMBER 30, 1993 AND 1994

Credit Risk Measures	1994	Peers	1993	Peers
Net loans and leases to assets	59.47%	60.11%	53.55%	58.82%
Loan loss provision to average total loans and leases	0.22	0.29	0.85	0.51
Loan loss allowance to total loans and leases	2.15	2.31	3.71	2.20
Loan loss allowance to nonaccrual loans	3.52	2.59	2.56	1.96
Loan loss allowance to net loss	5.33	7.41	19.38	5.92
Earnings coverage to net loss	7.92	11.70	33.15	9.38
Net loss to average loans and leases	0.41	0.27	0.19	0.34
Growth rate in net loans and leases	243.81	10.72	−0.56	4.71
Liquidity Ratios				
Net loans and leases to assets	59.47	60.11	53.55	58.82
Net loans and leases to total deposits	70.47	81.53	65.09	71.66
Securities with maturities less than 1 year to total assets	12.03	12.41	15.88	10.43
Volatile liabilities to assets	6.71	22.13	14.57	15.47
Core deposits to assets	81.20	66.40	75.82	75.57
(Securities with maturities less than 1 year volatile liabilities) to assets	5.32	−9.65	1.31	−4.56
Unused loan and lease commitments to assets	67.53	25.57	78.39	17.03
Standby letters of credit to assets	1.27	1.85	1.53	1.11
Interest Rate Risk				
(Rate-sensitive assets − rate-sensitive liabilities) to assets				
Within 3 months	−8.34	−12.74	NA	NA
Within 1 year	−2.21	−9.97	NA	NA
Rate-sensitive assets to rate-sensitive liabilities				
Within 3 months	0.80	0.85	NA	NA
Within 1 year	0.96	0.90	NA	NA
Capital Risk				
Equity (Tier 1 capital) average assets	8.36	7.37	7.73	7.58
Cash dividends to net income	NA	46.66	61.31	37.72
Tier 1 capital to risk-weighted assets	12.79	10.81	12.20	11.34
Tier 1 and Tier 2 capital to risk-weighed assets	14.84	12.81	13.48	12.82
Growth rate in Tier 1 equity capital	277.18	11.85	8.29	13.99
Equity growth less asset growth rate	65.57	3.33	12.47	8.17
Operating Efficiency Measures				
Average personnel expense per employee ($000)	$37.89	$36.32	$36.94	$33.45
Assets per employee ($ million)	$ 2.90	$ 2.62	$ 1.08	$ 2.39
Total overhead expense to assets	4.25%	3.60%	7.67%	3.70%
Personnel expense to average assets	1.30	1.44	3.44	1.44
Occupancy expense to average assets	0.34	0.44	1.14	0.45

Table 6.12   ✦   FINANCIAL ANALYSIS FOR PROVIDENT BANK OF MARYLAND, DECEMBER 1993 AND 1994

Overall Profitability Ratios	1994	Peers	1993	Peers
Return on equity (net income to equity)	**9.30%**	**15.55%**	**6.68%**	**15.52%**
Return on assets (net income to assets)	**0.69**	**1.21**	**0.47**	**1.18**
Equity multiplier (assets to equity)	13.48	12.85	14.21	13.15
Common Size Income Statement to Assets				
Interest revenue (tax equivalent)	7.13%	6.87%	6.97%	6.80%
Interest expense	3.27	2.69	3.15	2.52
Net interest margin (NIM)	**3.86**	**4.18**	**3.82**	**4.28**
Noninterest revenue	1.41	1.17	1.39	1.32
Noninterest expense	4.17	3.44	4.46	3.75
Types of noninterest expenses				
Personnel expense	2.30	1.56	2.56	1.55
Occupancy expense	0.62	0.44	0.63	0.46
Other operating expense	1.25	1.49	1.27	1.74
Burden	**2.76**	**2.27**	**3.07**	**2.43**
Provision for loan losses	**0.03**	**0.18**	**0.09**	**0.31**
Net income before gains and taxes	1.07	1.73	0.66	1.54
Gains/losses on securities	0.03	0.00	0.16	0.02
Net income after taxes and adjustments	**0.69**	**1.21**	**0.47**	**1.18**
Common Size Balance Sheet to Assets				
Assets				
Deposits at other banks	0.00	0.04	0.00	0.07
Fed funds sold and repos	0.00	1.72	0.00	2.58
Securities	**29.30**	**22.16**	**37.94**	**24.97**
Gross loans and leases	66.21	61.88	57.89	60.67
Allowance for loan and lease losses	1.06	1.17	1.19	1.20
Net loans and leases	**65.15**	**60.71**	**56.70**	**59.47**
Total loans and leases (as a percentage of gross loans and leases)				
Real estate loans	77.80	52.25	71.50	50.75
Commercial loans	9.60	18.52	14.11	19.38
Consumer loans	12.49	20.73	15.29	20.09
Other loans	0.11	8.50	0.00	9.78
Liabilities				
Demand deposits	5.29	13.54	5.58	14.15
Total deposits	68.13	79.08	72.71	82.72
Core deposits	66.75	71.02	71.50	75.21
Volatile liabilities	19.70	18.00	20.05	15.76
Average Yields Earned on Different Types of Assets				
Average yield on securities	6.45	6.04	6.57	6.26
Average yield on loans and leases	7.78	8.23	7.83	8.20
Average yield on real estate loans	7.46	8.20	7.49	8.13
Average yield on commercial loans	8.29	7.98	7.75	7.30
Average yield on consumer loans	8.80	9.03	9.80	9.74
Average Rates Paid on Different Types of Liabilities				
Average rate on interest-bearing deposits	3.44	3.34	3.63	3.27
Average rate on large, uninsured CDs	3.58	4.22	4.20	3.77
Average rate on other borrowed funds	4.69	4.12	2.61	2.66
Average rate on all interest-bearing liabilities	3.77	3.48	3.63	3.28

Table 6.13   ✦   CREDIT RISK ANALYSIS FOR PROVIDENT BANK OF MARYLAND, DECEMBER 1993 AND 1994

Credit Risk Measures	1994	Peers	1993	Peers
Net loans and leases to assets	65.15%	60.71%	56.70%	59.47%
Loan loss provision to average total loans and leases	−1.27	0.25	0.52	0.61
Loan loss allowance to total loans and leases	5.65	2.30	5.30	2.50
Loan loss allowance to nonaccrual loans	3.21	3.07	4.72	2.61
Loan loss allowance to net loss	360.22	7.89	18.37	5.90
Earnings coverage to net loss	348.47	13.82	11.25	9.00
Net loss to average loans and leases	0.00	0.23	0.12	0.38
Growth rate in net loans and leases	1.19	11.41	64.13	9.61
Liquidity Ratios				
Net loans and leases to assets	66.15	60.71	56.70	59.47
Net loans and leases to total deposits	89.46	79.97	99.82	74.20
Securities with maturities less than 1 year to total assets	3.80	9.34	1.18	9.84
Volatile liabilities to assets	28.91	19.38	23.36	16.02
Core deposits to assets	62.09	69.63	68.42	74.71
(Securities with maturities less than 1 year volatile liabilities) to assets	−25.11	−9.04	−22.18	−6.00
Unused loan and lease commitments to assets	10.81	17.98	13.60	17.74
Standby letters of credit to assets	0.58	1.13	0.64	1.07
Interest Rate Risk				
(Rate-sensitive assets − rate-sensitive liabilities) to assets				
Within 3 months	−11.55	−10.63	NA	NA
Within 1 year	−8.02	−9.06	NA	NA
Rate-sensitive assets to rate-sensitive liabilities				
Within 3 months	0.66	0.75	NA	NA
Within 1 year	0.82	0.85	NA	NA
Capital Risk				
Equity (Tier 1 capital) average assets	7.42	7.78	7.04	7.60
Cash dividends to net income	21.01	47.57	21.89	48.67
Tier 1 capital to risk-weighted assets	10.35	11.29	9.25	11.35
Tier 1 and Tier 2 capital to risk-weighed assets	11.61	12.72	10.50	12.85
Growth rate in Tier 1 equity capital	26.53	9.68	7.99	12.46
Growth rate in assets	23.84	7.61	13.02	6.47
Equity growth less asset growth rate	2.69	2.07	5.03	5.99
Operating Efficiency Measures				
Average personnel expense per employee ($000)	$45.69	$35.30	$45.74	$33.95
Assets per employee ($ million)	$2.39	$2.64	$1.94	$2.50
Total overhead expense to assets	4.17%	3.44%	4.46%	3.75%
Personnel expense to average assets	2.30%	1.56%	2.56%	1.55%
Occupancy expense to average assets	0.62%	0.44%	0.63%	0.46%

Selected References

English, William B., and William R. Nelson. "Profits and Balance Sheet Developments, at U.S. Commercial Banks in 1997." *Federal Reserve Bulletin* 84 (June 1998): 391–419.

Hempel, George H., Donald G. Simonson, and Alan B. Coleman. *Bank Management: Text and Cases*, 4th ed. New York: John Wiley & Sons, 1994.

Koch, Timothy W. *Bank Management*, 3rd ed. New York: Dryden Press, 1995.

McCoy, John B., Larry A. Frieder, and Robert B. Hedges, Jr. *Bottomline Banking: Meeting the Challenges for Survival & Success*. Chicago: Probus, 1994.

Nelson, William R., and Ann L. Owen. "Profits and Balance Sheet Developments at U.S. Commercial Banks in 1996." *Federal Reserve Bulletin* (June 1997): 465–489.

Sinkey, Joseph F., Jr. *Commercial Bank Financial Management*, 5th ed. Englewood Cliffs, NJ: Prentice-Hall, 1998.

Sheshunoff Bank Quarterly. Austin, Texas: Sheshunoff Information Services Inc.

Chapter 6 Internet Exercise

Depository Institution Performance and Risk Analysis

The Appendix to Chapter 6 gives the Uniforma Bank Performance Report for Nationsbank, N.A. of Bethesda, MD. This bank is no longer in existence, but you find out what happened to it and can locate the performance report for Nationsbank, N.A., Charlotte, N.C.

1. Go to the Federal Financial Institutions Examination Council home page at: http://www.ffiec.gov/nic.

2. Under "Acquisition/Institution History" click on "What Happened to an Institution." Enter "Nationsbank" and Bethesda, Maryland and submit. On the next page, click on "Nationsbank, N.A." You will then get a page that shows that Nationsbank, N.A., Maryland was merged with Nationsbank, N.A., Virginia, which in turn was merged with Nationsbank, N.A., North Carolina.

3. Click on Nationsbank, N.A., Charlotte, N.C. and you will be taken to a page that will enable you to find the performance report. On this page under "Financial Information" select performance report. Note that you can select to see data for up to four quarters. This report is not a complete report, but does give you the information for a Peer 1 group comparison.

The text provides an in depth analysis of the performance report of Wells Fargo. The FDIC Institution Directory provides a convenient online way to compare Wells Fargo with its peer institutions. Go to the FDIC Institution Directory at: http://www2.fdic.gov/id.

Enter certificate number 3511 for the main Wells Fargo institution headquartered in San Francisco. Select performance and condition ratios and at the bottom of the page click on "Compare Cert 3511 to Other Institutions."

On this page, then in "Group" select the category "Assets more than $5 billion" then click "Find." At the top of this page, again select "Performance and Condition Ratios" and click "Run Report."

You will then have a comparison for the latest quarter between Wells Fargo and aggregate data on institutions over $5 billion in assets.

Other useful sites for financial institution data:

Sheshunoff
www.sheshunoff.com/banking.htm

Thomson Bank Watch
www.bankwatch.com/

User's Guide to Uniform Bank Performance Report available from FFIEC
www.ffiec.gov/UBPR.htm

Wells Fargo
www.wellsfargo.com

Appendix 6a

SAMPLE UNIFORM BANK PERFORMACE REPORT

CERT # 12883 DSB # 05241075   NATIONSBANK, NATIONAL ASSOCIATION   BETHESDA, MD
CHARTER # 22546 COUNTY: MONTGOM   September 30, 1994 UNIFORM BANK PERFORMANCE REPORT
FPU#018566-0001

INFORMATION

INTRODUCTION

THIS UNIFORM BANK PERFORMANCE REPORT COVERS THE OPERATIONS OF YOUR BANK AND THAT OF A COMPARABLE GROUP OF PEER BANKS. IT IS PROVIDED FOR YOUR USE AS A MANAGEMENT TOOL BY THE FEDERAL FINANCIAL INSTITUTIONS EXAMINATION COUNCIL. DETAILED INFORMATION CONCERNING THIS REPORT IS PROVIDED IN "A USER'S GUIDE FOR THE UNIFORM BANK PERFORMANCE REPORT" FORWARDED TO YOUR BANK UNDER SEPARATE COVER. TO OBTAIN ADDITIONAL USER'S GUIDE OR OTHER UBPR MATERIALS, CALL THE NUMBER INDICATED AT RIGHT FOR ORDERING ASSISTANCE.

AS OF THE DATE OF PREPARATION OF THIS REPORT, YOUR BANK'S FEDERAL REGULATOR WAS THE OFFICE OF THE COMPTROLLER OF THE CURRENCY.

YOUR CURRENT PEER GROUP # 01 INCLUDES ALL INSURED COMMERCIAL BANKS HAVING ASSETS IN EXCESS OF $10 BILLION.

FOR THE DEFINITION OF OTHER UBPR PEER GROUPS, REFER TO THE UBPR USER'S GUIDE.

ADDRESSEE

CHIEF EXECUTIVE OFFICER
NATIONSBANK, NATIONAL ASSOCIATION
REG. REL. GRP. - 5TH FLR - 600 PEACHTREE ST. N.E.
ATLANTA, GA
30302-0000

NOTE

THIS REPORT HAS BEEN PRODUCED FOR THE USE OF THE FEDERAL REGULATORS OF FINANCIAL INSTITUTIONS IN CARRYING OUT THEIR SUPERVISORY RESPONSIBILITIES. ALL INFORMATION CONTAINED HEREIN WAS OBTAINED FROM SOURCES DEEMED RELIABLE. HOWEVER NO GUARANTEE IS GIVEN AS TO THE ACCURACY OF THE DATA OR OF THE CALCULATIONS DERIVED THEREFROM. THE DATA AND CALCULATIONS IN THIS REPORT DO NOT INDICATE APPROVAL OR DISAPPROVAL OF ANY PARTICULAR INSTITUTION'S PERFORMANCE AND ARE NOT TO BE CONSTRUED AS A RATING OF ANY INSTITUTION BY FEDERAL BANK REGULATORS. USERS ARE CAUTIONED THAT ANY CONCLUSIONS DRAWN FROM THIS REPORT ARE THEIR OWN AND ARE NOT TO BE ATTRIBUTED TO THE FEDERAL BANK REGULATORS.

THE REPORTS OF CONDITION AND INCOME FOR THIS BANK CONTAIN ADDITIONAL INFORMATION NOT INCLUDED IN THIS PERFORMANCE REPORT, SUCH AS AN OPTIONAL NARRATIVE STATEMENT BY THE BANK.

TABLE OF CONTENTS

SECTIONS .... PAGE NUMBER

SUMMARY RATIOS..............................01

INCOME INFORMATION:
   INCOME STATEMENT - REVENUES AND EXPENSES ($000)......02
   NONINTEREST INCOME AND EXPENSES ($000) AND YIELDS....03

BALANCE SHEET INFORMATION:
   BALANCE SHEET - ASSETS, LIABILITIES & CAPITAL ($000)....04
   OFF-BALANCE SHEET ITEMS..................................05
   BALANCE SHEET - % COMPOSITION OF ASSETS & LIABILITIES...06
   ANALYSIS OF LOAN & LEASE ALLOWANCE AND LOAN MIX.........07
   ANALYSIS OF PAST DUE, NONACCRUAL & RESTRUCTURED LN&LS...08
   MATURITY AND REPRICING DISTRIBUTION.....................09
   LIQUIDITY AND INVESTMENT PORTFOLIO......................10
   CAPITAL ANALYSIS..11

LAST-FOUR-QUARTERS INCOME ANALYSIS.................12

FOR ORDERING ASSISTANCE PHONE: (800) 945-2186
   (IN THE WASHINGTON, DC AREA: (202) 898-7108)

QUESTIONS REGARDING CONTENT OF REPORTS: (202) 634-6526

BANK AND BANK HOLDING COMPANY INFORMATION

CERTIFICATE # 12883   BANK # 241075   CHARTER # 22546

NATIONSBANK CORPORATION
(HOLDING CO. # 610)
CHARLOTTE   NC
(HOLDING COMPANY REFERS TO TOP HOLDER)

CERT # 12883 DSB # 05241075   NATIONSBANK, NATIONAL ASSOCIATION   BETHESDA, MD
CHARTER # 22546 COUNTY: MONTGOM   SUMMARY RATIOS   PAGE 01

	09/30/94 BANK	PEER 01	PCT	09/30/93 BANK	PEER 02	PCT	12/31/93 BANK	PEER 02	PCT	12/31/92 BANK	PEER 02	12/31/91 BANK	PEER 02
AVERAGE ASSETS ($000)	18609076**			4348838			4347201			4130801		4157124	
NET INCOME ($000)	199880			11026			8308			1701		-47515	
NUMBER OF BANKS IN PEER GROUP	56			127			128			128		131	

EARNINGS AND PROFITABILITY

PERCENT OF AVERAGE ASSETS:	09/30/94 BANK	PEER 01	PCT	09/30/93 BANK	PEER 02	PCT	12/31/93 BANK	PEER 02	PCT	12/31/92 BANK	PEER 02	12/31/91 BANK	PEER 02
INTEREST INCOME (TE)	6.34	6.25	57	5.33	6.76	08	5.31	6.69	11	6.56	7.28	8.50	8.59
- INTEREST EXPENSE	2.28	2.47	33	2.21	2.49	30	2.21	2.46	30	3.08	3.11	4.86	4.70
NET INTEREST INCOME (TE)	4.06	3.76	61	3.12	4.29	08	3.10	4.27	10	3.49	4.21	3.64	3.99
+ NONINTEREST INCOME	1.65	1.87	42	1.05	1.66	20	1.05	1.70	10	1.19	1.76	1.12	1.62
MEMO: FEE INCOME	0.17	0.58	10	0.14	0.48	05	0.13	0.49	06	0.17	0.52	0.24	0.45
- NON-INTEREST EXPENSE	3.91	3.72	59	3.41	3.79	32	3.72	3.81	50	3.97	3.91	3.44	3.77
- PROVISION: LOAN&LEASE LOSSES	-0.71	0.15	01	0.21	0.37	27	0.15	0.34	25	1.21	0.63	0.99	0.99
= PRETAX OPERATING INCOME (TE)	2.51	1.79	84	0.55	1.86	06	0.28	1.90	05	-0.51	1.55	-2.28	0.97
+ REALIZED GAINS/LOSSES SECS	0.00	0.00	52	0.01	0.02	53	0.03	0.02	62	0.02	0.04	-0.51	0.06
= PRETAX NET OPERATING INC(TE)	2.51	1.79	84	0.56	1.96	05	0.31	1.99	05	0.02	1.65	-1.76	1.10
NET OPERATING INCOME	1.43	1.14	77	0.34	1.28	06	0.19	1.30	05	0.04	1.08	-1.14	0.70
ADJUSTED NET OPERATING INCOME	0.71	1.09	19	0.44	1.31	11	0.24	1.29	06	-0.94	1.12	-0.01	0.83
ADJUSTED NET INCOME	1.18	1.15	50	0.44	1.33	11	0.26	1.28	10	-0.98	1.08	-0.65	0.78
NET INCOME	1.43	1.14	77	0.34	1.28	04	0.19	1.31	05	-0.04	1.10	-1.14	0.71

MARGIN ANALYSIS:

	09/30/94 BANK	PEER 01	PCT	09/30/93 BANK	PEER 02	PCT	12/31/93 BANK	PEER 02	PCT	12/31/92 BANK	PEER 02	12/31/91 BANK	PEER 02
AVG EARNING ASSETS TO AVG ASSETS	91.68	90.00	70	90.52	91.38	37	91.03	91.29	48	92.36	91.10	92.54	91.12
AVG INT-BEARING FUNDS TO AVG AST	71.50	73.41	36	74.30	75.87	34	74.50	75.72	37	77.87	77.14	79.26	78.76
INT INC (TE) TO AVG EARN ASSETS	6.91	6.91	57	5.89	7.42	07	5.83	7.35	09	7.11	8.03	9.18	9.46
INT EXPENSE TO AVG EARN ASSETS	2.49	2.73	33	2.45	2.73	29	2.42	2.70	30	3.33	3.42	5.25	5.17
NET INT INC-TE TO AVG EARN ASSET	4.42	4.16	57	3.44	4.71	09	3.41	4.69	10	3.78	4.64	3.93	4.41

LOAN & LEASE ANALYSIS

	09/30/94 BANK	PEER 01	PCT	09/30/93 BANK	PEER 02	PCT	12/31/93 BANK	PEER 02	PCT	12/31/92 BANK	PEER 02	12/31/91 BANK	PEER 02
NET LOSS TO AVERAGE TOTAL LN&LS	0.03	0.31	10	0.26	0.53	28	0.27	0.55	30	4.31	0.99	3.89	1.36
EARNINGS COVERAGE OF NET LOSS(X)	100.77	13.70	98	7.22	7.49	51	4.06	7.19	33	0.31	3.88	0.45	2.42
LN&LS ALLOWANCE TO NET LOSSES(X)	181.08	8.50	98	19.75	5.13	89	19.28	4.48	92	0.94	2.73	1.28	2.04
LN&LS ALLOWANCE TO TOTAL LN&LS	5.65	2.30	33	5.30	2.50	92	5.33	2.33	96	4.45	2.56	5.62	2.48
NON-CURRENT LN&LS TO GROSS LN&LS	2.24	1.26	94	4.13	1.82		3.42	1.50		5.47	2.13	6.81	2.79

LIQUIDITY

	09/30/94 BANK	PEER 01	PCT	09/30/93 BANK	PEER 02	PCT	12/31/93 BANK	PEER 02	PCT	12/31/92 BANK	PEER 02	12/31/91 BANK	PEER 02
VOLATILE LIABILITY DEPENDENCE	6.56	25.06	14	-22.95	13.16	02	-27.77	11.56	03	-4.34	10.95	5.78	15.55
NET LOANS & LEASES TO ASSETS	52.06	59.22	24	38.75	59.77	10	36.75	59.41	08	44.52	58.81	49.95	61.01

CAPITALIZATION

	09/30/94 BANK	PEER 01	PCT	09/30/93 BANK	PEER 02	PCT	12/31/93 BANK	PEER 02	PCT	12/31/92 BANK	PEER 02	12/31/91 BANK	PEER 02
TIER ONE LEVERAGE CAPITAL(***)	8.78	6.95	89	6.12	7.39	12	6.03	7.31	09	6.29	6.97	5.30	6.22
CASH DIVIDENDS TO NET INCOME	157.60	57.49	96	0.00	36.44	21	0.00	48.42	14	0.00	31.57	NA	49.25
RETAIN EARNS TO AVG TOTAL EQUITY	-7.98	6.57	03	5.65	9.37	31	3.18	7.97	28	0.70	9.37	-21.04	3.38

GROWTH RATES

	09/30/94 BANK	PEER 01	PCT	09/30/93 BANK	PEER 02	PCT	12/31/93 BANK	PEER 02	PCT	12/31/92 BANK	PEER 02	12/31/91 BANK	PEER 02
ASSETS	360.58	10.10	98	-2.04	7.81	12	2.88	7.67	34	-0.86	4.99	-5.94	3.20
TIER ONE CAPITAL(***)	501.31	10.37	98	4.03	14.91	21	3.53	13.43	18	17.33	16.00	-7.61	9.52
NET LOANS & LEASES	518.81	9.91	91	-18.34	7.01	03	-15.07	9.81	01	-11.64	2.32	-21.92	-1.30
TEMPORARY INVESTMENTS	130.49	6.98	98	89.45	29.97	75	105.69	18.64	85	21.44	22.97	257.97	16.00
VOLATILE LIABILITIES	447.72	16.21		5.92	13.16	38	34.67	19.44	68	-23.58	-3.08	-39.38	-12.17

**PRE-MERGER DATA HAS BEEN EXCLUDED FROM ALL AVERAGE CALCULATIONS AS A RESULT OF MERGERS/CONSOLIDATIONS.

(***) TIER ONE CAPITAL FOR 12/31/93 EXCLUDES FASB 115 NET UNREALIZED HOLDING GAIN ON AVAILABLE-FOR-SALE SECURITIES.

CERT # 12883 DSB # 05241075
CHARTER # 22546 COUNTY: MONTGOM

NATIONSBANK, NATIONAL ASSOCIATION
INCOME STATEMENT - REVENUES AND EXPENSES ($000)

BETHESDA, MD

PAGE 02

	09/30/94	09/30/93	12/31/93	12/31/92	12/31/91	PERCENT CHANGE 1 YEAR
INTEREST AND FEES ON LOANS	634197	104401	138068	179199	230255	507.46
INCOME FROM LEASE FINANCING	2871	389	535	793	1378	638.05
FULLY TAXABLE	623242	104142	137687	178871	229742	498.45
TAX-EXEMPT	13826	648	916	1121	1891	+ ##
ESTIMATED TAX BENEFIT	7189	328	376	582	983	
INCOME ON LOANS & LEASES (TE)	644257	105118	138979	180574	232616	512.89
U.S. TREAS & AGENCY SECURITIES	181239	45568	61511	66432	64546	297.73
TAX-EXEMPT SECURITIES INCOME	65	0	0	0	8432	NA
ESTIMATED TAX BENEFIT	33				4384	
OTHER SECURITIES INCOME	11210	313	451	665	28156	+ ##
INVESTMT INTEREST INCOME (TE)	192547	45881	61962	67097	105518	319.67
INTEREST ON DUE FROM BANKS	48	9	11	3191	5622	433.33
INT ON FED FUNDS SOLD & RESALES	47899	22880	29746	20320	9505	109.35
TRADING ACCOUNT INCOME	27	0	0	0	0	NA
TOTAL INTEREST INCOME (TE)	884779	173888	230698	271182	353261	408.82
INT ON DEPOSITS IN FOREIGN OFF	7867	NA	NA	NA	NA	NA
INT ON CD'S OVER $100M	12606	3874	4732	12008	39473	225.40
INTEREST ON ALL OTHER DEPOSITS	179779	55167	72664	100949	143778	225.88
INT ON FED FUNDS PURCH & REPOS	88004	12730	17967	13204	16330	591.31
INT BORROWED MONEY (+NOTE OPT)	29528	453	561	905	2445	+ ##
INT ON MORTGAGES & LEASES	909	0	0	0	0	NA
INT ON SUB NOTES & DEBENTURES	0	0	0	24	0	NA
TOTAL INTEREST EXPENSE	318693	72224	95924	127090	202026	341.26
NET INTEREST INCOME (TE)	566086	101664	134774	144092	151235	456.82
NONINTEREST INCOME	230555	34107	45489	49053	46438	575.98
ADJUSTED OPERATING INC (TE)	796641	135771	180263	193145	197673	486.75
NON-INTEREST EXPENSE	545262	111217	161551	164188	149385	390.27
PROVISION: LOAN & LEASE LOSSES	-98800	6700	6700	49856	142873	- ##
PROV: ALLOCATED TRANSFER RISK	0	0	0	0	0	
PRETAX OPERATING INCOME (TE)	350179	17854	12012	-20898	-94584	+ ##
REALIZED G/L HLD-TO-MATURITY SEC	408	376	1285	21591	21331	8.51
REALIZED G/L AVAIL-FOR-SALE SEC	19	NA	NA	NA	NA	NA
PRETAX NET OPERATING INC (TE)	350606	18230	13297	692	-73253	+ ##
APPLICABLE INCOME TAXES	143503	6876	4613	-1591	-31106	
CURRENT TAX EQUIV ADJUSTMENT	7223	328	376	110	0	
OTHER TAX EQUIV ADJUSTMENTS	0	0	0	472	5367	
APPLICABLE INCOME TAXES (TE)	150726	7204	4989	-1008	-25738	+ ##
NET OPERATING INCOME	199880	11026	8308	1701	-47515	+ ##
NET EXTRAORDINARY ITEMS	0	0	0	0	0	
NET INCOME	199880	11026	8308	1701	-47515	+ ##
CASH DIVIDENDS DECLARED	315007	0	0	0	0	NA
RETAINED EARNINGS	-115127	11026	8308	1701	-47515	- ##
MEMO: NET INTERNATIONAL INCOME		NA	NA	NA	NA	NA

CERT # 12883 DSB # 05241075
CHARTER # 22546 COUNTY: MONTGOM

NATIONSBANK, NATIONAL ASSOCIATION
OFF-BALANCE SHEET ITEMS

BETHESDA, MD

PAGE 05

	09/30/94	09/30/93	12/31/93	12/31/92	12/31/91	PERCENT CHANGE 1 QTR	1 YEAR
UNUSED COMMITMENTS							
HOME EQUITY (1-4 FAMILY)	639183	143658	141473	147658	148866	-0.06	344.93
CREDIT CARD	0	0	0	0	0	NA	NA
COMMERCIAL RE SECURED BY RE	203972	40988	54378	71576	85207	37.50	397.64
COMMERCL RE NOT SECURED BY RE	42984	226	346	16211	9284	-25.07	+##
ALL OTHER	286235	516456	513197	619650	584854	3.56	454.98
MEMO:UNUSED COMMIT W/MAT GT 1 YR	2880903	458650	439051	163270	177247	7.03	528.13
STANDBY LETTERS OF CREDIT	688554	155743	146246	136008	173097	8.81	342.11
AMOUNT CONVEYED TO OTHERS	0	0	0	0	3605	NA	NA
COMMERCIAL LETTERS OF CREDIT	25617	1824	380	448	948	-55.18	+##
INTEREST RATE CONTRACTS							
NOTIONAL VAL OF INT RATE SWAPS	4831512	21152	16604	38247	112331	0.40	+##
FUTURES AND FORWARD CONTRACTS	38567	0	0	0	0	NA	NA
OPTION CONTRACTS	372634	0	0	0	100000	-13.00	NA
FOREIGN EXCHANGE RATE CONTRACTS							
NOTIONAL VAL OF EXCHANGE SWAPS	4136	0	0	0	0	32.01	NA
COMMITMENTS TO PUR FOREIGN CUR	0	0	0	0	0	-100.00	NA
OPTION CONTRACTS	0	0	0	0	0	NA	NA
PRINCIPAL BALANCE OF MTG POOLS	6338	0	0	0	0	-9.37	NA
AMOUNT OF RECOURSE EXPOSURE	198	0	0	0	0	0.00	NA
ALL OTH OFF-BALANCE SHEET ITEMS	2229	0	317	0	49954	0.00	+##
GROSS OFF-BALANCE SHEET ITEMS	9721961	880047	872941	1029798	1264541	-0.64	+##

	09/30/94 BANK	PEER 01	PCT	09/30/93 BANK	PEER 02	PCT	12/31/93 BANK	PEER 02	PCT	12/31/92 BANK	PEER 02	12/31/91 BANK	PEER 02
PERCENT OF TOTAL ASSETS													
UNUSED COMMITMENTS													
HOME EQUITY (1-4 FAMILY)	3.41	1.96	77	3.53	2.05	75	3.36	1.96	75	3.60	1.84	3.60	1.77
CREDIT CARD	0.00	4.06	40	0.00	3.57	28	0.00	3.91	28	0.00	3.52	0.00	3.46
COMMERCIAL RE SECURED BY RE	1.09	1.00	52	1.01	1.05	48	1.29	1.10	59	1.75	0.90	2.06	1.16
COMMERCL RE NOT SECURED BY RE	0.23	0.20	57	0.01	0.05	54	0.01	0.04	55	0.40	0.05	0.22	0.05
ALL OTHER	15.28	26.88	22	12.68	12.18	51	12.18	12.44	51	15.13	12.62	14.16	13.95
TOTAL LN&LS COMMITMENTS	20.01	38.11	12	17.22	23.87	30	16.84	24.80	31	20.88	23.34	20.05	24.34
SECURITIES UNDERWRITING	0.00	0.00	78	0.00	0.00	93	0.00	0.00	94	0.00	0.00	0.00	0.00
STANDBY LETTERS OF CREDIT	3.67	5.37	35	3.82	2.07	75	3.47	2.00	71	3.32	2.35	4.19	2.61
AMOUNT CONVEYED TO OTHERS	0.00	0.37	14	0.00	0.04	53	0.00	0.04	52	0.00	0.06	0.09	0.05
COMMERCIAL LETTERS OF CREDIT	0.14	0.80	14	0.04	0.24	25	0.01	0.22	18	0.01	0.25	0.02	0.27
INTEREST RATE CONTRACTS													
NOTIONAL VAL OF INT RATE SWAPS	25.76	33.76	47	0.52	9.76	25	0.39	10.28	21	0.93	6.67	2.72	6.24
FUTURES AND FORWARD CONTRACTS	0.21	8.80	31	0.00	0.25	63	0.00	0.19	62	0.00	0.17	0.00	0.50
OPTION CONTRACTS	1.99	11.37	36	0.00	0.61	53	0.00	0.54	51	0.00	0.51	2.42	0.62
FOREIGN EXCHANGE RATE CONTRACTS													
NOTIONAL VAL OF EXCHANGE SWAPS	0.02	0.07	70	0.00	0.09	92	0.00	0.00	93	0.00	0.00	0.00	0.00
COMMITMENTS TO PUR FOREIGN CUR	0.00	18.95	14	0.00	0.09	44	0.00	0.12	43	0.00	0.10	0.00	0.14
OPTION CONTRACTS	0.00	0.51	47	0.00	0.00	92	0.00	0.00	94	0.00	0.00	0.00	0.00
PRINCIPAL BALANCE OF MTG POOLS	0.03	0.01	70	0.00	0.00	77	0.00	0.00	76	0.00	0.00	0.00	0.00
AMOUNT OF RECOURSE EXPOSURE	0.00	0.01	64	0.00	0.00	77	0.00	0.00	77	0.00	0.00	0.00	0.00
ALL OTH OFF-BALANCE SHEET ITEMS	0.01	2.27	22	0.00	0.36	43	0.01	0.24	51	0.00	0.13	1.21	0.18
GROSS OFF-BALANCE SHEET ITEMS	51.83	145.56	14	21.61	49.95	14	20.72	50.09	13	25.14	44.29	30.61	44.98

CERT # 12883 DSB # 05241075
CHARTER # 22546 COUNTY: MONTGOM

NATIONSBANK, NATIONAL ASSOCIATION
BALANCE SHEET - PERCENTAGE COMPOSITION OF ASSETS AND LIABILITIES
BETHESDA, MD
PAGE 06

	09/30/94 BANK	09/30/94 PEER 01	09/30/94 PCT	09/30/93 BANK	09/30/93 PEER 02	09/30/93 PCT	12/31/93 BANK	12/31/93 PEER 02	12/31/93 PCT	12/31/92 BANK	12/31/92 PEER 02	12/31/91 BANK	12/31/91 PEER 02
ASSETS, PERCENT OF AVG ASSETS													
TOTAL LOANS	54.17	58.70	31	41.37	59.90	10	40.63	59.22	13	49.36	59.50	56.72	62.62
LEASE FINANCING RECEIVABLES	1.05	1.06	56	1.16	0.56	69	1.15	0.58	68	1.29	0.70	1.35	0.77
LESS: LN&LS ALLOWANCE & ATRR	3.38	1.37	94	2.09	1.48	77	2.09	1.44	77	2.86	1.52	2.21	1.51
NET LOANS & LEASES	51.85	58.63	22	40.44	59.98	11	39.69	59.30	12	47.79	59.54	55.87	62.60
INTEREST-BEARING BANK BALANCES	0.00	1.56	21	0.00	0.35	32	0.00	0.35	29	1.53	0.65	2.36	0.93
FEDERAL FUNDS SOLD & RESALES	8.95	3.61	82	19.27	2.85	97	19.65	2.93	98	12.91	3.32	3.78	3.33
TRADING ACCOUNT ASSETS	0.02	1.16	19	0.00	0.06	54	0.00	0.07	53	0.00	0.08	0.00	0.15
HELD-TO-MATURITY SECURITIES	22.91	11.23	82	30.44	22.51	71	31.02	23.05	71	26.19	21.03	26.93	18.08
AVAILABLE-FOR-SALE SECURITIES	4.13	5.80	38	NA	NA		NA	NA		NA	NA	NA	NA
TOTAL EARNING ASSETS	87.86	88.22	42	90.15	89.50	60	90.36	89.59	62	88.42	88.57	88.94	88.28
NONINT CASH & DUE FROM BANKS	5.20	5.74	36	6.33	5.49	64	6.17	5.51	62	6.88	6.09	5.84	6.34
PREMISES, FIX ASSTS & CAP LEASES	1.24	1.35	40	1.17	1.26	41	1.15	1.27	39	1.23	1.27	1.26	1.30
OTHER REAL ESTATE OWNED	0.80	0.23	91	0.92	0.35	84	0.88	0.32	84	1.24	0.50	1.09	0.56
ACCEPTANCES & OTHER ASSETS	4.90	3.99	70	1.43	2.66	10	1.44	2.65	09	2.23	2.73	2.86	2.80
SUBTOTAL	12.15	11.78	61	9.85	10.50	39	9.64	10.41	37	11.59	11.43	11.06	11.72
TOTAL ASSETS	100.01	100.00		100.00	100.00		100.00	100.00		100.01	100.00	100.00	100.00
STANDBY LETTERS OF CREDIT	3.52	5.43	35	3.59	2.10	73	3.56	2.04	74	3.52	2.41	4.07	2.76
LIABILITIES, PERCENT OF AVG ASST													
DEMAND DEPOSITS	18.44	15.36	73	16.85	15.09	64	17.02	15.36	64	16.56	15.13	14.96	14.57
ALL NOW & ATS ACCOUNTS	9.25	6.68	70	12.66	9.09	82	12.70	9.12	82	11.85	8.16	9.52	6.99
MONEY MARKET DEPOSIT ACCOUNTS	9.90	10.75	45	14.63	13.85	58	14.42	13.73	57	15.01	14.25	11.55	12.98
OTHER SAVINGS DEPOSITS	14.05	6.82	82	13.13	8.01	81	13.21	7.77	82	12.06	6.34	9.62	5.30
TIME DEP < $100M	12.56	10.86	59	18.09	18.06	50	17.67	17.41	50	21.37	19.59	24.52	21.83
CORE DEPOSITS	64.20	55.20	61	75.29	68.92	69	75.03	68.52	71	76.87	68.56	70.17	66.10
TIME DEP OVER $100M	2.95	3.47	36	3.92	5.10	36	3.75	5.02	37	6.61	6.51	13.93	9.51
DEPOSITS IN FOREIGN OFFICES	1.64	7.70	30	NA	2.06		NA	2.08		NA	1.76	NA	1.67
TOTAL DEPOSITS	68.80	68.54	50	79.21	77.14	56	78.78	76.69	56	83.48	78.40	84.10	79.42
FEDERAL FUNDS PURCH & REPOS	14.53	10.17	68	13.06	9.30	67	13.44	9.56	71	8.72	9.24	7.71	9.09
OTHER BORROWINGS INCL < 1 YR	1.24	5.26	14	0.72	2.44	32	0.69	2.74	29	0.82	1.91	1.19	1.93
VOLATILE LIABILITIES	20.47	31.45	33	17.69	21.54	39	17.89	21.91	38	16.15	22.35	22.83	25.48
OTHER BORROWINGS > 1 YR	3.81	1.16	78	NA	NA		NA	NA		NA	NA	NA	NA
ACCEPTANCES & OTHER LIABILITIES	1.36	2.38	26	0.77	1.64	12	0.83	1.65	17	1.03	1.77	1.67	1.76
TOTAL LIABILITIES(INCL MORTG)	89.75	91.52	14	93.75	92.04	95	93.74	92.00	95	94.05	92.69	94.68	93.53
SUBORDINATED NOTES & DEBENTURES	0.00	1.23	19	0.00	0.33	42	0.00	0.32	42	0.00	0.21	0.00	0.12
ALL COMMON & PREFERRED CAPITAL	10.25	7.16	94	6.25	7.39	11	6.26	7.41	10	5.95	6.88	5.32	6.14
TOTAL LIABILITIES & CAPITAL	99.99	100.00		100.01	100.00		100.00	100.00		100.00	100.00	99.99	100.00
MEMO: ALL BROKERED DEPOSITS	0.66	0.22	75	0.41	0.31	63	0.38	0.31	62	0.95	0.43	2.36	1.09
INSURED BROKERED DEP	0.51	0.09	77	0.00	0.03	68	0.00	0.04	65	0.07	0.05	0.15	0.14

CERT # 12883 DSB # 05241075
CHARTER # 22546 COUNTY: MONTGOM

NATIONSBANK, NATIONAL ASSOCIATION
ANALYSIS OF LOAN & LEASE ALLOWANCE AND LOAN MIX
BETHESDA, MD
PAGE 07

CHANGE: LN&LS ALLOWANCE ($000)	09/30/94			09/30/93			12/31/93			12/31/92		12/31/91	
	BANK	PEER 01	PCT	BANK	PEER 02	PCT	BANK	PEER 02	PCT	BANK	PEER 02	BANK	PEER 02
BEGINNING BALANCE	87166			84995			84995			122900		75891	
GROSS LOAN & LEASE LOSSES	47965			11373			14144			99141		99347	
RECOVERIES	45542			8018			9624			8899		3483	
NET LOAN & LEASE LOSSES	2423			3355			4520			90242		95864	
PROVISION FOR LOAN & LEASE LOSS	-98800			6700			6700			49856		142873	
OTHER ADJUSTMENTS	599062			-9			-9			2481		0	
ENDING BALANCE	585005			88331			87166			84995		122900	
NET ATRR CHARGE-OFFS	NA			NA			NA			NA		NA	
OTHER ATRR CHANGES (NET)	NA			NA			NA			NA		NA	
AVERAGE TOTAL LOANS & LEASES	10361579			1726935			1700663			2093055		2467130	
ANALYSIS RATIOS													
LOSS PROVISION TO AVERAGE ASSETS	-0.71	0.15	01	0.21	0.37	27	0.15	0.34	25	1.21	0.63	3.44	0.99
LOSS PROVISION TO AVG TOT LN&LS	-1.27	0.25	01	0.52	0.61	46	0.39	0.56	37	2.38	1.05	5.79	1.56
NET LOSS TO AVERAGE TOTAL LN&LS	0.03	0.31	10	0.26	0.53	28	0.27	0.55	30	4.31	0.99	5.89	1.36
GROSS LOSS TO AVERAGE TOT LN&LS	0.62	0.60	49	0.88	0.85	54	0.83	0.87	50	4.74	1.28	4.03	1.57
RECOVERIES TO AVERAGE TOT LN&LS	0.59	0.27	92	0.62	0.28	89	0.57	0.28	86	0.43	0.25	0.14	0.18
RECOVERIES TO PRIOR PERIOD LOSS	429.31	28.99	98	10.78	23.20	10	9.71	24.21	06	8.96	18.29	18.81	16.83
LN&LS ALLOWANCE TO TOTAL LN&LS	5.65	2.30	94	5.30	2.50	92	5.33	2.33	96	4.45	2.56	5.62	2.48
LN&LS ALLOWANCE TO NET LOSSES(X)	181.08	8.50	98	19.75	5.13	89	19.28	4.48	92	0.94	2.73	1.28	2.04
LN&LS ALL TO NONACCRUAL LN&LS(X)	2.69	2.49		1.31	2.07		1.59	2.32		0.89	1.64	0.85	1.17
EARN COVERAGE OF NET LOSSES (X)	100.77	13.70	98	7.22	7.49	51	4.06	7.19	33	0.31	3.88	0.45	2.42
NET LOSSES BY TYPE OF LN&LS													
REAL ESTATE LOANS	-0.29	0.23	05	-0.18	0.29	02	-0.11	0.31	04	5.96	0.64	3.70	0.88
COMMERCIAL AND INDUSTRIAL LOANS	-0.07	0.14	23	-0.98	0.46	73	-0.76	0.48	67	2.42	1.08	7.65	1.56
LOANS TO INDIVIDUALS	1.30	0.83	68	1.16	0.94	63	1.15	0.98	60	2.10	1.39	2.37	1.71
AGRICULTURAL LOANS	0.00	0.02	64	NA	-0.01		NA	0.01		0.00	0.00	0.00	0.03
LEASE FINANCING	0.00	-0.01	63	0.00	0.04	60	0.00	0.07	53	0.04	0.30	0.57	0.42
ALL OTHER LOANS & LEASES	-0.23	0.00	08	-1.85	0.02	02	-1.16	0.02	02	1.94	0.07	0.00	0.12
MEMORANDA:													
LOANS TO FOREIGN GOVERNMENTS	0.00	-0.07	90	0.00	0.00	81	0.00	0.00	81	0.00	0.03	0.00	0.24
CREDIT CARD PLANS	2.77	2.11	67	3.52	2.27	75	3.39	2.23	76	3.76	2.93	3.54	3.26
LOANS TO FINANCE COMML REAL EST	-0.04	-0.05	36	-0.20	0.01	07	-0.28	0.01	08	10.74	0.15	24.26	0.64
CONSTRUCTION & LAND DEV	-0.62	-0.40	12	-0.59	0.41	04	-0.22	0.44	11	2.53	1.26	14.15	1.82
SECURED BY FARMLAND	-1.48	0.01	04	0.00	0.00	80	-0.30	0.00	00	0.00	0.01	0.00	0.01
SINGLE & MULTI FAMILY MORTGAGE	-0.14	0.08	03	-0.43	0.09	00	-0.25	0.10	00	0.48	0.18	0.06	0.20
HOME EQUITY LOANS	0.00	0.04	41	-0.35	0.06	84	-0.15	0.08	68	0.25	0.06	0.09	0.06
1-4 FAMILY NON-REVOLVING	-0.27	0.07	03	-1.02	0.08	00	-0.62	0.08	00	0.58	0.15	0.04	0.16
MULTIFAMILY LOANS	-0.06	0.14	12	0.26	0.05	76	0.55	0.09	79	0.95	0.37	0.00	0.24
NON-FARM NON-RESIDENTIAL MTG	-0.36	0.51	05	0.29	0.35	52	0.13	0.37	36	14.15	0.76	1.38	0.83

CERT # 12883   DSB # 05241075   COUNTY: MONTGOM
CHARTER # 22546   COUNTY: 22546   MONTGOM

NATIONSBANK, NATIONAL ASSOCIATION
ANALYSIS OF LOAN & LEASE ALLOWANCE AND LOAN MIX

BETHESDA, MD

PAGE 07A

LOAN MIX, % AVERAGE GROSS LN&LS	BANK	PEER 01	PCT	BANK	PEER 02	PCT	BANK	PEER 02	PCT	BANK	PEER 02	BANK	PEER 02
CONSTRUCTION & DEVELOPMENT	3.90	2.19	84	9.10	3.39	92	9.12	3.21	93	10.37	4.08	11.89	5.88
1 - 4 FAMILY RESIDENTIAL	16.95	19.34	40	24.81	21.19	67	24.11	21.43	63	23.36	18.80	19.68	16.93
HOME EQUITY LOANS	7.07	3.17	85	9.87	3.69	92	9.74	3.54	91	9.80	3.37	8.48	3.14
OTHER REAL ESTATE LOANS	25.35	10.82	98	23.95	15.10	85	24.10	14.92	86	23.71	14.04	20.94	13.92
FARMLAND	0.20	0.09	75	0.06	0.12	49	0.06	0.12	49	0.09	0.13	0.10	0.13
MULTIFAMILY	2.52	1.01	89	1.68	1.12	67	1.55	1.10	64	1.78	0.98	1.57	0.79
NON-FARM NON-RESIDENTIAL	22.63	9.67	98	22.21	13.36	89	22.50	13.21	89	21.84	12.51	19.26	12.56
TOTAL REAL ESTATE	46.20	34.34	77	57.86	42.82	79	57.34	42.89	80	57.44	40.58	52.51	39.41
FINANCIAL INSTITUTION LOANS	9.90	0.93	94	0.00	0.27	25	0.00	0.30	21	1.35	0.50	0.88	0.66
AGRICULTURAL LOANS	0.03	0.00	33	0.00	0.00	25	0.00	0.21	24	0.00	0.18	0.00	0.18
COMMERCIAL & INDUSTRIAL LOANS	18.80	27.49	29	16.10	22.37	31	16.53	22.29	31	13.67	24.01	17.22	26.15
LOANS TO INDIVIDUALS	17.13	13.69	68	20.22	19.22	53	20.28	19.11	55	20.83	19.04	22.96	18.58
CREDIT CARD LOANS	6.61	3.18	70	5.01	3.30	67	4.99	3.30	68	4.79	3.39	4.26	3.43
MUNICIPAL LOANS	2.72	0.89	94	0.89	1.45	35	0.97	1.40	39	0.99	1.82	1.03	2.05
ACCEPTANCES OF OTHER BANKS	0.00	0.00	70	0.00	0.00	78	0.00	0.00	77	0.00	0.01	0.00	0.00
FOREIGN OFFICE LOANS & LEASES	0.00	2.22	31	0.00	0.00	77	0.00	0.00	76	0.00	0.01	0.00	0.02
ALL OTHER LOANS	3.32	4.96	42	2.21	1.92	59	2.14	1.94	58	3.18	2.13	3.07	2.20
LEASE FINANCING RECEIVABLES	1.90	1.74	56	2.73	0.94	76	2.75	0.99	75	2.54	1.16	2.32	1.23
SUPPLEMENTAL:													
LOANS TO FOREIGN GOVERNMENTS	0.11	0.23	59	0.01	0.00	79	0.01	0.00	79	0.05	0.00	0.04	0.01
LOANS TO FINANCE COMML REAL EST	1.16	0.97	59	1.62	0.35	84	1.51	0.36	83	1.45	0.38	2.30	0.47
MEMORANDUM (% OF AVG TOT LOANS):													
COMMERCIAL PAPER IN LOANS	0.00	0.00	92	0.00	0.00	92	0.00	0.00	93	0.00	0.00	0.00	0.00
LOAN & LEASE COMMITMENTS	37.37	68.39	12	43.88	42.40	51	45.03	44.45	48	45.40	41.86	36.88	40.56
LOANS SOLD DURING THE QUARTER	NA	NA	NA	NA	0.47	27	NA	0.45	27	0.00	0.54	0.03	0.48
OFFICER, SHAREHOLDER LOANS	0.08	0.78	22	2.19	1.14	75	2.31	1.26	73	0.02	0.47	0.05	0.02
OFFICER, SHAREH LOANS TO ASSETS	0.04	0.43	22	0.86	0.63	57	0.86	0.71	57	0.01	0.01	0.02	0.01
OTHER REAL ESTATE OWNED % ASSETS													
CONSTRUCTION & LAND DEVELOPMENT	0.50	0.03	96	0.44	0.07	85	0.43	0.06	86	0.48	0.10	NA	NA
FARMLAND	0.00	0.00	82	0.00	0.00	82	0.00	0.00	84	0.00	0.00	NA	NA
1-4 FAMILY	0.08	0.02	84	0.15	0.03	94	0.13	0.03	93	0.22	0.04	NA	NA
MULTIFAMILY	0.01	0.00	73	0.00	0.01	52	0.00	0.01	53	0.00	0.01	NA	NA
NON-FARM-NON-RESID.	0.21	0.11	68	0.32	0.18	67	0.30	0.17	70	0.44	0.24	NA	NA
FOREIGN OFFICES	0.00	0.00	83	NA	0.00		NA	0.00		NA	0.00	NA	NA
SUBTOTAL	0.80	0.23	92	0.91	0.35	84	0.86	0.32	84	1.24	0.50	NA	NA
DIRECT AND INDIRECT INV.	0.00	0.00	89	0.01	0.00	96	0.02	0.00	97	0.00	0.00	NA	NA
TOTAL	0.80	0.23	91	0.92	0.35	84	0.88	0.32	84	1.24	0.50	NA	NA
MORTGAGE SERVICING % ASSETS													
MORTGAGES SERV. UNDER GNMA	0.00	0.18	63	0.00	0.01	74	0.00	0.03	73	0.00	0.02	NA	NA
MORTGAGES SERVICED UNDER FHLMC	0.00	1.38	42	0.00	0.52	53	0.00	0.57	52	0.00	0.50	NA	NA
MORTGAGES SERVICED UNDER FNMA	0.00	1.51	43	0.00	1.05	52	0.00	1.01	49	0.00	0.75	NA	NA
OTHER MORTGAGE SERVICING	0.00	1.35	42	0.00	0.44	49	0.00	0.47	48	0.00	0.42	NA	NA
TOTAL	0.00	5.94	36	0.00	3.52	44	0.00	3.44	43	0.00	3.21	NA	NA

PAGE 08

CERT # 12883 DSB # 05241075
CHARTER # 22546 COUNTY: MONTGOM

NATIONSBANK, NATIONAL ASSOCIATION   BETHESDA, MD
ANALYSIS OF PAST DUE, NONACCRUAL & RESTRUCTURED LOANS & LEASES

NON-CURRENT LN&LS ($000)	09/30/94	09/30/93	12/31/93	12/31/92	12/31/91
90 DAYS AND OVER PAST DUE	15302	1542	1319	9021	4482
TOTAL NONACCRUAL LN&LS	217208	67285	54672	95520	144453
TOTAL NON-CURRENT LN&LS	232510	68827	55991	104541	148935
RESTRUCTURED LN&LS 90+ DAYS P/D	0	0	0	0	0
RESTRUCTURED LN&LS NONACCRUAL	28854	457	27	476	0
CURRENT RESTRUCTURED LN&LS	41905	0	0	0	12187
ALL OTHER REAL ESTATE OWNED	136914	32103	28474	42019	65423

% OF NON-CURR LN&LS BY LN TYPE	09/30/94 BANK	PEER 01	PCT	09/30/93 BANK	PEER 02	PCT	12/31/93 BANK	PEER 02	PCT	12/31/92 BANK	PEER 02	12/31/91 BANK	PEER 02
REAL ESTATE LNS-90+ DAYS P/D	0.08	0.21	22	0.12	0.23	39	0.06	0.18	31	0.64	0.26	0.18	0.39
-NONACCRUAL	3.56	1.66	82	5.26	1.95	88	4.32	1.60	85	5.30	2.28	8.40	3.15
-TOTAL	3.64	1.97	80	5.37	2.31	86	4.38	1.90	82	5.94	2.77	8.59	3.69
COML & INDUST LNS-90+ DAYS P/D	0.20	0.05	87	0.05	0.11	43	0.09	0.06	63	0.21	0.12	0.01	0.18
-NONACCRUAL	2.03	0.92	80	4.59	1.68	87	3.36	1.34	88	5.29	2.22	13.05	2.70
-TOTAL	2.23	1.01	83	4.63	1.93	85	3.45	1.57	88	5.50	2.52	13.05	3.07
LOANS TO INDIVDLS-90+ DAYS P/D	0.14	0.31	29	0.10	0.46	21	0.10	0.38	23	0.30	0.49	0.44	0.64
-NONACCRUAL	0.11	0.16	49	0.11	0.13	51	0.11	0.10	57	0.28	0.18	0.41	0.25
-TOTAL	0.25	0.58	22	0.21	0.75	22	0.21	0.61	25	0.57	0.87	0.84	1.08
AGRICULTURAL LNS-90+ DAYS P/D	0.00	0.00	75	NA	0.00		NA	0.00		NA	0.00	0.00	0.00
-NONACCRUAL	0.00	0.76	32	NA	0.30		NA	0.21		NA	0.42	0.00	0.42
-TOTAL	0.00	0.99	30	NA	0.36		NA	0.23		NA	0.51	0.00	0.57
OTHER LN&LS-90+ DAYS P/D	0.28	0.02	89	0.00	0.01	55	0.19	0.01	85	0.01	0.02	0.07	0.04
-NONACCRUAL	0.39	0.19	71	5.18	0.27	96	5.32	0.19	97	17.98	0.35	0.00	0.51
-TOTAL	0.67	0.29	73	5.18	0.37	96	5.51	0.27	97	17.99	0.46	0.07	0.65
GROSS LN&LS-90+ DAYS P/D	0.15	0.20	42	0.09	0.32	21	0.08	0.25	24	0.47	0.32	0.20	0.45
-NONACCRUAL	2.09	1.02	87	4.04	1.32	92	3.34	1.08	89	5.00	1.61	6.60	2.17
-TOTAL	2.24	1.26	84	4.13	1.82	90	3.42	1.50	86	5.47	2.13	6.81	2.79
SUPPLEMENTAL: FOREIGN GOVT LNS-90+ DAYS P/D	47.05	0.00	97	NA	0.00		NA	0.00		0.00	0.00	0.00	0.00
-NONACCRUAL	0.00	0.02	70	NA	0.26		NA	0.00		0.00	1.25	0.00	0.36
-TOTAL	47.05	0.10	97	NA	0.26		NA	0.00		0.00	1.25	0.00	0.36
CREDIT CARD PLANS-90+ DAYS P/D	0.46	0.50	47	0.02	0.52	18	0.07	0.50	19	0.01	0.62	0.45	0.77
-NONACCRUAL	0.16	0.01	78	0.00	0.00	74	0.00	0.00	76	0.01	0.01	0.00	0.01
-TOTAL	0.62	0.64	47	0.02	0.62	14	0.07	0.59	16	0.03	0.77	0.45	0.92
LEASE FINANCING-90+ DAYS P/D	0.00	0.00	62	0.00	0.00	66	0.00	0.00	70	0.00	0.01	0.22	0.02
-NONACCRUAL	0.00	0.06	44	0.00	0.08	55	0.00	0.05	55	0.00	0.15	0.00	0.30
-TOTAL	0.00	0.10	33	0.00	0.14	41	0.00	0.09	43	0.00	0.23	0.22	0.45

CERT # 12883 DSB # 05241075
CHARTER # 22546 COUNTY: MONTGOM

NATIONSBANK, NATIONAL ASSOCIATION
ANALYSIS OF PAST DUE, NONACCRUAL & RESTRUCTURED LOANS & LEASES
MEMORANDA INFORMATION

BETHESDA, MD

PAGE 08A

NON-CURR LN&LS BY LN TYPE($000)	09/30/94	09/30/93	12/31/93	12/31/92	12/31/91
LNS FIN COML RE-90+ DAYS P/D	194	0	0	0	0
-NONACCRUAL	3210	5814	5435	17851	10167
-TOTAL	3404	5814	5435	17851	10167
CONST & LAND DEV-90+ DAYS P/D	491	67	5	0	0
-NONACCRUAL	48511	29401	19747	35188	79263
-TOTAL	49002	29468	19752	35188	79263
SINGLE & MULTI MTG-90+ DAYS P/D	1564	823	481	2248	2259
-NONACCRUAL	23962	8620	8229	9634	22922
-TOTAL	25526	9443	8710	11882	25181
NON-FARM/RESI MTG-90+ DAYS P/D	1547	172	56	5025	0
-NONACCRUAL	95252	9983	10704	14848	1405
-TOTAL	96799	10155	10760	19873	1405

% NON-CURRENT LN&LS BY LN TYPE	09/30/94 BANK	PEER 01	PCT	09/30/93 BANK	PEER 02	PCT	12/31/93 BANK	PEER 02	PCT	12/31/92 BANK	PEER 02	12/31/91 BANK	PEER 02
LNS FIN COML RE-90+ DAY P/D	0.19	0.00	89	0.00	0.00	84	0.00	0.00	91	0.00	0.00	0.00	0.00
-NONACCRUAL	3.16	1.46	71	31.63	1.20	95	32.09	0.53	97	43.88	1.45	29.44	1.48
-TOTAL	3.35	1.66	67	31.63	1.39	95	32.09	0.64	97	43.88	1.71	29.44	1.84
CONST & LAND DEV-90+ DAYS P/D	0.14	0.09	65	0.05	0.07	63	0.00	0.04	56	0.00	0.12	0.00	0.32
-NONACCRUAL	14.21	5.10	85	20.16	4.42	86	13.12	3.32	85	17.40	5.73	33.05	7.68
-TOTAL	14.36	5.63	83	20.20	5.21	85	13.12	3.96	82	17.40	6.68	33.05	8.82
SINGLE & MULTI MTG-90+ DAYS P/D	0.08	0.17	35	0.21	0.19	58	0.13	0.16	46	0.43	0.20	0.45	0.32
-NONACCRUAL	1.18	0.63	84	2.18	0.67	87	2.28	0.59	88	1.85	0.82	4.55	0.89
-TOTAL	1.25	0.90	77	2.39	0.92	86	2.41	0.84	87	2.28	1.16	5.00	1.32
NON-FARM/RESI MTG-90+ DAYS P/D	0.07	0.19	37	0.05	0.16	46	0.01	0.09	43	1.24	0.15	0.00	0.23
-NONACCRUAL	4.09	3.06	62	2.65	3.08	48	2.76	2.57	54	3.66	3.11	0.29	3.69
-TOTAL	4.16	3.45	57	2.70	3.43	43	2.77	2.83	50	4.89	3.66	0.29	4.31

OTHER PERTINENT RATIOS:

	09/30/94 BANK	PEER 01	PCT	09/30/93 BANK	PEER 02	PCT	12/31/93 BANK	PEER 02	PCT	12/31/92 BANK	PEER 02	12/31/91 BANK	PEER 02
ENC-LOANS TO TOTAL LOANS	0.58	0.60	49	0.46	0.57	11	0.45	0.55	20	0.46	0.59	0.56	0.71

% CURRENT RESTRUCT LN&LS BY TYPE:

	09/30/94 BANK	PEER 01	PCT	09/30/93 BANK	PEER 02	PCT	12/31/93 BANK	PEER 02	PCT	12/31/92 BANK	PEER 02	12/31/91 BANK	PEER 02
LOANS SECURED BY REAL ESTATE	0.89	0.05	87	0.00	0.04	57	0.00	0.05	55	0.00	0.06	0.99	0.01
COMMERCIAL AND INDUSTRIAL LNS	0.00	0.00	71	0.00	0.00	72	0.00	0.00	69	0.00	0.00	0.00	0.00
LEASE FINANCING RECEIVABLES	0.00	0.00	94	0.00	0.00	97	0.00	0.00	97	0.00	0.00	0.00	0.00
AGRICULTURAL LOANS	0.00	NA	96	NA	0.00		NA	0.00		NA	0.00	NA	0.00
ALL OTHER LOANS & LEASES	0.00	0.00	91	0.00	0.00	92	0.00	0.00	92	0.00	0.00	0.00	0.00

CERT # 12883 DSB # 05241075   NATIONSBANK, NATIONAL ASSOCIATION   BETHESDA, MD
CHARTER # 22546 COUNTY: MONTGOM   MATURITY AND REPRICING DISTRIBUTION AS OF 09/30/94   PAGE 09

CUMULATIVE AMOUNT AS A PERCENT OF ASSETS

ASSETS	TOTAL			PERCENT REPRICED WITHIN 3 MONTHS			PERCENT REPRICED WITHIN 12 MONTHS		
	BANK	PEER 01	PCT	BANK	PEER 01	PCT	BANK	PEER 01	PCT
LOANS AND LEASES (EXCL NONACC)	54.14	59.99	29	33.31	30.56	68	35.76	39.28	42
FIXED RATE BY MATURITY	25.41	27.14	43	6.97	5.87	56	7.75	8.80	42
FLOATING RATE BY REP INTERVAL	28.73	30.76	42	26.34	23.41	64	28.01	28.47	47
DEBT SECURITIES	25.96	17.66	73	2.02	1.26	66	7.46	4.20	75
FIXED RATE BY MATURITY	24.22	15.15	80	0.30	0.45	42	5.72	1.93	82
FLOATING RATE BY REP INTERVAL	1.74	1.26	59	1.72	0.53	73	1.74	1.21	59
FEDERAL FUNDS SOLD(OVERNIGHT)* / SECURITIES PURCHASED UNDER AGREEMENT TO RESELL*	7.98	2.73	82	7.98	2.73	82	7.98	2.73	82
INTEREST-BEARING BANK BALANCES*	0.20	0.28	57	0.20	0.28	57	0.20	0.28	57
TRADING ACCOUNT ASSETS*	0.00	1.49	26				0.00	1.49	26
	0.00	0.98	14	0.00	0.98	14	0.00	0.98	14
TOTAL INT-BEARING ASSETS(IBA)	88.27	88.83	36	43.51	42.25	52	51.39	57.68	29
LIABILITIES									
DEPOSITS IN FOREIGN OFFICES**	2.11	8.73	30						
CD'S OF $100,000 OR MORE	2.83	3.18	43	1.14	1.51	36	2.04	2.43	40
FIXED RATE BY MATURITY	2.81	3.13	43	1.11	1.47	40	2.01	2.39	38
FLOATING RATE BY REP INTERVAL	0.03	0.02	70	0.03	0.01	75	0.03	0.01	70
OTHER TIME DEPOSITS	12.41	11.02	57	3.40	2.98	52	8.81	7.48	64
MONEY MARKET DEPOSIT ACCOUNTS*	9.53	10.25	49	9.53	10.25	49	9.53	10.25	49
OTHER SAVINGS DEP (EXCL MMDA)**	13.83	6.67	82						
NOW ACCOUNTS*	9.10	6.38	71	9.10	6.38	71	9.10	6.38	71
FEDERAL FUNDS PURCH(OVERNIGHT)* / SECURITIES SOLD UNDER AGREEMENT TO REPURCHASE*	10.23	6.70	70	10.23	6.70	70	10.23	6.70	70
OTHER BORROWED MONEY***	4.46	2.21	71	4.46	2.21	71	4.46	2.21	71
SUB NOTES & DEBENTURES**	3.70	6.84	38				0.15	5.33	14
TREASURY NOTES*	0.00	1.24	21						
	0.44	0.74	43	0.44	0.74	43	0.44	0.74	43
TOTAL INT-BEARING LIABS (IBL)	68.65	75.51	17	38.29	36.41	56	44.75	48.89	33

NET POSITION (NOT CALCULATED FOR THE FFIEC 031 CALL REPORTER.)

*INDICATES ITEMS THAT ARE NOT REPORTED BY MATURITY/REPRICING INTERVAL, HOWEVER, REPRICING ASSUMPTIONS WERE MADE.
**INDICATES ITEMS THAT ARE NOT REPORTED BY MATURITY/REPRICING INTERVAL, HOWEVER, NO REPRICING ASSUMPTIONS WERE MADE.

PLEASE NOTE: DURING THE CURRENT QUARTER THIS BANK HAS PARTICIPATED IN INTEREST RATE CONTRACTS MARKET.

CERT # 12883 DSB # 05241075 NATIONSBANK, NATIONAL ASSOCIATION BETHESDA, MD
CHARTER # 22546 COUNTY: MONTGOM LIQUIDITY AND INVESTMENT PORTFOLIO PAGE 10

	09/30/94			09/30/93			12/31/93			12/31/92		12/31/91	
	BANK	PEER 01	PCT	BANK	PEER 02	PCT	BANK	PEER 02	PCT	BANK	PEER 02	BANK	PEER 02
TEMPORARY INVESTMENTS	2931649			1271947			1456517			708116		583118	
CORE DEPOSITS	12169051			3079473			3118749			3230501		3090128	
VOLATILE LIABILITIES	3816892			696875			785791			583508		763560	
NON-CUR DEBT SECURITIES & OTH ASSETS:													
-90+ DAYS P/D	0			0			0			0		0	
-NONACCRUAL	0			0			0			0		0	
-TOTAL NON-CURRENT	0			0			0			0		0	
CURRENT-RESTRUCTURED DEBT SEC	0			0			0			0		0	
PERCENT OF TOTAL ASSETS													
TEMPORARY INVESTMENTS	15.63	14.04	57	31.23	11.61	94	34.57	12.46	96	17.29	11.01	14.11	9.65
CORE DEPOSITS	64.88	53.78	63	75.62	67.48	72	74.01	68.02	66	78.87	69.58	74.79	68.55
VOLATILE LIABILITIES	20.35	32.13	31	17.11	22.82	32	18.65	22.18	41	14.25	21.01	18.48	22.89
LIQUIDITY RATIOS													
VOLATILE LIABILITY DEPENDENCE	6.56	25.06	14	-22.95	13.16	02	-27.77	11.56	03	-4.34	10.95	5.78	15.55
BROKERED DEPOSITS TO DEPOSITS	0.81	0.31	71	0.34	0.35	62	0.34	0.34	59	0.76	0.41	1.82	0.95
TEMP INV TO VOLATILE LIABILITIES	76.81	47.46	80	182.52	57.31	87	185.36	62.40	85	121.35	63.06	76.37	46.54
TEMP INV LESS VOL LIAB TO ASSETS	-4.72	-16.94	84	14.12	-10.31	97	15.92	-9.14	96	3.04	-8.50	-4.37	-12.11
NET LOANS & LEASES TO DEPOSITS	74.42	86.49	24	49.09	80.53	07	47.66	79.62	06	53.39	76.94	58.80	77.59
NET LN&LS TO CORE DEPOSITS	80.23	113.77	15	51.24	90.32	06	49.66	89.22	06	56.45	86.44	66.79	90.93
NET LN&LS & LEASES TO ASSETS	52.06	59.22	24	38.75	59.77	10	36.75	59.41	08	44.52	58.81	49.95	61.01
NET LN&LS & SBLC TO ASSETS	55.73	64.68	19	42.57	62.94	11	40.23	62.44	10	47.84	62.17	54.14	64.45
SECURITIES MIX													
HELD-TO-MATURITY % TOTAL SECS													
U.S. TREAS & GOVT AGENCIES	40.20	11.47	77	94.54	34.93	96	97.66	36.43	97	80.59	35.40	42.16	28.61
MUNICIPAL SECURITIES	2.46	3.99	43	0.00	5.43	11	0.00	5.58	10	0.00	6.05	0.00	7.14
PASS-THROUGH MTG BACKED SECS	0.30	5.97	42	0.00	14.64	13	1.92	15.19	13	0.00	15.07	27.02	18.41
CMO & REMIC MTG BACKED SECS	43.23	4.32	96	5.10	15.95	37	1.92	14.82	28	19.01	13.66	24.04	13.52
OTHER DOMESTIC DEBT SECS	0.53	1.58	50	0.00	4.58	18	0.00	4.01	18	0.00	4.45	4.87	6.48
FOREIGN DEBT SECURITIES	0.07	0.11	54	0.06	0.03	68	0.07	0.04	65	0.00	0.04	0.00	0.09
INVESTMENTS IN MUTUAL FUNDS	NA	NA		0.00	0.00	85	0.00	0.00	84	0.00	0.00	0.00	0.00
OTHER EQUITY SECURITIES	NA	NA		0.30	0.82	27	0.35	0.85	31	0.41	0.72	1.93	0.68
LESS: UNREALIZED LOSS (MES)	NA	NA		0.00	0.00	97	0.00	0.00	97	0.00	0.00	0.00	7.14
TOTAL HELD-TO-MATURITY	86.77	53.34	87	100.00	100.00	99	100.00	100.00	99	100.00	100.00	100.00	100.00
AVAILABLE-FOR-SALE % TOTAL SECS													
U.S. TREASURY & GOVT AGENCIES	10.90	15.71	45	NA	NA		NA	NA		NA	NA	NA	NA
MUNICIPAL SECURITIES	0.00	0.01	64	NA	NA		NA	NA		NA	NA	NA	NA
PASS-THROUGH MTG BACKED SECS	0.00	5.08	36	NA	NA		NA	NA		NA	NA	NA	NA
CMO & REMIC MTG BACKED SECS	0.00	2.25	45	NA	NA		NA	NA		NA	NA	NA	NA
OTHER DOMESTIC DEBT SECURITIES	0.03	0.90	36	NA	NA		NA	NA		NA	NA	NA	NA
FOREIGN DEBT SECURITIES	0.00	0.38	56	NA	NA		NA	NA		NA	NA	NA	NA
INVESTMENTS IN MUTUAL FUNDS	1.13	0.01	98	NA	NA		NA	NA		NA	NA	NA	NA
OTHER EQUITY SECURITIES	1.16	1.08	57	NA	NA		NA	NA		NA	NA	NA	NA
TOTAL AVAILABLE-FOR-SALE	13.23	46.66	12	NA	NA		NA	NA		NA	NA	NA	NA
DEBT SECURITIES UNDER 1 YEAR	28.73	29.28	56	46.25	29.53	76	40.46	31.32	69	16.86	23.86	0.01	21.26
DEBT SECURITIES 1 TO 5 YEARS	36.43	32.28	49	48.63	31.41	76	57.61	31.20	87	64.05	30.80	39.98	26.15
DEBT SECURITIES OVER 5 YEARS	34.84	33.88	43	5.12	34.31	12	1.93	32.48	12	19.08	37.71	60.01	45.39
OTHER SECURITIES RATIOS:													
APP(DEP) IN HTM SEC TO HTM SEC	-3.08	-2.12	32	0.42	2.11	07	0.03	1.01	16	1.21	1.85	4.15	3.44
APP(DEP) IN HTM SEC TO EQY CAP	-6.90	-2.81	15	2.62	6.58	22	0.15	2.80	21	5.74	5.83	19.08	11.08
PLEDGED SECURITIES TO TOT SEC	78.62	61.61	73	42.49	46.82	45	54.44	47.37	59	44.71	46.54	41.06	49.67

CERT # 12883 DSB # 05241075   NATIONSBANK, NATIONAL ASSOCIATION   BETHESDA, MD
CHARTER # 22546 COUNTY: MONTGOM   CAPITAL ANALYSIS   PAGE 11

END OF PERIOD CAPITAL ($000)	09/30/94	09/30/93	12/31/93	12/31/92	12/31/91
+ PERPETUAL PREFERRED	0	0	0	0	0
+ COMMON STOCK	432892	20073	20073	20073	18573
+ SURPLUS	1504777	144413	144413	144413	115636
+ UNDIVIDED PROFITS	-56732	101986	99268	90960	81295
+ UNREALIZED G/L AVAIL SALE SECS	-10628	NA	-832	0	0
+ CUMMULATIVE FOREIGN CURR. ADJ.	0	NA	NA	NA	NA
TOTAL EQUITY CAPITAL	1870309	266472	264586	255446	215504
LIMITED LIFE PREFERRED	0	0	0	0	0
SUBORDINATED NOTES & DEBENTURES	0	0	0	0	0
CHANGES IN TOTAL EQUITY ($000)					
BALANCE AT BEGINNING OF PERIOD	264586	255446	255446	215504	233263
+ NET INCOME	199880	11026	8308	1701	-47515
+ SALE OR PURCHASE OF CAPITAL	1708478	0	0	28241	0
+ MERGER & ABSORPTIONS	0	0	0	0	0
+ CUMUL ACCTG. CHANGES	0	0	0	0	0
+ CORR. MATERIAL ACCTG. CHG.	0	0	0	0	0
+ TRANS. WITH PARENT	23233	0	0	10000	18000
- DIVIDENDS	315007	0	0	0	0
+ NET OTHER INCREASE (DECREASE)	-10861	0	832	0	11756
BALANCE AT END OF PERIOD	1870309	266472	264586	255446	215504
INTANGIBLE ASSETS					
MORTGAGE SERVICING RIGHTS	0	0	0	0	0
+ PURCH CRED CARD RELATION.	0	0	0	0	NA
+ OTHER INTANGIBLES	115392	2117	1966	2596	0
+ GOODWILL	175943	0	0	0	0
TOTAL INTANGIBLES	291335	2117	1966	2596	NA
MEMO:					
GRANDFATHERED INTANGIBLES	0	0	0	0	NA

	09/30/94			09/30/93			12/31/93			12/31/92		12/31/91	
CAPITAL RATIOS	BANK	PEER 01	PCT	BANK	PEER 02	PCT	BANK	PEER 02	PCT	BANK	PEER 02	BANK	PEER 02
PERCENT OF TOTAL EQUITY:													
NET LOANS & LEASES (X)	5.22	8.01	10	5.92	7.84	18	5.85	7.88	18	7.14	8.08	9.58	9.57
SUBORD NOTES & DEBENTURES	0.00	17.78	21	0.00	4.80	44	0.00	4.49	45	0.00	4.35	0.00	1.82
LONG TERM DEBT	0.31	18.78	14	0.12	5.48	26	0.12	5.04	30	0.12	5.14	0.00	2.99
COM RE & RELATED VENTURES	155.38	114.83	73	215.40	143.28	83	221.18	138.62	83	270.98	156.41	384.53	212.37
PERCENT OF AVERAGE TOTAL EQUITY:													
NET INCOME	13.85	16.06	29	5.65	17.46	09	3.18	17.68	05	0.70	15.73	-21.04	10.81
DIVIDENDS	21.83	8.79	94	0.00	6.15	23	3.18	8.29	16	0.70	4.16	-0.00	4.71
RETAINED EARNINGS	-7.98	6.57	03	5.65	9.37	31	3.18	7.97	28	0.70	9.37	-21.04	3.38
OTHER CAPITAL RATIOS:													
DIVIDENDS TO NET OPER INCOME	157.60	57.46	96	0.00	37.27	21	0.00	49.05	14	0.00	31.16	NA	49.27
EQUITY CAPITAL TO ASSETS	9.97	7.14	91	6.54	7.53	20	6.28	7.53	10	6.24	7.14	5.22	6.31
GROWTH RATES:													
TOTAL EQUITY CAPITAL	601.88	9.06	98	3.74	14.65	17	3.58	14.31	19	18.53	14.96	-7.61	9.43
EQUITY GROWTH LESS ASST GROWTH	241.30	0.88	98	5.78	6.04	46	0.70	7.20	29	19.39	9.74	-1.67	5.37
INTANG ASSETS % TOTAL EQUITY													
MORTGAGE SERVICING RIGHT	0.00	0.20	57	0.00	0.02	73	0.00	0.02	72	0.00	0.06	0.00	0.07
GOODWILL	9.41	2.24	85	0.00	0.52	42	0.00	0.77	37	0.00	0.38	0.00	0.35
PURCH CREDIT CARD RELATION	0.00	0.01	71	0.00	0.00	80	0.00	0.00	81	0.00	0.00	NA	NA
ALL OTHER INTANGIBLES	6.17	1.12	85	0.79	0.44	68	0.74	0.44	66	1.02	0.48	0.00	0.74
TOTAL INTANGIBLES	15.58	5.60	77	0.79	2.93	31	0.74	3.35	27	1.02	2.86	0.00	3.02

CERT # 12883 DSB # 05241075
CHARTER # 22546

NATIONSBANK, NATIONAL ASSOCIATION
RISK-BASED CAPITAL ANALYSIS

BETHESDA, MD
PAGE 11A

RISK-BASED CAPITAL ($000)	09/30/94	09/30/93	12/31/93	12/31/92	12/31/91
TIER ONE CAPITAL(***)					
COMMON EQUITY	1880937	266472	263754	255446	215504
+ NONCUMULATIVE PERP PREFD STOCK	0	0	0	0	0
+ MINORITY INTEREST UNCONS SUBS	0	0	0	0	0
- INELIGIBLE DEF. TAX ASSETS	0	0	0	NA	NA
- INELIGIBLE INTANGIBLES	291335	2117	1966	2596	0
NET TIER ONE	1589602	264355	261788	252850	215504
TIER TWO CAPITAL					
+ ALLOWABLE SUB DEBT & LTD LIFE	0	0	0	0	0
+ CUMULATIVE PREFERRED STOCK	0	0	0	0	0
+ MANDATORY CONVERTIBLE DEBT	0	0	0	0	0
+ ALLOWABLE LN&LS LOSS ALLOWANCE	161113	27629	28181	30834	36671
+ AGRICULTURAL LOSS DEFERRAL	0	0	0	0	0
+ NET WORTH CERTIFICATES	0	0	0	0	0
NET ELIGIBLE TIER TWO*	161113	27629	28181	30834	36671
TOTAL RBC BEFORE DEDUCTIONS	1750715	291984	289969	283684	252175
- TIER ONE & TIER TWO	0	0	0	0	0
- RECIPROCAL CAPITAL HOLDINGS	0	0	0	0	0
TOTAL RISK-BASED CAPITAL	1750715	291984	289969	283684	252175
RISK-WEIGHTED ASSETS					
ON-BALANCE SHEET					
CATEGORY TWO - 20%	1225321	145549	211423	211847	246615
CATEGORY THREE - 50%	403199	74262	46377	10065	31977
CATEGORY FOUR - 100%	9539784	1629644	1654272	2050857	2372984
TOTAL ON-BALANCE SHEET	11168304	1849455	1912072	2272769	2651576
MEMO: CATEGORY ONE - 0%	2879181	1654747	1495465	1050717	584445
OFF-BALANCE SHEET					
CATEGORY TWO - 20%	14636	2230	2836	2225	3459
CATEGORY THREE - 50%	13626	2245	13	105	490
CATEGORY FOUR - 100%	1983830	358570	341555	194225	278226
TOTAL OFF-BALANCE SHEET	2012092	363045	344404	196555	282175
MEMO: CATEGORY ONE - 0%	12139	0	0	0	0
ADJUSTMENTS TO RISK-WEIGHTED ASSETS					
RISK-WEIGHTED ASSET BEFORE DED	13180397	2212501	2256477	2469325	2933751
- INELIGIBLE DEF. TAX ASSETS	0	0	0	NA	NA
- INELIGIBLE INTANGIBLES	291335	2117	1966	2596	0
- RECIPROCAL CAPITAL HOLDINGS	0	0	0	0	0
- EXCESS ALLOWABLE LN&LS LOSS AL	423891	60701	58984	54160	86228
- ALLOCATED TRANSFER RISK RESERV	0	0	0	0	0
TOTAL RISK-WEIGHTED ASSETS	12465170	2149682	2195526	2412568	2847523

RISK-BASED CAPITAL(***)	BANK	PEER 01	PCT	BANK	PEER 02	PCT	BANK	PEER 02	PCT	BANK	PEER 02	BANK	PEER 02
TIER ONE RBC TO RISK-WGT ASSETS	12.75	8.87	92	12.30	10.60	73	11.92	10.56	72	10.48	9.96	7.57	8.30
TOTAL RBC TO RISK-WEIGHT ASSETS	14.04	11.69	89	13.58	12.65	67	13.21	12.52	63	11.76	11.82	8.86	9.87
TIER ONE LEVERAGE CAPITAL	8.78	6.95	89	6.12	7.39	12	6.03	7.31	09	6.29	6.97	5.30	6.22
OTHER CAPITAL RATIO:													
DEF TAX ASSET TO T1 CAP	6.75	5.00	57	0.00	4.66	22	0.00	4.37	27	NA		NA	

*NET ELIGIBLE TIER TWO RISK-BASED CAPITAL CANNOT EXCEED NET TIER ONE RISK-BASED CAPITAL.

(***) TIER ONE CAPITAL AFTER 12/31/93 EXCLUDES FASB 115 NET UNREALIZED HOLDING GAIN/LOSS ON AVAILABLE-FOR-SALE SECURITIES.

CERT # 12883   DSB # 05241075   NATIONSBANK, NATIONAL ASSOCIATION   BETHESDA, MD   PAGE 12
CHARTER # 22546   COUNTY: MONTGOM   LAST-FOUR-QUARTERS   SEPTEMBER 30TH

INCOME ANALYSIS (OCTOBER 1ST THROUGH SEPTEMBER 30TH)

EARNINGS AND PROFITABILITY

	1993-1994 BANK	PEER 01	PCT	1992-1993 BANK	PEER 02	PCT	1991-1992 BANK	PEER 02	PCT	1990-1991 BANK	PEER 02	1989-1990 BANK	PEER 02
PERCENT OF AVERAGE ASSETS:													
INTEREST INCOME (TE)	5.06	6.21	16	5.56	6.74	10	6.90	7.60	23	8.91	8.84	9.50	9.53
- INTEREST EXPENSE	1.84	2.43	16	2.27	2.52	31	3.56	3.49	59	5.17	5.06	5.71	5.80
NET INTEREST INCOME (TE)	3.22	3.75	28	3.30	4.25	12	3.34	4.18	15	3.74	3.90	3.79	3.84
+ NONINTEREST INCOME	1.30	1.92	17	1.01	1.68	17	1.22	1.76	25	1.11	1.55	1.05	1.45
MEMO: FEE INCOME	0.14	0.60	03	0.16	0.49	07	0.20	0.51	16	NA	NA	NA	NA
- NON-INTEREST EXPENSE	3.20	3.73	28	3.51	3.84	35	4.32	3.93	67	3.11	3.61	3.14	3.34
= PROVISION: LOAN&LEASE LOSSES	-0.53	0.18	01	0.43	0.41	54	1.87	0.75	86	3.32	1.09	0.62	0.91
= PRETAX OPERATING INCOME (TE)	1.85	1.74	60	0.36	1.78	08	-1.63	1.38	03	-1.58	0.88	1.09	1.05
+ REALIZED GAINS/LOSSES SECS	0.01	0.01	60	0.01	0.03	50	-0.85	0.07	98	-0.15	0.04	0.02	0.01
= PRETAX NET OPERATING INC(TE)	1.86	1.75	62	0.37	1.89	08	-0.77	1.50	05	-1.43	0.95	1.11	1.07
NET OPERATING INCOME	1.06	1.14	42	-0.22	1.24	07	-0.55	0.97	05	-0.80	0.60	0.73	0.69
ADJUSTED NET OPERATING INCOME	NA	1.09		-0.68	1.28	03	-0.18	1.06	07	-0.67	0.85	1.03	0.94
ADJUSTED NET INCOME	NA	1.09		-0.54	1.25	03	-0.30	1.04	08	-0.06	0.76	0.86	0.86
NET INCOME	1.06	1.14	42	-0.22	1.25	07	-0.55	0.98	05	-0.80	0.61	0.73	0.69
MARGIN ANALYSIS:													
INT INC (TE) TO AVG EARN ASSETS	NA	6.95		6.14	7.48	07	7.45	8.40	13	9.63	9.73	10.25	10.49
INT EXPENSE TO AVG EARN ASSETS	NA	2.73		2.50	2.78	26	3.84	3.84	49	5.59	5.58	6.16	6.41
NET INT INC-TE TO AVG EARN ASST	NA	4.17		3.64	4.73	10	3.60	4.62	10	4.04	4.29	4.09	4.23

LOAN & LEASE ANALYSIS

	1993-1994 BANK	PEER 01	PCT	1992-1993 BANK	PEER 02	PCT	1991-1992 BANK	PEER 02	PCT	1990-1991 BANK	PEER 02	1989-1990 BANK	PEER 02
NET LOSS TO AVERAGE TOTAL LN&LS	NA	0.40		3.20	0.68	93	2.84	1.12	86	3.04	1.30	0.51	1.03
EARNINGS COVERAGE OF NET LOSS(X)	NA	9.66		0.59	6.30	03	0.16	3.34	03	0.86	2.56	4.67	3.07
LN&LS ALLOWANCE TO NET LOSSES(X)	NA	6.56		1.55	4.17	14	2.04	2.43	39	1.40	2.06	3.53	2.24

CAPITALIZATION

	1993-1994 BANK	PEER 01	PCT	1992-1993 BANK	PEER 02	PCT	1991-1992 BANK	PEER 02	PCT	1990-1991 BANK	PEER 02	1989-1990 BANK	PEER 02
CASH DIVIDENDS TO NET INCOME	NA	60.09		0.00	40.58	18	NA	33.06	06	NA	52.45	58.52	55.64
RETAIN EARNS TO AVG TOTAL EQUITY	NA	6.37		3.70	9.11	25	-9.61	8.27		-16.06	1.86	5.11	3.60

YIELD ON OR COST OF:

	1993-1994 BANK	PEER 01	PCT	1992-1993 BANK	PEER 02	PCT	1991-1992 BANK	PEER 02	PCT	1990-1991 BANK	PEER 02	1989-1990 BANK	PEER 02
TOTAL LOANS & LEASES (TE)	NA	7.73		8.28	8.26	55	8.67	9.05	32	9.87	10.24	10.64	11.00
LOANS IN DOMESTIC OFFICES	6.56	7.54	17	8.45	8.10	65	8.81	8.94	43	10.00	10.17	10.75	10.93
REAL ESTATE	6.34	7.70	05	7.82	7.94	43	8.35	8.80	26	10.03	10.04	11.28	10.66
COMMERCIAL & INDUSTRIAL	7.20	7.21	49	10.23	7.08	92	7.23	7.75	32	8.94	9.53	10.52	10.72
INDIVIDUAL	NA	9.36		9.49	10.12	38	11.34	11.22	51	11.15	12.01	11.43	12.21
AGRICULTURAL	NA	7.19		NA	7.54		NA	8.22		13.48	9.98	13.16	10.89
LOANS IN FOREIGN OFFICES	5.39	5.63	37	5.38	5.51	15	NA	6.25		NA	8.19	NA	9.14
TOTAL INVESTMENT SECURITIES (TE)	4.00	5.92	05	5.37	6.36	18	6.92	7.65	19	9.59	8.84	9.38	9.07
U.S. TREASURIES & AGENCIES	4.03	5.54	08	NA	6.10		6.80	7.49	22	9.17	8.77	9.09	8.89
STATE & POLITICAL SUB (BOOK)	3.68	6.74	03	NA	6.55		-36.24	6.83	00	8.03	7.11	7.17	6.96
STATE & POLITICAL SUB (TE)	NA	9.99		NA	9.54		-55.08	9.78	00	11.66	10.21	10.90	10.02
OTHER SECURITIES	NA	5.82		5.47	6.23	33	7.03	7.36	96	9.42	8.40	9.12	8.78
EQUITY SECURITIES	3.33	5.88	17	7.01	5.66	84	4.67	5.88	84	10.69	6.03	10.13	5.99
INTEREST-BEARING BANK BALANCES	11.67	4.79	94	16.00	3.67	95	3.79	4.99	36	6.69	7.22	9.31	8.65
FEDERAL FUNDS SOLD & RESALES	3.69	3.76	38	2.94	3.14	77	4.70	4.09	10	6.40	6.50	6.94	8.43
TOTAL INT-BEARING DEPOSITS	NA	3.05		3.10	3.32	37	4.70	4.58	59	6.58	6.44	7.21	7.26
TRANSACTION ACCOUNTS	1.65	1.49	58	2.06	2.02	56	3.19	3.02	67	4.65	4.51	5.09	4.79
MONEY MARKET DEPOSIT ACCOUNTS	2.20	2.35	30	2.59	2.63	41	4.09	3.74	83	5.81	5.62	6.36	6.37
OTHER SAVINGS DEPOSITS	2.04	2.14	46	2.50	2.64	38	3.52	3.65	36	4.94	5.00	5.02	5.10
LARGE CERTIFICATES OF DEPOSIT	2.49	3.74	12	2.64	3.90	09	5.64	5.18	70	7.42	7.17	8.62	8.31
ALL OTHER TIME DEPOSITS	2.92	3.96	16	4.71	4.45	64	6.10	5.71	71	7.71	7.35	8.33	8.30
DEPOSITS IN FOREIGN OFFICES	NA	3.86		NA	3.09		NA	4.18		NA	6.64	NA	8.15
FEDERAL FUNDS PURCH & REPOS	2.71	3.63	11	2.76	2.96	22	3.56	3.87	14	6.19	6.36	7.90	8.19
OTHER BORROWED MONEY	3.54	3.99	37	1.81	2.94	21	3.62	4.01	39	4.81	5.81	5.47	7.38
SUBORDINATED NOTES & DEBENTURES	NA	6.50		NA	6.67		NA	7.51		NA	8.49	NA	8.84
ALL INTEREST-BEARING FUNDS	NA	3.27		3.02	3.30	24	4.55	4.47	57	6.50	6.39	7.24	7.44

SUMMARY INFORMATION FOR BANKS IN STATE OF MARYLAND
AVERAGE FOR ALL INSURED COMMERCIAL BANKS IN STATE

	12/31/94	12/31/93	12/31/92	12/31/91	12/31/90	BANKS WITH ASSETS - $MILL 0-25	25-100	100+	STAVG (12/31/94)
EARNINGS AND PROFITABILITY									
PERCENT OF AVERAGE ASSETS:									
INTEREST INCOME (TE)	7.29	7.43	8.12	9.28	9.96	NA	7.48		7.16
- INTEREST EXPENSE	2.61	2.74	3.55	4.97	5.59	NA	2.72		2.54
NET INTEREST INCOME (TE)	4.63	4.59	4.50	4.26	4.37	NA	4.74		4.56
+ NONINTEREST INCOME	0.62	0.63	0.63	0.58	0.52	NA	0.51		0.69
MEMO: FEE INCOME	0.14	0.12	0.12	0.11	NA	NA	0.09		0.18
- NON-INTEREST EXPENSE	3.31	3.29	3.28	3.21	3.16	NA	3.25		3.28
- PROVISION: LOAN&LEASE LOSSES	0.11	0.20	0.36	0.38	0.40	NA	0.15		0.10
= PRETAX OPERATING INCOME (TE)	1.90	1.81	1.59	1.29	1.37	NA	1.84		1.99
+ REALIZED GAIN/LOSS SECS	0.00	0.01	0.04	0.00	0.00	NA	0.00		0.00
= PRETAX NET OPERATING INC (TE)	1.87	1.85	1.68	1.32	1.38	NA	1.80		1.97
NET OPERATING INCOME	1.17	1.16	1.05	0.82	0.84	NA	1.12		1.23
ADJUSTED NET OPERATING INCOME	1.21	1.24	1.23	0.94	1.07	NA	1.22		1.23
ADJUSTED NET INCOME	1.21	1.25	1.19	0.94	1.02	NA	1.20		1.24
NET INCOME	1.17	1.19	1.06	0.84	0.85	NA	1.13		1.23
MARGIN ANALYSIS:									
AVG EARNING ASSETS TO AVG ASSETS	93.88	93.98	94.18	93.95	94.07	NA	93.73		94.18
AVG INT-BEARING FUNDS TO AVG AST	76.04	77.04	78.15	78.60	77.78	NA	77.19		75.62
INT INC (TE) TO AVG EARN ASSETS	7.76	7.87	8.60	9.86	10.59	NA	8.00		7.56
INT EXPENSE TO AVG EARN ASSETS	2.80	2.93	3.79	5.33	5.98	NA	2.91		2.71
NET INT INC-TE TO AVG EARN ASSET	4.94	4.88	4.78	4.53	4.65	NA	5.08		4.83
LOAN & LEASE ANALYSIS									
NET LOSS TO AVERAGE TOTAL LN&LS	0.11	0.20	0.33	0.37	0.27	NA	0.09		0.13
EARNINGS COVERAGE OF NET LOSS(X)	28.71	16.31	12.23	8.25	10.95	NA	28.27		31.43
LN&LS ALLOWANCE TO NET LOSSES(X)	16.23	9.23	5.93	4.42	6.43	NA	12.83		17.41
LN&LS ALLOWANCE TO TOTAL LN&LS	1.52	1.62	1.59	1.36	1.29	NA	1.37		1.63
LIQUIDITY									
VOLATILE LIABILITY DEPENDENCE	-2.37	-7.66	-6.20	-2.76	-1.75	NA	-4.85		-0.53
NET LOANS & LEASES TO ASSETS	64.94	61.47	62.32	64.63	66.27	NA	67.78		62.43
CAPITALIZATION									
TIER ONE LEVERAGE CAPITAL	9.71	9.31	8.99	8.62	8.71	NA	10.02		9.33
CASH DIVIDENDS TO NET INCOME	29.16	25.62	25.30	31.95	31.90	NA	21.87		34.56
RETAIN EARNS TO AVG TOTAL EQUITY	7.98	8.59	7.95	6.00	6.31	NA	8.38		8.01
GROWTH RATES									
ASSETS	4.15	4.62	6.86	7.90	8.37	NA	5.36		3.40
TIER ONE CAPITAL	8.79	9.87	10.12	7.62	NA	NA	9.18		8.49
NET LOANS & LEASES	11.05	4.42	4.90	5.02	7.07	NA	12.50		9.25
TEMPORARY INVESTMENTS	-16.53	17.70	2.60	1.72	-4.32	NA	-21.52		-9.29
VOLATILE LIABILITIES	22.09	4.67	-19.64	-4.44	13.34	NA	16.51		25.46
% NON-CURRENT LOANS & LEASES:									
GROSS LN&LS-90+ DAYS PAST DUE	0.12	0.16	0.22	0.32	0.32	NA	0.13		0.11
-NONACCRUAL	0.41	0.61	0.76	0.68	0.49	NA	0.26		0.56
-TOTAL	0.70	0.97	1.24	1.35	1.02	NA	0.56		0.82
TOTAL ASSETS ($MILLIONS)	53907	51979	53083	54722	56937	70	2352		51483
EQUITY CAPITAL ($MILLIONS)	4540	4474	3924	3431	3324	8	228		4302
NET INCOME ($MILLIONS)	633	401	337	290	-230	-0	25		608
NUMBER OF BANKS IN TABULATION	93	94	96	102	103	3	36		54

"I prefer credit unions. Credit unions treat members well and offer the lowest average fees and the most competitive rates on deposits and on loans."

Eleanor Swanson
Professor Regis University and Credit Union Member (1998)

"The credit unions have enjoyed a free ride on the nation's taxpayers. The credit unions have overstepped their common bonds."

Barbara Walker
Executive Director of the Independent Bankers of Colorado,
"Credit Unions Launch Intense Lobbying Effort: Supreme Court Decision Prompts Action." *Denver Business Journal*,
February 27–March 5, 1998, 5A.

"The thrift segment has been particularly hard hit. From 1960 to the beginning of 1993, the number of thrifts dropped from 6,835 to 2,529. By the end of the century . . . the distinctions between thrifts and banks will probably have disappeared."

Richard D. Crawford
New Visions Financial, Inc.; William W. Sihler, Professor, Darden School, University of Virginia, *Financial Service Organizations: Cases in Strategic Management*. New York: Harper Collins College Publishers, 1994, 1.9.

"Fannie Mae and the creation of Freddie Mac marked the beginning of a new era for thrifts in the financial system. Today the functions of origination and servicing are still lodged in thrifts (although real estate brokers and finance companies are competing for this business), but over 50% of all new residential mortgage originations flow into the secondary market and the market continues to grow."

Professors Carliss Y. Baldwin and Benjamin C. Esty
Harvard University, "Lessons from the Thrift Crisis." ed. Samuel L. Hayes, III. *Financial Services: Perspectives and Challenges*.
Boston, Mass.: Harvard Business School Press, 1993, 39.

7

CREDIT UNIONS AND SAVINGS INSTITUTIONS

On February 27, 1998, many credit unions (CUs) and consumer advocates were shocked by the Supreme Court's decision that the National Credit Union Administration (NCUA) had exceeded its jurisdiction by allowing federal CUs to expand their original "common bond" requirement for membership. In 1982 the NCUA had reinterpreted the Federal Credit Union Act of 1934 to permit federal

CUs to diversify their membership to serve other local employee groups and associations and to set up their own definitions for membership. NCUA felt that this expansion of CUs' "common bond" was vital for their subsequent success and continued operations. During the severe recession of the early 1980s, many CUs faced potential liquidation when their sponsor firms experienced financial problems. Moreover, unless several businesses were allowed under one CU, a number of businesses were too small to start their own CUs. NCUA's new policy gave CUs a more diversified member base, and CUs expanded rapidly between 1983 to 1998, with a large commitment to capital improvements, branch expansion, and additions of personnel and equipment.

Community bankers challenged this expansion of membership as unfair, since tax-exempt CUs were acting like, but not being taxed like, banks. Some CUs, such as the AT&T Family Federal Credit Union, for instance, had members from 150 unrelated companies, with only 35% of its members employed by AT&T and its affiliates.[1]

The Supreme Court's 1998 decision threatened CUs with grave consequences, since almost a third of the industry had committed to large capital improvements, allowing greater economies of scale and the ability to provide a larger variety of services to credit union members. In response to a letter-writing campaign by credit union members and an appeal by CUs that this decision threatened their existence, the U.S. House of Representatives passed H.R. 411–8 in April, 1998; this bill was intended to open credit union membership to multiple groups. In July of 1998 the Senate voted 92 to 6 in favor of a bill granting CUs limited authority to expand their memberships. This bill was adopted by the House as an amendment and signed into law by President Bill Clinton in early August. The NCUA approved new field of membership rules in early 1999, and they continue to be controversial.[2]

Thrifts faced legislative challenges in the 1990s as well. After major losses and failures in the 1980s and more stringent regulations under the Financial Institutions Reform, Recovery, and Enforcement Act (FIRREA) of 1989, thrifts underwent a major restructuring and consolidation. In 1997 alone, 107 thrift acquisitions were announced, totaling $130 billion in assets and a price-to-earnings multiple of about 25. The viability of thrifts was threatened by house legislation that included a 1995 proposal to eliminate the thrift charter altogether and force stock thrifts to convert to banks. Other legislation attacked the diversification ability of one savings and loan holding companies (OSLHCs) by proposing that diversified OSLHCs be forced to convert to bank holding companies (BHCs); such a conversion would have forced the former OSLHCs to refrain from activities impermissible to BHCs. Although these proposals failed to pass, Congress continues to propose new bills that would merge the bank and thrift deposit insurance funds, halt new OSLHCs, and place current OSLHCs under the Federal Reserve's regulation. Furthermore, tax legislation enacted under the Small Business Jobs Protection Act of 1996 eliminates tax impediments for thrift-to-bank conversions, making bank acquisitions and conversions of thrifts to banks more attractive. Thus, the possibility that the federal thrift charter may be eliminated in the next few years re-

---

[1] Phillip C. Meyer, "High Court Decision Is Awaited on Credit Union 'Common Bond.'" *Banking Policy Report*, 16, October 20, 1997, 1, 12–14.

[2] The banking industry, in turn, attempted to fight the new legislation by taking it back to the Supreme Court. See Linda Greenhouse, "Supreme Court Rules for Banks in a Fight to Limit Credit Unions." *New York Times*, February 26, 1998, A1-C2.; Edward Felsenthal and Matt Murray, "Justices Deal Credit Unions Major Set Back." *Wall Street Journal*, February 26, 1998, A3; John R. Wilke, "Senate Passes Bill Allowing Credit-Union Growth." *Wall Street Journal*, July 29, 1998, A4; Donald Blount, "Credit Union Growth OK'd." *Denver Post*, July 29, 1998, C1; "House Votes to Let Credit Unions Expand Their Memberships, *New York Times*, April 2, 1998, C5; Paul Nylian, "House OKs New Growth for Credit Unions." *Rocky Mountain News*, April 2, 1998, 16b. "Bankers Ready Themselves to Stage Another Fight Against Credit Unions," *Banking Policy Report* 17, August 17, 1998, 2–3; "NCUA's D'Amours Says Field of Membership Rule Needs Improvement," *Banking Policy Report* 18, March 1, 1999, 6–7.

mains, and thrifts, like CUs, are subject to regulatory and legislative uncertainties.[3]

Thrifts were originally chartered to provide home mortgages, a need that was not being served by other financial institutions. Today, however, thrifts face increased competition, not only from commercial banks, mortgage banks, and finance companies, which have increased their home-mortgage lending, but also from government-owned or sponsored enterprises that now originate and securitize (package and sell as securities) mortgage loans. The latter include the Government National Mortgage Association (Ginnie Mae) and the publicly owned Federal National Mortgage Association (Fannie Mae). These institutions have lower costs, since they are not subject to reserve requirements, deposit insurance premiums, capital requirements, and other more stringent regulations of depository institutions. As government or quasi-government agencies, they also have low financing costs and compete with thrifts for home mortgage loans. As Baldwin and Esty (1993)

point out, new technology and standardization that allowed the creation of national mortgage markets and mortgage securitization dramatically changed the role of thrifts.[4] Many thrifts now operate more like mortgage banks, originating and then selling or securitizing home mortgages and receiving fee income for servicing loans. These activities require a great deal more sophistication on the part of managers. Thrifts have merged to cut costs and gain economies to compete with other financial-service providers.

This chapter provides a brief history of the development of CUs and thrifts and describes the industry structure, operations, and differences in the balance sheets and income statements between banks, CUs, and thrifts. The chapter also discusses trends in profitability for the different types of depository institutions over time, along with trends in depository institution failures and government concerns over potential deposit market contagion.

✦ ✦ ✦

SAVINGS INSTITUTIONS: A BRIEF HISTORY AND RECENT REGULATORY CHANGES

Savings institutions, often called thrifts, are the second largest depository institution. In 1997, about 1,653 thrifts with 9,979 total branches existed, holding about $1 trillion in assets. As the name suggests, thrifts traditionally promote "thriftiness" and cater to individual small savers, in contrast to commercial banks, which were originally established to cater to larger commercial customers. Two major types of thrifts exist: savings banks, often called mutual savings banks, and savings and loans (S&Ls).

---

[3]Cynthia J. Nickerson. "Mergers and Acquisitions: 1997 Acquisitions Cross Industries and Signal New Strategies." *Banking Policy Report*, January 19, 1998, 7.

"Financial Restructuring: Thrift Charter Is Still Under Siege in Budget Debate and Separate Bills." *Banking Policy Report*, December 18, 1995, 5.

Thomas P. Vartanian, Alan S. Kaden, and Matthew P. Haskins. "Tearing Down the Tax Wall Between Banks and Thrift Institutions." *Banking Policy Report*, October 16, 1995, 1. Ira L. Tannenbaum, "Thrift Powers: House Legislation Attacks Diversified Savings and Loan Holding Companies." *Banking Policy Report*, November 6, 1995, 2–4.

Ira L. Tannenbaum. "Bad Debt Legislation Clears Way for Thrifts Converting to Banks." *Banking Policy Report*, August 19, 1996, 15–18.

[4]Carliss Y. Baldwin and Benjamin C. Esty. "Lessons from the Thrift Crisis," in *Financial Services Perspectives and Challenges*, ed. Samuel L. Hayes, III. Boston, Mass: Harvard Business School Press, 1993, 39.

The differences between the two and their brief histories are discussed in the following sections.[5]

Differences Between Savings Banks and S&Ls

Savings banks arose in the 1700s because no existing institutions were willing to accept savings deposits from a growing population of workers. But by the time the population moved west, commercial banks had turned their attention to individuals as well as business customers, so the savings bank movement was never established outside the Northeast. Furthermore, a new type of institution with a dual interest in promoting thrift and home ownership emerged by the 1800s; this was the forerunner of the modern S&L. S&Ls originally were formed as building societies with members pooling funds to buy houses. Therefore, they were often formed as mutual associations. This new institution spread nationwide with the population.

Important regulatory and operating differences have separated S&Ls and savings banks for most of their history. Savings banks could issue demand deposits and make commercial loans in limited amounts. Unlike other depositories, they could also invest in corporate stock. In contrast, S&Ls' asset choices were greatly restricted until 1980 because a combination of regulations and tax laws virtually assured that more than 80% of their assets were mortgage-related. Under the Depository Institution Deregulation and Monetary Control Act (DIDMCA) and the Garn–St. Germain Depository Institution Act (G-ST G), both types of thrifts could invest a small percentage of their assets in commercial loans and issue traditional demand deposits. With minor exceptions, however, thrifts, like commercial banks, are now prohibited from investing in corporate stock. In the 1980s, however, many state-chartered thrifts operating as OSLHCs in liberally regulated states could invest through service corporations in the equity of other companies. Financial Corporation of America (FCA) in 1984, for instance, had large stock investments in the Disney Corporation. With FIRREA, such privileges were removed, and state-chartered thrifts had to abide by regulations similar to those governing federally chartered institutions.

In the past, chartering and insurance regulations differed markedly for the two types of thrifts. In 1989, FIRREA's overhaul of the regulatory structure produced further changes. With the abolition of the Federal Home Loan Bank Board (FHLBB), chartering for all federal thrifts, whether savings banks or S&Ls, is handled by the Office of Thrift Supervision (OTS). States may still charter both types of thrifts , although the activities allowed by states for state-chartered thrifts may be no more permissive than those allowed to comparable federally chartered thrifts.

All federally chartered thrifts and state-chartered S&Ls are insured by SAIF (Savings Institution Insurance Fund), but state-chartered savings banks are insured by BIF (Bank Insurance Fund) under the Federal Deposit Insurance Corporation (FDIC). The differences between being under SAIF versus BIF are significant. FIRREA imposed higher deposit insurance premiums initially under SAIF than BIF, mandating that thrifts formerly insured by the Federal Savings and Loan Insurance Corporation (FSLIC) (and now insured by SAIF) must partially pay the cost of cleaning up the industry. This cost for S&Ls included paying for the outstanding Fi-

---

[5]Sources: *Sheshunoff S&L Quarterly*. Austin, Texas: Sheshunoff Information Services, Inc., 1997. *Thomson Savings Institution Directory*. Skokie, Illinois: Thomson Financial Publishing Company, 1997. For more details on the history of thrifts, see Barth (1991); White (1991); Brumbaugh (1988), and Kane (1989).

nancing Corporation bonds used to finance S&L bailouts under the Competitive Equality in Banking Act (CEBA) of 1987. To prevent existing federal thrifts from switching en masse to become state-chartered savings banks, FIRREA also imposed a five-year moratorium on switching insurance funds, except in special circumstances specifically approved by FDIC officials.

With higher premium costs for S&Ls, thrifts initially lost deposits as they faced a competitive disadvantage compared with banks and BIF thrifts and a "backlash" from the S&L crisis. To avoid further S&L losses, Congress passed legislation assessing a large one-time insurance premium on all savings institutions in 1996. This hurt the profitability for thrifts in 1996 but reduced premiums for future years. Thrift premiums continue to be $\frac{1}{5}$ the rate of SAIF insured deposits. A decision whether to merge SAIF and BIF will be made after 2003.[6]

Tax Impediments for Conversions of Thrifts to Banks

Before 1996, the different treatment of bad debt reserves for banks and S&Ls presented a major impediment to Congressional proposals to merge the bank and thrift industries. Until 1951, S&Ls, like CUs, were exempt from federal income tax. The 1951 Revenue Act subjected S&Ls to corporate taxes, but allowed them more liberal tax deductions than banks for their yearly additions to bad debt reserves. Under prodding from the commercial banking industry, limits were placed on S&Ls' bad debt deductions, resulting in a gradual rise in the taxes that S&Ls paid. However, until 1996, S&Ls were allowed to deduct as much as 8% from their income, which meant that they still had a much larger bad debt reserve deduction than commercial banks. For thrifts to be eligible for this deduction they had to meet an IRS qualified thrift lender (QTL) test. The logic of this requirement was that the IRS's subsidy for QTLs could be passed on to home borrowers. The special tax treatment, however, reduced the diversification potential of S&Ls and discouraged thrifts from converting to banks. Prior to 1996, if thrifts converted to banks, they not only lost their special tax treatment for bad loans but also had to recapture their excess special bad debt reserves. Thus, a conversion to a bank charter was costly.

1996 Tax Legislation Encouraging Conversions of S&Ls to Banks

In contrast to past policies, the provisions passed under the Small Business Jobs Protection Act of 1996 promote S&L conversions to banks. Under the new tax legislation, the preferential bad debt reserve treatment previously available to S&Ls under Section 593 of the Internal Revenue Code was repealed. S&Ls are now subject to the same federal tax provisions as commercial banks of the same size.[7] Regardless of whether S&Ls convert to bank charters or remain as federally chartered S&Ls, the act requires S&Ls to recapture as taxable income the bad debt reserve attributed to the

---

[6]Thomas P. Vartanian, Alan S. Kaden, and Matthew P. Haskins. "Tearing Down the Tax Wall Between Banks and Thrift Institutions." *Banking Policy Report*, October 16, 1995, 1 and *Banking Policy Report,* March 15, 1999, 3–8.

[7]Ira L. Tannenbaum, "Bad Debt Legislation Clear Way for Thrifts Converting to Banks." *Banking Policy Report*, August 19, 1996, 15–18. Tannenbaum (1996) reports that experts estimate that approximately 80% of all excess bad debt reserves for taxes for thrifts as a group are pre-1988 reserves. The recapture of excess reserves could be deferred for 1996 and 1997 for thrifts meeting a newly developed residential mortgage origination test during these years.

special reserve method since 1988, spread out over a six-year period after 1996. Consequently, S&Ls no longer surrender any federal tax advantages prematurely by converting to bank charters on a federal tax level. Deposits of stock S&Ls that convert to banks remain insured by SAIF, until a suggested merger of SAIF and BIF occurs after 2000. With this legislation, the number of S&Ls converting to banks is expected to rise.

A Relaxation of Some S&L Product Restrictions in 1996

FIRREA of 1989 reinstated provisions limiting investment alternatives for thrifts. However, since S&Ls no longer have an incentive to meet the IRS's more stringent QTL test, they have more flexibility in structuring their asset portfolios as well as incentives to convert to banks. The Economic Growth and Regulatory Paperwork Reduction Act of 1996 also amends the investment restrictions of the Home Owners' Loan Act and the FHLBB's QTL test to allow federally chartered thrifts to originate credit card and educational loans without investment restrictions. S&Ls can invest an additional 10% of their assets in loans to small businesses and farms while maintaining their current authority to invest 10% of their assets in commercial loans and up to 400% of capital in loans secured by commercial real estate. On September 30, 1996, the OTS amended its lending regulations to reduce regulatory burden, including no longer aggregating the commercial loans of service corporations with those of the parent thrift for the purpose of computing the maximum commercial lending limits for federally chartered thrifts. Hence, federal S&Ls that wish to act more like community banks can adjust their assets and business to do so. Federal S&Ls, however, unlike banks, still must hold a significant percentage of their portfolio in consumer, small business, and mortgage loans under the regulatory QTL test, which allows them favorable borrowing privileges from the FHLBB. Currently, regulators are concerned about S&Ls' movement into new types of more risky home equity consumer loans, with this liberalization in the QTL test to include consumer lending.[8]

Will Favorable Regulation and Privileges for OSLHCs Continue?

As discussed in Chapter 4, federally chartered OSLHCs have greater flexibility than BHCs. Thrifts enjoy free interstate branching privileges, regardless of state laws, if they meet the state QTL test or qualify for statutory exceptions. Additionally, OSLHCs can engage in any line of business, including insurance, underwriting, securities brokerage, real estate brokerage and development, and other commercial businesses. The service corporations of federal thrifts can engage in any activity the OTS deems reasonably related to thrifts, such as real estate development and insurance, as long as they are well-capitalized and state laws do not prohibit this activity. Currently about 40 to 50 OSLHCs engage to some degree in activities that are impermissible to BHCs. The 1995 house legislation that attacked diversified OSLHCs did not pass, but similar legislation halting the unitary thrift charter and forcing OSLHCs to be regulated by the Federal Reserve continues to be proposed.[9]

---

[8]Ibid.

[9]"Financial Restructuring: Thrift Charter Is Still Under Siege in Budget Debate and Separate Bills." *Banking Policy Report*, December 18, 1995, 5. Ira L. Tannenbaum, "Thrift Powers: House Legislation Attacks Diversified Savings and Loan Holding Companies." *Banking Policy Report*, November 6, 1995, 2–4.

A Brief History of CUs

Credit unions originated in the mid-nineteenth century in Germany; the concept was brought to the U.S. in the early 1900s. The first CU gained legal status in Manchester, New Hampshire, through a special act of the state legislature; Massachusetts passed a similar act the same year. CUs were set up as "cooperative associations" to promote thrift among their members. During the 1920s and the Great Depression of the 1930s, CUs grew rapidly, reflecting the rapid development of consumer activism and labor organizations under a "common bond" concept. CUs provided an alternative to loan sharks and traditional thrifts and banks. In 1934, Congress passed the Federal Credit Union Act to charter federal CUs. CUs at this time were often no more than groups of farmers who pooled their money to make each other tractor loans or groups of servicemen who could not leave their military base to go to a traditional bank. Because CU profits go to individual members in the form of dividends, cheap loans, and higher interest rates on deposits, CUs are not taxed. During the first three years of their existence, federal CUs paid state taxes, but technical differences between CU shares and deposits meant that their tax burden was quite high in some states. In 1937, Congress decided that the cooperative movement was best served by exempting federal CUs from taxation. This tax exemption has been under renewed scrutiny in recent years, but it survived attempted tax reforms in 1986, 1993, and 1996. Opponents argue that the increasingly loose common bond requirements for credit union membership have eroded the principal reason for their not-for-profit status and that CUs' exemption from taxes represents a subsidy by taxpayers.[10]

Membership Requirements and Regulations

To join a CU, a person must be within its field of membership. Typical fields of membership include employee groups, associations, religious or fraternal affiliations, and residential areas. Many CUs depend heavily on volunteer labor and donated facilities. Like other depositories, CUs may choose either state or federal charters. Federally chartered CUs are regulated by NCUA and insured by the National Credit Union Share Insurance Fund (NCUSIF), a fund similar to the FDIC. State-chartered CUs may choose to obtain share insurance through NCUSIF, and most do. As of 1970, all CUs must be insured under the law creating NCUSIF. The NCUSIF is funded by fees and assessments from CUs. NCUA also provides a Central Liquidity Facility (CLF) as a lender of last resort. As a quasi-public organization, the CLF has the authority to borrow from public sources and has a credit line with the US Treasury department.

HR 411–8 passed in August 1998, allowing CU's extensions of their common bond requirement and extended member business loans up to 12.25 percent of CU assets. Accordingly, it also contains prompt corrective action provisioning comparable to those for banks and thrifts under the Federal Deposit Insurance Corporation Improvement Act (FDICIA).

As nonprofit, nontaxed organizations, CUs can offer lower average fees and more competitive rates on deposits, loans, and other products. The Bank Rate Monitor in North Palm Beach, Florida, for instance, a monitor of industry rates, found that banks paid on average 1.15% annually on interest-bearing checking accounts versus 2.08% for CUs and that loan rates for CUs were typically more competitive

---

[10]See citations in Note 2.

Table 7.1 ◆ Year End 1996

Percent of Credit Unions Offering Selected Services by Asset Size°

$ millions	$0–$.2	$.2–$.5	$.5–$1	$1–$2	$2–$5	$5–$10	$10–$20	$20–$50	$50–$100	$100–$200	$200+	All CUs
Once a member, always a member	72.1%	81.6%	85.7%	92.3%	94.8%	96.5%	96.2%	96.9%	95.8%	98.4%	96.5%	93.0%
Common bond includes family members	80.9%	89.4%	93.8%	94.3%	97.0%	97.9%	97.3%	98.4%	97.9%	99.2%	97.7%	95.8%
Service package for retirees	2.2%	1.0%	1.1%	2.1%	5.8%	13.1%	21.9%	34.3%	42.4%	52.9%	54.4%	16.0%
Special program for youth	7.9%	4.6%	6.2%	6.8%	13.2%	18.3%	28.4%	40.6%	51.2%	52.3%	53.0%	21.5%
Multiple groups including SEGs	5.0%	6.6%	11.7%	16.7%	25.3%	39.1%	51.6%	61.3%	66.1%	77.5%	77.5%	36.3%
Stock/bond brokerage	0.0%	0.2%	0.8%	0.6%	1.9%	4.0%	7.7%	16.6%	33.2%	43.5%	55.0%	8.8%
Mutual funds	0.0%	0.6%	1.0%	0.7%	1.5%	2.4%	6.4%	13.8%	31.6%	42.1%	56.8%	7.9%
Savings bonds	0.4%	0.6%	2.0%	2.8%	5.3%	11.6%	16.9%	29.2%	40.9%	51.6%	50.0%	14.2%
Life savings insurance	64.7%	67.8%	67.1%	65.2%	62.4%	58.6%	56.9%	54.9%	47.3%	46.4%	41.8%	59.5%
Direct Deposit												
Federal recurring payments	5.1%	9.8%	16.2%	31.7%	55.1%	78.8%	89.0%	95.0%	94.9%	96.5%	97.6%	61.8%
Net pay	11.6%	19.3%	22.8%	35.0%	54.8%	76.9%	85.2%	92.6%	94.3%	96.9%	97.6%	62.5%
Home Banking												
Audio Response	0.0%	1.3%	1.0%	1.5%	4.6%	22.0%	45.3%	76.8%	88.8%	96.7%	96.8%	30.1%
PCs	0.7%	1.1%	0.4%	0.7%	0.6%	1.3%	5.0%	10.8%	21.6%	33.6%	47.2%	5.9%
Wire Transfer	2.2%	5.2%	7.1%	17.5%	42.1%	66.1%	81.5%	92.1%	94.4%	96.5%	98.8%	53.4%
Money orders	2.2%	3.7%	5.1%	13.9%	27.2%	45.8%	62.5%	74.5%	81.0%	82.6%	80.8%	40.6%
Travelers Checks	0.4%	3.5%	6.1%	19.3%	43.5%	67.8%	82.4%	92.8%	93.1%	96.9%	96.9%	53.9%

Safe deposit boxes	0.9%	1.0%	0.4%	0.9%	1.0%	2.9%	11.8%	28.1%	50.2%	58.8%	64.7%	12.1%
Remedial financial counseling	12.1%	10.8%	11.9%	17.3%	23.4%	33.1%	39.4%	45.0%	53.5%	57.4%	66.3%	30.5%
Formal financial planning	2.6%	2.7%	2.7%	3.8%	4.4%	5.5%	10.8%	20.7%	37.2%	42.9%	58.6%	11.4%
ATM cards	0.0%	0.6%	0.4%	2.6%	18.0%	46.6%	70.9%	88.8%	92.7%	97.7%	99.2%	41.5%
Credit cards	0.0%	1.2%	1.6%	4.6%	20.0%	49.6%	75.1%	87.8%	93.1%	96.5%	97.7%	43.0%
Share drafts	0.9%	1.3%	4.6%	16.3%	43.2%	71.2%	87.3%	94.5%	96.2%	98.4%	98.4%	54.9%
Overdraft Protection	0.0%	0.0%	1.5%	8.2%	23.7%	42.4%	57.5%	72.0%	79.5%	87.5%	90.5%	37.6%
Certificates	7.5%	12.4%	22.5%	37.7%	58.5%	74.4%	86.5%	92.8%	95.5%	97.7%	97.2%	62.7%
IRAs	0.9%	4.1%	9.7%	21.6%	42.3%	66.1%	84.2%	90.7%	93.8%	98.4%	98.4%	54.1%
SEP IRAs	0.5%	1.0%	0.7%	5.0%	11.6%	20.3%	28.5%	31.8%	37.4%	48.2%	46.0%	18.2%
Business checking	0.4%	0.6%	2.6%	8.3%	19.1%	37.5%	47.8%	55.5%	50.9%	52.2%	44.6%	29.0%
Trust services	1.3%	1.6%	2.1%	2.9%	4.7%	8.5%	11.0%	14.8%	18.2%	23.9%	23.8%	8.4%
First mortgages	1.8%	5.8%	6.7%	10.1%	20.7%	34.7%	57.1%	75.5%	85.3%	91.8%	96.8%	37.9%
Stock secured loans	6.2%	9.2%	9.0%	11.1%	13.3%	20.5%	24.7%	35.5%	47.1%	55.3%	56.9%	21.8%
Plane/boat/R.V. loans	15.8%	43.3%	57.1%	70.7%	80.1%	85.9%	89.5%	91.1%	95.7%	95.3%	96.4%	77.6%
Guaranteed student loans	0.4%	2.2%	2.1%	5.5%	9.2%	17.2%	26.2%	34.6%	40.2%	46.2%	51.6%	17.9%
Other Student Loans	2.3%	5.5%	4.3%	7.8%	9.6%	15.8%	22.9%	29.7%	35.5%	39.9%	49.6%	16.9%
Balloon Auto Loans	0.0%	3.3%	2.7%	4.0%	5.2%	7.9%	11.4%	20.1%	24.0%	25.9%	27.9%	9.9%
Auto Leasing	0.0%	0.8%	1.7%	2.2%	3.5%	7.9%	12.3%	21.4%	31.7%	34.3%	38.1%	10.3%

ᵃData taken from December 1996 CUNA Yearbook Survey, p. 5 Credit Union Report, 1996, CUNA and P Affiliates.

Source: Credit Union Report, 1996, page 5 Table: CUNA and P Affiliates.

than banks' loan rates in 1996. The Credit Union National Association also reported in 1996 that 64% of CUs offered free checking, while most banks charge customers for falling below required minimum balances.[11]

Many large CUs offer services that rival those at many large banks, as shown in Table 7.1, including credit cards, ATMs, mutual funds, stock/bond brokerage, life insurance, and formal financial planning. Through corporate CUs, smaller CUs are also able

Table 7.2 ✦ Share of Consumer Savings and Consumer Loans by Financial Institutions

Distribution of Consumer Savings

| | $ BILLIONS | | | | | |
| | December 1996 | | December 1995 | | | |
	Outstanding	Market Share	Outstanding	Market Share	Change in 96	
Commercial Banks	$1,925.8	53.8%	$1,856.5	54.1%	$69.3	3.7%
Savings Institutions	634.5	17.7%	657.6	19.1%	−23.1	−3.5%
MMMFs	538.1	15.0%	456.3	13.3%	81.8	17.9%
Credit Unions	295.4	8.2%	278.8	8.1%	16.6	5.9%
U.S. Savings Bonds	187.0	5.2%	184.8	5.4%	2.2	1.2%
Total	$3,580.7		$3,434.0		146.8	4.3%

Share of Auto Loans Outstanding by Selected Lenders

| | $ BILLIONS | | | | | |
| | December 1996 | | December 1995 | | | |
	Outstanding	Market Share	Outstanding	Market Share	Change in 96	
Commercial Banks	$154.0	40.4%	$149.1	42.1%	$4.9	3.3%
Finance Companies	73.2	19.2%	70.6	19.9%	2.6	3.7%
Credit Unions	88.3	23.2%	79.3	22.4%	9.0	11.3%
Pool of Securitized Assets	51.2	13.4%	44.4	12.5%	6.8	15.3%
Savings Institutions	14.2	3.7%	10.7	3.0%	3.5	32.9%
Total	$380.8		$354.1		26.8	7.6%

Share of Installment Credit Outstanding by Selected Lenders

| | $ BILLIONS (NOT SEASONALLY ADJUSTED) | | | | | |
| | December 1996 | | December 1995 | | | |
	Outstanding	Market Share	Outstanding	Market Share	Change in 96	
Commercial Banks	$530.1	43.3%	$507.8	44.9%	$22.3	4.4%
Pool of Securitized Assets	271.9	22.2%	214.4	18.9%	57.5	26.8%
Finance Companies	154.5	12.5%	152.6	13.4%	1.9	1.2%
Credit Unions	144.2	11.8%	131.9	11.7%	12.3	9.4%
Savings Institutions	44.7	3.6%	40.1	3.5%	4.6	11.5%
Nonfinancial business	79.7	6.5%	85.1	7.5%	−5.4	−6.3%
Total	$1,225.1		$1,131.9		93.2	8.2%

Source: Credit Union Report, Year-End 1996, Madison, Wisconsin: CONAP Affiliates, p. 7.

---

[11]Karen Hube and Matt Murray. "Credit Unions Still Top Banks on Deals for Basic Service." *Wall Street Journal*, March 3, 1998, C1, C25; and *Credit Union Report, 1996, Year-end*. Madison, Wisconsin: CUNA & Affiliates, 1997.

to offer many of these services as well. In addition, CUNA has a mortgage corporation, a service corporation, a brokerage corporation, and an insurance agency. State CU organizations also provide services. For instance, the estimated 1.3 million members of state CUs in Colorado can access a statewide ATM network, use state CU service centers for financial planning, and apply for CU leasing, credit cards, and debit cards.

The market share of CUs at the end of 1996 was 8.2% of consumer savings versus 53.8% for banks and 17.7% for thrifts (Table 7.2). For auto loans, CUs had about a 23% share versus 40% for banks; for installment credit, CUs had about a 12% share versus 43% banks. CUs have a significant share of consumer deposits and consumer loans, despite being only about 7% of the asset size of commercial banks.

Support Systems for CUs

Credit unions enjoy the benefits of strong trade organizations. Because so many CUs are small, they often need facilities and managerial expertise that larger depositories develop in-house. Figure 7.1 shows the pyramid support structure for CUs. The largest of the trade organizations is the Credit Union National Association and its affiliates. Among the most important affiliates is the Corporate Credit Union (CCU) Network, a group of CUs for CUs, with about $20.481 billion in assets at the end of 1996. Individual CUs own interest-earning shares in CCUs; the latter pool the funds of small CUs and invest in money and capital market instruments. CCUs

Figure 7.1   ✦   NCUA Organizational Chart

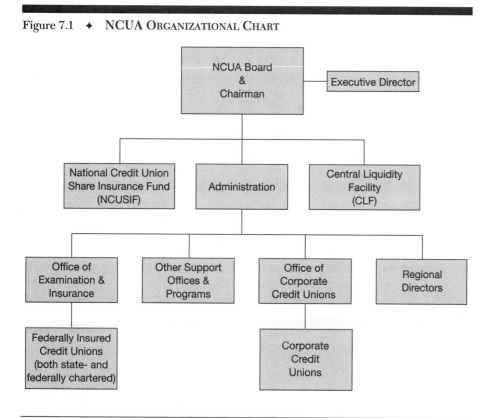

Source: Taken from Exhibit 1.4. David Walker. "Credit Union Insurance and Regulation." Washington, D.C. Georgetown University Center for Business-Government Relations, p. 9.

also function similarly to correspondent banks, offering advice, cash management, check processing, and the assistance necessary for the operation of individual CUs.

They also act as bankers' banks, accepting deposits and lending to CUs as needed. Further up the support ladder is the U.S. Central Credit Union (USC), established in the 1990s in Overland Park, Kansas, of which CCUs are themselves members. The USC and the 42 CUs are often referred to as the Corporate Network. This large CCU, with assets of $ 17.925 billion at year-end 1996, manages investments and provides a wide array of other services for CUs, including liquidity, custody, and payment services, as well as product research and development.[12]

COMPARISON OF INDUSTRY STRUCTURES: BANKS, THRIFTS, AND CUS

Size and Industry Structure of Commercial Banks

To understand the performance of the different depository institutions, it is important to compare their industry structures. Panel A of Table 7.3 provides the size and distribution of insured commercial banks, thrifts, and CUs. The industry structure of commercial banks is constantly changing. The number of banks in the U.S. reached a peak in 1980 of 15,190 banks with 41,000 branches. Since that time a massive consolidation has occurred, with the number of commercial banks shrinking 35% to about 9,692 at the end of 1997. However, bank assets grew about 6% annually during this period, rising from $1,704 trillion to $5,229 trillion at the end of 1997. The number of branches also grew by 46% to about 59,893 branches. Banks employ about 1.5 million individuals in the U.S.

As shown in the middle panel Table 7.3, about 85% of the total number of banks at the end of 1996 were small, with assets of less than $250 million. Nonetheless, larger banks dominate the U.S. banking industry. Banks with assets greater than $1 billion control about 78% of total bank assets. Banks with assets between $1 and $10 billion held $1 trillion in assets (21.89% of bank assets) and banks with assets over $10 billion owned $2.58 trillion in assets (56% of bank assets) at the end of 1996. Compared with other nations, the U.S. banking industry is not concentrated, but it is slowly becoming more concentrated with the creation of a greater number of megabanks. For example, NationsBank, the nation's third largest bank, grew 25% to $284 billion between 1996 and 1997. As a result of NationsBank's merger with BankAmerica in 1998, the new combined BankAmerica has over $570 billion in assets and $45 billion in equity. Similarly, Citicorp's merger with Travelers Group in 1998 creates the largest financial group in the world with $700 billion in assets. The regional bank merger of First Chicago and Banc One in the Midwest in 1998 created one of the largest regional banks with $279 billion in assets. The majority of banks are subsidiaries of holding companies. In early 1997, 5,163 holding companies held 90% of bank assets and owned 7,123 banks.[13]

---

[12]See Walker (1997). CUNA and Affiliates Annual Report, 1996, 1997, Madison, WI, and Barbara A. Good, "The Credit Union Industry—An Overview." *Economic Commentary: Federal Reserve Bank of Cleveland* , May 15, 1998, 1–4.

[13]See Robert B. Avery, Raphael W. Bostin, Paul S. Calem, and Glenn B. Canner, "Changes in the Distribution of Banking Offices." *Federal Reserve Bulletin*, September 1997, 706–725. *FDIC Statistics on Banking: A Statistical Profile of the United States Banking Industry*. Washington, D.C.: FDIC Division of Research and Statistics, 1996. "Mega-Merger Mania Strikes U.S. Banks," *The Banker*, May 1998, 4–5.

Table 7.3 ✦ **Comparison Industry Structure Thrifts, Commercial Banks, Credit Unions: Year-end 1996**

Panel A: Thrifts, banks, and credit unions have a wide distribution of asset sizes, with the largest firms holding the majority of assets.

TOTAL DEPOSITORY INSTITUTION ASSETS, YEAR-END 1996: $6.123 TRILLON

Appr. Total Industry Assets: Thrifts: $1.028 tril. 16.79% Banks: $4.758 tril. 77.71% Credit Unions: $.337 tril. 5.50%

Size Category	Thrifts Firms in Category		Banks Firms in Category		Size Category	Credit Unions in Category	
$10 mil. & under	69	4.19%	224	2.30%	$10 mil. or under	7,604	64.00%
>$10 mil. to $25 mil.	120	7.28%	1,332	13.86%	>$10 mil. to $20 mil.	1,478	12.40%
>$25 mil. to $50 mil.	254	15.41%	2,193	22.75%	>$20 mil. to $50 mil.	1,473	12.39%
>$50 mil. to $100 mil.	389	23.60%	2,402	24.92%	>$50 mil. to $100 mil.	648	5.45%
>$100 mil. to $250 mil.	413	25.06%	2,085	21.63%	>$100 mil. to $200 mil.	368	3.10%
>$250 mil. to $1 bil.	292	17.72%	675	7.00%	Over $200 mil.	316	2.66%
Over 1 billion	111	6.74%	727	7.54%			
Total Institutions Included	1,648	100%	9,638	100%	Total Firms	11,887	100.00%
	Thrifts	Branches	Banks	Branches			
Total Firms & Branches 1997	1,653	9,979	9,809	59,893			

Source: Thomson Savings Directory. Skokie, Illinois: Thomson Publishing Co., 1996, 1997. *Credit Union Report* 1996, Madison, WI.: CUNA.

Panel B: Nation's Largest Thrifts, February 1998   Nation's Largest Banks, December 31, 1996

Rank	Institutions	Total Assets (bils.)	Rank	Institutions	Total Assets (bils.)
1	Washington Mutual	$97.10	1	Citicorp	$281
2	H. F. Ahmanson	$55.50	2	Chase	$336
3	Merger Proposed Golden State/Calif. Fed.	$51.30	3	NationsBank	$228
4	Golden West Financial	$39.60	4	BankAmerica	$251
5	California Federal	$31.60	5	Wells Fargo	$109
6	Dime Bancorp	$21.80	6	Banc One	$107
7	Charter One Financial	$19.80	7	First Union	$140
8	Golden State Bancorp	$19.70	8	J.P. Morgan	$222
9	Sovereign Bancorp	$17.60			
10	GreenPoint Financial	$13.10			
11	Bank United	$12.50			
	Total Assets of 11 Largest Thrifts	$379.60		Total Assets 8 Largest Banks $1,674	

Source: Timothy O'Brien, "California Merger to Form No. 3 S&L," *New York Times,* February 6, 1998, C1, C4. and *Banking Policy Report* 16 (April 21, 1997), p. 7.

Size and Industry Structure of Savings Institutions

The first column of the upper panel of Table 7.3 shows that at the end of 1996, about 1,653 thrifts operated with 9,979 branches and about $1.028 trillion in assets. Thus, thrifts represent about 17% of all banks operating and about 22% of the asset size of the banking industry. Of the two types of thrifts, S&Ls dominate the industry, holding about $769 billion or about 77% of thrift industry assets. At the end of 1997, there were 1,211 S&Ls with $777 trillion in assets. About 56% of thrifts are federally chartered, holding 75% of thrift assets. The approximately 840 state-chartered thrifts tend to be smaller institutions. Federal charters have been preferred in the 1990s, since they have been given more favorable regulations (see above) including free interstate branching. In the late 1990s, thrifts holding about $201 billion in assets (about 25% of thrift assets) operated in two or more states, with 1,178 (about 39%) of a total of 3,038 branches operating outside of their home states.[14]

To raise capital and to compete with other bank and nonbank financial institutions, a large number of thrifts converted to stock form in the mid-1980s. To demonstrate how dramatic this change was, in 1980 only about 20% of all S&Ls were stock-chartered, with about a 27% share of industry assets. Today about 61% of S&Ls are stock, controlling over 71% of thrift assets. Another wave of conversions occurred in the early 1990s as thrifts struggled to meet higher capital requirements under FIR-REA. Thrifts must be stock-chartered to merge or convert to commercial banks. The larger stock thrifts are OSLHCs. In 1997, an estimated 700 OSLHCs existed.[15]

Like commercial banking, the thrift industry has a wide variety of very large and very small thrifts. The majority of thrifts are relatively small; more than 75% have assets of less than $250 million (Table 7.3, upper panel). Only 111 (6.74%) thrifts have assets of more than $1 billion. However, these 6.74% of thrifts hold about 37% of thrift assets. In February, 1998, the largest 11 thrifts held $379.6 billion in assets (Table 7.3, lower panel). With the help of more than 20 acquisitions, the nation's largest thrift, Washington Mutual, grew from $7.6 billion in assets in 1990 to $97.1 billion (about 12% of the industry total) in assets in 1997, earning an average compound return on equity (ROE) of 30.5%.

Despite its rapid growth, in 1997 Washington Mutual was only about 34% of the size of the largest commercial bank, Citicorp, which had $281 billion in assets. However, following a merger with H. F. Ahmanson in the spring of 1998, Washington Mutual grew to about $152.6 billion, making it at that time the seventh largest depository (including banks) in the U.S. With this merger, Washington Mutual is expected to underwrite approximately one of every eight adjustable-rate mortgage loans and to have major interests in consumer lending as well.[16] Ironically, Washington Mutual fought H. F. Ahmanson to become a white knight victor in the hostile takeover by Ahmanson of another huge California thrift, Great Western S&L, in 1997.

The nation's largest thrifts tend to be concentrated on the West Coast, particularly in California, partly because of previous favorable state regulations. Mega-savings banks also exist in New York; these were created in the mid-1800s to serve immigrants. In 1998, several giant savings banks merged with other banks or thrifts, such as Dime Savings' ($21.8 billion in assets) merger with HUBCO, a New Jersey bank with over $3 billion in assets. The concentration among the mega-thrifts in the U.S., along with mergers and conversions to commercial banks, is continuing.

---

[14]Sources: *Sheshunoff S&L Quarterly*. Austin, Texas: Sheshunoff Information Services, Inc., 1997 and 1998. *Thomson Savings Institution Directory*. Skokie, Illinois: Thomson Financial Publishing Company, 1997. Cebenoyan, Cooperman, Register, and Bauer (1997).

[15]Ibid.

[16]"OTS Is Promoting Appeal of Federal Thrift Charter." *Banking Policy Report*, January 6, 1997, 17. Timothy O'Brien. "California Merger to Form No. 3 S&L." *New York Times*, February 6, 1998, C1, C4. "Biggest S&L's in the Country Agree to Merge: $9.9 Billion Deal Latest in Industry Reshaping." *New York Times*, March 18, 1998, A1. Ralph T. King, Jr. "California Federal and Golden State to Combine in a Coup for Perelman." *Wall Street Journal*, February 6, 1998, A3, A6. "Washington Mutual to Buy Ahmanson: Value of Stock-Swap Plan Is Put at $10.03 Billion; More Consolidation Seen." *Wall Street Journal*, March 18, 1998, A3.

Size and Industry Structure of CUs

At the end of 1996, 71.4 million CU members belonged to 11,887 CUs; of these, 4,738 had state charters and 7,149 had federal charters.[17] By the end of 1997 the number of CUs was 11,659. CUs held about $.337 trillion in assets (less than 5.50% of total depository institution assets). In 1997, assets increased to $.361 trillion. Although CUs are the smallest of the three types of depository institutions, they have grown enormously. Federal CUs, for instance, with $.361 trillion in assets at the end of 1997, had assets of only $12.5 billion in 1971. This represents an annual compound growth rate of 14%, the fastest growth among the depository institutions.

Since 1982 federally chartered CUs have been allowed to be more flexible in their extension of a common bond among members, enabling greater CU consolidation and asset growth. With an extension of common bond definitions, CUs have experienced considerable consolidation. The number of CUs fell from a peak of 17,507 in 1979 to 11,659 in 1997. In the early 1980s a number of CUs were liquidated as a result of the recession-related financial problems of employers. In contrast, after 1982, with the extension of the common bond requirement by the NCUA, much of the decline in the numbers of CUs resulted from consolidation as CUs attempted to gain greater economies of scale and to offer a greater variety of services to compete with other bank and nonbank competitors. With rapid consolidation under more generous common bond requirements, the number of CUs fell from 15,891 in 1983 to 11,659 in 1997, a decline of over 39%, while assets grew 299%.

While the majority of CUs are very small, with 64% having assets of $10 million or less, other CUs are relatively large, although still small in comparison with other depositories. The third column of the upper panel of Table 7.3 shows that CUs range from tiny firms with less than $10 million in assets (some less than $200,000) to very large institutions, such as the Navy Federal Credit Union in Vienna, Virginia, which has $9 billion in deposits and 1.8 million members (despite a general downsizing of the U.S. military in the early 1990s). Only 316 (2.66%) CUs have over $200 million in assets. Over time, with greater consolidation, the largest CUs have grown in size, while the smallest category of CUs has shrunk. For instance, the assets of CUs greater than $200 million grew 12.6% in 1996; the smallest (less than $200,000) shrank by 9.1%.

COMPARISON OF ASSETS AND LIABILITIES: BANKS, THRIFTS, AND CUS

Comparison of Assets

The upper panel of Figure 7.2 compares the different types of assets held by banks, thrifts, and CUs at year-end 1996. Commercial banks have the most diversified asset portfolio (see Chapter 5), with a wide variety of different types of loans. Thrifts are the least diversified. At the end of 1996, the average thrift was a QTL, holding the majority (about 62%) of assets in real estate loans (primarily home mortgages), 4% in consumer loans, and 1% in commercial loans. At the end of 1997, as a percentage of

---

[17]For an excellent report on this structure and other information about the current credit union industry and regulation, see Walker (1997). Other sources include Crawford and Sihler (1994) and the CUNA Annual Report, 1996.

Figure 7.2 ✦ BALANCE SHEETS OF DEPOSITORY INSTITUTIONS, YEAR-END 1996

A visual comparison of banks, thrifts, and CUs shows banks to be the most and thrifts to be the least diversified of depository institutions.

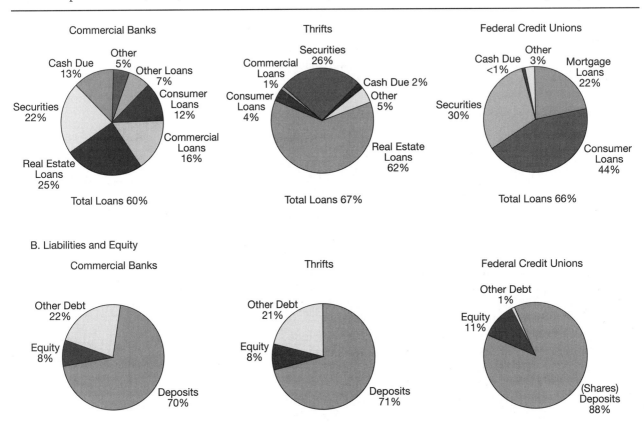

Sources: For banks and savings institutions, FDIC Statistics on Banking, 1996. (Figures Rounded to %). For Federally Insured Credit Union Administration, as cited by David Walker, Credit Union Insurance and Regulation, 1997.

total loans, S&Ls held 8.3% consumer loans, 2.1% commercial loans, 72.5% in home mortgages, and 17.1% in other types of construction and land, dwelling, and commercial real estate loans. The average fractions of consumer and commercial loans were well below the maximum regulatory limits allowed. Such a concentration of real estate loans exposes thrifts to changing economic conditions within their regions and the real estate market. Since the majority of home mortgage loans tend to be long-term and fixed rate, thrifts are also subject to greater interest rate risk than other depositories. Even when long-term real estate loans have variable rates, the rates still change less often over the life of the loan than the rates on the thrifts' deposits, which tend to be short-term. However, larger thrifts, such as Washington Mutual, have increased their consumer lending activities, and large OSLHCs have entered nontraditional areas through nonthrift subsidiaries. [18] As a result of in-

[18]Kenneth N. Gilpin. "Behind a Huge S&L Empire, A Low-Key Superstar." *New York Times*, March 19, 1998, C8. Timothy L. O'Brien. "Biggest S&Ls's in the Country Agree to Merge: $9.9 Billion Deal Latest in Industry Reshaping." *New York Times*, March 18, 1998, A1, C2.

creased regulatory stringency, the loan-to-asset ratio of thrifts fell dramatically from an average of 82% in 1991 to 67% in 1996. In contrast, the loan-to-asset ratio for banks is 60% and for CUs, 65%. Thrifts hold less cash than banks, with an average of 2% cash to assets versus 13% for the average bank. With the exception of mega-thrifts, thrifts generally have fewer off-balance sheet items than banks.

Credit Unions have greater diversification than thrifts, but less diversification than banks. CUs had on average about 44% consumer loans (new and used auto, home equity, and other loans), 22% home mortgage loans (first or secured mortgage loans), and 3% other loans. These percentages were fairly stable for CUs through the 1990s. CUs have the least interest-rate risk of all depositories, since the majority of their assets are short-term consumer loans financed by short-term deposits.

Comparison of Liabilities

Deposits provide the majority of financing for all depository institutions. Like banks, the percentage of deposit financing of thrifts has declined over the years to about 71% of asset financing. The deposit-to-asset ratio for thrifts in 1991 was 79%. In contrast, CUs have had a stable deposit-to-asset ratio of 88% (Figure 7.2, lower panel). CUs used only 1% financing with other debt, compared with 21%–22% for banks and thrifts. This liability composition gives CUs an advantage in terms of lower interest expense, although CUs by their nature try to give members (depositors) more favorable rates.

CUs and thrifts have similar types of deposits to banks (see Chapter 5). However, CU deposits are typically called *shares*, rather than deposits. Transaction deposits, equivalent to Negotiated Order of Withdrawal (NOW) accounts, are called *share drafts*, and certificates of deposit, *share certificates*. CUs also offer money market accounts and savings accounts. At the end of 1996, CUs had on average about 11% of deposits in share draft accounts and 23% in certificate accounts; the average annual compound growth rate in deposits was about 5.8%. CUs also have liabilities to other creditors, including borrowing from the Central Liquidity Fund, an agency of the NCUA that provides funds to meet CUs' needs for liquidity and other operating funds.

Thrifts, like banks, can offer traditional demand deposits (called noninterest NOWs or NINOWS), as well as NOWs, Money Market Deposit Accounts (MMDAs), passbook accounts, and CDs of all types. NINOWS are of virtually no importance to thrifts as they have few commercial loans. NOWs, however, have become more significant for thrifts since their nationwide authorization in 1980. MMDAs have also greatly increased in importance since 1982, and passbook accounts have correspondingly declined with the rise in new transaction and market-rate savings vehicles. Because depositories abandoned passbook savings in favor of market-sensitive deposits, the cost of funds to thrifts skyrocketed during the 1980s, when market interest rates were relatively high compared with previous decades. With lower interest rates in the 1990s, thrift profitability improved tremendously.

Thrifts have greater liquidity problems relative to CUs, since in the eyes of depositors, a thrift's liabilities are highly liquid, whereas its assets, in the eyes of homeowners whose mortgages are those assets, are quite illiquid. Managing the net interest margin of a thrift is clearly a challenge in a deregulated environment.

The major component of other liabilities for borrowed money for S&Ls is advances from the regulators, especially the Federal Home Loan Banks, which are used to meet liquidity and other operating needs. For BIF-insured savings institutions other liabilities for borrowed money are less important, since they lack access to this source of funding. Other items in other liabilities for borrowed money are subordinated notes and debentures issued by stockholder-owned thrifts. As with commercial banks, only the largest thrifts find a market for subordinated notes and debentures, and these liabilities are a relatively small proportion of the liabilities of the industry as a whole. Other liabilities include items comparable with accounts payable and accrued expenses on a nonfinancial balance sheet.

Mutually owned thrifts are permitted to issue long-term debt securities called **mutual capital certificates (MCCs)**. MCCs are securities with a minimum denomination of $100,000 and a minimum maturity of 10 years. They are similar to subordinated notes and debentures and were first authorized under DIDMCA. Their claim in income and assets is subordinate to that of depositors and other creditors. MCCs were intended to supplement undivided profits and reserves as a source of net worth for a mutually owned institution. However, regulators deemed them to be less effective than common stock or retained earnings in protecting the interests of the insurance funds. Thus, they serve a relatively minor role in institutional management.

Comparison of Equity-to-Asset Ratios and Trends

Equity to assets improved for each of the depositories from 1991 to 1996. In 1991, the equity-to-asset ratio for CUs was 7.6%, 4.1% for thrifts, and about 6.3% for banks. With higher capital requirements under FIRREA for thrifts and FDICIA for banks, equity-to-asset ratios improved dramatically in the 1990s. In 1996, CUs had an equity-to-assets ratio (including loan loss reserves) of about 11% versus about 8% for commercial banks and thrifts (Figure 7.2). At the end of 1997 banks had an average equity to assets ratio of 8.4% and S&Ls of 7.5%.

CU Capital

Because of their not-for-profit form of organization and the common bond requirement, CUs have limited access to funds except through the savings of members or retained earnings. Like other depositories, the balance sheets of CUs contain reserve accounts, or portions of retained earnings designated to serve as cushions against which future loan and investment losses can be charged. Earnings retained in excess of those officially designated as reserves are called undivided earnings, similar to undivided profits in commercial banks. The total of reserves and undivided earnings is equal to the capital or net worth of the CU.

Thrift Capital

Equity or net worth (since many thrifts are mutual) includes the reserves and retained earnings accounts of all institutions as well as the common stock, preferred stock, and paid-in capital accounts of stockholder-owned institutions. For mutual thrifts, retained earnings (or undivided profits or reserves) serve an identical function to common equity in a shareholder-owned firm. Although preferred stock issues have historically been more popular for banks than for thrifts, in 1984, the FHLBB enabled mutual as well as stockholder-owned S&Ls to sell preferred stock through affiliated service corporations. Many have done so.[19]

---

[19]See Kane (1989), Barth (1991), and White (1991) for a more detailed discussion of the capital of thrifts.

Capital Accounting Gimmicks for Thrifts in the 1980s

In the 1980s equity also included regulatory net certificates, which were used by regulators to keep technically insolvent thrifts from failing, along with accounting gimmicks that produced positive capital ratios under regulatory accounting practices (RAP). But according to Generally Accepted Accounting Practices (GAAP), hundreds of thrifts in the 1980s were technically insolvent, many with tangible equity-to-assets ratios lower than −20%. RAP superseded GAAP to allow what Kane (1989) calls "zombie" thrifts to continue to operate. In 1985, for instance, about 461 S&Ls had negative equity-to-asset ratios as evaluated by GAAP. RAP equity included goodwill, net worth certificates (NWCs), fees on loans, and appraisal items, among other gimmicks, while GAAP equity included only tangible equity capital consisting of retained earnings and common stock accounts.[20] Regulators gave NWCs that counted as capital to failing thrifts that met established guidelines in exchange for a promissory note from the insurer.[21] To encourage healthy thrifts to take over other failing thrifts, they were allowed to include a large amount of tangible goodwill as an asset from the acquisition boosting equity (value of assets less liabilities). Under FIRREA and FDICIA, RAP accounting practices were abolished, and thrifts were required to meet the same capital requirements as commercial banks. Significant goodwill as an asset was phased out, which caused some thrifts significant problems. An example is Glendale Federal, which lost $800 million in assets and equity with this ruling. Ten years later, in 1999, a federal judge ordered the U.S. to pay $908.9 million to Glendale based on a previous promise of goodwill when Glendale took over a failing S&L in the 1980s (see Schmitt, 1999). With lower interest rates in the 1990s, an economic expansion, closures of technically insolvent thrifts, and consolidation and recapitalization of the industry, thrifts had a much healthier 8% average equity-to-asset ratio at the end of 1996.

Trends in Market-to-Book Values for Thrifts

Figure 7.3 shows the trends in market-to-book values for large publicly traded thrifts between 1987 to 1995. Market value is equal to the stock price for thrift times its number of outstanding shares; book values are the equity values for thrifts reported on thrifts' balance sheets. With book value accounting in the 1980s, market values, which reflected what investors thought about thrifts, were much lower than book values. Thrifts had market-to-book values less than 1 from 1987 until 1992. In contrast, during this period nonfinancial firms always had market-to-book values greater than 1.[22] With the abolishment of RAP accounting, closures of less solvent thrifts, lower interest rates, and improved profitability, market-to-book values rose dramatically in the 1990s, indicating more favorable assessments for thrifts by investors. Recent empirical studies find thrifts and banks with low charter values (proxied by mar-

---

[20]Ibid.

[21]As a thrift's earnings improved, it could repay the promissory note and this liability would be removed, as would the NWC. For greater detail on the accounting provisions for capital for thrifts, see Barth (1991), Brumbaugh (1988), and White (1991). Also see Lee Berton, "Accounting at Thrifts Provokes Controversy as Gimmickry Mounts." *Wall Street Journal*, March 29, 1985, 1, 13.

[22]See Keeley (1990), and Galloway, Lee, and Roden (1997) for market-to-book values for bank holding companies and Cebenoyan, Cooperman, and Register (1998) for thrifts during these periods.

Figure 7.3 ✦ MARKET TO BOOK VALUES FOR LARGE PUBLICLY-TRADED THRIFTS 1987 TO 1995

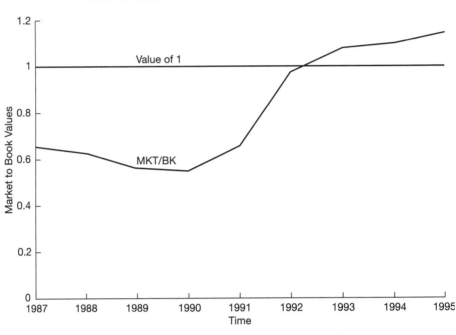

Source: Cebenoyan, Cooperman, and Register (1998). Ratios are for samples of large publicly traded thrifts. Ratios represent the aggregate market values of all corporations in each sample divided by the aggregate book value year-end.

ket-to-book values below 1) take on greater risk than other depository institutions. This suggests that market values of equity are more relevant measures of capital than book values and that low market to book institutions have a greater propensity to take on excessive risk under a federal deposit insurance system. Studies also found stock-chartered thrifts with low charter values to take on greater risk in the mid- to late 1980s and early 1990s.[23]

PERFORMANCE OF DEPOSITORIES: A COMPARISON

Annual Compound Growth Rates in Assets

Banks As shown in Table 7.4, the three types of depositories have experienced different rates of asset growth over time. From 1985 to 1990, both domestic commercial banks and thrifts had a significant fall in their average annual growth rate. The asset growth of banks slowed to an annual compound rate of 5.85% between

---

[23]These studies include Esty (1996), Cordell (1993), Keeley (1990), Cebenoyan, Cooperman and Register (1999), among others. See citations in Note 21. For an excellent discussion of the role of capital and banking, including a discussion of market versus book values, see Kaufman (1992).

Table 7.4 ✦ Panel A: Compound Growth Rates in Assets of Depositories 1960 to 1996

	1960–65	1965–75	1975–80	1980–85	1985–90	1990–96
Banks—Domestic	8.36%	8.91%	10.02%	9.47%	5.85%	7.06%
Banks—For. Subs.	4.68%	7.77%	61.13%	7.80%	20.40%	9.85%
Saving & Loans	12.25%	10.09%	13.32%	11.20%	.72%	
Savings Banks	7.57%	7.44%	7.48%	4.55%	3.98%	−3.35%°
Credit Unions	11.88%	12.85%	12.87%	14.75%	10.04%	8.69%

°1990–96 figure is for both S&Ls and Savings Banks.
Source: Data from Board of Governors of the Federal Reserve System, Flow of Funds Accounts, CUNA Annual Reports as cited in David A. Walker, "Credit Union Insurance and Regulation," Georgetown University 1997, p. 7.

The large growth rates for foreign subsidiaries and credit unions reflect a low starting asset base relative to the other depository institutions. The negative growth rate for thrifts in 1990–1996 reflects the closures of hundreds of thrifts in the early 1990's.

PANEL B: TRENDS IN BANK FAILURES 1933 TO 1996

Year	Number of Bank Failures
1933	4,004
1940–49	99
1950–59	28
1960–69	46
1970–79	76
1980–89	1,082
1990–92	208
1994–96	22

Commercial Bank failures were their highest during the Great Depression of 1933, with 4,004 failures. In the 1980s, the second largest number of failures occurred with 1,082 failures between 1980 and 1989. With a more prosperous economy in the 1990s, bank failures fell. In 1991, 88% of banks were profitable. In 1996, 96% were profitable.
Source: Austin, Texas: *Sheshunoff Bank Quarterly,* various issues, Austin, Texas: Sheshunoff Information Services, Inc., and Bank Management, 4th edition, by George H. Hempel, Donald G. Simonson, and Alan B. Coleman, New York: John Wiley & Sons, Inc., 1994.

1985 and 1990, and a rash of bank failures led to a decline in the industry's growth. During the decade from 1980 to 1989, 1,082 banks failed (Table 7.4, lower panel). Bank failures were particularly dramatic among some of the nation's biggest banks in Texas and New England. The growth rate in assets for banks, however, rose between 1990 and 1996 to 7.05%. Banks expanded by purchasing thrifts under FIRREA's liberalized acquisitions rules, and an economic expansion after 1992 increased bank loan and asset growth. Asset growth rates for banks do not include off-balance sheet items, which have grown tremendously for the nation's largest banks. Hence, the average bank growth rate in the 1980s and 1990s is significantly understated. Note that foreign bank subsidiaries grew rapidly in the late 1970s and 1980s. The large growth rates, although dramatic, reflect a small initial asset base for foreign banks.

S&Ls   Annual asset growth among S&Ls during recent decades was extremely variable, ranging from a high of 13.3% in the late 1970s to a low of −3.35% for all thrifts between 1990 and 1996. S&Ls, in particular, had a −6.3% growth rate during this time. The "go-go" days for S&Ls subsided, and the industry shrank in response to regulatory closures of insolvent S&Ls under FIRREA. Figure 7.4 graphs S&L and

Figure 7.4 ✦ SAVINGS & LOAN AND CREDIT UNION FAILURES. 1985-1995

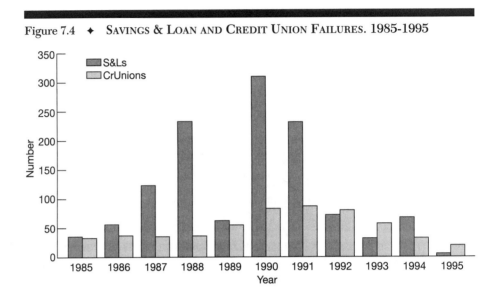

Sources: David Walker. "Credit Union Insurance and Regulation." Washington, D.C. Georgetown University and *Shesunoff S&L Quarterly.* Austin, Texas: Shesunoff Information Services.

CU closures over time. About 320 S&Ls were closed in 1990 and about 230 in 1991 (Figure 7.4). Thrifts attempting to meet higher capital requirements in the 1990s also merged with other thrifts and commercial banks. Other thrifts converted to bank charters. Between 1988 and 1996, the total assets of S&Ls fell from a peak of $1.391 trillion in 1988 to $769 billion, a decline of about 81%. In 1997, assets grew only 1.04% to $777 billion and the number of S&Ls fell 14.4% to 1,211 with about 205 mergers with banks and other thrifts and conversions to banks.

CUs Between 1990 and 1996, CUs grew at a 7.66% annual compound growth rate. In 1997, assets grew 7.1%, although the number of CUs fell about 2% with mergers. Although CUs grew at the fastest rate of depository institutions, as the smallest depository, CU growth in dollars did not exceed the dollar asset increases at banks. CUs have had a very low number of failures over time (Figure 7.4).

Relative Profitability of Depository Institutions

Thrifts Decline in the 1980s and Rebound in the 1990s Profitability has been the greatest difference among depositories. Figure 7.5 presents the return on assets (ROA) for S&Ls, banks, and federal CUs from 1980 to 1996. The profitability of S&Ls was low at best and negative at worst. In contrast, by the time S&Ls hit the bottom of the earnings charts in 1989, banks had rebounded from their earlier low. For most of the period, in fact, bank profitability was much more stable than were thrift earnings. The exception was 1987, when the problems among large Texas banks, as well as among large New York City banks with significant losses on loans to Latin American nations, depressed earnings for the entire industry. Federal CUs prospered during the later 1980s after regulatory ceilings on loan rates were lifted in

Figure 7.5   ✦   PROFITABILITY OF DEPOSITORY INSTITUTIONS

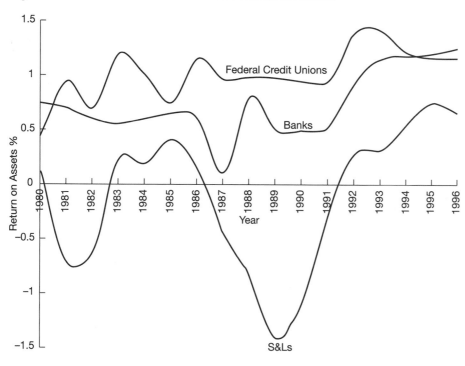

Source: Prepared by the Authors from National Credit Union Administration Annual Reports, *Federal Reserve Bulletins,*
    Shesunoff S&L and Bank Quarterly, CUNA & Affiliates Credit Union Reports.

1980, freeing them to charge market rates. CUs experienced a downturn in 1988,
however, as some institutions grew more rapidly than their relatively unsophisticated
managers could handle. CU regulators immediately increased their examination
forces to forestall problems.

Several additional reasons can be offered for these trends. Changes in the regulatory and economic environment for depositories did not affect the net interest
margin (NIM) of all institutions equally. Thrifts with asset maturities substantially
longer than liability maturities had difficulty, since interest rates on short-term liabilities rose in the early 1980s while interest rates on long-term, fixed-rate real estate
assets did not, thus reducing NIMs. With rising interest rates in the early 1980s,
thrifts suffered severe losses. Regulators kept hundreds of "zombie" thrifts alive,
hoping that interest rates would fall, improving thrift NIMs.

Unfortunately, interest rates did not fall and deposit rate deregulation and the
severe downturn in business activity, which produced the highest unemployment
rate since the Great Depression, also hurt thrift profits. Delinquencies on residential
mortgages reached unprecedented levels in the mid to late 1980s and early 1990s,
further reducing thrift earnings. Loan losses for commercial banks during this period
were also high relative to historical levels, but the portfolio of the industry as a whole
was more diversified than that of thrifts.

Despite the overall difficulties in the industry, prospects for some individual savings institutions seemed brighter during the 1980s because they were able to replace

maturing fixed-rate mortgages with adjustable-rate mortgages (ARMs) on which yields are more closely tied to market yields. For most of 1988, ARMs were about 50% of new mortgage loans. By 1992, however, the proportion of new mortgage loans with adjustable rates fell to 25%.[24] Although few ARMs can be repriced as often as MMDAs, for example, on which costs can change once a month or more often, the ability to shorten asset maturities is an important tool for improving the profitability of thrifts. Despite greater asset restrictions, which reduced the diversification ability of thrifts in the 1990s under FIRREA, thrift profitability improved after 1992. With the closure and merger of weaker thrifts, lower interest rates, and an economic expansion, ROAs rose after 1991, although they were low relative to banks and CUs. However, with the closure of sick thrifts and consolodation of the industry, along with lower interest rates and an expansion in the 1990s, ROAs improved. In 1997, the average ROA for S&Ls was .84% and ROE 10.36%—a considerable improvement from previous periods, and a 29% rise in the ROA from .30% in 1993 and a 22% rise from a 4.72% average ROE in 1993.

Some Banks Suffer, But Rebound Too The average bank ROA fell in the 1980s, largely because of the difficulties of the 17 largest banks and of banks with assets of less than $100 million. The largest banks, which controlled about 40% of industry assets, faced increased competition for business customers from nondepository lenders. In 1987, a number of large banks took on very large loan loss provisions for loans to less developed countries, severely reducing earnings. Smaller banks suffered from large loans to small business and agriculture as well as rising noninterest expenses during 1980 to 1985. In contrast, some banks, especially midsized regional banks, performed relatively well. By the end of 1988, profitability improved for banks to levels that exceeded the previous decade. Large banks led the recovery, with lower loan loss provisions relative to levels before 1988. Smaller banks benefited from improvements in the agricultural sector. From 1989 to 1991, however, the average ROA fell subsequent to an economic recession and continued large loan losses in some regions of the country. New England banks, in particular, suffered from a decline in regional real estate values after several years of increases. These losses, along with further deterioration in the value of loans to Mexico and other less developed countries, resulted in disappointing earnings for the banking industry from 1989 to 1991.

From 1992 to 1996, profits for banks on average soared as a result of lower interest rates, lower noninterest expenses gained from restructuring, and improved noninterest revenues as banks entered nontraditional activities, including banks acquiring security firms, having proprietary mutual funds, providing cash management services to small businesses, among numerous other fee-generating activities. By 1997, the average ROA for banks was 1.30% and average ROE 15.46%.

Federal CUs Generally Thrive after the Mid-1980s In the early 1980s CUs suffered losses as high interest rates drove up deposit costs and dampened members' loan demand. During the 1981–1982 recession, occupationally based CUs were hit

---

[24]See "The Primary Mortgage Market." *Freddie Mac Reports*, various issues and Vanessa Bush. "Low Rates Limit Lending Routes." *Savings Institutions*, 113, January 1992, 18–23. The percentage of ARMS originated varies considerably. Generally, when the general level of rates is high, ARM originations rise, perhaps because borrowers are reluctant during those times to lock into high fixed rates.

hard by unemployment and experienced savings outflows and increasing delinquencies on loans. By 1984, however, loans were again on the rise and CUs thrived. Since 1982, the average ROA of CUs has generally exceeded those of banks and thrifts. However, some selected CUs have had financial difficulties, such as the corporate CU in Lanham, Maryland, which, in 1995, handled investments for the White House and Pentagon Employees Credit Unions. In the late 1980s and 1990s, performance has been good for CUs.

As discussed earlier in this chapter, CUs have successfully extended the definition of common bond to allow greater diversification for borrowers and savers. However, this extension has not always been successful. For instance, the American Association of Retired Persons (AARP) created a federal CU with a common bond to anyone over 50 years old, intended to serve 29 million members. In 1990, the AARP, after considerable pressure from competitors and challenges to the AARP's tax-exempt status, closed its CU.

Industry observers suggest CUs should capitalize on high satisfaction levels and attempt to become their customers' primary financial institution by offering electronic and other more sophisticated banking services. CCUs have allowed smaller CUs to do this. Following this advice, CUs in California experimented with shared branching. Since CUs do not compete for customers, very large CUs with widely dispersed memberships have realized that they can share branching facilities and serve customers more conveniently, allowing expansion without incurring excessive costs. CUs have gained many customers that feel disenfranchised by large bank mergers by out-of-state banks in their state.[25]

Comparison of Simplified Income Statements by Depository Institution Type

To understand the reasons for differences in ROAs among S&Ls, banks, and CUs, it is helpful to compare the simplified income statements for 1996 shown in Table 7.5. In 1996, S&Ls had a before tax ROA of 0.87% compared with 1.1% for CUs and 1.95% for banks. The lower ROA for S&Ls is a result of their low NIM (2.83% versus 3.90% for CUs and 3.95% for banks). The low S&L NIM, in turn, was caused by lower average interest revenue on assets and a much higher average interest-expense-to-assets ratio in 1996. Thus, S&Ls have a NIM disadvantage compared with banks and CUs.

Despite having similar mean NIMs and provisions for loan losses, the average bank outperformed the average CU in 1996 because of a much higher average noninterest revenue-to-assets ratio. The average bank would have suffered a loss without the high average noninterest revenue to assets because the average NIM just about

---

[25]Jim McTague. "In the Capital, It's Motherhood, Apple Pie, and Credit Unions." *American Banker*, March 29, 1993, 14. Greg Crandell. "The Outlook for Credit Unions in a Restructured U.S. Financial System." *Southern Business and Economic Journal*, 15, January, 1992, 69–72. Lynn Asinov. "Looking for Better Rates and Lower Fees? Credit Unions Are Favorites These Days." *Wall Street Journal*, September 2, 1992, C1, C14. Robert E. Taylor, "Retired Persons Association Launches Credit Union for Its 29 Million Members." *Wall Street Journal*, May 11, 1988, 14; Bill Atkinson. "AARP's Retreat: Credit Unions Breathe Easier." *American Banker*, April 3, 1990, 1, 6. Barbara A. Good, "The Credit Union Industry—An overview." *Economic Commentary: Federal Reserve Bank of Cleveland*, May 15, 1998, 1–4.

Table 7.5 ✦ Comparison Simplified Common-Size Income Statements of Depository Institutions, 1996

% Average Assets 1996
S&Ls had the smallest net interest margin, resulting in a lower ROA than the other depository institutions in 1996.

	% S&Ls	% Credit Unions	% Banks
Interest Income	7.17%	7.47%	7.56%
Interest Expense	−4.34	−3.57	−3.61
Net Interest Margin	2.83	3.90	3.95
Provisions for Loan Losses	−0.27	−0.34	−0.38
Net Interest Margin after PLL	2.56	3.56	3.57
Noninterest Expense	−2.58	−3.23	−3.78
Noninterest Income	0.89	0.77	2.16
Burden	−1.69	−2.46	−1.62
ROA before taxes/adjustmts.	0.87%	1.10%	1.95%
ROA after taxes/adjustmts.	0.64%	1.10%	1.24%
Equity Multiplier	12.56	9.26	12.01
ROE	8.04%	10.19%	14.89%

Source: Sheshunoff Bank and S&L Quarterly, December 1996, Austin, Texas: Sheshunoff Information Services. Credit Union Report, 1996 Year-end. Madison, Wisconsin: CUNA & Affiliates.

equaled the noninterest expense to assets and provision for loan loss. Banks have increasingly invested in subsidiary businesses (investment banking, mutual funds, and other types of nonbank firms) to generate greater noninterest revenue, as NIMs from traditional banking activities have decreased with greater competition. Smaller banks have provided greater fee income services for business and retail customers.

MORE ON THE THRIFT CRISIS OF THE 1980s

In discussing the profitability of thrifts from the 1980s to 1990s, it is important to discuss in a little more depth the thrift crisis, which resulted in a government bailout that cost taxpayers close to half a trillion dollars if interest payments are included.[26] In some ways, the crisis resembles more recent crises in the 1990s for financial institutions in Asia in terms of evidence of fraud and mismanagement by financial institutions. However, part of the thrift crisis was caused by the fact that thrifts perform a maturity intermediation function by transforming short-term deposits into long-term, fixed-rate home mortgage loans. By their nature, thrifts have considerably greater interest rate risk than other financial institutions. This situation was aggravated by the fact that thrifts were not allowed to make ARMs until the early 1980s. Consequently, when interest rates rose in the inflationary environment of the 1970s

---

[26]See Cebenoyan, Cooperman, and Register (1998), Note 1. The GAO estimated a price tag including interest costs for the crisis to be $480.9 billion, with total direct bailout costs to taxpayers of $152.6 billion. *New York Times,* July 15, 1996, BB1.

and thrifts attempted to offer implicitly higher deposit rates to curb deposit disintermediation, interest expense rose, but interest revenues did not.

In the early part of the 1980s, thrifts continued to suffer severe losses as the result of rising interest expenses on short-term deposits while interest revenues on fixed-rate assets changed very little. In 1980, the Federal Reserve had attacked inflation by slowing the growth rate of the money supply, which caused short-term interest rates and interest rates on thrift liabilities to rise. As shown in the upper panel of Table 7.6, the average NIM fell from 2.16% during 1976 to 1979 to 0.84% during 1980 to 1993. With higher noninterest expense as well, the average ROA fell from 0.68% to –0.24%. Losses resulted in a deterioration in capital, and the average equity-to-assets ratio plunged from 5.7% to 3%, i.e., a rise in the equity multiplier (EM) from 17.54 to 33. The average ROE fell from 11.93% to –8%.[27]

Table 7.6   ✦   The S&L Crisis of the 1980's: Trends in Profitability & Losses, 1980–1996

Panel 1: Average Profitability Over Different Periods

	1976–1979	CHANGE rates	1980–1983	CHANGE rates	1984–1987	CHANGE rates	1988–1991	CHANGE rates	1992–1995	CHANGE rates	1996
Int. Rev%	7.84%	1.89%	9.73%	0.38%	10.11%	−1.45%	8.66%	−1.80%	6.86%	0.31%	7.17%
Int. Exp%	5.68%	3.21%	8.89%	−.96%	7.93%	−.79%	7.14%	−3.03%	4.11%	0.23%	4.34%
NIM %	2.16%		0.84%		2.18%		1.86%		2.75%		2.83%
Non-interest Exp.	1.21%		1.40%		1.91%		1.98%		2.27%		2.58%
Non-interest Rev.	N/G		N/G		0.48%		0.60%		0.72%		0.89%
%Reposs. Assets & Other Real Estate for last year of period:					1.54%		2.38%		0.31%		0.27%
ROA %	0.68%		−0.24%		0.07%		−0.91%		0.46%		0.64%
Eq/Assets RAP	*5.7%		3.00%		4.09%		2.84%		6.35%		7.40%
Eq/Assets GAAP			2.57%		0.79%		2.00%		6.35%		7.40%
EM*	17.54		33.33		24.43		35.21		15.75		13.51
ROE	11.93%		−8.00%		1.71%		−32.04%		7.24%		8.64%
No. S&Ls	N/G		3,544		3,242		2,951		1,807		1,416
% Not Profitable	N/G		N/G		23.75%		33.50%		9.75%		14.00%

Panel 2: Statistics for Last Year in Periods Examined for Insolvent Thrifts & Thrift Resolutions

	1983	1987	1989
End of Period No. Insolvent Operating	16.37%	21.35%	17.96%
End of Period Assets of Insolvent S&Ls	$234 bil.	$336 bil.	$283 bil.
End of Period No. of S&Ls Insolvent	515	672	517
Total Number of Resolutions for Period	138	145	242
Total Assets (bils.)	$37.659	$33.796	$110.322
Estimated Present Value of Cost (bils.)	$2.004	$8.491	$36.788

*Estimated based on Regulatory Accounting Principles. Under GAAP, ratios would be lower.

Source: George J. Benston. "An Analysis of the Causes of Savings and Loan Association Failures." Monograph Series in Finance and Economics, Salomon Brothers Center for the Study of Financial Institutions, New York University, 1985, p. 11; Barth (1991) and Kane (1989).

Other Sources: *Sheshunoff S&L Quarterlys*. Sheshunoff Information Services, Austin, Texas. Federal Home Loan Bank Board and U.S. League of Savings Associations, before 1988, Office of Thrift Supervision after 1988 for early years as cited in Exhibit 18.1, Kidwell, Peterson, and Blackwell. Financial Institutions, Markets, & Money. New York: Dryden Press, Fifth Edition, 1993. James R. Barth. The Great Savings and Loan Debacle. Washington, D.C.: AEI Press, 1991. See Barth (1991) Table 3.1 for greater detail concerning thrift resolutions and insolvencies, cited in this table.

---

[27]See Barth (1991).

To forestall closing hundreds of insolvent thrifts, thrift regulators practiced regulatory forbearance, allowing NWCs and other regulatory accounting principles to give thrifts positive equity values so they could continue to operate. With dwindling insurance reserves, regulators hoped that interest rates would fall, allowing thrifts to become solvent again. Congress passed emergency powers under the Garn-St. Germain Act of 1982 that permitted failing thrifts to merge with banks and other nonthrift institutions and interstate mergers. Regulators lowered capital-to-asset requirements under RAP to 3%.[28]

Unfortunately, regulators created a **moral hazard** for insolvent stock thrifts. Since stockholders of technically insolvent thrifts had already lost their investment, they had nothing to lose and everything to gain by taking on risky assets under **"bet the bank"** strategies and rapidly expanding to grow their way out of insolvency. Moreover, low capital requirements meant that owner-managers had the potential to make an exorbitant return on a small equity investment.

State regulators in several states, including California, Florida, Texas, and Ohio, adopted lenient laws concerning the types of investments a thrift could engage in. In California, for instance, state-chartered thrifts could invest in service corporations for real estate, land loans, construction development loans, and direct equity investments[29]. Consequently, low capital thrifts in these states had opportunities to take on risky nontraditional assets. These assets and high growth were often financed with insured jumbo deposits of $100,000 that offered above market yields. Many large thrifts marketed these deposits nationwide through brokers. Since these "brokered deposits" were insured, investors were willing to put funds into weak institutions in return for high yields. To match high deposit yields, thrifts were pressured to invest in even riskier assets. Owner-managers of severely insolvent thrifts also had incentives for looting types of behavior, such as paying high dividends, salaries, and other perks, and engaging in outright fraud, knowing that their thrift would eventually close and putting this cost to the deposit insurer.[30]

In the mid-1980s losses on risky assets finally came to light. In 1984, the nation's largest thrift, FCA, suffered severe loan losses as well as losses on interest-rate gambles. As a result, severe deposit runs by uninsured and "jumbo" depositors ensued. FCA's crisis threatened the solvency of the FSLIC, which had insufficient reserves. The FSLIC at this time also faced difficulties finding merger partners for failed thrifts, since with the entry of nonbank banks, taking over a failed thrift became a less attractive entry option. To resolve this crisis and the crisis of many other large insolvent thrifts in the mid-1980s, regulators instituted a Management Consignment Program whereby federal regulators replaced managers with regulator-picked CEOs or placed insolvent thrifts under the management of solvent S&Ls.[31]

Despite such measures to conserve FSLIC funds, in 1987 the Government Accounting Office (GAO) announced that the FSLIC was technically insolvent. By 1987, 672 (21.35%) S&Ls were technically insolvent, the percentage of repossessed

---

[28]See Brumbaugh (1988).

[29]See Benston (1985), Kane (1989), Akerlof and Romer (1993).

[30]See Kane (1989) and Akerlof and Homer (1993).

[31]See Brumbaugh (1988) and Cooperman, Wolfe, Verbrugge and Lee (1998). See also Flannery (1998), which provides a survey of studies of market discipline. Studies of market discipline during the thrift crisis include Golding, Hannan, and Liang (1989), Hirschhorn (1989), Cook and Spellman (1991), Cooperman, Lee, and Wolfe (1992), and Park and Peristiani (1998).

assets rose to 1.54% on average per year from 1984 to 1987, and the average GAAP equity-to-asset ratio fell to 0.79%. Panel A of Table 7.7 shows that the FSLIC between 1980 and 1998 had used funds to liquidate or assist in 91 liquidations, 541 assisted mergers, 333 supervised mergers, and 95 management consignment cases. Despite band-aid measures to recapitalize the FSLIC, by 1988 the situation was so severe that a huge bailout was required.

President Bush ordered insolvent thrifts to be closed, and in 1989 Congress passed FIRREA, which formalized the bailout and a forced recapitalization of the industry. FIRREA mandated closures of severely undercapitalized thrifts that could not meet higher capital requirements by 1991. Despite over 200 thrift closures in 1988, 517 insolvent S&Ls (17.96% of the industry) continued to operate in 1989. The Resolution Trust Company faced a tremendous challenge to resolve the problem of the enormous number of insolvent S&Ls. Panel B Table 7.7 shows that, between 1988 and 1996, over 1,001 thrifts exited, either through assisted transactions or closures, with the majority occurring in 1988, 1990, and 1991. In 1995 and 1996, with the industry profitable again, only two thrifts were closed each year and in 1997 no thrifts were closed.[32]

Table 7.7   ✦   Attrition of Federally Insured S&Ls, 1934 to 1988

Panel A: Attrition of Federally Insured S&Ls, 1934 to 1988

Source: James R. Barth. *The Great Savings and Loan Debacle.* Washington, D.C.: AEI Press, 1991, pp. 32–33.

Year	Liquidated	Assisted Mergers	Supervised Mergers	Management Consignment	Non-Failed Voluntary Mergers	Total Attrition
1934–79	13	130	0	0	0	143
1980	0	11	21	0	63	95
1981	1	27	54	0	215	297
1982	1	62	184	0	215	462
1983	5	31	34	0	83	153
1984	9	13	14	0	31	67
1985	9	22	10	23	47	111
1986	10	36	5	29	45	125
1987	17	30	5	25	74	151
1988	26	179	6	18	25	254
Total	91	541	333	95	798	1,858

Panel B: Closures of S&Ls & Federally Assisted Transactions, 1988–1996

	1988	1989	1990	1991	1992	1993	1994	1995	1996	Total
Assisted Transactions	207	54	246	153	42	19	34	0	0	755
Closures	26	6	68	78	26	8	30	2	2	246
Total	233	60	314	231	68	27	64	2	2	1,001

Sources: Sheshunoff S&L Quarterly, 1990–1996. Austin, Texas: Sheshunoff Information Services, Inc.

---

[32]See Barth (1991) and Shesnuoff S&L quarterlys.

ARE DEPOSITORY INSTITUTION FAILURES CONTAGIOUS?

The thrift crisis of the 1980s and the failures of several large banks during this time have created concern over whether public deposit runs will occur at other banks or thrifts if a large bank or S&L fails. Weaknesses in deposit insurance funds for both banks and thrifts in the 1980s have increased concerns over potential contagion. Although federal insurance funds incorporate an implicit guarantee by the government to rescue insurance agencies if they fail, this guarantee has been kept off the budget, and until CEBA of 1997, this implicit guarantee was not explicitly stated. Concern over possible contagion also occurred for thrifts because of their very low or negative capitalization in the 1980s.

Several studies have found evidence of risk premiums on jumbo CDs for low capital thrifts in the 1980s, suggesting that depositors demanded a higher rate for greater institution risk for low-capital thrifts, even for insured deposits. As Kane (1989) notes, when insurance funds and depository institutions are undercapitalized, depositor confidence may waver and silent runs, or the threat of silent runs, may occur for less solvent banks and S&Ls. If a small percentage of depositors threaten to withdraw funds, poorly capitalized banks and S&Ls may be able to retain funds by paying a higher deposit rate, which makes "customers willing to live with their growing doubts." A study of FCA's crisis found some evidence to suggest investor contagion for other Western thrifts with insured deposits during the period when the FSLIC's insolvency was threatened. Similarly, another study finds a sudden rise in federally insured CD-rate premiums for Ohio thrifts during the privately insured Ohio thrift crisis in 1985.[33]

For commercial banks, as the largest type of depository, the possibility of deposit market contagion is often considered undesirable for the financial system as a whole. This view arises from fears of a public run on other depository institutions when one fails, forcing solvent institutions to close, not because their net worth has vanished but because they lack the cash to pay off all depositors on demand. Fear of contagion was especially high in the 1980s, when 1,082 banks failed, including a number of very large banks. For this reason, prior to FDICIA, bank regulators implicitly adopted a "too big to fail" (TBTF) policy, generally rescuing mega-banks from failure.

An example is Continental Illinois's crisis in 1984, a few months before that of FCA. Continental Illinois National, one of the ten largest banks in the U.S. at that time, had assets exceeding $40 billion. Like FCA, Continental Illinois engaged in liability management, depending on short-term borrowings and uninsured deposits for liquidity. When bad news in terms of large loan losses appeared for the bank, Continental Illinois lost large uninsured deposits and was unable to get short-term borrowings renewed, suffering a severe liquidity crisis and teetering on the brink of failure.[34]

---

[33]See Kane (1989), Cooperman, Wolfe, Verbrugge, and Lee (1998), and Cooperman, Lee, and Wolfe (1992).

[34]Wall and Peterson (1990) and Swary (1986). Swary finds some evidence of deposit market contagion for other large liability-managed, less well-capitalized banks during the pre-rescue period of the Continental Illinois crisis. Wall and Peterson, however, find such contagion to be informationally based for other banks with problems similar to Continental Illinois.

Rather than closing the bank, federal regulators kept it afloat by the FDIC purchase of $1 billion of Continental preferred stock to shore up the bank's net worth. The insurance agency also purchased several billion dollars' worth of problem loans from Continental, enabling it to strengthen its balance sheet. This type of regulatory assistance was almost unprecedented and was interpreted to mean that the nation's largest banks would not be allowed to fail.[35] This federal assistance was given despite widespread belief that the bank's top management executives, all of whom were later removed from office, were responsible for the bank's precarious financial condition.

Similarly, in 1988, the FDIC provided an interim financial assistance package of $1 billion and provided assurances of protection to all bank depositors and creditors to rescue the two largest subsidiaries of First Republic Bank Corporation of Dallas, which had 41 subsidiary banks and assets of $32.5 billion, making it the largest BHC in Texas and the fourteenth largest in the U.S. When it became clear that the bank could not recover on its own, the FDIC entered into an agreement with NCNB Corporation (now NationsBank) of Charlotte, North Carolina, to create NCNB Texas National Bank. This **bridge bank** was to be managed by NCNB. New equity capital of $1.05 billion was invested, with 80% provided by the FDIC and 20% by NCNB. The North Carolina bank was given an exclusive five-year option to buy out the FDIC's 80% share. Regulators appeared to endorse the position that the failure of large institutions is more detrimental to the financial industry than the failure of small ones.

Research examining abnormal stock market reactions surrounding large bank failures generally finds evidence of stock market declines for banks with similar problems to a large failing bank, but not for other banks. This suggests that investors or depositors act on new information concerning problems at their individual bank but do not sell shares or remove deposits for unrelated solvent banks.[36]

Regulatory capital requirements are partly based on the fear of possible contagion by depositors. Under FIRREA of 1989 for thrifts and FDICIA of 1991 for banks, the previous TBTF policy of regulators was eliminated, and regulators were mandated to close all severely undercapitalized banks and thrifts. With the emergence of megabanks in the late 1980s, such as the Travelers/Citicorp group, analysts are concerned that the given economic importance of these large institutions' regulators may have to relapse to TBTF policies. These acts also imposed a system of new risk-based capital requirements. These requirements will be discussed in greater detail in Chapter 8.

---

[35]Comptroller of the Currency C. Todd Conover stated in Congressional testimony on September 9, 1984, that none of the 11 largest banks would be allowed to fail. Tim Carrington. "U.S. Won't Let 11 Biggest Banks in Nation Fail." *Wall Street Journal*, September 20, 1984, 2.See O'Hara and Shaw, 1990. O'Hara and Shaw find a positive stock price wealth effect for these "11" biggest banks on the days surrounding this announcement.

[36]See Kaufman (1994) and Aharony and Swary (1996). Aharony and Swary find that distance and capital adequacy are negatively related to the magnitude of the contagion effect for abnormal stock market returns for 33 Southwestern BHCs in response to large bank failures in the Southwest in the mid-1980s. Kaufman (1994) provides an excellent review of studies investigating contagion.

SUMMARY

This chapter focuses on thrifts and CUs by providing a brief history and describing regulatory changes and trends that affect these institutions along with a continued discussion of banks. A comparison is made among the industry structures, growth rates, balance sheets, income statements, failure rates, and financial performance of the three types of depository institutions. In contrast to banks and CUs, thrifts have had severe profitability problems as the result of their maturity intermediation function of making long-term, fixed-rate loans for home mortgages financed by short-term deposits. They also face increased competition for originating home mortgages from government and quasi-government specialized mortgage agencies as well as from banks and other nonthrift institutions. In the 1980s thrifts suffered a severe financial crisis. Hundreds of thrifts were closed and hundreds of mergers have occurred. In the 1990s, after regulatory closures, mergers, and restructuring, thrifts have generally become profitable again.

Credit unions, in contrast, which make short-term consumer loans financed by short-term deposits, have low interest-rate risk. They also have closer relations with customers, who are employees of the same firm or members of a group with a common bond, so have lower credit risk. Under an extended common bond definition, CUs have grown rapidly and are generally profitable nonprofit organizations, passing on returns to depositor owners in the form of higher deposit rates and lower loan rates. Many small CUs, however, do not have the professional expertise that professional managers of thrifts and banks have. CCUs allow smaller CUs to offer products that other depositories offer, although sometimes with not as high level of sophistication.

The chapter also discusses the thrift crisis, which was magnified in the 1980s by regulators who allowed technically insolvent thrifts to continue to operate, creating moral hazard problems. Many owners of thrifts took on risky assets in attempts to bet the bank and regain solvency. Despite the fact that the GAO estimates that taxpayers ultimately paid almost $0.5 trillion to resolve the S&L failures alone, the thrift industry became profitable again after the implementation of more stringent regulatory policies and a cleanup by the Resolution Trust Corporation in the early 1990s. With similar financial crises occurring in Asia in the late 1990s and a banking crisis in Russia, lessons can be learned from the causes and cure for the thrift crisis in the U.S. of the 1980s.

Questions

1. Identify the most important distinctions among banks, thrifts, and CUs. What differences do they have in terms of assets and liabilities? What similarities are there among thrifts, small banks, and CUs?

2. Explain why the thrift industry's heavy investment in fixed-rate mortgage loans exposed the industry to greater interest-rate risk than commercial banks face. How did FIRREA increase or reduce this exposure? What recent regulatory changes also enhanced thrifts' greater product flexibility?

3. How does the nonprofit status of CUs affect their performance compared with that of commercial banks and thrifts? How did that status become more controversial in the 1990s? Why did the NCUA extend the common bond requirement for CUs in 1982? What are the arguments for and against this extension?

4. What threats has the thrift charter faced? What advantages do OSLHCs have that BHCs do not? How were these advantages attacked in the 1990s?

5. What types of financial institutions besides thrifts offer home mortgages? How has mortgage securitization changed the thrift industry? What tax law changes have encouraged conversions and mergers with banks by thrifts?

6. Compare the growth rates and industry structures of CUs, banks, and thrifts. Why have numerous mergers occurred for thrifts and CUs? Give some examples of recent mergers.

7. What kind of regulatory and support groups do CUs have? What is a *CCU* and what services does a CU provide?

8. Compare S&L profitability during the 1980s and 1990s with the financial performance of banks and CUs. What factors contributed to their differences in profitability? Do you expect these trends to continue or to change in the near future? How important was noninterest revenue in 1996 to the profitability of banks?

9. Discuss the trends in capitalization for banks, thrifts, and CUs in the 1980s to 1990s. Why did regulators allow thrifts to remain so undercapitalized in the 1980s? What effect did regulatory gimmicks to keep "zombie" thrifts solvent have on thrift risk-taking?

10. Discuss the thrift crisis of the 1980s in terms of interest-rate risk and credit risk for the thrift industry.

11. What is the difference between the market value and the book value of equity for depository institutions? What were the trends in market value to book values for thrifts in the 1980s and 1990s?

12. Discuss the notion of *deposit market* or *investor contagion*. Have empirical studies found evidence of contagion? Why did regulators in the 1980s adopt TBTF policies? How was this changed under FDICIA of 1991?

Sources for Suggested Cases

Harvard Business School Publishing Co., www.hbsp.harvard.edu, 1-800-545-7685.

Also see dardencases@virginia.edu. Internet: http://www.darden.virginia.edu/case/bib, 1-800-246-3367 for Darden Case Bibliography, University of Virginia, Management Cases and Notes.

Suggested Case for Thrifts: Financial Analysis and Changing Role of Thrifts

"Metropolitan Savings and Loans." Harvard Business School Publishing. This case provides an opportunity for financial analysis and also deals with the changing nature of thrifts. Three former investment bankers have purchased the thrift in 1989 and are attempting to transform it into more of a mortgage bank, originating and securitizing mortgage loans and attracting nationwide deposits, yet still attempting to meet Community Reinvestment Act requirements.

Suggested Case for Thrifts: Thrift Mergers and Strategies

"Case 7: Great Western Bank." Darden School, University of Virginia: Richard D. Crawford and William W. Sihler. *Financial Service Organizations: Cases in Strategic Management.* New York: Harper Collins College Publishers, 1994, 7.1. This case also provides the opportunity for financial analysis and deals with a potential merger of a savings bank in the northeast with a large California S&L in 1988, at the peak of the S&L crisis.

Suggested Case for CUs in Association with Chapter 8 Capital Management: CUs/Capitalization

"Case 9: Navy Credit Union." Darden School, University of Virginia: Richard D. Crawford and William W. Sihler. *Financial Service Organizations: Cases in Strategic Management.* New York: Harper Collins College Publishers, 1994, 9.1. This case appraises the capital adequacy and strategic policies of Navy Credit Union in 1991, at a time when the military was downsizing.

Suggested Cases for Banks Discussing interest Rate Risk and Merger Trends

Financial Analysis & Bank Investment Portfolio Management and Interest Rate Risk

"Case 2: Quigley Bank Corporation." Darden School, University of Virginia: Richard D. Crawford and William W. Sihler. *Financial Service Organizations: Cases in Strategic Management.* New York: Harper Collins College Publishers, 1994, 2.1. Financial Analysis and Developing a Strategy for a Community Bank

"Case 8: Indiana Bank (A)." Darden School, University of Virginia: Richard D. Crawford and William W. Sihler. *Financial Service Organizations: Cases in Strategic Management.* New York: Harper Collins College Publishers, 1994, 8.1.

Selected References

Aharony, J. and I. Swary. "Additional Evidence on the Information-based Contagion Effects of Bank Failures." *Journal of Banking and Finance*, Vol. 20, No. 1 (January 1996), 57–69.

Akerlof, G. A. and P. M. Romer. "Looting: The Economic Underworld of Bankruptcy for Profit." *Brookings Papers on Economic Activity*, 1993, 1–73.

Baldwin, Carliss Y. and Benjamin Esty. "Lessons from the Thrift Crisis," in *Financial Services Perspectives and Challenges*, ed. Samuel L. Hayes, III, Boston, Mass: Harvard Business School Press, 1993.

Barth, J. R. *The Great Savings and Loan Debacle.* Washington, D.C.: The American Enterprise Institute, 1991.

Benston, G. J. *An Analysis of the Causes of Savings and Loan Association Failures.* New York University Graduate School of Business, Salomon Brothers Center for the Study of Financial Institutions Monograph Series, No. 4/5, 1985.

Brickley, J. A. and C. M. James. "Access to Deposit Insurance, Insolvency Rules, and the Stock Returns of Financial Institutions." *Journal of Financial Economics*, (July 1986), 345–371.

Brumbaugh, R. D., Jr. *Thrifts Under Siege: Restoring Order to American Banking.* Cambridge, MA.: Ballinger Publishing Co, 1988.

Cebenoyan, A. S., E. S. Cooperman, and C. A. Register. "Deregulation, Reregulation, Equity Ownership and S&L Risk Taking." *Financial Management*, 24 (Autumn 1995), 63–76.

Cebenoyan, A. S., E. S. Cooperman, and C. A. Register. "Ownership Structure, Charter Value, and Risk-Taking

Behavior for Thrifts," *Financial Management*, Spring 1999, 43–60.

Cebenoyan, A. S., E. S. Cooperman, C. A. Register, and D. L. Bauer. "Interstate Savings and Loans in the 1990s: A Performance and Risk Appraisal." Working Paper, University of Colorado at Denver, 1997.

Cook, D. O. and L. J. Spellman. "Federal Financial Guarantees and the Occasional Market Pricing of Default Risk." *Journal of Banking and Finance*, 15 (1991), 1113–1130.

Cooperman, E. S., W. B. Lee, and G. A. Wolfe. "The 1985 Ohio Thrift Crisis, The FSLIC's Solvency, and Rate Contagion for Retail CDs." *Journal of Finance*, 57 (July 1992), 919–941.

Cooperman, E. S., G. A. Wolfe, J. A.Verbrugge, and W. B. Lee. "Further Evidence on Equity Market Contagion: The FSLIC's Solvency and the Liquidity Crisis of Financial Corporation of America." *The Financial Review*, 33, November, 1998, 93–106.

Cordell, Lawrence R., Gregor D. MacDonald, and Mark E. Wohav. "Corporate Ownership and the Thrift Crisis." *Journal of Law and Economics*, 36, 1993, 719–756.

Crawford, Richard D. and William W. Sihler. *Financial Service Organizations: Cases in Strategic Management.* New York: Harper Collins College Publishers, 1994.

Esty, Benjamin C. "A Case Study of Organizational Form and Risk Shifting in the Savings and Loan Industry" *Journal of Financial Economics*, Vol. 18, April 1997, 57–76.

Flannery, Mark J. "Using Market Information in Prudential Bank Supervision: A Review of the U.S. Empirical Evidence." *Journal of Money, Credit and Banking*, 30 (August 1998, Part 1), 273–305.

Galloway, T. M., W. B. Lee, and D. M. Roden. "Bank's Changing Incentives and Opportunities for Risk Taking." *Journal of Banking and Finance*, 21 (April 1997), 509–527.

Golding, E. L., T. H. Hannan, and J. N. Liang. "Do FSLIC-Insured Institutions Pay Risk Premia for Insured Deposits?" Working Paper, Federal Reserve Board, 1989.

Hirschhorn, E."Depositor Risk Perceptions and the Insolvency of the FSLIC. "Working Paper, Office of Thrift Supervision, 1989.

Kane, E. J. *The S&L Insurance Mess: How Did It Happen?* Washington D.C.: Urban Institute Press, 1989.

Kaufman, G. G. "Bank Contagion: A Review of the Theory and Evidence." *Journal of Financial Services Research*, Vol. 8, No. 2 (1994), 123–150.

Kaufman, G. G. "Capital in Banking: Past, Present, and Future." *Journal of Financial Services Research*, Vol. 5, No. 4 (1992), 385–402.

Keeley, M. C. "Deposit Insurance, Risk, and Market Power in Banking." *American Economic Review*, (December 1990), 1183–1200.

O'Hara, M. and W. Shaw. "Deposit Insurance and Wealth Effects: The Value of Being Too Big to Fail." *Journal of Finance*, (December 1990), 1587–1600.

Park, Sangkyun and Stavros Peristiani. "Market Discipline by Thrift Depositors." *Journal of Money, Credit and Banking*, 30 (August 1998, Part 1), 347–364.

Schmitt, Richard B. "Judge Orders U.S. to Pay $908.9 Million to California Thrift Glendale Federal," *The Wall Street Journal*, April 12, 1999, A4.

Swary, I. "Stock Market Reaction to Regulatory Action in the Continental Illinois Crisis." *Journal of Business*, (July 1986), 451–473.

Wall, L. D. and D. R. Peterson. "The Effect of Continental Illinois' Failure on the Financial Performance of Other Banks." *Journal of Monetary Economics*, (August 1990), 77–99.

Walker, David A., Principal Investigator. "Credit Union Insurance and Regulation." Center for Business-Government Relations, Georgetown University, 1997.

White, Lawrence J. *The S&L Debacle: Public Lessons for Bank and Thrift Regulation.* New York: Oxford University Press, 1991.

Chapter 7 Internet Exercise

Credit unions and savings institutions

The FDIC provides Reports of Condition and Income (Call Reports) and Thrift Financial Reports beginning in 1998. These can be found at:

http://www2.fdic.gov/call_tfr_rpts/default.asp

As an example, you can look up the most recent Call Report information for Nationsbank, National Association based in Charlotte, NC. The FDIC Certificate number is 15802. From the FDIC page cited above, enter the certificate number 15802. You will then see the following schedules:

Schedule RI—Income Statement

Schedule RI-A—Changes in Equity Capital

Schedule RI-B—Charge-Offs and Recoveries on Loans and Leases and Changes in Allowance for Credit Losses

Schedule RI-D—Income from International Operations

Schedule RI-E—Explanations

Schedule RC—Balance Sheet

Schedule RC-A—Cash and Balances Due from Depository Institutions

Schedule RC-B—Securities

Schedule RC-C—Loans and Lease Refinancing Receivables

Schedule RC-D—Trading Assets and Liabilities

Schedule RC-E—Deposit Liabilities

Schedule RC-F—Other Assets

Schedule RC-G—Other Liabilities

Schedule RC-H—Selected Balance Sheet Items for Domestic Offices

Schedule RC-I—Selected Assets and Liabilities of IBFs

Schedule RC-K—Quarterly Averages

Schedule RC-L—Off-Balance Sheet Items

Schedule RC-M—Memoranda

Schedule RC-N—Past Due and Nonaccrual Loans, Leases, and Other Assets

Schedule RC-O—Other Data for Deposit Insurance and FICO Assessments

Schedule RC-R—Regulatory Capital

Special Report—Loans to Executive Officers

Optional Narrative Statement—Bank Management Statement

1. To get information on derivatives activities of Nationsbank for the most recent filing period, click on "Schedule RC-D." Schedule RC-D is to be completed only by banks with $1 billion or more in total assets or with $2 billion or more in par/notional amount of off-balance sheet derivative contracts (as reported in Schedule RC-L, items 14.a through 14.e, columns A through D). Click on "back" on your browser to return to the Call Report page for Nationsbank.

2. To find call report data for a credit union, go to:

http://www.ncua.gov/data/

3. Click on "Custom Reports." When the page comes up, in the first "Field to search on" click on the arrow and highlight "charter number." To the right, enter 162. This is the charter number for the Department of the Treasury Federal Credit Union.

4. Click GO! at the bottom of the screen. On this page, the name and charter number are already checked. Just click GO! again. The next page will say "1 matches found." Click on the charter number "162" and you will proceed to a page that gives basic information about the Treasury Federal Credit Union. You can choose to see the entire financial report and can also select the date of the report. The defaults are the "Entire Statement of Financial Condition" for the most recent quarter.

5. Click GO! to see the "Entire Statement of Financial Condition."

Other useful sites for financial institution data:

Nationsbank, soon to be BankAmerica with their merger in 1998:
http://www.nationsbank.com/

Chapter 7 Internet Exercise

Credit Unions:
Federal Credit Union Act
http://www.ncua.gov/ref/fcu_act/fcu_act.html

Credit Union National Association
http://www.cuna.org/

National Credit Union Administration
http://www.ncua.gov/

Government Owned or Sponsored Mortgage Enterprises:
Government National Mortgage Association (Ginnie Mae)
http://www.ginniemae.gov/

Federal National Mortgage Association (Fannie Mae)
http://fanniemae.com/

Federal Home Loan Mortgage Corporation (Freddie Mac).
http://www.freddiemac.com/

Office of Federal Housing Enterprise Oversight (OFHEO)
http://www.ofheo.gov/

Bank Regulatory Agencies:
Federal Deposit Insurance
http://www.fdic.gov/

Federal Financial Institutions Examination Council
http://www.ffiec.gov/

Board of Governors of the Federal Reserve
http://www.bog.frb.fed.us/

Office of the Comptroller of Currency
http://www.occ.treas.gov/

U.S. Treasury
http://www.ustreas.gov/

Bank Web Site
http://www.mybank.com/

American Bankers Association
http://www.aba.com/aba/

Thrift Sites:
Federal Home Loan Bank
http://www.fhlbanks.com/

Office of Thrift Supervision
http://www.ots.treas.gov/

"Stronger banks are favored under the new risk-based capital and insurance frameworks. These institutions receive more favorable treatment in their application for mergers and new product powers. Additionally, strong firms will face relatively less regulatory oversight. . . . Strong, well-capitalized institutions can acquire. Those that are not, cannot."

John B. McCoy
CEO, Banc One Corporation; Larry A. Frieder, Professor, Florida A&M University; and Robert B. Hedges, Jr., Executive Vice President, Consumer Banking Group, Shawmut National Corporation. *BottomLine Banking*. Chicago: Probus Publishing Company, 1994, 80.

"It should be clear who will win the battle for supremacy at the top of the financial services business. The large banks start with a big advantage in . . . market capital."

Arnold Danielson
President, Danielson Associates, Bank Consulting Firm, *Banking Policy Report*, Vol. 16, April 27, 1997, 6.

"The troubled Japanese banks face major problems of low capitalization which will be exacerbated as they make bad-loan provisions. Elsewhere in Asia, loan business is booming for fast-growing banks, which also face capitalization problems, although these are in many cases much less deep-seated."

"Asian Banks: A Crisis of Capital." *Euromoney*, December, 1995, 90.

8

CAPITAL REGULATIONS AND MANAGEMENT

*A*s the quotations above note, capital has been crucial for financial institutions in the 1990s. In response to the large number of bank failures and the thrift crisis of the 1980s, new capital requirements were instituted for banks and thrifts in the 1990s. Thus, many undercapitalized institutions had to scramble to raise new capital to meet new requirements or be acquired by or merge with other banks or thrifts. In the later 1990s capital became increasingly important to allow financial institutions to acquire other financial institutions to become major na- tional or international players. For Asian banks that suffered large losses in the late 1990s, having sufficient capital to absorb such losses became critical for their survival.

By their nature, financial institutions have high fi- nancial leverage (low capital ratios), which magnifies their profits but also increases their risk of bankruptcy. Low capital leaves less of an equity cushion to absorb losses. Hence, the management of financial institution capital is crucial. This chapter discusses the role of capi- tal, capital regulatory requirements, and capital management for financial institutions, focusing on depository institutions that have the most stringent capital regulations.

The following section briefly discusses market versus book value definitions of capital. This section is followed by a discussion of the importance of capital and the determination of its adequacy. The next section out-lines preferences of different agents and theories for the optimal amount of capital. A presentation is then made of regulatory capital requirements and definitions of capital. Finally, capital management strategies used by individual depository institutions are outlined, along with dividend policies.

✦ ✦ ✦

MARKET VERSUS BOOK VALUE DEFINITIONS OF CAPITAL

The majority of the assets and liabilities of all depositary institutions are in their book (historical) values versus market values. Consequently, book equity-to-asset ratios may be deceptive if the market value of assets and liabilities encompass losses in value based on interest rate changes. For instance, if assets are long-term, fixed rate loans and liabilities are short-term deposits, the market value of equity will fall if interest rates rise, since the value of assets will fall more than the value of liabilities. The book value of equity, in contrast, will stay the same.

Figure 8.1 shows the difference between using book and market values to measure the capital for the Market King Bank. For simplicity, the Market King Bank has three assets: cash, 3-month Treasury bills (T-bills), and consumer automobile loans with a four-year maturity and 10% rate. In this example, all deposits are variable rate, so their market values remain the same as their original book values.

In Panel A, equity capital is measured as the book value of assets less the book value of liabilities. Market King Bank has $4.2 million in equity or a book-valued based equity-to-asset ratio of 6%.

In Panel B, equity capital is measured as the market value of assets less the market value of liabilities, i.e., the present values of cash flows on assets less the present value of liabilities. Panel B assumes that after the loans were made, the market rate for auto loans rose to 13%. With a higher discount rate for the present value of future loan payments, the market value of the loans falls from $50,000,000 to $47,269,757. With the market value for the liabilities unchanged, the market value of equity (market value of assets less market value of liabilities) falls from $4,200,000 to $1,469,757 or by $2,730,243, a decline of about 65%! If Market King sold its loans, it would have a significant loss. The market value equity-to-asset ratio is now 2.18% versus a 6% book value-to-equity ratio, which assumes that the value of assets remains the same despite the drop in their market value.

Similarly, as shown in Panel C, if loan rates on similar auto loans fell to 7.5%, the market value (present value of future cash flows) for Market King's loans would rise significantly to $52,447,757, resulting in a rise in the market value of equity to $6,647,757, a 58% rise over the book value shown in Panel A. The bank's new market value equity-to-asset ratio would rise to 9.18% versus the book value-to-equity ratio that investors see, with book value accounting for only 6%.

Difficulties in Calculating Market Values.

As Figure 8.1 shows, market value capital measures are superior to book measures. However, problems exist in calculating the market value of assets and liabilities.

Figure 8.1   ✦   BOOK VALUE VERSUS THE MARKET VALUE OF CAPITAL

The market value of assets (and, therefore, of equity) reflects changing economic conditions. In this example, changing interest rates cause the market value of loans to fall (Panel B) or to rise (Panel C) when compared with their book value. Equity worth falls or rises correspondingly.

A. Book-Value Accounting:

Assets		Liabilities and Equity	
$ 1,000,000	Cash	$ 65,800,000	Deposits
19,000,000	T-Bills	4,200,000	Equity
50,000,000	10% Loans[a]		
$ 70,000,000	Total	$ 70,000,000	Total

Equity/Total Assets = 6.00%

[a]Amortizing these loans over 48 months at a monthly rate of 10%/12 = 0.833% results in expected monthly payments of $1,268,129.20. That is, the present value of $1,268,129.20, discounted at 0.833% for 48 months, is $50,000,000.

B. Market-Value Accounting (loan rates rise to 13%):

Assets		Liabilities and Equity	
$ 1,000,000	Cash	$ 65,800,000	Deposits
19,000,000	T-Bills	1,469,757	Equity
47,269,757	10% Loans[b]		
$ 67,269,757	Total	$ 70,000,000	Total

Equity/Total Assets = 2.18%

[b]The present value of the monthly payments discounted at 13%/12 = 1.0833.

C. Market-Value Accounting (loan rates fall to 7.5%):

Assets		Liabilities and Equity	
$ 1,000,000	Cash	$ 65,800,000	Deposits
19,000,000	T-Bills	6,647,757	Equity
52,447,757	10% Loans[c]		
$ 72,447,757	Total	$ 72,447,757	Total

Equity/Total Assets = 9.18%

[c]The present value of the monthly payments discounted at 7.5%/12 = 0.625%.

Some assets, for instance, may have no markets. For a stockholder-owned institution, the market value of common stock can be used (stock price—number of shares). However, many depository institutions are privately held or their stock is infrequently traded, so the market/book value assessments are unavailable. Thrift regulators proposed a plan for measuring the market value of assets on several occasions, but Congress declined in the Financial Institutions Reform, Recovery, and Enforcement Act (FIRREA) to require mark-to market accounting for depositories. Congress revised its position, however, and included provisions in the Federal Deposit Insurance Corporation Improvement Act (FDICIA) of 1991, requiring regulatory agencies to develop policies for market value disclosures in the quarterly reports required to be filed with their regulators. At about the same time, the Chairman of the Securities Exchange Commission began to advocate more extensive market-value reporting for depository institutions.[1]

The Financial Accounting Standards Board (FASB) embarked on a study of market-value accounting in 1986. The first result of its efforts was FASB Rule 107, issued in 1991 and effective for financial statements prepared by large firms on or after December 15, 1992. The new rule required banks, other financial institutions, and nonfinancial firms with assets of $150 million or greater to disclose in footnotes to their financial statements the fair market value of all financial instruments on their balance sheets—assets as well as liabilities. Smaller firms had three extra years before complying under the new rules. In early 1993, FASB issued another final rule on market value accounting, this time requiring firms to report—on the balance sheet—the market value of securities in the investment portfolio likely to be sold before maturity. Only securities being held to maturity can be reported under historical cost accounting rules. Other real estate owned similarly must be reported at market value. As discussed in Chapter 4, the market values of derivatives must also be reported. Although the new FASB rule affects all firms, they are particularly challenging for banks and other financial institutions because of the large proportion of financial securities they hold. Pressures for greater market value accounting for depository institutions will continue in the future.[2]

Why Capital?

As the thrift crisis of the 1980s and regulatory concerns over deposit market contagion at this time revealed, capital plays a crucial role for depository institutions. Capital fulfills several functions, including providing long-term funds for long-term investment and growth in assets, building confidence for depositors and other debtholders, and providing a cushion against future losses. The role of capital in building confidence by serving as a cushion against losses is illustrated in the following section.

The Role of Capital As a Cushion Against Losses

To understand the role of capital as a cushion against losses, observe the following balance sheet for the Majestic Savings Bank:

MAJESTIC SAVINGS BANK BALANCE SHEET

Assets	Deposits & Capital
Treasury bills $30 million	Deposits: $92 million ($80 million insured)
Mortgage Loans $70 million	Capital $8 million
Total: $100 million	Total: $100 million

---

[1] See Mondschean (1992); Moore (1992); David Siegel, "Disclosures to Herald Accounting's New Age," *American Banker*, September 21, 1992, 1, 18; Ford S. Worth, "The Battle of the Bean Counters," *Fortune*, June 1, 1992, 117–126; Lee Berton, "FASB Adopts Rule Requiring Updated Values," *The Wall Street Journal*, December 17, 1991, A3, A4; Mengle and Walter (1991); Kane and Unal (1990); Berger, Kuester, and O'Brien (1989); and Benston (1989).

[2] See Mondaschean (1992).

Suppose a major employer in town announces that it is transferring out of state, and many employees who have home mortgages with Majestic will lose their jobs. Majestic Bank's uninsured depositors may begin to evaluate whether their thrift could fail if delinquent loan payments reduce mortgage income and the value of loans, which would result in a fall in the value of the thrift's equity. They may think about pulling out their deposits, but may be reassured by Majestic's $8 million in capital. The value of Majestic's assets would have to fall by $8 million (i.e., $8 million/70 million, or 11.43%) before the depositors' interests would be threatened. Since such large a percentage decline in the value of Majestic's assets is unlikely, depositors may stay put.

If Majestic had only $2 million in capital, however, a small change in the value of assets ($2 million/$70 million, or 2.86%) would wipe out the thrift's equity. Hence, large depositors would be more likely to withdraw funds. Majestic would have a liquidity crisis if this happened and would have to liquidate assets to meet large deposit withdrawals or try to find some alternative borrowing sources. A large percentage of illiquid loans and low confidence would make finding other borrowing sources difficult, and Majestic could fail before managers had time to resolve the thrift's financial problems. In 1995 Continental Illinois suffered a similar liquidity crisis that led to its closure and takeover by regulators.

Although higher capital provides a cushion against losses and greater confidence for depositors, different parties have different preferences for how much capital should be held by a financial institution. Capital also has other uses: It supports growth and long-term fixed investments as well as reduces moral hazard. These preferences and uses are discussed in the following sections.

PREFERENCES BY DIFFERENT AGENTS FOR CAPITAL AND ITS USES

Preferences of Stockholders

For a financial institution with a positive return on assets (ROA) and an interest expense that does not rise excessively with a rise in debt (such as depository institutions with insured deposits), the higher its financial leverage (i.e., the lower its equity-to-capital ratio), the higher its return on equity (ROE). Basically, stockholders employ the funds of depositors and other debtholders to generate higher returns for them on a smaller investment. Debt also provides a tax subsidy, since interest expense is tax deductible. Moreover, debt provides an additional insurance subsidy for insured depositories, since insured depositors generally do not impose a penalty in the form of a risk premium on debt. The more risky, less capitalized an insured institution is, the higher the value of this insurance subsidy.

Studies show that the average equity-to-asset ratio for banks prior to deposit insurance was about 30% compared with 8% today. The fact that stockholders of insured depository institutions prefer greater financial leverage, i.e., greater capital risk, creates a moral hazard problem for the deposit insurer.[3]

---

[3]See Buser, Chen, and Kane (1981). See Kaufman (1992) and the *Journal of Banking and Finance*, 19, 1995 (*Special Issue on Bank Capital*) for surveys of research on the effect of deposit insurance on bank capital.

Moral Hazard Problems with Deposit Insurance   The following illustration demonstrates the moral hazard problem of deposit insurance. Consider an institution that begins with assets of $5 million in cash; the source of the cash is $5 million of capital. The cash can be used to make loans with a 50% probability of default (i.e., the entire $5 million could be lost) and a 50% probability of producing a $5 million profit after all expenses are paid. The expected dollar return on the investment is:

$$0.5 \, (-\$5 \text{ million}) + 0.5 \, (\$5 \text{ million}) = \$0$$

The expected rate of return to stockholders is 0%, and stockholders would encourage managers to seek better investments.

However, suppose the depository institution is funded by $4 million in insured deposits at a cost of 10% ($400,000 interest expense) and $1 million in capital. The most that stockholders can lose is $1 million, and their expected dollar profit on the loans is now:

$$0.5 \, (-\$1,000,000) + 0.5 \, (\$5,000,000 - \$400,000) = \$1,800,000$$

Their expected rate of return is 180%, not 0%, even though the investment is the same. The lower the amount of capital, the less incentive stockholders have to monitor the actions of management to prevent excessive risk taking. Stockholders have less to lose if things go poorly and more to gain if things go well. Similarly, if creditors are insured, creditors have little incentive to monitor the institution. All things being equal, then, stockholders of a federally insured depository with less capital will have stronger incentives to take excessive risks than a better capitalized institution.[4]

Purposes of Capital and Some Incentives for Stockholders to Hold Capital   On the other hand, from a current stockholder's perspective, retaining earnings and increasing equity capital permits a depository to grow and acquire other firms without having to issue additional external equity, which can be expensive and dilute current stockholders' earnings. It also prevents greater regulatory interference concerning branching or merger decisions. Using capital to finance additional fixed assets or additional growth is also less risky than financing long-term assets with short-term deposits. Paying for permanent assets with short-term liabilities would be unwise because it would require additional long-term capital, which can be more expensive for less well-capitalized depositories. Studies also show that better capitalized banks have a lower cost of uninsured funds and a lower weighted average cost of capital as well as generating higher ROEs than other banks. A significant positive relation between market-to-book values and capitalization for banks appeared in the 1980s, suggesting that better capitalized banks sell at a larger premium than other banks.[5]

Preferences of Uninsured Debtholders and Managers

In contrast to stockholders, who generally prefer lower capital ratios, uninsured debtholders prefer higher capital ratios as a cushion against potential losses to protect against loss of the funds they lent to the bank. Institutional investors also may be forbidden to invest in low capital stocks under a "prudent man" rule. Consequently, undercapitalized institutions may be penalized by uninsured investors and have to offer

---

[4]This illustration is similar to one used by Furlong and Keran (1984).
[5]See Kaufman (1992) for a survey of these studies.

a risk premium to attract uninsured debt. Managers may also fear losing their jobs if their institution fails, and so may generally prefer higher capital ratios as a cushion against loss and may demand higher salaries to work for a less well-capitalized bank. Some studies suggest, however, that the interests of managers become aligned with those of external stockholders for lower capital if managers have significant stock ownership or are under a compensation plan that is based on stock performance.[6]

Preferences of Regulators

Regulators prefer greater capital to protect deposit insurance funds and taxpayers' money. Also, because capital promotes confidence, it is more likely that depositors will not remove deposits all at once from a bank if the bank receives bad news. Because capital suppliers have a subordinate claim on the depository's income and assets, their investment helps to reassure uninsured creditors. Even if the institution has financial difficulty, uninsured depositors know the extent to which the value of assets can shrink before they are in danger of not recovering all their funds: that amount is equal to the total capital of the institution. The more capital, the more protection is afforded to uninsured depositors, the government in terms of insured deposits, and other short-term creditors, making a run on the institution less likely. Regulators are more likely to interfere in an institution's plans for an acquisition or additional branches if the institution is not well capitalized. The following section presents a model of how regulators influence the optimal capital structure decision for an insured depository institution.

BALANCING SHAREHOLDERS' AND REGULATORS' INTERESTS

The Optimum Capital Structure with Deposit Insurance and Regulation

Based on the preferences of stockholders discussed above, Buser, Chen, and Kane (1981) suggest that stockholders of insured depository institutions prefer as much debt financing as possible. Since stockholders receive both a tax subsidy and deposit insurance subsidy that increase in value as more debt is taken on, the optimal capital structure would be infinite debt, as shown in Figure 8.2 as V_L. This is in contrast to a depository with uninsured deposits. With a tax deduction from debt, the value of the firm rises as debt rises, but eventually the value V_o falls as uninsured debtholders demand a higher risk premium for greater risk and the cost of debt becomes excessive. Hence, uninsured depository institutions would have a much lower optimal debt-to-asset ratio (D_o).[7]

Buser, Chen, and Kane demonstrate that regulators of insured depository institutions dampen stockholders' incentives for excessive debt-to-asset ratios by imposing implicit regulatory costs for excessive financial leverage, including greater regulatory interference, the threat of closure, restrictions on growth, and other implicit costs. Although regulators could charge higher explicit deposit insurance premiums, this would discourage depositories from buying deposit insurance, since the tax ben-

---

[6]For instance, see Cebenoyan, Cooperman, and Register (1993) and studies discussed in Jensen (1998).

[7]See Buser, Chen, and Kane (1981).

Figure 8.2 ✦ RELATIONSHIP BETWEEN CAPITAL STRUCTURE AND VALUE

Many finance theorists believe that there is an optimal capital structure. Too little or too much debt capital can result in a lower value for the firm than if managers find the ideal range. The optimal capital struecture in depositories is also influenced by the deposit insurance system and capital regulations.

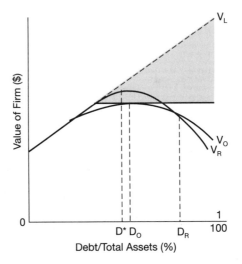

Source: Adapted from Buser, Chen, and Kane 1981.
V_L = optimal capital structure (debt/assets) with insured debt financing and no regulatory interference
V_O = optimal capital structure with uninsured debt financing, whereby the cost of funds rises and value of the firm falls as it takes on too much debt
V_R = optimal capital structure based on regulatory interference, insured deposits, and regulatory minimum capital requirements

efits of debt would be less than the combined explicit cost of insurance premiums and the burden of greater regulation for insured firms.

Hence, to provide incentives for institutions to choose deposit insurance, despite the added regulation it entails, regulators allow depositories to capture some of the value in the shaded area in Figure 8.2 by setting minimum capital requirements, allowing a higher debt-to-asset ratio at D_R and underpricing insurance. The minimum capital requirement then becomes the implicit deposit insurance premium, which most depository institutions will abide by to avoid extra scrutiny of their operations. At this minimum regulatory level, depositories have incentives to choose deposit insurance because the value of the firm at D_R will be higher than the value of the uninsured firm, which has a lower optimum debt ratio at D_o.

Under this theory, minimum capital requirements are a cost of being allowed deposit insurance. Fears of closure and greater regulatory interference along with a minimum capital requirement to reduce the incentives of stockholders for excessive risk-taking. Research has shown that the average depository institution chooses a capital-to-asset ratio close to the regulatory minimum.[8] The capital requirements that regulators historically and currently impose are discussed next.

---

[8]See Larry D. Wall and David R. Peterson, "Bank Holding Company Capital Targets in the Early 1990s: The Regulators versus the Markets." *Journal of Banking and Finance*, 19 (1995), 563–574.

Changes in Capital Requirements over Time

Before 1985, regulatory agencies generally set capital requirements on a case by case basis, allowing larger banks, as more diversified institutions, to have lower capital ratios. Consequently, capital ratios fell dramatically for large banks, from about 8.7% in 1984 to a little over 6% in 1980. Congressional concern over lower capital ratios led to the requirement of minimum capital-to-total assets ratios of 6% for large U.S. banks under the International Lending Supervision Act of 1983. As a result, capital ratios for large banks in the U.S. rose to an average of about 7% by 1988. Many large banks, however, shifted to off-balance sheet activities that did not, at that time, have capital requirements. International banks that competed with each other on a global basis had very different capital requirements, making it difficult for banks in countries that imposed more stringent capital regulations to compete. Regulators were also concerned about weaker international banks.

In response to these concerns, regulators for 12 major industrial nations agreed to introduce risk-based capital requirements for large international banks for Belgium, Canada, France, Germany, Italy, Japan, Luxembourg, the Netherlands, Sweden, Switzerland, the United Kingdom, and the U.S. This agreement, known as the Basle Accord of 1987, was implemented during 1990 to 1992.[9]

In the spirit of reducing moral hazard problems and preventing excessive risk taking, risk-based capital requirements, including capital requirements for off-balance sheet items, were also put into place for all U.S. banks and thrifts under FDICIA of 1991, which was implemented in January 1993. Risk-based deposit insurance premiums were put in place based on the capitalization of depository institutions in 1993 as well. Under FDICIA inadequately capitalized institutions are required to develop a plan to bring their capital back to regulatory standards. If a depository become severely undercapitalized, regulators are mandated to close that institution. Regulatory definitions of capital are discussed next.

Regulatory Definitions of Capital

Depository institutions have traditionally been allowed by regulators to hold two types of capital: **Tier 1, Core or Tangible Equity Capital**, and **Tier 2, Supplemental Capital**. These two types of capital and restrictions on each type are described in detail in Table 8.1 and in a simple form below.

> **Tier 1 Capital** = Common Stock Accounts and Retained Earnings (Common Equity)
>
> Perpetual Preferred Stock (up to 25% of Tier 1 Capital)
>
> Less Ineligible Intangible Assets
>
> **Tier 2 Capital** = Any Additional Perpetual Preferred Stock not allowed in Tier 1
>
> Limited Life Preferred Stock
>
> Subordinated Notes and Debentures (up to 50% of Tier 2 Capital)
>
> [original maturities of five years or more, amortized as they mature]
>
> Reserves for loan and lease losses (up to 1.25% of risk-weighted assets)
>
> Mandatory Convertible Subordinated Debt

---

[9]The Bask Accord also has an amendment that became effective in January of 1998 requiring commercial banks with significant trading activities to set aside capital to cover market risk exposure in their trading accounts based on the estimated value at risk. See Lopez (1998).

Table 8.1 ✦ Definitions for Tier 1 and Tier 2 Capital

U.S. banking regulators, along with regulators in 11 other nations, have recently agreed on the definitions of core and supplementary items used to determine institutions' capital adequacy.

Item	Description
Core (Tier 1) Capital	
Common stock	Aggregate par or stated value of outstanding common stock
Perpetual preferred stock	Aggregate par or stated value of outstanding perpetual preferred stock. Preferred stock is a form of ownership interest in a bank or other company that entitles its holders to some preference or priority over the owners of common stock, usually with respect to dividends or asset distributions in a liquidation. Perpetual preferred stock does not have a stated maturity date and cannot be redeemed at the option of the holder. It includes those issues that are automatically converted into common stock at a stated date
Surplus	Amount received from the sale of common or perpetual preferred stock in excess of its par or stated value
Undivided profits	Accumulated dollar value of profits after taxes that have not been distributed to shareholders of common and preferred stock as dividends
Capital reserves	Contingency and other capital reserves. Reserves for contingencies include amounts set aside for possible unforeseen or indeterminate liabilities not otherwise reflected on the bank's books and not covered by insurance. Capital reserves include amounts set aside for cash dividends on common and preferred stock not yet declared and amounts allocated for retirement of limited-life preferred stock and debentures subordinated to deposits
Minority interest in consolidated subsidiaries	Sum of the equity of the subsidiaries in which the bank has minority interest multiplied by the percentage ownership of the bank in the subsidiaries
Intangible assets[a]	Purchased credit card relationships and purchased mortgage servicing rights
Minus:	
All other intangible assets (primarily goodwill)	Generally these other intangible assets represent the difference between the purchase price and the book value of acquired institutions
Supplementary (Tier 2) Capital[b]	
Limited-life preferred stock	Preferred stock with an original maturity of 5 years or more
Subordinated notes and debentures[c]	Debt obligations of issuer, with original maturities of 5 years or more, that are subordinated to depositors in case of insolvency. Subordinated notes and debentures issued by depository institutions are not insured by the federal deposit insurance agencies
Reserves for loan and lease losses	Amount set aside to absorb anticipated losses. All charge-offs of loans and leases are charged to this capital amount, and recoveries on loans and leases previously charged off are credited to this capital account
Mandatory convertible subordinated debt	Debt issues that mandate conversion to common or perpetual preferred stock at some future date
Other items accepted as capital in international banking	Items such as "undisclosed reserves" that are similar to retained earnings but are not revealed on the balance sheet using accounting practices accepted in some nations

[a]The intangible assets regulators allow banks to include cannot total more than 50 percent of an institution's Tier 1 capital.
[b]Total supplementary capital cannot exceed the total of Tier 1 items.
[c]Subordinated debt may not exceed 50 percent of supplementary capital.

Tier 1 capital is defined as common stockholders' equity (common stock and retained earnings) plus perpetual preferred stock less any new goodwill incurred after new rules came into effect. **Tier 1 capital must be at least 50% of total capital.** Supplemental capital (Tier 2 capital) is included by regulators since it is subordinated to depositors in case of insolvency. Restrictions also exist concerning how much of different types of capital can be used. Perpetual preferred stock can only be up to 25% of Tier 1 capital, and subordinated debentures can be no more than 50% of Tier 2 capital. Reserves for loan losses can be included only up to 1.25% of risk-based assets.

Illustration of Tier 1 and Tier 2 Capital for Nationsbank of Maryland

To illustrate the calculation of Tier 1 and Tier 2 capital, Nationsbank's Maryland subsidiary figures in September of 1994 are shown below:

TIER ONE CAPITAL ($000)

Common Equity	$1,880,937
Less Ineligible Intangible Assets	291,335
Net Tier One	$ 1,589,602

TIER TWO CAPITAL ($000)

+ Allowable Subordinated Debt	$0
+ Cumulative Preferred Stock	0
+ Mandatory Convertible Debt	0
+ Allowable Loan & Lease Loss Allowance	161,113
Net Eligible Tier Two $161,113 For Tier 1 capital	

Nationsbank had no perpetual preferred stock, but it did have some ineligible intangibles to subtract, giving the bank $1,589,602 million in Tier 1 capital. For Tier 2 capital, Nationsbank did not have any allowable subordinated debt, preferred stock, or convertible debt, only an allowable allowance for loan losses, providing $161,113 million in additional Tier 2 capital. Hence, over 90% of Nationbank's total capital is Tier 1. Thus, total regulatory capital for Nationsbank is $1,750,715.

Minimum Regulatory Capital Requirements in 1993

Nationsbank must determine whether it meets the new risk-based regulatory requirements. The minimum capital ratios required are as follows as of January 1, 1993:

Leverage Ratio: Minimum Tier 1 capital-to-total assets ratio = 3%   (8.1)

Tier 1 capital-to-risk based assets ratio = 4%   (8.2)

Total Tier 1 + Tier 2 capital-to-risk based assets ratio = 8%   (8.3)

The first leverage ratio is based on total assets (i.e., Tier 1 capital divided by total assets). The second two ratios are based on risk-based assets (i.e., Tier 1 capital divided by risk-based assets and Tier 1 + Tier 2 capital divided by risk-based assets). The calculation of risk-based assets, which includes converted risk-based off-balance sheet assets, is discussed next.

CALCULATING RISK-BASED ASSETS AND RISK-BASED OFF-BALANCE SHEET ASSETS

Under the new risk-based capital requirements, capital is required to be held on assets based on their credit risk. Assets are classified into four risk categories that have higher or lower weights according to their credit risk. Risk-based assets are equal to the sum of the total assets for each risk class times their respective risk weights. The four risk categories have respective weights of 0%, 20%, 50%, and 100%. Thus, depository institutions do not have to hold any capital for risk-free assets with 0% weights, only capital for 20% of assets with low risk, only capital for 50% of assets with moderate risk, and capital on 100% on more risky assets. The basic types of assets that fit into each of the four categories are listed below:

Category 1 (0% weight): Federal Reserve balances, U.S. government securities, and some U.S. agency securities

Category 2 (20% weight): Cash items in the process of collection, U.S. and the Organization for Economic Cooperation and Development (OECD) interbank deposits and guaranteed claims, some non-OECD bank and government deposits and securities, General Obligation Municipal Bonds, Fed Funds Sold, some mortgage-backed securities, claims collateralized by the U.S. Treasury, and some other government securities

Category 3 (50% weight): municipal revenue bonds, secured mortgage loans on 1–4 family residential properties, and other securitized assets

Category 4 (100% weight): Commercial and consumer loans, corporate bonds, commercial paper, and other assets not included in other categories

Risk-based off-balance sheet assets must also be calculated and added to get total risk-based assets for risk-based capital ratios. To do this, off-balance sheet items must first be converted to credit equivalent assets.[10] These credit equivalent assets are then placed in respective risk-based categories, like other assets. The risk-based categories for off-balance sheet items are generally as follows:

Category 1 (0% risk weight): for unused commitments with an original maturity of one year or less or conditionally cancelable commitments

Category 2 (20% risk weight): for commercial letters of credit, bankers acceptances conveyed and other short-term self-liquidating trade-related items

Category 3 (50% risk weight): for standby letters of credits, other performance warranties and unused commitments with original maturities exceeding one year, and revolving underwriting facilities

---

[10]For details on how individual off-balance sheet items are converted into equivalent on-balance sheet items, see Saunders (1997), Chapter 19. For loan commitments and letters of credit, regulators generally give a conversion factor for individual off-balance sheet contingent or guaranty contracts. The conversion factor for a direct credit substitute standby letter of credit is 100%, for a performance-related standby letter of credit, 50%, for the unused portion of loan commitments with original maturities of more than one year, 50%, for commercial letters of credit, 20%, for bankers acceptances conveyed, 20%, and for other loan commitments, 0%. Once credit equivalent amounts are calculated, off-balance sheet items are placed in risk categories and multiplied by risk weights to get risk-based asset amounts. For other off-balance sheet items, conversions are much more technical. Details can be found in Saunders (1997) 411–414.

Category 4 (100% risk weight): for direct credit substitutes including general guarantees, sale and repurchase agreements with recourse, and forward agreements to purchase assets.

Example: Finding Risk-Based Assets for Nationsbank

To illustrate calculating risk-based assets, Nationsbank in 1994 classified its on-balance sheet risk-based assets as follows:

NATIONSBANK, SEPTEMBER 1994

On Balance Sheet ($000)	Assets in this Category	Risk-weighted Assets
Category 1: 0% weight	$2,879,181	$ 0
Category 2: 20% weight	6,126,605	1,225,321
Category 3: 50% weight	806,398	403,199
Category 4: 100% weight	9,539,784	9,539,784
Total On-Balance Sheet Risk-Based Assets		$11,168,304

Multiplying the amounts in each category by their appropriate weights, the risk-based assets for each category are calculated and then summed, resulting in total on-balance sheet risk-based assets of about $11.168 billion.

Credit equivalent amounts of off-balance sheet items are then calculated and placed in similar risk-weighted categories:

NATIONSBANK EQUIVALENT (CONVERTED) OFF-BALANCE SHEET (OBS) ITEMS ($000s)

Risk Category	Equivalent OBS	Weight—Equivalent OBS
Category 1: 0%	$ 12,139	$ 0
Category 2: 20%	73,180	14,636
Category 3: 50%	27,252	13,626
Category 4: 100%	1,983,830	1,983,830
Total Off-Balance Sheet Risk-Based Assets		$2,012,092

Multiplying each of the risk-based classes of off-balance sheet items by the appropriate weights and summing them, the total off-balance sheet risk-based assets equals about $2.012 billion.

Taking the sum of both on- and off-balance sheet risk-based assets, the total is:

Total Risk-Based Assets Before Adjustments =
Balance-Sheet Risk-Based Assets + Off-Balance Sheet Risk-Based Assets

$11,168,304 + $2,012,092 = $13,180,397

In reality, Nationsbank also had some very technical adjustments to make that resulted in somewhat fewer risk-based assets and total assets as follows:

Total Risk-Based Assets After Adjustments = $12,465,170

Total Assets After Adjustments = $18,756,337

Risk-based assets are much less than total assets. The next section calculates the regulatory capital ratios for Nationsbank by using the three required ratios shown in [8.1], [8.2], and [8.3].

Table 8.2 ✦ Calculating a Risk-Based Capital Ratio for Mega Bank

Capital standards are based in part on the riskiness of an institution's assets and on the degree of its off-balance sheet involvement. Depositories with lower-risk assets and lower-risk off-balance sheet activities will have more favorable capital ratios than higher-risk institutions.

(1)	(2)	(3)	(2) × (3)
Risk Category	Amount (in thousands)	Risk Weight	Risk-Based
On-Balance Sheet Assets			
Cash and Treasury securities	$ 20,000	0.00	$ 0
Repos and fed funds	30,000	0.20	6,000
Mortgages	10,000	0.50	5,000
Commercial loans and fixed assets	40,000		40,000
Total on-balance sheet items	$100,000		$51,000
Contingent Liabilities (Off-Balance Sheet Items)			
Cancellable short-term loan commitments	$ 5,000	0.00	$ 0
Commercial letters of credit	20,000	0.20	4,000
Long-term loan commitments	10,000	0.50	5,000
Selected forward agreements	15,000	1.00	15,000
Total off-balance sheet items	$ 50,000		$24,000
Total risk-weighted value			$75,000
Core (Tier 1) capital	$5,000		
Risk-based total assets ($5,000/$75,000)	6.67%		

Example: Find Capital Ratios for Nationsbank

By using the risk-based assets and total assets for Nationsbank and its Tier 1 and Tier 2 and Total Tier 1 and Tier 2 capital calculated earlier, Nationsbank's capital ratios can be expressed as:

Tier 1 to Risk-Based Assets   (8.1)

$1.5896/$12.465 = 0.1275 or 12.75%

Tier 1 to Total Assets   (8.2)

$1.5896/$18.756 = 8.48%

(Tier 1 + Tier 2) to Risk-Based Assets   (8.3)
$1.7507/$12.465 = 14.04%

Thus, Nationsbank has ratios considerably above the minimum regulatory ratios. Table 8.2 shows an additional example for the calculation of risk-weighted assets and the Tier 1 capital ratio for MegaBank. MegaBank has $5,000 in Tier 1 capital. Its total risk-based assets are $75,000, so its Tier 1 to risk-based assets ratio is $5,000/$75,000, or 6.67%.

DEFINITIONS OF CAPITAL ADEQUACY

In addition to the risk-based standards, U.S. bank regulators have identified levels of capital characterizing well-capitalized and undercapitalized banks. Banks in any of the three undercapitalized categories (see Table 8.3) face severe penalties and regulatory intervention. Banks just meeting minimum standards are considered adequately capitalized. To be classified as well capitalized—which qualifies banks for less regulatory scrutiny, lower deposit insurance premiums, and other benefits—institutions must have substantially higher capital. As you can see, Nationsbank is well capitalized, with a total capital ratio of 10% or higher, Tier 1 capital ratio greater than 6%, and leverage ratio greater than 5%. A depository institution's **Capital, Asset, Quality, Earnings, Liquidity, and Interest Rate Sensitivity** (CAMELS) rating reflects the examiner's evaluation of other characteristics and also affects regulatory actions. Finally, the rate of growth in a bank's assets is a factor that regulators consider in determining a bank's capital adequacy.

Institutions in the three undercapitalized categories find themselves subject to intense scrutiny by regulators. Undercapitalized banks must restrict growth, prepare plans to restore capital, and receive approval from regulators before expanding operations, making acquisitions, or opening new branches. Significantly undercapitalized banks face more strict limitations, including prohibitions on increases in compensation to senior executives. Finally, Congress requires regulators to take prompt corrective action against critically undercapitalized banks. If managers cannot correct deficiencies, regulators are required to place banks in receivership (**Federal Deposit Insurance Corporation** [FDIC] control) within 90 days. These policies reflect the view that severely undercapitalized institutions have little incentive to control risk, and thus expose the deposit insurance system to substantial moral hazard.

Exceptions for Capital for Federally Chartered Thrifts

As of October, 1989, the Office of Thrift Supervision announced capital definitions that are largely identical to those for banks. A few exceptions should be noted. Besides the components of core capital accepted by bank regulators, thrift regulators include certain nonwithdrawable customer deposits that really are more like perpet-

---

Table 8.3 ✦ Definitions of Capital Adequacy

Regulators have identified levels of capital characterizing well-capitalized and undercapitalized banks. Banks in any of three undercapitalized categories face severe penalties and regulatory intervention.

Category	Total Capital Ratio[a]		Tier 1 Capital Ratio[b]		Leverage Ratio[c]
Well Capitalized	10% or higher	and	6% or higher	and	5% or higher
Adequately Capitalized	8% − less than 10%	and	4% − less than 6%	and	3% − less than 5%
Undercapitalized	6% − less than 8%	or	3% − less than 4%	or	Less than 3%
Significantly Undercapitalized	Less than 6%	or	Less than 3%	or	More than 2% but less than 3%
Critically Undercapitalized					2% or less

[a]Tier 1 capital + Tier 2 capital/risk-adjusted assets.

[b]Tier 1 capital/risk-adjusted assets.

[c]Tier 1 capital/average total assets. Institutions with poor CAMEL ratings must have higher leverage ratios.

Source: Richard Cantor and Ronald Johnson, "Bank Capital Ratios, Asset Growth, and the Stock Market," *Quarterly Review* (Federal Reserve Bank of New York) 17 (Autumn 1992): 11–12; Kenneth H. Bacon, "FDIC Proposed Curbs on Banks' Loans for Real Estate, Seek Capital Levels," *The Wall Street Journal,* June 24, 1992, A5; and Catherine Lemieux, "FDICIA Mandated Capital Zones and the Bank Industry," *Financial Industry Trends* (Federal Reserve Bank of Kansas City) (1993): 11–14.

ual preferred stock; that is, they have no maturity and the institution's obligation to pay can be suspended. Furthermore, thrifts' goodwill, acquired in supervisory mergers during the 1980s, could count as part of core capital, in limited declining amounts, until December 31, 1994. Like commercial banks, thrifts may also count selected intangible assets arising from the sale of mortgages. Although the exact regulations are too complicated to be summarized here, supplementary capital for thrifts also includes mutual capital certificates, and thrifts must deduct from total capital the value of certain investments—such as direct holdings of real estate—that are not permitted to national banks.[11]

View of Capital for Federal Credit Union Regulators

Since every credit union (CU) is organized as a type of mutual association with CU members as the effective owners, measuring capital is considerably simpler than for other depositories. CU capital consists entirely of undivided earnings and reserves from past operations. Allowance for loan losses is almost always viewed as part of capital in determining capital adequacy by regulators. Reserves are amounts set aside from earnings each year to cover future losses on investments or loans; undivided earnings are those retained in excess of reserves. Since CUs cannot issue stock or bonds, capital is also increased through reserves and undivided earnings. In 1992, the National Credit Union Administration (NCUA) implemented risk-based capital requirements for corporate CUs that are similar to risk-based capital requirements for banks.[12]

In contrast to corporate CUs, the NCUA approach to capital adequacy differs from the plans of both banking and thrift regulators because it is based on the size and age of the CU and does not identify risk weights for different categories of assets. In general, federal CUs are expected to focus on the ratio of reserves to total risk assets. Risk assets are defined by the NCUA to be total assets minus cash, Treasury securities, and loans not considered subject to default risk, such as federally guaranteed student loans and loans to members backed by their personal share accounts. Institutions four years old or older with more than $500,000 in assets or those less than four years old must have a ratio of 10%. Special restrictions are placed on very small CUs not meeting the 10% requirement. CUs are also subject to CAMEL ratings, which affect how much capital they need to hold. CAMEL ratings range from 1 (highest) to 5 (lowest). Table 8.4 summarizes the individual components of CAMEL ratings for CUs. In 1996, of 11,392 CUs, about 19% had a CAMEL rating of 1; 58%, a rating of 2; 21%, a rating of 3; 2.4%, a rating of 4; and 0.23%, a rating of 5.[13]

---

[11]Office of Thrift Supervision, "Regulatory Capital: Interim Final Rule," 12 CFR, Parts 561, 563, and 576, October 27, 1989; Robert M. Garsson, "Government Loses Case on Goodwill Writedowns." *American Banker*, August 9, 1990, 1, 18; and Mike McNamee, "Nobody Is Laughing About This Funny Money Now." *Business Week*, May 4, 1992, 168.

[12]See Walker (1997) and Crawford and Sihler (1994) Case 9: "Navy Federal Credit Union," 9–1.

[13]Ibid.

Table 8.4   ✦   CAMEL Rating Components for Credit Unions

<u>C</u>apital adequacy, which is a measure of the ability of the institution's reserves to support its own risk; it is a reassurance to the members that the organization will continue to provide financial services even when interest rates, asset values, deposits and earnings fluctuate.

<u>A</u>sset quality is an indication of the riskness of a credit union's assets. This rating considers asset quality, portfolio risk, and lending and investment policies and procedures.

<u>M</u>anagement assessment is based on business strategy/financial performance, internal controls, management conduct, and service to members. These four management areas help determine whether a credit union is able to diagnose and respond to financial stress.

<u>E</u>arnings represents the ability of a credit union to generate an appropriate return on its assets and thereby have funds to satisfy withdrawals, support expansion, sustain competitiveness, and replenish and/or increase capital.

Asset/<u>L</u>iability management is the identification and control of interest-rate risk, sensitivity, and exposure; reliance on short-term sources of funds; availability of liquid assets; and technical competence relative to asset/liability management. (In the CAMEL system for banks the "L" stands for liquidity; however, it encompasses similar financial considerations.)

Source: "Credit Union Insurance and Regulation," David Walker, Georgetown University Center for Business Government Relations, 1997, p. 69.

Unresolved Issues in Capital Requirements

Interest Rate Risk and Capital Standards   FDICIA mandated that by mid-1993 regulators incorporate interest rate risk into bank capital requirements. A number of proposals were made by the Federal Reserve Board, the FDIC, and the Comptroller of the Currency. These proposals focused on the potential change in value of assets and liabilities and the change in a bank's net worth with a change in interest rates. Any bank that would suffer a significant change in net worth would be placed in a risky category and be required to hold additional capital. The Office of Thrift Supervision also proposed similar models for adjusting capital requirements for additional interest rate risk. However, these explicit proposals were not implemented. An additional factor, the "S" in revised CAMELS ratings implemented in 1996, however, includes a market sensitivity factor (i.e., an interest rate risk component) for ratings, and institutions with poor CAMEL ratings must have a higher leverage (i.e., Tier 1 capital to total assets) ratio. Banks and thrifts must have an interest rate risk policy that defines the strategy that the bank's management pursues when managing the bank's balance sheet and its interest rate risk. This policy includes a scenario analysis of net income and present value of equity projections with a change of 2% rise or fall in interest rates.

Capital Standards and the Credit Crunch of the Early 1990s   One major criticism of risk-based capital standards is that they can change the optimum allocation of assets for banks to favor assets with lower credit risk, such as U.S. government securities, home mortgages, and mortgage-backed securities versus traditional commercial loans. Some critics blamed the new risk-based capital requirements for the credit crunch of the early 1990s, when average security holdings for banks rose and commercial loans fell. Financial economists disagree over whether the contraction in credit at this time was due to a recession and reluctance of banks to take on risky loans or to the emergence of risk-based capital requirements for large banks or to other factors. Whether capital-based risk requirements led to different asset allocations for banks to reduce capital requirements is still subject to debate.[14]

The Road Ahead: Unresolved Issues in Capital Regulation Other criticisms of current capital requirements remain. One important issue is that current rules continue to focus on book-value rather than market-value measures. Thus, capital ratios do not accurately indicate a bank's exposure to risk of failing because the bank can no longer meet its obligations in the marketplace. Another criticism is that current ratios emphasize credit risk but place little emphasis on other types of risk. Poor portfolio diversification, for example, might result in losses for a thrift that holds only securities issued by a single state and home mortgages issued within that state. Because these assets are ordinarily defined as low to moderate risk, the institution could be allowed to maintain relatively small amounts of capital, and regulators might not see a problem caused by a failing regional economy soon enough to intervene.

Other unresolved issues focus on risk weights, which are somewhat arbitrary for different types of assets and contingent liabilities, regardless of their actual credit (default risk). Such weights create incentives for banks to innovate with new assets and off-balance sheet items that look as if they are low to moderate risk but that may actually be higher risk (and thus potentially more profitable) than other items. As regulations become more technical to prevent regulatory avoidance, such a system becomes more cumbersome and more costly to enforce.

Questions are also raised concerning competitive fairness and economic efficiency. Some observers believe that basing banks' capital rules on their assets and in part on their contingent liabilities places them at an unfair disadvantage compared with securities firms, insurance companies, and finance companies, which are not subject to the same rules. Finally, researchers have yet to determine if capital requirements impose costly regulatory taxes on depository institutions, making it more difficult for them to compete with nondepository institutions that have much lower capital requirements. To the extent that a greater-than-optimal level of capital is directed to the banking system and away from more productive uses, economic efficiency is thwarted.

BEYOND REGULATORY REQUIREMENTS

Management of Capital and Growth

Depository institutions must be well capitalized to acquire other financial institutions. Regulators approve acquisitions more easily for well-capitalized institutions, and such institutions can afford to make acquisitions and maintain required regulatory equity-to-asset ratios without having to issue additional, expensive common stock. Large financial institutions with higher earnings and market capital have a tremendous advantage in terms of being able to make acquisitions more easily and quickly than institutions that are only moderately well capitalized. Table 8.5 lists top

---

[14]See John Wagster, "The Basle Accord of 1988 and the International Credit Crunch of 1989–1992." Working Paper, Wayne State University, October 1997.

Table 8.5   ✦   BATTLE FOR THE TOP IN FINANCIAL SERVICES

(December 31, 1996 or Latest Available)

	Market	Equity	Assets	Income	ROE
			(In billions)		
Commercial Banks					
Citicorp°	$48	$20	$281	$3.7	18.80%
Chase	39	21	336	2.5	11.94
NationsBank°	38	16	228	2.8	17.91
BankAmerica°	36	21	251	2.8	14.04
Wells Fargo	25	15	109	1.3	8.82
Banc One	22	10	107	1.6	16.82
First Union	20	9	140	1.4	16.32
J.P. Morgan	18	11	222	1.5	14.32
Insurance Companies					
AIG	$51	$21	$145	$2.8	—
Travelers°	29	22	142	2.3	—
Allstate	26	13	72	2.0	—
Aetna	12	7	84	1.0	—
Cigna	11	8	97	1.0	—
Investment Banks					
Morgan Stanley/DW	$19	$11	$206	$1.8	18.63%
Merrill Lynch	13	7	208	1.5	23.27
Salomon Inc.°	5	5	169	.8	16.69
Bear Stearns	3	3	96	.7	19.57
Lehman Brothers	3	3	127	.4	9.89
Finance Companies					
GE Capital	—	$14	$204	$2.7	21.27%
American Express	$27	8	107	1.7	22.62
Ford Motor Credit	—	8	100	1.3	17.31
GMAC	—	8	96	1.2	14.82
Associates	4	5	48	.8	17.77
Financial Specialties					
MBNA	$9	$2	$16	$.4	34.62%
Charles Schwab	6	1	12	.2	31.06
Green Tree Financial	5	1	3	.3	28.71

Source: SNL Securities L.P., Charlottesville, VA., and Standard & Poor's Stock Guide, New York, N.Y.
°Indicates firms that merged in 1998.

financial service firms in terms of both market and book value of equity as of December 31, 1996. Note that with mergers these rankings have changed somewhat today. Note that a number of large banks had market values of equity over $20 billion, which places them in an excellent position to make acquisitions. Among nonbanks, only American Express and three insurance companies—American International Group, Travelers, and Allstate—have market values of equity over $20 billion. In fact, if the next three largest investment houses, the biggest independent finance company other than American Express, and the country's largest discount broker combined their market capital, they would still have less capital than the sixth most highly capitalized commercial bank—Banc One.[15] As depository institutions seek acquisitions to increase their noninterest revenues, the well-capitalized firms have a decided advantage. Large well-capitalized depository institutions also have easier and cheaper access to external equity. Smaller depository institutions have fewer choices of capital, relying primarily on retained earnings for capital growth.

Determining the Optimal Capital Structure

From a real-world standpoint, how much capital is adequate for a depository institution depends on a combination of (1) regulatory requirements, (2) an institution's risk profile, and (3) other practical considerations. In a discussion of capital management for banks, Donald Davis and Kevin Lee (1997) of Bank of America[16] point out that the process of developing an optimal capital structure for banks encompasses the economic risk of banks and regulatory requirements as well as practical considerations. These considerations are discussed in the following sections.

Capital Allocations Based on Economic Risk

Economic risk is the risk of a bank having significant losses. The amount of capital a bank needs to hold depends on its credit risk, market risk, business risk, and targeted equivalent bond rating. Banks with a higher risk profile than similar-size (peer) banks need to hold higher capital ratios. Very large money center banks often employ a **RAROC (risk-adjusted return on capital)** approach. Under RAROC, each asset is given a capital charge based on the amount of capital that needs to be held on the asset according to its risk, with a higher equity-to-asset percentage allocated to more risky assets. Hence, more risky assets require a higher return to cover the cost of the extra capital that has to be held for them. An example of RAROC pricing for a bank's commercial loans is shown below.[17]

EXAMPLE: RAROC PRICING OF COMMERCIAL LOANS FOR THE HARD ROCK BANK

Source	Component	Example
Funds Transfer Cost of Funds	5.45%	Funds Transfer Pricing System
Required Loan Loss Provision	1.25%	Credit Risk Model
Plus:		
Direct Expense	0.70	Customer/Product Cost
Indirect Expense	0.45	Accounting System
Overhead	0.40	
Total Charges before Capital Charge	8.25%	
Plus:		
Capital Charge (RAROC)	3.00%°	
°Allocated equity/asset = 12%		
Total Required Loan Rate	11.25%	

°RAROC: allocated equity/assets = 12%; opportunity cost of equity = 15%; after-tax capital charge = 15% × .12 = 1.80%; marginal tax rate = 40%; pretax capital charge = 1.80%/0.6 = 3.0%

---

[15]See Danielson (1997).
[16]See Davis and Lee (1997).
[17]This example comes from Kimball (1998). For a more detailed discussion of a practical application for RAROC, see Zaik, Walter, Kelling, and James (1996).

As shown above, to price its commercial loans, the Hard Rock Bank has allocated a transfer cost of funds that includes a profit markup, a loan loss provision, and other administrative expenses that must be covered to the loan, plus a RAROC charge based on capital that must be held on commercial loans. With a 100% equity capital requirement for commercial loans under risk-based capital requirements and an additional allocation for the estimated market risk of commercial loans, a target equity-to-capital ratio is set for the loans of 12%. Based on an expected after-tax cost of equity capital of 15%, the after-tax capital charge for the loans is equal to 15% × .12 or 1.8%. Since the bank's marginal tax rate is 40%, this becomes 1.80%/(1–0.4), or 3% on a before-tax basis. Adding the 3% capital charge to the other costs that must be covered, including a profit markup, the required loan rate is 11.25%. Whether a bank could charge this rate or not would depend on competitive conditions and the rates that other banks offer.[18]

Because of higher capital requirements, banks must earn a higher return on traditional commercial lending activities than for government securities or home mortgage loans, which would have a lower risk-based capital allocation. This makes traditional lending less attractive than other types of activities, such as brokerage and investment banking, which have much higher spreads, averaging about 20%. Hence, it is not surprising that banks have been active in entering nontraditional activities.[19]

Other Capital Allocation Techniques

While very large money center banks use detailed historic market data to determine equity-to-asset allocations under RAROC, different capital allocation methods are used by other banks. In a recent *Federal Reserve Bank of Boston New England Economic Review* article, Ralph Kimball (1998) provides examples of similar methods for allocating equity to assets according to the risk of a bank's different business lines. For instance, a bank might allocate equity that needs to be held for a particular line based on the average equity-to-asset ratio held by peer banks in that business. Such a peer group approach for the Consolidated Amalgamated Bank is shown below.[20]

Line of Business	Assets	Equity	Equity to Assets
Credit Cards	$20,261	$2,018	9.96%
Mortgage Banking	11,314	1,949	17.23%
Subprime Lending	5,072	1,666	32.77%
Total	$36,647	$5,633	15.37%

In the table above capital is allocated according to the average equity-to-asset ratio maintained by peer groups in each of the respective businesses. The overall equity-to-asset ratio for the bank is the total of the equity allocated to each line of business divided by total assets, which in this example is 15.37%. This approach can be problematic, however, since some business lines may have few peers for comparison. Also, peer capital ratios, although they reflect common practice, may not actually reflect the insolvency risk of a particular line of business.

---

[18]This material and example comes from Kimball (1998).
[19]See Crawford and Sihler (1994), Case 16.1 and Note to Case 16.1, National Bank of Los Angeles.
[20]This material and example comes from Kimball (1998).

An alternative allocation method Kimball presents is based on the standard deviation of the ROA for a particular line of business and a bank's probability of insolvency ratio (Z), defined as:

$$Z = (ROA° + K) / Std (ROA) \qquad (8.4)$$

where ROA° is the pretax expected ROA, K is the ratio of equity capital to assets, and Std (ROA) is the standard deviation of ROA. The Z-ratio is a function of the bank's normal profit margin, the variation in its profit margin, and the capital available to absorb that variation. The Z-ratio gives the number of standard deviations by which ROA would have to fall before the bank's book value of equity capital would be exhausted, with a lower Z-ratio showing greater insolvency risk. Under this alternative allocation approach, K° is solved for as the required capital-to-asset ratio to achieve a target Z°-ratio that the bank desires for each of the bank operations, as follows:

$$K° = [Z \times Std (ROA)] - ROA° \qquad (8.5)$$

The table below shows a simplified example for the Consolidated Amalgamated Bank that assumes an equal probability of solvency for each area of operations of 13.80, the initial Z-ratio of the credit card business:

Line of Business	ROA %	Std (ROA)	Z°-Ratio	Equity/Assets (%)	Equity (mils.)
Credit Cards	4.94	1.08	13.80	9.96	$2,018
Mortgage Banking	4.96	2.78	13.80	33.40	3,779
Subprime Lending	14.67	7.96	13.80	95.18	4,827
Total Bank	5.99	1.29	13.80	28.99	$10,624

Required equity capital for bank to achieve Z° = 13.80
K = (13.80) (1.29) − 5.99 = 11.81%
Equity capital = (0.1181) ($36,647 assets) = $4,328 million

This approach results in much higher capital allocated to each line of business than would be allocated by using the peer allocation method, and a much higher equity ($10,624 million) and equity-to-asset ratio for the total bank of 28.99% based on these allocations. However, the correlation in ROAs for the different businesses are ignored. As noted at the bottom of the table, the Std (ROA) for the total bank's operations based on the bank's overall standard deviation is much lower than the standard deviation of individual operations, resulting in a much lower required equity-to-asset ratio of 11.81% and hence lower equity capital needs to be held of $4,328 million.

The overall risk of the bank is lower than the risk of each of its operations because of the negative correlations between them. To address this fact, each equity-to-asset allocation could be reduced proportionately for each type of capital, so that the sum of the various equities required for each line of business equals $4,328 million, the required equity capital for the entire bank. Since the sum of total capital under this allocation plan totals $10,624 million based on individual standard deviations of returns but is only $4,328 million based on the standard deviation of returns for the entire bank, the initial allocation of equity for each business line needs to be reduced by multiplying the initial equity allocated by 4,328/10,624 or 0.4074, as follows:

Line of Business	Equity Allocated	Diversification	New Equity	Equity per (mils.)	Effect Allocated (mils.) Asset (%)
Credit Card	$2,018		0.4074	$ 822	4.06
Mortgage Banking	3,779		0.4074	1,539	13.61
Subprime Lending	4,827		0.4074	1,967	38.78
Total Bank		$ 10,624	0.4074	$4,328	11.81

With these reductions in equity for each line of business, the equity required for the bank goes down to $4,328 million. The equity allocated for each type of asset is also significantly lower for use with a RAROC-type pricing. Since banks must price loans competitively, this type of allocation is very important. If the allocation of equity to assets is too high and results in too high a price, the loan may not be priced competitively. Similarly, in strategic decision making, when allocating scarce resources or when deciding to enter or exit a business line, managers compare the expected ROE for the business to its cost of equity considering the amount of equity capital that needs to be allocated to that business line. For instance, if the banks cost of equity capital is estimated as the before tax ROE investors expect [ROE/(1-t)] and the expected ROE is 15%, with a marginal tax rate of 28%, the before-tax cost of equity 20.83%. Since only a 4.06% equity-to-asset ration is required for the credit card business, its equity cost of capital is 20.83% × .0406 = .85%. In contrast, the cost of equity capital for sub-prime lending would be 20.83% × .3878 = 8.08%. If the ROA for sub-prime lending is only 3%, its return would not be sufficient to cover this cost.[21]

These allocation methods are used for the purpose of illustration. Other types of allocations of capital are used that range from highly technical methods based on the distribution of a business lines' historic returns to simple allocation methods based on subjective consensus estimates of a business unit's risk. As these examples illustrate, such allocation methods may provide dramatically different allocations of equity for different lines of business.

A Practical Approach to Capital Structure

Davis and Lee (1997) point out that in practice depository institution managers consider practical factors in setting target capital ratios as well as including the capital ratios of peers, the risk appetite of the bank—balancing specific assets, markets, and ownership of a depository institution—and the benefits and costs of achieving a specific debt rating if a bank is large enough to qualify. They present the following steps for determining a firm's capital structure.[22]

1.   **Start with the Economic Risk Approach**
     Bank managers should allocate appropriate levels of loan loss reserves based on different lending activities and capital according to the volatility and risk of the

---

[21]This analysis assumes that all capital financing is equity and is based on an economic assessment by the firm for the amount of capital that should be held based on the risk of a business line. This analysis excludes risk-based capital requirements, which also affect a bank's equity-to-asset allocations.

[22]The material that follows comes from David and Lee (1997).

bank's individual operations, as discussed above. In deciding how much equity capital should be allocated, bank managers need to consider the volatility and risk of the bank's operations, along with their risk tolerance. How much protection do managers and owners want against the possibility of a significant business disruption (e.g., a 95% confidence level, a 99.7% confidence level?). Such a disruption could consist of a disruption by regulators or a higher cost of capital resulting from a lower stock price or lowering of a bank's credit rating.

2. **Maintain a Comfortable Margin above Regulatory "Well-Capitalized" Levels**

    Bank managers need to determine a comfortable margin over regulatory well-capitalized ratios. If they are planning growth or acquisitions, this margin should be higher both to assure sufficient capital for growth and for regulatory approval. The volatility revealed by a RAROC model can help to define the appropriate comfort margin, as can regulatory advice, particularly if a bank seeks regulatory approval to undertake "certain activities."

3. **Reality Check with a Peer Group Comparison**

    After economic and regulatory analysis for appropriate capital ratios, a bank's target capital ratio should be compared with ratios of comparable banks by using a peer group of banks with a similar asset mix, loan concentration, and regional economy. Analysts could be suspect of a bank that had capital ratios significantly below its peers in terms of its ability to "weather a significant downturn."

4. **Consider Future Prospects and Needs**

    In considering the bank's future prospects and needs, the bank should consider whether its target capital ratio will accommodate its specific growth plans. In particular, a bank needs to look at its **internal capital generation capacity**. A shorthand measure for this is:

    Internal growth rate equity = ROE (1 - D)   (8.6)

This internal growth rate is a function of a bank's ROE and its earnings retention ratio (1 - D), where D is a bank's dividend payout ratio (dividends/net income). The internal growth rate depends on a bank's ability to control its net interest margin (NIM) and burden to produce net income, the bank's equity-to-asset ratio, and its retention of earnings (1 - D). If the equity growth rate is below the growth rate of assets, the bank may be forced to raise expensive external equity capital to maintain its required leverage (equity-to-asset) ratio. If the bank does not have sufficient equity in reserve to support future strategic purchases, it could lose them. Finally, the bank needs to establish a mix of "capital," which can include debt, preferred stock, and equity. A bank needs to consider the optimal mix of capital within its regulatory definition. Available types of capital depend on the size of the institution. The relative costs of different types of capital need to be considered.

5. **Consider Rating Agency Requirements**

    For a bank that is rated or plans to become rated, the effect of any change in its capital ratio on the rating agencies needs to be considered, particularly if a bank is at the lower end of a rating range or plans to issue public debt. Rating agencies tend to focus on long-term performance versus particular ratios, but the effect of a change in capital structure on the risk of the bank and rating agencies' opinions still need to be considered.

6. **Finally, Establish a Mix of "Capital"**

    Management also needs to consider the optimal mix of capital it wants to have while remaining within the definition of a well-capitalized bank. Richard Crawford and William Sihler (1994) identify the maximum capital structure weights based on the regulatory restrictions discussed earlier as follows:[23]

CAPITAL STRUCTURE WEIGHTS

Class of Capital	Percent of Tier 2	Percent of Tier 1 & Tier 2 Capital
Loan loss reserve	31.25%	15.625%
Subordinated debt	50.00%	25.000%
Balance: other types capital	18.75%	9.375%
Tier 2 Capital	100.00%	50.000%
Class of Capital	**Percent of Tier 1**	**Percent of Tier 1 & Tier 2 Capital**
Perpetual Preferred Stock	25.00%	12.500%
Common Equity	75.00%	37.500%
Tier 1 Capital	100.00%	50.000%

Based on regulatory limits, 75% of Tier 1 capital or 37.5% of total capital must be common equity. A maximum of 50% of Tier 2 capital can be subordinated debt or 25% of total capital. Based on a maximum Tier 2 capital-to-asset ratio of 4% for a total capital ratio of 8% and a maximum loan loss reserve of 1.25% of total assets, the maximum loan loss reserve would be approximately 1.25%/4%, or 31.25% of total Tier 2 capital. Thus, there are limits to holdings of cheaper debt capital, which has a tax subsidy. Equity capital and additional loan loss reserves, in contrast, have a higher opportunity cost for stockholders and a higher cost of capital. A bank's weighted after-tax cost of capital can be calculated by taking the sum of the fraction of each type of capital relative to total capital times its respective cost. The table below provides an example. The bank has calculated the following costs of capital for each type of capital. The bank is holding its maximum allowable subordinated debt and preferred stock as cheaper forms of capital. The weighted average cost of capital is 10.656%:[24]

WEIGHTED AVERAGE COST OF CAPITAL

Capital Component	Weight	Cost of Capital Component	Weighted Cost
Loan Loss Reserve	15.625%	14%	2.1875%
Subordinated Debt	25.000%	5%	1.25%
Preferred Stock	21.875%	9%	1.9688%
Common Equity	37.500%	14%	5.250%
Sum Weighted Average Cost of Capital 10.656%			

HOW MUCH CAPITAL SHOULD BE RETURNED TO SHAREHOLDERS?

Dealing with Excess Capital in the 1990s

In the early 1990s, banks and thrifts faced a diminishing capital base as they sought additional capital to meet higher regulatory requirements during a time of low earnings. Small depository institutions that could not raise external capital to com-

---

[23]The capital structure weights that follow come from Crawford and Sihler (1994), Case 9, Instructor's Manual.

[24]See Crawford and Sihler (1994) as cited above.

ply with the "capital is king" rule were forced to boost earnings and/or reduce dividend payout ratios. Banks in the past have typically been associated with a shareholder clientele that preferred high dividend payout ratios, making such a reduction in dividend payout ratios difficult. With lower interest rates, higher NIMs, and higher ROAs and ROEs for banks, however, capital as a percentage of assets rose rapidly after 1992. The rise in capital ratios reflects the rise in ROAs and ROEs over the 1990s, as shown below. Capital ratios rose from 6.75% in 1991 to 8% in 1993 and 8.41% in 1997.[25]

COMMERCIAL BANK INCOME AND CAPITAL GROWTH, 1989 TO 1997

	Assets (bils.)	ROA	Capital Ratio	ROE
1997	$5,229	1.30%	8.41%	15.46%
1995	4,810	1.24%	8.29%	14.95%
1994	4,540	1.19%	8.08%	14.72%
1993	4,219	1.17%	8.00%	14.63%
1992	3,911	1.14%	7.83%	14.56%
1991	3,414	0.53%	6.75%	8.01%
1990	3,369	0.50%	6.47%	7.89%
1989	3,288	0.51%	6.23%	7.82%

Source: Sheshunoff Bank Quarterly 1997, 1992, and FDIC Reports of Conditional Income. Although not quite as high, a similar rise in ROAs occurred for thrifts in the 1990s with a rise in ROA from 0.30% in 1993 to 0.84% in 1997, a rise in ROE from 4.72% in 1993 to 10.38% in 1997, and a rise in capital- to-assets ratio from 6.36% in 1993 to 8.09% in 1997.

With the surge in earnings and modest growth for banks in the mid to later 1990s, the capital ratios of banks increased dramatically. But as bank consultant Arnold Danielson points out, although additional capital is a good thing from the perspective of safety, if the additional capital cannot be put to good use, with excess equity, ROEs will fall. Also, excess capital can tempt banks, such as the overcapitalized savings banks in the Northeast in the 1980s, to invest in overbuilding or other unprofitable projects in attempts to boost earnings on a larger equity base to increase otherwise lower ROEs.

Responses to excess capital include: (1) increased dividends and stock repurchases to reduce capital; (2) over-leveraging the balance sheet (taking on more loans or other higher revenue-producing assets) or increasing off-balance sheet activities to boost asset utilization and ROA to compensate for a higher equity base; and (3) acquiring other banks or nonbanks with cash to reduce capital-to-asset ratios (which leaves a bank with substantial goodwill amortization) or, for a smaller bank, selling out to a larger bank. Arnold Danielson notes that excess capital puts pressure on publicly traded depository institutions to sell as they "struggle with declining returns on average equity." It also leads to many large banks taking on more acquisitions, many of which may be "wrong bets," and hence to increased consolidation in the industry.[26]

---

[25]See Danielson (1994) and *Sheshunoff Bank & S&L Quarterly.* Austin, Texas: Sheshunoff Information Services, 1992, 1997.

[26]See Danielson (1994).

Stock Buybacks As a Means of Reducing "Excess" Total Capital in the 1990s

With excess capital in the 1990s, almost all of the 25 largest U.S. banks have stock buyback (repurchase) programs for the purposes of (1) adjusting capital ratios to reach a defined target; (2) returning capital to stockholders when marginal investment opportunities fall below the bank's relevant cost of capital (i.e., when capital cannot be effectively employed, so taking on such projects would reduce the value of the firm); (3) attempting stock price corrections (e.g., when management believes that its stock price is undervalued, such as when a bank can purchase its shares at $20 a share in one year and issue shares a few years later for $40); (4) driving out unhappy or weak shareholders, which provides a type of preliminary takeover defense; and (5) reducing the equity base to increase ROE and earnings per share. Stock repurchases have an advantage over dividends in terms of allowing shareholders the choice of selling or not selling their shares and only being taxed on cash they receive if they sell their shares. With dividends, shareholders must take the cash and be taxed, even when they would prefer that the money be kept with the firm. Although a sudden leverage change with a repurchase can increase financial risk and the risk premium associated with a firm's stock price, for a very well-capitalized bank, such an increase in leverage can enhance the bank's ROE and increase its stock price.[27]

Despite the advantage of stock buybacks, some stockholders prefer dividends, as David Coulter, Chairman and CEO of Bank of America, states:

> "The final necessary condition for creating value is to focus on effective capital management. We tried to set the tone early on with our dividend increase and large stock buy-back program. Our business is now generating a large amount of cash flow. We would love to be able to redeploy all that capital in revenue-producing activities. But if we determine that those opportunities won't earn the cost of capital, then we will pay it back to the shareholder. And I'm a strong believer that the best way to give money back to the shareholder is through buybacks rather than dividends. But the reality is that we have a large number of investors that continue to want dividends. So, you can theorize all you want about dividends, but when you go to the annual meeting, you will hear lots of people telling you to increase your dividend. With respect to our buyback program, we're a believer that you buy back stock at any price as long as you don't have a near-term effective use for your capital. There is no price at which you stop buying back stock if you're generating lots of excess capital."[28]

MANAGEMENT OF CAPITAL: DIVIDEND POLICY

Dividend Policies in the 1990s

As noted in the previous section, bank stockholders in the past have typically self-selected banks as high dividend yield, low capital gains stocks. Although capital gains increased for many bank stocks with mergers and acquisitions, the stockholder clientele of banks generally includes stockholders that prefer dividends. Many smaller

---

[27]See Danielson (1994), Coulter (1997), Cline (1996), and Davis and Lee (1997).
[28]See Coulter (1997), 69.

Figure 8.3 ♦ **EARNINGS AND COMMON STOCK DIVIDENDS FOR COMMERCIAL BANKS 1991 TO 1996**

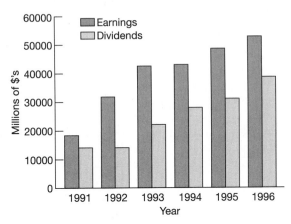

Source: FDIC Statistics on Banking, 1996. Put in figure form by the authors.

banks are also closely owned, and owners depend on dividends for income. Dividend payout ratios for banks averaged about 30% to 40% of net income in the 1980s. In 1987, when banks suffered low earnings, the average dividend payout ratio was more than 200% of earnings. Banks have generally kept stable dividends, even when earnings fall.

Figure 8.3 graphs dollar earnings and dividends from 1991 to 1996. With excess capital available in the 1990s, dividend payouts increased, averaging about 60%. In 1996, the average dividend payout ratio for all FDIC-insured banks was 74%, and 73% for Savings Institution Insurance Fund-insured thrifts. Banks greater than $1 billion had an average payout of about 79.8% compared with 53% for smaller banks. Similarly, in 1997, average capital ratios at large bank holdings companies (BHCs) declined as a result of very large dividend payouts and stock repurchases. For instance, in 1997, the 25 largest BHCs dividend payments rose 5% and the dollar value of repurchase agreements rose almost 70%, with total payouts exceeding net income by 10%. Large depositories paid out higher dividends to reduce excess capital. James H. Hance, Jr., chief financial officer of Nationsbank in 1996, points out that a more efficient use or "velocity of capital" resulted from large banks having reduced growth in traditional on-balance sheet lending and having greater growth in noninterest off-balance sheet revenue. This excess capital could then be returned in the form of higher dividends or a stock repurchase program.[29]

Dividend Theories and Considerations for Bank Policies

Under corporate dividend theory, financial markets favor stable dividend policies. Dividends often signal changes in a firm's earnings prospects. Consequently, it is often argued that unless a firm can maintain a higher dividend for the long-term,

---

[29]See Cline (1996) and Hirtle (1998).

dividends should not be raised, because investors will penalize the firm later if the dividend must be lowered. As a compromise, banks can engage in a share repurchase program or give special one-time dividends, which they carefully inform shareholders are one-time events, to avoid shareholder disappointment later. Clientele effects, such as discussed earlier, whereby many banks have stockholders that consider banks to be income-producing rather than growth stocks, also affect a bank's dividend policy.

From the standpoint of regulators, dividend payout is constrained by capital adequacy requirements and the ability of the bank to maintain sufficient capital given its risk. In 1985, for instance, federal banking regulators publicly warned against the payment of high cash dividends in certain economic environments and threatened enforcement actions against institutions defying their advice. In 1990, regulators repeated warnings in light of deteriorating loan quality and the onset of higher capital requirements. High dividend payouts by failing thrifts in the 1980s were seen by regulators as a form of looting at the expense of taxpayers. Under FDICIA, regulators have the right to curtail dividend payouts for undercapitalized depositories. Hence, management's ability to use dividends as a signal of future prospects for depository institutions is constrained by regulatory concerns that regulators believe are socially optimal but may not be optimal to stockholders of individual depository institutions.[30]

SUMMARY

This chapter examines capital regulations and management for depository institutions, the purposes of capital, market versus book value capital, and preferences of different agents within a firm for more or less capital. Capital management became increasingly important for banks and thrifts in the early 1990s as they were required to meet more stringent regulatory capital requirements. The optimal capital structure for a depository institution is affected by deposit insurance, which provides a larger subsidy for firms with high financial leverage. New risk-based capital regulations are presented, along with their benefits and limitations. The chapter presents a practical structure for determining a depository institution's optimal capital structure, which includes keeping a comfortable cushion of capital above well-capitalized regulatory standards, capital allocations based on a RAROC approach, and other practical considerations including capital ratios of peer banks, achieving a given bond rating, future prospects and needs for capital, and the best mix of different types of capital.

Capital-to-asset ratios rose in the 1990s as depository institutions became more profitable, and larger banks faced the unusual problem of having excess capital. Consequently, larger institutions devised new policies for stock repurchases and higher dividend payouts to return excess capital to stockholders. Bank dividend policies are affected by stockholders, who often prefer high dividends, and by regulatory policies that discourage higher dividend payouts, particularly for undercapitalized institutions. Capital management has become an important part of depository institution management to maximize shareholder value. In the 1990s, with more efficient use of capital through the generation of revenues from off-balance sheet activities, the "velocity" or efficient use of capital by very large depository institutions has increased. Hence, managers of very large banks, such as Nationsbank/BankAmerica, suggest that excess capital that cannot be put into endeavors that offer higher returns than a bank's marginal cost of capital should be returned to stockholders.

Questions

1. Why is the market value of equity so different from the book value of equity for depository institutions? What hap-

---

[30]For a summary of corporate dividend theory, see Brigham and Gapenski (1997).

pens to the market value of equity for a depository institution with long-term fixed-rate assets financed by short-term liabilities when interest rates rise? When interest rate fall? Explain why.

2. What is the purpose of capital? Why is capital particularly important for depository institutions?

3. What is the preference of stockholders for a depository institution's capital structure? What incentives do stockholders of depository institutions have for holding more capital? How does deposit insurance create a moral hazard problem in terms of stockholders' preferences for higher financial leverage?

4. What preferences do uninsured debtholders, managers, and regulators have for a depository institution's optimal capital structure? Briefly discuss Buser, Chen, and Kane's (1981) theory of the optimal debt ratio that will occur under deposit insurance.

5. Briefly discuss how capital requirements for banks have changed over time. Why were more stringent capital regulations imposed under the Basle Accord of 1987 and FDICIA of 1991? What advantages and limitations do the new risk-based capital requirements have?

6. In your own words, describe how risk-based assets and off-balance sheet assets are calculated. What are the current minimum leverage ratio and Tier 1 and Tier 2 risk-based capital ratios? What are the different classes of capitalization in which depository institutions are placed? What enforcement measures can be taken if institutions are undercapitalized?

7. Why do regulators allow supplementary Tier 2 capital to be included in the definition of total capital for depository institutions? Under what conditions does a depository institution's long-term debt qualify as capital? What are the advantages and disadvantages of using long-term debt to fulfill the functions of capital?

8. How are CAMEL(S) ratings combined with current risk-based capital requirements to determine when regulatory action is needed? How are regulatory capital ratios for CUs determined?

9. What are some current weaknesses of risk-based capital requirements?

10. Why are better capitalized financial institutions more likely to be winners in the acquisition game of the 1990s and the upcoming decade?

11. What is RAROC? How does RAROC help in allocating capital for a bank's economic risks? How is it used to price loans? Discuss the peer group method versus the volatility method for allocating capital-to-asset ratios for different lines of a bank's business. What are the respective advantages and disadvantages of each method?

12. Briefly discuss Davis and Lee's (1997) practical approach to capital structure. What are the five different steps? What practical considerations need to be made?

13. For small banks in particular, why is a bank's internal generation capacity so important? What options does a bank have to increase this capacity?

14. How have risk-based capital requirements increased the need for managers to understand their cost of capital? How is this cost of capital calculated? Why do types of assets in higher risk categories have to earn higher spreads to support the cost of capital? What types of nontraditional activities become more attractive in terms of having larger spreads that support the cost of capital?

15. How did bank capital ratios change from the 1980s to the 1990s? Explain why this change occurred.

16. Why did large banks wish to reduce their excess capital in the 1990s? Discuss ways to do this. How did dividend payout policies change in the 1990s?

17. Discuss factors that need to be considered by banks in setting their dividend policies.

Problems

1. The Sammy Sosa Savings Bank has the following balance sheet (book values):

Assets		Liabilities & Equity	
Cash	$ 300,000	Deposits	$40,500,000
T-bills	7,000,000	Equity	1,800,000
Consumer Loans	35,000,000	Total	$42,300,000
Total	$42,300,000		

All consumer loans have a 12% annual rate with amortized monthly payments (1% monthly rate) and are for 36 months.

a. If the market rate for similar consumer loans rises to 15%, what is the new market value of the consumer loans? If the market value for liabilities remains the same, what is the new market value of equity?

b. What is the book value of equity to assets? What is the new market value of equity to assets? Explain why they differ.

c. Do a and b again, but assume that similar consumer loans fall to an 8% rate.

2. The Mark McGwire Metropolitan Bank has Tier 1 capital of $60 million and Tier 2 capital of $15 million. The bank's assets and off-balance sheet items are listed below:

Assets (000)	Risk-Based Assets	Risk-Weights
Cash	$ 10,000	
Short-term Treasury securities	28,000	
Long-term Treasury securities	243,500	
Municipal bonds (GOs)	150,000	
Other long-term securities	50,000	
Residential mortgages	400,000	
Consumer loans	200,000	
Commercial loans	520,000	
Off-balance sheet items:		
Long-term loan commitments	$200,000	0.50
Interest-rate swap agreements	30,000	0.50
Total Risk-Based Assets $		

   a. Fill in the risk-weights in the table above for assets and calculate the bank's risk-based assets and off-balance sheet items.
   b. Calculate Tier 1 capital to assets, Tier 1 capital to risk-based assets, and Tier 1 + Tier 2 capital to risk-based assets.
   c. In which category of capital adequacy does the M.M.M. bank fall? What advice would you give to management?

3. The Titantic Savings and Loan has the following balance sheet (in millions):

Assets		Liabilities and Equity	
Cash & Reserves	$ 20	Deposits	$850
Treasury Securities	75	Subordinated debt	15
Mortgages	740	Common Stock	10
Fixed Assets	70	Retained Earnings	30
Total	$905		$905

   Off-balance Sheet Items: (assume 50% risk-based weights)

Long-term loan commitments	$500 million
Interest-rate swap agreement	$100 million

   Because of severe economic difficulties in Titantic's region, $50 million of the mortgages are in default.

   a. Calculate Titantic's risk-based assets, Tier 1 capital, Tier 2 capital, risk-adjusted capital, and leverage ratios. Is Titantic adequately capitalized?
   b. Suppose Titantic reduced its long-term loan commitments to $100 million. What would its new capital ratios be?

4. The Oakleigh-Roscoe Bank, with total assets of $850 million and an assets/equity multiplier (EM) of 11.5, expects to earn a ROE of 15%. Dividends will be 40% of net income, which is projected at $9 million. Risk-based off-balance sheet items total $200 million. The bank has $150 million in cash and Treasury securities. All other assets are commercial loans and fixed assets.
   a. What is the bank's equity-to—risk-based asset ratio and leverage ratio? Is the bank adequately capitalized?
   b. What internal growth rate in equity is expected?
   c. If deposits increase by 7%, what asset growth rate is expected? If these expectations materialize, explain why, without doing any calculations, the EM will be higher or lower than 11.5 next year. Calculate the EM and see if you are correct.
   d. If the bank paid out a 0% dividend, what would the new EM be? What would the EM be with a 100% dividend?
   f. If the bank pays a dividend payout of 40% and any new assets are invested in commercial loans with no new off-balance sheet items, what will be the new equity-to-risk-based asset ratio? Explain why the results change compared with part a.

5. The management of the Leonardo DiCaprio Savings and Loan forecasts a 5% growth in assets for the coming year and a 5.5% growth in liabilities.
   a. The equity-to-total assets ratio is now 8%. What rate of growth in equity is expected next year? At this rate, will the EM rise, fall, or remain the same? Do these plans make sense?

b. Suppose instead that asset growth is planned at 7.5%. If liabilities grow 2%, how much must equity grow to achieve this planned asset growth? If liabilities grow 10%, how much must equity grow to achieve the planned asset growth? Do you see any parallels between the results of this analysis and the financial condition of some thrifts in the late 1980s? Explain.

6. The management of the Caroline-Lizzie Bank and Trust is pleased about the bank's capital adequacy. Therefore, management has decided to increase the rate of growth in assets for the coming year by pursuing more aggressive liability management. A 15% growth rate in liabilities is projected, and a stable dividend payout ratio are projected.

Last year, the firm earned net income of $18 million and paid dividends of $12 million. It expects the same ROE and payout to prevail this year. Management will invest all new funds in consumer loans during the coming year. Total assets are $1.5 billion ($350 million in cash and Treasury securities, with the rest in consumer loans); total liabilities are $1.4 billion; equity is $100 million.

a. What is the current capital-to-risk-adjusted assets ratio?
b. Calculate the expected growth in percentages and dollars in equity and assets.
c. What capital-to-risk-based assets ratio is expected next year?
d. If this ratio is unacceptably low to management, suggest ways to improve it.

7. The Terrell-Albee Bank has a marginal tax rate of 35%, a current dividend of $2.00, and an expected growth rate of 5%. The stock is selling for $30. The yield to maturity for subordinated debt is 8%. Preferred stock has a price of $100 and a dividend of $8.00. The bank's Tier 1 and Tier 2 capital is given below:

% of Total Capital	Cost of Capital
Common equity	$300,000,000
Perpetual preferred stock	100,000,000
Subordinated debt	50,000,000
Loan loss reserve	50,000,000

a. Calculate the percent of each type of capital to total capital, the cost of each type of capital, and the weighted average cost of capital.
b. Suppose management has $70 million of subordinated debt and equity of $150 million. Recalculate the weighted average cost of capital.

Suggested Cases Dealing with Capital Requirements: Bank/Basle Capital Requirements/Cost of Capital and Strategies

Case 16: "National Bank of Los Angeles." Richard D. Crawford and William W. Sihler. *Financial Service Organizations: Cases in Strategic Management*. New York: Harper Collins College Publishers, 1994, 16.1. This case provides an opportunity for bank financial analysis and computing risk-based capital requirements and the cost of capital for a large bank in Los Angeles attempting to implement new risk-based capital requirements.

Case 9: "Navy Federal Credit Union." Same citation as above. This case examines a Navy Credit Union's capital strategy, subject to a decline in membership with the closure of naval bases in the early 1990s.

References

Benston, George J. "Market-Value Accounting: Benefits, Costs, and Incentives." In *Proceedings of a Conference on Bank Structure and Competition*, 547–563. Chicago: Federal Reserve Bank of Chicago, 1989.

Berger, Allen N., Kathleen A. Kuester, and James M. O'Brien. "Some Red Flags Concerning Market Value Accounting." In *Proceedings of a Conference on Bank Structure and Competition*, 515–546. Chicago: Federal Reserve Bank of Chicago, 1989.

Brigham, Eugene F. and Louis C. Gapenski. *Financial Management: Theory and Practice*, 8th ed. New York: Dryden Press, 1997.

Buser, Stephen A., Andrew H. Chen, and Edward J. Kane. "Federal Deposit Insurance, Regulatory Policy, and Optimal Bank Capital." *Journal of Finance*, 36 (March 1981), 51–60.

Cebenoyan, A. S., E. S. Cooperman, and C. A. Register. "Deregulation, Reregulation, Equity Ownership, and S&L Risk Taking." *Financial Management* (Autumn 1995), 63–76.

Cline, Kenneth. "The Velocity of Capital." *Banking Strategies* (November/December 1996), 37–42.

Coulter, David. "Managing for Shareholder Value at Bank of America." *Bank of America Journal of Applied Corporate Finance*, 10 (Summer 1997), 68–71.

Crawford, Richard D. and William W. Sihler. *Financial Service Organizations: Cases in Strategic Management.* New York: Harper Collins College Publishers, 1994.

Danielson, Arnold G. "Too Much Capital: Banking's Next Problem." *Bank Management* (September/October 1994), 18–20.

Danielson, Arnold G. "National Trends: Bankers' Choice: Adapt to the New Direction or Wait for Last Dance." *Banking Policy Report*, 16 (April 21, 1997), 7.

Davis, Donald and Kevin Lee. "A Practical Approach to Capital Structure for Banks." *Bank of America Journal of Applied Corporate Finance*, 10 (Spring 1997), 33–43.

Furlong, Frederick T., and Michael W. Keran. "The Federal Safety Net for Commercial Banks: Part II." *Weekly Letter* (Federal Reserve Bank of San Francisco), August 3, 1984.

Hirtle, Beverly. "Bank Holding Company Capital Ratios and Shareholder Payouts." *Current Issues in Economics and Finance*, Federal Reserve Bank of New York, Vol. 4, September, 1998, 1—5.

Kane, Edward J. and Haluk Unal. "Modeling Structural and Temporal Variation in the Market's Valuation of Banking Firms." *Journal of Finance*, 45 (March 1990), 113–136.

Kaufman, George G. "Capital in Banking: Past, Present, and Future." *Journal of Financial Services Research*, 5 (April 1992), 385–402.

Kimball, Ralph C. "Economic Profit and Performance Measurement in Banking." *New England Economic Review: Federal Reserve Bank of Boston* (July/August 1998), 35–53.

Jensen, Michael C. *Foundations of Organizational Strategy.* Cambridge, Mass., 1998.

Lopez, Jose A. "Methods for Evaluating Value at Risk Estimates," Federal Reserve Bank of New York *Economic Policy Review*, October 1998, 119–124.

McCoy, John B., Larry A. Frieder, and Robert B. Hedges. *BottomLine Banking.* Chicago: Probus Publishing Company, 1994.

Mengle, David L. and John R. Walter. "How Market Value Accounting Would Affect Banks." In *Proceedings of the Conference on Bank Structure and Competition*, 511–533. Chicago: Federal Reserve Bank of Chicago, 1991.

Mondschean, Thomas. "Market Value Accounting for Commercial Banks." *Economic Perspectives* (Federal Reserve Bank of Chicago), 16 (January/February 1992), 16–31.

Saunders, Anthony. *Financial Institutions Management: A Modern Perspective*, 2e. Chicago: Irwin, 1997.

Walker, David A. Principal Investigator. "Credit Union Insurance and Regulation." Center for Business-Government Relations, Georgetown University, 1997.

Zaik, Edward, John Walter, Gabriela Kelling, and Christopher James. "RAROC at Bank of America: From Theory to Practice." *Bank of America Journal of Applied Corporate Finance*, 9 (Summer 1996), 83–93.

Chapter 8 Internet Exercise

Capital regulation and management

Risk-based Capital Model for Bankers

The Risk-based Capital Model for Bankers, a microcomputer-based program to estimate a national bank's risk-based capital ratio, is available from the OCC. The model has been revised to reflect recent changes to the regulation and proposed changes to the call reports. The model operates in a Windows environment.

1. To access this program, go to the "Useful links and software" page at the OCC at:

   http://www.occ.treas.gov/useful.htm

2. To get an idea of the process involved in the filling out of Call Report data, you can go to the FDIC site on BANK REPORTS at:

   http://www.fdic.gov/banknews/fils/1997/fil9793.html

3. At the bottom of the page, click on the link "Regulatory Capital Worksheet Part I." This work sheet shows how to calculate eligible Tier 1 capital, Tier 2 capital, risk-adjusted weights, and risk-based capital ratios. Using the information from the call report for Nationsbank from Chapter 7, you can now calculate the capital ratios yourself as an exercise. The worksheet provides the information on where to find the item in the Call Reports. As an example, the first line of the worksheet is:

CALCULATION OF ELIGIBLE TIER 1 CAPITAL

Components of Tier 1 Capital:

1. RC 24 plus 25 —— Common stock and surplus

   If you go to Schedule RC, line 24 you will find "Common stock" and line 25 is "surplus."

4. Complete the worksheet and you will have an idea of the time involved by a bank in preparing its quarterly report. Of course, banks employ software programs to do this for them, and it is not necessarily done by hand, though it may be for small banks.

Other useful sites for financial institution data:

An Overview of Capital Adequacy
http://risk.ifci.ch/00013409.htm

Darryll Hendricks and Beverly Hirtle "Bank Capital Requirements for Market Risk: The Internal Models Approach"
http://www.ny.frb.org/rmaghome/econ_pol/1297hen.htm

Ralph C. Kimball "Economic Profit and Performance Measurement in Banking"
http://www.std.com/frbbos/economic/pdf/neer498c.pdf

"As the progressive deregulation . . . of the industry continues, banks are choosing to provide an increasingly diverse set of products and services. The real innovation in . . . new performance evaluation methods (such as RAROC) lies in their ability to allocate banks' capital among their expanding array of nontraditional fee-based activities—many of which do not involve any direct use of capital at all."

Edward Zaik, John Walter, and Gabriela Kelling
Bank of America, and Christopher James, Professor of Finance, University of Florida. "RAROC At Bank of America: From Theory to Practice." *Bank of America Journal of Applied Corporate Finance*, 9 (Summer 1996), 85.

"Revenue growth from other products, services, and revenue sources may not be enough to shore up for slow net interest income growth. Currently the top 50 banks generate noninterest income that comprises 33 percent of total revenues. . . . Some of the industry's proposed answers to the profitability challenge are to recapture revenues from population shifts. Due to an aging baby boomer population, borrowers have become savers, but the preferred savings vehicle has become mutual funds. While banks are scrambling to introduce investment products, do they have the systems in place to properly promote those products without overselling? Will the customers balk at dealing with banks without the insurance coverage of the FDIC?"

John B. McCoy
Chairman and CEO, Banc One Corporation; Larry A. Frieder, Professor, Florida A&M University; and Robert B. Hedges, Jr., Executive Vice President, Consumer Banking Group at Shawmut National Corporation. *Bottomline Banking: Meeting the Challenges for Survival and Success.* Chicago: Probus Publishing Co., 1994.

"The investment management and trust business of banks represents some $75 billion of shareholder value, or about 20% of the total market capitalization of the industry. Most of its component activities have above-average hurdle-rate ROEs and above-average earnings growth rates. As this is not the case for many other bank activities, the business could easily account for as much as 35% of total industry capitalization by decade-end."

Robert M. Tetenbaum
Executive Vice President, First Manhattan Consulting Group. "Investment Management: Fulfilling the Promise." *Bank Management*, (May/June 1995), 49.

9

MANAGING NONINTEREST REVENUES AND
ASSOCIATED RISKS: TRADITIONAL AND
NONTRADITIONAL SOURCES OF FEE INCOME, RISK
MANAGEMENT—VALUE AT RISK AND ECONOMIC
VALUE ADDED, SECURITIZATION, AND OTHER
OFF-BALANCE SHEET ITEMS

In the face of declining net interest margins (NIMs), depository institutions have entered new product areas over the past two decades, moving from traditional lending to areas that generate noninterest revenues. In particular, in the later 1970s, money center banks faced declining lending opportunities as Fortune 500 customers found it cheaper to issue commercial paper versus taking on bank loans. To compensate for lost interest revenue, money center banks changed their strategic focus to include wholesale investment and trading activities and corporate services. Bankers Trust in the late 1970s, for example, divested its branches and became an international merchant bank. Bankers Trust provides wholesale banking services to corporate customers, including cash management, merger and acquisition assistance, and other advisory services. It also trades and underwrites securities, engages in trust and investment management activities, and provides venture capital. By 1988, over 40% of its revenues were from noninterest sources. In 1997 Bankers Trust acquired a prestigious

investment bank in Baltimore, Alex Brown and in 1998 Bankers Trust merged with Deutsche Bank.[1]

Other large regional and nationally focused banks have created new fee income products or acquired nontraditional firms that provide high fee income. Banc One, for instance, acquired First USA, Inc. in 1997, "catapulting" Banc One from 11th to third place among credit card issuers, a very fee-oriented business.[2] As discussed in Chapter 4, starting in the 1980s, banks entered the discount brokerage and mutual fund business through joint types of ventures with mutual fund and discount brokerage firms. In 1992 regulators allowed banks to broker and manage their own affiliate mutual funds, and banks captured 14% of total mutual fund assets by 1995.[3] Some banks, such as Mellon Bank, which purchased Dreyfus in 1994, acquired mutual fund companies or securities firms; others started their own proprietary funds and created their own brand names. Even small banks have increased their fee income by providing working capital management and other personal banking services for small businesses and by expanding their

---

[1]Kelley Holland. "Banking On Fees." *Business Week*, January 18, 1993, 72–73; Anita Raghavan. "Bankers Trust Agrees to Buy Alex Brown As Merger Blitz Grows." *Wall Street Journal*, April 7, 1997, A1-A5. Also see "Bankers Trust New York Corporation." Boston: Harvard Business School, Case 9–286–005, 1995, and Clyde P. Stickney. *Financial Statement Analysis: A Strategic Perspective.* Harcourt Brace Jovanovich Publishers, 1990, 406–430.

[2]See Steven Lipin and Matt Murray. "Bigger than Big: The Superregional as a Banking Model Has Passed Its Prime." *Wall Street Journal*, April 13, 1998, A1, A14.

[3]See Gallo, Richardson, and Apilado (1996); Benston and Kaufman (1997); and Kaufman (1995).

trust business. In the mid-1990s, for example, Colorado Business Bank (CBB), a small business bank holding company in Denver with $264 million in assets, inaugurated cash management services and personal computer (pc) banking services for small firms. CBB also established a trust operation. These operations increased fee income for the bank. For 1997, CBB earned noninterest revenues to average assets of 0.81%, contributing to its very healthy operating return on assets (ROA) of 2.52%.[4]

Thrifts and credit unions (CUs) also offer mutual funds and other products and services to generate fee income. CUs do this through corporate CUs (CCUs), as noted in Chapter 7. Noninterest revenue management has its place for depository institutions of all types and sizes; however, it is most significant for the nation's largest banks. For large banks, sources of considerable fee income include loan sales, securitization, and other off-balance sheet activities, to be discussed later in this chapter.

As the opening chapter quotations suggest, new product areas that depository institutions are entering provide new opportunities, but they create new risks that need to be carefully monitored and managed. U.S. money center and regional banks have increased their security underwriting, derivative, and trading activities in recent years, activities that entail significant selling and market risk. Bankers Trust experienced tremendous losses on high-risk derivatives in the mid-1990s. As the result of tumultuous global markets in the summer of 1998, Bankers Trust, J. P. Morgan, and Bank

*America suffered severe foreign currency and bond trading losses as global markets.[5] In the third quarter of 1998, to protect their financial investment, large European and U.S. financial firms including Bankers Trust, J. P. Morgan, Chase Manhattan, UBS A.G. of Switzerland, and Dresdner Bank A.G. of Germany, among 14 financial firms, contributed $3.6 billion to bail out Long-Term Capital Management, L.P., an unregulated, highly levered, investment fund (known as a **hedge fund**) that invested in stocks, bonds, currencies, and other financial instruments for wealthy individuals.[6] Citigroup, Inc. (the financial-services giant formed with the merger of Citicorp and Travelers Group) lost $1 billion in the third quarter of 1998 resulting from trading activities in Russian government bonds and other investments in Russia by its Salomon Smith Barney investment-banking unit.[7] With depository institutions taking on greater risks, regulators require that institutions have risk management systems in place for many activities. Large financial institutions have developed their own systems for measuring the outstanding risk that they face on their trading and investment risk exposure as well. Institutions have tried to better price risk by allocating capital and its cost to different activities based on their risk by using a risk-adjusted return on capital (RAROC) method discussed previously in Chapter 8 and have used other risk management techniques, including value at risk (VAR) and economic value added (EVA), which are discussed later in this chapter.[8]*

---

[4] See *Sheshunoff Bank and S&L Quarterly 1997*. Austin, Texas: Sheshunoff Information Services, 1997.

[5] See Paul Beckett. "Bankers Trust Appears Back on the Hot Seat." *Wall Street Journal*, September 4, 1998, C1-C2, and Katharine Fraser. "BankAmerica Now Says It Lost $330M in Trading." *American Banker*, September 16, 1998, 1, 4.

[6] While some hedge funds do not take speculative risks, other hedge funds, such as Long-Term Capital Management, L.P., use short positions (i.e., they bet that prices will fall) to offset their other security holdings, and they frequently use borrowed money in an effort to boost returns. Because of the risks, securities laws only allow participation by individuals with at least $200,000 ($300,000 per couple) or net worth of $1 million in recent years. Limits are also placed on the number of investors, generally no more than 100, or up to 500 investors if each has an investment portfolio valued at $5 million or more. See Joseph Kahn and Peter Truell. "Europe Hard Hit as More Banks Post Losses from Hedge Fund." *New York Times*, September 26, 1998, B1-B2; Ruth Simon. "What Are Hedge Funds and Who Are They For?" *Wall Street Journal*, September 30, 1998, C1, C11; and Mark Gerson and Thomas Lehrman. "Most Hedge Funds Play It Safe." *Wall Street Journal*, October 1, 1998, A2.

[7] See Paul Beckett. "Citigroup Launched with Profit Warning." *Wall Street Journal*, October 9, 1998, A3.

[8] See Kimball (1998) and Zaik, Walter, Kelling, and James (1996).

In addition to the risk implications of entering new product areas, banks also face cultural clashes. For example, while traditional lending activities are usually made in a conservative culture to ensure the likelihood that loans will be repaid, investment banking activities embody the negotiation of large deals entailing a more aggressive, deal-making culture, often cited as a gun-slinger culture. Compensation is generally higher for investment bankers than traditional lenders, which can cause jealousies within a holding company. Other problems include ensuring regulatory-mandated separation or "fire walls" between activities, if required. Successful bankers must implement management policies that encourage harmony across different activity areas and develop a high performance, selling culture within their institution.[9]

This chapter provides an overview of different sources of noninterest income for depository institutions, including an overview of securitization, and other major off-balance sheet activities. Overall risk management strategies are also briefly discussed, along with examples of cultural problems involved in the management of nontraditional activities. The following sections begin by discussing the motivation for depository institutions to earn greater fee income, and the extent of bank noninterest revenue activities in the 1990s.

✦ ✦ ✦

WHY FEE INCOME?

As pointed out by William R. Robertson,[10] deputy chairman of National City Corporation in Cleveland, Ohio, in 1994, banks have been almost obsessed with fee income in the past decade for several good reasons. Fee income businesses:

- represent ways to increase competitiveness
- help to replace lost market share in traditional banking
- provide a diverse source of income
- help create consistent earnings
- require a small capital investment

Fee income enables banks to offer complementary, improved lending products and to meet customers' demands for new products, such as mutual funds. These new products, in addition to generating fee income, make banks more competitive with other banks and nonbanks that offer a wide array of services and products. With banks' NIMs highly dependent on interest-rate movements and economic cycles, fee income provides diversification and greater stability for bank profits. Fee income can also boost a bank's return on equity (ROE) and ROA, since activities generating fee income often do not require a large investment in fixed assets, and banks are often not required by regulators to hold additional equity capital for these activities, as they would for loans. Banks with fee income have more diversification and stable income, so they often have higher stock market values than banks that depend solely on traditional interest revenues. Many fee-based services, such as cash management services for corporate customers or

---

[9]See "Bankers Trust New York Corporation." Boston: Harvard Business School, Case 9-286-005, 1995. Other types of financial institutions have had similar problems as well including General Electric Corporation in its attempt to integrate Kidder Peabody into GE Capital's more conservative, transactional culture (see Case 6, General Electric Financial Services, Inc., in Crawford and Sihler, 1994).

[10]This section and the following section are from Robertson (1994).

mortgage servicing agreements, also have few risks. The following section briefly describes the successful implementation of a few-based program by National City Bank Corporation.

Implementation of a Fee-Income Strategy by National City Bank Corporation

As described in a recent article by deputy chairman William R. Robertson, National City Corporation (NCC), a large regional bank holding company operating in Ohio, Indiana, and Kentucky, decided to engage in a fee-income strategy in 1980. At that time NCC received only 20% of its revenue from noninterest sources. Implementing this strategy within a decade, NCC's fee income grew at double-digit rates to 40% of its total revenues. NCC changed its strategic focus to encompass products that generated fee income not to replace its primary function as a traditional banking institution, but to provide more consistent earnings and diversification as a buffer against economic swings. NCC developed three primary forms of fee income:

(1)   an item processing division,
(2)   a trust operation, and
(3)   a mortgage-servicing division.

Of the three, the crown jewel, National City Processing, is responsible for the largest growth in fee income. This division provides integrated, complementary products including:

(1)   the handling of approximately 70% of the receivables for the airline industry (the payments from customers to travel agents and airlines),
(2)   providing merchant bank-card services and retail lockbox processing, and
(3)   check guarantee, verification, and collection services.

National City Processing also entered other ventures, such as the electronic provision of food stamps and other welfare benefits through "smart cards," providing an entry into electronic banking.

National City's second most successful fee income generator is its trust operation, which managed more than $60 billion in trust assets with revenues of $120 million by 1994, ranking it 25th among U.S. banks. In addition to consolidating back-office operations to operate more efficiently on a single data processing system, the trust area provides a family of mutual funds with a pool exceeding $2 billion. Its mortgage-servicing business includes $12 billion in servicing assets, ranking the firm among the top 30 mortgage-servicing companies in the country. This area complements its mortgage lending operations. By setting up 25 retail mortgage origination offices up and down the East Coast unrelated to its bank branches, NCC could originate a greater volume of mortgages; these provide significant fee income from servicing contracts (contracts whereby a bank receives fee income for collecting and processing mortgage payments for other parties).

Furthermore, NCC initiated other sources of fee income, including service charges on checking accounts, fees for retail brokerage services, fees for credit life insurance, commissions on annuity sales, and credit-card fees. NCC also entered the venture capital arena, providing funds for promising small businesses. In the future NCC plans to grow fee-income businesses through acquisitions of compatible business areas and expand existing fee-generating businesses. NCC began a program to cross-sell fee income products to its existing customers. The keys for NCC's success with its fee-income strategy include:

(1) **being selective in choosing appropriate businesses**, focusing on areas that provide real value that the bank understood—realizing that "banks can't be all things to all people";

(2) **realizing that the appropriate mix** of nontraditional and traditional services will vary—with percentages changing over time as one business does better than another;

(3) **creating a culture that encourages cross-selling** by employees, being careful of any anti-tying laws that prevent cross-selling or tying in of sales for different products;

(4) **being aware of special considerations in acquiring fee business**—for instance, some fee income businesses may not be profitable if generous fringe benefits for other banking businesses are offered; and

(5) **using effective measurements to evaluate performance**—some fee income businesses have higher operating costs associated with them than traditional activities; hence, efficiency ratios (such as operating expense less fee income expense as a percentage of net interest income) may indicate lower operating efficiency. In contrast, overhead ratios (such as the percentage of total fixed costs to assets) demonstrate greater bank operating efficiency with the acquisition of such businesses, since fee-income businesses often have low operating costs relative to assets.

As summarized by William R. Robertson:

"fee-income businesses can provide tremendous advantages. As a complement to traditional banking, fee-income businesses can help a banking company become better positioned to deliver exceptional results on a more consistent and predictable basis. And as such, they can be a strong weapon in the competitive fight."[11]

HOW MUCH NONINTEREST REVENUES DO BANKS PRODUCE?

In 1997 the national averages for banks for different revenue and expense items relative to average assets were as follows:

NIM	3.90%
Noninterest Income	2.24%
Overhead Expense	(3.70%)
Provision for Loan Losses	(.42%)
ROA	1.30%
ROE	15.46%

With average assets in 1997 of $5.229 trillion, noninterest revenues were about $0.1171 trillion or $11.71 billion. The ratio of noninterest income to average assets increased about 16%, from 1.93% in 1994 to 2.24% in 1997. As shown by the figures above, as a percentage of average assets, the average NIM for U.S. banks in 1997 of 3.90% did not cover the total costs of overhead expenses and provision for loans losses

---

[11]See Robertson (1994) 18.

of 4.12%. Hence, the 2.24% noninterest revenues was crucial for U.S. banks to be profitable. The ten largest banks in the U.S. had average noninterest income to assets of 2.12% in 1997, only 64 basis points lower than their average NIM of 2.76%.[12] Noninterest revenues have increased phenomenally as a source of revenue for banks. In the first quarter of 1998, 39.7% of bank earnings were attributable to noninterest sources, rising from 24.7% in 1984. Many of the gains in noninterest revenue for larger banks have come from investment banking, trading, and brokerage activities, which are more market sensitive than other traditional sources.[13] However, banks with significant traditional trust activities generating fee income, particularly custodial business, such as Bank of New York and Northern Trust, had less of a fall in stock prices than other banks during a market downturn from July to September 1998.[14]

A BRIEF OVERVIEW OF TRADITIONAL FEE-BASED SERVICES

Some sources of fee income have been available to depositories for many years, but have recently taken on a more dominant position in the overall financial management strategies of banks. These include deposit service charges, credit card fees, and fees associated with electronic funds transfers (EFTs). Credit card fees have grown in recent years to the largest single source of noninterest income for many retail banks, even with the low annual fees and rates on cards that resulted from the price wars in the 1990s. Credit cards have been a major profit center for many large banks, including Citicorp, First Chicago NBD, and Banc One. At the end of 1997, Citicorp was the number one credit card company, with 45.5 million accounts and outstanding credit card loans of $64.86 billion. With the merger of First Chicago and Banc One, the combined institution will be number two, with 39.5 million accounts and $56.56 billion in credit card loans.

Trust and Personal Planning Services

Overview of the Trust Business of Banks in the U.S. The investment management and trust business of banks represented $75 billion of shareholder value or about 20% of the total market capitalization of the banking industry in 1995. In 1997, the 50 largest banks in the trust business boosted their discretionary trust assets (assets managed for wealthy individuals) by 22% to $3.5 trillion. Fiduciary assets (assets managed for pension funds, estates, or other trusts) also increased 28% to $18.3 trillion as this group of banks gained better selling and client retention. Gross trust income increased by 16%. The component activities for bank trust services also generally had above average earnings growth rates, with higher returns than many other types of nonfee income activities. For instance, pretax returns on revenue in personal trusts

---

[12]Information taken from *Sheshunoff Bank & S&L Quarterly 1997*. Austin, Texas: Sheshunoff Information Services, Inc.1998; *FDIC Statistics on Banking 1996*. Washington D.C.: FDIC Division of Research and Statistics, 1996; and William B. English and William R. Nelson. "Profits and Balance Sheet Developments at U.S. Commercial Banks in 1997." *Federal Reserve Bulletin*, June 1998, 391–419.

[13]See Tetenbaum (1995); Yvette D. Kantrow. "With More Fees from Risky Lines, Banks Tighten Focus on 'the Mix.'" *American Banker*, August 13, 1998, 1,6; and Katharine Fraser, "Trust Assets at Biggest Banks Grew 22% Last Year." *American Banker*, July 21, 1998, 1, 11.

[14]See Karen Talley. "Custody Business Keeps Losses in Check." *American Banker*, September 17, 1998, 30.

and pension management services for top providers were, respectively, 40% and 30%.[15] This was not always the case; in the 1970s trust services were often "loss leaders." Banks provided trust services at a loss to attract wealthy customers. Many customers viewed the trust department as an added convenience of doing business with a particular institution and not as a source of high investment returns.

With deregulation and competition from mutual funds and investment firms, bank trust departments must generate returns on portfolios comparable to those achieved by other asset managers. Bank trust department returns are publicized, and money managers must make good returns to attract funds from wealthy investors and corporate pension plans. Most banks charge explicit fees for trust services, often based on the principal value of the client's assets. Some banks assign the management of the portfolio to outside managers, including hiring a competitor mutual fund to manage clients' money. In addition, depository institutions generate fee income from personal financial planning services, assisting individuals with decisions on budgeting, taxes, investments, retirement, estate planning, and other financial matters. Since these services can be costly in terms of hiring and training individuals, fees must be commensurate with the cost of producing the service. Some institutions offer low-cost computerized plans that can be generated cheaply for a low price by using the customer's characteristics (such as age, income, family size, and assets). Since the cost to customers is low, banks must do plans for a high volume of customers for this product to be profitable. With the rapid growth of corporate defined contribution (401k) plans, management of plan assets is a high growth area for banks.

The investment management and trust businesses of banks can be divided into two aspects: asset management and accounting/record keeping. Asset management includes personal funds management: personal trust and retail mutual funds, defined benefit and defined contribution pensions, and corporate money management.[16] The account businesses include master trust, global custody, domestic custody, and corporate trust and paying agencies, including American Depository Receipts.[17] While banks have a considerable role in the accounting lines, many of these are low-margin, limited growth activities. In contrast, bank asset management businesses have higher margins and faster growth. In 1995, banks held over half the corporate money management (nonpension) market, about two-thirds of the $1.1 trillion personal trust market, about 30% of the $3.2 trillion defined benefit pension market, and about 25% of the rapidly growing defined contribution market. The 401(k) segment of the defined contribution pension area has grown at the highest annual rate. Banks often provide record-keeping

---

[15]This section comes from Tetenbaum (1995). Tetenbaum points out that in managing pension plans, banks often assume one of four roles as reseller, assembler, subcontractor, or integrated provider. Small banks may act as resellers by passing a customer's plans to other larger financial institutions. A bank may also just act as an assembler, performing some in-house functions, but primarily subcontracting out the management of funds to another party. Subcontractors generally must have a good brand name and may need scale if their chief expertise is in recordkeeping. In contrast, an integrated provider does everything and needs scale, sales skills, investment knowledge, and a brand name.

[16]Defined benefit pension plans are corporate plans to which corporations make contributions and invest the contributions for employees to provide a promised benefit for employees at retirement, taking all the investment risk. In contrast, under defined contribution plans, employers contribute a fixed amount and employees choose the investment vehicle and take all the responsibility for the funds they will have available at retirement.

[17]American Depository Receipts are certificates of ownership issued by a U.S. bank that represent a claim on underlying foreign securities (for more detailed information, see Eiteman, Stonehill, and Moffett [1992]).

and technical assistance in structuring 401(k) plans for customers or else outsource these functions. They also provide education and support services for businesses in setting up 401(k) plans.[18] Banks have an advantage through their lending relationships of gaining business in this area for small and midsized companies; however, mutual funds have been stronger contenders in recent years for these firms.

Office of the Comptroller of the Currency Allows Nationwide Trust Operations

In response to a request by Banc One, in December of 1995 the Office of the Comptroller of the Currency (OCC) issued an opinion that removed state restrictions, permitting U.S. national banks to provide trust services nationwide. National banks also gained relief from state laws specifying that deposits must be placed with state authorities for the protection of private and court trusts. However state-chartered banks within a state must abide by these laws. A national bank may engage in fiduciary activities in another state simply by opening an office in that state. This ruling allows national banks to centralize their trust management and administration and in this way to gain economies of scale.[19]

OCC-Federal Reserve System Guidelines for Managing Trust Risk

With greater competition and more sophisticated, knowledgeable trust customers, banks have developed more sophisticated products and investment strategies, including products that have potentially greater risk and higher expected returns. They also often offer wrap accounts that provide a mix of financial planning, brokerage, and asset management services for a single fee. Consequently, regulators have been concerned about whether the risks associated with these activities are properly measured and managed. Both the OCC and Federal Reserve System (Fed) issued risk management guidelines in 1996 for bank fiduciary operations. One point of the guidelines is that a bank's trust operations should be integrated fully into a bank's risk management process. The OCC guidelines also direct management at the minimum to "verify the integrity of risk measurement and control, related management reporting systems, and compliance with approved investment policies and procedures." The Fed's guidelines instruct examiners to emphasize how effectively institutions are managing risks associated with fiduciary functions.[20]

Ways Banks Can Become More Competitive

Although banks have made significant headway in generating traditional fee income, Robert Tetenbaum, Executive Vice President of First Manhattan Consulting, a distinguished New York bank consulting group, points out that for banks to remain competitive with other financial institutions, they need to expand their product breath and to improve sales, relationships, servicing, and investment know-how. Many wealthy customers are particularly concerned over principal maintenance, institutional reputation, and personal services. Integrated providers with their own brand name that manage their own funds

---

[18]See Tetenbaum (1995). The 401(k) plan derives its name from Section 401(k) of the Internal Revenue Code, which allows employees to have a portion of compensation contributed to a qualified retirement plan as part of the Revenue Act of 1978 (see Ambachtsheer and Ezra [1998], 200). Also see Vince DiPaolo. "Vista Funds: Chase Applies Formula to Funds Management." *Bank Management*, March/April 1995, 13–14.

[19]William Campbell Ries and Leilani Costa. "OCC Opens the Door for Nationwide Trust Operations." *Bank Management*, July/August 1996, 62–64, 71.

[20]Kim E. Lowry and Eric J. Woodstrom. "Risk Management Process: Implications for the Evolving Trust Business." *Bank Policy Report*, 15, September 2, 1996, 1, 13–15.

have a better chance of winning 401(k) retirement accounts from corporations and of creating spillover effects to sell other bank products. Other wealthy entrepreneurs, executives, and professionals prefer accounts that offer a variety of services, including financial planning, brokerage, and diversified asset management under a single "wrap" account for an annual fee as a percentage of assets, generally 1% to 3%. Banks that do not have this type of depth may be at a competitive disadvantage.

Banks may also be at a disadvantage in terms of paying less to the average bank investment sales representative. Banks pay an average of $63,000 a year, less than two-thirds of the salary for an average retail broker. Banks need better coordination between private banking and trust personnel as well. Often bank personnel managing fiduciary assets for trusts and pension plans work at cross purposes with personnel managing discretionary investment portfolios for wealthy individuals. All personnel need to be more integrated in their approach to clients. Finally, banks need to advertise nonbank products more and, with the boom in demand for customized financial planning, to offer customized financial planning services for both affluent and less affluent clients. As discussed later in the section on bank mutual funds, banks have gained economies by transferring trust assets into bank mutual fund accounts. In 1996, this was allowed to be a tax-free transfer.[21]

CORRESPONDENT BANKING

Correspondent banks sell management and administrative services, such as check clearing, wire transfer, securities transfer and clearance and safekeeping, federal funds trading, loan participation, and investment advisory services to smaller financial institutions (respondents) that do not have the personnel or economies of scale to provide these services for themselves. Correspondent banks receive significant fee income in return for these services. Of these services, check clearing has generally led in terms of profitability, followed by data processing and short-term lines (overlines) to respondents.[22] The heart of banking involves clearing billions of checks a day, so larger banks that provide processing services can reap significant income. Competition for these services includes the speed of processing as well as efficiency and accuracy and low cost per check cleared.

Competition for Correspondent Bank Check-Clearing Services

Pricing Before DIDMCA   Prior to DIDMCA (Depository Institutions Deregulation and Monetary Control Act), respondent banks were asked to hold compensating demand deposits balances with their correspondent banks along with being charged fees for services. Hence, the cost of services included the opportunity cost of lost interest income on those deposits in addition to other fees. In addition to fees, correspondent banks received cheap deposit funding for loans and other investments. Like trust customers, respondents were willing to forgo lost interest income in exchange for convenience and management expertise. Often correspondents offered a bundle of services for a single fee, a deposit balance requirement, or both, with no explicit fees listed for services.

---

[21]See Tetenbaum (1995).
[22]"Correspondent Products: Which is No. 1?" *ABA Banking Journal*, 1988 Survey.

Pricing After DIDMCA   The DIDMCA of 1980 changed the practice of bundling services for a single fee. DIDMCA mandated universal reserve requirements and access to Fed services for all depositories and the explicit pricing of Fed services. Previous to DIDMCA, many large banks that were Fed members used the Fed's free services and then charged their smaller nonmember respondents explicit fees for the same services. After DIDMCA, small and medium-sized depository institutions gained access to Fed services. The Fed was also required to publish explicit pricing lists for individual services, such as the cost per checked cleared, along with the average time to clear checks. Thus, small and medium-sized depository institutions had a choice between directly using the Fed's check clearing services, using a correspondent bank's services, or a combination of the two. In response to the Fed's explicit pricing, correspondent banks began offering similar unbundled price lists and competitive pricing for services as well as efficient check-clearing times. Studies by the American Bankers Association indicate that large correspondent banks consider the Fed their strongest competitor. Some observers point out that the Fed's entry into traditional correspondent banking has produced more efficient markets for these services.[23]

Entry of Other Competitors   The entry of thrifts and CUs into the business of offering transaction accounts after DIDMCA added a layer of complexity to correspondent banking. Initially, because they were relatively small, few thrifts or CUs established their own check-clearing systems, but many devised a much less expensive way of clearing checks through check imaging and check truncation. Instead of going through the expensive process of processing checks and then mailing them back to customers with monthly deposit account statements, some small thrifts and CUs used imaging machines, which capture check images as checks are sorted. In place of the actual checks, images are sent with monthly statements to customers, saving the labor-intensive task of sorting and returning canceled checks. As customers have gradually accepted this practice, many banks have begun to move to such a check truncation system as well. Since traditional check clearing by correspondent banks seldom provided a truncation feature, the Federal Home Loan Bank (FHLB) system soon began offering check-clearing services, including check truncation. Hence, the FHLB captured a great share of thrifts' check-clearing business. Under DIDMCA, CUs and CCUs are eligible to purchase Fed services as well. CCUs serve in a similar capacity as correspondent banks to small CUs, providing technology, expertise, and security safe-keeping services at a relatively lower cost. The volume of correspondent services provided by CCUs has grown rapidly.[24]

Bankers' Banks   Analogous to CCUs are **bankers' banks**, which are simply banks for banks. The first bankers' bank was formed in Minnesota in 1975. By the 1990s, about 2,834 small banks nationwide used bankers' bank services. Operating similarly to CCUs, bankers' banks provide low-cost services for groups of small banks that own stock in the bankers' bank, so are in effect owners of their service institution. Bankers' banks provide check clearing services, securities safekeeping, and other correspondent services. Also, like CCUs, bankers' banks have access to Fed services and provide additional competition for correspondent banks.[25]

---

[23]See Evanoff (1984).

[24]See *Credit Union National Association Annual Reports*.

[25]For more information on the functions of and laws governing bankers' banks, see Frisbee (1984), and A. Joseph Newman, Jr. "Pennsylvania Bankers' Bank Exemplifies A Vibrant Breed." *American Banker*, August 23, 1990, 2, 5.

The 1970s brought inflation and a high cost of funds, and corporations developed new techniques to manage and conserve cash within their organizations. Banks, in particular, developed fee income services to satisfy the needs of corporate customers for managing their cash, including reducing collection float, the time it takes for corporate customers to receive and invest funds from customers. These working capital management services provide significant noninterest revenue for depository institutions as well as making the bank more attractive for an overall lending relationship for corporate customers. Some of these services are described in the following section.

CORPORATE CASH MANAGEMENT AND MANAGEMENT CONSULTING

Several fee-based services closely related to correspondent banking have developed over the last two decades. Of particular importance are cash management services for nonfinancial corporations that are offered by commercial banks with which businesses maintain close financial relationships. Cash management services include assisting customers with collecting accounts, disbursing expenditures, forecasting cash balances, and investing temporarily idle cash in money market instruments. Although traditionally the province of large banks, the field is also promising for small institutions. Banks provide **lockbox** systems to customers, whereby customers send payments to a post office box managed by a bank, which opens, processes, collects, and deposits checks within an hour of their receipt, so interest can be earned on checks as quickly as possible. Customers receive a fax and other type of notification quickly as well, so they can manage their cash balances each day.

Banks also provide personalized services for both large and small companies, moving (**sweeping**) funds from savings accounts that earn interest to transaction accounts that do not earn interest as firms need to make disbursements. Bank employees monitor customers' accounts and contact them when additional funds are needed for upcoming disbursements and make daily EFTs for customers as needed. Large corporate customers often have cash concentration systems with lockboxes at key banks or branches of a bank with a national presence in different customer locations. These banks, in turn, routinely transfer funds to a centrally located **concentration bank**. This allows corporate cash managers a larger available cash pool to manage and makes funds at one central location easier to keep track of and manage.[26]

Many institutions have broadened their range of corporate services to include management consulting, data processing and information systems, or other technological services. Management consulting services allow corporate customers to purchase expert advice to address a variety of management problems. Information systems and software marketed by banks assist clients in collecting, analyzing, and reporting data effectively and efficiently. Among the most popular new technological services are **electronic data interchange (EDI) systems,** which generally refer to the practice of direct electronic information exchange between all types of businesses. Financial EDI allows the electronic transfer of financial information and funds between parties. Thus, corporations can exchange accounts receivable and accounts payable records electronically as well as transfer funds automatically to settle these accounts. This eliminates the cost of handling, mailing, and issuing paper checks. For payrolls, for instance, a bank can be authorized to take funds electronically from a corporation's checking account each month and deposit

---

[26]See Ross, Westerfield, and Jordan (1996), 436–440.

checks electronically through the **Automated Clearing House System** within minutes to employees accounts. EDI allows bills to be sent electronically as well, reducing mailing costs and time. Banks, in turn, receive fee income for these services. Corporate service activities provide more consistent fee income than other noninterest revenue activities, since fees are steady and less cyclical. Bank of New York, for instance, has a securities- and cash-processing business that constitutes 40% of its earnings. Although these types of services do not appear as exciting as other sources of noninterest revenue, such as security trading when other banks faced severe trading losses from volatility in global markets in the third quarter of 1998, Bank of New York's earnings remained stable.[27]

A BRIEF OVERVIEW OF NEWER FEE-BASED ACTIVITIES: SECURITIES, INSURANCE BROKERAGE, MUTUAL FUNDS, REAL ESTATE, AND OTHER ACTIVITIES

As discussed in Chapter 4, banks in the last two decades have been allowed to engage in greater securities, brokerage, annuities, mutual fund, and insurance activities as regulators have liberalized their interpretation of the Glass-Steagall Act of 1933. The Financial Modernization Bill, currently on hold in the Senate, allows securities and insurance firms to be affiliated with banks. A chief area of contention of the bill is whether banks would be allowed to engage in such activities through operating subsidiaries (Op-Subs) of national banks regulated by the OCC under the Treasury Department or only by separate Section 20 subsidiaries authorized and regulated by the Fed. Op-Subs provide greater opportunities for smaller banks to engage in such nontraditional activities. Many states have passed "wild card" bills to ensure that state-chartered banks will at least have the range of powers available for their federally chartered competitors through the year 2000. To date only five states and the District of Columbia do not have some form of wild card or parity provision for their state-chartered banks.[28]

Additional State Powers   States have continued to create new financial institution charters and to provide new opportunities for state-chartered banks to provide additional products and services to customers that the states fear may be repealed with the national financial modernization legislation. Maine, for instance, created a new merchant bank charter that allows state merchant banks to be funded through equity and borrowings versus deposits and to have trust, lending, and investment powers similar to commercial banks. Maine also created a universal charter that allows all Maine-chartered financial institutions to conduct any financial activities, including buying, selling, and underwriting investment and equity securities, making venture capital investments up to 20% of the institution's capital, and offering a broad range of trust services. The new Maine law also eliminates ownership restrictions, thus allowing a broad choice of ownership structures, including stock, mutual, limited liability partnerships, limited liability corporations, and limited partnerships.

Table 9.1 lists types of extended activities and the states that allowed them in 1998. These include securities brokerage, municipal securities underwriting, real estate brokerage activities, real estate development, real estate equity participation, and

---

[27]See Paul Beckett. "Bank of New York Stands Out Among Rivals By Dint of Scoring With Pedestrian Businesses." *Wall Street Journal*, October 9, 1998, A2.

[28]See "States Want to Protect Their Powers to Approve New Banking Activities." *Banking Policy Report*, 17, August 17, 1998, 6–9.

Table 9.1 ✦ Permissible Activities (beyond powers of national banks) by States

(state abbreviations are given for each type of activity)

State-chartered depository institutions have greater privileges in many states.

Activity	Permitted in
Securities Brokerage (discount or full)	AL, AK, AZ, AR, CO, CT, DE, FL, GA, IL,IN, IA, KS, KY, LA, ME, MD, MA, MI, MN, MS, MO, NE, NV, NH, NJ, NY, NC, ND, OR, PA, SC, TN, UT, VT, WV, WI, WY
Municipal Securities Underwriting (general obligation or revenue)	AZ, CO, CT, DE, FL, IN, IA, KS, LA, ME, MA, MI, MS, MO, NE, NJ, NY, NC, OH, PA, PR, TN, TX, UT, VT, WV
Real Estate Brokerage	AZ, CA, FL, IN, IA, LA, ME, MA, MN, NE, NJ, NC, WI
Real Estate Development	AK, AZ, AR, CA, CO, FL, IA, KY, LA, ME, MA, MI, MN, MO, NV, NJ, NM, NC, OH, OR, PA, RI, TN, UT, VA, WV, WY
Real Estate Equity Participation	AK, AZ, CA, CO, FL, HI, IL, IA, KY, LA, ME, MA, MN, NJ, NC, OH, OR, RI, TN, UT, VA, WV, WI
Insurance Brokerage	AL, AZ, CA, CO, CT, DE, HI, ID, IL, IN, IA, LA, ME, MD, MI, MS, NE, NV, NJ, NM, NY, NC, ND, OH, OR, PA, RI, SC, SD, UT, VA, WI

Source: "States Want to Protect Their Powers to Approve New Banking Activities," *Banking Policy Report,* 17 (August 17, 1998), Table 1, p. 7.

insurance brokerage activities. In a recent ruling, the Federal Reserve Board issued a legislative interpretation that permits state-chartered savings banks to sell annuities and other insurance products and allows bank Op-Subs of these banks to offer these products, which previously only national banks and thrifts have been allowed to offer.[29]

Performance and Risk of Banks Entering Securities Activities   The desire by banks to enter the investment business can be seen from Figure 9.1, which shows pretax ROEs for the securities industry. The average pretax ROE was 25.83% between 1980 and 1996. However, returns in the securities industry can also be volatile, as demonstrated by the –0.7% ROE in 1990 during a market downturn. Since depository institutions' major entrance into the securities arena has occurred within the current decade, research on profit contributions and risk has been generally speculative. Breakdowns of sources of noninterest revenue are difficult to come by. Many analysts, however, assume that the dramatic rise in noninterest revenues to

---

[29]Ibid. See also Jaret Seiberg. "Fed Lets State Savings Banks Market Insurance Products." *American Banker*, July 2, 1998, 2. See Chapter 4 for a discussion of recent regulatory developments that allow banks greater entry into security underwriting and brokerage activities. Thrifts have entered security brokerage services using owned service cooperation. Some thrifts have also affiliated with discount or full service brokers or developed inhouse brokerage facilities. The savings community Bankers of America also has mutual funds that savings institutions an offer to customers. CUNA Brokerage executes trades for individual comembers.

Figure 9.1   ✦   PRE-TAX ROEs FOR SECURITIES INDUSTRY (IN PERCENT %)

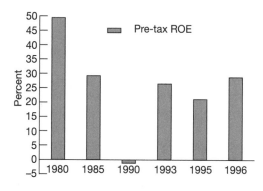

Source: Security Industry Trends. New York Securities Industry Association, 1997.

39.7% of total revenues for banks in the first quarter of 1998 came from investment banking, trading, and brokerage activities. These activities are much more market sensitive than trust fees and service charges for typical noninterest income. For instance, the *American Banker* reported that newly acquired brokerage firms bolstered profits at BankAmerica Corporation, Fleet Financial Group, and U.S. Bancorp in the first two quarters of 1998, a bull market period. The commissions earned by BankAmerica's Robertson Stephens investment banking unit helped to increase noninterest income by 29% to $1.84 billion in the second quarter of 1998. Similarly, Fleet and U.S. Bancorp cited fees from their respective Quick & Reilly and Piper Jaffray's brokerage firm acquisitions as contributing to respective 35% and 38% rises in noninterest revenue in the first half of 1998.[30]

However, with a decline in the stock market later in the third quarter of 1998, the financial press reported that first-time investors were pulling out of bank stock and mutual funds. Consequently, banks faced the reality of the cyclical nature of securities businesses. With volatile security markets, some analysts argue that it is too early to look at brokerage activities and other nontraditional securities activities as a solution to smooth out income for banks in the face of cyclical lending cycles. Hence, many bankers have recently focused on the right combination of fee-based businesses. For instance, a bank enjoying increased revenues from mortgage, investment banking, or mutual fund areas during a bull market might want to invest more in mortgage servicing, securities processing, mutual fund processing, insurance, or cash management, which will provide more consistent annuity-like fees during future bear markets.

Bank for International Settlements Study   Although few studies have evaluated the benefits of banks getting into the securities business, one recent study conducted by the Bank for International Settlements, "Commercial Banks in the Securities Business," provides evidence that the benefits outweigh the risks of allowing

---

[30]See "Broker Units Lift B of A, Fleet, U.S. Bancorp Profits." *American Banker*, July 16, 1998, 1–4, and Yvette D. Kantrow. "With More Fees from Risky Lines, Banks Tighten Focus on 'the Mix.'" *American Banker*, August 13, 1998, 1, 6.

banks to engage in the securities business. The study finds that commercial banks take on few additional risks by engaging in underwriting and other capital market activities, assuming the banks have the appropriate organization and adequate capitalization. The Bank for International Settlements study suggests that banks gain efficiency through economies of scale in the production and consumption of financial services through securities activities, providing diversification and alternative sources of revenue. Banks are also able to recapture customers who had previously sidestepped banks by financing in the direct capital markets by offering investment banking activities.[31]

Bank Mutual Funds   Given that banks' involvement in mutual funds is fairly recent, banks have made significant headway. In 1987, banks had only 4% of mutual fund assets. By 1994 bank-sponsored mutual fund assets grew to more than 14% of total mutual fund assets, with $312.8 billion in assets under management for all bank proprietary funds and banks accounting for more than 40% of mutual fund sales. As of June 30, 1998, bank-managed mutual fund assets were $755 billion, a 36% rise from June, 1997 figures.[32] Much of this rise was associated with a dramatic rise in the stock market in the first half of 1998. With a fall in the stock market during the third quarter of 1998, banks later faced some significant withdrawals from less sophisticated investors in bank funds. Recent industry marketing research, however, finds that there is considerable inertia in the movement of money out of mutual funds, with investors "hesitant" to move out of funds once an initial investment is made. Mutual funds not only provide significant fee income for banks through fees for advice and selling funds, but they also help banks to retain customers who might otherwise leave the bank in search of higher yielding investments. This was particularly the case when interest rates were very low in the 1990s, and bank deposits earned very low rates.

Roles of Banks in Mutual Fund Management   Banks are linked to mutual funds in several ways. Banks serve as **brokers for nonproprietary (unrelated) mutual funds**, acting as a sales-force marketing channel. They also serve as **investment advisors to proprietary (their own) mutual funds**, organized and distributed by the sponsoring bank's brokerage affiliate (to satisfy Glass-Steagall). Annuities that are sold to customers are often tied to mutual funds as well. Initially, in the later 1980s, banks served as a distribution network for mutual fund companies, such as Fidelity, receiving part of the sales load for selling the funds. As Pozen (1998) in the *Mutual Fund Business* states, by 1993 almost a third of all available mutual funds could be purchased through a bank, and about 100 banks sold 1,000 proprietary funds. By 1994, this figure was closer to 125 banks offering 1,400 proprietary mutual funds, with more large banks developing and managing their own proprietary funds. However, to manage a family of mutual funds, some studies suggest that a critical mass of $10 to $25 billion is needed to reap economies of scale and survive competition from other fund families.[33]

---

[31]See "Study Supports Commercial Banks to Engage in Securities Activities." *Banking Policy Report*, 17, August 3, 1998, 2.

[32]See Pozen (1998); Niamh Ring. "Banks' Fund Assets Surge 36%, Beating S&P, Rivals." *American Banker*, August 13, 1998, 1, 7; Gallo, Apilado, and Kolari (1996); Laderman (1997); Fortune (1997); and Gallo, Richardson, and Apilado (1996).

[33]Ibid.

Hence, **third-party funds** became popular, whereby **a bank outsourced its fund management** to an outside fund company that provided management and support for a fund or class of funds that used the bank's own "brand name." At first, banks received much of the money for proprietary bank mutual funds from a conversion of trust funds to mutual funds managed by banks. In 1996, banks also benefited from a provision in the Small Business Jobs Protection Act that allows a tax-free conversion of common trust funds into mutual funds. Prior to this act transfers were generally considered as a sale, requiring investors to pay a capital gains tax. This act benefits trust account holders who may prefer the greater liquidity and diversification of bank mutual funds versus separate trust accounts. Banks reap economies from commingled funds by being able to manage funds for wealthy and small investors together, capturing greater management fees. Minimum fees for investment in funds through vehicles like IRAs can be lower than the minimum for many nonbank mutual funds.[34]

The average size of bank mutual funds has been generally small, making it difficult to compete for funds from mutual funds with large families, such as Fidelity and Vanguard. A Goldman Sachs report indicated that 51 U.S. banks had proprietary mutual-fund families with more than $1 billion under management at the end of 1993.Banks initially offered plain vanilla proprietary funds of bond, money market, or equity types. Third-party funds were used to create a more sophisticated variety of funds for the needs of different investors, with fees coming from a share in the load (fee) charged to customers for entering these funds. Many bank customers who have never purchased investment products before can be reluctant to purchase funds directly from mutual fund companies and are more reassured by buying funds face to face with a service representative at a bank. Not surprisingly , such customers often prefer low risk funds. In a 1996 Deloitte and Touche investor survey 61% of the 750 investors surveyed said they would buy funds from their banks if they offered a financial planner and related services. However, when asked what services investors would be most interested in, 70% of investors also stated that they would like a full range of mutual funds and investment products.

Strategies by Larger Banks to Compete with Fund Families   Larger banks have created their own brand names and fund families. Mellon Bank's acquisition of Dreyfus Corporation allowed it to acquire a brand name. Dreyfus manages over $77 billion in assets in 147 portfolios, predominantly money market and bond funds. Wells Fargo took a different approach, creating a new family of mutual funds (called the Stagecoach Funds) to sell through its branches. Wells Fargo was able to reap fee income as both manager and investment adviser to its 11 funds. BayBank in Boston, Massachusetts, developed a similar brand of funds called "BayFunds" to build an association between BayBank and its funds, creating synergies from the bank's strong reputation and financial strength. First Union and Fleet Financial spent considerable advertising funds to build a brand identity for their funds to better compete with nonbank mutual funds that have well-known brand names. Banks

---

[34]See Pozen (1998); Hunting F. Deutsch. "Winning with Mutuals: Performance Is Not Enough." *Bank Management*, March/April 1994, 13–15; Eric Thebner. "Bridging the Needs Gap." *Banking Strategies*, November/December 1996, 59–69; and "Mutual Funds: Tax-Free Conversion of Common Trust Fund Finally Clears Congress. *Bank Policy* Report, 15, September 2, 1996, 12.

using mutual fund brokers to sell their funds particularly need to have a strong brand name to compete with well-known nonbank fund families, such as Vanguard and Fidelity.[35]

Banks generally offer load funds whereby banks reap income from sales fees. However, to attract customers, fees have often been waived or no-load funds offered as well. Chase Manhattan in June, 1998, launched a new family of funds that would be no-load on a pilot basis to self-directed retail customers. Such no-load funds in the past had been offered to institutional retirement clients, including 401(k) plans with assets under management for main banks, swelling 55% to $650 million in 1998 from 1997. This retail type of fund is in contrast to Chase Vista funds, which are distributed for fees for providing advice on fund selection. A 1994 Deloitte and Touche study surveying banks and thrifts found that in contrast to commercial banks, which were split in their offerings of no-load and load funds, thrifts had almost exclusively load funds.[36] The majority of the depository institutions surveyed cited marketing as the most difficult mutual-fund component to manage as well as being the most important success factor. To compete with other mutual funds, some large bank funds offer a toll-free number, providing customers with 24-hour service, seven days a week.

Regulatory Concerns   Regulators have been particularly concerned that investors in bank funds know that they are not insured by the Federal Deposit Insuran Coroporation (FDIC) and that such funds can be risky. Regulators have also been concerned about banks' confusing customers by selling uninsured products within the bank versus in a separate service office. Similarly, they have feared that banks with brand name funds may also confuse customers into thinking that these funds are insured. Banks have generally received excellent ratings in recent years for informing customers of the risks involved in mutual fund investing. Pozen (1998), for instance, reports that Baybank in its first year of operating its own mutual funds spend 20% of its time addressing regulatory issues, including requests from regulatory bodies concerning its proprietary funds. Baybank notified its customers 17 times in that first year that is their mutual funds were not FDIC insured.[37]

Since banks' mutual fund investors are often first-time stock/bond market investors, they also may run a greater risk of having funds withdrawn more quickly during stock/bond market downturns. First-time customers may be very risk

---

[35]See Pozen (1998) for a detailed discussion of Baybank's strategy.

[36]Niamh Ring. "Some Banks Spending to Construct 2nd Brand Identify for Fund Families." *American Banker*, August 32, 1998, 1, 8; Debra Cope. "Wells Fargo's Mutual Fund Brands Are Riding High." *American Banker*, January 20, 1993, 6; "Nationwide Study: Bankers Forsee Surge in Mutual Fund Activity." *Bank Management*, March/April 1994, 16–17; and Katharine Fraser. "In a Test, Chase to Offer No-Load Fund Family." *American Banker*, June 9, 1998, 15. Fraser points out that about 29 of the 103 bank proprietary fund families sold in the U.S. have no front-end charges, according to Lipper Analytical Service, Inc., Summit, New Jersey. Most banks have sales charges or loads because customers traditionally targeted have been willing to pay extra for advice on selecting investments. Citicorp also eliminated sales charges on its mutual funds last year with the introduction of a new family of funds, CitiSelect. Some bank funds that switched to no-load returned to load status, including Fleet Financial Group, Inc. and Key-Corp. Often banks waive sales charges for trust, 401(k), and other large clients who have already paid management fees.

[37]See Pozen (1998). Pozen points out that Congress proposed such a bill in 1994. Pozen provides an excellent case study for the marketing strategy of mutual funds by BayBank.

averse and, hence, if the risks involved in a mutual fund investment are not explained well, customers may be distraught when the value of their investments goes down, particularly when interest rates go up and net asset values go down for what appears to be very safe government bond funds. Banks with mutual funds or other securities activities are subject to the governance of the Security Exchange Commission, which has monitored banks' the marketing of their proprietary funds. The National Association of Securities Dealers has also had the right to approve some types of advertising and sales literature for bank fund programs. In early 1994, federal regulatory agencies issued guidelines for banks in terms of advertising claims, explicit rules for the disclosure of information about funds, and the qualifications and training necessary for personnel in terms of recommending or referring customers to funds, including detailed written disclosure statements. Although bank branch staffs can now sell funds, most banks require that only licensed personnel sell funds; nonlicensed personnel may be allowed to let customers know that funds are available without actively selling them. To give investment advice, an individual needs to be registered with the National Association of Securities Dealers and to be sponsored by a broker-dealer. At the minimum, to sell mutual funds an employee must have a Series 6 license, which permits giving advice on mutual funds and annuities only. To advise customers on other investments, an employee would need a Series 7 license. Congress has proposed bills that would put stricter standards on the selling of mutual funds by banks, including restricting nonlicensed personnel from making referrals.[38]

Profitability Trends and Performance for Bank Mutual Funds.   One recent study suggests that banks that diversified into mutual funds during 1987 to 1994 have enjoyed enhanced profitability and lower risk. A second study also finds that bank funds have performed close to market benchmarks. However, banks have often given fund fee waivers to increase fund sales, which reduces banks profit potential on funds. The study suggests that banks have generally done a poor job of marketing funds by not offering greater fund selection and more services, as fund families do. To generate greater fees to cover the expenses involved in managing and selling funds, banks need to generate greater asset volume. Investors in bank funds tend to be more risk averse than other mutual fund investors; consequently, money market mutual funds dominate in the industry, with 57% of fund assets invested in money market securities in 1994. These money market securities earn lower fees than higher-risk funds that invest in stocks and long-term bonds. Banks have often had to subsidize some funds with profits from other funds to provide a variety of funds for customers.[39]

Real Estate Activities.   All depository institutions can lend money secured by real property, but few can invest in real estate directly. In the 1980s many savings and loan (S&L) holding companies did invest in commercial real estate through service corporations, and many suffered large losses when commercial real estate prices fell in the later 1980s. Given the risk of direct equity investments, direct equity par-

---

[38]See Pozen (1998). Congress proposed such a bill in 1994.

[39]See Gallo, Apilado, and Kolari (1996); Gallo, Richardson, and Apilado (1996); W. Plasencia and D. Cope. "Banks Lose Their Lead in Growth of Fund Assets." *American Banker*, February 15, 1996, 2A; and Hunting F. Deutsch. "Winning with Mutuals: Performance Is Not Enough." *Bank Management*, March/April, 1994, 13–15.

ticipations were curtailed for thrifts under Financial Institutions Reform, Recovery, and Enforcement Act (FIRREA). As shown in Table 9.1, some state-chartered banks enjoy real estate brokerage, real estate development, and real estate equity participation privileges. Historically, regulations prohibited most national banks and their bank holding companies (BHCs) from owning real property, either directly or through subsidiaries. In early 1987, the Fed revised Regulation Y to permit BHCs to own real estate subsidiaries, with limitations tied to a BHC's capital ratios. National banks and their BHCs are prohibited from operating subsidiaries for either property management or residential real estate brokerage.[40]

Bank Insurance Activities   As noted in Chapter 4, until recently, most banks were limited to offering **credit life insurance** (insurance to pay a loan in the event of the borrower's death) to borrowers and the sale (but not the underwriting) of annuity policies to customers of all types. Under the Garn-St. Germain Act, Congress gave BHCs with total assets of less than $50 million in towns of less than 5,000 unlimited rights to engage in insurance activities, but other larger BHCs were prohibited from acting as underwriters or brokers of all insurance products, except credit life, accident, health, or unemployment insurance.[41]

Court Rulings Have Allowed Banks Greater Entry Into Insurance Activities
In recent years, the legal status of insurance activities in depositories has been less clearly defined, and changes are occurring rapidly under the proposed Financial Modernization bill, which would allow insurance companies and banks to be affiliated. In 1992, the Supreme Court approved a ruling that established the right of banks of all sizes to sell insurance nationally from small towns. The insurance activities of state-chartered commercial banks and savings banks are left to state laws, and many state laws are more liberal, allowing savings banks and some state-chartered commercial banks to engage in various aspects of the insurance business (see Table 9.1). In 1988, voters in California approved provisions under Proposition 103 that allowed state-chartered commercial banks to sell insurance. This opened the door for Security Pacific, Wells Fargo, First Interstate, and Bank of America to establish insurance operations in their previously owned state-chartered subsidiaries or newly acquired state-chartered banks. A federal appeals court in 1991 overturned a Fed

---

[40]Some depositories may own real estate not of their own choosing through foreclosures, i.e., other real estate owned (OREO), which does not violate laws prohibiting equity positions in real estate property, although limits are placed on the length of time the property can be held before sale. For more details on laws and regulations applying to banks, see Felgran (1988).

[41]The Garn-St. Germain Act also contained a "grandfather clause" that permitted large BHCs with any other kind of insurance services allowed by the Fed before May 1, 1982, to retain them. For more details on Garn-St. Germain insurance provisions, see Felgran (1985). The OCC ruled in 1986 that banks could sell insurance nationwide from banking offices located in towns with populations of less than 5,000. Following this ruling, several large institutions began to set up nationwide distribution systems in very small towns. However, a test case ruling by a court of appeals in 1992 brought these activities to a halt, stating that national banks did not have the authority to sell insurance at all, even from small towns. In 1993, the U.S. Supreme Court gave banks a long-awaited victory by overturning the Court of Appeals ruling, thus establishing the right of banks to sell insurance from small towns.

ruling and allowed out-of-state banks to purchase state-chartered banks and sell insurance nationwide as allowed by state law in Delaware.[42]

In 1995, the Supreme Court ruled in favor of the legality of national banks selling annuities in *NationsBank v. Variable Annuity Life Insurance Company*. Also, a 1996 Supreme Court decision called *Barnett* allows national banks to sell most types of insurance anywhere from an office in any location with a population of 5,000 or less, regardless of state laws that would otherwise prohibit such activities. Hence, affiliates of BHCs can enter and conduct insurance activities in other states if they operate in a town with such a population. Although the *Barnett* decision did not rule explicitly on whether national banks may market insurance products outside the small towns in which they are operating, other U.S. Court of Appeals decisions in 1993 and 1995 ruled that national banks may market insurance products outside the small towns in which their offices are located. In 1997 the OCC supported a proposal by First Union Corporation to conduct insurance agency activities (acting as a broker versus underwriting insurance) through subsidiaries of its affiliate national banks.

Recent Activities   Banks have been purchasing independent insurance agencies recently, and acquisition prices as a multiple of revenues have risen as banks vie for a limited number of agencies that are successful and growing. In June of 1998, agencies fetched about 1.3 times revenues on average, up from 1 times revenues less than a year before.[43] A few large banks are also planning strategies to put them in the forefront of bank insurance programs. BankBoston, for instance, is attempting to integrate its insurance sales with the bank's retail operations, emulating the European *bancassurance* model. By using this model of a joint bank/insurance company, European financial institutions such as Lloyds TSB in the United Kingdom, Credit Agricole in France, and Banco Bilbao Vizcaya in Spain have profitably cross-sold insurance to greater than 25% of their customers, generating a return greater than 20% on sales. In 1998, BankBoston sold term life and several other policies using direct mail and licensed specialists. On the retail side, it also sold annuities. The bank's insurance chief plans to enlist branch employees and even the internet to broaden the

---

[42]In contrast to California, many states that had fewer restrictions on insurance activities by banks were unit banking states that did not allow branching. Laws were more liberal based on the rationale that unit banks provide less competition for existing insurers than do banks with extensive branch networks. See Sam Zuckerman. "Banks Gain New Insurance Powers." *American Banker*, February 26, 1990, 1, 13, and Yvette D. Kantrow. "First Interstate Targets Insurance." *American Banker*, April 11, 1990, 21. Some smaller states, including Delaware and South Dakota, developed creative laws to encourage financial institutions to come to their states, allowing out-of-state depository institutions to purchase state-chartered banks and set up insurance operations that could be marketed outside of their states. The Fed was not amused and forbid any non-out-of-state banks from entering the insurance market through this loophole. However, a federal appeals court overturned the Fed's prohibition in Delaware in 1991 and ruled that selling insurance by Delaware-chartered banks was permissible nationwide. See William Gruber. "Fed Blocks Citicorp on Insurance." *Chicago Tribune*, August 2, 1985, Sec. 2, B1; Wade Lambert and David B. Hilder. "Banks Cleared to Underwrite, Sell Insurance." *The Wall Street Journal*, June 11, 1991; Melanie L. Fein. "Insurance Powers Gains of Barnett Decisions Clouded by 7th Circuit." *Banking Policy Report*, 15, June 17, 1996, 1, 12; and Brian W. Smith, Diane E. Ambler, and Charles M. Horn. "The Barnett Decision: Another Step Toward Expanded Bank Powers." *Banking Policy Report*, 15 May 16, 1996, 1, 17.

[43]See Michael O'D. Moore. "Insurance Agencies Grow Hungry for Bank Buyouts." *American Banker*, June 16, 1998, 1, 14.

distribution of the bank's insurance products. The bank also plans to administer small-business HMO (health maintenance operation) plans.

BankBoston's new strategy is in contrast to most banks, which have not entered the insurance marketplace in the wake of the Supreme Court's favorable 1996 decision. Fleet began an insurance unit in 1994, but recently scaled back by closing the unit, firing its 50 telephone-based life insurance agents, and folding its modest insurance program into retail operations.[44]

Other banks have joint ventures with insurance companies to sell insurance to their customers. For example in 1998 Comerica, Inc. decided to team up with American Direct Business Insurance in Windsor, Connecticut, to market insurance to the bank's smallest commercial customers instead of buying it. BankAmerica and Chase Manhattan, among others, also opted to have marketing arrangements with property and casualty brokers or underwriters to sell directly to bank customers. A survey by Risk Management Associates for the American Bankers Association and the Independent Insurance Agents of America found that 41% of 307 banks thinking about entering the insurance business preferred forming joint ventures with agencies and 35% preferred acquisitions. Acquisitions are often too expensive to build or buy in cases in which products are best sold by phone to thousands of very small customers.[45]

Insurance Activities of Thrifts and CUs   In 1967, federally chartered S&Ls were permitted to broker all types of insurance except private mortgage insurance and to engage in limited underwriting through affiliated service corporations. For state-chartered institutions, regulations varied widely. Under FIRREA, state-chartered thrifts were only allowed to engage in activities similar to federally chartered firms. Some states that restrict commercial bank entry into insurance give savings banks considerable authority to pursue insurance. Savings banks in Massachusetts, Connecticut, and New York have a long and successful involvement in life insurance, rooted in their origin as depositories for the urban working class. By eliminating agent commissions, the nearly 300 savings banks in these states offer customers life insurance at a lower cost than comparable policies marketed by insurance companies. Many CUs have offered insurance similar to credit life for several years, as well as other types of life and property/liability insurance policies as sources of fee-based income. For nationally chartered CUs, insurance must be offered through CU Service Organizations (CUSOs). CUSOs may offer policies underwritten by other insurance providers. Among the largest underwriters with which CUSOs deal is the CUNA Mutual Insurance Group. CUNA Mutual, founded by CUs for CUs, is a major national provider of credit life insurance, based on dollar volume of coverage in force. It also underwrites a variety of other insurance products for CU members nationwide.

Liability and Regulatory Risks for Depository Institutions Entering the Insurance Arena   Large banks, by virtue of their size and power and, hence, often a negative opinion by consumer groups, are particularly vulnerable to lawsuits and regula-

---

[44]See Michael O'D. Moore. "BankBoston Going Full Bore with Insurance Plan." *American Banker*, July 28, 1998, 1, 10, and John Garabedian and David Taylor. "Raising Aspirations." *Bank Strategies*, May/June 1998, 39–46. Garabedian and Taylor point out that critical factors to the success of bancassurers include the commitment of senior management to bancassuarance as a core strategy, a well-trained "generalist" sales force that is integrated with a bank's branches, simplified products that appeal to consumers, and a good incentive structure for both branch managers and salespeople.

[45]Michael O'D. Moore. "Agency Alliances Seen Gaining on Buyouts." American Banker, June 16, 1998, 15.

tory complaints as they begin marketing insurance products. For example, when Nationsbank entered the Texas insurance market by selling insurance through a branch in Hutchins, Texas, a town with less than 5,000 people near Dallas and Fort Worth, it received a consumer complaint when its literature listed an 800 phone number to an out-of-state affiliate. The consumer argued that by having customers for insurance call the nationwide number versus the Hutchins branch, Nationsbank was violating "the small town branch" requirement that allowed the bank to sell insurance nationwide.

Traditional insurers, such as Prudential, have also had class action lawsuits caused by agents trying to persuade customers to switch policies to generate commissions for the agents. Consequently, banks, like other insurers, need to dedicate resources and attend to the quality of their agents and their insurance business. In particular, as pointed out in a recent *Banking Strategies* article by Linda Corman, banks need to analyze the political culture in each state in which they are operating to avoid the sale of inappropriate products and to carefully train and monitor agents, including monitoring the licensing of agents in each state.[46] Banks also need to be careful about agents who pressure customers to purchase products. States also have various laws concerning whether insurance products can be sold to customers with loans pending at a bank or the specification that if such a product is sold that the acceptance of such a bank loan is not contingent on this sale. In some states, such as Texas, an agent may need numerous different licenses to sell different types of insurance products. Some states even demand that telemarketers must be licensed. Use of information in loan files to find insurance customers by a bank may also be forbidden. Rebates on insurance premiums in return for buying other bank products may also be illegal, and tying products to the acceptance of a loan is universally illegal. Banks must inform customers in every state that insurance products such as annuities are not FDIC insured. In effect, banks need to be careful in selling insurance products and making sure that a product is needed by a customer. Given complicated state laws for insurance operations, banks often benefit by having strategic alliances with insurance firms that have expertise in selling insurance products in different states.[47]

Movements Toward Comprehensive Risk Management

As banks enter new product areas that generate noninterest revenue, banks and regulators have been concerned about developing comprehensive new approaches to risk management. The value at risk (VAR) approach has become widely accepted by practitioners and regulators. In August 1996, U.S. Bank Regulatory Agencies adopted a market risk amendment (MRA) voted on by International regulators to the 1988 Basle Capital Accord. This MRA became effective in January 1998. It requires that banks with significant trading activity set aside captial to cover market risk exposure based on a bank's own value at risk estimates. However, many critics point out that while VAR is a useful tool, it needs to be used with caution as a measure for bank risk. Banks need to have a risk management program that encompasses broader efforts to control risk, including developing appropriate incentives and internal controls within a financial institution.[48]

---

[46]See Linda Corman. "The Liability Trap." *Banking Strategies*, July/August 1998, 23–26.
[47]Ibid.
[48]The following section on VAR models draws particularly from Simons (1996). See also Culp, Miller, and Neves (1998); Venkataraman (1997); and Saunders (1997).

What is VAR? Essentially, VAR asks "how much could the value of a bank's portfolio decline over a given period of time with a given probability?," i.e., how much money might the bank lose in a specified length of time? For example, a bank might want to know, based on a 99% probability using historical data on interest rate changes, what the expected loss would be on its bond portfolio in a given day or a given week. Similarly, if the bank does foreign exchange trading or has a portfolio denominated in a foreign currency, it might want to estimate its expected loss on its foreign exchange portfolio based on historical variation in currency rates. Hence, the bank needs to:

(1) designate a given time period to examine, such as a day or a few days
(2) designate a given probability of loss, based on a given statistical distribution, such as the normal distribution;[49] and
(3) obtain historic data on the volatility of interest rates, foreign exchange rates, or stock price movements, etc., to calculate expected price changes for the bank's investments or trading activities in these areas.

J.P. Morgan's RiskMetrics Model One of the most extensively used VAR techniques is RiskMetrics, developed by J.P. Morgan. This technique estimates the market risk of fixed income securities, foreign exchange, and equities based on a huge volume of historic data.[50] Under this model Daily Earnings at Riask is defined as the dollar value of a particular position (bonds, stock, foreign exchange) times the potential adverse change in that value on a daily basis. Generally, a distribution of price movements (e.g., the normal distribution) is used, and potential adverse changes are calculated based on the historic standard deviation in prices at a 99% or 95% confidence level. Historic simulations and the correlations between different types of assets that reduce a bank's total portfolio sensitivity are also incorporated to calculate the total risk for all the bank's positions. For instance, taking the dollar value of each of the bank's positions times the expected price volatility on a daily basis in that market, a bank might be expected to lose $50,000 on its fixed income portfolio, $30,000 on foreign exchange positions, and $100,000 on its equity positions on a daily basis. Its total DEAR is the sum of these, $180,000. However, if price movements for each of the positions are negatively correlated (move in opposition to each other) the DEAR for the entire bank portfolio will be lower, since the opposite movements in prices will reduce the expected earnings at risk. Consequently, adjusting for negative correlations, the DEAR for the entire portfolio may be $150,000 instead.[51]

Limitations of VAR Although VAR techniques have been widely accepted and used, in recent years analysts have criticized these models for being deemed a *panacea*

---

[49]For a discussion of other types of distributions and estimation techniques that might be used, see Venkataraman (1997).

[50]For a detailed description of J. P. Morgan's *RiskMetrics*, see Saunders (1997). As Saunders points out, J. P. Morgan's *RiskMetrics* calculates DEAR in three areas: fixed income, foreign exchange, and equities. J. P. Morgan has made its model available to the public, including data to estimate daily earnings at risk on the Internet. The Bank for International Settlements Basle Committee on Banking Supervision proposed a bank trading risk model discussed in detail in Saunders (1997).

[51]See Saunders (1997) for a detailed mathematical example for calculating the portfolio DEAR for a bank that incorporates the correlation between different bank positions.

versus being considered what they are, one useful tool. Limitations are that VAR models focus on a single point in a distribution of potential profits and losses versus looking at an entire distribution. Models also do not include information on how risks would be managed in extreme market crises, since data is based on normal situations. VAR is not very useful for long-term bank assets and liabilities that are infrequently traded, such as deposits and loans. Other methods may be more useful for depository institutions and other financial institutions such as insurance companies, which also have long-term assets. Similarly, banks have many other types of risk besides market risk, including credit risk, liquidity risk, operational risk, and legal risk, as discussed in Chapter 6.[52]

A well-known bank consultant, Edward Furash, chairman of Furash & Co., argues that banks must develop a comprehensive risk management system to ensure that they can take and be paid for greater risk without suffering more losses than competitors that take less risk. As he states:

> "The goal of a comprehensive risk management system is to apply a bank's risk-taking capacity profitably. To this end, senior management must aggregate and quantify its risk management resources—its 'risk budget' so to speak—in order to allocate these resources to areas of greatest potential."[53]

Unfortunately, most banks have a fragmented risk assessment system that evaluates and manages risk within each line of business at a line management level. Few banks have a formal, comprehensive, institution-wide risk assessment system to optimize and prioritize a bank's resources for risk management.

A Different Concept for Risk-Profitability Management: EVA

EVA is an overall risk management and profitability measure that has been used for over a decade by industrial companies. In recent years, financial institutions have begun adopting this technique. EVA is similar to the concept of RAROC discussed in the previous chapter. Under RAROC, greater amounts of equity capital are allocated to riskier bank activities, and accordingly the return on any activity must be sufficient to compensate for the total cost of this activity including the weighted capital allocation. Similarly, EVA provides an overall dollar measure of a firm's profit after the cost of the capital employed for all activities is subtracted:

$$\text{EVA} = \text{NOPAT} - (\text{Financial Capital Employed Cost of Capital}) \qquad (9.1)$$

---

[52]Simons (1996). Culp, Miller, and Neves (1998) point out alternative measures for risk that may be more useful to corporations and financial institutions, including cash flow volatility, RAROC (discussed in Chapter 8), and a shortfall technique to estimate the probability that the value of assets will fall below that of liabilities and require a contribution by the plan sponsor for pension plans.

[53]See Furash (1995). Also, see John P. Drzik. "CFO Survey: Moving Toward Comprehensive Risk Management." *Bank Management*, May/June 1995, 38–39. Drzik points out that a 1995 BAI Risk Management Survey showed that banks had made significant progress in developing and implementing risk measures that were used not only for risk control purposes, but also for performance measurement and pricing. Seventy-five percent of participants answered that the primary determinant for important consideration in most business decisions should be risk-adjusted profitability measures. Only 40% of respondents employed a risk capital concept in a survey performed four years earlier.

NOPAT is the bank's operating profits before any costs paid to investors and excluding any accounting conventions that misrepresent cash flows. The Cost of Capital (total financial capital supplied for the bank's operations—its cost as a rate) is subtracted from NOPAT to get EVA.

For instance, if a bank had a NOPAT of $50 million and $60 million of capital was supplied with a weighted average cost of capital of 15%, then:

$$\text{EVA} = \$50 - \$60\,(0.15) = \$50 - \$9 = \$41 \text{ million}$$

EVA implies that bank managers must generate sufficient revenues to cover both operating expenses and the returns demanded by investors based on the capital allocated for the banks' activities. EVA ensures that managers realize their obligations to stockholders as well as long-term debtholders. It also provides a formal mechanism by which to quantify the bank's overall risk structure in terms of the amount of capital allocated and its cost.

In addition to providing an overall measure of economic value created by a firm's operations, EVA can be used for individual decisions, such as determining whether different types of bank operations are profitable, with capital allocated to based on the risk of these activities. By using a dollar figure versus a percentage return ratio, as in RAROC, the actual incremental profitability of individual activities can be determined based on the size of the capital investment in a particular activity. Equity capital is allocated to different activities according to an activity's risk, so more risky activities will have a higher dollar cost of capital associated with them. In an article on EVA applied to banks, Dennis G. Uyemura, Charles C. Kantor, and Justin M. Pettit of Stern Stewart & Co. point out that EVA provides advantages by being:

> a 'top-down' process in that it can provide management and the Board of Directors with valuable comparative risk-and-return metrics for each of the major lines of businesses, product lines, and customer segments within the consolidated company. . . . The EVA Financial Management System encompasses the calculation and use of EVA for all aspects of financial measurement and decision-making at all levels of the organization. These activities include, but are not limited to, budgeting, strategic planning, product pricing, financial reporting, internal and external communications, and acquisition pricing. It also entails calculating EVA at various hierarchical levels and in various dimensions, including lines of businesses, functional departments, products, customer segments, and customer relationships. . . . Moreover, it is possible to discern which aspects of each detailed activity are most important in the EVA outcome of the analysis. This type of analysis is referred to as an 'EVA drivers' analysis in that it identifies the specific aspects and parameters of any product or service that are key to realizing a sustainable, positive EVA.[54]

In contrast to the more commonly used, conventional, fragmented systems at banks that come from the bottom up, EVA provides a way of integrating risk and return analyses for a bank and provides an overall top down system. EVA can be also used for objective goal-setting for incentive compensation plans in which officers are rewarded for the economic value added that they provide to providers of capital incorporating the cost of risk capital needed for different ventures.

---

[54]See Uyemura, Kantor, and Pettit (1996), 103. This provides detailed examples of how a bank can implement the EVA financial system for different types of activities.

Models based on EVA or RAROC quantify the dollar profitability or dollar return on a bank's different activities (including commercial lending, securities trading, and other investment activities) based on their risk by providing a charge for the capital required to support each activity. Thus, bank managers are involved in all aspects of risk management including "identification, quantification, and pricing." Banks, in turn, can use these models as strategic decision tools to evaluate business decisions, such as whether to enter or exit a given product line. Other more sophisticated models may be more effective in dealing with risks that are more complex. Innovative uses of technology can also be used to improve banks' monitoring of different types of risk.[55]

BANKS' ENTRANCE INTO NONTRADITIONAL FEE-GENERATING ACTIVITIES AND CULTURAL CLASHES

As banks have entered new nontraditional activities, they have often faced cultural clashes. When Bankers Trust changed its focus from being a traditional commercial bank to becoming an international merchant bank, it put in place incentive compensation plans to encourage individuals, including loan officers, to generate profits associated with Bankers Trust's new goals. Underlying a new RAROC system to measure employee performance, Bankers Trust hoped to develop a more "entrepreneurial" culture whereby employees would show more initiative to find and take advantage of new opportunities for profits. The bank also desired, however, that employees in different areas would work together for a common purpose, such as loan officers in the banking area referring corporate customers to the corporate services and investment banking areas.

Problems occurred, however, with occasional fights over who would receive credit for a transaction that involved a referral. Other problems involved developing a common incentive compensation scheme across the bank. For instance, traders were held to a high risk-adjusted rate of return on capital, but at the same time they could make unlimited compensation. A top successful trader could in effect receive compensation higher than the chairman of the bank. Investment bankers in corporate finance had to be paid higher salaries than commercial lenders to be able to attract quality employees. However, Bankers Trust also included bonuses for cooperation with commercial banking officers to develop a sense of common purpose across the bank. Commercial lenders were also given large bonuses for directing business to the corporate finance area. In this way Bankers Trust was able to provide a more seamless integration and prevent some jealous noncooperation between the very different commercial lending and corporate finance cultures. Other banks that have purchased securities firms and have not paid close attention to cultural differences have been less successful and have found themselves subject to serious defections on the part of valuable employees.[56]

---

[55]Ibid.

[56]See Susan Crevoor, Dwight B. Crane, and Robert G. Eccles. "Bankers Trust New York Corporation." Samuel L. Hayes, III, and David M. Meerschwam, eds. *Managing Financial Institutions: Cases Within the Financial Services Industry*. New York: Harcourt Brace (Dryden Press), 1992, 27–47; Kreps, Daniel J. "Risk-Based Strategic Planning." *The Bankers Magazine*, March/April 1994, 52–54.

Fee Income From Off-Balance Sheet Activities

Banks also receive fee income from a number of off-balance sheet items including loan commitments, note issuance facilities, letters of credit, foreign exchange services, and derivative activities (contracts for futures, forwards, interest rate swaps, and other derivative contracts). While many of these activities are limited to very large banks, loan brokerage, including loan sales and securitization, have become more accessible to medium-sized and small depository institutions as well. This final section provides a brief overview of some of these activities, with particular emphasis on loan securitization and loan sales. Derivative activities will be discussed later in Chapters 17 and 18.

Loan Commitments, Letters of Credit, Note Issuance Facilities, and Foreign Exchange Services[57]

Loan Commitments   **Loan commitments** are legally binding agreements by banks promising to guarantee that a certain amount of funds will be available for a borrower over a given time period for a given rate. Banks charge a fee for this guarantee. They often charge an additional back-end fee for any unused balances that the firm does not draw down from the given amount. For instance, a bank could charge a 0.25% fee for the total amount to be borrowed plus a 0.25% back-end fee on the unused amount.

Letters of Credit   **Letters of credit** include standby and commercial letters of credit. Standby letters of credit provide a promise by a bank that it will perform a contract in the event that the buyer of the letter of credit defaults, i.e., a letter of credit substitutes a bank's credit for that of the buyer of the standby letter of credit. Standby letters of credit are bought by institutions, such as a company issuing commercial paper or other securities, as well as individuals. By buying a standby letter of credit, a firm can have a stronger credit rating for an issue and accordingly a lower risk-premium on the cost of its securities. Commercial letters of credit are similar but guarantee the credit standing of a buyer for an international trade transaction. These letters of credit make importing/exporting easier by substituting the bank's credit for that of an importer. For taking the risk that the contract might not be fulfilled, the bank receive a fee, such as 0.25% of the amount guaranteed.

Note Issuance Facilities   Banks often facilitate private placement transactions for foreign investors through note issuance facilities. If a borrower has a problem obtaining financing at some time over the contract period involved, often two to seven years, the bank will buy the short-term notes. Thus, the bank has issued in effect a time of loan commitment for a note issuance contract. In return for this commitment, banks receive fees from 0.25% to 0.75%.

Foreign Exchange Transactions   Large banks provide services in foreign exchange markets by making currency exchanges and receiving brokerage fees. Similarly, banks offer traveler check services for a fee by selling traveler's checks in different currencies. They also make forward arrangements by promising to buy or sell

---

[57]See Saunders (1997); Koch (1995); and Sinkey (1998).

foreign currency for a given price at a given future date, receiving a brokerage fee for these services. These services facilitate transactions for businesses and individuals, and in return banks make fees.

These activities provide significant income for large banks but also additional risks, for instance, if a buyer of a standby letter of credit defaults. Fees are priced to compensate for the contingent risks involved in these activities. As noted in Chapter 5, such off-balance sheet item activities have grown enormously in the past decade.

LOAN SALES

Banks have been active in the past decade as loan brokers, negotiating large loans and selling them or selling portions of them to other financial institutions, including pension funds, insurance companies, and other depository institutions. The sales help customers by allowing them to maintain their relationship with their bank, which goes through the credit analysis and loan approval process, but allowing much longer-term loans to be made that can be sold to life insurance companies or pension funds, which have longer-term investment horizons than the bank. The bank benefits by allowing it to take longer-term loans off its balance sheet, reducing the bank's interest rate risk, yet at the same time satisfying customers who want longer-term loans. Also, by selling the loan without recourse, legally, the bank is no longer responsible for the loan and is no longer subject to the credit risk associated with the loan. By acting as a broker the bank also receives fee income, and the loan that it has made has no effect on the required capital it must hold on assets if the loan is sold without recourse.[58]

There are different types of loan sales. The most common form is *the participation* whereby the originating bank continues to hold the formal contract between the bank and the borrower. The originating bank continues to service the loan, collecting payments, overseeing the collateral, and keeping the books. In the case of a silent participation, the borrower may not be aware of the sale. A less common type is *the assignment*, in which the debtor-creditor relationship is transferred to the loan buyer, which gives the purchaser the right to take actions against the borrower if payments are not made. The originating bank, however, may retain the lien on any collateral backing the loan or some other obligations. The novation, the least common type of arrangement, transfers all rights and obligations of the selling bank to the buyer, and the originator is completely free from any legal obligations to either the borrower or the loan buyer. Nonetheless, selling a loan is generally less of a "clean break" than the sale of other types of assets. Even if loans are sold without recourse, banks implicitly have responsibilities to the buyer of the loan in terms of maintaining the reputation of the bank. If a bank simply sold its worse loans to other institutions, it would lose its reputation and goodwill with those institutions.[59]

However, banks can sell troubled loans to investors at large discounts. For instance, in the mid-1980s banks that had excessive loan exposure to Latin America and Mexico sold loans to other financial institutions and investors, taking a significant loss. To make such loans more sellable, the U.S. government has provided loan guarantees for several years to investors purchasing such loans. Under the U.S. Treasury's 1989 Brady plan, countries were also allowed to the exchange original

---

[58]See Koch (1995); Joseph G. Haubrich. "The Evolving Loan Sales Market." *Economic Commentary* (Federal Reserve Bank of Cleveland), July 15, 1993, 1–5.

[59]Ibid.

loans they made that were nonconforming at U.S. banks for long-term bonds with longer maturities and more favorable terms. These debt-to-debt swaps are known as Brady Bonds. By the mid-1980s, a strong secondary market for trading less-developed country debt emerged with large commercial banks and investment banks serving as brokers and dealers. Less-developed country debt brokers also made arrangement to swap debt for equity investments that could benefit foreign investors who wished to make fixed capital investments in their respective countries.[60]

SECURITIZATION

Loan securitization, which is similar to loan sales, involves removing loans from a bank's balance sheet and selling them to investors. However, before being sold, the loans are packaged into securities with characteristics that make them attractive to large and small investors. The mechanics of securitization are subject to a variety of tax, securities, regulatory, and accounting laws.

Structure of a Securitization   Figure 9.2 shows a brief outline of the mechanics for securitization for automobile loans. On a nonrecourse basis, a depository institution originating the loans sells a pool of loans and collateral values to a limited-purpose corporation. The limited-purpose corporation, often a subsidiary of an investment bank setting up the deal or a special subsidiary of the originating bank, exists solely to act as an intermediary between the buyer and seller to transfers assets to a trust. The trust purchases loans from the limited-purpose company and packages the loans into certificates that can be sold to investors. If the trust has no recourse with the originating bank for loan losses, the bank can then remove the loans sold from its balance sheet. To make the certificates that represent "fractional and undivided" interests in the pool of assets more attractive to investors, an insurance company surety bond or a bank letter of credit is purchased to guarantee a portion of the loan pool.

The trust generally also asks an agency to rate the certificates. With a portion of the pool guaranteed and the originating bank putting aside part of its future servicing income from the loan as security to back the pool, a high rating, the AA or AAA required by many investors, is often given if the loans are randomly selected and of decent quality. Standard and Poor's often requires for a AAA rating that the third-party credit enhancement and excess servicing fee put in trust be at least 8% of the value of the underlying loan portfolio if a bank has a history of losses of about 40 basis points per year. The trust generally hires an underwriter to set the initial price and market the securities to the public. The bank continues to service the loans and collect servicing fees for doing this. Collections of principal and interest net of the originating bank's servicing fees are deposited each month with the trustee, which in turn passes payments to investors as interest. All principal payments are passed on to the investor as well. Mortgage loans are securitized in a similar way (discussed in greater detail in Chapter 19). However, often government agencies such as the Government National Mortgage Association or quasi-government agencies, such as the Federal National Mortgage Association or Federal Home Loan Mortgage Corporation, provide the trust, investment banker, and guarantor roles.[61]

---

[60]See Saunders (1997), Chapter 15, 291–322.
[61]This section draws heavily from *Bank Performance Annual* (1988), 107–111.

Figure 9.2   ✦   MECHANICS OF SECURITIZATION

Structure of an Automobile Loan Securitization

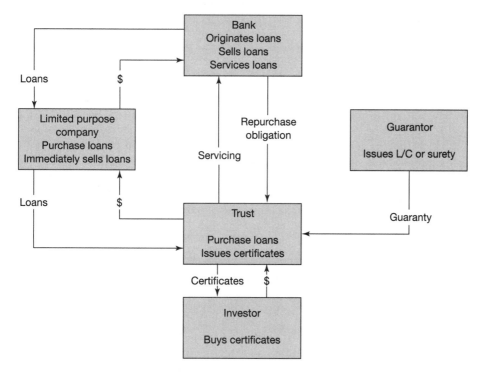

Cash Flows of Hypothetical Automobile Loan Securitization

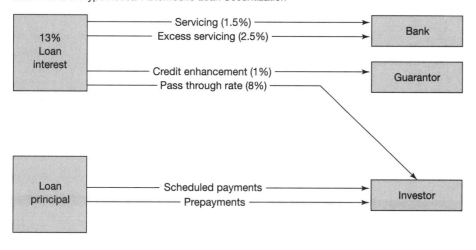

Source: Bank Performance Annual. (1988), Figure 3, p. 108, and Figure 4, p. 109.

Example of Cash Flows in a Hypothetical Securitization   The lower panel of Figure 9.2 shows the mechanics of a securitization. Automobile loans with a 13% interest rate are sold. The originating bank receives 1.5% of the loan amount for servicing the loans plus a 2.5% excess servicing fee that is reserved for future losses on the loans. If losses do not occur over the life of the securities, the bank is entitled to this excess fee as well. The guarantor receives 1% for the letter of credit. The remaining 8% is the pass-through interest rate that investors receive who purchase the certificates for automobile receivables (CARS).

Table 9.2 shows the cash proceeds based on automobile receivables of $100 million with a coupon rate of 8% with monthly payments and a maximum maturity of four years. The average life of the CARS is actually only two years, because borrowers are likely to prepay their loans early, particularly if rates fall. Hence, investors in effect are purchasing securities that have an expected life of two years. There is some prepayment risk because if the security is prepaid the investors will have to reinvest the principal payments that they receive early at a lower rate. This prepayment risk is particularly serious for mortgage securities, so investors will generally demand a premium on the rate they receive over comparable securities.

Table 9.2 ✦ **Pricing Summary of Hypothetical Automobile Loan Securitization**

Collateral

Type	Automobile receivables
Face amount	$100 Million
Amortization method	Effective interest
Weighted average APR	13%
Servicing fee	1.5%
Payment frequency	Monthly
Maturity range	18–48 Months
Weighted average maturity	24 Months

Asset-Backed Security

Face amount	$100 Million
Coupon	8% (Monthly)
Maximum maturity	4 Years
Average life	2 Years

Proceeds

Gross (sold at par)	$100,000,000
Underwriting fee	−500,000
Issuing expenses	−250,000
First-year credit enhancement	−100,000[1]
	$ 99,150,000

Net

Present value of excess servicing flows	+4,300,000[2]
Net present value	$103,450,000[3]

---

[1]Assumes a letter of credit for 10 percent of the transaction size at a cost of 1 percent.

[2]This can be reported as income at the time of sale under GAAP (but *not* RAP) after deduction of appropriate loan loss and prepayment provisions.

[3]This figure would be slightly less after deduction for cost of subsequent credit enhancement. This added cost would be a function of the amount of actual outstandings in years two, three, and four.

Source: Bank Performance Annual (1988), Table 2, p. 110.

The originating bank sells the loans for $100,000,000. After paying $500,000 for the underwriting fee, $250,000 for issuing expenses, and $100,000 for the first-year credit enhancement, the bank receives a net of $99,150,000. However, taking the present value of future servicing fees, the bank actually receives a net present value for the securitization of $103,450,000. This example shows securitizations to be quite profitable. In addition, banks no longer have to hold capital on these loans or pay interest on the deposits used to finance such loans. The bank has new-found liquidity and has cash to make new loans if it wishes. Banks can also get rid of long-term loans, such as home mortgage loans, to adjust their interest rate gaps and reduce their interest rate risk positions. For the loans to be completely off the bank's balance sheet for regulatory and accounting purposes, the loans must be sold with no recourse. Because packaged loans must have similar maturities, loan rates, and other characteristics, commercial loans that are tailor-made are difficult to securitize. Congress has recently discussed the possibility of developing agencies to help securitize small business loans to make more capital available from banks to small businesses. Securitizations are packaged in many innovative ways to make them more attractive to investors with different maturity and prepayment risk preferences. Collateralized Mortgage Obligations (Chapter 19) are repackaged mortgage securities that are made more attractive to investors.[62]

SUMMARY

The focus of this chapter was the increasingly important role of fee-based services in depository institution management. Fee income services help depository institutions to be more competitive by offering new types of services and products. Fee-based products also often require only a small capital investment. Experience also suggests that some sources of fee income are steady, providing reliable income for banks during downturns in traditional lending. Fee-based products include traditional ones, such as trust departments and correspondent banking, and new ones, such as securities underwriting, mutual funds, brokerage activities, insurance, securitization, and other off-balance sheet activities. Many banks have developed comprehensive fee-income strategies that involve a variety of activities that often complement each other. Noninterest revenue has become a much larger source of total revenues for depository institutions in the last two decades, rising from about 25% in 1984 to almost 40% in the first quarter of 1998.

Regulatory changes in recent years have allowed depository institutions to engage in greater securities, insurance, mutual fund, and brokerage activities that generate considerable fee income. These new activities entail new risks that depository institutions need to monitor. Regulators have been particularly concerned over such new risks and have issued guidelines for banks to follow to control risks. Depository institutions need to develop comprehensive risk management techniques. VAR is a method used to measure a bank's overall trading investment exposure on different types of investments and foreign currency. VAR is a useful tool, but it fails to consider many other bank risks, such as credit, liquidity, operational, and legal risks. EVA provides a more comprehensive risk measure for a depository institution's overall profitability based on the risk of different types of activities. It can also be used to evaluate the profitability of new activities that a depository plans to enter. An EVA analysis allocates a capital cost to different activities based on their respective risk, similar to the RAROC method.

Off-balance sheet items including security options, letters of credit, loan commitments, and loan sales provide banks with significant fee income.

As depository institutions hire personnel for new activities or acquire nonbank firms, they need to develop policies to prevent cultural clashes and promote cooperation between divisions within their organizations.

---

[62]Ibid. Also, see Saunders (1997), Chapter 26, and Koch (1995), Chapter 17.

Suggested Cases

Case 9-286-005, Harvard Business School: Bankers Trust New York Corporation, 1985.

This case deals with cultural clashes between Bankers Trust's traditional banking divisions and its investment banking divisions as it attempts to shift from being a traditional commercial bank to becoming an international merchant bank. The case also introduces Bankers Trust's attempt to create a risk-adjusted performance compensation system for different types of activities and the development of the first RAROC system.

"Case 14: Signet Bank Corporation." Darden School, University of Virginia: Richard D. Crawford and William W. Sihler. *Financial Service Organizations: Cases in Strategic Management*. New York: HarperCollins College Publishers, 1994.

This case analyzes Signet's decision to develop a mutual fund product to support a consumer banking strategy. It deals with some of the realities that banks face in organizing and selling mutual funds, including how to compensate bank employees to cross-sell funds and how to integrate trust activities and mutual fund management activities within the regulatory framework when banks were first allowed to manage their own funds in the early 1990s.

"Case 3: CARS (Certificates for Automobile Receivables)." Darden School, University of Virginia: Richard D. Crawford and William W. Sihler. *Financial Service Organizations: Cases in Strategic Management*. New York: HarperCollins College Publishers, 1994. This case provides an overview of the history of loan securitization and an introduction to the characteristics and structure of asset-backed securities, focusing on CARs.

Questions

1. Why have depository institutions taken on greater fee-income businesses in the past decade? On average, what percentage of total revenue has come from noninterest revenue for U.S. banks in recent years?
2. How did National City Corporation implement a fee-income strategy? Was this strategy successful? Explain NCC's keys for success.
3. Who are the major banks in terms of credit card accounts and loans? What is a credit card bank? Using MBNA as an example, do credit card banks appear profitable?
4. What are the two primary aspects of a bank's investment management and trust businesses? What types of activities are most profitable? When were national banks allowed to engage in nationwide trust operations? How can banks become more competitive—what types of services do trust customers want?
5. Explain how correspondent banks' pricing techniques have evolved in the past decade. What factors influenced the change? What types of services do correspondent banks provide to smaller banks? Who are their competitors?
6. What is a banker's bank? Explain the check truncation system used by CUs and some thrifts. How does this reduce check-clearing costs?
7. Describe new corporate management services that bankers have begun to offer in recent years.
8. Why do banks want to enter new securities activities? What are the benefits and what are the risks? Give some specific examples of risks that banks have faced recently.
9. Describe the strategies used by commercial banks to enter the mutual fund industry. What benefits are these banks seeking? Explain the difference between bank proprietary funds and third-party funds. Why is it to a bank's advantage to use third-party funds?
10. What concerns do regulators have about banks' entry into mutual fund activity? How are bank mutual funds regulated?
11. How have bank insurance activities expanded in recent years? If a bank wishes to sell insurance products, what alternatives does it have? What types of strategies have recently been adopted? What liability and regulatory risks do depository institutions entering insurance activities face in different states?
12. Define VAR. Give an example of its use. What are its advantages and disadvantages? What is DEAR? RiskMetrics? Explain their advantages and disadvantages.
13. Define EVA. How does EVA provide a comprehensive risk measure? How is it similar to RAROC? Can you think of any weaknesses it might have?
14. Using Bankers Trust or another firm, give an example of cultural clashes between traditional bank operations and new types of activities, such as securities. What types of different personality types are attracted to the two different types of businesses?
15. Define loan commitments, letters of credit, and note issuance facilities. How do these activities provide fee income for banks? What foreign exchange services do banks provide for fees?
16. What are the different types of loan sales? How do banks benefit from loan sales? How were loan sales handled in the 1980s for troubled less-developed country loans on large banks' balance sheets?
17. Diagram the process involved with securitization. How do depository institutions achieve high credit ratings on securitizations? Why is this important? How do depository institutions make profits on securitizations? What benefits do securitizations provide for depository institutions? What other types of financial institutions benefit?
18. Briefly explain prepayment risk. How do CARS and mortgage securities entail prepayment risk? What do investors demand in return for this risk? What characteristics do loans need to be securitized?

Selected References

Ambachtsheer, Keith P. and D. Don Ezra. *Pension Fund Excellence: Creating Value for Stakeholders.* New York: John Wiley and Sons, Inc., 1998.

Benston, George J. and George G. Kaufman. "Commercial Banking and Securities Activities: A Survey of the Risks and Returns." in *The Financial Services Revolution: Understanding the Changing Roles of Banks, Mutual Funds, and Insurance Companies.* ed. Clifford E. Kirsch, Chicago: Irwin Professional Publishing Co., 1997, 3–28.

Crawford, Richard D. and William W. Sihler. *Financial Service Organizations: Cases in Strategic Management.* New York: Harper Collins College Publishers, 1994.

Culp, Christopher L., Merton H. Miller, and Andrea M. P. Neves. "Value at Risk: Uses and Abuses." 10, Winter 1998, 26–38.

Eiteman, David K., Arthur I. Stonehill, and Michael H. Moffett. *Multinational Business Finance,* 6th ed. New York: Addison-Wesley Publishing Company, 1992.

Evanoff, Douglas D. "Priced Services: The Fed's Impact on Correspondent Banking." *Economic Perspectives (Federal Reserve Bank of Chicago)* 9, September/October 1984, 31–44.

Felgran, Steven D. "Bank Participation in Real Estate: Conduct, Risk, and Regulation." *New England Economic Review (Federal Reserve Bank of Boston),* November/December 1988, 57–73.

Felgran, Steven D. "Banks as Insurance Agencies: Legal Constraints and Competitive Advances." *New England Economic Review (Federal Reserve Bank of Boston),* September/October 1985, 34–49.

Fortune, Peter. "Mutual Funds, Part I: Reshaping the American Financial System." *New England Economic Review (Federal Reserve Bank of Boston),* July/August 1997, 45–72.

Furash, Edward E. "Risk Challenges and Opportunities." *Bank Management,* May/June 1995, 35–38.

Gallo, John G., Vincent P. Apilado, and James W. Kolari. "Commercial Bank Mutual Fund Activities: Implications for Bank Risk and Profitability." *Journal of Banking and Finance,* 20, December 1996, 1775–1791.

Gallo, John G., Gary M. Richardson, and Vincent P. Apilado. "The Performance of Bank-Sponsored Equity Mutual Funds: Implications for Bank Profitability." Working Paper, University of Nevada, May 1996.

Kaufman, George G. *The U.S. Financial System: Money, Markets, and Institutions,* 6th ed. Englewood Cliffs, New Jersey: Prentice Hall, 1995.

Kimball, Ralph C. "Economic Profit and Performance Measurement in Banking." *New England Economic Review (Federal Reserve Bank of Boston),* July/August 1998, 35–53.

Koch, Timothy. *Bank Management,* 3rd ed. New York: Dryden Press, 1995.

Laderman, Elizabeth. "Banks and Mutual Funds." Article 7 in *Readings on Financial Institutions and Markets.* Chicago: Irwin, 1995, 80–82.

Lopez, Jose A. "Methods for Evaluating Value at Risk Estimates," Federal Reserve Bank of New York *Economice Policy Review,* October 1998, 119–124.

Pozen, Robert C. *The Mutual Fund Business.* Cambridge, Mass.: MIT Press, 1998.

Robertson, William R. "The Fee-Income Phenomenon." *Bank Management,* 70 July/August 1994, 13–18.

Ross, Stephen A., Randolph W. Westerfield, and Bradford D. Jordan. *Essentials of Corporate Finance.* Chicago: Irwin, 1996.

Saunders, Anthony. *Financial Institutions Management: A Modern Perspective,* 2nd ed. Chicago: Irwin, 1997.

Simons, Katerina. "Value at Risk—New Approaches to Risk Management." *New England Economic Review (Federal Reserve Bank of Boston),* September/October 1996, 3–13.

Sinkey, Joseph F., Jr. *Commercial Bank Financial Management,* 5th ed. Upper Saddle River, New Jersey: Prentice Hall, 1998.

Tetenbaum, Robert M. "Investment Management: Fulfilling the Promise." *Bank Management,* May/June 1995, 49–53.

Uyemura, Dennis G., Charles C. Kantor, and Justin M. Pettit. "EVA for Banks: Value Creation, Risk Management, and Profitability Measurement." *Bank of America Journal of Applied Corporate Finance,* 9, Summer 1996, 94–113.

Venkataraman, Subu. "Value at Risk for a Mixture of Normal Distributions: The Use of Quasi-Bayesian Estimation Techniques." *Economic Perspectives (Federal ReserveBank of Chicago),* March/April 1997, 2–13.

Zaik, Edward, John Walter, Gabriela Kelling, and Christopher James. "RAROC at Bank of America: From Theory to Practice." *Bank of America Journal of Applied Corporate Finance,* 9, Summer 1996, 83–93.

Chapter 9 Internet Exercise

Noninterest Revenues and Associated Risks

1. J. P. Morgan, in RiskMetrics, provides a free program for Estimating Value at Risk at:

   http://www.riskmetrics.com/rm/index.html

2. On the left frame, click on VaR calculator. This page allows a user to use subsets of the RiskMetrics datasets to Calculate Portfolio VaR. Select assets from the categories in the above frame. For each asset class, choose whether you want All or a Selection of items. If you choose Selection, you will be prompted to make further choices. When you have completed your selections click on the "Portfolio Values" market value of items in your portfolio. When you are ready, click on "Calculate VaR". The Total VaR of your portfolio as well as Incremental and Marginal VaR of each instrument will be calculated. For a more complete discussion of Value at Risk models see Anthony Saunders, *Financial Institutions Management: A Modern Perspective*, 2nd ed. Chicago: Irwin, 1997.

3. A good discussion of the concept of Economic Value Added as an overall risk management and profitability measure can be found at:

   http://www.evanomics.com/study.shtml

4. To view a Power Point Presentation on the concept of Economic Value added go to:

   http://www.evanomics.com/intro/introindex.shtml

5. For a discussion of Economic Value Added for a small Business, go to:

   http://www.evanomics.com/evasmall/evasmallindex.shtml

Other useful sites for financial institution data:

National City Corporation (NCC)
http://www.nationalcity.com/

Thomson Bank Watch
http://www.bankwatch.com/

Management Issues and Performance Analysis of Nondepository Institutions

III

- ⬙ INSURANCE COMPANY FINANCIAL MANAGEMENT ISSUES

- ⬙ INVESTMENT BANKS, RETAIL SECURITY FIRMS, AND VENTURE CAPITALISTS

- ⬙ MUTUAL FUND AND PENSION FUND MANAGEMENT

- ⬙ MANAGING NONBANKS: FINANCE COMPANIES, FINANCIAL SERVICE FIRM

"Clearly, the most significant crisis the [insurance] industry faces right now is how to deal with catastrophes—natural disasters, hurricanes, earthquakes, and tidal waves."

General Robert T. Herres
Chairman and CEO-United Services Automobile Association (USAA) in Charles B. Wendel. *The New Financiers*. Chicago: Irwin Professional Publishing Co. (1996), 127.

"A number of life insurance companies recently have been funding a significant portion of [long-term] assets with relatively short-term liabilities, mostly guaranteed investment contracts, thus raising both interest sensitivity and liquidity concerns. Property-liability companies are also vulnerable to increases in interest rates, since their claims are relatively short-term and irregular. Higher interest rates lower the value of their assets, which may have to be sold to meet claims. The capitalization of property-liability companies has fallen significantly in the past 30 years, while their risks have not diminished. Capital ratios of life companies have remained essentially constant, but many life companies have undertaken investments that are riskier with respect to both possible default and vulnerability to interest rate increases."

Richard E. Randall
Vice President and Richard W. Kopcke, Vice President and Economist, Federal Reserve Bank of Boston. "The Financial Condition and Regulation of Insurance Companies: An Overview." *New England Economic Review* (May/June 1992), 32–43.

10

INSURANCE COMPANY FINANCIAL MANAGEMENT ISSUES

As the quotation above suggests, in the 1980s and early 1990s, insurance companies took on greater interest rate and liquidity risk by moving into annuities and guaranteed investment contracts that pay a specified fixed return over a specified period. To ensure a given return, investment companies often funded these investments with higher yielding, riskier investments.

Consequently, annuity purchasers, as well as insurers, were subject to greater default risk. For instance, Herbert D. Engle, senior vice president of Transamerica Occidental Life Insurance, invested $100,000 in a supposedly "safe" life insurance annuity product sold by Executive Life Insurance Company (EXEC) in 1983. EXEC funded its annuities by investing in junk bonds and commercial real estate *mortgages. With the collapse of the markets for these instruments in 1989, EXEC had huge losses and was seized by regulators in 1991. Although Mr. Engle recovered some of his investment, the investment return he received was significantly below the promised "guaranteed" rate for the annuity.[1]*

In addition to greater risk from investing in new investment products, property/liability (P/L) insurance companies faced significant losses from catastrophic events in the 1990s, including Hurricanes Andrew (1992), Opal and Fran (1995), and George and Mitch (1998), the Oakland fire of 1991, the blizzards of 1993 and 1996, the earthquakes of Northridge in 1994 and Columbia in 1999, and 163 tornadoes in Tennessee, Arkansas, and Missouri in January of 1999. As noted by Cornett and Saunders (1999), on an inflation-adjusted basis, Hurricane Andrew cost insurers $15.9 billion and 41 major catastrophes in 1996 cost $7.35 billion![2]

Despite these pressures, some major P/L insurers, such as State Farm weathered the decade's losses and even increased capital reserves during the most difficult periods. Similarly, despite failures and losses by many life insurance companies, other life insurers, such as Massachusetts Mutual, performed well. As the result of problems in the early 1990s, all insurance firms faced greater regulatory scrutiny as the decade progressed.

Factors that accounted for differences in insurers' financial strength included better financial and investment management. Executive Life had more than 60% of its investment portfolio concentrated in junk bonds. Many P/L firms, in contrast, relied on more stable investment income to offset large catastrophic losses in the 1990s. The financial opportunities and problems that insurers face are both similar to and different from those faced by the institutions discussed in previous chapters. Like depository institutions, insurance companies hold financial assets that are subject to interest rate, liquidity, and default risk. However, they have liabilities that are potential claims against the company by policyholders or their beneficiaries. Insurers are also subject to state regulations under the McCarron Ferguson Act.

This chapter addresses similarities and differences between insurance firms and other types of financial institutions, with the recognition that in recent years insurers and depositories have entered each other's arenas. The responses of insurers to economic challenges, competition, and regulatory developments, and the accompanying financial management techniques, are addressed as well.

Before discussing in more detail a financial analysis of insurance companies, it is worthwhile to present an overview of the their operations.

✦ ✦ ✦

OVERVIEW OF THE OPERATIONS OF INSURANCE COMPANIES

As pointed out by J. Francois Outreville in the *Theory and Practice of Insurance* (1998), insurance is an interesting process of financial intermediation because of its reverse production cycle with payment made before a service (the payment of claims) is provided. **Gross written premiums** provided by policyholders are used to cover the costs of commissions and administrative expenses, with the "ultimate service" or output of the firm, the claim paid, determined in the event of a loss. Because claims are not always made in the same year as premiums are received, **reserves** are put aside as commitments by the insurer for the insured policyholders and invested in securities of maturity equivalent to contracts. Similarly, a portion of premiums received in a given year may be used to cover claims incurred within that

---

[1] Richard S. Teitelbaum. "How Safe Is Your Insurance?" *Fortune* (September 9, 1991), 137–141.

[2] See Cornett and Saunders (1999), 91–92 and Greg Steinmetz, et. al. "In Wake of Hurricane, Insurers Face Financial and Regulatory Tests." *The Wall Street Journal* (September 2, 1992), A1, A4, and Property/Casualty Insurance Facts, 1998.

year. Insurers receive income each year from **premiums** and from **returns earned on investments**. Insurers make profits whenever premium and investment income exceeds the amount needed to cover all expenses, claims, and proper provisions (reserves) for liabilities to policyholders.[3]

Source of Revenues   Table 10.1 shows typical common-sized income statements for life insurance and property casualty insurance companies. During the past decade, on average, life insurers' **premium income contributed about 67%** of revenues with **investment income supplying the remaining 33%.**[4] For P/L insurers, premium income contributes a larger share, about **87% of revenues**, with investment income **contributing 13%.** P/L insurers depend more on premium income because they have shorter-term (unexpected payoff) contracts and thus cannot invest in higher yielding long-term assets as life insurers with long-term contracts can.

Details on Life Insurer Revenues   For life insurance companies, premium income comes from three sources: (1) life insurance premiums; (2) health insurance premiums; and (3) annuity considerations. As shown in Table 10.2, life insurance premiums over time have become a less significant percentages of total U.S. life insurance receipts (about 28% in 1997), with annuities contributing the largest share of revenues (about 49%) and health insurance premiums the lowest (about 23%). Although premiums from individuals for life and health insurance and annuities continue to be the largest percentage of premiums (50% in 1997), group insurance premium income has grown over time and contributed 49% of premiums. The rate of

---

Table 10.1   ◆   TYPICAL COMMON SIZE INCOME STATEMENTS FOR INSURANCE COMPANIES

% TOTAL REVENUES LIFE INSURANCE COMPANIES		% TOTAL REVENUES P/L INSURANCE COMPANIES	
Revenues:	% Revs.	Revenues:	% Revs.
Premium Payments	67%	Earned Premiums	87%
Net Investment Earnings	33%	Net Investment Earnings	13%
Expenses:	% Exps.	Expenses:	% Exps.
Benefit Payments	60%	Loss Expenses	74%
Additions to Policy Reserves	25%	Operating Expenses	25%
Operating Expenses	11%	Policyholder Dividends	1%
Taxes	2%		
Dividends to Stockholders	2%		
Addition to Surplus	2%		

Sources: American Council of Life Insurance Fact Books and Insurance Information Institute Property/Casualty Insurance Facts

Note: This represents a typical allocation, but %'s vary from year to year.

Typically life insurers receive a third or more of revenues from investment earnings while P/L insurers receive less.

The majority of life insurer expenses are benefit payments and then additions to policy reserves.

Loss expenses are the largest expenses of P/L insurers.

---

[3] See Outreville (1998).

[4] See *American Council of Life Insurance Life Insurance Fact Book* (1998).

Table 10.2 ✦ TRENDS IN INCOME FOR U.S. LIFE INSURANCE COMPANIES (MILS.)

	1986	% Income	% Prems.	1995	% Income	% Prems.	1997	% Income	% Prems.
Life Insurance Premiums	$66,213	23%	34%	$98,925	19%	29%	$115,039	19%	28%
Annuity Considerations	$83,712	30%	43%	$159,935	31%	47%	$197,529	32%	49%
Health Insurance Premiums	$44,153	16%	23%	$80,352	16%	24%	$92,737	15%	23%
Total Premium Receipts	$194,078	**69%**		$339,212	**66%**		$405,305	**66%**	
Investment Income	$75,435	**27%**		$140,092	**27%**		$170,713	**28%**	
Other Income	$12,744	**5%**		$32,894	**6%**		$34,628	**6%**	
Total Income	$282,257	100%		$512,198	100.00%		$610,646	100%	
Rate of Investment Income	*1986*			*1995*			*1997*		
Net Rate									
Total Assets	9.35%			7.34%			7.17%		
General Account Only	9.64%			7.90%			7.71%		
Gross Rate									
Total Fixed Income Assets	11.14%			8.16%			8.00%		

Source: **American Council of Life Insurance: Life Insurance Fact Books 1997, 1998.**

General Accounts are undivided accounts in which life and health insurers formerly recorded all incoming funds.

Since the 1960s, life and health insurers have begun using other accounts as well.

Separate accounts are asset accounts maintained independently from the insurer's general investment account that is used primarily for pension plans and variable life products. The arrangement permits wider latitude in the choice of investments, particularly in equities.

return on life insurance assets shown in the lower panel of Table 10.2 fell significantly as interest rates decreased in the 1990s, falling from 9.35% in 1986 to 7.17% in 1997.

Types of Securities Held by Life and P/L Insurers   Before discussing insurer expenses, it will be helpful to look at the composition of insurer securities, which are about 94% of assets. As shown in Figure 10.1, both life insurers and P/L insurers hold the majority of their assets in fixed-income securities, notably bonds. Life insurers in 1997 held 56% of their assets in a mixture of government (15%) and corporate (41%) bonds, while P/C insurers held 70% in bonds, with a mix of government (18%), municipal (33%), and corporate (19%) bonds. Because P/C insurers have unexpected maturities on their insurance contracts, they hold short-term and intermediate-term bonds. In contrast, life insurers have long-term contracts with more predictable maturities, and therefore can hold longer-term, higher-yielding bonds. Since the investments of life insurers are not taxed, they hold fewer munies. Preferred and common stock investments were about 23% for life insurers and 21% for P/C insurers. Life insurers hold only a small percentage of cash and short-term securities (about 4% of assets compared with about 7% for P/L insurers).[5]

Trends in Security Holdings for Life Insurers   Figure 10.2 shows that the percentage holdings of different types of securities for life insurers changed dramatically between 1986 and 1997. In the 1990s, stock holdings rose as state regulators became more flexible in allowing stock investments, and insurers took advantage of a

---

[5] Ibid, and figures cited in Harrington and Niehaus, 1999 from *Best's Aggregates*.

Figure 10.1 ✦ LIFE INSURERS AND P/L INSURERS: A COMPARISON OF ASSETS, OBLIGATIONS, AND NET WORTH

A notable difference in the assets of life and P/L insurers is the proportion invested in government securities and policy loans. Both types of insurers have large policy reserve liabilities, but life insurers are more highly leveraged.

Panel A:

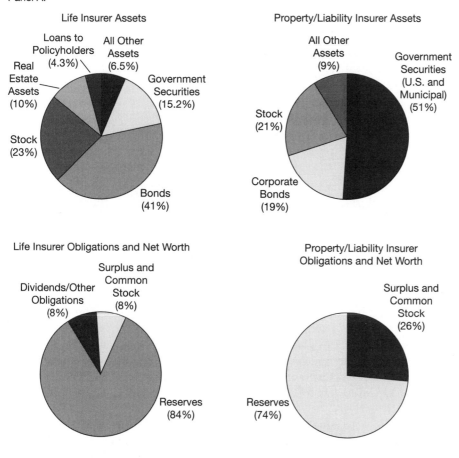

Source: Figures cited in Harrington and Niehaus, 1999 from *Best's Aggregates,* and *American Council of Life Insurance Fact Book,* 1998.

bull stock market. With large losses from real estate loans in the early 1990s, the percentage of mortgage and real estate holdings fell significantly, from 24% in 1986 to less than 10% in 1997.

Expenses of Insurers

Life Insurers   In contrast to depository institutions, in which the majority of expenses are interest expenses, the majority of expenses for life insurers are benefit payments and additions to policy reserves. These were approximately 85% of

Figure 10.2 ◆ TRENDS IN SECURITY HOLDINGS OF LIFE INSURERS

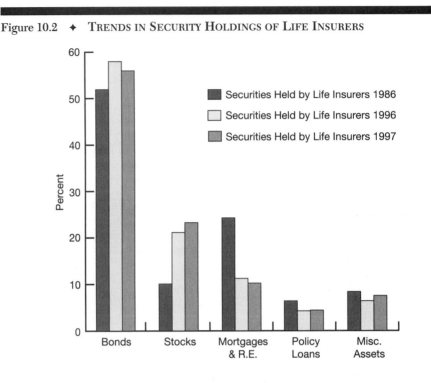

expenses in 1997 (see Figure 10.3). Operating expenses are a much smaller percentage of total expenses (11% in 1997). Dividends to stockholders of stock life insurance companies are about 2% of total expenses and taxes, 2%. Operating expenses include commissions to agents and costs such as depreciation, rent, and managerial salaries. Commissions to agents were about 3.9% of total expenses in 1997, and home and field-office expenses were 6.8%.

P/L Insurers   As shown in Table 10.1, the majority of expenses (about 74%) for property liability companies are loss expenses. Operating expenses, including commissions, are about 25%, and policyholder dividends, about 1%. Often, for many companies, total expenses are larger than revenues from premiums during periods of catastrophic losses. Consequently, P/L insurance companies often depend on investment revenues to make a profit.[6]

---

[6] See *Property/Casualty Insurance Facts 1998.* "Total premiums written" is often referred to in the industry as "net premiums written." These are premiums collected before deducting those paid but not yet earned. Accounting rules for unearned premiums on the income statement differ from unearned premium reserves on the balance sheet, which are often calculated under the assumption that services have been rendered for only one half of the amount of premiums paid during the year. As a result, unearned premium reserves on the balance sheet are often overstated and net worth understated for the industry. Some experts estimate the extent of reserve overstatement to be as much as 35%. See Vaughan (1982), 109, n. 7 and Mehr (1983), 470–471.

Figure 10.3   ✦   LIFE INSURANCE EXPENSES %

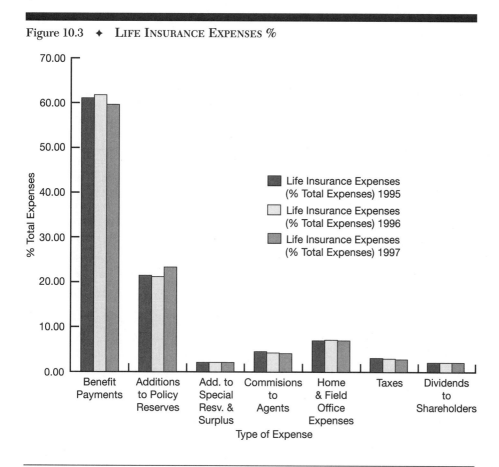

Source: American Council of Life Insurance Fact Book, 1998.

Statutory Accounting for Insurers   Interpreting financial data on P/L insurers is somewhat more difficult than for other financial institutions. Insurance companies are subject to two sets of accounting rules: regulatory principles that insurers call **statutory accounting** and generally accepted accounting principles (GAAP).

Statutory accounting is a combination of cash-based and accrual accounting; expenses are not recognized until earned. In general, it is a more conservative way of reporting financial results than GAAP. Statutory accounting affects balance sheets and income statements for all insurers, although differences between statutory accounting and GAAP are greater for P/L insurers than life insurers. Virtually all data on life insurers are consistent with GAAP; this is not true for P/L insurers. For instance, statutory accounting for P/Ls requires unrealized gains or losses on stock holdings to be reflected on the balance sheet, directly affecting both reported asset holdings and insurers' net worth. This is in contrast with GAAP, which requires the reporting of equity security holdings as the lower of either cost or market value. Also, for statutory accounting, P/L insurers may only include admitted assets in "other assets," which are assets that could be liquidated should the insurer face a financial emergency. This procedure differs from GAAP, in which "other assets" includes cash, but not premises. Thus, the reported net worth of P/L insurers is understated by nonadmitted assets that do not appear on the balance sheet.[7]

Overview of Insurance Company Balance Sheets

Life Insurers   Figure 10.1 provides an overview of common-size balance sheets of life and P/L insurers. Assets were discussed in a previous section. Reserves are the majority of total liabilities and equity for both types of insurers. Life insurers have policy reserves, security loss reserves, and also a dividend reserve. P/L insurers have a total loss and unearned premium reserve.[8] Surplus and common stock (equity accounts) to assets were about 8% for life insurers, on average, in 1997, and 26% for P/L insurers. Because of the potential for large catastrophic losses, P/L firms hold a larger capital cushion.

Details of Life Insurer Obligations and Surplus Funds   Table 10.3 shows trends and details for reserve and surplus accounts for life insurers. Policy reserves increased at an average 10% rate between 1987 and 1997. Policy reserves are estimated by taking the total present value of future financial obligations—that is, the total present value of expected death, medical, or lifetime income benefits that the company may be required to pay to current policyholders. The amount, determined actuarially, considers: (1) mortality and morbidity (disease) rates, reflecting the reasons future claims will be made; (2) the present value of future premium payments to be received from those currently insured; and (3) the expected rate of return on the company's investments. In sum, the reserves on a life insurer's balance sheet are the present value of expected claims, net of the present value of estimated receipts of premium and investment incomes. The largest percentage of outstanding reserves is often for annuity contracts.[9]

In addition to policy reserves, life insurers have a policy **dividend reserve** for mutual life insurance companies that provide refunds for **participating insurance policies** on premiums paid during the year if the loss experience, operating expenses, and investment income of the insurer are better than expected at the beginning of the year. In practice, to maximize the probability that dividends can be paid regularly, premiums on participating policies are higher than premiums on nonparticipating policies that provide similar coverage but that are not entitled to dividends.

Policy dividend accumulations are past dividends that policyholders have reinvested in interest-bearing accounts; **dividend obligations payable** are policy dividends declared during the current year but not yet paid to policyholders. Because policy dividends are considered refunds of previous payments, they are not

---

[7] See Harrington and Niehaus (1999).

[8] Life insurer policy reserves and P/L total loss and unearned premium reserve are liabilities, in contrast to other types of reserves, which are often included as equity.

[9] Reserves for annuities are included as the largest single category of policy reserves. Most of the annuity obligations of life insurers are from group pension plans established by employers for employees, although individual annuity policies can be purchased. Annuities provide protection against the risk of outliving one's accumulated financial resources. In exchange for a lump sum payment or a series of smaller payments relatively early in a policyholder's life, insurers provide a predetermined post retirement monthly income, either fixed or variable and usually lasting for the life of the policyholders. Actuaries project the cash outflows expected under an annuity policy, based on how long the policyholder may live after annuity payments begin. In 1997 group annuities were 35% of policy reserves and individual annuities, 32%. Life insurance was 29% and health insurance, 4%.

Table 10.3   ✦   Trends in Policy Reserves, Other Obligations and Surplus Funds for Life Insurers

	1987	% Total	1996	% Total	1997	% Total	ANNUAL AVERAGE % CHANGE 1987/97	1996/97
Policy Reserves	$862,133	82.54%	$1,965,790	83.99%	$2,164,559	83.79%	10.10%	9.60%
Policy Dividend Accumulations	15,837	1.52%	20,441	0.87%	20,456	0.79%	2.60%	0.10%
Funds set aside for Policy Dividends	12,043	1.15%	14,863	0.64%	16,197	0.63%	3%	9%
Other Obligations	71,063	6.80%	149,558	6.39%	174,359	6.75%	9.40%	16.60%
Asset Valuation Reserve (AVR)	16,013	1.53%	33,202	1.42%	36,159	1.40%	8.50%	8.90%
Interest Maintenance Reserve (MR)	N/A		9,360		11,398		N/A	21.80%
Surplus Funds	64,496	6.18%	144,247	6.16%	157,373	6.09%	9.30%	9.10%
Book Value of Capital Stock (stock comps)	2,874	0.28%	2,993	0.13%	2,713	0.11%	−0.60%	−9.40%
Total	1,044,459	100.00%	2,340,454	100.00%	2,583,214	100.00%	9.50%	10.40%

Source: American Council of Life Insurance 1998 Life Insurance Fact Book

N/A: Not Available

Beginning in 1992, the asset valuation reserve replaced the mandatory securities valuation reserve. 1987 data is for the mandatory securities valuation reserve.

Life Insurance Reserves by Policy Type (% Total) 1997

Type	%
Life	28.50%
Health	3.50%
Annuities	67.30%
Indiv.	32.20%
Group	35.10%
Suppl. Contracts	1.30%
Total	100.00%

Capital Ratios %

	1987	1996	1997
Including MSVR/AVR	8.90%	10.20%	10.60%
Excluding MSVR/AVR	7.20%	8.40%	8.70%

Note: Capital ratio is defined as capital plus surplus plus reserves.

AVR = asset valuation reserve divided by general acct. assets.

MSVR = mandatory securities valuation reserve.

taxable to the insured when paid. **Other obligations** include accrued expenses, prepaid premiums, and mandatory reserves for fluctuations in security values.

Asset valuation reserves are a type of reserve that makes provisions for credit-related losses on fixed-income assets (default component) as well as all types of equity investments (equity component). The **interest maintenance reserve** is a reserve that captures all realized, interest-related capital gains and losses on fixed-income assets. These gains and losses are amortized into income over the remaining life of the investment sold.

Surplus and common stock are the equity, or capital, of the life insurance industry. The surplus account is analogous to retained earnings. The common stock account is for shareholder-owned firms. The book value of an insurer's surplus plus common stock shows how much the book value of assets can shrink before estimated claims on the insurer exceed asset values. Often capital ratios are calculated only by using surplus and capital. At other times the asset valuation reserve and mandatory securities valuation reserve are included as part of capital. In 1997, with the inclusion of these reserves, the average capital ratio of life insurers was 10.6%. State regulators require that insurers meet minimum capital ratios. Calculations for risk-based ratios are shown later in the chapter.

PERFORMANCE EVALUATION OF LIFE INSURANCE COMPANIES

Similar to depository institutions, key ratios can be calculated to help analysts focus on critical aspects of an insurer's financial performance and risk. One ratio common to both types of insurers is the **Net Underwriting Margin (NUM),** which encompasses the main source of an insurer's revenues and expenses:

$$NUM = \frac{Premium\ Income - Policy\ Expenses}{Total\ Assets} \quad\quad [10.1]$$

Policy expenses include all benefit payments, additions to policy reserves, and operating expenses for life insurers and all loss expenses and operating expenses for P/L insurers. Policy expenses also include dividends to policyholders for mutual firms.

Sample Performance Analysis for a Life Insurance Company

Table 10.4 shows a financial analysis for trends in the Granite Life Insurance Company for 2004 and 2005. Like depository institution analysis, a Dupont analysis can be used, with the inclusion of NUM (versus net interest margin [NIM]) for a life insurer. Similar to depositories, life insurers have a small return on assets (ROA) but a high equity multiplier (EM), i.e., high financial leverage, which produces a higher return on equity (ROE).

Granite Life, for instance, has projected ROAs of 1.53% in 2004 and 0.71% in 2005. Its EM in 2004 is 14.43 (6.9% equity to assets). With a fall in equity to assets to 5.31% in 2005, the EM rises to 18.84. The higher EM has a positive effect on ROE, but with a much lower ROA in 2005, ROE falls from 22% in 2004 to 13.3% in 2005. The lower ROA is the result of cost efficiency problems. Although asset utilization rises in 2005 to 0.221 × from 0.193 ×, Granite's NPM falls from 7.91% in 2004 to 3.19% in 2005.

Because expenses rise 63% compared with revenues rising only 54%, net income falls by almost 38%. With premium expenses (benefit payments, additions to policy reserves, and operating expenses) much larger than premium revenues, Granite's NUM is −3.85% in 2004 and −6.25% in 2005, indicating net underwriting losses each year. Each expense item rises relative to assets in 2005. Benefit payments to assets rises from 10.6% to 11.87%, addition to policy reserves rise from 4.31% to 5.37%, and operating expenses rise from 2.41% to 3.67%. The average investment return (net investment revenues divided by earning assets) of 6.24% in 2004 and 7.94% in 2005 is responsible each year for Granite's having a profit.

Table 10.4   ✦   FINANCIAL PERFORMANCE ANALYSIS FOR GRANITE LIFE INSURANCE COMPANY
PANEL A. GRANITE LIFE INSURANCE COMPANY ASSETS & OBLIGATIONS, YEAR-END 2004 AND 2005 (MILS.)

Assets	2004	% Assets	2005	% Assets	Financial Ratios	2004	2005
Government Securities	$1,677	5.76%	$3,741	9.52%	Return on Equity	22.04%	13.27%
Corporate Securities					Return on Assets	1.53%	0.71%
Bonds	11,216	38.50%	$13,836	35.20%	Net Underwr. Margin	−3.85%	−6.25%
Stock	1,294	4.44%	3,215	8.18%	Net Profit Margin	7.91%	3.19%
Real Estate Loans	10,989	37.72%	12,411	31.57%	Asset Utilization	0.193	0.221
Real Estate Investments	971	3.33%	1,678	4.27%	Equity Multiplier	14.43	18.84
Loans to Policyholders	1,322	4.54%	1,953	4.97%	Ave Yld Erng Assets	6.24%	7.94%
Total Assets	**$29,134**	**100.00%**	**$39,309**	**100.00%**			
					Expenses to Assets		
Obligations & Net Worth					Benefits	10.60%	11.87%
Policy Reserves	$26,622	91.38%	$33,534	85.31%	Add Policy Rsvs.	4.31%	5.37%
Policy Dividend Obligations	595	2.04%	781	1.99%	Op. Expense	2.41%	3.67%
Other Obligations	1,898	6.51%	2,907	7.40%			
Total Obligations	27,115	93.07%	37,222	94.69%			
Total Net Worth (surplus & STK	**2,019**	**6.93%**	**2,087**	**5.31%**			
Total Obligations & Net Worth	$29,134	100.00%	$39,309	100.00%			

GRANITE LIFE INSURANCE COMPANY INCOME & EXPENSES FOR 2004 AND 2005 (MILS.)

Revenues:	2004	% Revs.	2005	% Revs.	% Change
Premium Payments	$3,930	69.89%	$5,760	66.33%	
Net Investment Earnings & Other Income	1,693	30.11%	2,924	33.67%	
Total Revenues	**$5,623**	**100.00%**	**$8,684**	**100.00%**	**54.44%**
Expenses:					
Benefit Payments	$3,091	54.97%	$4,666	53.73%	
Additions to Policy Reserves	1,258	22.37%	2,109	24.29%	
Operating Expenses	703	12.50%	1,443	16.62%	
Total Expenses	**5,052**	**89.85%**	**8,218**	**94.63%**	**62.67%**
Net Operating Income	$541	9.62%	$466	5.37%	
Taxes	126	2.24%	189	2.18%	
Net Income	**$445**	**7.91%**	**$277**	**3.19%**	**37.75%**

Table 10.5, Panel A, shows additional ratios often used by regulators. These include (1) additions to surplus, (2) change in premium payments, (3) commissions to premium payments, (4) real estate investments to total assets, (5) change in asset mix, and (6) change in product mix. Any decline in surplus or premiums alerts regulators to potential problems for an insurer. Commissions to premium payments is a cost efficiency measure. The other ratios represent signals of potential problems or strengths in terms of asset or product mix. Since real estate investments tend to be more risky than other types of assets, a large percentage of real estate investments signals greater risk. Granite has 37.7% of its assets in real estate investments in 2004 and 31.5% in 2005, which indicates a high proportion of more risky assets.

Table 10.5 ✦ SELECTED INSURANCE REGULATORY INFORMATION SYSTEM RATIOS

Panel A: The National Association of Insurance Commissioners developed the IRIS system for evaluating the performance of life and P/L insurers. These measures provide useful guidelines for industry analysts.

Property/Liability Insurers

1. Total Earned Premiums/Surplus
2. Change in Total Premiums Written/Total Earned Premiums in Prior Year
3. Net Investment Income/Average Invested Assets
4. Change in Surplus/Surplus
5. Liabilities/Liquid Assets

Life Insurers

1. Additions to Surplus
2. Net Income/Total Revenues
3. Commissions/Premium Payments
4. Real Estate Investments/Total Assets
5. Change in Premium Payments
6. Change in Asset Mix
7. Change in Product Mix

Source: Adapted from C. Arthur Williams and Richard M. Heins, *Risk Management and Insurance* (New York: McGraw-Hill, 1989), 617–618.

Panel B: Summary Sample Ratio Used by Best's to Evaluate P/L Insurers Profitability, Financial Leverage, Liquidity, and Loss Reserves Profitability:

Combined Ratio after Policy Dividends: Sum Loss, Expense, and Dividend Ratio
Loss Ratio: Incurred Losses & Loss Adjustment Expenses to Net Premiums Earned
Expense Ratio: Underwriting Expenses (including commissions) to Net Premiums
Policyholder Dividend Ratio: Dividends to Policyholders to Net Premiums Earned
Operating Ratio: Combined Ratio − (Net Investment Income to Net Prems. Earned)
Pretax ROR (Return on Revenue): Pretax Operating Income to Net Premiums Earned
Yield on Invested Assets: Net Investment Income to Cash and Net Invested Assets
Change in PHS: % Change in Policyholder Surplus
Return PHS (ROE): (Net Income & Unrealized Capital Gains) to Ave Policyholder Surplus
Leverage: Best's Capital Adequacy Relativity (BCAR): Company Capital Ratio/Peer Median Capital Ratio
NPW to PHS: Net Premiums Written to Policyholder Surplus
Net Liabilities to PHS: Net Liabilities to Policyholder Surplus
Liquidity: Overall Liquidity: Total Admitted Assets to Total Liabilities
Bonds to PHS: Noninvestment Grade Bonds to Policyholder Surplus
Loss Reserve Tests: Loss and LAE Reserves to PHS: Reported Loss and Loss Adjustment Reserves to Policyholder Surplus

Source: 1997 Best's Insurance Reports—Property/Casualty.

Sources of Financial Information

Sources of financial information on life insurance firms can be found in *Best's Aggregates and Averages, Life-Health Edition*, and for P/L insurers in *Best's Aggregates and Averages, Property-Liability Edition*. *Moody's Bank and Finance Manual* contains financial statements for large companies. *Best's* (Oldwick, N.J.: A. M. Best Company) also contains ratings for insurance companies and publishes monthly *Best Reviews* (life/health and P/L editions) that discuss current issues. SNL Securities in Charlottesville, Virginia (http://www.snl.com), also publishes *The SNL Insurance Quarterly*, which contains year-end financials on all covered insurance companies as well as managerial and institutional ownership data.

PERFORMANCE EVALUATION OF P/L COMPANIES

In addition to NUM, P/L companies have other underwriting efficiency ratios, including:

$$\text{Loss Ratio} = \text{Loss Expenses} / \text{Total Premiums Earned} \qquad [10.2]$$

where Total Premiums Earned are premiums received and earned on insurance contracts without a claim being filed (total premiums written less unearned premiums), and loss expenses include losses and adjustment expenses for settling losses.

$$\text{Expense Ratio} = \text{Operating Expenses} / \text{Total Premiums Written} \qquad [10.3]$$

$$\text{Combined Ratio} = \text{Loss Ratio} + \text{Expense Ratio} \qquad [10.4]$$

$$\text{Overall Profitability} = 100\% - (\text{Combined Ratio} + \text{Investment Yield}) \qquad [10.5]$$

where investment yield can be estimated as investment revenue/earning assets.[10]

The first two ratios reflect the two major expenses of P/L insurers: loss expenses and commissions and other operating expenses.

Interpretation of the Loss Ratio   If the loss ratio is >1 ($>100\%$), losses were greater than premiums earned. If the loss ratio is <1 ($<100\%$), then premiums earned were greater than loss expenses. Often loss ratios are calculated individually for particular lines of business for a P/L. As Cornett and Saunders (1999) point out, loss ratios have risen on average for the industry over time. The average loss ratio was about 60% in 1951; 64% in 1961; 67.5% in 1971; 76.8% in 1981; 81.1% in 1991; and about 80% in 1996.[11]

Interpretation of the Expense Ratio   Expense ratios, in contrast to loss ratios, have fallen for the industry over time; the average expense ratio was about 34% in 1951; 32% in 1961; 27% in 1971; 27% in 1981; 26.4% in 1991; and 26.2% in 1996.[10] P/L insurers have improved their efficiency in commission and other costs. Note that the premiums used in the denominators of the loss ratio and the expense ratio are different, so that losses incurred are related to premiums earned during the period, whereas operating expenses, most of which are agents' commissions, are related to premiums written during the same period.

---

[10] See Cornett and Saunders (1999); Saunders (1997); and Rejda (1995).
[11] See Cornett and Saunders (1999), 91–92.

Interpretation of the Combined Ratio   The combined ratio indicates the overall profitability in underwriting insurance for a P/L insurer or, if used for individual product lines, the profitability of a particular line of insurance. If the combined ratio is <1 (<100%), a P/L insurer has an underwriting loss with expenses greater than premium income. If the combined ratio is >1 (>100%), a P/L insurer has an underwriting profit. Trends in combined ratios or differences in combined ratios for different product lines can be evaluated. Also, a firm's combined ratio can be compared with similar firms writing similar lines of insurance. The combined ratio is also often calculated after dividends by subtracting dividends from premiums written. On average, P/L insurers have had underwriting losses in the last two decades. While the average combined ratio was 94.3% in 1951, in 1961 it was 96.5%; in 1971 it was 94.7%; in 1981 it was 104.1%; in 1991 it was 107.6%; and it continued to be greater than 100% in the 1990s, with a ratio of 105.9% in 1996, reflecting the continued rise in loss ratios.[12]

Overall Profitability   Since P/L companies on average have had underwriting losses, as indicated by their combined ratios, which have been greater than 100%, their profitability has depended on generating revenue from their investment portfolios. Taking 100% and subtracting the combined ratio (often after dividends) and the investment yield provides a measure of a P/L insurer's overall profitability.

Additional Performance Ratios

Table 10.5, Panel A shows some (of many) ratios that regulators consider for P/L companies. Many of these are similar to life insurer ratios, but others focus particularly on liquidity, which is more of a problem for P/L firms, especially liabilities/liquid assets. Changes in premium income and in surplus and total earned premiums/surplus indicate potential problems or improvements in premium income and surplus for companies. Net investment income/average invested assets provides the average yield on the insurer's investments.

Note on Financial Analysis for Insurance Companies

Many insurance companies are holding companies that offer both life and property/casualty insurance. Combined financial statements, such as those presented in *Best's* or *Moody's Bank & Finance Manual*, often aggregate information, making it difficult to calculate separate loss and expense ratios, or do not distinguish between premiums earned and premiums written. Hence, the financial analyst must adjust to these limitations. Insurers also often buy insurance from other insurance companies known as reinsurers, who reinsure a portion of an insurer's potential losses. With a growing trend toward consolidation in the insurance industries, combined statements often reflect many different lines of business. There are many other nuances and special accounts particular to different types of insurance companies, as well as complications with statutory versus GAAP accounting. With this caveat, the following section provides an illustration of an analysis for a P/L company. Panel B of Table 10.5 presents some of the ratios used by *Best's* for P/L insurers.

Sample Performance Analysis for a P/L Insurer

Table 10.6 provides information for Texas Farmers Insurance Company in Austin, Texas, for 1995 and 1996 from *Moody's Bank and Finance Manual*.

---

[12] Ibid.

Table 10.6 ◆ PERFORMANCE ANALYSIS FOR TEXAS FARMERS INSURANCE COMPANY (P/L INSURER)

(*Source:* Moody's Bank & Finance Manual, 1997, p. 5937)

NET PREMIUMS WRITTEN BY LINE OF BUSINESS

	1996	% Total	1995	% Total
Fire	920	1.17%	946	1.39%
Allied Lines	783	1.00%	713	1.05%
Multiple Peril Homeowners	**14,553**	**18.52%**	**13,022**	**19.20%**
Multiple Peril Commercial	889	1.13%	696	1.03%
Marine	719	0.92%	662	0.98%
Medical Malpractice	dr10	−.01%	dr163	−.24%
Earthquake	1480	1.88%	926	1.37%
Other Liability	44	0.06%	33	0.05%
Auto Liability	**41,104**	**52.32%**	**39,730**	**58.58%**
Auto Physical Damage	18,078	23.01%	11,254	16.59%
Total	78,560	100.00%	67,819	100.00%

Cons. Income Statements	1996	% Revs.	1995	% Revs.
Premiums Earned	**76,272**	**89.79%**	**65,801**	**88.91%**
Losses incurred	51,427	60.54%	49,688	67.14%
Loss Expenses Incurred	6,808	8.01%	5,342	7.22%
Other Underwriting Expenses	20,653	24.31%	17,498	23.64%
Total Underwriting Deductions	**78,889**	**92.87%**	**72,527**	**98.00%**
Net Underwriting Gain	**−2,617**	**−3.08%**	**−6,726**	**−9.09%**
Net Investment Income Ernd.	7,957	9.37%	8,232	11.12%
Net real capital gains	595	0.70%	2	0.00%
Other Income Received	839	0.99%	866	1.17%
Finance/Service Charges	−721	−0.85%	−894	−1.21%
Adj. Net Investment Income	**8,670**	**10.21%**	**8,206**	**11.09%**
Net Income Before Dividends	**6,053**	**7.13%**	**1,480**	**2.00%**
Dividends to Policyholders	0	0.00%	0	0.00%
Net Income Before Taxes	6,053	7.13%	1,480	2.00%
Taxes	1,818	2.14%	263	0.36%
Net Income	**4,235**	**4.99%**	**1,217**	**1.64%**
Total Revenues	**84,942**	**100.00%**	**74,007**	**100.00%**
Net Investment Revenues	**8,670**	**10.21%**	**8,206**	**11.09%**
Premium Revenues	**76,272**	**89.79%**	**65,801**	**88.91%**

FINANCIAL RATIOS

	1996	1995
Return on Equity	10.69%	3.44%
Return on Assets	3.50%	0.90%
Equity Multiplier	3.05	3.83
Net Profit Margin	4.99%	1.64%
Asset Utilization	.702 ×	.526 ×
Net Underwr. Margin	−2.16%	−4.98%
Loss Ratio	.76 ×	.84 ×
Expense Ratio	.27 ×	.27 ×
Combined Ratio	1.03 ×	1.11 ×
Ave Return Investmts	7.26%	6.18%
% Change Premiums	16%	
% Change in Assets	−10%	
Equity to Assets	32.73%	26.13%
Liabs./Liquid Assets	4.74 ×	2.27 ×
Short-term Investmts. to Assets	14.00%	32.00%

Consolidated Balance Sheet, as of Dec. 31 ($000)

Assets	1996	% Total	1995	% Total
Bonds	102,140	84.38%	88,883	65.83%
Cash	241	0.20%	940	0.70%
S.T. Inves.	**16,948**	**14.00%**	**43,025**	**31.87%**
Int. Due	1,371	1.13%	1,395	1.03%
Other	349	0.29%	772	0.57%
Total Assets	**121,050**	**100.00%**	**135,015**	**100.00%**
Liabilities				
Accrued Losses	28,371	23.44%	33,003	24.44%
Loss Adj. Expenses	10,444	8.63%	10,914	8.08%
Taxes, Licenses, Fees	968	0.80%	1,550	1.15%
Unearned Premiums	28,647	23.67%	26,715	19.79%
Other Liabilities	12,991	10.73%	27,547	20.40%
Total Liabilities	**81,421**	**67.26%**	**99,729**	**73.87%**
Equity Accounts	**39,629**	**32.74%**	**35,286**	**26.13%**
Total Liab. & Equity	121,050	100.00%	135,015	100.00%

Moody's shows the premiums written for fire, allied lines, multiple peril for homeowners, multiple peril for commercial businesses, marine, medical malpractice, earthquake, workmen's compensation, other liabilities, and automobile liabilities. Thus, Texas Farmers underwrites a number of different product lines of liability insurance. Liability insurance lines are often problematic for P/L insurers since they have a so-called **long tail of liability,** whereby insurers are forced to pay millions of dollars for claims arising from injuries that occurred decades earlier. The majority of net premiums written for Texas Farmers Insurance Company come from homeowners and auto insurance, which are liabilities that are more predictable and have less of a long tail problem.

A Dupont analysis shows that ROE rose from 3.44% in 1995 to 10.69% in 1996. The reason for the rise in ROE was a large rise in ROA, from 0.90% in 1995 to 3.5% in 1996. The EM fell with a rise in equity in 1996 (to 3.05 from 3.83) and thus did not contribute to the higher ROE. The higher ROA can be explained by both a higher asset utilization of 0.702 × in 1996 from 0.526 × in 1995 and a dramatically higher NPM of 4.99% versus 1.64% in 1995. AU rose as a result of both higher net premiums, which rose 16% in 1996, and a shrinkage of assets by about 10%.

Texas Farmer's NUM was negative in both years, which is typical of the P/L industry, but as the result of higher premiums earned in 1996, the negative NUM is much lower (−2.16% versus −4.98%). The operating expense ratio remained the same at 0.27, but the loss ratio fell to 0.76 in 1996 from 0.84 in 1995, resulting in a better combined ratio (1.03 versus 1.11 in 1995). Thus, Texas Farmers had a much lower net underwriting loss of 3% in 1996.

With a decline in investment assets, the average return on investment assets (excluding cash on hand and income due) rose to 7.26% in 1996 from 6.18% in 1995. In terms of investment mix, Texas Farmers reduced its cash on hand and short-term investments and increased its holdings of bonds, contributing to the higher average return on investments. With higher premiums earned relative to losses and other underwriting expenses and a higher average return on investments, Texas Farmers' performance improved significantly in 1996.

In terms of risk measures, the company's equity-to-asset ratio improved to 32.73% in 1996 from 26.13% in 1995. Liabilities to liquid assets, including cash and short-term investments, rose from 2.27 times in 1995 to 4.74 times in 1996. Similarly, the percentage of short-term investments to assets fell from 32% in 1995 to 14% in 1996. Thus, Texas Farmer's had greater liquidity risk in 1996.

Underwriting Cycles of P/L Insurers

The P/L business has always been subject to an **underwriting cycle,** which is characterized by two subperiods known as a soft market and a hard market. In the soft portion of the cycle, premiums are lowered and insurance coverage is amply available. During the hard market, insurers raise premiums and some customers may have difficulty obtaining coverage. In a soft market, because premiums received are invested in financial assets, increases in the general level of interest rates may give insurers an incentive to write more policies to increase investment income. Frequently, the desire to increase premium income to increase investment income results in price wars in which one company undercuts premiums charged by competitors.[13] If rate wars continue long enough, premium income may be insufficient to

---

[13] Ibid.

Figure 10.4   ✦   P/L Income, 1965–1991

Since the late 1970s, P/L insurers have not earned a profit on underwriting. Investment income has allowed the industry to report positive combined income, however. The cyclical nature of P/L underwriting results is also evident.

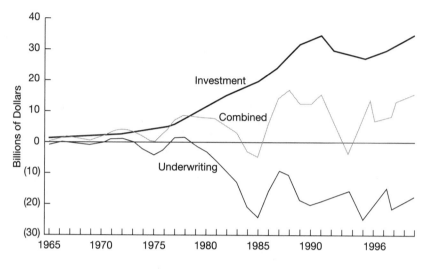

Source: Insurance Information Institute. *Property/Casualty Insurance Facts,* various issues.

cover underwriting expenses and policy claims during the year, resulting in a net underwriting loss.

When insurers raise rates to compensate for the losses, they encounter resistance from customers who like the lower rates, and this resistance postpones insurers' financial recovery. As customers balk against rate increases, insurers say the market turns "hard." If interest rates have fallen, investment income may not make up for continued underwriting losses. Eventually, however, the cycle turns back up as the balance between premium and investment income is restored and the industry regains profitability. Research suggests such cycles persist every six years and differ across lines of insurance. The cyclical nature of underwriting losses is shown in Figure 10.4[14]

SOCIAL AND ECONOMIC FORCES AFFECTING INSURERS

Factors Affecting P/L Insurers   Litigation began increasing in the U.S. in the 1960s, and as product liability suits, malpractice suits, and other suits have escalated,

---

[14] Outreville (1999) points out similar P/L cycles in other countries. See Sean Mooney. "How Insurance Cycles Work." *Insurance Review,* 15 (January 1990), 31–32. Cummins, Harrington, and Klein (1991) examine cycles and crises in P/L insurance markets, reviewing two possible explanations for market volatility: excessive price cutting by insurers, and external pressures to industry capital.

juries have increased awards to plaintiffs, putting P/L insurers at great risk.[15] To protect itself, the P/L industry often turns to reinsurers-insurance companies for insurance companies. Reinsurers agree, in exchange for a share of premium income, to assume responsibility for claims on policies written by other companies. Often insurance companies have a reinsurance subsidiary or captive insurer that provides reinsurance. The escalating costs of claims have required insurers to increase premium income, investment income, or both. These difficulties are compounded by the cost increases that occur during the downside of an underwriting cycle, a circumstance facing the industry by the mid-1980s. Adding to the challenge are increases in competition from depository institutions, which further inhibit premium increases to compensate for losses.

In 1985 and 1986, P/L companies and reinsurers responded to severe losses in key lines of insurance either by raising premiums or declining to sell some lines of insurance altogether. The industry also changed major features of some liability policies to protect itself against the so-called long tail of liability under which insurers were forced to pay millions of dollars for claims arising from injuries occurring decades earlier. This made liability insurance unaffordable for many public school systems, charitable organizations, municipal governments, hospitals, and physicians in high-risk specialties, such as obstetrics.[15]

Not surprisingly, customers and regulators were outraged, leading to major calls for reforms in the P/L industry and, in some instances, to outright customer revolt. Since the McCarran-Ferguson Act of 1945 permits federal regulation when (1) states fail to exercise their regulatory authority diligently or (2) when the industry itself engages in "boycott, coercion, or intimidation," the industry's refusal to insure some groups led to as yet unsuccessful attempts in the U.S. Congress to repeal or substantially modify McCarran-Ferguson to restore regulatory power to federal authorities and to bring the industry under antitrust rules. Currently, under McCarran-Ferguson, insurers are allowed to share information about losses so that actuaries can better estimate future costs. Industry opponents believe that the antitrust exemption simply makes it easy for insurers to collude to fix prices. Insurers argue that without access to shared data, small insurers could not survive because they could not afford to collect the necessary information on their own.

Consumer advocates have also passed legislation putting limits on the premiums that P/L insurers could charge. For instance, in late 1988, voters in California passed **Proposition 103,** which included (1) a 20% rate cut in automobile insurance premiums for all drivers and an additional cut for "good" drivers; (2) permission for banks in California to sell insurance; (3) prohibition against insurers' charging premiums based on driver residence; (4) repeal of insurers' protection against state antitrust laws; and (5) popular election of the state's insurance commissioner.[16] The California Supreme Court upheld Proposition 103 and its provisions took effect toward the end of 1989.

Reaction of P/L Insurers   In reaction to Proposition 103, a number of insurers believed they could not afford to operate and pulled out of the state. Similar actions

---

[15] A financial analyst needs to be careful in examining underwriting cycles, since many large P/L insurers are mutually owned and report only on a statutory basis. Statutory profits are often lower than they would be if reported on a GAAP basis, which may exaggerate downturns in the cycle, such as in Figure 10.4.

[16] See Marlys Harris. "Crisis in the Courts." *Insurance Review*, 47 (April 1986), 52–57, and Thomas S. Healey. "Insurers under Siege." *Insurance Review*, 47 (May 1986), 50–57. Also see various issues of *Property/Casualty Insurance Facts*.

occurred in other states where restrictions were imposed. P/L insurers began to rethink approaches to the problems of the 1980s, including actively promoting key changes in the way liability suits are handled.

Taking advantage of the fact that opinion polls showed trial lawyers to be the only group more despised by the public than insurers, the industry embarked on a campaign of tort reform across the nation.[17] **Tort laws** are established in each state concerning negligence and legal liability between citizens or between citizens and organizations and determine which suits can be brought and the methods by which damages may be awarded, including what factors can be considered by juries in making awards. Since 1986, dozens of states have enacted changes in their tort laws, some more sweeping than others. Insurers also promoted ways of reducing the cost of legal liability, including binding arbitration between plaintiff and defendant outside of court and a reduction of the percentage of damages a plaintiff's attorney may receive in a successful suit.

P/L insurers also publicized the skill and sensitivity with which many companies perform their services in times of trouble and developed new coverage and purchasing techniques, including **risk retention** groups and **purchasing** groups. Risk retention groups pool and share losses by entities with similar exposures. Purchasing groups negotiate coverage as a group to gain bargaining power. Insurers have also offered a claims-made form of liability insurance to escape the long tail of liabilities.[18]

Although P/L insurers were more profitable in the later 1990s, with a combined ratio of 1.01 for P/L insurers as a whole in 1997, problems occurred in the 1990s as well. For instance, consumers continued to be concerned over high premiums for auto insurance, which became a hot topic in gubernatorial races, such as New Jersey, where winning candidate Jim McGreevey promised a mandatory 10% rollback in premiums and an elected insurance commissioner. Earlier in the 1990s, with huge losses from catastrophes, insurers faced severe financial difficulties. Even Lloyd's of London, one of the oldest and most venerable English insurers and reinsurers, faced insolvency as the result of huge losses, including the explosion of an oil rig in 1988. Lloyd's did not regain an A-rating from *Best's* until 1997. Annual ROEs for P/L firms are typically lower than other financial institutions.[19]

Factors Affecting Life Insurers   Life insurers, particularly in the health insurance arena, have faced adverse public opinion as well. To reduce costs, many health care insurers have resorted to health maintenance organizations (HMOs), which limit services and the ability of the insureds to choose their own doctors or hospitals, visit emergency rooms without permission, and see specialists. Although HMOs in many cases have been very effective, others have not, and consumers have reacted adversely to such restrictions. With the advent of the AIDS epidemic, which

---

[17] See "Now Even Insurers Have a Hard Time Getting Coverage." *Business Week* (December 2, 1985), 128–129, and David B. Hilder. "Uncollectable Reinsurance Hurts Firms." *The Wall Street Journal* (April 1, 1986), 6.

[18] See Steven Waldman, Jennifer Foote, and Elisa Williams. "The Prop 103 'Prairie Fire.'" *Business Week* (May 15, 1989), 50–51, and "Proposition 103" and "Antitrust Issues" in *1990 Property/Casualty Insurance Facts,* 7–9.

[19] "Battle for the Cellar." *The Wall Street Journal* (August 28, 1988), and Peter Brimelow and Leslie Spencer. "The Plaintiff Attorneys' Great Honey Rush." *Forbes* (October 16, 1989), 197–203. As reported in the 1998 P/L Book, P/L companies had a 9.6% ROE compared to 16.5% for commercial banks, 18.5% for diversified financial firms, and 14% for Fortune 500 firms.

increased insurers' costs, some insurance companies began to require AIDS testing, along with tests for other illnesses, before insuring an individual. Many with such illnesses were left without the ability to be insured. Congress has consequently considered drastic reforms to the health insurance system and proposals that offer patients a bill of rights and choices in their medical provider. Although a national health care system was considered in the mid-1990s, legislation did not pass. Consequently, life insurers, like P/L insurers, have tried through advertisements to demonstrate the benefits they do provide to counter a reduction in their public image. Recent proposals in 1999 would set limits on deductions for advertising for annuities and other insurer expenses that could potentially further reduce insurer profits.

Other trends (discussed earlier in Chapter 4) include demutualization of both life and P/L insurance companies, with conversions to mutual holding companies or stock-owned companies, which would make raising capital easier for firms; concerns for companies over potential Year 2000 computer glitches; and numerous intra-industry and interindustry mergers (discussed in greater detail in Chapter 23). The best example of interindustry mergers is Travelers Group's purchase of two investment firms, Salomon Brothers and Smith Barney, as well as its merger with Citicorp in the late 1990s. Conesco, Inc., was a leader in intraindustry mergers in the later 1990s. Conesco purchased insurer Capitol American Financial Corporation, Colonial Penn Life Insurance Company, and Providential Life Insurance Company of Little Rock, Arkansas. It also assumed for reinsurance all the nonvariable business of Intramerica Life Insurance Co., and merged with Pioneer Financial Services Inc. Since 1982, Conesco completed 15 acquisitions, including 30 life insurers, growing from $3 million in assets to $36 billion in assets by the end of 1997, with an equity market capitalization of $9.2 billion. A number of international mergers occurred in 1997, including the merger of Swiss insurer Zurich Group with B.A.T. industries, creating a combined company with $342 billion in assets under management and $40 billion in gross premiums. Another Swiss banking giant, Credit Suisse, acquired Winterthur Group in a $9 billion stock swap, making Credit Suisse one of the world's largest financial service firms.

Insurance firms have entered the mutual fund business as well, either acquiring or starting their own funds or selling funds as agents for other fund companies.

Through the one savings and loan holding company loophole, insurers have entering the banking business by chartering or acquiring thrifts (see in Chapter 4). Insurers have also formed joint ventures with banks. Many banks, where allowed, have acquired independent brokerage businesses as subsidiaries.

Commerce Bancorp, a regional bank based in Cherry Hill, New Jersey, for instance, became a major player in the insurance industry by acquiring six independent brokerage businesses in 1996 and 1997. In contrast to focusing on retail customers for insurance sales, Commerce National Insurance Services focuses on commercial insurance for small and mid-sized businesses. This subsidiary contributed about $25 million in revenues and 10% to Commerce Bancorp's 1998 earnings and became in its first 17 months of operations one of the top 50 insurance brokerages in the nation.

Other insurers are majority partners in joint ventures in which a bank and insurer together establish a third company in which they both have interests. While the bank becomes the majority partner in a ***bancassurance*** venture (the sale of insurance products through bank distribution channels), the insurer becomes the majority partner in an ***assurbanking*** operation (a system of taking bank products and selling them through the insurer's distribution channels). With either arrangement, less capital is required than with a complete acquisition, but revenue must be shared and conflicts concerning distribution channels between partners resolved. Alternatively, insurers may want to become minority partners to gain new customers and new sources of revenues without losing independence. However, in this arrangement insurers forfeit the majority of the revenue in the venture and may later be bought out by the majority partner. Banks and insurers also may simply maintain distribution channels with each other without forming a separate firm, thus requiring less capital investment. Other opportunities involve an insurer's furnishing outsourcing services to a new virtual bancassurer (similarly, a bank could provide services to a new virtual assurbank). With such an arrangement, the service provider generates additional revenue from an existing infrastructure but does not require affiliation. However, a virtual firm can in the future become a direct competitor of an established firm.[20]

As discussed in Chapter 9, insurers face much more competition from banks as court rulings have allowed banks more product flexibility, particularly in the annuity and mutual fund business. By the first half of 1997, investment fee income at 2,250 banks and thrifts (excluding Mellon Bank and its Dreyfus Corp. mutual funds) was $1.5 billion versus only about $700 million in the first half of 1994 and exhibited a 31% rise compared with the same period in 1996. In 1997, banks accounted for about 15% of annuity sales ($19.4 billion) in the U.S. Life insurance sales, however, were less than 1% of total sales in 1997. In contrast, in Europe insurance distribution through banks is much higher, including 15% of insurance sales in England and 65% in France.[21]

Changes in Insurer Distribution Systems with Technology

Insurance policies in the past have been distributed (or sold) through a **direct writer** system, involving an agent representing a single insurer, or through the independent agent system, involving an agent representing multiple insurers. An independent agent is responsible for running an agency and for the operating costs associate with it. Independent agencies are compensated through commissions, but direct writers may receive either commissions or salaries. With this system, customers become associated with the independent agency versus the insurance company. Direct writers have the advantage of support from the insurance company.[22]

Recently, similar to large depository institutions and securities firms, insurers have used the internet as a distribution network to make sales. In 1998, about 73% of insurance agencies with more than $25 million in premiums reported an internet presence, ranging from a simple listing on a carrier or third party's site or an agency owning a site itself. Although many smaller agencies are hesitant to participate more on the internet because of costs and concerns about the value of internet access and its effect on employee productivity, others have jumped in. Chubb & Sons, a P/C company in Warren, New Jersey, that sells through independent agents, decided to give internet access to its 9,000 employees and estimates that 40% to 50% of its

---

[20] Purchasing groups and risk retention groups were permitted by the Risk Retention Act of 1986. See Barbara Bowers. "A Year of Profits, Mergers and Regulation Tussles." *Best's Review Life/Health Edition* (January, 1998), 36–41.

[21] This section relies heavily on information from Barbara Bowers. "Banking on Insurance." *Best's Review Life and Health Edition* (May, 1998), 28–34.

[22] Ibid.

agents "have Internet connectivity." Chubb found that its employee productivity improved as agents discovered many new online applications. In a 1998 automation and interface survey of agents by Acord, a nonprofit insurance association, 905 respondents agreed that automation had allowed their staffs to become more productive; 20% of agencies had a website, with 43% of those without a web site planning to have one within the next six months.[23]

Life insurers have also used the internet to make sales. For instance, a shopper can buy a life insurance policy over the internet from Zurich Kemper Life Insurance Company, whereby the applicant receives an instant quotation and is allowed to submit most of the application information online. Other products Zurich is considering include electronic billing for the product, e-mail notification, online account access, and the potential use of digitized or voice signatures. Zurich Kemper also offers online rate quotations for term life policies. Similarly, a customer can buy a variable annuity from Lincoln Financial Direct in Leesburg, Virginia, directly over the internet without any human intervention. Early in 1998, Kemper Insurance Company in Long Grove, Illinois, began allowing business customers to file claims notices through its web site. Business customers can also call up electronic versions of appropriate state forms for workers' compensation claims and general forms for other types of business insurance claims. Encrypted information can then be sent to Kemper through the internet.

Other life and P/L companies, such as Progressive Insurance Group in Ohio, have web sites that allow customers to check account status, make payments, get information about automobile policies, and view a state policy contract. This allows fast processing around the clock. All agents of Progressive must have Window NT operating systems and be connected to the internet by the end of 1999. Health insurers such as Aetna U.S. Healthcare have set ambitious goals to have transactions between insurer and doctors become paper-free by the end of 1999. Aetna's E-Pay system makes the promise to doctors that they'll receive payments in 15 days for problem-free claims submitted electronically. This compares with industry averages between 40 to 45 days. Currently, about 38% of all physicians submit bills electronically. Similar to the use of ATMs by banks, health care insurers hope to reduce transaction costs and improve efficiency.[24]

AN OVERVIEW OF INSURANCE OPERATIONS

Before looking at other details about insurers, this section provides a brief overview of major insurance company operations as presented by J. Francois Outreville in the *Theory and Practice of Insurance*, which includes:[25]

✦ **Product Design and Development.** The design of new products satisfies customer needs and allows insurance companies to compete with other financial institutions. The nature and size of the market for the product, potential competition, expected losses, legal and regulatory factors, costs, advertising, and strategic planning need to be considered.

---

[23] See Leslie Werstein Hann. "A Web of Changes"; Barbara Bowers. "The Long, Last Mile"; and "The Check Is in the E-mail." *Technology Supplement Best's Review* (November, 1998), 11–26.

[24] Ibid.

[25] See Outreville (1999), from which this section draws heavily.

✦   **Production and Distribution.** The firm's marketing managers must decide how the new product will be produced, distributed, promoted, and advertised.

✦   **Product Management.** Product management includes **rate-making**, **underwriting**, and **claims adjustment and settlement**.

1. **Rate-making** involves setting the price (rate) for the product, selecting and classifying risks associated with the product, including covering losses and other costs plus a profit markup (underwriting area), and the fair and prompt payment of claims (claims areas). Statistical and actuarial operations classify risks and calculate the probabilities of losses.

2. **Underwriting** is the avoidance of "adverse selection and the misclassification of risks." The overall underwriting policies of the firm determine what type of risks the company is willing to underwrite, depending on the firm's financial capacity, regulatory framework, technical skills and abilities, and the availability of reinsurance. Staff and line underwriting functions implement these policies.

3. **Claims Adjustment and Settlement** means paying for losses of claimants "fairly and promptly" and acting sincerely and with integrity, which in turn affects the firm's reputation and public image. As Outreville points out, an agent handling claims must be "a detective, a lawyer, a psychologist, a gentleman, and above all, an ambassador of good will and good public relations."[26]

✦   **Services.** Services include legal services, loss control, risk management and policyholder services, and educational services for consumers and employees.

✦   **Administration.** Administration includes general management, strategic planning, personnel management, branch management, accounting, and public relations.

✦   **Finance and Investment.** These functions include managing the company's investment portfolio and determining an investment strategy; the latter is often subject to regulatory supervision. Regulations include the percentage of different types of assets in which a company may invest and the valuation of securities. In different countries, valuation is based on the lower of book value, or market value. The National Association of Insurance Commissioners (NAIC) in the U.S. recommends that bonds be valued at their amortized values, adjusting book values for the difference between the coupon rate and the current market rate. Common stock values are often listed at market value in many countries, which in turn may reduce surplus and affect policyholder dividend decisions. Real estate is listed as the lower of market or book value, although the market value is difficult to estimate. In the U.S. restrictions on the fraction of different types of securities vary from state to state. In other countries, laws limit fraction holdings as well. In France, for example, laws limit real estate holdings to 40% of admitted assets, all loans to 35%, and cash balances to 15%, and further mandate that a minimum of 33% of assets be held in government securities.[27] *Best's* has recently created investment performance benchmarks (providing peer groups in similar insurance lines in terms of total investment returns for premiums.[28]

---

[26] See Outreville (1999), 226; quoted from Michelbacher and Roos (1970), 107.

[27] See Outreville (1999).

[28] See "Benchmarking Insurers' Investments." *Best's Review Life/Health Edition* (January 1998), 49–55. Insurers increased profits by taking gains on selling fixed income securities when rates fell in the 1990s. See also Robert W. Stein. "The Ups and Downs of Interest Rates." *Best's Review: Life and Health Edition* (June 1998), 80.

U.S. Risk-Based Capital Requirements

NAIC developed a formula for risk-based capital (RBC) requirements for life-health companies in December, 1992, and for P/L companies in December, 1993.

RBC requirements attempt to estimate the capital needed by a firm to safely absorb the losses to which it is subject. For P/L companies, four risk categories are given:

- Investment or asset risk
- Credit risk, such as reinsurance
- Off-balance sheet risk, such as separate accounts
- Underwriting risk, such as the loss ratio and reserve adequacy.

A RBC requirement is calculated for each category based on calculations of risk charges applying to potential risks for that category. These charges are weighted based on the importance of different types of risk and summed. Adjustments are then made for covariances to account for diversification to achieve the RBC requirement. Life insurance RBC is calculated in a similar fashion, but with a heavier weight on asset risk because of the risk of asset values falling.

In contrast, for P/L companies the risks of underestimating reserves and overestimating the profitability of incoming premiums are given heavier weights.[29]

---

[29] See Outreville (1999). For a more detailed discussion of RBC calculations for insurers, see Saunders (1997) and Cornett and Saunders (1999).

For assets, securities are given higher RBC requirements based on their NAIC ratings. U.S. government bonds have 0% weights, the highest-rated securities (AAA to A+) have a 0.30% weighting; BBB, a 1% weighting; BB, a 4% weighting; B, a 9% weighting; CCC, a 20% weighting; and in near default, a 30% weighting. Residential mortgages have a 0.5% weighting, commercial mortgages a 3% weighting, common stocks a 30% weighting, and preferred stock a 2% weighting. Similar weightings with some variations are given for P/L investments. After calculating the dollar values for risk for different categories, which include for life insurers asset risk (C1), insurance risk (C2), interest rate risk (C3), and business risk (C4), RBC is calculated as:

$$RBC = [(\ C1 + C3)^2 + C2^2]^{1/2} + C4$$

The formula sums risks for the different categories and adjusts for correlations among risks. This is the minimum required capital that the life insurer must hold. The insurer is below the RBC requirement and would be subject to regulatory scrutiny if, when comparing total surplus and capital that the insurer holds to this measure by dividing RBC into the insurer's total surplus and capital, the comparison is below 1. For P/L insurers, risk types include Ro, common stock and preferred stock investments in affiliates; R1, fixed income securities; R2, common and preferred stock securities; R3, reinsurance recoverables and other receivables for credit risk; R4, loss and loss adjustment expense reserves plus growth surcharges for underwriting risk; and R5, written premiums plus growth surcharges. For securities weights are similar, but somewhat different from those discussed for life insurers are used. RBC for P/L insurers is calculated as:

$$RBC = Ro + [R1^2 + R2^2 + R4^2 + R5^2]^{1/2}$$

Again, this ratio would be compared with the P/L insurer's total capital and surplus, similar to the example above, to determine whether capital was adequate.

REGULATORY MONITORING FOR SOLVENCY

Regulators use early warning systems to monitor insurance companies for solvency risk. Some states have their own systems, but most use the system developed through NAIC, which prioritizes insurers according to their risk for greater analysis and on-site regulatory examinations. Insurers also receive a normal detailed financial examination every 3 to 5 years. NAIC's Insurance Regulatory System (IRIS), which has been used since the mid-1970s, involves 11 financial ratios calculated for each insurer with reviews and analysis by an examiner team. A normal rate is established for each ratio based on historical data for failed versus nonfailed firms. Insurers are put into one of five categories for further analysis and/or actions. NAIC also developed a new solvency screening system for major insurers in the early 1990s known as FAST (Financial Analysis Tracing System) that has separate screening models for P/L, life, and health insurers and an expanded set of financial ratios with which each insurer is scored. FAST scores are used to prioritize how much regulatory scrutiny a major insurer needs; they are not available to the public.[30]

PRIVATE INSURER SOLVENCY RATINGS

Several agencies provide insurance company financial ratings based on subjective evaluations, including A.M. Best, Standard and Poor's, Moody's, and Duff and Phelps. Financial ratios, public information, news reports, private communications with managers, and visits with companies form the basis for these subjective evaluations. Best's gives ratings as Secure (A++ Superior, A+ Excellent, A−, B++ Very Good); Vulnerable (B, B− Adequate, C++, C+ Fair; C, C− Marginal); Very Vulnerable (D); Under Supervision (E); and In Liquidation (F).[31]

TYPES OF LIFE INSURANCE POLICIES AND THE DETERMINATION OF PREMIUMS

Life insurance products have changed over the years, as insurers have developed new products to compete with the investment products offered by other financial institutions. Different types of life insurance policies include:

✦ **Whole Life.** Policyholders pay fixed annual premiums over their lives in exchange for a whole life policy with a known death benefit, i.e., the face amount of the policy. A whole life policy is so named because it provides death protection for the policyholder's entire life. The insured beneficiary receives the full

---

[30] See Outreville (1999) and Harrington and Neuhaus (1999).

[31] Ibid and *Best's Insurance Reports*. Best's ratings evaluate a company's financial strength, operating performance, and market profile by using quantitative and qualitative standards. Best's evaluation of financial strength includes capitalization, capital structure and holding company, quality and appropriateness of reinsurance program, adequacy of loss/policy reserves, quality and diversification of assets, and liquidity. Operating performance includes profitability, revenue composition, management experience, and objectives. Market profile factors include market risk, competitive market position, spread of risks, and event risk.

face amount regardless of the date of death. Premiums are set based on the average actuarial premium amount needed to cover claims for a policyholder's entire life. Hence, policyholders pay premiums that are larger than actuarially needed in early years. Excess premiums above what is actuarially needed are invested at a fixed annual rate established at the time the policy is written (often states set a minimum yield). Policyholder builds up cash values based on the earnings for excess premiums that can be cashed in, in lieu of maintaining full death protections, or against which low rate loans can be made.

◆ **Term Insurance.** In contrast to whole life insurance, policyholders pay premiums that are based only on what is actuarially needed to protect their beneficiaries given the covered person's age and medical history. Hence, premiums are low for younger people and rise with age. There is no accumulated cash value for term policies. Under an alternative decreasing term policy, the premium remains constant but the amount of insurance coverage decreases with age. Other options are also available, and term policies are frequently offered as group plans as part of employee benefit packages.

◆ **Variable Life.** Variable life policies, first introduced in 1975, are like whole life policies in that they require premiums over a policyholder's lifetime. However, excess premiums that add to cash value earn variable rather than fixed rates of return; these rates are based on the insurer's yield on assets of the policyholder's choice. Thus, the policyholder bears the entire investment risk, but has the opportunity to earn higher returns than a fixed rate, providing protection against inflation. A minimum death benefit is specified in the policy, although there is no maximum. The actual payment to beneficiaries depends on yields earned on excess premiums.

◆ **Universal Life.** Universal life, like variable life is a flexible policy introduced in 1979 that combines the death protection features of term insurance with the opportunity to earn market rates of return on excess premiums and to take advantage of tax free investment accumulations. In this sense, universal life is often much more of an investment vehicle than an insurance vehicle. A lump sum premium can be paid for the investment or a series of payments with payments as high as the investor desires. Excess premiums are invested, and the policyholder builds up a cash value. Unlike whole or variable life policies, the face amount of guaranteed death protection in a universal life policy can be changed at the policyholder's option. With universal life, the cash value has a minimum guaranteed return. If the policy is variable universal life (first introduced in 1985), investors have the flexibility of investing excess premiums in different types of investments, such as mutual funds. Variable universal life, often called flexible premium life, also gives policyholders the greatest freedom to adjust death benefits, premium payments, and investment risk/expected return as their cash-flow and death protection needs change.[32]

Trends in Preferences for Different Types of Policies

In the early 1980s, whole life customers were earning relatively low rates on the cash buildups of their policies. Many policyholders switched to term insurance under the

---

[32] The tax-free status of universal life policies that serve more as investment vehicles than insurance vehicles has been under attack by Congress.

strategy that they could invest the excess premium paid on whole life insurance and earn a higher rate than they could get on whole life policies. Policyholders also borrowed at low rates against the whole life policies or allowed their policies to lapse. As a result, whole life insurance purchases declined steadily from 53% to 40% between 1972 and 1982, and term insurance rose from 41% to 60% of new insurance in force. This created greater uncertainty for insurers since steady fixed premiums on whole life were changed for varying premiums on term policies based on an investors' age. In response, insurers developed variable life and universal life policies that could offer higher return and tax-free savings for policyholders. Insurers also moved more into the annuity business. Policyholder loans wreaked havoc for insurers trying to meet liquidity demands in the late 1970s and early 1980s, when rates were high and policyholders could borrow at low rates. Many lobbied regulators to be able to offer higher rates on policy loans to discourage such loans. Policy lapses, particularly among customers with the least need for insurance, also resulted in lower premium income for insurers and declining NUMs.

The introduction of new investment vehicles also increased insurers' costs, since customers' satisfaction with new policies depended on the performance of the insurer's investment portfolio. Moreover, servicing the new policies cost more since policies are tailormade and require higher reserves for future policy obligations based on market rates. The cash inflows and outflows for the new policies are also much less predictable than for traditional whole life, which creates a need for asset liquidity that previously had not been significant for insurers. With underwriting margins squeezed, insurers sought new ways to reduce costs, including reducing a large sales force of agents who were paid huge commissions on the sale of new policies, often up to 100% of the first year's premiums. Insurers found new ways to market policies, such as renting space in local depositories or selling through the mail. Agents also had to be trained in the complex details of new policies and other new investment products offered by the insurer, often requiring security licenses by agents.[33]

Illustration of How Premiums Are Set

Regardless of the policy, the insurer begins calculating the premium by examining a mortality table (see Table 10.7).[34] Death rates per 1,000 are calculated conservatively, according to the number of insured men actually dying during the historical period examined, with an increase to allow for a margin of error. When setting premiums, an insurer uses actuarial estimates reflecting the most recent information available, including new causes of death, such as AIDS, or new treatments for formerly fatal diseases.[35]

---

[33] Furthermore, sophisticated computer systems are needed to maintain accurate records on new flexible, tailormade products. These expenses put further pressure on insurer earnings as their product mix changes.

[34] Mortaility tables, such as the Commissioners Standard Ordinary (see Table 10.7) are recommended as a basis for calculating required insurer reserves by NAIC. Death rates per 1,000 are calculated conservatively, according to the number of insured men actually dying during a period, such as 1970–1975.

[35] Because mortality rates for men and women differ, life insurers use separate tables to calculate premiums for each sex. P/L companies also use separate premium schedules for men and women drivers because women have had better driving records. These practices have been challenged in courts as discriminating against both sexes. Most insurers, however, object vigorously to so-called unisex pricing, believing that premium and benefit differences between the sexes are justified. The issue has also been raised in Congress; see Dennon (1988).

Table 10.7 ◆ Excerpts from Commissioners 1980 Standard Ordinary Mortality Table (Based on Death Rates of Males, 1970–1975)

Life insurance premiums are based on actuarial data. This Standard Ordinary Mortality Table indicates the probability of death for males of different ages and allows insurers to estimate the probability of paying cash benefits for a given category of customers.

(1) Age (Years)	(2) Number Living	(3) Number Dying	(4) Deaths per 1,000 [(3)/(2)] × 1,000
0	10,000,000	41,800	4.18
1	9,958,200	10,655	1.07
2	9,947,545	9,848	0.99
3	9,937,697	9,739	0.98
4	9,927,958	9,531	0.96
5	9,918,427	8,927	0.90
6	9,909,500	8,522	0.86
7	9,900,978	7,921	0.80
8	9,893,057	7,519	0.76
9	9,885,539	7,315	0.74
10	9,878,223	7,211	0.73
·	·	·	·
·	·	·	·
·	·	·	·
35	9,491,617	20,027	2.11
36	9,471,590	21,216	2.24
37	9,450,374	22,681	2.40
38	9,427,693	24,323	2.58
39	9,403,369	26,235	2.79
·	·	·	·
·	·	·	·
·	·	·	·
70	6,274,100	247,890	39.51
71	6,026,210	260,935	43.30
72	5,765,275	274,715	47.65
73	5,490,560	289,023	52.64
74	5,201,537	302,677	58.19
75	4,898,859	314,458	64.19
·	·	·	·
·	·	·	·
·	·	·	·
95	146,720	48,412	329.96
96	98,308	37,804	384.55
97	60,504	29,054	480.20
98	31,450	20,693	657.97
99	10,756	10,756	1,000.00

Source: Life Insurance Fact Book, 1997. A projected 2000 table is also included with lower percentage deaths per 1,000. For instance, a male policy holder, age 35 has a probabiltiy of a claim of .70% under the 2,000 projected table versus 2.11% under the 1980 table above.

Using Table 10.7, suppose the rate of death for men before age 36 is a rate of 2.11 men per 1,000 (i.e., of a population of 9,491,617 men, 20,027 died on average). So the probability of a claim's being made during the year a policyholder is 35 years old is .211%. To set premiums, the insurer estimates the rate of return to be earned on premium payments made in advance of claims. Because most states require insurers to use conservative assumptions about the rate they will earn on invested premiums, this example assumes a rate of 4% and assumes that any claims paid will be paid at the end of the year.[36] Hence, the premium on a $100,000, 1-year term policy would be:

$$\text{Pure Premium} = \text{Present Value of Face Amount} \times \text{Probability of a Claim} \quad [10.6]$$

$$= \frac{(\$100,000 \times .00211)}{1.04} = \$2,028.88$$

If someone were 70 years old and wished to purchase 1-year term insurance with a face value of $100,000, the pure premium would be:

$$\frac{(\$100,000 \times 0.0395)}{1.04} = \$3,799.04$$

based on a mortality probability of 3.95% (whereby 247,890 of 6,274,100 men that age had a claim). Thus, term premiums rise significantly with age. Note that the low 4% discount rate assumed on the insurer's investment produces a higher premium than if a higher discount rate were used. In the 1980s, for instance, life insurer returns were greater than 8%; however, insurers and state regulators justify the continued use of low rates in the interests of conservatism and the risk of claims not being met with lower premiums.[37]

For whole life policies, premiums are set based on the present value of the insurer's expected cash outflows over an individual's life adjusting for the probability that premium payments may not be made. Suppose that this premium amount is $1,260.43. For the individual who is 35 who takes out a whole life policy, the excess premium of $1,260.43 less $202.88 equal to $1,057.55 will increase the cash value of the policy and will be invested as excess premiums for the policyholder. Cash value increases based on the assumed interest rate. Regardless of the insurer's actual investment earnings, nonparticipating whole life policyholders earn a fixed rate, and their beneficiaries receive a fixed death benefit. In contrast, participating policyholders may receive dividends in good years.[38]

---

[36] Pure premiums are generally increased by a loading to cover operating expenses and profit for shareholders.

[37] Not every insurer would charge the pure premium plus the same loading. Individual insurance underwriters must decide what types of risks they are willing to bear. In some cases, if a company prefers to deal with one type of client (say, nonsmokers), it may undercharge them and overcharge smokers to make up the difference. As a result, policies with identical features may be priced differently, depending on the underwriter's risk preferences. For an example of the range of premiums on a given term policy, see Richard Morais. "Double Indemnity." *Forbes* 136 (November 18, 1985), 280.

[38] The present value of the expected outflow to the insurer is calculated as a lump sum, and the insurer calculates the probability of a customer' surviving his premium at the beginning of each policy year. The weighted number of premium payments expected considering the probability of death and the impact of lost interest is divided into the expected cost of insuring the individual for life, resulting in an annual pure premium of $1,260.43 without considering operating costs.

ASSET MANAGEMENT CONSIDERATIONS

Life Insurers Because the assets of life insurers are mostly stocks and bonds, insurers need to carefully analyze the default and interest rate risk to which bond portfolios are exposed. In fact, because so many of the corporate bonds held by life insurers are privately placed, assessment of default risk is paramount. As noted in the opening paragraphs of this chapter, the financial problems of Executive Life, which was taken over by regulators in 1991, have been traced to the firm's investments in high-risk bonds. With greater liquidity needs caused by guaranteed investment contracts and other new investment products, insurers may have to sell assets before maturity, so they need to be well acquainted with interest rate theories and hedging techniques, discussed in Chapters 14–17, as well as portfolio theory, discussed in investment courses. Immunization (protecting returns on fixed assets from interest rate swings) has become very important for insurers, particularly for insurers with substantial **separate accounts**, defined as groups of assets designated as backing for specific obligations. If an insurer manages pension fund obligations for an employer, separate accounts are often used to support these obligations. Also, reserves for variable and universal life policies are often backed by separate accounts. Like commercial banks, insurance firms have diversified into the pension and popular retirement annuity product management businesses.

Investment in real estate requires knowledge of real estate markets and finance. Earnings pressures have raised concerns both in and outside the industry as insurers have been tempted to invest in riskier than normal assets. Hence, risk management is very important. New performance measures, such as economic value added (EVA) and market value added (MVA) measures are sometimes used to evaluate publicly traded insurers, but some analysts do not think these measures adequately "accommodate" insurer's specialized capital needs. Table 10.8 lists the top 20 insurance companies ranked by MVA.[39]

P/L Insurers P/L insurers are also increasingly using the immunization techniques discussed in Chapters 14–17 to reduce interest rate and credit risk. Catastrophe futures discussed in Chapter 18 hedge against large losses. Industry publications stress the importance of estimating a firm's anticipated cash outflows resulting from policy claims, many of which may not actually occur until months or even years after a policy is written. If estimates are carefully made, asset portfolios can be selected with cash inflows to match the anticipated series of outflows. Thus, insurers can attempt to immunize at least portions of the balance sheet.[40] For hedging with futures positions (discussed in Chapters 17 and 18), NAIC requires that gains and losses on futures be directly reflected in net worth rather than being amortized over time. Still, in an environment of rising rates, profitable hedges can protect insurers against the shrinkage of net worth caused by a decline in portfolio values, which also must be directly written off against net worth. Interest-rate and risk management strategies are important for P/L firms.

---

[39] See Lee McDonald. "Reading the Market." *Best's Review, Life and Health Edition* (June, 1998), 73–74.

[40] See Jeffrey B. Pantages. "Negating the Interest Rate Risk." *Best's Review, P/L Edition* (May, 1984), 24–28, 120; Niehaus and Mann (1992); Charles P. Edmonds, John S. Jahera, Jr., and Terry Rose. "Hedging the Future." *Best's Review, Property Casualty Edition* (September, 1983), 30–32, 118; and Nye and Kolb (1986). For a discussion of catastrophe and credit risk futures, see Chapter 18.

Table 10.8   ✦   Top 20 Insurance Companies Ranked by 1997 Market Value Added (MVA) and Economic Value Added (EVA)

MVA is calculated by taking the Market Value (stock price × # shares) of Equity Less the Book Value of Equity
EVA is calculated as the Net Operating Profit After Taxes Less the Dollar Cost of Capital Financing Operations

Company	Rank in Assets	MVA (bils.)	MVA Rank	EVA (bils.)	EVA Rank
American International Group	2	$39.70	1	−$0.83	49
Travelers Group, Inc.	1	$27.83	2	−$0.71	47
Allstate Corp.	8	$25.59	3	$1.42	1
Aon Corp.	23	$7.44	4	$0.08	15
Equitable Cos. Inc.	3	$7.05	5	$0.22	5
Progressive Corporation-Ohio	33	$6.93	6	$0.32	2
Mgic Investment Corp.-Wisc.	45	$5.80	7	$0.16	8
Conesco Inc.	13	$5.42	8	$0.24	3
Cincinnati Financial Corp.	30	$5.37	9	$0.03	21
American General Corp.	7	$5.17	10	$0.13	11
Sunamerica Inc.	14	$5.16	11	$0.10	14
Lincoln National Corp.	9	$4.37	12	−$0.30	42
Alfac Inc.	16	$4.34	13	$0.15	9
Jefferson-Pilot Corp.	18	$4.08	14	$0.17	7
Torchmark Corp.	27	$3.66	15	$0.11	12
MBIA Inc.	29	$3.03	16	$0.02	25
Mercury General Corp.	48	$2.30	17	$0.11	13
Transamerica Corp.	11	$2.12	18	$0.23	4
Chubb Corp.	22	$2.09	19	$0.23	23
Unum Corp.	26	$1.88	20	−$0.04	31

Source: Stern Steward & Co's ranking, from Lee McDonald, "Reading the Market," Best's Review Life/Health Edition, June 1998, 73–74.

Note: Ranks are for the top 50 insurers (only top 20 are listed above).

MVA for the top 50 insurers increased by $119 billion in 1997.

EVA also rose as the result of reduction in fixed capital investments through mergers & acquisitions; improved profit margins by cutting costs; and higher leverage and reduction of excess capital through share repurchases.

Caveats in calculating EVA for MVA are biases in net operating profit after taxes (NOPAT) by failing to address reserving for long-tail losses. Also, companies that are underreserved will tend to look better under EVA, unless a separate adjustment is made.

This list includes P/L, multiline, and life/health and insurance brokerage firms.

Summary

Insurance companies are founded on probability estimation, better known to insurers as actuarial science. Premiums and reported obligations are based on estimates of the amount and timing of claims a firm will have to pay in the future. Successful financial management involves balancing premium income and investment income against benefits paid to policyholders. Life and P/L insurers have different financial characteristics that arise from the types of policies they write. They have structural characteristics in common, however, and all experienced earnings pressures in the past decade.

Life insurers have traditionally enjoyed predictable cash flows. Higher interest rates and changing consumer preferences, however, have forced insurers to develop alternative products, making premium income and obligations to policyholders subject to market conditions and policyholder preferences. Changes in operating conditions have made asset/liability management strategies increasingly important for life insurers.

P/L insurers have faced a similar need to adapt management strategies to changing market and economic conditions, although incentives for change are different. In recent years, the main influences on earnings of P/L insurers have been inflation, larger litigation awards, and consumer pressure for lower premiums. These factors, along with the traditional underwriting cycle, depressed underwriting income so strongly in the 1980s that even rapidly rising investment income could not protect earnings. As with life insurers, these operating changes require P/L insurers to adjust asset/liability management strategies.

Suggested Case

"Case 10: Rockhard Insurance." Darden School, University of Virginia: Richard D. Crawford and William W. Sihler. *Financial Service Organizations: Cases in Strategic Management*. New York: HarperCollins College Publishers, 1994.

This case provides an opportunity for financial analysis and also covers strategic issues for a traditional insurer's decision whether or not to diversify into new activities, building on its strengths.

Questions

1. Compare and contrast the characteristics of insurance coverage offered by life and P/L insurers. Explain how these characteristics are reflected in the asset and liability choices of the two types of insurers.
2. In the opening quotations, recent problems of insurers are discussed. Explain some of the problems in terms of catastrophic losses and interest rate and liquidity problems. Why did many of these problems increase in the past two decades?
3. What are the two sources of insurance companies' revenues? Explain why investment income has become a more important source of revenues in recent years.
4. What types of securities do life insurers and P/L insurers, respectively, hold? Explain reasons for their differences in

holdings. What changes have occurred between 1986 to 1997 in the security holdings of life insurers? Explain why.
5. What are the majority of expenses for life insurers? For P/L insurers? How does this differ from depository institutions?
6. Explain what statutory accounting is. How does it differ from GAAP accounting?
7. How do the assets and liabilities of both life and P/L insurers differ from depository institutions? How do services offered and fund sources result in balance sheet differences? What are policy reserves? How are they calculated for life insurers?
8. Explain how the NUM differs from the NIM. How similar a role do the two ratios play in financial management decisions?
9. Explain what the loss ratio, expense ratio, combined ratio, and overall profitability ratio indicate in terms of the profitability of a P/L insurer. Why are P/L insurers very dependent on investment yields? What is the long tail of liability? How has it affected the financial performance of P/L insurers?
10. What are underwriting cycles, and why do P/L insurers have them?
11. Why do P/L insurers have problems raising insurance premiums? Give an example of attempts by consumers to limit premiums. How have P/L insurers reacted to consumer revolts and high court settlements for lawsuits?
12. What issues have life insurers faced in the 1990s? What have insurers done to try to resolve these problems and to diversify? How has technology changed insurer distribution systems?
13. Discuss overall insurance operations and the importance of different areas, including product design and development, production and distribution, product management, administration, and finance and investment.
14. How do RBC requirements for insurers differ from those of depository institutions? How does NAIC monitor insurers for insolvency?
15. List some private rating agencies for insurers.
16. Explain the differences among whole life, term insurance, variable life, and universal insurance policies. How are premiums determined for whole life versus term insurance? Why have policyholders preferred term insurance? What implications does this have for the asset/liability management of insurers?
17. Briefly discuss recent asset management considerations for life and P/L insurers.

Problems

1. Do a Dupont analysis and calculate the NUM, loss ratio, expense ratio, combined ratio, and overall profitability ratio for the Town and Country Mutual Automobile Insurance Company for the two years given in Table P10.1. Explain precisely why the ROE and ROA changed in 2005; be sure to include a review of the common size financial statements. What additional information would you like to know about Town and Country for your analysis?

Table P10.1 ✦ FINANCIAL INFORMATION FOR PERFORMANCE ANALYSIS FOR TOWN AND COUNTRY MUTUAL AUTOMOBILE INSURANCE COMPANY, YEAR-END BALANCE SHEETS, YEAR-END 2004 AND 2005 (MILS.)

Assets	2004	% Assets	2005	% Assets
U.S. Treasury Bonds	1,169	7.60%	1,106	6.63%
Municipal Bonds	2,779	18.07%	3,505	21.02%
Other Bonds	4,161	27.06%	4,554	27.32%
Total Bonds	$8,109	**52.74%**	$9,165	**54.98%**
Common & Preferred Stock	3,192	**20.76%**	3,260	**19.55%**
Mortgages & Other Loans	2,422	**15.75%**	2,501	**15.00%**
Other Assets	1,652	**10.74%**	1,745	**10.47%**
Total Assets	**$15,375**	100.00%	**$16,671**	100.00%
Liabilities & Net Worth				
Total Loss & Unearned Premium Reserves	7,185	46.73%	7,879	47.26%
Total Surplus (Net Worth)	8,190	**53.27%**	8,792	**52.74%**
Total Liabs. & Net Worth	**$15,375**	100.00%	**$16,671**	100.00%

Income Statements for 2004 and 2005 (mils.)

	2004	% Revs.	2005	% Revs.
Revenues				
Total Premiums Written	$8,011	96.31%	$8,975	94.24%
Less Unearned Premiums	(375)	−4.51%	(473)	−4.97%
Total Earned Premiums	**$7,636**	**91.80%**	**$8,502**	**89.27%**
Net Investment Earnings & Other Income	**682**	**8.20%**	**1,022**	**10.73%**
Total Revenues	$8,318	100.00%	$9,524	100.00%
Expenses				
Loss Expenses	$6,077	73.06%	$7,276	76.40%
Policyholder Dividends	136	1.64%	4	0.04%
Operating Expenses	1,355	16.29%	1,511	15.87%
Total Expenses	$7,568	**90.98%**	$8,791	**92.30%**
Underwriting Results				
Earned Premiums	$7,636	**91.80%**	$8,502	**89.27%**
Less: Loss Expenses	(6,077)	−73.06%	(7,276)	−76.40%
Operating Expenses	(1,355)	−16.29%	(1,511)	−15.87%
Statutory Underwriting gain (loss)	$204	**2.45%**	$(285)	**−3.00%**
Less Dividends to Policyholders	(136)	−1.64%	$0	0.00%
Net Underwriting Gain (Loss)	**$68**	**0.81%**	**(289)**	**−3.00%**

2. Do a Dupont financial analysis for the RLI Corporation, shown in Table P10.2, for 1997 to 1998. Explain why the company's ROA improved in 1997 and why it fell in 1998. Include an evaluation of the GAAP combined ratio and common size statements.

3. Evaluate the ratios given from *Best's Insurance Reports: Property/Casualty Edition* for Gateway Insurance Company shown in Table P10.3. (Some ratios are particular to Best's and are defined in Table 10.5.) Do you agree with Best's rating of B++ for the company? Point out any strengths or weaknesses that you can find from the ratios given. What additional information would you like to have?

4. Evaluate the ratios given from *Best's Insurance Reports: Property/Casualty Edition* for Allstate Property and Casualty Insurance Company in Table P10.4. (Some ratios are particular to Best's and are defined in Table 10.5.) Do you agree with Best's rating of *Fair* for the company? Point out any strengths or weaknesses that you can find from the ratios given.

Table P10.2 ✦ RLI CORPORATION (MULTI-LINE INSURER) YEAR-END 1997 & 1988

Assets (in thous.)	1997	% Assets	1998	% Assets	Reported Financial Ratios	1997	1998
		Fiscal Year End					
Cash & Investments	603,857	66.23%	677,293	66.88%	Return on Average Assets	3.43%	2.93%
Reinsurance Assets	211,386	23.18%	274,707	27.13%	Return on Average Equity	12.93%	10.08%
Deferred Policy Acq. Costs	21,985	2.41%	22,510	2.22%	Investment Yield	4.66%	4.03%
Other Assets	74,516	8.17%	38,175	3.77%	Operating Income to Revenues	23.95%	22.76%
Total Assets	911,744	100.00%	1,012,685	100.00%	**Underwriting Measures:**		
Liabilities & Equity					GAAP Combined Ratio	86.8	88.2
Policy Reserves	532,807	58.44%	557,546	55.06%	Statutory Combined Ratio	90.4	N/A
Debt	24,900	2.73%	39,644	3.91%			
Other Liabilities	87,482	9.60%	121,536	12.00%			
Total Liabilities	645,189	**70.76%**	718,726	**70.97%**	**Balance Sheet Ratios:**		
Total Common Equity	266,555	**29.24%**	293,959	**29.03%**	Policy Reserves to Equity %	2.00%	1.90%
Total Liabilities & Equity	911,744	100.00%	1,012,685	100.00%	Debt + Rdm. Prfd. to Equity	9.34	13.49
					Debt to Total BkValue Capital	8.54	11.88
Income Statement							
Revenues:							
Policy Revenues	141,884	**83.28%**	142,324	**83.99%**			
Net Investment Income	24,558	**14.41%**	23,937	**14.13%**			
Net Realized Gains	2,982	1.75%	1,853	1.09%			
Other Revenues	951	0.56%	1,337	0.79%			
Total Revenues	**170,375**	100.00%	**169,451**	100.00%			
Expenses:							
Policy Expenses	61,252	35.95%	64,728	38.20%			
Other Expenses	66,053	38.77%	64,722	38.20%			
Interest Expense	1,548	0.91%	2,280	1.35%			
Total Expenses	**128,853**	75.63%	**131,730**	77.74%			
Net Income Before Taxes	**41,522**	24.37%	**37,721**	22.26%			
Provision for Taxes	11,351	6.66%	9,482	5.60%			
After-Tax Net Income	**30,171**	**17.71%**	**28,239**	**16.66%**			

Source: SNL Insurance Quarterly, SNL Securities, Charlottesville, Virginia, 1998.

5. Use the information from the Commissioners Standard Ordinary Table (abbreviated in Table 10.7) as well as an assumed rate of return on invested premiums of 6% to answer the following questions:
   a. What is the probability that a policyholder who is 30 years old will live to be 40?
   b. What is the pure premium on a $75,000, 1-year term policy for a 39-year old man?
   c. If the assumed rate of return on invested premiums were 9%, what would the pure premium be for the policy described in b?
   d. If, instead, the policyholder wished to take out a whole life policy with a face amount of $75,000, identify the additional steps needed to calculate the premium. Without doing any calculations, would the first year's premium on the whole life policy be higher or lower than the premium you calculated in part b? Explain why.
6. a. Using information from the Commissioners Standard Ordinary Table (abbreviated in Table 10.7) and an assumed rate of return of 8%, calculate the pure premium on a $1 million, 1-year term policy for a 4-year old boy. If you were the parent of a 4-year old boy, what factors might influence you to take out a life insurance policy on him? What type of policy would you prefer? Why?
   b. Calculate the premium on a $1 million, 1-year term policy for a 70-year old man. If you were 70 and had no life insurance, what type of policy would you choose? Why?

Table P10.3   ✦   GATEWAY INSURANCE COMPANY, INSURANCE FROM BEST'S 1997 INSURANCE REPORTS, PROPERTY/CASUALTY

Current Rating: B++ (Very good) reflecting the company's conservative operating strategy, favorable liquidity position, and strong capital support from its company. Management has geographically diversified operations outside of the northwestern/central region of the U.S. and additional licenses are being sought. Partially offsetting these positive factors is the company's fair return figures on its non-standard auto and taxicab business, lack of surplus growth, and modest debt service requirements at the holding company level. Management has continued to implement more efficient loss control measures to improve its financial position and support additional growth. With the improvement in operating earnings along with the available capital support from its parent, Best views the company's rating as stable.

| Key Financial Indicators | | | | | | |
Period Ending	Direct Premiums Written	Net Premiums Written	Pretax Op Income	Net Income	Total Admitted Assets	Policy-holders' Surplus
1992	8,386	8,004	296	260	12,001	3,359
1993	8,675	8,370	129	246	13,438	4,143
1994	8,961	8,858	602	467	14,757	4,481
1995	12,651	12,563	−930	−563	18,746	6,546
1996	12,218	12,119	273	362	18,854	6,942

Profitability

	Loss Ratio	Expense Ratio	Combined Ratio	Industry Ave	Investmt. Yield %	Industry Ave	Pretax ROR %	Industry Ave	Leverage BCAR %	NPW to PHS	Industry Ave.	Liquidity Overall Liquidity
1992	70.5	32.0	102.5	103.0	5.60%	5.40%	3.70%	4.70%		2.4	2.1	138.90%
1993	75.5	30.9	106.4	96.8	5.00%	5.50%	1.50%	10.10%		2.0	2.2	144.60%
1994	62.0	34.3	96.3	97.0	4.80%	5.20%	7.50%	9.50%	96.10%	2.0	2.3	143.60%
1995	72.3	36.7	109.0	100.9	4.80%	5.60%	−8.30%	6.50%	83.50%	1.9	2.3	153.70%
1996	68.2	36.9	105.1	99.0	5.60%	5.50%	2.20%	7.65%	104.40%	1.7	2.3	158.30%
5-Year	69.8	34.6	104.4	99.2	5.20%	5.40%	0.80%	7.70%				

1996 Business Production & Profitability ($000)

Product Line	Premiums Direct	Written Net	% of Total NPW	Pure Loss Ratio	Loss & LAE Res.
Private Auto Liability	6,862	6,862	56.60%	64.00%	3,151
Commercial Auto Lia.	3,612	3,513	29.00%	39.10%	2,655
Auto Physical	1,744	1,744	14.40%	70.30%	154
All Other				−7.90%	41
Totals	12,218	12,119	100.0	57.9%	6,001

Major 1996 Direct Premium Writings by State ($000):

Missouri $7,984 (65.3%); Louisiana $2,100 (17.2%); Indiana $921 (7.5%); Kansas $518 (4.2%)

Tennessee $355 (2.9%); and 3 other jurisdictions, $340 (2.8%)

Business Review

The overall business mix is 70% consumer and 30% commercial. The firm focuses on physical damage & liability coverage for non-standard personal autos & smaller size taxicab fleets. About 90% of all business is produced by MidAmerican General Agency. Most volume is concentrated in Missouri. Licensed in 22 states, management is hoping to add 6 additional states in the future.

Table P10.4 ✦ THE GARDEN STATE INDEMNITY COMPANY, INC., FREEHOLD, NEW JERSEY FROM BEST'S 1997
INSURANCE REPORTS, PROPERTY/CASUALTY

Current Rating: The firm is rated 4 (Fair) on a scale of 1 to 9 reflecting the firm's enhanced operating results, strengthened balance sheet and improved loss reserve development. Offsetting these positive factors is the firm's heavy reliance on reinsurance, low level of retained earnings, and higher operating leverage. Garden States primarily writes professional liability coverage for lawyers and accountants in New Jersey. (Mix 87% lawyers liability; 9% accountants, and 4% surety) The firm has been profitable in each of the past 4 years as the result of growth in net interest income & improved underwriting expenses. Underwriting has benefited from better risk selection, an extensive application process and increased rates. Pretax Return on Net Premiums Earned was favorable compared to peer commercial casualty carriers with < $10 mil. in policyholder surplus.

Profitability Analysis

Period Ending	Pretax ROR %	Industry Ave	Return on PHS	Industry Average	Combined Ratio	Industry Average	Operating Ratio	Industry Average
1992	−99.9	−3.2	−29.1	2.20	739.8	119.9	472.0	102.7
1993	39.1	3.2	17.2	11.4	74.1	112.2	61.8	95.7
1994	10.3	5.3	1.2	4.4	101.0	110.1	89.7	93.6
1995	9.6	6.4	7.1	16.1	102.1	110.5	88.8	93.3
1996	13.1	5.0	12.4	10.5	98.3	111.0	85.9	93.3
5-Year	12.9	3.4	4.4	9.2	101.3	112.7	87.7	95.7

Underwriting Experience — Loss Ratios — Expense Ratios

Period Ending	Underwriting Income (000)	Pure Loss %	LAE %	Loss & LAE %	Net Comms. %	Other Expenses %	Total Expenses %	Combined Ratio %
1992	−936	421.2	291.4	712.6	−15.6	42.9	27.3	739.8
1993	621	49.6	32.4	82	−33.6	25.7	−7.9	74.1
1994	−42	52.3	45.6	97.9	−23.0	26.1	3.1	101.0
1995	−153	54.0	37.4	91.4	−9.9	20.6	10.7	102.1
1996	98	42.5	47.7	90.2	−15.4	23.6	8.2	98.3
5-Year		50.8	43.4	94.2	−18.1	25.2	7.1	101.3

Leverage Analysis — **Liquidity Analysis**

Period	BCAR %	NPW/PHS	Industry	Overall Liquidity	Industry
1992		1.0	1.6	131.8	124.1
1993		0.9	1.5	146.3	126.0
1994	39.9	1.2	1.5	140.0	126.3
1995	52.7	1.4	1.4	135.2	128.4
1996	53.6	1.6	1.3	129.3	129.8

Source: 1997 Best's Insurance Reports—Property-Casualty 1997, 1949–1950.

Ceded Reinsurance Analysis

Ceded Reins. to PHS %

Period	Firm	Industry
1992	717.5	208.2
1993	568.0	196.4
1994	688.7	193.6
1995	709.6	175.7
1996	700.0	156.8

Ceded Reins. to PHS Ratio: Measures Company's dependence upon the security provided by reinsurers & its potential exposure to adjustments on such reinsurance. The larger the ratio, the greater the dependence on reinsurance versus policyholder surplus to cover losses.

Selected References

Altman, Edward I. and Irwin T. Vanderhoof. *The Financial Dynamics of the Insurance Industry*. New York: Irwin Professional Publishing, 1995.

Altman, Edward I. and Irwin T. Vanderhoof. *The Strategic Dynamics of the Insurance Industry: Asset/Liability Management Issues*. New York: Irwin Professional Publishing, 1996.

American Council of Life Insurance: Life Insurance Fact Book 1998. Washington D.C.: American Council of Life Insurance, 1998.

Cornett, Marcia Millon and Anthony Saunders. *Fundamentals of Financial Institutions Management*. New York: Irwin McGraw-Hill, 1999.

Crawford, Richard D. and William W. Sihler. *Financial Service Organizations: Cases in Strategic Management*. New York: Harper Collins, 1994.

Cummins, J. David and Joan Lamm-Tennant. *Financial Management of Life Insurance Companies*. Boston: Kluwer Academic Publishers, 1993.

Cummins, J. David, Scott E. Harrington, and Robert W. Klein. "Cycles and Crisis in Property/Casualty Insurance: Causes and Implications for Public Policy." *Journal of Insurance Regulation* (Fall, 1991), 50–93.

Dennon, A. R. "The Facts about Unisex Insurance." *Consumers' Research*, 71 (February, 1998), 25–27.

Harrington, Scott E. and Gregory R. Niehaus. *Risk Management and Insurance*. New York: Irwin McGraw-Hill, 1999.

Mehr, Robert I. *Fundamentals of Insurance*. Homewood, Illinois: Irwin, 1983.

Mehr, Robert I., and Sandra G. Gustavson. *Life Insurance: Theory and Practice*. Plano, Texas: Business Publications, Inc., 1984.

Michelbacher, G. F. and N. R. Roos. *Multiple-Line Insurers: Their Nature and Operation*. New York: McGraw-Hill Book Co., 1970.

Niehaus, Greg and Steven V. Mann. "The Trading of Underwriting Risk: An Analysis of Insurance Futures Contracts and Reinsurance." *Journal of Risk and Insurance*, 59 (December, 1992), 601–627.

Nye, David J. and Robert W. Kolb. "Inflation, Interest Rates, and Property-Liability Insurer Risk." *Journal of Risk and Insurance*, 53 (March, 1986), 144–154.

Outreville, J. Francois. *Theory and Practice of Insurance*. Boston: Kluwer Academic Publishers, 1998.

Property/Casualty Insurance Facts. New York: Insurance Information Institute, 1998.

Rejda, George E. *Principles of Risk Management and Insurance*, 5th ed. New York: Harper Collins College Publishers, 1995.

Saunders, Anthony. *Financial Institutions Management: A Modern Perspective*, 2nd ed. New York: Irwin, 1997.

Vaughan, Emmett J. *Fundamentals of Risk and Insurance*. New York: John Wiley and Sons, 1982.

Chapter 10 Internet Exercise

Insurance company financial management issues

1. A.M. Best Co. (http://www.ambest.com) was founded in 1899 with the purpose of performing "a constructive and objective role in the insurance industry towards the prevention and detection of insurer insolvency." This mission led to the development of Best's Ratings. Today, A.M. Best rates the financial strength of insurance companies and the security of holding company's debt and preferred stock. More than merely passing judgment on past performance, a Best's Rating gives an indication of how that company may be expected to perform in the future.

   A Best's Rating is an independent third-party evaluation that subjects all insurers to the same rigorous criteria, providing a valuable benchmark for comparing insurers, regardless of their country of domicile. Such a benchmark is increasingly important to an international market that looks for a strong indication of stability in the face of widespread deregulation, mergers, acquisitions and other dynamic factors.

   A.M. Best assigns to insurance companies one of two types of rating opinions, a Best's Rating (A++ to F) or a Financial Performance Rating (9 to 1). For an explanation of Best's rating system, go to:
   http://www.ambest.com/ratings/guide.html

2. Insurance company ratings from Standard and Poor's and Moody's are available through the Insurance News Network at
   http://www.insure.com/ratings/index.html

   From this page, click on "Standard and Poor's" to get the rating by type of company (life/health, property/casualty, etc.) For example, to find all life insurance companies in the U.S. with BB rating, then select:

   Type of company: life/health

   Rating: BB

   Country: U.S.

   Then click "Find the ratings."

   The resulting table listing the BB-rated insurance firms also provides information on "What the ratings mean" and whether there is a credit watch on the firm. An insurer rated 'BB' has MARGINAL financial security characteristics. Positive attributes exist, but adverse business conditions could lead to insufficient ability to meet financial commitments.

3. Know your insurance terms and also a crossword puzzle enthusiast? A crossword puzzle for insurance terms can be found at:
   http://www.bus.orst.edu/classes/ba535/crosswor.htm

Other useful sites for financial institution data:

American Risk and Insurance Association
http://www.aria.org/

BERKSHIRE HATHAWAY INC.
http://www.berkshirehathaway.com/

Insurance Industry Internet Network
http://www.iiin.com/index_frames.html

Insurance Information Institute
http://www.iii.org/

Progressive Insurance Online
http://www.progressive.com/

Traveler's Group
http://www.insuremarket.com/carrier/travelers/sh/index.htm

Wharton Risk Management and Decision Processes Center
http://grace.wharton.upenn.edu/risk/

"The only way to make investment banking more competitive would be to gouge eyes out."

Robert Baldwin
Partner at Morgan Stanley, 1960s, from Ron Chernow, *The House of Morgan*, New York: Touchstone, 1990, p. 587.

"I am not a yesterday person. I don't really care about yesterday. If we did well yesterday, that is history. What I am worried about is how we are going to perform five years from now."

David Komansky
President and Chief Operating Officer—Merrill Lynch & Co., Inc.
Quote from *The New Financiers: Profiles of the Leaders Who are Reshaping the Financial Services Industry,*
ed. Charles B. Wendel (Chicago: Irwin Professional Publishing, 1996), p. 143.

"Three years ago, it was an almost invisible blip: two years later, it was hard to miss. But the major brokerage firms continued to ignore the exploding phenomenon of online trading. Today, online trading has caught Wall Street's attention with a vengeance. Fueled by the bull market, Internet brokers have attracted a deluge of new customers. Online brokers' stocks have soared, with Ameritrade Inc. up 118% since January 4. Some 14 percent of all equity trades were executed online last year, up 50 percent since 1997. The online brokerage industry has doubled customer assets, to $420 billion, and doubled accounts, to 7.3 million, reports Piper Jaffray Inc."

Leah Nathans Spiro with Edward C. Baig
"Who Needs a Broker? *Business Week* (February 22, 1999), p. 113.

"The founder and former chief executive of Hambrecht & Quist, LLC has started a new company that will sell shares in IPO's over the Internet. While others have taken up that basic idea, Mr. Hambrecht is going a step further by using a 'Dutch auction' process both to set the offering price and allocate stock to individual investors. High bidders, not preferred investors, get the shares . . . And, theoretically, companies could raise more money by selling their shares closer to the price at which they begin trading on the market . . . . Just as the Internet has brought dramatic changes by lowering trading commissions and opening the door for new brokerages to attract individual investors, Mr. Hambrecht's concept . . . if it proves popular— could bring a new element of competition to Wall Street."

Lisa Bransten and Nick Wingfield
"New Company Aims to Shift IPO Playing Field," *The Wall Street Journal* (February 8, 1999), C1.

11

INVESTMENT BANKS, RETAIL SECURITIES FIRMS, AND VENTURE CAPITALISTS: MANAGEMENT AND ETHICAL ISSUES

*W*ith the advent of the information age, the traditional methods that investment banks and security firms use to distribute securities is changing dramatically. Online securities trading grew dramatically in the 1990s; Charles Schwab, an established discount brokerage firm, as well as new firms like E°Trade Group, Inc., and Ameritrade Holding Company offered low-cost trading on the Internet. Other traditional full service brokerage firms including Merrill Lynch, Citigroup Inc.'s Salomon Smith Barney, and Prudential Investments offer online research services to monitor and transfer accounts and to access pay-per-view research reports. Several traditional firms, such as Merrill Lynch, Morgan Stanley Dean Witter, and Prudential Securities also began offering online trading services as well, in 1998. As shown in Table 11.1, to take advantage of such services, customers often must have at least a $100,000 account with these respective firms. In early June 1999, Merrill Lynch, however, unveiled a new plan to offer online trading for as little as $29.95 a trade.[1]

Such traditional firms have been wary about offering Internet trading services to the public. Traditional brokerage firms face the dilemma of either competing with online rivals such as Charles Schwab, by quickly embrac-ing Internet trading and alienating their retail brokers, or not entering online trading and falling far behind what many believe is a "once-in a-generation technology breakthrough that will transform the investment world."[2] Donaldson, Lufkin & Jenrette's solution to this problem was to establish a separate subsidiary with a different name, DLJ Direct, as a separate Internet trading unit. Whether such ventures cannibalize current customers or bring in new customers is subject to question. For instance, Merrill Lynch noted that its temporary free research on the Internet in February 1999 attracted about 90,000 registered users, more than 2,000 of which became new clients for Merrill Lynch brokers. Other Merrill Lynch customers, however, have kept their brokerage accounts but used information they receive from their brokers to make trades with cheaper online discount brokers.[3]

Firms that do offer online trading are not always initially profitable. E°Trade, established in 1996 and now the third largest online broker, achieved 676,000 accounts in 1998. However, the firm lost $200,000 as a result of high advertising and other costs. It also faced a class action lawsuit by customers resulting from a three-day computer shutdown in February 1999. Similarly, Charles Schwab initially suffered a lower profit margin as it switched customers from telephone and

---

[1]See Rebecca Buckman. "More Old-Line Brokers Test Waters Online." *The Wall Street Journal* (January 6, 1999), C1; Charles Gasparino and Randall Smith. "Internet Trades Put Merrill Bull on Horns of a Dilemma." *The Wall Street Journal* (February 12, 1999), C1; and Rebecca Buckman. "Morgan Stanley Shows Caution in Promoting On-Line Trades." *The Wall Street Journal* (——, 1999) C1, C17; and McNamee (1999); and Rebecca Buckman, "Wall Street Is Rocked by Merrill's Online Plans," *The Wall Street Journal*, June 2, 1999, C1, C27.

[2]Charles Gasparino and Randall Smith. "Internet Trades Put Merrill Bull on Horns of a Dilemma." *The Wall Street Journal* (February 12, 1999), C1.

[3]See Rebecca Buckman. "More Old-Line Brokers Test Waters Online." *The Wall Street Journal* (January 6, 1999), C1.

broker trades to cheaper Internet trades costing as little as $29.95 for up to 1,000 shares traded.[4]

However, in the long run, both firms are poised for future success. E°Trade is pursuing a promising business model as a "pipeline" for all sorts of products and services, including 24-hour cross-currency trading, banking, and insurance, and in 1999 it received Securities and Exchange Commission (SEC) approval to sell

its own brand of mutual funds. E°Trade has invested heavily in Archipelago, a cutting-edge electronic trading system, opening the possibility of joint ventures with Goldman Sachs. E°Trade's pockets are deep: Japan's Softbank Corporation invested $400 million in the firm, and E°Trade is in a joint venture with Sanford Robertson, a well-known Silicon Valley Banker, to form an online investment banking firm and also acquired

---

Table 11.1   ✦   ONLINE TRADING COMPARISON WITH SERVICES OFFERED AND COSTS PER TRADE BY DIFFERENT SECURITY FIRMS

Here are how the Web offerings of three online brokers compare with those of three full-service brokers that do not have online trading:

ONLINE VS. OLD-LINE

Firm/Web Address	Costs	Research	Real-Time Quotes	Emergency Backup	Mutual Funds	Neat Features
Charles Schwab www.schwab.com	$29.95 per trade up to 1,000 shares, 3¢ per additional share	Hambrecht & Quist, Credit Suisse First Boston	100 per trade	800 number, 300 U.S. offices	Screen 1,500 funds, Morningstar data	Nearly every investment term on Schwab's pages is hyperlinked to a glossary
E°Trade www.etrade.com	$14.95 per market-order trade, up to 5,000 shares; 1¢ per additional share; Add $5 for limit orders or over-the-counter stocks	BancBoston/ Robertson Stephens	Unlimited	800 number (extra fee, may be waived in system failure)	Screen 4,300 funds, Morningstar data	Excellent charting for multiple stocks
DLJdirect www.dljdirect.com	$20 per trade up to 1,000 shares; 2¢ per additional share	Zacks Investment Research	100 per trade	800 number	Screen 6,500 funds, Lipper data	Offers chance to set up and track up to 20 model portfolios.
Morgan Stanley Dean Witter www.deanwitter.com	Asset-management fee: $40 per trade for $100,000 account, 56 trades per year	Proprietary; 248 analysts	Unlimited	438 U.S. offices	No online screening	CNBC video clips available online
PaineWebber www.painewebberedge.com	Asset-management fee: $43 per trade for $100,000 account, 52 trades per year	Proprietary; 92 analysts	None	303 U.S. offices	No online screening	Arrange to have up to 400 quotes E-mailed to you throughout the day
Merrill Lynch www.plan.ml.com	Asset-management fee: $56 per trade for $100,000 account, 27 trades per year June 1999, $29.95 per trade	Proprietary; 667 analysts	None	672 U.S. offices	No online screening	"Bullhorn" E-mails you when watch-list stocks hit target price

Source: Mike McNamee, "Who Needs a Broker?" *Business Week*, February 22, 1999, 124.

---

[4]Because of cost pressures some online broker fees rose in March 1999, including the online brokerage subsidiary of Fleet Financial Group, Suretrade; the discount brokerage unit of Lindner Funds; and the discount brokerage of Fidelity. See Rebecca Buckman. "Some Online Broker Fees Are Climbing." *The Wall Street Journal* (March 16, 1999), C21; Leah Nathans Spiro. "Will E°Trade Move Beyond E°Tragedy?" *Business Week* (February 22, 1999), 118; Rebecca Buckman. "E°Trade Hits Cyber-Bumps in Strategy." *The Wall Street Journal* (February 22, 1999), C1, C10; and Joseph Kahn. "Schwab Lands Feet First on Net." *The New York Times* (February 10, 1999); and Steven Lipin, Rebecca Buckman, and Paul M. Sherer, "E°Trade to Announce Pact for Telebans" *The Wall Street Journal*, June 1, 1999, A3, A6.

Telebanc Financial Corp. in June 1999, one of the few online banks.[5] Charles Schwab's profits took off in 1998, with about one in 20 stock trades in the United States passing through its system. Successfully converting itself into a full-line Internet brokerage firm, in 1999, Schwab opened an average of 6,400 new accounts and brought in $460 million in new net assets a day. Schwab also served as a selling syndicate member for a number of new stock issues.[6]

In addition to online trading, the nature of investment banking is changing dramatically in the Internet Age. In early February 1999, William Hambrecht, former chief executive officer and founder of Hambrecht & Quist, LLC, an innovative investment bank, announced the start-up of an Internet investment bank. This new firm offers initial public offerings (IPOs) on the Internet in Dutch auctions, as opposed to setting the price of an IPO as investment bankers currently do. High bidders,

rather than preferred investors (as is the common practice), are given shares. This new process should reduce the cost of underwriting issues for firms going public, including reducing current underpricing that occurs on average for issues. Under the new system, firms will be charged fees of 3 percent to 5 percent of the amount of money raised as opposed to the traditional 6 percent to 7 percent gross spread and fees collected by investment bankers. Hence, this new process may revolutionize current investment banking practices.[7]

The securities industry is constantly evolving. This chapter discusses the structure of the investment banking industry, the financial statements of firms in this industry and how to analyze them, the key activities for these firms, and changes that have occurred and are occurring. The chapter also presents a brief overview of the stock and bond underwriting process, and the activities of venture capital firms.

✦ ✦ ✦

STRUCTURE OF THE INDUSTRY, TYPES OF FIRMS, AND PROFIT CYCLES

The following sections present an overview of the structure of the investment banking and security firm industry, a brief history of investment banking and key areas of activity, and a review of financial statements and a financial performance analysis.

STRUCTURE OF THE INDUSTRY AND ITS CYCLES

Structure and Types of Firms In the late 1990s, about 8,000 securities firms in the United States had about 262,000 employees and more than $54 billion in equity capital, supporting assets of more than $1.25 trillion. In 1997 alone debt underwriting exceeded $1 trillion, and stock underwriting was greater than $150 billion.[8]

---

[5]Rebecca Buckman. "Ex-Robertson Stephens Official, Others See Unveiling Online Investment Bank." *The Wall Street Journal* (January 12, 1999), C20.

[6]See Sean Davis. "On-Line Brokers Set to Report Profit Growth." *The New York Times* (July 9, 1998), C15;, C1; and Rebecca Buckman. "Schwab Clients Increase Activity in Online Trading." *The Wall Street Journal* (February 17, 1999), C13.

[7]Under a traditional underwriting system, IPOs have on average been underpriced, with prices rising above the initial offering price on the date of the offering. Therefore, favored institutional investors, instead of the client firm, receive high returns. With the new Dutch auction process, underpricing should occur less often, and the client firm should get a more favorable price for shares. Lisa Bransten and Nick Wingfield. "New Company Aims to Shift IPO Playing Field." *The Wall Street Journal* (February 8, 1999), C1, C11; and Ruth Simon. "IPOs Over the Internet? Tread Carefully." *The Wall Street Journal* (February 24, 1999), C1.

[8]See *Securities Industry Trends* (1997, 1998).

The growth and size of the securities firm industry, however, is very cyclical, with rises during bull (upward) stock markets and falls during bear (downward) markets and periods of large trading losses. Frequently, layoffs occur during market downturns. For instance, in late September 1998, as the result of a "dearth of stock and bond deals" and huge trading losses, Wall Street Securities firms posted their worst quarterly results since the fourth quarter of 1994, and some major firms, including Merrill Lynch and Salomon Smith Barney, considered layoffs. As noted by Dean Eberling, an analyst at Putnam, Lovell, de Guardiola, and Thornton, a New York investment-banking boutique, "This [was] the wake-up call to remind people that . . . this business is cyclical."[9]

The extent of the cyclical nature of security firm profits is demonstrated in Table 11.2, which shows pretax return on equity (ROE) for different types of firms, including the following:

(1) National full line (firms offering both retail brokerage services and advice, along with corporate advisory and investment banking services and trading activities for customers and for the firm itself—principal transactions). Examples of full-line firms include Merrill Lynch and PaineWebber. National full line firms often receive the largest percentage of their revenues from brokerage commissions on security sales as well as from the net interest spread (interest revenues from loans to customers less interest cost to borrow). Customers are loaned securities that are in the firm's name for short-selling and provided with margin credit. Firms have the advantage of using low-cost customer balances as well. National full line firms also have a large number of employees with a national branch network.[10]

(2) Large investment banks that usually focus on wholesale (corporate) underwriting and advisory services, underwriting and distributing common stock and corporate and municipal debt; arranging private placements, acting as advisors in mergers and acquisitions, and providing other corporate services. Examples are Goldman Sachs in New York and Credit Suisse First Boston in Boston. Note that this category is not mutually exclusive, since many full-service and New York investment banks are also large.

(3) Regional securities firms based in a particular region, such as A. G. Edwards, Inc. and Morgan Keegan, Inc. that primarily provide brokerage service to clients in their region. These firms might also be involved in some regional investment banking activity, such as underwriting the stock or debt of select firms in their region and providing institutional investor and other services depending on the particular nature of the firm.

(4) New York City (NYC)-based investment banks, which include many large investment banks such as Goldman Sachs, Bear, Stearns, & Co., and Lehman Brothers that engage primarily in wholesale banking activities involving corporate underwriting and advisory services, and trading activities for both customers and principal transactions for the firm itself. Morgan Stanley would be included in this category; however, it recently became a full-service national firm with its acquisition of Dean Witter in 1997. NYC investment banks, generally as wholesale firms, receive a large percentage of their revenues from investment banking activities.

---

[9]Patrick McGeehan and Anita Raghavan. "Broker Profits Are Tumbling; Layoffs Mulled." *The Wall Street Journal* (September 22, 1998), A3.

[10]See Saunders (1997); Crawford and Sihler (1994); Marshall and Ellis (1994); Bloch (1989); and Friend et al. (1967).

Table 11.2 ✦ PROFITABILITY OVER TIME: SECURITY FIRMS OF DIFFERENT TYPES

PANEL A: PRE-TAX RETURN ON EQUITY (ROE) (IN PERCENT)

	National Full Line	Large Investment Bank	Regional	NYC-Based	Discounter	Total Firms°
1980	45.0	55.7	n.a.	n.a.	n.a.	49.2
1981	24.6	56.7	37.2	42.1	52.2	35.9
1982	29.7	54.8	36.0	43.3	53.9	40.5
1983	28.1	43.8	40.5	50.7	46.8	36.6
1984	(2.6)	31.1	6.8	19.9	0.8	13.3
1985	17.9	38.5	29.0	31.2	25.6	29.4
1986	20.3	34.2	32.7	38.3	49.5	28.6
1987	(2.1)	9.2	14.0	5.2	19.7	4.7
1988	(0.7)	18.2	5.4	15.0	5.0	9.6
1989	(0.3)	9.2	10.4	11.4	14.5	6.9
1990	(8.3)	5.4	1.0	3.1	15.4	(0.7)
1991	19.9	25.2	34.9	16.3	35.5	23.7
1992	21.4	23.7	40.0	8.9	33.7	22.8
1993	28.4	23.8	43.7	17.1	39.1	27.1
1994	4.8	(7.2)	21.7	(2.5)	26.4	3.3
1995	20.3	11.5	33.8	17.3	38.5	20.9
1996	28.2	26.2	40.2	17.3	42.6	29.1

°NYSE member firms doing a public business
Source: Securities Industry DataBank

PANEL B: PRE-TAX ROES AND PROFIT MARGINS BY INDUSTRY (IN PERCENT)

	1980	1985	1990	1993	1995	1996
Pre-tax ROE						
Securities Industry	49.2	29.4	(0.7)	27.1	20.9	29.1
Banking	20.8	17.1	11.4	23.6	22.6	22.2
Manufacturing	21.7	15.8	15.3	11.4	22.4	23.3
Mining	NA	NA	11.6	5.0	2.5	13.6
Retail Trade	NA	NA	15.1	16.5	16.7	18.4
Wholesale Trading	NA	NA	9.7	10.3	13.9	16.5
Pre-tax Profit Margin						
Securities Ind. (net)	18.0	14.5	(0.5)	15.3	12.7	15.9
Manufacturing	7.7	5.9	5.7	3.9	7.9	8.4
Mining	NA	NA	8.2	4.5	2.2	12.5
Retail Trade	NA	NA	1.9	2.5	2.7	3.0
Wholesale Trading	NA	NA	1.2	1.3	1.8	2.2

Source: Securities Industry Association, *Security Industry Trends* (New York).

(5) Discounter firms that trade for customers at low cost without offering investment advice, such as Quick & Reilly and Charles Schwab. Many discount firms receive commission fee income from selling mutual funds for mutual fund companies as well. The majority of discount firm revenues come from commissions on trades for retail customers.

Again, these categories are not mutually exclusive and are in constant flux. For instance, Charles Schwab has become a full-service brokerage firm recently. Other categories may include securities firms that are subsidiaries of other financial institutions, such as Prudential Securities, the investment subsidiary of Prudential Insurance Company; Alex Brown, a subsidiary of Bankers Trust/Deutsche Bank; Montgomery Securities, a subsidiary of NationsBanc; and Fidelity Brokerage, a subsidiary of the major mutual fund company Fidelity Investments. In the late 1990s many mutual funds began offering brokerage services, including Vanguard, T. Rowe Price, American Century, Dreyfus, Scudder, and USAA.[11] Finally, there are securities firms that are boutiques, such as Wasserstein and Perella, specializing in mergers and acquisitions, and merchant banking firms that take equity and debt interests in the firms that they advise for mergers and acquisitions and leveraged buyouts (taking a firm private with debt in the hopes of taking it public again when stock prices are high), such as Kohlberg, Kravis, and Roberts (KKR).

Prestigious and Nonprestigious Investment Banks   Investment banking firms also are often ranked as prestigious or nonprestigious firms based on their syndicate participation, as shown on advertisements for security issues, called Tombstone Ads because of the way they are laid out (see Figure 11.1). Lead underwriters in charge of an issue are listed first, followed by other underwriters based on their share of participation in the underwriting. Underwriters are selected for a syndicate based on their relationship with lead investment banks and their reputation in handling and selling an issue. Firms with continuous top rankings are deemed prestigious underwriters, such as Morgan Stanley Dean Witter, Merrill Lynch & Co., and Goldman Sachs. Prior to the 1970s prestigious firms were predominantly prominent New York wholesale investment banks. In the 1970s Merrill Lynch marked the entry of a full-service security firm into the prestigious ranks, thus, making them more competitive. A number of mergers occurred between wholesale and retail firms in the 1990s as well. For example, in 1997, Morgan Stanley, a wholesale firm, merged with Dean Witter, which has a large retail distribution chain. Online firms also began to be included in syndicates based on their ability to distribute securities to online customers, such as Schwab and E°Trade Securities, shown in the syndicate listing in the tombstone ad in Figure 11.1.[12]

---

[11]Fidelity's brokerage customers by March 1999 executed 71 percent of their stock trades online. See Vanessa O'Connell. "It's a Broker! It's a Banker! It's a Mutual-Fund Group!" *The Wall Street Journal* (February 19, 1998), C1, C27; Pui-Wing Tam. "Vanguard Group Flexes Its Brokerage Arm." *The Wall Street Journal* (October 13, 1998), C23; Anita Raghavan and Eleena De Lisser. "NationsBank, Montgomery Mine Client Ties," *The Wall Street Journal* (September 28, 1997), C1, C15; and Rebecca Buckman. "Some Online Broker Fees Are Climbing." *The Wall Street Journal* (March 16, 1999), C1, C21.

[12]See Hayes (1979); Hayes and Hubbard (1990); and Bloch (1989) for a more detailed discussion of prestigious versus nonprestigious investment bankers and syndicate rankings. Studies have shown greater IPO underpricing for nonprestigious investment bankers that take on riskier issues.

Figure 11.1 ✦ SAMPLE TOMBSTONE AD WITH SYNDICATE LISTING BY PARTICIPATION

Morgan Stanley Dean Witter is a service mark of Morgan Stanley Dean Witter & Co.

This announcement is neither an offer to sell nor a solicitation of an offer to buy any of these Securities. The offer is made only by the Prospectus.

7,475,000 Shares

perotsystems™

Class A Common Stock

Price $16 a Share

Copies of the Prospectus may be obtained in any State from only such of the undersigned as may legally offer these Securities in compliance with the securities laws of such State.

6,175,000 Shares

This portion of the offering is being offered in the United States and Canada by the undersigned.

MORGAN STANLEY DEAN WITTER

MERRILL LYNCH & CO.

WARBURG DILLON READ LLC

BEAR, STEARNS & CO. INC.

HAMBRECHT & QUIST

A.G. EDWARDS & SONS, INC.   E*TRADE SECURITIES   PAINEWEBBER INCORPORATED

PRUDENTIAL SECURITIES   SALOMON SMITH BARNEY

1,300,000 Shares

This portion of the offering is being offered outside the United States and Canada by the undersigned.

WARBURG DILLON READ

MORGAN STANLEY DEAN WITTER

MERRILL LYNCH INTERNATIONAL

BEAR, STEARNS INTERNATIONAL LIMITED

HAMBRECHT & QUIST

March 1, 1999

Source: New York Times, March: 1999, C14.

Trends in Profits   Under the classifications given in Table 11.2, the average security firm has been quite profitable, with an average ROE of 22.4 percent for all firms from 1980 to 1996. However, as shown in 1987 to 1990, and in 1994, pretax ROEs and profit margins have been volatile, particularly when compared with profit margins in other industries. With the stock market plunge in 1987, retail customers became wary of stocks, and fewer equity underwritings took place. With the recession, in 1990 securities firms had a −.5 percent NPM and a −.7 percent ROE. Similarly, in 1994, with a downturn in bond and stock underwriting by 31 percent from 1993, the average ROE for large investment banks fell to −7.2 percent. In 1995 and 1996 underwriting and brokerage activity picked up again during the bull market that continued in the later 1990s, resulting in high pretax profit margins and ROEs for the industry.[13]

A Brief Historic Overview of Security Firms

Table 11.3 provides a brief historic overview of security firms, emphasizing security firms in the United States. Trends over time are discussed in the following sections.[14]

16th, 17th, and 18th Centuries   Because of Catholic church dictums against lending, banking and investment firms were generally operated by non-Catholics; Catholic restrictions gradually weakened from the 16th to 18th centuries. Similar religiously based dictums against usury still exist in many Muslim countries, resulting in the growth of merchant banking in which investors take an equity interest in firms rather than debt. Prosperity and the need to finance government wartime activities in the late 18th century brought about the growth of major European family-run international banking houses, including the Rothchilds, Barings, and Warburgs.

19th Century   In the 19th century, investment banking firms prospered as they financed the Industrial Revolution and much of the railroad expansion in Europe and the United States. In the United States, in addition to extensions of European investment houses, including J.P. Morgan, immigrants such as Joseph Seligman and Goldman and Sachs started securities firms from scratch. During the mid-1800s, Jay Cooke and Co. devised the first syndication process to sell Union debt as bonds across the country during the Civil War. This opened up the field to small investors.

In the United States, the late 1800s was an era of railroad and financing tycoons. By the 1870s, large U.S. investment banks were actively influencing client policies by serving on corporate boards and financing committees. Investment banks also were often directors on each other's boards (interlocking directorates), preventing new entrants into capital markets. A severe contraction in 1893 caused more than 15,000 commercial firms and more than 600 banks to fail. Investment banks such as J.P. Morgan created trusts out of reorganized companies, transferring the majority of companies' stocks in particular industries to "voting trusts," controlled by the investment banking firm involved. Thus, by 1900, the nation's railroads were consolidated into six huge systems controlled by Wall Street bankers. From 1898 to 1902, the United States experienced a wave of horizontal mergers; the number jumped from

---

[13]See Saunders (1997); and Securitites Industry Association (1997, 1998).

[14]The information for this section relies heavily on Hayes and Hubbard (1990) and Chernow (1990), which provide excellent histories of the securities industry.

Table 11.3 ✦ **Brief Historic Overview of Security Firms Emphasizing U.S. Security Firms**

Time Period	Event
Prior to Renaissance	**Specialization in money lending business by non-Catholics**.
Renaissance 17th & 18th Centuries	Catholics adhered to dictums against lending; such church restrictions on commerce weaken in the Renaissance, and in the 17th and 18th centuries economic prosperity leads to the growth of public securities, banking, and merchant banking.
Late 18th Century	**Growth of major European family-run international banking houses** (Rothchilds, Baring brothers, Warburgs). Large European government needs to finance wartime activities brings rise of new merchant bankers.
19th Century	**Rise of London as financial capital;** large financings for Industrial Revolution; large railroad financings; emergence of large U.S. investment banks, such as J.P. Morgan. Immigrants start securities firms, such as Joseph Seligman and Goldman and Sachs; Jay Cooke & Co. uses **syndication process** to sell bonds to public during the Civil War. In the later 1800s era of financing tycoons, such as J.P. Morgan and development of oligopolistic behavior by prestigious Wall Street firms.
20th Century 1914–1950s	**New York becomes major financial center** during World War I, U.S. security firms assist in foreign and U.S. financings; during 1920s broader public interest in securities. Modernization of securities issue origination and distribution process with growth of telephone and telegraph. **1929: Stock market crash** followed by lawsuits and hearings against security firms; **1933: Glass Stegall** breaks up banks and security firms; poorly capitalized security firms with severe underwriting losses remain; mergers and cutbacks during the depression. **WWII:** Securities firms assist in government financings; anti–Wall Street sentiment ends; English merchant banks facilitate first postwar hostile takeovers.
1960s	**Dollar becomes principal currency of international trade.** With deficits in the United States, a stable international climate, the **1963 Interest Equalization tax** penalizing the sale of some foreign securities to American investors, and regulation Q preventing banks to offer market rates, banks and securities firms flock abroad, resulting in the development of the **Eurodollar and Eurobond market;** **London is reestablished as a major financial market.** **First Eurobond issue for the Italian Autostrade in 1963.** **Greater trading activities; new breed of impersonal traders.** Greater number of investment banks with international subsidiaries; high inflation; more active management of investments by institutional investors; securities firms develop **services for institutional investors** including block trading; this made firms like Salomon Brothers with large trading operations prominent.
1970s	**Former hierarchy in underwriting of prestigious underwriters is challenged** by full-service security firms, such as Merrill Lynch. Securities firms introduce production-oriented compensation to attract traders that creates new rivalries and tensions; entry of new type of "gunslinger"; development of research services area to attract investors.

Table 11.3   ✦   Brief Historic Overview of Security Firms Emphasizing U.S. Security Firms (*continued*)

Time Period	Event
	Dollar becomes a floating currency;
	1972: Merrill Lynch receives first license to have a security branch in Japan.
	Largest Japanese security firms expand overseas;
	first yen-denominated bond (samurai bond) issued by non-Japanese issuer.
	May 1, 1975: Fixed brokerage commissions abolished, making commissions competitively based; a few discount brokerage firms spring up, and security firms merge.
	High inflation leads to innovations to offer market rates, including cash management funds in 1977 by Merrill Lynch; other money and mutual funds followed.
1980s	**March 16, 1982:** Shelf Registration Rule (Rule 415) adopted by SEC, allowing corporations to register securities and issue them at any time over the next two years.
	SEC Rule 415 gives firms more flexibility to seek competitive bids for offerings, particularly debt offerings, which reduced underwriter gross spreads.
Mid-1980s	**Bull market; Go-Go Days; Great merger and acquisition activity; innovation of junk bonds by Drexel Lambert;** leveraged buyouts;
	dramatic growth in underwriting; industry grows from 5,248 firms in 1980 to 9,515 in 1987.
	Securitization rises.
	1986: "Big Bang" in London removes fixed commissions and other reforms, including development of a new international Stock Exchange Automated System (SEAQ), allowing 24-hour off-exchange trading.
Later 1980s	**October 1987: Stock Market Crash** resulting in lower underwriting and a loss of confidence by investors in equity markets.
	Insider trading and other scandals contribute to poor perceptions of security firms by the public.
	Profitability of securities industry declines with large drop in underwriting and brokerage commissions.
	Between 1987 and 1991, period of consolidation in the industry, mergers, and layoffs.
	Number of firms declines by about 20 percent.
	Movement into venture capital, real estate venture, mortgage-backed securities, and principal investing.
1990s	**Greater competition from major commercial banks with section 20 subsidiaries.**
	Recession; low profits; diversification into fixed income security and derivatives trading; securitization to offset decline in underwriting.
	1992 on: Bull stock market and rise in profits but severe drop in underwriting and profits in 1994.
	Industry expands to about 8,000 firms. Mid and Later 1990s: **Acquisitions by large banks** and other financial institutions and mergers of wholesale and retail firms.
	Trading scandals by rogue traders caused large losses, such as the 1995 Barings scandal and collapse.
	1992: European Economic Community harmonized regulations and allowed financial institutions to sell services throughout the EC.
	Lawsuits by customers and employees; greater oversight by SEC and exchanges. Innovations; growth of Internet services;
	Emergence of online brokerage firms and the first online investment bank.

Sources: Samuel L. Hayes III and Philip M. Hubbard, *Investment Banking* (Boston: Harvard Business School Press, 1990); Anthony Saunders, *Financial Institutions Management: A Modern Perspective*, 2d ed. (Burr Ridge, Ill.: Irwin, 1997); and Ron Chernow, *The House of Morgan* (New York: Touchstone (Simon & Schuster), 1990).

69 in 1897 to more than 1,200 by 1899, providing large fees for investment banks and power as new trusts were created for different industries.

Early to Mid 20th Century—Panics, World War I and Wall Street Primacy, the Stock Market Crash of 1929, Modernization, and Anti-Wall Street Sentiment
In the early 20th century, Wall Street suffered a panic in 1907, which led to clamor for bank reform and the emergence of the Federal Reserve system, along with later legislation breaking up the trusts. Hearings against the concentration of Wall Street bankers were held.

By 1914 New York investment banking firms were assisting in financing World War I. With economic prosperity in the United States and the dollar being the only remaining currency backed by gold, New York took over prominence from London as the world's financial capital. The growth of telephone and telegraph services helped to modernize the securities issue origination and distribution process and to attract greater public interest in stocks and bonds, and investment firms prospered in the 1920s.

This prosperity ended with the stock market crash of 1929. Following this crash, major investment/commercial banking firms faced a continuum of lawsuits. Congress also had a series of hearings attacking bank/securities firms for their monopoly power and their role in encouraging stock market speculation. During the depression of the1930s, anti-Wall Street public sentiment continued. This sentiment was expressed in the Glass Stegall Act of 1933, which forced commercial banks to divest their nonbank divisions. J. P. Morgan, for instance, became a commercial bank and its investment activities became a separate firm, Morgan Stanley. Poorly capitalized security firms with severe underwriting losses remained, leading to mergers and cutbacks during the depression. During World War II, investment banks helped in government financing, and by the mid-1950s, anti-Wall Street sentiment had diminished somewhat.

Globalization of Debt Securities and Institutionalization in the 1960s   The 1960s brought about greater internationalization of issues. Eurobond and Eurodollar markets emerged as a way to escape restrictions on the purchase of foreign securities under the 1963 Equalization tax in the United States, and on paying market rates for deposits by banks under Regulation Q. In 1963, the first Eurobond issue was for the Italian Autostrade, an Italian state highway authority with British, German, Dutch, and Belgian investment firms participating. The issue was listed on both the London and Luxembourg stock exchanges. With the development of international bond markets, investment banks cultivated international subsidiaries.

From the 1960s on, investment banking markets became more impersonal and competitive and less relationship oriented. Greater trading activities brought about a new breed of impersonal traders, and retail firms increased their competitive power by consolidating. Institutional investors became more active portfolio managers, and investment banks responded by offering more services for these investors, including block trading (trading of large blocks of securities), which made firms with large trading operations prominent, such as Salomon Brothers.

More Competition in the 1970s, Changes in Culture, and Globalization   In the 1970s the monopolistic underwriting ranks of prestigious wholesale underwriters eroded when Merrill Lynch, a full-service firm, entered the ranks as a major lead underwriter. Compensation became more production oriented in the industry, particularly to attract star traders. The culture of many investment banks changed to more of a "gunslinger" mentality, creating new rivalries and tension. Investment banks developed new research services, particularly to attract institutional investors.

Globalization of investment banks continued; Japan opened up its security markets to branches of foreign firms. In 1972 Merrill Lynch was the first foreign firm to receive a license for a branch in Japan. Soon other firms, such as Salomon Brothers, entered Japanese markets as well. Large Japanese firms also expanded overseas, and yen-denominated bonds (samurai bonds) were issued outside Japan by non-Japanese issuers. Brokerage fees became competitive as of May 1, 1975, often-called May Day, when fixed brokerage commissions were abolished.

Shelf Registration, Casino Day Prosperity, and Innovations in the 1980s   In 1982, the Shelf Registration Rule (Rule 415) adopted by the SEC made corporate underwriting more competitive by allowing corporations to register securities and then issue them at any time over the next two years. This gave firms more flexibility to seek competitive bids, particularly for debt offerings, resulting in lower underwriter gross spread for these issues.

The 1980s marked a period of "casino" or "go-go" days, characterized by a bull market, great merger and acquisition (M&A) activity, and junk bonds, an innovation by Drexel Burnham Lambert often used to finance leveraged buyouts. The securities industry grew dramatically from 5,248 to 9,515 firms in 1987. In London, fixed commissions were removed as well, and other reforms included the development of a domestic and international Stock Exchange Automated System (SEAQ) allowing 24-hour off-exchange trading. London gained preeminence again as a major financial market.

The 1980s was also a decade of innovations. With greater competition, investment bankers developed new types of securities to win clients and generate fee income. In 1982, Salomon Brothers created stripped zero-coupon issues from existing Treasury securities. In the uncertain interest rate environment of 1984, Merrill Lynch and Company and other investment bankers began giving investors puts on bonds, allowing investors to put securities back to issuers and receive par value, protecting investors against losses if interest rates rose. In late 1984, Salomon Brothers introduced securities backed by automobile loans (Certificates for Automobile Receivables, or CARs). Investment bankers led the development of mortgage-backed securities. And it was investment bankers who fueled the huge volume of leveraged buyouts with junk bonds and other innovative financing techniques. Securities firms also spurred growth in the interest rate swap market by matching suitable counterparties and sometimes even serving as counterparties themselves. They also developed other types of synthetic interest–rate hedging instruments discussed in Chapter 18. Securities firms also took advantage of great market volatility by developing new trading activities, such as program trading, whereby profits are made on differences in prices between stock market indexes and those on stock index futures by taking alternate positions in the two markets.[15]

The October 1987 Stock Market Crash and the Recession of the Early 1990s
The October 1987 stock market crash put an end to security firms' growth over the decade. With a loss of public confidence reducing brokerage activity and underwriting

---

[15]For further discussion of financial innovations and the securities industry, see Bloch (1989); Anthony Bianco. "The King of Wall Street." *Business Week* (December 9, 1985), 98–104; Norton (1987); Marshall and Ellis (1994); Stigum (1990); and Geisst (1995).

activity, profits fell for security firms dramatically until 1992, and the number of security firms fell by 20 percent. Public scandals, such as insider trading by Michael Milken, the junk bond king at Drexel Lambert Burnham, resulted in jail sentences for investment bankers, and in the case of Drexel Burnham, the firm's failure. Congress passed the Insider Trading and Securities Fraud Enforcement Act in 1988, which revised the definition of insider trading, clarifying that it is "the purchase or sale of securities while in possession of 'material' information that is not available to the general public." The Act stiffened civil and criminal penalties as well.[16]

Restrictions on bank and thrift holdings of junk bonds also led to a downtrend in junk bond underwriting. Securities firms compensated for lower underwriting profits by taking on greater trading activity, particularly for fixed income securities as interest rates fell in the 1990s. Larger investment banks also developed real estate and venture capital subsidiaries and engaged in securitization activities, greater principal trading, and mutual fund and investment management for wealthy clients.

The Bull Market of the 1990s, Harmonization of Regulations in Europe, Online Securities Firms, and Internet Day Trading After 1992 a bull stock market caused underwriting and brokerage activity to rise; however, it dropped significantly in 1994. The industry expanded to about 8,000 firms. In the mid and later 1990s, acquisitions by large banks and other financial institutions and mergers of wholesale and retail firms occurred. Trading scandals by rogue traders resulted in large losses, such as the 1995 Barings trading scandal and collapse. A number of securities firms faced lawsuits for not revealing the extent of the risk involved in different investments, including Merrill Lynch concerning the Orange County derivative trading losses and Prudential Investments for losses to retail customers on real estate investment products.

In 1992, the European Economic Community harmonized regulations and allowed financial institutions to sell services through the E.C. The advent of the euro in January 1999 also brought about new investment opportunities in Europe for European and U.S. financial firms. With the rapid spread of the Internet, securities firms entered the Information Age: Online brokerage firms grew quickly and the first online investment bank debuted, as discussed at the beginning of the chapter.

Regulators became particularly concerned in the later 1990s about the growth of less sophisticated day traders on the Internet and the effect of these traders on the volatility of market prices, which could reduce public confidence in financial markets. Day-trading firms, unlike online brokerage firms such as E°Trade, cater to individual investors who trade stocks full time over sophisticated computer systems at a firm's of-

---

[16]Anyone convicted of profiting from illegal insider trading can be required to pay up to three times the amount gained through the unlawful activity, and the maximum prison term for criminal penalties was increased to 10 years. The SEC was given greater authority to pursue offenders and is now allowed to pay to obtain information about potential violations. The 1988 act also placed a responsibility on securities firms to strengthen written policies and procedures designed to prevent the misuse of privileged material information. A firm failing to do so may itself face civil penalties if employees are found guilty of insider trading. Renewed emphasis was placed on the securities industry's long-standing tradition of maintaining so-called Chinese Walls, an imaginary barrier between the investment banking activities of a securities firm and its brokerage and trading arm. Under the law, a firm may not profit on trades for its own inventory or that of its customers by using information obtained through investment bankers' privileged contacts with clients.

fice instead of a home computer. However, in recent years day-trading firms have lured unsophisticated investors into the business by creating unrealistic expectations of becoming rich quickly. Often hefty upfront fees are charged before investors find out if they have an aptitude as a trader. Consequently, many new day traders fail. In 1999, the number of U.S. day-trading firms fell from 3,000 in 1998 to 2,000, with many failures.[17]

Regulators and securities firms have also been concerned about a crush of trading in Internet stocks, which have been subject to wild price swings, unbelievably high valuations, and rapid trading from novice investors. NASDAQ considered authorizing trading halts for such stocks under certain circumstances. DLJ Direct, Schwab, Salomon Smith Barney, and Waterhouse Securities have also set limits on customers wishing to borrow funds to buy such stocks.[18]

A Note on Changes in the Culture of Investment Banking and Breaches of Ethics

The culture of investment banking changed dramatically in the mid-1960s from a white-glove, genteel culture to a competitive, rather cutthroat one. As Chernow (1990) points out, by the mid-1960s as Morgan Stanley grew tremendously and diversified into new activities, "it no longer had the luxury of growing its own people and inculcating them with Morgan style. . . . To attract traders, the firm introduced production-oriented compensation, which eroded collegiality and generated new rivalries and tension."[19] As noted in the opening quote, with these changes, as Robert Baldwin, a Morgan Stanley partner in the 1960s, stated, "The only way to make investment banking more competitive would be to gouge eyes out."[20]

Chernow (1990) describes this cultural change for Morgan Stanley as follows: "Morgan Stanley kept up its gentlemanly aura only so long as nobody poached on its territory; once threatened, it retaliated with a vengeance. Both on Wall Street and in the City (London), the graceful, leisurely world of securities syndicates was being replaced by the predatory world of mergers and the freewheeling irreverent world of traders. Form was simply following function."[21]

These changes caused cultural clashes within investment banks and "underscored the paramount reality . . . that once-proud and all but omnipotent bankers were now subservient to their corporate clients."[22] With incentive systems changing to attract star traders, more senior partners were disgruntled that junior partner traders could make more than they could. Incentive systems were also "quite heavily loaded towards advocating takeovers. The bigger and more frequent the takeover, the more profit for Morgan Stanley. The new fee-for-service mentality directly related to the declining importance of underwriting"[23] and the greater importance of fees from M&A activity and

---

[17]Rebecca Buckman. "Day-Trading Firms Facing Tougher Rivalry, Scrutiny." *The Wall Street Journal*, C1, C18; and Sana Siwolop. "Day Traders Place Risk, Reward Above Job Security." *The Denver Post* (October 19, 1998), E1.

[18]David Barboza. "N.A.S.D. Chief Cautions Firms about Internet Trading Risks." *The New York Times* (February 10, 1999), C9; and "On-Line Investors Who Chase Market's Every Blip." *The New York Times* (October 1, 1998), D1; and Rebecca Buckman and Aaron Lucchetti. "Cooling It: Wall Street Firms Try to Keep Internet Mania from Ending Badly." *The Wall Street Journal* (February 24, 1999), A1, A10.

[19]Chernow (1990), p. 587.

[20]Chernow (1990), p. 587.

[21]Chernow (1990), p. 588.

[22]Chernow (1990), p. 589.

[23]Chernow (1990), pp. 595–596.

trading. Thus, high-paid superstar traders and M&A dealmakers became a prominent part of an investment bank's culture and profits. Investment banks faced a changing culture that suffered problems of "factionalism, ego, and avarice." As John Cassidy points out in a recent article on Goldman Sachs, "Investment banking, when you come down to it, is an information business. In any such industry, the key to success is getting talented people to work together and stay together. [W]orkaholism is the norm, and so is constant pressure to perform. Every person in the firm is continually assessed from three sides: by his bosses, by his subordinates, and by his peers."[24]

With these cultural changes and pressures to perform, ethical breaches became more common within the securities industry. Movies such as *Wall Street* and books such as *Liar's Poker* and *Barbarians at the Gate* portray tendencies for greed in creating takeover opportunities at the expense of ethical considerations concerning what is best for a firm, its customers, and employees. Trading scandals also became more frequent. For example, in 1991 Salomon Brothers attempted to corner the Treasury bond market by submitting false bids in its customers' names for a Treasury security auction. Under auction rules no single bidder was allowed to have more than 35 percent of the auction. By using false names, Salomon was able to win more than 90 percent of a two-year note issue. Upon discovery, Salomon Brothers was fined $290 million but only temporarily suspended as a government securities dealer. However, because reputation is a critical asset for investment banking, ultimately, market discipline imposes severe penalties for firms. Salomon's stock price dropped 30 percent. The firm also lost many of its relationships with customers and was subject to civil lawsuits, fines, penalties, and possible criminal charges. The firm's 80-year reputation for integrity and fair dealing was tarnished, so Salomon Brothers paid a heavy price.[25] The firm suffered years of lower profits, and eventually, in 1997 the Travelers Group took over Salomom Brothers.

The 1990 failure of Drexel Burnham Lambert is another good example of market discipline at work in the securities industry. Drexel had gained prominence in the 1980s as a result of its innovations in the junk bond and leveraged buyout markets. The aggressiveness of its dealmakers in these markets was legendary, and Drexel grew at a torrid pace for most of the decade. When it became clear in late 1988 that part of the firm's spectacular success was the result of fraud and mismanagement, and not of exceptional skill, the firm began to have difficulty getting financing to meet its liquidity needs. Ultimately, all market sources of cash dried up and Drexel's chief executive officer appealed to the Federal Reserve (Fed) and the SEC to bail the firm out of its troubles. Both agencies refused, and Drexel declared bankruptcy in February 1990. The financial markets absorbed news of the firm's end without panic, in considerable contrast to their reaction when Continental Illinois Bank almost collapsed, except for intervention from the Fed, in 1984.[26]

---

[24]See John Cassidy. "The Firm." *The New Yorker* (March 9, 1999), 28–36; Endlich (1999); Leah Nathans Spiro. "How Greed Changed Goldman." *Business Week* (March 15, 1999), 15.

[25]See Michael Siconolfi, et. al. "Salomon's Admission of T-Note Infraction Gives Market a Jolt," *The Wall Street Journal* (August 12, 1991); "Hidden Bonds: Collusion and Price Fixing in Market for Treasury Securities Have Been Rife for Years," *The Wall Street Journal* (August 19, 1991); and E. Gerald Corrigan. "Statement to Congress, September 4, 1991," *Federal Reserve Bulletin* 78 (November 1991): 887–902.

[26]See Brett Duval Fromson. "Did Drexel Get What It Deserved?" *Fortune* (March 12, 1990), 81–88; and Brett Duval Fromson. "The Last Days of Drexel Burnham." *Fortune* (May 21, 1990), 90–96.

Other ethical problems that securities firms faced in the 1990s included major lawsuits by investors for the failure of securities firms to warn them of the dangers associated with their investments, including a class action lawsuit against Prudential Investments concerning real estate investments sold to consumers and a lawsuit against Merrill Lynch concerning large losses in derivative trading by Orange County, a wealthy county south of Los Angeles. Both firms went through years of court battles and eventual large settlements.

Orange County's investment pool lost $1.5 billion by betting on a fall in interest rates in 1994. In addition to using reverse-repo agreements to finance five-year Treasury bond holdings (i.e., financing short-term to purchase longer-terms securities), Orange County purchased about $8 billion of inverse floater bonds from a group of investment bankers led by Merrill Lynch. Such inverse floater bonds have high payouts when interest rates fall, but large losses when interest rates rise. In the lawsuit, the county blamed the investment bankers for selling complex securities without fully explaining the full risk of these instruments.[27]

Charles Schwab Corporation also had to settle with 300 investors for $1.2 million in losses in association with unsuccessful attempts by investors to cancel orders for Theglobe.com, a hot Internet initial public offering in November 1998. Investors naively placed market orders for the stock instead of limit orders, which would limit the price they were willing to pay for the stock. Although the stock was set to trade for $9 the night prior, when it opened its price went up to $90 and closed at $63.50. When online investors who had placed orders prior to trading realized they could not afford the stock, they tried to cancel their orders. With 1,500 cancel orders, Schwab was not able to process about 300 of the orders that it received before the opening trading in the stock began, resulting in losses for these customers.[28] The old adage *caveat emptor*—let the buyer beware—was no longer sufficient in terms of selling securities to investors, and negative publicity tarnished Schwab's valuable reputation.

Other lawsuits in the 1990s include class-action gender discrimination lawsuits and diversity group lawsuits for more minorities and women to join Wall Street's upper ranks and for pay for women equal to men. In 1999, Goldman Sachs promoted two female partners to its prestigious management committee, as it moved to

---

[27]Morgan Stanley Dean Witter and Normura Securities International also agreed to pay a total of $117.5 million to end lawsuits filed by Orange County against the firms, and Merrill Lynch settled at $400 million. Orange County sued 20 brokers for their role in selling securities to the county and in lending the county money to buy those securities. It also sued some law and accounting firms and the Standard & Poor's credit rating agency. In a civil settlement for Credit Suisse First Boston, the firm paid $800,000 to resolve SEC claims that it negligently misrpresented and omitted material facts from its offering statement for more than $110 million of Orange County pension-obligation bonds in the fall of 1994 as well. See Arshadi and Karels (1997), pp. 480–482; Leslie Wayne and Andrew Pollack. "The Master of Orange County: A Merrill Lynch Broker Survives Municipal Bankruptcy." *The New York Times* (July 22, 1998), C1, C20; Andy Pasztor and Patric McGeehan. "SEC Tightens Disclosure Rules in Settling Orange County Case," *The Wall Street Journal* (January 30, 1998), C1; "2 Securities Firms Will Pay Orange County $117 Million." *The New York Times*, July 22, 1998, C20.

[28]Ruth Simon, "Schwab Settles with Investors Over IPO," *The Wall Street Journal*, March 11, 1999, C1.

go public. Firms have noted that it is easier to attract and retain female employees when women are in the upper ranks, making it a good policy for firms.[29]

In 1998, investment bankers were also accused of "spinning," giving venture capitalists and other individuals in a position to swap the company's decisions shares in their best initial public offerings (IPOs), expecting these individuals to pay them off and treat the investment bank in kind when they do a transaction. Although the practice of underwriters giving hot IPOs to institutions such as mutual-fund companies and pension funds, instead of "the little guy" investor is common, in this case spin shares do not go to a corporate customer but to individuals at a corporation who are in a position to swap the company's decisions. As a managing director at Salomon Inc. describes it, "It's a bribe, no question about it. . . . You pay them off and expect you're going to get treated in kind when they do the transaction."[30] Regulators soon imposed restrictions on this type of activity.

Deeply entwined in the business of investment banking is a banker's reputation. Firms that are being valued and taken public depend on a banker's good judgment and honesty. Hence, short-term, unethical abuses, including greed, ultimately hurt a firm and an individual's most valuable asset, this reputation.

The following sections look in more detail at the key areas of activities for security firms and provide an overview of their financial statements and financial analysis.

Overview of Key Areas of Activities for Security Firms and Financial Statements

As suggested by the brief history of securities firms, they have diversified into many different activities and benefitied from revenues from principal trading activities, for instance, in bear markets when commission and investment banking revenues are down. Key areas of activity for securities firms include the following:

(1) **Investment banking underwriting fees and gross spread (difference between the price paid for securities from a corporation and the offering price securities are sold for to the public) for** debt and equity securities; **private placements, management fees, M&A; restructuring, refinancing, advisory services, and so on.**

(2) **Principal transactions** involving trading and investments; for trading this involves making security, foreign exchange, or commodity trades that are profitable for the firm; for investing it means managing an investment portfolio to reap returns for the firm itself. Principal transactions also including revenues from mortgage-backed securities, swaps, derivative securities and hedging strategies, and so on.

(3) **Selling and dealing activities and trading for customers as an agent,** distributing securities and receiving commission income; making trades for customers in foreign exchange; commodities, bonds, or other instruments; and margin lending to customers.

---

[29]Eileen Gianton, "As Wall Street Firms Face Scrutiny, Goldman Sachs Promotes 2 Women," The Denver Post, March 6, 1999, C3; Other securities firms have been involved in sexual harassment lawsuits as well, see Peter Truell, "A Revised Pact Is Approved in Smith Barney Bias Case," *The New York Times*, July 25, 1998, B2.

[30]See Michael Siconolfi. "The Spin Desk: Underwriters Set Aside IPO Stock for Officials of Potential Customers." *The Wall Street Journal* (November 12, 1997), A1, A14.

(4) **Investing activities as an agent**—managing mutual funds and pension funds or portfolios for wealthy investors; receiving fee income for this activity.

(5) **Back office activities** including clearing and escrow services, research services, and advisory services, including M&A advice.

(6) **Other types of activities,** such as merchant banking, in which the securities firm takes an equity financing position in a merger or leveraged buyout (for instance; venture capital subsidiary activities) and real estate subsidiary activities, including real estate investment trust and real estate partnerships, among others.

Investment banks have entered many other new areas as well, including offering banking-type services-such as small business, consumer, and mortgage loans-and small business consulting services. Recently, investment banks have also entered the reinsurance business. For instance, in 1998 Lehman Brothers Holdings invested $500 million to set up a Bermuda-based reinsurance subsidiary that will write policies to cover a variety of risks that corporations face, which will be packaged and sold as securities to investors. Investors get a share of both the premiums and any losses according to formulas in the securities.[31]

Sources of Revenue

Financial Statements for security firms differ according to the type of firm and the activities it engages end. Sources of revenues have changed dramatically over time, as shown in the following table:

CHANGING REVENUE SOURCES

	1975	1996
Commissions	49.9%	15.4%
Principal Transactions	15.6	17.1
Underwriting Revenue	13.3	9.0
Margin Interest	7.8	5.8
Mutual Fund Sales	0.6	3.8
Commodities	3.0	1.3
All Other	9.9	47.6
Total Revenue	100.0%	100.0%

For the security industry as a whole, revenues have been spread over more different types of activities over the last two decades of the 20th century. With the elimination of fixed commission brokerage fees, commission income as the primary source of revenues for firms fell from 49.9 percent to 15.4 percent, with other activities providing 47.6 percent of revenues in 1996 compared with 9.9 percent in 1975. Other activities include M&A fees, private placements, market making and global investment management, with fee-based businesses increasing in importance. Fees for services to institutional investors also became a bigger source of revenue, with the share of institutional investor equity holdings rising from below 10 percent in 1965 to well over 43 percent in 1975, reaching 50 percent in 1996, and remaining at this level through the later 1990s, as shown in Figure 11.2. With globalization, U.S. gross

---

[31]Patrick McGeehan. "Investment Bankers Are Moving Fast to Offer Securities Backed by Pools of Insurance Policies." *The Wall Street Journal* (June 15, 1998), C4. Also see sources cited in Note 10.

Figure 11.2 ✦ TRENDS IN SECURITY HOLDINGS AND THE GROWTH OF MUTUAL FUND ASSETS

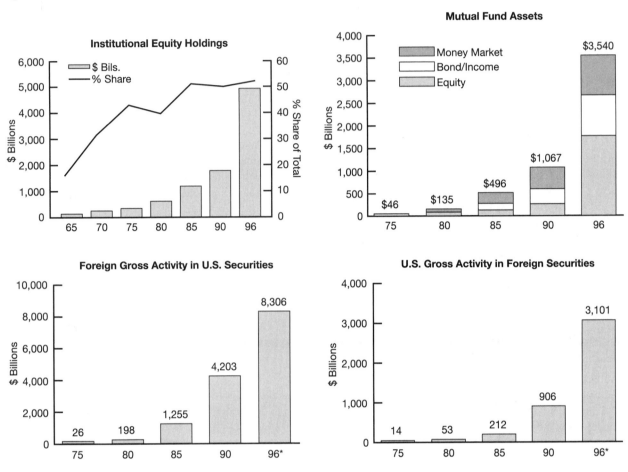

*Nine months annualized
Source: Securities Industry Association, *Security Industry Trends*, Vol. 23, No. 1, Jan. 31, 1997, pp. 14, 15, 17.

activity in foreign securities and foreign gross activity in U.S. securities grew dramatically, also shown in Figure 11.2. For example, in 1996, U.S. investors bought and sold about $3 trillion of stocks and bonds from non-U.S. issuers, a 1,500 percent growth rate since 1985, and U.S. institutions often hold 15 percent of their portfolio in foreign companies. Mutual funds also grew phenomenally, with assets growing from $36 billion in 1974 to $135 billion in 1980 to $1 trillion in 1990 and exceeding $3.5 trillion by 1996, as shown in Figure 11.2.[32]

Revenues grew from $5.88 billion in 1975 to $118.5 billion in 1996 or by 1,915 percent, about a 43 percent annual compound growth rate. Earnings grew from $801 million to $11,533 million, by 1,334 percent or at a 13.5 percent annual growth rate. There have been massive increases in trading volume, as the market rose to 10,000 by 1999, and more than a third of U.S. households are invested in the market through

[32]See Securities Industry Association (1998).

mutual funds, pension plans, 401(k)s, or direct stock holdings. In 1996, U.S. household assets invested 40 percent in stocks, 28 percent in banks, 18 percent in mutual funds, and 16 percent in bonds. In addition, the U.S. securities industry changed its business model to emphasize new lines of business and market opportunities.

Figure 11.3 demonstrates he rapid compound annual growth rate between 1975 and 1996 in other types of activities, including mutual fund and asset management (30 percent annual growth rate) and interest income, M&A, and private placements (23 percent annual growth rate). Over these years, numerous acquisitions have occurred to increase operating efficiency, increase the capital base of firms, and diversify lines of business. For instance, Paine Webber acquired Mitchell Hutchins and entered the institutional business in 1977. Merrill Lynch acquired White Weld to develop institutional business in 1978, Morgan Stanley acquired Dean Witter in 1997 to improve its retail business, and from 1979 to 1999 every leading firm was engaged in an acquisition.

Technology also brought forth a whole range of capabilities and competition for securities firms. Discount brokerage firms, including Schwab, Fidelity Discount Brokerage, Quick and Reilly, E°Trade, and others have also gained a larger share of retail commission income over time, moving from less than 2 percent of market share in 1980 to greater than 15 percent in the late 1990s. Securities firms have been innovative in making M&A deals, leveraged buyouts, bridge financing (temporary financing for corporations for takeover battles and other purposes), developing new retirement fund services and individual retirement accounts, managing money, and developing cash management and wrap accounts, in which a variety of services including financial planning, investment management, and brokerage services are offered for a single, comprehensive (wrapped) fee of about 3 percent of account value

Figure 11.3   ✦   **GROWTH RATES IN DIFFERENT SECURITY INDUSTRY BUSINESS LINES**

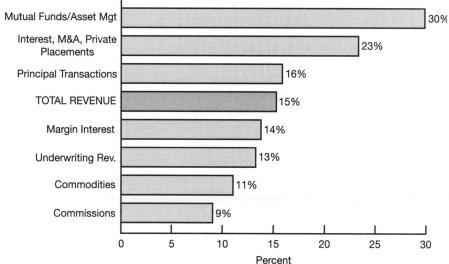

Source: Securities Industry Association, *Security Industry Trends*, Vol. 23, No. 1, January 31, 1997, p. 15.

annually for high-balance customers (usually minimum $100,000). They have also earned fees from developing new forms of securitization and derivatives to help corporations and other financial institutions hedge interest-rate risk.[33]

Examples of Financial Statements   Table 11.4 provides examples of typical financial statements for two different types of security firms: Morgan Keegan, Inc., a regional securities broker/dealer, and Morgan Stanley Group, prior to its merger with Dean Witter, when it was predominantly a large New York investment banking firm.

Income Statement   Reviewing the income statements in Panel A of Table 11.4, note that Morgan Keegan received a large percentage of its revenues from commissions. In contrast, Morgan Stanley received a very low percentage of revenues from commissions at this time and a larger percentage of revenues from trading. Although Morgan Stanley has a larger percentage of revenues from interest revenue than Morgan Keegan, when netted out against interest expense, the interest spread is small relative to revenues, about 2.53 percent compared with 5.63 percent for Morgan Keegan in 1996, which is typical of retail versus wholesale security firms.

Looking at expenses, the major expense (other than interest expense for Morgan Stanley, which nets out against interest revenues) is compensation. The industry is very labor intensive, and the labor environment is extremely sensitive to the state of the markets and the economy. For instance, in the bleak period of 1987 to 1990, the industry lost one in five of its employees and one in of every five firms .[34]

Top managers in the industry receive large salaries, as do super-traders. For instance, in 1998, the class of partners receiving partnership in 1996 at Goldman Sachs earned about $6 million each, with more senior partners getting larger sums, and Goldman's senior executives earning up to $20 million. In addition, with Goldman going public in 1999, top managers would receive equity stakes worth more than $150 million each, and each junior partner would receive stakes worth more than $15 million.[35] The danger with superstars is that they may leave the firm and take their customers with them. For example, in 1988 two M&A superstars at First Boston, Bruce Wasserstein and Joseph R. Perella, defected to start up their own M&A boutique, Wasserstein and Perella, taking a large number of corporate clients with them.[36]

Other expenses include fees for floor brokerage and clearance with exchanges and clearing corporations, communications, travel, promotion and business development, occupancy expense, and other operating expenses and taxes.

From Table 11.4, the pretax profit margin (income before taxes as a percentage of total revenue) for the regional securities brokerage firm, Morgan Keegan, is 18.30 percent, larger than that of the wholesale investment bank, Morgan Stanley, whose profit margin was 11.96 percent in 1996. Similar to wholesale money center banks, New York investment banks operate in competitive markets with smaller profit margins than smaller regional retail firms. For the securities industry as a whole, as shown in Table 11.2, the average pretax profit margin was about 15.9 percent in 1996.

---

[33]Some of these innovations, including interest rate caps, collars, and floors, are discussed later in Chapter 18; see Securities Industry Association (1998).

[34]See Securities Industry Association (1998).

[35]See John Cassidy. "The Firm." *The New Yorker* (March 9, 1999), 28–36.

[36]See Crawford and Sihler (1994), Case 11: First Boston, Inc., p. 11.1.

Table 11.4   ✦   **EXAMPLES OF TYPICAL FINANCIAL STATEMENTS FOR SECURITIES FIRMS**

PANEL A: TYPICAL INCOME STATEMENTS

Morgan Keegan, Inc., Regional Securities Broker/Dealer, incorporated 1984.
Focus: Retail Clients in Southeast U.S. and Institutional Investors Worldwide.
Incorporated in Tennessee
Consolidated Income Statement (Year-end July 31 in thous.)

Revenues	1996	% Revs.	1995	% Revs.	1994	% Revs.
Commissions	67,870	22.52%	46,162	20.24%	46,537	20.08%
Princ. Transactions	115,203	38.22%	87,110	38.19%	89,422	38.59%
Trading						
Investmts						
Investment Banking	50,301	16.69%	45,194	19.82%	55,832	24.09%
Interest Revenue	49,923	16.56%	37,780	16.56%	24,894	10.74%
& Dividends						
Asset Mgt & Adm.						
Other Revenue	18,109	6.01%	11,826	5.19%	15,035	6.49%
Total Revenue	301,406	100.00%	228,072	100.00%	231,720	100.00%
Expenses						
Compensation	158,352	52.54%	120,795	52.96%	125,205	54.03%
Floor Brokerage						
& Clearance	4,397	1.46%	3,724	1.63%	3,875	1.67%
Communications,						
Travel, & Promotion	7,336	2.43%	5,855	2.57%	5,721	2.47%
& Bus Dev, Prof. Servs.						
Occupancy & Equip.	11,812	3.92%	9,716	4.26%	8,320	3.59%
Interest Expense	32,930	10.93%	23,600	10.35%	14,393	6.21%
Other Taxes	7,006	2.32%	6,298	2.76%	4,972	2.15%
Other Oper. Expense	5,514	1.83%	3,774	1.65%	3,741	1.61%
Total Expenses	246,239	81.70%	189,724	83.19%	180,079	77.71%
Income before						
Income taxes	55,167	18.30%	38,348	16.81%	51,641	22.29%
Income Tax Expense	21,300	7.07%	14,500	6.36%	19,800	8.54%
Net Income (NPM)	33,867	11.24%	23,848	10.46%	31,841	13.74%

Morgan Stanley Group, Inc., originally incorporated 1935.
Focus: Investment Banking and Trading; prior to merger with Dean Witter in 1997; Wall Street Investment Bank
Consolidated Income Statement (in mils.)

Revenues	1996	% Revs.	1995	% Revs.	1994	% Revs.
Comms.	613	4.66%	437	4.79%	449	4.79%
Prin. Tran.	2,296	17.47%	1,224	13.42%	1,243	13.26%
Trading	2,210	16.81%	1,122	12.30%	1,104	11.77%
Investmts	86	0.65%	102	1.12%	139	1.48%
Inv. Bkg.	1,944	14.79%	1,211	13.27%	919	9.80%
Int. Revs.	7,701	58.59%	5,939	65.09%	6,406	68.32%
& Divs.						
Asset Mgt	582	4.43%	310	3.40%	350	3.73%
Other Rev	8	0.06%	3	0.03%	9	0.10%
Total Rev	13,144	100.00%	9,124	100.00%	9,376	100.00%

Table 11.4 ✦ EXAMPLES OF TYPICAL FINANCIAL STATEMENTS FOR SECURITIES FIRMS (*CONTINUED*)

Expenses						
Compens.	2,863	21.78%	1,795	19.67%	1,733	18.48%
Floor Brk. & Clear.	274	2.08%	211	2.31%	230	2.45%
Comms. Travel & Pr & Bus Dev	542	4.12%	349	3.83%	451	4.81%
Occ. Exp.	362	2.75%	276	3.02%	303	3.23%
Int. Exp.	7,368	56.06%	5,501	60.29%	5,875	62.66%
Other Exp	163	1.24%	109	1.19%	190	2.03%
Total Exp	11,572	88.04%	8,241	90.32%	8,782	93.66%
Income before tax	1,572	11.96%	883	9.68%	594	6.34%
Tax Exp.	543	4.13%	283	3.10%	199	2.12%
Net Inc. (NPM)	1,029	7.83%	600	6.58%	395	4.21%

PANEL B: TYPICAL BALANCE SHEET OF SECURITIES FIRMS

Morgan Keegan, Inc., Regional Securities Broker/Dealer, incorporated 1984
Consolidated Balance Sheet as of July 31 (thous.)

Assets	1996	% Assets	1995	% Assets
Cash	17,156	1.81%	22,287	2.53%
Segreg. Secs. at Mkt Value	225,200	23.79%	226,000	25.62%
Deposits with Clearing Organiz.	7,655	0.81%	7,655	0.87%
Receivables from Broker/Dealers	16,978	1.79%	25,046	2.84%
Receivables from Customers	314,436	33.22%	260,707	29.55%
Securities Purchased Under Agreement to Resell	69,278	7.32%	91,861	10.41%
Securities Owned at Mkt Value	229,278	24.22%	209,915	23.79%
Membership in Exchanges	719	0.08%	719	0.08%
Net Furniture & Equipment & Leasehold Improvements	18,492	1.95%	13,037	1.48%
Buildings & Equipment at Cost	19,908	2.10%	N/A	
Other Assets	27,548	2.91%	25,065	2.84%
Total Assets	946,648	100.00%	882,292	100.00%

Liabilities	1996	% Assets	1995	% Assets
Short-term Borrowings	31,400	3.32%	127,649	14.47%
Mortgage note payable	19,965	2.11%		
Commercial Paper	42,928	4.53%	7,468	0.85%
Payable to Brokers or Dealers & Clearing Organization	9,201	0.97%	5,387	0.61%
Payable to Customers	484,547	51.19%	438,518	49.70%
Customer Drafts Payable	14,456	1.53%	13,774	1.56%
Securities Sold Under Agreement to Repurchase	54,826	5.79%	35,360	4.01%
Securities Sold, Not Yet Purchased at market value	62,972	6.65%	68,430	7.76%
Other Liabilities	57,345	6.06%	46,249	5.24%

Table 11.4   ✦   EXAMPLES OF TYPICAL FINANCIAL STATEMENTS FOR SECURITIES FIRMS (CONTINUED)

Total Liabilities	777,640	82.15%	742,835	84.19%
Common Stock (par & surplus)	14,284	1.51%	13,317	1.51%
Retained Earnings	154,724	16.34%	126,140	14.30%
Total Equity	169,008	17.85%	139,457	15.81%
Total Liabilities & Equity	946,648	100.00%	882,292	100.00%

Morgan Stanley, Inc.
Consolidated Balance Sheet (mils.)

Assets	1996	% Assets	1995	% Assets
Cash & int.-bearing equivalents	4,545	2.31%	2,471	1.72%
Cash & Secs. with Clearing Ass.	3,164	1.61%	1,339	0.93%
U.S. Gov. & Non U.S. Gov. Secs	30,552	15.55%	26,272	18.28%
Cor. Debt & Currency Swaps	19,473	9.91%	13,792	9.59%
Corporate Equities	12,622	6.43%	13,185	9.17%
Derivative Contracts	11,220	5.71%	8,043	5.60%
Physical Commodities	375	0.19%	410	0.29%
Secs. borrowed or purchased under contract to resell	100,137	50.97%	72,955	50.75%
Receivables from Customers	5,761	2.93%	3,413	2.37%
Other Receivables	7,486	3.81%	3,063	2.13%
Net Property & Equipment	1,301	0.66%	1,286	0.89%
Other Assets	3,305	1.68%	626	0.44%
Total Assets	196,446	100.00%	143,753	100.00%

Liabilities	1996	% Assets	1995	% Assets
Short-term Borrowing	20,461	10.42%	11,703	8.14%
U.S. & Non U.S. Gov. & Agency Secs. Not Yet Purchased	16,709	8.51%	15,431	10.73%
Corp. Debt & Currency Swaps Sold	1,112	0.57%	1,076	0.75%
Corporate Equities Sold Not Yet Purchased	8,889	4.52%	3,585	2.49%
Derivative Contracts	9,982	5.08%	7,537	5.24%
Physical Commodities	476	0.24%	71	0.05%
Secs. loaned or sold under Repurchase Agreement	83,296	42.40%	60,738	42.25%
Securities Loaned	8,975	4.57%	9,340	6.50%
Accounts Payable	20,449	10.41%	15,792	10.99%
Interest & Dividends Payable	1,478	0.75%	1,019	0.71%
Other Liabilities & Accruals	2,718	1.38%	1,787	1.24%
Long-term Borrowings	14,498	7.38%	9,635	6.70%
Total Liabilities	189,043	96.23%	137,714	95.80%
Common & Preferred Stock	2,899	1.48%	2,224	1.55%
Retained Earnings	4,504	2.29%	3,815	2.65%
Total Equity	7,403	3.77%	6,039	4.20%
Total Liabilities & Equity	196,446	100.00%	143,753	100.00%

Source: Moody's Bank & Finance Manual, 1997

Typical ratios used to evaluate trends for securities firms based on the income statement include the following[37]:

✦ Commissions/revenues (%), which will be larger for retail firms;
✦ Principal transactions/revenues (%);
✦ Investment banking/revenues (%);
✦ Revenues/expenses (%);
✦ Portfolio revenue/investments (%), i.e., the average rate of return on the securities portfolio for the firm.
✦ Revenue per employee;
✦ Expenses per employee;
✦ Compensation and benefits per employee; and
✦ Number of employees.

Growth Rate in Expenses Relative to Growth Rate in Revenues Over Time

Wholesale investment banking firms will typically have fewer employees and higher revenue, expense, compensation, and benefits per employee. Trends in these ratios, as well as trends in common size income statements, as shown in Table 11.4 for Morgan Keegan and Morgan Stanley, can reveal changes in sources of revenues and expenses and their relationships. A faster growth in expenses than revenues, for instance, can indicate a serious problem.

Analyzing the Trends in Net Income   Looking at the common size income statements for Morgan Keegan, the firm's net income (NPM) fell in 1995 from 13.74 percent to 10.46 percent in 1995 and then rose in 1996 to 11.24 percent. The fall in 1995 can be seen to be a result of a fall in total revenue by 3,648,000 (a fall of 1.57 percent) and a rise in total expenses by 9,645,000 (a rise of 5.36 percent), i.e. expenses grew at a faster rate than revenues. Expenses to revenues increased from 77.71 percent to 83.19 percent. In particular, investment banking and other revenue declined, and travel and promotion and occupancy expenses particularly rose. In 1996 the NPM rose as total revenue rose 32 percent and total expenses rose less, by 29.8 percent. Expenses to revenues fell from 83.19 percent to 81.7 percent. Revenues from principal transactions, commissions, and other revenues rose particularly. The interest spread relative to total revenues was 4.53 percent in 1994, 6.21 percent in 1995, and 5.64 percent in 1996.

Morgan Stanley's NPM rose each year from 1994 to 1996. In 1995 total revenues fell with the growth rate in total revenues a −2.69 percent, but the growth rate in expenses was lower: −6.16 percent. Trading income and investment banking increased as a percentage of revenues. For expenses, compensation increased as a percentage of expenses, with other items falling relative to revenues in 1995. The net interest spread relative to total revenues in 1995 was 4.80 percent compared with 5.66 percent in 1994. In 1996, the growth in revenues was 44 percent compared with 40.4 percent for expenses. Principal transactions rose as a percentage of revenues, particularly for trading, as did investment banking and asset management. Compensation, travel, promotion, business development, and other expenses rose as a per-

---

[37]See SNL Securities (1994) and "Salomon Brothers' Strategic Review" in Hayes and Meerschwam (1992).

centage of revenues, and the net interest spread to revenues fell to 2.53 percent in 1996. However, overall, the expense-to-revenue ratio improved from 93.67 percent in 1994 to 90.32 percent in 1995 to 88.04 percent in 1996, resulting in the higher NPMs over time.

Balance Sheets   Panel B of Table 11.4 shows typical balance sheets for securities firms. The asset mix for each firm reflects the basic securities business. For trading and broker/dealer activities a large securities inventory is needed. Thus, a large percentage of assets are securities, including those that will be sold and those for the firm's investments. Other assets are predominantly receivables from customers and broker/dealers, with a relatively small percentage of fixed and other assets. As can be seen in Table 11.4, Panel B, Morgan Stanley, a large New York investment bank, is involved in many different activities holding derivative contracts, debt and currency swaps, and physical commodities as assets in addition to government and corporate bonds and equity.

Liabilities are primarily short-term; they include short-term borrowings and repurchase agreements and securities sold but not yet purchased, along with customer payables. Security firms generally have very high financial leverage, particularly wholesale investment banks. Morgan Stanley, for instance, had a 3.77 percent equity-to-asset ratio in 1996, implying an equity multiplier of 26.53. In contrast, Morgan Keegan is much better capitalized with an equity-to-asset ratio of 17.85 percent, implying a much lower equity multiplier of 5.60. For security firms, capital ratios are calculated using the market value of equity. Under the SEC's Rule C3–1 of 1975, the minimum equity-to-asset ratio for broker-dealers is 2 percent.[38]

Analyzing Trends in Asset and Liability Composition   Asset utilization (revenues/assets) for Morgan Keegan was .318 in 1996 compared with .259 in 1995. Whereas assets grew 7.29 percent, revenues grew 32.2 percent, hence, asset utilization improved. In terms of asset mix, there were few changes relative to total assets. Receivables from customers rose as a percentage of assets. Liability mix changed with a significant fall in short-term borrowings to assets and a rise in commercial paper to assets. Total liabilities to assets fell by almost 2 percent, as equity to assets rose by 2 percent.

For Morgan Stanley, asset utilization was .067 in 1995 compared with .063 in 1996. Assets grew by 36.7 percent and revenues grew by 44 percent, resulting in the slight rise in asset utilization. The asset composition relative to total assets remained relatively constant, with some small composition changes. Government and

---

[38]See Saunders (1997). As Saunders points out, the 2 percent represents a capital cushion for brokers-dealers sufficient to liquidate assets at market values and satisfy customer liabilities. Adjustments are made to book net work by subtracting out fixed assets and other assets that cannot readily be converted to cash and securities that cannot be readily sold. Other adjustments are made to reflect profits and losses that are unrealized, subordinated liabilities, contractual commitments, deferred taxes, options, commodities and commodity futures, and certain collateralized liabilities. High equity multipliers or leverage ratios are typical for securities firms on Wall Street. For instance, in October 1998, the leverage ratio for Merrill Lynch was 31.9; for Morgan Stanley Dean Witter 33.7; for Lehman Brothers 35.2; for Donald, Lufkin & Jenrette 29; and for the PaineWebber Group 25. See Patrick McGeehan and Gregory Zuckerman. "High Leverage Isn't Unusual on Wall Street." *The Wall Street Journal*, October 13, 1998, C1, C19.

nongovernment securities to assets fell 3 percent, as did corporate equities, whereas cash-related assets, other receivables, and other assets rose. On the liability and equity side, the equity-to-asset ratio fell from 4.20 percent to 3.77 percent in 1996. Short-term borrowings to assets rose slightly, as did corporate equities sold, along with other minor changes in liabilities.

Overall Dupont Analysis   Similar to other financial institutions, a Dupont Analysis can be used to provide an overall analysis of trends, as follows:

	Morgan Keegan		Morgan Stanley	
	1996	1995	1996	1995
Return on Equity	20.04%	17.10%	13.90%	9.94%
Return on Assets	3.58%	2.70%	.524%	.417%
Equity Multiplier	5.60	6.33	26.53	23.81
Net Profit Margin	11.24%	10.46%	7.83%	6.58%
Asset Utilization	.318	.259	.067	.063

Note that because of rounding errors, Dupont multiplied figures may be slightly different from actual return on assets (ROA) and ROE calculations. Using a Dupont Analysis for Morgan Keegan, the firm's ROE improved as the result of a higher ROA and despite a lower equity multiplier. The higher ROA was the result of both a higher NPM and higher asset utilization.

Morgan Stanley's ROE improved as a result of both a higher ROA and a higher equity multiplier. The higher ROA was primarily due to a higher NPM and slightly higher asset utilization. Comparing the two firms, Morgan Keegan, the regional brokerage firm, has a much higher NPM and asset utilization and lower financial leverage than did Morgan Stanley, the New York investment banking firm.

Recent Diversification Trend in the Securities Industry   Numerous mergers have occurred in the securities industry in the 1990s. Some firms have found that by diversifying, they can achieve more consistency and less variability in profit margins, which, as noted in Table 11.2 can be quite variable. However, mergers with different types of firms can create cultural problems, particularly if mergers are between very different types of firms. An example of a recently successful merger of diverse cultures is that between Morgan Stanley, a blueblood investment banking firm, with Dean Witter, a blue-collar brokerage firm spun off by Sears in 1997.[39] Morgan Stanley's lower profitability and capitalization than other firms at the time may have been an incentive for this merger. Although many bank analysts felt that cultural problems would arise and Morgan Stanley would be running the firm, Philip Purcell, from the Dean Witter side, was made the chief executive officer. He followed a policy of meshing the two companies very slowly, often at a slower rate than preferred by John Mack, his second in command at Morgan Stanley. He also resisted any attempts for co-management with John Mack. The company managed its risks by cutting its inventory of risky bonds after losing about $300 million on its portfolio of Russian debt, when Russia devalued the ruble, and avoided major losses from emerging market bond funds that other firms suffered. Dean Witter supplied advantages to Morgan Stanley, including its army of 11,000 brokers selling securities and Dean Witter mu-

---

[39]Randall Smith. "Dean Witter Holds Its Own at Morgan." *The Wall Street Journal* (March 10, 1999), C1, C16.

tual funds to investors, along with its Discover credit card, and Morgan Stanley helped to expand markets for Dean Witter and the Discover card globally.

Since this merger, Morgan Stanley's profits improved considerably, as shown in Figure 11.4. In 1998, Morgan Stanley Dean Witter had a growth rate in profits of 27 percent, with $3.28 billion in profits in 1998. This compares with a fall in profits of 3.1 percent at Goldman Sachs, a 72 percent fall at Salomon Smith Barney, and a 35 percent fall at Merrill Lynch. Other mergers for diversification, such as that between General Electric Financial Services and Kidder Peabody, discussed in Chapter 13, have had problems in mixing cultures and have been less successful. Also, as firms get larger and more diversified, they may have greater trouble providing oversight for different divisions and identifying and controlling costs. Studies examining for economies of scale and scope in the securities industry find no significant economies or diseconomies of scope for firms of different sizes and find scale economies but at a relatively small optimal size. Thus, the choice between operating as a diversified firm or a specialty firm does not seem to be related to performance but may be related to a reduction in overall risk or smoothing of earnings.[40]

Figure 11.4   ✦   **COMPARISON OF PROFITS OF MORGAN STANLEY DEAN WITTER AFTER ITS MERGER TO OTHER SECURITIES FIRMS**

Happy Marriage?
Earnings at the merged Morgan Stanley Dean Witter have held steadier than those of its largest rivals; figures for years ended in November except Merrill Lynch

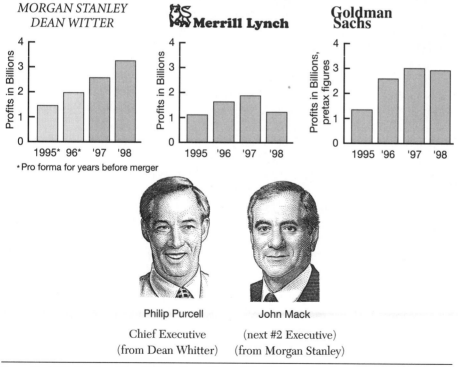

*Pro forma for years before merger

Philip Purcell
Chief Executive
(from Dean Whitter)

John Mack
(next #2 Executive)
(from Morgan Stanley)

Source: Randall Smith, "Dean Witter Holds Its Own at Morgan." *The Wall Street Journal*, March 10, 1999, C1, C16.

[40]See "Case 11: First Boston, Inc." and "Case 6: General Electric Financial Services, Inc." in Crawford and Sihler (1994).

Risk Management in Securities Firms

Trading Risk   As discussed in Chapter 9, in the 1990s, risk management has gained considerable importance for financial institutions and particularly for securities firms. Huge trading losses associated by individual traders resulted in a $370 million loss in mortgage-backed security strips for Merrill Lynch in 1987. Similarly, Kidder, Peabody lost $330 million of fictitious profits entered by Joseph Jett, the head of its bond trading department in the early 1990s. In 1995 Barings went under as the result of huge trading losses by a young trader in Singapore, Nick Lesson, on Japanese stock index futures; and a trader for Daiwa Bank, a leading Japanese investment bank, lost $1.1 billion through 30,000 unauthorized trades over 11 years as a senior manager in its New York Branch. Securities firms have attempted to develop better information on the risk exposure of traders using daily earnings at risk (DEAR) and value at risk (VAR) measures discussed in Chapter 9. They also have attempted to allocate greater capital and capital costs for potential losses associated with the risk of different activities using the risk–adjusted return on capital approach (RAROC) discussed in Chapter 8. Position limits for traders have also been devised based on the market risk of traders' portfolios, and compensation methods devised, so traders' returns are considered, along with the additional risk that riskier trades impose on the firm. Regulators including the Bank for International Settlements (an organization of the world's largest central banks) and the Fed have also proposed higher capital requirements for greater trading risk.[41]

Underwriting Risks   In addition to trading risks, investment banking firms have considerable underwriting risk, the risk of adverse price movements immediately after the issue of new securities. Under a negotiated offering, investment bankers purchase securities at a given price and sell securities at a higher offering price to the public. Thus, they receive a profit equal to the gross spread (offering price − price paid to the firm) plus any additional fees associated with the offering. To reduce this risk, syndicates of securities firms are often formed (as noted in Figure 11.1) to take on a portion of the offering and reduce the underwriting and selling risk of the lead underwriter. Table 11.5 shows an example of the distribution of gross spread for a hypothetical bond offering among syndicate members who take on underwriting risk and selling concession members who simply receive a commission for selling shares but have no underwriting risk (i.e., a best efforts arrangement). To retain prestige associated with being a leading firm in syndicates, firms must maintain a high profile by managing a large volume of new offerings, putting them at greater risk.

Underwriters have had greater risk with SEC 415 shelf registration deals; they are often asked to provide bids for an offering, particularly debt offerings that may have to be offered in just a few days. With a shelf registration, the SEC gives prior approval for an issue, and may take as little as two days to make a final approval based on the final price and contract rate for the offering. Consequently, underwriters may not have time to market the bond to institutional investors before making a bid. A bought deal is such an accepted bond transaction, often for Eurobond, whereby an investment bank has not had time to develop a syndicate or access market interest before submitting a bid. Such a deal places an underwriter at considerable risk. A kamikaze offer is an offer by a prospective underwriter for a bought deal at such a low yield that other underwriters may decline to participate in a syndicate for it. Such an offer may

---

[41]See Saunders (1997).

Table 11.5 ✦ EXAMPLE: DISTRIBUTION OF GROSS SPREAD ACROSS A SYNDICATE FOR A $100 MILLION BOND ISSUE

The lead manager receives a management fee, and an underwriter and selling concession fee for the firm's share in the underwriting. Syndicate members receive an underwriter discount and sales concession fee, while sales concession members receive only a sales concession fee.

EXAMPLE: PRELIMINARY DISTRIBUTION OF GROSS SPREAD

	Management Fee	Underwriter Discount	Sales Concession	Bonds Sold Direct to Public	Income
Manager	$2.00	$2.50	$5.50	30,000	$300,000
Syndicate Member	—	2.50	5.50	40,000	320,000
Group Member	—	—	5.50	30,000	165,000
					$785,000

Example: Bond Issue of $100 million.

Management Fee − $200,000 (20%); Underwriter & sales concession = $8.00 per bond

Sales commission = $5.50 per bond. Manager collects an additional $140,000 implicit management fee (equivalent of an additional 70,000 bonds worth).

Source: Richard D. Crawford and William W. Shiler. "Note to Case 18: Dakota Menska, Inc.," *Financial Service Organizations: Cases in Strategic Management*. New York: HarperCollins College Publishers, 1994.

be an effort for an investment bank to gain market share, at the expense of a loss. With shelf offerings, gross spreads for bond issues have fallen dramatically. However, underwriters may feel compelled to participate in an offering to retain other types of business from corporations. Technological innovations in the past decade have also allowed corporations to bypass security firms. In 1990, CapitaLink, a system through which blue chip corporations can issue bonds directly to institutional investors, became available. A company may request bids by computer for bonds it plans to issue; bids are received electronically and issuing costs are less than half the fees usually paid to underwriters. Such changes, along with new online investment banks discussed at the beginning of the chapter, diminish the potential profitability of services traditionally provided by investment bankers and increase their operating risk.[42]

Hedging of Underwriting Risks   Securities firms have not only developed hedging techniques for clients but have also developed hedging strategies to manage pricing risk for securities. One of the earliest and most widely publicized examples of hedging in the industry came in 1979, when Salomon Brothers underwrote an IBM bond issue. Just after the underwriting agreement was completed and the coupon rate was established, interest rates jumped sharply. The increase in market rates caused the bonds' market value to drop below Salomon's original estimates, wiping out expected profits. Industry observers assumed that Salomon had taken a big loss but soon learned that the deal had been hedged in the futures market, so the firm's

---

[42]See Carey, et al. (1993); and Smith (1989), which provides excellent anecdotes of the author's experience as an investment banker doing deals in Europe and Japan.

losses were limited (Hedging using futures is discussed in detail in Chapter 17; it basically entails taking a position on bonds in the futures market that will provide a gain to offset a loss on a spot position on bonds). In an increasingly competitive securities market with narrower gross spreads and commission fees, hedges are commonplace. In 1986, the SEC recognized the importance of integrated asset/liability management in the industry by permitting lower capital requirements for securities firms whose corporate bond holdings were hedged, although the agency began placing pressure on securities firms to strengthen their capital positions.[43]

Underwriters are allowed to use stabilization techniques during the first 30 days of a new stock issue, whereby they purchase or sell securities to stabilize the security's price. Often negotiated in an offering are overallotment options, often called green shoe provisions that allow a maximum of an additional 15 percent of the number of shares included in the basic offering. This option permits the underwriter to sell to the public more shares than it must purchase under the underwriting agreement, and to cover its "short position" used to stabilize the price of an issue by exercising the overallotment option. If the share price does rise considerably, it also offers additional profits to the underwriter, who can buy additional shares at the initial price and sell them at the higher market price. In a falling market, the lead manager may attempt to use overallotments to syndicate participants as a way to encourage sales efforts.[44]

Venture Capital and the Process of Taking a Firm Public

This final section provides a short overview of venture capital (VC) firms, investment firms that provide seed capital to firms just starting, start-up capital to firms beginning to operate or manufacture a product, and later stage capital and temporary (bridge) financing.

Many investment banks have VC firms as subsidiaries. VC firms' goal is to make a large return, averaging about 50 percent a year, for investors who are willing to take the risk of investing in relatively new companies. Returns required are higher depending on the risk and stage of the firm's growth. For instance, for firms just getting started (seed financing) an 80 percent return is required, 60 percent for a start-up actually beginning manufacturing, 50 percent for a first-stage firm making sales; 40 percent for a firm in a second major investment stage, 30 percent for a third-stage firm, and 25 percent for bridge, temporary financing. To make such an average return, VCs invest in a portfolio of firms with high growth potential, generally taking an equity interest. Their objective is to take a firm public or sell it in the relatively short time frame of five to seven years. Normally VC firms consider investments in excess of $2 million. Firms must give up a portion of control of the business, whereby the VC provides expertise and financial backing; VC firms have preferences for firms in such high-growth areas as biotech, software, media communications, and information technology. In 1997 of $12.2 billion invested, $2.6 billion was invested in software companies, $2.4 billion in communication companies, $.6 billion in electronics, and $6.4 billion in other industries.[45]

---

[43]"How Salomon Brothers Hedged the IBM Deal." *Business Week* (October 29, 1979), 50; and Cynthia S. Grisdella. "Capital Rules Eased for Securities Firms that Hedge Corporate Bond Holdings." *The Wall Street Journal* (November 5, 1986), 4.

[44]See Lipman (1994).

[45]Matt Richtel. "Venture Capital Is Alive, and Plentiful." *The New York Times* (April 6, 1998), C3.

Different types of venture capital firms include: (1) private VC firms, which are often subsidiaries of investment firms or other corporations; (2) angels, wealthy individuals who advance venture capital to entrepreneurs generally in businesses that they know; (Approximately 250,000 angels invest about $10 billion in over 30,000 firms a year, with the average investment $100,000 to $500,000 to early-stage firms.) (3) venture capital networks (VCNs) provide anonymous matching; (4) small business investment corporations (SBICs), which are funded by $4 of low-cost government debt for every $1 of stockholder equity that provide capital often in the form of convertible debenture debt for small businesses capable of an annual cash flow that will allow SBICs to cover their commitments; and (5) minority enterprise small business investment companies (MESBICs) that provide debt and equity to small businesses that are at least 51 percent owned by socially or economically disadvantaged persons. Like SBICs, MESBICs receive low-cost government debt financing.[46]

Capital deals are designed by VC firms with commitment letters, investment agreements, loan covenants, rewards for performance and penalties for failures. If goals are met, entrepreneurs reap financial rewards when the company goes public, is sold, or is refinanced. Through VC subsidiaries, investment banks can have access to promising firms to take public under initial public offerings (IPOs). A VC's subsidiary's portfolio of firms may have a number of firms that fail, but with diversification large returns on stellar firms can result in an overall high return for the portfolio.[47]

REGISTERING AND MARKETING THE TRADITIONAL IPO

In taking a firm public, an investment bank provides considerable advice and expertise to its client firm. Once an investment bank and a firm have decided to work together, they sign a letter of intent, which is not legally binding but does express a basic business understanding between the parties including the expected offering per share, amount of the underwriter's discount (gross spread) or commission in the case of a best efforts offering, the overallotment or green shoe option; and who is responsible for expenses including lawyers, accounts, printer and filing fees, and so on; and preferential rights on future financings by the investment bank, such as over a period of five years. An example of the pricing for the total fees for an offering is $400,000 for a $15 million offering, with an underwriter's discount (offering price − price paid to firm) of $1,050,000, amounting to a total of $1,450,000 in aggregate offering costs or about 10 percent of the $15 million offering disregarding the overallotment option. To determine the gross spread, the underwriter must determine the valuation of the company at the start of the IPO.[48]

Valuation of a Typical IPO   Typically underwriters determine procedures for the valuation of a company at the start of the IPO by looking at comparable companies that are public and determining their price earnings multiple (P/E) or their multiple on EBITDA (earnings before interest, taxes, depreciation, and amortization).[49]

---

[46]See Bygrave and Timmons (1992).

[47]Information on SBICs can be obtained from the National Association of Small Business Investment Companies, Suite 1101, 1156 15th St., N.W., Washington, D.C. 20005 and on MESBICs from the American Assn. of MESBICS, Suite 700, 915 15th St., N.W., Washington, D.C. 20005.

[48]See Lipman (1994).

[49]See Lipman (1994).

For example, if a comparable company has been public for a while and its market price is 14 times its trailing earnings; it will probably be valued at a 10 percent to 15 percent discount below the 14 multiple, say at a multiple of 12. Such a discount provides an incentive for institutional investors to buy the stock versus other more seasoned public companies in the industry. For instance, if the firm's adjusted earnings or EBITDA was $2 million using this multiple, the valuation would be as follows:

$$\text{Valuation} = \$2 \text{ million} \times 12 = \$24 \text{ million}$$

If the firm was financed totally with owners' equity, this would be the value of the equity of the firm. Hence, if the firm wanted to raise $12 million from the sale of stock in the IPO, the firm's overall valuation would be $12 million + $24 million = $36 million, and $33\frac{1}{3}$ percent ($\frac{12}{36}$) of the outstanding stock of the firm would be sold in the IPO.

If the firm was financed with debt, for instance $12 million, in the original valuation, the total value of the firm (debt + equity) would be equal to $24 million plus the value of its debt tax subsidy (Value of Debt $\times$ marginal tax rate of the firm). For instance, if the firm had a 30 percent marginal tax rate, its total value would be as follows:

$$\text{Valuation} = \$24 \text{ million} + \$12 \text{ million} (.30) = \$27.6 \text{ million},$$

and the Value of Equity would be the Valuation − the Value of Debt:

$$\text{Value of Equity} = \$27.6 \text{ million} - \$12 \text{ million} = \$15.6 \text{ million}$$

With an additional $12 million desired to be raised, the new total value of equity would be as follows:

$$\$12 \text{ million} + \$15.6 \text{ million} = \$27.6 \text{ million}$$

so the new offering would represent 43.48 percent (12/27.6) of the value of total equity.

Determining the Share Price and Total Number of Shares   Underwriters generally tend to price IPOs between $10 to $20 per share, although on occasion an IPO might be priced at a higher price to create prestige for an issue or based on demand for the issue. IPOs prices at less than $5 per share are often considered to be "penny stocks" subject to more onerous SEC and state (blue sky) rules. Institutional investors may also avoid "penny stock" issues. Underwriters also prefer 350,000 or more shares to make certain there is sufficient float or liquidity for an issue. Hence, for the offering in the preceding section, if after checking market conditions, a price of $15 was reasonable, the total number of shares for the $27.6 million value of total equity would be as follows:

$$\$27.6 \text{ million} / \$15 = 1.84 \text{ million shares}$$

and $12 million / $15 = $.8 million or 800,000 new shares would be sold to the public.

To achieve a price in the range of $10 to $20 million, the firm may have to change its initial stock capitalization by stock splits or the reverse of stock splits to achieve its desired IPO price based upon the valuation of the company and the proportion of the firm to be sold in the IPO.[50]

---

[50]See Lipman (1994) from which this example comes, and Brigham, Gapenski, and Ehrhardt (1999), Chapter 15. Under this model, basically, EBITDA (cash flows) are considered to be perpetuities, and the multiple can be considered as 1/ke, where ke is the cost of equity capital. Other valuation techniques are also often used in combination with this approach.

Other Steps in an IPO   After the valuation and letter of intent, the investment bank must perform an active due diligence process, basically interrogating the firm's managers and directors and making sure that all information in the registration statement for the offering is correct and that there are no significant omissions. This registration statements is submitted to the SEC and undergoes a minimum 30-day waiting period. The SEC submits a comment letter, often asking for revisions to statements and supplemental explanations, often requiring several amendments before it is willing to accept the registration statement.

Meanwhile, the investment bank can contact institutional and other investors to ask for verbal offers for the security, but no written offers. A tombstone ad can be placed and a syndicate formed, and a preliminary red herring prospectus can be published. Road shows around the country presenting the officers of the company to institutional investors for questions can be carried on. Registrations must be made to conform with state security laws. Some states have merit reviews allowing state administrators to determine the substantive fairness and merit of an issue to investors. Once an issue is a approved by the SEC, and the investment bank determines the market is ready for the offering, a pricing meeting is held, whereby the price for the IPOs is firmly established and negotiated between the firm and the investment banker. This meeting usually occurs after the close of the market on the day prior to the effect date of the registration statement or within a few days following. With the execution of the underwriting agreement and the effective date set for the offering, the underwriter legally binds itself to purchase the firm's securities. The closing is generally held during the first five business days after the execution of the underwriting agreement. At the closing the firm and other selling shareholders receive a check (typically in next-day funds) and the underwriter receives the firm's securities.

Once the IPO takes place, investment bankers practice stabilization techniques (buying or selling shares) to hold the price of the stock steady while it is in syndication, which is allowed for a period of 30 days following the issue. One stabilization technique is for the lead manager to allot less stock to the underwriters in a syndicate than originally indicated. For instance, an underwriter asked to underwrite 50,000 shares may only receive 45,000 on the allotment day. If that underwriter already sold 50,000, it must go to the market to buy 5,000 additional shares to cover its short position. Thus, the price of the common stock will be held steady or rise above its issue price. However, if the lead underwriter holds too much back, an usually large short position could drive the price too high or a small short position could drive the price down by not holding it steady enough. Typically, underwriters use the "greenshoe" provision that allows them to buy up to 15% additional shares at the offering price.[51]

This discussion provides a very simple description for an IPO. Actually, a number of valuation techniques may be used to value a firm, negotiation with the client firm, fact finding under due diligence, and road show schedule and marketing to institutional investors can be quite arduous. Although a great deal of publicity is given to successful IPOs and to typical underpricing for IPOs that brings favored investors huge returns, many IPOs have floundered, resulting in significant losses for underwriters, as IPO markets turn from hot markets to cold. Many new companies are also very difficult to value, having few comparative industries to draw from. Internet start-ups, for instance, were very hot in the later 1990s but very difficult to value, since they may have great potential but not have made a profit, as in the case of Amazon.com.[52]

---

[51]See Lipman (1994).

[52]See Rebecca Buckman and Aaron Lucchetti. "Wall Street Firms Try to Keep Internet Mania from Ending Badly." *The Wall Street Journal* (February 24, 1999), A1, A10.

A Brief Note on Other Activities   In addition to IPOs, underwriters are involved in secondary (seasoned offerings), mergers and acquisitions, and spinoffs of companies, among other activities that involve strong negotiation, people, and marketing skills as well as financial ones. Investment banks are also often called in to help with taking firms private and assisting in major privatizations for countries. With the crisis in Asia in 1997 and 1998, investment bankers were called in to help restructure debt offerings and have been called in as consultants to help countries to develop their financial markets and financial instruments. With the Latin American debt crisis of the 1980s, for instance, U.S. investment banks assisted with debt for equity swaps, whereby investment banks purchased troubled loans from U.S. banks and sold them to U.S. firms that could swap the debt for an equity investment in that country. They also assisted in debt for debt swaps (known as Brady bonds), in which bank debt was converted into longer-term, more liquid collateralized bonds, partially guaranteed by the U.S. government.[53]

SUMMARY

This chapter presents an overview of securities firms, which provide brokerage, trading, underwriting, merchant banking, and other financial services to wholesale and retail customers. Securities firms operate under unique regulatory guidelines in an increasingly competitive environment in which risk management is a necessary key to survival. The industry has been at the forefront of financial innovation in recent decades. With the Information Age, the industry is undergoing continued restructuring with the development of online trading and selling of securities on the Internet by electronic trading and recently established online investment banks.

The securities industry has faced increased competition and great volatility in earnings. Narrowing profit margins for traditional lines of business provided an incentive for securities firms to seek fee income by serving M&A clients and engaging in merchant banking activities, providing working capital and other services to small businesses, developing business in other countries, and engaging in greater trading activities. Security firms have attempted and develop better risk management techniques to measure to control for the risks associated with these activities. Some firms have become more diversified by becoming full-line service firms engaging in both retail and wholesale activities, which entails meshing very different cultures.

Some of the problems faced today by the securities industry were internally generated by the unethical and illegal insider trading activities of some industry partici-

pants. Congress responded to the growing number of violations by passing the Insider Trading Act of 1988, strengthening the regulatory authority of the SEC. The securities industry also has faced greater competition from commercial banks, who may pose even stronger challenges if the repeal of Glass-Steagall becomes a reality. Many mergers between securities firms and banks have occurred in recent years, as regulators have more liberally interpreted provisions allowing Section 20 investment subsidiaries for large, well-capitalized banks.

Questions

1. What advantages and disadvantages do online trading firms have compared to traditional brokerage firms? Why have traditional firms been reluctant to offer online trading to the public? Why has Charles Schwab been successful with its online trading while some other online firms have had problems with profits?

2. What would be the advantages and disadvantages of an online investment banking firm to a firm that is going public? To investors?

3. Why are earnings in the securities industry so cyclical? What factors affect security firm profits? Where do brokerage firms revenues and expenses chiefly come from? Where do investment banking firm revenues and profits come from? How do the different categories of securities firms differ in terms of sources of revenues and expenses?

4. What are prestigious investment banks and how have their ranks been changing?

---

[53]See Saunders, 1997.

5. Why were investment banking firms so important in the 19th century? How did trusts develop? In the 20th century, why was there anti-Wall Street sentiment? What factors led to the development of the Eurobond market and the globalization of the industry? What changes led to greater competition in the 1970s and 1980s?

6. Give some examples of innovations by securities firms. What factors encouraged these innovations? Look up articles in a recent *Wall Street Journal* and find an example of a recent innovation.

7. Discuss the October 1987 stock market crash. What led to the greed and fraud that occurred for many securities firms in the 1990s? How did the Insider Trading and Securities Fraud Enforcement Act attempt to reduce fraud and insider trading?

8. Why have many mergers between security firms occurred in the 1990s? Why was the harmonization of regulations for the European Economic Community important in 1992? What is day-trading? Why have regulators been concerned about day-trading and the crush of trading in Internet stocks?

9. Find a recent example of fraud by a securities firm or individual in the securities industry. Why is the security industry prone to fraud? Why is ethical behavior particularly crucial for firms in the securities industry? Give some examples of recent lawsuits that different firms in the securities industry faced in the 1990s. Can you suggest any solutions for reducing fraud?

10. What are the key areas of activity for security firms? Which areas have been more profitable in recent years? Look in *The Wall Street Journal* at ads by security firms. What are some new areas of activity that are advertised?

11. How have revenue sources been changing for the securities industry? Explain why. How did the industry become more profitable after the stock market crash of 1987?

12. Discuss typical assets and liabilities that would be found on the balance sheet of a regional securities firm versus an investment bank. Why do you think security firms have such high financial leverage on average?

13. What type of risks do security firms and investment banks respectively face? How does their interest rate risk compare to that of depository institutions?

14. How have investment firms attempted to reduce their risks in the 1990s?

15. Describe the venture capital process. What is an angel? A private venture capital firm? An SBIC? A MESBIC? What is the objective of the VC process?

16. List the steps associated with taking a firm public. Why do investment firms use syndicates? What is the gross spread? What is stabilization? What risks do lead managers of an issue face?

17. How did the Shelf Registration Rule SEC 415 make underwriting issues, particularly bond issues, more competitive for investment bankers? What has been the effect on gross spreads for bonds? What is a bought deal? A kamikaze offering?

18. Discuss the role of investment bankers internationally in the 1980s and 1990s. How did they assist in the Latin American debt crisis? In the Asian debt crisis? In privatizations in Russia and eastern Europe? What is a debt for debt swap? Debt for equity swap?

19. Find an article in *The Wall Street Journal* about recent international activities by U.S. investment banks or securities firms. What are recent trends?

Recommended Cases:

Darden School, University of Virginia (also in Richard D. Crawford and William W. Sihler, *Financial Service Organizations: Cases in Strategic Management*, New York: HarperCollins College Publishers, 1994.)

(1) **Case 11: First Boston, Inc.** Determining the Strategic Structure of a Major Investment Bank. Case analyses differences in the performance of full service firms versus wholesale investment banks and retail firms and some of the cultural problems within investment banking firms.

(2) **Case 17: Winson Furniture Company, Inc.** Underwriting a public issue of common stock; gives students practice in valuation issues.

(3) **Case 18: Dakota Menska, Inc.** Underwriting a public issue of debt. Information about changes in debt markets with the SEC's shelf registration process and the bond issuing process.

(4) **Case 4: Jefferies Group, Inc.** Case involving a securities firm that deals with over-the-counter and off-the-board competition in trading stock and new technology.

Harvard Business School Cases:

(5) **Salomon Brothers' Strategic Review:** 1987 (also in Hayes and Meerschwam, 1992). Strategic overview for Salomon Brothers at a time when it was facing financial problems.

(6) **Bankers Trust New York Corporation** (also in Hayes and Meerschwam, 1992). This case deals with cultural issues meshing a commercial bank with an investment bank culture.

(7) **Morgan Stanley: The Tokyo Branch** (also in Hayes and Meerschwam, 1992). Morgan Stanley's attempt and cultural problems in setting up a branch office in Tokyo.

(8) **CSFB and the International Capital Markets** (A) (also in Hayes and Meerschwam, 1992). History of Credit Suisse First Boston and strategic issues facing the firm, including a review of the Euro-Markets and the firm's competitive environment.

(9) **Alex Brown Incorporated,** Strategic Issues Facing a Regional Investment Banking Firm; also presents the trends in the industry.

Problems

1. Rene Gash, the famous research analyst, of the Whole Lot of Bucks Analytics, has asked you to do a financial analysis including a Dupont analysis for Charles Schwab, shown in Table 11P.1. She asks that you include an analysis of asset and liability mix. Discuss the primary sources of revenues and expenses for a discount brokerage firm. How does this differ from a wholesale investment bank, like Morgan Stanley in 1996?

Table 11P.1 ✦ **FINANCIAL STATEMENTS FOR CHARLES SCHWAB CORPORATION 1995 & 1996**

Business: Provide brokerage & related investment services to customers. Company's strategy is to attract and retain customers by focusing on retail brokerage, mutual funds, support services for independent investment managers, equity security market-making, online brokerage and 401(k) defined contribution plan. Competitive advantages include advertising and marketing programs that have created a national brand, a broad range of products and services, diverse delivery systems and an ongoing investment in technology.

CONSOLIDATED INCOME ACCOUNTS, YEARS ENDED DEC. 31 ($000):				
Revenues:	1996	% Revs.	1995	% Revs.
Commissions	954,129	51.55%	750,896	52.88%
Mutual Fund Service Fees	311,067	16.81%	218,784	15.41%
Interest Revenue	254,988	13.78%	210,897	14.85%
Principal Transactions	256,902	13.88%	191,392	13.48%
Other Revenues	73,836	3.99%	47,934	3.38%
Total Revenues	1,850,922	100.00%	1,419,903	100.00%
Expenses:				
Compensation & Benefits	766,377	41.41%	594,105	41.84%
Communications	164,756	8.90%	128,554	9.05%
Occupancy & Equipment	130,494	7.05%	110,977	7.82%
Commissions, Clearance & Floor Brokerage	80,674	4.36%	77,061	5.43%
Depreciation & Amortization	98,342	5.31%	68,793	4.84%
Advertising & Mktg. Developmt.	83,987	4.54%	52,772	3.72%
Professional Services	52,055	2.81%	41,304	2.91%
Other Expenses	80,174	4.33%	69,233	4.88%
Total Expenses Excluding Int.	1,456,859	78.71%	1,142,799	80.48%
Income before taxes	394,063	21.29%	277,104	19.52%
Taxes on Income	160,260	8.66%	104,500	7.36%
Net Income	233,803	12.63%	172,604	12.16%

Table 11P.1   ✦   FINANCIAL STATEMENTS FOR CHARLES SCHWAB CORPORATION 1995 & 1996 (CONTINUED)

CONSOLIDATED BALANCE SHEET, AS OF DECEMBER 31 ($000)

Assets	1996	% Assets	1995	% Assets
Cash & Equivalents	633,317	4.60%	454,996	4.31%
Cash & Investmts. Reqd to be Segregated	7,235,971	52.52%	5,426,619	51.43%
Receivables from brokers, dealers, & clearing orgs.	230,943	1.68%	141,916	1.34%
Receivables from customers	5,012,815	36.38%	3,946,295	37.40%
Securities owned at market value	127,866	0.93%	113,522	1.08%
Net Equipment & Property	315,376	2.29%	243,472	2.31%
Intangible Assets	68,922	0.50%	80,863	0.77%
Other Assets	153,558	1.11%	144,325	1.37%
Total Assets	13,778,768	100.00%	10,552,008	100.00%
Liabilities and Equity				
Drafts Payable	225,136	1.63%	212,961	2.02%
Payables to Brokers, Dealers, etc	877,742	6.37%	581,226	5.51%
Payable to Customers	11,176,836	81.12%	8,551,996	81.05%
Accrued exps. & other	360,683	2.62%	326,785	3.10%
Borrowings	283,816	2.06%	246,146	2.33%
Total Liabilities	12,924,213	93.80%	9,919,114	94.00%
Equity	854,555	6.20%	632,894	6.00%
Total Liabilities & Equity	13,778,768	100.00%	10,552,008	100.00%

Source: Moody's Bank & Finance Manual 1997

2. Marcel Arak, the super analyst at Golden Boulder Securities Company, has asked you do a financial analysis including a Dupont analysis for Alex Brown, shown in Table 11P.2, a regional investment banking firm prior to its merger with Bankers Trust. Include an analysis of any changes in asset and liability mix.

Table 11P.2   ✦   FINANCIAL STATEMENTS FOR ALEX BROWN, INC. 1995 AND 1996 (PRIOR TO BANKERS TRUST MERGER)

Business: Major Investment Banking and Securities Brokerage Firm located in Baltimore, Maryland

Income Statement	1996	% Revs.	1995	% Revs.
Revenues ($000)				
Commissions	201,896	19.06%	173,471	21.43%
Investment Banking	414,891	39.16%	293,375	36.25%
Prin. Transactions	167,815	15.84%	139,383	17.22%
Int. & Dividends	142,307	13.43%	105,544	13.04%
Advisory & other	132,512	12.51%	97,621	12.06%
Total Revenues	1,059,421	100.00%	809,394	100.00%

(continued)

Table 11P.2   ◆   **FINANCIAL STATEMENTS FOR ALEX BROWN, INC. 1995 AND 1996**
(PRIOR TO BANKERS TRUST MERGER) (*CONTINUED*)

Expenses ($000)

Comp. & benefits	554,711	52.36%	432,880	53.48%
Communication Expense	38,388	3.62%	33,934	4.19%
Occupancy & Equip	38,504	3.63%	39,758	4.91%
Interest Expense	50,668	4.78%	36,204	4.47%
Floor Brokerage, exch. & clearing fees	20,755	1.96%	18,646	2.30%
Other oper. expenses	97,013	9.16%	89,797	11.09%
Total Oper. Exps.	800,039	75.52%	651,219	80.46%
Erngs before income & taxes	259,382	24.48%	158,175	19.54%
Income taxes	105,237	9.93%	62,620	7.74%
Net Earnings	154,145	14.55%	95,555	11.81%

Balance Sheet	1996	% Assets	1995	% Assets
Assets ($000)				
Cash & equivalents	109,800	4.32%	62,103	4.32%
Customer receivables	1,487,041	58.49%	1,277,869	58.49%
Rec. from brokers, dealers & clrg. orgs.	368,099	14.48%	416,449	18.96%
Cur. state inc. tax	17,429	0.69%		0.00%
Other receivables	59,097	2.32%	62,056	2.83%
Firm Trading Secs.	210,412	8.28%	110,564	5.03%
Sec. purchased under Reale Agremt	15,510	0.61%	34,865	1.59%
Deferred income tax	46,433	1.83%	27,813	1.27%
Mmship in Exchgs.	323	0.01%	323	0.01%
Net off & equipment	48,079	1.89%	41,189	1.88%
Investment Secs.	56,889	2.24%	50,294	2.29%
Loans to employees to purch convertibles	54,454	2.14%	48,320	2.20%
Other Assets	69,009	2.71%	64,662	2.94%
Total Assets	2,542,575	100.00%	2,196,507	100.00%
Liabilities and Equity				
Bank Loans	29,900	1.18%	120,008	5.46%
Cash mgt. facil pay.	83,733	3.29%	70,338	3.20%
Customers, incl. free credit bals.	676,734	26.62%	506,993	23.08%
Brokers, dealers, & clrg. orgs. payable	495,947	19.51%	480,621	21.88%
Curr. fed & state inc. tax payable	1,840	0.07%	5,032	0.23%
Other payables	378,981	14.91%	294,643	13.41%

Table 11P.2 ✦ FINANCIAL STATEMENTS FOR ALEX BROWN, INC. 1995 AND 1996 (PRIOR TO BANKERS TRUST MERGER) (CONTINUED)

Sec. sold not yet purch. at market	48,223	1.90%	54,276	2.47%
Secs. sold under repur. agreement			2,460	0.11%
Senior Debt	183,315	7.21%	172,849	7.87%
Total Liabilities	1,898,673	74.68%	1,707,220	77.72%
Equity	643,902	25.32%	489,287	22.28%
Total Liabs. & Equity	2,542,575	100.00%	2,196,507	100.00%

Source: Moody's Bank & Finance Manual 1996

3. Stu Rosenstein and Scott Barnhart, investment managers of Big Country Securities, have asked you to perform a Dupont analysis for Legg Mason, Table 11P.3, a regional brokerage and investment firm in Baltimore, Maryland. Include an analysis of changes in asset and liability mix and primary sources of revenues and expenses.

Table 11P.3 ✦ FINANCIAL STATEMENTS FOR LEGG MASON, 1997 AND 1996

Business: Holding Company whose subsidiaries engage in securities brokerage and trading & investment management of individual & institutional accounts and company-sponsored mutual funds, investment banking for corporations & municipalities, commercial mortgage banking and provision of other financial services.

Income Statement	1997	% Revs.	1996	% Revs.
Revenues ($000)				
Commissions	189,980	29.70%	169,181	32.78%
Prin. Transactions	73,181	11.44%	65,870	12.76%
Investment Advisory & related fees	183,401	28.67%	144,790	28.06%
Investment Banking	77,062	12.05%	43,328	8.40%
Interest Revenue	84,076	13.14%	57,098	11.06%
Other Revenue	37,006	5.78%	35,776	6.93%
Total Revenues	639,706	100.00%	516,043	100.00%
Expenses:				
Comp. & Benefits	362,876	56.73%	299,562	58.05%
Occu. & equp. rental	43,043	6.73%	36,403	7.05%
Communications	30,528	4.77%	28,081	5.44%
Floor brokerage & clearing fees	5,912	0.92%	5,063	0.98%
Interest Expense	43,357	6.78%	26,177	5.07%
Other Expenses	58,788	9.19%	56,903	11.03%
Total Expenses	544,504	85.12%	452,189	87.63%
Earnings before tax	95,202	14.88%	63,854	12.37%
Income taxes	38,609	6.04%	25,987	5.04%
Net Earnings	56,593	8.85%	37,867	7.34%

(continued)

Table 11P.3 ✦ FINANCIAL STATEMENTS FOR LEGG MASON, 1997 AND 1996 (*CONTINUED*)

Balance Sheet	1996	% Assets	1995	% Assets
Assets: ($000)				
Cash & equivalents	150,976	8.04%	89,378	6.80%
Segregated cash & securities	442,305	23.54%	168,859	12.85%
Resale Agreements	132,801	7.07%	108,413	8.25%
Customer Receivbls.	527,456	28.07%	398,375	30.31%
Securities Borrowed	263,612	14.03%	196,569	14.95%
Secs. owned at market value	78,862	4.20%	84,219	6.41%
Investment Secs.	66,983	3.56%	83,497	6.35%
Net Prop & Equipmt	35,809	1.91%	33,339	2.54%
Intangible Assets	61,423	3.27%	67,370	5.13%
Other Assets	118,741	6.32%	84,481	6.43%
Total Assets	1,878,968	100.00%	1,314,500	100.00%
Liabilities & Equity				
Pay to Customers	960,646	51.13%	564,698	42.96%
Pay. to Brks & Dirs.	7,112	0.38%	3,854	0.29%
Securities Loaned	250,804	13.35%	170,829	13.00%
Sht-term Borrowings	13,400	0.71%	6,800	0.52%
Secs. sold, not yet purch. at mkt.	12,507	0.67%	10,693	0.81%
Accrued Compens.	58,893	22.28%	41,168	22.74%
Other Liabs.	57,396	3.05%	50,018	3.81%
Senior Notes	99,581	5.30%	99,534	7.57%
Subordinated Liabs.			68,000	
Total Liabilities	1,460,339	77.72%	1,015,594	77.26%
Common Stock	1,827	0.10%	1,538	0.12%
Additional Pd-in Cap.	192,817	10.26%	120,960	9.20%
Retained Earnings	223,752	11.91%	176,098	13.40%
Net unrealized appr. on invest. secs.	223	0.01%	310	0.02%
Total Equity	418,629	22.28%	298,906	22.74%
Total Liabs. & Equity	1,878,968	100.00%	1,314,500	100.00%

Source: Moody's Bank & Finance Manual 1997

4. Jim Verbrugge of Royal Gorge Securities, asks you to do a Dupont analysis for Paine Webber, (Table 11P.4) a national full-service securities firm. Include an analysis of changes in asset and liability mix and primary sources of revenues and expenses. How do profits compare Charles Schwab, a discount brokerage firm, and Legg Mason, the regional securities firm shown in the previous problems?

Table 11P.4 ✦ FINANCIAL STATEMENTS FOR PAINE WEBBER 1995 AND 1996

Business: One of the largest full-service securities and commodities firms in the industry.

Income Statement	1996	% Revs.	1995	% Revs.
Revenues:				
Commissions	1,381,475	24.21%	1,272,766	23.92%
Prin. Transactions	1,023,615	17.94%	914,201	17.18%
Investment Banking	391,164	6.86%	326,777	6.14%
Asset Management	453,267	7.94%	399,540	7.51%
Other Income	146,708	2.57%	150,056	2.82%
Interest Revenue	1,970,754	34.54%	1,969,811	37.03%
Total Revenues	5,705,966	100.00%	5,320,090	100.00%
Interest Expense	1,970,754	34.54%	1,969,811	37.03%
Net Revenues	3,735,212	65.46%	3,350,279	62.97%
Expenses:				
Employee comp. & related expenses	2,219,129	38.89%	2,004,585	37.68%
Office & equip. rental	267,006	4.68%	266,291	5.01%
Communications	153,301	2.69%	149,047	2.80%
Business Developmt.	75,981	1.33%	90,752	1.71%
Brokerage, clearing & exchange fees	87,839	1.54%	93,657	1.76%
Professional Servs.	108,123	1.89%	101,911	1.92%
Other Expenses	263,800	4.62%	541,359	10.18%
Total Expenses	3,175,179	55.65%	3,247,602	61.04%
Earnings before taxes	560,033	9.81%	102,677	1.93%
Prov. for Income Tax	194,649	3.41%	21,927	0.41%
Minority Interest	1,034	0.02%		0.00%
Net Earnings	364,350	6.39%	80,750	1.52%

Balance Sheet	1996	% Assets	1995	% Assets
Assets				
Cash & Cash Equivalents	383,856	0.73%	222,497	0.49%
Segregated cash & Securities	499,761	0.95%	427,068	0.94%
Trading assets at fair value	16,823,307	32.04%	14,095,446	30.86%
Secs. pur. under agrmt to resell	20,746,831	39.51%	16,699,295	36.56%
Securities borrowed	7,380,374	14.05%	7,226,515	15.82%
Client receivables	4,327,996	8.24%	4,070,599	8.91%
Broker & Dealer receivables	273,737	0.52%	279,676	0.61%
Dividends & int. receivable	350,796	0.67%	263,948	0.58%
Fees & other receivables	136,545	0.26%	200,444	0.44%
Office equip & lsehld improv.	313,261	0.60%	322,056	0.71%
Other Assets	1,277,036	2.43%	1,863,750	4.08%
Total Assets	52,513,500	100.00%	45,671,294	100.00%

(continued)

Table 11P.4 ✦ FINANCIAL STATEMENTS FOR PAINE WEBBER 1995 AND 1996 (*CONTINUED*)

Liabilities and Equity				
Short-term borrowings	1,337,646	2.55%	991,227	2.17%
Secs. sold but not yet purchsd. at market	6,621,891	12.61%	6,233,054	13.65%
Secs. sold under repur. Agree.	28,797,276	54.84%	25,199,377	55.18%
Securities loaned	3,459,860	6.59%	2,752,429	6.03%
Payable to clients	4,883,344	9.30%	3,698,477	8.10%
Payable to brokers & dealers	205,437	0.39%	155,118	0.34%
Dividends & int. payable	285,341	0.54%	256,338	0.56%
Other accr. liabs. & accts pay.	1,290,555	2.46%	1,639,403	3.59%
Accrued compen. & benefits	737,376	1.40%	570,786	1.25%
Total short-term Liabilities	47,618,726	90.68%	41,496,209	90.86%
Long-term Borrowings	2,781,694	5.30%	2,436,037	5.33%
Total Liabilities	50,400,420	95.98%	43,932,246	96.19%
Total Equity	2,113,080	4.02%	1,739,048	3.81%
Total Liabs. & Equity	52,513,500	100.00%	45,671,294	100.00%

Source: Moody's Bank & Finance Manual 1997

5. The Skye Wescott Securities Firm in Dallas, Texas has asked you to do a valuation for a new initial public offering for Sylvia's Shoe Company in Norfolk, Virginia.

Information is provided as follows. What is the value of equity? If the firm wants to issue $15 million in total equity, what is the new value of equity? If a share price of $20 is desired, how many shares should be issued? What percentage will the new shares be of the total value of equity?

AVERAGE EBITDA = $12 millionDEBT: $50 million

Industry Multiplier = 15 (use 20 percent discount); Marginal tax rate = 30 percent

Selected References

Arshadi, Nasser, and Gordon V. Karels. "Trends in Derivatives and the Management of Financial Risk," in Modern Financial Intermediaries & Markets. Upper Saddle River, N.J.: Prentice Hall, 1997.

Bartlett, Sarah. *The Money Machine: How KKR Manufactured Power & Profits.* New York: Warner Books, 1991.

Bloch, Ernest. *Inside Investment Banking,* 2d ed. Homewood, Ill.: Dow Jones-Irwin, 1989.

Brigham, Eugene F., Louis C. Gapenski, and Michael C. Ehrhardt. *Financial Management: Theory and Practice,* 9th ed. Fort Worth, Tex.: Dryden Press, Harcourt Brace College Publishers, 1999.

Bygrave, William D. and Jeffrey A. Timmons. *Venture Capital at the Crossroads.* Boston: Mass.: Harvard Business School Press, 1992.

Carey, Mark S., et al. "Recent Developments in the Market for Privately Placed Debt." *Federal Reserve Bulletin* 79 (February 1993): 77–92.

Chernow, Ron. *The House of Morgan.* New York: Touchstone Books (Simon and Shuster, Inc.), 1990.

Chernow, Ron. *The Warburgs.* New York: Vintage Press, 1993.

Crawford, Richard D. and William W. Sihler. *Financial Service Organizations: Cases in Strategic Management.* New York: Harper Collins College Publishers, 1994.

Endlich, Lisa. *Goldman Sachs: The Culture of Success.* New York: Knopf, 1999.

Geist, Charles. *Investment Banking in the Financial System.* Englewood Cliffs, N. J.: Prentice Hall, 1995.

Goldberg, Lawrence G., et al. "Economies of Scale and Scope in the Securities Industry." *Journal of Banking and Finance* (February 1991): 91–107.

Hayes, Samuel L., III. "The Transformation of Investment Banking." *Harvard Business Review* 57 (January/February 1979): 153–170.

Hayes, Samuel L., III, and Philip M. Hubbard. *Investment Banking: A Tale of Three Cities.* Boston: Harvard Business School Press, 1990.

Hayes, Samuel L., III. and David M. Meerschwam. *Managing Financial Institutions: Cases within the Financial Services Industry.* New York: The Dryden Press, 1992.

Kidwell, David S., et al. "SEC Rule 415: The Ultimate Competitive Bid." *Journal of Financial and Quantitative Analysis* 19 (June 1984): 183–196.

Langevoort, Donald C. *Securities Law Series: Insider Trading Legislation.* New York: Clark Boardman Co., 1988.

Lipman, Frederic D. *Going Public.* Rocklin, Calif.: Prima Publishing, 1994.

Marshall, John F. and M. E. Ellis. *Investment Banking and Brokerage.* Boulder, Colo.: Kolb Publishing Co., 1994.

McNamee, Mike. "Investor's Guide: How Do the Upstart Net Brokers Stack Up Against Traditional Firms Online?" *Business Week* (February 22, 1999), 120–124.

Norton, Robert E. "Upheaval Ahead on Wall Street," *Fortune* (September 14, 1987), 68–77.

Rogowski, Robert J., and Eric H. Sorenson. "Deregulation in Investment Banking: Shelf Registrations, Structure and Performance." *Financial Management* 14 (Spring 1985): 5–15.

Saunders, Anthony. *Financial Institutions Management: A Modern Perspective,* 2d ed. Burr Ridge, Ill.: Irwin Press, 1997.

SNL Securities. *Industry Review: Broker/Dealers.* Charlottesville, Va.: SNL Securities, 1994.

Securities Industry Association. *Securities Industries Trends.* New York, Various issues.

Selby, Beth. "The Twilight of the Syndicate." *Institutional Investor* 19 (August 1985): 205–209.

Smith, Roy. *The Global Bankers.* New York: Truman Talley Books/Plume, 1989.

Sprio, Leah Nathans and Edward C. Baig. "Who Needs a Broker?" *Business Week* (February 22, 1999), 113–118.

Stigum, Marcia. *The Money Market,* 3d ed. Homewood, Ill.: Dow Jones-Irwin, 1990.

Walter, Ingo, and Roy C. Smith. "Investment Banking in Europe after 1992." In *Proceedings of a Conference on Bank Structure and Competition.* Chicago: Federal Reserve Bank of Chicago, 1989, 312–317.

Chapter 11 Internet Exercises

1. Have concerns about a securities firm? The SEC has a large database of information on regulated securities firms. EDGAR, the Electronic Data Gathering, Analysis, and Retrieval system, performs automated collection, validation, indexing, acceptance, and forwarding of submissions by companies and others who are required by law to file forms with the U.S. SEC. Its primary purpose is to increase the efficiency and fairness of the securities market for the benefit of investors, corporations, and the economy by accelerating the receipt, acceptance, dissemination, and analysis of time-sensitive corporate information filed with the agency. The EDGAR database can be accessed from

http://www.sec.gov/edgarhp.htm

To do a search, click on "Search the Edgar Database." There are two kinds of basic searches: General and Special-Purpose. The General Search includes Quick Forms Lookup where you can look up common forms for a designated company. This is a very valuable search if you already know the exact name of a company but is less useful for entities such as mutual funds. You can also search the EDGAR Archives as a keyword (WAIS) search of all the header information in all the filings in the database.

There are six Special-Purpose Searches: (1) EDGAR CIK (Central Index Key) Lookup, the CIK is a unique identifier assigned by the SEC to all companies and people who file disclosure with the SEC; (2) Current Events Analysis of forms filed in the previous week; (3). Mutual Funds Retrieval; (4) Prospectus search; (5) Exhaustive Mutual Funds Search of all the filing mutual funds in the database; and (6) Executive Compensation Test.

2. There is no shortage of financial scandals, and you can find a guide with links to information sources

at http://www.ex.ac.uk/~RDavies/arian/scandals/. The site includes links for classic financial scandals, political corruption, organized crime, money laundering, and links to regulatory and anti-fraud organizations that combat these scandals. There are also links to financial scandals in fiction.

The classic financial scandals links is found at http://www.ex.ac.uk/~RDavies/arian/scandals/classic.html

This is a guide with lots of links to information on these and other lesser-known financial scandals. Although most of the cases in these pages involve real or suspected criminal activity, a few are included simply because the scale of the incompetence or greed makes them scandalous: BCCI, Barings, Daiwa, Sumitomo, Credit Lyonnais, Bre-X, Lloyds, NASDAQ, Savings and Loan, and others.

Useful Web Links

Investment Banks on the World Wide Web
http://FinanceHub.com/invbanks

Securities Industry Association
http://www.sia.com

National Securities Clearing Corporation
http://www.nscc.com/

Moody's Investor's Services
http://www.moodys.com

National Association of Securities Dealers
http://www.nasd.com

International Securities Exchange: The First Electronic Securities Exchange in the U.S.
http://www.iseoptions.com

"The mutual fund families are competing with the banks and the banks are competing with the brokers. There is going to be an awful lot of competition in this market."

Eric Kobren
Editor, *Fidelity Insight* (1992)

"There are no guarantees in this business. Sure you can look back at 60 years of data and say that, in general, small company stocks beat large. But you had better be prepared to be wrong for a couple of decades."

John Rekenthaler
Morningstar, Director of Research (1999) Quote from Charles A. Jaffe, "Recall your First Mutual Fund?"
The Denver Post (February 15, 1999), 3C.

12

MUTUAL FUND AND PENSION FUND MANAGEMENT

Portfolio managers have used computers to aid investment decision making for decades. But Bradford Lewis of Fidelity Investments, a large mutual fund company, has taken computerized investing one step farther. As the head of Fidelity's Disciplined Equity fund, Lewis has gained attention for his reliance on "neural network" investing. His personal computer is programmed to mimic the activity of the human brain so well that it tells him when to buy or sell large blocks of stock. Mr. Lewis's goal is for his computer's picks to beat market averages consistently, and he argues that his neural network can exercise judgment and "learn" from its mistakes, as can the human brain, without being subject to human emotions.

Colleagues at Fidelity confess to being bewildered at the complexity of Lewis's approach, but his motivation is a simple one: He wants to keep his job. "I'm flip-
ping burgers if I don't beat the Vanguard index fund," *he says, citing a major rival known for its passive investment strategies.[1]*

As of April 8, 1998, the Investment Company Institute, the national association of the investment company industry, reported 6,987 mutual funds, 437 closed-end funds, and nine sponsors of unit investment trusts in the United States, managing over $5 trillion assets, representing more than 62 million individual shareholders. By the end of 1997, about 37.4 percent of U.S. households owned shares in a mutual fund, up from 5.7 percent in 1980 and 25 percent in 1990.[2] The growth in assets managed by investment companies including money market funds, equity and stock mutual funds, and unit trusts in the last two decades of the 20th century has been phenomenal, as shown in Figure 12.1. In 1980 mutual funds held only about 3.68 percent of financial assets. By 1997, this share was 21.74

---

[1]Robert McGough. "Fidelity's Bradford Lewis Takes Aim at Indexes with His 'Neural Network' Computer Program." *The Wall Street Journal* (October 27, 1992), C1, C19.

[2]*1998 Mutual Fund Fact Book* (1998). The address for the Investment Company Institute is 1401 H Street, N.W., Washington, D.C. The Web site is http://www.ici.org.

Figure 12.1 ◆ ASSETS OF MUTUAL FUNDS, 1940–1998

Mutual funds have enjoyed great popularity in recent years, spurred by the development of MMMFs in the mid-1970s. Stock and bond funds also grew rapidly in the same period.

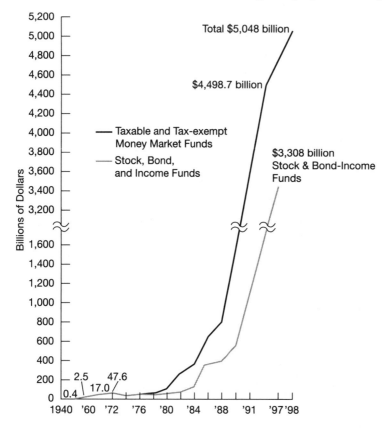

Source: Investment Company Institute, *1992, 1998 Mutual Fund Fact Book.* Reprinted with permission, and Robert McGough, "Bull Milestone: Mutual Funds Cross the $5 Trillion Mark," *The Wall Street Journal,* May 29, 1998, C1.

percent, and mutual funds became the second largest financial institution, next to banks, in the United States. Private and government pension funds (many of which are in fact mutual funds as well) similarly have grown tremendously, holding assets in excess of $1.5 trillion by the third quarter of 1998.[3] Not only does their size make these institutions important, their role in the flow of funds across economic sectors also is significant. Pension funds and mutual funds provide financial security for retirement. Investment companies also provide pro-

fessional investment management and diversified portfolios to small savers at reasonable costs.

The managers of these institutions face just as many challenges as do those of depositories, finance companies, securities firms, and insurance firms in the current economic environment. This chapter presents some of these challenges, along with information about the mutual fund and pension fund industries. The following section begins by discussing the investment companies that manage mutual funds.

◆ ◆ ◆

[3]Board of Governors of the Federal Reserve System, "Flow of Funds Assets and Liabilities," *Federal Reserve Bulletin,* Vol. 85 (February 1999), p. 141.

OVERVIEW OF THE MANAGEMENT STRUCTURE OF MUTUAL FUNDS

As discussed in Chapter 4, mutual funds are owned by investors who invest in the funds. In turn, companies that manage the funds are often owned by other companies or privately owned. Almost all mutual funds are externally managed, with operations conducted by investment companies and other affiliated organizations and independent contractors. Figure 12.2 shows the typical structure of a mutual fund. The key players in mutual fund areas follow[4]:

1.   **The board of directors.** The board of directors oversees the fund's activities, including approving contracts with management companies and other service providers. Directors are expected to exercise the care that a prudent person would take with his or her own business in overseeing and reviewing the performance of affiliates, including the investment adviser and the principal underwriter for the fund. Under a provision of the Investment Act of 1970, at least 40 percent of a board of directors must be independent of the fund's investment adviser or principal underwriter.

Figure 12.2   ✦   STRUCTURE OF A MUTUAL FUND'S MANAGEMENT

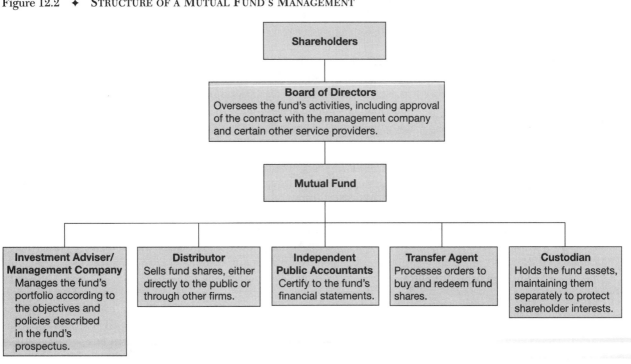

Source: 1998 Mutual Fund Fact Book, 38th ed. Washington, D.C.: The Investment Company Institute, 1998, p. 30.

---

[4]Information for this section comes from the *1998 Mutual Fund Fact Book,* (1998); and Fortune (1997).

2. **The investment adviser/management company.** The investment adviser/ management company manages the fund's portfolio according to the objectives and policies provided in a fund's prospectus. The investment adviser's job includes portfolio management and security trading. Traders place portfolio orders with broker-dealers and try to obtain the most expedient and lowest-cost execution of these orders. Contracts with investment advisers specify compensation, generally in terms of an annual fee based on the percentage of the fund's average net assets. Advisers are subject to numerous legal restrictions, including those on any transactions between the adviser and the fund it advises. The investment adviser affiliate often provides administrative services overseeing operations and accounting services, but this can be done through an unaffiliated party.

3. **The distributor or principal underwriter.** Mutual funds usually distribute their shares through separate organizations designated as principal underwriters. The principal underwriters are regulated as brokers and dealers to continuously offer new shares to the public and are subject to National Association of Securities Dealers, Inc. (NASD) rules governing the sales practices of mutual funds.

4. **The custodian.** By law mutual funds are required to place their securities with a custodian for protection. Almost all mutual funds use qualified bank custodians. Custodians are required to segregate mutual fund portfolio securities from other bank assets.

5. **The transfer agent.** A mutual fund employs a transfer agent to perform record-keeping and related functions, including maintaining record-keeping, calculating and disbursing dividends, and preparing and mailing shareholder account statements, tax information, and other notices. Some agents also prepare and mail statements confirming transactions and account balances and maintain customer service departments to respond to customer inquiries.

6. **Independent public accountants.** Independent public accountants are employed to certify the fund's financial statements.

Thus, the management of mutual funds not only includes portfolio management, but the careful management and timing of trades, meticulous record-keeping and correspondence, daily pricing, accounting, and custodial functions, along with intense customer service (often on a 24-hour basis), marketing, and promotion. Different affiliate groups perform these functions. Many funds also commission brokers and dealers or agents at banks, insurance companies, and securities firms to help distribute and sell fund shares. Affiliates may be part of a single company or be a collection of different companies. Investment companies also have diverse ownership structures, as discussed in the following section.

OWNERSHIP STRUCTURE OF AFFILIATES

Many investment companies are subsidiaries of other large corporations that may or may not engage in financial services. For instance, Kansas City Southern Industries, the holding company for the Kansas City Southern Railroad, owns several mutual fund companies including Janus Capital Corporation, Berger Associates, and American Century Funds. A profile for Janus Capital Corporation is shown in Figure 12.3. Based on its returns, Janus was acclaimed as the number 1 family of funds, with its

Figure 12.3 ✦ Profile for Janus Mutual Funds

Janus continues to win acclaim

Magazine names it, sister firm tops

By Donald Blount
Denver Post Business Writer

Janus Capital Corp., the dean of the Denver mutual fund companies, is white hot.

In its March issue, Mutual Funds magazine will name Janus and Berger Associates Inc. — both owned by Kansas City Southern Industries Inc. — the No. 1 and No. 2 "family of funds" in the country for 1998, based on return.

The company's assets under management broke the $100 billion mark for the first time ever this past December and have grown by an additional $23 billion since.

At the end of 1998, its top fund performers had annual returns of 73 percent, 58 percent and 57 percent.

And in its Jan. 11 issue, a Fortune magazine poll named Janus the 17th best place to work in the United States. The poll was based on employees' trust in management, pride taken in their work and workplace camaraderie.

All of this comes about as Janus waits for Kansas City Southern Industries Inc. to spin off its mutual funds unit later this year, a KCSI spokesman said. Kansas City Southern is primarily a railroad company, and a spin-off would create a new independent holding company.

Janus is named for the Roman god of gates, of beginnings and endings. One only needs to look at the beginning of the 1990s to see how far the company has come as the decade, and century, ends. In 1990, Janus had $2.2 billion in net assets. By the end of 1997, that number was at $67.3 billion.

It now has $123.4 billion under management and serves 1.5 million investors. Janus is the nation's fifth-largest mutual fund.

Janus' growth and success are results of the company's focus, said Claire Young, manager of the Olympus Fund.

At the end of 1998, the Olympus Fund had a one-year return of 56.97 percent, according to Morningstar, the Chicago-based analytical firm.

The Olympus Fund is a capital-appreciation fund, one with an objective of gaining long-term growth of capital.

For the 1998 fourth quarter, the Olympus Fund was the fourth-best-performing Colorado equity fund with a return of 32.66 percent.

Janus funds were also Nos. 3, 7 and 9.

The Enterprise Fund sported "only" a 33.75 percent return for the year and a 34.15 percent return for the fourth quarter.

But the Mercury Fund had a 58.41 percent return for 1998 and the Twenty Fund a 73.39 percent return for the year.

"I've never worked at another place, so I can't tell you how the other funds operate," said Young, sister of Helen Young Hayes, who manages Janus' Overseas and Worldwide funds. "But I can tell you what we do well, and that's picking stocks and companies that meet our investment criteria and not straying from our areas of strength."

She credits the research staff for much of the portfolio managers' success.

"I draw on our pool of analysts who gather information and come up with investment ideas," she said.

"Being in Denver helps us. We're not in Wall Street so we don't hear the buzz, we can be independent thinkers and can identify things that are going on with companies early," Young said.

Her portfolio is largely steeped in technology and pharmaceutical stocks. America Online, Cisco Systems, Microsoft Corp., Warner-Lambert Co. and Time Warner.

"It's an aggressive growth fund that does not have any sort of market capitalization restrictions so it can invest in any size company, domestic or international," Young said.

The companies she selects are usually first or second in their market "We're in a period where the strong get stronger. Those with the top positions can continue to grow their positions," she said.

Young is a Yale graduate with a degree in electrical engineering.

Working in financial services after studying the sciences isn't quite as much of a stretch as it may sound she said.

The companies she selects are usually first or second in their market "We're in a period where the strong get stronger. Those with the top positions can continue to grow their positions," she said.

Young is a Yale graduate with a degree in electrical engineering.

Working in financial services after studying the sciences isn't quite as much of a stretch as it may sound she said.

"Doing research on a stock, building a model and coming up with a conclusion is not different than being in a lab and writing a report. It's a different set of data."

She has worked at Janus since 1992 and has managed the Olympus fund since October 1997.

Young was brought to Janus by her sister Helen, who has previously been named by Morningstar as International Manager of the Year.

But Claire said she doesn't feel any pressure to measure up to her sister's success.

"Helen introduced me to Janus and the financial-services industry," she said.

"Every single manager here is an incredible stock picker with good records. My pressure is on myself to make sure I'm at the same caliber as my peers, . . . it's not because of Helen. I do not want to be the one Janus manager to let people down."

Janus' growth-fund performers

Janus Twenty has been flying high since fund manager Scott Schoelzel took over in mid-1997. But two other Janus funds, Mercury and Olympus, also are near the top of the large-capitalization growth class, and have done particularly well in recent months.

Mercury

Established: 1993
Manager: Warren Lammert
Assets: $3.1 billion
Top five holdings: Time Warner, Cisco Systems, Nokia, Comcast, America Online
Year-to-date total return/rank*: 9.8%/7
Three months: 42.2%/11
One year: 74.7%/16
Five years (annualized): 28.1%/7

Olympus

Established: 1995
Manager: Claire Young
Assets: $1.3 billion
Top five holdings: America Online, Cisco Systems, Microsoft, Warner-Lambert, Time Warner
Year-to-date total return/rank*: 9.7%/8
Three months: 43.8%/9
One year: 72.5%/19
Three years (annualized): 37.5%/7

Twenty

Established: 1985
Manager: Scott Schoelzel
Assets: $15.8 billion
Top five holdings: America Online, Dell Computer, Microsoft, Time Warner, Nokia
Year-to-date total return/rank*: 7.3%/19
Three months: 37.9%/21
One year: 85.1%/6
Five years (annualized): 31%/2

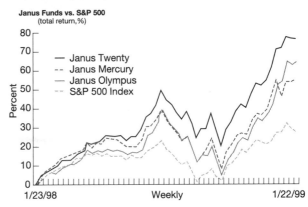

Janus Funds vs. S&P 500 (total return, %)

— Janus Twenty
-- Janus Mercury
— Janus Olympus
-- S&P 500 Index

1/23/98 — Weekly — 1/22/99

Source: Donald Blount, "Janus Continues to Win Acclaim," *The Denver Post*, January 31, 1999, 1K, 17K

sister company Berger, ranked as number 2. Denver, Colorado, far from Wall Street, has become a mutual fund capital with Janus, Berger, American Century, and Invesco, among other prominent funds, operating in the Denver metropolitan areas. Other large funds, such as Vanguard and Fidelity, have their investment management operations centered in the East Coast, with affiliates in other areas. For instance, Fidelity has affiliates in Kentucky and Texas.

In terms of ownership structure, Vanguard is one of the few funds mutually owned by its stockholders, which allows the company to keep its expenses low. Fidelity Investment Co. is privately owned by the Johnson family and its top executives and mutual fund managers.[5] Often fund families are subsidiaries of banks, insurance companies, or securities firms. Examples are Dreyfus Funds, a subsidiary of Mellon Bank; Marisco Capital Management, which is 50 percent owned by BankAmerica Corporation; Scudder Funds, a subsidiary of Zurich Insurance Corporation; and Merrill Lynch Funds. In 1998, a number of asset management firms that operated as partnerships considered taking their firms public with initial public offerings (IPOs). These include Neuberger and Berman in New York with $56 billion in mutual funds and Federated Investors with $96 billion in assets under management. This consideration was in response to high stock price multiples over earnings for other publicly traded investment companies, including T. Rowe Price Associates and Franklin Resources.[6]

RECENT DIVERSIFICATION AND CONSOLIDATION FOR MUTUAL FUNDS

In recent years investment companies have diversified the products that they offer, merged funds with other funds, and diversified internationally as well.

Product Diversification As noted in Chapter 4, many investment companies, such as Fidelity, have become "jacks of all trade," offering a wide variety of financial services including discount brokerage, automated bill paying, insurance, annuities, debit cards for automatic teller machines, check-writing services against funds, and even some Internet-based investing and home-banking services. As of February 1998, seven of the 10 largest direct marketing mutual funds (those that sell funds directly to the public; they are Fidelity, Vanguard, T. Rowe Price, American Century, Janus, Dreyfus, Scudder, USAA, Neuberger and Berman, and Strong), had brokerage services and five had debit card services; the Strong Group considered both.[7]

Consolidation Mutual funds have experienced a large number of mergers in the 1990s. As reported in Pozen (1998), in 1996 alone, 96 acquisitions occurred involving over $530 billion in assets. Some mergers involved large funds trying to fill out their line of products. Others involved institutional-oriented firms seeking a greater

---

[5]James S. Hirsch and Robert McGough. "Fidelity Denies Rumors of Intention to Sell Firm." *The Wall Street Journal* (June 12, 1998), C1, C26; Jonathan Clements. "Money Machine: While Brokers Suffer, a Mutual Fund Firm Thrives in Stock Surge." *The Wall Street Journal* (July 16, 1990), A1, A5.

[6]Robert McGough. "Neuberger, After Half Century, Considers IPO," *The Wall Street Journal* (April 22, 1998), C1.

[7]Vanessa O'Connell. "It's a Broker! It's a Banker! It's a Mutual Fund Group!" *The Wall Street Journal*, February 19, 1998, C1, C27.

retail investor distribution. For instance, Morgan Stanley's merger with Dean Witter provided the firm with a broader line of retail mutual funds. Fund groups have also merged their losing funds into long-term winning funds. For instance, in March 1999 the Invesco Funds Group proposed to eliminate 11 of its smaller funds that were not performing well and to merge them into other funds, allowing costs of operating funds to be spread over a large number of customers.[8]

International Diversification   In the late 1990s, many U.S. investment companies and security firms managing mutual funds entered new markets in Asia and Europe, where investors do not commonly invest in mutual funds. On December 1, 1998, Japan, in the process of deregulating its financial markets, began permitting mutual fund managers, banks, and life insurers to sell mutual funds, a privilege previously reserved only for brokers. A number of U.S. asset managers planned to sell funds in Japan, including Fidelity Investments, Putnam Investments, and Merrill Lynch & Co. Roger Servisonm, a Fidelity managing director, predicted that Fidelity's assets under management in Japan could rise in the next decade to $100 billion, with $10 trillion in savings held by Japanese individuals and more than half in bank accounts paying interest of less than .5 percent. In the late 1990s, mutual funds such as Fidelity and securities firms with mutual funds including Morgan Stanley Dean Witter, Goldman Sachs, Merrill Lynch, and Salomon Brothers/Smith Barney formed joint ventures with Japanese brokerage firms to sell their funds in Japan. This presented a challenge in educating individual investors on the benefits of diversification in a country where individual stock investments are generally preferred.[9]

U.S. investment companies including Fidelity and Vanguard also launched funds in Europe in the 1990s, where again mutual funds are not as widely used by individual investors as in the U.S. With the emergence of the Euro, European mutual funds have adapted their strategies, changing fund bylaws and launching new country sector funds as a means for European investors to diversify their holdings with limited foreign exchange diversification with the Euro. A study of mutual fund name recognition in continental Europe found that European mutual funds had name recognition in their own regions with little recognition across borders, while other funds such as Fidelity Investments of the U.S. and Fleming Asset Management of Britain had greater name recognition across countries.[10]

---

[8]Charles A. Jaffe. "Look for Fund Consolidation in '99." *The Denver Post* (January 4, 1999), 3C; and Al Lewis. "Invesco Group Wants to Close or Merge 11 Mutual Funds." *The Rocky Mountain News* (March 25, 1999), B2.

[9]Fund experts reported that in 1997 roughly 4 percent of Hong Kong households owned mutual funds, sliding to 2 percent in February 1998, as disappointed investors pulled out money from funds. About 3 percent of U.S. households hold investments in Real Estate Investment Trusts (REITs), and 30 percent own mutual funds. See Ellen E. Schultz. "Mutual Funds Get Cold Shoulder in Asia." *The Wall Street Journal* (February 17, 1998), C25. Pui-Wing Tam. "New Funds Continue to Appear in Asia." *The Wall Street Journal* (March 25, 1998), C23; Bill Spindle. "Japan's Great Mutual-Fund Battle Begins." *The Wall Street Journal* (November 30, 1998), C25; and Margaret Boitano. "Fund Companies' Overseas Ties Can Fray." *The Wall Street Journal* (March 3, 1999), C23.

[10]Robert Bonte-Friedheim, "Vanguard to Launch Funds in Europe," *The Wall Street Journal*, April 1, 1998, C27; Sara Callan, "European Funds Lack Broad Recognition," *The Wall Street Journal*, February 17, 1999, C23; and Robert Bonte-Friedheim, "European Funds Prepare Euro Strategies," *The Wall Street Journal*, April 22, 1998, C27.

BASIC GROUPS OF INVESTMENT COMPANIES

Investment companies are organized to permit investors to invest in a portfolio of assets. There are three broad groups or types of investment companies: open-end investment companies, closed-end investment companies, and unit investment trusts. **Open-end mutual funds** continuously sell shares to the public and are obligated to buy or sell their shares at a fund's net asset value (NAV) or share price, which is linked to prices of the firm's underlying assets as follows:[11]

$$NAV = \frac{\text{Market Value in Dollars of Funds Securities–Its Liabilities}}{\text{Number of Investor Shares Outstanding}} \tag{1}$$

The majority of mutual funds are open-end funds; fund share prices appear in the financial pages of most newspapers, as well as in a fund's semiannual and annual reports. Funds usually value exchange-traded securities using the most recent closing price from the exchange in which the securities are primarily traded. Fund accounting agents internally validate the prices received.[12] An example of a mutual fund price quote is as follows for Vanguard's S&P 500 Index Fund in *The Wall Street Journal* on February 17, 1999, p. 23:

Vanguard Index Fds	NAV	Net Change	YTD % Ret.
500	115.31	+1.09	+1.2%

Here the NAV per share is $115.31 with a rise of $1.09 from the previous day, and its year to date return (YTD) of 1.2 percent. *The Wall Street Journal* also often publishes reports on the largest mutual funds with their one-year, three-year, and five-year total returns. *Forbes, Business Week, Money Magazine*, and *Consumer Reports* provide annual mutual fund performance issues, which, in addition to reporting returns over longer holding periods, report risk measures for funds.

Section 22 (e) of the Investment Company Act of 1940 (1940 Act) requires that funds make payment of redemptions within seven days except when trading on the New York Stock Exchange is halted or when the Securities and Exchange Commission (SEC) issues an exemptive order. Open-end funds often honor redemption requests at the end of the day NAV and cut checks the next day. Since cash receipts from security sales are often delayed for several days, open-end funds often require liquidity either by holding cash or short-term securities (cash equivalents) or by borrowing from a line of credit with a bank. In recent years open-end funds have fewer liquid assets, depending more on bank credit lines or other short-term borrowing for liquidity.

In contrast, **closed-end funds** issue a fixed number of shares and do not redeem shares. Once issued, shares of a closed-end fund are traded on exchanges or over the counter like shares of individual companies, with supply and demand determining share price, which can be above or below NAV. Often closed-end fund shares trade at a discount, below NAV.

Unit investment companies often issue unit investment trusts (UITs) that offer interests in a fixed portfolio of securities that is held passively for an agreed upon period of time, whereby assets are distributed among the shareholders. Real estate investment trusts (REITs) similarly offer shares in real estate investments.

---

[11]Information for this section comes from the *1998 Mutual Fund Fact Book* (1998) and Fortune (1997).

[12]Ibid and Pozen (1998).

Unit trusts may redeem shares at NAV but may only redeem shares in large blocks. Hence, closed-end funds and UITs do not have the liquidity concerns of open-end funds that agree to redeem shares at NAV upon request.[13]

TYPES OF MUTUAL FUNDS

The three basic types of mutual funds are equity (stock) funds, bond and income funds, and money market funds. As shown in Figure 12.4, the distribution of total mutual fund assets has changed over time. For a total of $4.49 trillion invested in mutual funds at the end of 1997, $2.399 trillion or 53 percent was invested in stock funds, with $1.032 trillion or 23 percent in bond and income funds, and $1.06 trillion or 24 percent in money market funds. This was a dramatic change from 1991, when equity funds were only 27 percent of mutual fund assets and money market funds 40 percent. With a bull market in the mid to late 1990s and falling rates, investors pulled money out of lower-yielding money market and bond funds and invested more money in stock funds. In 1975, total investments in mutual funds were much lower, about $45 billion with the majority of investments in equity funds at that time. After 1975, money market funds grew phenomenally and dominated total mutual fund assets until the mid and late 1990s, when equity funds held the largest share. As shown in Figure 12.1, by May 29, 1998, mutual fund assets were above $5 trillion in assets.[14]

Mutual funds have been very creative with numerous different types of equity, bond, and money market funds. In 1997, more than 6,700 mutual funds existed with a wide variety of investment objectives from conservative to aggressive and a wide range of securities. The Investment Company Institute classifies funds into 21 broad categories by their basic investment objective, which are listed in Table 12.1. In addition,

---

Figure 12.4   ✦   PERCENTAGE ALLOCATION OF MUTUAL FUND ASSETS 1975, 1991, 1998

The proportion of industry assets held by stock funds was 81.7 percent in 1975, declining to 27.3 percent in 1991, and rising to 53 percent at the beginning of 1998.

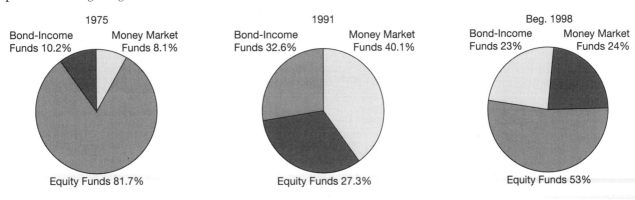

Source: Investment Company Institute, 1986, 1992, and 1998 *Mutual Fund Fact Books*. Reprinted with permission.

---

[13]Ibid.

[14]Ibid and see Robert McGough. "Bull Milestone: Mutual Funds Cross the $5 Trillion Mark." *The Wall Street Journal* (May 29, 1998), C1.

Table 12.1 ✦ TYPES OF MUTUAL FUNDS AS CLASSIFIED BY THE INVESTMENT COMPANY INSTITUTE IN 1998

Types of Equity Mutual Funds

Aggressive Growth Funds seek maximum capital growth; current income is not a significant factor. These funds invest in stocks out of the mainstream, such as new companies, companies fallen on hard times, or industries temporarily out of favor. They may use investment techniques involving greater-than-average risk.

Growth Funds seek capital growth; dividend income is not a significant factor. They invest in the common stock of well-established companies.

Growth and Income Funds seek to combine long-term capital growth and current income. These funds invest in the common stock of companies whose share values have increased and that have displayed a solid record of paying dividends.

Precious Metals/Gold Funds seek capital growth. Their portfolios are invested primarily in securities associated with gold and other precious metals.

International Funds seek growth in the value of their investments. Their portfolios are invested primarily in stocks of companies located outside the U.S.

Global Equity Funds seek growth in the value of their investments. They invest in stocks traded worldwide, including the U.S.

Income–Equity Funds seek a high level of income by investing primarily in stocks of companies with good dividend-paying records.

Types of Bond and Income Mutual Funds

Flexible Portfolio Funds allow their money managers to anticipate or respond to changing market conditions by investing in stocks or bonds or money market instruments, depending on economic changes.

Balanced Funds generally seek to conserve investors' principal, pay current income, and achieve long-term growth of principal and income. Their portfolios are a mix of bonds, preferred stocks and common stocks.

Income–Mixed Funds seek a high level of income. These funds invest in income-producing securities, including both stocks and bonds.

Income–Bond Funds seek a high level of current income. These funds invest in a mix of corporate and government bonds.

U.S. Government Income Funds seek current income. They invest in a variety of government securities, including Treasury bonds, federally guaranteed mortgage-backed securities, and other government notes.

GNMA (Ginnie Mae) Funds seek a high level of income. The majority of their portfolios is invested in mortgage securities backed by the Government National Mortgage Association (GNMA).

Global Bond Funds seek a high level of income. These funds invest in debt securities of companies and countries worldwide, including the U.S.

Table 12.1   ✦   TYPES OF MUTUAL FUNDS AS CLASSIFIED BY THE INVESTMENT
COMPANY INSTITUTE IN 1998 (*CONTINUED*)

Types of Equity Mutual Funds

Corporate Bond Funds seek a high level of income. The majority of their portfolios is invested in corporate bonds, with the balance in U.S. Treasury bonds or bonds issued by a federal agency.

High-yield Bond Funds seek very high yield, but carry a greater degree of risk than corporate bond funds. The majority of their portfolios is invested in lower-rated corporate bonds.

National Municipal Bond Funds–Long-term seek income that is not taxed by the federal government. They invest in bonds issued by states and municipalities to finance schools, highways, hospitals, bridges and other municipal works.

State Municipal Bond Funds–Long-term seek income that is exempt from both federal tax and state tax for residents of that state. They invest in bonds issued by a single state.

Types of Money Market Mutual Funds

Taxable Money Market Funds seek to maintain a stable net asset value. These funds invest in the short-term, high-grade securities sold in the money market, such as Treasury bills, certificates of deposit of large banks and commercial paper. The average maturity of their portfolios is limited to 90 days or less.

Tax-exempt Money Market Funds–National seek income that is not taxed by the federal government with minimum risk. They invest in municipal securities with relatively short maturities.

Tax-exempt Money Market Funds–State seek income that is exempt from both federal tax and state tax for residents of that state. They invest in municipal securities with relatively short maturities issued by a single state.

Source: 1998 Mutual Fund Fact Book, 38th ed. Washington, D.C.: The Investment Company Institute, 1998, 18–19.
   Reprinted with permission.

there are sector funds that invest in specialized industries or security market segments, such as biotech firms, small company growth funds, index funds, and social criteria funds. This broad selection enables investors to meet different financial objectives and goals. With the tremendous growth of mutual funds in recent decades, they have become a major player in the financial markets. At the end of 1997, mutual funds owned 19 percent of U.S. corporate equities, 8 percent of U.S. Treasury and agency securities, 10 percent of corporate and foreign bonds, and 32 percent of municipal securities.[15]

MUTUAL FUND FAMILIES

As reported by Peter Fortune in an excellent article on mutual funds in the Federal Reserve Bank of Boston's *New England Economic Review*, the majority of funds in

---

[15]Information for this section comes from the *1998 Mutual Fund Fact Book* (1998).

the U.S. are held by fund groups or families that allow for economies of scale and scope. Table 12.2 shows that 27 families accounted for about 63 percent of the industry's assets at the end of 1996. Of these fund families, Fidelity Advisors/Distributors is the largest family of funds, with more than 225 portfolios, 302 funds, and total assets greater than $427 billion. Fund families use a combination of **direct marketing**, in which investors directly contact the fund through 800 phone number to make investments, and sales through third parties, such as brokers, banks, and life insur-

Table 12.2 ✦ MAJOR MUTUAL FUND FAMILIES WITH 1995 ASSETS OVER $20 BILLION AND 1995–96 GROWTH

12/31/95 Rank	Complex	12/31/95 Assets ($million)	12/31/95 Number of Funds	12/31/95 Number of Portfolios	12/31/96 Assets ($million)	12/31/96 Number of Funds	12/31/96 Number of Portfolios	1995–96 Asset Growth (Percent)
1	Fidelity Advisors/Distributors	353,245	246	207	427,071	302	225	20.90
2	The Vanguard Group	184,833	84	84	245,518	87	87	32.83
3	Merrill Lynch Asset Mgt.	141,987	316	102	159,769	323	103	12.52
4	American Fund Distributors	138,320	30	30	174,362	30	30	26.06
5	Franklin Distributor	114,026	171	117	135,499	185	118	18.83
6	Putnam Financial Services	78,372	180	61	111,531	179	67	42.31
7	Dreyfus Premier/Service Corp.	73,924	263	154	77,008	262	147	4.17
8	Smith Barney Advisors	65,796	179	72	75,372	184	83	14.55
9	Federated Securities	63,480	179	115	66,457	204	119	4.69
10	Dean Witter Reynolds	63,382	80	80	72,061	85	85	13.69
11	T. Rowe Price Investment Svcs	50,872	66	66	67,825	70	70	33.32
12	IDS Financial Services	48,141	94	32	58,142	113	47	20.77
13	Oppenheimer Investors Svcs	46,115	149	69	58,631	152	60	27.14
14	American Century Investments	44,323	58	58	50,893	61	61	14.82
15	Prudential Securities	43,768	154	76	46,547	164	72	6.35
16	Zurich Kemper Investments	40,844	117	48	37,618	132	53	−7.90
17	AIM Distributors	39,998	53	28	58,011	55	29	45.03
18	Charles Schwab	31,613	24	24	43,091	30	30	36.31
19	Alliance Fund Distributors	27,138	142	58	32,916	161	60	21.29
20	Massachusetts Financial Svcs	26,436	128	58	33,024	131	56	24.92
21	Paine Webber	26,224	94	48	28,247	89	44	7.71
22	Van Kampen American Capital	25,781	106	39	29,534	108	41	14.56
23	Janus Funds, Inc.	24,181	19	19	35,680	23	23	47.55
24	First Union Nat'l Bank of NC	23,829	203	80	26,119	195	70	9.61
25	Scudder Investor Services	21,618	46	46	23,257	48	48	7.58
26	PIMCO Advisors	21,008	87	41	25,503	88	41	21.40
27	PNC Inst'l Management Corp.	20,081	49	39	21,536	44	35	7.25
	Total	1,839,335	3,317	1,851	2,221,222	3,505	1,904	20.76
	Industry Totals (ICI)	2,777,357	5,728	n.a.	3,535,330	6,235	n.a.	27.29
	Percent of Industry	66.2%	57.9%	n.a.	62.8%	56.2%	n.a.	n.a.

n.a. = not available

Note: The number of funds exceeds the number of portfolios when there are several classes of shares in the same portfolio.

Source: Peter Fortune, "Mutual Funds, Part I: Reshaping the American Financial System," *New England Economic Review*, (Federal Reserve Bank of Boston), (July/August 1997), 45–72. Reprinted with permission, Table 1, p. 49.

ance companies who receive a sales commission from the fund. Fidelity sells 90 percent of its funds through direct marketing, for instance, and the remaining 10 percent or $32 billion in 1996 through third parties. In 1996 Fidelity also managed about $20 billion in separate accounts for trusts and endowments.[16]

Fortune points out the typical structure of fund families using Fidelity. Fidelity is owned by FMR Corporation, which owns several affiliates that provide services to each fund, subject to the approval of trustees and shareholders. For Fidelity's Magellan Fund, its investment adviser is Fidelity Management and Research, its distributor is Fidelity Distributors Company, its transfer agent is Fidelity Service Company, and its custodian and accounting service is Fidelity Custody Services. Hence, most of Fidelity's funds have contacts with the same agents and trustees, which often serve on the boards of many funds.[17]

THE COSTS OF MUTUAL FUND OWNERSHIP

In addition to funds being classified as open-end, closed-end, or unit trust, mutual funds are also often classified as **no load**, **low load**, and **load funds**. Load funds are generally funds sold through brokers that have a front-load (upfront) sales charge or a back-end load, charged at the time of the fund's redemption. At times this back-end load is amortized so that it disappears if the fund is not redeemed for several years. With the SEC's approval of **Rule 12b-1** in 1980 allowing use of continuing annual charges to cover the cost of sales commissions and other marketing expenses, many previous no-load funds became low-load funds. Funds that are direct marketed are more likely to be no-load or low-load funds. The American Association of Individual Investors annually publishes an *Individual Investor's Guide to Low-Low Mutual Funds*, previously titled a *No-Load Guide*, reflecting the fact that few funds today have no loads.[18]

Other costs of mutual fund ownership are fees and commissions paid to agents responsible for mutual fund services including the adviser, distributor, custodian, and transfer agent. Fees vary widely according to types of securities held and fund turnover. Table 12.3 reports fees by type of funds. Management fees are ongoing fees to the fund's investment adviser for managing the fund and portfolio selection, generally averaging between .5 percent and 1 percent of the fund's assets annually. Front-end sales charges cannot be greater than 8.5 percent of the investment. The

---

[16]See Fortune (1997). Some in the industry share the belief that investors often are more concerned about the convenience and service provided by family of funds, such as the ease of switching to different funds, than on the financial performance of funds. See Woerheide (1982); Jeffrey M. Laderman, et. al. "The People's Choice: Mutual Funds." *Business Week* (February 24, 1986), 54–57; and Laderman and Smith (1993).

[17]See Fortune (1997) and James S. Hirsch and Robert McGough. "Fidelity Denies Rumors of Intention to Sell Firm." *The Wall Street Journal* (June 12, 1998), C1, C26.

[18]The SEC's 12b-1 rule permits mutual funds to charge advertising and selling expenses, including sales commissions to brokers, as an annual operating cost against the fund's assets instead of assessing new purchasers. In 1988 the SEC began requiring all funds to provide a hypothetical example of the dollar fees that would be charged on a $1,000 investment earning a 5 percent return over periods of one, five, and 10 years. Critics argued that the present value of fees should instead be used. See Fortune (1997) and Pozen (1998). Also see *The Individual Investor's Guide to Low-Load Mutual Funds*, 18 edition, 1999, Chicago, Illinois: The American Association of Individual Investors (1999).

Table 12.3 ✦ EXPENSES FOR MUTUAL FUNDS BY TYPE AND RELIANCE ON DIRECT MARKET SALES

PANEL A: MUTUAL FUND MEDIAN EXPENSE RATIOS

Percent of Net Assets, Where Noted

Fund Type		Advise/ Admin. (%)	EXPENSE TYPE		Custody/ Accting (%)	Adult ($000)	Other (%)	12b-1 (%)	Total Expenses (%)
			TRANSFER AGENT						
			(%)	($/ACCT)					
Equity Funds (No. of Funds)									
DIRECT-MARKET									
Cap Apprec.	(39)	.687	.184	$21.69	.021	$ 30.0	.021	.000	.964
Total Return	(21)	.501	.132	20.73	.014	44.0	.015	.004	.723
Int'l/Global	(13)	.767	.185	23.86	.081	62.0	.022	.000	.167
NONPROPRIETARY SALES FORCE									
Cap Apprec.	(58)	.683	.178	$21.09	.023	$100.5	.054	.360	1.246
Total Return	(31)	.491	.161	20.89	.016	85.0	.046	.216	.988
Int'l/Global	(25)	.860	.181	22.78	.103	129.0	.067	.419	1.670
BANK PROPRIETARY									
Cap Apprec.	(12)	.888	.064	$35.38	.017	$237.0	.024	.079	1.051
Total Return	(9)	.650	.045	35.61	.017	219.0	.018	.055	.827
Int'l/Global	(3)	.722	.017	78.52	.113	72.0	.049	.023	.901
Bonds Funds									
DIRECT-MARKET									
Corporate	(19)	.561	.112	$23.23	.023	$ 24.0	.030	.063	.806
Govt./GNMA	(28)	.454	.188	29.45	.026	25.0	.046	.003	.695
Muni-Long	(28)	.496	.087	33.76	.014	28.0	.018	.000	.607
High Yield	(7)	.514	.175	34.10	.014	25.5	.075	.055	.855
NONPROPRIETARY SALES FORCE									
Corporate	(26)	.503	.149	$20.21	.025	$ 35.0	.070	.290	1.069
Gov't/GNMA	(58)	.563	.154	26.70	.037	44.0	.073	.431	1.274
Muni-Long	(75)	.500	.080	25.77	.023	35.0	.060	.281	.982
High Yield	(36)	.600	.145	18.41	.027	39.0	.068	.405	1.287
BANK PROPRIETARY									
Corporate	(33)	.633	.043	$ n.a.	.034	$ 17.5	.060	.063	.811
Gov't/GNMA	(18)	.527	.083	38.22	.061	14.0	.074	.093	.860
Muni-Long	(16)	.461	.070	55.85	.026	14.5	.061	.124	.796

Table 12.3   ✦   EXPENSES FOR MUTUAL FUNDS BY TYPE AND RELIANCE ON DIRECT MARKET SALES (*CONTINUED*)

PANEL B: MUTUAL FUND RELIANCE ON DIRECT-MARKET SALES, BY TYPE OF FUND, 1995

Percent of Total Sales

High		Moderate		Low	
Precious Metals	77.6	Aggressive Growth	48.7	Muni Bond-Nat'l	37.6
Flexible Portfolio	61.8	Growth	44.4	Corporate Bond	37.2
Income-Equity	60.6	Growth & Income	42.5	U.S. Govt.-Income	30.3
Balanced	58.3	International	42.2	Income-Mixed	27.5
Ginnie Mae	56.1	Income-Bond	40.3	Global Bond	25.5
				Muni Bond-State	25.1
		Very Low			
		High-Yield Bond	13.7		
		Global Equity	12.3		

Source: Peter Fortune, "Mutual Funds, Part I: Reshaping the American Financial System" *New England Review: Federal (Reserve Bank of Boston),* (July/Aug. 1997), Tables 2 and 3, p. 54, 55. Reprinted with permission.

12b-1 fees deducted to compensate sales professionals and to pay for marketing and advertising by law cannot exceed 1 percent of the fund's average net assets per year. Exchange fees may be charged when transferring funds from one fund to another. Account maintenance fees are often charged for accounts with low balances.[19]

Total expenses are generally lower for funds that rely more on direct market sales. Direct market equity funds shown in Panel A of Table 12.3 had total expenses ranging from .167 to .964, and funds sold through a sales force ranged from .988 to 1.670. Similar for bond funds, direct market funds had lower total expenses. Note also that funds with more passive management and lower turnover, such as index funds, have lower total expenses. As shown in Panel B of Table 12.3, different types of funds have more reliance on direct sales. About 53.6 percent of the value of shares sold in 1995 was through a sales force channel, 37.7 percent was through a direct market channel, and 9.7 percent through a variable annuity channel. Often funds are distributed through more than one channel.[20]

Fund expenses are important for investors to monitor, because they can significantly lower net returns and result in negative net returns in down markets. Figure 12.5, Panel A, shows the differences between total returns and net returns after fees and loans for major mutual funds. The 12-month return as of July 31, 1998, for Fidelity Magellan, for instance, was 19 percent if unadjusted for fees and loads. With these adjustments, the return was closer to 13.5 percent.[21]

---

[19]See Fortune (1997).

[20]See Fortune (1997). Fidelity, for instance, distributes funds through direct market sales, as well as through brokers, insurance agents, and bank agents, who receive commissions for sales.

[21]See Charles Gasparino. "Pain of Mutual-Fund Fees Is More Acute When the Market Is Going Down Than Up." *The Wall Street Journal* (August 25, 1998), C1. Also see John Markese. "How Much Are You Really Paying for Your Mutual Funds?" *AAII Journal* (February 1999), 2–5; and Jonathan Clements. "Selecting a Fund? Expenses Can Be Crucial." *The Wall Street Journal* (July 24, 1991), C1, C10.

Figure 12.5　◆　MUTUAL FUND RETURNS LESS FEES AND MINIMUM INVESTMENT REQUIREMENTS

Taking a Bite Out of Returns
12-month returns, through July 31, for the five largest mutual funds

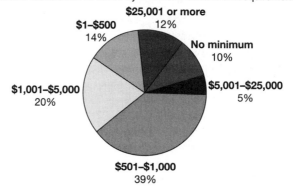

Source: Charles Gasparino, "Pain of Mutual-Fund Fees Is More Acute When the Market Is Going Down Then Up," *The Wall Street Journal* (August 25, 1998), C1.

Mutual Fund Minimum Investment Requirements, 1997
(percent distribution of funds by minimum investment requirement)*

$25,001 or more 12%

$1–$500 14%

No minimum 10%

$5,001–$25,000 5%

$1,001–$5,000 20%

$501–$1,000 39%

Source: Investment Company Institute, *Mutual Fund Fact Book, 1998*, p. 24. Reprinted with permission.

In recent years, funds have also increased their minimum investment requirement. Panel B of Figure 12.5 reports the percentage of funds with different minimum investment requirements in 1997. Only 10 percent of funds had no minimum, and a total of 24 percent of funds a minimum of $500 or less.[22]

---

[22]Information for this section comes from the *1998 Mutual Fund Fact Book* (1998).

Regulations for Mutual Funds and Regulatory Issues

The **National Securities Markets Improvement Act of 1996** transformed the regulatory structure for mutual funds by giving the SEC full regulatory oversight for securities with national versus local markets, eliminating state regulation of mutual funds. The act also eliminated the 1940 Investment Act's Section(d)(1)(B) provision that mutual funds could not invest in shares of other mutual funds, thus allowing mutual funds to issue shares in "funds of funds." Shares in unregistered private pools, such as hedge funds and venture capital funds, are also allowed to be offered in an unlimited amount to "qualified shareholders," defined as investors with more than $5 million in assets and institutions with greater than $25 million in assets, or a trust established by a qualified investor. Previously, hedge funds organized as limited partnerships were limited to 99 qualified shareholders to avoid being defined as an investment company under the 1940 Act.[23]

All mutual funds are subject to strict regulation and oversight by the SEC and are required to provide investors with complete disclosure concerning the fund in a written prospectus, including the fund's goals, fees, expenses, investment strategies, and risk, as well as information on purchasing and selling shares. The **Investment Act of 1933** mandates specific disclosures, and the **Securities Act of 1934** sets out antifraud rules covering the purchase and sale of fund shares. The **Investment Act of 1940** requires all funds to register with the SEC and to meet certain operating standards. Section 18 of the 1940 Act also addresses a mutual fund's capital structure with the intent of limiting the ability of a mutual fund to take on too much leverage. Open-end funds are prohibited from issuing senior securities and are allowed to borrow only from banks and to limit bank loans to no more than $33\frac{1}{3}$ percent of a fund's total assets. If a fund's assets fall below three times the outstanding loans, the loans must be paid immediately. In recent years the SEC has released interpretations of the Act to allow short-term borrowing other than bank borrowing, including the use repurchase agreements, options, writing short futures positions, lending securities for short-selling by broker-dealer clients, and short sales (included as senior securities in Section 18(g)). Stockholders and directors must approve the use of these instruments so that they are explicitly allowed in the prospectus, and they must be held in segregated account securities no less than equal to the value of the liabilities created and must be marked to market daily.[24]

Under **Subchapter M of the Internal Revenue Code:** Taxation of Investment Companies Registered with the SEC under the 1940 Act, pass-through taxation, whereby the company pays no tax on investment dividends, capital gains, or income, is allowed if it distributes 90 percent of these payments to shareholders. Several tests must also be met: (1) The **Short 3's Test**, whereby no more than 30 percent of gross income can come from the sale of securities held for less than three months; and (2) **Diversification Tests**, whereby no more than 25 percent of assets can be held in securities of any one issuer or if any two or more issuers are substantially identical, excluding government securities. Also, at least 50 percent of assets must be invested in cash-equivalents (cash or short-term securities) and other securities, subject to limitations.[25]

---

[23]See Fortune (1997) and Pozen (1998).
[24]Ibid.
[25]Ibid.

RECENT REGULATORY CONCERNS

With the boom in mutual funds in the 1990s, the SEC has been concerned about unsophisticated investors purchasing funds and being unaware of the risks involved. In response the SEC called for streamlined disclosure of risk/return relations in a mutual fund prospectus, greater due diligence on the part of fund directors, prevention of false advertising, and continued oversight by independent directors following fund mergers.

Streamlined Disclosure   In the 1990s the SEC was concerned about mutual fund prospectuses being too lengthy and difficult for fund investors to understand. With this in mind, the SEC updated rules for mutual fund prospectuses, known as the **modernized Form N-1A**, which went into effect on June 1, 1998. New prospectuses are less cluttered with technical and operational information discussed in a separate supplement; use shorter sentences and an active voice; and use tables or bullet points for presenting complex material. A brief risk/return summary must be included at the start of each prospectus with the fund's investment objectives and policies, a narrative risk summary, a bar chart showing annual return over 10 years, a table of performance figures, and a fee table. The prospectus is also required to contain information on the fund's highest and lowest return for any quarter and one-year, five-year, and 10-year returns contrasted against the returns of a benchmark index. The prospectus is also required to state what a portfolio's main investments are, so investors can more easily make comparisons.[26]

Oversight of Mutual-Fund Boards   In 1999, Arthur Levitt, the chair of the SEC, hosted a round table concerning the role of boards of directors in the governance of mutual funds, particularly encouraging boards to take a more active role and ensure that fund fees are fair and proper. This concern arose because while mutual funds "ballooned" almost sevenfold to about $5 trillion over the 1990s, the average mutual-fund expense ratio rose to 1.148 percent of assets up from .90 percent according to Lipper, Inc. With an expansion in fund assets, some industry experts and consumer activists argued that the expense ratio should have fallen as the result of economies of scale. With 40 percent of every fund's board required to be independent and the remaining "interested trustees" coming from the fund company itself, independent directors may have little incentive to confront fund advisers. A conflict of interest exists because the fund adviser pays directors' salaries, averaging $46,000 in 1997. Tufano and Sevick (1997) studied the composition and compensation of boards of directors of U.S. open-end mutual funds in 1992 and found evidence supporting such concerns. Funds with a greater fraction of independent directors and more professional directors who sit on a large number of a fund sponsor's other boards had lower fees. The study also found some evidence of higher shareholder fees for funds whose independent directors are paid relatively higher fees.[27]

---

[26]Pui-Wing Tam. "Mutual-Fund Documents Are Simply Put." *The Wall Street Journal* (June 12, 1998), C1; and Edward Wyatt. "Big Changes Expected in the Sale of Mutual Funds." *The New York Times* (March 7, 1998), B1.

[27]Over 66 million people invest in mutual funds. See "SEC Chairman Demands Mutual-Fund Accountability." *The New York Times* (February 23, 1998), B1; Charles Gasparino and Pui-Wing Tam. "Mutual-Fund Boards: No Comfort?" *The Wall Street Journal* (February 5, 1999), C1, C23 and Tufano and Sevick (1997).

Advertising Exaggerated Performance Claims   The SEC has also been concerned about exaggerated performance claims by funds. With baby-boomers in their peak income producing years, more professional money managers are used for portfolio management. To compete managers may zealously try to attract clients with enthusiastic advertising, such as intentionally exaggerating investment returns in newsletters, on internet postings, and performance sheets. In 1999, for instance, Meridian, one of the largest money management firms in Colorado, with $488 million in assets, failed to deduct some commissions and mutual fund sales loads that could be as large as 5.5 percent of customer's initial investment from advertised investment returns during 1993 to 1996. The SEC requires investor-paid fees such as commissions and finder's fees to be deducted from advertised performance data. Under terms of an SEC settlement, Meridian agreed to a fine of $70,000 and its president was fined $15,000.[28]

Concern Over Fund Mergers   Regulators have also been concerned over the effect of fund mergers on the independence of directors' decisions. Since the Investment Company Act of 1940 specifies that a change in control of an investment adviser terminates an advisory contract, the acquirer must have the approval of the independent directors of the relevant funds and the stockholders to renew an advisory contract. In effect, an acquiring firm with the ability to dismiss directors could buy independent directors' approval. Congress in 1970 enacted special rules for such an acquisition to ensure that such an acquisition did not impose an "unfair burden" on the involved mutual funds and that a minimum of 75 percent of the fund directors be independent for at least three years following an acquisition.[29]

MEASURING THE PERFORMANCE AND RISK OF MUTUAL FUNDS

Measuring the performance of mutual funds is often controversial. Based on a fund's objectives and the risks that it takes, it may have higher or lower returns than general market benchmarks, such as the S&P 500, although the S&P 500 would be a good benchmark for a stock index fund. Hence, benchmarks by fund categories are often more useful to investors and fund advisers.

Financial Press and Investor Association Benchmarks

Table 12.4, taken from *The Wall Street Journal* (January 29, 1999), p. C23, provides performance yardsticks by fund categories as well as overall market benchmarks. Individual funds of each class can then be compared with these averages. *Forbes, Business Week, Money Magazine, Consumer Reports,* among other financial publications, also provide fund rankings on performance and risk in up and down markets for different classes of funds. *Forbes,* for instance, gives rankings from A+ to F, for both up and down markets, in an annual survey. Based on fund expenses, Forbes also reports Best Buy rankings based on both risk-adjusted returns and fund expenses. Panel A of Table 12.5 shows rankings for fund families

---

[28]See "SEC Eyes Money Managers." *The Denver Post* (January 31, 1999),1K, 22K.
[29]See Pozen (1998) and Charles A. Jaffe. "Look for Fund Consolidation in '99," *The Denver Post* (January 4, 1999), 3C.

Table 12.4 ◆ Mutual Fund Performance Benchmarks Reported in the Final Press

Based on a fund's objectives and the risks it takes, it may have higher or lower returns than general market benchmarks, such as the SP500. Hence, benchmarks by fund categories are often more useful to investors.

PERFORMANCE YARDSTICKS
HOW FUND CATEGORIES STACK UP
ON A TOTAL RETURN BASIS

Investment Objective	Year-to-Date	Four Weeks	One Year	3 Yrs (annualized)	5 Yrs (annualized)
Capital Appreciation	+ 4.10%	+ 5.70%	+ 26.37%	+ 18.48%	+ 14.95%
Growth	+ 3.16	+ 3.63	+ 27.31	+ 23.91	+ 19.27
Small-Cap Stock	− 0.19	+ 3.00	+ 1.21	+ 13.07	+ 12.35
Mid-Cap Stock	+ 0.32	+ 3.46	+ 14.93	+ 16.73	+ 14.62
Growth & Income	+ 0.92	+ 0.88	+ 18.55	+ 22.23	+ 18.63
Equity Income	− 1.01	− 0.98	+ 10.65	+ 18.37	+ 16.04
Global (inc U.S.)	+ 1.18	+ 1.66	+ 13.76	+ 14.01	+ 10.93
International (non U.S.)	+ 0.47	+ 0.58	+ 10.73	+ 9.61	+ 6.72
European Region	+ 0.89	+ 0.57	+ 18.94	+ 21.45	+ 15.00
Latin America	− 13.70	− 13.03	− 41.71	− 7.47	− 10.62
Pacific Region	− 2.59	− 1.90	− 3.09	− 13.59	− 8.59
Emerging Markets	− 1.95	− 1.33	− 22.92	− 10.75	− 11.19
Science & Technology	+ 12.57	+ 13.74	+ 68.99	+ 28.98	+ 24.12
Health & Biotech	− 0.12	+ 1.69	+ 21.47	+ 18.09	+ 19.88
Natural Resources	− 5.86	− 4.27	− 24.90	− 1.64	+ 1.82
Gold	− 2.92	− 1.02	− 19.13	− 23.98	− 13.89
Utility	− 0.45	− 0.28	+ 17.27	+ 17.05	+ 13.51
Balanced	+ 0.87	+ 1.13	+ 14.45	+ 16.04	+ 13.66
Intermediate Corp. Debt	+ 0.50	+ 0.78	+ 7.54	+ 6.63	+ 6.26
Intermediate Govt	+ 0.39	+ 0.65	+ 7.75	+ 6.43	+ 5.88
Long-Term Govt	+ 0.45	+ 0.74	+ 8.54	+ 6.60	+ 6.31
High-Yield Taxable	+ 1.32	+ 1.45	− 1.06	+ 8.05	+ 7.30
Mortgage Bond	+ 0.48	+ 0.66	+ 5.93	+ 6.18	+ 5.85
Short-Term US	+ 0.36	+ 0.56	+ 6.21	+ 5.65	+ 5.29
Long Term	+ 0.61	+ 0.92	+ 7.10	+ 6.75	+ 6.60
General US Taxable	+ 0.48	+ 0.70	+ 2.24	+ 6.85	+ 5.92
World Income	− 0.53	− 0.22	+ 2.15	+ 5.77	+ 5.16
Short-Term Muni	+ 0.63	+ 0.72	+ 4.91	+ 4.60	+ 4.30
Intermed.-Term Muni	+ 1.05	+ 1.16	+ 6.05	+ 5.76	+ 5.11
General L-T Muni	+ 0.99	+ 1.10	+ 5.95	+ 6.41	+ 5.47
High-Yield Muni	+ 0.64	+ 0.72	+ 5.41	+ 6.86	+ 5.95
Insured Muni	+ 1.00	+ 1.11	+ 6.11	+ 6.14	+ 5.40

Table 12.4   ✦   MUTUAL FUND PERFORMANCE BENCHMARKS REPORTED IN THE FINAL PRESS (CONTINUED)

BENCHMARKS FOR MUTUAL-FUND INVESTORS
ON A TOTAL RETURN BASIS

	Year-to-Date	Four Weeks	One Year	3 Yrs (annualized)	5 Yrs (annualized)
DJIA (w/divs)	+ 1.13%	− 0.38%	+ 19.32%	+ 23.04%	+ 21.34%
S&P 500 (w/divs)	+ 3.02	+ 1.98	+ 31.40	+ 29.07	+ 24.17
Small-Co. Index Fund[1]	+ 0.47	+ 3.40	− 0.26	+ 13.35	+ 12.37
Lipper Index: Europe	+ 1.23	+ 0.78	+ 20.85	+ 23.20	+ 15.70
Lipper Index: Pacific	− 0.69	+ 0.57	− 2.59	− 11.26	− 6.73
Lipper L-T Govt[2]	+ 0.43	+ 0.69	+ 7.73	+ 6.44	+ 5.83

[1]Vanguard's: tracks Russell 2000
[2]Includes government agency debt

FUND LEADERS AND LAGGARDS
FOUR-WEEK PERFORMANCE

Leaders	Total Return	Laggards	Total Return
Internet-Internet Fund	+ 45.01%	Montgomery Fds:Latin Amer	− 31.71%
Perkins-Perkins Oppty	+ 35.43	Offitbank Fds:Latin Am Eq;Sel	− 20.66
ProFunds:UltraQTC;Inv	+ 30.50	Invesco:Latin Amer Growth	− 19.97
ProFunds:UltraOTC;Svc	+ 30.43	Excelsior Funds:Latin America	− 17.47
Amerindo: Technology;D	+ 29.50	ABN Amro Fds:Ltn Am Eq;Com	− 17.08

LARGEST STOCK AND BOND FUNDS
YEAR-TO-DATE PERFORMANCE

Stock	Total Return	Bond	Total Return
Fidelity Invest: Magellan Fund	+ 4.26%	Pimco Fds Instl: Tot Rtn;Instl	+ 0.50%
Vanguard Index Fds: 500 Index	+ 3.04	Vanguard Fds: GNMA	+ 0.65
American Fds: Wash Mutual Inv	− 1.76	American Fds: Bd Fd America	+ 0.98
Fidelity Invest: Growth & Income	+ 0.50	Franklin Class A: US Govt;A	+ 0.54
American Fds: Invest Co Amer	+ 2.45	Vanguard Index Fds: Tol Bd Mkt	+ 0.63
Fidelity Invest: Contrafund	+ 5.00	Vanguard Fds: Sht-Tm Corp	+ 0.63
Vanguard Fds: Windsor II	+ 0.17	Vanguard Fds: Hi Yld Corp	+ 1.37
Amer Century 20th: Ultra; Inv	+ 5.99	Morg Stan Dn Wt B:US Govt; B	+ 0.31
Fidelity Advisor T: Growth Opp	+ 0.18	MAS Funds Instit Cl:Fxd Inc	+ 1.02
Janus: Janus	+ 8.17	AARP Invst: GNMA	+ 0.51

Source: Lipper
Source: The Wall Street Journal (January 29, 1999), C23.

Table 12.5 ◆ FUND FAMILIES RECOMMENDED IN *FORBES*

PANEL A: FORBES' RATING OF PERFORMANCE FOR BIGGEST FUND FAMILIES, 1998

Fund Family	FAMILY VALUES			Cap-weighted 10-Year Performance[1,2]	Assets June 1998 ($bil)
	Average Lead	Average Expenses per $100[1]	Number of U.S. Stock Funds		
Fidelity Distributors	2.00%	$0.69	57	17.9%	$324.6
Vanguard Group of Investment Cos	0.34	0.30	20	16.3	181.2
American Funds Group	5.75	0.62	8	16.4	149.4
Putnam Mutual Funds	5.75	0.99	15	16.5	107.8
T Rowe Price Associates	0.05	0.82	19	15.5	53.6
AIM Distributors	5.70	1.07	11	16.9	53.5
American Century Investment	0.00	0.97	11	17.1	51.2
Franklin Templeton Distributors	5.41	1.06	17	12.7	44.5
Janus Capital	0.00	0.87	6	20.0	39.1
American Express Financial Advisors	5.00	0.84	12	16.6	37.3

Data are for U.S. equity funds covered in this survey. [1]Asset-weighted. [2]Annualized.

Which of the biggest fund families has the best performance? The lowest costs? We calculate a family's composite performance for each 12-month period over the past decade by looking at the stock funds available in each period and weighing the performance of each fund by its assets at the start of the 12 months. The ten-year numbers link the year-by-year averages. Asset weighting prevents a hot small fund from overshadowing a cold big fund. By our methods, Janus Capital is the best-performing family. Its six equity funds had a weighted ten-year annualized return of 20% versus 18.5% for the S&P 500.

Source: Steve Kichen and Thomas Easton, "Mutual Funds the Big Picture," *Forbes* (August 24, 1998), p. 114. Reprinted with permission.

Table 12.5   ◆   FUND FAMILIES RECOMMENDED IN *FORBES* (*CONTINUED*)

PANEL B: NO LOAD FUNDS OFFERED BY MUTUAL FUND FAMILIES

DOWN THE AISLE AT SOME MUTUAL FUND SUPERMARKETS

Supermarket Sponsor/Telephone	Web Site/www.	Total Funds Available	Total No-Load No-Fee Funds Recommended by Forbes†	AVAILABILITY OF MAJORITY OF RECOMMENDED FUNDS IN SELECTED FAMILIES						
				American Century	Fidelity	Invesco	T Rowe Price	Scudder	USAA	Vanguard
Muriel Siebert/800-872-0711	misiebert.com	7,069	70	■	▲	▲	■	▲	—	■
Jack White/800-233-3411	jackwhiteco.com	7,009	69	▲	■	▲	■	▲	—	■
Charles Schwab/800-435-4000	schwab.com	2,200	69	▲	▲	▲	■	▲	—	■
Fidelity Investments/800-544-8666	fidelity.com	3,400	69	■	▲	▲	■	▲	—	■
Waterhouse Securities/800-934-4410	waterhouse.com	7,100	63	▲	■	▲	■	▲	—	■
Scudder/800-700-0820	scudder.com	5,600	53	▲	■	▲	■	▲	—	■
Dreyfus/800-843-5466	dreyfus.com	7,100	49	▲	■	▲	■	▲	—	■
KeyCorp/888-715-8715	key.com	1,000	49	■	■	■	■	▲	—	■
National Discount Brokers/800-888-3999	ndb.com	7,840	49	▲	▲	▲	■	▲	—	▲
Vanguard°/800-992-8327	vanguard.com	500	46	●	▲	■	—	■	—	—
Prudential Securities/800-225-1852	prusec.com	300	45	■	—	●	—	●	—	—
T Rowe Price/800-638-5660	troweprice.com	3,700	39	●	—	■	—	■	—	—
Merrill Lynch/800-637-3863	ml.com	2,000	38	●	—	●	—	■	—	■
Bank of America/888-333-0639	bankamerica.com/ p-finance/mra	939	23	▲	—	—	—	—	—	—
Quick & Reilly/800-533-8161	quick-reilly.com	2,600	17	■	■	■	■	■	—	■
Accutrade/800-494 946	accutrade.com	6,757	11	■	■	■	■	■	■	■

▲ No load, no transaction fee.
■ No load, with a transaction fee.
● No load or transaction fee but subject to annual wrap fee.

°Not strictly a supermarket, shown for comparison. †From Best Buy and Honor Roll lists in this issue.

Source: William P. Barrett, "Mutual Fund Supermarkets," *Forbes* (August 24, 1998), p. 123. Reprinted with permission.

by *Forbes* in 1998, along with average expenses per $100, load percentage, number of U.S. stock funds, average 10-year performance, and total assets as of June 1998. Panel B lists recommendations for no-load funds, along with information on the transaction fees and annual wrap fees. Annual wrap fees are annual fees on top of fund fees for advice, brokerage, and other services on the value of all assets, which are often 1 percent or more. *Forbes* also provides information on the maximum cumulative loss for any period, which for most funds was in the fall of 1987, in association with the October 1987 stock market crash. *The American Association of Individual Investors Low-Load Mutual Fund Guide* provides betas for funds, standard deviations of historic returns, average returns during bear and bull markets, along with average annual returns for three-, five-, and 10-year periods. Morningstar and Lipper Analytical Services also provide information on funds and fund performance measures.[30]

RISK-ADJUSTED PERFORMANCE MEASURES

The SEC has been particularly concerned about improving descriptions of risk and performance for mutual funds. In response to a request for comments on such improvements, the agency received 3,600 comment letters from investors. A recent article by Katerina Simmons in the *New England Economic Review* of the Federal Reserve Bank of Boston noted several of the most commonly used measures, including the standard deviation of returns, value at risk, the Sharpe ratio, the Modigliani measure, Morningstar return and risk measures, betas, and asset class measures. These are briefly discussed in the following sections.[31]

Standard Deviation of Returns

The monthly standard deviation (STD) of returns (r) is often measured for mutual funds calculated as the square-root of [the sum of the squared differences between each monthly return (Ri) from the average monthly return (mean R)] divided by the number of observations (N):

$$STD = [1/N \times Sum (Ri - mean R)^2]^{1/2} \qquad (2)$$

For mutual funds, analysts are usually interested in the standard deviation of excess returns over the risk-free rate or some appropriate benchmark index based on the fund's objective. The standard deviation of the difference in returns between a fund and an appropriate benchmark index is sometimes referred to as a fund's tracking error. Table 12.6 shows an example for the XYZ Equity Fund, as reported in the Simmons article. The monthly standard deviation of returns for the fund is 3.27 percent or 11.34 percent annualized. Using excess returns over the risk-free rate, the monthly standard deviation is 3.28 percent or 11.36 percent annualized. If the excess

---

[30]See *Forbes*, Special Issue on Mutual Funds (August 24, 1998) and Pozen (1998).

[31]The following sections on risk/return measures all come from Simmons (1998). For more detailed information on mutual fund performance and performance rankings, see Treynor (1965), Sharpe (1966, 1992, 1997), Shukla and Trzcinka (1992), Modigliani and Modigliani (1997), Financial Economists Roundtable (1996), Jensen (1968), French and Henderson (1985), Hendricks, Patel, and Zeckhauser (1993), Lakonishok, Schleifer, and Vishny (1992), and Shulka and Trzcinka (1992).

Table 12.6 ✦ INFORMATION FOR RISK/RETURN MEASURES FOR XYZ FUND EXAMPLE: SHOWING CALCULATION OF RISK/RETURN MEASURES

XYZ EQUITY FUND MONTHLY RETURNS AND SUMMARY STATISTICS

Month	XYZ Return (%) (1)	Risk-Free Rate (%) (2)	Benchmark Return (%) (3)	XYZ Excess Return (%) (4)	Benchmark Excess Return (%) (5)	XYZ Excess Return over Benchmark (%) (6)
1	−1.66	.46	.16	−2.12	−.30	−1.82
2	3.37	.41	3.43	2.96	3.02	−.06
3	3.26	.43	1.87	2.83	1.44	1.39
4	4.61	.41	5.59	4.20	5.18	−.98
5	4.40	.43	3.93	3.97	3.51	.47
6	−1.45	.42	−3.79	−1.87	−4.21	2.34
7	−6.23	.44	−8.45	−6.67	−8.89	2.22
8	4.82	.44	5.94	4.38	5.50	−1.12
9	3.86	.43	3.76	3.43	3.33	.10
10	1.56	.44	−1.45	1.12	−1.89	3.01
11	4.36	.42	4.36	3.94	3.94	.00
12	3.51	.44	2.41	3.07	1.97	1.10
Geometric Mean (percent)						
Monthly	1.98		1.40	1.55	.97	.54
Annualized	26.53		18.11	20.26	12.22	6.72
Arithmetic Mean (percent)						
Monthly	2.03		1.48	1.60	1.05	.55
Annualized	24.41		17.77	19.25	12.60	6.64
Standard Deviation (percent)						
Monthly	3.27		4.06	3.28	4.06	1.43
Annualized	11.34		14.06	11.36	14.08	4.97

Source: Table 1 from Katerina Simons, "Risk-Adjusted Performance of Mutual Funds," *New England Economic Review* (Federal Reserve Bank of Boston) (Sept./Oct. 1998), p. 35. Reprinted with permission.

returns over a benchmark based on the fund's objective is used instead, the standard deviation or tracking error is much lower, 1.43 percent or 4.97 percent annualized.

VALUE AT RISK

As noted in Chapter 9, value at risk (VAR) is a popular risk measure, often used to measure a firm's trading risk, for derivatives and other securities. VAR provides an estimate of how much a firm's portfolio can decline with a given probability over a given time period. Hence, VAR reports the likely range of losses. If a 95 percent probability is selected, based on a normal distribution, 95 percent of all observations will occur within 1.96 standard deviations from the mean, with only 5 percent deviating from the mean, i.e., 2.5 percent falling below the mean. For instance, if XYZ Fund has a mean monthly return of 2.03 percent and a standard deviation of 3.27 percent, its monthly VAR would be 2.03 percent − (1.96)(3.27) = −4.38 percent, amounting to a 2.5 percent probability of losing no more than $43.80 a month for a $1,000 investment.

Although VARs are based on historical volatilities, estimated volatilities and correlations can be used. Risk managers at mutual fund companies can also find a VAR for underperforming a fund's selected benchmark, known as a "relative" or "tracking" VAR.

Sharpe Ratio

To calculate the Sharpe ratio or index, a fund's average excess return over the risk-free rate or an appropriate benchmark is divided by the standard deviation of the fund's excess return. For example, returning to Table 12.6, the monthly mean excess return of XYZ Fund is 1.60 percent and its monthly standard deviation for this excess return is 3.28 percent, indicating a monthly Sharpe ratio of .49. To annualize this ratio, annualized figures can be used or the monthly Sharpe ratio can be multiplied by the square root of 12. Multiplying XYZ's monthly ratio of .49 by 3.46 (the square root of 12), the annualized Sharpe ratio is 1.69. An alternative ratio often used is the Treynor index, which is a fund's average excess return divided by the beta of the fund portfolio. These ratios indicate measures of a fund's excess return adjusted for risk, providing a method to compare funds with different levels of risk.

The Sharpe and Treynor ratios are based on the capital asset pricing model (CAPM), which assumes that investors can achieve any level of risk by investing in the fund with the highest Sharpe ratio, regardless of the investor's particular degree of risk aversion. For a more risk-averse investor, the level of risk can be reduced by investing part of his or her portfolio in risk-free securities. An investor preferring greater risk can achieve a higher standard deviation and expected return by leveraging the investment, i.e., financing his or her investment by borrowing at the risk-free rate. Institutional investors and academics have universally accepted this model, but, as Katerina Simmons points out, the general public and financial advisers often do not understand or use this model.

Modigliani or M-Square Measure

Modigliani and Modigliani (1997) proposed a different measure that they believed would be easier for investors to understand; often known as the M-square measure, it measures a fund's performance relative to the market in percentage terms defined as follows:

$$\text{Modigliani Measure} = \frac{\text{Fund's Average Excess Return}}{\text{STD of Fund's Excess Return}} \times \text{STD of Index Excess Return} \qquad (3)$$

Modigliani and Modigliani propose to use the standard deviation of the S&P 500 or some other broad-based market index for the second term. The M-square provides a measure equivalent to the return the fund would earn if its risk was the same as the market index. Similar to the Sharpe ratio, the higher the M-square, the higher the fund's return for any level of risk. For example, as pointed out by Katerina Simmons, for the XYZ Fund in Table 12.6, if the annualized mean excess return is 19.25 percent, its annualized standard deviation is 11.36 percent, and the annualized standard deviation of the excess return on the S&P 500 market index is 15 percent, XYZ's M-square measure is 19.25 percent/11.36 percent × 15 percent = 25.42 percent. Investors could take on greater debt or financial leverage to increase the standard deviation of XYZ's portfolios return to that of the S&P 500 market index and achieve this 25.42 percent return.

MORNINGSTAR RATINGS

Morningstar, Inc., publishes its own risk return measures, which are used for its star ratings that have become very popular. Morningstar divides mutual funds into four asset classes: domestic stock funds, international stock funds, taxable bond funds, and municipal bond funds. An excess return is calculated for each fund adjusting for sales loads and subtracting the 90-day Treasury bill rate. This load-adjusted excess return is then divided by the average excess return for the fund's asset class as follows:

$$\text{Morningstar Return} = \frac{\text{Load} - \text{Adjusted Fund Excess Return}}{\text{Ave. Excess Return for Asset Class}} \tag{4}$$

A measure of downside risk is estimated by counting the number of months that a fund's excess return was negative, summing all negative returns, and dividing this sum by the total number of months over the measurement period. The same measure is calculated for the fund's asset class as a whole. The ratio of the two, Morningstar's risk measure, is as follows:

$$\text{Morningstar Risk} = \frac{\text{Fund's Average Underperformance}}{\text{Ave. Underperformance of Its Asset Class}} \tag{5}$$

To rate funds, Morningstar subtracts the risk score in Equation 12.5 from the return score in Equation 12.4 and ranks funds by this raw rating within their asset class. Stars are then assigned as follows: The top 10 percent rankings receive five stars, the next 22.5 percent four stars, the middle 35 percent three stars, the next 22.5 percent two stars, and the lowest 10 percent one star. Overall rankings are calculated by combining stars that are calculated for three-, five-, and 10-year periods. Category ratings for each fund are also calculated for more narrowly defined fund categories; however, these ratings are not adjusted for sales load and are only calculated for a three-year period.

Katerina Simmons performed a detailed study examining the relations among Sharpe, Modigliani, and Morningstar ratings. Sharpe and Modigliani rankings were identical, and Sharpe and Morningstar ratings were very highly correlated. In September 1996 at the Financial Economist Roundtable on risk disclosure for mutual funds, an information ratio was also suggested involving a Sharpe ratio calculating excess returns over a benchmark based on a fund's asset class divided by the standard deviation of these excess returns. Such a measure, in contrast to the other measures, would provide quite different rankings and might only be used to rank funds within a particular fund class.

Mutual fund portfolio managers often argue that they are unfairly judged by being compared with broad market indexes, such as the S&P 500, when the objectives for the fund are based on particular types of investment strategies. Different investment strategies include (1) value investing—attempting to find undervalued stocks that have low price/earnings ratios and high yields; (2) growth funds—seeking long—term capital appreciation-with dividend yields incidental; (3) equity income funds—seeking to provide a total return through income by investing in high yield stocks; (4) broad-based specialty funds—focusing on major market subsectors such as small company or international stocks; (5) concentrated specialty funds—investing in a single industry such as health care or internet companies; and (6) index funds—investing in stocks mimicking a stock index, such as the S&P 500. In the late 1990s index funds with a passive investment strategy, low turnover, and low fund expenses often surpassed the other types of funds that have done better or worse in other periods. More diversified mutual stock funds may at times have lower returns during certain periods than other strategies but lower losses during downturns.[32]

PENSION FUNDS, MUTUAL FUNDS' ROLE, AND THE RETIREMENT MARKET

Average life expectancy at birth for Americans has increased from an average of about 47.6 years in 1900 to about 76.5 years in 1995; therefore, individuals have had to plan more for retirement income. Today half of all full-time workers in U.S. commerce and industry and 75 percent of government civilian personnel are enrolled in retirement plans other than Social Security, including profit-sharing plans. The estimated number of participants is 50 million.[33] Retirement savings come from federal, state and local, and private pension funds; and from personal savings plans, often with savings contributed to tax-qualified plans such as individual retirement accounts (IRAs) and annuities.

In contrast to private plans, which accumulate assets, federal plans, the largest of which is Social Security, have historically relied on a "pay-as-you-go" system whereby collections from those currently employed are used to pay retirement benefits, and assets under management are quite small in comparison with the number of workers covered. With a large number of baby boomers retiring in upcoming decades, there has been much concern and debate on the adequacy of such a system. State and local retirement systems accumulate assets for retirement but differ in many ways from pension funds, because they are not regulated by the same federal laws that govern private pension plans. Management differs from state to state, depending on regulations and objectives. The following sections focus on private pension plans and tax-deferred personal savings plans. The growth in pension plans, ERISA, and types of plans are discussed first.

PENSION PLAN GROWTH, ERISA, AND TYPES OF EMPLOYER PENSION PLANS

Following World War II, with firms competing for workers, companies developed retirement benefits to attract workers. Support from labor unions contributed to the growth of pension plans. In 1949, the Supreme Court ruled that pension benefits could be included in collective bargaining agreements. The nation's largest unions took advantages of the ruling and during 1950 to 1960, the number of private plan assets and participants doubled. As pension plans grew, so did the possibility of sponsoring firms failing to meet their pension obligations. In 1964, for instance, the failure of Studebaker left most of the firm's employees with few or no pension bene-

---

[32]See Bogle (1994). For instance, value funds often had returns and risks that varied significantly from the market as a whole. Value funds performed very well in the 1980s but not as well as the market during the bull market of the 1990s. Bogle points out that by investing in value funds or a specialty fund, investors need to be aware that they are taking extra risk in accepting a lower level of diversification. Hence, the rewards of investing in such a fund that might rank in the top 10 percent of funds over a given period also implies the risk that they might perform in the bottom 10 percent of funds during a different period.

[33]See Steinberg and Dankner (1983) and *Life Insurance Fact Book,* 1998, Washington, D.C.: American Council of Life Insurance (1998).

fits. Congress passed the Employee Retirement Income Security Act (ERISA) in 1974 to prevent fund insolvencies, ensuring that employers work toward **full funding**, the equality of pension assets and accrued liabilities.[34]

Retirement plans offered by firms are generally classified as either **defined benefit (DB)** or **defined contribution (DC)** plans. A DB plan promises a specified benefit or income stream during retirement. Thus, employers take on all the investment risk of the plan, making contributions based on the age of the plan participant, the level of benefits promised, and the plan's expected investment returns. A pension plan is fully funded if the present value of its assets equals the present value of its future pension obligations minus the present value of future contributions, known as its **funding target**. Since the total amount of the fund's liabilities are not known with certainty, the fund's liabilities are estimated using actuarial methods based on the actuarial assumptions including the retirement age of covered employees, their expected salaries at retirement, how long they will live after retirement, and the interest rate that will be earned on assets. Employer contributions are based on these calculations. A major question in the management and regulation of defined benefit plans is whether an employer's contribution to the fund is sufficient to meet future pension liabilities. ERISA established the **Pension Benefit Guaranty Corporation (PBGC)** to assure within limits the payment of up to 85 percent of vested benefits if a defined benefit pension fund fails. The PBGC is supported by annual premiums based on the number of participants covered. If a plan is terminated, the PBGC becomes the trustee, taking control of the fund's assets and using them to pay as large a portion of the basic vested benefits as possible. The sponsoring company of a terminated plan may be held liable for unfunded benefits based on a formula established by Congress in the Single Employer Pension Plan Amendment Act of 1986.[35]

---

[34]Besides ERISA, the Multiemployer Pension Plan Amendments Act of 1980 affects plans jointly sponsored by more than one employer. As noted in Chapter 3, ERISA set standards for 100 percent vesting of benefits for most employees after 15 or fewer years of service; employees are entitled to vested benefits even if they leave the employer before retirement. ERISA also requires that fiduciaries make decisions for plans based on the prudent man rule, which requires a manager to make decisions with the same care and judgment that a prudent individual would use in handling personal investments. ERISA, however, did not place requirements on the level of benefits promised by an employer or on the dollar amount of employer contributions. Nor did ERISA require employers to establish pension plans. Rather, the intent is to protect employee interests once a plan has been established and benefits defined. Interpretations of ERISA's fiduciary requirements and the impact of ERISA are discussed in Cummins (1980), Pozen (1977), Ambachtsheer and Ezra (1998), and Logue and Rader (1998).

[35]In the late 1980s the PBGC was in poor financial condition. As a result of the termination of several underfunded plans, the PBGC had a deficit of almost $4 billion. After Congress raised insurance premiums, the deficit fell to about $1.5 billion by the end of 1987, when Congress again acted to assist the PBGC. In 1988 the premium structure was strengthened by another increase in the base rate, plus the ability to charge a risk-based premium related to a plan's unfunded vested benefit obligations. The PBGC also gained more hard-to-recover costs from firms terminating pension plans, even if the firms were in bankruptcy proceedings. For example, in 1990 the Supreme Court ruled that a firm could not transfer its existing pension liabilities to the PBGC, only to replace it with a new plan assuming future, not past, obligations. The PBGC has difficulties raising premiums for insurance, because profitable firms could discontinue their company-sponsored retirement plans to avoid the escalating cost of PBGC insurance, and riskier plans may not be able to pay higher risk-based premiums (see Abken 1992; Estrella and Hirtle 1988; Warshawsky 1988; Buynak 1987; Bodie 1985; and Munnell 1982).

With a DC plan, in contrast, the per-employee contributions made by the employer are specified, but the amount of retirement income generated is not defined or guaranteed. An employee's retirement income will instead depend on the plan's investment returns and the age and life expectancy of the plan's owner at retirement. Employees are often given a choice of funds to invest in and take on all of the investment risk. Employee-sponsored retirement plans include traditional DB pensions, **profit-sharing plans**, and **401(k)**, **403(b)**, and other similar plans. The 401(k) is a defined contribution employer-sponsored retirement savings program. Employers generally provide a choice of mutual funds in which employees may choose to invest. In 1997 employees were allowed pretax contributions up to $9,500. The 403(b) plans under the U.S. Internal Revenue Code for employees of a public school system or qualified charitable organize allowed pretax contributions also up to $9,500 in 1997.

ERISA also allowed individuals to set up their own **individual retirement accounts (IRAs)** if no private pension plans were available where an individual worked. As of 1982, the Economic Recovery Act of 1981 extended the eligibility for IRAs to persons covered by employer pension plans, with tax benefits associated with IRAs later limited under the Tax Reform Act of 1986. The Taxpayer's Relief Act of 1997 created the **Roth IRA**, which allows anyone to make a contribution regardless of whether they actively participate in a retirement plan; contributions are limited to $2,000, which are not tax-deductible. **Keogh or H.R. 10** plans allow self-employed individuals and proprietors of small businesses to set up individually defined contribution plans for themselves and their employees. The **Small Business Job Protection Act of 1996** also created simplified retirement plans: **SIMPLE IRAs** and **401(k)** plans for businesses with 100 or fewer employees.[36]

About 20 years ago, most employer retirement plan contributions went to DB plans; however, today the majority of contributions go to DC plans. For instance, according to Internal Revenue Service data, in 1994, 24.6 million participants were active in DB plans, whereas nearly double that figure, 40.3 million, were active participants in DC plans. In terms of assets, however, DB plans had $4.8 trillion in assets compared with $1.8 trillion in assets for DC plans, or 27 percent of the $6.6 trillion employer-sponsored market at the end of 1996.[37]

The Role of Different Financial Institutions in Managing Retirement Plan Assets

Figure 12.6 provides a summary of 1996 U.S. retirement market assets managed by financial institutions. About $1.24 trillion or 18.6 percent were managed by mutual funds (representing 35 percent of all mutual fund assets). The other $6.66 trillion were managed by pension funds, insurance companies, banks, and brokerage firms, with life insurance companies managing about $1 trillion.[38]

Panel B of Figure 12.6 shows that mutual fund retirement plan assets grew tremendously in the 1990s, including both IRAs and employer-sponsored plans. Mutual fund retirement assets rose by $245 billion or 25 percent in 1996, reflecting both

---

[36]See American Council of Life Insurance (1998); *1998 Mutual Fund Fact Book* (1998); and Pozen (1998).

[37]Ibid and see Ambachtsheer and Ezra (1998) and Logue and Rader (1998) for other statistics on pension funds. These plans simplify pension provisions and create a new simplified plan for small employers.

[38]Ibid.

Figure 12.6   ✦   MUTUAL FUNDS' SHARE OF THE RETIREMENT MARKET

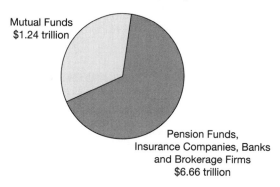

U.S. Retirement Market Assets, 1996

Mutual Funds
$1.24 trillion

Pension Funds,
Insurance Companies, Banks
and Brokerage Firms
$6.66 trillion

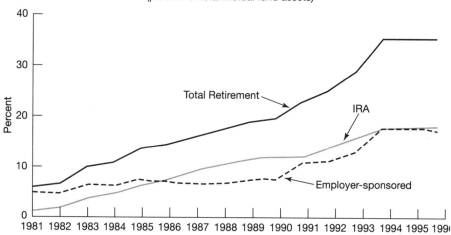

Mutual Fund Retirement Plan Assets
(percent of total mutual fund assets)

IRA PLAN ASSETS* (BILLIONS OF DOLLARS)

	1991	1992	1993	1994	1995	1996	% 1996
Commercial Bank Deposits	134.4	136.9	134.1	136.1	143.0R	143.7	10.66
Thrifts	91.1	85.3	76.6	71.6	72.8R	71.5	5.31
Life Insurance Companies	49.7	55.6	69.5	78.7	94.3R	105.6	7.84
Credit Unions	32.3	32.5	32.4	32.1	33.5R	33.2	2.46
Mutual Funds**	169.1	211.0	283.9	304.9	410.8	510.8	37.91
Brokers—Self-directed***	180.6	224.7	271.0	317.5	415.0	482.6	35.82
Total	657.2	746.0	867.5	940.9	1169.4R	1347.4	100.00

*Includes rollovers and Simplified Employee Pensions (SEPs).

**Does not include IRAs held in "street name" or omnibus accounts such as those that would arise through self-directed
IRAs.

***Includes only those self-directed items not included in other categories (including stocks, bonds, CDs sold by brokers,
and nonproprietary and other mutual funds not reported to Investment Company Institute for the mutual fund
category) and should not be interpreted as the total self-directed universe for IRAs.

Source: Federal Reserve Board, ACU, CUNA and Investment Company Institute special survey

Source: Investment Company Institute Mutual Fund Fact Book, 1998, pp. 44, 45, 47. Reprinted with permission.

the performance of underlying investments and new investments and the rapid growth in the defined contribution market. By 1997 mutual funds captured 32 percent of this market compared with less than 10 percent in 1985. As shown in the lowest panel of Figure 12.6, mutual funds also had the largest share of IRA plan assets relative to other financial institutions.

Panel C of Figure 12.7 shows the distribution of mutual fund plan assets. Mutual funds captured a greater share of 401(k) plan assets, which grew about 14 per-

Figure 12.7　◆　MUTUAL FUND RETIREMENT PLAN ASSETS

Legislation that went into effect on January 1, 1997, the Small Business Job Protection Act of 1996, created Sample IRAs and 401(k) plans for businesses with 100 or fewer employees. An Investment Company Institute survey in 1997 of mutual funds found these plans are becoming increasingly popular.

Mutual Fund Assets by Type of Retirement Plan
(billions of dollars)

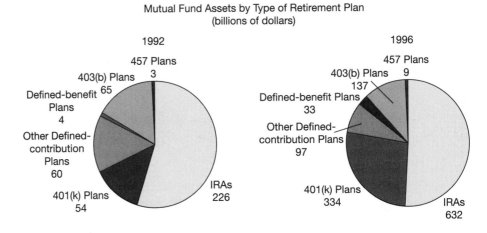

401(k) Plan Assets in Mutual Funds
(billions of dollars)

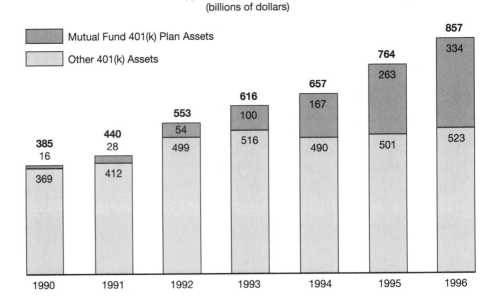

Source: Investment Company Institute *Mutual Fund Fact Book*, 1998, pp. 46, 48. Reprinted with permission.

cent a year between 1990 and 1996. Mutual funds only manage less than 1 percent of the DB plan market, although their share has increased dramatically since 1992. The performance of mutual funds accounted for about 75 percent of the rise in DC assets in 1996.[39]

MANAGEMENT ISSUES IN DEFINED BENEFIT PLANS

Although DC pension plans have dramatically increased in the United States, (managed by mutual fund companies, insurance companies, commercial banks, and other institutions as chosen by individual employees based on opportunities offered by employers), the majority, 73 percent, of pension assets remain in DB plans, in which the firm agrees to provide a given retirement benefit to employees at retirement, and the firm takes on all the investment risk. Key issues for pension fund managers include the following:[40]

1. What is the pension contract between all plan stakeholders?
2. How good is pension fund performance adjusted for risk and management costs?
3. Should an active or passive management policy be pursued?
4. What is the optimal allocation for pension assets?
5. Should pension smoothing techniques be used?
6. Who owns the surplus pension assets on termination?

Although these issues can easily cover volumes, they are briefly discussed in the following sections.

WHAT IS THE PENSION CONTRACT BETWEEN ALL STAKEHOLDERS?

As Ambachtsheer and Ezra (A&E) point out in their excellent book *Pension Fund Excellence*,[41] the stakeholders involved in a pension plan determine how a plan should be managed. In a DC pension plan the plan participant is ultimately the stakeholder, because the plan participant bears all the investment risk. However, with a DB plan, the firm and its stockholders who bear the investment risk of the pension plan are also stakeholders. If the investments for the pension plan perform well, the firm does not have to make as large a contribution to have the amount of capital promised available for employees at retirement.

As APE point out, pension funds, however, may have agency problems if pension fund fiduciaries do not have a strong motivation to create value for all the firm's stakeholders, including its stockholders and plan participants. Whether fiduciaries act in stockholders' as well as plan participants' interest depends on their view of what the pension contract is between all plan stakeholders. Investment returns on average contribute the majority of a pension plan's wealth; investment returns contribute about 80 percent to pension wealth and contributions only about 20 percent for firms in

---

[39]See *1998 Mutual Fund Fact Book* (1998).

[40]See Ambachtsheer and Ezra (1998) and Logue and Rader (1998) for an excellent and detailed discussion of these and other issues. This section on pensions draws heavily from these two sources.

[41]See Ambachtsheer and Ezra (1998).

North America, with variations during bear and bull markets.[42] Hence, as A&E point out, investment returns determine the wealth available for employees at retirement and contributions that a firm must pay to provide employees with retirement benefits. If fiduciaries consider stockholders as stakeholders, accordingly they should try to maximize returns for a pension fund, subject to risk and cost considerations, discussed in the following section.

How Good is Pension Fund Performance Adjusted for Risk and Management Costs?

A&E point out that the choice of an asset mix policy and the way in which such a policy is implemented depend on a number of different considerations, including the nature of the pension liabilities, risk tolerance of managers, the funded status of a pension plan, the prospects for long-term capital markets, and perceptions currently for the standard asset mix of pension funds. However, assessing how a plan has been implemented in terms of the return gained, operating costs, and incremental risk can be measured using a **risk-adjusted net value added (RANVA)** approach. Under this approach, (1) the gross annual return for an actively managed fund is estimated; (2) the expected annual compound return for the average passively managed fund (such as an index fund) is subtracted to solve for the **gross value added**; (3) the average annual incremental management cost is subtracted to get a **net value added**; (4) an average risk penalty based on the risk posture of the active management is then subtracted to get the RANVA.[43]

For instance, from 1992 to 1995, A&E estimate a 10.7 percent annual compound return for 98 North American pension funds. Subtracting 10.7 percent as the average annual compound return for other passively managed index funds, the gross value added from the active management was 0 percent. Subtracting a .2 percent average annual incremental active management cost, the net value added is −2 percent. Subtracting an average risk penalty of −.3 percent based on the risk posture of the active management, the RANVA is −.5 percent. As A&E point out, based on this perspective, the average pension fund would have done better undertaking a passive asset management policy, which would have entailed a lower management cost and lower active management risk. Whether a fund should undertake an active or passive management strategy is discussed in the following section.[44]

Should an Active or Passive Asset Allocation Management Policy Be Pursued?

As A&E point out, whether to implement an active or passive pension asset management policy depends on the performance return for a passive policy, the management cost entailed in following an active policy, and the additional risk entailed in following an active asset allocation management policy. Fiduciaries have trade-offs between seeking opportunity, which entails risks, and safety, which often implies lower returns. Often managers of defined pension plans follow long-term asset allocation strategies and do not change their policies unless a policy has changes in its li-

---

[42]Information in this section comes from Ambachtsheer and Ezra (1998).

[43]Information in this section comes from Ambachtsheer and Ezra (1998), who develop a RANVA approach and provide more details on this approach in *Pension Fund Excellence*.

[44]Ibid.

abilities, its objectives, or risk tolerance, or market conditions change. Most funds also have similar asset allocations as a result of trying to diversify. Whether a fund chooses to hold the average asset allocation (a passive approach) or to take advantage of asset mispricings within asset classes are decisions that should be made as long-term strategic decisions based on the goals and objectives of the fund.

Whether funds should be outsourced to other managers or managed within a firm is another important consideration. Larger funds have lower costs, so if funds are relatively small it makes sense to outsource both asset management and benefits record keeping to take advantage of cost savings in many cases. A&E again point out that ultimately asset strategy management decisions depend on being able to answer questions such as what was the return earned and did it justify the risks and investment costs involved?[45]

Although a passive investing strategy might seem more prudent from this perspective, on the other hand, a passive investment strategy with low costs because of infrequent monitoring might be considered by some to be imprudent. For example, infrequent monitoring might result in a manager being unaware of the potential bankruptcy of a company in which the fund has invested,. Hence, as pointed out by Logue and Rader (L&R) in their superb book *Managing Pension Plans*, a pension fund manager following such a policy would have a problem explaining why he or she was not aware of this firm's problems. Even if a passive policy is adopted, other decisions must be made in its implementation, including whether index funds should be invested in and, if so, which ones and how often these should be monitored. Passive policies also have other implications: Using index funds could preclude active corporate governance in terms of persuading specific companies included in an index fund to improve their performance. Choosing the right index includes estimating the costs of maintaining the fund and whether it has the proper risk/return mix for the pension fund and meets the fund's objectives.[46]

What is the Optimal Allocation for Pension Assets?

L&R point out that pension funds have a broad choice of assets, from investing in indexes for different asset classes to investing in publicly-traded stocks and bonds, the major investments of pension funds; to investing in the private bond or equity market or real estate market, among other choices. Other assets that a fund might invest in include emerging market stocks, limited partnerships with small firms, venture capital real estate, oil and gas, commodities, derivatives, managed futures, and market-neutral types of portfolios. The advantages of private equity market investments are higher potential returns, but fund managers must also consider the high costs in terms of greater risk from both a liquidity and default perspective. Funds may also receive greater total fund diversification with such private investments.[47]

Theoretical studies, including Sharpe (1976) and Harrison and Sharpe (1983), have proposed that DB pension plans, because they are partially insured by the PBGC, should take on more risky assets, holding the majority of their investments in stock. From the viewpoint of stockholders, because returns on stock are on average

---

[45]Ibid.

[46]See Logue and Rader (1998) and Ambachtsheer and Ezra (1998). Material in this section summarizes major points made by these authors.

[47]Ibid.

higher, if funds are invested in stock, the firm will not have to make as large a contribution to plans, maximizing shareholder value.

Alternatively, theoretical arguments by Black and Dewhurst (1981) and Tepper (1981) contend that the firm should sell any equities held by the pension fund, take the money from the sale and buy risky bonds. The firm should then borrow from the fund and use the proceeds to buy stock for the firm's own account, because stock is a tax advantage investment to the firm (70 percent of dividend income is excludable). In this way the firm achieves a type of tax arbitrage by using tax-deductible contributions to the pension fund in order to purchase a tax advantaged investment for the firm.[48]

From a more realistic standpoint, Logue and Rader (L&R) point out that asset allocations are quite different from these theoretical arguments and depend on the financial condition of the firm. For instance, they point out that in a study of 24,426 firms in 1977, Peterson found that (1) firms with more volatile earnings and higher financial leverage held lower percentages of equity and larger percentages of safe debt than other firms; (2) more profitable firms held a relatively higher percentage of equity in their pension portfolios than less profitable firms; and (3) firms with relatively young workforces tended to hold more debt in their plans than firms with older workforces. More recently, in 1996 Peterson examined 47,000 observations in 1988–1990 and found similarly that more profitable firms invested a greater portion of their assets in stocks, and riskier firms allocated a smaller portion to stock. He also found that less mature plans with a lower ratio of current benefits-to-asset size invested more in stocks. DB plans also invested more in stocks than DC plans. In 1980 Bodie and Associates studied 939 plans and found that the more highly funded a pension plan was, the greater its investment in bonds. With bull markets and pressure for funds to perform, allocations for stock have increased in recent years. For instance, the average allocation for public funds in stocks was over 50 percent in 1995 compared with 43 percent in 1991.[49]

Other Active Management Considerations   Other considerations involved in active asset management include investment style, management fees, derivatives, rebalancing, evaluation of money managers, and whether tactical asset allocation should be used. These issues are briefly discussed in the following subsections.

Investment Style   In addition to determining the best asset allocation policy in terms of the percentages of bonds, stocks, and other types of assets held, different money managers also have different investment styles, which L&R define as exper-

---

[48]This overview of studies summarizes major points made by Logue and Rader (1998). Also see Ippolito (1985, 1986), Sharpe (1976, 1987, 1990, 1992); Harrison and Sharpe (1983); Black and Dewhurst (1981); and Tepper (1981).

[49]These points come from Logue and Rader (1998). For a detailed discussion of previous studies, see their excellent book *Managing Pension Plans*. Pension funds have also been active in allocating a greater percentage of assets to real estate investments, although this has still been a small percentage of pension fund assets, about 2 percent. Critics have been concerned about fund managing entering areas where they have little expertise. The downturn in real estate in the late 1980s and early 1990s deterred some pension funds from further investing, although with an uptrend in real estate in the late 1990s, concerns have been expressed in the financial press again. See Richard D. Hylton. "How Real Estate Hit Pension Funds." *Fortune* (December 14, 1992), 123–131; Rosen (1982); Louargand (1992); and Bajtelsmit and Worzala (1995).

tise in some market sector, such as a subset of a larger investment class. The various styles that money managers offer can be pursued actively or passively. L&R point out that equity styles include growth, income, value, market capitalization, quality (which often includes special situations or turnarounds), and international or foreign equities including developed and emerging markets. Bond management styles for domestic or international bonds include true trading approaches, in which managers attempt to find under or overvalued bonds, and structured bond portfolios, in which managers adjust a portfolio in response to expected changes in interest rates or other market conditions. Other investment styles pertain to special classes of assets, including leveraged buyout funds, real estate funds, commodities, venture capital, managed futures, and market-neutral strategies. Hence, as L&R point out, pension fund managers must determine which if any of these strategies are appropriate, particularly if funds are outsourced to other money managers.[50]

Management Fees   L&R note that active management fees for a pension fund average about 50 basis points whereas passive fees for broad market index funds, for instance, average about 2 to 10 basis points and active index funds about 20 to 40 basis points. Mutual funds and other funds for managing employee pension plans have higher active equity fund expense ratios, averaging 100 basis points. Thus, pension managers need to monitor fees carefully as part of their due diligence.[51]

Derivatives   Pension funds' use of derivatives has been controversial; note, for example, the large investment losses incurred by Orange County's fund, which used derivatives to make bets on interest rates. ERISA guidelines discourages the use of derivatives for speculation. Policies must be implemented to specify how derivatives will be used for hedging or enhancing returns for risk management purposes. Policies also need to be put in place on monitoring derivative exposures. Managers must also understand the payoff structures and risks entailed upon undertaking different derivative positions.[52] **Managed futures** are baskets of commodity and financial futures held by an institution not for hedging purposes, but for investment purposes, generating their own return-risk contribution to a fund's performance. The managed futures portion of a fund may consist of a wide variety of short and long positions in a wide variety of short and long positions in a wide variety of derivatives, without regard to the remaining composition of the fund's assets. Beginning in 1991, managed futures attracted greater attention as the Virginia Retirement System announced that it was committing at least $100 million of its assets to managed futures. That a usually conservative public fund would adopt such a nontraditional approach to fund management spurred many private pension funds to consider managed futures as well. Managed futures often have been found to have a negative correlation with other assets in a funds pension plan, providing potential diversification without incurring the liquidity risk associated with other assets used for diversification, such as real estate.

Despite these attractions, not all observers are eager for pension funds to take large positions in managed futures. Critics point to the complexity of managed futures in multiple markets and to the additional costs, either in fees to hire new

---

[50]See Logue and Rader (1998) and Bogle (1994).
[51]See Logue and Rader (1998).
[52]Ibid.

futures managers or in training existing managers. They also worry that the higher return on managed futures does not adequately compensate for the volatility in futures positions. Thus managed futures have been a controversial pension fund activity.[53]

Rebalancing   Another important policy question for pension managers is when asset rebalancing should occur and if it is permitted. For instance, should trading occur to get allocation targets back to desired percentages when they fall outside their desired range by 5 percent or 10 percent? Also, should rebalancing occur once a year or over a shorter interval? Finally, can futures or options be used to achieve rebalancing? The cost of rebalancing in terms of transaction costs and time and effort need to be weighed against the benefits.[54]

Evaluation of Money Managers

Whether a pension fund is managed in-house or outsourced to external managers, managers should be rewarded for their performance based on their performance. However, it is important to compare a managers' performance based on a similar benchmark and the manager's investment style. As Bogle points out (1994), different categories of funds have different strategies and may perform differently in different markets. A value fund, for instance, which attempts to find undervalued stocks by focusing on stocks with above-average yields and below-average price-earnings ratios, should be judged against other value funds, rather than a market benchmark. Similarly a small firm growth fund, which takes greater risk than a fund that invests in blue chips, should be judged against a similar benchmark fund in terms of both risk and return. A&E note that too many fiduciaries depend on ranking lists published in newspapers or industry journals to compare managers with completely different management styles and may invest in funds based on a fund with a particular substyle that just happened to do well in one particular year. However, fiduciaries may also go overboard and try to create a benchmark for every manager, taking into account all of that manager's eccentricities to the point that the benchmark rationalizes a manager's behavior no matter what type of return he or she makes. Thus, finding the best benchmark can be problematic. When adjusting for risk, pension fund managers have used risk/return measures similar to those discussed for mutual funds, including the M-Square method and Sharpe and Treynor indexes.[55]

Tactical Asset Allocation   Some funds have used an active management strategy known as *tactical asset allocation*, in which money managers try to make timely movements among stocks, bonds, and cash based on complex quantitative models. These techniques were successful in shielding some funds from the 1987 crash but did not perform well during subsequent periods. In fact, comprehensive studies of pension fund performance indicate that high turnover and frequent reallocation of assets significantly hurt performance. Studies suggest that fund managers are better at selecting individual stocks than at timing the market. The explanation offered by

---

[53]See Stanley W. Angrist. "Virginia's Pension Plan Earmarks $100 Million for Futures Trading." *The Wall Street Journal* (April 26, 1991), C1, C5; "Futures Shock." *The Economist* (August 8, 1992), 69; Chicago Mercantile Exchange, "Roundtable for Pension Plan Sponsors on the Use of Managed Futures," (1991); and Chicago Board of Trade (1992).

[54]See Logue and Rader (1998).

[55]See Bogle (1994), Ambachtsheer and Ezra (1998), and Logue and Rader (1998).

many observers is that pension funds cannot beat the market because they *are* the market. In the late 1980s and the 1990s, the proportion of pension fund assets invested in stock and bond index funds—so named because the portfolios are deliberately selected to mirror the market as a whole—increased dramatically.[56]

Should Pension Smoothing Activities Be Used?

As pointed out by L&R, some companies are concerned about reducing the variability of pension returns by using techniques that have a rate of return equal to the assumed discount rate used to project pension benefit obligations. Such smoothing techniques reduce the plan's risk, although at the expense of higher potential returns. Smoothing techniques include the use of guaranteed investment contracts, dedicated bond portfolios, and a portfolio insurance strategy.

Guaranteed Investment Contracts   An alternative to active management is using guaranteed investment contracts (GICs), in which a pension fund contracts with a life insurer to earn a fixed rate of return over a specified period. The fund pays a lump sum to the insurer and receives annuity payments in return. The insurer provides the payments from earnings on its own bond portfolio. Although GICs are designed to reduce uncertainty in pension fund earnings, they are not risk-free. The guarantee is only as sound as the financial condition of the life insurer. This point was brought out dramatically when two large insurers, Executive Life and Mutual Benefit Life, became insolvent in the early 1990s. Although some corporations stepped in to make annuity payments to their retired employees after the insurers failed, others did not. Even when default risk on GICs is not high, interest rate risk can be a problem. If interest rates rise after a GIC contract is negotiated with an insurer, pension funds with a large volume of GIC investments are not able to profit from higher market yields.[57]

Dedicated Bond Portfolios   Dedicated bond portfolios are portions of bond portfolios that are designated to be immunized from changes in interest rates. The idea is to hold a portfolio of bonds whose present assets move exactly as the present

---

[56]See Robert A. G. Monks. "How to Earn More on $1 Trillion." *Fortune* (September 1985), 98–99; "The Forbes/TUCS Institutional Portfolio Report." *Forbes* (February 23, 1987), 156–157; and Lakonishok, Schleifer, and Vishny (1992). Also, see Coggin, Fabozzi, and Rahman (1993); Berkowitz, Finney, and Logue (1988); James A. White. "Asset Allocators Long for Glory Days of 1987." *The Wall Street Journal* (May 16, 1989), C1, C23; and Gary Weiss. "Index Funds: Getting More Bonds for the Buck." *Business Week* (September 21, 1987), 104. Despite large support for indexing, surveys report that 89.9 percent of pension fund managers believe they can beat the market, regardless of evidence to the contrary. See "The Abiding Faith in Active Management." *Institutional Investor* 20 (May 1986), 97, 100.

[57]See Nathans, "The New Breed of Pension that May Leave Retirees Poorer," 1989; Robert L. Rose. "GICs: Popular, Safe—But Are They Smart?" *The Wall Street Journal* (March 5, 1986), 33; and Larry Light, et al. "Are You Really Insured?" *Business Week* (August 5, 1991), 42–48. Ambachtsheer and Ezra (1998, p. 189) report that for defined contribution plans in the late 1990s, the use of GICs as an investment choice by employees has fallen, with assets moving more into stocks and a balance asset mix.

value of the projected benefit obligation for the pension plan. To do this a fund sponsor matches the duration (see Chapter 16) of the bonds to the holding period for the pension obligation. *Duration* is basically a measure of a bond's weighted average time to maturity. Duration for coupon bonds is less than equivalent zero-coupon bonds, because coupon income and the interest it earns reduces the time for an investor to get his or her money back. As L&R note, a dedicated portfolio technique works relatively well in immunizing a bond portfolio against interest rate risk. However, the fund does this at the expense of potentially higher returns that could be made on an unimmunized bond portfolio if rates move favorably. Risk is also not eliminated with such a strategy, because pension liabilities may change over time with changes in mortality and other demographic factors, as well as wage rates. Hence, the fixed returns on the dedicated bond portfolio may be insufficient to meet higher than expected pension obligations in the future.[58]

Portfolio Insurance or Insured Asset Allocation   Portfolio insurance or insured asset allocation attempts to maintain a basic asset value for a portfolio. Above this basic asset value, the portfolio manager may take on additional risks, such as risky assets proportionately to this basic value cushion. For instance, if stock prices, with stock as a risky asset, are rising, additional stocks can be purchased. But, if stock prices are falling, consuming the cushion above the basic asset value, stocks should be sold to reduce this risk exposure. L&R point out that portfolio insurance was widely used by institutional investors in the mid-1980s, but during the October 1987 stock market crash, the trading strategies that it relied on could not be executed, reducing the effectiveness of this strategy. However, they point out that from time to time this strategy of using insurance-like trading rules can be useful in more stable markets. Other techniques of reducing a portfolio's risk include hedging techniques using derivative securities, discussed later in Chapters 17 and 18. Basically, these techniques aim to produce a gain by taking a position in derivatives that will offset a potential loss anticipated if rates or prices moves the wrong way for securities in a fund's portfolio.[59]

WHO OWNS PENSION SURPLUS ASSETS?

During the mid-1980s, the relationship between fund performance and corporate sponsors achieved a new dimension. As the economy strengthened and financial assets rose in value, a larger number of pension funds became **overfunded**, i.e., the value of assets exceeded the estimated pension obligations, and the fund accumulated net worth, or a surplus of assets over liabilities. Some corporate executives took the position that any fund value in excess of the obligations to employees should accrue to the firm's shareholders in a more direct fashion than any considered thus far. By terminating an overfunded plan, the corporate sponsor could immediately capture the after-tax value of the excess assets. The terminated plan could be replaced by an identical plan or a defined contribution plan or by no plan at all with the purchase of annuities from an insurance company or other financial institution to fulfill the firm's previous obligations.

---

[58]See Logue and Rader (1998) See Chapter 16 for a detailed discussion of the use of duration for immunizing a dedicated bond portfolio.

[59]See Logue and Rader (1998).

Firms with large plan surpluses became merger targets as well, whereby an acquirer would later terminate the plan of the acquired firm and use the recaptured surplus assets from the plan to finance the merger. An example is when Carl Icahn and TWA acquired Ozark Airlines in 1986, terminated two of Ozark's pension plans, and recaptured for TWA $26 million. In response to such abuses, Congress passed a bill to discourage surplus recaptures by charging an excise tax of 50 percent of the amount of the surplus that is withdrawn that reverts to the employer.

Surpluses can also only be withdrawn if a plan is terminated. If an amount equal to a minimum of 20 percent of the reversion is first utilized to provide pro rata improvements to accrued benefits, or at least 25 percent of the terminated plan's excess is transferred to a replacement plan, the excise tax falls to 20 percent. These new regulations provided an impetus for corporate sponsors not to build up a surplus, such as reducing contributions if they are not needed.[60]

Actuarial Assumptions   The adequacy of contributions also depends on the actuarial assumptions, including the expected retirement age of covered employees and how long they live after retirement, and the discount rate used to find the present value of future liabilities. Similarly, it depends on the expected yield on the fund's assets over time. These assumptions resemble those used to establish reserves in the life insurance industry. Like life insurance actuaries, pension actuaries are cautious, preferring to err by overestimating future obligations rather than by underestimating them. When pension fund actuaries notify the corporate sponsor that a plan is overfunded, contributions may decrease, subsequently affecting pension fund management. For example, the stock market surge and falling interest rates between 1982 and 1986 increased the value of pension fund assets. Actuarial assumptions in some plans were changed, increasing the expected rate of return on assets in the future. Because this rate is used to discount future obligations, estimates of the present value of obligations decreased, and some corporations reduced contributions or terminated their pension plans to capture the excess assets.

The risks to corporate sponsors of changing actuarial assumptions to lower their contributions is clearly illustrated by General Motors' (GM) 1992 announcement that the assumptions it had recently adopted were not working and that its unfunded pension obligations were almost $2 billion higher than the firm had reported two years earlier. Two years earlier GM changed its actuarial assumptions to a more ambitious 11 percent expected return on assets versus a previous 10 percent and a retiree death rate two year earlier than mortality tables showed. After less than two years it was clear that these assumptions were unrealistic and that larger pension

---

[60]See Michael Tackett and Christopher Drew. "Pension Funds Become Bonanza for Companies." *Chicago Tribune* (December 4, 1989), Section 1, 1, 8; and Roger Thompson. "The Battle over Pension Surpluses." *Nation's Business* (August 1989), 66–67. Some state governments have raided their employees' pension funds, too, to balance operating budgets. See Alan Deutschman. "The Great Pension Robbery." *Fortune* (January 13, 1992), 76–78. See Logue and Rader (1998) for current rules and Ambachtsheer and Ezra (1998). Despite laws that discourage firms from terminating pension plans and taking pension assets, the issue of who is entitled to surplus pension assets remains controversial. See, for instance, Frances A. McMorris. "Sunbeam Unit Is Entitled to Surplus in Pension." *The Wall Street Journal* (April 5, 1999), B2.

contributions would have to be made to compensate for a shortfall. GM's lower contributions over the two-year period were ultimately not worth the added costs two years later.[61]

RECENT CONVERSIONS OF PENSIONS TO NEW CASH-BALANCE PLANS

In the late 1990s, hundreds of traditional plans converted to new **cash-balance plans (CBP)** and other account-style programs. A&E note that a CBP is somewhat of a blending of both a DC and DB plans. The defined benefit of such a cash plan is an agreement to a minimum rate of interest, such as the Treasury bill rate plus 1 percent on employees' retirement accounts. CBPs are insured by the PBGC and subject to ERISA fund regulations, similar to DB plans. Benefits are generally paid out as lump sums, but an employer may provide other options such as a standard life annuity from the employer or the option to defer payments until they are needed. Like a defined contribution plan, the employer contributes a minimum percentage of pay, such as 6 percent, into employees' retirement accounts. The employer also may include an option to occasionally credit additional contributions and interest to the accounts. Employees receive regular account statements of benefits, and employees can take these accrued benefits with them if they leave the employer.[62]

The advantage of CBPs to an employer are lower administration costs as a result of greater simplicity in record-keeping, lower legal exposure, and lower costs of educating employees with DC and DB plans. However, like DB plans, the employer continues to bear the investment risk. Although employees carry the risk of inflation and the risk of outliving the accrued benefits of their plans, similar to DC plans. Firms may use CBPs to save costs, to encourage early retirement or bring benefits in line with those of a firm they are merging with, and to boost employee stock ownership by tying the benefits of plans to company performance. Examples are IBM, which considered adopting a CBP in 1999, estimating savings of $200 million a year. Citicorp in 1999 converted 36,000 eligible U.S. employees in its Citibank unit from a traditional plan to a CBP to bring the firm's benefits in line with those of Traveler's Group in light of its merger and to tie employee benefits to the performance of the firm. Stock options will be given to all Citibank employees, and pension-plan contributions will not be only based on salary, but on total compensation, a plan Travelers Group already has in place. Analysts estimate that fixed costs for pension plans will

---

[61]See Ezra and Ambachtsheer (1985); Light (1989); Warshawsky (1988); Neal Templin. "GM Says Pension Liabilities to Exceed Estimates and Will Hurt Balance Sheet." *The Wall Street Journal* (September 25, 1992), A2; and Susan Pulliam. "Hopeful Assumptions Let Firms Minimize Pension Contributions." *The Wall Street Journal* (September 2, 1993), A1, A6. For more detailed discussions of actuarial assumptions, see Ambachtsheer and Ezra (1998) and Logue and Rader (1998).

[62]This material comes from Ambachtsheer and Ezra (1998) and Logue and Rader (1998), which provide more detailed discussions of cash balance plans; Paul Beckett. "Citigroup Makes Move to Change Pension Benefits." *The Wall Street Journal* (April 2, 1999), A4; and Ellen E. Schultz. "Your Pension May Be Changing; Go Figure How . . . If You Can." *The Wall Street Journal* (March 3, 1999), C1.

fall for Citibank, but if the firm's stock price rises, ultimately the company may pay more in benefits.[63]

As A&E point out, critics have argued that such a CBP can become a DC plan with a return that is not very competitive, which may not produce adequate income for a retiree. In addition, an employer may underfund plans relative to defined contribution plans, because the pension fund is one big account versus separate investment accounts for individual employees. With a conversion from a DB to a CBP, older employees with their pension benefit based on their average salary for their last five years before retirement may not fare as well with the new plan. Consequently, Citigroup and other firms have introduced "grandfathering" terms for older employees with significant years of service. The financial press has also criticized corporations for not giving employees sufficient information on how conversions from traditional plan to cash plans may reduce an employee's pension benefits. At times firms give employees a choice of a traditional and a cash plan, and employees do not have sufficient information to determine how benefits will be affected. The Senate Finance Committee in response drafted a requirement for companies to disclose whether pensions are being reduced and by how much.[64]

SUMMARY

This chapter examines financial management issues for mutual funds and pension funds. In recent years with changing demographics and aging baby boomers, these financial institutions have had dramatic asset growth. Mutual fund assets, for instance, in 1998 reached $5 trillion making mutual funds, the second largest financial institution in the U.S. Mutual funds are managed by a number of different types of affiliate firms including an investment management company, a principal underwriter or distributor, a custodian, a transfer agent, and independent public accountants, all of which contribute to the efficient operations of a fund. Many funds operate as fund families offering hundreds of different types of mutual funds. Mutual funds have diversified into a wide variety of financial services in recent years including discount brokerage, automated bill paying services, insurance, annuities, check-writing services, and Internet investing services, among others. Mutual funds have also undergone great consolidation, similar to other financial institutions, in the 1990s to make themselves more competitive. They have also diversified by offering their product outside the United States, including new markets for mutual funds in Asia and Europe.

With the tremendous growth in mutual funds, regulators have been concerned about mutual funds offering more streamlined disclosure to less sophisticated investors, and the SEC created a modernized simplified prospectus form that went into effect in June 1998. The SEC has also been concerned about the independence of mutual fund boards in protecting investors and reducing fund costs. Measuring the performance of mutual funds is often controversial, and the chapter discusses alternative measures for mutual fund performance and risk.

Private pension funds are responsible for investing money to be used later to pay retirement benefits. ERISA established the fiduciary responsibilities of

---

[63]See Paul Beckett. "Citigroup Makes Move to Change Pension Benefits." *The Wall Street Journal* (April 2, 1999), A4. The issue of relating pension assets to a company's performance is controversial, although it has been related more to funding plans by giving employees stock in the firm they work for. In January 1999, federal laws were changed to limit the percentage of retirement dollars that companies can force investors to invest in their own corporate stock. The 401(k) Pension Plan Protection Act in 1997, which took effect in 1999, forbids firms from requiring that employees invest more than 10 percent in their 401(k) assets in company stock. Voluntarily, however, employees may invest as much as they would like in their firm's stock. See Kathy Kristof. "Reforms Too Late to Prevent Some Workers' 401(k) Losses." *The Denver Post* (April 5, 1999), 2C.

[64]See cites in Note 62.

managers, funding standards, methods for guaranteeing benefits, and other important aspects of pension fund management. Most pension fund assets are invested in common stock and corporate bonds, and the funds' obligations are determined actuarially. The largest source of pension funds are earnings on assets, followed by plan contributions. DC plans are those in which firms make defined contributions and employees are responsible for choosing among a choice of investments, such as different mutual funds. Under a DC plan, the employee takes on all the investment risk. With DB plans the firm makes contributions and invests them in a pension fund, promising employees a given, defined benefit upon retirement. Hence, the firm takes on all the investment risk.

Management issues in DB plans include whether the firm wishes to maximize the wealth of shareholders as well as pension beneficiaries in terms of its investment policy. The firm's investment policy ultimately determines the risk and potential returns that the fund will make. By taking on greater risk, such as a larger percentage of equity investments, the firm has the potential to increase shareholder risk by reducing the necessary contributions to the plan that the firm has to make. Other issues include whether to pursue an active or passive management policy, and if an active policy is pursued, what the optimal allocation for pension assets is. The performance measurement of a pension portfolio needs to adjust for the risk of the plan and the management costs that are incurred, which can be significant with active management strategies. Recently hundreds of firms have converted to CBPs, which combine attributes of both DC and DB plans by making defined contributions to plan participants but guaranteeing a minimum return for these contributions. These plans have been controversial, however, because traditional plans may offer ultimately higher benefits to a participant at retirement.

Recommended Cases: Harvard Business School Publishing: Cases on Mutual Funds Companies & Pension Funds:

T. Rowe Price: Managing Money Market Funds

Keller Fund's Option Investment Strategy: Effect of Using Options on a Fund's Profit Profile and the Pricing of Multiple Option Strategies

Fidelity Investments, Spartan Florida Municipal Fund: Decision on Buying Portfolio Insurance

JKJ Pension Fund: Issuing for a Pension Fund in Valuation and Real Estate Portfolio Management

Useful Web Sites: SEC Tool to Calculate Cost of Funds

In an effort to help investors better understand mutual fund expenses, the SEC provides a new online tool to calculate the costs of fund investing known as the Cost Calculator, which is available on the SEC's Web site, www.sec.gov, or by going directly to: www.sec.gov/mfcc/mfcc-int.htm.

The cost calculator enables investors to evaluate and compare costs. The calculator provides a dollars-and-cents estimate of the cost of investing in a fund, which may be easier for many investors to grasp versus annual percentages or other comparisons. Investors using the calculator need to plug in actual costs, which are available in a fund's prospectus and project the number of years they will hold the fund, as well as estimating the average annual return. An example for the calculator is the finding in the article by Richard Oppel cited below that a fund held for 25 years with an annual expense ratio of .70 percent will leave an investor with 16 percent more than a fund with a 1.3 percent expense ratio. Hence, the calculator demonstrates the impact of fees on fund net returns. See Judith Burns, "SEC Tool to Calculate Costs of Funds," *The Wall Street Journal* (April 7, 1999), C27; and Richard A. Oppel, Jr. "SEC Web Site Now Offers Mutual Fund Fees Calculator," *The New York Times* (April 7, 1999), C10.

Questions

1. Explain reasons for the rapid growth of mutual funds in the 1990s. How much of this rise do you think is the result of higher fund performance in the 1990s, and how much is the result of demographic factors? Discuss some of these factors.

2. Explain the management structure for mutual funds as a group of affiliates. Explain what each of these affiliates do. Discuss the different ownership structures for affiliates, providing an example of a privately owned fund, a mutually owned fund, and a publicly owned funded. How does the type of ownership of fund affect its performance?

3. Discuss the recent trends that have occurred for mutual funds including product diversification, consolidation, and movement to markets outside the United States. Why have mutual funds carried out these trends?

4. What is the difference between an open-end mutual fund, a closed-end mutual fund, and a unit investment company? How do you calculate the NAV for an open-end mutual fund? How is the price determined for a closed-end mutual fund? Which of these funds has a larger liquidity management problem. Explain why.

5. Looking at Figure 12.3, how has the average asset allocation for mutual funds changed from 1975 to 1998; what are the reasons for this change? What is a fund family, and what advantages does a fund family have? Explain the dif-

ference between direct and indirect marketing strategies. Which strategy is more expensive?

6. Discuss the different types of expenses involved in operating a mutual fund. What is a Rule 12b-1 expense, a back-end load, and a front-end load? How can a back-end load be used to discourage investors from holding a fund for only a short period of time? What is the difference in the median expense ratio for a direct-market equity fund versus a direct-market bond fund, as shown in Table 12.4? Why are these expense ratios different? Why do funds have minimum investment requirements?

7. Who regulates mutual funds? Briefly list the major provisions for mutual funds under the National Securities Market Improvement Act of 1996, the Investment Acts of 1933 and 1940, and the Securities Act of 1934. What tests must mutual funds meet under Subchapter M of the Internal Revenue Code to be allowed pass-through taxation for dividends and capital gains?

8. What is the modernized Form N-1A for streamlined mutual fund disclosures that went into effect on June 1, 1998? Why is the SEC concerned over the oversight of mutual fund boards? What percentage of board members must be independent? How can independent board members be compromised by fund managers? What other concerns does the SEC have?

9. Discuss the differences between the different risk-adjusted performance measures in the chapter. What are their advantages and disadvantages? What are some sources of information on mutual fund performance? Why are mutual fund managers concerned about being compared with broad market indexes versus being compared with funds with similar types of investment strategy objectives?

10. Discuss the effects of ERISA on the fiduciary responsibility of pension fund managers. What is the difference between a DB and a DC plan? Which is partially insured by the PBGC? Why have corporations moved more to defined contribution plans? As an employee, which type of plan would you prefer?

11. Why has mutual funds' role in managing pension assets in-

creased in recent years? What other financial institutions manage large percentages of pension fund assets?

12. For DB plans do you think fiduciaries should consider stockholders as stakeholders in determining their investment decisions? Explain why or why not. What percentage of pension plan wealth is generally the result of investment performance, and what percentage is generally the result of firm contributions?

13. Explain the RANVA approach to judging fund performance for risk and management costs.

14. Discuss the advantages and disadvantages of an active versus a passive asset management policy for DB pension funds. For an active strategy, what are the theoretical arguments for holding more stock investments? For holding more bond investments? Based on actual pension holdings, why do you think funds with more volatile earnings and higher financial leverage hold lower percentages of equity and larger percentages of safe debt in their plans?

15. Explain what is meant by a money manager's investment style. Why is it important for funds that outsource their funds to money managers to be aware of these styles in relation to the pension fund's policies and objectives? What is the difference on average in the fees paid as a percentage of assets for active management versus passive management?

16. Why has pension funds' use of derivatives in the 1990s been controversial? Explain what managed futures are. How does this differ from the use of futures for hedging (i.e., reducing the risk of a fund's portfolio)?

17. Explain what tactical asset allocation is and what pension smoothing activities are. Give examples of different types of smoothing techniques.

18. How were pension surplus assets abused by firms in the 1980s? How did Congress attempt to stop this abuse?

19. Why are actuarial assumptions crucial in determining whether a DB plan has a surplus or a deficit? Use GM's change in assumptions in 1990 as an example.

20. What is a pension CBP? Why have so many conversions occurred from traditional plans to cash balance plans. Why have critics been concerned about these conversions?

Problems

1. Colorado adventurers, Dave and Liz Ingram, are trying to decide which mutual fund to invest in. They are trying to choose between investing in a S&P 500 Index Fund offered by Vanguard or an Aggressive Growth Fund A offered by Van Kampen Funds. *The Wall Street Journal* on April 5, 1999, reports the following information on the two respective funds: The Van Kampen Aggressive Growth Fund A has a maximum sales charge of 5.75 percent, an annual expense percent of 1.44 percent, a NAV of $17.14, a first quarter return of 18.6 percent, and a one-year return of 39.9 percent with an A performance rating. It is a new fund, so has no information on three-, five-, or eight-year performance, and has a minimum investment requirement of $500. The Vanguard 500 Index fund has a minimum investment of $3,000, no sales charge, and annual expense of .19 percent, and a NAV of $118.90. The first quarter return was 5 percent. The fund has A ratings for its one-, three-, and five-year returns with annual returns of 18.5 percent, 28 percent, and 26.2 percent and an eight-year average return of 19.4 percent.

a. Assuming that the average annual return for each fund is the same as in the past, 39.9 percent for the Van Kampen Aggressive Growth fund and 18.5 percent for the Vanguard Fund S&P 500 Index fund, and Liz and Dave invest $10,000, what would be the net return on each fund after sales charges and annual expense charges at the end of one year?

b. What other adjustments would Liz and Dave want to make if the Van Kampen Aggressive Growth Fund has greater risk than the Vanguard S&P Fund? Based on the discussion in the chapter, how could this be done?

2. Mark Williamson, the president, chief executive officer, and chairman for the Invesco Funds Group, a major mutual fund operating in Denver, Colorado, has asked Thomas Hurley, the super vice-president of Database Marketing and Research of Invesco Funds in Denver, to evaluate the performance of a potential fund for Invesco. The fund has a predicted monthly return of 3.00 percent with a monthly standard deviation of returns of 1.5 percent. At a 95 percent probability level, what would be the fund's monthly VAR? If an investor invested $1,000, with a 2.5 percent probability, what is the likely maximum monthly loss for the investor?

3. For the same fund in problem 2, Gail and Mike of Welpy International Funds ask you to calculate the Sharpe Ratio for monthly returns and an annualized Sharpe figure if the average monthly risk free rate is .44 percent, and the monthly standard deviation for this excess return is 1.75. Alternatively, calculate the Treynor Index if the average beta for the fund is 1.00. Explain what the Sharpe and Treynor Ratios indicate and how they are used.

4. Using the same example in problem 2, Gail and Mike ask you to use the standard deviation of the S&P 500 as an index for comparison as a benchmark. The average monthly return for the S&P 500 index is expected to be 1.20 percent, the monthly standard deviation of the fund's excess return over the benchmark is 1.5 percent, and the standard deviation of the excess return for the S&P Index is 1.3 percent, what is the M-square (Modigliani) measure for the fund's performance? (Hint: you might want to annualize all figures before calculating this measure.) What does this measure tell you? How is Morningstar's ratings measure different from this measure?

5. The MassMutual Participation Investors Company is a closed-end diversified management investment company whose investment objective is to maximize total returns by providing a high level of current income. As reported in Moody's Bank and Finance Manual, 1997, the fund's investment adviser is Massachusetts Mutual Life Insurance Company, and MassMutual is paid a quarterly advisory and administrative services fee equal to .90 percent of the value of the Trust's net assets on an annual basis. At the end of 1996, the fund's percentage of different types of securities in its fund, income, and balance sheets were as shown in Table P12.1.

a. What are the largest components of revenues and expenses on MassMutual Participation Investors' income statement? What changes occurred in the expense composition in 1996 versus 1995? What was the return on total assets? What was the return on net assets? How much did revenues grow in 1996? How much did expenses grow in 1996? How much did net investment income grow?

b. Given the asset allocations for the securities portfolio, what type of fund is MassMutual Participation Investors? What type of liabilities does the fund have? How much did net assets grow in 1996? How much did total liabilities and net assets grow? Comment on any changes between 1995 and 1996.

Table P12.1 ✦ **INFORMATION FOR PROBLEM 5 CHAPTER 12: MASSMUTUAL PARTICIPATION INVESTORS**

Securities	Value	Value	% Total
Corporate Restricted Securities	$72,985,477	72,985,477	71.17%
Convertible Bonds	2,297,838	2,297,838	2.24%
Bonds	16,040,232	16,040,232	15.64%
Warrants	60,250	60,250	0.06%
Common Stock	4,257,666	4,257,666	4.15%
Convertible Preferred Stock	1,994,917	1,994,917	1.95%
Commercial Paper	4,909,790	4,909,790	4.79%
Total Investments	$102,546,170	$102,546,170	100.00%

The consolidated income statements and balance sheets for 1995 and 1996 are shown below.

Table P12.1   ✦   **Information for Problem 5 Chapter 12: MassMutual Participation Investors (continued)**

CONSOLIDATED INCOME STATEMENT, DECEMBER 31 (IN $'S)

	1996	% Revs.	1995	% Revs.
Interest Income	8,784,434	98.35%	8,088,960	97.90%
Dividend Income	147,618	1.65%	173,463	2.10%
Total Income	8,932,052	100.00%	8,262,423	100.00%
Management fee	885,454	9.91%	822,845	9.96%
Trustees fees	55,690	0.62%	50,625	0.61%
Transfer agent exps.	48,500	0.54%	90,187	1.09%
Custodian fees			18,647	
Interest Expense	831,600	9.31%	378,840	4.59%
Reports to shrhldrs.	26,513	0.30%	56,787	0.69%
Audit & legal	42,935	0.48%	70,731	0.86%
Other Expenses	21,514	0.24%	32,075	0.39%
Total Expenses	1,912,206	21.41%	1,520,737	18.41%
Net Inv. Income	7,019,846	78.59%	6,741,686	81.59%
#Year-end shares	9,216,665		9,216,665	
NinvIncome per share	$0.78		$0.73	

CONSOLIDATED BALANCE SHEET (IN $'S)

Assets	1996	%	1995	%
Corporate restricted securities (fair value)	81,145,818	69.82%	69,576,592	63.09%
Corporate public securities (market value)	24,650,903	21.21%	26,399,294	23.94%
Short-term securities at cost	4,909,790	4.22%	11,611,375	10.53%
Total investments	110,706,511	95.25%	107,587,261	97.55%
Cash	4,414	0.00%	28,405	0.03%
Interest and Dividends Receivable	1,540,439	1.33%	1,804,874	1.64%
Receivable for Investments Sold	3,970,102	3.42%	866,010	0.79%
Total Assets	116,221,466	100.00%	110,286,550	100.00%
Liabilities	1996	%	1995	%
Dividends Payable	3,778,833	3.25%	1,751,358	1.59%
Payable for Investments Purchased	135,000	0.12%	500,000	0.45%
Management Fee Payable	218,596	0.19%	214,300	0.19%
Notes Payable	12,000,000	10.33%	12,000,000	10.88%
Interest Payable	170,940	0.15%	120,000	0.11%
Accrued Expenses	157,518	0.14%	160,000	0.15%
Accrued Taxes	2,606,720	2.24%	225,000	0.20%
Total Liabilities	19,067,607	16.41%	15,000,210	13.60%
Net Assets	97,153,859	83.59%	95,286,340	86.40%
Total Liabilities & Net Assets	116,221,466	100.00%	110,286,550	100.00%
Net Asset Value per Share	$10.54		$10.34	

Source: Moody's Bank & Finance Manual, 1997, p. 4348.

Selected References

Abken, Peter J. "Corporate Pensions and Government Insurance." *Economic Review* (Federal Reserve Bank of Atlanta) 77 (March/April 1992): 1–16.

Ambachtsheer, Keith P. and D. Don Ezra. *Pension Fund Excellence: Creating Value for Stakeholders.* New York: John Wiley & Sons, Inc., 1998.

The American Association of Individual Investors. *The Individual Investor's Guide to Low-Load Mutual Funds,* 18th ed. Chicago, 1999.

American Council of Life Insurance. *Life Insurance Fact Book, 1998.* Washington, D.C., 1998.

Bajtelsmit, Vickie L., and Elaine M. Worzala. "Real Estate Allocation in Pension Fund Portfolios." *Journal of Real Estate Portfolio Management* 1, No. 1 (1995), 25–38.

Berkowitz, Stephen A., Louis D. Finney, and Dennis E. Logue. *The Investment Performance of Corporate Pension Plans.* New York: Quorum Books, 1988.

Bodie, Zvi, et al. "Corporation Pension Policy: An Empirical Investigation." *Financial Analysts Journal* 41 (September/October 1985): 10–16.

Bogle, John C. *Bogle on Mutual Funds.* New York: Irwin Professional Publishing Co., 1994.

Black, Fischer, and Moray P. Dewhurst. "A New Investment Strategy for Pension Funds." *Journal of Portfolio Management* 7, No. 4 (1981), 26–34.

Buynak, Thomas M. "Is the U.S. Pension-Insurance System Going Broke?" *Economic Commentary* (Federal Reserve Bank of Cleveland), January 15, 1987.

Chicago Board of Trade. *Managed Futures: An Investment Opportunity for Institutional Investors.* Chicago, 1992.

Coggin, T. Daniel, Frank J. Fabozzi, and Shafiqur Rahman. "The Investment Performance of U.S. Equity Fund Managers: An Empirical Investigation." *Journal of Finance* 48 (July 1993): 1039–1055.

Cummins, J. David, et al. "Effects of ERISA on the Investment Policies of Private Pension Plans: Survey Evidence." *Journal of Risk and Insurance* 47 (September 1980): 447–476.

Estrella, Arturo, and Beverly Hirtle. "Estimating the Funding Gap of the Pension Benefit Guaranty Corporation." *Quarterly Review* (Federal Reserve Bank New York) (Autumn 1988): 45–59.

Ezra, D. Don, and Keith P. Ambachtsheer. "Pension Funds: Rich or Poor?" *Financial Analysis Journal* 41 (March/April 1985): 43–56.

Financial Economists Roundtable, "Statement on Risk Disclosure by Mutual Funds," September: http://www-sharpe.standord.edu/fer/htm.

Fortune, Peter. "Mutual Funds, Part I: Reshaping the American Financial System." *New England Economic Review* (Federal Reserve Bank of Boston), July/August 1997, 45–72.

French, Dan W., and Glenn V. Henderson, Jr. "How Well Does Performance Evaluation Perform?" *Journal of Portfolio Management* (Winter 1985): 15–18.

Harrel, David, "The Star Rating." http://text.morningstar.net/cgiin/GetNews.exe/NewsStory=MS/Investing101/StarRating/star.html

Harrison, J. Michael, and William F. Sharpe. "Optimal Funding and Asset Allocation Risks for Defined Benefit Pension Plans." In *Financial Aspects of the United States Pension System,* edited by Zvi Bodie and John B. Shoven. Chicago: University of Chicago Press, 1983, 91–103.

Hendricks, Darryll, Jayendu Patel, and Richard Zeckhauser, "Hot Hands in Mutual Funds: Short-Run Persistence of Relative Performance, 1974–1988." *Journal of Finance* 48 (March 1993): 93–130.

Ippolito, Richard A. "The Labor Contract and True Economic Pension Liabilities," *American Economic Review* 75, no. 6 (1985), 1031–1043.

———. *Pension, Economics and Public Policy.* Homewood, Ill.: Dow/Jones Irwin, 1986.

Jensen, Michael D. "The Performance of Mutual Funds in the Period 1945–1964." *Journal of Finance* 23 (May 1968): 389–416.

Laderman, Jeffrey M., and Geoffrey Smith. "The Power of Mutual Funds." *Business Week,* January 18, 1993, 62–68.

Lakonishok, Josef, Andrei Schleifer, and Robert Vishny. "The Structure and Performance of the Money Management Industry." *Brookings Papers on Economic Activity: Microeconomics.* Washington, D.C.: Brookings Institution, 1992.

Light, Larry. "The Power of Pension Funds." Business Week, November 6, 1989, 154–158.

Logue, Dennis E. and Jack S. Rader. *Managing Pension Plans: A Comprehensive Guide to Improving Plan Performance.* Boston: Harvard Business School Press, 1998.

Louargand, Marc A. "A Survey of Pension Fund Real Estate Portfolio Risk Management Practices." *Journal of Real Estate Research* 7 (Fall 1992): 361–374.

Modigliani, Franco and Leah Modigliani. "Risk-Adjusted Performance." *Journal of Portfolio Management* 23 (Winter 1997), 45–54.

Munnell, Alice H. "Guaranteeing Private Pension Benefits: A Potentially Expensive Business." *New England Economic Review* (Federal Reserve Bank of Boston) (March/April 1982): 24–47.

Mutual Fund Fact Book, 38th edition. Washington, D.C.: Investment Company Institute, 1998, and various other issues.

Pozen, Robert C. "The Prudent Person Rule and ERISA: A Legal Perspective." *Financial Analysts Journal* 33 (March/April 1977): 30–35.

————. *The Mutual Fund Business.* Cambridge, Mass.: The MIT Press, 1998.

Rosen, Kenneth T. "The Role of Pension Funds in Housing Finance." *Housing Finance Review* 1 (April 1982): 147–177.

Sharpe, William F. "Mutual Fund Performance." *Journal of Business Supplement on Security Prices*, 39 (January 1966), 119–38.

————. "Corporate Pension Funding Policy." *Journal of Financial Economics* 4, No. 2 (1976), 183–193.

————. "Integrated Asset Allocation." *Financial Analysts Journal* 43, No. 5 (1987), 25–32.

————. "Asset Allocation." In *Managing Investment Portfolios: A Dynamic Process*, 2nd ed., edited by John L. Magin and Donald L. Tuttle. New York: Warren, Gorman, and Lamont 1990, 7–1-7–70

————. "Asset Allocation, Management Style and Performance Measurement," *Journal of Portfolio Management* 18, No. 2 (1992), 7–19.

————. "Morningstar Performance Measures." http://www-sharpe.stanford.edu/stars0/htm.

Shukla, Ravi, and Charles Trzcinka. "Performance Measurement of Managed Portfolios." *Financial Markets, Institutions and Instruments* 1 (Number 4, 1992)

Simmons, Katerina. "Risk-Adjusted Performance of Mutual Funds." *New England Economic Review* (Federal Reserve Bank of Boston) (September/October 1998), 33–48.

Steinberg, Richard M., and Harold Dankner. *Pensions: An ERISA Accounting and Management Guide.* New York: John Wiley & Sons, 1983.

Tepper, Irwin. "Taxation and Corporate Pension Policy." *Journal of Finance* 36, No. 1 (1981): 1–13.

Treynor, Jack L. "How to Rate Management of Investment Funds." *Harvard Business Review* (January/February 1965): 131–136.

Tufano, Peter and Matthew Sevick. "Board Structure and Fee-Setting in the U.S. Mutual Fund Industry." *Journal of Financial Economics*, 46 (1997), 321–355.

Warshawsky, Mark J. "Pension Plans: Funding, Assets, and Regulatory Environment." *Federal Reserve Bulletin* 74 (November 1988): 717–730.

Woerheide, Walt. "Investor Response to Suggested Criteria for the Selection of Mutual Funds." *Journal of Financial and Quantitative Analysis* 17 (March 1982): 129–137.

Chapter 12 Internet Exercises

Insurance Company Institute Web site (http://www.ici.org/) contains basic information about mutual funds in the United States. To find the latest figures on the size of the mutual fund industry, click on "Mutual Fund Facts and Figures" and go to http://www.ici.org/facts_figures/index.html, which contains statistical releases, mutual fund developments, and a mutual fund fact book. Click on "Current Statistical Releases" to get the latest information on mutual fund trends for total assets, flows, and sales for open-end funds.

The SEC Mutual Fund Cost Calculator: A Tool for Comparing Mutual Funds can be found at http://www.sec.gov/mfcc/mfcc-int.htm To use the online JavaScript version of the program, you will need to have a JavaScript-enabled browser, such as Netscape Navigator™ 2.0 or higher, or Microsoft® Internet Explorer 3.0 or higher. The SEC Cost Calculator estimates the cost of investing in a mutual fund based on information you provide. The results should be compared for several funds or different classes of a single fund. Before you begin, take out the prospectus or profile for the funds you want to evaluate. You will need to plug in information from the expense section of these documents. Here is the information you will need to supply:

1. How many years do you plan to hold the fund?
2. Enter the dollar value of your investment.
3. What type of fund best describes what you want to analyze? (e.g., money market, bond, stock)
4. Enter the annual rate of return you expect to receive.
5. Enter the percentage sales charge on purchases for the amount of your investment.
6. Enter the percentage deferred sales charge at the end of the period you plan to hold your fund.
7. Does this fund convert from one share class to another by the end of the period you plan to hold your fund?
8. Enter the percentage total annual operating expenses or expense ratio for this fund.

You will be given the total dollar cost of holding the fund and the value of the investment for the length of period that you plan to hold the fund.

Other Useful Sites for Financial Institution Data:

Fortune, Peter "Mutual funds, part I: reshaping the American financial system." New England Economic Review (Federal Reserve Bank of Boston) (July 1997), pp. 45–72. http://www.std.com/frbbos/economic/pdf/neer497d.pdf

Janus Funds
http://www.janus.com

Vanguard Funds
http://www.vanguard.com

Fidelity Investments
http://www.fidelity.com

The American Association of Individual Investors
http://www.aaii.com

Pension Benefit Guaranty Corporation
http://www.pbgc.gov

"Just three months ago, stocks of specialty-finance companies such as credit card issuers and 'subprime' lenders were tumbling amid fears about aggressive accounting by some and about consumers' debt load. But now a spate of richly priced acquisitions has sent the stocks on a tear again, despite their undeniably high risks, as investors speculate that more deals will follow."

Gregory Zuckerman
"Deals Boost Specialty Finance Firms," *The Wall Street Journal* (April 17, 1998), C3.

"Nonbanks are quite simply redefining the financial services industry. GE Capital may be the most prominent example of a large company that takes pride in managing itself as a small entrepreneurial firm."

Charles B. Wendel
President, Financial Institutions Consulting, Inc. Quote from *The New Financiers*. Chicago: Irwin Professional Publishing, 1996, 2–3.

"By far the most important lesson that we have learned in making four or five acquisitions over the last two years is that you buy culture along with assets."

Samuel L. Eichenfield
Chairman, President & CEO, The FINOVA GROUP, INC. Quote from *The New Financiers*. Chicago: Irwin Professional Publishing, 1996, 95.

"This venture has been going for about nine years. It has been incredible to see our company grow from $25 million dollars in earnings in 1986 to about $1.6 billion in 1995."

Sanford I. Weill
Chairman & CEO, The Travelers Group Quote from *The New Financiers*. Chicago: Irwin Professional Publishing, 1996, 287.

13

MANAGING NONBANKS: FINANCE COMPANIES, FINANCIAL SERVICE FIRM CONGLOMERATES, AND MERGER CONSIDERATIONS

Depository institutions have faced growing competition from nonbank financial service firms, including finance companies and finan-cial conglomerates, over the last two decades of the 20th century. Many of the financial conglomerates ultimately started out as finance companies, such as Travelers

Group, which originally began as Primerica, the finance subsidiary of American Can Company. A number of large financial service firms that experimented with diversification in the 1980s, however, had problems and later spun off a diverse set of financial service subsidiaries in the early 1990s. Mega financial service firms continue to face problems of how to meld cultures and manage a diverse group of firms. Many analysts are skeptical about the success of diverse mega-financial institutions, although other argue that these institutions have a tremendous advantages over smaller firms that depend on a single source of revenue.[1]

Finance firms, as well as mega financial firms, were involved in a large number of mergers in the late 1990s. For instance, in the first three months of 1998, three huge mergers took place: Household International's purchase of Beneficial for $7.7 billion; Conseco's acquisition of Green Tree Financial for $7.6 billion; and First Union's acquisition of the Money Store for $2.1 billion. In anticipation of being future acquisition targets, other specialty finance firms' stock prices rose dramatically at that time. Similar to banks, finance companies are involved in a spread business, whereby they borrow and lend, making a profit on the spread. Increasing their size through mergers may lower two firm's overall costs of funds and increase this spread, in addition to providing other synergies or economies of scale.[2]

Finance companies have been reinventing themselves in recent decades, coming up with innovative products and strategies. Beneficial Finance Corporation, for instance in the early 1990s gave customers advances on expected tax refunds for $29. Beneficial submitted customers' tax forms electronically, so it received refunds in two weeks, earning significant fee income from more than 5 million customers who took advantage of this service.[3]

Other huge finance companies, like General Electric Capital, have acquired nonbank banks and are strong competitors in the credit card business. Some have bought thrifts, whereas others vie with banks to offer financial alternatives to corporate customers. Finance companies also initiated and assumed a leadership role in asset securitization.

This chapter discusses the nature, operations, and strategic considerations of finance companies and provides brief case histories of financial conglomerates and their successes and failures over the last two decades of the 20th century. The chapter begins with a discussion of finance companies including recent trends, and special characteristics of their financial statements.

◆ ◆ ◆

AN OVERVIEW OF FINANCE COMPANIES

Finance companies are like banks in that they make loans of different types. However, unlike banks, they do not have deposits as a source of funds. Finance companies finance their lending activities by issuing commercial paper or bonds or borrow-

---

[1]For an example of difficulties that mega-financial firms have had in blending cultures for diverse lines of business see Crawford and Sihler (1994), Case 6: General Electric Financial Services, Inc.

[2]Gregory Zuckerman. "Deals Boost Specialty Finance Firms." *The Wall Street Journal* (April 17, 1998), C1, C2. With high levels of risky consumer debt in 1998, some firms, such as Beneficial did not perform up to expectations. With high valuations, firms were under considerable pressure from stockholders to put themselves up for sale. See Steven Lipin and Jeff Bailey. "Beneficial Corp. Puts Itself on the Block as a Result of Pressure from Wall Street." *The Wall Street Journal* (February 17, 1998), A4; Laura M. Holson. "Beneficial May Put Itself Up for Sale." *The New York Times* (February 17, 1998), C1; and Richard Waters. "Money Store Acquired for $2.1 Billion." *The Rocky Mountain News* (March 5, 1998), B4. See Durkin and Elliehausen (1998) for a study of the cost structure of the consumer finance industry. They find little evidence of economies of scale, despite much anecdotal evidence in the industry. Also see Benston (1977).

[3]See Howard Rudnitsky. "Tax Play." *Forbes* (May 1, 1992), 48, 50.

total value. Securitizations rose dramatically, growing at an annual compound rate of 8.5 percent to $126 billion by the end of 1996.

For the largest captive finance companies, equipment loans and leases were about 60 percent of all receivables, motor vehicle loans 26 percent, retail loans 7 percent, and other 6.4 percent. In the 1990s there was a surge in leasing for motor vehicles, rapid growth averaging about 10 percent a year in consumer receivables, and a high growth rate of about 8 percent annually for equipment financing. Business receivables, however, only grew at a 4.7 percent annual rate. Mortgage loans and home equity loans grew rapidly, averaging 9.2 percent growth a year.

The fall in business loans can be seen more dramatically in Panel A of Figure 13.1. Between 1991 and 1998, business receivables fell from 52 percent to about 36

Figure 13.1   ✦   TRENDS IN AVERAGE U.S. FINANCE COMPANY ASSETS AND LIABILITIES

PANEL A: TRENDS IN ASSETS, YEAR-END 1991, AND 3RD QUARTER, 1998 (% TOTAL)

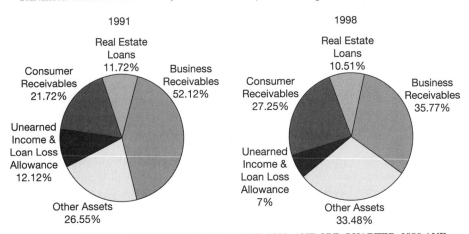

PANEL B: TRENDS IN LIABILITIES, YEAR-END 1991, AND 3RD QUARTER, 1998 AND EQUITY (% TOTAL)

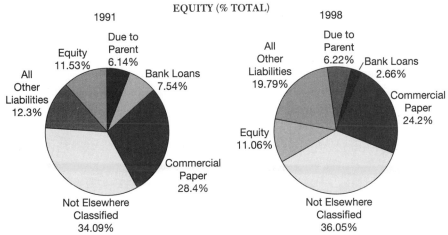

Source: Information from Federal Reserve Bulletins 79 (Jan. 1993), A35, and 85 (March 1999), A33.

percent of assets. In contrast, consumer receivables rose from about 22 percent to 27 percent of assets. Real estate receivables fell slightly, from about 12 percent to 10.5 percent of assets. As the economy improved in the late 1990s, relative to assets unearned income and loan loss allowances fell from 12 percent in 1991 to 7 percent in 1998. Unearned income and loan loss allowance losses is the sum of interest on discounted loans and the allowance for expected loan losses. Other assets relative to total assets rose from about 27 percent in 1991 to about 34 percent in 1998. Other assets include premises, cash, investments in subsidiary companies, and securities. The securities holdings of finance companies are conspicuous by their absence, providing one of the main differences between depositories and finance companies. Panel A of Table 13.1 shows the dollar figures for U.S. domestic finance companies as of March 1998 and a typical balance sheet.[15]

Panel B of Figure 13.1 depicts the sources of financing at finance companies, which changed between 1991 and 1998. Finance companies on average relied less on commercial paper and bank loans in 1998. The largest finance companies account for the majority of the commercial paper outstanding.[16] In 1991 finance companies on average financed with 6 percent bank loans, 28 percent commercial paper, and 6 percent debt due to parent and a total of 46 percent with other liabilities and not elsewhere classified debt. In 1998 bank loans fell to about 2.7 percent and commercial paper fell to 24 percent of total financing. Debt due to parent stayed about the same, but other liabilities and not elsewhere classified debt rose to about 56 percent of financing.

Other liabilities include short- and long-term borrowing, with larger firms relying more on bond financing.[17] "Due to parent" represents funds obtained by large captive finance companies to facilitate the sale of the parent's goods by providing financing to potential purchasers. Between 1991 and 1998, equity-to-asset ratios fell from 11.53 percent to 11.06 percent. Throughout the 1991–1998 period, the average equity-to-asset ratio was 11 percent, implying an equity multiplier (assets/equity) of about nine times. Large firms are more highly leveraged; small finance companies must rely on equity for almost half of their financing because they have limited access to the money and capital markets.

Because finance companies do not have depository insurance and often have customers with a higher risk profile than do depository institutions, they need to have more equity financing. The sources of funds for finance companies are banks and money and capital market borrowing. Hence, they are subject to market discipline by institutional investors and other lenders of funds.

One source of market discipline for finance companies is publicly disclosed risk ratings on their bonds and commercial paper. All the major rating agencies—Standard and Poor's Corporation, Moody's Investors Service, Duff and Phelps, Inc., and Fitch Investors Service, Inc.—focus heavily on asset quality, the determinants of earnings, and capital. A fall in such ratings for commercial paper and bonds means

---

[15]See *Federal Reserve Bulletins* 79 (January 1993), A35; and 85 (March 1998), A33.

[16]Because of the size of commercial paper issues and the methods of issuance, most commercial paper is held by institutional investors.

[17]Many long-term bonds issued by large finance companies are also held by large institutional investors. Through skillful negotiation with fund suppliers, large finance companies with access to both the commercial paper and long-term bond markets have opportunities to tailor the terms of their financing to conform to interest rate forecasts or to match the maturities of their planned asset structures.

Table 13.1 ✦ Average Financial Statements for U.S. Domestic Finance Companies, 1998

PANEL A: AVE. BALANCE SHEET IN 1998, 3RD QUARTER (IN BILS.)

Assets Receivables (loans):	$'s bils.	% Total	Liabilities & Capital Liabilities	$'s bils.	% Total
Consumer	255.3	27.25%	Bank Loans	24.9	2.66%
Business	335.1	35.77%	Commercial Paper	226.9	24.22%
Real Estate	98.5	10.51%	Debt:		
Less Reserves for unearned income	(52.4)	−5.59%	Owed to Parent	58.3	6.22%
Less reserves for losses	(13.2)	−1.41%	Not elsewhere classified	337.7	36.05%
Net Receivables	623.3	66.54%	All other liabilities	185.4	19.79%
Other Assets	313.6	33.48%	Equity	103.6	11.06%
Total Assets	936.8	100.00%	Total Liabilities & Capital	936.8	100.00%

Source: Federal Reserve Bulletin, Volume 85, March 1999, A32, A33.

PANEL B: SELECTED INCOME AND EXPENSE DATA FOR FINANCE COMPANIES: 1977–1989

Finance companies' profitability has fluctuated in recent years, although the industry has fared better than in the 1970s as managers have become more skillful in managing the spread.

Income Statement as % Assets	1977 (%)	1978 (%)	1979 (%)	1980 (%)	1981 (%)	1982 (%)	1983 (%)	1984 (%)	1985 (%)	1986 (%)	1987 (%)	1988 (%)	1989 (%)
Gross income/total assets	11.4	12.0	13.1	15.0	15.4	16.0	14.3	14.2	13.2	13.0	12.2	12.3	13.1
Operating expenses/total assets	4.6	4.5	4.6	5.3	4.5	4.6	4.5	4.6	4.6	5.0	4.4	4.8	4.8
Cost of borrowed funds/total assets	4.7	5.4	6.8	8.0	9.4	8.9	6.8	7.2	6.3	6.0	5.5	5.8	6.6
Net income/total assets (return on assets)	1.3	1.3	1.2	1.2	1.0	1.5	1.9	1.6	1.5	1.5	1.6	1.3	1.3
Net income/net worth (return on net worth)	11.2	11.3	10.6	9.6	8.6	12.2	18.3	15.4	16.2	16.2	17.7	13.7	13.7

Source: Ysabel Burns McAleer, "Finance Companies 1977–1989," *Finance Facts*, July 1990.

Typically finance company gross income includes interest and fee income on receivables (loans) and securitizations, as well as revenue from credit insurance payments and fees for other services. Operating expenses often range from 40 to 50% of expenses.

higher interest costs for finance companies, such as what occurred when companies had large loan losses in the 1980s. Finance company subsidiaries are also affected by the health of their parent companies. Some have faced higher liability costs when the rating agencies lower the risk ratings of the parent firm, even though the risk of the finance subsidiary may not have changed.

INCOME, EXPENSES, AND PROFITABILITY OF FINANCE COMPANIES

Little information is available on the income, expenses, and profitability of finance companies as a whole, because Fed surveys do not include income statement information. The American Financial Services Association (AFSA), a trade organization for finance companies, collected data from voluntarily reporting finance companies, but this database was discontinued after 1989. Panel B of Table 13.1 shows basic income statements items as a percentage of assets from 1977 to 1989, information from AFSA. Finance company gross income or revenues include interest and fee income on receivables and securitizations, as well as revenue from credit insurance payments and fees for other services. In 1989, the latest year reported, gross income was 13 percent of total assets. The largest expenses incurred are operating expenses, including provision for loan loss expenses and the cost of borrowed funds. As a percentage of assets, these were respectively 4.8 percent and 6.6 percent. Deducting for taxes and extraordinary items, the average net income as a percentage of assets was 1.3 percent, higher than the average for banks at this time. With an equity multiplier of about 10.5 percent in 1989, the average ROE was 13.7 percent. The lower ROEs in 1980 and 1981 (9.6 percent and 8.6 percent) reflect higher costs of borrowed funds at that time (9.4 percent in 1981). These costs rose higher than the rise in gross income to assets, resulting in a lower return on assets and equity. In 1982, however, interest costs relative to assets declined more than gross income to assets, resulting in a much improved return on assets (ROA) and ROE. Hence, finance company managers controlled the spread well enough between 1982 and 1989 to earn higher ROAs and ROEs than the early 1980s.

In a study titled "Finance Companies, Bank Competition, and Niche Markets," researchers Eli M. Remolona and Kurt C. Wulfekuhler of the Federal Reserve Bank of New York[18] compare the performance of a sample of the nation's largest finance companies with all insured commercial banks. As shown in Panel A of Figure 13.2, the finance company sample has a higher interest spread than do banks. Interest revenues to assets were much higher, with finance companies holding a larger proportion of higher-yielding consumer loans in their portfolio, despite higher interest expenses to assets. The researchers attribute the superior performance of the nation's largest finance companies to managers' ability to manage the spread and to the larger proportion of higher-yielding consumer loans.

Higher potential yields, however, also connote higher risk. By the late 1980s, the luster of the industry's profits dimmed as the rising tide of personal bankruptcies increased loan losses. As shown in Figure 13.2, which compares ROEs between commercial banks and consumer and diversified finance companies, returns were volatile. Consumer finance companies enjoyed the strongest performance, despite uncertainties introduced by revised bankruptcy laws. After 1982, both consumer and diversified finance companies reported higher ROEs than commercial banks. An increase in financial leverage for finance companies explains some of the growth in ROEs over the 1980's. Finance companies also escaped the default risk exposure banks encountered in agricultural lending, loans to oil producers, and international lending.

In a corporate scoreboard by *Business Week* in March 1999, a group composite of financial services firms, including 25 large finance firms and diversified financial firms (with a few large security firms included), showed an average ROE of 18.8 percent compared with 11.9 percent for a group composite of insurance firms, a 14.1 percent return for an industry composite of banks, and a 11.3 percent for large thrifts. Although somewhat biased, because large securities firms are included as well in this category, the returns suggest that the nation's largest finance firms are

---

[18]See Remolona and Wulfekuhler (1992). Figures for this section come from this article.

Figure 13.2   ✦   Comparisons Between Bank and Finance Company Profitability in the 1980's by Remolona and Wulfekuler, 1992

PANEL A: ANALYSIS OF INCOME FOR FINANCE COMPANIES AND BANKS, 1988–90 AVERAGE

PANEL B: RETURN ON EQUITY FOR FINANCE COMPANIES AND COMMERCIAL BANKS IN THE 1980S

Both consumer finance companies and diversified finance companies earned higher rates of return on net worth than did commercial banks during the 1980s.

Percent of Assets	Finance Company Sample	All Insured Commercial Banks
Interest revenues	11.36	9.48
Interest expenses	7.21	5.99
Interest spread	4.15	3.49
Other revenues	2.12	1.57
Other expenses	4.54	4.18
Income before taxes and extraordinary items	1.72	0.88
Income taxes and extraordinary items	0.55	0.27
Net income	1.17	0.62

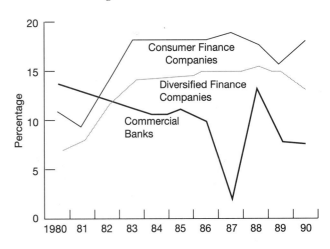

Source: Table 5, Remolona and Wulfekuler, 1992.

Source: Eli M. Remolona and Kurt C. Wulfekuhler, Federal Reserve Bank of New York, *Quarterly Review*, Summer 1992, 25–38.

Source: Remolona and Wulfekuhler 1992.

continuing to have higher returns than other types of financial institutions under more regulatory constraints.[19]

REGULATIONS FOR FINANCE COMPANIES

Finance companies are regulated almost entirely at the state level and are subject to all federal and state regulations on consumer, commercial, and mortgage credit, such as the Truth in Lending Act and Equal Credit Opportunity Act (Chapter 21), along with the Uniform Commercial Credit code. Most states require finance companies to demonstrate to authorities that a new branch office will provide "convenience and advantage" to customers. Finance companies are free from restrictions on interstate expansion. In the past, when banks did not have this freedom, finance companies had a competitive edge in reaching customers, and consequently, the largest finance companies built extensive nationwide branch networks. Recently, the cost of operating "brick and mortar" branches has risen, and finance companies have turned to less expensive ways, such as mail solicitations and credit cards to attract

---

[19]See "Corporate Scoreboard." *Business Week* (March 1, 1999), p. 85. Firms included in the financial services industry composite include a mixture of large diversified financial service firms.

customers and deliver services. The result is a decline in the number of branches operated by finance companies.[20]

Like other consumer lenders, finance companies are affected by state usury laws, which restrict the interest rates lenders can charge on specific types of loans. One impact of these ceilings was to make less credit available to borrowers. For instance, one study of finance company lending found that the ratio of consumer installment loans to total loans held by finance companies declined from 50 percent to 39 percent from 1965 to 1974, a period characterized by increasing usury ceilings in most states. Similarly, in 1981 Beneficial Corporation, at that time the second largest consumer finance company, closed 400 of its 1,900 offices in states with low usury interest rate ceilings. With many state usury laws rewritten in the 1980s to permit higher ceilings, finance companies faced fewer problems in being able to offer rates sufficient to cover costs and potential high loan losses.[21]

Personal bankruptcy laws also have a significant effect on the profitability of consumer finance companies in terms of their ability to collect on loans that default. In the first year the 1978 Bankruptcy Reform Act went into effect, making it easier for consumers to declare bankruptcy while retaining many of their assets, loan losses at finance companies more than doubled, and accordingly operating expenses rose in 1980. In 1981, profits for the industry as a whole fell 20 percent. GE Credit, for example, estimated that by 1982, 3,085 consumer borrowers per month were declaring bankruptcy.[22] In response finance companies have diversified away from unsecured consumer lending and moved into second mortgage lending for protection. In June 1984, a new federal bankruptcy law was passed after much lobbying by finance companies, making it more difficult for debtors to abuse their credit privileges by declaring bankruptcy. The new law encouraged the reentry of finance companies into the market for personal cash loans. However, the surge of personal bankruptcies continues, prompting Congress to consider bankruptcy reform legislation, although at the time of this writing, no action has been taken.[23]

PERFORMANCE INFORMATION AND MEASUREMENT

For publicly traded finance companies there is a wealth of public information available, including stock reports from sources such as ValueLine and financial statements from Moody's Financial Reports. *The Journal of Commercial Lending*, a publication of Robert Morris Association, compiles an annual performance report for

---

[20]See Benston (1977).

[21]See Benston (1977).

[22]See "A New Source of Mortgage Money." *Business Week* (March 23, 1981), 95; "Finance Companies Show the Strain." *Business Week* (March 22, 1982), 80–81; "The Allure of Second Mortgages." *Business Week* (March 16, 1981), 126; "Turning Back a Tide of Personal Bankruptcy." *Business Week* (June 14, 1982), 32; Johnson (1989); Staten (1989); Stephen Wermiel. "Court Clears Chapter 11 Use By Individuals." *The Wall Street Journal* (June 14, 1991), A2: and Stahl (1993).

[23]See Chapter 21 for a discussion of bankruptcy and consumer lending. In the second quarter of 1998, personal bankruptcies rose by 5.9 percent to 361,908 filings, up more than 20,000 from the first quarter. See Sougata Mukherjee. "American Flock to the Poor House: Bankruptcy Filings May Break Record." *Denver Business Journal* (August 27–31, 1998), 15-A.

the industry. The National Commercial Finance Association, a trade organization for asset-based lenders, compiles financial ratios annually to its members. The *Federal Reserve Bulletin* also does a comprehensive report on finance companies every few years. Dun and Bradstreet's Key Business Ratios is another source on the performance of finance companies given by quartiles for peer comparisons.

The performance of finance companies can be analyzed using a Dupont analysis similar to other financial institution firms and also by looking at the components of net income, as shown in Panel A of Figure 13.2 including the net interest margin, burden, provision for loan losses, and extraordinary items as a percentage of assets. Asset and liability mix, rate, and volume effects can also be reviewed, similar to depository institutions. Analysts also use particular selected performance measures for finance companies, as shown in Table 13.2 including information on maturing loans (receivables) and unused credit lines, as reported in *The Journal of Commercial Lending*.

The **liquidity ratios** reflect the particular nature of finance companies' financing and the ease with which the company's assets can be converted into cash. Because finance companies hold very few, if any, securities, cash relative to short-term

Table 13.2 ✦ SELECTED PERFORMANCE MEASURES FOR FINANCE COMPANIES

Some performance measures for finance companies differ from those used for depositories. In particular, analysts focus on key financial variables relative to total finance company receivables.

Ratio		Consumer Finance Industry Averages, 1991	Diversified Finance Industry Averages, 1991
Liquidity			
23.1	Cash/Short-Term Debt	NA[a]	NA
23.2	Receivables Maturing in 12 Months/Total Receivables	NA	37.50%
23.3	Unused Credit Lines/Open Market Debt	121.00%	125.50%
Credit Risk			
23.4	Direct Cash Loans/Gross Receivables	42.20%	9.70%
23.5	Net Charge-offs/Average Net Receivables	2.60%	1.70%
Leverage			
23.6	Total Debt/Net Worth	5.70 times	7.90 times
23.7	Interest Expense/Average Net Receivables	7.30%	6.90%
Efficiency/Productivity			
23.8	Operating Expenses (Exclusive of Loan Loss Expense)/Average Net Receivables	7.50%	3.20%
23.9	Average Monthly Principal Collections/Average Net Monthly Receivables	4.20%	NA
28.10	Annual Gross Finance Revenues/Average Net Receivables	19.60%	15.30%
Profitability			
23.11	Net Finance Profit/Average Net Receivables	3.40%	1.40%
23.12	Net Interest Margin = (Gross Finance Revenue − Interest Expense)/Average Net Receivables	12.30%	8.40%
23.13	Return on Net Worth = Net Income/Average Net Worth	18.70%	10.90%

[a]NA = not available.

Source: Mark C. Kramer and Raymond M. Neihengen, Jr., "Analysis of Finance Company Ratios in 1991," *Journal of Commercial Lending* 75 (September 1992): 39–47.

debt and the percentage of maturing receivables help to estimate potential liquidity for a firm. The unused credit line-to-open market debt ratio indicates the company's ability to generate cash from additional borrowing. Information on the finance company's unused credit lines can be found in footnotes to the firm's annual report.

The **credit risk** measures also reflect the particular nature of finance companies. Because personal cash loans are among the riskiest made, the ratio of these loans to total credit extended suggest the overall risk of the portfolio, as does the percentage of net charge-offs to total receivables (loans). Because interest is more expensive for finance companies, an additional **financial leverage** measure is interest expense to average net receivables, providing an indication of a firm's debt service burden and trends in that burden.

Operating expenses are some of the largest expenses for a finance company, so the **operating efficiency** ratios are very important. The average monthly principal collections to average net monthly receivables measure indicates the thoroughness of the firm's collection and loan monitoring policies. A declining trend indicates either that the firm is increasing the maturity of its loan portfolio and, hence, a smaller amount of principal is collected on loans made recently, or that efforts to collect are more lax than in the past. Either way questions need to be asked. Unfortunately, information on this ratio may be difficult to find. The annual gross finance revenues to average net receivables is an asset utilization measure for finance companies, revealing how much revenue was generated per dollar lent during a period. In 1991, for example, 19.6 cents of finance revenue was returned to the firm for every dollar of credit extended.

Profitability measures are similar to those used by depository institutions including an ROA and net interest margin figure. Commonly, net receivables (which are the majority of a finance company's assets) are used instead of total assets in the denominator.

The nation's largest finance companies are diversified finance companies with numerous financial service activities included in their financial statements, ranging from insurance activities, brokerage and other securities activities, activities related to thrifts, as well as finance company activities. The final section of this chapter provides a discussion and brief case study of some of these firms that began diversifying in the 1980's.

AN OVERVIEW OF DIVERSIFIED FINANCIAL FIRMS
WHAT ARE THEY?

Financial services is a term encompassing all the deposit, credit, investment, insurance, and risk management operations discussed in this book. In the 1980s and continuing in the 1990s, however, financial institutions have increasingly expanded their range of services, becoming financial service conglomerates. This trend is likely to continue into the 2000s, particularly if the Financial Modernization Act goes into effect. Table 13.3 summarizes the major provisions of the compromise bill as of May 6, 1999. Under the Compromise Financial Modernization bill, for the first time since 1933, insurance firms, security firms, and banks could operate as one company. Both the Treasury Department and the Fed would have veto powers over activities for firms. Financial activities would be allowed to be conducted in a bank as an operating subsidiary but must be conducted through a holding company with the Fed having the sole authority to establish how such activities are conducted. The SEC would

Table 13.3 ✦ Brief Summary of Some of the Major Provisions Of
Proposed Financial Modernization Bill as of May 1999

REGULATORY AUTHORITY

• **Both the Treasury Department and the Federal Reserve (Fed) would have authority to veto a certain activity** to be engaged in by a holding company or an operating subsidiary as nonfinancial. The Fed would have the sole authority to establish parameters for how merchant banking can be conducted.

• **The Securities and Exchange Commission (SEC) would have regulatory jurisdiction over all securities activities**, regardless of whether a holding company or affiliated operating subsidiary is used.

• **State insurance and licensing requirements** must be complied with for financial institutions engaging in insurance activities, subject to nondiscrimination requirements.

• **Holding Company Structure:** Large national banks ($1 billion) are required to have a holding structure to engage in new financial activities. Smaller national banks may use an operating subsidiary to conduct financial activities.

AFFILIATION AMONG SECURITIES FIRMS, INSURANCE COMPANIES, AND
DEPOSITORIES

• **Repeals Glass-Steagall Act prohibitions against banks affiliating with securities firms**, permitting holding companies to engage in securities underwriting and dealing without limitation, as well as sponsoring and distributing mutual funds

• **Repeals Bank Holding Company Act prohibitions on insurance underwriting**, allowing holding companies to underwrite and broker any type of insurance product

• **Expands permissible nonbanking activities** for holding companies from those "closely related to banking" to those that are **"financial in nature."**

• **Community Reinvestment Act (CRA):** All banks in a holding company must have a Satisfactory or better CRA rating in order to continue to engage in new financial activities.

• **Suitability:** Federal regulators are required to issue **regulations regarding the suitable standards for retail sales of non-deposit products.**

• **The number of wholesale financial institutions (WFIs) with membership in the Federal Reserve and allowed to use the Fed's payment system and discount window is limited to 10.**

• **Bank holding companies (BHCs) are prohibited from engaging in commercial activities.**

• **Consultative process involving the Federal Reserve Board and the Secretary of the Treasury will be used to determine which financial activities will be allowed.** Expanded financial activities must be approved and a notice filed with the Federal Reserve Board. The Fed is established as the umbrella regulator.

• **Well capitalized and well managed:** To be allowed to engage in expanded financial activities, all insured depository institutions of a bank holding company must be well managed and well capitalized.

• **Terminates the current unitary savings and loan company authority for all applications** other than those approved or pending as of February 28, 1999.

STREAMLINING SUPERVISION AND RESOLVING REGULATORY DISPUTES

• **The Federal Reserve will, where possible, accept existing reports that a BHC or subsidiary has provided to other Federal or State regulators or the SEC.**

• **The Fed may examine functionally regulated nondepository institution subsidiaries of bank holding companies only if reasonable cause exists to believe that the subsidiary is engaged in activities posing a material risk to an affiliated depository institution** or is not in compliance with statutory requirements.

(continued)

Table 13.3 ✦ Brief Summary of Some of the Major Provisions Of Proposed Financial Modernization Bill as of March 1999 (CONTINUED)

- **Federal and state regulators are directed to share information**, consult with each other on certain affiliation issues, and to preserve the confidentiality of information.
- **Federal and state dispute resolution:** Disputes between Federal regulators and State insurance regulators on insurance issues would be expedited at the Federal appellate court level, with equal deference given to both regulators.

REGULATORY IMPROVEMENTS

- Eliminates SAIF and BIF special reserves established in 1996. Additional time is given to determine whether to merge the two funds and consolidate regulators. BIF-insured deposits would continue to be $\frac{1}{5}$ the rate on SAIF insured deposits (1.30 bp versus 6.50 bp currently) for 3 years.
- Permits greater access to small banks for s-corporation treatment.
- Removes limitations placed on institutions that were covered under CEBA in 1987 with respect to permissible activities within the holding company and cross-marketing of products.
- Directs federal banking agencies to use plain language in all proposed and final rule-makings published in the Federal Register after January 1, 2000.

Source: Banking Policy Reports, Vol. 18 (February 1, 1999), 2–6 and March 15 and June 7, 1999, 3–4, 3–8, Washington, D.C.: Aspen Law and Business.

regulate all securities activities. Bank holding companies would be required to have a Satisfactory CRA rating, and new unitary savings and loan holding companies would not be allowed.[24]

As Arnold Danielson, a well-known financial service firm consultant, notes, with greater financial modernization in the 21st century, financial service firms are likely to experience rapid growth. Major events in 1998 radically changed the environment for financial institutions in 1998, including (1) the Citicorp-Travelers merger, which forced Congress to deal with the issue of allowing insurance-securities-banking activities to be conducted together; (2) the OTS's widespread approval of new unitary holding companies, which opened the banking-commerce debate: (3) the BankAmerica-NationsBank and other mega bank mergers and acquisitions of securities firms by commercial banks; (4) a contraction in net interest margins for banks favoring banks with greater sources of noninterest income; and (5) the emergence of the Internet, which allows financial services to be carried out in Web space. Financial institutions of all sizes will have to make serious adjustments to be able to participate in the expected financial boom in the 2000s associated with these events. He notes that the next wave of megamergers will likely be the largest financial service firms purchasing mutual fund companies.[25]

---

[24]*Source Banking Policy Reports*, Vol. 18 (February 1, 1999, 2–6 and March 15, 1999, 3–8, and June 7, 1999, 3–4). Washington, D.C.: Aspen Law and Business. At the time of this writing, problems arose in negotiations because Senator Graham, the Chairman of the Senate Banking Committee wished to do away with CRA requirements, which if done would be vetoed by President Clinton.

[25]See Danielson (1999).

Figure 13.3   ✦   The Emergence of the Travelers Group as a Mega Financial Institution, 1986 to 1998

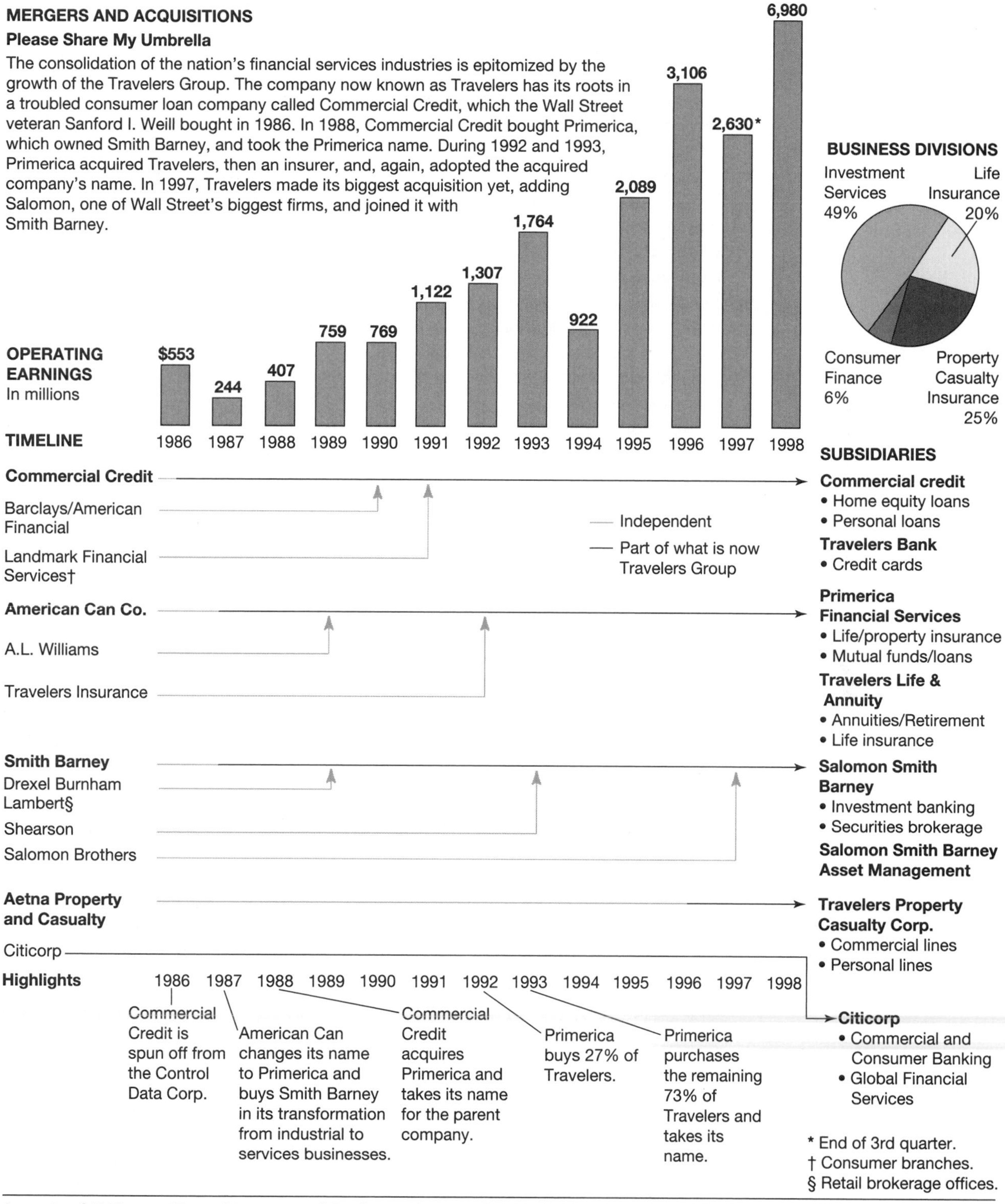

MERGERS AND ACQUISITIONS

Please Share My Umbrella

The consolidation of the nation's financial services industries is epitomized by the growth of the Travelers Group. The company now known as Travelers has its roots in a troubled consumer loan company called Commercial Credit, which the Wall Street veteran Sanford I. Weill bought in 1986. In 1988, Commercial Credit bought Primerica, which owned Smith Barney, and took the Primerica name. During 1992 and 1993, Primerica acquired Travelers, then an insurer, and, again, adopted the acquired company's name. In 1997, Travelers made its biggest acquisition yet, adding Salomon, one of Wall Street's biggest firms, and joined it with Smith Barney.

BUSINESS DIVISIONS

Investment Services 49%
Life Insurance 20%
Property Casualty Insurance 25%
Consumer Finance 6%

OPERATING EARNINGS
In millions

TIMELINE	1986	1987	1988	1989	1990	1991	1992	1993	1994	1995	1996	1997	1998
	$553	244	407	759	769	1,122	1,307	1,764	922	2,089	3,106	2,630*	6,980

SUBSIDIARIES

Commercial Credit

Barclays/American Financial

Landmark Financial Services†

Independent

Part of what is now Travelers Group

Commercial credit
• Home equity loans
• Personal loans

Travelers Bank
• Credit cards

American Can Co.

A.L. Williams

Travelers Insurance

Primerica Financial Services
• Life/property insurance
• Mutual funds/loans

Travelers Life & Annuity
• Annuities/Retirement
• Life insurance

Smith Barney

Drexel Burnham Lambert§

Shearson

Salomon Brothers

Salomon Smith Barney
• Investment banking
• Securities brokerage

Salomon Smith Barney Asset Management

Aetna Property and Casualty

Citicorp

Travelers Property Casualty Corp.
• Commercial lines
• Personal lines

Highlights

	1986	1987	1988	1989	1990	1991	1992	1993	1994	1995	1996	1997	1998

Commercial Credit is spun off from the Control Data Corp.

American Can changes its name to Primerica and buys Smith Barney in its transformation from industrial to services businesses.

Commercial Credit acquires Primerica and takes its name for the parent company.

Primerica buys 27% of Travelers.

Primerica purchases the remaining 73% of Travelers and takes its name.

Citicorp
• Commercial and Consumer Banking
• Global Financial Services

* End of 3rd quarter.
† Consumer branches.
§ Retail brokerage offices.

Source: Joseph B. Treaster, "Financial Services Consolidate, but Regulation Is Still Fragmented," *The New York Times*, January 2, 1998, D1, A5, Figure extended by authors for most recent merger.

In preparation for the continuing emergence of financial conglomerates, in April 1998, the Basle Committee on Banking Supervision, the International Organization of Securities Commissions, and the International Association of Insurance Supervisors released documents prepared by the Joint Forum on Financial Conglomerates to address some of the most crucial supervisory issues that have arisen with "the continuing emergence of financial conglomerates and the blurring of distinctions between the activities of firms in each of the banking, securities, and insurance sectors," including exchange of information among supervisors, assessing the capital adequacy of conglomerates, coordination among supervisors, and testing the fitness and propriety of managers, directors, and major shareholders of conglomerates.[26]

The Travelers Group-Citicorp merger in 1998 (see Figure 13.3) perhaps is the best representative of the financial conglomerate trend. Travelers Group, which began as a small finance firm, Commercial Credit, that was spun off from the Control Data Corporation and became a part of American Can in 1987, has come quite a long way. In 1987, American Can had $244 million in assets. With Traveler's merger with Citicorp, the combined financial conglomerate will have $698 billion in assets with operations in all aspects of financial services.[27]

This section explores diversified financial services firms and examines the implications for asset/liability management in the future. The following section discusses reasons for the development of financial conglomerates in the 1980s and in the 1990s. The experiences of several financial conglomerates are also discussed. The final section discusses implications of these firms' experiences for the management of diversified financial service firms in the future.

REASONS FOR THE DEVELOPMENT OF FINANCIAL CONGLOMERATES

The reasons for the emergence of both nonfinancial conglomerates and financial conglomerates have often been debated throughout the 1990s. Reasons include the following:

1. Firms can smooth their earnings by receiving interest and noninterest income from a variety of sources;
2. Smoother earnings allow firms to have greater debt capacity and a lower overall cost of funds;
3. Firms can achieve operating synergies including economies of scale and scope and more productive resource utilization;
4. Firms in maturing industries, such as the insurance or banking industries, can diversify for long-term survival and greater profitability and growth;
5. Managers can reduce unemployment risk by smoothing earnings or achieving greater ego satisfaction or compensation, if management compensation is related to growth; and

---

[26]See "International Group Addresses Supervision of Conglomerates." *Banking Policy Report*, 18 (March 15, 1999), 2.

[27]See Joseph B. Treaster. "Financial Services Consolidate, but Regulation is Still Fragmented." *The New York Times* (January 2, 1998), D1, D5; and David Greising, Peter Galuszka, Kathleen Morris, Andrew Osterland, and Geoffrey Smith. "Are Megabanks—Once Unimaginable, Now Inevitable—Better?" *Business Week* (April 27, 1998), 33–36.

6.   By applying management competencies, firms can improve the efficiency of inefficient firms in a related industry.[28]

Other less theoretical, but more practical, considerations include ease of entry, substitutability of products, perceived profitability, other synergies, spreading the cost of new technology over a wide variety of products and services, and a significant decline in traditional net interest margins, necessitating a move into new areas that provide greater noninterest revenues.

Ease of Entry   The cost of entering different aspects of the financial services industry can be low, because a major investment in capital may not be needed particularly for a firm in the information or retailing business. For instance, in the 1980s and 1990s some nonfinancial firms, such as retailers already offering credit cards, found it particularly easy to expand their financial services. Nordstrom, a major retailing firm, set up banking services in 1998 for its consumer customers through a nonbank bank. Telecommunication and computer firms such as TCI and Microsoft similarly found it easy to set up joint ventures with banks to offer bill-paying and mortgage shopping services. In 1999, three of the most popular banks for small businesses included major nonbank credit card issuers, Mountain West Financial, American Express, and Advanta Corporation, which moved easily into the small firm financing area. Merrill Lynch and Boston Financial Network, a new Internet firm, also provide loans, credit lines, cash management, and other banking type services for small firms. In 1999, Merrill Lynch hired 100 commercial bankers to work in regional offices around the country in cooperation with the firm's 14,000 brokers to provide counseling and loans to small businesses. By purchasing a cheap failed Florida savings and loan, Merrill Lynch can offer trust services in all states in the United States. Similarly, the Internet permits Boston Financial network, which has no branches for tellers to act as a bank, brokerage firm, bookkeeping, and bill-paying service for small businesses anywhere through a single Web site.[29]

Substitutability of Products   Financial products have commodity-like characteristics. It is hard to tell one ear of corn from another, and one savings account is similar to another, as is one whole life policy to another. A single provider rarely can corner a market at the expense of competitors, and all firms offering a service have an equal opportunity to succeed—or fail. If one financial service provider does not provide a service efficiently or does not serve a particular market segment, another firm can move in. For example, in the preceding section, Boston Financial Network, which provides business loans another financial services to firms over the Internet, started up because its chairman ran a small business for a while and could not get support from banks or brokerage firms. Similarly, Nordstrom has been able to provide cheaper consumer loans for its retail customers and check-cashing services.[30]

---

[28]See Lee and Cooperman (1989) for a summary of theoretical arguments for the reasons for conglomerate mergers.

[29]See Joseph Kahn. "Banking on the Unbanks." *The New York Times* (February 4, 1999), C1 and "Financial Services Coming to TV." *The Rocky Mountain News* (March 25, 1998), 1B, 5B.

[30]Ibid.

Perceived Profitability and Significant Decline in Traditional Profits   Many firms have entered new types of financial services businesses because they perceive it to be more profitable than their primary lines of business. An executive with JCPenney Company, a leading retailer with insurance and thrift subsidiaries, noted, "In general financial services are more profitable than retailing."[31] Sears also found entering the financial service arena to be profitable in the 1980s. Although many executives of financial services firms might quarrel with this thought, it has led several nonfinancial firms into the financial services business.

With a significant decline in traditional bank net interest margins, banks have also realized that they cannot depend on spread income for profits. As Arnold Danielson points out:

> Because of the declining importance of spread in income, traditional banking might be viewed as a modern day version of the railroads of the early 1900s. The railroads were once the dominant players in a transportation business that was exploding as travel and shipping needs grew, but the constraints of their iron rails kept them from keeping pace with automobiles, trucks, and airplanes. Being tied to traditional delivery systems, hampered by regulatory constraints, and the reduced need for deposit funded loans have created similarities for banks with the railroads of the early 20th century."[32]

He also notes that in the early 1990s banks and thrifts had very low growth in spread income. Although from 1995 to 1997, the annual increase in spread rose to 5.7 percent, during the first nine months of 1998, the annualized increase was only 3.3 percent, typical of the early 1990s. Thus, with this low growth if depository institutions continue to rely on spread income, they will suffer losses in their share of the overall financial services business. In contrast, the growth in bank noninterest revenue rose from a 4.4 percent annual growth rate between 1993 and 1995 to double-digit figures after 1995, reaching an annual growth rate of 16.1 percent in 1998. With growth in noninterest revenues rising at a faster rate than the growth of overhead, banks with significant noninterest revenues were profitable. Similarly, insurance firms in the last two decades of the 20th century have faced slower profit growth in a maturing industry and the need to diversify into areas with more rapid growth, such as mutual funds and annuity products.

Synergy   A final motivation for the move toward diversified financial services, espoused by firms that diversified by purchasing other firms, is a belief that the earnings of a diversified firm will exceed those of two or more firms operating separately and/or reduce the volatility of the earnings of the two individual firms. As a reporter for *The Wall Street Journal* put it in an article on diversified financial services firms in the 1980s," "With each acquisition, the word 'synergy' was used to the point of exhaustion."[33] Without synergy, of course, firm growth through diversification will not

---

[31]Steve Weiner and Hank Gilman. "Debate Grows on Retailers' Bank Services." *The Wall Street Journal* (May 18, 1984).

[32]See Danielson (1999), p. 15. Information in the next paragraph also comes from this article.

[33]See Hilder and Weiner (1985). In finance theory, a reduction of risk through diversification as a source of synergy is often not accepted, because stockholders can diversify their own portfolios. See Richard Booth. "Reducing Risk Doesn't Pay Off." *The Wall Street Journal* (March 15, 1999), A18, for a discussion of these arguments.

be valued by shareholders who can diversify their personal equity portfolios more cheaply and who recognize the high transaction costs incurred by diversifying corporations. Synergy has eluded some financial services firms and benefited others. In the preceding discussion, for instance, Merrill Lynch found synergies in offering loans and services to small businesses. Other firms, such as Sears, which attempted to offer a full range of financial services to its retail customers, did not find as much synergy in some cases, because customers did not necessarily wish to shop for clothes and goods and financial services at the same time, at least in the 1980s. A discussion of trends in financial service conglomerates and successful and less successful firms follows.

TRENDS IN FINANCIAL SERVICE CONGLOMERATES

Conglomerate Waves   Conglomerates seem to come in waves. For instance, for nonfinancial firms, Leonitades (1986) points out that there were several conglomerate waves including (1) a conglomerate wave from 1955 to 1968, when new conglomerates, fed by the expansion of the 1960s, "naively yet feverishly acquired firms in unrelated fields"; (2) a period of reevaluation from 1969 to 1976, in which time conglomerates were unprofitable during the recession of the mid-1970s; and (3) a third merger wave from 1977 to the early 1980s associated with the emergence of professional managers, the entry of more conservative firms, and a corporate repositioning and restructuring of many mature conglomerates. This stage included the divesting of unrelated subsidiaries, resulting in more focused inter-industry strategic groups, in contrast to the random diversification of the past.[34]

Similarly, financial conglomerates have come in waves with the emergence of a number of financial conglomerates in the late 1970s to mid 1980s, although some early financial conglomerates, such as Sears, began diversifying as early as 1911. The early 1990s is characterized as a time when many financial conglomerates divested or spun off subsidiaries that they had acquired in the 1980s. The reasons for these spin-offs included problems blending cultures, the failure of the stock market to reflect the full value of individual businesses, and the need to refocus on a firm's central lines of business. In the 1990s, new financial conglomerates such as Travelers Group, BankAmerica-Nationsbank, and DeutscheBank-Bankers Trust have emerged. Examples of successful and less successful financial conglomerates are discussed in the following section.[35]

SOME FIRMS ARE SUCCESSFUL, OTHERS ARE NOT: EXAMPLES

Although many financial services firms have continued to be successful in their diversification activities, such as the Travelers Group, Prudential, and Merrill Lynch, at times these firms have navigated rocky roads attempting to manage and integrate diverse acquisitions. Similarly, other firms, such as Sears, General Electric Financial Services (GEFS), and Merrill Lynch have found it worthwhile to divest financial

---

[34]This summary comes from Lee and Cooperman (1989), 45. See Leonitades (1986).
[35]Ibid.

service firms in some areas. The experiences of Sears, GEFS, Merrill Lynch, and Prudential are briefly summarized in the following sections.

Sears Sears entered the financial services business as early as 1911 by setting up a consumer finance subsidiary to provide credit to its customers. In 1931, Allstate was formed to market auto insurance to Sears customers, and in 1959 Sears formed a commercial real estate development and management firm. In the 1970s Sears also purchased a mortgage company and savings and loan. In 1981 Sears purchased a major real estate brokerage firm, Coldwell Banker, and a major securities brokerage firm, Dean Witter Reynolds. Sears intended to provide full-financial services within its retail stores, providing synergies in terms of cross-selling products with one-stop financial and retail shopping for its customers. Financial service revenues would also diversify the firm's profits, which was appealing because of stagnant retailing profits in the 1970s.

Unfortunately, by 1985, Sears found its financial centers offering insurance, brokerage, and real estate services did not generate as much business and profit as expected. Dean Witter suffered large operating losses and the exit of talented brokers. Also, one-stop financial shopping failed to appeal to customers. Customers in the 1980s appeared to reject the idea of purchasing socks, mutual funds, and banking products in the same location, despite the fact that Dean Witter at the time had about 6,600 brokers on its payroll, making it the second largest securities firm, next to Merrill Lynch, in terms of number of brokers. When Dean Witter management cut costs, they were made somewhat indiscriminately, further hurting morale at Dean Witter. Despite the poor performance of Dean Witter, performance for Allstate and Coldwell Banker was good relative to the industry. In 1984, Sears earned 57 percent of its income from retailing, 42 percent from Allstate Insurance, 5 percent from Coldwell Banker Real Estate, and had losses at Dean Witter and its Sears World Trade Center building.[36]

Despite much criticism, Sears introduced its Discover Card in 1985; it was marketed nationally by 1986. Sears had the informational advantage of having names, addresses, and credit histories of over 60 million customers with a Sears credit card, 28 million of whom were active users, to target its new credit card to. It offered favorable terms of no fee for two years for its card, compared with higher fees offered by Visa, MasterCard, and American Express. Sears also offered rebated of up to 1 percent on a customer's annual credit balance. It also undercut the fees competitors charged merchants to settle credit card transactions to get merchants to accept its card. With the card Sears hoped to be able to cross-sell products from Dean Witter and Sears Savings Bank by offering a Family Savings Account with the savings bank, which collected deposits by mail. Sears also offered tiered interest rates with larger deposits and individual retirement accounts to encourage customers to entrust their checks to the U.S. Postal Service.

To the surprise of analysts, Sears' Discover Card became quite a success, after initial losses in 1985 and 1986. By 1992, a healthy $239 million profit was earned, and Discover had more than 40 million cardholders, making Sears the second largest credit card issuer (behind Visa) at that time. Sears also planned on synergies with its Coldwell Banker and Dean Witter division by having mortgages on homes financed

[36]See Martin, Kensinger, and Gillan (1996); Williams (1985); and Crawford and Sihler (1994), Discover Card, Case 5.

by Sears, insured by private mortgage insurance, and packaged for resale by Dean Witter. However, when real estate and mortgage markets became troubled in the late 1980s and early 1990s, plans to be involved in more than 25 percent of all home sales and mortgages for those homes in the country failed to materialize. Sears' core merchandising business continued to deteriorate during this period as well.[37]

By 1989 several of its large institutional shareholders. including the California Public Employees Retirement System (CALPERS), expressed great concern over Sears' performance. Sears' stock price fell significantly in 1990. Pressure from institutional investors continued, and in 1992, Sears management announced a major restructuring, which involved selling Coldwell Banker spinning off 20 percent of Dean Witter and 20 percent of Allstate, and Sears refocusing on its core retail businesses, carried out in 1993. Later other interests in Allstate were spun off as a tax-free dividend in 1994, and in 1997 Morgan Stanley purchased Dean Witter/Discover. The stock price of Sears responded favorably to the spinoffs of its financial services firms. With considerable restructuring and a redefining of its retail business, Sears' stock price improved as well in the mid-1990s, although it faced some problems in 1998 and 1999, with a fall in retail profits.[38]

In recent years, banks such as Wells Fargo have placed financial service kiosks in supermarkets with considerable success, suggesting that customers in the 1990s accept doing banking and purchasing mutual funds while shopping for dinner. However, in the 1980s, this did not seem to be the case, when customers sent messages that they did not want one-stop financial shopping, preferring to shop around for financial services and products before making purchases. However, just as home banking was not successful in the 1980s but is becoming more successful in the 1990s for certain market segments, customer perceptions may change over time.

General Electric Financial Services, Inc. GEFS is an example of a very successful diversified financial services firm. As early as 1989, GEFS, a subsidiary of General Electric (GE) Company, was a global diversified financial services firm with $75 billion in assets and operations in over 17 different financial services businesses. In addition to serving as the captive finance company for GE to assist the customers of GE and other retail firms in financing purchases, it was active in other types of commercial finance activities, including leasing and equipment sales financing, and in accounts receivables financing. In 1998 GEFS purchased the First Factors Corporation, also entering the U.S. factoring commercial finance business. GEFS also has considerable property and casualty and reinsurance subsidiaries.

In 1985, GEFS acquired Kidder Peabody to provide synergies in terms of diversification, and to help GEFS with its financing and securitization of the loans that its finance subsidiaries made. In turn, GEFS provided a well-established customer base and financial strength for Kidder's investment banking business and future growth. Despite the potential synergies, the two firms had quite different cultures. GEFS had the more conservative, transaction-based culture of finance and insurance companies, whereas Kidder had the more deal-based, innovative, superstar, performance-based culture of an investment bank. Similarly, Kidder was involved in many

---

[37]Ibid.

[38]Ibid. Other sources on Sears include Haggerty (1984); Hilder and Weiner (1985); Williams (1985); Glynn (1985); Siconolfi (1991); Flynn, et al. (1992); Patterson and Schwadel (1992); and Schwartz (1985); Key (1985); Greising (1989); Ellis (1986); Schmeitzer (1993); Roosevelt (1992); Kantro (1992); and Steinmetz (1993).

activities, such as trading and deal-making, that had large potential returns and losses, which could not be readily controlled or observed by GEFS.

In 1986, Kidder suffered a scandal when one of its superstars was indicted in the Ivan Boesky insider-trading scandal, costing GEFS $25.3 million in fines to the SEC. With the 1987 stock market crash, Kidder also suffered losses. In response, GEFS exerted more cost controls over Kidder Peabody, including cutting over 1,500 jobs, resulting in management battles between Kidder and GEFS. This ultimately led to the resignation of Kidder's chief executive officer and other senior managers. Investment banking profits continued to be low in the early 1990s, and trading income supplemented declines in underwriting income. In 1994, Kidder suffered huge trading losses by a rogue trader, resulting in the collapse of the firm. GE was forced to sell most of Kidder's assets to Paine Webber in 1994 for $670 million in exchange for stock. Ironically, GE eventually made a larger return on its original investment in Kidder, with a gains on its holdings of Paine Webber stock of $1.33 billion in 1998. GEFS's difficulties with its Kidder Peabody acquisition demonstrates some of the problems that diverse financial services firms have in controlling and managing acquisitions of an entirely different culture from the acquiring firm.[39]

Merrill Lynch and Company   In the early 1970s Merrill Lynch's (ML's) chairman, Donald Regan, announced a plan to transform ML into, as *Business Week* termed it, a "womb to tomb" financial services firm.[40] In 1977, ML diversified by initiating the first Cash Management Account (CMA) , i.e., a money market fund from which checks could be written, offered through its brokerage subsidiary. By the early 1990s, ML had a range of mutual funds with assets managed by its subsidiaries. In 1979, ML formed Merrill Lynch Realty, Inc. to acquire local real estate agencies, particularly in the rapidly growing Sun Belt. By the end of 1986, ML Realty had 500 residential real estate offices. By late 1986, however, ML officials realized that the synergy expected from adding real estate to its product offerings had not materialized. By 1989 ML sold all its remaining interests in ML Realty. ML introduced insurance to its range of services in the mid-1970s with the acquisition of Family Life Insurance Company and two additional insurance firms. (The first was sold later in 1991.) Merrill Lynch Life Insurance Company was founded in 1986 to develop life and annuity products to be marketed exclusively to ML clients.[41]

In 1985, ML unveiled the first of its retail "financial centers" in downtown Manhattan. The center was staffed with financial consultants (no longer called brokers) and on-site specialists in taxation, insurance, and other aspects of personal finance, with the objective of providing clients with a wide range of financial services that could be purchased from ML. Costs were reduced by consolidating offices in different areas, with 500 offices located throughout the world by the early 1990s. Personnel costs were reduced by hiring sales assistants to serve small-account customers.

---

[39]See Crawford and Sihler (1994), Case 6: General Electric Financial Services, Inc. for an excellent case on GEFS and the its history acquiring Kidder Peabody. Also see Anita Rahhavan and Patrick McGeehan. "GE Scores Big With Kidder $3\frac{1}{2}$ Years After." *The Wall Street Journal* (May 14, 1998), C21.

[40]See "How They Manage the New Financial Conglomerates." *Business Week* (December 20, 1982), 50.

[41]See Merrill Lynch Annual Report, 1988, 37; Steve Swartz. "Merrill Lynch Real Estate Line Will Go Public." *The Wall Street Journal* (December 23, 1986), 2; and Merrill Lynch (1991), Form 10-K. Information from this section comes from these sources.

In 1991 alone, assets in individual client accounts rose almost 20 percent and represented about 2.5 percent of total household financial assets in the United States. ML's retail services were also enhanced by two nonbank banks, Merrill Lynch Bank and Trust in New Jersey and Merrill Lynch National Financial in Utah, which sell certificates of deposit (CDs), issue Visa cards, and offer consumer loans. Through Merrill Lynch Trust Company, personal trust services are offered throughout the United States.

In 1984 ML acquired the firm Becker Paribus to enhance its investment banking activities and became a major commercial paper dealer and among the largest underwriters of municipal and corporate bonds throughout the 1980s. ML also developed ties abroad to pursue its activities to Europe and Asia. ML is involved in international banking through its Merrill Lynch International Banks located in London, Geneva, Singapore, and other main financial centers.

On the domestic front, ML launched efforts to attract commercial customers from its bank competitors. In the late 1980s, ML began an aggressive campaign to attract more small business borrowers. By 1992, ML had loaned more than $500 million to small businesses and was attracting their deposits to its working capital management accounts. In the later 1990s with a surge in small businesses, ML provided a variety of consulting and banking services to small firms.[42]

Thus, ML has many strengths, including a major geographic presence with its worldwide offices, a huge retail customer base, cash management accounts with check writing privileges, its own nonbank banks, and international banking operations. The role of ML in investment banking strengthens its image in wholesale financial services. If the financial modernization bill passes, ML's relationships with corporate customers will make it a fierce competitor for their banking business. ML's training programs and incentive compensation schemes have developed an effective and skilled workforce. ML has lowered its consultant turnover rate and attempted to reduce its high level of operating costs. ML is also very careful in its recruiting policies and training to maintain its culture throughout the firm with a focus on the client, responsibility for the individual, teamwork, responsible citizenship, and integrity. As Daniel P. Tully, Chairman and CEO of ML in 1996 notes, "If you are a gunslinger, you are going to work somewhere else."[43] ML also adopted a very sophisticated, time-consuming career and succession planning system. Individuals who are too political and ambitious and who can only think of their own responsibilities under this system fall by the wayside. Consequently, ML has had fewer cultural problems in its investment banking division and in integrating different types of firms.

Prudential Insurance Company of America Prudential Insurance Company of America (Pru), one of the nation's largest life insurers has been operating since 1875. In 1981, Pru sent shock waves through the financial community with its purchase of the Bache Group, Inc., the nation's sixth largest securities firm. Negotiations lasted only 13 days, astonishing observers of the usually conservative insurer. Although

---

[42]See Lynn W. Adams. "Merrill Lynch Beckoning Bank Customers." *American Banker* (September 9, 1992), 10; and Randall Smith and Michael Siconolfi. "Merrill Quietly Folds a Big Lending Operation." *The Wall Street Journal* (March 31, 1993), C1, C13. Also see Taub (1986); and Steve Swartz and Laurie P. Cohen. "Merrill Lynch Will Sell Units in Real Estate." *The Wall Street Journal* (September 30, 1986), 3–4.

[43]See Tully (1996), p. 269; also see Komansky (1996). These chapters from the book *The New Financiers* provide excellent insights from executives of Merrill Lynch.

Bache was in some turmoil, Pru's management was optimistic that Bache's problems were past and believed the acquisition was an ideal way to enter the brokerage, mutual fund, and underwriting business.[44]

Performance of Bache　　　Unfortunately, in the 1980s and early 1990's the Bache acquisition failed to live up to the expectations of Pru's management. In 1984, the renamed securities firm, Prudential Bache, had one of the largest losses for a securities firm ever, exceeding $110 million. The firm became marginally profitable in the mid 1980s but suffered large losses in 1987 with the stock market crash. One of Bache's major problems was its low productivity, with, for instance, commissions and fees per employee nearly $15,000 less at Bache than at other leading brokers. New managers brought in unfortunately initially increased salaries even more and made costly cosmetic changes to the firm's offices. Undaunted, however, Pru's management decided to expand its securities business in 1989 by purchasing the brokerage segment of Thomson McKinnon, acquiring an additional 158 retail offices and 2,000 brokers. In 1989 Bache lost about $50 million, and finally in March 1990, after most other brokerage firms had laid off employees, layoffs were announced.

Rocked by class action lawsuits resulting against security brokers for not informing investors fully about the risks entailed with limited commercial real estate partnerships and a failed entry into investment banking, in 1991 Bache's CEO was replaced and its name was changed to Prudential Securities. Although performance improved in 1992, it was not attributed to the desired synergy and cross-selling. In 1990 Pru was forced to support Bache by transferring capital from the parent organization to increase Bache's equity capital. Finally, most investment banking activities were discontinued. Pru absorbed a few of the services into its Prudential Asset Management Group and Company, subsidiaries that offer investment operations, products, and services to commercial customers. Services range from asset management to loan originations to the purchase and management of private placements. As early as 1991, these operations were serving more than 800 institutional clients. Pru also owns a limited-service bank called Prudential Bank and Trust Company with services focused on individuals versus business customers. The performance of Prudential Securities improved with the bull market of the late 1990s.[45]

Insurance Company Performance　　　During the 1980s, like other life insurers, Pru faced problems, but it introduced the industry's first combination variable/universal life policy in 1985. Although popular with customers, this and other nontraditional products were less profitable than whole life policies, squeezing the firm's overall margin. Also problems plagued Pru's P/L subsidiary, PRUPAC, and the firm's reinsurance subsidiary, Pru Re, had significant losses through the mid-1980s. The original strategic plan at the time of the Bache acquisition called for brokers and insurance agents to work side by side, sharing client lists to increase sales. By the early 1990s, however, that desired synergy continued to be elusive. Although the insurance company manages almost $50 billion for customers, insurance agents in

---

[44]See Carol J. Loomis. "The Fight for Financial Turf." *Fortune* 104 (December 28, 1981), 55.
[45]See Moore (1983). The New York Stock Exchange fined Bache $400,000 for the incident, the largest fine ever for a member firm. See "New Bache Chief Pushes a Host of Changes, Including New Name, to Lift Firm's Image." *The Wall Street Journal* (October 29, 1982).

1991 referred only enough brokerage activity to the securities firm to generate $25 million in commissions.

Pru's insurance subsidiaries also suffered from scandals and large class action settlements. In March 1998, Prudential reported a 43.4 percent drop in profits as the result of depressed life insurance sales and the provision of $1.6 billion set aside to pay policyholders who contended that they were deceived by being sold insurance that they did not need. Analysts reported that the decline in Pru's life insurance sales was related to a fall in its reputation as the result of negative publicity surrounding large lawsuits.[46]

Further Diversification and Prospects for the Future   Since the move to diversification began, Pru has experienced frequent restructuring. Pru also acquired a variety of new diverse subsidiaries, including a "sick thrift" in 1989, a farm management firm, investment management firms, a home mortgage subsidiary, and a real estate brokerage. However, Arthur Ryan, Pru's CEO, hired in 1994 to try to turn the company around, attempted to focus the company more on its core insurance and investment products businesses. Consequently, he sold several holdings, including a mortgage company, a reinsurer, and billions of dollars worth of real estate holdings. In response to changes, profits rose in 1996, before problems occurred in 1997 and 1998, with a fall in policy sales and troubled health insurance units.[47]

Although Pru has diversified into securities brokerage, mutual funds, asset and investment management, banking through its thrifts, real estate investment and development, and other activities, its huge insurance business continues to dominate. In 1998, it ranked second in life and health insurance with a 5.1 percent share of the market and 28th in property and casualty insurance with .7 percent share of the market. At the end of 1996, premiums and other insurance-related income consisted of 69 percent of Pru's revenues, net investment income 29 percent, and other less than 2 percent.[48]

Pru's size and special features make it a major force in the financial markets, despite recent problems. Because of the insurance subsidiary's huge asset portfolio, the firm has substantial expertise in portfolio management, including real estate

---

[46]Michael Siconolfi and William Power. "Prudential Securities Seeks New Identity But Seems to Be Revisiting '80s Pitfalls." *The Wall Street Journal* (January 28, 1992), C1, C14; Chuck Hawkins. "The Mess at Pru-Bache." *Business Week* (March 4, 1991), 66–72; Matthew Winkler and William Power. "Gap Between Rich and Poor Brokerage Firms Widen." *The Wall Street Journal* (January 24, 1990), C1, C17; Hilder and Weiner (1985); William Power. "Wall Street Wields Ax Again as Woes Deepen." *The Wall Street Journal* (January 29, 1990), C1, C17; and Michael Siconolfi. "Prudential-Bache Plans to Eliminate Hundreds of Jobs." *The Wall Street Journal* (March 29, 1990), A4.

[47]See Paulette Thomas. "Prudential Cleared to Buy Sick Thrift." *The Wall Street Journal* (August 8, 1989), A3; The Prudential 1991 Annual Report; Larry Light. "How Much Prudence Is Good for Prudential?" *Business Week* (July 13, 1992), 124–126; Melody Petersen. "Prudential's Leader Knows His Way Around in New Jersey." *The New York Times* (February 13, 1998), C1, C3; and Joseph B. Treaster. "Prudential Profit Falls 43 percent on Life Insurance Problems." *The New York Times* (March 3, 1998), C2; Leslie Scism. "After the Fall: Prudential's Cleanup in Wake of Scandals Hurts Insurance Sales." *The Wall Street Journal* (November 17, 1997), A1, A6.

[48]See Joseph B. Treaster. "A $12 Billion Carrot for Prudential Policyholders." *The New York Times* (February 13, 1998), A1, C3.

development. Pru has established relationships with many major corporations, whose bonds it holds in private placements. The firm also enjoys relative freedom from geographic restrictions. In addition Pru has made the commitment to stick with a diversified strategy for the long haul and to build on even its most troubled acquisitions. Although in the past, Pru believed that its mutual form of organization gave it an edge over its competitors, in 1998 Pru's managers decided to convert the firm to a publicly owned company to gain greater access to capital. Similar to other large mutual insurers undergoing conversions to stock ownership in 1998, management felt that the cash infusion that would be gained with such a conversion would allow it to buy new growth and strength.[49]

MANAGERIAL IMPLICATIONS OF DIVERSIFIED FINANCIAL SERVICES FIRMS

The case histories for GEFS, Sears, ML, and Pru indicate that synergies in financial services may be easier to promise than achieve, at least in the 1980s. Managing diversified financial firms is challenging, especially when the business cultures of the combined firms ae not compatible. All four of the firms profiled have had problems, often selling or spinning off many of their acquisitions in later years. Each suffered serious financial and managerial setbacks on the path to diversification. Integrating and cross-selling services has at times been elusive. Without such integration, synergy which depends on a unified operating plan may not be realized. And because diversification without synergy is not valued by shareholders, the equity markets often react positively to some announced diversitures, such as the sale of Dean Witter by Sears or Kidder Peabody by GE. Recently, a number of nonfinancial firms have had initial public offerings to spin off diverse segments as separate firms. They did this based on the rationale that financial analysts are unable to determine the true value of a diversified firm, which results in a depression of their stock prices.[50]

The large size of a firm also does not always appear to be synonymous with efficiency, and larger firms may have more difficulty exerting control over different divisions, resulting in scandals for brokers, such as Pru and GE experienced. Without adequate risk management, the benefits of diversification in terms of smoothing earnings and reducing risk can be lost.

Likewise, the premise that customers prefer diversified financial service firms in terms of convenient, one-stop shopping can also be called to question. Sears in the 1980s learned that customers did not necessarily want to take care of all of their financial needs with one firm, preferring to shop around versus placing their money with one institution. The atmosphere they prefer for financial service dealings may be more staunch and conservative than that of a retail establishment, although this preference may be changing, as the popularity of bank branches in grocery stores is growing.

---

[49]Ibid and Leslie Scism. "Prudential's Plan to Go Public Reflects Industry Trend: More Mutual Life Insurers Need to Seek Outside Capital to Stay Competitive." *The Wall Street Journal* (February 18, 1998), B4.

[50]Martin, Kensinger, and Gillan (1996) find evidence of positive wealth effects for Sears stockholders in response to Sears' spinoff of Dean Witter. Also, see Crawford and Sihler (1997) General Electric Financial Services Inc., Case 6, for a discussion of this issue.

Thus, institutional value may be created from careful identification of market opportunities through careful identification of market opportunities; analysis of these opportunities, including assessments of risk and the expected impact on financial targets; and skillful execution, including the use of available risk-management tools. These principles hold regardless of the type, size, and location of the institution or its historical origins. In fact, financial deregulation has not changed the determinants of value at all; it has merely broadened the range of opportunities available to individual firms. Although diversified financial firms were not as a whole generally as successful as some other firms in the 1980s, some analysts think that market conditions are now right for these financial megaplayers, as discussed in the following section.

The Rationale for the Financial Megaplayers in the 21st Century

In 1986, four years after having trumpeted the rise of diversified financial services firms, *Business Week* flatly stated, ". . . the financial supermarket has been a conspicuous bust . . . the supermarket's advent was catalyzed not by the arguments of think-tank strategists but by such basic human emotions as insecurity, lust, and greed."[51] Similarly, in the late 1990s with new mergers creating financial megaplayers, reviews for diversified financial service firms are mixed.

For instance, in 1997, following Traveler Group's purchase of Salomon Brothers, Lenny Mendonca and Greg Wilson, partners at McKinsey & Co, a well-known consulting firm, published an article in *The Wall Street Journal* titled "Financial Megaplayers' Time Is Here."

In this article they point out economic rationale for mega financial service firms in the late 1990s, as well as the benefits to customers in terms of lower cost and higher quality financial products. Some of the economic reasons for the mega-mergers of the late 1990s they include are:[52]

1. The high valuation of large financial service companies such as Travelers, makes it cheaper to use stock to acquire another company "to get high-value customers, a choice distribution network, and market-tested skills rather than building these capabilities over time." In other words, more productive firms can purchase less productive and whip them into shape.
2. There is enormous potential for efficiency improvements with consolidation and the ability to enter new markets and geographic regions (because of relaxed regulations). Productivity for large firms, such as large banks, has improved by more than 13 percent as a result of a consolidation process.
3. Firms can have excess capital to do acquisitions. For instance, they suggest that $46 billion in excess capital for the banking industry at the end of 1996 would translate to over $1 trillion in future acquisitions.
4. With mergers across industry lines, new fee income can be gained from cross-selling products. For example, Fleet's acquisition of Quick & Reilly allows cross-selling between its bank and brokerage units; and Travelers' acquisition of Salomon brothers allows greater fee income for the firm;
5. Although the size of new mega-financial firms makes these new firms more complex and less nimble, the cost-benefit balance favors strong, skilled players. Only

---

[51]See Ford (1982) and Anthony Bianco. "How a Financial Supermarket Was Born." *Business Week* (December 23, 1985), 10.
[52]See Mendonca and Wilson (1997).

very large players can make enormous but necessary investments to increase revenues while managing costs without destroying the market valuation of their stock. For instance, large players can afford the major advertising and promotion needed to develop a "truly national brand." Also, they can afford the high costs of technology, such as more than $1 billion paid each year by the top 10 banks today. With millions of customers, these costs can be spread-out over a larger customer base.

Similarly, Arnold Danielson, a consultant at Danielson Association Inc., argues that size has become a great competitive advantage for banks and other financial service firms. He points out that BHCs over $50 billion in 1998 had a net operating expense-to-asset ratio of .64 percent compared with 2.22 percent for banks between $100 billion and $2 billion. They also generated 48 percent of their revenues from noninterest revenues, versus 19 percent for banks between $100 billion and $2 billion, and achieved a mean ROE of 17.29 percent versus 13.29 percent. He also points out that if large banks do not diversify, they will have difficulties competing with the largest "nonbanks," including AIG, GE Capital, and Morgan Stanley. Mega-financial services also have a comparative advantage by having more competitive prices and services and delivering services nationwide through new delivery systems, such as computer/Internet banking. In the information age, size and diversity may be more beneficial than in the past.[53]

A Brief Note about Pricing and Earnings Dilution with Financial Institution Mergers

Although generally a number of different pricing techniques are used for valuing mergers, often typical benchmark estimates are used based on pricing multiples including market value-to-book value (market/book) ratios and market price-to-earnings (price/earnings or P/E) ratios. For example, if a target has earnings of $500,000 and the typical P/E ratio for similar targets is 3, a starting valuation point would be 3 × $500,000 = $1,500,000. Similarly, if a target had a book value of equity of $750,000, and the typical Market to Book ratio was 2, a starting valuation using this method would be also 2 × $750,000 = $1,500,000. The premium percentage that is paid over book value could be calculated as the (market price/book value) − 1. In this case, with a market value of $1,500,000 and a book/value of $750,000, this premium would be (1,500/750) − 1, which equals 1 or a 100 percent premium. The larger the premium paid, the more difficult it will be for the acquirer to earn a return on the investment to justify the purchase price and the risk involved with the acquisition. The average merger premium, however, tends to follow trends. During periods when targets are in great demand, merger premiums can be quite high, such as from 1994 to 1997 for banks, when massive consolidation occurred with the advent of interstate branching, compared with the low multiples in the early 1990s when banks suffered low profits.

If a stock swap is used, whereby the target's shareholders receive shares in the acquiring firm as payment, the exchange ratio is calculated as the market price per share of the target firm/market price per share of the acquirer. For instance, in the previous example, if the market price for the target was $1,500,000 and the target had 100,000 shares, its market price per share would be $15. If the share price for

---

[53]See Danielson (1999).

the acquirer was also $15, then the exchange ratio would be 1 share of the acquirer for 1 share of the target.[54]

For diversified financial firms, price multiples used for valuations are often calculated by taking a weighted average of price multiples for a firm's different businesses. For instance, if a firm had 50 percent of its earnings from insurance, 25 percent from securities activities, 25 percent from finance company operations, and the respective market to book ratios for the three different industries were hypothetically 1.10, 1.46, and 1.30, the weighted average market to book ratio would be (.50) 1.10 + (.25)1.46 + (.25) 1.30 = 1.24, which could be used.[55]

Many financial institutions calculate expected earnings dilution measures as well. Earnings per share (EPS) dilution is calculated as follows:

$$\text{EPS dilution} = \frac{\text{EPS of acquirer} - \text{Expected EPS with consolidation}}{\text{EPS of acquirer}}$$

For example, if the acquirer has an expected EPS of $10 and the expected EPS with the consolidation is $8, then the earnings dilution expected is as follows:

$$\text{EPS dilution} = (\$10 - \$8) / \$10 = -.20 \text{ or } -20\% \text{ earnings dilution.}$$

As a rule of thumb, EPS dilution should not be greater than 5 percent to get a reasonable return on an acquisition.[56]

Pooling vs. Purchase Accounting

In April 1999, the Financial Standards Accounting Board ruled that companies in the future would no longer be allowed to use the favorable "pooling of interests" accounting method. This change was expected to result in a surge of mergers to take advantage of pooling.[57]

---

[54]See Koch (1995) for a more detailed discussion of bank merger premiums and earnings dilution. The average acquisition premium for bank/thrifts changes with the supply and demand for targets, as well as market conditions. In the 1970s and 1980s, with a seller's market, acquired banks had large premiums. From 1992 to 1993, the market was more of a buyer's market, with premiums declining since many of the best deals were taken. After 1994, premiums rose again with greater demand for targets. For instance, in 1997, bank stocks sold for about 12 times their earnings, which was much less than the 18 times its earnings that the average bank target was getting. See Saul Hansell. "Merger-Hungry Banks Find the Pickings Slim." *The New York Times* (January 2, 1997), C22.

[55]See Crawford and Sihler (1994), Primerica Corporation, Case 12 for an illustration of using a weighted average price/earnings ratio to value a diversified financial firm.

[56]See McCoy, Frieder, and Hedges (1994) and Koch (1995). Some studies find the average workout time for mergers in 1986 to 1990 to eliminate earnings dilution to be quite long, often greater than 20 years based on a 10 percent growth rate in net income, suggesting overpayment The average workout time for Bank One was about 10 years. High expected growth rates in earnings for the consolidated firm are needed to prevent such dilution. At times banks are willing to pay large premiums to gain access to strategic options.

[57]Under the pooling method, when two companies merge they simply add their balance sheets together line by line, making it difficult for investors to see the premium paid for assets acquired. With purchase accounting, the acquired company is treated as an investment asset with any premium paid over a target's value shown as goodwill which must be expensed (amortized) over several years.

SUMMARY

This chapter discusses finance companies and diversified financial service firms. Finance companies are diverse financial institutions grouped together under one industry classification. They share an emphasis on consumer and business lending, and they differ from depositories because they lack deposits as a source of funds. The industry was historically grouped into consumer and commercial finance companies, along with special function firms, but these distinctions are now blurred. Many firms that started out as finance companies are now diversified financial service firms, such as Travelers Group, American Express, and GEFS. Other diversified financial firms started out as banks or as securities firms or insurance firms, such as Merrill Lynch and Prudential Insurance Company.

Finance companies make loans like banks but finance these loans through borrowings versus deposits. Finance companies also take on a more risky group of borrowers than banks, and asset management includes managing this greater default risk. Finance companies have increasingly moved into securitization of all types of loans which increases their managerial flexibility and competitiveness with banks and other financial institutions.

The final sections of the chapter discuss the economic rationale for diversified financial firms and provides case histories of four. These firms faced difficulties developing synergies to create value for stockholders. Similarly, analysts often fail to identify the value of diversified divisions, resulting in depressed stock prices for these firms. As a consequence, many of the firms that diversified in the 1980s have divested many of their acquisitions to improve their stock prices and refocus on core businesses. Trying to integrate diverse cultures also created management problems for these firms. In the information age of the 1990s, with more liberal regulations, changes in delivery systems, and greater opportunities to create synergies, diversified financial institutions may have greater opportunities to create synergies and value than they had in the past. Some analysts point out that it may be essential for financial institutions to become megaplayers to have the economic backing to provide innovative services through technology, to create national brands to compete and to provide low-cost, high-quality products to consumers.

The valuation of acquisitions is complex, but often price earnings or market-to-book multiples are used based on the price paid for similar acquisitions. For diversified targets, weighted average of price earnings multiples are often used based on the percentage of earnings of each of the target's businesses. The premium paid over book value is equal to the market price divided by the target firm's book value minus 1. The higher this premium, the more difficult it will be to generate returns to cover the cost and risk of the acquisition. Earnings dilution measures are also often estimated as the expected earnings of an acquirer less the expected earnings of the consolidated firm as a percentage of the expected earnings of the acquirer. As a rule of thumb, if the earnings dilution is greater than 5 percent, an acquirer should be wary. The greater the earnings dilution and the higher the market-to-book premium, the longer it will take to reap benefits from the acquisition.

Recommended Cases

Harvard Business School (Case 9–292–089): MNC Financial: The Credit Card Business: This case provides an excellent overview of the credit card business, the credit card securitization process, and Maryland National Bank's initial public offering for MBNA, a specialized credit card bank.

Darden School, University of Virginia:

1. Primerica Corporation, Case 12 in Crawford and Sihler (1994). This case provides an excellent understanding of the development of a diversified financial service firm, the predecessor of Travelers Group. It also goes through the valuation process for such a firm, and strategic considerations.

2. General Electric Financial Services Inc. (GEFS), Case 6 in Crawford and Sihler (1994). This case looks at GEFS as a diversified financial service firm and its problems integrating Kidder Peabody into its corporate culture.

3. Discover Card, Case 5 in Crawford and Sihler (1994). This case looks at Sears' financial service businesses and its strategy in introducing its Discover Card to enter the consumer finance business.

Questions

1. What are the major types of finance companies and what types of loans do they make? Give some examples of each. What is the difference between a captive and an independent firm?

2. How are finance companies different and similar from depository institutions in their operations? Which type of institution has more interest rate risk? Default risk? Why do finance companies hold more capital than depository institutions?

3. What advantages does securitization provide for finance companies? Describe how securitization is used by credit card banks and by mortgage banks.

4. Discuss recent trends in the types of loans (receivables) that finance companies hold. Also discuss trends in the types of liabilities of finance companies between 1991 and 1998. Why do you think the mix of assets and liabilities has changed so much? Why have holdings of second mortgages and home equity loans increased?

5. How does the income statement for a finance company differ from that of a commercial bank? Explain why the average interest rate spread and return on equity of a large finance company typically higher than that of a commercial bank.

6. How are finance companies regulated? What was the impact of low ceilings on consumer loan rates established by some states in the 1960s and 1970s? What was the effect on finance companies of more lenient bankruptcy laws?

7. Explain how the financial analysis of finance companies resembles that of depository institutions. How is it different? What sources of industry performance information are available for finance companies?

8. Briefly discuss the five major events in 1998 that radically changed the environment for financial institutions in 1998. Explain how these events might favor megamergers between financial institutions.

9. How many different types of financial services is the Travelers Group involved in (see Figure 13.3)? Discuss advantages that Travelers-Citicorp might have by being involved in a variety of financial services. What disadvantages might Travelers have with this wide a degree of diversification?

10. Explain some of the theoretical and practical reasons for the development of financial conglomerates discussed in the chapter. Which explanations do you agree with most?

11. What stages occurred for nonfinancial conglomerates in terms of conglomerate waves in the 1970s to 1980s, as suggested by Leonitades (1986)? Do similar types of wave seem to have occurred for financial conglomerates? Explain.

12. Compare and contrast the diversification strategies used by GEFS, Sears, Prudential, and Merrill Lynch. Explain the similarities and differences in their responses to problems that occurred and how they implemented their diversification strategies. Which firms seemed more successful in their diversification?

13. Explain some of the advantages and disadvantages of diversification using GEFS, Sears, Prudential, and Merrill Lynch as examples. Why is diversification without synergy of little or no value to shareholders?

14. In the 21st century, do you expect a larger or smaller proportion of financial services delivered by diversified firms? Explain why or why not. What factors encouraged a greater number of diversification by financial institutions in the late 1990s?

15. Briefly discuss how targets can be valued using P/E or market-to-book value ratios. How is the percentage premium paid calculated? What is earnings dilution, and how is it calculated? Why is an estimation of expected earnings dilution so important?

Problems

1. As a financial analyst for Euphoria Securities, Phil and Roz Lerner ask you to do a Dupont financial analysis for the trends in the mortgage banking firm shown in Table P13.1. Look at changes in the firm's balance sheet to explain why profits improved in the latest year. Discuss differences in this mortgage bank's balance sheet and income statement compared to commercial banks. How do these differences reflect differences in the operations of a finance company compared to a bank?

2. Ann and Al Fox of Fox Famous Funds ask you to do a trend financial analysis for the Travelers Group's consolidated financial statements shown in Table P13.2. Explain precisely why the ROE went down in 1997. From what sources does the Travelers Group get most of its revenues? Where do most of its expenses come from? Does Travelers appear to benefit from its diversification?

3. Jerry and Rae Blumberg of Blumberg Boca Securities ask you to do a trend financial analysis for Ford Motor Credit shown in Table P13.3. Explain reasons for changes in Ford Motor Credit's performance in 1995 and 1996. How does your analysis differ from the analysis for a depository information? What additional information would you like to have?

4. MegaBank is thinking about acquiring Beta Bank. Mergers with similar banks have had a market to book ratio of 2.0. If Beta Bank has a book value of equity of $2 million, what would be its value based on this market to book ratio? What would be the premium that MegaBank would pay if it paid this amount? If consolidated EPS is expected to be $10 and Megabank's expected earnings is $9, what would be the earnings dilution with the merger?

Table P13.1 ◆ Financial Statements for Countrywide Credit Industries, Inc.

Consolidated Income Statement (thous)	1997	% Revs.	1996	% Revs.
Loan Origination Fees	193,079	17.36%	199,724	23.20%
Gain on Sale of loans, net of commt. fees	247,450	22.24%	92,341	10.73%
Loan Production Revenue	440,529	39.60%	292,065	33.93%
Interest Earned	350,263	31.49%	308,449	35.84%
Interest Charges	(316,205)	−28.42%	(281,573)	−32.71%
Net Interest Income	33,558	3.02%	26,876	3.12%
Total Servicing Income	773,715	69.55%	620,835	72.13%
Loan Amortization, net of serv. hedge gain	(101,380)	−9.11%	(342,811)	−39.83%
Servicing hedge gain (loss)	(125,306)	−9.11%	200,135	−39.83%
Loan admin. income, net	547,029	49.17%	478,159	55.55%
Commissions, fees & other income	91,346	8.21%	63,642	7.39%
Total Revenues	**1,112,462**	**100.00%**	**860,742**	**100.00%**
Expenses:				
Salaries and related expenses	286,884	25.79%	229,668	26.68%
Occupancy & other office expenses	129,877	11.67%	106,298	12.35%
Guarantee fees	159,360	14.32%	121,197	14.08%
Marketing expenses	34,255	3.08%	27,115	3.15%
Other operating expenses	80,188	7.21%	50,264	5.84%
Total Expenses	690,564	62.08%	534,542	62.10%
Earnings before income tax	421,898	37.92%	326,200	37.90%
Provision for income tax	164,540	14.79%	130,480	15.16%
Net Earnings	**257,358**	**23.13%**	**195,720**	**22.74%**

Balance Sheet Assets (thous.)	1997	% Assets	1996	% Assets
Cash	18,269	0.23%	16,444	0.19%
Receivables for Mtg. Loans				
Mtg. Loans Held for Sale	2,579,972	31.89%	4,740,087	54.75%
Finance Receivables, Net				
Other Receivables	1,451,979	17.95%	912,613	10.54%
Net Prop. Equipment, etc.	190,104	2.35%	140,963	1.63%
Capitalized Servicing fees rc.				
Mortgage Servicing Rights	3,023,826	37.38%	2,323,665	26.84%
Other Assets	825,142	10.20%	523,881	6.05%
Total Assets	**8,089,292**	**100.00%**	**8,657,653**	**100.00%**
Liabilities & Equity				
Notes Payable	4,713,324	58.27%	6,097,518	70.43%
Drafts pay with mfg. closings	221,757	2.74%	238,020	2.75%
Accounts payable & accurals	607,037	7.50%	505,148	5.83%
Thrift investment accts.				
Deferred income taxes	635,643	7.86%	497,212	5.74%
Convertible sub. Debentures				
Total Liabilities	6,177,761	76.37%	7,337,898	84.76%
Equity	1,911,531	23.63%	1,319,755	15.24%
Total Liabilities & Equity	**8,089,292**	**100.00%**	**8,657,653**	**100.00%**

Source: Moody's Bank & Finance Manual, 1997
Business: Mortgage Banking Business; Originates, Purchases, Sells & Services Mortgage Loans

Table P13.2 ◆ Consolidated Financial Statements (in mils.) for Travelers Group from Annual Report 1997

Consolidated Income Statement (mils.) Revenues	1997	% Revs.	1996	% Revs.
Insurance Premiums	8,995	23.92%	7,633	23.55%
Commissions and Fees	5,119	13.61%	4,637	14.31%
Interest and Dividends	16,214	43.11%	13,286	40.99%
Principal Transactions	2,504	6.66%	3,027	9.34%
Asset management & administration fees	1,715	4.56%	1,390	4.29%
Finance related interest & other charges	1,404	3.73%	1,163	3.59%
Other Income	1,658	4.41%	1,278	3.94%
Total Revenues	**37,609**	**100.00%**	**32,414**	**100.00%**
Expenses				
Policyholder benefits & claims	7,714	20.51%	7,366	22.72%
Non-insurance compensation & benefits	6,345	16.87%	5,804	17.91%
Insurance underwriting, acquisition & operating expenses	3,236	8.60%	3,013	9.30%
Interest Expense	11,443	30.43%	8,927	27.54%
Provision for consumer finance credit losses	277	0.74%	260	0.80%
Other Operating Expenses	3,582	9.52%	2,481	7.65%
Total Expenses	**32,597**	**86.67%**	**27,851**	**85.92%**
Gain (loss) on sale of subs. & affiliates			445	
Income before income taxes & minority interest	5,012	13.33%	5,008	15.45%
Provision for income taxes	1,696	4.51%	1,679	5.18%
Minority interest, net of income taxes	212	0.56%	47	0.14%
Income from continuing operations	3,104	8.25%	3,282	10.13%
Income from discontinued operations			−334	
Net Income	**3,104**	**8.25%**	**2,948**	**9.09%**

Balance Sheet (mils.) Assets	1997	% Assets	1996	% Assets
Cash & Equiv.	4,033	1.04%	3,260	0.94%
Investments	61,834	16.00%	56,509	16.33%
Repurchase Agreements	109,734	28.39%	97,985	28.32%
Brokerage Receivables	15,627	4.04%	11,592	3.35%
Trading Securities	139,732	36.15%	126,573	36.59%
Net Consumer Receivables	10,816	2.80%	7,885	2.28%
Reinsurance Recoverables	9,579	2.48%	10,234	2.96%
Value of Insurance in Force and deferred policy acq. costs	2,812	0.73%	2,563	0.74%
Cost of acqd businesses in excess of net assets	3,446	0.89%	3,060	0.88%
Separate & variable accounts	11,319	2.93%	9,023	2.61%
Other Receivables	5,733	1.48%	4,869	1.41%
Other Assets	11,890	3.08%	12,395	3.58%
Total Assets	386,555	100.00%	345,948	100.00%
Liabilities:				
Investment Banking & Brokerage Borrowing	11,464	2.97%	10,020	2.90%
Short-term Borrowings	3,979	1.03%	1,557	0.45%
Long-term Debt	28,352	7.33%	24,696	7.14%
Repurchase Agreements	120,921	31.28%	103,572	29.94%
Brokerage Payables	12,763	3.30%	10,019	2.90%
Trading Secs. not yet Purchased	96,166	24.88%	92,141	26.63%
Contractholder Funds	14,848	3.84%	13,621	3.94%
Insurance Policy & Claims Reserves	43,782	11.33%	43,944	12.70%
Separate & variable accounts	11,309	2.93%	8,949	2.59%
Accounts Payable & Other	19,418	5.02%	16,693	4.83%
Total Liabilities	**363,002**	**93.91%**	**325,212**	**94.01%**
Preferred Stock	2,660	0.69%	2,194	0.63%
Stockholders Equity	**20,893**	**5.40%**	**17,942**	**5.19%**
Total Liabilities & Equity	386,555	100.00%	345,948	100.00%

Table P13.3 ✦ FINANCIAL STATEMENTS FOR FORD MOTOR CREDIT CORPORATION

Consolidated Income Statement (mils.) Revenues	1997	% Revs.	1996	% Revs.
Operating Leases	8,223.60	49.50%	7300.8	48.68%
Retail Receivables	5000.7	30.10%	4522.7	30.16%
Wholesale Receivables	1645.8	9.91%	1875.2	12.50%
Diversified Receivables	84	0.51%	152.2	1.01%
Other Receivables	393.5	2.37%	354.9	2.37%
Total Financing Revenues	**15347.6**	**92.37%**	**14205.8**	**94.72%**
Insurance Premiums Earned	225.7	1.36%	0	0.00%
Investment & Other Income	1041.4	6.27%	791.4	5.28%
Total Revenues	**16614.7**	**100.00%**	**14997.2**	**100.00%**
Expenses				
Interest Expense	6224.2	37.46%	5998.3	40.00%
Depreciation	5537.6	33.33%	5235.1	34.91%
Operating Expense	1467.4	8.83%	1211	8.07%
Provision for Losses	993.3	5.98%	480.4	3.20%
Other Insurance Claims	207.3	1.25%	0	0.00%
Total Expenses	**14429.8**	**86.85%**	**12924.8**	**86.18%**
Equity in Income of Affiliates	55.3	0.33%	255.4	1.70%
Income before income taxes	**2240.2**	**13.48%**	**2327.8**	**15.52%**
Provision for income taxes	731.6	4.40%	682.9	4.55%
Income before minority interests	**1508.6**	**9.08%**	**1644.9**	**10.97%**
Minority interests	68	0.41%	65.5	0.44%
Net Income	**1440.6**	**8.67%**	**1579.4**	**10.53%**

Balance Sheet (mils.) Assets (mils.)	1997	% Assets	1996	% Assets
Cash	2716	2.23%	1478.1	1.33%
Security Investments	1324.8	1.09%	1914.3	1.72%
Net Finance Receivables	80848	66.43%	76376.7	68.65%
Notes Rec. from affiliates	30645.2	25.18%	25680.2	23.08%
Net Operating Leases	1133	0.93%	672.9	0.60%
Property, Plant, & Equipment	44.4	0.04%	1730.5	1.56%
Other Assets	4985	4.10%	3405.2	3.06%
Total Assets	121696.4	100.00%	111257.9	100.00%
Liabilities:				
Accounts Payable	5677.8	4.67%	3683.5	3.31%
Income Tax Payable	0	0.00%	0	0.00%
Subordinated Notes	325	0.27%	325	0.29%
Long-term Debt	0	0.00%	0	0.00%
Deferred Income Tax	4260.4	3.50%	3109.8	2.80%
Other Liabs. & Defd. Income	2929.9	2.41%	2340.2	2.10%
Total Liabilities	**110892.4**	**91.12%**	**101313.8**	**91.06%**
Minority Interest	**1313.8**	**1.08%**	**988.9**	**0.89%**
Total Stockholders Equity	**9205.7**	**7.56%**	**8670.7**	**7.79%**
Total Liabs. & Equity	121696.4	100.00%	111257.9	100.00%

Note: With rounding, sum of %'s may be less 100%.
Source: Moody's Bank & Finance Manual, 1997, 3366–3367

References

Aguilar, Linda. "Still Toe-to-Toe: Banks and Nonbanks at the End of the '80s." *Economic Perspectives* (Federal Reserve Bank of Chicago) 14 (January/February 1990): 12–23.

Benston, George J. "Rating Ceiling Implications of the Cost Structure of Consumer Finance Companies." *Journal of Finance* 21 (September 1977), 1169–1194.

Cantor, Richard and Rebecca Demsetz. "Securitization, Loan Sales, and the Credit Slowdown." *Federal Reserve Bank of New York Quarterly Review* (Summer 1993), 27–38.

Cauette, John B. "Securitization: What's Next?" In *Proceedings of a Conference on Bank Structure and Competition.* Chicago: Federal Reserve Bank of Chicago, 1992.

Crawford, Richard D. and William W. Sihler. *Financial Service Organizations: Cases in Strategic Management.* New York: HarperCollins Publishers, 1994.

Danielson, Arnold G. "Getting Ready for the 21st Century: A Look at Recent Banking Trends." *Banking Policy Report*, 18, March 15, 1999, 1, 13–20.

Dorgan, Richard J. "Banks Keen to Make Asset-Based Loans," *NCFA Journal* 40 (September 1984), 5–14.

Durkin, Thomas A. and Gregory E. Elliehausen. "The Cost Structure of the Consumer Finance Industry." *Journal of Financial Services Research* 13 (February 1998), 71–86.

Ellis, James E. "Sears' Discover Card Finds Its Way," *Business Week* (September 15, 1986), 166–167.

Ford, William F. "Banking's New Competition: Myths and Realities." *Economic Review* (Federal Reserve Bank of Atlanta) 67 (January/February 1982): 4–11.

Flynn, Julia, et al. "Small but Wiser." *Business Week* (October 12, 1992), 28–29.

Greising, David. "The Discover Card Is No Longer a Joker." *Business Week* (October 9, 1989), 138.

Haggerty, Alfred G. "Financial Centers a Big Success for Sears." *National Underwriter* (November 23, 1984), 56.

Harris, Maury. "Finance Companies as Business Lenders." *Quarterly Review Federal Reserve Bank of New York* 4 (Summer 1979), 35–39.

Hilder, David B. and Steve Weiner. "Big Brokerage Houses Are Problem Children for Their New Parents." *The Wall Street Journal* (September 13, 1985), 1.

Jenster, Per V. and John H. Lindgren, Jr. "The New Game in Retail Auto Financing." *Journal of Retail Banking* 10 (Winter 1988), 39–45.

Johnson, Robert W. "The Consumer Banking Problem: Causes and Cures." *Journal of Retail Banking* 11 (Winter 1989), 39–45.

Key, Janet. "New Card Chief Focus for Sears." *Chicago Tribune* (October 3, 1985), Section 3, 1, 6.

Koch, Timothy W. *Bank Management*, 3d ed. Fort Worth, Tex.: Dryden Press, 1995.

Komansky, David H. "Inheriting the Mantle." In *The New Financiers*, ed. Charles B. Wendel. Chicago: Irwin Professional Publishing Co., 1996, 133–151.

Lee, Winson B. and Elizabeth S. Cooperman. "Conglomerates in the 1980s: A Performance Appraisal," *Financial Management* (Spring 1989), 45–54.

Leonitades, M. *Managing the Unmanageable: Strategies for Success Within the Conglomerate.* Reading, Mass.: Addison Wesley Publishing Co., Inc., 1986.

Logan, John and Richard J. Dorgan. "Asset-Based Lending: You're Doing It, but Are You Doing It Right?" *Journal of Commercial Bank Lending* 67 (June 1984), 9–16.

Martin, John D., John W. Kensinger, and Stuart L. Gillan, "Value Creation and Corporate Diversification: The Case of Sears, Roebuck & Co.," Working Paper, University of Texas, August 6, 1996.

McCoy, John, Larry A. Frieder, Robert B. Hedges, Jr. *Bottomline Banking: Meeting the Challenges for Survival and Success.* Chicago: Probus Publishing Co., 1994.

Mendonca, Lenny and Greg Wilson. "Financial Megaplayers' Time Is Here." *The Wall Street Journal* (September 29, 1997), A22.

Moore, Thomas. "Ball Takes Bache and Runs With It." *Fortune* (January 24, 1983), 97–100.

Olson, Wayne. "Securitization Comes to Other Assets." *Savings Institutions* 107 (May 1986), 81–85.

Patterson, Gregory A. and Francine Schwadel. "Sears Suddenly Undoes Years of Diversifying Beyond Retailing Field." *The Wall Street Journal* (September 30, 1992), A1, A6.

Remolona, Eli M. and Kurt C. Wulfekuhler. "Finance Companies, Bank Competition, and Niche Markets." *Federal Reserve Bank of New York Quarterly Review* (Summer 1992), 25–38.

Roosevelt, Phil. "Sears to Pull Out of Banking." *American Banker* (September 30, 1992), 1, 7.

Schmeitzer, John. "3.9 Billion Loss Sears' Worst Ever." *Chicago Tribune* (February 10, 1993), Section 3, 1,3.

Schwartz, David M. "When Home Sweet Home Was Just a Mailbox Away." *Smithsonian* 16 (November 1985), 91–100.

Selden, Richard T. "Consumer-Oriented Intermediaries," in *Financial Institutions and Markets*, 2d ed., ed. Murray Polakoff and Thomas A. Durkin. Boston: Houghton Mifflin, 1981, 202–215.

Sellers, Patricia. "Why Bigger Is Badder at Sears." *Fortune* (December 5, 1988), 79–84.

Shapiro, Harvey D. "Securitizing Corporate Assets." *Institutional Investor* 19 (December 1985).

Siconolfi, Michael. "Dean Witter Proves an Asset to Sears, Confounding Pundits." *The Wall Street Journal* (March 15, 1991), A1.

SNL Securities. *Industry Review-Finance Companies*. Charlottesville, Va.: SNL Securities Corporation, 1996.

Stahl, David. "The Rising Tide of Bankruptcy." *Savings and Community Banker* 2 (May 1993), 14–20.

Staten, Michael. "Statistics: Bankruptcy Watch." *Journal of Retail Banking* 11 (Winter 1989), 65–69.

Steinmetz, Greg. "Sears' Allstate Unit Expects to Raise More than $2 Billion in Initial Offering." *The Wall Street Journal* (March 19, 1993), A3.

Taub, Stephen. "Sizing Up the Brokers." *Financial World* (January 8–21, 1986), 1–4.

Tully, Daniel P. "Reflections on Transforming a Company." In *The New Financiers*, ed. Charles B. Wendel. Chicago: Irwin Professional Publishing Co., 1996, 259–282.

Wendel, Charles B. *The New Financiers*. Chicago: Irwin Professional Publishing, 1996.

Williams, Monci Jo. "Sears Roebuck's Struggling Financial Empire." *Fortune* (October 14, 1985), 40–43.

Chapter 13 Internet Exercises

1. Information on a wide range of topics in securitization can be found at *http://www.asset-backed.com/*.

   A library of papers on securitization can be found at: *http://www.the-financier.com/finance/library.htm#four2*.

   The papers are catalogued by subject: corporate finance, risk management, project finance, securitization, public finance, emerging markets, and banking.

2. Corporate Finance Network: CorpFiNet's mission is to provide professionals and executives in the financial services industry the information and resources they need to develop and implement competitive strategies in a wired world.

   Go to *http://www.corpfinet.com/*

   from this page, click on "Securities Online" Then click on "Legislation" for significant legislation, regulations, and case law. Under case law you will find Significant Securities Law Court Decisions with links to some historically important opinions in the area of Securities Law. Although a list of important court decisions affecting the securities laws would make for a multi-volume treatise, there are a number of court decisions that are central to an understanding of the securities laws, and that have interpreted the statutes and rules that govern the securities industry.

Useful Links:

Survey of finance companies, 1996. James D. August, Michael R. Grupe, Charles Luckett, and Samuel M. Slowinski. Federal Reserve Bulletin (*July 1997*), *p. 543–556.*
http://www.bog.frb.fed.us/pubs/bulletin/1997/199707LEAD.pdf

Konstas, Panos. "Government-Sponsored Enterprises: Their Role as Conduits of Credit and as Competitors of Banking Institutions." FDIC Banking Review *Vol. 8 No. 2—Article II—Published: June 1995*
http://www.fdic.gov/databank/bkreview/1995sprg/rbr01a02.html

American Financial Services Association
http://www.americanfinsvcs.org/

The Conference on Consumer Finance Law
http://www.theccfl.com/

Interest Rate & Foreign Exchange Environments

IV

- INTEREST RATES EXCHANGE RATES, AND INFLATION: THEORIES AND FORECASTING

- TERM STRUCTURE THEORIES & MANAGEMENT APPLICATION

- INTEREST RATE RISK MEASUREMENT & IMMUNIZATION USING DURATION

"Two shekels of silver have been borrowed by Mas-Schamach, the son of A., from the sun-priestess Amat-Schamach, daughter of W. . . . At the time of the harvest he will pay back the sum and the interest upon it."

Translation from a business document of Babylonia and Assyria, circa 2000 B.C., from Sidney Homer and Richard Sylla. *A History of Interest Rates*, 3rd ed. New Brunswick: Rutgers University Press, (1991), 29.

"When the war ended, some people thought that . . . perhaps rates as high as 2½ % would vanish forever. Therefore, in 1945, after the war ended, purchases of the last (Treasury) issues of 2½ s approached $20 billion."

"The United States in the Twentieth Century: 1900–1945," from Sidney Homer and Richard Sylla. *A History of Interest Rates*, 3rd ed. New Brunswick: Rutgers University Press, (1991), 356.

"The rise of interest rates and market yields to record levels in the 1970s and early 1980s [such as the three-month Treasury bills rates rising to 15.5% in 1981] cannot be understood without reference to inflation and the economic concept of real interest rates. If a lender considers that a 4% real return, that is, a 4% gain in purchasing power or in dollars of constant value, is required in order to justify lending $100 for one year, then that lender will demand a nominal interest rate of 14.4% if the expected rate of inflation in that year is 10%.

"The United States in the Twentieth Century: 1900–1945," from Sidney Homer and Richard Sylla. *A History of Interest Rates*, 3rd ed. New Brunswick: Rutgers University Press, (1991), 429.

"But the bond-market turmoil that began in August, and led to the near-collapse of Paloma's Greenwich neighbor Long-Term Capital Management LP, also played havoc with Paloma (Partners LLC) . . . . The bulk of the losses came in bond arbitrage, which involves betting on the relationship between interest rates on a variety of bonds. In August, interest rates on the safest government bonds fell, while rates on riskier bonds shot up, spoiling the bets of many investors."

Mitchell Pagelle
"Paloma Sustained Hedge-Fund Losses of as Much as 25% in the Third Quarter." *The Wall Street Journal* (October 23, 1998), C15.

14

INTEREST RATES, EXCHANGE RATES, AND INFLATION: THEORIES AND FORECASTING

*A*s these quotations demonstrate, interest rates have been an important factor in individuals' and financial institutions' lives throughout history and are subject to great volatility. Exchange rates also have a critical effect on the business of financial institutions. Exchange rates can be exceptionally volatile, as noted in recent years. For instance, the U.S. dollar value of the Japanese yen fell more than 20 percent between June 1997 and June 1998.

On August 26, 1998, in response to Russian economic problems, the Russian ruble fell 69 percent relative to the German mark. With a similar plunge in the ruble's dollar value, the Russian government halted dollar trading.[1] In reaction to the 1998 Asian economic crisis, currencies in Korea, Malaysia, Thailand, and Indonesia also fell dramatically relative to the U.S. dollar (for the Indonesian rupiah, a drop of almost 70 percent). Such declines resulted in government imposition of currency controls in some countries, such as Malaysia. In contrast, the Mexican peso rose 24 percent relative to the dollar during 1998. Hence, in 1998 financial institutions with long positions in financial instruments denominated in falling currencies experienced tremendous losses, whereas institutions with short positions received extraordinary gains. Financial institution managers learned difficult lessons concerning the severity of foreign exchange risk.

Financial institution managers of institutions with significant European operations also faced significant complications in their foreign exchange management with the introduction of the euro on January 1, 1999, and the gradual phasing out of the different currencies of participating European Union member states by July 1, 2002. Such complications include overhauls to internal information systems and accounting procedures as well as legal implications for contracts in member currencies, including debt securities and derivatives contracts, such as foreign exchange swaps and currency option transactions based on member country currencies, which will be obsolete by July 2002. The advent of the euro will reduce exchange rate risk among the participating 11 nations (Austria, Belgium, France, Finland, Germany, Ireland, Italy, Luxembourg, Portugal, Spain, and the Netherlands) and foreign exchange risk for financial institutions with significant European Union exposure, but the transitional period and the risk entailed with the gradual curtailment of individual currencies could be painful.[2]

✦ ✦ ✦

[1]Andrew Higgins and Mark Whitehouse. "Russia Quits Fight to Back the Ruble: Moscow Halts Dollar Trading; Currency Drops 69% vs. Mark." *The Wall Street Journal* (August 27, 1998), A8; Christopher Rhoads. "European Bank Stocks Again Hit by Russia Woes." *The Wall Street Journal* (August 27, 1998), A8.

[2]Darren McDermott and Karby Leggett. "Jitters Grow over Currencies of Asia's Giants." *The Wall Street Journal* (June 12, 1998), A8; Bill Spindle. "Yen Falls Again Against Dollar: Data Awaited." *The Wall Street Journal* (June 12, 1998), A8; Darren McDermott and Leslie Lopez. "Malaysia Imposes Sweeping Currency Controls." *The Wall Street Journal* (September 2, 1998), A10; and Paul S. Tufaro. "European Economic and Monetary Union: A Continuity of Contracts." *Banking Policy Report* 17 (July 6, 1998), 1, 13.

OVERVIEW OF THE CHAPTER

Preceding chapters introduce unique characteristics of financial institutions, including the predominance of financial assets and liabilities and the resulting emphasis on the net interest margin (NIM). The interest rate environment is one of the most important influences on asset/liability decisions and institutional performance. Key determinants of success are managers' abilities to understand movements in interest rates and inflation and to interpret forecasts. And, although all financial institution managers must respond to interest rate changes, the growing globalization of financial markets creates additional requirements for some; they must make asset/liability decisions in reaction to changes in the value of the dollar compared with other currencies. Fortunately, managers have access to a growing array of risk management tools; but they must first understand the theories underlying interest rate and exchange rate movements. Similarly, managers must be able to calculate rates on different types of financial instruments. This chapter looks at trends in interest rates and exchanges rates and discusses theories that help managers of financial institutions to make critical decisions concerning future trends. The chapter also presents the calculation of yields on different types of money market instruments and quotations for money market rates and foreign exchange rates. Finally, implications of the introduction of the euro for financial institutions are briefly discussed. The first section discusses why theories are important to managers.

WHY THEORIES ARE IMPORTANT TO MANAGERS

Managers are rarely theoreticians; instead, they spend their time analyzing and making decisions critical to the future of their institutions. These decisions rely on often conflicting opinions about the direction of the economy and interest rates, nationally and internationally. To make better decisions, managers must be able to evaluate available data and forecasts. Those evaluations, in turn, require knowledge of the principles on which forecasts are based.

For example, the manager of the investment portfolio of a life insurance company can invest in variable-coupon bonds, zero-coupon bonds, or traditional fixed-rate instruments, among many other choices. The manager's expectations about interest rate movements will certainly influence the decision. In a period of declining rates, a variable-coupon instrument will be unattractive, but a zero-coupon bond (a bond that only makes a maturity payment) will lock in a higher rate if intermediate cash flows are not important. A bond denominated in British pounds will be undesirable if the value of the pound is expected to fall. Similarly, raising funds also must be guided by forecasts.

Often economists are unable to agree about the future direction of economic variables, and managers must exercise judgment in evaluating available forecasts. Theories concerning the economic, political, and behavioral factors that influence interest rates and exchange rates provide the foundation on which economic forecasters base their expectations about interest and exchange rate changes, which also affect managerial evaluation and decision making.

A HISTORICAL LOOK AT INTEREST RATES

Although interest rates are always changing, they have been particularly volatile over the past two decades, reaching historically high levels in 1980 and 1981. Ten years later, short-term Treasury securities were at their lowest yields, and interest rates on some savings accounts at banks and thrifts hovered at Great Depression levels. After rising in the mid-1990s, interest rates again plunged in the later 1990s and were exceptionally volatile. Figure 14.1 shows trends in rates for bonds of different rate classes over time, demonstrating this volatility. Rates on different bonds tend to follow each other, but the spread between risk-free (U.S. government securities) and more risky corporate bonds changes over time, generally becoming larger as economic recessions approach and smaller during expansions, when corporations have lower earnings risk.

Panel A traces yields on long-term bonds for several different default risk classes over the period 1930 to 1990. An upward trend in rates began in the late 1960s. After some dips in the 1970s, rates rose rapidly again in late 1979 and peaked about two years later, fueled by expectations of high inflation and government deficits. As discussed in the Appendix to Chapter 3, the Federal Reserve System's (Fed's) famous temporary policy change away from targeting interest rates as a part of monetary policy from October 1979 to October 1982 also led to greater rate volatility during the early 1980s. Even though yields declined in 1982, as inflation subsided, the volatility continued through the end of the decade.

Panel B of Figure 14.1 shows in more detail trends in both short-term and long-term rates from 1981 to the third quarter of 1998, with shaded areas showing recessionary years. Rates generally fall during recessions, such as 1981–1982 and 1990–1992, and rise during expansions. However, exceptions exist. For instance, in 1997 and 1998, years of expansion with low inflation, interest rates fell dramatically. Short-term rates also often lead long-term rates in terms of rising and falling, such as in 1990–1991, when short-term rates fell dramatically, but long-term rates did not fall until 1992–1993. However, long-term rates fell dramatically in 1997–1998, whereas short-term rates remained stable.

Rates are very difficult to predict and vary enormously, especially on a weekly or monthly basis. Panel A of Figure 14.2 shows samples of weekly, monthly, and hourly trends in bond yields that demonstrate considerable volatility. Although short-term rates are generally more volatile than long-term rates, long-term rates were extremely volatile in 1998. Note the hourly volatility in 30-year Treasury bond yields on September 17, 1998.

Panel B shows trends in the spreads between corporate and U.S. Treasury securities in recent years, which have varied widely. The spread between corporate and Treasury bonds widened in 1998, particularly as professional investors fled to Treasury bonds as a safe investment, following the financial crises in Russia and Asia. These financial crises also had a seemingly contagious effect on Latin American financial markets. Such a "flight to quality" created a liquidity crunch for investors holding corporate bonds, who found bidders for the long-term bonds that they held scarce at the end of September 1998. Liquidity for high-quality corporate bonds gradually improved in November of that year.[3] Traders speculating on risk spreads between Treasury and corporate bonds also experienced large losses during this period. Investment bankers hoping to assist corporations in issuing bonds or initial public offerings of stock faced very unreceptive markets and high borrowing costs, making firms reluctant to issue securities.

Hence, financial institution managers find the volatile interest rate environment a continuing challenge. Some institutions have maintained good performance

---

[3]Gregory Zuckerman and Greg Ip. "Ripple Effect: It Isn't Just Investors Who Are Smarting from Liquidity Crunch." *The Wall Street Journal* (November 6, 1998), A1, A9.

Figure 14.1 ✦ TRENDS IN INTEREST RATES

Over time, interest rates are variable. Although there are many different financial markets, interest rates in all markets tend to move in the same general direction at the same time.

PANEL A. LONG-TERM BOND YIELDS (PERIODIC AVERAGES)

Quarterly Averages, Trends in Rates, 1930-1990

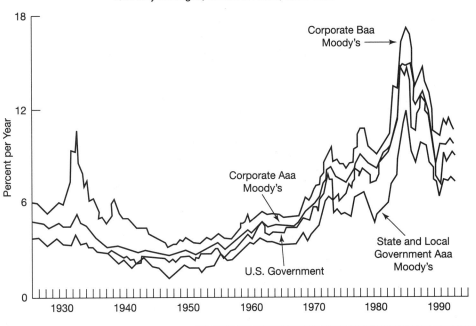

Sources: Board of Governors of the Federal Reserve System, *Historical Charts* and Federal Reserve Bank of Cleveland *Economic Trends.*

PANEL B. TRENDS IN RATES, 1981–1998 III

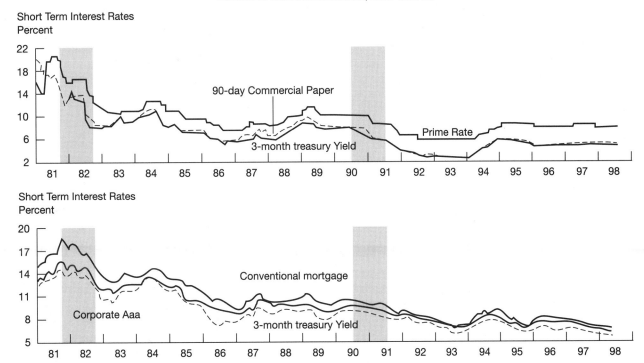

Source: Federal Reserve Bank of St. Louis, *Monetary Trends*, October 1998, p. 9. Shaded areas indicate recessionary periods.

Figure 14.2 ✦ RECENT TRENDS IN YIELDS

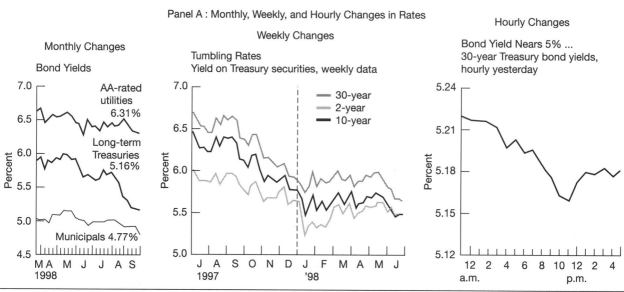

Sources: *The Wall Street Journal*, September 28, 1998, C19; *The Wall Street Journal*, June 29, 1998, C1; *The Wall Street Journal*, September 17, 1998, C1.

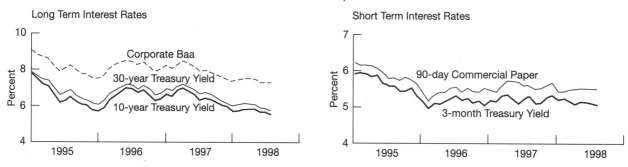

Source: *Federal Reserve Bank of St. Louis Monetary Trends*, October 1998, 9.

records, but many firms have faltered or failed. For example, at the end of 1987, First Bank System, Inc., at that time the nation's sixteenth largest bank holding company (now part of US Bancorp) announced a loss on its investment portfolio of more than $700 million. The reason? According to *The Wall Street Journal*, management's mistake was "betting heavily the wrong way on interest rates." Fortunately, the outlook is almost always brighter for institutions that successfully navigate choppy interest rate waters. In 1992, for example, Boatmen's Bankshares Inc. of St. Louis enjoyed hefty profits because, according to Chairman Andrew Craig, "We structured the balance sheet in anticipation of a downturn in rates." As the final quotation in the introduction to this chapter suggests, financial institutions continue to speculate on interest rate and exchange rate movements. In 1998 investment firms Long-Term Capital and Paloma Partners, LLC, hedge-funds that invest in stocks, bonds, currencies, and other financial instruments for wealthy investors, suffered severe losses from interest rate bets that went bad in volatile domestic and international bond markets. Bankers Trust (now part of Deutsche Bank), Citicorp, J. P. Morgan, Morgan Stanley Dean Witter, Barclays, Nomura Securities, and other large financial institutions that engaged actively in bond trading suffered severe losses. Many of these losses were associated with foreign exchange rates as well. When the ruble plunged on August 26, 1998, U.S. banks' exposure to Russia was about $6.8 billion, not including hedge-fund lending. Deutsche Bank, Dresdner Bank, Commerzbank, Credit Suisse, and other European banks with large loan exposure in Russia experienced significant declines in their stock prices on that date. Investment banks, such as Salomon Smith Barney, that held Russian treasury bonds, known as GKOs, received about 20 percent to 25 percent of the face value of the debt under the Russian government's restructuring plan at that time. Given the risk that financial institutions face, managers must have a theoretical knowledge of both interest ratesand exchange rates to assist them in predicting the advent of sudden interest rate and currency changes.[4]

The following sections discuss theories of interest rates that are helpful for financial institution managers as they attempt to decipher possible movements in interest rates that significantly affect their institutions' performance.

THE GENERAL LEVEL OF INTEREST RATES

Theories of interest rate determination follow several conventions. First, models usually focus on determination of the *equilibrium* level of interest. Equilibrium is a state of rest or the absence of forces for change. Actually, the financial markets are seldom, if ever, in equilibrium but are in the process of approaching equilibrium as they respond to the numerous factors that cause an imbalance between supply and demand.

Second, economic models rely on several assumptions required to simplify the real world. The objective is to develop a useful explanation without omitting factors crucial to achieving the purpose of the model.

Finally, theories explaining the general level of interest rates do just that: They focus on *the* rate of interest. Obviously, there are many interest rates for different types of securities. This chapter points out how differences in yields reflect term to maturity, default risk, taxability, and other characteristics of the underlying security. Still, compared over time, yields on securities tend to move in the same general direction. Although the correlation is not perfect, it is strong enough that economists are justified in focusing on *one* interest rate to build a model that explains movement in *all* rates.

---

[4]Jeff Bailey. "First Bank System Says Bond Portfolio Fell $700 Million as Interest Rates Rose." *The Wall Street Journal* (October 14, 1987), 17; Fred R. Bleakley. "Banks, Thrifts Scored as Interest Rates Fell, But Difficulties Loom." *The Wall Street Journal* (February 2, 1992), A1, A6; and Peter Truell. "5 Big Lenders Report Losses from Russia: At Citicorp, Profit Drain of $200 Million Is Seen." *New York Times* (September 2, 1998, C1; and Christopher Rhoads. "European Bank Stocks Again Hit by Russia Woes." *The Wall Street Journal* (August 27, 1998), A8.

LOANABLE FUNDS THEORY

Several compatible theories attempt to explain interest rate movements, although they are not equally useful for forecasting changes in rates. The loanable funds theory focuses on the amount of funds available for investment (the supply of loanable funds) and the amount of funds that borrowers want (the demand for loanable funds). It is particularly adaptable for use in forecasting and, therefore, is the one on which this discussion concentrates.

The Supply of Loanable Funds

The **loanable funds theory** categorizes borrowers and lenders into five distinct types: households or consumers; businesses; governments; the central bank, which has control over changes in the money supply; and the foreign sector. Governments supply almost no loanable funds, but it is important to understand the forces affecting the savings decisions of individuals, businesses, and foreign investors.

The Expected Rate of Return and the Decision to Save Economic units always have several choices for disposition of funds. They can *spend* money on consumable goods; they can *save* money by investing in financial assets; or they can choose to hold, or *hoard*, money. The motivation for consumption is self-evident. But once the amount of consumption has been determined, there is still a choice between investing and holding money.

A key motivation for saving is the expected rate of return. Because investors have a **time preference for consumption**, they will reduce current consumption to save money only if they receive some reward for doing so. That reward is the expected rate of interest, which must always be positive to induce substantial postponement of consumption.

Economists have also identified several other motivations for savings, discussed shortly, which suggest that some funds will be saved even if the expected rate of interest is zero.

Holding or hoarding cash requires postponement of consumption but, unlike saving, does not provide a positive rate of return. So why does anyone hold cash balances? Three motivations have been identified: the **transactions demand**, the **precautionary demand**, and the **speculative demand**.[5] Because individuals and businesses cannot always assume that the timing of cash inflows and cash expenditures will coincide, they usually need to maintain ready access to cash to handle transactions. Also, some cash will be held as a precaution against unforeseen contingencies. Neither of these motivations is tied to the expected rate of interest.

---

[5]These motivations for holding cash were introduced by the renowned economist John Maynard Keynes in *The General Theory of Employment, Interest, and Money* (1936). Actually, Keynes used them in the liquidity preference theory, an explanation of interest rates that is separate but compatible with the loanable funds theory. The liquidity preference theory focuses on the supply and demand for money, whereas the loanable funds theory focuses on the supply and demand for credit. Once consumption is determined, a household's decisions to hold cash (demand money) or to lend (supply credit) are not independent of one another; deciding to do more of one means deciding to do less of the other. Thus, it is easy to see how theories on the determination of interest rates can be approached by looking at either money or loanable funds.

The third demand for money—the speculative motivation—is sensitive to expected interest rates and is therefore especially important in understanding the supply of loanable funds. In the face of high expected rates on financial assets, funds suppliers will reduce cash balances as they invest; with low expected rates of return, they will hold cash in anticipation of better opportunities later. Thus, the expected rate of return is important in the decision to reduce speculative cash balances, which in turn increases the supply of loanable funds.

Other Factors Influencing Households   These relationships lead to a better but still incomplete understanding of the amount of funds available for borrowing. Factors other than interest rates affect the savings decision. For example, most people voluntarily save for future needs, either because they recognize that illness or other emergencies could jeopardize their financial position or because they will need funds to support themselves after retirement. Other people may be involved in involuntary savings programs, such as social security or required retirement programs for state and federal employees.

The income of a household is also significant. Low-income families often spend all available funds on the basic necessities of life, leaving nothing for alternative uses. At the opposite end of the spectrum, high-income families may be unable to consume all available funds even if they wanted to, so they must invest regardless of the expected interest rate.

Other Factors Influencing Businesses   Although businesses are usually demanders, they also supply some loanable funds. The primary sources of these funds are the depreciation tax shield and retained earnings from profitable past operations. Expected interest rates may have some bearing on the decisions of businesses to save by investing in financial assets, but other important factors are potential real asset investments, the nature of the business enterprise, and the philosophy of the firm's managers and owners.

The Money Supply   The supply of loanable funds is affected by changes in the total money supply (ΔM), which is influenced by Fed policy. An increase in the money supply makes more funds available for saving after consumption is satisfied.

The Foreign Sector   Funds available domestically are also influenced by the behavior of foreign investors. The key factor influencing funds provided by the foreign sector is not simply the expected rate of interest in the United States, but the difference between that rate and the expected rate available in other countries. Also, the stability of a country's currency may make investments in that country's securities more attractive to international investors. These relationships will be explained in more detail later.

The Supply of Loanable Funds Illustrated   The combined impact of these influences on the supply of loanable funds is shown in Figure 14.3. The supply curve (S_{LF}) is positively related to the expected rate of interest; that is, the quantity supplied is larger as the interest rate increases, but only moderately so. Even at a zero rate of interest, the supply of loanable funds exceeds zero because of nonrate factors influencing the savings decision.

The household sector is the only *net* supplier of loanable funds; that is, in a given period, households save more than they demand in the credit markets. For that reason, the borrowings of the household sector are usually netted against savings, and

Figure 14.3 ◆ SUPPLY OF LOANABLE FUNDS

The willingness of households, businesses, governments, and the foreign sector to supply loanable funds increases as the expected interest rate increases.

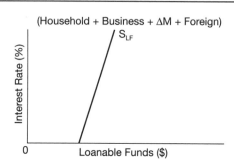

the S_{LF} curve is net of loanable funds demanded by households. Using this approach, households' savings equals income minus consumption minus household borrowing.

The Demand for Loanable Funds

The forces determining the demand for loanable funds—the total funds that households, businesses, government units, and the foreign sector want to borrow—is tied much more closely to expected interest rates than is the supply.

The Effect of Expected Interest Rates on Borrowing   Most business borrowing is sensitive to expected interest rates. The funds raised by nonfinancial firms will depend on their optimal budgets for investment in real assets. An optimal capital budget reflects a firm's investment opportunities. It occurs at the point where the marginal returns from investing in real assets are equal to the marginal costs of raising the funds, and the net present value of incremental investments is zero. At lower rates of interest, the capital budget will be larger, because a lower discount rate will be used for calculating net present value (the present value of the cash flows less the initial outlay cost of the project). The investment opportunity schedule and the resulting demand for loanable funds (D_{LF}) are inversely related to expected interest rates.

Noninterest Factors   As with the supply of loanable funds, noninterest factors motivate the demand for borrowing. For example, government units at the local, state, and federal levels often must borrow regardless of interest rates. Governments borrow whenever they face budget deficits or when they need to finance major construction of roads or government buildings.[6] In fact, government demand for credit is relatively inelastic with respect to interest rates.

---

[6]Many experts argue that the relationship between borrowing and interest rates is not the same for state and local governments as it is for the federal government, under the assumption that the former are more flexible in spending decisions and may postpone some projects to be financed by borrowing if interest rates are high. In addition, some state or municipal statutes actually prohibit government units from borrowing if expected interest rates exceed a certain critical level. For further discussion, see Polakoff (1981), 494.

Figure 14.4   ✦   DEMAND FOR LOANABLE FUNDS

The willingness of businesses, governments, and the foreign sector to borrow funds decreases as the expected interest rate increases.

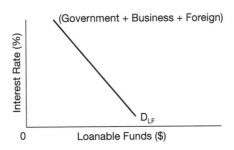

Demand by the Foreign Sector   Foreign borrowers also seek funds in the domestic credit markets. Foreign business borrowers are motivated by the same factors that affect domestic firms, but differences between interest rates in the United States and those abroad will determine where borrowing actually occurs. Foreign governments also borrow in U.S. markets for the same reasons that U.S. governmental units borrow. Recently, in fact, the domestic demand for loanable funds by foreign governments has been substantial.[7]

The Demand for Loanable Funds Illustrated   The demand schedule (D_{LF}) for loanable funds in Figure 14.4 is for total business, government, and foreign borrowing. As noted earlier, households do borrow, but their demand is usually netted against the funds they supply and is not included in the aggregate demand for loanable funds.

LOANABLE FUNDS THEORY AND INTEREST RATE FORECASTING

The loanable funds theory follows classical supply/demand analysis and explains the equilibrium rate of interest as the point of intersection of the supply and demand schedules. In Figure 14.5, i^* and Q^* represent the equilibrium rate of interest and the equilibrium quantity of loanable funds, respectively. Many analysts use the loanable funds framework to explain and anticipate the movement of interest rates.

Because the loanable funds theory explains the rate of interest as the point of intersection between supply and demand curves, the political, economic, or behavioral factors that shift either curve are expected to result in a change in interest rates.

---

[7] In recent years, the foreign sector as a whole has been a net supplier of funds to the U.S. credit market. In the past, however, it was a net borrower. See Board of Governors of the Federal Reserve System. *Flow of Funds Accounts, Financial Assets and Liabilities* (First Quarter, 1992).

Figure 14.5 ◆ Equilibrium Rate of Interest

The equilibrium level of interest rates is the rate at which the quantity of loanable funds demanded equals the quantity of loanable funds supplied.

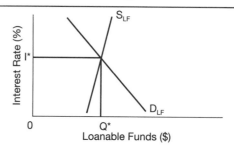

Changes in Supply or Demand

What forces could shift the supply or the demand curves? Government fiscal policy is one important force. The size of the federal budget deficit affects the demand for loanable funds. The more federal expenditures exceed federal revenues, the more frequently the government must enter the credit markets. Unless the change in government borrowing is offset by an equal and opposite change in demand for loanable funds by other sectors, the demand curve must shift, and the rate of interest will be higher. Furthermore, the supply curve may also be affected, as anticipated increases in government borrowing cause funds suppliers to increase their speculative balances in anticipation of higher interest rates.

Another fiscal policy, taxation, also has the potential for shifting the supply or demand curves. For example, an increase in corporate taxes reduces after-tax profits and thereby reduces the incentive for additional business spending. Smaller capital budgets lower the demand for borrowed funds.

Monetary policy, through its effect on the money supply, also affects interest rates. For example, an increase in the money supply relative to money demand leads to higher levels of savings, shifting the supply curve to the right. This subsequently leads to a lower interest rate, at least in the short run.[8] Research suggests another monetary policy effect: Volatility in money growth may lead to higher interest rates because it precipitates a reduction in the supply of loanable funds. High variability in monetary growth increases investors' uncertainty about future rates of return on financial assets. In response to that uncertainty, the suppliers of loanable funds will choose to hold more money, and the supply curve will shift to the left. Borrowers may also respond by reducing their demand for funds as they grow more uncertain about their borrowing costs.[9]

A shift in the demand curve could also result from a change in the state of the economy. As the economy moves into a recession, customer demand drops off, in-

---

[8]This effect is somewhat controversial; some analysts argue that growth in the money supply will lead to higher inflation so that the long-term effect on interest rates is uncertain. The effects of inflation are examined in subsequent sections.

[9]Mascaro and Meltzer (1983).

ventory surpluses accumulate, and expansion plans are postponed. Capital expenditures and the need for funds to support them decline.

Forecast of Future Interest Rates Illustrated

Suppose a recession is anticipated. The forecaster expects the quantity of funds required by the business community to decline in anticipation of reduced consumer demand. At the same time, estimates of lower federal tax revenues, as unemployment rises, lead to a forecast of larger deficits. The government sector, therefore, will demand more loanable funds.

In practice, an interest rate forecast requires detailed identification of all potential changes and their magnitude. As shown in Figure 14.6 (left panel), if the increase in the government's demand for funds is greater than the decrease in demand by the business sector, net demand will increase, and the demand curve (D_{LF}) will shift to the right to D_{LF}'. Thus, the new equilibrium interest rate (i') will be higher. However, as shown in the right panel, if the decrease in business demand is greater than the increase in government demand, aggregate demand for loanable funds will decline, and the demand curve will shift to the left. Hence, the forecast will be for a new lower equilibrium rate of interest. The supply curve also may shift as a result of changing conditions. This, too, would affect anticipated movements in interest rates.

Inflation and the Level of Interest Rates

The rate of inflation was of particular concern in the 1980s because of the volatility in and high levels of several different measures of price changes. By the early 1990s, a decline in annual inflation rates had some economists studying and writing about

---

Figure 14.6   ✦   **Shifts in the Demand Curve and Changes in the Equilibrium Rate of Interest**

If the demand for loanable funds increases, the equilibrium level of interest rates will increase. If the demand for loanable funds decreases, the equilibrium level of interest rates will fall.

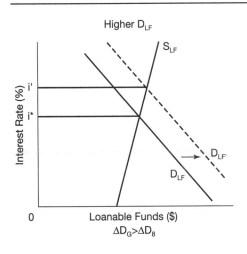
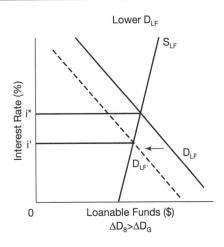

disinflation, or a reduction in the inflation rate to zero.[10] Because anticipated changes in the purchasing power of the dollar affect investors' yields, price-level changes have a role in theories of the general level of interest rates.

To illustrate, suppose a student's parents are saving for a graduation gift to be presented in one year. They are considering a one-year, $2,000 bank certificate of deposit (CD) in a federally insured institution that is expected to yield 10 percent. The expected yield at the time of investment is the nominal return. If there is no inflation during the coming year, the ex post real return will also be 10 percent. But if the price level increases during the year, say 5 percent, the $2,200 that the student receives is worth 5 percent less. Deflating the $2,200 by dividing by 1.05, it is worth only $2,095.24 in terms of real purchasing power. Thus, the ex post return on the investment in terms of what the student received in real terms over what his/her parents invested is only 4.76 percent [(2,095.24 − 2,000)/2,000 = 0.0476 or 4.76 percent], instead of the ex ante return expected of 10 percent.

Looking at this from a more practical perspective, let us say that a year prior to the investment, a compact disc cost $10. A year later, with a 5 percent rise in prices, a compact disc now costs 5 percent more, or $10 (1.05) = $10.50. With $2,000, the amount his/her parents invested, the student a year before could have bought 200 (i.e., $2,000/$10) compact discs. However, because of the 5 percent price rise over the year, when the student receives the $2,200 earned on the investment a year later, he or she can buy only $2,200/$10.50 = 209.52 compact discs. The profit on the investment in terms of additional purchasing is only 9.52 more compact discs, a return in terms of purchasing power of just 4.76 percent (i.e., 9.52 compact discs/200 compact discs).

Inflation and Financial Innovation

If inflation were uncommon, participants in the financial markets would pay relatively little attention to it in forecasting future events. Charts of historic movements in the Consumer Price Index (CPI) and the Producer Price Index (PPI) in Panel A for 1975 to 1990 and Panel B for 1981 to 1998 of Figure 14.7 demonstrate, however, that neither borrowers nor lenders can afford to ignore price levels and their potential impact on returns and costs.[11] Although inflation rates have subsided in recent years, as noted by the CPI inflation rate in Panel A, CPI inflation rates were close to 14 percent in 1975 in the United States and continue to be high in many countries. Many observers note that the demand for new financial products in the 1970s and

---

[10]Croushore (1992) reviews the arguments for and against the Fed's trying to reduce inflation to 0 percent and provides a comprehensive bibliography. See also Lawrence B. Lindsey. "The Case for Disinflation." *Economic Commentary: Federal Reserve Bank of Cleveland*, (March 15, 1992).

[11]There is no general agreement on how to measure inflation. The most widely used measures are the CPI, the PPI, and the implicit Gross National Product (GNP) Price Deflator. The first two track changes in the price level of "market baskets" of goods; the third attempts to reflect price changes in all components of the GNP. Wallace and Cullison (1979) provide a good discussion of the PPI and the GNP Price Deflator. For a description of the current components of the CPI, which has been undergoing revisions since 1981, see the monthly issues of "The CPI Detailed Report" from the U.S. Department of Labor, Bureau of Labor Statistics.

1980s can be attributed at least partially to expectations of inflation. Examples are adjustable-rate bonds and mortgages, zero-coupon bonds, deposit accounts that pay variable rates of interest, universal life insurance policies, interest rate swaps, inflation-adjusted Treasury securities, and inflation futures contracts. An entirely new type of financial instrument, the money market mutual fund, was created to allow investors to obtain yields that vary with daily changes in market conditions. Major deregulation of the financial system, through the Depository Institutions Deregulation and Monetary Control Act (DIDMCA), the Garn-St. Germain Act, and changes in state laws permitted institutions to meet this inflation-driven demand.

Inflation has deleterious effects on an economy. Hence, there are a number of different measures calculated for expected inflation (Figure 14.7, Panel B), including the Federal Bank of Philadelphia's survey of professional forecasters, the Federal Open Market Committee inflation range reported to Congress annually under the Humphrey-Hawkins Act, and the University of Michigan Research Center's Survey of Consumers. As Panel B shows, expected inflation and actual inflation as estimated by the CPI index often differ.

Figure 14.7 ✦ MEASURES OF EXPECTED INFLATION

PANEL A: COMPREHENSIVE PRICE MEASURES: CPI AND PPI

Inflation rates change over time. There are also many different ways of measuring inflation, such as the CPI, which focuses on the prices of goods most important to households, and the PPI, which tracks prices of goods especially important to businesses.

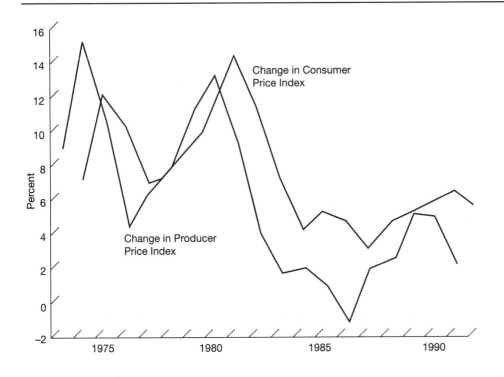

Source: Federal Reserve Bank of St. Louis, *Annual U.S. Economic Data.*

(continued)

Figure 14.7 ✦ **MEASURES OF EXPECTED INFLATION (*CONTINUED*)**

PANEL B: INFLATION AND INFLATION EXPECTATIONS

The shaded region shows the Humphrey-Hawkins CPI inflation range. CPI Inflation is the monthly percentage increase in the CPI for all urban consumers at an annual rate. Inflation expectations measures include the quarterly Federal Bank of Philadelphia *Survey of Professional Forecasters*, the monthly University of Michigan Research Center's *Survey of Consumers*, and Federal Open Market Committee ranges reported to Congress in testimony for the Humphrey-Hawkins Act.

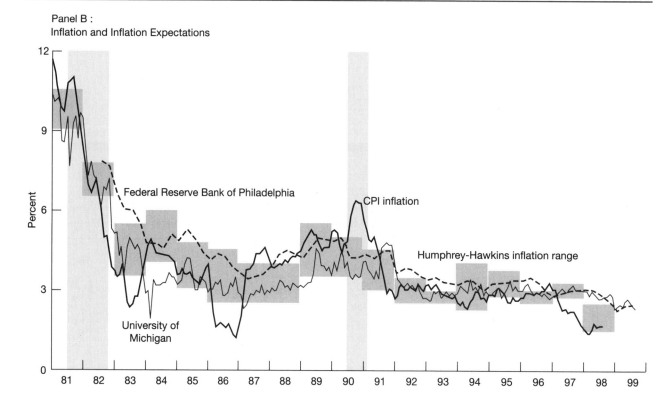

Panel B :
Inflation and Inflation Expectations

Sources: Federal Reserve Bank of St. Louis *Monetary Trends*, October 1998, p. 8.

The Fisher Effect

Although the basic principles of this real/nominal effect were first suggested in the eighteenth century, a twentieth-century economist, Irving Fisher, is widely credited with laying the foundation for the study of the relationship between interest rates and expected inflation.[12] Suppose, for instance, investors wanted a 2 percent real return, and inflation was expected to be to be 12 percent over the year. Basically, investors will demand a higher interest rate (an inflation premium) for expected lost purchasing power over the period of an investment. That relationship, frequently

[12]This discussion draws on the work of Santoni and Stone (March, 1981). For a discussion of the development of the theory of real and nominal rates, including Fisher's forerunners and his own contributions, see Humphrey (1983).

called the Fisher effect, is summarized as follows: The nominal rate of interest reflects the real rate of inflation and a premium based on the expected rate of inflation.[13] Stated as an equation:

$$(1 + i_N) = (1 + i_R)(1 + \text{Expected Inflation Rate}) \qquad [14.1]$$

Thus,

$$i_N = [(1 + i_R)(1 + \text{Expected Inflation Rate})] - 1$$

where i_N is the nominal interest rate demanded and i_R is the real rate of return desired. Note that when multiplying rates 1 is added to each rate and then subtracted. In effect, multiplying this out, the nominal rate asked will be a function of the real rate, the inflation rate, and the cross-product terms, the interaction terms between the real rate and the inflation rate. In practice, many analysts simply solve for **$i_N = i_R$ + Expected Inflation Rate,** eliminating the cross-product terms for ease of calculation if precision is not desired.

Using Equation 14.1, if the real rate of return desired is 2 percent and expected inflation is 12 percent, the nominal rate that should be charged to adjust for the 12 percent loss of purchasing power would be:

$$(1 + i_N) = (1.02)(1.12) = 1.1424$$

and

$$i_N = 1.1424 - 1 = .142, \text{ or } 14.2\%$$

Using the approximate formula, which eliminates the cross-product, the nominal rate would be just the real rate plus the inflation rate, or 2% + 12% = 14%.

The ***real ex post return*** that an investor actually gets, based on the actual inflation that occurred over the year, can be solved for by using Equation 14.1, as follows:

$$i_R = [(1 + i_N)/(1 + \text{Actual Inflation Rate})] - 1 \qquad [14.2]$$

Equation 14.2 shows that if inflation turned out to be 12 percent and the investor had charged 14.2 percent, the ex post real return would be equal to the desired return as follows:

$$i_R = [(1.142)/(1.12)] - 1 = 0.02, \text{ or } 2\%$$

EXPECTED INFLATION AND THE LOANABLE FUNDS THEORY

Changes in nominal interest rates can be examined in the context of the loanable funds theory. As shown in Panel A of Figure 14.8, an anticipated increase in price levels means that savers (the suppliers of loanable funds) will require a higher

---

[13]Economists have studied several relationships between yields and price levels. Fisher was interested in the relationship between security yields and *changes* in the price level. Another researcher, A.H. Gibson, studied the relationship between the actual level of prices and yields, noting that when prices are relatively high, so are interest rates, and when prices are low, yields also tend to be low. No conclusion has been reached about whether the Gibson relation is consistent with or in conflict with the Fisher effect. See Gibson (1923); Shiller and Siegel (1977); and John H. Wood and Norma L. Wood. *Financial Markets*. San Diego, California: Harcourt Brace Jovanovich (1985), 579–586.

Figure 14.8 ✦ **EFFECT OF INFLATION ON INTEREST RATES**

PANEL A: INFLATION AND THE EQUILIBRIUM RATE OF INTEREST

According to the Fisher theory of interest rates and inflation, if inflation is anticipated, the nominal equilibrium level of interest rates (i_N) will equal the real rate (i_R) plus a premium equal to the expected rate of inflation $[E(P)]$.

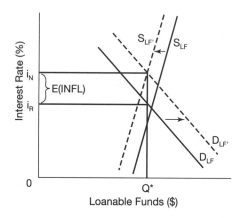

PANEL B: INFLATIONARY EXPECTATIONS AND THE REAL RATE OF INTEREST

Challengers of the Fisher theory argue that real rates are also affected by expected inflation. Thus, the supply of loanable funds may increase if inflation is anticipated, resulting in a decrease in the real rate.

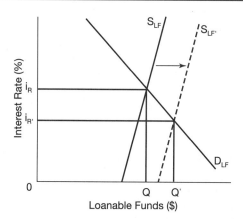

nominal rate of return equal to approximately the real rate plus the expected inflation rate at every quantity of loanable funds supplied. This change means that the original curve S_{LF} must shift to the left, to S_{LF}'. At the same time, however, borrowers (the demanders of loanable funds) will be willing to pay the higher nominal rate, realizing that they will be repaying their loans in "cheaper dollars," so the demand curve D_{LF} will shift to D_{LF}'. The result is a new point of intersection at a higher nominal rate of interest, with the increase in nominal interest rates, or the inflationary premium, equal to the expected rate of inflation. A key point is that the real rate of interest remains unchanged. The Fisher theory implicitly assumes that even in the face of inflationary expectations, the real rate, or the rate at which goods can be exchanged for goods, is unaffected.

Stability of the Real Rate   Alternatively, challengers to the stability of the real rate under the Fisher theory argue that real rates will not stay constant and will be affected by expected inflation, as shown in Panel B of Figure 14.8. With higher expected inflation, investors will reduce their cash holdings in the short-run to avoid an even greater loss of purchasing power and invest in a larger amount of interest-bearing assets. The additional money available for investments will increase the supply of funds available, causing the supply curve to shift to the right to (S_{LF}'). Under this scenario, the real rate of interest falls from i_R to i_R'.[14] Hence, if Equation 14.1 is used to estimate the new nominal rate, expected inflation would be adjusted to using a lower real rate, not the original one, and investors would set a lower nominal rate adjusted for inflation than under the Fisher theory, in which the real rate remains the same.

FURTHER EVALUATION OF THE FISHER THEORY

Fisher's theory is intuitively appealing and widely cited. During the 1980s, as inflation approached a modern peak of 13.6 percent in 1980 and Treasury bill (T-bill) yields were on their way to levels as high as 15.51 percent in the summer of 1981, the link between the two was emphasized even more than usual. Without actual reference to the Fisher theory, Fed officials publicly blamed high interest rates on inflation. Then Chairman Paul Volcker stated, "When the money supply is brought clearly under control and expectations of inflation dissipate, interest rates will tend to decline." His predecessor, G. William Miller, made a similar reference, stating, ". . . the recent and expected inflation also has been an extremely important factor underlying the increase in interest rates. . . ."[15] The Bush administration's chief economist, Michael Boskin, also acknowledged the linkage, stating, "The best step we can take to reduce pressure on inflation and interest rates is to negotiate a credible deficit-reduction package promptly."[16] (This statement is an implicit acceptance of the loanable funds theory.)

Historical Relationships   Empirical research on past interest rate movements and the rate of inflation has also been used to support the Fisher theory. Tracking historical changes in a rate-of-inflation measure such as the CPI against an interest rate measure almost always results in a positive correlation. For example, during the period 1966–1979, the correlation coefficient between the prime rate and the GNP Price Deflator was 0.70; when the commercial paper rate was used as the measure of

---

[14]Mundell (1963) and Tobin (1965). Recent empirical work also casts doubt on the stability of the real rate. See Rose (1988).

[15]See Cox (1980).

[16]David Wessel and Tom Herman. "Interest Rates Head Up Across the Board, but Brady Discounts New Inflation Fears." *The Wall Street Journal* (February 24, 1989), A2.

interest rates, the correlation was 0.81.[17] Although the relationship has been stronger in some periods than others, it encourages belief in the Fisher effect. However, observed correlation does not guarantee causality, because some unknown factor or factors could be affecting both interest rates and inflation in a similar fashion so that they appear to be related to one another but are actually both related to other things. In addition, these findings focus on historical inflation rates, whereas the Fisher effect addresses expected inflation rates.

Measurement Problems　　Other studies, including those by Fisher himself, have calculated ex post real rates of return by subtracting ex post inflation rates from nominal rates to solve for the real rate of return (i.e., real rate = nominal rate −ex post rate of inflation). Fisher found that ex post real rates were not stable, which suggests that inflationary expectations by investors were consistently incorrect. In later tests, he concluded that the inflation premiums imposed by the markets were strongly influenced by past rates of inflation and that past price changes were inadequate estimates of future inflation.[18]

Recent ex post analyses confirm that if the Fisher theory is true, inaccurate inflationary expectations persist. For example, Panel A of Figure 14.9 shows that during the period 1960–1986, the ex post real rate on three-month T-bills was sometimes negative. This means that nominal rates were less than actual rates of inflation in some years. However, investors appeared to have gained a lesson from these years and demanded higher nominal rates in most years in the 1980s and in the 1990s as well to cover the higher inflationary expectations that were realized. As shown in Panel C, with the exception of a period in 1992 and 1993, when real rates were close to zero, real rates were positive (see panels B and C of Figure 14.9).

Although nominal rates have seemed ex post to compensate for lost purchasing power in the 1990s, Fisher's theory is based on ex ante expectations. Researchers have had difficulty calculating desired ex ante real rates of return by investors, since neither the real rate of interest nor the expected rate of inflation is empirically observable. In general, expert observers assume the real rate of interest to be in the range of 2 percent to 4 percent, based on the average growth rate in the GNP. Estimates of real rates have included yields on T-bills, high-grade corporate bonds, and equity securities. Actual figures or lagged averages of one of several inflation measures, such as CPI or the GNP Price Deflator, have been used to estimate the inflationary premium. Not surprisingly, there is no uniform agreement on measurement or methodology, and the research findings are contradictory.[19]

Adjusting for the Tax Effect　　Another complicating factor is income taxes, which are levied on nominal rather than real returns. For example, suppose that the before-tax ex ante real return is 4 percent. For an investor in the 28 percent marginal tax bracket, an after-tax real rate of 4 percent ([1 − 0.28 = 2.88%] would be expected in the absence of inflation.[20]

---

[17]See Cox (1980), 22.

[18]A review of Fisher's initial empirical research is provided in Humphrey (1983).

[19]Examples of attempts to measure inflationary expectations and/or the real rate can be found in Fama (1975), Carlson (1977), Mullineaux and Protopapadakis (1984), and Leonard and Solt (1986).

[20]Key proponents of the tax effect are Darby (1975) and Feldstein (1976). A discussion of the potential effect of changing inflationary expectations on the real rate and the subsequent tax effects is provided in Holland (1984).

Figure 14.9 ✦ TRENDS IN INFLATION AND INTEREST RATES

PANEL A: EX POST NOMINAL AND REAL INTEREST RATES ON 3-MONTH T-BILLS: 1960–1986

If the actual (ex post) rate of inflation during a period exceeds the premium for expected (ex ante) inflation incorporated in nominal interest rates, the ex post real rate will be negative.

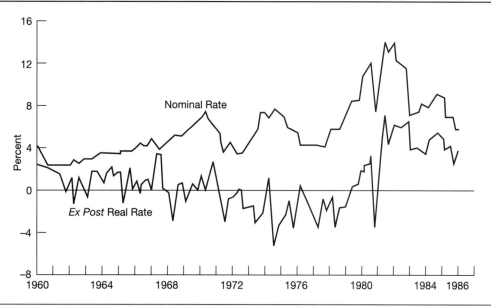

Source: Adapted from Carl E. Walsh, "Three Questions Concerning Nominal and Real Interest Rates," *Economic Review* (Federal Reserve Bank of San Francisco) (Fall 1987): 7.

PANEL B: ACTUAL INFLATION IN RECENT YEARS, 1989 TO MID-1998

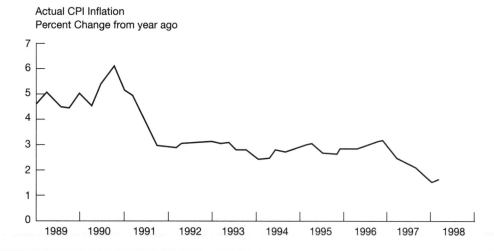

Source: Federal Reserve Bank of St. Louis *Monetary Trends*, October 1998, p. 8.

(continued)

Figure 14.9 ✦ **TRENDS IN INFLATION AND INTEREST RATES** (*CONTINUED*)

PANEL C: TREND IN REAL INTEREST RATES, 1981 TO MID-1998 (EX-POST RATES)

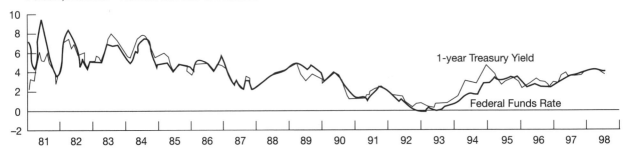

Real Interest Rates
Percent, Real rate = Nominal rate less CPI inflation

Note: Real Interest Rates are ex post measures, equal to nominal rates minus CPI inflation.

Source: Federal Reserve Bank of St. Louis *Monetary Trends*, October 1998, p. 8.

Now suppose that inflation is expected to be 4 percent, so ignoring the Fisher theory cross-product terms, investors ask for an approximate nominal rate of 8 percent (4 percent before-tax real rate + 4 percent expected inflation rate). However, since the investor will be taxed on the entire nominal rate, he or she will be taxed on the inflation premium as well as the real rate. Thus, the expected approximate real after-tax return would be the nominal rate after tax less the expected inflation rate, or 8.00 percent $(1 - 0.28) - 4$ percent = only 1.76 percent versus the 2.88 percent desired. Anticipation of this tax effect exerts a new upward pressure on the nominal rate, suggesting that the change in nominal yields will actually be greater than that predicted by Fisher to compensate for the tax on the investors' inflation premium. To protect after-tax real returns to an investor with a 28 percent tax rate (t), the approximate nominal yield must include a before-tax inflation premium inflated for the tax to be imposed on that premium by dividing the expected inflation ratio by $(1 - t)$, i.e.:

$$\text{Before-Tax Inflation Premium} = [\text{Expected Inflation Rate}] / (1 - t) \qquad [14.3]$$

Incorporating the before-tax inflation premium in the original Fisher equation (Equation 14.1), the nominal rate adjusted for taxes would be calculated as follows:

$$i_N = [(1 + i_R)(1 + \text{Before-Tax Inflation Premium})] - 1 \qquad [14.4]$$

where i_n = the nominal return before taxes and i_R = the real rate expected before taxes.

For the previous example, using Equation 14.3, the before-tax inflation premium would be:

$$4\% / (1 - 0.28) = 5.556\%,$$

and using Equation 14.4, the nominal rate that investors would charge would be:

$$i_N = (1.04)(1.0556) - 1 = 9.782\%$$

To prove that the tax-adjusted nominal rate compensates for both inflation and its tax effect, Equation 14.4 can be used to solve for the after-tax real return, $i_R (1 - t)$:

$$i_R (1 - t) = \{[(1 + i_N) / (1 + \text{Before-Tax Inflation Premium})] - 1\} (1 - t) \qquad [14.5]$$

If 4 percent inflation actually occurs, the ex post real rate after taxes that the investor will receive will be:

$$i_R (1 - t) = \{[(1.0978) / (1.0556)] - 1\} (0.72) = 0.0288, \text{ or } 2.88\%$$

The 2.88 percent is the original after-tax real rate of return the investor desired. The inflation adjustments, however, are based on ex ante rather than ex post inflation rates. Thus, again, if expected inflation is different than actual inflation, the investor may not get this desired ex post after-tax real return. Thus, the problem of protecting ex ante after-tax yields remains.[21]

Accuracy of Interest Rate Forecasting

As the opening paragraphs to this chapter suggest, the life of a forecaster of interest rates and inflation is difficult. Many variables must be considered before rates are predicted, and each variable is a possible source of error. Another problem is that forecasters cannot stop with a prediction of the real rate of interest; they are expected to estimate several different rates. At commercial banks, movements in T-bill and negotiable CD rates are of great concern. At a savings institution, trends in mortgage rates are just as crucial. Managers of insurance companies are interested in long-term bond yields, as are mutual fund and pension fund managers. Finance company managers focus on interest rates on consumer credit and commercial paper.

Professional Forecasts Based on the Loanable Funds Theory

The loanable funds framework is widely used by professional forecasters. They project changes in interest rates based on an analysis of credit demand by sector and by type of security offered as well as on the amount of loanable funds supplied and the types of securities investors will prefer. Resulting forecasts are crucial to managers who must choose what securities to issue or to purchase from among a variety with fixed and variable rates and different maturities.

Salomon Brothers' annual *Prospects for the Credit Markets* is perhaps the most widely quoted example of this approach to rate forecasting, but the American Council of Life Insurance, Morgan Guaranty Trust Company, Prudential Insurance Company, and others also make their forecasts available to financial intermediaries. Other analysts supply forecasts only on a proprietary basis. Large financial institutions often have staff economists who develop forecasts for managers. Managers of smaller firms gather information from many professional forecasters to assist in formulating asset/liability strategies appropriate for the interest rate environment.

---

[21]For more discussion, see Gordon J. Alexander and William Sharpe. *Fundamentals of Investments*. Englewood Cliffs, NJ: Prentice-Hall (1989), 102, and Peek (1988).

Economists use other more sophisticated time series or regression models for forecasts as well.[22]

This section discussed factors that are important in understanding and predicting the movements of interest rates. Before discussing theories for exchange rates, the following sections discuss how to read and calculate interest rates or yields for short-term money market securities, with which individual investors are often unfamiliar.

CALCULATING EFFECTIVE ANNUAL YIELDS

In its simplest form, a *yield is what you earned divided by what you paid for a security adjusted for how many times you could earn this yield during a year*. Since securities have different maturities, holding periods, and cash flows, *effective annual yields* are calculated to facilitate comparisons. The effective annual yield (y°) on an investment is the compound rate of return an investor would earn, given the asset's cash flow characteristics if the investor held it for exactly 365 days (366 days in leap years) and received the return at the end of that year. For long-term securities, in general the effective annual yield is calculated as the discount rate that makes the price of the security equal to the present value of its future cash flows, a definition with which students of financial management are familiar.[23]

Money market securities are unique in that they are short-term securities with maturities less than one year that generally sell as discount securities, requiring a single cash outflow from the investor, followed by a single cash inflow at a later date (much like a zero coupon bond that simply pays a maturity value). However, money

---

[22]VAR (vector autoregressive) models are discussed and illustrated in Eugeni, Evans, and Strongin (1992), and in "The Future Is Not What It Used To Be." *The Economist* (June 13, 1992), 75. Other models that have been used are multivariate regression models, in which the expected change in rate is a function of the unexpected change in a money supply measure, the unexpected change in the CPI, the unexpected change in the PPI, the unexpected change in the unemployment rate, the unexpected change in industrial production, the unexpected change in the trade balance, an intercept term, and a random error term. The model attempts to explain interest rate changes by using measures of the money supply, inflation, the level of business activity, and activity involving the foreign sector—all important components of the theoretical interest rate models discussed earlier in the chapter. See Dwyer and Haler (1989). The perils of economic forecasting are discussed in more detail in Van Dyke (1986) and Taylor (1992). A recent study at the Federal Reserve Bank of Cleveland showed that households' forecasts of inflation are more accurate than forecasts of professional economists. Some argue, however, that economists are improving through the use of techniques such as VAR. See Bryan and Gavin (1986). Many argue that in reasonably efficient markets, only those participants with private sources of information or with superior information-processing models unknown to other participants are in a position to earn potentially superior profits. Thus, if an economist is an exceptionally successful forecaster, it is not in his or her best interest to reveal that fact to others. See Urang (1988, 1989); Tom Herman. "How to Profit from Economists' Forecasts." *The Wall Street Journal* (January 22, 1993), C1, C6; Ronald Bailey. "Them That Can, Do; Them That Can't, Forecast." *Forbes* (December 26, 1988), 94–100; and Belongia (1987).

[23]The yield to maturity on a bond, for instance, is the discount rate that makes the bond's price equal to coupon payment (PVIFAn) + Maturity Value (PVIFn), where PVIFA = the present value annuity factor and PVIF, the single sum present value factor. See Arthur J. Keown, David F. Scott, John D. Martin, and J. William Petty. *Basic Financial Management*, Eighth Edition, New Jersey: Prentice Hall, 1999, Chapter 7.

market securities have maturities that are less than one year in maturity, so their yields have to be annualized for the number of times a year an investor could earn that yield. For instance, if an investor invests in a three-month T-bill, the investor could earn that yield 365 days / 90 days = 4.06 times a year. Hence, formally, the equation for the annual or often called **coupon equivalent yield** for a money market security is basically what the investor received over what he or she paid times the number of times a year this could occur:

$$y = \frac{\text{Par or (P1)} - \text{Po}}{\text{Po}} \left(\frac{365}{n} \right) \qquad [14.6]$$

where Po is the amount initially invested; Par (or P1) is the par value at maturity (Par) or price (P1) received if sold before maturity; and n is the number of days until maturity or until sold.

If the possibility of compounding over a full year is also considered, an **effective annual yield (y°)** can be calculated as follows:

$$y° = \left[1 + \frac{\text{Par (or P1)} - \text{Po}}{\text{Po}} \right]^{(365/n)} - 1 \qquad [14.7]$$

or simply

$$y° = [\text{Par (or P1)} / \text{Po}]^{(365/n)} - 1$$

This equation implicitly assumes that any money received will be reinvested at the given annual rate during the year, resulting in a higher effective annual rate at the end of the year. Hence, y° will always be greater than y.

In the real world, the yield on money market securities is generally quoted, however, as a percentage of the securities par (maturity) value of 100 percent. This is called a **bank discount yield**. This traditional method for quoting bills yields dates to 1929, when T-bills were first sold. At that time, traders found it easier to make computations considering a year as 360 days, and calculating yields as a fraction of 100 percent (par value) versus price (Po). The formula for calculating the bank discount yield (d) on T-bills is:

$$d = \frac{\text{Par} - \text{Po}}{\text{Par}} \left(\frac{360}{n} \right) \qquad [14.8]$$

Note that because bank discount yields are a fraction of par value versus price, discount yields (d) will always be lower then annual yield (y) or effective annual yields (y°).

Solving for the T-bill's price (Po) by using Equation 14.8, Po is:

$$\text{Po} = \text{Par} \times \left[1 - \frac{(d \times n)}{360} \right] \qquad [14.9]$$

The T-bill's price is the par value of 100 percent less the discount rate times n/360, adjusting for the T-bill's maturity in days relative to a-360 day year. Given the security's price (Po), y and y° can then be calculated by using Equations 14.6 and 14.7.

Example of Price and Yield Calculations

Money market securities are sold in both primary (original issuance) and secondary (for resale) markets. T-bills, for instance, are usually issued with one of three original maturity dates—92, 182, or 364 days—with typical minimum denominations of $10,000.

Weekly auctions are conducted by the Federal Reserve Bank of New York, with bids quoted as discount yields as a percentage of par value, as calculated in Equation 14.8. Approximately 40 large government security dealers (large banks and investment banks) authorized by the U.S. Treasury stand ready to purchase Treasury securities at every auction and often act as buyers and sellers in the secondary market. Thus, these dealers are frequently involved in trades for Fed open market operations.[24]

Figure 14.10, Panel A, shows the results of a typical T-bill auction as reported in *The Wall Street Journal*. Information for T-bill auctions are published on Tuesday after regularly scheduled Monday auctions. These data are for a T-bill auction on Monday, November 2, 1998. In this auction, as usual, many more bids were submitted than could be accepted, based on the volume of bills the Treasury had decided to sell. Noncompetitive bidders are assured of receiving bills, but the price they pay is determined by the average competitive bid that is ultimately accepted. Winning competitive bidders are those willing to pay the highest percentage of par value. Thus, noncompetitive bidders know their bids will be accepted but are unsure of the price, whereas competitive bidders know the price they will pay if they win but have no guarantee of delivery.

Published information on T-bill auctions includes the average, high, and low prices paid for bills, the bank discount rate, and the annual yield coupon equivalent yield. Standard and Poor's assigns the Committee on Uniform Securities Identification Procedures (CUSIP) to securities.

The auction price (rate) for the 13-week (91-day) T-bill is 98.881 (4.425 percent). The 98.881 is the price as a percentage of par, i.e., 98.881 percent. The 4.425 percent is the discount yield. Based on the discount yield of 4.425 percent for 13 week (91-day) T-bills, by using Equation 14.9, the T-bill's price was calculated using:

$$\text{Po} = \text{Par}\left(\left[1 - \frac{d \times n}{360}\right]\right) = 100\%\left[1 - \frac{(0.04425)(91)}{360}\right] = 98.881\% \text{ of par}$$

So, the price that must be paid is: $10,000 (0.98881) or $9,888.10.

---

[24]Primary dealers are involved in about 75 percent of the daily volume in T-bill trading, so they receive significant price information that provides them with a competitive advantage over other traders. In 1991 Salomon Brothers misused its power by submitting false bids in its customers' names to win more than 90 percent of a two-year Treasury note issue, in spite of the fact that Treasury auction rules are intended to prevent a single bidder from receiving more than 35 percent of any issue. Salomon was fined $290 million; these actions hurt the firm's reputation and, hence, profitability for many years. In 1992, the Fed instituted a single-price or Dutch auction system for selected two-year and five-year notes. This entails that all winning bidders in the auction pay the same price, unlike a traditional auction, in which securities are allocated to the highest bidders in descending order of price until all securities are allocated. Many experts believe that the traditional bidding system encourages primary dealers, who must bid at every auction, to collude in their efforts to minimize the "winners' curse." The Dutch auction system reduces such problems. In 1998 the U.S. Treasury announced that Treasury bond and note sales would be based on a Dutch auction format, with all bonds sold at the price offered by the highest bidder. Consumers can more easily purchase Treasury notes directly from the government under a recent Treasury Direct program by calling the Bureau of Public Debt at (202) 874–4000 and punching in 1 and then 241 to receive documents; by phoning (800) 943–6864; or by visiting the Bureau's Web site at http://www.publicdebt.treas.gov. Five-year notes are issued quarterly with interest on the notes paid semiannually and taxed in the year received. See Robert Heady. "'Safe' Options for Your Dollar." *The Denver Post* (November 15, 1998), 13L.

Figure 14.10 ✦ PUBLISHED INFORMATION ON TREASURY BILLS

PANEL A: RESULTS OF WEEKLY T-BILL AUCTIONS PUBLISHED IN *THE WALL STREET JOURNAL*, NOVEMBER 3, 1998, C18.
Data include the volume sold, the average price, and the discount (d) and coupon equivalent yields to purchasers.

PANEL B: DAILY DATA ON SECONDARY MARKET YIELDS FOR T-BILLS.
Information includes the maturity date and days to maturity, the bid discount yield at which investors can sell to dealers, and the asked discount yield at which investors must pay dealers. The Ask Yld. is the bond equivalent yield (y) based on the asked price.

Here are the details of yesterday's auction by the Treasury of 13-week and 26-week bills.
All bids are awarded at a single price at the market-clearing yield. Rates are determined by the difference between that price and the face value.

	13-Week	26-Week
Applications	$25,343,719,000	$22,628,149,000
Accepted bids	$8,001,177,000	$8,008,349,000
Accepted noncompet'ly	$1,321,145,000	$1,158,564,000
Auction price (rate)	98.881 (4.425%)	97.796 (4.360%)
Coupon equivalent	4.539%	4.520%
Bids at market yield	46%	66%
CUSIP number	912795BT7	912795BK6

Both issues are dated Nov. 5. The 13-week bills mature Feb. 4, 1999, and the 26-week bills mature May 6, 1999.

Here are the details of yesterday's 79-day Treasury cash-management bills. All bids are awarded at a single price at the market-clearing yield. Rates are determined by the difference between that price and the face value.

Applications	$53,976,620,000
Accepted bids	$25,000,370,000
Accepted noncompetitively	$7,620,000
Bids at market-clearing yield accepted	27%
Auction price (rate)	98.975 (4.67%)
Coupon equivalent	4.78%
Cusip number	912795AY7

The bills are dated Nov. 3, and mature Jan. 21, 1999.

TREASURY BILLS

Maturity	Days to Mat.	Bid	Asked	Chg.	Ask Yld.
Nov 05 '98	2	3.83	3.75	+ 0.13	3.80
Nov 12 '98	9	4.00	3.92	+ 0.29	3.98
Nov 19 '98	16	3.84	3.76	+ 0.47	3.82
Nov 27 '98	24	3.54	3.46	+ 0.19	3.52
Dec 03 '98	30	3.68	3.64	+ 0.14	3.70
Dec 10 '98	37	3.98	3.94	+ 0.32	4.01
Dec 17 '98	44	4.02	3.98	+ 0.25	4.05
Dec 24 '98	51	4.22	4.18	+ 0.19	4.26
Dec 31 '98	58	4.24	4.20	+ 0.17	4.29
Jan 07 '99	65	4.25	4.23	+ 0.15	4.32
Jan 14 '99	72	4.25	4.23	+ 0.10	4.33
Jan 21 '99	79	4.65	4.63	+ 0.20	4.74
Jan 28 '99	86	4.33	4.32	+ 0.12	4.43
Feb 04 '99	93	4.44	4.42	+ 0.16	4.53
Feb 04 '99	93	4.42	4.41	+ 0.10	4.52
Feb 11 '99	100	4.37	4.35	+ 0.19	4.46
Feb 18 '99	107	4.34	4.32	+ 0.18	4.44
Feb 25 '99	114	4.34	4.32	+ 0.17	4.44
Mar 04 '99	121	4.39	4.37	+ 0.21	4.50
Mar 11 '99	128	4.34	4.32	+ 0.16	4.45
Mar 18 '99	135	4.35	4.33	+ 0.17	4.46
Mar 25 '99	142	4.33	4.31	+ 0.19	4.45
Apr 01 '99	149	4.36	4.34	+ 0.17	4.48
Apr 08 '99	156	4.36	4.34	+ 0.16	4.48
Apr 15 '99	163	4.38	4.36	+ 0.17	4.51
Apr 22 '99	170	4.38	4.36	+ 0.17	4.51
Apr 29 '99	**177**	**4.38**	**4.37**	**+ 0.16**	**4.53**
May 06 '99	184	4.37	4.36	+ 0.17	4.52
May 27 '99	205	4.35	4.33	+ 0.18	4.49
Jun 24 '99	233	4.26	4.24	+ 0.14	4.40
Jul 22 '99	261	4.27	4.25	+ 0.16	4.42
Aug 19 '99	289	4.26	4.24	+ 0.17	4.41
Sep 16 '99	317	4.19	4.17	+ 0.15	4.35
Oct 14 '99	345	4.15	4.14	+ 0.15	4.33

Source: The Wall Street Journal, November 8, 1998, C20.

The coupon equivalent (or annual yield) for the T-bill given as 4.539 percent can be calculated by using Equation 14.6 as:

$$y = \frac{\text{Par} - \text{Po}}{\text{Po}} \left(\frac{365}{n} \right)$$

$$y = \frac{100\% - 98.881\%}{98.881} \left(\frac{365}{91} \right) = 0.04539, \text{ or } 4.539\%$$

The effective annual yield for the T-bill is not given, but can be calculated by using Equation 14.7:

$$y° = [\text{Par (or P1)} / \text{Po}]^{(365/n)} - 1 = [100\% / 98.881\%]^{(365/91)} - 1$$

so:

$$y° = (1.01132)^{4.01099} - 1 = 0.04618, \text{ or } 4.618\%$$

Panel B of Figure 14.10 shows data on T-bill yields in the secondary market for the same date, November 2, 1998. Besides the maturity date and days to security, the discount yield at which dealers are willing to buy (the bid price) and sell them (the asked price) are given on a bank discount basis. The dealer makes a profit on the spread between the asked and bid prices. Because there is an inverse relationship between bill prices and yields, dealers sell bills at higher prices (lower yields to buyers) than the prices at which they are willing to buy them. Given the January 28, 1999, maturity date bill shown in Panel B with 86 days to maturity and an asked discount rate of 4.32%, its price can be calculated by using Equation 14.9:

$$Po = Par \times \left[1 - \left(\frac{d \times n}{360} \right) \right] = 100\% \left[1 - \frac{(0.0432)(86)}{360} \right] = 98.968\% \text{ of par}$$

So, the price that must be paid is: $10,000 × 0.98968, or $9,896.80.

Hence, the effective annual rate (y°) for the bill can be computed by using Equation 14.7:

$$y° = [Par \text{ (or P1) } / Po]^{(365/n)} - 1 = [100\% / 98.968\%]^{(365/86)} - 1$$

so:

$$y° = (1.01043)^{4.2442} - 1 = .04502 \text{ or } 4.502\%$$

DIFFERENCES IN YIELDS FOR MONEY MARKET SECURITIES

Differences in yields on securities reflect differences in default risk, liquidity, denomination size, and maturity. Because Treasury securities are backed by the taxing and money-creation power of the federal government, they are in this sense free of default risk. The existence of secondary markets for investments and the size of those markets also affect an investor's assessment of risk. An investor wishing to sell a financial asset quickly obviously needs a market in which to sell it. The larger the market, the greater the seller's opportunity to obtain cash easily without substantial loss of value—that is, the greater the **liquidity**. As short-term securities maturing in less than a year, money market securities are subject to low price risk in terms of the present values of their cash flows falling with a change in rates. Securities with higher minimum denominations, such as money market securities, also tend to pay higher rates.

Figure 14.11 shows money rates for different types of money market securities including commercial paper, CDs, banker's acceptances, repurchase agreements, and T-bills. These securities are similar by having maturities less than one year, having low or no default risk, and generally being very liquid; that is, they can be sold easily with little or no loss of value. Since these money market securities are relatively homogeneous and substitutable, their rates tend to be close to each other. For instance, as shown on Figure 14.11, three-month CDs had a rate of 4.83 percent; 90-day commercial paper, 5.1 percent; 90-day banker's acceptances, 5.05 percent; and overnight repurchase agreements (repos), 4.83 percent. Differences reflect differences in default risk, maturity, minimum denomination, and the marketability of different securities in terms of having a strong or weak secondary market for trading.

Figure 14.11 ✦ MONEY MARKET YIELD QUOTATIONS

MONEY RATES

December 2, 1998

The key U.S. and foreign annual interest rates below are a guide to general levels but don't always represent actual transactions.

PRIME RATE: 7.75% (effective 11/18/98). The base rate on corporate loans posted by at least 75% of the nation's 30 largest banks.

DISCOUNT RATE: 4.50% (effective 11/17/98). The charge on loans to depository institutions by the Federal Reserve Banks.

FEDERAL FUNDS: 4 3/4% high, 3% low, 4 % near closing bid, 4 1/4% offered. Reserves traded among commercial banks for overnight use in amounts of $1 million or more. Source: Prebon Yamane (U.S.A.) Inc.

CALL MONEY: 6.50% (effective 11/18/98). The charge on loans to brokers on stock exchange collateral. Source: Telerate.

COMMERCIAL PAPER placed directly by General Electric Capital Corp.: 4.80% 30 to 37 days; 5.28% 38 to 47 days; 5.23% 48 to 65 days; 5.11% 66 to 97 days; 5.03% 98 to 125 days; 4.96% 126 to 153 days; 4.90% 154 to 190 days; 4.82% 191 to 208 days; 4.80% 209 to 270 days.

COMMERCIAL PAPER: High-grade unsecured notes sold through dealers by major corporations: 5.45% 30 days; 5.25% 60 days; 5.10% 90 days.

CERTIFICATES OF DEPOSIT: 4.78% one month; 4.79% two months; 4.83% three months; 4.97% six months; 4.95% one year. Average of top rates paid by major New York banks on primary new issues of negotiable C.D.s, usually on amounts of $1 million and more. The minimum unit is $100,000. Typical rates in the secondary market: 5.45% one month; 5.20% three months; 5.05% six months.

BANKERS ACCEPTANCES: 5.50% 30 days; 5.20% 60 days; 5.13% 90 days; 5.05% 120 days; 5.00% 150 days; 4.95% 180 days. Offered rates of negotiable, bank-backed business credit instruments typically financing an import order.

LONDON LATE EURODOLLARS: 5 5/8% - 5 1/2% one month; 5 3/8% - 5 1/4% two months; 5 9/32% - 5 5/32% three months; 5 1/4% - 5 1/8% four months; 5 3/16% - 5 1/16% five months; 5 1/8% - 5 % six months.

LONDON INTERBANK OFFERED RATES (LIBOR): 5.62375% one month; 5.27531% three months; 5.12813% six months; 5.07094% one year. British Bankers' Association average of interbank offered rates for dollar deposits in the London market based on quotations at 16 major banks. Effective rate for contracts entered into two days from date appearing at top of this column.

FOREIGN PRIME RATES: Canada 6.75%; Germany 3.64%; Japan 1.500%; Switzerland 3.500%; Britain 6.75%. These rate indications aren't directly comparable; lending practices vary widely by location.

TREASURY BILLS: Results of the Monday, November 30, 1998, auction of short-term U.S. government bills, sold at a discount from face value in units of $10,000 to $1 million: 4.435% 13 weeks; 4.410% 26 weeks.

OVERNIGHT REPURCHASE RATE: 4.83%. Dealer financing rate for overnight sale and repurchase of Treasury securities. Source: Telerate.

FEDERAL HOME LOAN MORTGAGE CORP. (Freddie Mac): Posted yields on 30-year mortgage commitments. Delivery within 30 days 6.57%, 60 days 6.63%, standard conventional fixed-rate mortgages; 5.625%, 2% rate capped one-year adjustable rate mortgages. Source: Telerate.

FEDERAL NATIONAL MORTGAGE ASSOCIATION (Fannie Mae): Posted yields on 30 year mortgage commitments (priced at par) for delivery within 30 days 6.57%; 60 days 6.61%, standard conventional fixed rate-mortgages; 5.55%, 6/2 rate capped one-year adjustable rate mortgages. Source: Telerate.

MERRILL LYNCH READY ASSETS TRUST: 4.67%. Annualized average rate of return after expenses for the past 30 days; not a forecast of future returns.

Source: Wall Street Journal, December 3, 1998, C20.

The minimum denominations are large for money market securities. For instance, the minimum T-bill has a face value of $10,000. Commercial paper ranges from a minimum of $25,000 upward. Negotiable CDs have a legal minimum of $100,000 but in practice usually are more than $1 million, and banker's acceptances come in denominations of $100,000 to $500,000. Consequently, small investors may choose to hold shares in a money market fund (holding a portfolio of money market securities) with a $500 to $2,500 minimum. The different types of securities are summarized in Table 14.1.

Figure 14.12 shows how a banker's acceptance is created, a process with which individual investors are often unfamiliar. Basically, an importer arranges with his or her bank to have a letter of credit (L/C) from the bank guaranteeing that the importer will pay. This L/C is delivered to the exporter's bank, which notifies the exporter, upon which the exporter sends the goods to the importer, along with shipping documents and a time draft, asking for payment in a certain number of days. When the bank accepts this draft, it becomes a banker's acceptance. If the bank pays the draft, the importer owes the bank this sum. The banker's acceptance can be sold by the bank at a discount and traded among investors like other money market securities, to be paid after the bank is paid by the importer at maturity.

Some money market securities, including Fed funds and Negotiable CDs, rather than selling for a discount and paying a higher maturity value, sell at par value and pay interest and principal at maturity. Effective rates are calculated similar to those for T-bills. In this case Po is the par value of amount invested and P1 is the

Table 14.1 ◆ SUMMARY OF CHARACTERISTICS: DIFFERENT TYPES OF MONEY MARKET SECURITIES

Repurchase Agreements

Money market transactions in which securities (usually Treasury securities) are sold by one party to another, with the agreement that the seller will repurchase the securities at a specified price on a specified date. For the seller, the transaction is called a repo and for the buyer, a reverse repo. Repurchase agreements are commonly used by large government security dealers to finance their inventories. The daily volume of repurchase agreements sometimes reaches $1 trillion, with many transactions as short as one day. Repos are used by the Fed as part of open market operations to temporarily decrease the amount of reserves available in the banking system by selling Treasury securities with agreements to repurchase them later or to increase reserves by buying Treasury securities from banks under agreements that the banks will repurchase them later. In the mid-1980s crises occurred in the repo market with the collapse of government security dealers with large reverse repos with financial institutions. There is no secondary market for reverse repos.

Commercial Paper

Commercial paper are corporate short-term borrowings in the open market by major and lesser known companies. Commercial paper has a maturity of less than nine months; issues of longer maturity sold in the U.S. must be registered with the SEC, which increases the borrower's cost and time required to raise funds. Commercial banks, S&Ls, insurance companies, mutual funds, and other large financial institutions are main purchasers of commercial paper. The paper, like T-bills, is bought on a discount basis and redeemed at par on maturity. Minimum denominations range from $25,000 upwards, depending on whether the purchase is made through a dealer or directly from the borrowing firm. Finance companies are large issuers. Most commercial paper is held to maturity, and the secondary market is somewhat limited compared with T-bills, but the growth of money market funds enlarged the market.

Banker's Acceptance

Banker's Acceptance are negotiable securities that arise out of bankers' accepting payment in association with international trade. Thus, banker's acceptances serve not only as short-term assets to money market investors but also as short-term sources of funds to large banks that finance international transactions. Similar to T-bills, banker's acceptances are sold to money market investors at a discount from the face value, and yields are quoted on a banker's discount basis.

Negotiable Certificates of Deposit

Negotiable CDs developed as a loophole to Regulation Q, which prevented banks from offering market rates on deposits. Negotiable CDs have face values with a legal minimum of $100,000, but in practice are usually more than $1 million. They can be sold in secondary markets. Innovations in the CD market include variable-rate CDs, on which the maturity is fixed but the interest rate varies every 30 days. Also, Eurodollar CDs—which are dollar-denominated negotiable CDs issued primarily by London-based branches of American, Japanese, British, or other foreign banks—are popular. The secondary market for Eurodollar CDs is smaller than the secondary market for negotiable CDs issued in the U.S. Because the first $100,000 of each domestic negotiable CD is eligible for federal deposit insurance, but Eurodollar CDs are uninsured, yields are usually higher on Eurodollar CDs than domestic CDs.

Federal Funds

Excess reserves required by the Fed lent by one institution to another are federal funds (Fed funds). They are the assets of the lending institution and liabilities of the borrowing firm. Typically, Fed Funds transactions are very short-term; in fact, many are overnight, similar to repo/reverse repos. Fed Funds are borrowed either through direct negotiation with the lending institution or through New York brokers. The lending institution instructs the Fed or its own bank to transfer the agreed-on balances to the borrower. Because most Fed Funds transactions are overnight, the transaction is reversed the next day, including one day's interest. The Fed Funds rate is extremely important in monetary policy decisions on a daily basis. To make short-term adjustments in the supply of funds, the New York Fed will be instructed by the Fed to keep the Fed Funds within a desired range by buying or selling funds.

See Marcia Stigum. *The Money Market*. Homewood, IL: Dow Jones-Irwin, 1990; Marcia Stigum. *Money Market Calulations: Yields, Breakevens, and Arbitrage*. Homewood, IL: Dow Jones-Irwin, 1981 for in depth discussions of money market securities and yields.

Figure 14.12   ✦   **EXAMPLE OF BANKERS' ACCEPTANCE FINANCING OF U.S. IMPORTS: A BANKERS' ACCEPTANCE IS CREATED, DISCOUNTED, SOLD, AND PAID AT MATURITY**

Mechanically speaking, bankers' acceptances are among the most complex money market instruments. In this example, a banker's acceptance is created as a result of a purchase of imported goods by a U.S. firm. The purchaser's bank, assumed to be Chase Manhattan, initially extends credit to pay for the goods. Chase, in turn, borrows the funds from a money market investor by issuing a bankers' acceptance. When the acceptance matures, Chase repays the investor, using funds repaid to it by the importer.

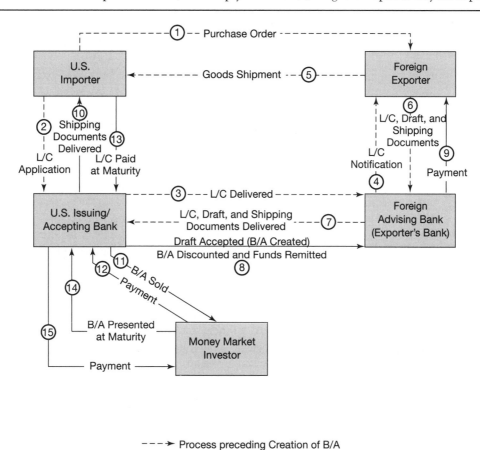

Source: Adapted by the authors from Eric Hill, "Bankers' Acceptances," in *Instruments of the Money Market* (Richmond, Va.: Federal Reserve Bank of Richmond, 1986), 127.

amount received at maturity, equal to the interest earned at the quoted rate (d) on the CD as a function of a 360-day year, as follows:

$$P1 = \text{Amount Invested}\left(1 + \frac{d \times n}{360}\right) \qquad [14.10]$$

For example, if a 180-day negotiable CD had a face value of $1 million and a coupon rate (d) of 3.5 percent, the investor would receive at maturity P1, as follows:

$$P1 = \$1\text{ million} \times \left[1 \times \frac{(0.035)\,(180)}{360}\right] = \$1.0175\text{ million}$$

The effective annual rate $(y°)$ for the bill can be computed by using Equation 14.7:

$$y° = [\text{Par (or P1)} / \text{Po}]^{(365/n)} - 1 = [1.0175 / 1]^{(365/180)} - 1$$

SO:

$$y° = (1.0175)^{2.0278} - 1 = .03581., \text{ or } 3.581\%$$

CURRENCY EXCHANGE RATES

Financial institutions active in international markets face **exchange rate risk**, or variability in NIM caused by fluctuations in currency exchange rates. Exchange rate risk increased significantly in 1971 when, as explained in the Appendix to Chapter 3, the United States officially abandoned the gold standard and allowed its currency exchange rate to float. Although many other currencies had been pegged to the value of the U.S. dollar, since 1973 most have been allowed to float. As a result, institutions that have foreign branches, issue banker's acceptances, purchase foreign securities, accept deposits in foreign currencies, or provide loans in the international markets are exposed to exchange rate risk.

Panel A of Figure 14.13 tracks exchange rates for two foreign currencies against the U.S. dollar between 1990 and 1992. The fluctuations illustrate the uncertainty faced in international finance. For example, during this relatively short period, the graph shows that a U.S. dollar could have been exchanged for more than 155 Japanese yen at one time, only to be worth as little as 123 yen less than two years later. The rates plotted are **spot rates**, or rates for immediate exchanges between currencies. In the foreign exchange markets, spot rates are distinguished from forward rates, which are agreed on today for currency exchanges that will occur at a future date. Differences between forward and spot rates are discussed later.

Panel B shows exchange rates for the mark and yen to the U.S. dollar for a more recent period, 1996 until the third quarter of 1998. With greater joint intervention by governments, the monthly exchange rate was less volatile than in the early 1990s. However, as shown by Panel A of Figure 14.14, on a weekly and daily basis, such apparently smooth exchange rates can be quite unstable. With problems in Japan in the second half of 1998, the weekly and daily Japanese yen to the dollar spot rate was quite volatile. The last ten-day patterns for October 28, 1998, and November 3, 1998, demonstrate this extreme volatility. Panel B shows the dramatic plunge in the value of the Russian ruble on August 27, 1998, and the Malaysian ringgit in 1997 and 1998.[25]

---

[25]See Marianne Sullivan. "Russia's Crisis Affects Latin America As Several Currencies There Weaken." *The Wall Street Journal* (August 27, 1998), C17; Andrew Higgins and Mark Whitehouse. "Russia Quits Fight to Back the Ruble." *The Wall Street Journal International Edition* (August 27, 1998), C1; Darren McDermott and Leslie Lopez. "Malaysia Imposes Sweeping Currency Controls." *The Wall Street Journal International* (September 2, 1998), A10; Darren McDermott and Raphael Pura. "Malaysian Currency Controls Roil Asia Markets." *The Wall Street Journal International* (September 3, 1998), A14; and "Japan's 6-Month T-Bill Yield Is Negative." *The Wall Street Journal* (November 6, 1998), C1, C19.

Figure 14.13   ◆   Spot Exchange Rate Trends

PANEL A: SPOT EXCHANGE RATES, 1990–1992

Exchange rates among currencies fluctuate, sometimes considerably. In recent years, the value of the U.S. dollar has changed frequently in relation to other major currencies.

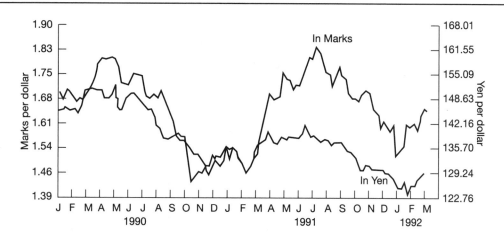

Source: Federal Reserve Bank of Cleveland, *Economic Trends*.

PANEL B: SPOT EXCHANGE RATES, 1996–1998Q3

With greater joint government intervention, dollar, mark, and yen rates were less volatile in 1996–1998Q3 than 1990–1992 on a monthly basis.

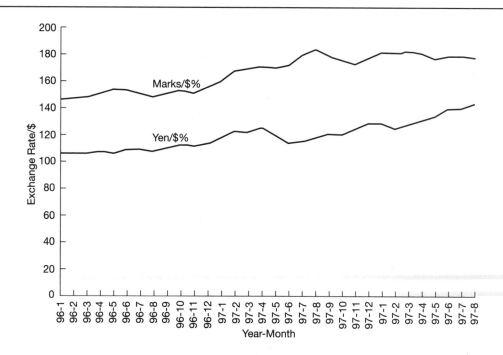

Source: Compiled by the authors using Exchange Rate Data from the *Federal Reserve Bulletins,* 1996 to 1998. Mark/$ rates are multiplied by 100 to be compatible to the yen for this figure.

Figure 14.14 ✦ **EXCHANGE RATES**

PANEL A: RECENT WEEKLY AND DAILY CHANGES IN YEN TO DOLLAR

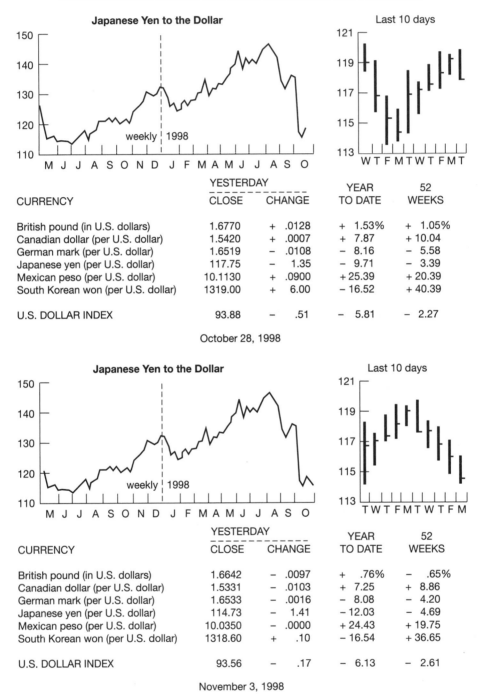

CURRENCY	YESTERDAY		YEAR TO DATE	52 WEEKS
	CLOSE	CHANGE		
British pound (in U.S. dollars)	1.6770	+ .0128	+ 1.53%	+ 1.05%
Canadian dollar (per U.S. dollar)	1.5420	+ .0007	+ 7.87	+ 10.04
German mark (per U.S. dollar)	1.6519	− .0108	− 8.16	− 5.58
Japanese yen (per U.S. dollar)	117.75	− 1.35	− 9.71	− 3.39
Mexican peso (per U.S. dollar)	10.1130	+ .0900	+ 25.39	+ 20.39
South Korean won (per U.S. dollar)	1319.00	+ 6.00	− 16.52	+ 40.39
U.S. DOLLAR INDEX	93.88	− .51	− 5.81	− 2.27

October 28, 1998

CURRENCY	YESTERDAY		YEAR TO DATE	52 WEEKS
	CLOSE	CHANGE		
British pound (in U.S. dollars)	1.6642	− .0097	+ .76%	− .65%
Canadian dollar (per U.S. dollar)	1.5331	− .0103	+ 7.25	+ 8.86
German mark (per U.S. dollar)	1.6533	− .0016	− 8.08	− 4.20
Japanese yen (per U.S. dollar)	114.73	− 1.41	− 12.03	− 4.69
Mexican peso (per U.S. dollar)	10.0350	− .0000	+ 24.43	+ 19.75
South Korean won (per U.S. dollar)	1318.60	+ .10	− 16.54	+ 36.65
U.S. DOLLAR INDEX	93.56	− .17	− 6.13	− 2.61

November 3, 1998

Note the enormous changes in spot rates for some currencies in 1998 including the Mexican peso and South Korean won.

Source: The New York Times, October 28, 1998, C10 and November 3, 1998, C10.

Figure 14.14 ✦ EXCHANGE RATES (*CONTINUED*)

PANEL B: EXAMPLES OF VOLATILE EXCHANGE RATE CHANGES IN 1998

The Rubie Plunges...
Rubies per U.S. dollar, daily data, inverted scale

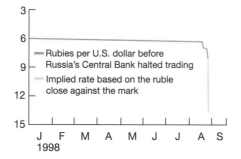

Russian Stocks Decline...
Daily close of the RTS index

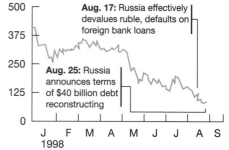

Germany's Exposure Is Greatest...
Countries with the largest bank claims on Russia, in billions of U.S. dollars, at year end 1997

And Investors Show Concern
Frankfort shares of three German banks, and their exposure to Russia*; reindexed, June 3=100

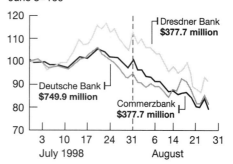

A Deflated Currency and...
U.S.-dollar value of Malaysia's ringgit

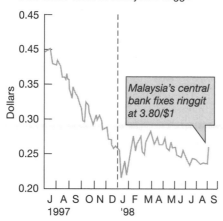

...An Economy Officially in Recession
Year-to-year percentage change in Malaysia's gross domestic product

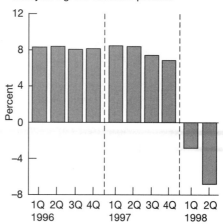

Source: Andrew Higgins and Mark Whitehouse, "Russia Quits Fight to Back the Ruble," The Wall Street Journal International Edition, August 27, 1998, C1.

Source: Darren McDermott and Raphael Pura, "Malaysian Currency Controls Roiz Asia Markets," *The Wall Street Journal International*, September 3, 1998, A14.

Exchange Rate Risk

Whenever a financial institution negotiates an international transaction involving a transfer of funds at a later date, so that the rate at which foreign currencies and U.S. dollars will be exchanged is unknown when the transaction is negotiated, exchange rate risk is present. For example, suppose that a U.S. bank agreed in August 1998 to finance a U.S. importer of Swiss chocolates. The cost of the imported chocolates, in Swiss francs (SF), was 25 million; the exporter agreed to pay back the loan in Swiss francs and did not have to pay back funds until November 2, 1998. As shown in Panel A of Figure 14.15 under the column labeled "U.S. $ equiv.," the spot exchange

Figure 14.15 ✦ FOREIGN EXCHANGE RATES

Spot and forward exchange rates between the U.S. dollar and other currencies are reported daily in the financial pages. Both direct (U.S.$ equivalent) and indirect (currency per U.S.$) rates are listed.

PANEL A:

CURRENCY TRADING

EXCHANGE RATES
Monday, August 24, 1998

The New York foreign exchange selling rates below apply to trading among banks in amounts of $1 million and more, as quoted at 4 p.m. Eastern time by Telerate and other sources. Retail transactions provide fewer units of foreign currency per dollar.

Country	U.S. $ equiv. Mon	U.S. $ equiv. Fri	Currency per U.S. $ Mon	Currency per U.S. $ Fri
Argentina (Peso)	1.0007	1.0007	.9993	.9993
Australia (Dollar)	.5803	.5839	1.7232	1.7126
Austria (Schilling)	.07918	.07918	12.630	12.630
Bahrain (Dinar)	2.6525	2.6525	.3770	.3770
Belgium (Franc)	.02701	.02692	37.020	37.150
Brazil (Real)	.8513	.8511	1.1747	1.1749
Britain (Pound)	1.6407	1.6365	.6095	.6111
1-month forward	1.6377	1.6337	.6106	.6121
3-months forward	1.6326	1.6284	.6125	.6141
6-months forward	1.6252	1.6209	.6153	.6169
Canada (Dollar)	.6455	.6486	1.5493	1.5418
1-month forward	.6458	.6490	1.5484	1.5409
3-months forward	.6462	.6494	1.5474	1.5398
6-months forward	.6467	.6499	1.5464	1.5387
Chile (Peso)	.002112	.002109	473.55	474.15
China (Renminbi)	.1208	.1208	8.2799	8.2797
Colombia (Peso)	.0007106	.0007186	1407.27	1391.55
Czech. Rep. (Koruna) .	....	....	....	....
Commercial rate	.03093	.03093	32.335	32.335
Denmark (Krone)	.1462	.1461	6.8385	6.8460
Ecuador (Sucre)	....	....	....	....
Floating rate	.0001858	.0001858	5383.00	5383.00
Finland (Markka)	.1831	.1830	5.4606	5.4633
France (Franc)	.1662	.1659	6.0175	6.0266
1-month forward	.1665	.1662	6.0066	6.0157
3-months forward	.1671	.1668	5.9847	5.9938
6-months forward	.1679	.1677	5.9553	5.9644
Germany (Mark)	.5569	.5564	1.7955	1.7973
1-month forward	.5581	.5574	1.7919	1.7939
3-months forward	.5600	.5594	1.7858	1.7875
6-months forward	.5628	.5622	1.7768	1.7786
Greece (Drachma)	.003265	.003298	306.30	303.23
Hong Kong (Dollar)	.1291	.1290	7.7475	7.7493
Hungary (Forint)	.004518	.004518	221.33	221.33
India (Rupee)	.02355	.02349	42.465	42.570
Indonesia (Rupiah)	.00008734	.00008547	11450.00	11700.00
Ireland (Punt)	1.3972	1.3893	.7157	.7198
Israel (Shekel)	.2686	.2689	3.7234	3.7188
Italy (Lira)	.0005650	.0005637	1770.00	1774.00
Japan (Yen)	.006924	.006907	144.42	144.78
1-month forward	.006951	.006937	143.87	144.15
3-months forward	.007017	.006999	142.51	142.88
6-months forward	.007083	.007093	141.19	140.98
Jordan (Dinar)	1.4065	1.4065	.7110	.7110
Kuwait (Dinar)	3.2552	3.2552	.3072	.3072
Lebanon (Pound)	.0006609	.0006609	1513.00	1513.00
Malaysia (Ringgit)	.2379	.2375	4.2028	4.2103
Malta (Lira)	2.5478	2.5478	.3925	.3925
Mexico (Peso)	....	....	....	....
Floating rate	.1032	.1027	9.6900	9.7400
Netherland (Guilder)	.4940	.4933	2.0241	2.0270
New Zealand (Dollar) .	.4925	.4929	2.0305	2.0288
Norway (Krone)	.1282	.1296	7.7978	7.7178
Pakistan (Rupee)	.02196	.02196	45.540	45.540
Peru (new Sol)	.3401	.3401	2.9407	2.9407
Philippines (Peso)	.02313	.02345	43.240	42.645
Poland (Zloty)	.2727	.2650	3.6675	3.7738
Portugal (Escudo)	.005440	.005435	183.81	183.99
Russia (Ruble) (a)	.1401	.1428	7.1400	7.0050
Saudi Arabia (Riyal)	.2665	.2666	3.7519	3.7507
Singapore (Dollar)	.5669	.5655	1.7640	1.7685
Slovak Rep. (Koruna)	.02791	.02791	35.830	35.830
South Africa (Rand)	.1588	.1577	6.2960	6.3400
South Korea (Won)	.0007658	.0007692	1305.80	1300.00
Spain (Peseta)	.006562	.006555	152.39	152.55
Sweden (Krona)	.1214	.1225	8.2342	8.1600
Switzerland (Franc)	.6664	.6655	1.5005	1.5027
1-month forward	.6688	.6677	1.4952	1.4976
3-months forward	.6731	.6721	1.4857	1.4879
6-months forward	.6792	.6784	1.4723	1.4741
Taiwan (Dollar)	.02873	.02883	34.809	34.690
Thailand (Baht)	.02401	.02404	41.650	41.605
Turkey (Lira)	.00000365	.00000365	273640.00	273640.00
United Arab (Dirham)	.2723	.2722	3.6725	3.6731
Uruguay (New Peso)	....	....	....	....
Financial	.09341	.09390	10.705	10.650
Venezuela (Bolivar)	.001734	.001736	576.62	575.87

SDR	1.3252	1.3256	.7546	.7544
ECU	1.0999	1.0981	....	....

Special Drawing Rights (SDR) are based on exchange rates for the U.S., German, British, French, and Japanese currencies. Source: International Monetary Fund.

European Currency Unit (ECU) is based on a basket of community currencies.

a-Russian Central Bank rate. Trading band lowered on 8/17/98.

The Wall Street Journal daily foreign exchange data for 1996 and 1997 may be purchased through the Readers' Reference Service (413) 592-3600.

Source: The Wall Street Journal, August 25, 1998, C18.

rate prevailing on Monday, August 24, 1998, for Switzerland (Franc) was 0.6664. In other words, one Swiss franc would buy $0.6664 U.S. dollars, the **direct rate**, or dollars per unit of foreign currency. Under the column headed "Currency per U.S. $," the spot rate is quoted as an **indirect rate**, or units of foreign currency per dollar: SF/$1.5006. Thus, one U.S. dollar would buy 1.5006 Swiss francs. Direct and indirect rates are reciprocals.

The Swiss funds that the bank lent to the importer in dollars on August 24, 1998, would have cost the bank SF25,000,000 × $.6664 = $16,660,000. The bank faced uncertainty because the SF25,000,000 would be paid back approximately two months later, and the actual dollar value of the Swiss currency that the bank would receive could be worth more or less than $16,660,000. In fact, Panel B of Figure 14.15 shows that on Monday, November 2, 1998, the direct spot rate was 0.7402 and the indirect spot rate was 1.3510. The value of the dollar had fallen, and SF25,000,000 received from the customer would now be worth SF25,000,000

Figure 14.15   ✦   **FOREIGN EXCHANGE RATES** (*CONTINUED*)

PANEL B:

CURRENCY TRADING

EXCHANGE RATES
Monday, November 2, 1998

The New York foreign exchange selling rates below apply to trading among banks in amounts of $1 million and more, as quoted at 4 p.m. Eastern time by Telerate and other sources. Retail transactions provide fewer units of foreign currency per dollar.

Country	U.S. $ equiv. Mon	U.S. $ equiv. Fri	Currency per U.S. $ Mon	Currency per U.S. $ Fri
Argentina (Peso)	1.0001	1.0001	.9999	.9999
Australia (Dollar)	.6243	.6237	1.6018	1.6033
Austria (Schilling)	.08604	.08571	11.622	11.667
Bahrain (Dinar)	2.6525	2.6525	.3770	.3770
Belgium (Franc)	.02934	.02923	34.080	34.210
Brazil (Real)	.8383	.8430	1.1930	1.1863
Britain (Pound)	1.6640	c1.6738	.6010	c.5974
1-month forward ...	1.6609	c1.6710	.6021	c.5984
3-months forward ...	1.6568	c1.6662	.6036	c.6002
6-months forward ...	1.6507	c1.6566	.6058	c.6037
Canada (Dollar)	.6522	.6479	1.5332	1.5435
1-month forward ...	.6522	.6479	1.5332	1.5435
3-months forward ...	.6523	.6479	1.5330	1.5434
6-months forward ...	.6524	.6479	1.5329	1.5435
Chile (Peso)	.002168	c.002162	461.15	c462.50
China (Renminbi)	.1208	.1208	8.2779	8.2779
Colombia (Peso)	.0006340	.0006367	1577.19	1570.50
Czech. Rep. (Koruna) .	....	....	....	....
Commercial rate	.03473	.03446	28.795	29.021
Denmark (Krone)	.1591	.1591	6.2850	6.2865
Ecuador (Sucre)	....	....	....	....
Floating rate	.0001494	.0001494	6693.00	6692.50
Finland (Markka)	.1991	.1983	5.0230	5.0430
France (Franc)	.1803	.1803	5.5451	5.5477
1-month forward ...	.1806	.1805	5.5368	5.5396
3-months forward ...	.1811	.1810	5.5212	5.5242
6-months forward ...	.1817	.1816	5.5036	5.5077
Germany (Mark)	.6048	.6045	1.6535	1.6543
1-month forward ...	.6057	.6054	1.6510	1.6519
3-months forward ...	.6074	.6070	1.6464	1.6474
6-months forward ...	.6093	.6088	1.6411	1.6425
Greece (Drachma)	.003588	.003556	278.70	281.25
Hong Kong (Dollar)	.1292	.1291	7.7429	7.7455
Hungary (Forint)	.004645	.004614	215.28	216.73
India (Rupee)	.02364	.02362	42.297	42.330
Indonesia (Rupiah)	.0001250	.0001299	8000.00	7700.00
Ireland (Punt)	1.5069	1.5065	.6636	.6638
Israel (Shekel)	.2319	.2339	4.3128	4.2761
Italy (Lira)	.0006112	.0006109	1636.00	1637.00
Japan (Yen)	.008699	.008610	114.95	116.15
1-month forward	.008740	.008646	114.42	115.65
3-months forward ...	.008822	.008728	113.36	114.57
6-months forward ...	.008931	.008835	111.98	113.19
Jordan (Dinar)	1.4094	1.4094	.7095	.7095
Kuwait (Dinar)	3.3113	3.3179	.3020	.3014
Lebanon (Pound)	.0006629	.0006629	1508.50	1508.50
Malaysia (Ringgit-b) ..	.2632	.2632	3.8000	3.8000
Malta (Lira)	2.6954	2.6774	.3710	.3735
Mexico (Peso)	....	....	....	....
Floating rate	.09928	.09928	10.073	10.073
Netherland (Guilder) ..	.5363	.5362	1.8647	1.8650
New Zealand (Dollar) .	.5311	.5295	1.8829	1.8886
Norway (Krone)	.1363	.1361	7.3373	7.3458
Pakistan (Rupee)	.02000	.02000	50.010	50.010
Peru (new Sol)	.3274	.3276	3.0546	3.0525
Philippines (Peso)	.02480	.02480	40.330	40.330
Poland (Zloty)	.2920	.2906	3.4250	3.4413
Portugal (Escudo)	.005900	.005863	169.48	170.56
Russia (Ruble) (a)	.06321	c.06246	15.820	c16.010
Saudi Arabia (Riyal) ..	.2666	.2666	3.7505	3.7505
Singapore (Dollar)	.6162	.6154	1.6229	1.6250
Slovak Rep. (Koruna) .	.02856	.02860	35.019	34.960
South Africa (Rand) ...	.1773	.1767	5.6405	5.6600
South Korea (Won)	.0007583	.0007583	1318.70	1318.80
Spain (Peseta)	.007117	.007113	140.51	140.58
Sweden (Krona)	.1283	.1281	7.7970	7.8039
Switzerland (Franc) ...	.7402	.7395	1.3510	1.3523
1-month forward ...	.7428	.7420	1.3463	1.3477
3-months forward ...	.7477	.7468	1.3374	1.3390
6-months forward ...	.7540	.7531	1.3263	1.3278
Taiwan (Dollar)	.03083	.03080	32.440	32.470
Thailand (Baht)	.02702	.02723	37.005	36.725
Turkey (Lira)	.00000349	.0000350286820.00	285770.00	
United Arab (Dirham) ..	.2723	.2723	3.6725	3.6730
Uruguay (New Peso) ..	....	....	....	....
Financial	.09368	.09346	10.675	10.700
Venezuela (Bolivar) ...	.001760	.001759	568.13	568.50
SDR	1.4093	1.4083	.7096	.7101
ECU	1.1874	1.1898	....	....

Special Drawing Rights (SDR) are based on exchange rates for the U.S., German, British, French, and Japanese currencies. Source: International Monetary Fund.
European Currency Unit (ECU) is based on a basket of community currencies.
a-Russian Central Bank rate. Trading band lowered on 8/17/98. b-Government rate. c-Corrected.
The Wall Street Journal daily foreign exchange data for 1996 and 1997 may be purchased through the Readers' Reference Service (413) 592-3600.

× \$0.7402 = \$18,505,000. In this example, the bank benefited from the rise in the Swiss franc relative to the dollar, receiving \$1,845,000 more back than it lent (\$18,505,000 − \$16,660,000 lent). However, the bank could just as easily have seen a fall in the value of the Swiss franc and received less than it lent. If the SF25,000,000 had been due only one trading day earlier, on Friday, October 30, when the direct exchange rate for Swiss francs was .7395, the bank would have received SF25,000,000 × 0.7395 U.S. \$ equivalent) = \$18,487,500, or \$17,500 less than it received on the following trading day, Monday, November 2, 1998. The fall in the value of the dollar relative to the Swiss franc over this period was associated with economic events, including the Fed's lowering of its discount rate from 5 percent to 4.75 percent in mid-October 1998. As explained in a later section, changes in relative interest rates among major economies often lead to changes in the relative values of their currencies on the worldwide market. In this instance, the U.S. dollar fell in value relative to other currencies during November and December in a response to this rate cut and other factors. Because they can rarely forecast with precision the actions of regulators or other market participants over whom they have no control, financial institution managers face exchange rate variability, such as that illustrated here, whenever they engage in international commerce.[26]

The Forward Currency Market

A discussion of exchange rate risk would be incomplete without mention of a mechanism heavily used by investors, nonfinancial firms, and financial institutions to reduce the uncertainty about exchange rates during a planning period—the **forward currency market**. A forward exchange is an agreement between two parties to exchange a specified amount of one currency for another, at a specified future date and a specified rate of exchange. The forward rate that is agreed on may differ from the spot rate at the time of negotiation and also from the spot rate at the time the exchange actually occurs.

Forward rates are quoted daily along with spot rates. For many currencies, rates for 30-, 90-, and 180-day forward exchanges are reported. In Figure 14.15, all three forward rates are quoted for the Swiss franc. As of August 24, 1998, the direct forward rates were more than the spot rate. If the U.S. bank, in its agreement to finance the Swiss chocolate importer, had wanted to lock in a rate in the forward market to protect against a fall in the value of the Swiss franc relative to the dollar, it could have negotiated an agreement. Since the loan was due in about two months, the bank would have wished to negotiate a forward contract for 60 days. Such a forward rate is not quoted but could be negotiated with a foreign exchange dealer, such as another large bank, guaranteeing a given forward exchange rate. For instance, if the 60-day rate had been the average of the posted one-month and three-month forward rates shown for the Swiss franc on August 24, 1998, the forward rate may have been 0.6710 U.S. \$ equivalent and 1.4904 Currency per U.S. \$. Locking in this rate, the bank would have been able to convert the SF25,000,000 × 0.6710 U.S. \$ equivalent to \$16,775,000, closer to the dollar value of the funds lent on August 24, 1998, of \$16,660,000. The forward rate is favorable compared with August's spot rate, and the bank could base its plans on this figure. The uncertainty about the dollar commitment

---

[26]Details on the microstructure of foreign exchange markets and illustrative transactions (using the colorful vocabulary of the markets) are found in Flood (1991).

in August would have been eliminated. A forward transaction could, however, lock a financial institution into an exchange rate less desirable than the spot rate that actually prevailed on November 2, 1998. Still, the potential for a favorable movement in rates could have been traded for certain knowledge of the rate of exchange. Of course, as things turned out on November 2, 1998, the bank was happy that it did not lock in this forward rate. However, if the direct rate for the Swiss franc had fallen during this period, the bank might have had losses as large as its current gains.

On average, forward rates are reasonably good indicators of future spot rates, so in this instance managers might have predicted that spot rates in November for Swiss francs would be greater than those in August. But averages, by definition, are based on the results of many transactions occurring above and below the mean. In this case, in fact, spot rates in November were actually higher for the Swiss franc than for the 30- or 90-day forward rates predicted in August. As these examples suggest, to determine whether spot or forward exchange transactions are appropriate, managers must understand the reasons behind exchange rate fluctuations.

Theories of Exchange Rate Determination

Exchange rate variability has been the focus of much academic research. Some theories focus on supply/demand relationships for goods and services; others focus more specifically on comparative inflation rates or interest rates among nations.

Supply and Demand for Goods and Services   A fundamental factor influencing exchange rates is the demand for goods and services produced in one country relative to the demand for goods and services produced in another. Imbalances may lead to trade or balance-of-payments deficits that eventually affect currency exchange rates. Suppose, for example, that the demand for California wine in France is greater than the demand for French wine in the United States. The demand for U.S. dollars with which to buy California wine will exceed Americans' demand for French francs to buy French wine. An excess supply of French francs will develop in the currency markets, and the value of the franc will fall. The reverse would apply if Americans demanded relatively more French wine; the value of the dollar would fall compared with the franc. In brief, an increase in the demand for a country's goods and services should lead to an increase in the value of that country's currency, and a decrease in demand for its goods and services should lead to currency depreciation.

Under a managed floating exchange rate system, such as that described in the Appendix of Chapter 3, trade imbalances leading to exchange rate fluctuations are somewhat self-correcting. If the value of the French franc falls because the French are exchanging their money to buy California wine, California wine will begin to seem more expensive. Even if the dollar price of California wine does not change, subsequent wine purchases by the French will cost more because more francs will be required to purchase the same amount of dollars. Eventually, the demand for California wine may diminish among the French and they will begin to purchase more French wine. As fewer francs are changed into dollars, the supply of francs in the currency markets will fall, and the value of francs will rise relative to the dollar.

Relative Inflation Rates   The preceding illustration assumed no change in the dollar prices of California wines, but changes in the prices of goods *do* occur. The **purchasing power parity theorem** ties exchange rates to differential inflation rates across countries. The theorem states that relatively high inflation in one country will be accompanied by a *depreciation* of its currency relative to currencies in countries with lower inflation rates. In other words, there is an inverse relationship between differences in inflation rates and changes in currency values.

Suppose that a drought in the western United States greatly reduces harvests on most agricultural products, including Chardonnay grapes, which are used to produce some of California's finest white wines. Even with no increase in demand, the price of California wine will increase, along with the price of most goods dependent on agriculture. More francs must be exchanged to import California wines and other U.S. products, not because the exchange rate has changed, but because U.S. prices have increased. If French goods of comparable quality are less expensive because they escape the drought, French *and* U.S. citizens will increase their demand for French products. As more dollars are exchanged for francs and fewer francs are exchanged for dollars, the value of the dollar will fall. The purchasing power parity theorem holds that the value of the dollar will decline because inflation in the United States exceeds that in France.

Relative Interest Rates   Yet another theory suggests that exchange rates are closely tied to interest rates. The previous two theories have focused on consumption goods and services, but currencies also travel among countries as a result of the purchase and sale of financial assets. The **interest rate parity theorem** asserts that

Figure 14.16 ✦ RELATIVE INTEREST RATES IN GERMANY, JAPAN, AND THE UNITED STATES

During the early 1990s, the German central bank raised its discount rate as central banks in the United States and Japan lowered theirs. Market interest rates in the three countries followed the lead of central bank rates. These differences in interest rates affected currency exchange rates.

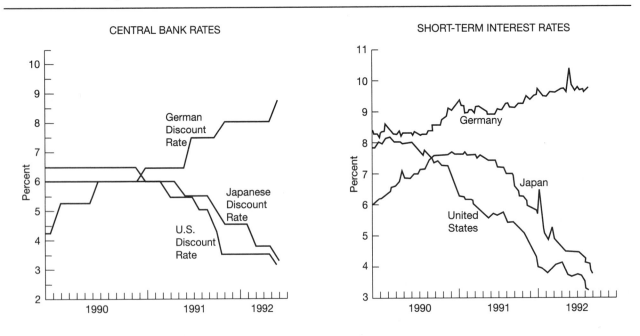

Source: Federal Reserve Bank of Cleveland, *Economic Trends* (August 1992): 18.

interest rates and exchange rates are interdependent: If interest rates in one country differ from those in another, supply and demand for the currencies of the two countries can be affected. According to this theory, when interest rates in the United States are high relative to those in other countries, foreign investors will demand U.S. dollars so that they can take advantage of more desirable rates of return. Exchange rates will then adjust to reflect the interest rate differentials; in this example, the value of the dollar will increase as demand exceeds supply.

Figure 14.16 provides a concrete example of the workings of interest rate parity. As the top panel shows, for many months before September 1992, the German discount rate had been rising as Japanese and U.S. central bank rates were falling. Market rates in the three countries followed the lead of central bank rates (lower panel). Thus, investors all over the world were changing U.S. dollars into Deutschmarks to take advantage of high yields on German securities. Central banks in other European countries had also kept their interest rates high to maintain their currencies' value relative to the Deutschmark. But many of these currencies were mired in recessions, so the higher rates were hurting them domestically even as they helped in the foreign exchange markets. Finally, under pressure from its G-7 trading partners (the United States, Canada, France, Great Britain, Italy, Japan, and Germany, which agreed to coordinate efforts to keep the U.S. dollar within a specified trading range relative to other currencies) the German central bank cut its discount rate by 1/4% (not shown in Figure 14.6). Because the spread between U.S. and German rates narrowed, the immediate reaction in world markets was to increase the value of the U.S. dollar. Although the long-term effects of the German bank's action are more complex and beyond the intent of this chapter, the importance of relative interest rates to exchange rate determination is clear.

Figure 14.17 shows more recent trends (from 1996 to the third quarter of 1998) in central bank rates and short-term interest rates for the United States, Germany, and Japan. In contrast to the earlier period (Figure 14.16), central bank rates and interest rates were fairly stable, as were exchange rates (see Panel B of Figure 14.15 for exchange rates), at least on a monthly basis. The United States cut its discount rate 25 basis points in mid-October, 1998. With this change short-term interest rates in the United States fell, along with a fall in the value of the dollar relative to other European currencies, such as the Swiss franc. It is interesting to note that at this time Japan faced severe economic problems; on November 6, 1998, Japan's six-month T-bills were actually selling at prices above par, whereby investors receiving par at maturity in effect locked in a small loss. Traders at this time noted that some foreign investors were betting that the yen would appreciate against other currencies over the six-week period, thus offsetting the small loss they would incur by holding the Japanese T-bills. Because U.S. and European banks also had large amounts of yen on their books as the result of foreign-exchange arbitrage trades, they were willing to tie up this money in safe Japanese T-bills even though the price was at a premium.[27]

Prior to the advent of the EURO, participating countries started to cordinate central bank actions. In a surprise move, on December 3, 1998, the central banks of the 11 countries participating in the coming European Monetary Union issued coordinated

---

[27]The colorful activities of currency traders in several large U.S. commercial banks are profiled in Randall Smith. "How Currency Traders Play for High Stakes against Central Banks." *The Wall Street Journal* (September 18, 1992), A1, A5.

Figure 14.17 ✦ COMPARISON OF RATES

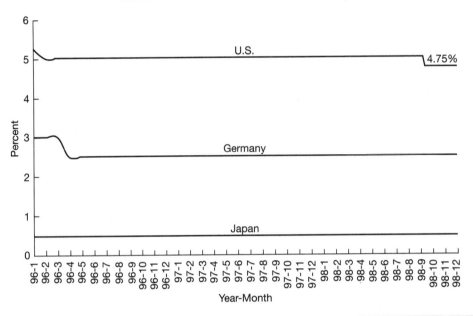

PANEL A: CENTRAL BANK RATES 1996–1998Q3

Source: Compiled by authors using data from AGO. International statistics, 3.26 Discount Rates of Foreign Central Banks and A.22 Domestic Financial statistics, 1.35 Interest Rates, *Federal Reserve Bulletins*, 1996 to 1998. Note in October 1998 the Fed lowered its discount rate to 4.75%, not shown.

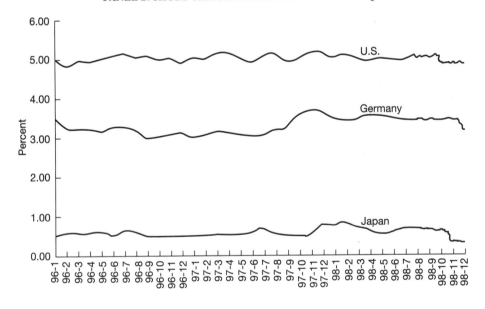

PANEL B: SHORT-TERM INTEREST RATES 1996–1998Q3

Figure 14.18 ✦ THE FIRST COORDINATED INTEREST RATE CUT BY THE EUROPEAN MONETARY UNION

Inflation Subsides...
Year-to-year percentage change in consumer prices

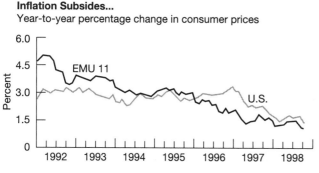

But Unemployment Remains High...
Monthly rate

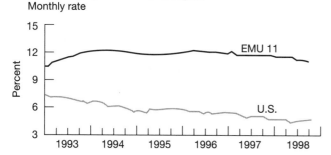

And Growth Is Forecast to Slow...
Consensus forecasts for 1999 gross domestic product

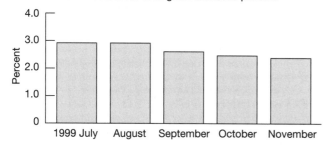

So Rates Are Cut
Key interest rates for the 11 member countries of Europe's economic and monetary union

	PREVIOUS	NEW
Austria	3.20%	3.00%
Germany, France, Netherlands, Belgium, Luxembourg	3.30	3.00
Finland	3.40	3.00
Spain	3.50	3.00
Ireland	3.69	3.00
Portugal	3.75	3.00
Italy	4.00	3.50

Source: Silvia Ascarelli, Dagmar Aaland, and David Wessel, "European Monetary Union Leaps to a Fast Start as 11 Nations Order a Coordinated Rate Cut," *The Wall Street Journal* December 4, 1998, A16.

lower interest rates in response to softening economic conditions. Italy lowered its interest rate to 3.5 percent, with a promise of a further reduction in the weeks ahead. The other ten countries lowered their key interest rates to 3 percent. This was the first joint act of the new monetary union prior to the introduction of the Euro on January 1, 1999. Figure 14.18 shows rate-cut and other information about the 11 member countries.

A Complex Puzzle

It is obvious that integrating these three explanations of changes in currency exchange rates requires some thought. Thus far, one can conclude that greater demand for a nation's goods and services leads to appreciation in the value of its currency, assuming no change in the price level. But this limited scenario is insufficient when inflation or deflation occurs. The purchasing power parity theorem says that higher inflation in one country will lead to a *depreciation* of its currency, and the interest rate parity theorem states that higher interest rates in a country will lead to an *appreciation* of its currency. Yet the Fisher effect says that inflation rates and interest rates are directly related!

What may seem confusing can actually be resolved by recalling Fisher's distinction between nominal and real rates of interest. Suppose that nominal rates in the United States increase as a result of expected inflation. Although the interest rate parity theorem would seem to predict that the U.S. dollar would appreciate as a result of higher interest rates, the purchasing power parity theorem helps managers recognize that increases in interest rates caused by inflation will ultimately result in depreciation, not appreciation, of the U.S. dollar. However, relatively high U.S. nominal rates that result from an increase in the real rate, signifying greater potential return on investment in goods and services, should strengthen the value of the dollar as investment in U.S. assets is seen as being more desirable.[28]

The Role of Expectations Finance experts recognize that no forecasts are complete acknowledging the role of expectations. Some of the ideas discussed previously focus on market participants' reactions to what *is*, but both consumers and investors also react to what they believe *will be*. Indeed, the existence of the forward market is a testimony to the influence of expectations in foreign currency exchanges. The role of expectations is so important in interest rate (and thus exchange rate) forecasting, in fact, that it is explored in greater detail in the next chapter.

The final section of this chapter discusses the process for introducing the euro under the under the new European Monetary Union, which will dramatically change the currency landscape of Europe, eventually reducing transaction costs between member nations.

BRIEF OVERVIEW OF THE PROCESS FOR INTRODUCING THE EURO

In addition to the 11 members participating in the European Monetary Union, five countries are members of the European Economic Union, including Britain, Sweden, Denmark, and Greece. Greece's economy was too weak to meet the requirements for membership, and Britain, Sweden, and Denmark declined to be part of the initial monetary union. As of January 1, 1999, the fiscal management of the euro will be assumed by the European Central Bank, headquartered in Frankfurt, Germany, and the euro will be the currency of the participating members. The old national currencies will remain as legal tender until no later than July 1, 2002, when the euro will become the only legal tender for participating member nations. The euro will be divided into 100 cents, and national currency units will be defined as

---

[28]Further discussion of the parity theorems is found in Kubarych (1983), Shapiro (1983), and Giddy and Dufey (1975). Reconciling the theories is considered in Reuven Glick. "Global Interest Rate Linkages." *Weekly Letter, Federal Reserve Bank of San Francisco* (May 25, 1990) and Strongin (1990).

subdivisions of the euro, thus establishing "a legal equivalence between the euro unit and the national currency unit."[29] Fixed irrevocable exchange rates for old member currencies will be set on that date. New issues of government debt will be denominated in euros, and the euro will be used for commercial transactions, including noncash transactions such as checks, credit card transactions, wire transfers, and other electronic payments. As of January 1, 1999, financial institutions may use the euro unit to make credit transfers before the euro banknotes and coins are introduced and begin to use the euro as a book-entry noncash form. By January 1, 2002, at the latest, the euro will be introduced for all retail activities; on this date, euro notes and coins will be introduced and bank accounts will be switched to euros. For a six-month period, both the euro and national currencies will be accepted. euro banknotes and coins will have legal tender status and start to circulate alongside the national notes and coins. As the circulation of euro notes and coins increases, national notes and coins will be withdrawn and cease to be legal tender within six months following the introduction of the euro notes and coins. As of that deadline, the changeover to the euro will be complete, and the currencies of the 11 countries will no longer be legal tender.

Preparations in the United States and Europe for the Euro's Introduction

European companies and financial institutions have been preparing for years for the euro's introduction. The estimated costs to financial institutions for the euro's conversion have been estimated at hundreds of millions of dollars and hundreds of employee hours for systems conversions (including developing system changes to handle a single currency), along with potential lost revenues for exchanging currencies and other foreign exchange activities. Companies with cross-border operations will benefit most from the euro.

Carol Beaumier, a partner of the Secura Group, a Washington, DC, financial services consulting firm, notes a brief list of negative effects for European financial institutions:: (1) a loss of intra-Europe foreign exchange trading; (2) a consolidation of bank correspondent markets; (3) declines in revenues for banks as corporate cash management is simplified; (4) a loss of perceived or real competitive advantage in terms of "knowing" particular member country marketplaces; and (5) an unpredictable effect on consumer preferences for financial institutions within an individual country to have financial institution relationships across national boundaries. Beaumier notes possible benefits as well: (1) potential revenues from a larger customer base and perhaps currency transaction savings for businesses and consumers; (2) perhaps a more robust economy with lower inflation that should result in lower interest rates; and (3) savings from consolidation and reduced currency risk. Beaumier predicts that a proportionately small number of financial institutions will compete on a truly global basis in Europe; superregionals will operate on a pan-European basis, and smaller institutions may rely on being niche players in their own countries. A number of mergers and alliances have already occurred between European financial institutions.[30]

---

[29] The information from this section comes from Paul S. Tufaro. "European Economic and Monetary Union: A Continuity of Contracts." *Banking Policy Report* 17 (July 6, 1998), 1, 13.

[30] See Carol M. Beaumier. "Countdown to the Euro: How Europe and the U.S. Are Preparing for the Change." *Banking Policy Report* 17 (July 6, 1998), 6–8.

Carol Beaumier points out that U.S. financial institutions with foreign exchange trading and conversion services must also prepare for the euro. First, they may need to reassess their operations and how they deliver services in Europe. They may also face risk management issues during the transitional period for the new currency and set new position and concentration limits for the euro. Institutions also face contractual and market issues concerning the effect of the euro on the value of outstanding financial contracts and the risk of problems if counterparties are unprepared. Other areas of concern are training and communicating with customers, employees, and vendors about changes and the renovation of internal systems to interface with new euro systems. Banks involved in European markets supervised by the Fed are required to have conducted an assessment of the effect of the euro on their operations and to have developed a "euro project plan" for their operations to be reviewed and approved by their Board of Directors. Accordingly, examiners were asked to review and assess the level of euro risk (high, medium, or low), and the strength of a bank's risk management process (strong, acceptable, or weak) for handling this risk.[31]

SUMMARY

Because the NIM is the key variable in asset/liability management, understanding the behavior of interest rates is important. In increasingly global markets, the NIM is also affected by the value of one currency relative to others. This chapter discusses the general level of interest rates and currency exchange rates. It also discusses institutional details concerning money market securities and their prices and yields as well as exchange rate pricing. A brief overview is given of changes that will occur with the introduction of the Euro.

Because all interest rates tend to move in the same direction, a forecast for the general level of interest rates is a starting point for estimating future rates on specific assets and liabilities. The most widely used explanation for movements in the general level is the loanable funds theory, based on the motivations for saving and borrowing. Although other factors also affect the decision, the dollar amount individuals are willing to save is positively related to interest rates, and the demand for borrowing is inversely related to interest rates. The equilibrium general level of interest rates is determined by the intersection of the supply and demand curves for loanable funds.

Economists have also hypothesized that expected inflation influences the general level of interest rates. In fact, the Fisher effect suggests that nominal market rates of interest reflect a real rate of interest plus a premium equal to the expected rate of inflation. Although this theory is difficult to validate empirically, most researchers agree that inflationary expectations affect the general level of rates. Because they attempt to predict an unknown future, interest rate forecasts, no matter how carefully they are made, are subject to error. So, besides theories, financial institution managers must be aware of techniques to minimize the impact of forecasting errors on their institution's performance.

Exchange rate risk, or the rate variability at which one currency can be converted to another, is significant for all institutions participating in international markets, particularly for those that negotiate transactions today for execution at a later date. Such transactions may occur either at subsequent spot rates or at forward rates determined today. Several theories have been advanced to explain exchange rate variability. In general, the value of a nation's currency should increase if demand increases for its goods and services or if interest rates are relatively high compared with those in other countries. The value of a country's currency should decrease, however, if its rate of inflation is relatively high. Both interest rates and exchange rates are influenced not only by contemporary developments but also by market participants' expectations of the future.

Questions

1. The Greg and Mary McArthur Investment Company runs a bond mutual fund. Describe the direction and volatility

---

[31]Ibid.

of interest rate movements during the past two years. Discuss the expected effects of this interest rate environment on the management of their bond fund.

2. What choices are available to Greg and Mary's bond fund for their use of funds? Why would the fund hold cash balances? Do interest rates affect these motives? If so, how?

3. Explain to Greg and Mary what economic sector is a net supplier of loanable funds. How are the savings decisions of this sector affected by noninterest factors?

4. As a financial economist for a major bank, suppose you see a survey of consumer savings patterns in the United States revealing that Americans save less disposable income than in the past. Based on your knowledge of the loanable funds theory, explain to the bank's president, Marilyn Taylor, the potential effect of this trend on U.S. interest rates (assuming no increase in loanable funds from international investors).

5. Continuing as the financial economist for the major bank, explain to Bob Taylor, the bank's investment manager, why the federal government's demand for loanable funds is relatively inelastic with respect to interest rates.

6. Baine Kerr, the comptroller of the major bank, asks you how the business sector's demand for loanable funds relates to interest rates. Explain this to Baine. If corporate taxes are lowered, also explain to Baine how the demand curve for loanable funds would be affected.

7. You are a financial planner. A client, Patty Hamilton, asks you to explain the difference between the nominal rate and the real rate of interest. She also asks how inflation affects the real, ex post rate of return to investors. Explain this to Patty.

8. Beverly Walker, an artist and client of your financial planning firm, astutely asks you if the ex post real rate could be negative. Give an example to Beverly of this happening.

9. Explain to Gail Welply, president of a diversified financial firm in France, Fisher's theory of the relationship between the nominal rate of interest and expected inflation. Why would this relationship be important for Gail to know? Also, explain why Fisher's belief that the ex ante real rate of interest is constant has become controversial.

10. Doug Walker, your boss at the Rock Island Railroad Bank, has criticized you for your recent interest rate forecast. Explain some of the difficulties economists face in developing forecasts.

11. Your friend, Carl Weeks, is thinking of investing in a money market mutual fund. Explain to Carl the difference between money market securities and longer-term capital market securities. What special characteristics do money market securities have? What affects differences in yields for different types of money market securities?

12. Carl, your friend and a business college student, also asks you the following questions; What is a yield? How is it calculated for a money market security? What is the difference between a discount yield, annual yield, and effective annual yield?

13. Explain to Bud Fogerty, owner of a Colorado importing firm, what a banker's acceptance is and how it is created. Why is this information important to Bud?

14. Hugh Ruppersburg, a Georgia exporter, asks you what the difference is between spot and forward rates in the foreign currency markets. He also asks you how a forward exchange agreement could assist him in reducing his exchange rate risk exposure. Explain this to Hugh.

15. How do changes in the supply of and demand for goods and services affect exchange rates between the currencies of two countries? How do relative changes in interest rates and inflation effect exchange rates between the currency of two countries? Why would these relations be important for Hugh, an exporter, to know?

Problems

1. Graph the supply and demand curves for loanable funds. What is meant by the equilibrium rate of interest?

2. Using the graph from Problem 1, show the effect on the equilibrium rate of interest if government borrowing increases while the demand for loanable funds from other sectors remains constant.

3. If the demand for loanable funds by the business sector decreases because of a recession and the demand for loanable funds by the government increases but by a smaller amount, how will the equilibrium interest rate be affected? Sketch the change on the same graph used in Problems 1 and 2.

4. Within the framework of the loanable funds theory, illustrate how inflation affects the equilibrium rate of interest.

5. Ignoring taxes, use the Fisher equation to calculate the nominal yield required by investors when the real rate of interest is 4 percent and the expected inflation rate is 5 percent. What will be the ex-post real rate of return to an investor if inflation actually turns out to be 8 percent?

6. Do the same problem in Problem 5 assuming you want a 4 percent real rate of return after taxes and considering the investor has a marginal tax rate of 28 percent.

7. Suppose your favorite uncle expected to earn a real after-tax rate of return of 4.5 percent and demanded a nominal rate of 12.79 percent.
   a. What rate of inflation was he expecting? His marginal tax rate is 28 percent.
   b. Considering the fact that his actual after-tax real rate of return was only 2.5 percent, what was the ex post rate of inflation?

8. Several years ago, a Texas bank offered a 30-year CD with an annual return indexed to inflation. The rate offered was the annual percentage increase in the CPI plus 4 percent. Suppose that you are in the 28 percent marginal tax bracket and require a 5 percent real return after taxes. Suppose also that the annual inflation rate last year was 3 percent, so this year's annual rate on the CD investment is set at 7 percent.
   a. Show the after-tax real return you would earn, assuming that the inflation rate stays at 3 percent and the CD rate offered is 7 percent.
   b. What ex ante nominal rate should you require instead to keep your after-tax real yield at 5 percent?
9. State College's Credit Union bid noncompetitively for a $10,000, 91-day T-bill. The average discount yield for the auction was 3.4 percent.
   a. What price did the credit union pay for the T-bill?
   b. What was the annual effective yield for the T-bill? Annual yield?
10. What is the effective annual yield on a 52-week T-bill selling at 93.27 percent of par with a 100 percent par value? The bank discount yield?
11. The discount yield on a ten-day, $100,000 reverse repurchase agreement is quoted in the market as 5.95 percent. Calculate the expected annual yield and effective annual yield for the reverse repo.
12. Robert Cooperman, president of Snow City Bank, plans to invest $4 million in a negotiable CD for 180 days. The bank offers a discount rate of 6.2 percent. What is the effective annual yield on the CD?
13. Refer to the exchange rates reported in Figure 14.15.
   a. Suppose that on August 25, 1998, your firm needed to pay a French exporter for goods received. The bill was 750,000 French francs. The direct rate for French francs was $.1662. What was the cost in dollars on August 25?
   b. If, on the same day, a Japanese corporation needed to pay your firm $3.5 million, what was the cost in yen? The direct rate for Japanese yen is $.006924.
   c. If the bill was due on November 3, 1998, what would be the change in the dollar value of 750,000 French francs with the direct rate for French francs changing to $.1806? What would be the change in the yen value of $3.5 million? The direct rate for Japanese yen has changed to $.008699.
14. Suppose a midwestern auto dealer must convert $2 million into yen to buy Japanese cars currently priced at 220 million yen.
   a. Calculate the implied direct rate of exchange between dollars and yen given these prices and the implied indirect exchange rate?
15. Suppose that the importer in the Problem 14 had earlier locked in a forward exchange agreement at a direct rate for the yen of $0.0094. Under that agreement, how many U.S. dollars must be converted to cover the cost of the imported automobiles?
16. Suppose it is August 25, 1998, and the Crazy Boris Export Company plans to receive 200,000 British pounds in November 1998. Based on the August 24 direct exchange rate of $1.6407, what does the company expect to receive? Looking at the top panel of Figure 14.15, what would the firm receive in dollars if it took out a three-month forward contract for this amount? Note that the three month forward direct rate is $1.6377 per British pound. What would it receive in dollars if it did not take out a contract and instead received the pounds on November 3, 1998? Note that the direct rate for the pound has changed to $1.6640 in November.

Selected References

Barth, James R., and Michael D. Bradley. "On Interest Rates, Inflationary Expectations and Tax Rates." *Journal of Banking and Finance* 12 (June, 1988), 210–220.

Belongia, Michael T. "Predicting Interest Rates: A Comparison of Professional and Market-Based Forecasts." *Review* (Federal Reserve Bank of St. Louis) 69 (March, 1987), 915.

Bryan, Michael F., and William T. Gavin. "Comparing Inflation Expectations of Households and Economists: Is a Little Knowledge a Dangerous Thing?" *Economic Review* (Federal Reserve Bank of Cleveland) (Quarter 3, 1986), 1419.

Carlson, John A. "Short-Term Interest Rates as Predictors of Inflation: Comment." *American Economic Review* 67 (June, 1977), 469–475.

Clarida, Richard D., and Benjamin M. Friedman. "The Behavior of U.S. Short-Term Interest Rates since October, 1979." *Journal of Finance* 39 (July, 1984), 671–682.

Cox, William N., III. "Interest Rates and Inflation: What Drives What?" *Economic Review* (Federal Reserve Bank of Atlanta) 65 (May/June, 1980), 20–23.

Croushore, Dean. "What Are the Costs of Disinflation?" *Business Review* (Federal Reserve Bank of Philadelphia) (May/June, 1992), 3.

Darby, Michael R. "The Financial and Tax Effects of Monetary Policy on Interest Rates." *Economic Inquiry* 12 (June, 1975), 266–276.

Dwyer, Gerald P., Jr., and R. W. Hafer. "Interest Rates and Economic Announcements." *Review* (Federal Reserve Bank of St. Louis) 71 (March/April, 1989), 34–46.

Eugeni, Francesca, Charles Evans, and Steven Strongin. "Making Sense of Economic Indicators: A Consumer's Guide to Indicators of Real Economic Activity." *Economic Perspectives* (Federal Reserve Bank of Chicago) 16 (September/October, 1992), 232.

Fama, Eugene A. "Short-Term Interest Rates as Predictors of Inflation." *American Economic Review* 65 (June, 1975), 269–282.

Feldstein, Martin. "Inflation, Income Taxes and the Rate of Interest: A Theoretical Analysis." *American Economic Review* 66 (December, 1976), 809–820.

Fisher, Irving. *The Theory of Interest.* New York: Macmillan (1930).

Flood, Mark D. "Microstructure Theory and the Foreign Exchange Market." *Review* (Federal Reserve Bank of St. Louis) 73 (November/December, 1991), 52–70.

Friedman, Benjamin. "Price Inflation, Portfolio Choice and Nominal Interest Rates." *American Economic Review* 70 (March, 1980), 32–48.

Gibson, A. H. "The Future Course of High Class Investment Values." *Bankers Magazine* (London) 115 (January, 1923), 15–34.

Giddy, Ian H., and Gunter Dufey. "The Random Behavior of Flexible Exchange Rates." *Journal of International Business Studies* 6 (Spring, 1975), 1–32.

Hakkio, Craig S. "Interest Rates and Exchange Rates—What Is the Relationship?" *Economic Review* (Federal Reserve Bank of Kansas City) 71 (November, 1986), 33–43.

Holland, A. Steven. "Real Interest Rates: What Accounts for Their Recent Rise?" *Review* (Federal Reserve Bank of St. Louis) 66 (December, 1984), 18–29.

Humphrey, Thomas M. "The Early History of the Real/Nominal Interest Rate Relationship." *Economic Review* (Federal Reserve Bank of Richmond) 69 (May/June, 1983), 2–10.

Keane, Michael P., and David E. Runkle. "Are Economic Forecasts Rational?" *Quarterly Review* (Federal Reserve Bank of Minneapolis) 13 (Spring, 1989), 26–33.

Keynes, John Maynard. *The General Theory of Employment, Interest, and Money.* New York: Harcourt, Brace, and World (1936).

Kubarych, Roger M. *Foreign Exchange Markets in the United States,* 2nd ed. New York: Federal Reserve Bank of New York (1983).

Leonard, David C., and Michael E. Solt. "Recent Evidence on the Accuracy and Rationality of Popular Inflation Forecasts." *Journal of Financial Research* 9 (Winter, 1986), 281–290.

Mascaro, Angelo, and Allen H. Meltzer. "Long- and Short-Term Interest Rates in a Risky World." *Journal of Monetary Economics* 12 (November, 1983), 485–518.

McNees, Stephen K. "Consensus Forecasts: Tyranny of the Majority?" *New England Economic Review* (Federal Reserve Bank of Boston) (November/December, 1987), 15–21.

Mullineaux, Donald J., and Aris Protopapadakis. "Revealing Real Interest Rates: Let the Market Do It." *Business Review* (Federal Reserve Bank of Philadelphia) (March/April, 1984), 3–8.

Mundell, Robert. "Inflation and Real Interest." *Journal of Political Economy* 71 (June, 1963), 280–283.

Peek, Joe. "Inflation and the Excess Taxation of Personal Interest Income." *New England Economic Review* (Federal Reserve Bank of Boston) (March/April, 1988), 46–52.

Polakoff, Murray E. "Loanable Funds Theory and Interest Rate Determination." In *Financial Institutions and Markets.* 2nd ed. Edited by Murray E. Polakoff and Thomas A. Durkin. Boston: Houghton Mifflin (1981), 483–510.

Rose, Andrew K. "Is the Real Rate Stable?" *Journal of Finance* 43 (December, 1988), 1095–1112.

Rosenblum, Harvey, and Steven Strongin. "Interest Rate Volatility in Historical Perspective." *Economic Perspectives* (Federal Reserve Bank of Chicago) 7 (January/February, 1983), 10–19.

Santoni, G. J., and Courtenay C. Stone. "Navigating Through the Interest Rate Morass: Some Basic Principles." *Economic Review* (Federal Reserve Bank of St. Louis) 63 (March, 1981), 11–18.

Santoni, G. J., and Courtenay Stone. "What Really Happened to Interest Rates?" *Economic Review* (Federal Reserve Bank of St. Louis) 63 (November, 1981), 3–14.

Shapiro, Alan C. "What Does Purchasing Power Parity Mean?" *Journal of International Money and Finance* (December, 1983), 295–318.

Shiller, Robert J., and Jeremy J. Siegel. "The Gibson Paradox and Historical Movements in Real Interest Rates." *Journal of Political Economy* 85 (October, 1977), 891–907.

Strongin, Steven. "International Credit Market Connections." *Economic Perspectives* 14 (July/August, 1990), 2–10.

Taylor, Herbert. "Interest Rates: How Much Does Expected Inflation Matter?" *Business Review* (Federal Reserve Bank of Philadelphia) (July/August, 1982), 3–12.

"The Livingston Surveys: A History of Hopes and Fears." *Business Review* (Federal Reserve Bank of Philadelphia) (January/February, 1992), 15–27.

Tobin, James. "Money and Economic Growth." *Econometrica* 33 (October, 1965), 671–684.

Urang, Sally. "The Economists' Scoreboard." *Institutional Investor* 22 (March, 1988), 251–256, and 23 (March, 1989), 211–216.

Van Dyke, Daniel T. "Why Economists Make Mistakes." *Bankers Magazine* 169 (May/June, 1986), 69–75.

Van Horne, James C. *Financial Market Rates and Flows*, 2nd ed. Englewood Cliffs, NJ: Prentice-Hall (1984).

Wallace, William H., and William E. Cullison. *Measuring Price Changes*, 4th ed. Richmond, VA: Federal Reserve Bank (1979).

Wood, John H. "Interest Rates and Inflation." *Economic Perspectives* (Federal Reserve Bank of Chicago) 5 (May/June, 1981), 3–12.

Yohe, William P., and Denis Karnosky. "Interest Rates and Price Level Changes, 1952–1969." *Review* (Federal Reserve Bank of St. Louis) 51 (December 1969), 18–39.

Chapter 14 Internet Exercise

Interest Rates, Exchange Rates, and Inflation: Theories and Forecasting

1. Dr. Ed Yardeni's Economic Network:
   http://www.yardeni.com/

   Dr. Ed Yardeni is the Chief Economist and Global Investment Strategist of Deutsche Bank Securities in New York. His site contains a wealth of information, such as quick access to the dates for economic indicators such as income, consumption, and so on.. From the main home page, click on "Weekly Forecasts" under Economic Indicators. The information is provided for the current month and is updated regularly. The chart also provides the Deutsche Bank Securities forecasts for those dates in the future.

2. Survey of Professional Forecasters:
   http://www.phil.frb.org/econ/spf/spfpage.html

   The Survey of Professional Forecasters is the oldest quarterly survey of macroeconomic forecasts in the United States. The survey began in 1968 and was conducted by the American Statistical Association and the National Bureau of Economic Research. The Federal Reserve Bank of Philadelphia took over the survey in 1990. To get the most recent forecasts summary, click on the highlighted quarter under News Release. This will provide a short summary of the forecasters'

consensus on economic growth, interest rates, inflation expectations, and long-term expectations for real GDP growth and productivity. The main site also includes links for historical data on median forecasts, the forecasts by individual forecaster, and mean forecasts. Since the data go back to 1968, some of the files are available only in zipped format. In addition, there are tables for short-term inflation forecasts (over the next year) and long-term forecasts (over the next ten years). Finally, there is a useful bibliography of academic articles using the data from the survey.

Useful Links

NBER Macrohistory Database: Historical economic data for the United States.
http://www.nber.org/databases/macrohistory/contents/index.html

Fed in Print: An index to articles published by the Federal Reserve System
http://www.frbsf.org/system/fedinprint/index.html

The Federal Reserve Euro Resource Page: Information on the European Monetary System
http://www.frbchi.org/consumer/euro.html

15

THE TERM STRUCTURE OF INTEREST RATES

*A*n investor with idle funds in mid-1989 would have faced nothing but frustration in soliciting professional advice about how long to invest those funds. Consider the recommendations given simultaneously to a reporter for The Wall Street Journal: *"Shorter is better right now,"* said Michael D. Hirsch, chief investment officer of Republic Bank of New York. *"People should be lengthening their maturities now,"* advised James Riepe, director of investment services at T. Rowe Price, a large mutual fund group. *"Intermediate-term bonds offer the possibility of price appreciation and good rates,"* opined William E. Donoghue, chairman of Donoghue Organization, an investment research group. The reason behind the confusion? The yield curve, often used as an indicator of the course of future interest rates, was "flat"—that is, expected rates of return were almost equal regardless of how long one invested one's money. Similarly, a decade later, in 1998, over the course of the year, the yield curve

flattened somewhat for securities with maturities from one to ten years.[1] This situation in both 1989 and 1998 made economic forecasting even more difficult than usual.

The previous chapter points to the importance of understanding how both the supply and demand for credit and inflationary expectations affect the general level of interest rates. The preceding paragraph, as well as the opening quotation, point to another important influence on institutional performance—the **term structure of interest rates,** often called the **yield curve**. All else equal, the term structure of interest rates is the relationship, at a specific time, between yields on securities and their maturities. For example, yields on 182-day Treasury bills (T-bills) almost always differ from those on 25-year Treasury bonds (T-bonds).

Just as there are theories explaining how the general level of interest rates is determined, there are also theories explaining the term structure. Because

---

[1]Georgette Jasen. "High-Yield Hunters Now Face a Decision." *Wall Street Journal* (May 3, 1989), C1.

financial institutions simultaneously participate in the markets for securities of many different maturities, theories of the term structure can assist man- *agers in making decisions that commonly confront them. Some of these decisions are illustrated later in the chapter.*

✦ ✦ ✦

The Term Structure Defined: A Closer Look

As noted, the term structure of interest rates is the relationship between security yields and maturities, *all else equal*. "All else equal" is an important qualifying phrase. To isolate the effect of maturity on yield, one must remove the potential effects of other factors. Comparing a bank's existing yields on a six-month T-bill and a 20-year loan to a developing nation would say little about the effect of maturity on yields but a great deal about default risk. It would also be misleading to compare a T-bill yield with the tax-exempt yield on bonds of the City of Dallas or to compare General Motors' 90-day commercial paper rate with the yield on its preferred stock and then draw conclusions about the effect of maturity on expected return.

Identifying the Existing Term Structure

It is generally agreed that comparing yields on Treasury securities of different maturities is the best way to control for extraneous factors. Existing term structures are obtained by observing spot rates, i.e., current market yields, on T-bills, Treasury notes (T-notes), and T-bonds. A daily listing of yields and maturities is found in the "Treasury Issues" column of major newspapers; an example is shown in Figure 15.1. The few Treasury issues that are callable or have special estate tax features, called flower bonds, must be eliminated. Standardized calculations must be used so that bank discount yields for T-bills with maturities of one year or less are not erroneously compared with bond-equivalent yields.[2]

---

[2]For a theoretically correct determination of the "true" term structure, the securities used should all be pure discount, zero-coupon bonds of varying maturities. The growing market for stripped Treasury securities may eventually introduce new practices, but currently coupon-bearing as well as discount security yields are used to estimate existing term structures, especially when the analyst is fitting a curve visually. Also, bonds with different coupon rates are usually used to construct a yield curve, causing some distortion. The yields and prices for T-bills are discussed in Chapter 14. The prices for T-bonds in Figure 15.1 are prices as 100 percent of par value. For example, an ask price of $100\frac{1}{32}$ would be 100.03125 percent times the bond's par value. The yield for a long-term bond is its their "yields to maturity" (YTM), the rate that makes the present value of the bond's coupon payments and maturity value equal to its current ask price. This implied discount rate can be calculated using a financial calculator or trial and error approach.

Figure 15.1

Yields of Treasury Securities of varying maturities are found in the daily financial pages. These data are the basis for estimating the current shape of the yield curve.

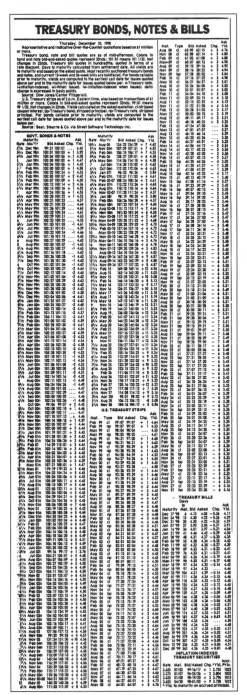

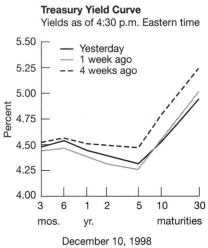

Treasury Yield Curve
Yields as of 4:30 p.m. Eastern time

December 10, 1998

A Historical Look at Term Structures

Just as the general level of interest rates differs over time, so does the term structure. In March, 1989, for example, yields on short-term Treasury securities exceeded those on long-term Treasuries. A plot of this relationship is shown in Figure 15.2. A yield curve with this shape is often described as **downward sloping** or **inverted**. In contrast, Figure 15.3 shows an upward-sloping relationship in March 1992. Figure 15.4 shows an almost constant (flat) relationship between yields and maturities in December 1988.

Figure 15.5 gives a long-term view of short- and long-term rates, showing yields on T-bills and T-bonds over a period of approximately 28 years. During this period, no single relationship between short- and long-term rates prevailed, although long-term rates exceeded short-term rates most of the time. In fact, the prevalence of

Figure 15.2   ✦   YIELDS OF TREASURY SECURITIES, MARCH 31, 1989

The yield curve in March 1989 was downward-sloping, or inverted: Short-term rates were higher than long-term rates.

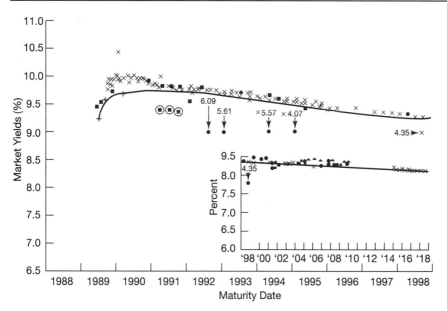

Note: The curve is fitted by eye and is based only on most actively traded issues. Market yields on coupon issues due in less than 3 months are excluded.

× Fixed maturity coupon issues less than 12%
■ Fixed maturity coupon issues of 12% or more.
● Callable coupon issues less than 12%.
▲ Callable coupon issues of 12% or more.
   Note: Callable issues are plotted to the earliest call date when prices are above par and to maturity when prices are at par or below.
+ Bills. Coupon equivalent yield of the latest 13-week, 26-week, 52-week bills.

Source: Treasury Bulletin, June 1989, 55.

Figure 15.3   ◆   YIELDS OF TREASURY SECURITIES, MARCH 31, 1992

The yield curve in early 1992 was upward-sloping, or normal: Short-term rates were lower than long-term rates.

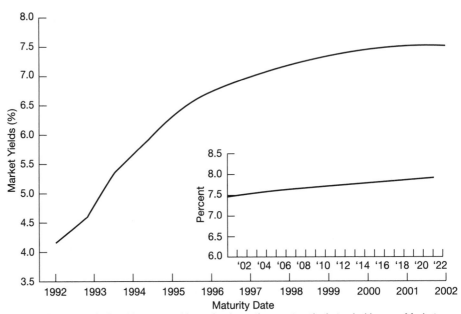

Note: The curve is fitted by eye and based only on the most actively traded issues. Market yields on coupon issues due in less than 3 months are excluded

Source: Treasury Bulletin, June 1992, 78.

upward-sloping yield curves during much of the early twentieth century led to them being dubbed **"normal" yield curves**, which is why downward-sloping curves have been called "inverted."[3]

Figure 15.6 shows more recent changes in yield curves during the second half of 1998. The yield curve changed dramatically over this period, flattening in August and September and becoming steeper in October. It is interesting to note that on several dates, such as November 6, 1998, securities with maturities of two- to five-years actually had lower yields than three-month T-bills, whereas securities with maturities of ten years or greater had consistently higher yields. To be able to anticipate changes in interest rates, financial institution managers need to understand relations between yield curves and different stages of the business cycle.

---

[3]Inverted yield curves appeared more frequently in the 1970s and early 1980s than in previous periods, although they are not evident in Figure 15.5, which shows only annual averages.

Figure 15.4   ✦   YIELDS OF TREASURY SECURITIES, DECEMBER 31, 1988

The yield curve in late 1988 was almost flat: Short-term and long-term rates were approximately equal.

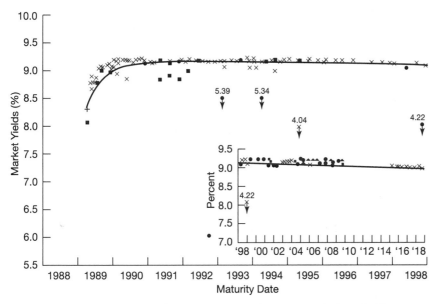

Note: The curve is fitted by eye and is based only on most actively traded issues.
Market yields on coupon issues due in less than 3 months are excluded.

× Fixed maturity coupon issues less than 12%
■ Fixed maturity coupon issues of 12% or more.
● Callable coupon issues less than 12%.
▲ Callable coupon issues of 12% or more.
   Note: Callable issues are plotted to the earliest call date when prices are above par
   and to maturity when prices are at par or below.
+ Bills. Coupon equivalent yield of the latest 13-week, 26-week, 52-week bills.

Source: Treasury Bulletin, March 1989, 59.

The Term Structure and the General Level of Interest Rates

Another feature of Figure 15.5 is important because it suggests a historical relationship between the general level of economic activity and the shape of the yield curve. The dates labeled on the graph denote months when there were peaks in the business cycle.[4] A downward sloping yield curve often appears at these peaks, such as November 1973. Investors seem to be anticipating the end of an expansion and beginning of a recession that will result in a lower demand for funds and a fall in rates.

---

[4]Peaks shown are as delineated by the National Bureau of Economic Research, U.S. Department of Commerce, *Business Conditions Digest*.

Figure 15.5 ✦ LONG- AND SHORT-TERM INTEREST RATES

Short-term rates have been lower than long-term rates most of the time in this century. Periods when short-term rates were higher have often coincided with peaks in the business cycle, leading to subsequent recessions.

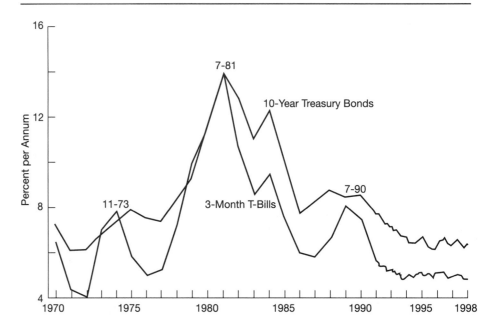

Source: Board of Governors of the Federal Reserve System, *Federal Reserve Bulletin*, various issues.

During periods of sluggish economic performance but toward the end of a recession, such as the mid-1970s, the yield curve has often been upward sloping as investors anticipated the end of a recession and a rise in future rates. This same pattern occurred in anticipation of the recession of 1981–1982 with a downward slope curve prior to July 1981, followed by an upward sloping curve as the economy moved out of the recession.[5]

The next downward-sloping curve appeared for a brief period in 1989 (recall Figure 15.2). At the time, some economists suggested that an inverted term structure might no longer signal a recession. Previously, recessions were the only times that market participants seemed to expect interest rates to decline. But surveys of financial institution managers at this time revealed expectations of a prolonged decline in the rate of inflation, particularly relative to inflation in the early part of the decade. Some experts suggested that the downward-sloping curve meant only that a smaller inflationary premium would be built into future short-term rates, not that a recession was at

---

[5]From the beginning of World War II until 1951, Federal Reserve policies actually kept the term structure independent of the level of economic activity. Controls were lifted under President Harry Truman, and rates were free to move according to the supply of and demand for funds. For more discussion of this policy and the accord that brought it to an end, see Wallich and Keir (1979).

Figure 15.6 ◆ Yɪᴇʟᴅ Cᴜʀᴠᴇꜱ Dᴜʀɪɴɢ 1998

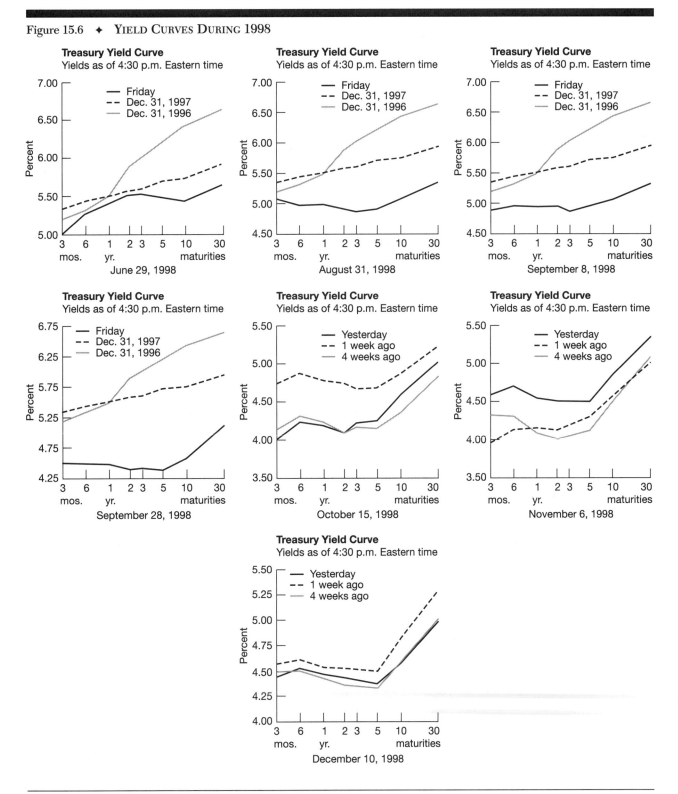

Source: The Wall Street Journal, for the dates given, C17, C17, C23, C19, C21, C19, C22.

Figure 15.7 ✦ YIELD CURVES FOR HIGH-GRADE CORPORATE BONDS, 1900–1929 AND 1930–1982

When the general level of interest rates is relatively high, yield curves are usually downward-sloping. When the general level is relatively low, the yield curve often slopes upward.

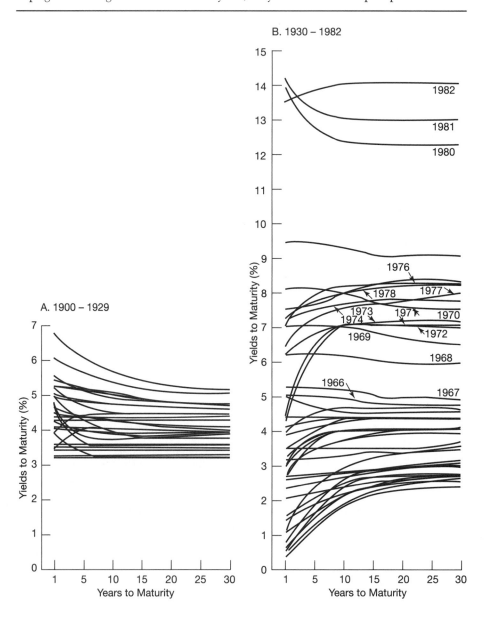

Source: John Wood, "Do Yield Curves Normally Slope Up? The Term Structure of Interest Rates, 1862–1982," *Economic Perspectives* (Federal Reserve Bank of Chicago) 7 (July/August 1983): 18.

hand.[6] This alternate interpretation of the inverted yield curve proved, of course, to be incorrect. The U.S. economy fell into a prolonged recession in the early 1990s, confirming once again the difficulties encountered by economic forecasters. Yield curves again became steeper and upward sloping toward the end of the 1990–1991 recession, with short-term rates falling more than long-term rates, and the economy expanded.

Another perspective on historical term structures is shown in Figure 15.7. When the general level of rates has been relatively high, term structures have tended to slope downward, and they have sloped upward when the general level has been relatively low. From 1900 to 1929, as the general level of rates drifted upward, yield curves gradually changed shape from flat to inverted. From 1930 to 1981, as rates gradually moved higher, yield curves also shifted from upward sloping to downward sloping. Scholars have inferred from these historical curves that the financial markets may periodically revise their opinions of what represents a high general level of rates. Before the 1930s, for example, a 7 percent short-term rate may have been considered high, but by the 1970s such a rate was considered relatively low. In this context, the 1982 normal curve was an aberration from recent history. As Figures 15.2, 15.3, and 15.4 indicate, during the late 1980s and early 1990s the general level of interest rates fell and yield curve levels appeared similar to those from the 1960s and 1970s.

One important difference observed in the early 1990s, however, was the extremely steep slope of the yield curve. As shown in Figure 15.8, although short-term

Figure 15.8   ✦   Yields of Treasury Securities, 1991 and 1992

The term structure of interest rates exhibited a very steep slope in 1991 and 1992, presenting a strong contrast to earlier periods when the differential between short-term and long-term rates was much smaller.

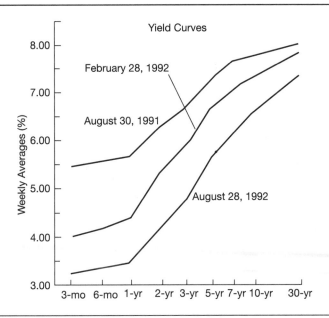

Source: *Economic Trends* (Federal Reserve Bank of Cleveland) (September 1992): 5.

---

[6]See Furlong (1989) and Stevens (1989).

interest rate levels were similar to those prevailing in the 1960s, the relative differential between short-term and long-term rates was most unusual. By August 1992, when the yield on three-month T-bills was just above 3 percent, the yield on 30-year T-bonds was more than twice that, at 7.3 percent. Experts attributed this differential to investor uncertainties about long-term economic conditions, including the outlook for inflation and stability in the world currency markets.[7]

UNBIASED (PURE) EXPECTATIONS THEORY

Historical patterns and the reasons for their existence provide clues about when to expect shifts in the term structure, but they are no substitute for a theoretical understanding of the yield curve. Understanding how the term structure is determined is complicated by economists' lack of agreement on any single explanation. The existence of several theories should not be discouraging, however, because each provides insights the others lack. The body of knowledge is valuable for managers who make decisions involving assets and liabilities of different maturities. Perhaps the most influential of the term structure theories is the **unbiased (pure) expectations theory**, hereafter reffered to as the pure expectations theory, which holds that observable long-term yields are the average of expected, but directly unobservable, short-term yields.[8] For example, this theory argues that the spot rate on 20-year T-bonds is the average of expected annual yields on short-term Treasury securities over the next 20 years. Theoretically, there is no best definition of "short term" or "long term." For simplicity, most of the following examples define short term as one year; however, the pure expectations theory also holds that the observed yield on one-year securities is the average of expected rates on shorter-maturity securities during the year. *Short-* and *long-term* can therefore be defined as the decision maker desires.

Assumptions of the Pure Expectations Theory

The pure expectations theory rests on the following important assumptions about investors (lenders or demanders of securities) and markets:

1. All else equal, investors are indifferent between owning a single long-term security or a series of short-term securities over the same time period. In other words, maturity alone does not affect investors' choice of investments.
2. All investors hold common expectations about the course of short-term rates.
3. On average, investors are able to predict rates accurately. Their expectations about future rates are unbiased in the *statistical* sense, i.e., they are neither consistently low or consistently high.
4. There are no taxes, information costs, or transaction costs in the financial markets. Investors are free to exchange securities of varying maturities quickly and without penalty.

---

[7]For more discussion, see Wood (1983); Blalock (1993); and Cogley (1993).

[8]Irving Fisher, discussed in Chapter 14 in connection with inflation and the general level of rates, is often credited with the first statement of the pure expectations hypothesis in 1896. The theory was not fully developed until several decades later, however, when both J. R. Hicks (1946) and Frederick Lutz (1940) pursued it. More recent discussions are found in Malkiel (1966) and Meiselman (1962).

The main implication of the pure expectations theory follows directly from these assumptions. *For a given holding period, the average expected annual yields on all combinations of maturities will be equal.*[9] For example, the theory holds that the average annual yield on a series of one-year investments over a specific five-year period will be the same as the average annual yield on a single three-year investment followed by two one-year investments *and* the same as the average annual yield on a single five-year security. Because investors are assumed to be indifferent about the maturity of their holdings and because they have common and accurate predictions about future rates, they will demand securities at prices that equalize average annual yields over the period. Investors simply have no incentive to prefer one combination of maturities over another. Annual yields currently available on long-term securities will be the average of expected annual yields on shorter-term instruments.

Mathematics of the Pure Expectations Theory

Mathematically, the theory is expressed by the following formula:

$$1 + {}_1r_n = [(1 + {}_1r_1)(1 + {}_2\gamma_1) \ldots (1 + {}_n\gamma_1)]^{1/n} \qquad [15.1]$$

The "average" of rates referred to earlier is not the simple arithmetic average, but a **geometric average** that is equal to the nth root (or 1/n power) product of one plus the current r and one plus the expected [γ] short-term interest rates during the life of the long-term bond issued today with n years to maturity. Rates are fractions, so one is added to each of the rates before taking the product and added to the long-term rate on the left-hand side of the equation as well. The left subscript in each term identifies the beginning of a particular time period. The right subscript in each term indicates the maturity to which a particular yield applies. Thus, for example, the term $({}_1r_1)$ refers to the observed yield of a one-year security (right subscript) at the beginning of period 1 (left subscript). The term $_2\gamma_1$ refers to the expected yield of a one-year security (right subscript) at the beginning of period 2 (left subscript), where the r term refers to actual rates and the γ term to expected rates. Equation 15.1 states that the *observed* yield in period 1 for a security with n years to maturity $({}_1r_n)$ is the **geometric average** of a series of one-year current and *expected* yields over this period.[10]

Table 15.1 contains investors' expectations for one-year yields during a hypothetical period January 2000 to January 2003. The first three columns are used in the following examples. The fourth column of liquidity premiums is used later.

According to the unbiased expectations theory and from these expectations alone, Equation 15.1 can be used to calculate the required yield to maturity on a

---

[9]Recently, some scholars have argued that this implication holds strictly only for a specific holding period of instantaneous duration and that it is incompatible with other versions of the expectations hypothesis, such as the statement that long-term spot rates are the average of expected short-term rates. See Cox, Ingersoll, and Ross (1981).

[10]The notation for pure expectations mathematics is invariably confusing. Present and compound value calculations usually emphasize end-of-period cash flows, so t = 1 usually means the end of period 1, and t = n means the end of period n. That usage prevails in most chapters in this book. The pure expectations theory focuses on beginning-of-period expectations; however, t = 1 means the beginning of period 1 (or the end of period 0), and the notation t = n means the beginning of period n.

Table 15.1 ✦ Observed and Expected 1-Year Yields and Premiums as of January 2000

These hypothetical data on observed and expected 1-year rates and liquidity premiums can be used to estimate the shape of a yield curve.

BILL PURCHASED	BILL MATURES	OBSERVED OR EXPECTED ANNUAL YIELD (%)	LIQUIDITY PREMIUM (%)
January 2000	January 2001	8.50% observed ($_1r_1$)	0.00% (on 1-year security)
January 2001	January 2002	9.50% expected ($_2r_1$)	0.35% (on 2-year security)
January 2002	January 2003	11.00% expected ($_3r_1$)	0.45% (on 3-year security)
January 2003	January 2004	11.75% expected ($_4r_1$)	0.50% (on 4-year security)

four-year Treasury security bought in January 2000 (the beginning of period 1) and maturing in January 2004:

$$1 + {_1}r_n = [(1 + {_1}\gamma_1)(1 + {_2}r_1)\ldots(1 + {_n}\gamma_1)]^{1/n}$$

$$1 + {_1}r_4 = [(1 + {_1}r_1)(1 + {_2}\gamma_1)(1 + {_3}\gamma_1)(1 + {_4}\gamma_1)]^{1/n}$$

$$1 + {_1}r_4 = [(1.0850)(1.0950)(1.1100)(1.1175)]^{1/n}$$

$${_1}r_4 = 1.10180 - 1 = 0.10180 = 10.180\%$$

Using the Equation 15.1, it is possible to calculate spot yields on securities with two- and three-year maturities as of January 2000 as follows:

$$1 + {_1}r_2 = [(1 + {_1}r_1)(1 + {_2}\gamma_1)]^{1/2}$$

$$1 + {_1}r_2 = [(1.0850)(1.0950)]^{1/2}$$

$${_1}r_2 = 1.08999 - 1 = 0.08999 = 8.999\%$$

$$1 + {_1}r_3 = [(1 + {_1}r_1)(1 + {_2}\gamma_1)(1 + {_3}\gamma_1)]^{1/3}$$

$$1 + {_1}r_3 = [(1.0850)(1.0950)(1.1100)]^{1/3}$$

$${_1}r_3 = 1.09662 - 1 = 0.09662 = 9.662\%$$

As shown in Figure 15.9, the pure expectations theory implies that investors' expectations of rising short-term yields will result in an upward-sloping yield curve for Treasury securities as of January 2000.

If the pure expectations theory is correct, the average annual yield an investor could obtain over the period 2000–2004 is the same, regardless of the investment strategy chosen. If the investor decides to buy four one-year securities, the average annual yield over the holding period (i_H) will be 10.180 percent. If, instead, the investments are a two-year security in January 2000 (annual yield of 8.999 percent) and two successive one-year T-bills in 2002 and 2003 (expected yields of 11.000 percent and 11.750 percent, respectively), the average annual yield for this strategy is as follows:

$$1 + i_H = [(1.08999)(1.08999)(1.1100)(1.1175)]^{1/4}$$

$$1 + i_H = 1.10180 - 1 = 10.180\%$$

Or, if an investor buys a 3-year T-note in 1994 (annual yield of 9.662 percent), followed by a 1-year bill in 1997 (11.750 percent expected yield), the average annual yield for the holding period is as follows:

$$1 + i_H = [(1.09662)(1.09662)(1.09662)(1.1175)]^{1/4}$$

$$1 + i_H = 1.10180 - 1 = 10.180\%$$

Figure 15.9   ✦   Hypothetical Observed Yield Curve, January 2000

Because long-term yields are the average of expected short-term yields, if short-term rates are expected to increase, the pure expectations theory holds that the term structure will be upward-sloping.

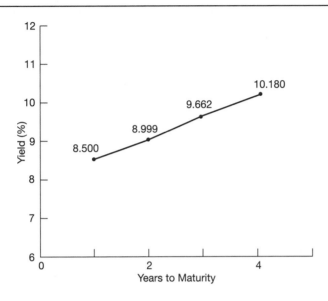

Under the assumptions of investor indifference to maturity and unbiased expectations of future short-term rates, any combination of maturities over the period will result in an average annual yield of 10.180 percent. This will be true as long as all proceeds are reinvested and expectations of future rates remain constant during the period. In other words, the 10.180 percent average four-year yield would be expected as long as investors do not revise their one-year predictions for 2002, for example, at some point after 2000.

Modifications of the Unbiased Expectations Theory

The unbiased expectations theory succinctly explains the shape of any term structure: Lenders' expectations of rising short-term rates produce an observable upward-sloping yield curve; expectations of falling short-term rates produce a downward-sloping term structure; and expectations of unchanging rates produce a flat yield curve. Changes in the shape of the curve over time can easily be explained by changes in expectations. Also, the theory appeals to researchers because its mathematical form provides testable hypotheses as well as the opportunity to develop models for predicting interest rates.

CRITICISMS OF THE PURE EXPECTATIONS THEORY

The pure expectations theory is not without its critics, however, who focus on its restrictive assumptions as serious shortcomings. In particular, investors' assumed indifference between short- and long-term securities ignores the fact that a long-term investment may be riskier than a series of short-term investments. Risk, brought about by the passage of time alone, is rarely a matter of indifference. Even for two securities of the same issuer with equal initial default risk, the probability of default may increase on the long-term security over time. Furthermore, investors are never certain that personal circumstances will allow them to follow initial investment strategies throughout the holding period. If emergencies arise, they may have to sell long-term securities at a loss.[11]

A second assumption that troubles critics is that, according to the theory, issuers of securities have no influence on the term structure. This appears to contradict the negotiation process that actually occurs between borrowers and lenders in many financial markets. It is important to remember that no theory should be judged on the realism of its assumptions. The test of a theory is how well it explains "real-world" relationships, and the theory enjoys some qualified empirical support. However, these criticisms have led to some theoretical modifications.

The Liquidity Premium Hypothesis

The belief that most investors find long-term securities to be riskier than short-term securities has led to the **liquidity premium hypothesis**. According to this theory, today's long-term rates reflect the geometric average of intervening expected short-term rates *plus* a premium that investors demand for holding long-term securities instead of a series of short-term, less risky investments. The hypothesized effect of these liquidity premiums, also called **term premiums**, can be illustrated by looking at the fourth column on Table 15.1.[12]

In the previous example using the pure expectations theory, spot rates of 8.99 percent, 9.66 percent, and 10.18 percent were calculated earlier for two-, three-, and four-year maturities. According to the liquidity premium hypothesis, the following yields would be expected to be observed instead, using Equation 15.1 with the liquidity premiums added:

$$1 + {}_1r_2 = [(1.0850)(1.0950 + 0.0035)]^{1/2}$$

$$
{}_1r_2 = 1.0917 - 1 = 0.0917 = 9.17\%
$$

$$1 + {}_1r_3 = [(1.0850)(1.0950 + 0.0035)(1.1100 + 0.0045)]^{1/3}$$

$$
{}_1r_3 = 1.0993 - 1 = 0.0993 = 9.93\%
$$

$$1 + {}_1r_4 = [(1.0850)(1.0950 + 0.0035)(1.1100 + 0.0045)(1.1175 + 0.0050)]^{1/4}$$

$$= 0.1050 = 10.50\%$$

---

[11]For an investor who holds the investment throughout the planned holding period, another element of risk must be considered: the potential for unexpected changes in short-term yields. If such changes occur, the investor faces uncertainty from periodic reinvestment rates. This source of risk is discussed in more detail in Chapter 16.

[12]Presentations of the liquidity premium hypothesis can be found in Hicks (1946); and Kessel (1965). Although it is easy to incorporate given liquidity premiums into the basic pure expectations equation, it is more difficult to specify the structure of liquidity premiums themselves. Scholars disagree about how to model them, but for illustrative purposes, liquidity premiums in these examples are considered to increase with time. A brief review of alternative specifications is provided later in the chapter.

Because investors are no longer indifferent among maturities, the same expectations are supplemented by a premium for holding long-term securities. As shown in Figures 15.10 to 15.12, this term structure has a steeper slope than curves based on the same expectations but assumed no liquidity premiums.

A general restatement of the term structure including liquidity premiums is seen in Equation 15.2:

$$1 + {}_1r_n = [(1 + {}_1r_1)(1 + {}_t\gamma_1 + L_t)]^{1/n} \qquad [15.2]$$

where

L_t = liquidity premium for holding a t-period security instead of a one-year security.

By definition, $Ld_1 = 0$, since investors will not demand a liquidity premium for a one-year security.

The liquidity premium hypothesis does not rule out the possibility of downward-sloping yield curves, although some economists believe that it explains why they are less common. If investors expect future short-term rates to fall sharply, the pure expectations theory holds that a steeply downward-sloping curve should be observed in the spot markets. If investors also demand a premium for investing long-term, the observed yield curve might still be inverted, but it would be more gently sloped than if determined by expectations alone, as shown in Figure 15.10.

It is even possible, according to the liquidity premium hypothesis, that a yield curve reflecting expectations of falling rates could appear to be upward sloping if investors demanded a relatively high premium on long-term issues. Such a situation is illustrated in Figure 15.11.

Figure 15.10   ✦   PURE EXPECTATIONS AND LIQUIDITY PREMIUMS

If short-term rates are expected to decrease sharply and if investors also demand a premium for holding long-term securities, the slope of the yield curve will be less steep than if expectations alone are considered.

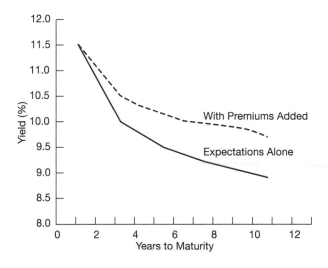

Figure 15.11 ✦ TRANSFORMATION OF AN INVERTED CURVE

If short-term rates are expected to decrease slightly and if investors also demand a premium for holding long-term securities, the yield curve could be slightly upward-sloping.

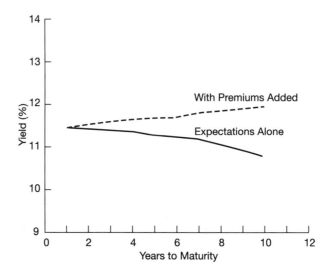

Figure 15.12 ✦ HYPOTHETICAL YIELD CURVE WITH LIQUIDITY PREMIUMS

If short-term rates are expected to increase and if investors demand a premium for holding long-term securities, long-term yields will be higher than if expectations alone are considered.

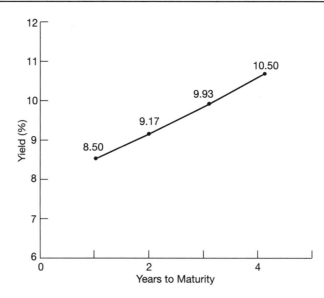

Incorporating the Role of Lenders

Other theories of the term structure are distinguished from the pure expectations approach because they include a role for lenders in the determination of spot rates, and they discard the assumption of indifference between maturities.

The Modified Expectations Theory   One theory is sometimes called the **modified expectations theory** to reflect support for the idea that expectations of future rates do, in fact, determine today's yields.[13] As this argument goes, if interest rates are expected to rise in the future, lenders may wish to lend short-term to avoid locking in today's lower spot rates. Such a long-term commitment would not only prevent reinvestment of principal at the expected higher rates, but it also would subject lenders to capital losses should they sell their investments before maturity. However, borrowers will wish to borrow long-term to avoid expected higher interest costs.

According to the theory, the common expectations of borrowers and lenders and their conflicting maturity preferences put pressure on long-term rates, producing an upward-sloping curve. Conversely, when all parties expect interest rates to fall, lenders wish to lend long, but borrowers prefer to roll over a series of short-term loans at progressively lower expected rates. This places upward pressure on short-term rates, resulting in an inverted term structure. Thus, the conclusions of the modified expectations theory are the same as those for the unbiased expectations theory: Expectations of rising rates produce an upward-sloping curve, whereas expectations of falling rates produce a downward-sloping relationship. The main difference between the theories is the motivations that determine spot rates.

The Segmented Markets Theory   Relying heavily on the existence of market imperfections, the **segmented markets theory** argues that there really is no term structure. The segmentation theory has gained especially strong support among market participants.[14] It suggests that different spot rates on long- and short-term securities are explained not by any common set of market expectations, or by a liquidity premium to induce lenders to switch from short- to long-term securities, but rather by separate supply/demand interactions in the financial markets. According to this theory, short-term yields result from interactions of individuals and institutions in the short-term market segment; the same is true of yields on long-term securities. Because laws, regulations, or institutional objectives prevent many market participants from borrowing or lending in every segment, some maturities are of little concern.

One justification for the segmented markets theory is that it reflects the preference of financial institutions to match the maturities of their assets and liabilities. Commercial banks, for example, have traditionally concentrated on lending in the short-term markets while obtaining funds from depositors in that same segment of the market. Similar segmented supply/demand factors may affect long-term rates. Life insurance firms expect long-term payment inflows from customers and invest those funds heavily in instruments with long maturities.

According to the segmented markets theory, what might seem to be a downward-sloping yield curve is really many distinct—and theoretically unrelated—market interactions, as shown in Figure 15.13. Notice the similarities between this

---

[13]Smith (1960). The modified expectations theory produces the same mathematical model as the pure expectations theory (Equation 15.1).

[14]See Culbertson (1957).

Figure 15.13 ✦ YIELDS IN SEGMENTED MARKETS

The segmented markets theory holds that the term structure is not continuous. Instead, supply and demand in separate financial markets determine the yields in those markets.

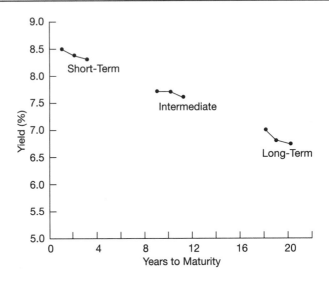

hypothetical curve and the actual term structure of interest rates shown in Figure 15.14. For example, proponents of the market segmentation theory believe that the yield curve on December 31, 1969, clearly reveals distinct financial market segments. This theory has implications for interest rate forecasting that are quite distinct from those of the expectations hypothesis. It returns forecasting solely to supply/demand in market segments and relies on forecasting methods similar to those discussed in Chapter 14.

The Preferred Habitat Theory   Closely related to the segmented markets theory is the **preferred habitat theory**, which assumes that although investors may strongly prefer particular segments of the market, they are not necessarily locked in to those segments. These strong preferences for certain maturities arise not from legal or regulatory reasons but, rather, from *consumption preferences*.[15] In other words, investors' time preferences for spending versus saving influence their choice among securities. They will lend in markets other than their preferred one, but only if a premium exists to induce them to switch. This argument differs from the liquidity premium theory in that it does not assume that all lenders prefer short-term securities to long-term ones. There may well be lenders who prefer to lend long but who can be induced to lend short for a yield premium, or vice versa.

---

[15]See Modigliani and Sutch (1966). Cox, Ingersoll, and Ross (1981) argue instead that risk aversion, not time-related consumption preferences, will create preferred habitats. In particular, they interpreted a habitat "as a stronger or weaker tendency to hedge against changes in the interest rate" (p. 786).

Figure 15.14 ✦ Yields of Treasury Securities, December 31, 1969

The shape of the yield curve in December 1969 has been used by some as support for the segmented markets theory; yields seemed to cluster rather than being continuously distributed across the spectrum of maturities.

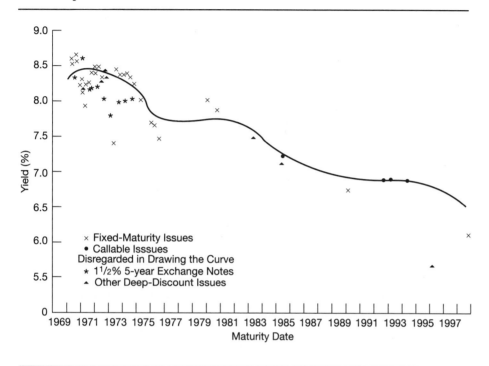

Source: Treasury Bulletin, January 1970, 83.

Although the preferred habitat theory recognizes that some lenders may not be persuaded to depart from their preferred habitats at any price, it holds that the markets are only partially segmented because many participants are willing to switch maturities if properly rewarded. Short- and long-term yield differentials are only partially explained by the expectations hypothesis; supply/demand imbalances in various markets may result in positive or negative premiums added to the pure expectations rate to induce shifts from one segment to another. Thus, the preferred habitat theory differs from the segmented markets theory in the following ways:

1. It relies less on the maturity preferences of the suppliers of securities in the determination of spot rates.
2. It acknowledges that many investors consider developments across the spectrum of maturities before making their decisions.

Emerging Theories of the Term Structure

Since the mid-1980s, several new formulations of the term structure have emerged. Although still in their formative stages and yielding conflicting results in empirical tests, these models are gaining support in some circles at the expense of the expectations theory and its modifications.[16] They have by no means supplanted the more traditional theories, however.

Best known of the new models is the work of Cox, Ingersoll, and Ross. Their model bears some similarity to the expectations theory in that it, too, recognizes the influence of interest rate expectations. The newer approach, however, focuses on the factors determining those expectations, such as inflation, uncertainty, and productivity.

Researchers continue to explore adjustments, applications of, and empirical verification of the new models, although their complexity has made empirical testing difficult. Experts agree that investigation of these term structure theories will continue to be a fertile area of research.

EMPIRICAL TESTS OF THE TERM STRUCTURE THEORIES

A full review of empirical tests of term structure theories would fill a book, because research interest in the subject spans almost a century. Nonetheless, no single theory has prevailed.

A Familiar Research Problem: Measuring Expectations

As the oldest of the theories, the pure expectations model has received the greatest attention. Particularly troublesome, however, is a problem also faced in tests of the Fisher effect: measuring market expectations to be compared with subsequent actual rates. Researchers have used several alternatives. Some have used ex post rates as a proxy for expected rates. The conclusions are similar to those drawn by students of the Fisher theory: Even though, after the fact, expectations are not always correct, they still influence observed term structures.[17]

For example, some researchers have developed an "error learning" model, which argues that investors continually revise their expectations in response to earlier errors. This model implies that past and present experiences affect investors' response to new information. Other researchers have argued that investors' expectations are "regressive," i.e., when the general level of rates is high, people expect them to fall, and when the general level is low, they expect rates to increase.

Quite a different approach uses interest rate forecasts of professional investors and analysts as proxies for interest rate expectations. Some researchers have also recognized that the financial futures markets may provide a good method for estimating interest rate expectations and have turned to those markets for continuation of empirical tests. Others have investigated the influence of monetary policy on expectations and the slope of the yield curve.[18] Regardless of the chosen measurement,

---

[16]See Cox, Ingersoll, and Ross (1981, 1985) and Ho and Lee (1986). Abken (1990) offers a comprehensive summary and evaluation of the newer models and results of empirical tests.

[17]Examples of these studies include Van Horne (1965); Kessel (1965); Meiselman (1962); Wood (1983); Walz and Spencer (1989); Froot (1989); and Dua (1991).

[18]See Kane and Malkiel (1967); Friedman (1979); Hafer and Hein (1989); and Cook and Hahn (1990).

many studies of the U.S. Treasury securities market have concluded that expectations play a major role in determining the term structure.[19]

Research on the expectations theory increasingly reflects globalization of financial markets. Scholars have noted that investors' expectations may be directed not only toward rates in their home country but also toward rates in other financial markets in which they customarily interact. Thus, some recent studies have tested the expectations theory on contemporaneous data from several countries. Although the evidence by no means supports a definite conclusion that long-term rates in one country reflect expectations of short-term rates in other countries, this avenue of term structure research will undoubtedly be continued in the next decade.[20]

Evidence on Liquidity Premiums

Many researchers have concluded that investors also demand liquidity premiums, although they do not agree on the nature of these premiums. The disagreement centers on whether the premium demanded by investors is affected by the general level of interest rates (i.e., whether the premium increases or decreases when rates are considered to be relatively high or low) and whether it is stable or rises monotonically with maturity. There is considerable evidence that the liquidity premium *does* vary with the general level of interest rates, but there is no agreement on whether the relationship is positive or negative.[21] In other words, some research indicates that when rates are higher than normal, the liquidity premium required by investors is smaller than usual, whereas other results suggest that it is larger.

The debate over the nature of the liquidity premium has implications for tests of the expectations hypothesis and for its usefulness as a forecasting model. Because it is difficult to determine the size and pattern of liquidity premiums, it is difficult to isolate an expected "pure" interest rate from a premium attached to it. Some research has suggested that liquidity premiums range from 0.54 percent to 1.56 percent, but other studies have concluded that premiums are less than 0.50 percent, even for long maturities. Some researchers have even concluded that liquidity premiums decrease, rather than increase, with maturity.[22]

Research on Segmented Markets and Preferred Habitats

Research on the segmented markets and preferred habitat theories is extremely contradictory. Some researchers have reported findings of discontinuities in the yield curve, supporting the market segmentation theory; some have concluded that preferred habitats exist.[23] In contrast, other studies, including those supporting the expectations and liquidity premium theories, argue that the financial markets function

---

[19]There are serious critics. For example, one study concludes that the use of the simple expectations theory "to forecast the direction of future changes in the interest rate seems worthless." See Schiller, Campbell, and Schoenholtz (1983). Belongia and Koedik (1988) also fail to find support for the expectations hypothesis.

[20]See Belongia and Koedik (1988) and Kool and Tatom (1988).

[21]See Nelson (1972); Van Horne (1965); Friedman (1979); and Dua (1991).

[22]For further information on empirical research addressing the liquidity premium hypothesis, see McCulloch (1975); Lee, Maness, and Tuttle (1980); Roll (1970); and Throop (1981).

[23]See Modigliani and Sutch (1966). Also see Dobson, Sutch, and Vanderford (1976); Echols and Elliott (1976); Roley (1981); and Heuson (1988).

more efficiently than the segmented markets theory or preferred habitat theory recognizes. In other words, investors are more willing to move funds back and forth between maturities to maximize returns than either of these theories implies.

APPLICATION OF TERM STRUCTURE THEORIES TO FINANCIAL INSTITUTIONS MANAGEMENT

Most managers do not personally intend to resolve these theoretical and empirical debates, but they are interested in using the fruits of research to make better decisions. Fortunately, although no one has written the definitive word on yield curves, ample insights are available from existing theory to assist a knowledgeable manager. Some of the most important problems for which term structure theories are useful are illustrated in the following discussion.

It is important to appreciate the perspective from which managers view the term structure. Instead of confronting the raw material of yield curves—investors' expectations, liquidity premiums, and supply/demand relationships in the financial markets—managers observe the finished products, such as the actual term structures depicted in Figures 15.2 through 15.4. Term structure theories attempt to explain how observed term structures came about. The information a manager obtains by applying theory to an existing yield curve can assist in making decisions, such as forecasting interest rates, setting a mortgage loan rate, or trading securities for the institution's portfolio.

INTEREST RATE FORECASTING

Of particular importance to interest rate forecasting is the pure expectations theory. The mathematical expression of the pure expectations theory itself provides a forecasting model. To illustrate, suppose that in June 2000, the spot Treasury yields shown in Table 15.2 for a five-year maturity horizon are observed.

Forward Rates   If it is currently June 2000, according to the pure expectations theory, the two-year spot rate (i.e., the existing yield on a security maturing in June 2002) is the geometric average of the expected yield on a one-year Treasury security (a rate that can be directly observed from the existing yield curve maturing in 2001) and the expected annual yield on one-year securities issued a year later in June 2001 (a rate not directly observable). That relationship was modeled mathematically in Equation 15.1.

Table 15.2 ✦ HYPOTHETICAL SPOT RATES ON TREASURY SECURITIES AS OF JUNE 2000

These hypothetical data on observed yields can be used to infer 1-year forward rates.

MATURITY DATE	SPOT YIELD (%)	NOTATION
June 2001	12.50%	$_1r_1$
June 2002	11.85%	$_1r_2$
June 2003	11.00%	$_1r_3$
June 2004	10.90%	$_1r_4$
June 2005	10.50%	$_1r_5$

Using data from Table 15.2,

$$1 + {}_1r_2 = [(1 + {}_1r_1)(1 + {}_2\gamma_1)]^{1/2}$$

$$1 + 0.1185 = [(1.1250)(1 + {}_2\gamma_1)]^{1/2}$$

where ${}_2\gamma_1$ = unobservable expected 1-year rate at the beginning of period 2.

If the pure expectations theory is correct, one can infer the expected one-year rate at the beginning of period 2 by solving Equation 15.1 for ${}_2\gamma_1$.

$$(1 + {}_2\gamma_1) = (1 + {}_1r_2)^2 / (1 + {}_1r_1) \qquad [15.3]$$

$$(1 + {}_2\gamma_1) = (1.1185)^2 / (1.1250)$$

$$(1 + {}_2\gamma_1) = 1.1120 - 1 = 0.1120 = 11.20\%$$

An implied expected rate calculated from an existing yield curve is a **forward rate**. The one-year forward rate or expected rate at the beginning of period 2 is 11.20 percent. This rate is expected to prevail on investments made in June 2001 and maturing in June 2002. It is lower than the one-year T-bill yield in 2000 because the spot yields in Table 15.2 suggest market expectations for falling rates. If an institution's managers use the pure expectations theory, this forward rate can serve as a specific forecast for short-term T-bill rates for future years.

The general formula for a one-year forward rate as of the beginning of period t is as follows where observable bond rates with n years to maturity are used.

$$(1 + {}_t\gamma_1) = (1 + {}_1r_n)^n / (1 + {}_1r_{n-1})^{n-1} \qquad [15.4]$$

Equation 15.4 allows calculation of the one-year forward rate as of the beginning of any future period (t). It is more useful than Equation 15.3, which solves only for the one-year forward rate as of the beginning of period 2.

Incorporating Liquidity Premiums Many managers may not accept the unbiased expectations theory as the only explanation for the term structure. Fortunately, it is possible to incorporate liquidity premiums into a forecasting model. If liquidity premiums exist, spot rates for two-, three-, four-, and five-year securities in Table 15.2 are affected not only by expectations but also by premiums on long-term investments.

For example, suppose a manager believes that investors expect a premium of 0.5 percent for holding a two-year security in 2000. That belief can be incorporated into a forecast of future short-term rates by solving Equation 15.2 for the forward rate as of the beginning of period 2:

$$1 + {}_1r_2 = [(1 + {}_1r_1)(1 + {}_2({}_{1+}L_2))]^{1/2} \qquad [15.5]$$

$$1 + {}_2\gamma_1 = [(1 + {}_1r_2)^2 / (1 + {}_1r_1)] - L_2$$

Under the assumption of liquidity premiums, the estimate for the forward rate in June, 2001 becomes the following:

$$(1.1185)^2 = (1.1250)(1 + {}_2\gamma_1 + 0.005)]$$

$$1 + {}_2\gamma_1 + 0.005 = (1.1185)^2 / (1.1250)$$

$$1 + {}_2\gamma_1 + 0.005 = 1.1120$$

$$1 + {}_2\gamma_1 = 1.1120 - 0.005 = 1.1070$$

$$1 + {}_2\gamma_1 = 0.1070 = 10.70\%$$

This one-year rate expected to prevail in 2001 is lower than the forward rate of 11.20 percent calculated earlier with only the pure expectations theory as a basis for forecasting. The difference is the assumed liquidity premium required for two-year loans. If liquidity premiums exist, their effect on actual long-term rates will cause the results of Equations 15.3 or 15.4 to be biased upward. Equation 15.5 adjusts for that bias.

Using the pure expectations theory with liquidity premiums, the general equation for calculating the one-year forward rate in period t is as follows:

$$1 + {}_t\gamma_1 = [(1 + {}_1r_t)^t / (1 + {}_1r_{t-1})^{t-1}] - L_t \qquad [15.6]$$

Equation 15.6 allows estimation of the forward rate as of the beginning of any future period, adjusted for a liquidity premium. In contrast, Equation 15.5 applies only to the forward rate as of the beginning of period 2.

Setting Institutional Interest Rates

A financial institution manager frequently faces simultaneous decisions about short- and long-term interest rates. For example, if short-term deposits such as one-year certificates of deposit (CDs) are to be used to finance long-term assets such as mortgages, care must be taken to establish both rates so that the cost of financing does not exceed the yield on the mortgages. Using the pure expectations theory, a manager who observes an upward-sloping Treasury security term structure can infer that most investors expect increasing short-term rates over the next several periods. The cost of one-year CDs is therefore likely to increase during the period when mortgage loans made today have a constant yield.

According to the liquidity premium theory, existing Treasury rates may also include liquidity premiums, and the manager may also believe that a premium for default risk should be required for holding mortgages instead of Treasury securities. Furthermore, the segmented markets and preferred habitat theories suggest that competitive pressures from other depository institutions should be considered in setting both rates. For example, if there is strong competition for one-year CDs, a savings and loan association (S&L) may be forced to pay an even higher yield than the expectations hypothesis would suggest.

Estimating the Cost of Deposits   Sample calculations and estimations involved in this decision are provided in Table 15.3. For simplicity, it is assumed that mortgages made today will mature in five years. Because the source of funds is one-year CDs, the manager would begin by calculating a series of one-year forward rates implied in the existing yield curve by using Equation 15.4. Using Equation 15.6, liquidity premiums embedded in the current term structure would be removed to avoid overestimating expected one-year CD rates in future periods. Because the institution plans to issue one-year CDs each year, it would not have to offer liquidity premiums to its depositors.

The resulting series of forward rates (given in Column 5) is used to set initial and anticipated one-year CD rates. Specifically, the initial CD rate is based on the first rate in this series (8 percent), with subsequent forward rates serving as the basis for estimating the future annual interest cost of the deposits. After obtaining these costs, the manager would increase them as needed to account for the administrative costs of servicing deposits (Column 6). In addition, adjustments might be made to account for premiums necessary to meet competitors' offerings. Column 6 contains

Table 15.3   ✦   Using Term Structure Theories to Set Institutional Interest Rates

These hypothetical data on observed yields, liquidity premiums, administrative costs, risk premiums, and profit markups can be used to estimate the appropriate rate to charge on a mortgage loan.

(1) MATURITY (YEARS)	(2) OBSERVED YIELD ON TREASURY SECURITIES	(3) UNADJUSTED 1-YEAR FORWARD RATE (FROM EQUATION 7.4)	(4) ESTIMATED LIQUIDITY PREMIUM	(5) ESTIMATED 1-YEAR RATE WITH LIQUIDITY PREMIUM REMOVED (COLUMN 3 − COLUMN 4)
1	0.0800	0.0800	0.0000	0.0800
2	0.0825	0.0850	0.0050	0.0800
3	0.0950	0.1204	0.0100	0.1104
4	0.1025	0.1253	0.0250	0.1003
5	0.1100	0.1405	0.0350	0.1055

(6) ANNUAL CD COST (COLUMN 5 + ADMINISTRATIVE MARKUP OF 0.25% PER YEAR)	(7) ESTIMATED PREMIUM REQUIRED TO HOLD MORTGAGES	(8) ESTIMATED ANNUAL REQUIRED RETURN (COLUMN 6 + COLUMN 7 + PROFIT MARKUP OF 0.75% PER YEAR)
0.0825	0.0100	0.1000
0.0825	0.0250	0.1150
0.1129	0.0300	0.1504
0.1028	0.0400	0.1503
0.1080	0.0450	0.1605

(9)
ESTIMATION OF REQUIRED ANNUAL YIELD ON MORTGAGES
(USING EQUATION 7.1 ON DATA FROM COLUMN 8)

$$i_m = \sqrt[5]{(1.1000)(1.1150)(1.1504)(1.1503)(1.1605)} - 1$$
$$i_m = 0.1350 = 13.50\%$$

estimated total interest plus noninterest costs of issuing one-year CDs each year for five years.

Setting the Mortgage Rate   The manager would then set the five-year mortgage rate by estimating the risk premium necessary to compensate the institution for holding mortgages (Column 7). Finally, a desired profit markup of 0.75 percent per year is added to allow for a return to owners in a stockholder-owned firm or to provide for additions to net worth in a mutual institution. The resulting figures in Column 8 are the estimated annual returns required to cover all costs, including the cost of funds, noninterest costs, and a target rate of profit. Finally, the geometric average of the five rates is calculated by using Equation 15.1. This rate, 13.50 percent in Table 15.3, is the appropriate annual interest rate to charge on a mortgage made at the beginning of the five-year period. If the institution earns 13.50 percent annually for five years and if actual costs equal estimates, the desired profit markup over the life of the mortgage will be earned. Of course, an institution's ability to charge this rate is constrained by competition, but competing institutions would also be aware of the need to recover long-term costs.

It is important to remember that even such careful forecasting and rate setting include a great deal of uncertainty. As the review of empirical research suggests, expectations embedded in the term structure are not always fulfilled, and additional sources of error are introduced in the estimation of the liquidity premium. Such errors can be costly, because once the long-term mortgage rate has been established, it may not be subject to renegotiation, and profits will disappear if interest rates move to such a high level that costs cannot be recovered. Many thrift institutions, in particular, learned this lesson the hard way in the early 1980s. Institutions must also maintain sufficient flexibility to respond when forecasts prove to be incorrect. Increasingly sophisticated techniques for managing interest rate risk are discussed in chapters that follow.

USING FORWARD RATES ESTIMATED FROM YIELD CURVES TO SET LOAN CREDIT RISK PREMIUMS

Another use for yield curves is to set risk premiums for loans based on risk premiums set in bond markets for corporate bonds.[24] Under this technique, which is based on the pure expectations theory of interest rates, Equation 15.3 is used to calculate the one-year expected rates, i.e., forward rates, for next year's one-year Treasury bond and a corporate bond with some credit classification (for instance, BBB). The probability of no default for the BBB bond is then calculated by taking the ratio between (1 + forward rate for the Treasuries) / (1 + forward rate for the corporate bonds). For example, hypothetically suppose in the year 2002, you are a loan pricing analyst, and the *Wall Street Journal* quotes a two-year Treasury bond to have a 4.62 percent yield and a one-year Treasury bond to have a 4.28 percent yield. Similarly, the *Wall Street Journal* shows a two-year BBB Corporate bond to have a 5.18 percent yield and a one-year corporate BBB bond to have a 5.00 percent yield. By using Equation 15.3, the respective forward rates for one-year Treasury and corporate bonds issued next year can be calculated, as follows:

$$(1 + {_2}\gamma_1) = (1 + {_1}r_2)^2 / (1 + {_1}r_1)$$

$$\text{Expected 1 yr Tbill} = (1.0462)^2 / (1.0428) - 1 = 4.961\%$$

$$\text{Expected 1 yr Corporate rate} = (1.0518) / (1.0500) - 1 = 5.360\%$$

By taking the ratio of one plus the Treasury forward rate to one plus the risky bond rate, the expected probability of the corporate bond defaulting can be calculated. Taking the ratio of (1 + Treasury forward rate)/ (1 + corporate forward rate) is equal to the following:

$$(1.04961) / (1.0536) = 0.9962$$

Hence, the expected probability of the BBB corporate bond of defaulting is 1 − 0.9962 = 0.0038 = 0.38 percent. Based on this, the risk premium for similar

---

[24]This use of forward rates to calculate probabilities of bonds not defaulting comes from. Saunders (1997), who provides a detailed description of the term structure derivation of credit risk.

one-year loans with a probability of default of only 0.38 percent should be similar to the risk premium for the corporate bond over the Treasury bond of about (5.36 percent − 4.961 percent) = 0.40 percent, or 40 basis points (1 basis point = 0.01 percent). For longer-term bonds, risk premiums can be calculated by finding the respective forward rates for each year and the ratio of forward rates to find the probability of no default for each year. The joint probabilities, i.e., the product of the probabilities of no default for each year, can then be calculated for the life of the bond, and the joint probability of default [1 − (p1)(p2), and so on] can be calculated for bonds of different maturities. A term structure of default risk can then be graphed to show the increase in default risk for securities of different maturities.

MANAGING THE SECURITIES PORTFOLIO

Term structure theories are also useful in managing the institution's securities portfolio. A common trading strategy is searching for undervalued or overvalued securities. This strategy assumes that, although the pure expectations theory applies in general and investors price securities to make the expected annual yield the same regardless of the maturities selected over a holding period, the markets are sometimes in temporary disequilibrium. According to this line of thinking, if a security's yield exceeds those on securities of equal maturity and risk, the security is underpriced. If the institution does not own the security, it can purchase it immediately. When the market returns to equilibrium, the price of the security should rise, lowering its yield to the appropriate level. The institution can expect to profit from the capital gain.

Conversely, if a security's yield is less than those on securities of comparable maturity, the security is overpriced and should be sold. The pure expectations theory suggests that its price will fall as the market returns its yield to the level proper for its maturity. Analysts sometimes attempt to identify under- or overvalued securities in the Treasury market, for example, by studying yield curves such as the one in Figure 15.2. The issues circled left of the center of the graph have lower yields than securities of similar maturity (approximately two years). A manager who believed that the market was in temporary disequilibrium would sell the issues before the anticipated drop in price increased their yields.

Such a strategy would reflect not only a belief that the pure expectations theory correctly describes interest rate movements in the long run but also a recognition of the role of **arbitrage** in the financial markets. Arbitrage is trading to profit from temporary price discrepancies in otherwise identical assets. As noted, the pure expectations theory assumes that investors are indifferent among equally risky securities of varying maturities. If the theory is correct, investors holding the relatively lower-yielding two-year securities circled in Figure 15.2 would possess arbitrage opportunities. They could attempt to improve returns by selling the circled securities and either purchasing higher-yielding two-year securities or purchasing a series of shorter-term securities over a two-year period. These arbitrage selling and buying activities would, in turn, cause the price of the circled securities to decline and the prices of purchased securities to rise. Because of the inverse relationship between prices and yields, the expected return to subsequent owners of the circled securities would rise. Ultimately, then, the actions of arbitrage traders should cause the yields on securities of similar maturity to converge.[25] The relationship between prices and yields is explored further in Chapter 16.

SUMMARY

The term structure of interest rates is the relationship at a specific time between the yields and maturities of securities of comparable default risk. Historically, this relationship has varied. The variation is related both to the general level of interest rates and to the pace of economic activity.

Economists have developed several theories to explain term structures. Researchers agree that the financial markets' expectations of future short-term rates play a large role in determining existing yields on long-term securities. Other factors, such as investors' varying preferences for liquidity, their policies and attitudes, or regulation in the financial markets, appear to have less influence on the term structure.

Knowledge of term structure relationships is useful in asset/liability management. Understanding the role of expectations allows managers to develop interest rate forecasts to use in institutional planning and in trading strategies for the securities portfolio. Also, knowledge of expectations, liquidity preferences, and supply/demand interactions can help managers establish the prices of financial products such as deposits and loans.

Questions

Suppose you are interviewing for a job with a mutual fund company. Jim Moser, the financial economist interviewing you, wants to see if you understand how yield curves are created and used. Answer the following questions for him.

1. Explain the term structure of interest rates and the relationships measured. Why must all securities plotted on a given term structure have equal default risk?

2. Historically, what has been the relationship between the slope of the yield curve and the level of economic activity? Between the slope of the yield curve and the general level of interest rates?

3. In a recent issue of the *Wall Street Journal* or other major newspaper, find yield quotations for U.S. Treasury securities. Using data for T-bills, bonds, and notes, sketch the prevailing term structure.

4. According to the pure expectations theory, what determines the slope of the term structure of interest rates? On what important assumptions is this theory based? Using this theory, what expectations about future interest rates are reflected in the term structure you plotted for Question 3?

5. An investor who accepts the pure expectations theory and its underlying assumptions has been offered two six-year investment plans. One plan is a series of three two-year instruments, whereas the other plan is a series of six one-year T-bill purchases. Ignoring any fees and assuming no liquidity premiums, which alternative would be preferable? Why?

6. Explain how the liquidity premium hypothesis differs from the pure expectations theory. Which of the pure expecta-

---

[25]This discussion refers to arbitrage in general and not to a specific trading strategy used by some securities firms called "yield-curve arbitrage." The latter phrase refers to simultaneous trading in short-term interest rate futures and long-term bonds to profit from the fact that short-term interest rates (thus, the "short" end of the yield curve) fluctuate more than long-term rates. For more information, see Craig Torres. "'Yield-Curve Arbitrage' Rewards the Skillful." *The Wall Street Journal* (July 27, 1989), C1, C10. For the sake of brevity, basic applications are considered here for financial institutions. As noted in the introduction to the chapter, yield curves are commonly used to forecast stages of the business cycle and the future movements of rates as well. For instance, in the past the end of a business expansion has often been accompanied by a downward sloping yield curve. Although the downward slope is not always a reliable indicator, it would suggest that a financial institution might think about investing in long-term bonds, because under the expectations theory, investors are expecting rates to fall. Similarly, a rising yield curve is often present at the end of a recession (start of an expansion), which under the expectations theory suggests that investors are expecting rates to rise. If this is thought to be the case, a financial institution might want to shorten the maturity of its securities to avoid capital losses on fixed income securities. If an expansion does begin, it will often be accompanied by rising rates as the demand for funds by businesses grows.

tions assumptions is rejected under the liquidity premium hypothesis?

7. Assume that the yield curve you plotted in Question 3 includes liquidity premiums that gradually increase as maturity increases. Sketch an estimate of the prevailing pure expectations term structure.

8. According to the modified expectations theory, what role do borrowers play in determining the relationship between short-term and long-term interest rates?

9. What market imperfections are recognized in the segmented markets hypothesis? What are its assumptions about the maturity preferences of borrowers and lenders?

10. How does the preferred habitat theory characterize the maturity preferences of borrowers and lenders? Under what conditions will investors switch from one maturity to another? Does the preferred habitat theory support the concept of a continuous yield curve? Why?

11. Which theory of the term structure do you find most plausible? Which is the least plausible? By integrating ideas from all term structure theories, state briefly how you believe the term structure is determined.

12. Briefly summarize the difficulties in measuring interest rate expectations and liquidity premiums for tests of the pure expectations theory.

13. Explain how estimates of forward rates may be used by financial institution managers as they set long-term loan and deposit rates.

14. How are estimates of forward rates used to set risk premiums for loans?

Problems

1. Jeff and Lori Cooperman, your financial planning consultant has adopted the followed expectations for short-term interest rates:

   1-year rate prevailing January 2000: 6.7%
   1-year rate prevailing January 2001: 7.8%

   Based on these expectations and assuming no liquidity premiums, what rate do your consultants expect you to earn on a 2-year security purchased in January 2000?

2. Your mother, who watches her investments closely, has sent a newsletter reporting yields currently available on various Treasury securities. As of January 1, 2000, a T-bond with exactly 3 years to maturity carries a yield of 7.65 percent, while a 4-year bond (maturing January 1, 2004) offers a yield of 7.30 percent. Assuming no liquidity premiums, what is the 1-year forward rate expected to prevail as of January 1, 2003 (the beginning of Year 4)?

3. If you estimate that a liquidity premium of 0.0025 (0.25 percent) on a 4-year investment is included in the yields quoted in Problem 2, what is your revised estimate of the 1-year forward rate expected to prevail at the beginning of Year 4?

4.

TREASURY BILL PURCHASED	TREASURY BILL MATURES	EXPECTED ANNUAL RATE %
January 2000	January 2001	9.35% (observed)
January 2001	January 2002	8.95
January 2002	January 2003	8.15
January 2003	January 2004	7.50

   a. Using the preceding information and the pure expectations hypothesis, calculate the yield to maturity as of January 2000 for each of the following:
      1) a 2-year security
      2) a 3-year security
      3) a 4-year security
   b. Using your calculations in Part a, sketch the term structure of interest rates prevailing in January 2000.
   c. Calculate the expected average annual yield for each of the following investment strategies:
      1) investment in a 2-year security followed by investment in a 2-year security
      2) investment in a series of four 1-year T-bills
   d. Explain how your answers to Part c support the pure expectations theory.

5.

TREASURY BILL PURCHASED	TREASURY BILL MATURES	EXPECTED ANNUAL RATE %	LIQUIDITY PREMIUM AS OF JUNE 1996 %
June 2002	June 2003	4.25% (observed)	0.00%
June 2003	June 2004	5.95	0.15 (on 2-year security)
June 2004	June 2005	6.75	0.25 (on 3-year security)
June 2005	June 2006	7.95	0.30 (on 4-year security)

a. Based on the preceding information and using the pure expectations and liquidity premium hypotheses, calculate the yield to maturity as of June 2002 for each of the following
  1) a 2-year Treasury security
  2) a 3-year security
  3) a 4-year security
b. Using your calculations in Part a, sketch the observed term structure of interest rates as of June 2002.
c. Calculate the expected average annual yield for each of the following investment strategies:
  1) investment in a 4-year Treasury security
  2) purchase of a 1-year T-bill followed by investment in a 3-year Treasury security
  3) investment in a series of four 1-year T-bills

6.

TREASURY BILL PURCHASED	TREASURY BILL MATURES	EXPECTED ANNUAL RATE %
June 2000	June 2001	6.75% (observed)
June 2001	June 2002	7.30
June 2002	June 2003	8.05
June 2003	June 2004	8.95

a. Calculate the expected average annual yield for each of the following investment strategies:
  1) investment in a series of three 1-year securities, with the investments made in June of each year from 2000 through 2002 (beginning of the month)
  2) investment in a 2-year security in June 2000 followed by investment in a 1-year T-bill in June 2001
b. Calculate the expected average annual yield for each of the following investment strategies:
  1) investment in a 1-year security in June 2000 followed by investment in a 3-year security in June 2001
  2) investment in a series of four 1-year T-bills, with the investment made in June of each year from 2000 through 2003
c. Recalculate your answers for Parts a and b under the liquidity premium hypothesis, given the following liquidity premiums as of June 2000:

MATURITY OF SECURITY	LIQUIDITY PREMIUM
1 Year	0.00%
2 Years	0.12
3 Years	0.18
4 Years	0.22

7. Assume it is now May 2001 and that the following yields prevail:

TREASURY SECURITY MATURITY DATE	SPOT YIELD AS OF MAY 1995 %
May 2002	11.05%
May 2003	10.50
May 2004	10.05
May 2005	9.45
May 2006	8.95

    a.   Calculate the 1-year forward rate as of May 2004 (the beginning of Period 4).
    b.   Calculate the 1-year forward rate as of May 2003 (the beginning of Period 3).

8.   For these problems, use the information on maturity dates and spot yields from Problem 7 and the liquidity premiums in the following table:
    a.   Calculate the 1-year forward rate with liquidity premium removed as of May 2004 (the beginning of Period 4).
    b.   Calculate the 1-year forward rate with liquidity premium removed as of May 2005 (the beginning of Period 3).

MATURITY OF SECURITY	LIQUIDITY PREMIUM AS OF MAY 1995 %
1 Year	0.00%
2	0.15
3	0.21
4	0.26
5	0.29

9.   Charles Register, the president of the Alligator Bank of Trust is in the process of setting rates on 1-year certificates of deposit and on 4-year, fixed-rate automobile loans, in which newly acquired funds will be invested. The yield curve is presently upward sloping, suggesting that these fixed-rate loans should be priced carefully. Based on the following information and the pure expectations hypothesis, what rate should the bank charge on a 4-year loan? (Hint: Calculate the expected rates for future 1-year CDs first.) Assume liquidity premiums equal 0.

TREASURY SECURITIES:

Maturity	Observed Annual Yield %
1 Year	4.50
2	5.25
3	5.75
4	6.50

Administrative Markup:
$1\frac{1}{2}\%$ per year

Risk Premium Required
for Holding Auto Loans:

Year 1	2.0%
Year 2	2.5
Year 3	3.0
Year 4	3.5

10. Zunan Cebenoyan of the Big Apple National Bank is evaluating its charges on 5-year balloon mortgages. The mortgage rate is fixed for 5 years, but the bank acquires funds primarily by issuing 1-year CDs. Using the following information, estimate rates for future CDs and the appropriate 5-year mortgage rate.

<table>
<tr><td colspan="2" align="center">**TREASURY SECURITIES:**</td></tr>
<tr><td>Maturity</td><td align="center">Observed Yield</td></tr>
<tr><td>1 Year</td><td align="center">9.00%</td></tr>
<tr><td>2 Years</td><td align="center">9.75</td></tr>
<tr><td>3 Years</td><td align="center">10.15</td></tr>
<tr><td>4 Years</td><td align="center">10.95</td></tr>
<tr><td>5 Years</td><td align="center">11.40</td></tr>
</table>

Administrative Cost

Percentage (Markup) on CDs:
1% per year

ESTIMATED RISK PREMIUMS REQUIRED FOR HOLDING MORTGAGES:	
Year 1	1.0%
Year 2	1.8
Year 3	2.5
Year 4	3.2
Year 5	3.8

In addition to this information, bank management estimates that the following liquidity premiums are included in observed long-term yields:

MATURITY	PREMIUM
1 Year	0.00%
2	0.10
3	0.16
4	0.21
5	0.25

Selected References

Abken, Peter. "Innovations in Modeling the Term Structure of Interest Rates." *Economic Review* (Federal Reserve Bank of Atlanta) 65 (July/August 1990), 2–27.

Belongia, Michael T., and Kees G. Koedik. "Testing the Expectations Model of the Term Structure: Some Conjectures on the Effects of Institutional Changes." *Review* (Federal Reserve Bank of St. Louis) 70 (September/October 1988), 37–45.

Blalock, Joseph. "Whither the Yield Curve?" *Savings and Community Banker* 2 (April 1993), 36–38.

Cogley, Timothy. "Interpreting the Term Structure of Interest Rates." *Weekly Letter* (Federal Reserve Bank of San Francisco) (April 16, 1993).

Cook, Timothy and Thomas Hahn. "Interest Rate Expectations and the Slope of the Money Market Yield Curve." *Economic Review* (Federal Reserve Bank of Richmond) 76 (September/October 1990), 3–26.

Cox, John C., Jonathan E. Ingersoll, Jr., and Stephen A. Ross. "A Re-Examination of Traditional Hypotheses about the Term Structure of Interest Rates." *Journal of Finance* 36 (September 1981), 769–799.

Cox, John C., Jonathan E. Ingersoll, Jr., and Stephen A. Ross. "A Theory of the Term Structure of Interest Rates." *Econometrica* 53 (March 1985), 385–408.

Culbertson, John M. "The Term Structure of Interest Rates." *Quarterly Journal of Economics* 71 (November 1957), 485–517.

Dobson, Steven W., Richard C. Sutch, and David E. Vanderford. "An Evaluation of Alternative Empirical Models of the Term Structure of Interest Rates." *Journal of Finance* 31 (September 1976), 1035–1065.

Dua, Pami. "Survey Evidence on the Term Structure of Interest Rates." *Journal of Economics and Business* 43 (1991), 133–142.

Echols, Michael E., and J. Walter Elliott. "Rational Expectations in a Disequilibrium Model of the Term Structure." *American Economic Review* 66 (March 1976), 28–44.

Friedman, Benjamin M. "Interest Rate Expectations versus Forward Rates: Evidence from an Expectations Survey." *Journal of Finance* 34 (September 1979), 965–973.

Froot, Kenneth A. "New Hope for the Expectations Hypothesis of the Term Structure of Interest Rates." *Journal of Finance* 44 (June 1989), 283–305.

Furlong, Frederick T. "The Yield Curve and Recessions." *Weekly Letter* (Federal Reserve Bank of San Francisco) (March 10, 1989).

Hafer, R.W., and Scott E. Hein. "Comparing Futures and Survey Forecasts of Near-Term Treasury Bill Rates." *Review* (Federal Reserve Bank of St. Louis) 71 (May/June 1989), 33–42.

Heuson, Andrea J. "The Term Premia Relationship Implicit in the Term Structure of Treasury Bills." *Journal of Financial Research* 11 (Spring 1988), 13–20.

Hicks, J. R. *Value and Capital.* London: Oxford University Press (1946).

Ho, Thomas, and Sang-Bin Lee. "Term Structure Movements and Pricing Interest Rate Contingent Claims." *Journal of Finance* 41 (December 1986), 1011–1029.

Kane, Edward J., and Burton G. Malkiel. "The Term Structure of Interest Rates: An Analysis of a Survey of Interest Rate Expectations." *Review of Economics and Statistics* 49 (August 1967), 343–355.

Kessel, Reuben A. *The Cyclical Behavior of the Term Structure.* New York: National Bureau of Economic Research (1965).

Kool, Clemens J.M., and John A. Tatom. "International Linkages in the Term Structure of Interest Rates." *Review* (Federal Reserve Bank of St. Louis) 70 (July/August 1988), 30–42.

Lee, Wayne, Terry S. Maness, and Donald Tuttle. "Non-Speculative Behavior and the Term Structure." *Journal of Financial and Quantitative Analysis* 15 (March 1980), 53–83.

Lutz, Frederick. "The Structure of Interest Rates." *Quarterly Journal of Economics* 30 (November 1940), 36–63.

Malkiel, Burton. *The Term Structure of Interest Rates: Theory, Empirical Evidence, and Applications.* Princeton, NJ: Princeton University Press (1966).

McCulloch, Huston J. "An Estimation of the Liquidity Premium Hypothesis." *Journal of Political Economy* 83 (January/February 1975), 95–119.

Meiselman, David. *The Term Structure of Interest Rates.* Englewood Cliffs, NJ: Prentice-Hall (1962).

Modigliani, Franco, and Richard Sutch. "Innovation in Interest Rate Policy." *American Economic Review* 66 (May 1966), 178–197.

Nelson, Charles R. *The Term Structure of Interest Rates.* New York: Basic Books (1972).

Roley, V. Vance. "The Determinants of the Treasury Yield Curve." *Journal of Finance* 36 (December 1981), 1103–1126.

Roll, Richard. *The Behavior of Interest Rates.* New York: Basic Books (1970).

Saunders, Anthony. *Financial Institutions Management: A Modern Perspective*, 2d ed. Burr Ridge, IL: Irwin (1997).

Schiller, Robert J., John Y. Campbell, and Kermit L. Schoenholtz. "Forward Rates and Future Policy: Interpreting the Term Structure of Interest Rates." In *Brookings Papers on Economic Activity, I: 1982.* Washington, DC: Brookings Institution (1983), 173–223.

Smith, Warren L. *Debt Management in the United States.* Study Paper 19, Joint Economic Committee of the 86th Congress (January 1960).

Stevens, E. J. "Is There a Message in the Yield Curve?" *Economic Commentary* (Federal Reserve Bank of Cleveland) (March 15, 1989).

Throop, Adrian. "Interest Rate Forecasts and Market Efficiency." *Economic Review* (Federal Reserve Bank of San Francisco) (Spring 1981), 29–43.

Van Horne, James. "Interest Rate Risk and the Term Structure of Interest Rates." *Journal of Political Economy* 73 (August 1965), 344–351.

Wallich, Henry C., and Peter M. Keir. "The Role of Operating Guides in U.S. Monetary Policy: A Historical Review." *Federal Reserve Bulletin* 65 (September 1979), 679–691.

Walz, Daniel T., and Roger W. Spencer. "The Informational Content of Forward Rates: Further Evidence." *Journal of Financial Research* 12 (Spring 1989), 69–81.

Wood, John H. "Do Yield Curves Normally Slope Up? The Term Structure of Interest Rates, 1862–1982." *Economic Perspectives* (Federal Reserve Bank of Chicago) 7 (July/August 1983), 17–23.

Chapter 15 Internet Exercise

The Term Structure of Interest Rates

Risk Library International Finance and Commodities Institute (IFCI)

IFCI site is designed to help the user navigate his or her way through the sea of regulatory documents on international finance. The online documents have been selected by IFCI's Advisory Committee because they are regarded as essential to understanding the current status of various aspects of financialregulation and risk management. They provide the answers to the "why and how of where we are" and point to future trends ininternational finance.

1. Go to: http://risk.ifci.ch/RiskDocuments.HTM

2. From the Risk Library page, click on "Core Documents."

The table provides a linked list of articles on international finance, and then in the columns, the key finance concepts discussed in the article are marked with an "X." For example, the article "Sound Practices for Loan Accounting, Credit Risk Disclosure, and Related Matters," published by the Basle Committee of the Bank for International Settlements (BIS), the concepts of credit risk, risk control, and accounting and disclosure. This site provides a wealth of information about key concepts in international finance and articles that can help you understand the real-world application of those concepts.

Estimating the Term Structure of Interest Rates

1. Go to http://www.bundesbank.de/en/monatsericht/bericht10/97/termstu.htm

The German Central Bank (Bundesbank) provides information on a new way to estimate the term structure of interest rates. The term structure of interest rates shows the relation between the interest rates and maturities of zero-coupon bonds without risk of default. In the monetary policy context, it is primarily of interest as an indicator of the market's expectations regarding interest rates and inflation rates. Its slope can provide information about the expected changes in interest rates or inflation rates. Hitherto, this constellation was captured by way of approximation in the publications of the Deutsche Bundesbank by an (estimated) yield curve. From

(continued)

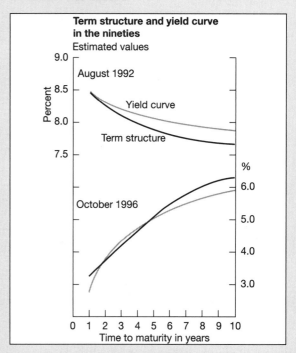

Term structure and yield curve in the nineties
Estimated values

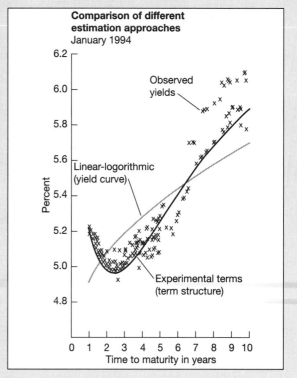

Comparison of different estimation approaches
January 1994

Chapter 15 Internet Exercise

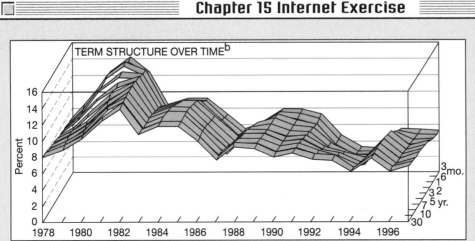

TERM STRUCTURE OVER TIME[b]

twists and shifts up and down over time. A 3-D perspective indicates that the big rise in 1994 was not a parallel shift. It also shows how the high but inverted curve of 1981 first steepened in 1982 and then dropped downward. On the other hand, it allows us to see how inversions occurred as a result of short rates rising, not long rates falling.

now on that approach is to be replaced by a direct estimation of the term structure of interest rates. This approach is being adopted increasingly in the international context. In principle, it allows a more precise presentation and analysis of expectations and ensures enhanced cross-country comparability of the estimation results. Moreover, (implied) forward rates can be calculated directly from the term structure of (spot) rates. Although such forward rates contain the same information as the term structure of interest rates, in principle they make it easier to separate expectations for the short, medium, and long term.

Term Structure of Interest Rates over Time

1. Go to http://www.clev.frb.org/research/aug96et/charts/intrat1c.HTM

   Tracking the yield curve is fundamentally a three-dimensional problem, because the curve both

FinanceWise http://www.financewise.com/
FinanceWise does not aim to index the Internet in its entirety, only sites that possess content of interest to the financial world.

"Movements in the term structure of interest rates."—Robert R. Bliss
FEDERAL RESERVE BANK OF ATLANTA. Economic Review. Q IV, 1997 , pp. 16–33.
http://www.frbatlanta.org/publica/eco-rev/rev_abs/4th 97.html

"Models of the term structure of interest rates."—John Y. Campbell and Andrew W. Lo and A. Craig MacKinlay
FEDERAL RESERVE BANK OF PHILADELPHIA. Working Papers. No. 94–10. May, 1994
http://206.79.163.3/library/index.HTM

16

INTEREST RATE RISK MEASUREMENT AND IMMUNIZATION USING DURATION

As the preceding quotations suggest, managing interest rate risk is a crucial part of managing a financial institution, and interest rates are volatile and difficult to predict. Many managers faced a critical dilemma in the early 1990s as market rates fell to levels not seen in three decades or more, while the upward-sloping term structure was much steeper than usual; that is, the spread between what could be earned on long- versus short-term assets was relatively large. Decision makers at Collective Savings Bank in Egg Harbor, New Jersey, decided to structure the institution's assets on the assumption that the rate decline was temporary: They chose a preponderance of short-term investments so as not to be "locked in" if rates rose suddenly. But managers of other depositories, such as Boatmen's Bancshares in St. Louis, took an entirely opposite tack and lengthened asset maturities to take advantage of the high spread between long- and short-term rates.

Considering how many of each bank's asset returns and liability costs were affected by these decisions about an unknowable future, the risks of betting wrong were enormous for both groups of managers. In 1998, investors experienced a similar flat yield curve for securities with three-month to five-year maturities, with yields on five-year securities below yields on shorter-

621

term securities, but a steeper rising slope for securities with maturities longer than five years. Interest rate movements were volatile and difficult to predict, and a number of securities firms and banks involved in securities activities suffered large losses in 1998 as a result of incorrect predictions for movements in interest rates.[1]

This chapter examines concepts of interest rate risk for financial institutions, including reinvestment risk and market price risk. It also discusses duration, an overall measure of interest rate risk and applications for financial institution management. The first section begins by discussing interest rate yields.

◆　◆　◆

INTEREST RATE RISK DEFINED

Risk is a fact of life. Risk for securities is the potential variation in the returns from an investment. This chapter explains and illustrates one of the most significant risks faced by financial institutions today: potential variation in returns caused by unexpected changes in interest rates, or **interest rate risk**.

Note the use of the word *unexpected*. Investors can and do incorporate expected changes in interest rates into their investment decisions. The risk they face, then, arises not from changes they correctly anticipate at the time investment decisions are made, but from changes they do not anticipate. Because even the most astute forecasters err, no investors are protected against potential variation in returns, even if forecasting is a part of their decision making.

THE PRICE/YIELD CONNECTION

Although unexpected changes in interest rates affect virtually all financial institutions, they do not affect them equally. Differences in interest rate risk occur because of the type of instrument, maturity, size and timing of cash inflows, and planned holding period relative to the asset's maturity. To understand interest rate risk, however, it is first necessary to understand the fundamental principles of financial asset prices. Financial markets are characterized by many participants and much publicly available information. Generally, an individual investor, as only one of many buyers and sellers, is unable to influence the price of a financial asset. A manager considering the purchase of a Treasury bill (T-bill) knows that an institution must pay the going market price. The supply and demand for an asset are also important (see the loanable funds theory in Chapter 14). Risk aversion is also critical. All else equal, the price of a riskier asset will be lower than that of a less risky one because most financial market participants are risk averse. Risk aversion causes investors to demand higher expected rates of return from riskier investments.

---

[1]Fred R. Bleakley. "Banks, Thrifts Scored as Interest Rates Fell, But Difficulties Loom." *The Wall Street Journal* (February 12, 1992), A1, A6; Steven Vames. "Bond Prices Fall Despite Favorable CPI Report." *The Wall Street Journal* (December 16, 1998), C20; and Jonathan Fuerbringer. "A Flatter Yield Curve Indicates Investors May Be Expecting a Significant Slowing of the Economy." *The New York Times* (December 10, 1998), C9.

PUTTING THEM TOGETHER

The effects of these influences on security prices are incorporated in the general equation for the effective annual yield on a financial asset:

$$P_o = \sum_{t=1}^{n} \frac{C_t}{(1 + y^\circ)^t} \qquad [16.1]$$

where y° is the discount rate that makes the sum of the present value of the assets' cash flows (C_t) equal to its price (P_o). This expression reveals the relationship between price and yield. It is evident that, all else equal, price changes must be accompanied by yield changes, and vice versa, with prices and yields changing simultaneously in the opposite directions. If the price of an asset falls (rises), its yield rises (falls). Similarly, if y° rises, which will usually occur when investors become more risk averse and require a higher market rate, the price of the security falls. If y° falls, for example, as the result of a rise in the supply of loanable funds, the price of the security rises.

THE PRICE/YIELD RELATIONSHIP ILLUSTRATED

Calculating Ex Ante Effective Annual Yield (Y^*) for Bonds

For a bond, the yield to maturity or ex ante effective annual yield (y°) that an investor expects to receive over the life of the bond is the discount rate that makes the present value of the bond's future cash flows equal to its current price. For a coupon bond, solving for y° entails using the bond price formula as follows:

$$P_o = \text{Coupon Payment (PVIFA } y^\circ, n) + \text{Maturity Value (PVIF } y^\circ, n) \qquad [16.2]$$

where P_o is the price (market value of the bond), PVIFA is the present value of the annuity factor $\{[1 - 1/(1 + y^\circ)^n]/y^\circ\}$ (used to find the present value of the coupon payments), and PVIF is the present value factor, $\{1/(1 + y^\circ)^n\}$ (used to find the present value of the maturity value). This yield assumes that the bond will be held to maturity and that each coupon payment will be invested at the y° rate over the life of the bond.[2]

As an example, see the price information for bonds traded on Wednesday, December 16, 1998, presented in Figure 16.1. Under NYSE bonds, find the highlighted

---

[2]To find the approximate rate by using the trial and error method, an approximation formula can be initially used, where

$$\text{YTM} = \frac{\text{Coupon Payment} + [(\text{Maturity Value} - \text{Price})/n]}{(\text{Maturity Value} + \text{Price})/2}$$

This represents the approximate yearly benefit received from a bond divided by its average price over its life. This YTM (yield to maturity) should be plugged into the bond formula to see if it is correct, which is more likely if the bond is selling close to par value. Otherwise, it is a good starting point. Interpolation can also be used, in which the bond's price is calculated at a high and too low rate (i.e., by using a discount rate in which the bond's price is too low and by using a lower discount rate in which the bond's price is too high). Through interpolation, the yield can be found between these two rates as the following:

$$\text{the low rate} + \frac{(\text{High Price} - \text{Price}) \times 1\%}{(\text{High Price} - \text{Low Price})}$$

Figure 16.1 ✦ SAMPLE BOND PRICES, DECEMBER 16, 1998

STOCK EXCHANGE BOND TRADING

WEDNESDAY, DECEMBER 16, 1998

NYSE BONDS

Company	Cur. Yld	Vol	Price	Chg
AES05	...	27	96 7/8	−5 1/8
AMR 9s16	7.4	5	121 3/4	...
AON 6 7/8 99	6.9	25	100 1/2	...
ATT 5 1/8 01	5.1	45	99 3/4	...
ATT 7 1/8 02	6.8	63	105 1/8	...
ATT 6 3/4 04	6.3	20	107 3/8	+ 1/4
ATT 7s05	6.5	10	108 1/2	− 1/4
ATT 8.2s05	7.9	66	104	− 1/8
ATT 8 1/8 22	7.5	43	109	− 1/2
ATT 8 1/8 24	7.5	22	109	...
Aames 10 1/2 02	18.8	115	56	−2
AlldC zr09	...	30	50 7/8	...
Allwst 7 1/4 14f	cv	51	10	...
Alza 5s06	cv	46	138	−3
ARetire 5 3/4 02	cv	105	82	...
Amresco 8 3/4 99	9.0	25	97	...
Amresco 10s03	13.7	50	72 7/8	+ 3/8
Amresco 10s04	13.7	108	73	+1
AnnTaylr 8 3/4 00	8.6	15	101 3/8	+ 3/8
Argosy 12s01	cv	45	101 1/2	+ 1/2
Argosy 13 1/4 04	11.9	28	111	+ 7/8
BkrHgh zr08	...	2	65	−1
BankAm 8 1/2 99	8.5	15	100 5/8	...
BellPa 7 1/8 12	7.0	15	101 1/4	− 1/4
BellsoT 6 3/8 04	6.0	35	105 1/2	+ 1/4
BellsoT 7 7/8 32	7.2	75	109 1/2	...
BellsoT 7 1/2 33	6.8	15	109 5/8	...
BellsoT 6 3/4 33	6.5	102	103 1/2	− 1/8
BethSt 8.45s05	8.5	94	100	− 1/4
Bevrly 9s06	8.7	40	103 1/8	+ 1/4
Bluegrn 8 1/4 12	cv	10	93	+1
Bordn 8 3/8 16	8.2	5	102	− 3/8
BosCelts 6s38	10.0	104	60	+ 1/2
BrnGp 9 1/2 06	9.0	69	105 5/8	+ 1/8
BurNo 3.20s45	6.1	3	52 3/4	− 1/8
Capstar 4 3/4 04	cv	4	70	...
Caterplnc 6s07	6.0	16	99 1/2	+ 1/8
Caterplnc 9 3/4 19	9.1	11	107 1/4	...
ChaseM 8s04	7.9	20	101 3/4	+1
ChaseM 6 3/4 08	6.4	5	106	−1 1/8
CPWV 7 1/4 13	7.1	2	102 1/4	+ 5/8
ChespkE 9 5/8 05	11.7	4	82	−3
ChespkE 9 1/8 06	12.0	115	76 1/4	−3 5/8
ChckFul 7s12	cv	46	98 3/4	+ 1/4
ChryF 6 5/8 00	6.6	15	101	− 3/8
Clardge 11 3/4 02f	...	100	72	+ 1/2
ClrkOil 9 1/2 04	9.3	57	101 3/4	+ 3/8
CoeurDA 7 1/4 05	12.1	40	59 7/8	...
Coeur 6 3/8 04	cv	166	58 1/2	+ 3/4
CmwE 7 5/8 03F	7.5	8	101 1/4	−1 1/2
CompUSA 9 1/2 00	9.3	226	101 7/8	+ 1/8
CompMgt 8s03	cv	5	21	+1
ConPort 10 1/2 04	16.4	20	64	−3
ConPort 10s06	14.3	80	70	...
Convrse 7s04	cv	70	34	+1 1/4
DR Hrtn 10s06	9.4	6	106	− 1/8
DVI 9 7/8 04	10.0	15	98 7/8	− 1/8
DataGen 6s04	cv	1	98	−1
DelcoR 8 5/8 07	8.5	5	102	...
DukeEn 8s99	7.9	20	101 3/4	...
DukeEn 5 7/8 01	5.8	10	100 3/4	− 7/8
DukeEn 6 5/8 03	6.3	13	105 1/2	+ 3/4
DukeEn 6 1/4 04	6.2	10	101 1/8	− 3/8
DukeEn 6 3/8 08	6.3	20	100 5/8	− 5/8
DukeEn 6 7/8 23	6.8	7	101 1/2	...
FedNM zr19s	...	1	30	+1
FordCr 6 3/8 08	6.1	15	104 1/8	...
GBCB 8 3/8 07	8.4	14	100	+ 1/4
GEICap 7 7/8 06	7.0	15	111 5/8	+ 1/4
GMA 8.40s99	8.3	2	101 3/4	− 5/8
GMA 5.60s99	5.6	12	99 25/32	...
GMA 9 3/8 00	9.0	5	103 3/4	− 7/8
GMA 7s00	6.9	25	101 3/4	− 1/8
GMA 5 1/2 01	5.5	35	99 3/4	+ 1/8
GMA 7s02	6.7	6	104	+ 1/8
GMA 6 5/8 02	6.4	5	103 1/4	− 1/2
GMA 8 1/2 03	7.7	5	110	+ 7/8
GMA 5 7/8 03	5.9	3	100 1/4	...
GMA dc6s11	6.0	32	99 1/2	+1 1/2
GMA zr12	...	44	398 1/2	+2 7/8
GMA zr15	...	3	333	+ 1/4
GenesisH 9 3/4 05	9.9	20	98 1/8	−1 7/8
Gerrity 11 3/4 04	11.6	5	101	...
GrnTrFn 10 1/4 02	9.4	5	109	+1 5/8
HRPT 7 1/2 03	cv	30	97	...
HlthcrR 6.55s02	cv	3	92	...
HewlPkd zr17	...	2	54 5/8	+ 3/8
Hexcel 7s03	cv	10	85	+1 1/4
Hills 12 1/2 03	24.0	608	52	+2
Hilton 5s06	cv	194	90 1/2	− 1/2
Hollngr 8 5/8 05	8.1	5	106	...
Hollngr 9 1/4 06	8.9	17	103 3/4	−1 1/4
IRT Pr 7.3s03	cv	23	94 3/4	− 5/8
IllBell 7 5/8 cld	...	17	100 11/16	− 1/16
IBM 6 3/8 00	6.3	324	101 3/4	...
IBM 7 1/4 02	6.8	50	107 3/8	+ 1/4
IBM 7 1/2 13	6.5	25	116	...
IBM 8 3/8 19	6.8	1	123 3/8	...
IBM 7s25	6.3	38	111	+1 3/8
IBM 6 1/2 28	6.3	1	103 1/8	+ 1/2
IPap dc5 1/8 12	5.9	15	86 3/4	+ 3/4
IntShip 9s03	8.8	30	102 1/2	+ 3/4
JumboSp 4 1/2 00	cv	10	11	...
KCS En 8 7/8 08	14.8	100	60	...
KaufB 9 3/8 03	9.2	511	102 1/4	+ 1/8
KaufB 7 3/4 04	7.6	51	102 1/4	...
KaufB 9 5/8 06	9.0	125	106 3/4	+ 1/4
KentE 4 1/2 04	cv	150	79 1/8	− 1/8
Kolmrg 8 3/4 09	cv	12	102	+1
LeasSol 6 7/8 03	cv	28	30	...
Leucadia 8 1/4 05	7.9	15	104 1/4	...
Leucadia 7 3/4 13	7.7	79	100 3/4	−1 1/8
Loews 3 1/8 07	cv	99	81	+1 1/2
MBNA 8.28s26	8.1	15	102	+ 1/4
MDC Hld 8 3/8 08	8.5	46	98 1/2	+ 3/4
MacNS 7 7/8 04	cv	10	91 1/2	+ 1/2
MarO 7s02	6.9	25	102 1/8	+ 5/8
Mascotch 03	cv	76	80	− 1/4
Medtrst 7 1/2 01	cv	116	92 1/2	+ 1/2
MichB 7scld	...	10	101 13/32	− 1/32
MKT 5 1/2 33f	...	40	88	−1 1/8
MPac 5s45f	...	20	65	− 3/8
Mobil 8 3/8 01	7.9	50	106 5/8	+ 1/4
Motrla zr13	...	43	73 1/2	−1 1/8
Nabis 8.3s99	8.3	2	100 11/32	− 1/32
Nabis 8s00	7.8	8	102	...
NatData 5s03	cv	140	97	+4
NStl 8 3/8 06	8.3	50	100 7/8	+1 5/8
NETelTel 6.15s99	6.1	23	100 1/4	...
NETelTel 4 5/8 05	4.7	25	98	...
NETelTel 6 1/8 06	6.1	15	100 3/8	...
NJBTl 7 3/8 12	7.2	5	102	− 7/8
NYTel 6 1/2 05	6.2	25	105	...
NYTel 6 1/8 10	5.8	50	105	+2 1/2
Noram 6s12	cv	29	96 1/2	+ 1/4
Novacr 5 1/2 2000	cv	347	70 1/2	− 1/4
OcciP 10 1/8 01	9.3	44	109 1/4	...
OcciP 10 1/8 09	8.3	5	122 1/2	+ 3/8
OffDep zr07	...	19	87 1/8	+1 3/4
OffDep zr08	...	6	74 5/8	−2 3/8
OhBIT 7 7/8 13	7.7	3	101 25/32	...
OreStl 11s03	10.6	231	103 1/2	− 1/8
Oryx 7 1/2 14	cv	25	99 3/8	...
PacBell 6 1/4 05	6.0	53	104 3/4	...
PacBell 7 1/2 33	7.0	5	106 3/8	...
PacBell 6 5/8 34	6.4	1	103 1/2	...
ParkElc 5 1/2 06	cv	30	85	− 1/2
ParkerD 5 1/2 04	cv	494	64 1/2	+1 1/4
Pennzl 4.9s08	cv	4	95	−4
Pennzl 4.95s08	cv	45	98	+ 1/4
PepBoys 4s99	cv	2	99 1/4	+1
PepBoys zr11	...	25	52 1/2	− 1/2
PhilEl 7 3/8 01	7.3	1	101 3/4	− 1/4
PhilEl 5 5/8 01	5.7	8	99 1/2	−1 1/4
PhilEl 7 1/4 24	7.0	15	103	+ 1/4
PhilPt 7.92s23	7.5	54	105 1/8	− 3/8
PhilPt 7.2s23	7.0	20	102 1/2	−1 1/8
PhnxInv 6s15	cv	22	112	+6 1/2
PotEl 5s02	cv	2	97 1/2	+1 1/2
PotEl 7s18	cv	14	98 1/2	−2 1/2
Pride 6 1/4 06	cv	5	83	...
PSEG 7 5/8 00	7.5	5	101 7/8	− 1/8
PSEG 6s00	5.9	9	101 1/8	+ 1/2
PSvEG 6 1/8 02	6.0	25	102 3/4	+ 1/2
Quanx 6.88s07	cv	10	93 1/8	−1 7/8
RJR Nb 8 5/8 02	8.3	3	104 5/8	− 3/8
RJR Nb 7 5/8 03	7.6	915	100 1/4	− 1/2
RJR Nb 8 3/4 05	8.4	92	103 3/4	− 1/4
RJR Nb 8 3/4 07	8.5	25	102 7/8	− 3/8
RJR Nb 9 1/4 13	8.8	41	105 3/8	− 3/8
RJR Nb 8.3s99	8.3	16	100 5/16	− 1/16
RJR Nb 8 3/4 04	8.5	40	103 1/2	+ 1/2
Rallys 9 7/8 00	12.8	25	77 1/2	− 1/8
RalsP 8 1/8 23	7.5	10	109	+1 1/2
Revl 9 1/2 99	9.4	65	101	+ 1/4
Ryder 8 3/4 17	8.6	4	102 1/8	+1 1/8
Safwy 10s01	9.1	48	109 1/2	...
Safwy 9.3s07	8.0	7	115 3/4	−2 7/8
Sequa 9 3/8 03	9.1	40	102 1/2	...
SvcMer 8 3/8 01f	...	83	44	−29
SvcMer 9s04f	...	5925	16 1/2	−15 1/2
Shoney zr04	...	20	25	+3
Simula 8s04	cv	20	87	−1
Sizeler 8s03	cv	9	94 7/8	+2 7/8
SoCG 6 7/8 25	6.8	10	100 3/4	+1
SwBell 6 3/8 01	6.2	6	102 5/8	− 1/8
SwBell 7 1/4 25	6.9	60	105 5/8	− 3/8
StdCmcl 07	cv	46	73 1/2	−1 3/4
StdPac 10 1/2 00	10.1	4	104	+ 1/4
StoneC 11 1/2 99	11.3	99	101 3/8	+ 3/8
StoneC 9 7/8 01	9.8	226	101 3/8	...
StoneC 11 1/4 02A	11.2	75	100 1/4	− 5/8
StoneC 11 1/2 04	10.9	5	105 3/4	...
StoneCn 6 3/4 07	cv	58	80 5/8	− 1/2
SunCo 9 3/8 16	8.4	5	112	+1
SwiftE 6 1/4 06	cv	10	76	...
TVA 6 1/8 03	6.0	75	101 1/4	...
TVA 8.05s24	8.0	133	101 1/4	+ 1/8
TVA 8 5/8 29	8.0	280	107 5/8	− 1/2
TVA 8 1/4 34	8.1	65	101 5/8	− 1/8
TVA 7 1/4 43	6.8	14	106	+ 1/8
TVA 6 7/8 43	6.6	106	104	− 5/8
Tenet 05	cv	25	87 1/8	− 1/8
Tenet 8s05	7.7	20	104 1/4	+ 1/4
Tenet 8 5/8 07	8.3	26	104 1/2	+ 7/8
TmeWar 9 1/8 13	7.3	26	124 7/8	− 1/8
TmeWar 9.15s23	7.1	35	128 1/4	− 3/4
TollCp 9 1/2 03	9.2	54	103 1/4	− 1/2
TollCp 8 3/4 06	8.4	121	104 1/8	− 3/4
US Timb 9 5/8 07	9.5	10	101 1/4	+ 1/4
US Filt 4 1/2 01	cv	142	93 1/2	− 1/8
WsteM 4s02	cv	85	117	+4
Webb 9 3/4 03	9.5	20	102 1/2	+ 1/4
Webb 9 3/4 08	9.5	20	102 3/8	+ 7/8
WebbDel 9 3/8 09	9.6	319	98	− 1/8
Weirton 11 3/8 04	12.6	176	90	...
Weirton 10 3/4 05	12.6	60	85	+1
WhlPit 9 3/8 03	8.6	17	108 5/8	...
WldColor 9 1/8 03	8.6	13	106	+2 1/8
WldColor 07	cv	83	98 1/2	−1 1/2

BOND TABLES EXPLAINED

Bonds are interest-bearing debt certificates. Their value is usually quoted as a percentage, with 100 equaling par, or face value. This table shows the issuing company, then the original coupon rate (interest rate) and the last two digits of the maturity year.

Current yield represents the annual percentage return to the purchaser at the current price. The **Price** column refers to the bond's closing price, and **Chg** is the difference between the day's closing price and the previous daily closing price. A majority of bonds, and all municipal or tax-exempt bonds, are not listed on exchanges; rather they are traded over the counter

Other footnotes:

- **cv** Bond is convertible into stock under specified conditions
- **cld** Called
- **dc** Selling at a discounted price
- **f** Dealt in flat — traded without accrued interest
- **k** Treasury bond, non resident aliens exempt from witholding tax
- **m** Matured bonds
- **na** No accrual of interest
- **p** Treasury note, non-resident aliens exempt from witholding tax
- **r** Registered
- **rp** Reduced principal
- **st** Stamped
- **t** Floating rate
- **x** Ex interest
- **vj** In bankruptcy or receivership or being reorganized under the Bankruptcy Act, or securities assumed by such companies
- **wd** When distributed
- **wi** When issued
- **zr** Zero coupon issue

AMEX BONDS

Company	Cur. Yld	Vol	Price	Chg
AltLiv 5 1/4 02	cv	20	104	...
ArchCm 10 7/8 08f	...	57	60	+5
AssisLiv 5 5/8 03	cv	25	73	−4
AssisLiv cv02	7.9	50	76	+ 1/2
ChckFul 8s06	cv	28	101	...
FruitL 7s11	7.5	24	93 1/2	−2 1/2
Greyhnd 8 1/2 07	cv	45	100 1/2	...
HaltMar 4 1/2 04	cv	128	60	−2
HlthCh 10 3/8 99	cv	16	53	−2
MagHunt 10s07	11.6	25	86	+1
MercAir 7 3/4 06	cv	10	112	−3 1/2
MLAmexOil 00	...	5	101 1/2	− 1/2
Paxson 11 5/8 02	11.4	15	102 1/2	...
SwBell 6 7/8 11	6.8	20	101 1/4	...
TrnsLux 7 1/2 06	cv	55	94	−1
TWA 11 1/2 04	13.4	10	86	− 1/2
Trump 11 3/4 03f	...	164	80 1/2	−1 5/8
US Cell zr15	...	8	41	− 1/2
Viacom 8s06	7.7	161	104 1/4	...

Source: New York Times, December 17, 1998, C17.

IBM bond maturing in 2013 (15-year maturity) that has a coupon rate of $7\frac{1}{2}$ percent and sells for a price of 116 percent of its par value of \$1,000, or \$1,160 (1.16 × \$1,000). The yield listed is the coupon yield of 6.5 percent (the coupon payment divided by the bond's price, not y*). The effective annual yield (y*) for the bond is the discount rate that makes the present value of the coupon payments and maturity value equal to \$1,160:

$$\$1{,}160 = \$75\,(\text{PVIFA}\ y^{*}, 15) + \$1{,}000\,(\text{PVIF}\ y^{*}, 15)$$

Because the bond is selling at a higher price than its par value, we know that $y° <$ 7.5 percent, the annual coupon rate. Using trial by error or a financial calculator, $y°$ can be found to be 5.87 percent. At a 5.87 percent discount rate, the bond's price is equal to the present value of its cash flows:

$$\$75 \,(9.79528) + \$1,000 \,(0.4250) = \$1,160$$

However, an investor will only receive an annual effective yield of 5.87 percent if this bond is held to maturity and coupons can be reinvested at a 5.87 percent rate each year.

Calculating Ex Post (Actual) Effective Annual Yield

The premise that an investor will receive an actual effective annual yield of 5.87 percent if he or she holds the bond until maturity and reinvests the coupon payments at 5.87 percent can be demonstrated by solving for the ex post effective annual yield (EAY). The ex post EAY is the future value (FV) of all cash flows from our investment divided by the price we paid, annualized by taking this to the 1/nth power and then subtracting 1 to subtract out our original investment that was included as part of our future value, as follows:

$$EAY = (FV/Po)^{1/n} - 1 \qquad [16.3]$$

The FV of the cash flows received at the end of the life of a bond includes the future value of all the coupons reinvested at some rate $y°$ each year plus the bond's maturity value:

$$FV = \text{Coupon PMT} \,(FVIFA \, y°, n) + \text{Maturity Value} \qquad [16.4]$$

$$FV = \$75 \,(FVIFA \, 5.87\%, 15) + \$1,000$$

$$= \$75 \,(23.047) + \$1,000 = \$2,728.50$$

where FVIFA is the future value of an annuity factor $\{[\,(1 + y°)^n - 1 \,]/y°\}$. Here we are assuming that $y°$ stays the same over the life of the bond, and the coupons can be reinvested each year at that market rate of 5.87 percent.

Hence, the investor will receive $2,728.50 at the end of 15 years if the bond is held until maturity and the coupon payments are reinvested each year at 5.87 percent. Using Equation 16.3 to solve for the realized annual effective rate (EAY) shows that it is indeed equal to 5.87 percent:

$$EAY = (\$2,728.50 \,/ \,\$1,160)^{1/15} - 1$$

$$EAY = (2.35185)^{0.0667} - 1 = 0.0587, \text{ or } 5.87\%$$

Thus, if all coupon payments are reinvested at the $y°$ rate and the bond is held until maturity, the EAY will be equal to the ex ante effective annual rate, $y°$.

Reinvestment and Price Risk

The ex ante effective annual rate $y°$ will only equal the realized rate EAY, however, if the bond is held to maturity and all coupons can be reinvested at the $y°$ rate. If this is not the case, the realized return that the investor will receive can be quite different. If the investor has to sell the bond prior to maturity, he or she may sell the bond for a gain or loss and receive more or less than the maturity value. Similarly, if interest rates fall or rise, the investor may receive more or less interest income than expected on reinvesting coupon payments by the end of year 15. Thus, investors in fixed-income securities always face interest rate risk, that is, the risk of not achieving their desired ex ante yield y^*.

THE TWO SIDES OF INTEREST RATE RISK

Interest rate risk consists of two components:

1. **Reinvestment risk**, the risk of interest rates falling and having to reinvest coupon payments at a lower rate than y^*, resulting in a lower ex post yield, and
2. **Price or market value risk**, the risk of rates rising and the market price of the bond falling if the bond must be sold prior to maturity, also resulting in a lower ex post yield.

Example of Reinvestment Risk   Looking at the bond in the previous example, suppose that market rates fall after the purchase of the bond and that rates are, on average, only 5 percent over the life of that bond.[3] The FV at the end of 15 years can now be calculated as follows:

$$FV = \$75 \ (FVIFA\ 5\%, 15) + \$1,000$$

$$= \$75 \ (21.579) + \$1,000 = \$2,618.39$$

The ex post EAY (using Equation 16.3) now becomes

$$EAY = (\$2,618.43 / \$1,160)^{1/15} - 1$$

$$EAY = (2.2573)^{.0667} - 1 = 0.0558, \text{ or } 5.58\%$$

Thus, because of reinvestment risk, the investor has a lower ex post yield on his or her bond than the expected y^* of 5.87 percent. This yield may not seem very much lower, but if a portfolio manager invested $1.16 million in bonds, the difference in the ex post terminal amount received at the end of year 15 is $2.2573 million, which is $471,200 lower than the expected $2.7285 million. If the investor was the portfolio manager of a fixed income portfolio for a mutual fund, a pension fund, or an insurance fund with a guaranteed income certificate (GIC) promising a given annual return to investors, he or she could suffer a serious shortfall.

Example of Market Price Risk   Suppose for the bond discussed in the preceding section that rates instead stay at 5.87 percent on average for the first five years of the bond but rise to 6.5 percent at the end of year 5. Also, suppose that the investor needs to sell the bond at the end of year 5. Because of the rise in interest rates, the bond's price will fall to

$$Price = Coupon\ Payment\ (PVIFA\ r, n) + Maturity\ Value\ (PVIF\ r, n)$$

$$Price = \$75 \ (PVIFA\ 6.5\%, 5) + \$1,000 \ (PVIF\ 6.5\%, 5)$$

$$= \$75 \ (4.1557) + \$1,000 \ (0.7299) = \$1,041.48$$

---

[3] This is a very simplified assumption, but the same results can be demonstrated if one assumes that the market rate changes each year over the life of the bond.

Thus, the investor has a capital loss of $1,160 − $1,041.58 = −$118.42. Again, this may not seem like a significant loss, but if a portfolio manager invested $1.16 million in the bonds, the loss would be a potentially significant $118,420.

Based on the assumption that the investor reinvested the coupon payments at the 5.87 percent rate for five years and then sold the bond for $1,041.58 at the end of year 5, the terminal FV that the investor received is as follows:

$$FV = \$75 \ (FVIFA \ 5.87\%, 5) + \$1,041.58$$

$$= \$75 \ (5.6225) + \$1,041.58 = \$2,504.85$$

and the ex post EAY (using Equation 16.3) now becomes

$$EAY = (\$2,504.85 \ / \ \$1,160)^{1/15} - 1$$

$$EAY = (2.15935)^{0.0667} - 1 = 0.0527, \text{ or } 5.27\%$$

Because of market price risk, the annual effective yield the investor received ex post of 5.27 percent for the five years was 0.50 percent, or 50 basis points lower than the expected annual effective yield of 5.87 percent.

Reinvestment Risk Versus Price Risk

Thus, interest rate risk has two facets: potential variation from unexpected changes in the rate at which intermediate cash flows can be reinvested—**reinvestment risk**—and potential variation from unexpected changes in market prices of financial assets—**market value** or **price risk**. For a given change in market conditions, the two types of interest rate risk have opposite effects. A decline in market rates lowers reinvestment income but increases prices (potential capital gains); an increase in market rates improves reinvestment income but decreases prices (potential capital losses). It is not surprising, then, that interest rate risk is so hard to manage successfully.

Because interest rate risk is so difficult to manage, it is important to understand as much as we can about how joint effects of reinvestment and price risk affect the prices of fixed income securities. Some well-known bond theorems can lay a foundation for understanding duration, an overall measure of interest rate risk for such securities. These theorems are discussed in the following sections.

BOND THEOREMS

In 1962, as part of an article on the term structure of interest rates, Burton Malkiel proposed and proved mathematically a series of theorems on the relationship between the yields and prices of fixed-income securities. These theorems have become known as "the bond theorems." By using calculus, Malkiel differentiated a bond price equation with respect to yield and maturity and drew the following conclusions[4]:

Theorem I. Bond prices must move inversely to bond yields. The implications of Theorem 1 were explained earlier in the chapter. When bond prices rise (fall), yields fall (rise) and vice versa.

---

[4]The bond theorems are discussed and proven in Malkiel (1962), pp. 201–206.

Theorem II. Holding the coupon rate constant, for a given change in market yields, percentage changes in bond prices are greater the longer the term to maturity of a bond.[5] In informal terms, with a change in interest rates longer-term bonds will have bigger capital losses and capital gains than short-term bonds. Longer-term bonds have cash flows further into the future, so the present value of their cash flows and, hence, their market values fall and rise more with a change in rates than do shorter-term bonds.

Theorem III. The percentage price change for a bond will increase at a decreasing rate as N increases. The longer the time to maturity, the less the difference in percentage price changes. For example, when yields change, the price of 15-year bonds will change by a greater percentage than the prices of ten-year bonds, but the difference is less than the difference between the price changes of a five-year bond and a ten-year bond.

Theorem IV. (Convexity Theorem) Starting with a given market yield $y°$, holding other factors constant, the rise in price with a fall in $y°$ will be greater than the fall in price with the same absolute value rise in $y°$. Price changes in bonds with a change in rates are asymmetric. For a given change in $y°$, a fall in rates will result in a larger capital gain than the capital loss with the same absolute value rise in $y°$. This property is known as *convexity*. This relation benefits investors, because for a given change in rates, capital gains will be greater than capital losses.[6]

Theorem V. Holding N constant and starting from the same $y°$, the higher the coupon rate, the smaller the percentage change in price for a given change in yield.[7] This principle is illustrated in Figure 16.2, which shows the percentage price changes of three eight-year bonds plotted against changes in yields, starting from a 12 percent base. As yields drop (rise) from a 12 percent level, the percentage changes in the price of a 6 percent coupon rate, eight-year bond are greater than the percentage price changes for a 12 percent or 18 percent coupon-rate bond of comparable maturity. Hence, lower coupon bonds have greater interest rate risk.

Implications of the Bond Theorems

The bond theorems show that changes in market rates will not affect all bond portfolios in the same way. In periods of volatile market rates, portfolios heavily invested in long-term securities have greater price fluctuations than portfolios concentrated in money market securities. The value of portfolios heavily invested in low-coupon instruments is more changeable than portfolios of high-coupon bonds. If (a big if) managers forecast market changes correctly and understand the bond theorems, they can position their institutions to profit from anticipated rate movements. Judging a bond's interest rate risk depends on the current level of market rates ($y°$) and

---

[5]Theorem II is true for bonds selling at or above par at the time of a change in market yields but not for all discount bonds. Malkiel observed this but did not examine why it was so, as other authors have done subsequently.

[6]Although coupon bonds have positive convexity, mortgage securities can actually have negative convexity because if rates fall dramatically, prepayments will be reducing the present value of the security's future cash flows. Thus any rise in value with a fall in rates will be dampedned by the fall in value associated with greater mortgage prepayments.

[7]Theorem V holds for all bonds except perpetuities and bonds with one period to maturity.

Figure 16.2 ✦ BOND THEOREM V: AS COUPON RATE INCREASES, PERCENTAGE PRICE CHANGES DECREASE AS YIELDS CHANGE

With term to maturity held constant, the higher the coupon rates, the lower the percentage price changes on bonds as market yields change.

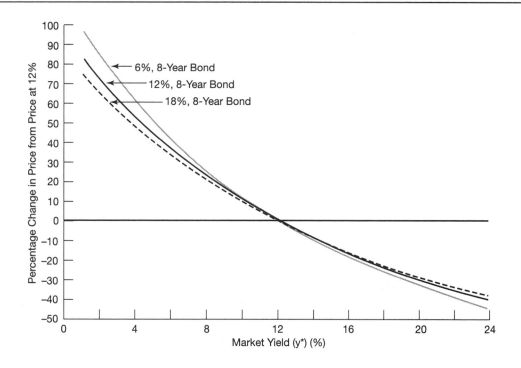

the coupon rate of a bond as well as its time to maturity. The concept of duration enables a manager to develop an overall measure of interest rate risk that includes the effect of coupon rate, level of interest rates, and time to maturity, discussed later in the chapter.

IMPLICATIONS FOR FINANCIAL INSTITUTIONS

Financial institutions have so many interest-bearing assets and liabilities that the effect of changing market interest rates is very important to them. For instance, higher reinvestment rates for investors mean changing costs for financial institutions. However, if market yields fall unexpectedly, the interest costs of a financial institution will fall if it has incurred variable rate liabilities. If market rates rise unexpectedly, the reverse is true. Either way, the net interest margin is subject to unexpected variation.

In Chapter 6, a financial institution's funding gap is presented as rate sensitive assets-rate sensitive liabilities. This serves as a measure of an institution's reinvestment (refinancing) risk for a given time period. Recall that if the funding gap is positive, the financial institution risks a lower net interest income (NII) if interest rates fall, because interest revenues will fall more than interest expenses. If the funding gap is negative, the financial institution risks a lower NII if interest rates rise, because interest expenses will rise more than interest revenues. The approximate change in NII with a change in interest rates was described as

$$(\Delta NII = (\Delta \text{ in interest rates}) \times (\text{Funding Gap})$$

The funding gap, however, only measures one side of interest rate risk for a financial institution: reinvestment (refinancing) risk. It does not consider the time value of money, and the effect of a change in the market value of assets and liabilities on a financial institution's balance sheet. Financial institutions that hold long-term financial assets and liabilities also have market price risk, that is, the risk of a decline in the market value of assets being greater than the decline in the market value of liabilities, and, hence, a decline in the market value of equity (equal to the market value of assets − market value of liabilities). A duration gap, discussed later in the chapter, provides a better overall measure of interest rate risk including market price as well as reinvestment risk.

EFFECTS OF INTEREST RATE CHANGES ON COMMON STOCK

"Fed Move Ignites Explosive Stock, Bond Rallies," read a *Wall Street Journal* headline on Friday, April 10, 1992.[8] The story centered on the behavior of common stock prices after the Fed's April 9, 1992, cut in the discount rate. A similar story followed the Fed's cut in October 1998. Because common stocks are financial assets, their prices behave similarly to those of bonds. As market yields fall, yields on common stock also fall and their prices rise. As market yields rise for other financial assets, the yields on common stock rise and their prices fall. In 1998, analysts suggested one reason for the booming stock market was that low interest rates on bonds prompted investors to seek better returns elsewhere. These analysts theorized that investors were willing to take on more risk by investing in stock and to put a low price on that risk because their alternative investment bonds offered very low yields.[9] Research shows that financial institutions and other nonfinancial firms that have more fixed rate assets than liabilities (i.e., larger interest rate risk) are more sensitive to unexpected changes in interest rates than other firms. Hence, for financial institutions, the relationship between interest rates and stock prices is particularly important.[10]

---

[8]Randall Smith and Robert Steiner. "Fed Move Ignites Explosive Stock, Bond Rallies." *The Wall Street Journal* (April 10, 1992), C1. The Dow's reactions to discount rates over a 20-year period are discussed and illustrated in Douglas R. Sease. "Are Five Fed Rate Cuts Enough?" *The Wall Street Journal* (December 2, 1991), C1, C2.

[9]Greg Ip. "Low Interest Rates Pave the Road to Risk." *The Wall Street Journal* (December 14, 1998), A1.

[10]See Fogler and Tipton (1981); Christie (1981); Flannery and James (1984); and Sweeney and Warga (1986). Flannery and James found that the interest rate sensitivity of a firm's common stock is related to the net fixed-rate asset position of the firm, or the amount by which long-term, fixed-rate assets exceed long-term, fixed-rate liabilities. The effect was confirmed in Scott and Peterson (1986) and Bae (1990). Neuberger (1992) found that commercial real estate loans have a strong effect on bank stock returns. In the 1990s banks have made greater use of interest rate hedging strategies; therefore, more recent studies find that many banks have less interest rate sensitivity for stocks.

DURATION: AN IDEA AHEAD OF ITS TIME

Duration is a measure of overall interest rate risk. It is difficult to find a recent scholarly article on financial institution management that does not mention duration, and many fixed-income mutual funds are listed as high- or low-duration funds. It would be easy to conclude that duration is a new idea, but, in fact, it was first developed more than 50 years ago by Frederick Macaulay. Similar concepts were developed shortly thereafter, but Macaulay's duration has only recently been widely appreciated for the power it brings to the management of interest rate risk.[11]

Duration Defined

Duration is the weighted average time over which the cash flows from an investment are expected, where the weights are the relative time-adjusted present values of the cash flows. It is an alternative to maturity for expressing the time dimension of an investment. Focusing on maturity ignores the fact that, for most securities, some cash benefits are received *before* the maturity date. Benefits received before maturity are often substantial, especially for bonds with relatively high coupon rates or annuities. It can be argued, therefore, that ignoring the time dimension of cash benefits before maturity is unwise.

The importance of the time dimension is evident in the basic expression for the market value (Po) of an investment shown earlier (Equation 16.1):

$$P_o = \sum_{t=1}^{N} \frac{C_t}{(1 + y^*)^t}$$

Because the market value of an investment equals the present value of expected benefits and because the discount factors $(1 + y)^t$ are exponential functions of time, early payments are discounted less than those received later. Differences in discounted value become more pronounced as t increases. In essence, the *effective* maturity—that is, the time period over which the investor receives cash flows with relatively high present value—may differ from the *contractual*, or legally specified, maturity. Duration is a measure of this effective maturity. Duration is also a measure of the interest rate risk or responsiveness of a bond's market price to a change in market rates. Securities with higher durations will have a greater change in market value with a change in market rates.

The formula for duration is shown as follows:

$$\text{DUR} = \frac{\sum_{t=1}^{N} \frac{tC_t}{(1 + y^*)^t}}{\sum_{t=1}^{N} \frac{C_t}{(1 + y^*)^t}} \qquad [16.5]$$

The equation used to solve for duration is the sum of the weighted present value of a bond's cash flows, each weighted by being multiplied by t, the time each cash

---

[11]Macaulay (1938). One early work based on a property similar to duration was Samuelson (1945). Several scholars have also attributed an idea virtually identical to duration to J. R. Hicks in his *Value and Capital* (1939). For a review of the intellectual history of duration, see Weil (1973).

flow comes in, divided by the sum of the present value of the cash flows (i.e., the bond's price, Po). Duration can also be calculated as sum [(present value of each cash flow / Po) × t]. Hence, duration represents the weighted contribution of a cash flow to the market value or present value of a bond. A bond with larger cash flows coming in later will have a higher duration than a bond with larger cash flows coming in earlier that can be reinvested earlier at the market rate (y°) by the investor.

Example: Calculation of Duration for Bonds

Duration is perhaps best understood through examples. Consider the following three bonds:

✦ Bond 1 has an 8 percent coupon rate, $1,000 maturity value, n = 6 years.
✦ Bond 2 is a zero-coupon bond with a $1,000 maturity value, n = 6 years.
✦ Bond 3 has a 6 percent coupon rate, $1,000 maturity value, n = 6 years.

The market rate y° for bonds of similar risk to these bonds is 8 percent. Which bond has the least overall interest rate risk, that is, the shortest duration?

Calculating duration is often easiest by using a table, as in the following:

BOND 1: 8% COUPON RATE, $1,000 MATURITY VALUE, 6 YEARS TO MATURITY, Y° = 8%

Year	Cash Flow	PVIF 8%	PV Cash Flow	t × PV Cash Flow
1	$80	0.9259	$74.07	$74.07
2	80	0.8573	68.58	137.16
3	80	0.7938	63.50	190.50
4	80	0.7350	58.80	235.20
5	80	0.6806	54.45	272.25
6	1080	0.6302	680.62	4,083.72
			Sum $1,000.00	4,992.90

Duration = Sum (t × PV Cash flow) / Sum (PV Cash flow)
= $4,992.90 / $1,000.00 = 4.993 years

BOND 2: $1,000 MATURITY VALUE, NO COUPONS, 6 YEARS TO MATURITY, Y° = 8%

Year	Cash Flow	PVIF 8%	PV Cash Flow	t × PV Cash Flow
1	$0	0.9259	0	0
2	0	0.8573	0	0
3	0	0.7938	0	0
4	0	0.7350	0	0
5	0	0.6806	0	0
6	$1,000	0.6302	$630.20	$3,781.20
			Sum $630.20	$3,781.20

Duration = $3,781.2 / $630.20 = 6 years

PORTFOLIO IMMUNIZATION

Interest rate risk, both with respect to changing market values and reinvestment rates, means that the realized yield on an investment will often differ from the expected yield at the time of investment. For some investors, accepting this risk may be extremely unappealing if they have financial goals or obligations that depend on attaining a certain amount of cash at the end of a holding period. For example, a pension fund may have known obligations to retirees, and cash must be accumulated by the due date. Or an individual may retain the services of a bank trust department and require that his or her funds increase enough by a given date that they will cover the cost of a child's Harvard education.

In the 1970s, a duration-based strategy for portfolio management was introduced and has since been widely adopted by financial institutions.[20] The strategy is known as **immunization** because it makes a portfolio "immune" to the "disease" of interest rate risk over a given holding period. Immunization is a portfolio management strategy to achieve a realized annual rate of return at the end of a holding period that is no less than the expected annual yield at the beginning of the period. Within the constraints addressed later in the chapter, a portfolio is immunized if its duration is equal to the holding period.

Immunization Illustrated

Suppose an insurance company issues a $1 million guaranteed investment contract that guarantees an annual effective yield of 8 percent ($y°$) for five years. In other words, the investor is promised that he or she will receive $1 million $(1.08)^5 = \$1.4693$ million in five years, that is, an 8 percent annual realized return on the investment:

$$r = (FV / PV)^{1/n} - 1 = (1.4693 / 1 \text{ mil.})^{1/5} - 1 = 0.08, \text{ or } 8\%.$$

The company is considering two alternatives:s

1. **Bond 1: six-year bonds with an 8% coupon rate** and $1,000 par value, which sell for $1,000 per bond, with $y° = 8\%$.
2. **Bond 2: five-year bonds with an 8% coupon rate** and $1,000 par value, which sell for $1,000 per bond, with $y° = 8\%$.

The duration for Bond 1, as we calculated earlier, is equal to 4.993 years. The duration for Bond 2, can be calculated by using a table as follows:

Year	Cash Flow	PVIF 8%	PV Cash Flow	t × PV Cash Flow
1	$80	0.9259	$74.07	$74.07
2	80	0.8573	68.58	137.16
3	80	0.7938	63.50	190.50
4	80	0.7350	58.80	235.20
5	1080	0.6806	735.05	3,675.25
			Sum $1,000.00	$4,312.18

$$\text{Dur} = \$4,312.18 / \$1,000 = 4.312$$

---

[20]Fisher and Weil (1971). The authors acknowledge their indebtedness to the ideas of writers dating back to the 1970s. In an interesting history of the use of immunization by institutional portfolio managers, Leibowitz (1983) notes that despite previous academic research, immunization was not put into practice until financial markets faced unprecedented events in the late 1970s. Academics, however, benefited from the use of the technique in the real world. Advanced applications are discussed in more detail in Leibowitz (1981) and Bierwag (1987).

or you can use the short Equation 16.6:

$$\text{Dur} = N - \{[\text{Coupon Pmt} / (\text{Po} \times y°)]\,([N - (1 + y°)\,(\text{PVIFA } y°, N)]\}$$
$$5 - \{[80/80] - [5 - (1.08)(3.9927)]\} = 5 - 0.68788 = 4.312$$

If the insurance company's portfolio manager selected a maturity match strategy, Bond 2 would be selected. In contrast, Bond 1 would be selected under a duration match strategy.

To see which choice immunizes the portfolio manager's investment to ensure an 8 percent effective annual yield, we need to calculate the **ex post** effective annual rate (EAY) for each bond under different interest rate scenarios. These are shown in Table 16.1. The first panel shows the duration matching strategy. Under this strategy, the six-year bond will be held until the end of year 5 and then sold for a price equal to the present value of the remaining coupon and maturity value at that time [\$1080 / (1 + y°)]. Under each of the scenarios (rates staying the same, rates rising, or rates falling) the ex post effective annual (realized) rate will be 8 percent. This is because reinvestment risk exactly offsets market price risk for each of the strategies. For instance, in Scenario 2, if rates rise, the portfolio receives higher reinvestment income from the coupons for the first five years, but the bond will be sold for a loss that just offsets the rise in reinvestment income, leaving a realized return of 8 percent. In Scenario 3, if rates fall, the portfolio receives lower reinvestment income from the coupons for the first five years; however, the bonds can be sold for a gain at the end of year 5, offsetting the lower reinvestment income. Thus, an effective annual yield of 8 percent is again realized. In effect, with duration matching the bond portfolio is immunized and an 8 percent effective annual return is locked in. Of course, there is an opportunity cost, associated with Scenario 2, in which the higher reinvestment income is offset by the lower price that the bond is sold for at the end of year 5.

The second panel of Table 16.1 shows the results of Strategy 2: maturity matching. Under this strategy, the portfolio achieves a greater than 8 percent realized annual rate if interest rates rise, as in Scenario 2, because at the end of year 5, the portfolio receives higher reinvestment income from the coupon payments plus the maturity value. However, if interest rates fall (Scenario 3), the portfolio will receive a lower realized annual yields as the result of lower reinvestment income (with no offsetting capital gain) as in the duration matching strategy.

Hence, only under the duration-matched strategy is the bond portfolio immunized. For a portfolio of bonds with several different durations, the weighted average duration of the bond portfolio would be constructed to be equal to the desired holding period horizon.[21]

Immunization: Assumptions and Limitations

Under certain assumptions, a bond with a duration equal to the desired holding period results in exactly offsetting market value and reinvestment risks, as suggested for Bond 1 in the previous illustration. With a flat initial yield curve and with only one unexpected parallel shift in the curve immediately after the beginning of the pe-

---

[21]The weighted average duration would simply be the sum of (the market value of each bond / total market value of the portfolio) (its duration). For development and proof of the additive property of duration, see Bierwag (1987), pp. 84–86 and 109–110.

Table 16.1   ✦   ILLUSTRATION: DURATION AND PORTFOLIO IMMUNIZATION

With immunization, the expected return on a portfolio is protected from both reinvestment and market value risk. In this example, holding bonds with a duration of five years will lock in an annual rate of return of 8% over a holding period of five years. Suppose, for instance, that an insurance company issues a $1 million guaranteed investment contract (GIC) that guarantees an annual effective yield of 8% ($y°$) for five years. The portfolio manager would like to immunize this yield regardless of what interest rates do.

STRATEGY 1: DURATION MATCH; BUY 8% BOND WITH A APPROXIMATELY 5-YEAR DURATION:

Bond 1: six-year bonds, with an 8% coupon rate, and $1,000 par value that sells for $1,000/bond, with $y° = 8\%$, Dur = 4.993 years.

Coupon payments reinvested at $y°$ and bond sold at end of year 5

Scenario (1) Market interest rates stay at $y° = 8\%$ for the five years.

   Ex post effective annual rate for Bond 1:

FV of cash flows per bond at end of year 5 = $80 (FVIFA 5, 8%) + $1,080 / (1.08) = $80 (5.8666) + $1,000 = $1,469.33

   Ex post effective annual rate is $(1469.33 / 1000)^{.20} - 1 = .08$ or 8%.

Scenario (2) Market interest rates rise to $y° = 9\%$ for the five years.

   Ex post effective annual rate for Bond 1:

FV of cash flows per bond at end of year 5 = $80 (FVIFA 5, 9%) + $1,080 / (1.09) = $80 (5.9847) + $990.83 = $1,469.61

   Ex post effective annual rate is $(1469.61 / 1000)^{0.20} - 1 = 0.08$ or 8%.

Scenario (3) Market interest rates fall to $y° = 7\%$ for the five years.

   Ex post effective annual rate for Bond 1:

FV of cash flows per bond at end of year 5 = $80 (FVIFA 5, 7%) + $1,080 / (1.07) = $80 (5.7507) + $1,009.35 = $1,469.41

   Ex post effective annual rate is $(1469.41 / 1000)^{0.20} - 1 = .08$ or 8%.

Summary for Duration Matching Strategy: Regardless of the yield scenario, the duration matching strategy achieves an annual effective yield of 8%, because reinvestment and price risk offset one another.

STRATEGY 2: MATURITY MATCH: BUY 8% BOND WITH MATURITY OF FIVE YEARS.

Bond 2: five-year bonds, with an 8% coupon rate, and $1,000 par value that sells for $1,000/bond, with $y° = 8\%$, Dur = 4.312 years.

Coupon payments reinvested at $y°$ and bond held to maturity

Scenario (1) Market interest rates stay at $y° = 8\%$ for the five years.

   Ex post effective annual rate for Bond 2:

FV of cash flows per bond at end of year 5 = $80 (FVIFA 5, 8%) + $1,000 = $80 (5.8666) + $1,000 = $1,469.33

   Ex post effective annual rate is $(1469.33 / 1000)^{.20} - 1 = .08$ or 8%.

Scenario (2) Market interest rates rise to $y° = 9\%$ for the five years.

   Ex post effective annual rate for Bond 2:

FV of cash flows per bond at end of year 5 = $80 (FVIFA 5, 9%) + $1,000 = $80 (5.9847) + $1,000 = $1,478.78

   Ex post effective annual rate is $(1478.78 / 1000)^{.20} - 1 = .0814$ or 8.14%.

Scenario (3) Market interest rates fall to $y° = 7\%$ for the five years.

   Ex post effective annual rate for Bond 2:

FV of cash flows per bond at end of year 5 = $80 (FVIFA 5, 7%) + $1,000 = $80 (5.7507) + $1,000 = $1,460.06

   Ex post effective annual rate is $(1460.06 / 1000)^{.20} - 1 = .0786$ or 7.86%.

Summary for Maturity Matching Strategy: the portfolio manager will not achieve an 8% effective annual yield if rates fall, because of lower reinvestment income on coupon payments. Hence, a maturity matching strategy does not immunize the bond against reinvestment risk if interest rates fall.

riod, the realized annual return over the holding period will *exactly* equal the expected annual yield. However, market yield changes can occur in the middle of the investment period, and an investor may be less than perfectly immunized. Also, although not considered in the example, interest rate changes are so common and so unpredictable that single parallel shifts in the yield curve are the exception rather than the rule.[22] Still, empirical tests of duration and maturity strategies over 44 years suggest that the dispersion of realized returns is consistently smaller when durations rather than maturities are matched with holding periods.

Another limitation of immunization is that it is difficult to find an investment with a duration exceeding 10 years.[23] Thus, investors with lengthy desired holding periods may be unable to use the strategy. Although zero-coupon bonds may not be available, the stripped securities introduced in 1982 by divisions of Merrill Lynch and Salomon Brothers have alleviated this limitation. Stripped securities are created when the originators "strip" ordinary T-bonds of their coupon payments and sell one or more coupon payments or the par value separately to investors wanting single cash inflows at specified dates. The acronyms given to these securities include CATS (Certificates of Accrual on Treasury Securities), Salomon Brothers' version of a strip, and TIGRS (Merrill Lynch's Treasury Investment Growth Receipts), among others.[24] In 1985, to facilitate the issuance of strips, the Treasury Department decided that each coupon payment on specified Treasury issues may be registered in a separate name. The program is called Separate Trading of Registered Interest and Principal of Securities (STRIPS). Treasury issues eligible for the program may be presented to the Treasury for stripping; subsequently, each expected cash flow may be sold as if it were a separate security. This broadening and deepening of the market reduced the liquidity risk of owning strips for investors forced to sell before maturity. As expected, STRIPS have been exceptionally popular, with outstanding volume exceeding $113 billion by the end of 1990.[25] The Tax Reform Act of 1986 allowed the stripping of municipal bonds for the first time, and large securities firms began doing so within minutes of the signing of the law. Mortgage lenders have fashioned stripped securities based on cash flows from expected mortgage payments. Each new type of strip has addressed a market need, such as the desire to minimize taxes or to immunize particular kinds of cash flow obligations.[26]

---

[22] See Yawitz (1977); Bierwag, Kaufman, and Toevs (1983); and Ott (1988).

[23] The behavior of duration for bonds with very long maturities is discussed and illustrated in Fisher and Weil (1971). They note that for bonds selling at or above par, duration is bounded by $(y° + m) / (m \times y°)$, so the maximum duration for a bond paying interest twice a year (m = 2) with a yield of 10 percent, regardless of coupon or maturity, would be $(0.10 + 2) (2 \times 0.10) = 2.10 / 0.20 = 10.5$ years. For bonds selling at a discount, duration actually decreases for maturities of more than about 50 years. The mathematical expression of the maximum duration for a discount bond is more complex and is presented in Hopewell and Kaufman (1973). Because, as a practical matter, few institutions have investment planning periods exceeding 50 years and because few, if any, bonds with contractual maturities of more than 50 years are available, the limitations of this property are not considered further.

[24] See Becketti (1988).

[25] See Livingston and Gregory (1989) and Gregory and Livingston (1992).

[26] Ann Monroe. "Goldman Sachs and Salomon Brothers Scramble for Sales of Stripped Municipal Bonds." *The Wall Street Journal* (October 23, 1986), 50 and Sherlock and Chen (1987).

FINANCIAL INSTITUTIONS AND IMMUNIZATION

Immunization of Security Portfolios

As the previous example illustrates, one way in which financial institutions use immunization is to offer it as part of an array of portfolio management services to customers. Commercial bank trust departments, securities firms, and investment companies are among those institutions for which knowledge of immunization is important. Yet even institutions that do not sell portfolio management services can benefit from understanding immunization. If an institution has promised to make cash payments to others at specified dates in the future, as is the case with pension funds and life insurance companies, a way to enhance the probability that cash will be available to meet those payments is to invest in assets with a weighted average duration equal to that of future cash obligations. Asset portfolios selected for their duration and designed to help meet future cash outflows are called **dedicated portfolios**.

Despite its usefulness, immunization presents difficulties for institutions. Ideally, immunization locks in a yield for a desired holding period by protecting against both sides of interest rate risk. But immunized portfolios are not protected from default risk, nor is there a guarantee against changes in anticipated yields as a result of unanticipated changes in tax laws. Finally, immunization eliminates the possibility of unexpected gains when interest rates change. In other words, it is a *hedging*, or risk-minimization, strategy, not a profit-maximization strategy. If rates rise to 9 percent, as in the example, the second strategy is the most desirable, but an immunizer forgoes that opportunity. Thus, immunization is appropriate for portfolio managers who wish to avoid rate forecasting or who are willing to trade potential unexpected gains for protection from potential unexpected losses.

DURATION GAP: MEASURING AN INSTITUTION'S OVERALL INTEREST RATE RISK

In addition to locking in returns on fixed income portfolios through immunization, depository institutions also use their duration gap as an overall measure of the bank's interest rate risk and to immunize the market value of equity for the institution. A depository institution's duration gap has an advantage over its funding gap by considering not only reinvestment (refinancing) risk and the effect of possible changes in NII with a change in rates, but also market value risk, i.e., the effect of possible change in interest rates on the market value of the depository institution's assets and liabilities, as well as potential changes in the market value of the institution's equity (market value of assets − market value of liabilities).

A depository institution's duration gap (DGAP) is the difference between the duration of its assets (Dur_A) minus the duration of its liabilities (Dur_L) multiplied by the fraction of liabilities held to assets:

$$DGAP = \left[Dur_A - \left(\frac{\text{Liabilities}}{\text{Assets}} \right) (Dur_L) \right] \qquad [16.10]$$

Hence, a depository institution's duration gap is a function of the duration of its assets, the duration of its liabilities, and the percentage of the institution's debt financing. If the institution has a positive duration gap, it has assets with a higher duration (more interest rate risk) than its liabilities. If interest rates rise, the market value of its assets will fall more than the market value of liabilities, and the value of equity will fall. Similarly, if interest rates fall, the market value of equity will rise. If the institution has a negative duration gap, its liabilities will have a higher duration than its assets, and if interest rates rise, the value of its equity will rise; in contrast, if interest rates fall, the value of equity will fall. Note that a positive duration gap implies a negative funding gap (more long-term assets and fewer rate-sensitive assets than liabilities). Similarly, a negative duration gap implies a positive funding gap (more long-term liabilities and fewer rate-sensitive liabilities than assets). A percentage change in the value of the depository institution's equity-to-assets ratio can be found just as one would find a change in any other security:

$$\Delta \text{Value Equity} / \text{Total Assets} = -\text{DGAP} \left[\Delta y° / (1 + y°) \right] \qquad [16.11]$$

where $y°$ is the average rate on assets. The Duration of Assets for a balance sheet is the weighted average of the duration of the assets as follows:

$$\text{Dur}_A = \left[\text{Dur}_{A1} \left(\frac{A_1}{TA} \right) + \text{Dur}_{A2} \left(\frac{A_2}{TA} \right) \right. \qquad [16.12]$$
$$+ \ldots \text{Dur}_{AN} \left(\frac{A_N}{TA} \right)$$

where A_i is the dollar value of Asset_i and TA is the total dollar value of assets.

Similarly, the Duration of Liabilities for a balance sheet is the weighted average of the duration of the liabilities:

$$\text{Dur}_L = \text{Dur}_{L1} \left(\frac{L_1}{TL} \right) + \text{Dur}_{LZ} \left(\frac{L_2}{TL} \right) \qquad [16.13]$$
$$+ \text{Dur}_{LN} \left(\frac{L_N}{TL} \right)$$

where L_i is the dollar value of Liability_I and TL is the total dollar value of liabilities.

Difficulties in Calculating Durations

Durations are often difficult to calculate for some depository institution balance sheet items. For instance, do demand deposits have a duration of 0, because they mature at any time, or a duration of the average time they turn over in a year? What is the duration of a variable-rate loan? Often the time frame to which the loan is subject to change is used; thus, a variable-rate loan, subject to change every six months, would have a duration of 0.50. Also, remember that with any market rate change, the duration of an asset or liability will also change, so durations must be constantly updated and monitored.

EXAMPLE: CALCULATING A BANK'S DURATION GAP

Information for Excelsior Bank is shown on Table 16.2, Panel A and as follows.

Calculating the Duration Gap for a Simplified Bank, Excelsior (in mils.)

ASSETS		
Cash	Dur = 0	$ 10,000
6-month T-bills $y° = 6\%$	Dur = maturity = 0.5 years	$40,000
10-year Fixed-Rate Loans, 10%	Dur = ?	$ 50,000
amortized	Total Assets	$100,000

LIABILITIES AND EQUITY

Transaction Deposits rate = 2%	Dur = 0	$40,000
1 Year CDs°, rate = 7%	Dur = 1	50,000
Equity		10,000
	Total Liabilities and Equity	$100,000

°interest and principal paid at maturity for 1 year CDs.

Duration of Excelsior's Assets   To calculate the duration of Excelsior's assets, we first calculate the duration of the 10-year amortized loans with equal loan payments of $8,137.27 per year as follows. First we calculate the duration of the 10-year amortized loans with an annual loan rate of 10 percent, where the loan payment is:

PMT = Loan Amount / (PVIFA 10%, 10) = $50,000 / 6.1446 = $8,137.27 per year:

Year	Cash Flow	PVIF 10%	PV Cash Flow	t × PV Cash Flow
1	$8,137.27	0.9091	$7,397.59	$ 7,397.59
2	8,137.27	0.8264	6,724.65	13,449.28
3	8,137.27	0.7513	6,113.53	18,340.59
4	8,137.27	0.6830	5,557.76	22,231.02
5	8,137.27	0.6209	5,052.43	25,262.16
6	8,137.27	0.5645	4,593.49	27,560.93
7	8,137.27	0.5132	4,176.05	29,232.33
8	8,137.27	0.4665	3,796.04	30,368.29
9	8,137.27	0.4241	3,451.02	31,059.15
10	8,137.27	0.3855	3,136.92	31,369.18
		Sum°	$50,000.00	$236,270.52

Duration of Loans = $236,270.52 / $50,000 = **4.73 years**

°Note: the present value of the loan should be $50,000, but because of PVIF rounding errors, the sum when adding up the PVCFs is slightly off.

Similarly, the formula for short duration (Equation 16.6) could be used, as follows:

Dur = N − {[Coupon Payment / Loan Amount × y°] × [N − (1 + y°) (PVIFA y°, N]}

Dur = 10 − {8.137.27 / (50,000 × 0.10] × [10 − (1.10)(6.1446)]} =

$$10 - \{1.6275 \ (3.241\} = 4.73 \text{ years}$$

Because the loan is amortized, paying equal amounts each year, in contrast with a bond that pays only interest and then principal the final year, the duration years of the loan are much lower than the loan's maturity. The duration of the T-bills is six months, because all cash flows are paid at maturity, and the duration of cash is zero. Thus, the **weighted average duration of Bank Excelsior's assets, Dur$_A$,** using Equation 16.12 is as follows:

($10,000 / $100,000) 0 + ($40,000 / $100,000) 0.5 + ($50,000 / $100,000) 4.73
= (0.10) 0 + (0.40) 0.5 + (0.50) 4.73 = 2.565 years

Table 16.2 ✦ ILLUSTRATION OF IMMUNIZING A BANK'S DURATION GAP

PANEL A: BANK EXCELSIOR'S BALANCE SHEET (UNIMMUNIZED)

Assets	Maturity	Rate y°	Duration	Mkt Value	Liabs/Eq.	Maturity	Rate y°	Duration	Mkt Value
Cash	0	0%	0 years	$10,000	Tran. Deps	0	2%	0 years	$40,000
T-bills	6-months	6%	.5 years	40,000	1Yr CD's	1 year	7%	1 year	50,000
Loans	10-years	10%	4.73 years	50,000	Equity				10,000
Total Assets				$100,000	Total Liabilities & Equity				$100,000

Information on Assets: T-bills pay interest & principal at maturity, so Duration = .5 years

Loans are amortized, so Annual Loan PMT = $50,000/(PVIFA 10%, 10) = $50,000/6.1446 = $8,137.27

Information on Liabilities: CDs pay interest and principal at maturity, so duration = 1

Assume 0 maturity and duration for transaction deposits.

Sample Duration Calculation for Loans:

$DUR = N - \{[\text{Loan PMT} / (Po \times y°)] \times [N - (1 + y°)(\text{PVIFA } y°, N)]\}$

$10 - \{8137.27 / (50,000 \times .10)] \times [10 - (1.10)(6.1446)]\} = 4.73$ years

Calculation of DGAP

$DUR_{Assets} = (10,000 / 100,000) 0 + (40,000 / 100,000) .5 + (50,000 / 100,000) 4.73 = 2.565$ years

$DUR_{Liabs} = (40,000 / 90,000) 0 + (50,000 / 90,000) 1 = .5556$ years

$DGAP = DUR_{Assets} - (\text{Liabilities/Assets}) \times DUR_{Liabs} = 2.565$ years $- (90,000 / 100,000) .5556$ years $= 2.065$ years

---

Expected Net Interest Income = 40,000(.06) + 50,000(.10) − 40,000(.02) − 50,000(.07) = $7,400 − $4,300 = $3,100 mil.

6-month funding gap = RSA − RSL = $40,000 − 0 = $40,000

1-year funding gap = $40,000 − $50,000 = −$10,000

PANEL B: HYPOTHETICAL RISE IN INTEREST RATES 100 BASIS POINTS (1%): NEW BALANCE SHEET (MILS.)

Assets	Maturity	Rate y°	Duration	Mkt Value	Liabs/Eq.	Maturity	Rate y°	Duration	Mkt Value
Cash	0	0%	0 years	$10,000	Tran. Deps	0	2%	0 years	$40,000
T-bills	6-months	7%	.5 years	39,807	1Yr CD's	1 year	8%	1 year	49,537
Loans	10-years	11%	4.73 years	47,922	Equity				8,192
Total Assets				$97,729	Total Liabilities & Equity				$97,729

Approximate Change in Equity Using DGAP = −DGAP (chg y°) / (1 + y°) × Total Assets = −2.065 (.01) / (1.074) × $100,000 = −$1,922.72

Actual Change in Value of Equity = Change in Value of Assets − Change in Value of Liabilities = −2.271 − (−463) = −$1,808

New Net Interest Income = $40,000(.03) + 40,000(1.03)(.035) + 50,000(.10) − 40,000(.02) − 50,000(.07) = $7,642 − $4,300 = $3,342 [$3,342 − $3,100 = $242 higher net interest income]

°In this scenario with a positive 6-month funding gap, NII went up when rates rose.

However, with a positive duration gap, the market value of equity fell when rates rose.

Note: Changes in balance sheet items are calculated by taking the present value of future cash flows for each item. See Koch (1995) for a more thorough example of Duration Gap immunization, which this example is derived from.

Table 16.2   ✦   Illustration of Immunizing a Bank's Duration Gap (*continued*)

PANEL C: IMMUNIZED BALANCE SHEET FOR EXCELSIOR BANK (MILS.)

Assets	Maturity	Rate y°	Duration	Mkt Value	Liabs/Eq.	Maturity	Rate y°	Duration	Mkt Value
Cash	0	0%	0 years	$10,000	Tran. Deps	0	2%	0 years	$40,000
T-bills	6-months	6%	.5 years	40,000	5Yr CD's	5 years	8%	5 years	50,000
Loans	10-years	10%	4.73 years	50,000	Equity				10,000
Total Assets				$100,000	Total Liabilities & Equity				$100,000

DUR-Assets = same as previously, no change = 2.565 years
DUR-Liabilities = (40,000 / 90,000) 0 + (50,000 / 90,000) 5 = 2.78 years
DGAP = DUR-Assets − (Liabilities/Assets) × DUR-Liabs = 2.565 − (90,000 / 100,000) 2.78 years = 2.565 − 2.502 = .063
Expected NII = 40,000(.06) + 50,000(.10) − 40,000(.02) − 50,000(.08) = $7,400 − $4,800 = $2,600 mil.
6-month & 1 year funding gaps = $40,000 − 0 = $40,000

PANEL D: HYPOTHETICAL RISE IN RATES OF 1% BASED ON IMMUNIZED BALANCE SHEET

Assets	Maturity	Rate y°	Duration	Mkt Value	Liabs/Eq.	Maturity	Rate y°	Duration	Mkt Value
Cash	0	0%	0 years	$10,000	Tran. Deps	0	2%	0 years	$40,000
T-bills	6-months	7%	.5 years	39,807	1Yr CD's	1 year	9%	1 year	47,749
Loans	10-years	11%	4.73 years	47,922	Equity				9,980
Total Assets				$97,729	Total Liabilities & Equity				$97,729

Approximate Change in Equity Using DGAP = −.063 (.01 / 1.074) × $100,000 = $58.65
Actual Change in Value of Equity = −$2,271 − (−2,251) = − $20
Net Interest Income = Interest Revenue − Interest Expense
NII = $40,000(.03) + 40,000(1.03)(.035) + 50,000(.10) − 40,000(.02) − 50,000(.08) = $7,642 − $4,800 = $2,842
In this scenario, the value of equity is much better protected, but at the cost of a higher interest expense and a lower net interest income.

Duration of Excelsior's Liabilities   The **weighted average duration of Bank Excelsior's liabilities**, Dur_L, can be calculated by using Equation 16.13:

$$(40,000 / 90,000) \, 0 + (50,000 / 90,000) \, 1 = 0.5556 \text{ years}$$

Duration Gap for Excelsior   The duration gap for Excelsior can be calculated by using Equation 16.14:

$$\text{DGAP} = \text{Dur}_A \left(\frac{\text{Liabilities}}{\text{Assets}} \right) \text{Dur}_L$$
$$= 2.565 \text{ years} - (90,000 / 100,000) \, 0.5556 \text{ years} = 2.065 \text{ years}$$

Effect on the Value of Equity of a 1% Rise in Rates

Table 16.2, panel B, shows the actual effect on the balance sheet and the value of equity for Excelsior if interest rates rise 1 percent. A 1 percent rise in interest rates means that the change in value of equity for Excelsior will be as follows:

$$\Delta \text{Value Equity to Total Assets} = - \text{DGAP} \left[\Delta y° / (1 + y°) \right]$$
$$(\Delta \text{Value Equity to Total Assets} = - 2.065 \left[0.01 \times 1.074 \right]° = -0.0192 \text{ or } - 1.92\%$$

Note: the weighted average rate on assets = (0.4) 6 percent + (0.5) 10 percent = 7.4 percent should be used for y^*. Multiplying the fraction change by Total Assets, we get the following:

$ Δ Value Equity is approximately: (− 0.0192) × $100,000 mil. = − $1,920 mil.

With a positive duration gap of 2.065, the market value of Excelsior's equity will fall by about $1,920 million, or $1.92 billion, for the $100 billion bank. Note that the actual change in the market value of equity is −$1,808 million (see Table 16.2, Panel B). The duration gap formula, which does not adjust for convexity, somewhat overestimates the fall in the bank's equity value.

IMMUNIZATION AND ITS COST

If Bank Excelsior's managers expect rates to rise and wanted to have a duration gap closer to zero, they have several alternatives. They could shorten the duration of the bank's assets, such as by issuing variable-rate loans. Alternatively, they could issue longer-term certificates of deposit (CDs) to lengthen the bank's liabilities. However, there is a price to pay for either strategy. If Bank Excelsior issues variable-rate loans, its customers will demand a lower loan rate, because they will in effect be taking on the upcoming interest rate risk. This will lower Bank Excelsior's interest revenues and NII. Similarly, if Bank Excelsior lengthens the duration of its liabilities to match that of its assets, it will have to offer a higher CD rate for longer-term deposits for customers to be willing to take on the additional interest rate risk of locking into a longer-term CD rate when rates might rise.

Panel C of Table 16.2 shows a scenario of immunizing the balance sheet by lengthening the duration of liabilities so the duration gap is closer to zero. As shown in Panel D, the bank switched to longer-term, five-year CDs. The duration of liabilities rises to 2.78, and the Duration Gap is now .063. Under this scenario the value of equity does not change very much with a rise in rates. However, the net interest revenue for the bank is lower than when it had a positive duration gap because of the higher interest expense for five-year CDs of 8 percent versus 7 percent for one-year CDs used in Panel A.

With immunization, the bank misses any opportunities of a higher value of equity if interest rates fall instead. Thus, bank balance sheet immunization brings with it an opportunity cost. Hence, many bank managers do not aim for a zero gap but rather position the bank with a duration gap based on their confidence in interest rate forecasts. For instance, a number of banks in the 1990s, a period of low, falling interest rates, had positive duration gaps. Other banks have gaps that hinge largely on customer preferences for different types of assets and liabilities, accepting interest rate risk as part of the risk/reward of banking. Still, other banks hedge using off-balance sheet methods, including securitization, discussed earlier in Chapter 8, and derivatives (futures, options, interest rate swaps, caps, collars, and floors), which are discussed in Chapters 17 and 18.

Simulation and Scenario Analysis

One weakness of both funding gaps and duration gaps is the assumption that assets and liabilities remain the same after an interest rate rise or fall. In reality, with a fall in rates, for instance, loan customers may prepay their fixed loans and refinance at

Table 16.3   ✦   PANEL A: EARNINGS AND ECONOMIC EXPOSURE TO CHANGES IN INTEREST RATES—MARCH 31, 1997

1997 NET INCOME				1998 NET INCOME				PRESENT VALUE EQUITY		
Change in Basis Points	Net Income	% Change		Change in Basis Points	Net Income	% Change		Change in Basis Points	Net Income	% Change
−200	947,285	−9.73%		−200	1,049,435	−17.42%		−200	8,229,473	−4.13%
−150	974,583	−7.13%		−150	1,093,400	−13.96%		−150	8,342,986	−2.81%
−100	1,002,811	−4.44%		−100	1,156,205	−9.01%		−100	8,454,402	−1.51%
−50	1,030,674	−1.79%		−50	1,219,582	−4.03%		−50	8,555,311	−0.33%
0	1,049,407	0.00%		0	1,270,749	0.00%		0	8,583,900	0.00%
50	1,090,599	3.93%		50	1,353,001	6.47%		50	8,698,321	1.33%
100	1,130,970	7.77%		100	1,417,080	11.52%		100	8,809,193	2.62%
150	1,169,383	11.43%		150	1,474,793	16.06%		150	8,900,457	3.69%
200	1,207,417	15.06%		200	1,531,015	20.48%		200	8,982,353	4.64%

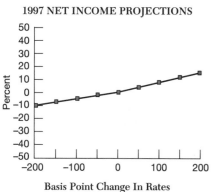

1997 NET INCOME PROJECTIONS

Basis Point Change In Rates

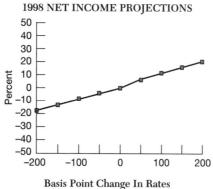

1998 NET INCOME PROJECTIONS

Basis Point Change In Rates

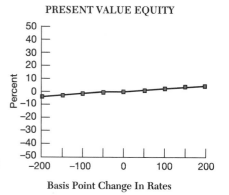

PRESENT VALUE EQUITY

Basis Point Change In Rates

PANEL B: CURRENT EXPOSURE / RISK LIMIT ANALYSIS—MARCH 31, 1997

Net Interest Income Exposure	
Current Rolling 12 Month NII Exposure (−200 bp)	6.1%
Current Net Interest Income Limit	N/A
Exposure to Limit Ratio	N/A

Present Value Equity Exposure	
Current Present Value Equity Exposure (−200 bp)	4.1%
Current Present Value Equity Limit	N/A
Exposure to Limit Ratio	N/A

Income Exposure Analysis

EXPOSURE TO FALLING RATES

	Base Case	−200 bp	Exposure
Net Interest Income	3,777,812	3,548,569	6.1%
Net Income	1,175,915	1,022,323	13.1%
ROA	1.89%	1.65%	13.0%
ROE	16.70%	14.66%	12.2%

Present Value Equity Exposure Analysis

1) The change in economic value, given a 200 basis point change in rate	354,427
2) The change in economic value as a percentage of total assets.	0.58%
3) The change in economic value as a percentage of total market value equity.	4.13%
4) Pre-shock present value ratio: Present value equity as a percentage of present value assets.	13.99%
5) Post-shock (200 bp) present value ratio: Post shock present value equity as a percentage of present value assets.	13.42%
6) Change in present value ratio (#4 - #5).	0.58%

their bank or with another bank. Thus, the bank's mix of loans may change considerable if rates fall significantly. Similarly, deposit customers may withdraw funds from CDs and be willing to take withdrawal penalties to be able to reinvest funds in higher-yielding assets when rates rise. However, with static duration and funding gap measures, mix and volume changes in assets and liabilities are not considered.

Hence, most depository institutions use simulation or scenario analysis packages that consider mix and volume changes in assets and liabilities and changes in the institution's net interest margin under different scenarios. Sheshunoff, for instance, has such a package.[27] Similarly, regulators ask institutions to perform such an analysis with the interest rate sensitivity (S) component of their regulatory CAMELS rating (Capital, Assets, Management Quality, Earnings, and Liquidity). Table 16.3 shows such an interest rate scenario analysis. Note that net income is projected, and the present value of equity for different interest rate scenarios, from −2 percent (200-basis-point fall) to a +2 percent (200-basis-point rise), is included. The lower panel quantifies the effect on return on assets and return on equity based on a 200-basis-point change in rates, along with the percentage of the value of equity relative to total assets with a 2 percent change in rates. The exposure to falling rates is shown in the bottom panel for this bank which has a positive funding gap and, hence, a negative duration gap.

SUMMARY

Managing interest rate risk is a crucial part of financial management for a financial institution. Managers need to understand interest rate risk and to have an overall method of measuring that risk. Interest rate risk can be divided into two components: reinvestment risk and market value (or price) risk. Reinvestment risk is most serious when an investor plans to hold an asset to maturity. Market value risk can be severe when an investor plans to sell an asset before maturity. Changes in market yields cause changes in market value in the opposite direction. The bond theorems further define the effect of interest rate changes on market value. The magnitude of fluctuations in value for a given change in market yields varies with the term to maturity, size of the security's coupon rate, and direction of the change in yields. The theorems hold important implications for financial institutions: In managing a given asset/liability mix, one must recognize varying degrees of sensitivity to shifts in market yields.

Equity securities are also sensitive to changes in interest rates, but the nature of the relationship is more difficult to identify. Recent research indicates an inverse relationship between shifts in interest rates and prices of common stock, so even institutions primarily involved with the management of equity portfolios are susceptible to interest rate risk.

Duration is the foundation for analyzing an investor's and a financial institution's overall exposure to both reinvestment and market price risks. It is a measure superior to contractual maturity for comparing the riskiness of debt instruments because it also captures the effects of differing coupon rates and market yields. An important property of duration is that it is directly proportional to percentage changes in asset prices that result from a change in market yields. Thus, duration can be used to calculate an investment's interest rate elasticity.

Portfolio immunization is a strategy that balances reinvestment risk and market risk to protect a portfolio from the effects of an unexpected shift in interest rates. An immunized portfolio is one with a duration equal to the planned holding period for the investment. The demand for immunization through longer-duration assets has led to the development of a new type of financial asset: the stripped Treasury security.

Duration is also used to calculate the duration gap as a comprehensive measure for the overall interest rate risk of a depository institution. The duration gap for an institution is the duration of its assets less the duration of its liabilities times the proportion of assets financed by liabilities. In contrast to the traditional funding gap measure, which considers only reinvestment (refinancing)

---

[27]Sheshunoff Information Services, Inc., Austin, Texas.

risk, the duration gap considers both reinvestment and market price risk.

Depository institutions also use scenario and simulation analysis in their analysis of interest rate risk. Scenario and simulation analysis allow for potential mix and volume changes in an institution's assets and liabilities that neither the funding nor duration gap measures include. Regulators now require institutions to specify under the S, the "sensitivity to interest" rate measure of CAMELS, what will happen to their net interest margin, net income, and market values of equity with a 200-basis-point rise or fall in rates. Sheshunoff and other private bank services offer packages for such simulations.

Questions

1. Suppose you are a bond portfolio manager for a major insurance company and are training a new assistant. Explain how the ex ante annual effective yield to maturity differs from a bond's ex post (realized) ex ante yield. Also explain under what assumptions the two are the same.
2. What are the two components of interest rate risk? If a portfolio manager has invested in 10-year bonds to be held until maturity and the proceeds expected of $1 million will be needed for a new corporate venture, explain how this position is exposed to interest rate risk.
3. A small insurance company's board of directors has asked for an explanation of the effect of interest rate changes on bond values and on the choices between high- and low-coupon bonds or between long- and short-term maturities. Based on the bond theorems, what should the directors be told about the ideal composition of a bond portfolio when market yields are rising? When they are falling?
4. Using the bond theorems, but without doing any calculations, explain which bonds would fluctuate more assuming their other characteristics are the same (high or low coupon bonds, short- or long-term maturity bonds or zero-coupon bonds) given a rise or fall in market rates of 2 percent. If rates are expected to fall, would it be better to have a longer- or shorter-term bond?
5. What is the relationship between interest rates and stock prices? Why do the bond theorems not provide a sufficient explanation of this relationship? Why do the stock prices of financial firms tend to be more affected by changes in market interest rates than other stocks?

6. In your own words, explain what duration measures are and why duration is more useful than time to maturity for evaluating the interest rate risk of an investment.
7. Under what circumstances are the duration of a bond and its contractual maturity the same? Why?
8. How can a security's interest rate elasticity be calculated by using its duration? Explain what a security's interest rate elasticity is. What is modified duration, and how is it used?
9. What are the limitations of duration? What adjustments can be made for these? What is the property of convexity for bonds?
10. How can duration be used to immunize a fixed-income bond portfolio? Explain how a given rate of return is locked in. Why will a maturity matching strategy not work in terms of immunizing a portfolio from interest rate risk?
11. The bond portfolio manager of a small life insurance company emphasizes immunization as a primary goal. Explain whether the manager is following a hedging or a profit-maximizing approach. Identify the limitations that prevent immunization from providing total protection against interest rate risk. What is a dedicated portfolio? When is a dedicated portfolio useful?
12. What are STRIPS? Why are STRIPS and zero-coupon bonds popular choices for immunized portfolios?
13. Explain the difference between a depository institution's funding gap and its duration gap. Why is the duration gap a better overall measure? How is a duration gap calculated?
14. What limitations do both funding gaps and duration gaps have in terms of changes in volume and mix in assets and liabilities for a depository institution when interest rates change? How can simulation and scenario analysis provide a depository institution with a better picture of its overall interest rate risk?
15. Explain the options available to managers for restructuring the balance sheet under either funding gap or duration gap immunization. What are the advantages and disadvantages of each? How do customers' preferences influence a depository institution's ability to manage its gap?
16. For an institution with a positive funding gap (negative duration gap) that uses using active GAP management (adjusting the gap to make larger profits when interest rates rise or fall), what adjustments should managers make under expectations of declining rates? under expectations of rising rates?
17. Explain how a depository institution's efforts to manage interest rate sensitivity through the loan portfolio might also affect its profits and default risk exposure. If you were a depository institution manager, would you try to achieve a zero gap for the institution? Why or why not?

Problems

1. Your broker, Sue Tracy has brought three bond portfolios to your attention. Each has
   a. annual interest payments, a 9 percent rate, and a par value of $1,000. The portfolios differ in that they are for 10-, 20-, and 30-year bonds. Calculate and compare the change in values in each of the bonds with a fall in rates from 9 percent to 6 percent.

2. Hostess International Corporation issued zero-coupon bonds 10 years ago with an initial time to maturity of 25 years and a par value of $1,000. Today, 10 years later, you can buy one of these bonds for 23.455.
   a. What yield to maturity $(y°)$ is the market expecting on the bonds today?
   b. What will the percentage change in price in the bond be if market yields rise to 14 percent immediately after you buy the bonds?
   c. Explain why a zero-coupon bond is particularly exposed to market price risk but not reinvestment risk if it must be sold prior to maturity.

3. You purchase a 13.5 percent coupon rate bond with annual interest payments and a market value of $1,170, par value of $1,000, and yield to maturity of 10.49 percent and plan to hold it for nine years when it matures. If market yields change just after you buy the bond and fall drastically to 8 percent, what will be your ex post (realized) annual return on the investment? Explain why the realized yield is lower than the expected yield to maturity when you bought the bond.

4. Your father is preparing for his 25th wedding anniversary celebration. He wants to have $5,000 on July 1, 2010, and has set up an annuity to reach that goal. He will invest $869.46 on July 1 of each of five years from 2006 to 2010 and estimates that he will earn an average annual yield of 7 percent.
   a. Show that if market yields of 7 percent prevail, your father will reach his investment goal of $5,000 by July 1, 2010.
   b. Suppose that market yields drop to 5 percent immediately after the first $869.46 investment and that they remain there until July 1, 2010. Calculate the future value of the investment and realized return. What type of risk does this problem demonstrate?

5. Calculate the duration of the following bonds with $1,000 par values, annual interest payments, and $y° = 8$ percent to determine which bond has the most interest rate risk:
   a. 6 percent coupon rate, three years to maturity, market price = $94.846
   b. 10 percent coupon rate, two years to maturity, market price = $103.567
   c. 14 percent coupon rate, five years to maturity, market price = $123.956

6. A bond mutual fund manager is considering adding two bonds to the portfolio: (a) a 4 percent coupon rate bond trading at 85 and (b) a 5 percent coupon rate bond trading at 94. Both bonds have nine years remaining until maturity, annual interest payments, and a par value of $1,000. Calculate the duration of each bond and its elasticity. Which bond has greater interest rate risk?

7. As a new analyst for a large insurance firm's investment division, you have been assigned to assist the firm's asset/liability management committee. Durations are calculated for all assets to evaluate risk.
   a. As your first assignment, estimate duration and interest rate elasticities for the following corporate real estate loans ($y° = 9$ percent):
   1. $10,000, five-year amortized loan with a 9 percent annual interest rate
   2. $10,000, five-year loan with a 9 percent annual interest rate. This loan is not amortized. It pays interest only at the end of each year and then the $10,000 principal at the end of year 5.
   Which loan has more interest rate risk? Why?

8. Suppose you need to earn 7.18 percent on your investment portfolio of $100,000 each year to reach a goal of $200,049 in 10 years. You have a choice between the following bonds with annual coupon payments:
   a. 7.18 percent coupon bond that matures in 10 years, with $1,000 par value, selling at par value now (i.e., $y° = 7.18$ percent).
   b. 7.18 percent coupon bond that matures in 16 years, with $1,000 par value, also selling at par value now (i.e., $y° = 7.18$ percent).
   c. 7.18 percent zero-coupon bond that matures in 10 years.
   Find the duration for each bond. Also find the realized annual yield that you would earn under each strategy if rates fall to 6 percent after you purchased the bond and remain at 6 percent for the next 10 years. Which strategies would be appropriate to immunize your annual 7.18 percent return, regardless of what interest rates do? Explain why.

9. Texas Independence Bank has the following balance sheet in millions:

Assets		Liabilities and Equity	
3-year fixed rate loans (9%)	$35	Demand Deposits (0%)	$12
30-year fixed rate mortgages (10%)	11	Fed Funds Purchased (7%)	30
Land and Buildings	4	Equity	8
Total Assets	$50	Total Liabilities and Equity	$50

a. What is the bank's expected NII next year?

b. What is its one-year funding gap? How large is this gap relative to assets? Without doing any calculations but looking at the maturity of assets and liabilities, decide whether the bank has a positive or negative duration gap.

c. Assuming Fed Funds Purchased have an average 0.50 (half a year duration), and demand deposits a 0 duration, what is the duration of the bank's liabilities?

d. Suppose both the three-year and 30-year loans are amortized loans. Find their annual loan payments and durations (assume $y° =$ the rate given for each loan). Assuming the land and buildings have 0 duration, what is the duration of the bank's assets, and what is the bank's duration gap?

e. If interest rates rise 1 percent over the year, what will be the effect on NII and net interest margin?

Based on the bank's duration gap, what will be the effect on the value of assets relative to the value of liabilities and the value of the bank's equity?

10. A balance sheet analysis and the average duration of each account for the Blumberg Savings Bank is shown in the following table:

THE BLUMBERG SAVINGS BANK
BALANCE SHEET ANALYSIS (MILS.)

Assets		Liabilities and Net Worth	
Short-term securities and adjustable-rate loans; Duration: 3 months	$210	Short-term and floating-rate funds Duration: 1 month	$580
Fixed-rate loans		Fixed-rate funds:	
Duration: 8 years	650	Duration: 35 months	280
Nonearning assets	80	Core capital (net worth)	80
Total Assets	$940	Total liabilities and net worth	$940

---

a. Calculate the bank's duration of assets and liabilities and its duration gap.

b. Currently, the average rate or return on assets is 10 percent. If the general level of interest rates increases by 1 percent, how much will the value of the bank's net worth change?

c. Suppose that the expected change in the value of net worth is unacceptable to management. Suggest several actions that could be taken to counteract this expected change. What are the advantages and disadvantages of each action?

d. Show the effect on the bank's capital if interest rates fall by 1 percent instead.

11. The Sofia National Bank has the following balance sheet (in mils):

Assets		Liabilities and Net Worth	
Short-term securities and adjustable-rate loans; Duration: 3 months	$660	Short-term and floating-rate funds Duration: 1 month	$210
Fixed-rate loans		Fixed-rate funds:	
Duration: 8 years	220	Duration: 35 months	650
Nonearning assets	80	Core capital (net worth)	80
Total Assets	$940	Total liabilities and net worth	$940

---

a. Calculate Sofia's duration gap.

b. If the average rate on Sofia's assets is 10 percent and the general level of interest rates increases by 100 basis points (1 percent), by how much will Sofia's net worth change? If you were the bank manager, would you be pleased with this result? Why?

c. Now suppose that interest rates fell sharply by 300 basis points. By how much will Sofia's net worth change? If you were Sofia's manager, would be pleased with this result? Why?

d. Notice that Sofia National's assets and net worth are identical to the assets and net worth of the Blumberg Savings Bank in the previous problem, as are the durations of both institutions' assets and liabilities. Compare the results for the two banks. Can you see why managing institutions with large positive duration gaps can be stressful?

12. Consider the Mardi Gras National Bank's balance sheet:

THE MARDI GRAS NATIONAL BANK

Assets	Rate	Liabilities and Equity		Rate
Cash	$441.67	Demand Deposits	$2,000	
Consumer		CDs		
Loans	$4,814.55	0.10	$12,000	0.08
Commercial				
Loans	$9,743.78	Equity	$1,000	
Total Assets	$15,000	Total Liabilities and Equity	$15,000	

Each of the loans are amortized loans that have equal payments of principal and interest each period. The consumer loans pay $2,774.10 per year for two years, and the commercial loans pay $2,570.92 per year for five years.

On the liability side, the CDs have a one-year maturity and pay principal of $12,000 and the annual interest payment at maturity in one year.

a. Calculate the duration of each of the assets and liabilities.
b. Calculate Mardi Gras Bank's duration of assets, duration of liabilities, and duration gap and the expected change in the value of equity if rates rise by 1 percent.
c. How could the bank reduce its duration gap? What would be the effect on profits?

Selected References

Bae, Sung C. "Interest Rate Changes and Common Stock Returns of Financial Institutions: Revisited." *Journal of Financial Research* 13 (Spring 1990), 71–79.

Becketti, Sean. "The Role of Stripped Securities in Portfolio Management." *Economic Review* (Federal Reserve Bank of Kansas City) 73 (May 1988), 20–31.

Benesh, Gary A., and Stephen E. Celec. "A Simplified Approach for Calculating Bond Duration." *Financial Review* 19 (November 1984), 394–396.

Bierwag, Gerald O. *Duration Analysis.* Cambridge, Massachusetts: Ballinger Publishing Co. 1987.

Bierwag, Gerald O., George G. Kaufman, and Alden Toevs. "Bond Portfolio Immunization and Stochastic Process Risk." *Journal of Bank Research* 13 (Winter 1983), 282–291.

Bisignano, Joseph, and Brian Dvorak. "Risk and Duration." *Weekly Letter* (Federal Reserve Bank of San Francisco) (April 3, 1981).

Caks, John, et al. "A Simple Formula for Duration." *Journal of Financial Research* 8 (Fall 1985), 245–249.

Christie, Andrew A. "The Stochastic Behavior of Common Stock Variances: Value, Leverage, and Interest Rate Effects." *Journal of Financial Economics* 5 (December 1981), 407–432.

Chua, Jess B. "A Closed-Form Formula for Calculating Bond Duration." *Financial Analysts Journal* 40 (May-June 1984), 76–78.

Dietz, Peter O., H. Russell Fogler, and Anthony U. Rivers. "Duration, Non-Linearity, and Bond-Portfolio Performance." *Journal of Portfolio Management* 7 (Spring 1981), 37–41.

Fabozzi, Frank J. *Bond Markets, Analysis and Strategies*, 2d ed. Englewood Cliffs, N.J.: Prentice-Hall, Inc., 1993.

Fisher, Lawrence. "An Algorithm for Finding Exact Rates of Return." *Journal of Business* 39 (January 1966), 111–118.

Fisher, Lawrence, and Roman Weil. "Coping with the Risk of Interest Rate Fluctuation: Returns to Bondholders from Naive and Optimal Strategies." *Journal of Business* 44 (October 1971), 408–431.

Flannery, Mark J. and Christopher M. James. "The Effect of Interest Rate Changes on the Common Stock Returns of Financial Institutions." *Journal of Finance* 39 (September 1984), 1141–1153.

Fogler, Russell H. "Bond Portfolio Immunization, Inflation, and the Fisher Equation." *Journal of Risk and Insurance* 51 (June 1984), 244–264.

Gregory, Deborah W., and Miles Livingston. "Development of the Market for U.S. Treasury Strips." *Financial Analysts Journal* 48 (March-April 1992), 68–74.

Hempel, George H., Donald G. Simonson, and Alan B. Coleman. *Bank Management: Text and Cases*, 4th ed. New York: John Wiley & Sons, 1995.

Hess, Alan C. "Duration Analysis for Savings and Loan Associations." *Federal Home Loan Bank Board Journal* 15 (October 1982), 12–14.

Hicks, J. R. *Value and Capital.* Oxford: Clarendon Press, 1939.

Hopewell, Michael C., and George G. Kaufman. "Bond Price Volatility and Term to Maturity: A Generalized Respecification." *American Economic Review* 63 (September 1973), 749–753.

Kaufman, George G. "Measuring and Managing Interest Rate Risk: A Primer." *Economic Perspectives* (Federal Reserve Bank of Chicago) 8 (January/February 1984), 16–29.

Kaufman, George G., G. O. Bierwag, and Alden Toevs, eds. *Innovations in Bond Portfolio Management: Duration Analysis and Immunization.* Greenwich, Conn.: JAI Press, 1983.

Koch, Timothy W. *Bank Management,* 3rd Edition. Fort Worth, TX: Harcourt Brace, 1995.

Leibowitz, Martin L. "Bond Immunization: A Procedure for Realizing Target Levels of Return." In *Financial Markets: Instruments and Concepts,* ed. John R. Brick. Richmond, Va.: Robert F. Dame, 1981, pp. 443–454.

Leibowitz, Martin L. "Financial Theory Evolves into the Real World-or Not: The Case of Duration and Immunization." *Financial Review* 18 (November 1983), 271–280.

Leibowitz, Martin, et al. "A Total Differential Approach to Equity Duration." *Financial Analysts Journal* 45 (September/October 1989), 30–37.

Livingston, Miles, and Deborah Wright Gregory. *The Stripping of U.S. Treasury Securities.* New York: Salomon Brothers Center for the Study of Financial Institutions, 1989.

Macaulay, Frederick R. *Some Theoretical Problems Suggested by the Movements of Interest Rates, Bond Yields, and Stock Prices in the U.S. since 1856.* New York: National Bureau of Economic Research, 1938.

Malkiel, Burton, G. "Expectations, Bond Prices, and the Term Structure of Interest Rates." *Quarterly Journal of Economics* 76 (May 1962), 197–218.

Moser, James T., and James T. Lindley. "A Simple Formula for Duration: An Extension." *Financial Review* 24 (November 1989), 611–615.

Neuberger, Jonathan A. "Bank Holding Company Stock Risk and the Composition of Bank Asset Portfolios." *Economic Review* (Federal Reserve Bank of San Francisco) 3 (1992), 53–62.

Ott, Robert A., Jr. "Duration Analysis and Minimizing Interest Rate Risk." In *Managing Interest Rate Risk: Selected Readings.* Atlanta: Federal Home Loan Bank of Atlanta, 1988, pp. 31–34.

Reilly, Frank K., and Rupinder S. Sidhu. "The Many Uses of Bond Duration." *Financial Analysts Journal* 36 (July-August 1980), 58–72.

Rosenberg, Joel L. "The Joys of Duration." *Bankers Magazine* 169 (March-April 1986), 62–67.

Samuelson, Paul. "The Effects of Interest Rate Increases on the Banking System." *American Economic Review* 35 (March 1945), 16–27.

Saunders, Anthony. *Financial Institutions Management: A Modern Perspective,* 2d ed. Burr Ridge, Ill.: Irwin, 1997.

Scott, William L., and Richard L. Peterson. "Interest Rate Risk and Equity Values of Hedged and Unhedged Financial Intermediaries." *Journal of Financial Research* 9 (Winter 1986), 325–329.

Sherlock, Patricia M., and Le In Chen. "Stripped Mortgage Backed Securities: The Sum Is Greater than the Parts." *Mortgage Banking* 47 (June 1987), 61–68.

Smith, Donald J. "The Duration of a Bond as a Price Elasticity and as a Fulcrum." *Journal of Financial Education* 17 (Fall 1988), 26–38.

Sweeney, Richard J. and Arthur D. Warga. "The Pricing of Interest Rate Risk: Evidence from the Stock Market." *Journal of Finance* 41 (June 1986), 393–410.

Weil, Roman L. "Macaulay's Duration: An Appreciation." *Journal of Business* 46 (October 1973), 589–592.

Yawitz, Jess B. "The Relative Importance of Duration and Yield Volatility on Bond Price Volatility." *Journal of Money, Credit, and Banking* 9 (February 1977), 97–102.

Chapter 16 Internet Exercise

Interest Rate Risk Measurement and Immunization Using Duration

The Olson Research site provides a Risk Measurement Digest for banks. (http://www.olsonresearch.com), including information on interest rate risk, liquidity risk, asset quality risk, capital adequacy, earnings performance, and balance sheet mix. The data are analyzed in multiple ways. The site provides a full explanation of the data, the bank samples, methodologies and assumptions utilized, as well as Treasury yield curves.

The site also allows you to do your own analysis of risk measurement for an individual bank for data that they provide.

1. Go to: http://www.olsonresearch.com/RMD963Q/detailbankinfo.htm.

2. You must download the detailed bank information in Microsoft Excel format (or Adobe PDF format). The file is saved as Excel version 5.0.

The site of the Chicago Mercantile Exchange provides a wealth of educational resources. At the Chicago Mercantile Exchange Library you can find the Daily Futures News Index: http://www.cme.com/educational/library/: This is a chronological list of news items relating to the futures market.

The CME Strategy and Research Papers can be found at: http://www.cme.com/educational/papers.html. These are research papers in either HTML or Adobe Portable Document Format on the following topics: interest rates, indices, currencies, emerging markets, or institutional. For example, in the institutional category you will find papers on topics such as futures and options trading for pension plans, derivatives, hedge funds, and European Union regulations.

The Bank for International Settlements site (http://www.bis.org) provides a number of useful publications. Especially important are those authored by the BIS standing committees such as the Basle Committee on Banking Supervision, the Committee on Payment and Settlement Systems, and the Euro-currency Standing Committee. The publications are available in either HTML or Adobe Portable Document Format. For example, the Committee on Banking Supervision has policy pieces on public disclosure of derivatives activities of banks and securities firms, the supervision of financial conglomerates, operational risk management, and enhancing bank transparency.

Useful Links

Finance Sites:
http://www.cob.ohio-state.edu/~fin/journal/jofsites.htm#edres

Chicago Mercantile Exchange
http://www.cme.com/

17

INTEREST RATE RISK MANAGEMENT: INTEREST RATES AND FOREIGN CURRENCY FUTURES

Professor Merton Miller, winner of the Nobel Prize for financial economics and recognized for his contributions to the development of financial futures, commented to a Chicago Tribune reporter on the innovations in the financial markets. Miller believes that the wonderment of Rip Van Winkle as he awoke after 20 years would pale in comparison with the astonishment felt by a banker or financial services professional who fell asleep in 1970 and awoke in the 1990s to the radically changed financial environment. In fact, the rapidity with which new markets and instruments are introduced is challenging even to those who are wide awake!

In 1992, the futures markets embraced another major technological innovation. In a joint venture, the Chicago Board of Trade (CBOT) and the Chicago Mercantile Exchange (CME) inaugurated Globex, a computerized futures trading system designed to link futures markets around the world with 24-hour trading. As the first bid and offer popped onto his screen, a trader in New York described the system as similar to a video game, except with real money involved. But Globex is *very different from the chaos of the "live" trading pits, and some participants found it challenging to remain alert all night. Experts predicted a more exciting environment with increased volume and market participants, but some European traders were less than excited about the prospect of being asked to work the "graveyard shift." Nonetheless, computer screen-based systems have also rapidly developed in Europe for derivatives, including the German-Swiss exchange Eurex.[1]*

Although 24-hour markets may require some schedule adjustments for traders, no one doubts that automation and globalization will continue to bring changes to the financial markets and will make the futures markets an ever more integral part of every financial manager's daily environment. In fact, in a complex economic environment, financial institutions and their managers need complex strategies; and duration, discussed in Chapter 16, is only one of many essential risk management techniques.

Other risk management techniques that are explored in this chapter and Chapter 18 include financial futures contracts and options on financial futures. All are relatively new; for example, the interest rate futures

contract was created in 1975 at the CBOT, and stock index futures began trading in 1982. Since the introduction of futures and options, financial institutions have recognized their potential for improving asset/liability management. This chapter focuses on interest rate and foreign currency futures.

Futures are not without their own risks. The inherent dangers have attracted the attention of regulators and legislators and in some cases have resulted in restrictions on their use by financial institutions. A number of financial institutions, including Banc One and Bankers Trust, had large losses associated with the use of derivatives in the early 1990s. Scandals were also associated with derivatives for Orange County, California, and Barings, Inc., in London. Futures have also presented some new financial reporting problems. In 1990, in response to early concerns, the Financial Accounting Standards Board (FASB) issued FAS 105, which requires firms and financial institutions to disclose their exposure in derivative instruments.[2] Thus, the integration of futures into asset/liability management has, by necessity, moved somewhat slowly, with the largest institutions often serving as the trend setters.

♦ ♦ ♦

---

[1]*Chicago Tribune* (January 20, 1992), Section 4, 1, 2; William B. Crawford, Jr. "Globex Takes Off." *Chicago Tribune* (June 26, 1992), Section 3, 1, 3. Terzah Ewing. "'Open-Outcry' Trading Faces Threat from Electronic Rivals." *The Wall Street Journal* (December 24, 1998), C1.

[2]For a summary of the Orange County crisis, see Keith Sill. "The Economic Benefits and Risks of Derivative Securities." *Federal Reserve Bank of Philadelphia Business Review* (January/February 1997), 15–25. The Orange County Investment Pool (OCIP) for Orange County, California, had losses amounting eventually to $1.7 billion, resulting in the county declaring bankruptcy. OCIP's losses were largely the result of bad bets on interest rates staying the same or falling, whereby the fund would profit by borrowing short-term funds at a low rate to buy higher yielding long-term bonds. When interest rates rose in 1994, this strategy resulted in severe losses in the value of bonds and higher short-term borrowing costs. OCIP also invested in interest rate derivative securities called inverse floaters, which gain value when interest rates fall and lose value when they rise.

For a summary of Banc One Corporation's use of derivatives in the mid-1980s to early 1990s, see Esty, Tufano, and Headley (1994). Banc One suffered a steep decline in its stock price in 1993. Chief executive officer John B. McCoy attributed this decline to investor concern over Banc One's large and growing interest rate derivatives portfolio, which, ironically, was intended to hedge the bank's overall interest rate risk.

See Chaudhry and Reichert (1998) for a summary of FASB concerns. FASB recommends that firms and institutions provide detailed information regarding the specific transactions for which risk is being hedged but contains no specific guidelines identifying the degree of risk inherent in various types of derivative activities.

Financial Institutions and Financial Futures

Although financial futures have received a great deal of attention, in 1987 only about 400 U.S. commercial banks, of more than 13,000, actually held a position in the interest rate futures market. As Carter and Sinkey (1998) point out, however, by mid-1997, the notational amount of derivatives held by all commercial banks was a phenomenal $15.8 trillion, with banks holding almost 68 percent of the $23.3 trillion total derivatives outstanding. The amount of derivatives held by banks in mid-1997 was also four times the industry's total assets. However, 25 very large banks held 98.6 percent of the total bank-held derivatives and 98.1 percent of the interest-rate derivatives. These 25 very large banks also are involved in market making or brokering derivatives. Medium-sized banks' increased in the 1990s, but only for about 279 large community banks, with interest rate derivatives used by only about 250 banks per year. The relatively low level of participation can be partially traced to unfavorable regulatory and accounting rules for futures. Carter and Sinkey's study examining the use of derivatives by banks with total assets between $100 million and $1 billion from 1990 to 1993 also shows that better capitalized banks tend to use some types of derivatives (interest rate swaps), which suggests that market and/or regulatory discipline have some effect on assuring that end users of derivatives are well capitalized. Carter and Sinkey also find the use of derivatives to be positively related to an institution's interest-rate risk, indicating that medium-sized banks use derivatives to hedge this risk.[3]

Data on nonbank financial institutions' use of financial futures are sparser. Research from the 1980s suggests that some members of the thrift, life insurance, and pension fund industries participated in the futures markets. As is true in the commercial banking industry, the evidence indicates that large institutions are the major players.[4]

Futures Contracts

Futures contracts on agricultural products have existed for more than a century; the first organized market for them was the CBOT, also the birthplace of the interest rate futures contract in October 1975. The International Monetary Market, a branch of the CME, introduced the first financial futures contracts on foreign currencies in 1972.[5]

---

[3]See Carter and Sinkey (1998). Also, see Jeffery W. and Thomas F. Siems. "Who's Capitalizing on Derivatives?" *Federal Reserve Bank of Dallas Financial Industry Studies* (July 1995), 1–8. This study of banks from 1991 to 1994 finds derivative usage among U.S. banking organizations to be surprisingly low. The authors suggest that a primary reason may be the large amount of intellectual and reputational capital required to develop and maintain a knowledgeable trading function. They also find that banks with the highest capital ratios use derivatives to the greatest extent.

[4]See Koppenhaver (1990); Booth, Smith, and Stolz (1984); Hurtz and Gardner (1984); Lamm-Tennant (1989); and Hoyt (1992).

[5]For details on the birth of the first financial futures contract at the International Monetary Market, see Miller (1986).

Futures Contracts Defined

A *futures contract* is a commitment to buy or sell a specific commodity of designated quality at a specified price and date in the future (the delivery date). The specified price is an estimate of the commodity price that is expected to prevail at that future time. A distinguishing feature of futures trading is that the two sides of a futures contract do not trade directly with one another but, rather, with a clearinghouse. This feature of futures markets is explained in more detail later in the chapter.

A commodity may fall into one of many categories; the number continues to expand in these innovative markets. However, five categories, three of which are financial, include the vast majority of commodities on which contracts are traded: agricultural products, metallurgical products, interest-bearing assets, stock indexes and other market indexes, and foreign currencies. The last two, although not specifically focused on interest rate risk, have emerged as tools of asset/liability management for some institutions. Foreign currency futures are discussed later in this chapter and stock index futures in Chapter 18.

Hedging Versus Speculation

One reason that futures contracts developed is to avoid risk. Wheat or soybean farmers can use futures agreements to reduce uncertainty about the prices they will receive for their products. A grower, by agreeing through a futures contract to deliver a certain amount of wheat at a specified future date and price, avoids exposure to unfavorable price movements during the intervening period. Thus, futures contracts, like immunization (discussed in Chapter 16), can be used to hedge, or minimize, risk.

On the other side of the farmer's contract may be a **speculator**, someone willing to accept the risk of price fluctuations with the intention of profiting from them. The counterparty to the farmer could also be a hedger who needs the farmer's wheat at the designated time and is minimizing the risk that wheat will be in short supply at the time. Alternatively, both parties in a futures contract could be speculators, each hoping to profit from price fluctuations.

Thus, the distinction between hedging and speculation comes not from the side of a futures contract one takes but from the motivation for entering into the contract. With few exceptions, because of regulatory limitations, financial institutions use the financial futures markets only for hedging.

Financial Futures Contracts

In a financial futures contract, the underlying commodity promised for future delivery is one of three financial commodities: an interest-bearing asset, a stock or bond index, or a foreign currency. Since 1972, contracts on many financial assets have been introduced with varying levels of success. For example, contracts on Treasury bills (T-bills) have been widely accepted, but futures contracts on commercial paper were tried without success. Interest-bearing or discount securities on which contracts written include T-bills, Treasury notes (T-notes), Treasury bonds (T-bonds), and Eurodollar deposits, among others. The instruments span the entire yield curve, giving managers important flexibility.

Role of the Clearinghouse   All trading is conducted through the **clearinghouse** of each exchange. In effect, the clearinghouse acts as a buyer to every seller and a seller to every buyer; it does not simply match buy and sell orders. This procedure eliminates the need for direct contact between traders. The clearinghouse guarantees the performance of the contract and, instead of the seller, assumes responsibility for the creditworthiness of buyers. The willingness of participants to rely on the financial stability of the clearinghouse is an important characteristic of the futures markets, and the fact that the clearinghouses have so far consistently performed as promised testifies to the validity of their role. At the end of each trading day, the clearinghouse settles all accounts, paying profits earned by some traders and collecting payments due from others.

Because the contracts are standardized and default risk is assumed by the clearinghouse, the original owner of a futures contract can easily offset or cancel the contract before its delivery date. Few financial futures contracts (less than 2 percent) are carried to an actual physical transfer of assets, and traders make an offsetting trade to close out their positions rather than delivering or accepting the commodity.[6] The bookkeeping and associated transactions are handled by the exchange clearinghouse.

If the commodity is an agricultural product, movements in the market price of the product affect the contract value. If the commodity is a T-bill, a change in short-term interest rates affects the price of bills in the spot market and also affects the value of a T-bill contract. Similarly, the value of bond futures contracts is tied to changes in long-term yields.

The standardization of futures contracts allows the market to function efficiently. For interest rate futures, the contract size, maturity, and (except for discount securities) coupon rate are predetermined to facilitate efficient trading. For example, a T-bill contract is traded in a standard size of $1 million, based only on a 90-day maturity. T-bond futures contracts are standardized at $100,000 with an 8 percent coupon. The contract size is the face value of the underlying securities.

THE DEVELOPING GLOBAL MARKETPLACE

The rapid growth in the volume of futures contract trading on the exchanges in Chicago has not gone unnoticed in other countries. In the 1980s, in fact, international markets for trading futures and other risk management securities opened in strategic locations around the world; at least 18 have originated since 1985. These newer exchanges include the **London International Financial Futures Exchange (LIFFE)**, the **Marché a Terme International de France (MATIF)**, the **Tokyo International Financial Futures Exchange (TIFFE)**, and the **Sydney Futures Exchange (SFE)**. The **Deutsche Terminbourse (DTB)** opened in Frankfurt in 1990, along with futures exchanges in Austria, Belgium, and Italy; other exchanges opened in Asia in the mid- and later 1990s. Many recent exchanges have developed as electronic, computer-based systems versus the more traditional "open outcry" trading of the CBOT, the CME, and the relatively high-tech Chicago Board Options Exchange. The all-electronic German-Swiss exchange Eurex, for example, has been highly successful, managing to take a high volume of futures contracts on the German bund away from its "open outcry" counterpart in London. Even the CME has moved somewhat electronically with one contract, the Standard & Poor's

---

[6]The Chicago Board of Trade. *A Guide to Financial Futures at the Chicago Board of Trade,* 29.

500 index future, which trades electronically "24 hours per day" on the CME's Globex 2 system.[7]

Several of the international exchanges, in addition to offering more automated trading methods than the U.S. exchanges, also offer greater flexibility. For example, LIFFE allows traders to settle their positions in a variety of currencies, whereas the Chicago markets are almost entirely dollar-based. Market participants responded favorably to this flexibility, and by 1992, the volume of financial futures trading in Europe was beginning to challenge the dominance of the Chicago markets.

For the most part, expert observers view the emergence of these new markets as a positive development for market participants. The increased competition across international borders has brought the exchanges under pressure to control transaction costs, making futures trading more efficient for participants. Traders can now participate in more than one market simultaneously and enjoy greater liquidity and longer trading hours. In addition, the new exchanges are highly automated and are setting new standards for the use of technology in futures trading.

The growth of these international markets was one of the motivating factors behind the 's creation of Globex. As noted in the opening paragraphs of this chapter, Globex is to be a 24-hour, computerized trading network. Traders in London, Paris, New York, and Chicago can transmit buy and sell orders for most of the popular interest rate and foreign currency futures contracts to each other in seconds. However, although many futures market professionals view Globex as a system with great potential, they acknowledge that its debut has been disappointing. The average daily volume of trading on the system during its first six months was less than 1 percent of the average daily volume on the CBOT or CME. Activity was so low, in fact, that some brokerage firms discontinued their involvement, citing the high cost of 24-hour trading and low customer interest. Globex suffered further from technical problems that halted trading entirely several times in its early months. Nevertheless, some firms remained loyal and indicated a commitment to stay involved. Hopes remain that Globex will eventually constitute a truly global, 24-hour market that will lower trading costs, despite the fact that currently electronic orders are still a small percentage of trading orders filled on both the CME and CBOT.

Besides the advantages noted previously, futures market expansion carries increased risks, most notably the potential for problems in the clearing process. Although all international futures exchanges have clearinghouses, the settlement of claims may involve counterparties operating under different legal and payment systems. In the view of most experts, however, the increased opportunities clearly outweigh the additional risk exposure.[8]

---

[7]Terzah Ewing. "'Open-Outcry' Trading Faces Threat from Electronic Rivals." *The Wall Street Journal* (December 24, 1998), C1.

[8]For more information on the development of international markets, see Remolona (1992–1993); Napoli (1992); Scarlata (1992); Abken (1991); David Greising. "Has Chicago Lost Its Edge?" *Business Week* (March 9, 1992), 76–78; William B. Crawford, Jr. "London's Exchange to Sign On to Globex." *Chicago Tribune* (September 28, 1992), Section 4, 1, 2; Jeffery Taylor. "Globex System Is Vexed by Low Trading Volume, Overseas Competition, and Technology Glitches." *The Wall Street Journal* (December 14, 1992), C1; Peter J. W. Elstrom. "Sleepy Globex May Start Trading Earlier." *Crain's Chicago Business* (January 18, 1993), 3.

CHARACTERISTICS OF FINANCIAL FUTURES TRANSACTIONS

Financial futures markets have several unique features, as explained in the following sections.

The Margin   Futures traders are required to post an initial margin to support their positions. The margin serves as a deposit in good faith. It may be in the form of cash, a bank letter of credit, or short-term Treasury securities. The margin required is quite small in comparison with the face value of the securities underlying the financial futures contract; the initial deposit is often no more than 5 percent of the contract face value. The margin is set by the exchange; it depends on the type of contract and whether the trader is a hedger or speculator. The price volatility of the underlying instrument is an influencing factor on the margin: The higher the volatility in the underlying instrument, the higher the margin.[9]

    At the end of each day, the clearinghouse requires a trader to settle the account; if there are losses on a given day, they are charged against the trader's margin account. If the charges reduce the account to a balance below the required minimum, the trader must immediately produce additional cash. Futures trading involves some cash flow on every trading day, and many observers believe that the daily resettlement makes the futures markets much safer than they would be otherwise. The daily resettlement or "mark to market" is also viewed as a justification for the relatively small initial cash required to trade contracts with a much higher face value. Nevertheless, managers of institutions trading futures contracts must manage cash carefully, because they must be ready each day to make deposits into their margin accounts.

Limits on Price Changes   To control traders' exposure to risk the exchanges set a maximum amount by which the price of a contract is allowed to change. When that limit is reached on a given day, the price cannot move farther, and subsequent trades will take place only if they are within the limits. Risk exposure still exists, however. For example, the maximum price fluctuation allowed by the CBOT on T-bond and T-note contracts is 3 percent of par value, so the price can move by as much as $3,000 on any one day. Several days of "limit moves" in a row could add up to substantial losses.

INTEREST RATE FUTURES

For most **interest rate futures contracts**, interest-bearing or discount securities are the underlying commodity. Recently, contracts based on movements in an interest rate such as the Fed funds rate have been developed. Should a trader hold such contracts to maturity, they would be settled in cash rather than by delivery of an underlying security. Because they are an important component of asset/liability management, techniques involving interest rate futures trading will be examined in detail. First, however, it is important to introduce the characteristics of contracts commonly traded by financial institutions.

---

[9]Legislation pending in Congress in late 1992 would transfer to the Federal Reserve Board the authority to set margins for some types of futures contracts. The CBOT and CME opposed the legislation containing this provision.

Terms of Selected Interest Rate Futures Contracts

As in any field in which change is the rule rather than the exception, a comprehensive list of interest rate futures contracts is virtually impossible. Undoubtedly, contracts that were unheard of—perhaps even unimagined—at the time this book was written may be traded regularly by the time it is read. Nonetheless, it is clear that certain interest rate futures contracts, such as those for Treasury securities, have had staying power over the years, and it seems reasonable to assume that they will continue to be popular. Table 17.1 summarizes features of these popular contracts as well as other cash-based instruments.

Although the importance of individual features will become clear as applications of futures in asset/liability management are presented, the table shows that interest rate futures contracts are available in a wide range of face values on underlying instruments or indexes with a variety of maturities. The table also indicates that futures contracts have standardized delivery dates in the rare event that delivery is actually made or taken. By convention, then, a contract with a delivery date of the last trading day in June is known as a "June contract." The varied features provide important flexibility for interest rate risk management in financial institutions.

Table 17.1 ✦ FEATURES OF SELECTED INTEREST RATE FUTURES CONTRACTS

Interest rate futures are available on a variety of underlying instruments. Face values and other specifications differ, and the choice of contract depends on the cash instrument to be hedged.

Name of Contract	Underlying Instrument	Face Value of Contract	Daily Price Limits	Standard Delivery Months
T-bill futures	13-week T-bills	$1 million	None	March, June, September, December
3-month Euro-dollar futures	None; settled in cash based on prevailing rate on 3-month Eurodollar time deposits	$1 million	None	March, June, September, December
T-note futures	2-year, 5-year, or 10-year T-notes	$100,000 or $200,000	Varies: 1 to 3 points	March, June, September, December
T-bond futures	8% T-bonds, minimum maturity of 15 years	$100,000	3 points ($3,000 per contract)	March, June, September, December
Municipal bond index	None; settled in cash based on Bond Buyer Municipal Bond Index	$1,000 times value of index	$3,000	March, June, September, December
30-day interest rate futures	None; settled in cash based on monthly average of daily fed funds rate	$5 million	150 basis points from previous settlement price	Every month
LIBOR[a]	None; settled in cash based on prevailing LIBOR rate on 1-month Eurodollar time deposits	$3 million	None	First 6 consecutive months, beginning with current month

Source: Adapted from Patrick J. Catania, ed., *Commodity Trading Manual* (Chicago: Chicago Board of Trade, 1989), updated by authors; Chicago Board of Trade, "30-Day Interest Rate Futures," 1992; Chicago Mercantile Exchange, "CME Interest Rate Futures," 1991.

[a]LIBOR is an acronym for the London Interbank Offered Rate, a short-term European interest rate.

Interest Rate Futures as a Hedging Device

By definition, a hedge is a position taken in the futures market to offset risk in the cash or spot market position. The preceding chapters stressed the inverse relationship between changes in market values of interest-earning assets and changes in market yields. Because the value of a futures contract depends on the market value of its underlying commodity, the prices of interest rate futures contracts also change inversely with interest rates. Thus, a financial institution can use futures to reduce its exposure to adverse rate changes.

For example, a decline in interest rates, which lowers the reinvestment rate on an insurance company's bond portfolio, increases the price of interest rate futures contracts. Profits from the futures transactions could reduce the negative effect of the interest rate reduction on the bond portfolio. Futures can provide similar protection in times of interest rate increases.

FUTURES PRICES AND MARKET YIELDS: AN ILLUSTRATION

When interest rates rose in 1998 between mid-November and the end of December, the prices on Treasury securities fell, as did the prices of outstanding futures contracts. Portions of *The Wall Street Journal* quotations of futures prices for Thursday, November 12, 1998, and Monday, December 28, 1998, are shown in Figure 17.1. On November 12, a T-bond contract for March 1999 delivery had a settlement price (listed under the column heading "Settle") of 127–18. The settle price is a representative closing price for that date. The open interest reflects the volume of contracts outstanding for that contract.

Futures contracts on T-bonds and T-notes, like the prices of their underlying instruments, are quoted in 32nds of a percent, so 127–18 means $127\frac{18}{32}$ percent of the face value of a contract, or \$127,562.50 on a \$100,000 contract. (Recall that Table 17.1 indicates the face value of T-bond and T-note contracts as \$100,000.) Each $\frac{1}{32}$ change is a dollar change of \$31.25 [\$100,000 (($\frac{1}{32}$ (0.01)]. At the close of trading on December 28, 1998, the March contract price was 127–03, a decrease of $\frac{15}{32}$, or 0.37 percent of face value. The dollar change was \$468.75—down to \$127,093.75. Price changes for other futures contracts in Figure 17.1 were also negative, so traders who owned contracts for future delivery lost on their positions, whereas traders with short positions (owning contracts to sell T-bonds for future delivery) gained on their positions. Those who lost on their positions were required to settle with the clearinghouse, including the possibility of adding cash to their margin accounts if the loss eroded their balances below acceptable levels.

Toward the bottom of Figure 17.1 data commonly associated with trading for T-bill futures is provided. Like T-bill prices, T-bill futures are quoted as discount yields (d), with the quoted price as (100 percent − d). Hence, for November 12, the March 1999 T-bill futures contract had a discount yield settle of 3.98 percent and a quoted price of 96.02 percent. The actual price for a \$1 million contract would be the par value [1 − (dn/360)], where (n) is the number of days maturity. Hence, since T-bill futures are based on 90-day maturity T-bills, the actual price on November 12, 1998, was \$1 million [1 − (0.0398) (90/360)] = \$990,050. On December 28, 1998, with a rise in rates, the new discount settle rate was 4.37 percent, implying a new actual price of \$1 million [1 − (0.0437) (90/360)] = \$989,075, or a fall in price of \$975.

Figure 17.1 ◆ INTEREST RATE FUTURES PRICES: NOVEMBER 12, AND DECEMBER 28, 1998

Information on interest rate and other futures contracts is reported daily in the financial pages of major newspapers. The most recent prices and the total volume of contracts outstanding (open interest) are included.

INTEREST RATE

TREASURY BONDS (CBT)-$100,000; pts. 32nds of 100%

	Open	High	Low	Settle	Change	Lifetime High	Low	Open Interest
Dec	127-17	128-08	127-11	127-28	+ 18	135-08	103-13	638,270
Mr99	127-08	127-29	127-00	127-18	+ 18	134-26	103-04	147,016
June	126-27	127-08	126-25	127-01	+ 18	134-02	110-07	3,448
Sept	....	....	....	126-16	+ 18	131-06	115-11	4,342

Est vol 375,000; vol Tu 399,668; open int 793,111, −7,401.

TREASURY BONDS (MCE)-$50,000; pts. 32nds of 100%

	Open	High	Low	Settle	Change	Lifetime High	Low	Open Interest
Dec	127-18	128-08	127-11	127-26	+ 18	135-08	118-30	14,855

Est vol 6,000; vol Tu 5,439; open int 14,978, +11.

TREASURY NOTES (CBT)-$100,000; pts. 32nds of 100%

	Open	High	Low	Settle	Change	Lifetime High	Low	Open Interest
Dec	118-27	119-04	118-22	118-28	+ 11	123-19	111-10	442,589
Mr99	119-00	119-11	118-31	119-04	+ 12	123-22	112-04	49,964
June	....	....	....	118-23	+ 11	120-20	113-18	2,548

Est vol 140,000; vol Tu 146,951; open int 495,101, −3,398.

5 YR TREAS NOTES (CBT)-$100,000; pts. 32nds of 100%

	Open	High	Low	Settle	Change	Lifetime High	Low	Open Interest
Dec	113-12	113-18	113-07	113-12	+ 7.0	116-07	108-30	331,176
Mr99	113-28	113-28	13-215	113-25	+ 7.5	116-15	112-10	18,345

Est vol 54,000; vol Tu 70,060; open int 349,546, −235.

2 YR TREAS NOTES (CBT)-$200,000; pts. 32nds of 100%

	Open	High	Low	Settle	Change	Lifetime High	Low	Open Interest
Dec	105-23	05-265	105-22	05-237	+ 3.50	7-025	04-047	37,634

Est vol 2,500; vol Tu 3,722; open int 37,654, −47.

30-DAY FEDERAL FUNDS (CBT)-$5 million; pts. of 100%

	Open	High	Low	Settle	Change	Lifetime High	Low	Open Interest
Nov	95.075	95.085	95.075	95.080	+.010	95.780	94.270	10,328
Dec	95.16	95.16	95.14	95.15	....	95.34	94.25	8,776
Ja99	95.19	95.19	95.18	95.18	....	95.40	94.25	5,534
Feb	95.36	95.38	95.36	95.37	+.02	95.71	94.31	3,310
Mar	95.38	95.39	95.37	95.38	....	95.78	94.38	1,399
Apr	95.42	95.43	95.42	95.43	+.02	95.76	94.43	418
May	95.41	95.42	95.41	95.42	+.02	95.82	94.61	137

Est vol 2,222; vol Tu 2,684; open int 29,902, +2.

MUNI BOND INDEX (CBT)-$1,000; times Bond Buyer MBI

	Open	High	Low	Settle	Change	Lifetime High	Low	Open Interest
Dec	125-03	125-28	125-00	125-15	+ 12	130-07	123-07	22,019
Mr99	125-00	125-15	124-23	125-05	+ 12	129-27	123-15	302

Est vol 2,200; vol Tu 1,620; open int 23,321, −14.
The index: Close 125-00; Yield 5.35.

TREASURY BILLS (CME)-$1 mil.; pts. of 100%

	Open	High	Low	Settle	Chg	Discount Settle	Chg	Open Interest
Dec	95.67	95.70	95.66	95.70	+.03	4.30	− .03	1,702
Mr99	96.04	96.06	96.02	96.02	−.02	3.98	+.02	346

Est vol 144; vol Wed 30; open int 2,077, −5.

LIBOR-1 MO. (CME)-$3,000,000; points of 100%

	Open	High	Low	Settle	Chg	Discount Settle	Chg	Open Interest
Nov	94.75	94.75	94.73	94.73	−.01	5.27	+.01	13,242
Dec	94.54	94.55	94.53	94.53	+.02	5.47	−.02	11,816
Ja99	95.05	95.05	95.04	95.05	....	4.95	....	4,847
Feb	95.15	95.16	95.13	95.15	+.01	4.85	− .01	2,907
Mar	95.23	95.23	95.19	95.20	....	4.80	....	635
Apr	....	....	....	95.29	....	4.71	....	1,012
June	95.35	95.35	95.33	95.31	+.01	4.69	− .01	100

Est vol 4,323; vol Wed 281; open int 34,639, +101.

INTEREST RATE

TREASURY BONDS (CBT)-$100,000; pts. 32nds of 100%

	Open	High	Low	Settle	Change	Lifetime High	Low	Open Interest
Mar	126-15	127-10	126-10	127-03	+ 25	134-26	103-04	592,251
June	125-31	126-27	125-31	126-20	+ 25	134-02	111-24	12,614
Sept	....	....	....	126-06	+ 25	131-00	111-15	4,994
Dec	....	....	....	125-24	+ 25	128-28	111-06	244

Est vol 100,000; vol Thu 94,010; open int 623,712, −430.

TREASURY BONDS (MCE)-$50,000; pts. 32nds of 100%

	Open	High	Low	Settle	Change	Lifetime High	Low	Open Interest
Mar	126-17	127-13	126-13	127-12	+ 35	134-28	124-22	12,308

Est vol 1,000; vol Thu 640; open int 12,975, −203.

TREASURY NOTES (CBT)-$100,000; pts. 32nds of 100%

	Open	High	Low	Settle	Change	Lifetime High	Low	Open Interest
Mar	118-07	118-19	117-31	118-18	+ 15	123-22	112-04	496,354
June	118-08	118-17	118-08	118-17	+ 15	120-21	113-00	7,806

Est vol 25,000; vol Thu 42,166; open int 515,714, +996.

5 YR TREAS NOTES (CBT)-$100,000; pts. 32nds of 100%

	Open	High	Low	Settle	Change	Lifetime High	Low	Open Interest
Mar	112-20	112-27	112-07	12-255	+ 10.0	116-15	109-23	307,700

Est vol 15,000; vol Thu 52,559; open int 327,330, +7,752.

2 YR TREAS NOTES (CBT)-$200,000, pts. 32nds of 100%

	Open	High	Low	Settle	Change	Lifetime High	Low	Open Interest
Dec	105-11	05-145	105-11	05-145	+ 7.5	07-025	04-047	1,177
Mr99	05-115	05-155	05-107	05-155	+ 5.0	106-30	105-08	40,083

Est vol 750; vol Thu 1,838; open int 41,260, +930.

30-DAY FEDERAL FUNDS (CBT)-$5 million; pts. of 100%

	Open	High	Low	Settle	Change	Lifetime High	Low	Open Interest
Dec	95.220	95.230	95.220	95.220	+.01	595.340	94.350	6,707
Ja99	95.13	95.13	95.13	95.13	+ .01	95.40	94.25	8,598
Feb	95.29	95.29	95.28	95.28	....	95.71	94.37	6,667
Mar	95.28	95.29	95.28	95.28	....	95.78	94.44	4,860
Apr	95.30	95.31	95.30	95.31	+.01	95.76	94.43	455
May	95.31	95.31	95.31	95.31	+.01	95.82	94.61	224

Est vol 2,300; vol Thu 1,249; open int 27,575, +277.

MUNI BOND INDEX (CBT)-$1,000; times Bond Buyer MBI

	Open	High	Low	Settle	Change	Lifetime High	Low	Open Interest
Mar	123-26	123-26	123-05	123-22	+ 3	129-17	123-15	23,207

Est vol 1,000; vol Thu 1,275; open int 23,207, +349.
The index: Close 124-10; Yield 5.39.

TREASURY BILLS (CME)-$1 mil.; pts. of 100%

	Open	High	Low	Settle	Chg	Discount Settle	Chg	Open Interest
Mar	95.62	95.66	95.61	95.66	+ .30	4.37	+ .09	1,875

Est vol 767; vol Th 427; open int 1,875, +242.

LIBOR-1 MO. (CME)-$3,000,000; points of 100%

	Open	High	Low	Settle	Chg	Discount Settle	Chg	Open Interest
Jan	95.01	95.02	95.00	95.00	....	4.99	+.01	14,878
Feb	95.03	95.08	95.02	95.03	....	4.97	+.04	9,370
Apr	....	....		95.08	....	4.94	+ .10	1,168
June	....	....	....	95.06	....	4.97	+ .15	143

Est vol 1,351; vol Th 1,090; open int 28,129, −225.

Source: The Wall Street Journal, November 13, 1998, C14; and December 29, 1998, C14.

The approximate change in price with a change in the discount rate for T-bills can also be approximated as $25 (the number of basis points change in the discount rate, here, 39 basis points (4.37 percent − 3.98 percent = 0.39 percent). Thus, the approximate price change was 39 − $25 = $975.

SHORT VERSUS LONG HEDGES

A financial institution using futures to hedge can choose either a short hedge or a long hedge. A short hedge means that the trader *sells* a futures contract, incurring an obligation either to deliver the underlying securities at some future point or close out the position through the clearinghouse before the delivery date by buying an off-setting contract. When interest rates rise, as they did in December 1998, the value of both interest-earning assets and outstanding futures contracts falls. A trader who has contracts to sell T-bills or T-bonds in the future can buy them at the lower price for an immediate profit. If, instead, the futures contract is bought before the delivery date, the contract selling price will be higher than the purchase price. Either way, the trader benefits from a short position if interest rates rise.

A long hedge, in contrast, means that the trader buys a futures contract, incurring an obligation either to take delivery of the securities at the preestablished price on some future date or to sell the contract, closing out the position through the clearinghouse before the delivery date. If interest rates fall in the intervening period, either obligation can be met at a profit. A trader who actually takes delivery on securities can sell them at an immediate profit over the purchase price written into the futures contract. If, instead, the futures contract is sold before the delivery date, the contract selling price will be higher than the purchase price. Either way, the trader benefits from a long position if interest rates decline.

It is important to emphasize that neither the long nor the short position is a hedge unless the futures transaction is undertaken to offset interest rate risk in an existing portfolio. Traders also should know that transaction costs and brokers' commissions reduce the proceeds of both long and short hedges.

The Long Hedge Illustrated

Suppose that, in June 2001, the manager of a money market portfolio expects interest rates to decline. New funds, to be received and invested in 90 days (September 2001), will suffer from the drop in yields, and the manager would like to reduce the effect on portfolio returns. The appropriate strategy under this forecast is a long hedge, because long futures positions profit from falling rates.

Gains and losses on cash and futures market transactions are summarized in Table 17.2. The money manager expects an inflow of $10 million in September. The discount yield currently available on 91-day T-bills is 10 percent, and the goal is to establish a yield of 10 percent on the anticipated funds. Because contracts on 91-day T-bills have face values of $1 million, 10 contracts are needed to hedge the cash position. Assuming that the initial margin requirement is 2 percent of the contract price, the cash required in June will be slightly less than $20,000. The market value of the contracts purchased for future delivery in September is $9.75 million. If the funds were available now for the T-bill investment at a discount yield of 10 percent, the cost would be $9,747,222.

Suppose interest rates have fallen by the time the new funds arrive in September. The 91-day T-bill yield is down to 8 percent, and it now costs $9,797,778 to purchase bills with a face value of $10 million. The higher price results in an "opportunity loss" to the portfolio manager of $50,556, but the long futures hedge offsets most of that loss. With the decline in market yields, the September contracts have risen in value from $9.75 million to $9.8 million. Their sale provides a gain of $50,000 (the difference between the actual new and old prices, or $25 (the 200-basis-point change in the discount yield (10 contracts), which almost equals the loss in the cash market. The effective discount yield on T-bills purchased, including the effect of the hedge (calculated as the net amount earned as a percentage of par value × the number of times this could be earned a year) is 9.978 percent, very close to the desired discount yield of 10 percent.

Table 17.2 ✦ THE LONG HEDGE (FORECAST: FALLING INTEREST RATES)

A long hedge is chosen in anticipation of interest rate declines and requires the purchase of interest rate futures contracts. If the forecast is correct, the profit on the hedge helps to offset losses in the cash market.

I.

Cash Market	Futures Market
June	
T-bill discount yield at 10%	Buy 10 T-bill contracts for September delivery
Price of 91-day T-bills, $10 million par:	at 10% discount yield
$9,747,222[a]	Value of contracts:
	$9,750,000[b]
September	
T-bill discount yield at 8%	Sell 10 September T-bill contracts at 8%
Price of 91-day T-bills, $10 million par:	discount yield
$9,797,778	Value of contracts:
	$9,800,000

II.

Cash Market Loss		Futures Market Gain	
June cost	$9,747,222	September sale	$9,800,000
September cost	9,797,778	June purchase	9,750,000
Loss	($ 50,556)	Gain	$ 50,000
	Net Loss: ($556)		

III.

Effective Discount Yield with the Hedge

$$\frac{\$10,000,000 - (\$9,797,778 - \$50,000)}{\$10,000,000} \times \frac{360}{91} = 9.978\%$$

---

[a]At a discount yield of 10%, the price of a 91-day T-bill is

$$P_0 = \$10,000,000 \left[1 - \frac{0.1(91)}{360} \right] = \$9,747,222$$

[b]T-bill futures contracts are standardized at 90-day maturities, resulting in a price different from the one calculated in the cash market.

By definition, a hedge is undertaken to offset potential losses in an institution's existing or planned portfolio of financial assets. Buying long futures contracts when no future investment in T-bills was planned would be speculation, not hedging, because the contract purchase would be an attempt to earn a pure profit on futures.

The Short Hedge Illustrated

If a financial institution stands to lose under forecasts of rising rates, it can undertake a short hedge. For depository institutions, many liability costs are tied to yields on short-term Treasury securities, and an increase in interest rates can raise the cost of funds significantly. Profits on a short hedge may be used to lock in a lower cost of funds.

For deposit costs pegged to the T-bill rate, T-bill futures provide a good vehicle for the short hedge. Suppose that in September a savings institution wants to hedge

$5 million in short-term certificates of deposit (CDs) whose owners are expected to roll them over in 90 days. If market yields go up, the thrift must offer a higher rate on its CDs to remain competitive, reducing the net interest margin (NIM). The asset/liability manager can reduce these losses by the sale of T-bill futures contracts. With a subsequent increase in rates, the value of contracts declines, and when the position is closed out through the clearinghouse, a profit will be realized.[10]

The short hedge illustrated in Table 17.3 is designed to offset the increase in CD rates from 7 percent to 9 percent; the interest paid on the CDs will increase by $25,000 for the three-month period. In September, the savings and loan association (S&L) sells five December contracts at a discount yield of 7 percent. To close out the position in December, after rates have risen to 9 percent, the hedger buys five T-bill contracts from the clearinghouse. They have declined in value, resulting in a $25,000 profit on the futures position. In the simplified world of this example, the institution's returns are protected from interest rate fluctuations because the dollar

---

Table 17.3   ◆   THE SHORT HEDGE (FORECAST: RISING INTEREST RATES)

A short hedge is chosen in anticipation of interest rate increases and requires the sale of interest rate futures contracts. If the forecast is correct, the profit on the hedge helps to offset losses in the cash market.

I.

Cash Market	Futures Market
September	
CD rate: 7%	Sell 5 T-bill contracts for December delivery at 7% discount yield
Interest cost on $5 million in deposits (3 months):	Value of contracts:
$87,500	$4,912,500
December	
CD rate: 9%	Buy 5 December T-bill contracts at 9% discount yield
Interest cost on $5 million in deposits (3 months):	Value of contracts:
$112,500	$4,887,500

II.

Cash Market Loss		Futures Market Gain	
September interest	$ 87,500	September sale	$4,912,500
December interest	112,500	December purchase	−4,887,500
Loss	($ 25,000)	Gain	$ 25,000
	Net Result of Hedge: $0		

III.

Net Interest Cost and Effective CD Rate

$112,500 − $25,000 = $87,500

$$\frac{\$87,500}{\$5,000,000} \times \frac{360}{90} = 0.07 = 7.0\%$$

---

[10]This example assumes that the thrift has at least $5 million more short-term liabilities than short-term assets and thus meets regulatory requirements for hedges. This example also ignores the tax consequences of short hedges, which worsened after an IRS ruling in early 1993. See William B. Crawford, Jr. "IRS Rule Change Putting Futures Hedging at Risk." *Chicago Tribune* (February 21, 1993), Section 7, 1, 10.

interest cost for the quarter, netted against the gain on the hedge, is the desired $87,500. Again, transaction costs, brokers' fees, and the opportunity cost of the margin deposit are not included.

As with the long hedge, the short hedge is undertaken only to protect an existing financial position. Attempting to gain a pure profit from rising rates would be speculation.

RISK AND THE FINANCIAL FUTURES MARKETS

The preceding scenarios are extremely simplified. For example, they assume that the changes in spot and futures yields are identical. They also do not address several decisions that investors must make before entering the market, such as the type and number of contracts to be purchased or sold and the length of the hedge. The examples also assume that the interest rate forecasts are accurate and timely. The more complex aspects of hedging and the risks they introduce are discussed in this section.

Incorrect Rate Forecasts

The preceding examples illustrate that rate forecasts are an integral part of every hedge but that their accuracy determines management's satisfaction with the results. The assumption made in Table 17.2 was that interest rates would fall and that funds received and invested after three months would earn a lower yield. If interest rates had not fallen, the portfolio manager could have maintained or even increased returns through the cash market position alone. The long hedge would result in a loss, because the contracts owned would decline in value. The loss on the futures hedge would reduce the otherwise favorable returns on the securities investment. The protective hedge limits the institution's loss from an unfavorable interest rate change, but it also limits the potential gains from a favorable movement in rates. Thus, hedging is indeed a risk-minimization strategy that is intended to reduce potential variation in the NIM.

Basis Risk

An influence on both the type and number of contracts to be traded is the **basis**. Basis is the difference between the spot price of the underlying financial asset and the price of a futures contract at time t:

$$\text{Basis} = P_{St} - P_{Ft} \qquad [17.1]$$

To execute a perfect hedge, one in which the cash market loss is exactly offset by the futures market profit, the hedger must predict the basis accurately and adjust the size of the hedge accordingly. In the simplified world of Table 17.2, the discount yield on the T-bills equals the effective discount yield at which the T-bill contract traded. The difference in the cash and futures market results arose from the futures market convention of pricing T-bill contracts based on 90 rather than 91 days. In reality, however, although cash yields and futures market yields are closely related, they are not perfectly correlated because each market has its own supply/demand interactions. The possibility of unexpected changes in the relationship between spot and futures market prices introduces another element of risk, known as **basis risk**.

Basis Risk Illustrated[11]   When a hedger closes out cash and futures positions, the gains and losses from each are netted. These calculations are shown at the end of Tables 17.2 and 17.3. Presenting them in a different format clarifies the importance of the basis.

At the close of a hedge, the results from the cash market transactions are determined by the number of securities bought or sold and their cost, $Q(P_{St})$. In Table 17.2, the trader bought 10 bills with a total par value of $1 million:

$$Q(P_{St}) = 10 \times \$979{,}777.80 = \$9{,}797{,}778$$

The result of the futures transaction alone is the proceeds from the sale (at $t = 1$) minus the cost of the purchase (at $t = 0$):

$$Q(P_{F1}) - Q(P_{FO}) = Q(P_{F1} - P_{FO})$$

For the long hedge,

$$Q(P_{F1} - P_{FO}) = 10 \times (\$980{,}000 - \$975{,}000) = 10 \times \$5{,}000 = \$50{,}000$$

The net cost of the bills purchased can be expressed as the difference between their spot price in September—the amount the institution would actually pay for the bills—and the profits from the futures trade:

$$\text{Net Cost} = Q(P_{St}) - Q(P_{F1}(P_{FO}) \qquad [17.2]$$

$$= 10 ((\$979{,}77.80)(10 - \$980{,}000.00 \times \$975{,}000.00) = \$9{,}797{,}778 - \$50{,}000 = \$9{,}747{,}778$$

Rearranging, the net cost is also

$$\text{Net Cost} = Q(P_{S1} - P_{F1}) + Q(P_{FO})$$

$$= 10(\$979{,}777.80 - \$980{,}000.00) + (10 \times \$975{,}000.00)$$

$$= -\$2{,}222 + \$9{,}750{,}000 = \$9{,}747{,}778$$

In other words, the basis at the time the position is closed out—the quantity $(P_{S1}(P_{F1})$—determines the success or failure of the hedge. If there were no uncertainty about the basis, a hedge in the futures market would involve much less risk. In reality, at the time the hedge is undertaken, the trader does not know P_{S1} or P_{F1} or the difference between the two that will prevail in the future. As the basis fluctuates, so does the potential gain or loss on the hedge.

The top panel of Figure 17.2 shows prices on a popular futures instrument, T-bond contracts, as well as prices on T-bonds during the period 1978–1988. The high positive correlation in price movements is evident from the bottom line, which is the basis over that period. Although the basis does not fluctuate greatly, it is not stable. Traders who hedge positions in the cash markets with futures incur basis risk, a fact that must be considered in the hedging decision. As the top of Figure 17.2 illustrates, however, basis risk exposure on the futures position may be lower than price risk exposure in the cash market, especially when the cash and futures instruments are identical or very closely related. The variability in the basis in the top panel is clearly much smaller than the variability in prices on 30-year T-bonds.

---

[11]The following section draws on Van Horne (1990), 160–161.

Figure 17.2 ✦ Prices of 30-Year Bonds and T-Bond Futures Contracts

The basis is the difference between the current price of a hedged asset and the current price of a futures contract. The more nearly identical the characteristics of the hedged asset and the futures contract, the more stable the basis.

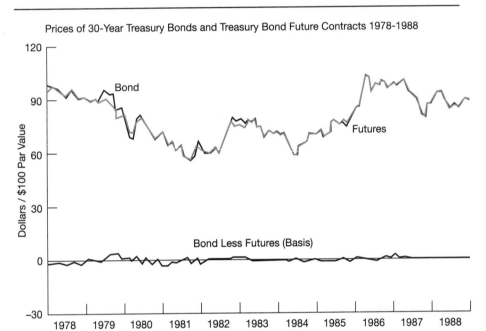

Prices of 30-Year Treasury Bonds and Treasury Bond Future Contracts 1978-1988

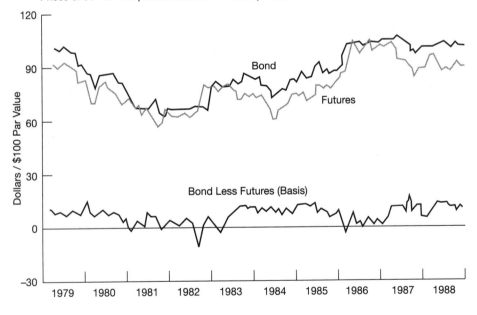

Prices of 30-Year Corporate Bonds and Treasury Bond Futures Contracts 1979-1988

Source: Adapted from Charles S. Morris, "Managing Interest Rate Risk with Interest Rate Futures," *Economic Review* (Federal Reserve Bank of Kansas City) 74 (March 1989): 13.

The Cross Hedge and Basis Risk

In Table 17.2, the money market portfolio manager protected yields on an anticipated T-bill investment with a T-bill futures contract. In many hedging decisions, however, the limited variety of futures contracts available makes it impossible to hedge a cash instrument with a contract for future delivery of the same security. Whenever a futures hedge is constructed on an instrument other than the cash market security, as would be the case when hedging a corporate bond portfolio, the hedge is considered a **cross hedge**. The basis risk for these positions is even greater than when the same security is involved in both sides of the transaction, as the bottom panel of Figure 17.2 demonstrates.

Figure 17.2 shows that from 1979 to 1988, the prices of T-bond futures contracts and the prices of a typical high-grade corporate bond differed more than the prices of T-bond futures and T-bonds. If a portfolio manager had hedged a corporate bond portfolio with T-bond futures during this period, the basis risk would have been higher than if the manager were hedging a T-bond portfolio. The basis in the cross hedge, however, would still have been less variable over the period than the price of the unhedged corporate bond.

If a short-term instrument was hedged with a futures contract on a long-term security, or vice versa, the basis risk would be even greater. A change in the slope of the yield curve would produce changes of differing magnitudes for long- and short-term yields. In that case, the changes in spot and futures values would certainly diverge, and, consequently, the effectiveness of the hedge would be more uncertain.

The cross hedge exposes the hedger to basis risk for another important reason. Even if the changes in yields were the same on two securities, the resulting price changes could very well differ. The bond theorems and duration discussions in Chapter 16 demonstrate that a given basis-point change in yields will not affect the prices of securities in the same way if they have different coupon rates or terms to maturity, differences likely to occur in a cross hedge. As market interest rates fluctuate, the goal of a hedge—minimizing NIM fluctuations by realizing a profit on the futures trade that exactly offsets the cash market loss—is difficult to achieve with a cross hedge.

CHOOSING THE OPTIMAL NUMBER OF CONTRACTS

An asset/liability manager faces additional uncertainties in determining the size of the futures position. The objective of hedging is to offset as closely as possible potential losses on a cash instrument with gains on futures, but price changes on the two types of instruments are seldom exactly proportional to one another. Therefore, simply dividing the total value of the cash portfolio to be hedged by the face value of a single futures contract on an appropriate instrument would give a misleading signal about the number of futures contracts a hedger should buy or sell. Selecting the number of contracts to trade is particularly difficult in a cross hedge, because face value, coupon, and maturity characteristics may all differ between cash and futures instruments.

The first step in structuring the hedge is to identify the assets or liabilities (or both) to be protected. The volume and interest rate characteristics of the instrument to be hedged are the foundation for the futures decision.[12]

---

[12]The development of an institutional hedging strategy is a major aspect of asset/liability management. The futures position may revolve around either a macro or micro hedge, terms that refer to the magnitude of the futures position in relation to the institution's balance sheet.

The Hedge Ratio   Before the optimal position in the futures market can be determined, a **hedge ratio** must be estimated. Although there are other ways of defining a hedge ratio, many experts prefer a definition that focuses on the relative variability of the prices of the cash and futures instrument involved in a contemplated hedge. This definition assumes that the objective of the hedge is to minimize the variability in price/yield changes to which the hedger is exposed[13]:

$$HR = \frac{\text{Cov}\,(\Delta P_S, \Delta P_F)}{\sigma^2\,\Delta P_F} \qquad [17.3]$$

where HR is the hedge ratio, Cov $(\Delta P_S, \Delta P_F)$ is the covariance between changes in spot prices and change in future prices, and $\sigma^2 \Delta P_F$ is the variance in changes in future prices.

The covariance is a statistic that measures the extent to which two variables move together. Students of regression analysis may also realize that the covariance between two variables, divided by the variance of one of the variables, is the beta coefficient in a simple regression model between the two variables. Thus, the hedge ratio as defined previously can be estimated by regressing past price changes in the cash instrument to be hedged against past price changes in a futures instrument. The beta of such a regression is the hedge ratio for the proposed hedge.[14]

Suppose that a securities portfolio manager, anticipating a decline in interest rates over the next three months, wishes to protect the yield on an investment of $15 million in T-bills and that a T-bill futures contract is now selling for $989,500. If the hedge ratio between price changes in T-bills and T-bill futures contracts has been estimated through regression to be 0.93, the number of contracts to be used in the hedge can be determined by

$$N_F = \frac{V \times HR}{F} \qquad [17.4]$$

where

N_F = the number of futures contracts to be purchased or sold,

V = the total market value of securities to be hedged, and

F = the market value of a single futures contract.

In this example, the number of contracts to be purchased (a long position is needed because the forecast is for falling rates) is as follows:

$$\frac{\$15,000,000}{\$989,500} \times 0.93 = 14.098$$

Several factors will affect the outcome of the hedge. If the *past* covariance between changes in T-bill prices and changes in T-bill futures prices is not the same as the covariance between those price changes *during* the hedge, the number of contracts calculated by using Equation 17.4 will not result in a position that minimizes the hedger's risk exposure. Also, it is not possible to trade fractional amounts of futures contracts, so the hedger in this instance would need to purchase 14 contracts.

---

[13]For further discussion of hedge ratios, including alternative definitions, see Kolb (1988); Schwartz, Hill, and Schneeweis (1986); and Chance (1989).

[14]Note the similarity between this process and estimating the beta coefficient on common stock.

Thus, even if past and future covariances between price changes were equal, the manager would still expect a less-than-perfect hedge. This inability to trade fractional futures units or, for that matter, fractions of a T-bill explains why the hedge results in Table 17.2 are imperfect. Although many financial theories assume perfect divisibility of financial assets, it seldom exists in practice.

The appendix shows an alternative hedge ratio model using duration.

FUTURES AS A SUPPLEMENT TO GAP MANAGEMENT

Macro Hedges Versus Micro Hedges

The hedging examples described have been **micro** hedges, designed to hedge the risk of a loss in the spot market for a particular asset or liability. For instance, suppose a bond portfolio manager has some bonds maturing in three months that he or she wants to reinvest in the bond market but fears that interest rates will fall and the prices of bonds will rise over this time period. The bond manager could set up a micro hedge for the dollar worth of the bonds to be purchased by purchasing futures contracts to buy bonds at a given price in three months. If bond prices rise, the futures contract will have a gain that will offset the higher cost of the bonds in the spot market three months from now. Similarly, suppose the manager of a depository institution expects to make a loan in three months and is concerned that the interest rate of CDs used to fund the loan will rise during that time. He or she could set up a micro hedge for the dollar worth of the CDs to be financed by purchasing futures contracts to sell CDs (or T-bills of similar maturity) at a given price in three months. If CD rates rise (prices fall), the futures contract will have a gain that will offset the higher interest expense for the CDs three months from now.

An institution, however, may be more concerned over its overall interest rate risk as reflected by its funding gap or duration gap, and wish to hedge this entire gap, i.e., use a **macro** hedge. With a negative funding gap (i.e., a positive duration gap), if interest rates rise, the institution's net interest income and the market value of its equity will fall.

With a proper number of futures contracts, the financial institution could hedge this loss by taking a short position in futures that would produce a gain equal to the institution's expected loss if interest rates rise. Similarly, if the institution had a positive funding gap (i.e., a negative duration gap), exposing it to losses if interest rates fall, it could hedge this loss by taking a long position in futures that would produce a gain equal to the institution's expected gain if interest rates fall.

Example of a Macro Hedge: Hedging a Funding Gap

Suppose a bank has a funding gap of −$100 million over the next three months. This implies that if interest rates rise 100 basis points (1 percent), its loss in net interest income will be: Funding Gap $\times \Delta y° = -\$100$ million $\times$ (0.01×90 days/360) = $25,000. By using Equation 17.4, hedging with future contracts on three-month T-bills and assuming a hedge ratio of 1, the bank manager would purchase 100 contracts to sell T-bills in three months at a given discount rate of 8.55 percent. If, three months later, both spot and futures rates rose 100 basis points, the approximate gain on the futures with a discount rate of 9.55 percent now would be $25.00 per basis point rise, or 100 basis points × $25 × 100 contracts = $25,000. Here, we are assuming a perfect hedge, which of course may not be the case if spot and futures prices do not move by the same amount over this period. Of course, the bank also has an opportunity cost with this hedge if interest rates fall, whereby its gain in net interest income will be offset by an equal loss on its futures position. A duration gap hedge could also be implemented. Note that a macro hedge requires detailed knowledge of a bank's total exposure to interest rate risk and requires a relatively large transaction in the futures market because it is designed to protect the value of or the earnings generated by the entire asset and liability portfolio. The institution makes a significant commitment to its interest rate forecast.[15]

INTEREST RATE FUTURES: REGULATORY RESTRICTIONS AND FINANCIAL REPORTING

The risks accompanying the futures markets have led regulators to focus attention on policies governing institutional involvement. For state-regulated institutions, there may be as many different policies as there are state regulators. In contrast, federally chartered or federally insured institutions in each industry do have uniform regulations. In general, regulators disapprove of futures transactions that increase the institution's risk exposure. Instead, they expect an institution to assume a futures position that will desensitize the balance sheet to interest rate changes. Because commercial bank balance sheets are less homogeneous than thrift balance sheets, thrift regulators have set more specific rules on the use of futures. Bank regulators have followed a model similar to that used by securities industry regulators by emphasizing a self-policing approach.

In any case, depositories cannot use futures as income-generating investments for speculative purposes. Regulators also expect a high-level management committee, often including members of the board of directors, to establish a hedging policy for the institution, including a set of guidelines for establishing hedges and monitoring the results.

In addition to futures, options and other derivatives (financial instruments whose value derives from an underlying security) are traded by security firms. With several highly publicized crises, such as the involvement of Barings, Inc., and Daiwa in Japan in derivative trading activities, and more recent losses in 1998 by Long-Term Capital Management, L.P., which led to a $3.6 billion Federal Reserve-brokered bailout, Congress and regulators since the mid-1990s have contemplated greater oversight over the derivatives market and financial institutions' use of derivatives. Regulators have also established examiner guidance on bank derivatives activities, including Federal Reserve Guidelines issued in 1993 that are applied to all trading activities, including derivatives and other financial instruments. Examiners also began assigning a for-

---

[15]See Saunders (1997) for more details on hedging a duration gap. Basically, the formula for the number of futures contracts to purchase is as follows:

$$NF = [(DGAP \times Assets) / (DFUT \times Price \ of \ 1 \ Futures \ Contract)] \times beta$$

where DGAP is the institution's duration gap and DFUT is the duration of the bond underlying the futures contract. The ratio is multiplied by a beta to adjust for basis risk differences; beta represents $[\Delta R / (1 + R)] / [\Delta R_f / (1 + R_f)]$, where R represents the average market yield on the bank's assets and R_f the futures prices' yields. A similar duration approach is shown for other hedges in Appendix 17A.

mal rating to a bank's overall risk management capabilities as part of the management component of the CAMELS (regulatory ratings on Capital, Asset Quality, Management, Earnings, and Liquidity) rating for safety and soundness. Similarly, examiners for the Office of the Comptroller of the Currency are required to determine whether bank managers understand the risks associated with derivatives.

Managers are required to implement controls to quantify and manage these risks effectively. Such controls include written policies setting limits on various risks and procedures and internal controls to ensure that policy limits are enforced. They also include a risk management system to quantify the risks associated with a position and to provide the means to manage that risk effectively. Examiners must ensure the accuracy of the models used to measure and monitor the risk, including analyzing earnings of the position (i.e., the gains and losses associated with given hedges) and comparing them with the expected result. Internal and external audits also must be performed, focusing particularly on the effectiveness of internal controls and the adequacy of the management information system.[16]

Accounting Rules   Guidelines for reporting futures transactions have also received much attention. The accounting profession has addressed two areas of controversy: what distinguishes a hedge from a speculative trade and how to report a futures position. FASB rules designate a futures transaction as a hedge when two conditions are met:[17]

1.   The asset or liability to be hedged exposes the institution to interest rate risk.
2.   The futures contract chosen reduces interest rate risk, is designated as a hedge, and has price movements highly correlated with the instrument being hedged.

FASB recommends more favorable accounting methods for future hedges linked to identifiable cash market instruments (micro hedges) than for more general hedges (macro hedges). In other words, hedging a portfolio of six-month adjustable rate mortgages with T-bill futures contracts (a micro hedge) qualifies for more favorable reporting than a macro hedge that lowers the total rate of the institution but cannot be linked to a specific asset or liability.

Unless an institution can identify a specific asset or liability for which a hedge has been selected, accounting rules require the results of the hedge to be reported as gains or losses on the income statements before the final futures position is closed out. Because changes in interest rates during the course of a hedge may produce temporary losses that are ultimately recovered, reporting hedging results before the position is closed can increase variability in reported earnings. The results of micro hedges, in contrast, must be reported only when closed out,

---

[16]For more details on the guidelines established for commercial banks and bank holding companies, see Chicago Board of Trade (1990), 94–95; Parkinson and Spindt (1985), 469–474; and Koppenhaver (1984). Also, see Chorafas (1998); Dominic Casserley and Greg Wilson. "Managing Derivatives-Related Regulatory Risk." *Bank Management* (July/August, 1994), 27–32; and Susan M. Phillips. "Derivatives and Trading: No Quarantine Necessary." *Banking Strategies* (September/October, 1996), 39–42.

[17]See Drabenstott and McDonley (1984), 24–25, and Chicago Board of Trade (1990), 100–101. The FASB rules became effective December 31, 1984. Also, see Chorafas (1998) for details of the 1996 Market Risk Amendment by the Basle Committee of Banking Supervision, which includes a section on hedge accounting and more sophisticated hedge ratios.

and they can be amortized over the life of a hedged asset or liability. Not surprisingly, managers often favor micro hedges for accounting reasons alone as well as the flexibility to structure bank services to meet the needs of a particularly desirable customer.

For reporting the results of hedges, institutions prefer to wait until a futures position is closed, and FASB permits transactions meeting its definition to be reported at that time, i.e., after the results are known. Some regulators prefer contemporaneous reporting and require institutions to use a mark-to-market approach. For example, the Comptroller of the Currency requires national banks to report the market value of their futures positions before closure and thus before any gains or losses are realized. During the course of a hedge, the value of a futures contract may fluctuate substantially as financial market conditions change, although the institution's financial position is not actually affected until a contract is closed out. Thus, many bank managers believe that mark-to-market futures reporting may provide misleading information.

Thrift regulators have allowed savings institutions to use a deferral rather than a mark-to-market approach for several years. Any transactions that do not meet the FASB criteria are considered speculative and must be reported by mark-to-market. Banks, however, must use different methods to report futures transactions to two different audiences.

The risks inherent in the interest rate futures markets, as well as additional regulatory and accounting standards, mean that futures strategies require careful planning and monitoring after they are implemented. Most financial institutions that are successful hedgers have established objectives and safeguards to control the additional risk exposure.

Limitations of Futures in Asset/Liability Management

Setting the appropriate hedge ratio and selecting the most effective futures instrument are difficult problems for any type of hedge. For many assets held by depositories, no futures contracts exist, forcing institutions to cross hedge and increase basis risk. These decisions are less complex for a micro hedge, however, because only one instrument and one maturity are involved. Monitoring the institution's futures position is also time-consuming, especially in a micro strategy that may involve many individual hedges. Finally, the daily cash settlements required for futures trading place additional liquidity demands on the institution, especially if rate forecasts prove to be incorrect. The disadvantages must be weighed against the additional flexibility that futures provide.

Other synthetic or derivative techniques used for hedging—including interest rate swaps, caps, collars, floors and options on interest rate futures—are discussed in Chapter 18.

FOREIGN CURRENCY FUTURES

Financial institutions active in international markets face exchange rate risk, or variability in NIM caused by fluctuations in currency exchange rates. Foreign currency futures are instruments used to hedge exchange rate risk, just as interest rate futures are used to hedge interest rate risk. Hedging strategies useful to institutions financing international transactions are similar to the choices available for hedging against interest rate fluctuations.

Figure 17.3   ♦   FOREIGN EXCHANGE RATES AND FUTURES PRICES

Panel A: Foreign Exchange Rates: Spot and forward exchange rates between the U.S. dollar and other currencies are reported daily in the financial pages. Both direct (U.S. $ equiv.) and indirect (currency per U.S. $) rates are listed. [December 24, 1998]

Panel B: Foreign Currency Futures Prices: December 24, 1998. Prices and other information on foreign currency futures contracts are reported daily in major newspapers.

CURRENCY TRADING

EXCHANGE RATES

Thursday, December 24, 1998

The New York foreign exchange mid-range rates below apply to trading among banks in amounts of $1 million and more, as quoted at 4 p.m. Eastern time by Telerate and other sources. Retail transactions provide fewer units of foreign currency per dollar.

Country	U.S. $ equiv. Thu	U.S. $ equiv. Wed	Currency per U.S.$ Thu	Currency per U.S.$ Wed
Argentina (Peso)	1.0002	1.0002	.9998	.9998
Australia (Dollar)	.6108	.6109	1.6372	1.6369
Austria (Schilling)	.08473	.08497	11.802	11.769
Bahrain (Dinar)	2.6525	2.6525	.3770	.3770
Belgium (Franc)	.02881	.02897	34.706	34.520
Brazil (Real)	.8321	.8321	1.2018	1.2018
Britain (Pound)	1.6723	1.6783	.5980	.5958
1-month forward	1.6712	1.6771	.5984	.5963
3-months forward	1.6687	1.6746	.5993	.5972
6-months forward	1.6670	1.6728	.5999	.5978
Canada (Dollar)	.6449	.6445	1.5507	1.5515
1-month forward	.6452	.6448	1.5500	1.5508
3-months forward	.6453	.6450	1.5497	1.5505
6-months forward	.6456	.6453	1.5489	1.5497
Chile (Peso)	.002113	.002109	473.15	474.25
China (Renminbi)	.1208	.1208	8.2784	8.2782
Colombia (Peso)	.0006816	.0006816	1467.04	1467.04
Czech. Rep. (Koruna)				
Commercial rate	.03334	.03334	29.990	29.990
Denmark (Krone)	.1562	.1571	6.4020	6.3665
Ecuador (Sucre)				
Floating rate	.0001524	.0001524	6562.50	6562.50
Finland (Markka)	.1955	.1965	5.1157	5.0880
France (Franc)	.1773	.1781	5.6410	5.6160
1-month forward	.1776	.1784	5.6296	5.6049
3-months forward	.1782	.1790	5.6122	5.5875
6-months forward	.1790	.1798	5.5855	5.5618
Germany (Mark)	.5945	.5972	1.6820	1.6744
1-month forward	.5957	.5984	1.6787	1.6711
3-months forward	.5976	.6002	1.6735	1.6660
6-months forward	.6003	.6030	1.6657	1.6583
Greece (Drachma)	.003549	.003565	281.80	280.47
Hong Kong (Dollar)	.1291	.1291	7.7455	7.7436
Hungary (Forint)	.004657	.004657	214.75	214.75
India (Rupee)	.02351	.02351	42.535	42.535
Indonesia (Rupiah)	.0001274	.0001290	7850.00	7750.00
Ireland (Punt)	1.4804	1.4843	.6755	.6737
Israel (Shekel)	.2391	.2391	4.1820	4.1821
Italy (Lira)	.0006002	.0006031	1666.00	1658.00
Japan (Yen)	.008608	.008600	116.17	116.28
1-month forward	.008648	.008640	115.63	115.75

CURRENCY

	Open	High	Low	Settle	Change	Lifetime High	Low	Open Interest
JAPAN YEN (CME)-12.5 million yen; $ per yen (.00)								
Mar	.8665	.8730	.8658	.8720	+ .0054	.8935	.6997	59,978
June	.8810	.8820	.8810	.8823	+ .0055	.9015	.7066	3,997
Sept	....	....	....	.8921	+ .0055	.9076	.7680	1,347
Dec	....	....	....	.9018	+ .0055	.9069	.8690	141
Est vol 5,576; vol Tue 13,580; open int 65,463, +1,590.								
DEUTSCHEMARK (CME)-125,000 marks; $ per mark								
Mar	.6009	.6022	.5993	.6001	— .0008	.6300	.5540	58,571
June	....	....	....	.6028	— .0007	.6285	.5620	1,222
Sept	....	....	....	.6056	— .0004	.6300	.5979	138
Est vol 8,280; vol Tue 9,561; open int 59,991, −1,601.								
CANADIAN DOLLAR (CME)-100,000 dlrs.; $ per Can $								
Mar	.6443	.6438	.6447	.6447	+ .0004	.7247	.6290	36,012
June	.6449	.6457	.6449	.6452	+ .0004	.7170	.6300	2,222
Sept	.6462	.6462	.6451	.6457	+ .0004	.7080	.6310	698
Dec	.6455	.6470	.6455	.6462	+ .0004	.6695	.6320	712
Est vol 2,384; vol Tue 6,419; open int 39,710, +4,5.								
BRITISH POUND (CME)-62,500 pds.; $ per pound								
Mar	1.6760	1.6788	1.6716	1.6738	— .0018	1.7150	1.5950	42,677
June	....	....	....	1.6712	— .0014	1.7060	1.5880	1,207
Sept	....	....	....	1.6700	— .0006	1.6980	1.6270	230
Est vol 2,205; vol Tue 2,732; open int 44,144, −136.								
SWISS FRANC (CME)-125,000 francs; $ per franc								
Mar	.7398	.7413	.7380	.7394	— .0006	.7890	.6635	33,450
June	....	....	....	.7456	— .0006	.7930	.6700	385
Sept	....	....	....	.7516	— .0006	.7646	.7420	230
Est vol 4,210; vol Tue 10,934; open int 34,227, +1,682.								
AUSTRALIAN DOLLAR (CME)-100,000 dlrs.; $ per A.$								
Mar	.6132	.6159	.6095	.6100	— .0032	.6490	.5785	16,226
Est vol 614; vol Tue 2,319; open int 16,234, +170.								
MEXICAN PESO (CME)-500,000 new Mex. peso, $ per MP								
Mar	.09595	.09630	.09550	.09557	— 0037	.10565	.07550	15,140
June	.09030	.09035	.08980	.08977	— 0040	.10220	.06900	3,432
Sept	.08530	.08545	.08530	.08510	— 0020	.09510	.06350	688
Est vol 1,228; vol Tue 2,223; open int 19,301, − 13.								
BRAZILIAN REAL (CME)-100,000 Braz. reals; $ per reals								
Jan	....	....	....	.08260	....	.08260	.07430	2,351
Feb	.08110	.08117	.08110	.08117	....	.08120	.06805	7,198
Mar	.07970	.07970	.07961	.07961	....	.08090	.06900	913
Est vol 765; vol Tue 332; open int 12,033, +212.								

Source: The Wall Street Journal, December 28, 1998, C14.

At the end of 1998, futures contracts were available on exchange rates between the U.S. dollar and the German mark, the Japanese yen, the Swiss franc, the British pound, the French franc, the Australian dollar, the Canadian dollar, the Mexican peso, and the Brazilian real. As seen in Figure 17.3 (upper panel), these contract prices are quoted as direct rates, or dollars per unit of the foreign currency (i.e., the value of a foreign currency in American dollars). Thus, when the value of the dollar declines, the values of a foreign currency and futures contracts on that currency rise.

In early 1992, the CME introduced futures contracts on currency **cross rates**. (Cross rates are rates of exchange between two nondollar currencies.) The first contract of this type approved for trading was the mark/yen futures contract. The contract price is quoted as yen per mark; contracts are settled in yen. As the value of the mark increases against the yen, the mark/yen contract price rises; when the yen appreciates against the mark, the price of the contract falls.

COMPARISON OF FORWARD AND FUTURES MARKETS

Like foreign currency futures, forward markets provide a mechanism for avoiding the uncertainty of exchange rate fluctuations over a given planning period. Before illustrating the use of foreign currency futures to hedge exchange rate risk, it is useful to distinguish between futures and forward contracts.

Forward contracts are not standardized and can be customized to the needs of each trader. For example, they can be negotiated in any currency, in any denomination, and for any maturity. Currency futures contracts, like interest rate futures contracts, are available only in standard denominations and maturities. Forward contracts are arranged electronically by means of a foreign currency dealer or through large financial institutions, especially money center banks. Currency futures contracts are traded on the futures exchanges. As a result, the holder of a forward contract faces default risk, whereas the clearinghouse assumes that risk in the futures markets. Because there is no secondary market for forward contracts, they are less liquid than currency futures, a position that can be offset before maturity. However, as with interest rate futures, currency futures contracts require that a trader's margin account be marked to market daily (i.e., losses must be taken against the margin deposited on a contract). Nonetheless, because of the default and liquidity risks faced in the forward markets, usually only very large traders participate.

Currency Futures Illustrated

Suppose a U.S. bank made a formal commitment on December 24, 1998, to loan a German customer 1 million marks in six days. At that time, the bank plans to convert dollars into marks, but management recognizes the risk of exchange rate fluctuations over the period. With the upcoming advent of the euro on January 1, 1999, there was particular concern over a possible decline in the value of the dollar, which would result in a higher dollar cost for the marks. Figure 17.4 shows the conversion rates for the currencies of the 11 countries participating in the euro when they were set on December 31, 1998. As shown in Panel A of Table 17.3, on December 24, 1998, the direct exchange rate between marks and dollars was $0.5945; the indirect rate was 1.6820 marks per dollar. In other words, one mark cost $0.5945, and one U.S. dollar would buy 1.6820 marks. The bank could negotiate a one-month forward rate, currently quoted as $0.5947 for large banks in amounts of $1 million or more.

Instead of negotiating a forward contract to permit the Exchange at a known rate 30 days hence, suppose the bank decides to use futures contracts to hedge against the risk of appreciation in the value of the mark. Because the hedge is undertaken to protect against the appreciation of the mark (that is, against decline in the value of the

Figure 17.4   ✦   11 MEMBERS OF EUROPEAN UNION TIE THEIR CURRENCIES TO EURO

After years of preparing, an idea first conceived in the 1950s, the euro was launched on January 1, 1999, as a way to unify Europe and prevent another world war. Based on exchange rates on December 31, 1998, the exchange rates of the 11 participating countries in this figure were set, providing the euro a value of about $1.17 on January 1, 1999. Banks, stock exchanges, and securities traders across Europe had to scramble to adapt their computer systems to the euro's introduction. Euro notes and coins will not circulate until Jan. 1, 2002, but banks and stock exchanges must carry out all noncash transactions in euros. European banks converted their systems to offer euro-denominated bank accounts for any customer desiring them.

National currencies will remain in circulation until July 1, 2002, and they will trade in lockstep to the euro until they phase out. In foreign exchange tables, the euro exchange rate is now included.

BY THE NUMBERS

For What It's Worth . . .

The conversion rates involving the 11 countries participating in the euro were set today. The worth of the euro as of today:

13.76	Austrian schillings
40.34	Belgian francs
2.20	Dutch guilders
5.95	Finnish markkas
6.56	French francs
1.96	German marks
0.79	Irish punts
1,936.27	Italian lire
40.34	Luxembourg francs
200.48	Portuguese escudos
166.39	Spanish pesetas

The euro is expected to start trading on Monday at $1.17.

Euro exchange rates are listed in the foreign exchange tables in Business Day.

■ European Union countries adopting the euro

▓ European Union countries not adopting the euro

The New York Times

Source: Edmund L. Andrews, "11 Countries Tie Europe Together in One Currency." *New York Times*, A1, A10, January 1, 1999.

dollar), a long futures position is indicated. Table 17.3, Panel B shows that on December 24, 1998, the settlement price for a March 1999 futures contract for German marks was 0.6001. Each mark futures contract has a face value of 125,000 marks, so eight contracts (1,000,000/125,000 = 8) will be required to hedge against the entire 1,000,000-mark transaction. Table 17.4 presents the details of the hedge.

Table 17.4 ✦ HEDGING WITH CURRENCY FUTURES CONTRACTS (FORECAST: FALLING DOLLAR)

Currency futures contracts may be used to protect against a decline in the value of the dollar. A long hedge, requiring the purchase of currency futures, results in a gain if the value of the dollar falls against the currency on which the futures contract is written, but results in a loss when the value of the dollar strengthens.

I. Hedging in December	
Cash Market	Futures Market
December 24	
Dollars required to purchase 1 million marks at $0.5945	Buy 8 March contracts at $0.6001
$594,500	Value of contracts:
	125,000 × 8 × $0.6001 = $600,100
Results in January	
January 24	
Dollars required to purchase 1 million marks at $0.6725	Sell 8 September contracts at $0.6730
$672,500	Value of contracts:
	125,000 × 8 × $0.6730 = $673,000

II.

Net Results of Hedge in January

Cash Market Gain		Futures Market Loss	
December "cost"	594,500	December purchase	$600,100
January cost	−672,500	January sale	683,500
Loss	− 78,000	Gain	$ 83,400
	Net Gain: $5,400		

This hedge assumes that in January, the mark rose in the spot market to $.6725 and the futures contract price for the mark rose to $.6730.

Suppose, as shown in Table 17.4, that the actual spot exchange rate on January 24, 1999, rose to 0.6725 dollars per mark (or 1.4870 marks per dollar). The mark had actually depreciated relative to the dollar, as the bank managers feared. Suppose the value of the March mark contract, also shown in Table 17.4, had risen to 0.6730. If bank management had chosen not to hedge, the institution would have had only a higher cost of $78,000 to convert the dollars to marks. However, the bank receives a gain on the futures contract of $83,400. This results in a net gain of $5,400, becausethe gain on the futures contract is larger than the higher dollar cost for the marks. Of course, if the mark had fallen in value instead, this could have been a net loss, and the bank would have had more money if it did not hedge. Transaction costs, which are ignored here, would actually result in a somewhat lower net gain. It is important to remember that in December, no one knew whether the mark would appreciate or depreciate relative to the dollar. This uncertainty is precisely the reason for a hedge.[18]

---

[18]For more information on currency futures, see Kolb (1988) and Fieleke (1985).

SUMMARY

Tools for managing interest rate risk include two types of financial futures: interest rate and foreign currency futures. They allow managers to adopt a hedging strategy, through which expected profits on the institution's existing financial position are protected against unfavorable changes in interest rates or foreign exchange rates. Hedging is a risk-minimization approach; it does not allow an institution to profit from unexpected favorable changes. Futures are traded on organized exchanges, facilitating their liquidity, and the clearinghouse plays an important role in transactions.

An interest rate futures contract is an agreement between a buyer and seller to exchange a fixed quantity of a financial asset at a specified price on a specified date. The buyer has a long futures position and purchases a contract when interest rates are expected to fall. The seller of a futures contract takes a short position in anticipation of rising rates. Because the prices of futures contracts move in the same direction as prices on underlying financial assets, falling interest rates coincide with rising prices for futures contracts, and rising rates coincide with falling futures prices. The hedger uses profits earned on futures transactions to offset losses incurred on other financial assets. Additional markets permit institutions to hedge against the risk of changes in currency exchange rates.

The most compelling reasons to use futures contracts are the low transaction costs of initiating and closing out a hedge, the flexibility to take either a long or short position, and the minimal default risk exposure because of the clearinghouse. Problems faced in futures hedging include the cash-flow requirements from daily margin calls, basis risk, and the difficulty of determining the best hedge ratio. Financial institutions must also be careful to follow regulatory and accounting rules governing the use of futures contracts.

Questions

1. Describe the characteristics of an interest rate futures contract. Consult a current issue of *The Wall Street Journal* or other major newspaper to find price quotations on interest rate futures contracts. Are there any contracts written on any financial instruments not shown in Figure 17.1?

2. What features of futures contracts distinguish them from other financial instruments? What are the important differences between forward markets and futures markets? What is the role of the clearinghouse in the futures market? Why do clearinghouses set margin requirements?

3. Explain the difference between using financial futures in a hedging strategy and using futures to speculate. Explain why futures are called derivatives. With the Orange County and Long-Term Capital Hedge Fund crises, derivatives were used to place interest-rate bets. How can futures be used to speculate if the consensus is that interest rates are going to fall? If interest rates are going to rise?

4. Identify interest rate forecasts or investment situations in which each of the following would be appropriate: (a) short hedge, (b) long hedge, and (c) cross hedge.

5. Find a current article on one or more of the futures exchanges located outside the United States. What is the rate of growth in trading volume? How do policies and trading mechanisms compare with those in U.S. markets such as the CBOT or CME? How much closer are we to a truly global futures market?

6. What is meant by the term *basis risk*? What types of hedges have the greatest exposure to basis risk?

7. What does the hedge ratio measure? Why is the hedge ratio needed to determine the number of contracts to trade? What factors make it difficult to construct a perfect hedge? What is the difference between a micro and a macro hedge?

8. What types of restrictions have regulators and accountants developed to control the risk exposure of financial institutions participating in futures markets? Why in recent years have regulators asked banks to have an overall risk management strategy for derivatives?

9. If you were charged with managing exchange rate risk for a U.S. commercial bank operating in international markets, in which types of situations might you prefer to enter into a forward contract? Trade foreign currency futures contracts? What different risks would you face with the different contracts?

10. Consult the financial pages of *The Wall Street Journal* or another major newspaper. Find the price quotations for foreign currency futures contracts. Have any new currencies been added to those shown in Figure 17.3, Panel B? Do currency futures contracts exist for the euro, discussed in Figure 17.4? Based on the current settlement prices you find, is the value of the dollar higher or lower against foreign currencies than it was in late 1998? How do you think the euro will affect futures trading when it becomes a true currency in 2002, and other currencies mentioned in Figure 17.4 no longer exist?

11. Suppose it is your responsibility to manage exchange rate risk for a large German bank with activities in the European Community, the United States, and Asia. How does the development of cross rate futures contracts facilitate the bank's exchange rate risk management?

12. What are some limitations in using futures to hedge a financial institution's overall risk that might explain why the

majority of users of futures are very large financial institutions? If a depository institution performs an overall macro hedge for a negative funding gap, would the institution take a long or short position? What would happen to the basis risk of the hedge if rates go down and mortgage customers prepay their mortgages (i.e., if overall volume or mix changes occur that change the institution's funding gap during the hedging period)?

Problems

1. A portfolio manager will trade futures contracts to protect the value of a $150 million portfolio invested in short-term securities. Calculate the number of contracts that should be traded for the following instruments and hedge ratio estimates. Refer to Table 17.1 to determine the face value (minimum amount) for each of the different types of contracts: (a) T-bond contracts; hedge ratio = 0.85. (b) T-bill contracts; hedge ratio = 0.82. (c) 30-day interest rate futures contracts; hedge ratio = 0.91.

2. A money market portfolio manager needs to hedge against an expected drop in interest rates that could occur before a large inflow of funds is received and invested. The manager plans to buy 10 T-bill futures contracts at a price of 97 percent (i.e., one less the discount yield). If the contracts are sold three months later at 96.25 percent, what will be the gain or loss on the futures position? What if the contracts are sold at 97.63 percent?

3. The manager of a large thrift forecasts an increase in interest rates over the next two months. The thrift currently has $20 million in CDs costing 6 percent. The manager hedges against the expected increase in interest rates by trading twenty 90-day T-bill futures contracts.
   a. Should a long or short hedge be used? Why?
   b. Based on the following information, calculate the gain or loss on the hedge:

	CD Cost	T-bill Futures Settlement Price
Current	6.0%	$983,750
Futures (2 months later)	7.5%	$979,950

4. The executive vice president of a large bank believes that a forecasted increase in T-bill rates will occur, forcing the bank to pay higher interest on its MMDAs (money market demand accounts). She decides to hedge $20 million of its deposit accounts by trading T-bill futures contracts.
   a. Should the executive vice president assume a long or short futures position?
   b. If she estimates a hedge ratio of 0.97, how many contracts should she buy or sell?
   c. Suppose the T-bill futures contracts are trading at 98.13 percent today but are priced at 98.01 percent one month from today, when the position is closed out. What will be the profit or loss on the futures transactions?
   d. Suppose the bank's MMDA costs rise from 2 percent to 8 percent between the beginning and end of the one-month period. What will be the net effect on the monthly interest cost for the institution resulting from the hedge and the change in interest rates?

5. After studying market forecasts, the investment manager of a property/liability insurer anticipates an interest rate decline over the next three months. He expects to receive $100 million in new funds in 90 days, which he will invest in T-bills. In an effort to avoid the adverse effect of the interest rate decline on expected yield, he hedges in the futures market.
   a. Should he assume a short or a long position?
   b. Based on the following information, calculate the resulting gain or loss on the hedge.

	T-Bill Discount Yield	T-Bill Futures Settlement Price
January	9.85%	$979,200
April	8.80%	$982,000

   c. Suppose the manager's interest rate forecast is incorrect and interest rates increase. By April the discount yield on T-bills is 10.50 percent, and the settlement price on the contracts held is 97.75. What is the resulting gain or loss on the hedge?

6. A finance company is planning to issue $50 million in commercial paper in four months. Forecasts of interest rate movements over the intervening period are contradictory, so the firm's manager decides a T-bill futures hedge should be assumed. Fifty T-bill futures contracts are sold at 98.94. The firm estimates that the rate currently required on its commercial paper is 7 percent. Four months later, when the finance company closes out its futures position, the contracts are trading at 98.80 and the company issues commercial paper at a rate of 8.45 percent. Calculate the net interest cost to the firm on its 30-day paper and the effective interest rate it is paying on this short-term debt.

7. Metropolitan National Bank regularly extends loans to importer/exporter customers. In March, management agrees to finance a shipment of cameras for an importer who does not have to pay for the merchandise until it arrives in June. The current cost of the cameras in Japanese yen is 200 million. The prevailing exchange rate is $/yen 5 0.008639 and yen/$5 115.75. The bank's economists anticipate that the value of the dollar will fall over the next three months and recommend a hedge with foreign currency futures. Using the following information, calculate the gain or loss on the hedge.

a. The most recent settlement price on a June yen futures contract was 0.008642, and the standard size of a Japanese yen futures contract is 12.5 million. Given the economists' forecasts, what position should management assume in the futures market to hedge its foreign currency risk? How many contracts will be traded?

b. In June, the bank closes out its position. The spot rate ($/yen) is 0.008333, and June yen futures are trading at 0.008345. Calculate the gain or loss on the hedge. Did the hedge work as expected?

c. Suppose instead that the June spot rate is 0.008929 $/yen and yen futures trade at 0.008928. Calculate the results of the hedge. Comment.

8. A German exporter will receive payment in U.S. dollars for a candle shipment made to an American firm. The current spot rate between Deutsche marks (DM) and dollars (currency per U.S. dollar) is DM/$ = 1.718, and the U.S. dollar equivalent rate (value of a DM in dollars) is $/DM = $0.5820. The exporter will receive $5 million in exactly two months (July). Given the uncertainty about the DM/$ exchange rate that will prevail in July, the German firm decides to hedge with foreign currency futures.

a. Anticipating a decline in the value of the dollar (rise in the value of the DM), will the German firm buy or sell DM futures? The prevailing price on DM futures is $0.5810. How many contracts will be traded? DM futures contracts are written for 125,000 DM.

b. In July the spot rate is 0.6011 $/DM, and DM futures trade at 0.5995. Calculate the gain or loss on the hedge.

c. In general, should you buy or sell currency futures on a foreign currency (priced at U.S. $ equivalent rates, i.e., the currency's value in dollars) if you have a long position in that currency and want to protect its value? Should you buy or sell if you have a short position in that currency, i.e., a future liability in that currency?

9. An American importer buys French wine. The wine shipment will arrive in 30 days, at which time payment is due. If the payment due is 4 million francs and the value of the dollar is expected to fall, how could the importer use the forward currency market to hedge? What cost, in U.S. dollars, would the firm be obligated to pay if the current 30-day forward rate is 0.1942 $/franc? What risks is the firm assuming by using the forward market? If the spot rate between dollars and francs at the time payment is due is 0.1875 $/franc, would the forward agreement achieve its purpose? Explain.

10. Turn to the duration-based hedging example in the appendix to this chapter. Suppose that the initial price of the instrument to be hedged is $955. The expected position of the cash instrument is a YTM of 10.14 percent and a price of $1,008.76, the same as in Table 17A1. Turn to the duration-based hedging example in the appendix to this chapter. Suppose that the initial price of the instrument to be hedged is $955. The expected position of the cash instrument is a yields to maturity of 10.14 percent and a price of $1,008.76 with a duration of 4.148, the same as in Table 17A1. Suppose that in May 2007, the expected duration of T-bond futures is 10.06 and the expected yield on futures is 8.50 percent. The expected futures price is 96–24. Calculate the number of futures contracts needed as well as the results of the new hedge.

Suggested Case Study of Macro Hedging for a Depository Institution

Esty, Ben, Peter Tufano, and Jonathan Headley. "Banc One Corporation: Asset and Liability Management." *Bank of* *America Journal of Applied Corporate Finance* (Fall 1994), 33–65.

Selected References

Abken, Peter A. "Globalization of Stock, Futures, and Options Markets." *Economic Review* (Federal Reserve Bank of Atlanta) 76 (July/August 1991), 1–22.

Booth, James R., Richard L. Smith, and Richard W. Stolz. "Use of Interest Rate Futures by Financial Institutions." *Journal of Bank Research* 14 (Spring 1984), 15–20.

Carter, David A., and Joseph F. Sinkey, Jr. "The Use of Interest Rate Derivatives by End-users: The Case of Large Community Banks." *Journal of Financial Services Research* 14 (July 1998), 17–34.

Chance, Don M. *An Introduction to Options and Futures*, 2d ed. Hinsdale, Ill.: The Dryden Press, 1992.

Chaudhry, Mukesh K., and Alan K. Reichert. "Interest Rate Derivatives and Bank Risk." Working Paper, Cleveland State University, 1998.

Chicago Board of Trade. *Treasury Futures for Institutional Investors*. Chicago: Board of Trade of the City of Chicago, 1990.

Chicago Mercantile Exchange. *Trading and Hedging with Currency Futures and Options*. Chicago: Chicago Mercantile Exchange, 1985.

Drabenstott, Mark, and Anne O'Mara McDonley. "Futures Markets: A Primer for Financial Institutions." *Economic Review* (Federal Reserve Bank of Kansas City) 69 (November 1984), 17–33.

Esty, Ben, Peter Tufano, and Jonathan Headley. "Banc One Corporation: Asset and Liability Management." *Bank of America Journal of Applied Corporate Finance* 7 (Fall 1994), 33–65.

Federal Reserve Bank of New York. *Clearing and Settlement Through the Board of Trade Clearing Corporation.* New York, 1990.

Fieleke, Norman S. "The Rise of the Foreign Currency Futures Markets." *New England Economic Review* (Federal Reserve Bank of Boston) (March/April 1985), 38–47.

Goldstein, Henry S. "Foreign Currency Futures: Some Further Aspects." *Economic Perspectives* (Federal Reserve Bank of Chicago) 7 (November/December 1983), 3–13.

Hansell, Saul. "The Computer that Ate Chicago." *Institutional Investor* 23 (February 1989), 181–188.

Hieronymous, Thomas A. *Economics of Futures Trading.* New York: Commodity Research Bureau, Inc., 1971.

Howard, Charles T., and Louis J. D'Antonio. "Treasury Bill Futures as a Hedging Tool: A Risk-Return Approach." *Journal of Financial Research* 9 (Spring 1986), 25–39.

Hoyt, Robert E. "Use of Financial Futures by Life Insurers." *Journal of Risk and Insurance* 56 (December 1992), 740–748.

Hurtz, Rebecca M., and Mona J. Gardner. "Surviving in a New Environment." *Best's Review (Life/Health Edition)* 85 (September 1984).

Kolb, Robert W. *Understanding Futures Markets.* Glenview, Ill.: Scott, Foresman and Co., 1988.

Kolb, Robert W., and Raymond Chiang. "Improving Hedging Performance Using Interest Rate Futures." *Financial Management* 10 (Autumn 1981), 72–79.

————. "Duration, Immunization and Hedging with Interest Rate Futures." *Journal of Financial Research* 5 (Summer 1982), 161–170.

Koppenhaver, Gary D. "An Empirical Analysis of Bank Hedging in Futures Markets." *Journal of Futures Markets* 10 (February 1990), 1–12.

————. "Futures Market Regulation." *Economic Perspectives* (Federal Reserve Bank of Chicago) 11 (January/February 1987), 3–15.

————. "Trimming the Hedges: Regulators, Banks and Financial Futures." *Economic Perspectives* (Federal Reserve Bank of Chicago) 8 (November/December 1984), 3–12.

Lamm-Tennant, Joan. "Asset/Liability Management for the Life Insurer: Situation Analysis and Strategy Formulation." *Journal of Risk and Insurance* (September 1989), 501–517.

Miller, Merton H. "Financial Innovation: The Last Twenty Years and the Next." *Journal of Financial and Quantitative Analysis* 21 (December 1986), 459–471.

Morris, Charles S. "Managing Interest Rate Risk with Interest Rate Futures." *Economic Review* (Federal Reserve Bank of Kansas City) 74 (March 1989), 3–20.

Napoli, Janet A. "Derivative Markets and Competitiveness." *Economic Perspectives* (Federal Reserve Bank of Chicago) 16 (July/August 1992), 13–24.

Parkinson, Patrick, and Paul Spindt. "The Use of Interest Rate Futures by Commercial Banks." In: *Proceedings of a Conference on Bank Structure and Competition.* Chicago: Federal Reserve Bank of Chicago (1985), 457–489.

Remolona, Eli M. "The Recent Growth of Financial Derivative Markets." *Quarterly Review* (Federal Reserve Bank of New York) 17 (Winter 1992–1993), 28–43.

Saunders, Anthony. *Financial Institutions Management: A Modern Perspective,* 2d ed. Burr Ridge, Ill.: Irwin, 1997.

Scarlata, Jodi G. "Institutionalization Developments in the Globalization of Securities and Futures Markets." *Economic Review* (Federal Reserve Bank of St. Louis) 74 (January/February 1992), 17–30.

Schwarz, Edward D., Joanne M. Hill, and Thomas Schneeweis. *Financial Futures: Fundamentals, Strategies, and Applications.* Homewood, Ill.: Dow Jones-Irwin, 1986.

Smirlock, Michael C. "Hedging Bank Borrowing Costs with Financial Futures." *Business Review* (Federal Reserve Bank of Philadelphia) (May-June 1986), 13–23.

Van Horne, James. *Financial Market Rates and Flows,* 3d ed. Englewood Cliffs, N.J.: Prentice-Hall, 1990.

Appendix 17A

A DURATION-BASED FUTURES HEDGE

In a cross hedge, Equation 17.4, used for calculating the appropriate number of futures contracts to trade, could suggest an inappropriate number of contracts because of the unequal price reactions in instruments with different coupons and maturities, even if yields are perfectly correlated. Including the duration of the cash and futures instruments provides a better estimate of the required number of contracts:

$$N_{DUR} = \frac{R_F P_C D_C}{R_C FP_F D_F} \qquad [17A.1]$$

where

N_{DUR} = the number of contracts to be traded for each cash market instrument being hedged

R_F = 1 + the rate expected to prevail on the instrument underlying the futures contract,

R_C = 1 + the expected yield to maturity on the asset to be hedged,

F_{PF} = the price agreed on in the futures contract,

P_C = the expected spot price of the asset to be hedged as of the hedge termination date,

D_C = the expected duration of the asset to be hedged as of the termination date, and

D_F = the expected duration of the instrument underlying the futures contract as of the termination date.

This approach to estimating N was developed in Kolb and Chiang (1981, 1982). For additional discussion, see Chance (1992).

The duration-based equation adjusts the size of the futures position for potential differences in the maturity and coupon rates of the cash and futures securities. For example, consider the decision facing a bond portfolio manager in February 2002, when he anticipates an $8 million cash inflow in May 2002 and forecasts a

---

Table 17A.1 ✦ DURATION-BASED ESTIMATION OF THE FUTURES POSITION

Expected Cash Inflow (May 2002)	$8,000,000
Cash Instrument to be Hedged	Corporate bonds: $10\frac{3}{8}$ of 02
	Current YTM (February 1997): 11.14%
	Current price: $971.83
Number of Bonds if Purchased at Current Price	8,231
Expected Position of Cash Instrument in May 2000	Expected YTM: 10.14% (R_C = 1 + 0.1014)
	Expected market price: $1,008.76 ($P_c$)
	Duration at expected YTM: 4,148 (D_c)
February 2002 Price on T-Bond Futures (10.12% Yield)	83–24 = 83.75% of par = $83,750 ($FP_F$)
Expected Position of T-Bond Futures in May 2000	Price: 91–16 = 91.5% of par = $91,500
	Yield: 9.12% (R_F = 1 + 0.0912)
	Duration: 9.871 (D_F)
Duration-Based Number of Contracts	

$$N_{DUR} = \frac{R_F P_C D_C}{R_C FP_F D_F} \qquad [17A.1]$$

$$N_{DUR} = \frac{(1.0912)(\$1,008.76)(4.148)}{(1.1014)(\$83,750)(9.871)} = 0.005015 \text{ per cash instrument}$$

Total Number of Contracts = 0.005015(8,231) = 41.28 = 41 contracts

---

decline in corporate bond yields over the intervening period. The manager is watching a bond issue that matures in 2002; he expects the yield on these bonds to be 10.14 percent in May, down from the February level of 11.14 percent. At that yield, their duration in May would be 4.148 years. If funds were available in February, 8,231 bonds ($8 million ($971.83 per bond) could be purchased at the current market price. By May, however, the price is expected to have risen to $1,008.76, and $8 million will buy only 7,930 bonds.

Table 17.A1 shows the calculation of a duration-based hedge position to fit this situation. Because there are no futures contracts on corporate bonds, a cross hedge is required. T-bond futures are a reasonable choice. However, because they are standardized at an 8 percent coupon, with at least 15-year maturities, the duration of the cash and futures securities will differ. Constructing a hedge by simply comparing the market values of the cash and futures instruments would lead to a less than optimal hedge. The appropriate long position for this hedge is to buy 41 T-bond contracts, which can later be sold at a profit if rates fall.

Table 17.A2 shows the results of a long hedge with 41 T-bond contracts. Assuming the manager's expectations are perfectly fulfilled, the net gain on the hedge is $13,779, more than offsetting the opportunity loss from the decline in market yields during the period in which investment must be delayed. Nothing guarantees a perfect hedge, but performance is improved if the coupon and maturity of the instrument to be hedged are matched closely to the security underlying the futures contract. As with any duration measure, the hedge protects against only one interest rate movement, so it must be adjusted frequently as market conditions change.

Table 17A.2 ✦ RESULTS OF THE DURATION-BASED HEDGE

I.

Cash Market		Futures Market	
February			
Corporate bond yield: 11.14%		Buy 41 T-bond contracts for September delivery	
Price: $971.83		at 83–24	
Total available if purchased in February 2000		Yield: 10.12%	
8,231 bonds		Cost: $3,433,750	
May			
Funds received and invested: $8,000,000		Sell 41 September T-bond contracts at 91–16	
Corporate bond yield: 10.14%		Yield: 9.12%	
Price: $1,008.76		Price: $3,751,500	
Total purchase: 7,930 bonds			

II.

Cash Market Loss		Futures Market Gain	
February cost (8,231 bonds)	$7,999,133	May sale	$3,751,500
May cost (8,231 bonds)	−8,303,104	February purchase	−3,433,750
Loss	($ 303,971)	Gain	$ 317,750
	Net Gain: $13,779		

18

INTEREST RATE RISK MANAGEMENT: INDEX FUTURES, OPTIONS, SWAPS, AND OTHER DERIVATIVES

*I*n the early 1990s, members of the financial press anointed a small group of securities experts as Wall Street "Rocket Scientists." These experts—most of whom work for securities exchanges or securities firms—are a new breed of inventors who study financial markets, sources of risk, and the needs of market participants. These "scientists" then devote their creative energy to developing financial instruments capable of satisfying these needs.

For the most part, the rocket scientists are working with **derivatives,** the name given to instruments whose value is derived from prices and price fluctuations in some underlying asset. Financial futures contracts on Treasury bills (T-bills) and bonds (T-bonds),

introduced in the previous chapter, are just one category of derivative securities; futures contracts and options are now available on many other instruments. As the rocket scientists have continued their inventive work into the early 1990s, new derivatives are introduced almost daily.

What continues to drive these innovations? The most important factor is risk. Uncertainty about interest rates, exchange rates, price fluctuations in stock and bond markets around the world, even air pollution—all are categories of risk that market participants want to escape. The rocket scientists are constantly searching for a better means of allowing them to do so. This chapter continues the discussion of hedging *techniques begun in Chapter 17 by introducing a variety of new derivative instruments and compares and contrasts several strategies used for managing risk by financial institutions.*[1]

◆ ◆ ◆

STOCK INDEX FUTURES

Like interest rate and currency futures, **stock index futures** are instruments for hedging exposure to changes in market values, specifically exposure to the change of values in equity portfolios. Participants in the stock index futures markets include commercial bank trust departments, insurance companies, pension funds, equity mutual funds, and securities firms. In contrast to the contracts discussed in Chapter 17, stock index futures do not protect against changes in interest rates, but instead their value is pegged to movements in one of several aggregate measures of stock market performance. Their origins in the wild and woolly commodities markets, coupled with their appeal to conservative financial institutions, led to an early nickname of "pin-striped pork bellies."[2]

As of 1993, futures contracts were traded regularly on groups of domestic stocks such as the Standard and Poor's (S&P) 500, the New York Stock Exchange (NYSE) Index, the Value Line Composite Index, the Mini Value Line Index, and the Major Market Index (MMI) of 20 large firms, designed to emulate the Dow Jones Industrial Average (DJIA). An attempt by the Chicago Board of Trade (CBOT) to offer a contract based on the Dow was met by a lawsuit from the Dow Jones Company, thwarting introduction of that futures contract. Indexes tracking the performance of non-U.S. equities have also been introduced—most notably the Nikkei 225.

As is true of interest rate futures, developments in the stock index futures market are rapid. New contracts come into the market and old ones leave relatively often, and the array of available contracts is likely to change with time. An example is the development in 1998 by the Kansas City Board of Trade of futures and options contracts on the ISDEX, an index of 50 stocks that receive their revenues from the internet.

THEORETICAL BASIS OF STOCK INDEX FUTURES

Stock index futures are based on capital market theory as reflected in the capital asset pricing model (CAPM) and the **efficient markets hypothesis** (EMH). CAPM models the price of an individual asset or portfolio as a function of its beta coefficient, which, in turn, is a function of the covariance between the asset's expected returns and the expected returns on the market portfolio. The market portfolio, with a beta of 1, is a fully diversified combination of assets that represents the standard of

---

[1]Donald Katz. "Wall Street Rocket Scientists." *Worth* (February/March, 1992), 68–74; "Derivatives Sprout Bells and Whistles." *Euromoney* (August, 1992), 29–39.

[2]Kathleen Kerwin. "Pin-Striped Pork Bellies: Why Stock Index Futures Are Red Hot." *Barron's* 14 (February 14, 1983), 32–34.

comparison for all others. EMH argues that given the wide availability of information to market participants and the speed with which prices react to it, investors with well-diversified portfolios cannot consistently earn returns higher than those on the market portfolio. Investors who choose portfolios with more or less risk than the market portfolio, as measured by beta, should expect to earn a return commensurate with the risk of the portfolio they choose.

Although not perfect, some stock indexes are used as surrogates for the stock market as a whole; the portfolio of stocks underlying such an index is assumed to have a beta of 1. The performance of many professional portfolio managers is evaluated through comparison to a market index, and those who earn lower returns are soundly criticized. Other indexes may reflect a segment of the market. For example, the Chicago Mercantile Exchange (CME) introduced the S&P MidCap 400 Index in 1992, tracking the performance of a portfolio of firms with market values between $300 million and $5 billion. Smaller investors, who may be prevented by brokerage fees, commissions, or funds limitations from holding a well-diversified portfolio, often use "the market" or a market segment as a standard of comparison for interpreting their own results. Later examples indicate why using a stock index as a benchmark of performance is useful to managers hedging equity portfolios.

HISTORY AND CHARACTERISTICS OF STOCK INDEX FUTURES

The first stock index futures contract, based on the Value Line Composite Index, was traded on the Kansas City Board of Trade in February, 1982. Within three months, an S&P 500 contract was trading at the CME, and a NYSE contract was trading on the New York Futures Exchange. The indexes are similar in that they are composite measures of the prices of several stocks, but there are also important differences. Table 18.1 compares the composition and calculation of several indexes, including some developed expressly for use in the index futures and options markets. Because the indexes are not identical, they do not behave identically, although their movements are similar. For example, during the period 1987 through 1991, the MMI had a 0.99 correlation with the DJIA.[3]

Impossibility of Delivery   In comparison with almost all other futures contracts, stock index futures have a distinguishing characteristic: It is not possible to make or take physical delivery of an index. If closure does not occur before the delivery month, the contract's settlement level is the same as the level of the index on a given date in either March, June, September, or December, the four months during the year when index futures contracts expire. As with other futures contracts, a trader's account is marked to market daily and cash settlement is required.

Value of a Contract   The value of a stock index contract is calculated as the level of the index multiplied by an established amount, usually $500. The dollar multiplier for each index is given in daily price quotations in major newspapers. For example, Figure 18.1, showing January 5, 1999, data for index futures from *The Wall Street Journal* of the next day, indicates that the settlement price on an S&P 500 Index contract scheduled to expire in June, 1999, was 1264.90 (note that decimals must be

---

[3]Chicago Board of Trade. *MMI Futures and Options* (1991).

Table 18.1 ◆ Composition of Selected Stock Market Indexes

Some popular futures contracts and options are based on commonly watched indicators of general stock market activity. A wide variety of market indexes is regularly published in the financial pages. Each index is based on a different group of securities. There are many ways of calculating index values.

Index	Composition
S&P 500 Index	Measures value of 500 representative stocks listed on national and regional exchanges. The index is a weighted average; the weights reflect the total market value of all outstanding shares.
NYSE Composite Index	Measures the value of all common stocks listed on the NYSE (more than 1,500 stocks). The index is a weighted average; the weights reflect the total market value of all outstanding shares.
Value Line Composite Index	Measures the value of most stocks listed on the NYSE and some traded on other regional exchanges or the over-the-counter markets. The index is a geometric average; all values are equally weighted.
Dow Jones Industrial Average	Measures the value of 30 blue-chip industrial stocks. The index is a simple average; all prices are equally weighted, with the divisor adjusted for stock splits and stock dividends.
Major Market Index	Measures the price of 20 blue-chip stocks traded on the NYSE, 17 of which are in the DJIA. The index is a simple average.
AMEX Market Value Index	Measures value of all stocks traded on the American Stock Exchange (approximately 850).
S&P 100 Index	Measures value of 100 stocks, selected from and designed to mirror the S&P 500. The index is value-weighted.
Wilshire Index	Measures the value of all NYSE and AMEX stocks plus the most actively traded over-the-counter stocks. The index is a weighted average; the weights reflect the total market value of all outstanding shares.
NASDAQ 100 Index	Measures the value of the 100 largest nonfinancial firms traded over the counter.
S&P MidCap 400 Index	Measures value of 400 stocks—none of which is included in the S&P 500—with firm market values between $300 million and $5 billion. The index includes firms in four main industrial groups. The index is a weighted average like the S&P 500 but is quoted as a percentage of its base value on December 31, 1990.
Nikkei 225 Index	Measures the value of 225 large publicly traded Japanese firms. Historically the index was price-weighted, but it was recently revised to reflect market value weights.
Dow Jones World Stock Index	Measures value of 2,200 stocks traded in 10 countries. The index is calculated in four major currencies: dollar, mark, pound, and yen. It is value-weighted and quoted as a percentage of its base value on December 31, 1991.

inserted in this price by looking at the actual S&P 500 index, which was 1244.78 on this date). Multiplying the futures price index by $500, the settlement price is:

$$1264.90 \times \$500 = \$632,450$$

Note that because January 5, 1999, was not a contract expiration date, the closing settlement level on the futures contract on the S&P index for June (1264.90) was not the same as the closing level of the actual S&P 500 Index in the spot market (1244.78), suggesting that investors expect a rise in the market between January and June.

Figure 18.1   ✦   STOCK INDEX FUTURES AND STOCK MARKET INDEXES

Data on index futures contracts and on the indexes underlying popular futures contracts are found daily in the financial pages of major newspapers.

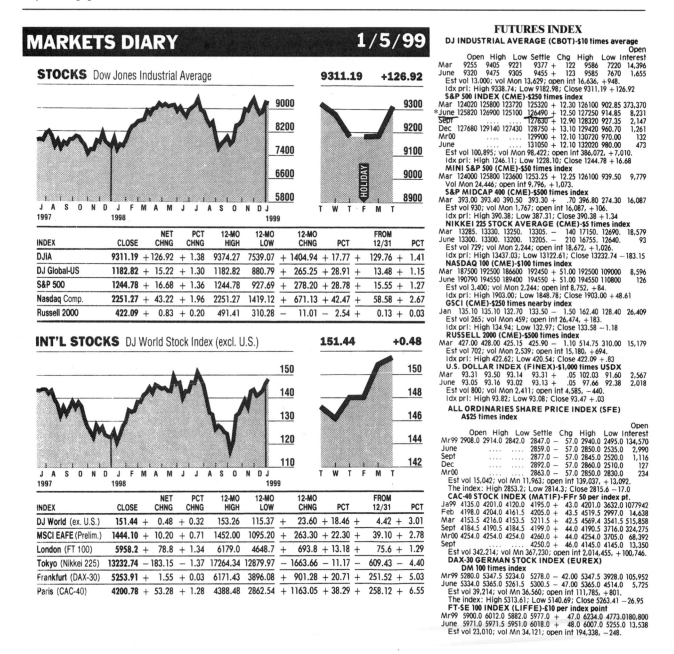

Limits on Price Movements   Until after the stock market crash of 1987, stock index futures contracts had no limits on daily price movements. Since the crash, however, most index futures contracts have been subject to daily trading limits. Each exchange has handled the limits somewhat differently. The limits on S&P 500 futures contracts, for example, are pegged to price movements on the underlying stocks. In contrast, daily limits on other indexes at times are based in part on movements away from the previous day's contract settlement price and in part on movements in the DJIA. Limits on other stock index futures contracts are different still.

Besides overall price movement limits, most contracts also require minimum price movements from trade to trade. In general, the limit is 0.05 times the dollar multiplier on the contract. For example, the minimum movement on a contract may be $25 because, as shown in Figure 18.1, the dollar multiplier may be $500 (0.05 × $500 = $25).[4]

Greater Price Volatility   Observers of stock index futures have identified another distinguishing characteristic. The price volatility of each index futures contract, measured by the standard deviation of daily percentage price changes, is greater than the volatility of the underlying index. Such a relationship suggests that basis risk exposure can be significant for institutions using index futures to hedge their equity portfolios.[5] These early findings, however, have not dampened investor interest in these markets.

FINANCIAL INSTITUTIONS AND STOCK INDEX FUTURES

Because of regulatory restrictions and unfamiliarity with index futures, institutions at first engaged in only limited trading. As risk management strategies used by financial institutions have become increasingly sophisticated, their involvement in the index futures markets has accelerated.

Hedging Against a Decline in the Market

A direct use of stock index futures is as a hedge for an equity portfolio, designed to protect against swings in the market that could reduce returns. The most obvious need for a hedge occurs when a market downturn is anticipated. The manager of a large equity position naturally wants to avoid a substantial decline in portfolio value if a **bear market** is forecast—one in which prices in general are expected to fall.

One way to avoid losses is to sell large portions of the portfolio before the decline, but transactions costs could be considerable. Another drawback is the time required to choose the stocks to be sold. As an alternative, the manager could hedge against market price declines with a short hedge by selling stock index futures. If the market indexes do indeed fall, so will the value of the contracts, resulting in a profit when the position is closed out and offsetting losses in the stock portfolio.

Again, as with interest rate futures, an increase in expected market yields (decline in prices) suggests a short hedge. The small margin requirements on index futures contracts allow an institution to assume a significant position with a small amount of cash.

---

[4]Chicago Board of Trade. *MMI Futures and Options*.
[5]See Hill, Jain, and Ward (1987), 10–11.

Importance of the Number of Contracts

A main determinant of the effectiveness of the hedge, as in any other futures position, is the number of futures contracts used. Besides the size of the portfolio, the number of contracts is affected by the volatility of returns on the portfolio relative to the market indexes on which futures contracts are available. Beta is a relative measure of volatility. Because the portfolio of stocks underlying a market index is assumed to have a beta of 1, if the portfolio to be hedged has a beta greater or less than 1, changes in the value of the hedged portfolio will be more or less than changes in the index underlying the futures contract. Thus, the number of contracts must be adjusted to structure an effective hedge.

The Number of Contracts When Portfolio Beta Is 1   Suppose that a pension fund manager holds a stock portfolio of $450 million in January, and the NYSE index is at 600.24. The equity market has been on the upswing, but the surge is expected to end soon. Rather than liquidating portions of the portfolio, the manager chooses to sell NYSE stock index futures. The previous day's index settlement level on March futures was 602.75. Assuming that the portfolio beta is 1, the number of contracts to sell is:

$$NF = \frac{\text{Value of Stock Portfolio}}{\text{Futures Index} \times \text{\$ Multiplier}} \times Bp \qquad [18.1]$$

$$= \frac{\$450,000,000}{602.75 \times \$500} \times 1 = 1,493 \text{ contracts}$$

Equation 18.1 divides the value of the portfolio the manager is attempting to hedge by the value of one index futures contract at the current settlement level. It then adjusts for the relative riskiness of the cash portfolio as compared with the risk of the market index. In this case, the cash portfolio has a beta of 1, as does the NYSE index.

Now suppose that by March, the market index falls, as anticipated, to 585.23, a decline of 2.5 percent. Results of the hedge are summarized in Table 18.2. The value of the portfolio falls by 2.5 percent to $438,750,000, or a loss of $11,250,000 on the spot position. The value of the futures contracts, with a settlement level now also down by 2.5 percent to 587.68, falls to:

$$587.68 \times \$500 \times 1,493 \text{ contracts} = \$438,703,120$$

When the position is closed out, the profits before transactions costs are $11,249,755 on the futures contracts. Netting out the loss on the portfolio and gain on the futures contract, the net loss is only ($245). The hedge is not perfect because the manager cannot trade fractional contracts; the custom of rounding index values to two decimal places also affects results.

The Number of Contracts When Beta Is Not 1.   What are the consequences of the hedge if the price volatility of the portfolio exceeds that of the market index? Suppose that the portfolio beta is 1.3. When the market index declines by 2.5 percent, the portfolio value declines by 1.3×2.5 percent = 3.25 percent, a dollar decline of $450,000,000 \times 0.0325 = \$14,625,000$. A hedge with only 1,493 NYSE Index contracts would be insufficient protection, because the gain on a hedge using that number of contracts is only $11,249,755. The net result of the hedge would be a loss of more than $3 million.

Table 18.2 ✦ THE SHORT HEDGE: PORTFOLIO BETA OF 1.0 (FORECAST: BEAR MARKET)

A short hedge with index futures is used when falling securities prices are forecast. The profit on the short futures position can be used to offset losses in a portfolio of stocks.

Cash Market	Futures Market
January	
NYSE Index: 600.24	NYSE Index settlement level: 602.75
Stock portfolio value:	Sell 1,493 contracts
$450,000,000	602.75 × $500 × 1,493 = $449,952,875
March	
Market decline = 2.5%	NYSE Index settlement level:
NYSE Index: 585.23	602.75 (1 − 0.025) = 587.68
Stock portfolio value:	Close out position by buying 1,493 contracts:
$450,000,000 (1 − 0.025) = $438,750,000	587.68 × $500 × 1,493 = $438,703,120

Cash Market Loss		Futures Market Gain	
January value	$450,000,000	January sale	$449,952,875
March value	438,750,000	March purchase	438,703,120
Loss	($ 11,250,000)	Gain	$ 11,249,755

Net Loss ($245)

A better hedge position would adjust for the beta coefficient:

$$NF = \frac{\$450,000,000}{602.75 \times \$500} \times 1.3 = 1,941 \text{ contracts}$$

As shown in Table 18.3, with a short hedge of 1,941 contracts, the decline in the NYSE settlement price to 587.68 produces a gain of $14,625,435 and a net gain on the hedge of $435. Both short hedge examples assume that price movements in the hedged portfolio and the futures contract are perfectly correlated; in practice, the correlation would not be perfect, introducing basis risk exposure.

Hedging When An Upturn Is Anticipated

A stock index futures hedge in anticipation of a stronger equity market would be more unusual but still possible. For example, a long hedge may be undertaken when a trust department has good reason to expect a large inflow of funds at some future point, funds that can be invested only after an expected upswing. The invested funds will miss the benefits of the **bull market**, one in which price increases are anticipated. If the manager buys stock index futures contracts, they will increase in value during the bull market. When the position is later closed out by selling the contracts, the increase in value produces a profit that compensates for the higher prices at which new stock must be purchased. Once again, the effectiveness of the hedge is based on the price volatility of the stock purchased relative to the price volatility of the futures contract.

Table 18.3 ◆ The Short Hedge: Portfolio Beta of 1.3 (Forecast: Bear Market)

Short hedges with index futures must take into account the market risk (as measured by beta) of the hedged portfolio. Portfolios with high betas must be hedged with a larger number of index futures contracts than portfolios with lower betas.

Cash Market	Futures Market
January	
NYSE Index: 600.24	NYSE Index settlement level: 602.75
Stock portfolio value:	Sell 1,941 contracts:
$450,000,000	602.75 × $500 × 1,941 = $584,968,875
March	
Market decline = 2.5%	NYSE Index settlement level:
Stock portfolio value change:	600.25 (1 − 0.025) = 587.68
−2.5% × 1.3 = −3.25%	
Stock portfolio value:	Close out position by buying 1,941 contracts:
$450,000,000 (1 − 0.0325) = $435,375,000	587.68 × $500 × 1,941 = $570,343,440

Cash Market Loss		Futures Market Gain	
March value	$435,375,000	January sale	$584,968,875
January value	450,000,000	March purchase	570,843,440
Loss	($ 14,625,000)	Gain	$ 14,625,435

Net Gain $435

Program Trading: Index Arbitrage

The term **program trading** encompasses several modern investment strategies. The narrowest definition is the simultaneous placement of buy and sell orders for groups of stocks totaling $1 million or more. A common and controversial form of program trading is the simultaneous trading of stock and stock index futures to profit from changes in the spread between the two, sometimes called **index arbitrage**.[6]

Table 18.4 illustrates a simple example of index arbitrage using the MMI (see Table 18.1), which was used widely for arbitrage in the late 1980s. Suppose that on February 26, a manager buys 2,000 shares of each stock in the MMI, simultaneously selling 18 MMI futures contracts. Hypothetically, the MMI is at 311.74, and the futures settlement level is 313.55 on that date. The contracts expire on March 21, and the manager knows, as is true of all index futures, that the contract settlement level and the MMI itself will converge by the expiration date, even though they differ on February 26.

On March 21, the stock portfolio will be liquidated and the short futures position closed out. Regardless of the actual level of stock prices on that day, the manager profits. If prices rise, the value of the stock will increase more than the loss on

---

[6]These and other definitions can be found in "The Realities of Program Trading." *Market Perspectives (Chicago Mercantile Exchange)* (January/February, 1990). The example in Table 18.4 is similar to one in Jeffrey Laderman. "Those Big Swings on Wall Street." *Business Week* (April 7, 1986), 32–36.

Table 18.4 ✦ INDEX ARBITRAGE

Index arbitrage is the simultaneous trading of index futures and stocks composing the underlying index. Computer programs are used to determine when stocks and futures should be bought or sold to profit from temporary price discrepancies in the two markets.

Cash Market	Futures Market
February 26	
MMI:	MMI settlement level: 313.55
311.74	Sell 18 contracts:
Buy 2,000 shares of each MMI stock:	313.55 × $500 × 18 = $2,821,950
Value = $2,749,000	
If Prices Increase by March 21	
MMI increase = 5.238%	MMI settlement level:
MMI:	328.07, an increase of 4.631%
328.07	Close out position by buying 18 contracts:
Stock portfolio value:	328.07 × $500 × 18 = $2,952,630
$2,893,000	

Cash Market Loss		Futures Market Gain	
3/21 value	$2,893,000	2/26 sale	$2,821,950
2/26 value	2,749,000	3/21 purchase	2,952,630
Gain	$ 144,000	Loss	($ 130,680)

Net Gain $13,320

Cash Market	Futures Market
If Prices Decrease by March 21	
MMI decrease = 5.238%	MMI settlement level: 295.41, a decrease of 5.785%
MMI: 295.41	Close out position by buying 18 contracts:
Stock portfolio value:	295.41 × $500 × 18 = $2,658,690
$2,605,000	

Cash Market Loss		Futures Market Gain	
3/21 value	$2,605,000	2/26 sale	$2,821,950
2/26 value	2,749,000	3/21 purchase	2,658,690
Loss	($ 144,000)	Gain	$ 163,260

Net Gain $19,260

the futures contract, resulting in a net profit. If prices fall, the value of the stock will fall less than the value of the futures contracts. This is true because both the index and the contract settlement value must be the same on March 21, but the contract settlement value is higher on February 26. The gain on the futures contracts will exceed losses on the stock portfolio, again resulting in a net profit.

Index arbitrage and other forms of program trading differ from hedging because hedgers use futures to offset adverse changes in a portfolio held in the normal course of operations. Index arbitragers, however, choose and manage portfolios based solely on the characteristics of available futures contracts, with the intention of profiting from fluctuations in the basis.

Program Trading and the Crash of 1987

Because program trading involves buying and selling large quantities of stocks, it has been blamed for wide fluctuations in stock prices in recent years. In the early days of index arbitrage, price swings were particularly noticeable on the four trading days each year in which stock index futures contracts expired, as large numbers of traders closed out positions in stocks, index futures, or both. A widely quoted study in 1986 concluded, however, that small investors could potentially benefit from institutions' use of program trading because they would know in advance when price volatility would be high and could avoid the market on those days.[7]

When the DJIA fell by 508 points to 1,738.74 (a 22.6 percent drop) on October 19, 1987, the debate over the effect of program trading on stock price volatility escalated. The **Brady Commission**, a blue-ribbon panel appointed by President Reagan to investigate causes of the crash, concluded in 1988 that computerized trading by large institutions played a major role in the downward spiral of the market. The commission recommended that the stock and futures markets be brought under a single regulator (the Federal Reserve System [the Fed]) and that the two markets institute coordinated "circuit-breaker" programs to halt trading in both markets when price movements exceeded specified limits. Other observers suggested that the Securities and Exchange Commission (SEC) be given oversight authority for both stock and stock index futures markets. Some critics even called for a complete regulatory ban on computerized trading.

Other experts have come to very different conclusions. They believe that the computerized trading of stocks and stock index futures improves the liquidity of the markets and contend that the 1987 crash was actually caused by the NYSE's antiquated system of trading. As stock prices fell during the day on October 19, traders who wished to purchase stock at "cheap" prices were unable to do so because their orders could not be executed. Had the NYSE's computers been more up-to-date, these observers argue, the market decline would have been considerably slowed.[8]

Since 1987, the debate over program trading has continued. In fact, it escalated in 1990 when Japanese investors and officials blamed U.S. securities firms for contributing to the steep decline in the Tokyo stock market by using index arbitrage. Some large securities firms, although not condemning the practice, succumbed to pressure from politicians and regulators and curtailed—or even abandoned—index arbitrage for their own accounts. (Many will still engage in it on behalf of clients.) Still, by 1993, no formal ban on program trading had been contemplated. Most experts recognize that financial and technological innovations, and the regulatory avoidance they spawn, virtually ensure that no amount of regulation will eliminate institutions' efforts to profit from market opportunities. Instead, it is likely that regulators' efforts will focus on potential abuse of innovation rather than its elimination. In fact, as technology and innovation have increased market efficiency, potential profits from program trading have declined, and the volume of activity has declined as well.

---

[7]See Stoll and Whaley (1986). Other studies have questioned the conclusion that program trading increases price volatility. See James T. Moser. "Trading Activity, Program Trading, and the Volatility of Stock Returns." Unpublished Working Paper, Research Department, Federal Reserve Bank of Chicago (September, 1992).

[8]Excerpts from the Brady Commission Report, as well as analyses by the commission's critics, can be found in Barro, et al. (1989).

OTHER INDEX FUTURES

An institution's ability to hedge against portfolio declines through index futures is not limited to stock index futures. For example, the CBOT introduced Bond Buyer Municipal Bond Index futures contracts in 1985. This contract was motivated by the relatively poor historical results for cross hedges of municipal bond portfolios that used T-bond futures. Using a recently created index of 40 municipal bonds, daily settlement prices are calculated as $1,000 times the index level. Institutions with diversified holdings of municipals, such as commercial banks, mutual funds, securities firms, and property/liability insurers, view the contracts as holding much promise for protecting against broad-based declines in the bond markets.

Other index futures contracts have been developed to protect investors against exchange rate risk in general, i.e., for those not wishing to hedge against a particular currency (U.S. Dollar Index and European Currency Unit Index), as well as against changes in the value of precious metals (Commodity Research Bureau Index). Stock index futures for stocks traded on the London, Sydney, Tokyo, Singapore, and Hong Kong exchanges have also been developed; most are traded only on foreign stock exchanges, but several are approved on U.S. exchanges.

OPTIONS ON FINANCIAL ASSETS

Another financial innovation, the **option**, is enjoying greater acceptance as a hedging instrument for financial institutions, including options on stock indexes and stock index futures, T-bonds and T-bond futures, and foreign currencies. Although options are similar to futures contracts, important differences separate the two types of hedging mechanisms. Like futures, options can be used for speculation, but this discussion emphasizes hedging.

Options on individual stocks have existed for some time. When they were concentrated in the over-the-counter markets, trading was relatively infrequent. The move in 1973 to offer standardized instruments on the organized exchanges has improved liquidity, and newer types of options have attracted a wider group of market participants.

Options Defined

An option is an agreement giving its holder the right to buy or sell a specified asset, over a limited time period, at a specified price. The option itself is created by an **option writer**, someone who stands ready to buy or sell the asset when the holder wishes to make a transaction. The price written into the option agreement is the **exercise** (or **strike**) **price**. Because options are traded on organized exchanges, they may also be sold to other investors before they expire.

Although options are similar to futures agreements, there are differences. As the name suggests, an option does not obligate the holder to undertake the purchase or sale. Depending on movements in the value of the underlying asset, the holder may choose not to exercise the option to buy or sell. If so, the option expires at maturity and becomes worthless. Another difference is that most options (those called **American options**) can be exercised at any point during their lives; with futures contracts, in contrast, an exchange of securities takes place only on the specified delivery date. (A few options, including options on the S&P 500 Index, are **European options**, which can be exercised only at expiration.)

Call Options   A **call option** is an agreement in which the option writer sells the holder the right to buy a specified asset on or before a future date. The buyer of a call option expects the price of the asset to increase over the life of the option, eventually exceeding the exercise price. If the asset price rises, the value of the option also rises, and the option holder has the additional opportunity to sell it at a profit before it expires.

Put Options   A **put option** is the opposite of a call. Puts give the holder the right to sell an asset at the strike price, and the option writer is obligated to buy it if the holder desires to sell. The buyer of a put option expects the asset's price to fall below the strike price. If the price falls, the put option becomes increasingly valuable.

Premiums   If market prices do not move as the option buyer forecasts, the option is allowed to expire. There is no obligation to exercise it if market conditions make it unprofitable to do so. The cost, however, is the original price (the **premium**) of the option. If the option is not exercised, that cost cannot be recovered; the writer of the option, i.e., the seller, realizes a gain.

Option Values Illustrated

The value of an option over time is influenced by the difference between the market and exercise prices of the underlying asset. Other influences are the time to expiration of the option and the volatility in the price of the underlying asset.

Figure 18.2 shows the value of options on several indexes at the close of trading on December 21, 1998. As with futures contracts on indexes, it is not possible for investors to take physical delivery of the index when an option or an option on a futures contract is exercised; therefore, index options are settled with cash. The holder of a call option on a stock index is really purchasing the right to "buy" cash, based on the difference between the strike price (in this case a designated value for the S&P 100 Index) and the actual value of the index at the end of trading on the expiration date. The amount the holder receives in cash is determined by the difference between the actual index value and the strike price times the dollar multiplier assigned to that index. For options on indexes, by far the most common dollar multiplier is $100.

In Figure 18.2, call options for the S&P 100 Index are shown with strike prices ranging from 510 to 640. On December 21, 1998, the call option with a strike price of 570 and an expiration date of January, 1999, traded for a premium index of 33, or a total premium cost of $33 \times \$100$ multiplier $= \$3,300$. Hence, based on the strike settlement price of $570 \times \$100 = \$57,000$, the premium cost is about 5.79 percent of the value of the settlement price. As shown in Panel B of Figure 18.2, the index itself closed at 596.16 on December 21, 1998. If the index were still at that level at expiration (an unlikely event), the holder of the option would exercise the option and receive a gain of $(596.16 - 570) \times \$100 = \$2,616$. However, this gain would not be large enough to cover the premium cost. Consequently, to cover the premium cost, the price would have to move considerably higher than the current closing price. This call option, with a strike price below the market index value, is said to be **in the money;** when the strike price of a call option is greater than the index value, the call is **out of the money.**[9] In Figure 18.2, even call options that are out of the money

---

[9]Because put holders benefit when underlying asset or index values fall, put options are in the money when their strike prices exceed the market value of the underlying asset or index; puts are out of the money when the value of the asset or index exceeds the put strike price.

Figure 18.2 ✦ INFORMATION FOR INDEX OPTIONS AND ACTUAL INDEXES

INDEX OPTIONS — MONDAY, DECEMBER 21, 1998

S.& P. 100 (CBOE)   Close: 596.16

Strike Price	Calls Jan	Feb	Mar	Puts Jan	Feb	Mar
510	93	r	r	7/8	43/8	93/8
520	811/2	r	s	11/8	55/8	83/4
525	r	s	s	13/8	s	s
530	73	r	83	17/16	r	93/8
535	r	s	s	13/4	s	s
540	r	r	r	2	8	117/8
545	563/4	s	s	2	s	s
550	52	617/8	r	23/4	91/8	14
555	48	s	s	27/8	s	s
560	42	53	r	33/4	101/8	r
565	391/4	s	s	4	s	s
570	33	421/2	463/4	51/4	121/4	17
575	291/4	391/2	s	61/4	131/4	s
580	243/4	343/4	43	7	16	191/2
585	211/4	311/2	r	81/4	r	211/4
590	171/2	301/2	323/4	93/4	183/4	231/4
595	141/2	s	r	115/8	191/2	s
600	113/8	235/8	301/4	14	23	28
605	85/8	s	r	163/8	s	s
610	65/8	16	23	171/8	s	s
615	43/4	s	s	s	s	s
620	31/4	113/4	151/2	251/2	r	r
625	21/4	s	s	s	s	s
630	11/2	81/4	s	311/8	s	s
640	11/16	43/4	105/8	s	441/4	r

Prev call vol..22,469 Call open int...99,443
Prev put vol..27,930 Put open int...119,382

S.& P. 500 (CBOE)   Close:1202.83

Strike Price	Calls Jan	Feb	Mar	Puts Jan	Feb	Mar
995	r	s	r	1	61/4	111/2
1005	r	s	2231/2	1	61/2	111/2
1025	r	r	r	11/2	81/8	14
1050	r	170	r	21/16	91/2	171/2
1065	r	s	s	27/8	s	s
1070	r	s	s	23/4	s	s
1075	1353/4	r	162	3	123/8	191/4
1100	115	r	1361/2	41/2	15	221/4
1125	92	r	1161/2	61/2	183/8	29
1140	80	s	s	7	s	s
1145	s	s	s	75/8	s	s
1150	67	r	r	9	225/8	311/2
1155	r	s	s	121/4	s	s
1160	r	s	r	107/8	s	35
1175	51	70	r	14	263/4	401/2
1180	451/2	s	s	151/2	s	s

1185	r	s	s	17	s	s
1190	38	s	s	155/8	s	s
1200	29	49	63	211/2	37	47
1225	151/4	371/2	49	33	441/4	55
1250	71/4	231/4	36	487/8	571/4	70
1275	21/4	151/2	25	r	80	r
1300	7/8	s	17	851/2	s	985/8
1315	s	s	1/4	s	r	r
1350	3/16	2	6	138	137	139

Prev call vol..22,501 Call open int. 579,080
Prev put vol..30,755 Put open int. .594,266

Nasdaq 100 (CBOE)   Close:1787.30

Strike Price	Calls Jan	Feb	Mar	Puts Jan	Feb	Mar
1400	s	s	s	s	113/8	s
1420	s	s	s	23/4	s	r
1440	s	s	s	3	s	r
1480	r	s	r	43/8	s	r
1500	s	s	s	4	15	s
1540	s	s	s	55/8	s	s
1560	s	s	s	7	s	s
1600	r	s	r	103/4	s	r
1620	r	s	r	12	s	s
1640	1661/8	s	r	13	s	r
1660	1473/4	s	r	18	s	r
1680	1301/8	s	197	201/4	s	r
1700	s	s	s	23	s	s
1700	r	s	1773/8	253/4	s	69
1720	973/4	s	r	301/2	s	r
1740	841/2	s	s	36	s	s
1740	s	s	s	35	s	s
1760	733/8	s	r	r	s	s
1760	s	s	s	40	s	s
1780	621/4	s	130	50	s	983/4
1780	58	96	s	483/4	781/4	s
1800	481/8	88	s	56	s	106
1820	423/4	s	s	s	s	s
1840	30	s	s	s	s	s
1860	24	s	s	s	s	s

Prev call vol. ...742 Call open int. ....
Prev put vol. ...398 Put open int. ....

DJ Inds (1/100) (CBOE)   Close: 89.88

Strike Price	Calls Jan	Feb	Mar	Puts Jan	Feb	Mar
68	s	s	r	1/8	r	r
70	s	s	s	1/8	s	s
72	r	s	r	r	3/8	r
76	s	s	r	r	r	11/8
80	11	r	123/4	r	7/8	11/2
81	10	s	s	r	s	s
82	r	s	s	r	11/16	s
84	61/2	s	r	r	r	21/8
85	61/2	s	s	1/2	s	s
86	57/8	6	s	5/8	17/8	s
87	43/8	s	s	13/16	s	s
88	35/8	53/8	61/4	11/16	21/2	31/4
89	27/8	s	s	11/2	s	s
90	2	37/8	47/8	13/4	213/16	33/4
91	11/2	31/2	s	23/8	s	s
92	11/8	27/8	35/8	21/2	r	43/4
93	r	s	s	33/8	r	s
94	9/16	13/8	s	r	s	s
95	5/16	17/16	s	41/8	61/4	s
96	3/16	1	2	51/4	r	61/4
98	r	r	s	71/8	s	s
100	r	r	13/16	91/8	s	91/4
108	s	s	9/16	s	s	r

Prev call vol. ..2,360 Call open int. ..65,265
Prev put vol. ..2,192 Put open int. .104,442

Japan Index (A)   Close: 146.52

Strike Price	Calls Jan	Feb	Mar	Puts Jan	Feb	Mar
130	s	s	r	r	13/4	r
135	s	s	16	r	s	43/8
145	r	r	r	33/8	53/4	r
150	215/16	r	63/8	r	r	r
155	r	s	45/8	r	s	121/2
160	9/16	r	33/8	r	s	r
165	s	s	21/16	r	s	s
170	r	11/4	s	s	s	s

Prev call vol. ..3,056 Call open int. ..16,954
Prev put vol. ....411 Put open int. 3,035

STOCK MARKET INDEXES

	High	Low	Close	Chg	% Chg	52 Wk % Chg	YTD % Chg	12/8 1994* % Chg
DOW JONES								
Industrials	9150.54	8874.28	8988.85	+ 85.22	+ 0.96	+14.96	+13.66	+143.88
Transportation	3088.06	2987.90	3025.52	+ 16.48	+ 0.55	− 3.93	− 7.09	+119.64
Utilities	316.73	310.80	314.36	+ 1.07	+ 0.34	+17.43	+15.12	+75.02
Composite	2860.57	2778.87	2813.83	+ 21.23	+ 0.76	+10.04	+ 7.92	+129.85
STANDARD & POOR'S								
Industrial	1448.58	1420.94	1438.59	+ 17.65	+ 1.24	+30.51	+28.29	+172.23
Transportation	665.53	654.86	654.86	− 0.61	− 0.09	− 2.70	− 4.98	+94.38
Utilities	262.53	260.49	261.27	+ 0.27	+ 0.10	+13.17	+10.80	+73.92
Financial	131.23	128.52	130.67	+ 2.03	+ 1.58	+11.91	+10.00	+223.04
Mid-Cap 400	361.04	354.39	361.04	+ 6.65	+ 1.88	+12.33	+ 8.30	+121.59
Small-Cap 600	168.00	166.17	167.98	+ 1.81	+ 1.09	− 4.31	− 7.28	+89.57
100 Stocks	600.75	589.84	596.16	+ 6.32	+ 1.07	+31.37	+29.62	+187.20
500 Stocks	1210.88	1188.03	1202.84	+ 14.81	+ 1.25	+26.12	+23.95	+170.03
NEW YORK STOCK EXCHANGE								
Composite	581.01	571.79	577.70	+ 5.63	+ 0.98	+15.43	+13.01	+136.96
Industrial	720.37	708.85	714.20	+ 4.91	+ 0.69	+15.88	+13.30	+132.61
Transportation	463.84	452.81	459.21	+ 6.40	+ 1.41	+ 1.72	− 1.51	+113.48
Utility	441.75	429.94	440.61	+ 9.81	+ 2.28	+33.08	+31.45	+121.28
Finance	520.20	511.86	518.71	+ 6.40	+ 1.25	+ 6.73	+ 4.59	+171.21
NASDAQ								
Composite	2143.81	2104.19	2138.03	+ 51.89	+ 2.49	+39.55	+36.15	+197.31
Industrials	1252.78	1238.19	1252.03	+ 20.10	+ 1.63	+ 5.92	+ 2.54	+73.54
Financial	2413.24	2379.40	2412.71	+ 42.80	+ 1.81	− 0.98	− 3.63	+188.84
Banks	1791.97	1784.57	1788.90	+ 4.33	+ 0.24	−11.89	−14.13	+163.40
Insurance	1739.96	1721.14	1735.00	+ 18.85	+ 1.10	− 1.40	− 3.50	+98.41
NMS Composite	974.06	955.81	971.41	+ 23.86	+ 2.52	+40.21	+36.75	+203.57
NMS Industrial	515.91	509.67	515.60	+ 8.56	+ 1.69	+ 5.47	+ 2.02	+76.57
OTHER INDEXES								
American Exch	655.45	651.18	654.12	+ 2.87	+ 0.44	− 1.35	− 4.45	+54.71
Russell 2000	402.15	397.42	401.83	+ 4.41	+ 1.11	− 4.98	− 8.05	+70.20
Value Line Arith	890.16	880.88	888.10	+ 7.22	+ 0.82	+ 4.09	+ 1.28	+104.60
Wilshire 5000			10956.28	+137.72	+ 1.27	+20.41	+17.83	+149.72

Source: New York Times, December 22, 1998, C7, C12.

have a positive value, indicating the possibility that by the expiration date the index value could rise above the strike price.

Call Option Values, Strike Prices, and Expiration Dates   Given an underlying asset or index and holding the expiration date constant, call options with higher strike prices have lower values. For example, premiums for call options expiring in January, 1999, ranged in value from 93 for a strike price of 510 to $\frac{11}{16}$ (0.6875) for a strike price of 640. The higher the strike price, the less likely the index value will rise above the strike price, so the less valuable the option.

Holding strike price constant, call options with more distant expiration dates are more valuable. For the single strike price of 570, the call option value ranged from 33 for a January expiration to $46\frac{3}{4}$ for a March expiration. The longer time to maturity increases the chances that the actual index value will eventually exceed the strike price.[10]

A final factor that influences option prices in general is unobservable in the data for the S&P 100 options in Figure 18.2. All else equal, the greater the price volatility of an underlying asset, the greater the value of an option on that asset. For a call option, for example, the greater the asset price volatility, the greater the probability that the price will eventually exceed the strike price; and the higher the asset's price, the higher the value of the option. Yet the minimum value to which an option can fall, no matter how volatile the price of the underlying asset, is zero. If an option's value falls to zero, the holder will simply not exercise it, losing the premium but nothing else. The fact that losses to option holders are limited but gains are not is illustrated in more detail later in the chapter.

Put Option Values, Strike Prices, and Expiration Dates   For put options, holding the expiration date constant, the higher the strike price, the higher the value of the put option; this is in contrast to call options. Puts on physical assets give the holder the right to sell an asset at the option strike price if its market value falls below the strike price. Because one cannot sell an index, the holder of a put option on an index buys the right to receive cash if the index value falls below the strike price by the expiration date.

In Figure 18.2, the premium cost of a put on the S&P 100 Index with a January, 1999, expiration date ranged from 7/8 at a strike price of 510 to $31\frac{1}{8}$ for a strike price of 630. The higher the exercise price, the more likely it will be above the actual index value at the expiration date. As with call options, however, holding strike price constant, put values are higher for more distant expiration dates. Again, the chance that the option will eventually be profitable for the holder is greater the longer the time to maturity. The value of put options is also positively related to volatility in the price of the underlying asset.

OPTIONS AND FINANCIAL INSTITUTIONS

Options on assets other than common stock originated in 1982. Table 18.5 lists many of the nonstock options that have been traded. Options are written both on various financial assets (such as bonds or stock) and on a variety of futures contracts. The list

---

[10]The increase in value with more distant expiration dates holds for most options, with exceptions. For more details, see Chance (1992), Chapter 3.

Table 18.5 ✦ OPTION INSTRUMENTS AND MARKETS

Options are available on financial assets *and* on futures contracts. New options come and go according to the needs of the marketplace. The table lists a representative group of options traded on financial assets.

Options on Financial Assets	Options on Financial Futures Contracts
Interest Rate Options	*Options on Interest Rate Futures*
Chicago Board Options Exchange	CBOT
Short-term Interest Rates	T-bonds
Long-term Interest Rates	Municipal Bond Index
Stock Index Options	2-year T-notes
American Stock Exchange	5-year T-notes
LEAPS MMI	CME
Computer Technology Index	Eurodollar
Eurotop 100 Index	LIBOR
Institutional Index	T-bills
S&P MidCap Index	London International Financial Futures Exchange
Japan Index	Eurodollar
Chicago Board Options Exchange	Long Gilt
Russell 2000	
S&P 100 Index	*Options on Stock Index Futures*
S&P 500 Index	CBOT
LEAPS—S&P 500 Index	MMI
LEAPS—S&P 100 Index	CME
CAPS—S&P 500 Index	S&P 500 Index
CAPS—S&P 100 Index	Nikkei 225 Stock Average
NYSE	S&P MidCap 400
NYSE Index	New York Futures Exchange
Philadelphia Exchange	NYSE Composite Index
Gold/Silver Index	
Value Line Index	*Options on Foreign Currency Futures*
O-T-C Index	CME
Pacific Exchange	Australian dollars
Financial News Index	British pounds
Wilshire Index	Deutschemarks
	Swiss francs
Foreign Currency Options	Japanese yen
Philadelphia Exchange	Canadian dollars
Australian dollars	Mark/Yen Cross Rate
British pounds	FINEX
British pound/German mark cross rate	U.S. Dollar Index
Canadian dollars	
French francs	
German marks	
German mark/Japanese yen cross rate	
Japanese yen	
Swiss francs	
European Currency Units	

Source: The Wall Street Journal, various issues.

of options on financial instruments is in a state of flux. Based on trading volume, stock index options often attract the largest group of traders, but this, too, may well change as the markets mature.

Regulation of Options Trading

Writers and holders can both use options for speculative purposes. Either party can profit by correctly forecasting price movements on the underlying asset. Some financial institutions, however, may use options only to hedge against adverse movements in the prices of existing assets. As with futures, federal bank regulators disapprove of options trading that increases risk exposure. For example, buying stock options without owning stock would increase risk and thus be disallowed. Also, regulators may question banks that write, rather than buy, options.

Thrifts are permitted broader authority both to write and to purchase options as long as they report their positions to regulators and as long as the positions are related to financial instruments in which an institution can legally invest. Federal credit union regulations permit purchase of put options written on several categories of secondary mortgage market securities. Thus credit unions making mortgage loans are able to hedge against increases in market rates.[11]

HEDGING WITH OPTIONS

The choice of options depends on the portfolio to be hedged. The manager of an equity mutual fund might hedge with options on stock indexes or stock index futures. For managers protecting the value of interest-bearing assets, options on debt instruments or interest rate futures are a logical choice.

When Options Make a Good Hedge Options are a particularly good hedging choice when a financial institution faces potential declines in profitability at the discretion of its customers. In other words, an institution may enter the organized options markets to hedge against the effects of the options it has made available to its customers. For example, a commercial bank may make a commitment to lend in the future at a fixed rate negotiated today. Falling rates can cause the borrower to ignore the commitment; but if interest rates rise, the borrower is almost certain to complete the transaction, and the bank's net interest margin will decline when its deposit costs increase. Or, if mortgage rates are expected to decline, existing customers may choose to prepay their mortgages, borrowing at new lower rates and lowering a thrift's interest revenues.

A bank can hedge its commitment to lend in the future by buying a put option on a T-bond. If rates go up, bond values will fall, and the bank can exercise its right to sell bonds at the strike price. The profit on the hedge can be used to offset liability costs that will increase as market rates increase. However, if rates decline, the value of T-bonds will rise, and the bank will not exercise the put. The option premium is the price the lender pays for protecting the spread against rising rates. Since a large price change is necessary to cover the cost of the option premium, instruments with large expected price changes are better to hedge with options. Futures, in contrast, do not have a premium cost, so do not need as large a price change to be profitable.

---

[11]See Koppenhaver (1986) and Christopher (1989).

A thrift can protect itself against potential mortgage prepayments in the face of falling rates by purchasing a call option on T-bonds. As rates fall and the value of bonds rises, the call option will also rise in value. Profits from selling the option can be used to offset a decline in interest revenues as mortgages are prepaid. If rates rise instead, the option premium is the price paid for attempting to protect the spread.

A Put or a Call   As suggested by the preceding examples, the decision to use options for hedging depends on the choices that customers have been offered by the institution. Once the decision to use options has been made, however, managers still must decide whether to use calls or puts. This choice depends on the anticipated direction of market changes. For example, consider the alternatives faced by an equity fund manager who expects a reversal in the market. With a bear market forecast, a stock index put option is indicated. If the market index does, in fact, decline, the option value will increase as the index falls below the strike price. A put option is also the proper choice for hedging an existing portfolio of interest-bearing assets if rates are expected to rise. If the forecast is accurate, the put's value will increase, offsetting the existing portfolio's decline in value.

Or a LEAP?   Options on equity securities are a relatively short-term hedge; most expire within 90 days. Some institutional investors, however, have desired an alternative offering longer-term protection. In the early 1990s, a new instrument was introduced to meet that need. These options—called long-term equity anticipation securities, or LEAPS—are traded on approximately 100 stocks and several stock indexes. LEAPS have expiration dates several years into the future and have less price volatility than traditional options. The longer maturity also gives investors more time to determine the best course of action for managing an options hedge (i.e., selling or exercising the option).[12]

An Option on an Asset or on a Futures Contract?   The choice between an option on a financial asset itself or an option on a financial futures contract is influenced by several factors. One of the most important is that not all option markets are equally liquid. For example, although options on T-bonds are available, the market is small compared with the market for options on T-bond futures contracts. Thus, many managers using options to hedge bond portfolios will prefer options on T-bond futures.

If option markets for an underlying asset and a futures contract on the same asset are equally liquid, the option choice is influenced by whether the manager intends to exercise the option. To exercise an option on T-bonds, for example, funds must be available to purchase securities at the strike price. To exercise an option on a futures contract, however, only a relatively small margin requirement is needed to buy the contract.[13] The appropriate hedge strategies, under various market forecasts,

---

[12]Stanley W. Angrist. "Taking Leaps with Treasuries to Buffer Sell-Off." *The Wall Street Journal* (June 5, 1992), C1, C14; Joan Warner. "A Different Kind of Hedge." *Business Week* (September 7, 1992), 94–95.

[13]Another reason for preferring one type of option over another is the difficulty of determining the appropriate size of the hedge. Because T-bond futures contracts are standardized with an 8 percent coupon, they sometimes trade at deep discounts, and the number of contracts (or options on contracts) must be adjusted to reflect that discount. For options on the T-bonds themselves, however, the difference between coupon and current market rates is seldom as large, because T-bond and T-note options are traded on issues with many different coupons.

Table 18.6   ✦   **MARKET FORECASTS AND OPTIONS HEDGES**

Managers hedging with options choose calls (giving them the right to buy assets or futures contracts) or puts (giving them the right to sell assets or futures contracts), depending on their forecasts for the financial markets. Falling stock prices or rising interest rates suggest the use of puts. Rising stock prices or falling interest rates suggest the use of calls.

	HEDGE			
	Option on Index or Index Futures		Option on T-Bonds or Interest Rate Futures	
Forecast	Call	Put	Call	Put
Increase				
Stock prices	X			
Interest rates				X
Decrease				
Stock prices		X		
Interest rates			X	

are summarized in Table 18.6. Again, a futures contract by itself without an option does not require as large a price change as an option to be profitable, since an option has a large premium cost that must be covered by a gain if the option is exercised. However, a futures contract must be carried through, while an option on a futures contract does not have to be exercised.

Hedging With Options: An Illustration

Suppose that in June, 2002, the bond portfolio manager for a large insurance firm forecasts a sharp decline in interest rates over the next three months. Because of several new products developed by the company, a large inflow from sales of insurance policies in August is also expected. The manager wants to hedge the opportunity loss on the investment of those premiums.

On the other side of town, however, the manager of a money market fund holds the opposite expectation for interest rate movements; she is willing to write a call option on T-bond futures contracts. Suppose T-bond futures for September delivery ($100,000 face value) are currently trading at 75.5 (75.5 percent of face value). The call option has a strike price of 76, a premium of $1,187.50, and an expiration date of August, 2002. Table 18.7 summarizes the effect of the hedge on the position of the insurance company under three different interest rate scenarios.[14]

First, if interest rates go up instead of down, the bond manager will not exercise the option because the market value of the futures contract will be less than the strike price. The company will lose the $1,187.50 option premium. Second, if interest rates do fall but not by a significant amount, the value of the T-bond futures and the

---

[14]Specifications on options vary considerably. Options on T-bond futures contracts expire in the month before the futures contract delivery month. See Chicago Board of Trade (1986b).

Table 18.7 ✦ HEDGING WITH OPTIONS ON T-BOND FUTURES CONTRACTS

An option provides the opportunity to limit losses to the amount of the option premium if forecasts are incorrect. If forecasts are correct, gains on a hedge can be used to offset losses in cash markets.

Treasury Bond Call Option

Premium:	$1,187.50
Strike price:	76
Expiration date:	August 2002
Security:	Treasury bond futures contract for September delivery
	$100,000 face value
	Current market value: 75.5

Scenario 1: Interest Rates Rise
T-bond futures contract market value: <76
Call option not exercised
Results of hedge: −$1,187.50 (premium)

Scenario 2: Interest Rates Fall Slightly
T-bond futures contract market value: 77
Call option exercised: Contract purchased at 76 and sold at 77
Results of hedge:

$1,000.00	Profit on futures trade
− 1,187.50	Premium
($187.50)	Loss

Scenario 3: Interest Rates Fall Significantly
T-bond futures contract market value: 81
Call option exercised: Contract purchased at 76 and sold at 81
Results of hedge:

$5,000.00	Profit on futures trade
− 1,187.50	Premium
$3,812.50	Gain

T-bond futures option will increase. But the rise in value—for example, to 77—will be insufficient to recover the entire purchase premium. The bond manager will suffer an opportunity cost on the investment of the new funds received in August, and this cost will be increased by the additional loss of $187.50 on the options transactions.

Finally, suppose interest rates drop sharply. The value of the T-bond futures contract rises sharply to 81. The bond portfolio manager exercises the call at 76 and immediately resells the futures contracts at 81, for a $5,000 profit. That profit is still offset somewhat by the cost of the option, but the hedge has now provided a net gain of $3,812.50, compensating for the lower return on the newly invested funds. The larger the drop in interest rates, the higher the profits earned. The bond manager could also choose to sell the option before its expiration date, also at a profit, although that hedge would require the purchase of a larger number of options. Finally, the manager could retain ownership of the futures contracts and take delivery on the T-bonds at a yield reflecting the higher levels that were available in June.

OPTIONS AND FUTURES HEDGING: A COMPARISON

A financial institution manager needing to hedge unfavorable market movements must evaluate the relative advantages and disadvantages offered by options and futures. The most important differences are the size and nature of the investment required and the potential size of losses and gains on the two instruments.

Investment Required

The margin requirements on positions in the futures market are discussed in Chapter 17. They are established by the clearinghouse as a percentage of the contract value and must be maintained on a daily basis. For purchasers of options, however, the investment required is the price of the option. It must be paid when the option is purchased, and no further payments are required unless the option is exercised. Option writers must post margin and mark their positions to market daily.

Potential Risk and Return

A more important distinction between options and futures is the different risk exposures for an option purchaser and a futures hedger. The potential profits or losses on futures transactions are virtually unlimited, but the loss on the purchase of an option is limited to the option price, and profits are offset by the option premium.[15]

Table 18.8   ✦   HEDGING WITH T-BOND FUTURES CONTRACTS

Futures hedges also provide opportunities to gain if forecasts are correct. If forecasts are incorrect, however, losses on a futures position can be larger than losses on comparable options hedging strategies.

The Long Hedge
T-bond futures contract
$100,000 face value
Current market value: 75.5

Scenario 1: Interest Rates Rise
T-bond futures contract market value: 70
Position closed at loss of 5.5 per contract
Results of hedge: −$5,500

Scenario 2: Interest Rates Fall Slightly
T-bond futures contract market value: 77
Position closed at profit of 1.5 per contract
Results of hedge: $1,500 profit

Scenario 3: Interest Rates Fall Significantly
T-bond futures contract market value: 81
Position closed at profit of 5.5 per contract
Results of hedge: $5,500 profit

---

[15]Theoretically, losses on futures contracts are halted when the value of the contract falls to zero.

A comparison of a long hedge with T-bond futures contracts and the T-bond futures call option just illustrated should clarify the differences in risk/return exposure.

The insurance company manager with a forecast of falling rates could have assumed a long hedge in T-bond futures, buying at a price of 75.5. The results of the futures hedge are summarized in Table 18.8. If interest rates move against the manager's forecasts, his or her losses have no ceiling except for those imposed by the movement of interest rates. If interest rates rise sharply and the contract value falls to, for example, 70, there will be a significant loss when the position is closed. The greater the increase in interest rates, the greater the loss on the long hedge. Losses on the hedge will offset the returns gained from investing the new funds at the higher market rates.

Figure 18.3 ✦ COMPARISON OF RISK EXPOSURE IN FUTURES AND OPTIONS HEDGES

The two left panels show that the losses to option holders are limited to the option premium, whereas profits are limited only by movements in the underlying asset's price. In contrast, the right panels illustrate that losses, as well as profits, on futures contracts depend on the price behavior of the underlying asset.

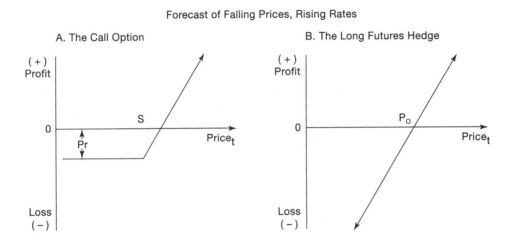

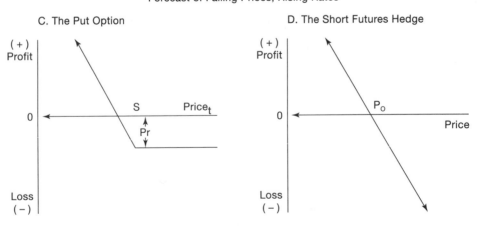

However, if the manager's forecasts for lower interest rates are correct, there is no purchase premium to reduce the profits from the hedge. If the value of the T-bond futures contract rises to 81, there will be a profit of $5,500 per contract instead of the gain of $3,812.50 shown in Table 18.7.

Figure 18.3 depicts the differences in risk exposure between futures and options hedges. The top half of the figure assumes a forecast of falling rates. With a call option (Panel A), the loss is equal to the option premium (Pr) until the underlying asset price reaches the strike price (S). As the asset price increases, returns on the option increase, eventually becoming positive after the premium is recovered. With a long futures contract hedge (Panel B), a change in the price of the contract after purchase at P_0 is translated into a gain or loss because no premium must be recovered. Thus, hedging with futures is riskier than hedging with options.

The lower half of the figure compares a put option with the sale of futures contracts under a forecast of rising rates. Panel C shows that the purchaser of a put suffers a loss equal to the premium until the market price of the underlying asset falls below the strike price. As the asset's price continues to fall, the option holder's position improves and becomes profitable once the cost of the premium has been earned. In contrast, any change in the price of a futures contract translates directly into a profit or loss for the contract holder (Panel D).

INTEREST RATE SWAPS

Investors' thirst for new risk management strategies may be unquenchable. Despite the wide range of alternatives offered by futures, options, and options on futures, new hedging techniques are constantly under development and finding a place in the financial management policies of financial institutions. One of these—**interest rate swaps**—had become a mainstay of risk management by the early 1990s. In fact, interest rate swaps account for the majority of derivative activity by banks.[16]

A swap agreement, in its basic form, is an exchange of cash flows between two parties (or **counterparties**, in the standard terminology of swaps). An interest rate swap is a transaction in which each of two parties agrees to pay the interest obligations on a specified debt obligation of the other party. In the simplest type of interest rate swap, one counterparty exchanges a fixed-rate payment obligation for a floating-rate one, while the other counterparty exchanges floating for fixed.[17]

---

[16]See David A. Carter and Joseph F. Sinkey, Jr. "The Use of Interest Rate Derivatives by End-users: The Case of Large Community Banks." *Journal of Financial Services Research* 14 (July, 1998), 17–34. For their sample of banks between $100 million and $1 billion, swaps accounted for 69 percent of bank derivative activity, options for 23 percent, and futures/forwards for 8 percent. Other studies have also shown that interest rates swaps have been used more often in hedging activities by very large banks as well.

[17]Further discussions on the development and purposes of swaps are provided in Brown and Smith (1993); Abken (1991[a and b]); Smith, Smithson, and Wakeman (1991); Litzenberger (1992); Marshall (1990, 1991); Wall, Pringle, and McNulty (1990); Wall and Pringle (1988, 1989); Smith, Smithson, and Wakeman (1988); Felgran (1987); Whittaker (1987); Bicksler and Chen (1986); Loeys (1985); Hutchinson (1985); Baldoni and Isele (1986); and Roy C. Smith. "Swaps and Synthetic Securities." *Working Paper Series* Number 489, Salomon Brothers Center for the Study of Financial Institutions, New York University (September, 1988).

MOTIVATIONS FOR SWAPS

A government agency introduced interest rate swaps to the United States, although currency swaps had previously been introduced in international markets. The Student Loan Marketing Association, known as Sallie Mae, pioneered swap programs in the United States in 1982 because of an asset structure heavily dominated by floating-rate student loans and advances. Investors supplying funds to Sallie Mae preferred to lock in the high rates prevailing at that time. The agency preferred to fund its rate-sensitive assets with sources of funds of a similar nature. Hence, Sallie Mae sought a swap to meet both its and its investors' needs. In the intervening years, the popularity of interest rate swaps has increased at a phenomenal rate. By 1992, the interest rate swap market, including financial and nonfinancial institutions, was estimated to involve liabilities with principal values of almost $3 trillion. The market for all swaps and swap-related products increased by 50 percent between 1989 and 1991, and no evidence suggests that the growth will moderate in the near future.[18]

For a financial institution, the objective of an interest rate swap is to trade one form of rate sensitivity on liabilities for another that better matches its asset structure. Federal savings and loans (S&Ls), for example, are permitted by regulation to seek swaps only to trade rate-sensitive deposit costs for fixed costs, and not the reverse. A swap allows a thrift to reduce its rate sensitivity and to lock in a spread on long-term, fixed-rate assets. Conversely, a multinational commercial bank that borrows in the long-term Eurodollar market may, if most of its assets are rate-sensitive, prefer to swap fixed-rate interest obligations on Eurodollar deposits for floating-rate payments.

Nonfinancial firms also participate in the interest rate swaps market; they benefit from the ability to tailor interest obligations to suit their cash-flow patterns without having to restructure existing balance sheets. This flexibility may save substantial transactions costs. Also, nonfinancial firms, if they find a substantial rate differential between short-term and long-term interest rates, often engage in interest rate swaps to reduce the effective cost of borrowing. By swapping interest payments with a counterparty experiencing similar but opposite rate differentials, a firm can lower the costs of its liabilities.

SWAPS AS A HEDGING TOOL

Plain Vanilla Swap

The most basic type of interest rate swap is known as a **plain vanilla swap**. The mechanics of a swap of this type are shown in the diagram in Figure 18.4. The example involves a savings institution that has interest rate risk from a large proportion of fixed-rate mortgages on its balance sheet. The S&L needs a source of funds with similar interest rate characteristics, but its liabilities are primarily short-term with floating rates. The S&L finds a large commercial bank counterparty with the ability to borrow at fixed rates. The S&L and bank agree to swap interest rate obligations on $50 million of liabilities, called the **notional principal** of a swap.

---

[18]Remolona (1992–1993); Pat Widder. "Trillions at Stake in the Swaps Market." *Chicago Tribune* (June 22, 1992), Section 4, 1, 2; and William Glasgall. "Swap Fever: Big Money, Big Risks." *Business Week* (June 1, 1992), 102–106.

Figure 18.4   ◆   EXCHANGE OF OBLIGATIONS IN AN INTEREST RATE SWAP

This swap involves an S&L that exchanges its variable-rate interest obligations for the fixed-rate interest obligations of a counterparty commercial bank. The cost of the swap is the initially higher interest payments the S&L must make.

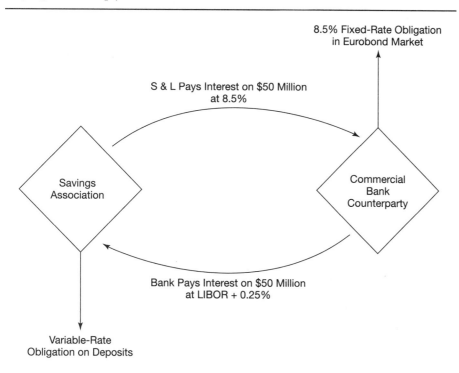

Exchanging Interest Obligations   The flow of funds is evident in Figure 18.4. The S&L agrees to pay interest on the notional principal at a rate of 8.5 percent; it will receive cash flows from the bank at the London Interbank Offered Rate (LIBOR) plus 25 basis points. Initially, this floating rate will probably be lower than the fixed rate of 8.5 percent. That relationship could change over the life of the swap as interest rate levels fluctuate. The swap allows the S&L to lock in its cost of liabilities, resulting in a more stable net interest margin on its fixed-rate mortgage portfolio.

Costs and Benefits of a Swap Agreement   As with any hedging tool, interest rate shifts can make a swap agreement costly or beneficial. Also, as noted above, it is quite common for the fixed rate agreed on when the swap is initiated to be higher than the floating rate. In the context of this example, that differential is the "insurance premium" paid by the thrift to transfer interest rate risk exposure to its commercial bank counterparty.

Important Factors in a Swap

Maturity   The maturity of an interest rate exchange can vary from a relatively short period to as long as 20 years. The longer maturities available in the swap market make swaps suitable hedges when futures or options contracts are not. If interest rate forecasts underlying the swap prove to be incorrect, however, five or 10 years is a long time to pay for one's mistakes. For this reason, shorter swaps are more popular, and termination clauses are usually included in the original agreement. The party that "unwinds" (the swap market term for ending a swap early) must pay a penalty, but that may be cheaper than the consequences of continuing the swap under an unfavorable interest rate scenario. Many participants in the swap market make arrangements to reverse a swap, in the event of unfavorable rate movements, by agreeing to a swap that offsets the original one. The growing market for options on swaps, discussed later in this chapter, presents an increasingly popular alternative for early termination. A secondary market in swap agreements has also developed.

Interest Rate Index   Another important issue for negotiation is the index by which floating-rate interest payments will be adjusted. In the example, the S&L would prefer a payment stream positively correlated with the rate on its short-term deposits and at least equal to the average deposit cost. There is no guarantee that the anticipated relationship will materialize.

The LIBOR rate is the predominant index, but the T-bill rate and the prime rate, among others, are also used. Increased competition for deposits may change the effectiveness of a given index.

The Role of Brokers and Dealers   Interest rate swaps are often arranged through brokers or dealers. Although it is possible for a small depository to find a swap partner on its own, the process is time-consuming and may be expensive. Most market participants prefer to use an intermediary.

In 1984, the Federal Home Loan Bank Board (FHLBB) formally recognized the potential benefits of swaps for thrift institutions and allowed the district FHLBs to serve as brokers and counterparties to member institutions. Thus, member associations can take advantage of reduced transactions costs if they work through the FHLBB system.

Many large banks in the United States and Great Britain, as well as large Japanese securities firms, act as brokers and dealers in the swap markets, earning substantial fees for arranging and servicing swaps. As brokers, institutions bring two parties together, but as dealers they may even take the position of counterparty in a swap agreement. In many dealer arrangements, the intermediary guarantees the continuation of the cash flows for the swap, even if one counterparty defaults on the agreement. Thus, the dealer may be exposed to considerable credit risk, while the individual counterparties benefit from greater confidence that their cash flows will be uninterrupted.

Credit Risk   A financial institution must evaluate the counterparty's credit position, because some confidence is needed that there will be no default. When a dealer actually becomes a principal in an agreement or guarantees the payment streams, the financial position of the dealer is the most important issue.

Concern about controlling credit risk escalated when Beverly Hills Savings and Loan failed in 1985. It had previously made a swap with one of the subsidiaries of Renault, the French automaker. When the thrift failed, the Federal Savings and Loan Insurance Corporation (FSLIC) and Renault disagreed about who had claim to the $2 million in collateral pledged by Beverly Hills to secure the swap. Although counterparties with weak financial positions had become accustomed to pledging collateral to improve their chances of finding swap partners, the Beverly Hills incident provoked concern from stronger market participants and regulators about access to assets pledged. In the early 1990s, regulators' apprehensions about the swap market were rekindled in the aftermath of the failures of the Bank of New England and Drexel Burnham Lambert, Inc. These two failures alone left behind swaps with more than $30 billion in notional value, and one European official claimed that the entire global payments system was almost upset.[19]

Although debate continues about the legal and systemic risk exposure in swap agreements, credit risk does appear to be limited. If a counterparty defaults on an agreement, the other party has responsibility only for its own debt obligations, not for the counterparty's. If the default occurs in an unfavorable interest rate environment, however, the loss of the protective hedge could be expensive.

Regulatory and Accounting Issues

As swaps have grown in popularity, regulators and accountants have focused attention on appropriate means for controlling and reporting the potential risk to which swap counterparties are exposed. Regulatory controls on depositories' swap activities have been imposed in the form of the risk-based capital standards discussed in Chapter 8. The Financial Accounting Standards Board now requires that firms involved in financial agreements with off-balance-sheet risk, including interest rate swaps, disclose details about these agreements and the potential loss that could occur should a counterparty fail to perform. Since 1993, firms have been required to disclose unrealized gains and losses from swap agreements.

Stock Price Risk Issues

One interesting risk that appeared for Banc One was the risk of investors not understanding the institution's use of interest rate swaps. Analysts reported concern over Banc One's interest rate swap exposure. This, in turn, led to a decline in the bank's stock price in April, 1993, from a high of $48\frac{3}{4}$ to just $36\frac{3}{4}$, as well as a fall in the corporation's credit rating based on its derivative exposure. Esty, Tufano, and Headley report in a case study on Banc One that one analyst stated that "Banc One's investors are uncomfortable with so much derivative exposure. Buyers of regional banks do not expect derivatives involvement. . . . Heavy swaps usage clouds Banc One's financial image [and is] extremely confusing. . . . It is virtually impossible for anyone on the outside to assess the risks being assumed." These reports occurred despite the consistent reporting by Banc One of unrealized losses and gains on its swap portfolio and its sending a brochure explaining its swap activity to investors. Nevertheless, Banc One's use of swaps for hedging was considered by some analysts to be speculative.[20] Hence, public misconceptions of speculative derivative activity by a large regional bank using interest rates swap for macro hedging did cause some market valuation problems.

---

[19]For more discussion of the risks in the swap market, see Hansell and Muering (1992); Glasgall. "Swap Fever." and Jonathan R. Laing. "The Next Meltdown?" *Barron's* (June 7, 1993), 10–11, 30–34.

[20]See Ben Esty, Peter Tufano, and Jonathan Headley. "Banc One Corporation: Asset and Liability Management." *Bank of America Journal of Applied Corporate Finance* 7 (Fall, 1994), 33–65. The quotation used in this paragraph is from George Salem. "Rating for Banc One Reduced to Hold from Buy Based on Confusion from Heavy Exposure to Interest Rate Swaps." *Prudential Securities* (November, 1993), 2.

MORE EXOTIC SWAPS

Market participants have recognized the swap concept as one of the most flexible and effective tools for managing many types of financial risks. As a result, many innovations have appeared. A representative (but not exhaustive) sample of those available in the early 1990s is presented in Table 18.9. The variety and complexity of the swap market are apparent.

Two emerging categories of swaps not shown in the table are **commodity swaps** and **equity swaps**. Commodity swaps allow exchange of risks due to price fluctuations of raw materials or other production inputs. One or both counterparties

Table 18.9 ✦ VARIETIES OF INTEREST RATE AND CURRENCY SWAPS

By the early 1990s, swap dealers and brokers were offering a vast array of agreements, all much more complex than the original plain vanilla swap.

Type of Swap	Description
Interest rate swaps	
Amortizing swap	Used to hedge interest rate risk on mortgages or other amortized loans; the notional principal diminishes over the life of the swap
Accreting swap	Used to hedge interest rate risk on agreements with a rising principal value, such as construction loans; notional principal increases over the life of the swap
Seasonal swap	Notional principal may vary up or down over the life of the swap. Also known as roller coaster swap
Basis swap	Exchange of floating rate payments between counterparties, but with interest rates based on different indexes
Zero-coupon swap	All cash flows of the swap occur at the end of the life of the agreement; payment obligations are compounded to future maturity
Yield curve swap	A subset of the basis swap; involves exchange of interest payments indexed to a short-term rate for payments indexed to a long-term rate
Participating swap	Allows the fixed rate to be adjusted downward during the life of the swap, depending on the level of the floating-rate index. Allows counterparty paying fixed to participate in benefit of declining rates
Reversible swap	Allows counterparty to change status from floating-rate payer to fixed-rate payer, and vice versa
Asset swap	Effectively transforms an asset into an asset of another type, such as converting a fixed-rate bond into a floating-rate bond. Results in what is known as a "synthetic security"
Forward swap	Used when new debt is to be issued at a future date; allows issuer to hedge against an undesirable increase in rates before the securities are issued
Forward rate swap	Reduces default risk by establishing, at the time the swap is executed, a schedule for adjusting the fixed rate over the life of the swap
Mark-to-market swap	Reduces default risk by allowing the fixed rate to be reset when fixed and floating rates diverge substantially after the beginning of the swap
Currency swaps	
Currency-coupon swap	Used to hedge currency and interest rate risk; a fixed rate is paid in one currency while a floating rate is paid in another
ECU swap	Used to transform principal and coupon payments denominated in European Currency Units into another currency, and vice versa

Source: Adapted from Abken 1991(a and b); Litzenberger 1992; Brown and Smith 1993.

may lock in a price on future commodity purchases, depending on the terms with the swap dealer. The equity swap allows a portfolio manager to convert interest flows on a debt portfolio to cash flows linked to an equity index, such as the S&P 500. Thus, managers can realize the benefit of returns on different asset categories without paying transactions costs.

SWAPS VERSUS FUTURES HEDGING

Table 18.10 summarizes important differences between hedging with futures and hedging with interest rate swaps. In general, the swap market is less complex, and agreements do not require the daily monitoring necessary in futures trading. Swaps allow management more flexibility in negotiating the initial size and maturity of a hedge, but futures hedges are easier and less costly to reverse once in place. Currently, the futures markets are larger, more liquid, and more competitive, although growth in dealer activity and development of a secondary market are facilitating the use of swaps. Thus, the choice between futures and swaps depends on the expertise of managers and the regularity with which hedges will be managed.

SWAP OPTIONS AND FUTURES

Despite the fact that swaps are used as a hedging tool by many market participants, swap dealers and some counterparties continue to feel the effect of interest rate risk exposure. Consequently, mechanisms in the form of swap options—**swaptions**—and futures are now available to assist in more precise management of those risks. As is true of other options, swaptions provide the buyer with the right to exercise some choice during the life of the option. In the early 1990s, options on plain vanilla swaps were most common; the swaptions market had reached a volume of almost $100 billion by 1990.

A call swaption gives the buyer an opportunity to enter into a swap agreement in the future to receive a fixed rate and pay a floating rate. A put swaption gives the buyer the right to make a future swap agreement to receive a floating rate of interest

Table 18.10   ✦   COMPARING INTEREST RATE FUTURES AND INTEREST RATE SWAPS

These comparisons show that swaps are more flexible hedging tools than futures, but futures markets are larger, more well-developed, and more standardized.

Feature	Futures	Swaps
Maturities available	$1\frac{1}{2}$ to 2 years	1 month to 20 years
Costs	Margins and commissions	Brokers' or dealers' fees
Size of hedges available	Standardized contract values	Any amount over $1 million
Contract expiration dates	Fixed quarterly cycle	Any dates
Difficulty of management	Complex	Simple
Termination of positions	Closed out with opposite contract	Unwound or reversed
Transactions completed through	Organized exchanges	Commercial or investment banks

Source: Adapted from Robert Baldoni and Gerhard Isele, "A Simple Guide to Choosing between Futures and Swaps," *Intermarket* 3 (October 1986): 16; and Vivian Lewis, "Stop and Swap," *Bankers Monthly* 106 (October 1989): 82–84.

while paying a fixed rate. If a swaption is exercised, the swap will begin at a stipulated future date with a predetermined rate of interest. Most swaptions are of the European variety, meaning that they can only be exercised at the option's expiration date.

A put swaption would be exercised if the option would allow the buyer to pay a rate of interest lower than the level of interest rates prevailing on similar swaps at the swaption's maturity. If the buyer does not really need the swap agreement, the low fixed-rate swap could be sold at a gain to another counterparty.

The swaption market also effectively gives counterparties the opportunity to cancel or otherwise alter a swap agreement before maturity, if interest rate movements are unfavorable. This method of cancellation can be less costly than unwinding a swap before the end of the agreement. A swap can be bundled together with a swaption to allow the holder to terminate the agreement. For example, a counterparty paying the fixed rate can bundle the swap with a call swaption; if interest rates have declined by the time the swaption matures, the swaption can be exercised and the agreement cancelled. Such a combination is known as a **callable swap**. Other types of swaptions allow the holder to exercise the right to extend a swap agreement **(extendable swaps)** or reverse the obligation to pay floating and fixed rates (another way to achieve a reversible swap).

Swap Futures

The CBOT introduced a swap futures contract in 1991. The "cash instruments" on which such futures contracts are based are generic, plain vanilla swaps with three- or five-year lives, with a variable rate indexed to LIBOR. The price of the futures contract reflects expectations about the fixed rate required for such a swap. At maturity, the price of a swap futures contract is determined by the prevailing fixed rate on swap agreements at that point in time.

Swap futures were primarily designed to offer protection to swap dealers, who face risk exposure in many swap agreements. Dealers, besides assisting in structuring agreements, often serve as counterparties. As such, they face risk from unfavorable fluctuations in interest rates, as well as credit risk from potential nonperformance of counterparties. The swap futures contracts provide a mechanism for managing the interest rate risk exposure of the counterparty paying the fixed rate.[21]

INTEREST RATE CAPS, FLOORS, AND COLLARS

The final interest rate risk management tool introduced in this chapter is a group of relatively new products called **interest rate caps**, **floors**, and **collars**. These are designed to limit exposure to interest rate fluctuations on existing assets, liabilities, or payment obligations in a swap agreement. For example, institutions can purchase interest rate caps to limit increases in their cost of funds in a volatile rate environment.

---

[21]Unfortunately, because swaptions are so new, terminology is not yet standardized. Readers may even find conflicting definitions in different sources. For more information on these emerging markets, see Beidleman (1991); Chicago Board of Trade. *CBOT Swap Futures: The Reference Guide*. Chicago: Chicago Board of Trade (1991); William B. Crawford, Jr. "CBOT's Planting a New Hedge." *Chicago Tribune* (June 18, 1991), Section 4, 1, 4; Abken 1991(a and b); and Brown and Smith (1991).

Likewise, a cap could serve as an effective ceiling to limit potential increases in floating rate payments required by an existing swap agreement.

Interest rate caps are similar to call options. The purchaser pays a premium for the right to limit the cost of its liabilities to a specified rate (the strike level), just as purchasers of call options pay a premium for the right to buy an asset at the strike price. If the current rate on the index underlying the cap (usually the LIBOR rate, the prime, the T-bill rate, the prime commercial paper rate, or a certificate of deposit index) rises above the strike level, it will be profitable to exercise the cap. If interest rates remain below the strike level, the cap expires unused, and its price serves as an insurance premium.

Alternatively, interest rate floors can be purchased to protect against the possibility that returns on variable-rate instruments will fall so low that they no longer exceed the cost of funding sources. Floors could also be used to protect against the possibility that floating payments received from a swap agreement fall below the existing fixed obligations. Floors are similar to put options. For a premium, institutions that purchase floors own the right to receive interest payments at the strike level, just as put buyers own the right to receive a specified sales price for an underlying asset. If interest rates fall below the strike level, it becomes profitable for the floor owner to exercise the option. If interest rates remain above the strike level, the floor expires unused.

For example, consider a swap agreement with a fixed rate of 7.5 percent. As interest rates rise, the floating rate could easily reach a level several hundred basis points above the fixed rate. By purchasing a cap, the floating-rate counterparty could effectively limit the rate paid to, say, 9 percent. If the indexed rate rises above 9 percent, the cap is exercised and the party who sold it is obligated to pay the difference between the cap rate and the actual rate.

An interest rate floor can protect the recipient of the floating-rate payments. The floor would be exercised if the index rate falls below the strike rate, and the writer of the interest rate floor would again be obligated to pay an amount sufficient to cover the shortfall. Buyers of caps and floors pay a premium, just as is true in the purchase of options.

Finally, some market participants may purchase both caps *and* floors or may purchase a cap and sell a floor. These strategies hedge against both increases and decreases in interest rates or provide some premium income to offset the cost of purchasing the cap. Such arrangements, known as **interest rate collars**, attempt to stabilize the net interest margin within a defined range.

Risks in the Market for Caps and Floors

The market for interest rate caps and floors is similar to the interest rate swap market, in that it is over-the-counter and dominated by large commercial and investment banks acting as dealers or brokers. Many of these dealer/broker institutions purchase caps and floors as part of their own interest rate risk management plans and also write caps and floors for others. Like swaps, caps and floors are tailored to individual user's needs. For every cap or floor purchaser entitled to receive payments if the cap or floor goes in the money, there is a cap or floor writer (seller) who is obligated to make those payments. Thus, the purchaser faces the possibility that the writer may default on the promised obligations. Furthermore, the purchaser also faces basis risk when attempting to hedge assets or liabilities whose returns or costs are not perfectly correlated with an index on which caps or floors are available.

Data on the volume of caps and floors outstanding are sparse, but most purchasers appear to be banks and other financial institutions, as well as nonfinancial firms using caps to hedge against increases in short-term borrowing costs. Transactions are large, with a typical minimum notional principal amount of $5,000,000. Thus, many purchasers are highly sophisticated businesses whose managers are aware of the risks inherent in the market. Interestingly, however, caps can also be attractive hedging vehicles for weaker institutions with poor credit ratings that are unable to find a willing counterparty in the interest rate swap market. Because the writer of a cap bears no default risk, the credit standing of the purchaser is of no consequence.

Given their relatively low risk levels, caps and floors are enjoying increasing acceptance among financial institution managers. The market has been strengthened by their association with swap agreements. Along with swaptions and swap futures contracts, caps, floors, and collars are the most recent examples of financial innovation and engineering. Fed estimates suggest their collective volume exceeded half a trillion dollars by 1991, with even greater growth predicted in the future.[22]

OTHER NEW DERIVATIVES FOR FINANCIAL INSTITUTION MANAGEMENT

New types of financial innovations are constantly being made to assist managers of financial institutions. Two new types of derivatives that do this are insurance derivatives as a new hedging tool for the insurance industry and credit derivatives, including credit swaps, to assist financial institutions in managing their credit risk for loans.

Insurance Derivatives

Options Contracts for Insured Losses from Catastrophic Events   On September 29, 1995, the CBOT began trading options contracts that are based on the Property Claims Services' (PCS) indices, which track the aggregate amount of insured losses that result from catastrophic events that occur in given regions and risk periods. Each index represents total losses that occur in a region during a risk period. For an index based on seasonal catastrophes, the risk period is quarterly and the options trade in March, June, September, and December. For regions with nonseasonal catastrophes, such as earthquakes, the risk period is annual, with only a December contract traded. The index begins by being zero and rises one point for each $100 million of insured property damage that occurs over a time period. Contracts are also available for trading in a "loss development" period of either six or twelve months after a risk period. Options can be traded on "small cap" or "large cap" contracts, where small cap options track aggregate insured losses from $0 to $20 billion, and large cap options track losses from $20 billion to $50 billion. Caps limit the amount of losses that are included under each contract, protecting the seller of an uncovered call. For instance, if the damage in a region is $25 billion dollars (250 index points), the seller of a 150 call will need to pay only $10,000 $(200 - 150) \times$ $200 for each call spread written versus $20,000 $(250 - 150) \times$ $200. These caps

---

[22]For more information on caps, floors, and collars, see Remolona (1992, 1993); Abken (1991a and b); Abken (1989); and Spahr, Luytjes, and Edwards (1988).

play an important role since traders otherwise would not be willing to write out-of-the-money calls for a small premium while bearing the risk of unlimited losses. Market participants, however, recognize that even these caps do not provide enough protection against large losses, so they commonly trade call spreads, in which a seller sells a call at one strike value and simultaneously buys another call of the same expiration at a higher strike value, limiting the potential loss to the difference between the strike prices of the two options. Puts can be traded on all indices, but they are rarely traded. There are also no underlying futures contracts for trading the PCS catastrophe indices, making PCS options the first contracts ever listed on the CBOT that lack an underlying futures contract. Insurance derivatives are an alternative for a property-casualty (p/c) insurers to buying a traditional layer of reinsurance from a reinsurer (another insurance company whose business is to insure some of other insurers' risk), reducing the p/c companies' exposure to the credit risk of the reinsurer. Similarly, reinsurers could purchase PCS options to reduce their layers of risk.[23]

Credit Derivatives

New risk management tools that transfer credit risk from one party to another are called credit derivatives. Credit derivatives come in different types, but they all have common features in terms of retaining assets on the books of originating institutions while transferring some portion of the credit exposure underlying these assets to other parties. Credit derivatives have advantages in terms of not requiring the sale of assets, which would weaken relationships with borrowers. Also, credit derivatives allow the reshaping of an institution's credit exposure by improving diversification, such as when an institution has too large a loss exposure in one region. A credit risk swap, for instance, reduces the institution's concentration in that area, allowing the firm's loan portfolio to be more diversified. Two of the major types of credit derivatives are total return swaps and credit swaps. Figure 18.5 illustrates each of these types of swaps.[24]

Total Return Swaps   With a total return swap shown in Panel A of Figure 18.5, cash flows are exchanged between a total return payor and a total return receiver. The total return payor pays out a return based on the return from its holdings of a risky debt obligation or portfolio of risky debt obligations, based on an interest income

---

[23]This section is based on Canter, Cole, and Sandor (1997). Other derivative-type instruments to reduce p/c insurers' risk are catastrophe-linked bonds (cat bonds), which constitute an exchange of principal for periodic coupon payments whereby the payment of the coupon and/or return of the principal are linked to the occurrence of a specified catastrophic event. An insurance company establishes an offshore special purpose vehicle (SPV) reinsurer from which it will buy a reinsurance contract. In turn, the SPV issues a bond that cedes that reinsured risk to the capital markets. The insurance company pays a reinsurance premium to the SPV, which is passed on as a premium to investors in the form of a coupon. In return, investors pay the notational amount of the bond equal to the maximum loss, which is placed in a trust invested in short-term Treasuries. Hence, the risk that the investors bear is fully collateralized, eliminating any credit risk. If a catastrophic event occurs that exceeds a given amount in a given region, the investors lose a portion or all of their principal. If not, the investor will earn the coupon plus the risk-free rate. The buyer of the bonds in effect is writing a call spread, whereby the investor shares proportionately in the maximum loss of a catastrophic event. Also see Doherty (1997).

[24]This and the following sections comes from Moser (1998). Also see Wall and Shrikhande (1998).

Figure 18.5 ◆ **EXCHANGE OF OBLIGATIONS IN A TOTAL RETURN SWAP AND CREDIT SWAP**

Panel A: Total Return Swap

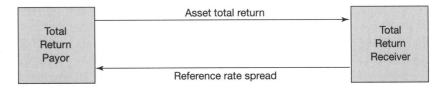

Panel B: Credit Swap

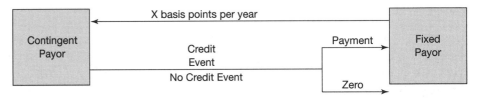

Source: James T. Moser, "Credit Derivatives: Just-in-Time Provisioning for Loan Losses." *Federal Reserve Bank of Chicago Economic Perspectives* (Fourth Quarter 1998), 2–11.

stream and changes in the market value of debt. If a bond defaults, returns from the bond and its market value will be affected. The counterparty, the total return receiver, bases what it pays on a default-free obligation less a negotiated compensation for taking on the exposure to risky debt and receives the return from the underlying risky debt. In essence, the total return payor receives an income stream appropriate for a default-free obligation and the total return receiver obtains the income stream appropriate for holdings of risky debt. The income stream reconfiguration occurs contractually without any exchange of assets. The swap allows participation in the return stream of the underlying debt without having to purchase a risky bond itself.

Credit Swaps   Compared with return swaps, credit swaps are more like insurance contracts, whereby a fixed payor insures against credit events by periodically paying a fixed percentage of the loan's par value, as shown in Panel B of Figure 18.5. If a credit event such as a loan default occurs, the contingent payor makes a payment that compensates the insured for part of its loss, but otherwise the contingent payor pays zero. As Moser (1998) points out, credit swaps are in effect a technique of just-in-time loan provisioning. Financial institutions, instead of holding liquid assets against future loan losses, could use credit swaps instead, whereby a portion of their credit risk is in effect insured against losses. This derivative method of provisioning may be more cost effective in many cases, although regulators, in their treatment of credit derivatives, do not currently view them as a means of reducing risk; thus, institutions receive limited relief from capital requirements. The global size of the primarily "privately negotiated" credit derivatives market was about $100 to $200 billion by the end of 1996. However, market participants estimate that the trading volume will reach 1 to 2 trillion by the year 2000.[25]

---

[25]See Tavakoli (1998), who provides a detailed guide for credit derivatives.

SUMMARY

This chapter concludes the material on tools for managing interest rate risk by discussing index futures; options; interest rate and other swaps; swaptions; swap futures; and interest rate caps, floors, and collars and other new derivatives. Like other financial futures, stock index futures are used to hedge against declines in existing financial positions, especially in equity portfolios. Procedures governing their use are similar to those for all futures contracts. Futures contracts have also been developed for market indexes on other financial instruments.

Options are also available for hedging. An option enables the holder to purchase or sell a financial asset or a futures contract at the strike price. A call option is purchased in anticipation of rising asset prices or falling interest rates. If the forecast is incorrect, losses are limited to the option premium. In contrast to the call option, the holder purchases a put in anticipation of falling asset prices or rising interest rates.

Hedging with futures and hedging with options are popular risk management tools. In general, financial futures present more risk to the hedger but can be more profitable.

Interest rate swaps allow two parties to exchange cash flows on debt obligations. The most common form of such agreements involves an exchange of fixed-rate payment obligations for floating-rate payments. Swaps allow market participants to manage exposure to interest rate uncertainties. Many forms of interest rate swaps have been developed; currency, commodity, and equity swaps are also increasingly popular risk management tools. Although the futures markets continue to have a higher volume of participation, swap market volume grew exponentially in the late 1980s and early 1990s.

Two very new risk management tools complement the swaps market: swaptions and swap futures contracts. Swaptions are a form of option agreement; when exercised, the holder has the right to enter into a swap with a predetermined fixed rate. Depending on interest rate changes after the option is written, swaptions may provide beneficial interest rate terms for the holder. The swaps futures contract, introduced in 1991, has a value determined by expectations about the fixed rate available on a hypothetical three- or five-year swap agreement.

Finally, interest rate caps, collars, and floors allow risk managers to limit their exposure to interest rate fluctuations. Caps can be used to create a ceiling for the costs of deposits or other liabilities of financial institutions. They can also be used to limit increases in floating-rate obligations of a rate swap. An interest rate floor serves the opposite function, limiting potential decreases in returns on variable-rate assets or in the floating-rate payments to be received in a swap agreement.

New types of financial innovations are constantly appearing. Recent innovations include options to insure against catastrophic events, which help managers of p/c insurers to reduce their risk, and credit derivatives, which help to insure the risk of credit losses for financial institutions.

Suggested Case

Ben Esty, Peter Tufano, and Jonathan Headley. "Banc One Corporation: Asset and Liability Management." *Bank of America Journal of Applied Corporate Finance* 7 (Fall, 1994), 33–65. This case examines Banc One's interest swap strategy and its solution to the dramatic fall in its stock price related to analysts' opinion of its swap exposure.

Questions

1. Give an example of a stock index and another market index. Why are these indexes computed, and what benefits do they offer to financial market participants?

2. What are stock index futures contracts? Compare and contrast their use by financial institutions for interest rate risk management with the use of interest rate futures contracts.

3. Explain the importance of the correlation between movements in an institution's stock portfolio and movements in the stock index used for hedging. How are the risks posed by this relationship similar to the risks posed by a cross hedge in the interest rate futures market?

4. Given a forecast of a bear market, why might the manager of an equity portfolio hedge with stock index futures rather than adjusting the cash portfolio? What are the advantages and disadvantages of each strategy?

5. Compare and contrast the delivery terms of stock index and interest rate futures contracts. How do the delivery characteristics of stock index futures affect hedging positions in those markets?

6. Suppose that a portfolio manager structures a stock index futures hedge based on an estimated portfolio beta equal to 1. What is the implicit assumption about the volatility of the returns on the portfolio? If the portfolio beta was 1.25, would the number of contracts traded rise, fall, or remain the same? Why?

7. What is meant by the term *index arbitrage*? Could this trading technique work in the T-bill or T-bond futures market? Why? What conclusion did the Brady Commission draw about the relationship between program trading and the stock market crash in 1987? What alternative

explanation has been offered by proponents of program trading?

8. Describe the characteristics of an option. Compare a call option and a put option. Under what equity market forecast would a hedger buy a call option? A put option? Why?

9. What is the difference between American and European options?

10. Two call options have equal strike prices, but one has a more distant expiration date. Which option would trade at a higher value? Why? Is price volatility of the underlying asset positively or negatively related to option values? Why?

11. Under what interest rate forecast would a hedger buy a call option on debt instruments such as T-bonds? A put option? Why?

12. Explain why an asset/liability manager might choose a financial futures hedge rather than an options hedge. When is the options hedge preferred? Compare the risk exposure of the two alternatives.

13. What is the maximum loss exposure to the purchaser of a call option? To the writer of a call option?

14. Describe in your own words a plain vanilla interest rate swap. Draw a simple diagram of a typical swap agreement. Explain the terms *notional principal* and *counterparty*.

15. Examine recent forecasts of interest rates for the coming year. How might the manager of a large savings institution heavily invested in fixed-rate mortgages use a swap agreement to hedge interest rate risk? What additional risks may be encountered?

16. Compare and contrast the credit risk exposure in swap agreements and futures contracts.

17. Explain how the market for interest rate swaps is organized, and describe the roles of brokers and dealers.

18. Suppose you were charged with managing interest rate risk exposure for a large commercial bank that is heavily invested in intermediate term securities and loans (i.e., those with maturities of approximately five years). Evaluate the relative advantages and disadvantages of hedging with futures versus swaps.

19. Explain a basic call swaption. Does the holder of a call swaption benefit from an interest rate increase or decrease? Give an example.

20. Explain how a swaption and a swap can be combined to give a market participant flexibility in terminating a swap obligation.

21. Describe the interest rate forecast under which it would be beneficial to buy a call option on an interest rate futures contract. Is this the same forecast under which you would buy a call swaption? Why or why not?

22. What is a swap futures contract? What determines the changes in value of swap futures?

23. What are caps and floors? Discuss the similarities between these instruments and options. Give an example of a scenario in which a financial institution manager might buy an interest rate cap.

24. What is an interest rate collar? What is its role in risk management? Could a similar hedge be structured using swaps and swaptions? Explain.

25. Briefly explain how an option contract for insured losses from catastrophic events works. How does a credit swap work? What is a return swap?

Problems

1. John Turner of the Risk-Be-Gone Property/Liability Insurance Company, manages a $700 million stock portfolio. In June, he is watching the stock market carefully and anticipates a downturn in the next two months. He knows that liquidating part of the portfolio will involve transactions costs, so he instead chooses a hedge with stock index futures. The S&P 500 stock index is currently at 1244.78. Yesterday's settlement level for a September S&P index futures was 1256.30. He expects the market index and futures prices to fall by 6.5 percent over the next two months. He has estimated that the company's portfolio has a beta of 1.25.
   a. Calculate the number of contracts required and the resulting gain or loss on the hedge, assuming that the market index and futures prices fall by 6.5 percent as predicted.
   b. Suppose futures prices and cash prices are not perfectly correlated so that futures prices fall by 6.2 percent when the market falls by 6.5 percent. Recalculate the gain or loss on the hedge.
   c. Now suppose that John's forecast is incorrect and that stock prices rise by 2 percent after he places the hedge. Assuming a 2 percent rise in futures prices as well, calculate the gain or loss on the hedge. What potential disadvantages of hedging are revealed by this situation?
   d. Now suppose again that cash and futures positions are not perfectly correlated and that futures rise by 3 percent when stock prices rise by 2 percent. Recalculate the net results of the hedge. If John anticipated this possibility, what might he do at the time the hedge is placed?

2. Pam Lowry, Titan Corporation's pension fund manager, is expecting a $50 million cash inflow three months from now that she must invest in the equity market. Economists forecast an upswing in the stock market over the next three months. Knowing that the expected funds will miss the upswing and resulting benefits, Ms. Lowry has decided to hedge by using stock index futures. The DJIA index currently stands at 9311.19. Yesterday's settlement level for the DJIA (CBOT) futures index for settlement in three months was 9377, and economists predict an increase of 4.5 percent in the index during the same period. The average beta of the stocks in which the incoming funds will be invested is 0.87.

a. Recommend the number of futures contracts to be traded.

b. Calculate the gain or loss on the hedge if the economists' forecasts are correct.

c. Calculate the gain or loss if the market falls by 4 percent and futures fall by 5 percent.

3. Lisa Brown, a commercial loan officer, has made a commitment to one of her best clients to provide a fixed-rate loan for $100,000 in three months at the rate prevailing today. However, she forecasts rising rates in the interim. She recommends to the bank's portfolio manager that the position be hedged by buying a put option on T-bond futures contracts. Assume Ms. Brown's bank will exercise the put if it is profitable to do so. The following information is available:

T-bond futures	Face value $100,000
	Current price: 97–16
Put option	Strike price 97–12
	Premium $2,000

Calculate the gain or loss on the hedge under the following conditions:

a. Interest rates decrease; T-bond futures rise to 99.

b. Interest rates increase; T-bond futures fall to 95–28.

c. Interest rates increase; T-bond futures fall to 94.

4. Suppose John Turner, whose situation is described in Problem 1, can buy a stock index futures put option for a premium of $1,000 with a strike price of 420. Assume the number of options purchased is equal to the number of contracts that would be involved in a futures hedge. Also, assume a multiplier for the strike price of $250.

a. Calculate the gain or loss on the options transaction under each of the following conditions that could prevail when options expire:

    1) the index futures continue to trade at 423.75.

    2) the index futures settlement level drops to 400.

    3) the index futures settlement level rises to 440.

b. Calculate the gain or loss on the futures hedge described in part a of Problem 1 under each of the three scenarios in part a of this problem.

c. Compare the futures results to the gains or losses on the options hedge and assess the risk exposure of the two alternatives. Note: This problem does not require you to calculate the net result of the options or futures hedges; that is, no calculations are required for the stock portfolio results.

5. Return to the index arbitrage example in Table 18.4. Show that the portfolio manager will gain on the transaction even if the market falls by 20 percent before the expiration date. (Hint: Remember that the futures settlement level and the index must be equal at expiration.)

Selected References

Abken, Peter. "Interest-Rate Caps, Collars, and Floors." *CME Financial Strategy Paper*, Chicago Mercantile Exchange (1991a).

———. "Beyond Plain Vanilla: A Taxonomy of Swaps." *Economic Review (Federal Reserve Bank of Atlanta)* 76 (March/April, 1991b), 12–29.

———. "Interest-Rate Caps, Collars, and Floors." *Economic Review (Federal Reserve Bank of Atlanta)* 74 (November/December, 1989), 2–24.

Baldoni, Robert, and Gerhard Isele. "A Simple Guide to Choosing between Futures and Swaps." *Intermarket* 3 (October, 1986), 15–22.

Barro, Robert J., et al. *Black Monday and the Future of Financial Markets*. Homewood, Illinois: Richard D. Irwin (1989).

Beidleman, Carl R., ed. *Interest Rate Swaps*. Homewood, Illinois: Business One Irwin (1991).

Bicksler, James, and Andrew H. Chen. "An Economic Analysis of Interest Rate Swaps." *Journal of Finance* 41 (July, 1986), 645–655.

Brown, Keith C., and Donald J. Smith. "Default Risk and Innovations in the Design of Interest Rate Swaps." *Financial Management* 22 (Summer, 1993), 94–105.

———. "Forward Swaps, Swap Options, and the Management of Callable Debt." In *New Developments in Commercial Banking*, ed. Donald Chew. Cambridge, Massachusetts: Blackwell Publishers (1991).

Canter, Michael S., Joseph B. Cole, and Richard L. Sandor. "Insurance Derivatives: A New Asset Class for the Capital Markets and a New Hedging Tool for the Insurance Industry." *Bank of America Journal of Applied Corporate Finance* 10 (Fall, 1997), 69–83.

Chance, Don M. *An Introduction to Options and Futures.* 2nd ed. Chicago: The Dryden Press (1992).

Chicago Board of Trade. *Commodity Trading Manual.* Chicago: Board of Trade of the City of Chicago (1989).

———. *MMI Futures and Options.* Chicago: Board of Trade of the City of Chicago (1991).

———. *Stock Index Futures.* Chicago: Board of Trade of the City of Chicago (1987).

———. *NASDAQ-100 Index Futures.* Chicago: Board of Trade of the City of Chicago (1986a).

———. *An Introduction to Options on Treasury Bond Futures.* Chicago: Board of Trade of the City of Chicago (1986b).

———. *Options on U.S. Treasury Bond Futures for Institutional Investors.* Chicago: Board of Trade of the City of Chicago (1985).

Chicago Mercantile Exchange. *Using S&P Index Futures and Options.* Chicago: Chicago Mercantile Exchange (1985).

Christopher, Benjamin B. "Recent Developments Affecting Depository Institutions." *FDIC Banking Review* 2 (Spring/Summer, 1989), 37.

Doherty, Neil A. "Financial Innovation in the Management of Catastrophe Risk." *Bank of America Journal of Applied Corporate Finance* 10 (Fall, 1997), 84–95.

Felgran, Steven D. "Interest Rate Swaps: Use, Risk, and Prices." *New England Economic Review (Federal Reserve Bank of Boston)* (November/December, 1987), 22–32.

Goodman, Laurie. "New Options Markets." *Quarterly Review (Federal Reserve Bank of New York)* 8 (Autumn, 1983), 35–47.

Hansell, Saul, and Kevin Muehring. "Why Derivatives Rattle the Regulators." *Institutional Investor* (September, 1992).

Hill, Joanne M., Anshuman Jain, and Robert A. Ward, Jr. *Portfolio Insurance: Volatility Risk and Futures Mispricing.* New York: Kidder Peabody and Co. (1987).

Hutchinson, Michael M. "Swaps." *Weekly Letter (Federal Reserve Bank of San Francisco)* (May 3, 1985).

Koppenhaver, G. D. "Futures Options and Their Use by Financial Intermediaries." *Economic Perspectives (Federal Reserve Bank of Chicago)* 10 (January/February, 1986), 18–31.

Litzenberger, Robert. "Swaps: Plain and Fanciful." *Journal of Finance* 47 (July, 1992), 831–850.

Loeys, Jan G. "Interest Rate Swaps: A New Tool for Managing Risk." *Business Review (Federal Reserve Bank of Philadelphia)* (May/June, 1985), 17–25.

Marshall, John F. "Futures Versus Swaps: Some Considerations for the Thrift Industry." *Review of Business* 12 (Winter, 1990–1991), 15–22, 44.

Merrick, John J., Jr. "Fact and Fantasy about Stock Index Futures Program Trading." *Business Review (Federal Reserve Bank of Philadelphia)* (September/October, 1987), 13–25.

Moser, James T. "Credit Derivatives: Just-in-time Provisioning for Loan Losses." *Federal Reserve Bank of Chicago Economic Perspectives* (Fourth Quarter, 1998), 2–11.

Napoli, Janet A. "Derivative Markets and Competitiveness." *Economic Perspectives (Federal Reserve Bank of Chicago)* 16 (July/August, 1992), 13–24.

Remolona, Eli M. "The Recent Growth of Financial Derivative Markets." *Quarterly Review (Federal Reserve Bank of New York)* 17 (Winter, 1992–1993), 28–43.

Smith, Clifford W., Jr., Charles W. Smithson, and Lee Macdonald Wakeman. "The Market for Interest Rate Swaps." *Financial Management* 18 (Winter, 1988), 34–44.

———. "The Evolving Market for Swaps." In *New Developments in Commercial Banking*, ed. Donald Chew. Cambridge, Massachusetts: Blackwell Publishers (1991).

Spahr, Ronald W., Jan E. Luytjes, and Donald G. Edwards. "The Use of Caps as Deposit Hedges for Financial Institutions." *Issues in Bank Regulation* 12 (Summer, 1988), 17–23.

Stoll, Hans R., and Robert E. Whaley. *Expiration Day Effects of Index Futures and Options.* New York: Salomon Brothers Center for the Study of Financial Institutions (1986).

Tavakoli, Janet M. *Credit Derivatives: A Guide to Instruments and Applications.* New York: John Wiley & Sons, Inc. (1998).

Wall, Larry D., and John J. Pringle. "Interest Rate Swaps: A Review of the Issues." *Economic Review (Federal Reserve Bank of Atlanta)* 73 (November/December, 1988), 22–40.

———. "Alternative Explanations of Interest Rate Swaps: A Theoretical and Empirical Analysis." *Financial Management* 18 (Summer, 1989), 59–73.

Wall, Larry D., John J. Pringle, and James E. McNulty. "Capital Requirements for Interest Rate and Foreign-Exchange Hedges." *Economic Review (Federal Reserve Bank of Atlanta)* 75 (May/June, 1990), 14–29.

Wall, Larry D., and Milind M. Shirkhande. "Credit Derivatives." *Working Paper, Federal Reserve Bank of Atlanta* (Fall, 1998).

Whittaker, J. Gregg. "Interest Rate Swaps: Risk and Regulation." *Economic Review (Federal Reserve Bank of Kansas City)* 72 (March, 1987), 3–13.

Interest Rate Risk Management: Index Futures, Options, Swaps, and Other Derivatives

The Chicago Board of Trade (CBOT) *http://www.cbot.com/* was formed in 1848 by 82 merchants. The purpose was to promote commerce in the city by providing a place where buyers and sellers could meet to exchange commodities. In 1865, the CBOT took steps to formalize grain trading by developing standardized agreements called futures contracts. By the late 19th and early 20th centuries, growth in futures trading increased as more and more businesses adopted the practice into their business plans. The fixed exchange rate between U.S. and West European currencies, estab-lished after World War II, began to unravel in the early 1970s. To meet the demands of this new economic environment, the CBOT expanded its contract offerings, giving financial institutions the opportunity to manage price risk. CBOT provides a great deal of data on the futures market. From the main page, click on "Market Information." Volume data can be found in Microsoft Excel® format.

1. To download the latest data, go to "Statistical reports and Databases" and under "Daily" select "Estimated Volume." The table can be saved to disk and viewed in Excel®.

CHICAGO BOARD OF TRADE
ESTIMATED VOLUME
WEDNESDAY, MARCH 17, 1999

Agricultural Futures	Estimated Volume	Record Daily Volume		Record Open Interest	
Wheat	27,000	56,420	Feb. 25, 99	136,419	Oct. 08, 98
Corn	90,000	170,660	Jun. 27, 95	525,063	Feb. 14, 96
Oats	2,000	11,961	Feb. 25, 94	22,865	Feb. 05, 25
Soybeans	80,000	129,186	Sep. 13, 83	224,578	Dec. 09, 80
Soybean Meal	23,000	56,672	Jun. 23, 98	148,091	Oct. 01, 98
Soybean Oil	34,000	58,019	Apr. 28, 98	170,031	May 05, 98
Rough Rice	600	2,892	Dec. 29, 98	9,485	May 29, 98

2. The Chicago Board of Trade offers a wide variety of financial products. The complete list can be found at: *http://www.cbot.com/ourproducts/financial/contracts.html* Some examples areas follows: Treasury Bond Futures, Fed Fund Futures, and Treasury Bond Futures Options.

A recent innovation is Catastrophic futures, which have arisen to help with the risks associated with catastrophic events. Catastrophe options are standardized, exchange-traded contracts that track Property Claim Services (PCS) catastrophe loss indices. PCS provides each index daily based on its own widely accepted estimates of insured catastrophe losses.

PCS provides nine loss indices to the CBOT: a National index; five regional indices covering Eastern, Northeastern, Southeastern, Midwestern, and Western exposures; and three state indices covering catastrophe-prone Florida, Texas, and California. With this geographic diversity, CBOT catastrophe options can help meet the risk-transfer needs of insurers and reinsurers no matter what their geographic risk exposure. Information on the Catastrophic futures can be found at: *http://www.cbot.com/ourproducts/financial/pcs_intr.html*

3. Daily options volatility summary is available from PM Publishing *http://www.pmpublishing.com.*

Chapter 18 Internet Exercise

You can get a free daily volatility summary by clicking on the icon. This provides essential end-of-day data for 39 markets. The information included provides historical v. implied volatilities, volatility skew graphs, futures movement implied by options market deltas, vegas, gammas, and ticks over fair value.

As an example, from *http://www.pmpublishing. com/volatility/index.html* click on NYMEX to go to the New York Mercantile Exchange data. Click on "heating oil" to get the futures prices of heating oil and the implied volatilities.

Other useful sites for financial institution data:

Applied Derivatives Trading Magazine
http://www.adtrading.com/

Chicago Board Options Exchange
http://www.cboe.com/

Coffee, Sugar & Cocoa Exchange, Inc.
http://www.csce.com/

The Smart Money™ — JAVA Market Map is a unique way of presenting a graphical view of the U.S.A. stock market. The mapping changes with market conditions throughout the day. http://www.dfin. com/stockmap/stock_map.htm

Particular Asset/Liability Management Problems: Depository Institutions

V

▨ ASSET MANAGEMENT: LIQUIDITY RESERVES AND THE SECURITIES PORTFOLIO

▨ DEPOSIT AND LIABILITY MANAGEMENT

▨ ASSET MANAGEMENT: COMMERCIAL, CONSUMER, AND MORTGAGE LENDING

▨ GLOBAL FINANCIAL CRISES AND INTERNATIONAL MANAGEMENT ISSUES

19

ASSET MANAGEMENT: LIQUIDITY RESERVES AND THE SECURITIES PORTFOLIO

Asset management has changed dramatically for financial institutions in the past two decades. In the mid to late 1980s, with deregulation and rising interest expense costs, many depository institution managers took on high risk investments to gamble for high returns. Unfortunately, some of these institutions made "bad bets" and failed. Columbia Savings and Loan in Beverly Hills, California, for example, had at its zenith over 40 percent of its assets in high yielding, noninvestment grade junk bonds (a practice allowed at the time for state-chartered thrifts in California). By 1990, the junk market collapsed, resulting in a $1 billion decline in Columbia's junk bond portfolio, and Congress outlawed junk bonds as thrift investments. In 1991, Columbia was closed, costing taxpayers $2 billion, and its CEO, Thomas Spiegel, awaited trial on a 55-count indictment on charges of misappropriation, fraud, and lying to federal reglators.[1] Similar

---

[1] Kathleen Kerwin. "He Who Lives by the Junk Bond...." *Business Week* (December 25, 1989), 46–47; Richard B. Schmitt. "Spiegel Indicted in Case Stemming from S&L Failure." *The Wall Street Journal* (June 25, 1992), B4.

stories have occurred for other types of financial institutions that took on high-risk investments in the 1980s.

In 1990, investments in below-investment grade (junk) bonds and commercial real estate came to roost for several life insurance companies, including First Executive, the sixteenth largest U.S. life insurance holding company, with $18 billion in assets, and Travelers, the seventh largest life insurance firm, with more than $36 billion in assets. The stock prices of these institutions fell dramatically upon the announcement of bond portfolio losses, including a 42 percent price drop for First Executive and a 21 percent drop for Travelers. Other insurance companies' stock prices were also adversely affected, which researchers found to be associated with an institution's liquidity risk. This suggests some contagion in terms of investors' fears of future policyholder disintermediation for weaker institutions with liquidity problems.[2]

Almost all financial institutions, by their nature, are subject to investment management and liquidity problems related to potential withdrawals by liability holders, including policyholders for insurance companies, depositors for depository institutions, and investors for mutual funds and security firms. How managers respond to new asset investment opportunities and how they manage liquidity are both determined by the institution's long-term goals, and decisions are influenced by the preferences of shareholders, regulators, customers, and managers themselves. In this chapter and those to follow, liquidity, security management, liability management, and lending management are examined, focusing predominantly on depository institutions, which face the greatest liquidity risk and challenges in terms of security, liability, and loan management in terms of satisfying a nexus of regulations. The final challenge of financial institution management is to coordinate decisions in separate areas into an overall asset/liability management strategy for the institution, addressing the risk and return preferences of all parties. This chapter examines aspects of liquidity and securities management for depository institutions. Financial institutions have not always been successful in these areas, such as in the cases of Columbia S&L and First Executive Life, which both failed, providing sobering lessons. But managers continue to adapt and to innovate in an effort to outperform the competition and stay ahead of regulators.

◆ ◆ ◆

IMPORTANCE OF LIQUIDITY IN DEPOSITORY INSTITUTIONS

As one expert explained, depository institution liquidity is "the ability . . . to raise a certain amount of funds at a certain cost within a certain amount of time."[3] Access to cash is important in the financial management of all businesses, but because providing liquidity for customers is an intermediation function, a depository institution's own liquidity is even more important. Institutions obtain many deposits under promise of immediate or almost immediate repayment on demand, so the investment and financing decisions for a depository are inseparable. In other words, obtaining deposits and deciding how to invest them are closely intertwined.

---

[2]George W. Fenn and Rebel A. Cole. "Announcements of Asset-Quality Problems and Contagion Effects in the Life Insurance Industry." *Journal of Financial Economics* 35 (April, 1994), 181–198.

[3]See Burns (1971), 1.

Regulators Require Liquidity

Because deposits—especially some transactions accounts—can be volatile, government regulatory agencies emphasize depository institution liquidity. Most depositories operate under a set of liquidity requirements established at either the state or the federal level. Also, after the Depository Institutions Deregulation and Monetary Control Act (DIDMCA) extended Federal Reserve System (Fed) reserve requirements to all depository institutions, all but the smallest institutions must meet standards set by more than one regulator—the Fed's and those of their chartering or insuring agency.

Depositors Require Liquidity

Besides the requirements of regulators, liquidity needs are affected by the expectations of depositors. The nation's largest depositories explicitly recognize this fact. A recent annual report of the First Chicago Corporation states, "The Corporation has traditionally viewed liquidity quite simply as the ability to meet all present and future financial obligations in a timely manner."[4] One of Citicorp's annual reports presents a similar view: "Citicorp defines adequate liquidity as having funds available at all times to repay fully and promptly all maturing liabilities in accordance with their terms, including customer demand deposits."[5]

Borrowers Require Liquidity

Depository institutions generate most of their interest income from loans and strive to develop a strong base of loan customers. To retain the loyalty of customers, a lender must be able to provide funds for all loan applications that meet its credit standards. Thus, an institution needs to maintain liquidity to support expected loan demand in addition to meeting obligations arising from its liabilities. To maintain a favorable credit rating, which lowers a financial institution's cost of funds, a firm must have adequate liquidity as well.

LIQUIDITY: THE RISK/RETURN TRADE-OFF

With many compelling reasons to maintain liquidity, one might think that liquidity can be easily managed by keeping a large quantity of cash or marketable securities in the asset portfolio. However, a well-recognized trade-off is that liquid assets contribute relatively little to the firm's net interest margin (NIM), because they ordinarily offer a low rate of return. The conflict between the risk of illiquidity and a desire to maintain a high NIM is the heart of liquidity management. The challenge is to maintain enough liquidity to avoid a crisis but to sacrifice no more earnings than absolutely necessary. Although the need for liquid assets arises for a variety of reasons, and all demands must be met simultaneously, each need presents a separate problem. First, reserve requirements must be met, but since deposits with the Fed and cash held for reserve requirements can not be used to meet liquidity needs for deposit withdrawals and loan demand, liquidity needed for such normal and unexpected demands must also be estimated.

---

[4]First Chicago Corporation, *1982 Annual Report*, 25.
[5]Citicorp, *Citicorp Worldwide: 1988 Report*, 34.

Estimating Liquidity Needs for Reserve Requirements

The first reserve requirements for depository institutions were established on deposits of commercial banks with national charters in the National Currency and National Banking Acts of 1863 and 1864.[6] These reserves, established as a percentage of deposits and other liabilities, were required as either cash or interbank deposits, depending on the location of the bank. The rationale for reserve requirements was to protect the liquidity of the banking system to promote public confidence. The Federal Reserve Act of 1913 revised but continued reserve requirements. At the time of its passage, the motivation for the reserve provisions remained prevention of liquidity crises in individual institutions or geographical regions.

New Rationale

The establishment of the Fed discount window in 1913, through which member banks had access to short-term borrowed funds, provided a source of liquidity that had previously been lacking. With the discount window to protect liquidity, the Fed revised its view of the purpose of reserve requirements. By 1931, they were recognized as a tool for controlling the amount of credit extended by banks, and by the 1950s, they had become an important element of monetary policy. In the 1970s the Fed argued that existing reserve requirements, applying only to Fed-member commercial banks, limited the Board's ability to achieve monetary policy goals. That view finally prevailed in the passage of DIDMCA, and reserve requirements were extended to all depositories, both state and federally chartered.[7] While the Fed sought greater control over reserve requirements in DIDMCA, many observers have lamented the fact that the requirements are an unproductive regulatory tax that either reduces funds available for lending and investing or is passed along to customers in the form of higher loan rates and fees. In the 1990s, the Federal Reserve Board itself has seemed to agree with its critics: reserve requirements have been lowered several times, to 0 percent in some cases. Note, however, that in less developed countries such as Mexico with money markets that are not very well developed, so that central bank open market operations cannot take place, large reserve requirements for banks are more crucial for implementing monetary policy.

Reserve Requirements Since 1980

Although the rationale for imposing reserve requirements on depository institutions is no longer solely to protect the liquidity position of the financial system, meeting the requirements continues to be a key issue in individual institutions. Table 19.1

---

[6]For a discussion of the history of reserve requirements, on which the historical information in this chapter is based, see Feinman (1993) and Goodfriend and Hargraves (1983). An earlier survey treatment of this topic is Knight (1974). A good recent article arguing that **no** rationale for reserve requirements is convincing enough to justify them is Stevens (1991).

[7]In one DIDMCA provision, Congress established a range of 8 percent to 14 percent for the marginal reserve requirements on transactions accounts. It gave the Fed the authority to set a higher percentage for monetary policy reasons but stipulated that the Fed must pay interest on those reserves. The authority has never been exercised. For further details, see "The Depository Institutions Deregulation and Monetary Control Act of 1980"; and Cacy and Winningham (1980).

Table 19.1   ✦   RESERVE REQUIREMENTS OF THE FEDERAL RESERVE SYSTEM

Reserve requirements vary according to the amount of deposits held by institutions and are set at different levels for different categories of deposits. Requirements have been altered several times in the 1990s and are less burdensome for depositories than in past decades.

REQUIREMENTS		
Type of Deposit and Deposit Interval	% of Deposits	Effective Date
Net transactions accounts[a]		
$0 million—$46.5 million	3	12/31/98
More than $46.5 million	10	12/31/98
Nonpersonal time deposits by original maturity		
Less than $1\frac{1}{2}$ years	0	12/27/90
$1\frac{1}{2}$ years or more	0	10/6/83
Eurocurrency liabilities, all types	0	12/27/90

[a]0% bracket as of 1999 was $4.9 million.
Source: Federal Reserve Bulletin, 1999.

contains Fed reserve requirements as of 1999. Since 1980, reserve requirements have fallen. Table 19.1 points out that in 1999, the 10 percent requirement applied to total transactions accounts in excess of $46.5 million, with a 3 percent requirement for the first $46.5 million. Also, under the Garn-St. Germain Act of 1982, an annually adjusted amount of reserve deposits are exempt, initially $2 million and as of 1999, $4.9 million (see note to Table 19.1). This provides a reprieve to the nation's smallest banks.[8]

Managing the Reserve Position

Required reserves must be held as vault cash or as deposits at a district Federal Reserve Bank. The Fed requires weekly reports from large depositories; a quarterly schedule applies to institutions with total deposits below an amount specified in Federal Reserve **Regulation D**. If an institution's reserves are 4 percent below the daily average minimum reserve required, it is subject to a penalty imposed by the Fed. Reserves that are 4 percent below the minimum can be carried over as a deficit into the next period, with 4 percent more reserves needed to be held that period. Similarly, if reserves are 4 percent higher than the minimum, this excess can be carried over to the next two-week reserve period. The Fed does not pay interest on reserve deposits, so reserve balances are nonearning assets for depositories. Because of the interest penalty plus regulatory intervention exacted for having too few reserves and the loss of income from having too many, depositories must estimate their reserve requirements as accurately as possible.

---

[8]More details on the comparison between lagged reserve accounting and contemporaneous reserve accounting may be found in the following articles, some of which also serve as the sources for the description of CRA in the paragraphs that follow: Rosenbaum (1984); Hamdani (1984); and Tarhan (1984). Also, major portions of the December, 1983, and January, 1984, issues of *Roundup*, Federal Reserve Bank of Dallas, were devoted to the change in reserve accounting procedures. See also Stevens (1991).

Contemporaneous and Lagged Reserve Accounting   From 1968 until early 1984, calculating reserve requirements was relatively straightforward. An institution knew a week in advance the amount of reserves needed, because they were based on average deposits for the week ending seven days earlier, a system called **lagged reserve accounting (LRA)**. The chief problem for management was deciding the most efficient way to obtain this known quantity of funds.

The Fed, however, viewed the lagged system as an impediment to effective monetary control. In October, 1979, the Fed revised its monetary control procedures, placing greater emphasis on depository reserves as a way of achieving monetary growth targets. Subsequently, on February 2, 1984, the Board of Governors instituted a procedure known as **contemporaneous reserve accounting (CRA)** for transaction deposits. The new system has complicated reserve management. CRA applies only to institutions reporting weekly; others continue to compute required reserves under a lagged system. However, recently, regulators have considered proposals to go back to LRA for transaction deposits to make reserve management easier for depository institutions. LRA is used for reserve requirements on nonpersonal nontransaction accounts (see Table 19.1). However, currently the requirements are 0 percent, which were instated in 1990 when there was a credit crunch in the banking system to stimulate lending, and are still 0 percent.

CRA Rules   Under CRA, an institution's required reserves on transactions deposits are determined by deposit levels in the same period, rather than in a previous period, as is the case under the lagged system. The **maintenance period** is the time during which reserve balances must be on deposit. It lasts two weeks, extending from a Thursday to a Wednesday 14 days later. The reserve **computation period** is also two weeks, but it begins on a Tuesday (two days prior) to the maintenance period and ends two days earlier (on the Monday 14 days later). The average daily level of reserves during the maintenance period must meet the required percentages on the average level of deposits during the computation period.[9]

These rules, which sound (and are) confusing, are illustrated in Figure 19.1. On the calendar at the bottom of Figure 19.1, the computation period on transactions deposits extends from day 15 to day 28, and the maintenance period covers days 17 to 30. As deposits fluctuate, reserve balances must be adjusted almost simultaneously. Depository institutions must carefully monitor large depositors. Large banks must coordinate deposit withdrawals and deposits for many branches. Fed funds can be bought and sold to compensate for reserves under or over an institution's minimum reserve requirement. Reserve requirements must be met with an average daily balance held for the two-week period, so adjustments can be made if reserves are too low for any given day. A LRA schedule, in contrast, would involve a computation period two weeks prior to the maintenance period in days 1–14.

Forms in Which Reserves Are Held   Reserves can be held in vault cash or deposits with the Fed, or for nonmember institutions, with designated institutions

---

[9]Average cash balances counted toward reserve requirements had been based on the same computation period as that used for reserves against nontransactions balances. See Rosenbaum (1984). For cash balances, the computation period was altered from days 1–14 to days 15–28 in 1992.

Figure 19.1 ✦ RESERVE REQUIREMENT COMPUTATION: CONTEMPORANEOUS
RESERVE ACCOUNTING

Under contemporaneous reserve requirements, the reserve computation period for transactions accounts and the reserve maintenance period overlap substantially, increasing the difficulty of managing reserves.

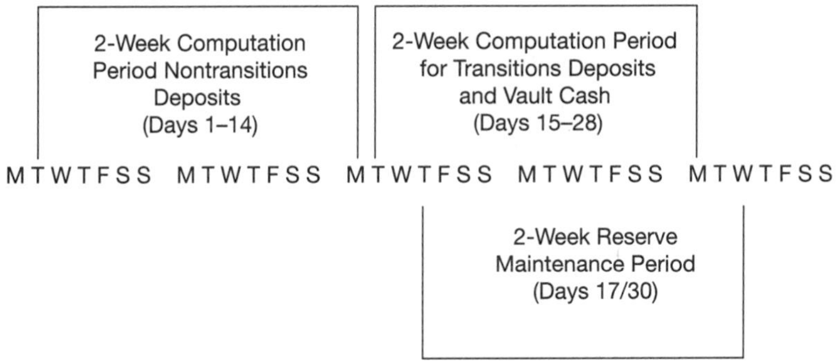

2-Week Computation Period Nontransitions Deposits (Days 1–14)	2-Week Computation Period for Transitions Deposits and Vault Cash (Days 15–28)

M T W T F S S   M T W T F S S   M T W T F S S   M T W T F S S   M T W T F S S

2-Week Reserve Maintenance Period (Days 17/30)

Reserve Management Calender

M	T	W	T	F	S	S	
	1	2	3	4	5	6	Lagged Computation
M	T	W	T	F	S	S	Period
7	8	9	10	11	12	13	(Days 1–14)
M	T	W	T	F	S	S	Contemporaneous Computation
14	15	16	17	18	19	20	Period (Days 15–28)
M	T	W	T	F	S	S	Maintenance
21	22	23	24	25	26	27	Period (Days 17–30)
M	T	W	T	F	S	S	
28	29	16	17	18	19	20	
M	T	W	T	F	S	S	
35	35	37	38	39	40	41	
M	T	W					
42	43	44					

Source: Adapted from Mary Susan Rosenbaum, "Contemporaneous Reserve Accounting: The New System and its Implications for Monetary Policy," *Economic Review* (Federal Reserve Bank of Atlanta), 69 (April 1984): 47; and "Contemporaneous Reserves Change Accounting Procedures," *Roundup* (Federal Reserve Bank of Dallas), December 1983. Updated by the authors.

(pass-through balances), such as correspondent banks. Knowing the exact amount of cash and reserves available to meet reserve requirements is complicated by the check-clearing process. As checks are cleared through the district Fed banks, the Fed transfers funds from the account of one bank to the account of another. At any time, then, an institution's total reserves contain **clearing balances**, which may be subsequently transferred as a result of customers' transactions. Conversely, reserves from other institutions may be transferred in.

Calculating Required Reserves

Table 19.2 provides an example of calculating required reserves under CRA. The institution is a hypothetical commercial bank, but the process would be similar for any institution subject to CRA rules. The days correspond to the reserve management calendar in Figure 19.1, and all dollar amounts are in millions. The lagged computation period is a two-week span (days 1–14) that ends one day before the contemporaneous computation period (days 15–28) begins.

Calculating the CRA Requirements for Transaction Deposits   Since the current requirement for nontransaction liabilities is 0 percent, only reserve requirements on transaction accounts need to be calculated. Transaction accounts include all deposits for which a depositor may withdraw funds through a negotiable or transferable instrument or make more than three monthly withdrawals by telephone or preauthorized fund transfers. This includes demand deposits, NOW accounts, and credit union (CU) share draft accounts. Time deposits, personal savings deposits, and money market deposit accounts are typically deemed nontransaction accounts. In calculating reserve requirements, total transaction account balances are reduced by demand balances due from other U.S. depository institutions and cash in the process of collection (CIPC) to get the net transaction account balance.

Looking at Table 19.2, this bank's daily average vault cash is $9.671 million and its net average daily transaction account balance is $1,135.286 million (over any exempt amount) during the contemporaneous computation period, i.e., days 15–28. The lower panel shows that to calculate the bank's reserve requirement, the first $46.5 million of the net daily transaction balance is multiplied by 0.03, and the $1,088.79 million is multiplied by 0.10. The remaining total $110.274 million is reduced by the average daily vault cash of $9.671 million to calculate the average daily balance required of $100.603 million. Multiplying this amount by 14 gives the total cumulative reserves required for the contemporaneous computation period equal to $1,408.442 million.

As shown in the top panel, the reserve balance held during the maintenance period for the last 12 days is $1,191.00 million. Subtracting this from the $1,408.442 million required to be held over the 14-day maintenance period equals $217.442 million. Thus, the bank must hold on average for the remaining two days of the maintenance period $108.721 million ($217.442). The maximum deficit that the bank can carry over to the next period without penalty is the bank's average daily requirement of $100.603 × 0.04, or $4.024 million. If the bank has held excess reserves in the previous maintenance period, management would use the positive carryover privilege to cover some of the current required balances.[10]

---

[10]CRA research published by the Federal Reserve Bank of New York shows that most institutions do, in fact, hold excess reserves most of the time, with smaller institutions holding larger reserves, perhaps because they have fewer sources of short-term external borrowing in the capital markets and can not afford a full-time manager to keep reserves at the lowest possible level, as large banks can. Research conducted at the Federal Reserve Bank of St. Louis concluded that forecasting errors could be large enough to justify an increase in the positive/negative carryover privilege to 5 percent from the 2 percent used initially. As noted, the carryover privilege *was* increased in 1992. See Gilbert (1980) and Hamdani (1984).

Table 19.2 ✦ Reserve Balance Computation (millions)

Under contemporaneous reserve accounting, management of reserve balances involves complex relationships. The last two days of the maintenance period are particularly important for assuring that the average required minimum balance is achieved.

LAGGED COMPUTATION PERIOD			CONTEMPORANEOUS COMPUTATION PERIOD				MAINTENANCE PERIOD		
Day #	Day	Non-Transactions Liabilities	Day #	Day	Vault Cash	Transactions Deposits	Day #	Day	Reserve Balances
1	T	$450	15	T	$9.5	$1,082			
2	W	485	16	W	9.3	1,090			
3	T	460	17	T	9.6	1,055	17	T	$93
4	F	445	18	F	9.8	1,085	18	F	99
5	S	445	19	S	9.8	1,108	19	S	104
6	S	445	20	S	9.8	1,115	20	S	101
7	M	440	21	M	9.1	1,100	21	M	97
8	T	425	22	T	9.5	1,110	22	T	103
9	W	465	23	W	9.2	1,112	23	W	105
10	T	450	24	T	9.8	1,150	24	T	96
11	F	475	25	F	9.9	1,155	25	F	98
12	S	475	26	S	9.9	1,138	26	S	94
13	S	475	27	S	9.9	1,256	27	S	102
14	M	460	28	M	10.3	1,338	28	M	99
							29	T	
							30	W	
Average:		$456,786			$9,671	$1,135,286	12-day total:	$1,191,000	
							12-day average:	$99.250	

A 10% requirement applies to all transactions deposits of over $46.5 million.

Required average daily reserve balance for $1,135.286 mil. transaction deposits:

0% of nontransactions liabilities (lagged)	$0.000
+3% of first $46.5 mil. in transactions deposits (contemporaneous)	$1.395
+10% of remaining transactions deposits (contemporaneous)	$108.879
− Average vault cash	($9.671)
Average daily balance required	$100.603[a]

Reserve adjustment required:

Cumulative total reserves required (daily average × 14):	$1408.442
Less cumulative total achieved in first 12 days:	$1,191.000
Total amount required for last two days	$217.442
Average balance required for each of last two days ($217.442):	$108.721

Maximum negative carryover allowed:

Daily requirement × 0.04	$4.024

[a]Does not add because of rounding; slight rounding differences may also affect other calculations.

Estimating Liquidity Needs Above Reserve Requirements

Besides meeting standards set by government regulators, depository institutions need liquid funds to meet customer loan demand and deposit withdrawals.[11] Commercial banks, having offered transactions accounts and short-term commercial loans longer than other depositories, have traditionally been more concerned with liquidity needs arising from operations, but nonbank depositories now pay increased attention to liquidity because they, too, now offer transactions accounts. Liquidity management is closely related to liability management. If a large money center bank, for instance, has multiple sources for short-term borrowing, it requires less liquidity in terms of short-term assets on its balance-sheet. However, ultimately, the amount of liquidity needed depends on predicted loan demand, deposit withdrawals adjusted for cyclical and seasonal factors, and growth. Also, the amount of liquidity needed depends on how much of a cushion a bank wants for unexpected loan demand and deposit withdrawals and the risk preferences of stakeholders in the institution.

DISCRETIONARY AND NONDISCRETIONARY FACTORS

The balance sheet of a depository can be divided into discretionary and nondiscretionary items.[12] Discretionary items include those over which management can exert considerable influence, such as the use of repurchase agreements. Nondiscretionary items are those beyond the short-run control of an institution, such as deposit fluctuations, loan demand, and reserve requirements. Some nondiscretionary items—such as deposit increases or maturing loans—are sources of liquidity, but others are drains on liquidity.

Managers must understand the implications of nondiscretionary items for their institutions. A depository that derives most of its revenues from loans does not really wish to deny loans to good customers based on liquidity shortages. Such actions would undermine customer relationships built over long years of service and damage profit potential. Refusing to honor customer requests for deposit withdrawals would surely have even more severe consequences. These operations-based liquidity demands are an important part of the planning process. The better an institution can predict its expected loan demand and deposit withdrawals, the lower excess liquidity it needs to hold.

---

[11]Thrift regulators have typically set minimum liquidity requirements as a percentage of a thrift's withdrawable accounts. Under the Financial Institutions Reform, Recovery, and Enforcement Act (FIRREA), the director of the Office of Thrift Supervision was given the authority to establish minimum liquidity requirements, but Congress mandated that they be between 4 percent and 10 percent of an association's total short-term liabilities, including a thrift's withdrawable accounts (i.e., transactions accounts, money market deposit accounts, passbook accounts, and short-term CDs, plus borrowings repayable on demand or within one year). Liquid assets, however, include a variety of investments, including fed funds sold, municipal bonds, selected mutual fund holdings, short-term MBSs, and even certain types of home mortgage loans. Since FIRREA, different liquidity requirements may be set for different categories of savings associations, depending on size, location, type, or other institutional characteristics. FIRREA allows the Office of Thrift Supervision to penalize institutions not complying with prescribed liquidity standards. See Conference Report on H.R. 1278 (1989).

[12]This dichotomy was proposed in Luckett (1980), 12–13.

Estimating Liquidity Needs for Operations: An Example

The estimation of liquidity needs arising from anticipated volatility in deposits and expected loan demand involves several techniques, ranging from managerial judgment to quantitative models. Table 19.3 presents a simplified example of estimating a liquidity surplus or deficit over a single planning period.[13] The first step is to estimate total balances in each main asset and funding source category.

Liquid and Illiquid Assets   Asset categories are divided into liquid or illiquid components; liquid assets in this context are those available to meet operational needs. For example, at the top of Table 19.3, the institution's total cash balances

---

Table 19.3   ✦   ESTIMATING LIQUIDITY NEEDS FOR OPERATIONS

Institutions need to forecast potential liquidity positions and plan to avoid deficits. The approach illustrated identifies the volatility of funds sources and estimates whether liquid assets could cover large outflows and meet additional loan demand.

	Total (Millions)	Liquid (%)	Liquid	Illiquid
I. Original Assumptions				
Assets				
Cash	$ 209.7	10%	$ 21.0	$ 188.7
Investments	1,037.6	59	609.4	428.2
Loans	1,214.4	0	0.0	1,214.4
Other assets	171.0	0	15.0	156.0
Total	$2,632.7		$645.4	$1,987.3
		Volatile (%)	Volatile	Nonvolatile
Funds sources				
Deposits	$1,755.0	7%	$130.0	$1,625.0
Other liabilities	674.0	82	549.7	124.3
Equity	203.7	0	0.0	203.7
Total	$2,632.7		$679.7	$1,953.0

Liquidity deficit (liquid assets − volatile funds):
$645.4 − $679.7 = ($34.3)

	Total (Millions)	Liquid (%)	Liquid	Illiquid
II. Additional Loan Demand				
Assets				
Cash	$ 209.7	10%	$ 21.0	$ 188.7
Investments	1,037.6	59	609.4	428.2
Loans	1,214.4	−1	(12.1)	1,226.5
Other assets	171.0	9	15.0	156.0
Total	$2,632.7		$633.3	$1,999.4

Liquidity deficit (liquid assets − volatile funds):
$633.3 − $679.7 = ($46.4)

---

[13]This example is similar to one in Kaufman and Lee (1977).

during the next period are estimated to be almost $210 million. But because of reserve requirements and daily transactions, total cash balances are never entirely available to meet deposit withdrawals or increased loan demand. In fact, management has estimated that only $21 million could be used to fulfill these needs. Within the investments category, liquid investments are those that can be sold easily, without great loss of value, during the planning period. Sources of funds are also maturing securities and loans.

More about managing the securities portfolio to allow for operational liquidity appears later in the chapter. Longer-term securities are not liquid, but they can be used as a form of stored liquidity for unexpected loan demand or deposit withdrawals; however, they may have to be sold at a loss if interest rates have risen since their initial purchase.

Volatile and Nonvolatile Sources of Funds   Drains on liquidity can be estimated by examining funds sources. In this institution, most deposits are considered relatively stable, so only $130 million are judged to be volatile. In contrast, other liabilities for borrowed money, including negotiable certificates of deposit, repurchase agreements, and federal funds purchased, are quite volatile. Management assumes that most could be withdrawn or become unavailable on short notice. The equity of the institution is entirely nonvolatile in the short run.

A liquidity deficit is projected for the upcoming period because liquid assets are less than volatile funds sources by $34.3 million. If management's estimates are correct, the institution must somehow generate additional cash in that amount.

Additional Drains on Liquidity   The first panel of Table 19.3 adjusts for normal loan demand and deposit supplies. It assumes that next period's loan demand can be completely met by maturing loans or stable deposits; that is, the loan portfolio is viewed neither as a source of liquidity nor as a drain on liquidity. A more conservative approach would build in coverage for unexpected loan demand by assigning a *negative* balance to the liquid loan category, reflecting the drain on liquidity from increased loan demand. Suppose that management wishes to allow for additional loan demand equal to 1 percent of that already forecast, or a total of $12.1 million. The liquidity deficit from operations would then rise to $46.4 million (bottom panel of Table 19.3).

Other more detailed liquidity gaps estimate all funding sources and funding uses (including all maturing loans and securities, unused loan commitments, expected deposit withdrawals, and maturing deposits) to derive a more precise liquidity gap for an upcoming period, including unexpected loan demand and deposit withdrawals. The liquidity gap is then compared with contingent borrowing sources or other sources of stored liquidity.

Incorporating Quantitative Models   A more quantitative method of estimating liquidity needs is to forecast from a regression analysis of past data. For example, in the analysis of expected loan demand, management could use a model relating past loan demand, D, to time, t: $D = f(t)$. The resulting regression equation can serve as a basis for projecting a range of future demand that incorporates past volatility and knowledge of other economic or seasonal factors that may cause a change from past trends. An even better forecast might be generated with multiple regression, because loan demand is also affected by factors such as economic conditions, interest rates, and competition from other institutions, to name just a few, and each institution must identify its relevant set of variables. Similar analyses can be performed for all nondiscretionary items that affect liquidity.

Sophistication in forecasting techniques is positively related to the size of depository institutions; this is not surprising because it is expensive to employ forecasting specialists.[14] Regardless of how forecasts are generated, they are an important part of the liquidity management solution. These estimates combine with estimates of required reserves to represent a target level of liquid funds for the planning period.

MANAGING THE LIQUIDITY POSITION

Table 19.2 presents a bank's reserve dilemma; the bank has a potential reserve deficiency and needs immediate access to liquid funds to bring the two-week daily average balance in line with the Fed requirements.[15] The institution in Table 19.3 needs liquidity as a result of operational factors. Whatever the reason, managers must act.

Borrowing Versus Selling Securities

Two general liquidity management strategies are available. First, management can borrow funds, either from the regulators or from nondeposit creditors in the financial markets. Obtaining nondeposit sources of cash, a technique used more often by large commercial banks than by other depositories, is called **liability management**. Because the use of nondeposit funds, such as federal funds and Euromarket borrowing, has implications far beyond liquidity management, full discussion of liability management is deferred until Chapter 20. This chapter discusses borrowing from regulators as a source of liquidity. Larger institutions with greater sources of borrowing can engage in greater liability management than smaller institutions that are often limited to Fed Funds Purchased or borrowing from regulators.

A second strategy is to use asset management and liquidate assets from the securities portfolio. High market interest rates can make this approach undesirable. Also, depositories hold securities for purposes other than liquidity, so trade-offs are involved in this approach to liquidity management. Some of these are discussed later in the chapter.

Factors Influencing Liquidity Management

The choice between borrowing or selling securities (i.e., between liability management and asset management) is influenced by several factors, including the size of

---

[14]A survey of forecasting techniques revealed that the percentage of large banks (deposits in excess of $400 million) that use sophisticated forecasting techniques (such as multiple regression, time series forecasting, and simulation) was higher than among smaller banks. A large number of institutions of all sizes, however, rely on managerial judgment—either alone or in combination with quantitative methods—for estimating future deposit levels and loan demand. See Giroux (1980).

[15]Management of the reserve position is not limited to the problem of covering reserve deficiencies. Depositories may also find themselves with *excess* reserves toward the end of the maintenance period. When the institution has excess reserves, management may choose to lend them in the federal funds market. The asset thus created is defined as "federal funds sold."

the institution, its financial stability, its industry, and the risk/return preferences of managers and owners:

+ **Size and Financial Stability**. Small or financially weak institutions are especially likely to look to the securities portfolio, not to liability management, for generating liquidity. Within the asset portfolio, too, liquidity is influenced by institutional size. As discussed more fully later, active portfolio management is expensive; thus, a smaller institution is likely to keep larger proportions of readily marketable short-term securities and higher excess reserve balances.

+ **Industry Membership**. Another influence over which a depository institution usually has little control is its industry. Regulatory policies governing an industry limit its operations—including the composition of its securities portfolio, the proportion of liquid assets held, and the sources of short-term loans for liquidity purposes. Recently, however, regulators have provided depository institutions with more freedom to change from one industry to another by simplifying the process of applying for new charters.

+ **Risk/Return Preferences**. Managers' and owners' risk preferences also influence liquidity management. For a variety of reasons (explored in Chapter 20), liability management exposes an institution to greater risks than does a strategy of selling securities when cash is needed. Furthermore, some strategies for managing the securities portfolio are riskier than others.

Borrowing From Regulators as a Source of Liquidity

The carryover privilege on Fed reserve requirements is useful in meeting small deficiencies in liquid assets. For example, if deposits fluctuate unexpectedly toward the end of the maintenance period, an institution can postpone major reserve adjustments until the next period as long as the fluctuations are not too large. However, if deficiencies are large or frequent, the institution can turn to federal regulators for other sources of cash for liquidity management.

The Discount Window   The Fed discount window was originally available only to member commercial banks, but DIDMCA opened it to all depositories subject to Fed reserve requirements. Commercial banks remain by far the largest users, because Fed policy requires other depositories to exhaust traditional sources of regulatory borrowing before turning to the discount window.

The Fed administers discount window borrowing under its **Regulation A**, which permits institutions to borrow under three conditions: to meet temporary liquidity needs, such as those illustrated in Table 19.2; to meet seasonal credit demands, such as those arising around Christmas or, for many rural banks, during planting season; and for special "extended credit" purposes, often after disasters such as Hurricane Andrew or the Los Angeles riots, both in 1992, which make unforeseeable demands on institutions. The Fed may also provide extended credit if an institution experiences unusually heavy withdrawals and regulators fear a "run," such as occurred with the near-failure of Continental National Bank in 1984.

The interest cost and availability of these borrowings are major factors in the decision to use the window. Ordinarily, discount-window borrowings are very short-term, used only to meet genuine liquidity emergencies and not as additional funds for expanding the loan portfolio. Officials at the Fed monitor an institution's use of the window and may ask management to discontinue borrowing should norms for the amount and frequency of borrowing be exceeded. Thus, frequent borrowing at the window has negative connotations that managers are careful to avoid.[16]

FHLB Advances   Before FIRREA, federal savings institutions facing a shortage of qualifying liquid assets could apply for advances from the Federal Home Loan Banks (FHLBs). This FHLB lending program was originated in the Federal Home Loan Bank Act of 1932 and modeled after that of the Fed. Advances from the FHLBs tended to be longer term than the Fed's discount-window loans, and the interest rate was sometimes adjusted by the Bank System in an effort to alter the volume of mortgage lending that thrifts were undertaking.

FIRREA made important changes to the FHLB advance program. Under certain circumstances, commercial banks and CUs are now eligible for advances from the FHLBs. In general, however, longer-term advances are made only to enable an institution to meet unmet demand for mortgage loans and not to provide a more-or-less permanent source of cash. Advances must be collateralized by low-risk assets, and the volume of advances is limited by an institution's level of net worth. Furthermore, the FHLBs must consider an institution's reinvestment in the community and its willingness to lend to first-time homebuyers in deciding whether to grant a requested advance.

FIRREA also specified conditions under which institutions with emergency cash shortages can obtain short-term advances from the FHLBs. Eligible institutions must be solvent and must present substantial evidence that they can repay the debt.[17] With these guidelines, Congress hoped to prevent a recurrence of the situation prevailing immediately before FIRREA, in which the insolvent portion of the industry owed regulators millions of dollars borrowed during the period of extreme forbearance, which it could never realistically repay.

Sources of Borrowing for Credit Unions   For CUs, three sources of short-term funds are available, two of these from regulatory sources. One source of liquidity was authorized by Congress in 1978, when it approved the creation of the Central Liquidity Facility (CLF) as an arm of the National Credit Union Administration. The CLF functions as the lender of last resort for CUs voluntarily choosing to join it. In contrast to FHLB advances, CLF loans are made for liquidity purposes only. Besides interest, the CLF requires borrowing CUs to pay a commitment fee of $\frac{1}{4}$ of 1 percent. Fed discount-window loans are also available to CUs offering transactions deposits or nonpersonal time deposits. Finally, a CU that is a member of a Corporate Credit Union (CCU) may borrow from the CCU.[18]

THE SECURITIES PORTFOLIO AS A SOURCE OF STORED LIQUIDITY

Managing the securities portfolio—in particular, choosing an optimal combination of liquid versus higher-yielding assets—is an integral part of liquidity management for financial institutions, particularly small and medium-sized depositories. Under a

---

[16]Details on the administration of the window can be found in Mengle (1986a) and Sprong (1990).

[17]See McKenna, Conner, and Cuneo (1989), 49–50.

[18]See Pearce (1984) and *NCUSIF Annual Report* (1991).

stored liquidity approach, institutions keep a pyramid of reserves, with cash above reserve requirements as **primary reserves**, short-term marketable securities that are not pledged for public deposits (such as Treasury and agency bills) as **secondary reserves**,[19] and mortgage-securities and other longer-term securities as **tertiary reserves** that can be sold if necessary—although possibly at a loss if interest rates have risen since their purchase. Tertiary reserves are primarily for income-producing purposes, particularly counter-cyclical income when loan demand is down.

Most depository institutions use a combination of stored liquidity and liability management for their liquidity needs. Again, the more borrowing sources that an institution has and the better it can forecast its liquidity needs, the less stored liquidity it has to keep. Other ways of maintaining liquidity are securitization and loans sales, which are discussed in Chapter 9 on Managing Noninterest Revenues.

SECURITIZATION OF LOANS AND LOAN SALES AS LIQUIDITY SOURCES

Depository institutions with institutional investor networks can sell loans for liquidity to long-term investors, such as pension funds and insurance companies. In addition to shortening their funding gaps by removing long-term fixed assets from the balance sheet and reducing credit risk if loans are sold without recourse, such loan sales provide a stream of liquidity that can be used to fund new loan demand or deposit withdrawals. Similarly, if loan securitization processes are set in place for a depository institution through a subsidiary or a correspondent bank, or for home mortgages through a government or quasi-government agency, the depository institution has a steady source of liquidity and fee income. In addition, if the depository institution removes loans from the balance sheet, it can use the funds received from securitization or loan sale to pay off deposits (i.e., shrink the size of the bank), reducing its deposits, and, hence, its reserve requirements as a regulatory tax. With fewer assets, capital requirements, also as a regulatory tax, can be reduced.

LIQUIDITY RISK OF OTHER FINANCIAL INSTITUTIONS

Although depository institutions have the largest liquidity risk of financial institutions, since deposits as liabilities have instantaneous maturities and can be withdrawn at any time, life insurance companies and other types of financial institutions have liquidity risks as well.

Insurance Companies   Although life insurance companies have long-term contracts and therefore have much lower liquidity risk than other financial institutions, they still have some liquidity risk when they have large investment losses, such as First Executive Life in 1990. Policyholders and annuity-holders and investors in

---

[19]Institutions receiving deposits from the U.S. government and many state and municipal governments, such as tax deposits, are required to pledge collateral against deposits in excess of the $100,000 FDIC insurance ceiling, i.e., invest deposits greater than $100,000 in only certain assets, such as U.S. government, state, or local securities that qualify as collateral. In addition, institutions serving as major dealers in money market assets must keep an inventory of **trading account securities** to make trades with customers.

guaranteed investment contracts (GICs) have at times engaged in runs to cash in policies and investments to try to obtain what they could before a troubled institution's closure. Similarly, property/casualty insurance companies (P/Cs) must keep sufficient liquidity to make payouts for contingencies for damages to personal property or individuals. Since policy coverages are shorter-term than life insurance companies, P/Cs must keep a larger percentage of shorter-term assets. They are also exposed to the liquidity risk of policyholders canceling or not renewing policies, which reduces cash flow from incoming premiums, and to potential liquidity crises from catastrophic events, such as Hurricane Mitch in 1998.

Mutual Funds   Mutual funds are also subject to liquidity risk in the event of an investor panic in the expectation of a large market downturn. However, as Peter Fortune, a senior economist at the Federal Reserve of Boston, points out, research shows that even during the stock market crash of 1987, mutual fund outflows were relatively small compared with their liquidity on hand, and very few funds experienced problems. Such stability is often attributed to the relatively high income profile of the median shareholder for mutual funds, with investments predominantly for retirement, suggesting a longer-term investment time horizon and some degree of sophistication.[20]

Open-end funds are obligated to buy back their shares in any quantity offered generally at the net asset value on the day the redemption is requested. As Fortune notes, "Thus, their shares are similar to demand deposits at financial institutions, redeemable at short notice although at a variable price."[21] To bridge the gap between the settlement period until liquidity can be replenished by selling securities, mutual funds typically hold cash-equivalent assets, such as cash and Treasury securities.

A number of factors have resulted in mutual funds holding lower liquidity ratios in the 1990s, falling to 5.5 percent cash equivalents to assets for equity and mixed bond/stock funds and 4 percent for bond funds at the end of 1996. These factors include a shorter settlement period (from five to three days for securities), which requires less cash to bridge the gap between redemptions and receipts from security sales; a larger average size of mutual funds, which provides economies of scale in cash balances; the availability of lines of credit with banks as a source of liquidity, which was not readily available prior to October, 1987; and greater competitive pressures, which encourage fund managers to hold less liquidity to achieve higher fund returns.[22]

---

[20]This section comes from Peter Fortune. "Mutual Funds, Part I: Reshaping the American Financial System." *Federal Reserve of Boston New England Economic Review* (July/August 1997), 1–72. According to a 1996 Investment Company Institute study, the median shareholder in a mutual fund had household income of $60,000 and held $50,000 in financial assets, with $18,000 in mutual funds. About 60 percent of shareholders had completed college and over 54 percent also held individual stocks. Over 60 percent of shareholders responding indicated that they invested for at least a six-year horizon, and 35 percent indicated a horizon of more than 10 years.

[21]Ibid, 64.

[22]Ibid, 64. For equity and mixed funds, the liquidity-to-asset ratio averaged about 10 percent during the mid to late 1980s, peaking in 1990 to 13 percent, and then dramatically falling to 5.5 percent at the end of 1996. Bond funds have typically had lower liquidity ratios, generally above 5 percent but declining to 4 percent by the end of 1996.

Other Financial Institutions   Finance companies, securities firms, and other types of financial institutions have liquidity concerns as well, since they are all highly financially levered institutions and rely on public confidence. Government security dealers, security traders, and investment bankers have to finance security inventories with short-term sources of financing such as repurchase agreements and other short-term borrowings, and thus are subject to great liquidity risk as well if securities are not sold quickly. Similarly, finance companies often finance loans with short-term borrowings and commercial paper, which must be paid back in less than a year. Better capitalized institutions and institutions with greater reputational capital are able to attract larger sources of short-term financing.

DEPOSITORY INSTITUTION INVESTMENT PORTFOLIO MANAGEMENT

The preceding sections have discussed different aspects of liquidity management for depository institutions, including reserve management, estimating liquidity needs, and alternative strategies for achieving liquidity through stored liquidity, securitization and loan sales, and short-term borrowing (liability management).

In contrast to other financial institutions that rely on portfolio management and other strategies taught in investment courses for investment management, depository institutions are subject to much greater regulation on the type of securities that they can hold; to pledging requirements (collateral that must be held in the form of government or other very safe securities for U.S. government and often state and municipal deposits greater than the $100,000 ceiling on deposit insurance); and to greater liquidity needs. Depository institutions are also subject to interest-rate risk considerations. A depository, by its nature, often has a negative funding gap and must use its security portfolio to reduce that gap, since customer preferences may restrict an institution from shortening the duration on its loans, such as fixed-rate home mortgage loans. The investment portfolio may also used by depository institutions to reduce the institution's tax burden. As Hempel, Simonson, and Coleman state in their well-regarded text on bank management, bank managers have to establish general criteria and objectives for portfolios, including:[23]

- ◆ Providing liquidity, either through the maturing of securities or as stored liquidity
- ◆ Providing income, particularly countercyclical income to keep funds fully employed
- ◆ Satsifying pledging requirements
- ◆ Reducing taxes through tax swaps or holding municipal securities
- ◆ Using the portfolio to make adjustments for the bank's asset and liability position, including the bank's overall capital and interest rate risk.

Types of Securities That Depository Institutions Can Hold

Regulatory Restrictions   Although during the 1980s permissive states allowed thrifts and in some cases banks that were state-chartered to hold risky securities, under the Federal Deposit Insurance Corporation Improvement Act (FDICIA) of

---

[23]See George H. Hempel, Donald G. Simonson, and Alan B. Coleman. *Bank Management: Text and Cases*. 4th ed. New York: John Wiley & Sons, Inc. (1994).

1991, state-chartered banks and thrifts were placed under the same rules as nationally chartered banks.

Banks are not generally allowed to hold equity securities in their investment portfolio. Consequently, their investments are predominantly fixed-income securities of different types. Regulators classify securities into three groups. The first class, or Type 1 securities, are securities that carry very low or no default risk. These include U.S. Treasuries, federal agency, and general obligation municipals that are backed by the taxing power of the state or municipal government that issues the bonds. Type 2 securities includes quasi-public federal and municipal agency securities and selected state agencies associated with public projects, such as housing or universities, with the restriction that no more than 15 percent of a bank's capital plus surplus can be invested in any single issuer. Type 3 securities encompasses investment grade securities (BBB/Baa ratings or better), with no more than 10 percent of capital and surplus in any single issue invested in any single issue and any issues underwritten or dealt in by a bank disallowed. There are no specific restrictions on maturity, but as a rule of thumb, banks often do not like to hold securities greater than 10 years, since they often have long-term loans and long-term securities would increase their interest-rate risk.[24]

Liquidity Restrictions

Since the investment portfolio is held partially for liquidity reasons, the liquidity portion of the portfolio needs to be identified. Different investment strategies are used to provide for liquidity and investment returns, including a matching cash flow, ladder of maturities, and barbell strategy, which are discussed in the following sections.

Matching Cash Flows   One school of thought for protecting liquidity argues that a depository institution should carefully analyze its deposit structure and loan demand to forecast the timing and quantity of cash needs. Maturities of the investment portfolio should then be chosen to coincide with those forecasts. In other words, investments should mature, providing a cash inflow, at just the time an institution needs liquid funds. The relative proportion of primary, secondary, and tertiary sources of asset liquidity would be determined by cash-flow forecasts. A problem with this policy is that forecasts contain errors, so there could still be a liquidity crisis.

Ladder of Maturities   An alternative investment strategy is the **ladder of maturities**, which spreads the maturity of securities held for liquidity purposes evenly throughout a given period. For example, suppose that a savings bank decided the maximum maturity of its tertiary reserves should be five years. In the ladder-of-maturities strategy, an equal proportion of the portfolio would mature during each planning period. Cash received at maturity would be reinvested in assets with a five-year term to maturity. One way of conceptualizing the ladder of maturities is as a conveyor belt. Assets move along the belt for five years toward their maturity date; when they reach the end of the line (maturity), the funds are placed back at the beginning through reinvestment if they are not immediately needed for liquidity purposes.

---

[24]Ibid. See also Timothy W. Koch. *Bank Management*. 3rd ed. Fort Worth, Texas: Dryden Press/Harcourt Brace College Publishers (1995).

Perhaps the most serious criticism of the ladder portfolio is that it does not attempt to optimize investment returns for the institution. It is a relatively passive approach to investment management; no real effort is made to distinguish between secondary and tertiary reserves. Consequently, the institution may forgo investments that could increase returns without also incurring unacceptable liquidity risks. But for institutions without personnel to manage the securities portfolio, it may be a viable strategy.

Barbell Strategy   An alternative to the ladder-of-maturities strategy is to invest funds at either end of the yield curve but not in the middle, a strategy called the **barbell** or **split-maturity** portfolio. This approach retains some very liquid assets as secondary reserves but (assuming an upward-sloping yield curve) allows a larger investment in higher-return, long-term securities. To manage a barbell portfolio efficiently, however, the institution must devote resources to interest rate forecasting, because the anticipated direction of rate movements plays an important role in the proportionate investments at either end of the yield curve.

For example, under expectations of falling rates, the portfolio manager would want to increase the investment at the long-term end of the portfolio. The manager would be locking in current high rates, and the market value of the securities would benefit from the declining rates if long-term tertiary reserves had to be liquidated. With the opposite interest rate scenario, more funds would be invested in short-term assets. Consequently, knowledge of interest rate theories, the bond theorems, and duration would play an integral role in the management of liquidity reserves.

Buffer Portfolio

A fourth alternative is the **buffer portfolio strategy**, under which most of the investment in securities is concentrated in the short-term end of the maturity schedule, allowing the portfolio to serve as a buffer against even the slightest risk of cash shortages. With this approach, most secondary reserves and even some tertiary reserves would be invested in short-maturity assets. The average maturity under this strategy is considerably lower than under either the ladder-of-maturities or barbell strategies.

Choosing a Strategy

The ladder-of-maturity, barbell, and buffer portfolio strategies are illustrated side by side in Figure 19.2 for a hypothetical $100 million securities portfolio. The choice of a strategy depends on the institution's risk and expected return objectives. Risk arises from several sources. The risk of illiquidity is obviously the primary concern. But exposure to interest rate risk under a ladder-of-maturities or buffer portfolio is quite different from that of the barbell. A ladder-of-maturities or buffer portfolio, with a regular reinvestment schedule, poses extreme exposure to reinvestment risk but little or no risk from fluctuations in market value, because securities are held to maturity. In the barbell portfolio, the exposure to market-value risk could be severe, especially if the portfolio is heavily invested at the long end of the term structure. As interest rates change, returns could fluctuate significantly if it becomes necessary to liquidate securities. Yet if managers correctly anticipate interest rate movements, adjusting portfolio maturities in advance of rate changes can allow them to take advantage of favorable price changes. Such regular monitoring of the portfolio and interest

Figure 19.2 ✦ THE LADDER-OF-MATURITIES, BARBELL, AND BUFFER PORTFOLIO STRATEGIES

Depending on their risk/return objectives, depository institutions managers may choose either the ladder-of-maturities, barbell, or buffer portfolio strategies as part of liquidity management. The figure shows how a $100 million portfolio might be allocated across maturities under the three strategies.

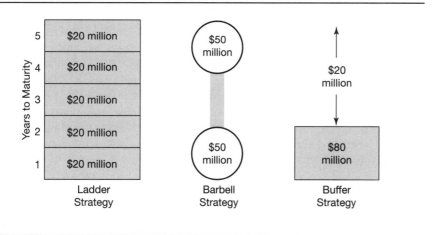

rate forecasts requires a larger commitment of resources. Smaller banks often receive investment advice from larger correspondent banks.[25]

Real World Considerations in Investment Strategies

For depository institutions face a number of real world considerations in their investment strategies that other financial institutions do not. Depository institutions are in the business of making loans, which generally offer higher returns than securities. Consequently, a bank's loan policies restrict its investment strategies.

Limitations on Investment Maturity Strategies for Banks   During expansions banks' security portfolios shrink and loan portfolios expand as investments are sold to meet expanding loan demand. Similarly, during recessions with lower loan demand, the investment portfolio expands as banks have more liquid funds available to invest in securities to attempt to generate countercyclical income. Typically, during the beginning of an expansion (ending of a recession) the yield curve is upward sloping, suggesting under the expectations theory that rates are expected to rise. Ideally, under a barbell-type maturity strategy, banks would hold a larger percentage of short-term securities that could be reinvested at higher rates when loan demand

---

[25]An early discussion of the split-maturity portfolio (but called spaced maturity) is included in Robinson (1962), 370–375. Another good source on alternatives for managing liquidity through the investment portfolio is Watson (1972). The descriptions of the ladder-of-maturities and barbell portfolios also draw on Watson. A recent discussion geared to thrift managers is Tom Parliment. "Barbell Strategy Helps to Manage the Yield Curve." *Savings Institutions* 113 (May, 1992), 38–39.

picks up and interest rates rise. However, bank investment managers during such a time period may be pressured to invest in longer-term securities that offer higher yields to make up for low profitability at the end of a recession.

Similarly, at the peak of an expansion (beginning of a recession) a downward yield curve often appears, indicating that investor expect rates to fall. Ideally, an investment manager following a barbell strategy would lock in high yield by purchasing long-term bonds. However, at this time the bank will be likely loaned up, with little cash available to purchase securities. Hence, maturity strategies may not be able to be optimally implemented for many banks.[26]

Limitations on Diversification of the Investment Portfolio for Banks Similarly, a bank investment manager may desire greater geographic diversification for the bank's portfolio, such as by purchasing municipal securities from different areas of the country. Real world considerations may, however, may limit this decision as well. For community relations reasons, a bank may feel obligated to support its municipality or community by purchasing local municipal bonds. Also, a bank investment manager may have better knowledge of the quality of bonds within its own area versus out-of-state munies.

Limitations on Tax Swap Strategies Strategies to reduce a bank's taxable income include tax swaps, whereby a bank sells a bond that has a loss and invests in another higher yielding bond. To see whether this would be a viable strategy, a bank manager would compare the present value of the higher coupon income with the new bond to the present value of the lower maturity value of the new bond, as the result of investing less money to invest in the new bond compared with the old bond's maturity value, as the result of the old bond's after-tax loss. Other considerations, such as a difference in maturity or credit risk for the new bond versus the old bond, would complicate this analysis.

In reality, a bank may be hesitant to take a loss and make a tax swap that would improve the bank's profitability in the future, because investors may misinterpret such a loss as a reflection of poor management. Similarly, the bank may not have a sufficient capital cushion to absorb the losses involved with a large tax swap.

Similarly, other considerations might affect a bank's strategy to reduce taxable income by investing in municipal securities, the income for which is not taxed at the federal level. Additionally, some states do not tax the income generated by state-issued municipal securities in the issuing state. Some of these considerations include a stipulation in the Tax Reform Act of 1986 that does not allow banks to deduct the interest cost of funds raised to purchase munies. Interest rate and default risk also must be considered. Most municipals are long-term and expose an institution to considerable interest-rate risk. Furthermore, there is the risk of a bond rating downgrade by rating agencies that would reduce the market value of munies. For instance, Moody's bond rating service reduced the credit ratings of more issues between 1978 and 1983 than it increased, and fear of greater default risk on municipals has discouraged investment at times.[27]

---

[26]See note 24.

[27]These trends are discussed in Rodrigues (1993). See also Steven Lipin. "Are Banks Playing a Dangerous Game?" *The Wall Street Journal* (June 30, 1992), C1, C9, and Fred R. Bleakley. "Banks Turn to Government Securities in Basic Reassessment of Profitability." *The Wall Street Journal* (October 1, 1991), A2.

Investment Accounting Rule Restrictions

Investment accounting rules require banks to clearly distinguish between "investment" securities, presumably to be held until maturity, and "securities available for sale" that are held to earn potential profits if their prices increase. Investment securities can be shown on the balance sheet at historical cost, but securities held for sale are supposed to be shown at the lower of cost or market value. This classification somewhat reduces managers' ability to respond intelligently and prudently to changing market conditions in terms of tax or other types of swaps for securities that are classified as "held to maturity."[28]

The requirements of liquidity, regulations, and real world considerations make depository institution investment management a challenge. However, the development of new types of securities, such as mortgage-backed securities (MBSs) and collateralized mortgage obligations (CMOs), among others, allow depository institutions a wide choice of securities. The following section provides a brief description of the average commercial bank's investment portfolio as of the end of 1996.

THE TYPICAL BANK INVESTMENT PORTFOLIO

Table 19.4 shows the different types of securities held by the average commercial bank at the end of 1996. By far the largest investment held (55.17 percent for all banks) were U.S. agency securities, most of which (see "Memoranda" in Table 19.4) were MBSs. The next largest investment was U.S. Treasury securities (21.11 percent), followed by municipal securities (9.35 percent), domestic debt securities (6.27 percent), and foreign debt securities (5.37 percent). The remaining 3 percent of assets were in equity securities, predominantly for very large banks of $1 billion or more. This reflects special cases as normally commercial banks are not allowed to hold equity investments.

The largest banks ($1 billion or more) have a larger percentage of their portfolio as securities available for sale. The largest banks also hold fewer municipals and Treasuries and a larger percentage (totaling about 16 percent) of other domestic and foreign debt securities. They appear to receive more government deposits with a larger percentage of pledged securities and to hold a much larger percentage of MBSs (50.56 percent), compared with 28 percent for the medium-sized banks ($100 million to $1 billion). This difference reflects a willingness to take on riskier types of securities that require more sophisticated investment management strategies. The largest banks also have more assets in trading accounts.

The lower portion of the table shows the percentage of securities by different maturity classes. On average, commercial banks hold about 28 percent of their portfolio in securities of one year or less, with about 40 percent invested in maturities over five years, and 32.67 percent between one to five years. The largest banks, on average, hold a larger percentage of securities in the over five-year range than the medium-sized banks do.

---

[28]Tom Parliment. "Overall, TB 52 Is a Welcome Tool for Portfolio Managers." *Savings Institutions* 113 (April, 1992), 38–39; Lee Berton. "SEC Pushes Market-Value Accounting on Banks Reaping Big Investment Gains." *The Wall Street Journal* (April 29, 1992), A2, A3; Martha Brannigan. "NationsBank Is Reclassifying Part of Portfolio." *The Wall Street Journal* (June 9, 1992), A2; Lee Berton. "Accounting Body Backs Modified Rules on the Valuation of Securities by Banks." *The Wall Street Journal* (July 16, 1992), A2, A6; David Siegel. "FASB Votes to Adopt Mark-to-Market Rule." *American Banker* (April 14, 1993), 1, 20.

Table 19.4   ✦   SECURITIES OF FDIC-INSURED COMMERCIAL BANKS (IN MILS. $s)

	Total Commercial Banks	% Total	$1 Billion or More	% Total	$100 Mil. to $1 Bil.	% Total
Total Securities	$800,827	100%	$525,878	100%	$191,858	100%
Securities Held to Maturity	174,227	21.76%	89,693	17.06%	58,215	30.34%
Securities Available for Sale	626,600	78.24%	436,186	82.94%	133,643	69.66%
(held to maturity at amortized cost; available for sale at fair value)						
By Security Type						
U.S. Treasury Securities	169,027	21.11%	100,296	19.07%	47,069	24.53%
U.S. Agency Securities	441,856	55.17%	291,587	55.45%	105,323	54.90%
Municipal Securities	74,897	9.35%	33,082	6.29%	28,419	14.81%
Other Domestic Debt Securities	50,213	6.27%	42,063	8.00%	6,266	3.27%
Foreign Debt Securities	42,981	5.37%	42,526	8.09%	453	0.24%
Equity Securities						
Investments in Mutual Funds	2,655	0.33%	1,353	0.26%	984	0.51%
Other Marketable Equity Securities	5,175	0.65%	4,394	0.84%	692	0.36%
Other Equity Securities	14,025	1.75%	10,579	2.01%	2,650	1.38%
Memoranda:						
Pledged Securities	355,981	44.45%	259,150	49.28%	71,600	37.32%
Mortgage-Backed Securities	336,045	41.96%	265,878	50.56%	53,719	28.00%
Certificates of Participation						
in Pools of Residential Mortgages						
Issued or Guaranteed by U.S.	221,347	27.64%	177,789	33.81%	33,421	17.42%
Privately Issued	2,642	0.33%	2,419	0.46%	171	0.09%
Collateralized Mortgage Obligations						
Issued by FNMA or FHLMC (includes REMICs)	89,954	11.23%	65,584	12.47%	18,473	9.63%
Privately Issued	22,102	2.76%	20,086	3.82%	1,654	0.86%
Maturity and repricing data for selected debt securities:						
Total	777,942	100%	508,529	100.00%	187,526	100.00%
With remaining maturity or repricing interval of:						
3 months or less	109,327	14.05%	74,767	14.70%	24,558	13.10%
Over 3 months through 12 months	107,583	13.83%	65,331	12.85%	28,730	15.32%
Over 1 year through 5 years	254,136	32.67%	138,773	27.29%	77,035	41.08%
Over 5 years	306,896	39.45%	229,657	45.16%	57,203	30.50%
Assets held in trading accounts	240,978		240,612		295	

Source: FDIC Statistics on Banking for 1996, published April 1997

The Typical Thrift Investment Portfolio

Table 19.5 shows a similar table for the security portfolio of savings institutions (savings and loans and mutual savings banks). Like commercial banks, savings institutions hold the majority of their assets in agency securities that are dominantly MBSs. In fact, for all savings institutions, 73.59 percent of assets are held in MBSs, consisting of 45.16 percent in certificates of participation in pools of residential mortgages

Table 19.5   ✦   SECURITIES OF FDIC-INSURED SAVING INSTITUTIONS (SAVINGS & LOANS AND SAVINGS BANKS)

	Total Savings Institutions	% Total	$1 Billion or More	% Total	$100 Mil. to $1 Bil.	% Total
Total Securities	**$262,383**	**100%**	**$186,478**	**100%**	**$66,983**	**100%**
By Security Type						
U.S. Treasury Securities	10,230	3.90%	5,773	3.10%	4,075	6.08%
U.S. Agency Securities	202,606	77.22%	141,382	75.82%	53,934	80.52%
Municipal Securities	2,068	0.79%	920	0.49%	949	1.42%
Other Domestic Debt Securities	39,352	15.00%	34,311	18.40%	4,664	6.96%
Foreign Debt Securities	59	0.02%	22	0.01%	37	0.06%
Equity Securities	8,657	3.30%	4,070	2.18%	3,915	5.84%
Memoranda:						
Pledged Securities	12,875	4.91%	10,846	5.82%	1,915	2.86%
Mortgage-Backed Securities	193,079	73.59%	152,094	81.57%	36,785	54.92%
Certificates of Participation in Pools of Residential Mortgages						
Issued or Guaranteed by U.S.	118,485	45.16%	87,965	47.17%	27,059	40.40%
Privately Issued	21,002	8.00%	20,209	10.84%	757	1.13%
Collateralized Mortgage Obligations	53,592	20.43%	43,920	23.55%	8,970	13.39%
Assets Held in Trading Accounts	55	0.02%	24	0.01%	23	0.03%

Note: Total %'s may have rounding errors.

Source: FDIC Statistics on Banking for 1996, published April 1997

issued or guaranteed by the U.S. and 8 percent in privately issued certificates of participation. Thrifts held 20.43 percent of assets in CMOs (these are discussed in the following section). The largest thrifts (those with assets greater than $1 billion) held 81.57 percent MBSs compared with 54.92 percent for medium-sized thrifts. Larger thrifts held more domestic debt securities as well (18.4 percent versus 6.96 percent). U.S. Treasuries and municipals are a very small part of the average thrift's investment portfolio.

Under the FDICIA, thrift can have no more than 35 percent of their assets invested in bonds, commercial paper, and consumer loans. Also, the average maturity of the bond portfolio is limited.

As discussed in Chapter 7, the "qualified thrift lender" (QTL) provision of the IRS tax code allowed QTLs that invest 65 percent of assets in home mortgages or housing-related securities a larger tax deduction for additions to bad-debt reserves than banks could have. However, as noted in Chapter 7, this provision is being phased out. QTL thrifts also have special borrowing privileges at the FHLB, one reason for a larger percentage of MBSs.

Credit Union Investment Portfolios

Federal CUs can invest in Treasury and agency securities, insured accounts at other depositories, and Eurodollar deposits and bankers acceptances without restriction. They can also invest in municipal securities, up to 10 percent of capital plus surplus. Beyond this, federal CUs may invest only in securities of organizations providing services associated with the routine operations of CUs, up to 1 percent of capital plus surplus. In 1991, further restrictions were placed on CUs when they were prohibited from holding several types of complex MBSs. Hence, CUs hold the majority of their investments, beyond cash and deposits and Fed Funds and Repos (representing 58 percent of their cash and securities portfolio) in Treasury Issues (17.9 percent), and Federal Agency Issues (23.3 percent).[29]

Since agency securities and in particular mortgage-backed agency securities are the predominant investment for depository institutions in the 1990s, they are discussed in greater detail in the following section, including peculiar characteristics that financial institution managers should be aware of.

Agency Securities and Mortgage-Backed Securities

As shown in Tables 19.4 and 19.5, the largest holdings by banks and thrifts were predominantly mortgage-backed agency securities. There are a number of different federal agencies to achieve different purposes. These agencies are backed by the U.S. government with the primary purpose of reducing the cost and increasing the accessibility of funds to particular sectors. They are funded by the Treasury and can borrow from the Federal Financing Bank, a subdivision of the Treasury. Many of these federal agencies were later privatized and became quasi-public agencies or so-called government-sponsored agencies. Although government-sponsored agencies are owned by private investors, most investors implicitly assume that these agencies will be bailed out by the U.S. government if they get into trouble. Consequently, they generally have a lower cost of funds than other private firms. The Government National Mortgage Association (GNMA, or Ginnie Mae), is a federal government agency owned by the U.S. government, as are the Federal Housing Administration (FHA), and the Export-Import Bank. The Federal National Mortgage Association (FNMA, or Fannie Mae), and the Federal Home Loan Mortgage Corporation (FHLMC, or Freddie Mac) are privately owned, government-sponsored agencies.

GNMA, FNMA, and the FHLMC are active in the mortgage security market. GNMA does not create mortgage securities, but since 1968 it has sponsored MBS programs instituted by banks, thrifts, and mortgage banks and provides guarantees to investors for the timely pass-through of interest and principal payments for these securities. GNMA, however, only backs mortgage loans that have their credit risk insured by any one of three government agencies, the Federal Housing Administration (FHA), the Veteran's Administration (VA), or the Farmer's Home Administration (FMHA), which target low income borrowers and veterans. Caps for the maximum mortgage amount are included for loans to be included in GNMA securitizations, although these caps are frequently raised to adjust for higher home prices.[30]

---

[29]See the Federal Credit Union Act (1983), 5–6; and National Credit Union Administration *Annual Reports* (1984 and 1991). These averages are based on 1992, but have been similar in recent years.

[30]See Note 24. See also Anthony Saunders. *Financial Institutions Management: A Modern Perspective.* 2nd ed. Chicago: Irwin (1997); Frank J. Fabozzi. *Bond Markets, Analysis and Strategies.* 2nd ed. Englewood Cliffs, New Jersey: Prentice Hall (1993); Clifford E. Kirsch, ed. *The Financial Services Revolution.* Chicago: Irwin Professional Publishing (1997); and David S. Kidwell, Richard L. Peterson, and David W. Blackwell. *Financial Institutions, Markets, and Money.* 6th ed. Fort Worth, Texas: Dryden Press (1997).

The FNMA, created in 1938, is now a stock-owned, publicly traded firm. In contrast to GNMA, FNMA creates pass-through securities itself by purchasing conventional mortgages, as well as FHA/VA loans from banks and thrifts. Conventional loans must have 80 percent collateralization ratios (i.e., 20 percent down payments for new loans). Otherwise, they must have private credit insurance. Such purchases are financed by selling MBSs created from these mortgages to investors, including large institutional investors such as insurers, pension funds, banks, thrifts, CUs, and mutual funds that desire MBSs. Like GNMA, FNMA provides guarantees for the timely payment of interest and principal on these bonds. With these guarantees, these securities are very marketable in the capital markets. Although FHLMC, originally owned by the Federal Home Loan Mortgage Corporation, is now a publicly traded quasi-government agency, Congress stills selects a portion of FHLMC's Board of Directors. FHLMC, like FNMA, purchases conventional and insured mortgages from financial institutions and creates MBSs. Both the FHLMC and FNMA also swap MBSs for mortgage loans with financial institutions as well. This enables institutions to have greater liquidity and geographic diversification in their asset portfolios.

Mortgage-Backed Security Securitization Process   Similar to the mechanics of the loan securitization process that is described in Figure 9.3 of Chapter 9, Figure 19.3 illustrates the process for the creation of mortgage securities. GNMA, FNMA, and FHLMC provide guarantees, in place of a private credit enhancer, shown in a credit card receivables or automobile loan securitization. A custodian is designated to maintain mortgage documentation, and a mortgage servicer (which could be the selling bank in a GNMA securitization, for instance, or another financial institution) receives payments of principal and interest from borrowers. After deducting a

Figure 19.3   ✦   STRUCTURE OF SECURITIZING MORTGAGE LOANS

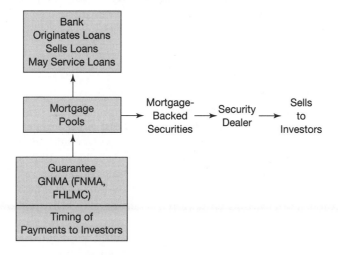

Note: The mortgage servicer (which could be the selling institution or another institution) receives payments of principal and interest from the borrowers for the sold loans and pays principal and interest (less servicing fees received) to the investors who own the mortgage-backed securities.

servicing fee, the mortgage services passes on these payments to the investors owning the MBSs.

Different Types of Mortgage-Backed Securities   MBSs include **mortgage-backed bonds**, **certificates of participation in pools of residential mortgages** (either issued or guaranteed by the U.S. government or privately issued), and **CMOs**. Mortgage-backed bonds are simply bonds collateralized by mortgages on a financial institution's balance sheet, and thus are not securitizations. Banks, for instance, can offer bonds with a lower coupon rate because they are collateralized by specific mortgage assets on the bank's balance sheet. This arrangement provides investors with a primary claim on these assets if the institution goes under.

Mortgage pass-through securities or certificates of participation in pools of residential mortgages, in contrast, are securitizations (as described in the following section) whereby shares in the interest and principal payment on a pool of mortgages are passed on to investors who purchase these securities.

CMOs, like stripped securities, are securities created from mortgage pass-through securities designed to have more favorable characteristics than the pass-throughs, or they can simply be pass-throughs originally packaged into several classes (tranches) of securities with different characteristics for each tranche appealing to different types of investors. The FHLMC introduced CMOs in 1983. Under the Tax Reform Act of 1986, the IRS removed regulations that previously imposed irksome costs on the issuers and investors in CMOs, resulting in rapid growth for CMOs. An issuer of CMOs takes a pool of mortgages and converts them into different maturities by allowing the first or A-class or tranche of bonds to be repaid their principal payments first when mortgage-holders prepay their mortgages in a pool of mortgages. B-class investors would be paid off next, then C-class, and so on. Consequently, A-class investors have mortgage securities with the lowest expected maturity, B-class the next, and later classes, the highest maturities. In this way, investors have less prepayment uncertainty than they would with an ordinary pass-through security. Also, investors have a better estimate in terms of the likely maturity and yield that should be offered on a particular type of CMO relative to a similar maturity Treasury security that has no prepayment risk.

Different Types of CMOs

A plain vanilla CMO may have four tranches, A, B, C, and Z, with A receiving prepayments first and having the shortest maturity, then B and C. Class Z, in contrast to A, B, and C, which receive interest payments, receives no periodic interest until the other three tranches are retired. At that time, the cash flow payments from the remaining underlying collateral (remaining mortgage pool) are utilized to pay principal plus accrued interest to investors with Z-bonds (often called accrual bonds). Hence, Z-bonds are like zero-coupon bonds that receive principal and interest, but at some unknown approximate maturity date. Z-tranches have the most interest-rate risk.

A **planned amortization class** (PAC) bond is a CMO that has lower risk by having a fixed amortization schedule, so investors can better predict when a particular tranche of bonds will mature. If actual prepayment rates differ from that the expected prepayment rates, principal payments to designated tranches are reduced or increased to ensure that PAC CMOs mature as scheduled.

Stripped mortgage-backed securities separate securities into classes of interest only (IO) paying securities and principal only (PO) paying securities. With prepayment risk, POs and IOs are very interest-rate sensitive. If interest rates decline significantly, IOs decline in value, since the maturity of the security is shortened with prepayments, indicating fewer interest payments for the investor. In turn, if rates rise significantly, then prepayment risk will decrease significantly, and the value of the IO will rise because the expected maturity rises. When interest rates fall significantly, the market value for POs rises since the principal payments are discounted at a lower rate and are expected to come in sooner. When interest rates rise significantly, PO market value falls since the principal payments are discounted at a higher rate and are expected to come in later. Thus, IOs and POs are very risky, and regulators have discouraged their use.[31]

The Prepayment Risk and Pricing of Mortgage-Backed Securities

As mentioned above in connection with CMOs, MBSs have considerable prepayment risk, particularly during periods of falling rates. When interest rates fall approximately 2 percent below the average mortgage-rate on a pool of securities, prepayments rise for that pool as mortgage borrowers rush to refinance their loans at lower rates. Consequently, holders of pass-through mortgage securities receive a return of principal at a time when interest rates are low, and they must reinvest this return of principal at a lower rate. In this sense, a pass-through mortgage security is like a callable bond. Because of their prepayment risk, pass-through MBSs often demonstrate negative convexity, with smaller capital gains than other conventional bonds when interest rates fall, but smaller capital losses than other conventional bonds when interest rates fall. This is because although the present value of cash flows rises for MBSs when interest rates fall, their prepayment risk rises, shortening their expected duration. Similarly, when interest rates rise, the present value of cash flows fall, but the lower prepayment risk lengthens their expected duration.

Pricing Prepayment Risk   Investors in pass-through securities demand a higher coupon rate for their prepayment risk. Different factors affect how much prepayment risk a pass-through mortgage security has, including the coupon rate relative to current mortgage coupon rates, the age of the mortgage pool, the region where mortgages are originated, whether a mortgage is assumable, and the demographic characteristics of the borrowers in the pool of mortgages, among many other factors. Several models have been developed to estimate the prepayment risk of specific mortgage security pools, including the Public Securities Association model, which estimates the average prepayment risk of a pool based on the experience of previous FHA-insured mortgage pools. Accordingly, mortgage securities are priced relative to similar Treasury securities based on their prepayment risk.[32]

INVESTMENTS IN MUTUAL FUNDS

Table 19.4 shows a small amount of investment in mutual funds by commercial banks. Regulators have permitted banks to own mutual funds for securities that they are allowed to hold, including U.S. government and agency bonds, investment grade

---

[31]See sources cited in Note 30. For a detailed discussion of other types of CMOs, see Fabozzi
(1993), as cited in Note 30.
[32]See sources in Note 30.

bonds, and MBSs. Banks are limited to holding mutual fund assets of up to 10 percent of a bank's capital and surplus. Shares must be marked to market, which has discouraged banks from investing in mutual funds despite the diversification benefits that they could reap.[33]

DECLINE IN INVESTMENTS IN GOVERNMENT SECURITIES

As shown in Tables 19.4 and 19.5, banks and thrifts hold a very small percentage of municipal securities today, since they no longer can deduct their interest expense for funds borrowed to purchase municipals, making municipals an unattractive investment. Other real world considerations that have made municipals less attractive were discussed in an earlier section. U.S. Treasuries are invested in, predominantly for liquidity purposes, although as default-free securities they offer lower yields than other securities. With competition, higher liability costs, and, hence, narrower NIMs, banks have moved away from Treasury securities, which previously dominated their investment portfolios, into other types of securities, such as MBSs, which offer higher yields.

Other Changes in Bank Investment Portfolio Management

Larger banks have become much more sophisticated in their asset management, including derivatives among their investments, with swaps to protect against changes in interest rates and the yield curve to lock in spreads between asset returns and liability costs. They have also responded to the need for improved portfolio diversification, realizing that improved diversification can lower their requirements for economic capital by up to 25 percent. With increasing liquidity for banks as the result of loan sales and securitization, large banks have expanded investments in high quality, large corporate debt. As pointed out in a recent article in *Banking Strategies*, "the takeoff of credit derivatives is creating new possibilities for risk transformation through innovative structures such as credit-linked notes, default swaps and collateralized loan obligations. One recent example of the later is J. P. Morgan's 'Bistro' deal, in which the bank essentially paid investors to assume the default risk on a $9.7 billion pool of large corporate credits."[34]

The article also points out that an important consequence of the rise in market liquidity for banks is a "convergence of traditional fixed income and corporate lending activities," whereby banks are coming to view loans and bonds as complementary products in the same asset class, and credit, bond, and derivative exposures to the same borrowers can be managed as a single portfolio. Derivatives, in turn, are being used as means for transforming credit risk, and larger banks have switched to active portfolio management models to adjust their interest rate and credit risks across their entire asset portfolio of loans and securities.[35]

---

[33]See Andrew Kuritzkes. "Transforming Portfolio Management." *Banking Strategies* (July/August, 1998), 57–60.

[34]Andrew Kuritzkes. "Portfolio Management Strategies." *Bank Management* 70 (1994), 56–60.

[35]With recent laws on derivatives, large banks and investment banks have made concerted efforts to develop risk management strategies for their investment portfolios, including derivatives.

SUMMARY

Liquidity, or the ability to obtain cash with little risk of financial loss, is one of the most important concerns of depository institutions. Sufficient liquidity is necessary for two reasons: to meet regulatory requirements, and to ensure uninterrupted operations in the face of unexpected loan demand or deposit withdrawals. With the growth of asset sales and loan securitization, many large banks have, however, been faced with excess liquidity. Liquidity can be managed by having stored liquidity in terms of holding short-term securities on a bank's balance sheet or through liability management, whereby depository institutions have many short-term borrowing sources to meet liquidity needs. Most banks use a combination of the two techniques.

The Federal Reserve Board influences institutional liquidity through reserve requirements on transactions accounts and time deposits. Because deposit levels fluctuate constantly, estimating liquidity needs is a challenge for management. Contemporaneous reserve accounting for transaction deposits accelerates the need for forecasting tools in depository institution management. Besides meeting Federal Reserve specifications, some depositories must comply with liquidity requirements set by states or other federal regulators.

Depositories also require liquidity to meet unexpected loan demand or deposit withdrawals. To avoid selling assets at a loss when these needs arise, management should maintain liquid assets in excess of those required by regulators. Because liquid assets are often low yielding, however, liquidity needs must be balanced against profitability. Other financial institutions have also demonstrated the need to have sufficient liquidity in the event of unusual events including life insurers, property-casualty insurers, and mutual funds.

Unlike other financial institutions that can manage their investment portfolios to maximize returns based on a desired risk level, depository institutions must insure that liquidity needs are met, provide countercyclical income when loan demand is down, satisfy pledging requirements for large government deposits, and use the investment portfolio to make adjustments for the bank's asset and liability position, including the bank's overall capital and interest rate risk. Depository institutions are also generally limited by regulations to hold debt securities that are investment grade or better. Consequently, depository institutions often rely on maturity strategies, such as barbell or ladder strategies, to ensure liquidity as well as to maximize returns if possible. With the invest-

ment portfolio as a complement to a depository institution's loan portfolio, depository institutions are also subject to a number of real world limitations on their investment strategies.

In recent years, to improve returns, depository institutions have moved away from holding predominantly Treasury and municipal securities to holding MBSs, and for very large banks, to corporate debt securities as well. This movement necessitates a greater degree of sophistication from institution investment managers in terms of understanding the special risks entailed in MBSs, including considerable prepayment risk. Larger banks have also come to use derivatives more in their overall investment strategies, a practice that also necessitates greater sophistication by investment managers.

Suggested Cases

"Case 3: CARs (Certificates for Automobile Receivables)." Darden School, University of Virginia: Richard D. Crawford and William W. Sihler. *Financial Service Organizations: Cases in Strategic Management*. New York: HarperCollins College Publishers (1994). This case provides an overview of the history of loan securitization and an introduction to the characteristics and structure of asset-backed securities, focusing on CARs.

"Case 2: Quigley Bank Corporation" Darden School, University of Virginia: Richard D. Crawford and William W. Sihler. *Financial Service Organizations: Cases in Strategic Management*. New York: HarperCollins College Publishers (1994). This case, in addition to providing a format for financial analysis for a bank, also focuses on the investment management of a bank's portfolio and its interest-rate risk, including difficulties trying to forecast interest rates.

Questions

1. Providing liquidity is one of the functions of a financial intermediary. How does the intermediation role of depository institutions affect their liquidity needs?

2. Explain the historical rationale for the reserve requirements first imposed on national banks in the 1860s and continued after the creation of the Federal Reserve. Since that time, how has the Fed's monetary policy role affected the breadth and management of reserve requirements for all depository institutions? Why do other countries that do not have a strong money market have high reserve requirements for banks?

3. Explain the most important differences between CRA and LRA. How do CRA provisions affect liquidity management in depository institutions? How does the carryover privilege assist in reserve management? What policy objectives provided the motivation for implementing CRA?

5. A key problem for depository managers is accurately estimating their liquidity needs for operations. How is this effort affected by the relative proportion of volatile and nonvolatile funds? By changes in economic conditions and return to depositors on alternative investments?

6. Depository institution managers may rely on both sides of the balance sheet to ensure adequate liquidity. Compare and contrast the potential effects on risk and return that result from asset sources of liquidity as compared with that from liability sources. How does an institution's size and financial soundness affect its liquidity management options?

7. Explain the functions of the Federal Reserve discount window. Contrast the Regulation A provisions governing use of the window to FHLB advances and to sources of CU liquidity.

8. Evaluate the differences in interest rate risk exposure from the ladder-of-maturities, the buffer, and the barbell portfolio investment strategies. Compare the relative rates of return that managers might expect from the three strategies under upward-sloping, flat, and downward-sloping yield curves.

9. Why can't bank managers simply manage a bank's investment portfolio from a risk/return respective? What are some other objectives for a bank's investment portfolio? What are some real world considerations that prevent bank managers from focusing only on risk and return in their investment strategies?

10. What restrictions to regulators impose on banks in terms of the types of securities that they can hold? What special restrictions do thrifts and CUs have?

11. Looking at Tables 19.4 and 19.5, what are the most important distinctions between bank and thrift portfolios? Explain how differences in regulations, tax policies, and financial objectives have influenced asset holdings in banks and thrifts.

12. Do you consider the restrictions on bank and thrift investment in equity securities and junk bonds justified? What rationale would you offer for retaining or revising these regulations?

13. Explain the rationale for requiring firms—including depository institutions—to report the market value of financial assets on the balance sheet. Describe the different accounting procedures allowed by the Financial Accounting Standard Board for securities held for sale and for investment. What might be the potential effect on bank portfolio management?

14. What are GNMA, FNMA, and FHLMC? How do these agencies help increase the amount of mortgage credit available in the U.S.? What characteristics must mortgage loans have to be securitized? Why do depository institutions hold such a large percentage of MBSs?

15. Explain what a mortgage security is and what a CMO is and how they are created and priced. What is a PAC, an IO, and a PO? How does prepayment risk affect the value of MBSs when rates rise? when rates fall?

16. Why have very large banks in the later 1990s had so much excess liquidity to invest? How have these large banks transformed their approach to portfolio management? Do you think this is a good idea? Explain why.

Problems

1. J. C. Bosch, CEO, just placed you in charge of managing the Rockies Riviera Banks reserve position. It is now the morning of day 29 of the maintenance period. Your immediate responsibility is to set reserve deposit levels for days 29 and 30. You have been given the following information:

Days 15–28 Average vault cash	$4 million
Days 1–14 Average nontransaction liabilities	$220 million
Days 15–18 Average Transactions Balances	$625 million
Days 17–28 Average Reserve Balances	$61 million

   a. Using the current reserve requirements in Table 19.1, compute the average reserve balances required for the maintenance period (days 17–30).
   b. Compute the average balances required for the last two days if the carryover privilege is **not** used.
   c. Compute the average balance needed for the final two days of the maintenance period, assuming the bank uses its carryover privilege.

2. Using the data from Problem 1, suppose that in the next reserve maintenance period, average transactions balances during days 15–28 fall to $475 million and average reserve balances during days 17–28 fall to $66 million. Other balances remain the same. Compute the average reserve balances needed for the maintenance period and the total needed for the last two days. What alternatives are available to the bank in this situation?

3. One of your major responsibilities at the Ski Fine Bank is calculating Fed reserve requirements. Your supervisor Jim Morris has provided the following data for your bank and for another subsidiary of the holding company. Calculate the average daily reserve target balance and the minimum reserve balances required for the final two days of the maintenance period using the information in Figure P19.1.

Figure P19.1 ✦ Algonquin National: Forecast for Average Reserves on Transactions Deposits—$97,000,000

Day #	Day	Nontransactions Liabilities (in millions)
1	T	$440
2	W	460
3	Th	460
4	F	435
5	Sat	450
6	S	445
7	M	445
8	T	445
9	W	480
10	Th	475
11	F	490
12	Sat	490
13	S	450
14	M	440

CONTEMPORANEOUS COMPUTATION PERIOD				MAINTENANCE PERIOD		
Day #	Day	Vault Cash (in millions)	Transactions Deposits (in millions)	Day #	Day	Reserve Balances (in millions)
15	T	$7.5	$860			
16	W	7.4	864			
17	Th	7.6	875	17	Th	$90
18	F	7.6	880	18	F	84
19	Sat	7.7	880	19	Sat	82
20	S	7.7	880	20	S	82
21	M	7.2	850	21	M	88
22	T	7.4	850	22	T	90
23	W	7.3	862	23	W	92
24	Th	7.6	865	24	Th	88
25	F	7.2	920	25	F	85
26	Sat	7.1	940	26	Sat	84
27	S	7.1	940	27	S	84
28	M	7.7	980	28	M	88
				29	T	
				30	W	

4. Extra practice: do the same calculations for Bayou National Bank in Figure P19.2.
5. a. Western Slope Bank must estimate its liquidity needs over the next two months. Using the following information given for that period, estimate the bank's liquidity surplus or deficit:

Assets	Millions	Liquid
Cash	$266.25	12%
Commercial loans	1,002.27	0%
Consumer loans	539.68	0%

Figure P19.2 ✦ Bayou National: Forecast for Average Reserves on Transactions Deposits—$39,450,000

Day #	Day	Nontransactions Liabilities (in millions)
1	T	$150
2	W	140
3	Th	135
4	F	160
5	Sat	155
6	S	155
7	M	130
8	T	135
9	W	150
10	Th	145
11	F	160
12	Sat	135
13	S	135
14	M	140

CONTEMPORANEOUS COMPUTATION PERIOD				MAINTENANCE PERIOD		
Day #	Day	Vault Cash (in millions)	Transactions Deposits (in millions)	Day #	Day	Reserve Balances (in millions)
15	T	$2.10	$350			
16	W	2.00	355			
17	Th	2.40	370	17	Th	$43
18	F	2.30	364	18	F	38
19	Sat	2.50	340	19	Sat	40
20	S	2.50	340	20	S	40
21	M	2.60	370	21	M	48
22	T	2.80	380	22	T	45
23	W	2.30	320	23	W	43
24	Th	2.30	322	24	Th	39
25	F	2.60	335	25	F	39
26	Sat	2.75	345	26	Sat	43
27	S	2.10	345	27	S	43
28	M	2.10	390	28	M	48
				29	T	
				30	W	

Investments	1,317.45	45%
Other Assets	217.15	17%
Total	$3,342.80	
Sources of Funds	**Millions**	**Volatile**
Deposits	$2,228.38	10%
Other Liabilities	885.79	75%
Equity	258.63	0%
Total	$3,342.80	

b. Assume instead that 65 percent of investments are liquid and that 65 percent of nondeposit liabilities are volatile. Recalculate the liquidity surplus or deficit. Compare the advantages and disadvantages of this situation to that in part a.

c. Assume that Western Slope Bank wants to be prepared for an increase in commercial loan demand of 1 percent and an increase in consumer loan demand of 2 percent during the next two months. Using the data in part a, recalculate the bank's liquidity surplus or deficit under these assumptions.

6. Glen Wolfe, a famous bank portfolio manager holds a 12-year, 10 percent coupon T-bond with a par value, the bond's original price of $1,000, a current price of $990, and a pretax yields to maturity (YTM) of 10.15 percent. The bank has a marginal tax rate of 30 percent. A municipal bond in the bank's state has a coupon rate of 10.15 percent and sells for $1,000 with a pretax YTM of 10.15 percent (note that its tax equivalent coupon rate since coupon payments are not taxed is the coupon rate / $[1 - t]$ or 10.15 percent / $[1 - 0.30]$ = 14.5 percent).

a. Calculate the tax savings if the T-bond is sold (the current price − the original price) (t), i.e., the tax deduction for the loss on the bond. Add this to the $990, which will equal the total amount the bank manager will have to invest if the bond is sold.

b. Calculate the present value of the change in coupon payments for the 12 years if the T-bond is sold and the municipal bond is purchased. Assume a discount rate of 10.15 percent $(1 - t)$ = 10.15 percent $(1 - 0.3)$ = 7 percent.

c. Calculate the present value of the change in the principal payment at year 12 if the T-bond is sold, where the difference in principal payment will be the $1,000 that would have been received less the new principal payment, which will be the amount available to invest in the new bond calculated in a.

d. Add the present value of the change in coupon payments to the present value of the change in principal payments to get the net present value for the swap decision. If it is positive the swap will be value-enhancing. If it is negative, the swap will value-reducing.

e. Based on your answer in d, should the tax swap be made? What other considerations should be taken into consideration in determining whether to undertake this tax swap?

7. **Minicase:** The Sunny Side Bank, a small bank operating in Boca Raton, Florida, is having an investment committee meeting on Thursday, January 14, 1999, to see how it should adjust its investment portfolio. Attending the meeting are Charles A. Register, the senior vice president in charge of investments, Patty Moran, a member of an investment firm in Miami that handles many of the bank's investment orders, and Sinan Cebenoyan and Fatma Cebenoyan, the vice-president and investment manager, respectively, of the Alligator Bank of Miami. The Alligator Bank, a family-owned, but prominent regional bank in Miami, is Sunny Side's primary correspondent.

Before the meeting Charles Register glances at the Thursday morning *Wall Street Journal* to read the report on credit markets for the previous. Figure P3 summarizes the current yield curve on the page from the preceding day and the movement of interest rates that Register observes. On the preceding day markets had been volatile in the wake of Brazil's devaluation of its currency. Consequently, many international investors shifted into Treasuries on that date to seek safety amid sizable losses in global stock markets and emerging bond markets. This resulted in a rise in Treasury security prices (fall in rates). For instance, the price for the bellwether 30-year T-bond rose $1\frac{6}{32}$ or $11.875 for a bond with a $1,000 face value, selling at $101\frac{24}{32}$, a fall in the yield to 5.126 percent. Two-year T-note prices rose even more, by $\frac{7}{32}$, to a yield of 4.54 percent. Such a short-term flight to quality was short-lived, with traders selling bonds when they reached market highs. However, speculation that the Brazilian situation might fuel rate cuts by the Federal Reserve resulting in a buying trend in Treasuries, but a rebound in the stock market during the day quelled buying by reducing hopes of a rate cut at the Federal Open Market Committee's next meeting. Despite the market turmoil, Freddie Mac, with Goldman Sacs and J.P. Morgan and Salomon Smith Barney as joint lead managers, sold $3 billion worth of five-year notes, priced to yield about 0.56 percent over U.S. Treasury yields, with 25 percent of the demand coming from international investors.

Register also glances at a recent copy of *The Federal Reserve Bank of St. Louis Monetary Trends* with trends in interest rates provided as shown in Figure P.4. News on the radio that morning suggested that inflation and unemployment continued to be low in the U.S. However, after such a long expansion, some security analysts predicted a downturn, and some corporations were announcing large layoffs. These analysts suggested buying long-term bonds, since if a recession occurs, interest rates tend

Figure P3   ✦   TREASURY YIELD CURVE AND RECENT MOVEMENT IN SHORT-TERM INTEREST RATES FOR JANUARY 13, 1998

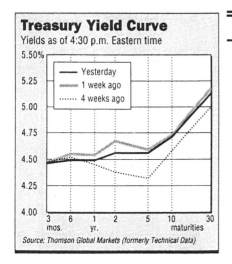

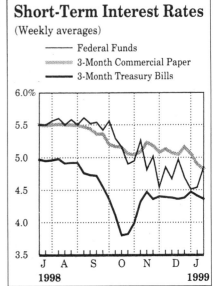

YIELD COMPARISONS

Based on Merrill Lynch Bond Indexes, priced as of midafternoon Eastern time.

	1/13	1/12	–52 Week– High	Low
Corp.-Govt. Master	5.36%	5.42%	6.13%	4.84%
Treasury 1-10yr	4.73	4.79	5.77	4.19
10+ yr	5.40	5.46	6.12	4.86
Agencies 1-10yr	5.40	5.46	6.19	4.71
10+ yr	5.76	5.81	6.44	5.22
Corporate				
1-10 yr High Qlty	5.46	5.52	6.27	5.08
Med Qlty	6.05	6.11	6.53	5.59
10+yr High Qlty	6.18	6.25	6.81	5.91
Med Qlty	6.72	6.79	7.22	6.46
Yankee bonds(1)	6.24	6.30	6.69	5.87
Current-coupon mortgages (2)				
GNMA 6.00%	6.21	6.25	6.81	5.79
FNMA 6.00%	6.28	6.33	6.77	5.87
FHLMC6.00%	6.29	6.34	6.80	5.89
High-yield corporates	10.02	9.96	10.81	8.17
Tax-Exempt Bonds				
7-12-yr G.O. (AA)	4.23	4.28	4.86	4.07
12-22-yr G.O. (AA)	4.70	4.73	5.25	4.50
22+yr revenue (A)	4.97	5.00	5.37	4.67

Note: High quality rated AAA-AA; medium quality A-BBB/Baa; high yield, BB/Ba-C.
(1) Dollar-denominated, SEC-registered bonds of foreign issuers sold in the U.S. (2) Reflects the 52-week high and low of mortgage-backed securities indexes rather than the individual securities shown.

Source: *Wall Street Journal*, January 14, 1999, C21.

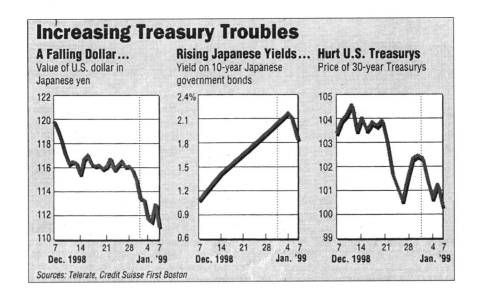

Source: *Wall Street Journal*, January 8, 1999, C1.

Figure P4 ✦ TRENDS IN INTEREST RATES, AS OF DECEMBER 1998

Short Term Interest Rates

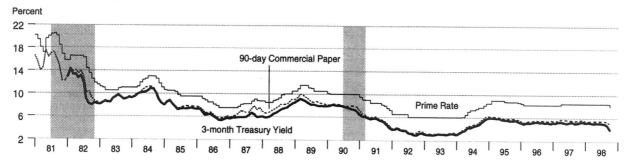

Long Term Interest Rates

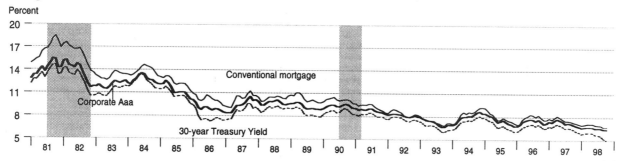

Long Term Interest Rates

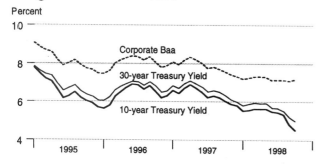

Short Term Interest Rates

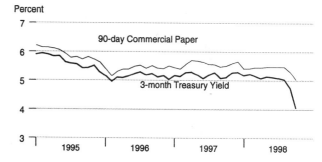

FOMC Expected Federal Funds Rate and Discount Rate

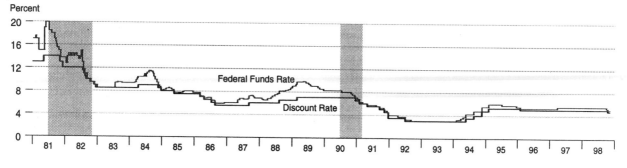

Source: Monetary Trends: The Federal Reserve Bank of St. Louis, December 1998.

to fall. Other analysts predicted that the economy in the U.S. would continue to be strong. The dollar had fallen sharply the previous week relative to the Japanese Yen. As shown in the lower panel of Figure P3, this was the result of a rise in Japanese bond yields, resulting in a sell-off of U.S. T-bonds by Japanese investors and day traders, causing U.S. Treasury security prices to fall, and hence yields to rise. This week, however, with intervention by the bank of Japan, the dollar had risen.

Register shakes his head in confusion. Bond market prices were much too volatile for his liking. How could a small bank manage its investment portfolio in such a global economy, where events in Brazil and Japan had a dramatic effect on Treasury security yields and, hence, the bank's investment portfolio? He had always thought of Treasuries as a risk-free investment, but in terms of interest-rate risk, they certainly were not.

The investment portfolio for the Sunny Side Bank is depicted below, with estimated maturities, fair value, amortized cost, and weighted average yields of securities by type.

	MATURITY DATE					
	1999	2000	2001	2006	2007+	
Tax-Exempt Securities Held to Maturity						
Amortized Cost	$76	$87	$59	$89	$38	
Fair Value	$81	$91	$63	$95	$41	
Weighted Ave Yield (tax equivalent)	6.54%	7.08%	6.65%	6.50%	5.58%	
All Other Securities						
Amortized Cost	$26	$9	$9	$80		
Fair Value	$27	$9	$9	$79		
Weighted Ave Yield	6.88%	6.51%	6.83%	7.42%		
Total Amortized Cost	$102	$96	$68	$169	$38	
Total Fair Value	$108	$100	$72	$174	$41	
Total Unrealized Gains	$6	$4	$4	$5	$3	$22

	MATURITY DATE				
	1999	2000	2001	2006	2007+
Securities Available for Sale					
U.S. Treasury Securities					
Amortized Cost	$351	$392	$452	$911	$3
Fair Value	$349	$392	$437	$904	$3
Weighted Ave Yield	5.37%	6.24%	5.41%	6.33%	7.47%
Government-Sponsored MBSs					
Amortized Cost	$955	$1,905	$959	$1,763	$164
Fair Value	$967	$1,934	$972	$1,757	$165
Weighted Ave Yield	6.66%	6.92%	7.19%	6.95%	7.66%
Corporate Bonds					
Amortized Cost	$9	$121	$11	$57	$92
Fair Value	$10	$121	$11	$57	$93
Weighted Ave Yield	6.47%	6.06%	8.03%	7.48%	6.67%
Total Amortized Cost	$1,315	$2,418	$1,422	$2,731	$259
Total Fair Value	$1,326	$2,447	$1,420	$2,718	$261
Total Unrealized Gain or Loss	$11	$29	($2)	$2 ($13)	$42 ($15)
Net Unrealized Gain on Held for Sale Securities					$27

Note: Dollar amounts are in thousands.

Note: Annual Reports and *Moody's Bank & Finance Manual* often provide this information.

As shown by the investment portfolio unrealized gains/loss above, with falling rates in the 1990s the security portfolio is posting gains. Based on the information above, answer the following questions.

a. Based on the maturities for the securities given, does the portfolio seem to be engaged in any type of maturity strategies (i.e., barbell, ladder, or buffer)? Explain why. Does Sunny Side's strategy seem appropriate for a small bank?

b. Based on trends shown in Figure P4, why do you think the securities portfolio is posing net gains?

c. Compare Sunny Side's percentage holdings in Treasury securities, municipals, MBSs, and corporate bonds to the percentages held by the average $100 million to $1 billion dollar bank (see Table 19.4).

d. Based on the recent information listed from the *Wall Street Journal* and from Figures P2 and P3, what do you think rates will be like during 1999 (disregard what actually happened)? How have recent international events at the time of the case affected interest rates on T-bonds? Why is it so difficult to predict interest rates?

e. Would you recommend any changes in Sunny Side's investment portfolio management strategy?

f. Would your recommendation change if you thought strongly that interest rates were going to rise? What would your recommendation be if you thought strongly that interest rates were going to fall?

g. The bank could swap a current $100,000 of eight-year T-bonds with par values of $1,000 each with 4 percent coupon rates for a recently issued eight -year T-bonds with 5 percent coupon rates selling at $1,000 par. If the bank has a 30 percent marginal tax rate, should it make the swap? Assume the par value of the T-bond is $1,000 (Hint: you will need to calculate the prices of the current bond using the new 5 percent yield as the discount rate and find the present value of the change in coupons and change in maturity values).

h. Why do you think Sunny Side, like other banks, holds a large percentage of MBSs? What benefits do MBSs have over other bonds? What disadvantages do they have?

Selected References

Burns, Joseph E. "Bank Liquidity—A Straightforward Concept but Hard to Measure." *Business Review (Federal Reserve Bank of Dallas)* (May, 1971).

Cacy, J. A., and Scott Winningham. "Reserve Requirements under the Depository Institutions Deregulation and Monetary Control Act of 1980." *Economic Review (Federal Reserve Bank of Kansas City)* 65 (September/October, 1980), 3–16.

Cook, Timothy and Timothy D. Rowe, eds. "The Discount Window." In *Instruments of the Money Market.* 6th ed. Richmond, Virginia: Federal Reserve Bank of Richmond. (1986b).

Dietz, Peter O., H. Russell Fogler, and Donald J. Hardy. "The Challenge of Analyzing Bond Portfolio Returns." *Journal of Portfolio Management* 6 (Spring, 1980), 53–58.

Evanoff, Douglas D. "Reserve Account Management Behavior: Impact of the Reserve Accounting Scheme and Carry Forward Provision." Federal Reserve Bank of Chicago, WP-89–12. (1989).

Feinnan, Joshua N. "Reserve Requirements: History, Current Practice, and Potential Reform." *Federal Reserve Bulletin* 79 (June, 1993), 569–589.

Gilbert, R. Alton. "Lagged Reserve Requirements: Implications for Monetary Control and Bank Reserve Management." *Review (Federal Reserve Bank of St. Louis)* 62 (May, 1980), 7–20.

Giroux, Gary. "A Survey of Forecasting Techniques Used by Commercial Banks." *Journal of Bank Research* 11 (Spring, 1980), 51–53.

Goodfriend, Marvin, and Monica Hargraves. "A Historic Assessment of the Rationales and Functions of Reserve Requirements." *Economic Review (Federal Reserve Bank of Richmond)* 69 (March/April, 1983), 3–21.

Haberman, Gary, and Catherine Piche. "Controlling Credit Risk Associated with Repos: Know Your Counterparty." *Economic Review (Federal Reserve Bank of Atlanta)* 70 (September, 1985), 28–34.

Hamdani, Kausar. "CRR and Excess Reserves: An Early Appraisal." *Quarterly Review (Federal Reserve Bank of New York)* 9 (Autumn, 1984), 16–23.

Homer, Sidney, and Martin Leibowitz. *Inside the Yield Book.* New York: Prentice-Hall and the New York Institute of Finance (1972).

Kaufman, Daniel J., Jr., and David R. Lee. "Planning Liquidity: A Practical Approach." *Magazine of Bank Administration* 53 (November, 1977), 55–63.

Knight, Robert E. "Reserve Requirements, Part I: Comparative Reserve Requirements at Member and Nonmember Banks." *Monthly Review (Federal Reserve Bank of Kansas City)* 59 (April, 1974), 3–20.

Luckett, Dudley G. "Approaches to Bank Liquidity Management." *Economic Review (Federal Reserve Bank of Kansas City)* 65 (March, 1980), 11–27.

McKenna, Conner, and Cuneo. *An Analysis of the Financial Institutions Reform, Recovery, and Enforcement Act of 1989.* New York: McKenna, Conner, and Cuneo. (1989).

Mengle, David. "The Discount Window." *Economic Review (Federal Reserve Bank of Richmond)* 72 (May/June, 1986a), 2–10.

Pearce, Douglas K. "Recent Developments in the Credit Union Industry." *Economic Review (Federal Reserve Bank of Kansas City)* 69 (June, 1984), 10–12.

Proctor, Allen J., and Kathleen K. Donahoo. "Commercial Bank Investment in Municipal Securities." *Quarterly Review (Federal Reserve Bank of New York)* 8 (Winter, 1983–1984), 26–37.

Robinson, Roland I. *The Management of Bank Funds.* New York: McGraw-Hill (1962).

Rodrigues, Anthony P. "Government Investments of Commercial Banks." *Quarterly Review (Federal Reserve Bank of New York)* 18 (Summer, 1993), 39–53.

Rosenbaum, Mary Susan. "Contemporaneous Reserve Accounting: The New System and Its Implications for Monetary Policy." *Economic Review (Federal Reserve Bank of Atlanta)* 69 (April, 1984), 46–57.

Saunders, Anthony, and Thomas Urich. "The Effects of Shifts in Monetary Policy and Reserve Accounting Regimes on Bank Reserve Management Behavior in the Federal Funds Market." *Journal of Banking and Finance* 12 (December, 1988), 523–535.

Sealey, C. W., Jr. "Valuation, Capital Structure, and Shareholder Unanimity for Depository Financial Intermediaries." *Journal of Finance* 38 (June, 1983), 857–871.

Sprong, Kenneth. *Banking Regulation.* Kansas City: Federal Reserve Bank of Kansas City. (1990).

Stevens, E. J. "Is There Any Rationale for Reserve Requirements?" *Economic Review (Federal Reserve Bank of Cleveland)* 27 (Quarter 3, 1991), 2–17.

Stigum, Marcia. *The Money Market.* 3d ed. Homewood, Illinois: Dow Jones-Irwin (1990).

Tarhan, Vefa. "Individual Bank Reserve Management." *Economic Perspectives (Federal Reserve Bank of Chicago)* 8 (July/August, 1984), 17–23.

Tschinkel, Sheila S. "Overview." *Economic Review (Federal Reserve Bank of Atlanta)* 70 (September, 1985), 5–9.

Watson, Ronald D. "Bank Bond Management: The Maturity Dilemma." *Business Review (Federal Reserve Bank of Philadelphia)* (March, 1972), 23–29.

Chapter 19 Internet Exercise

Asset Management: Liquidity Reserves and the Securities Portfolio

1. Extending credit to depository institutions to accommodate commerce, industry and agriculture is a principal function of Federal Reserve Banks. The Fed's discount window plays an important role in liquidity management by banks, especially in times of financial crisis when liquidity must be supplied to the system. An overview of the function of the Fed's discount window can be found at: *http://www.frbchi.org/loans/overview.html*. Depository institutions that maintain reservable transaction accounts are entitled to borrowing privileges at the Discount Window. Adjustment credit is available on a short-term basis to help eligible depository institutions meet temporary requirement for funds or to cushion outflow of funds while adjustments are made to institutions balance sheet, or when funds are not reasonably available in the money markets or from usual sources. Seasonal credit is available to institutions that can demonstrate a clear pattern of recurring intra-yearly swings in funding needs, which are generally reflected by decreases in deposit and increases in loan activity. Only after all other funding sources are exhausted, the Federal Reserve may provide longer-term funds to institutions experiencing liquidity strain or difficulties arising from special circumstances. The Board of Governors may authorize a Reserve Bank to provide emergency credit to individuals, partnerships and corporations that are not depository institutions. Such lending may occur when lending is not available from other sources and failure to provide credit would adversely affect the economy. This type of lending has not occurred since the mid-1930s.

2. The Federal Reserve Bank of New York provides a useful summary of all banking regulations at: *http://www.ny.frb.org/pihome/regs.html*. For example, Regulation D imposes uniform reserve requirements on all depository institutions with transaction accounts or nonpersonal time deposits; defines such deposits and requires reports of deposits to the Federal Reserve. Regulation DD requires depository institutions to disclose the terms of deposit accounts to consumers.

3. The Federal Reserve Bank of New York provides a useful summary of the role of reserve requirements in monetary control and financial stability at: *http://www.ny.frb.org/pihome/fedpoint/fed45.html*. As of September 1996, the reserve requirement was 10 percent on transaction deposits, and there were zero reserves required for time deposits.

Other useful sites for financial institution data:

NCUA-FCUA Central Liquidity Function
http://www.ncua.gov/all_docs/ref/fcu_act/ACT-3.html

Federal Home Loan Bank System
http://www.fhlbanks.com/

Federal Home Loan Bank of Chicago
http://www.fhlbc.com/

Liquidity Model: (You will need Excel® 97 to open this file.)
http://www.fhlbc.com/models.htm

"Bankers face the unappetizing choice of watching dollars run out of certificates of deposit into such alternative investments as mutual funds and annuities, or actively offering those alternatives and accelerating the trend."

Douglas Freeman
Chief Corporate Banking Executive, Barnett Banks, Quoted in Jeffrey Marshall, "Rolling the Dice on Asset Management," *U.S. Banker* (March 1994), p. 33.

"(A) myth has grown—even among many who should know better—that checks are going away. However, while the rate of check growth is slowing—and may eventually result in a modest percentage rate of decline—checks will still be used in huge quantities well into the next century."

Donald R. Hollis
Executive Vice President-Operations, First Chicago Corporation "The Payments System Evolution at the Crossroads," *Bank Management* (July/August 1994), 49.

"Customer service is a key competitive intangible—a factor that will profoundly affect the future of competition in financial services. . . . When we talk about reputation risk, we are referring to how well banks fare . . . at the court of public opinion. Bankers have suffered reputation risk because the public does not perceive banks generally as outstanding service providers. . . . Whether particular fees are justified or not, in too many cases, they have been imposed and raised without adequate explanation . . . and without calculating the trade-off between short-term income and long-term reputation risk."

Julie L. Williams
Acting Comptroller of the Currency "Regulatory Policy: OCC's Williams: Banks Must Improve Customer Service . . . Or Else," *Bank Policy Report* 17 (December 14, 1998), 7–10.

"Banking's traditional organizational model, based on full-service branches, absorbs up to 65 percent of banks' operating expenditures today. Yet it fails to provide what our non-bank competitors deliver— 'convenience, simplicity, and value.' This is costing us dearly. According to BAI analysis, banks are losing money on 20 percent of our customers, and merely breaking even on another 60 percent. Furthermore, customer profitability relates directly to the frequency of branch visits: It costs about 50 percent more to serve a customer in a lobby than by remote means. . . . Direct access (or electronic delivery of service) provides personal service 24 hours a day—yet limits costly

human resources . . . (but) direct access needs a complex information infrastructure and a thorough reengineering of banking processes."

William M. Randel
Senior Vice President, Huntington Bancshares, Inc., Ohio "Delivering the Future: Redefining the Role of Banks in a New Competitive Environment," *Bank Management* (January/February 1995), p. 46.

"The banking and computer industries anticipated huge growth and cost savings with the increased availability of electronic banking. But consumers have not been so quick to embrace the service. . . . Consumers care about cost more than technology."

The New York Times, August 24, 1998, C3.

20

DEPOSIT AND LIABILITY
MANAGEMENT

As the preceding quotes suggest, depository institutions have faced and continue to face dramatic changes in their deposit and liability management. Bank deposit financing fell from 92 percent of assets in 1950 to about 65 percent of assets in 1998,[1] as investors moved funds out of deposits with low rates into higher yielding investments banks also increased their equity financing with higher capital requirements. Yet depository institutions are still strongly in the deposit-taking and clearing business, which has represented the heart of a bank's operations and which encompasses a large percentage of bank costs.

Although some institutions have moved away from the deposit business, such as Bankers Trust (soon to merge with Deutsche Bank); Nationsbank-BankAmerica and other large regional banks have developed national or regional networks of branches. Other large banks including BankBoston and Bank One have taken advantage of economies of scale and gained fee income by offering deposit check-writing and clearing services for nonbank financial institutions. A number of banks and thrifts, such as TeleBank Financial Corporation of Arlington, Virginia, are virtual banks, attracting deposits by mail, phone, and the Internet. An increasing number of cyberbanks and thrifts—for example CompuBank in Houston, Texas—can offer higher deposit rates, because they do not have the cost of branches.

In the 1970s, to compensate for lost deposits as depositors defected to money market funds that could offer higher rates, larger banks developed new money market types of securities that provide sources of nondeposit funds, including bankers acceptances and negotiable CDs. Being allowed to offer money market funds in the 1980s helped banks to recapture lost deposits. However, with the deregulation of interest rates in the 1980s, depository institutions have had to be much more active in finding creative ways to compete with other depository and nondepository institutions for

---

[1]Source: *Federal Reserve Bulletin,* various issues 1997, 1998.

funds. Depository institution managers have developed a new marketing focus.

Managers have come up with innovative deposit products to attract deposit customers. These include certificates of deposits (CDs) that are indexed to savings goals, such as the cost of education or inflation. For more gaming customers, depository institutions offer CDs with premiums that rise based on the results of football games, elections, or more conventional investments, such as the price of gold or stock market indexes. By offering annuities, mutual funds, and other types of investment services, depository institutions are able to retain customers who prefer one-stop investment shopping. Although such offerings may cannibalize other deposit accounts, they generate fee income and retain some customer deposits. Similarly, by offering cash management, personal banking, and other corporate services, banks have been able to retain deposits of corporate customers.

Depository institutions have also tried to retain deposit customers by offering better service, including automated 24-hour telephone services that provide customers with account information. In addition to reducing labor-intensive costs of having to hire employees to answer hundreds of phone calls, this service provides a way to attract deposits and allows depository institutions to compete with mutual funds that offer such services. Although in the past larger depository institutions charged for this service, many institutions, including community banks, are now offering this service free of charge. Depository institutions have also developed new low-cost deposit-gathering mechanisms that are more convenient for customers through supermarket branches. For instance, Wells Fargo and TCF National Bank in Minneapolis have taken advantage of liberalized interstate branching rules by establishing kiosks in supermarkets in different states, which means the banks avoid the expense of building new branches.

Depository institutions have become more sophisticated in their advertising and marketing campaigns, as well, and in creating favorable publicity by sponsoring community funding raising events. National advertising including letter-writing campaigns, newspaper ads, and radio and television ads have allowed depository institutions to attract funds across the country.

The payment system for banks is also evolving, with the development of check imaging systems, which significantly reduce bank costs in terms of having to compile and mail canceled checks to customers. Banks have also become leaders in electronic check presentment (ECP), which is a hybrid, electronic/paper method of expediting check collections. Under this system, check data are exchanged in advance of presenting actual checks, speeding up the payment system, and reducing operational expenses for banks. New computer systems and software allow even small community banks to reduce the cost of processing checks and speed up the check-clearing process. When you think of depository institutions clearing billions of checks each day and spending $4 billion annually just to handle checks, new systems have simplified the lives of harried bankers dramatically and lowered costs for many banks in the late 1990s.[2]

With about 25 percent of households owning a personal computer in the late 1990s, a number of banks have entered or thought of entering online banking. By June 1997, a General Accounting Office (GAO) survey showed that although 50 percent of banks planned to have online banking by 1998, only 7 percent of U.S. banks at that time offered online banking services, allowing customers to check balances and transfer between accounts using a computer at home or at work. Another survey by Inteco Corporation, which publishes the Directory of Home Banking and On-Line Financial Services, found that in 1997 individuals 18 years of age or older doing online banking made up about 4.6 percent of the population (lower than the 5.5 percent predicted by experts, but a significant increase from 2.8 percent in 1996). Analysts attribute the slowdown to large industry mergers, which require a melding of sometimes very incompatible computer systems. Banks also were limited by systems built around personal finance software, for which customers frequently had to purchase upgrades and that limited the design of services. An industry-wide shift to Internet-based systems, with robust encryption security available, reduces such

---

[2]See Buddy Massengill and Ned Miltko. "NCHA: Private Check-Clearing Alternative," *Bank Management* (March/April 1995), 47–50; J.D. Carreker. "Electronic Check Presentment: Capturing New Technology." *Bank Management* (March/April 1995), 33–44; and William M. Randle. "Delivering The Future: Redefining the Role of Banks in a New Competitive Environment." *Bank Management* (January/February 1995), 45–48.

problems. *Previously, many consumers had been reluctant to tackle online banking because of expensive software, unreliable service, limited technology support, and unproven security of financial data, as well as high fees. Large banks like Citicorp have recently lowered or gotten rid of such fees.*[3]

The entry of banks into online banking has concerned regulators in terms of how banks will be able to handle technology risk. For instance, one of the 10 banks that the GAO surveyed did not have basic virus-detection software on their systems. Consequently, the Office of the Comptroller of the Currency (OCC) issued new guidelines in 1998 for examiners to follow when reviewing a bank's technology risk management plan.[4]

Despite dramatic improvements in customer service and products, as noted in the quote by Julie L. Williams, Acting Comptroller of the Currency in 1998, banks and thrifts have suffered from the perception that they are charging fees and low deposit rates that are not justified from a cost perspective.[5] *With the deregulation of interest rates in the 1980s, banks and thrifts began charging explicit or implicit fees for deposit services. Additional fees were imposed in the early 1990s to improve falling profitability. Depository institution managers have often failed to provide an adequate explanation for new fees. Consumers are not aware of regulatory costs including the implicit cost of reserve and capital requirements and explicit cost of deposit insurance premiums that depositories must pay. With mergers resulting in larger banks, service has fallen for many large banks because of difficulties integrating different bank cultures and computer systems. The thrift crisis of the 1980s still haunts the thrift industry as well. Hence, banks and thrifts face a challenge in their deposit management in terms of courting public opinion in their favor.*

This chapter examines the liability management of depository institutions, including the current liability structure and typical types of deposits, and the history of liability management. Liability management entails the active use of nondeposit funds to meet liquidity needs, enhance profits, or achieve growth. The chapter also provides greater detail on different types of nondeposit funds and how they are typically used. Concepts of liability mix, pricing, and the effects of deposit insurance on depository institution behavior are also discussed. The following section briefly discusses factors that depository institutions need to consider in their deposit management and the typical deposit structure.

◆ ◆ ◆

---

[3]See Aldo Svaldi. "Online Banking Moves Ahead," *Denver Business Journal*, March 6–12, 1998, 8A; and David J. Wallace. "Mergers and Year 2000 Slow On-Line Banking." *The New York Times* (August 24, 1998), C3. In October 1997, Citibank introduced an Internet-based system for its Direct Access electronic banking service, which was first offered in 1984. In 1997, Citibank had about 300,000 electronic-banking clients, with a jump in customers when Citibank eliminated its fee.

[4]See "Electronic Banking: OCC Issues New Guidance to Ensure Banks Can Handle Technology Risks." *Banking Policy Report* 17 (March 2, 1998), 13–18. The OCC guidelines evaluate whether senior management has significant knowledge and skills to manage the bank's use of technology, including significant involvement of the board of directors in the planning process to manage the bank's technology risk. Banks also must closely scrutinize the operations of vendors to ensure that systems work properly and are secure, and that consumer information is protected.

[5]For an example of consumer criticism, see Robert Heady. "Benefits of Rate Cuts Elusive." *The Denver Post*, January 10, 1999, p. 9K. This article points out that in response to rate cuts by the Fed in 1998, savings rates came down twice as fast as personal loan rates on average for banks and thrifts.

FACTORS TO CONSIDER IN DEPOSIT AND LIABILITY MANAGEMENT

Type of Business a Depository Is In   Whether a bank or thrift can attract different types of deposits is affected by the type of bank it is and the market segment it serves. For instance, a bank that provides consumer loans will also attract more consumer deposits than a bank that primarily focuses on commercial loans. Credit unions are financed by consumer deposits because they make loans to consumers.

However, a bank focusing on commercial loans will attract more business demand deposits, which, at the time of this writing, are not allowed to pay interest, although there is lobbying to change this in the future. Banks often give such business loan customers the choice of paying fees or holding compensating balances in the form of demand deposits (in effect charging implicit interest) or a combination of the two. They also provide sweep accounts for businesses, so they can earn interest on savings accounts until funds are needed, when they are swept to demand deposit accounts. Wholesale banks, like Bankers Trust, that have few or no branches, in contrast, must rely on nondeposit funds for financing. Thus, in terms of a bank's market segment and the type of loans it makes, asset management is closely related to its deposit and liability management.

More Sophisticated and Less Loyal Customers   With the deregulation of interest rates in the 1980s, the dramatic growth in money market and mutual funds, and the greater availability of information for consumers, depositors have become more sophisticated and less loyal to particular financial institutions. Consequently, retail CDs have became much more interest-rate sensitive, with CD depositors willing to pull funds out, despite withdrawal penalties, if other institutions or funds offered higher rates. This has been particularly the case for large, insured, CDs of $100,000 (often called jumbo CDs), discussed in a later section. Investors have also invested more in mutual fund bond and stock funds that have offered higher returns. Hence, banks and thrifts must competitively price such interest-sensitive deposits, which are often repriced weekly based on T-bill rates and the rates offered by competitors. The best savings rates are readily available to savers on the Internet, in published newsletters, and in magazines and newspapers, such as the column shown in Figure 20.1 for *The Denver Post*. Companies such as the Bank Rate Monitor collect and publish CD rate data in a weekly report (www.bankrate.com).

As shown in Figure 20.1, in early January 1999, the average money market deposit account (MMDA) rate for banks and thrifts was 2.24 percent, but rates varied. For instance, Providian National Bank, a direct mail deposit bank, offered a 5.26 percent rate. Similarly, CD rates averaged from 4.16 percent to 4.49 percent depending on maturity, but some banks offered rates that were more than 100 basis points (1 percent) higher, although minimum deposits vary. The bottom panel shows that stock market returns during this time were much larger (although much more volatile), with an average 16.1 percent return for the Dow Jones in 1998. Looking at Figure 20.2, banks had a hard time with falling rates over the 1990s competing with a rising stock market. Consequently, as shown in the upper panel of Figure 20.2, banks and thrifts lost time deposits, and nondeposit liabilities, such as repurchase agreements, rose.

More National Advertising to Attract Funds Across the Country and More Competition for Funds   As pointed out in Figure 20.1, consumers have greater access to rates across the country. Although consumers may prefer to have transaction

Figure 20.1 ◆ Average and Best Savings Rates for Bank/Thrift Deposit Accounts

Best Savings Rates

Annual percentage yields offered by the largest-asset banks and thrifts as of Dec. 28 for the lowest minimum deposit. Minimums may vary.

DENVER		NATIONAL	
MONEY-MARKET DEPOSIT ACCOUNTS			AVG. 2.24%
Liberty Savings Bank	3.60	Providian Nat., Tilton, N.H. (4)	5.26
FirstBank of Colorado	3.25	Providian Bank, Salt Lake City (3)	5.26
Guaranty Bank	2.99	Imperial T&L, Glendale, Calif. (4)	5.25
Bank of Cherry Creek	2.89	Key Bank USA, Albany, N.Y. (5)	5.23
Colorado Business Bank	2.80	Net.Bank, Alpharetta, Ga. (4)	5.13
Union Bank & Trust	2.80		
Vectra Bank	2.80		
6-MONTH CDS			AVG. 4.16%
Liberty Savings Bank	4.90	Cross Country, Wilmington, Del. (3)	5.55
FirstBank of Colorado	4.55	Net.Bank, Alpharetta, Ga. (4)	5.35
First National Bank of Niwot	4.45	New South Fed., Birmingham, Ala. (3)	5.27
U.S. Bank	4.35	Arkansas Nat., Bentonville, Ark. (2)	5.25
Key Bank	4.25	Providian Nat., Tilton, N.H. (4)	5.23
1-YEAR CDS			AVG. 4.27%
Liberty Savings Bank	5.00	Cross Country, Wilmington, Del. (3)	5.71
Mountain States Bank	4.68	Net.Bank, Alpharetta, Ga. (4)	5.40
World Savings Bank	4.62	Providian Nat., Tilton, N.H. (4)	5.35
FirstBank of Colorado	4.60	Providian Bank, Salt Lake City (3)	5.35
First National Bank of Niwot	4.58	Southern Pacific, Los Angeles (4)	5.34
Guaranty Bank	4.58		
2.5-YEAR CDS			AVG. 4.35%
Liberty Savings Bank	5.10	Capital One, Glen Allen, Va. (4)	5.52
Guaranty Bank	4.78	Providian Nat., Tilton, N.H. (4)	5.51
World Savings Bank	4.72	Providian Bank, Salt Lake City (3)	5.51
Commercial Federal Bank	4.55	Key Bank USA, Albany, N.Y. (5)	5.50
Citywide Banks	4.53	Southern Pacific, Los Angeles (4)	5.44
5-YEAR CDS			AVG. 4.49%
Liberty Savings Bank	5.10	Capital One, Glen Allen, Va. (4)	5.77
Citywide Banks	4.84	Providian Nat., Tilton, N.H. (4)	5.71
World Savings Bank	4.77	Providian Bank, Salt Lake City (3)	5.71
U.S. Bank	4.70	Eastern Svgs., Hunt Valley, Md. (1)	5.65
FirstBank of Colorado	4.65	Key Bank USA, Albany, N.Y. (5)	5.65

Rates in blackened area are national average. Numbers are based on account-opening minimums. Figures in parentheses rate financial strength, on a scale of 1 to 5, with 5 the strongest as determined by Bank Rate Monitor. A U indicates an institution is too new to rate. Source: Bank Rate Monitor, North Palm Beach, Fla. (800) 327-7717, www.bankrate.com

Source: The Denver Post, January 3, 1999, 5K.

Figure 20.1 ✦ AVERAGE AND BEST SAVINGS RATES FOR BANK/THRIFT DEPOSIT
ACCOUNTS (*CONTINUED*)

A Turbulent but Profitable Year
Investors who stuck with United States stocks in 1998 were rewarded, defying expectations by
many Wall Street professionals that the market would falter on the uncertainty of economic
turbulence abroad. The Nasdaq market rose nearly 40 percent on the strength of Internet and
technology stocks. The Standard & Poor's index rose more than 20 percent for a record fourth
consecutive year.

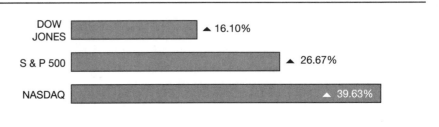

Source: The New York Times, January 1, 1999, A1.

accounts in nearby depository institutions that offer convenient national automated
teller machine (ATM) networks, make branches less of a priority. With the advent of
interstate banks, such as Nationsbank-Bank America, it is easier for depositors using
such banks to deposit and cash checks nationwide. With national advertising and the
advent of cyberbanks and direct banks, it is also easier for banks to attract funds
from different regions. Nonbanks, such as security firms, also offer money market
funds and resource management accounts with check-writing privileges and other
services. Similarly, mutual fund companies offer check writing, and some companies—including Fidelity, American Century, Dreyfus, Scudder, and USAA—offer
debit cards.[6] Credit unions, which have lower costs and are not taxed, also are formi-
dable competitors for banks and thrifts, with the ability to offer lower fees and at
times more attractive deposit rates.

Need to Estimate Marginal Cost of Funds   With declining NIMs in the later
1980s, banks and thrifts became more aware of the need to reduce operating expenses, including the major costs entailed with administering deposit accounts. Loan
rates are often priced from a bank's marginal cost of funds, which includes administrative and processing costs for deposits. When these costs can be lowered, loans can
be more competitively priced.

Greater Use of Nondeposit Funds   With the decline in bank and thrift deposits in
the 1970s, which has continued into the 1990s, banks have needed more nondeposit
funds. Purchased funds have a higher interest cost and can be very interest-rate sensitive, as discussed in Chapter 6. Liability management and different types of nondeposit
funds are discussed in greater detail later in this chapter. Before discussing nondeposit
funds, the deposit structure of banks and thrifts is presented in the following section.

---

[6]Vanessa O'Connell. "It's a Broker! It's a Banker! It's a Mutual-Fund Group!" *The Wall Street
Journal* (February 19, 1998), C1.

Figure 20.2 ✦ PERCENTAGE CHANGES IN DEPOSITORY INSTITUTION DEPOSITS AND PERFORMANCE STANDARD POOR'S 500 INDEX AND INTEREST RATE TRENDS

Checkable and Savings Deposits

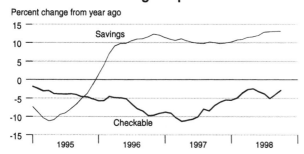

Time Deposits

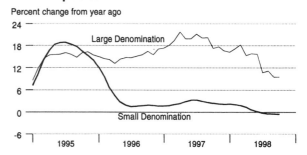

Repurchase Agreements and Eurodollars

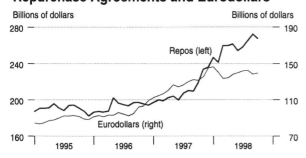

Money Market Mutual Fund Shares

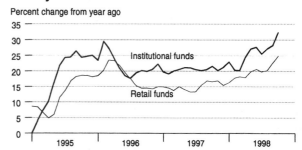

Standard and Poor's 500

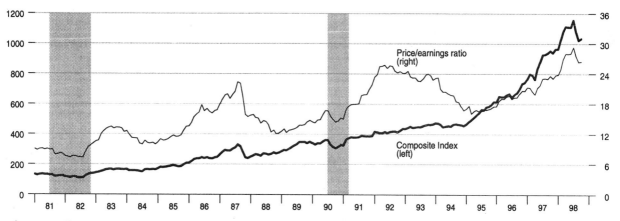

Interest Rates

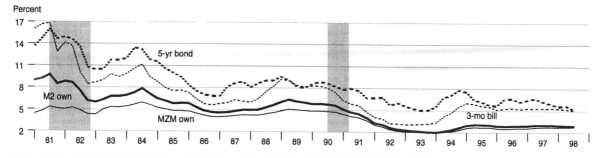

Source: St. Louis Fed Reserve, December 1998, *Monetary Trends*, pp. 5, 12, 15

Deposit Structure for Banks and Savings Institutions

Deposits as a Percentage of Total Liabilities   Commercial banks have on average about 76 percent of their liabilities in deposits, compared with 78 percent for savings institutions and 88 percent for credit unions. Banks with assets greater than $1 billion have 71 percent of their liabilities in deposits compared with 97 percent for the smallest banks (assets less than $100 million) and 92 percent for midsize banks (assets between $100 million and $1 billion). Similarly, for the largest savings institutions, 73 percent of liabilities are deposits compared with 88 percent for thrifts between $100 million and $1 billion, and 94 percent for the smallest institutions. Thus, deposits remain the majority of depository institution liabilities, with larger institutions engaging more in liability management.[7]

Deposit Structure for Banks   Table 20.1 shows details on the deposit structure for all FDIC-Insured Commercial Banks as of the end of 1996. Banks held about $3.197 trillion in deposits, $2.724 trillion (85 percent) of which were domestic deposits, 62.6 percent of which were insured (83 percent for banks with assets between $100 million and $1 billion and 55 percent for banks with assets greater than $1 billion). For banks with $1 billion or more in assets, 20 percent of their deposits were foreign deposits. For domestic deposits, about 29 percent were transaction accounts and about 71 percent nontransaction accounts, with a similar distribution across different sizes of banks. The majority of the transaction accounts for larger banks were demand deposits, reflecting their wholesale nature, with a more diversified transaction deposit base for banks with less than $1 billion in small assets between NOW accounts and demand deposits. Nontransaction deposits consist of a fairly equal distribution of savings deposits and time deposits. Banks of $1 billion or more had a larger percentage of jumbo CDs ($100,000 or more) than smaller sized banks. Only a very small percentage (4.75 percent) of domestic deposits are in IRAs and Keogh Plan accounts for banks on average.

Brokered Deposits   The percentage of **brokered deposits**, deposits obtained when a depository engages a broker to raise funds, is only 1.48 percent of total domestic deposits. With brokered deposits, the broker (often a broker for a securities firm) receives a commission and may solicit money on a national or even international basis, usually ensuring that the total funds raised to individual accounts is fully insured up to $100,000 each. In the 1980s weak banks and thrifts depended heavily on brokered funds (which can leave an institution at any time, since depositors are investing for higher yields); weak firms ultimately failed, leaving the federal deposit insurers with a huge bailout. Legislation in FIRREA in 1989 and Federal Deposit Insurance Corporation Improvement Act (FDICIA) in 1991 forbids institutions that do not meet minimum capital requirements from accepting brokered deposits. Under FDICIA even firms deemed to have "adequate" capital are required to obtain permission from regulators before seeking brokered funds. Regulators are also authorized to impose interest rate ceilings on brokered deposits to prevent a reoccurrence of the excessive and risky growth

---

[7]Source: FDIC Statistics on Banking, 1996 and David A. Walker. "Credit Union Insurance and Regulation." Center for Business-Government Relations, Georgetown University, Washington, D.C., 1997.

Table 20.1 ✦ **DEPOSIT LIABILITIES OF FDIC-INSURED COMMERCIAL BANKS (MILS.)**

	All Commercial Banks		$100 Mil. to $1 Bil.		$1 Billion or More	
Total Deposits	3,197,234		593,572		2,360,968	
Total Foreign Deposits	473,544		2,655		470,861	
Total Domestic Deposits	2,723,690		590,917		1,890,107	
Structure of Total Domestic Deposits (% of Total Domestic Deposits)						
Total Transaction Accounts	798,883	29.33%	171,036	28.94%	555,253	29.38%
NOW Accounts	192,389	7.06%	70,436	11.92%	87,580	4.63%
Demand Deposits	603,312	22.15%	99,305	16.81%	466,681	24.69%
Total Nontransaction Accounts	1,924,807	70.67%	419,881	71.06%	1,334,854	70.62%
Structure of Total Nontransaction Deposits (% Total Domestic & Foreign Deposits)						
Total Time and Savings Deposits	2,120,378	66.32%	491,612	82.82%	1,423,426	60.29%
Savings Deposits	1,083,117	51.08%	222,973	45.36%	775,606	54.49%
Money Market Deposit Accts.	560,600		81,566		455,154	
Total Time Deposits	1,037,261	48.92%	268,639	54.64%	647,820	45.51%
Time CDs $100,000 or more	322,049		70,653		223,336	
Selected Components of Total Domestic Deposits (% Total Domestic Deposits)						
IRAs and Keogh Plan Accounts	151,876	4.75%	35,994	6.06%	102,418	4.34%
Brokered Deposits	47,225	1.48%	4,614	0.78%	41,642	1.76%
Estimated Insured Deposits	2,001,885	62.61%	488,230	82.25%	1,300,187	55.07%
Total Time Deposits	1,037,261		268,639		647,820	
Maturity and Repricing Data for Time Deposits						
CDs of $100,000 or more	322,049	31.05%	70,653	26.30%	223,336	34.48%
Repriced in 3 months or less	162,524	50.47%	31,642	44.79%	119,524	53.52%
Over 3 months through 12 months	103,434	32.12%	27,893	39.48%	63,057	28.23%
Over 1 year through 5 years	50,994	15.83%	10,735	15.19%	36,105	16.17%
Over 5 years	5,096	1.58%	382	0.54%	4,650	2.08%
CDs of Less than $100,000	715,212	68.95%	197,987	73.70%	424,484	65.52%
Repriced in 3 months or less	200,387	28.02%	55,246	27.90%	118,479	27.91%
Over 3 months through 12 months	311,797	43.60%	89,081	44.99%	179,171	42.21%
Over 12 months	203,028	28.39%	53,660	27.10%	126,834	29.88%

Figures for year-end December 31, 1996.
Source: FDIC Statistics on Banking, 1996

strategies used by some thrifts in the 1980s. Well-capitalized depositories, however, can continue to seek brokered deposits.[8]

---

[8]Severely undercapitalized savings and loans in California and the Southwestern U.S. took advantage of deposit insurance by offering very high rates in the 1980s to attract funds to finance rapid growth, in an attempt to grow their way out of insolvency. To cover the higher rates on brokered deposits, these institutions had to invest in very high yielding, risky loans, many of which were subject to default in the later 1980s. Studies have shown evidence of some rate contagion, whereby other solvent thrifts and banks had to offer higher rates as well, in order to compete with weakened thrifts for deposits. Because of the moral hazard problem of deposit insurance, depositors did not often care about the solvency of an institution because deposits were insured, allowing sick thrifts to capture new deposits. See FDIC Annual Report, 1991 and Moore (1991).

Table 20.2 ✦ DEPOSIT LIABILITIES OF SAVINGS INSTITUTIONS (MILS.)

	All Savings Institutions		$100 Mil. to $1 Bil.		$1 Billion or More	
Total Deposit Liabilities	$727,994		$212,580		$479,225	
Estimated Insured Deposits	687,082	94.38%	201,903	94.98%	450,725	94.05%
Memoranda:						
Demand Deposits	33,065	4.54%	7,948	3.74%	24,028	5.01%
Time CDs of $100,000 or more	86,400	11.87%	22,429	10.55%	60,004	12.52%
Selected Components of Total Domestic Deposits:						
IRAs and Keogh plan accounts	73,036	10.03%	22,033	10.36%	47,808	9.98%
Brokered Deposits	10,994	1.51%	2,036	0.96%	8,738	1.82%

Figures for Year-end December 31, 1996
Source: FDIC Statistics on Banking, 1996

Maturity of Time Deposits   In the lower panel of Table 20.1, the maturity of time deposits is shown. For jumbo CDs of $100,000 or more, 50.47 percent of CDs had remaining maturities of three months or less, and 32.12 percent had maturities of three months to one year, suggesting very short-term volatile deposits. For retail CDs of less than $100,000, about 44 percent are between three months and one year, with about 28 percent over one year and 28 percent with maturities of three months or less. Thus, the majority of both retail and jumbo CDs are short term, with 82 percent of jumbo CDs and 72 percent of retail CDs maturing in one year or less.

Deposit Structure for Saving Institutions   Table 20.2 shows deposit liabilities for savings institutions at the end of 1996. The FDIC Statistics on Banking does not include as much detail for these institutions. As can be seen from the table, savings institutions have a larger percentage of insured deposits, averaging 94 percent of deposits. Jumbo CDs average only about 12 percent of deposits. Hence, as mortgage lender thrifts have a larger percentage of core (insured) less volatile deposits. Demand deposits are also a very small percentage of deposits, averaging 4.54 percent. IRAs and Keogh plan accounts are about 10 percent of deposits on average, a somewhat higher percentage than commercial banks have. Brokered deposits are 1.51 percent of deposits, similar to commercial banks, with a slightly larger percentage (1.82 percent) for thrifts with assets of $1 billion or more.

Special Features of Deposit Accounts   Table 20.3 summarizes characteristics and special features of deposit accounts that were mentioned in Chapter 5. Super-NOW accounts are also offered, which require a higher minimum balance and pay a higher rate than NOW accounts. Different institutions also offer variations to these basic types of accounts, in addition to savings accounts, discussed in Chapter 5. The following section discusses liability management and types of nondeposit funds.

BRIEF HISTORY OF LIABILITY MANAGEMENT

As early as 1961, money-center banks began to develop alternatives to traditional deposits. The active search for nondeposit funds to meet liquidity needs, enhance

Table 20.3   ✦   CHARACTERISTICS OF DEPOSIT ACCOUNTS

Depository institutions offer accounts with a wide variety of interest rates and other characteristics. Few regulatory restrictions remain.

Account	Minimum Maturity	Interest Rate Characteristics	Reserve Requirements	Special Features
Demand deposits (noninterest negotiable orders of withdrawal at thrifts)	None; payable on demand of the depositor	No explicit interest permitted	3% on first ≈ $46.8 million total of demand deposits and NOW accounts; 10% on total thereafter	May not be offered by federal CUs
NOW accounts (share drafts at CUs)	Institution *may* reserve the right to require 7 days' advance notice before withdrawal	Fixed or variable; no restrictions at banks and thrifts[a]	Same as demand deposits	Unlimited number of transactions; may not be offered to businesses
Money market deposit accounts (MMDAs)	Institution *must* reserve the right to require 7 days' advance notice before withdrawal	Fixed or variable; no restrictions	None	Preauthorized transfers to and from account limited to 6 per month, including 3 by check; unlimited in-person, mail, or automatic teller transactions
Passbook savings (savings shares at CUs)	Same as MMDAs	Same as MMDAs	Same as MMDAs	No check-writing privileges
Non-negotiable certificates of deposit, or share certificates at CUs	7 days	Same as MMDAs	Same as MMDAs	Forfeiture penalties imposed on withdrawals within the first 6 days; additional penalties may be imposed on nonpersonal accounts with original maturities of 18 months or more
Individual retirement accounts (IRAs)	Depends on type of plan; MMDA-type plan has no legal minimum; CD-type plan has minimum based on maturity	Depends on plan selected	None	Depositors with income below specified levels may make tax-deferred additions to these accounts up to a maximum of $2,000 per year per individual; interest earned on accounts is tax-deferred, regardless of depositor income; penalties for withdrawal before age $59\frac{1}{2}$
Negotiable CDs (Jumbos)	7 days	Same as MMDAs	Same as MMDAs	$100,000 minimum denomination; depositor can sell the deposit to a buyer before maturity, price is market-determined; no federal insurance on amount over $100,000

[a]Federal law sets a 6% ceiling for CU interest on deposits, but the NCUA may override it. As of 1992, the NCUA had imposed no interest ceiling for CU deposits.

Source: Prepared by the authors from information in Board of Governors of the Federal Reserve System, "Regulation Q: Interest on Deposits," as amended effective January 1, 1984; "Insured Accounts for Savers," pamphlet, Federal Reserve Bank of Richmond, April 1988; and *Federal Reserve Bulletin,* various issues.

profits, or achieve growth is called *liability management*. Although liability management arose primarily because large institutions wished to grow more quickly than traditional strategies allowed, it accelerated in the late 1960s because of constraints imposed by Regulation Q and the absence of interest-bearing demand deposits. Even without Reg Q, liability management is a vital part of the strategies of many institutions.[9]

HISTORY OF LIABILITY MANAGEMENT

Commercial banks ended World War II with about 75 percent of their assets in cash and T-bills; thus, it took considerable time—in fact, until the late 1950s—for them to run out of assets to liquidate to meet postwar loan demand. By the early 1960s, however, money-center banks needed additional loanable funds. The shortage of funds was exacerbated by improvements in corporate cash management, which caused large firms to reduce demand deposit balances to the bare minimum, investing surplus cash in T-bills and commercial paper.

Precipitating Events At this time First National City Bank of New York (now Citibank) developed the negotiable CD in response to changed customer preferences. Although large CDs had been sold by major banks before this time, the key to First National City's success was an agreement by securities dealers to create a secondary market, permitting corporations to invest in the CDs and yet maintain liquidity. The negotiable CD became a tool for keeping current depositors as well as attracting new ones, allowing a bank's loan portfolio to grow. Soon, other nondeposit funds were used for the same purposes. Large banks so actively sought cash in the financial markets, rather than by liquidating assets, that managed liabilities went from 0 percent of new funds at large banks in 1960 to almost 30 percent by 1974. In the 1970s, a few large savings institutions also began to use the technique.

Expanded Objectives Today liability management serves several purposes. It plays a role in managing the reserve position and in meeting loan demand.[10] It is also used by institutions to balance the maturity and interest rate sensitivity of liabilities with those of the asset portfolio, discussed earlier in the text. The first two motivations for liability management, the tools used to achieve them, and the risks and rewards are discussed in this section.

USING LIABILITIES TO COVER RESERVE DEFICIENCIES

One of the motivations for liability management is to maintain liquidity, an issue explored in Chapter 19 from the asset side of the balance sheet. As explained in that chapter, for many years depository institutions looked for liquidity solely in their asset portfolios. But that approach to liquidity management may not coincide with the risk/expected return preference of managers and owners, so institutions have increasingly turned to nontraditional deposits and other liabilities as sources

---

[9]For an early discussion of liability management, see Schweitzer (1974).
[10]See Kane (1979). Note these are the same reasons for liquidity identified in Chapter 19.

of liquidity.[11] If one categorizes funds as either discretionary or nondiscretionary, nontraditional deposits and other liabilities (along with short-term investment securities) are discretionary items. They can be actively used to adjust a depository's liquidity position.

The main categories of discretionary liabilities are the Fed's discount window and borrowings from other regulators; the Fed funds market; and the issuance of repurchase agreements, large CDs, liabilities collateralized by the institution's assets, and Eurodollar deposits. Borrowing from regulators is ordinarily used only to cover reserve deficiencies and not to expand assets; it is discussed in the sections on reserve position management in Chapter 19. Remaining tools of liability management are discussed in the following sections.[12]

Federal Funds Purchased   Unlike the discount window, regular use of which is discouraged by the Fed, the Fed funds market is used by many depositories, some on a daily basis. Fed funds play a main role in reserve requirement management.[13] As early as 1970, more than 60 percent of all member banks were reportedly involved.

Like discount-window borrowings, Fed funds are not considered deposits, so no reserves must be held against them. The lending institution instructs the Fed or its correspondent bank to transfer agreed-upon balances to the borrower instantaneously through Fedwire, the Fed's communication system. Because most fed funds transactions are **overnight loans**, the transaction is usually reversed the next day, including one day's interest calculated at the Fed funds rate. The yield on these transactions is illustrated in Chapter 14.

Because the Fed funds rate changes daily, a major problem with Fed funds as a regular source of financing is estimating the cost. This problem has escalated since late 1979, when the Federal Reserve Board began placing less emphasis on the Fed funds rate as a target of monetary policy. As shown in Figure 20.3 the Fed funds rate increased after 1979, and Fed funds have usually been more expensive than discount-window borrowings, although the spread between the two is not constant. When the differential becomes too great, institutions sometimes try to substitute one source of funds for the other, complicating the Fed's efforts to manage the discount window.

Fed funds are readily available, but the cost is difficult to forecast, as suggested by all panels of Figure 20.3. An institution borrowing fed funds and investing them in assets on which yields do not change daily increases potential variability in its net interest margin. For this reason, a relatively small market exists for **"term" Fed funds** transactions, with maturities of one week to six months, or sometimes even longer.

---

[11]For more discussion of the choice between asset liquidity and liability liquidity, see McKinney (1980).

[12]The following discussion relies on Stigum (1990); Brewer (1980); and Goodfriend and Whelpley (1986).

[13]Research on reserve position management has suggested that managers are risk-averse and borrow Fed funds early in a maintenance period to avoid emergency borrowing at the end. Thus, excess supplies may be accumulated by the end of a period, and the funds rate may be lower than at earlier points. For a review of this literature, see Wood and Wood (1985), Chapter 9.

Figure 20.3 ♦ THE FEDERAL FUNDS RATE VERSUS THE DISCOUNT RATE, 1930–1992 AND RECENT TRENDS

The fed funds rate is usually higher than the Federal Reserve discount rate, although the spread fluctuates. The fed funds rate became more volatile after 1979, increasing the complexity and riskiness of liability management.

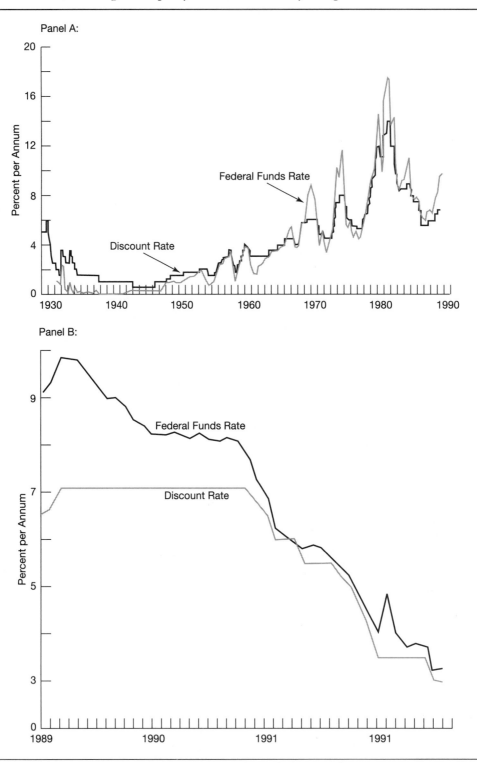

Source: Board of Governors of the Federal Reserve System, *1989 Historical Chart Book*, 98; *Federal Reserve Bulletin*, various issues.

Figure 20.3   ✦   THE FEDERAL FUNDS RATE VERSUS THE DISCOUNT RATE, 1930–1992 AND RECENT TRENDS (*CONTINUED*)

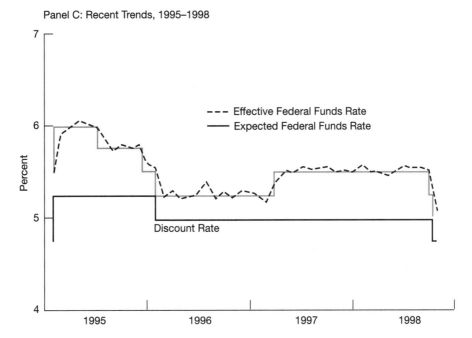

Panel C: Recent Trends, 1995–1998

Source: The Federal Reserve Bank of St. Louis Monetary Trends, December 1998, p. 3.

USING LIABILITIES TO MEET LOAN DEMAND OR PURSUE GROWTH

Institutions can also use liability management to obtain cash when a valued customer has an unplanned need to borrow or when a customer withdraws a large deposit unexpectedly. Customers who might disintermediate may be persuaded not to if the institution can offer an attractive alternative. An institution can also bid aggressively for funds in the financial markets to expand its size and customer base, even when disintermediation of existing customers is not a problem. The characteristics of discount-window borrowing and Fed funds make them inappropriate for these purposes, so alternative ways of raising funds have been developed.

Negotiable CDs   Negotiable CDs, called **jumbos** by thrifts, are large-denomination ($100,000 or greater) time deposits with a minimum maturity of seven days, for which there is a secondary market. They can be marketed aggressively when an institution needs cash. As noted, when first created, they helped stem the flow of corporate deposits from large banks and enabled the banks to meet new loan demand. But after the mid-1960s, because Reg Q ceilings were below market rates more often than not, negotiable CDs were not competitive with T-bills, and the loss of these deposits contributed to disintermediation at money-center banks. In a move sympathetic to large institutions, the Fed temporarily suspended ceilings on negotiable

CDs in 1970 and finally removed them altogether in 1973. Thus, for many years, they have been a tool for aggressive liability managers.

Most negotiable CDs are issued directly to customers, although some large institutions issue them to dealers, who then sell them to other investors. Dealer participation allows institutions to obtain funds with fewer delays. The high face value of the CDs means that the portion in excess of $100,000 is not federally insured. Consequently, institutions in financial difficulty find that this source of funds may increase in cost or even evaporate, a particular problem if CDs are habitually used to fund reserve deficiencies or are invested in long-term loans to customers.

Continental Illinois (now part of Nationsbank/BankAmerica), in 1984 among the 10 largest banks in the country, serves as an extreme example. In the spring of that year, the bank's financial problems surfaced as a result of large loan losses. Large CDs were almost 75 percent of its deposits worldwide, and depositors reacted quickly by withdrawing large volumes of these uninsured deposits. Only an unprecedented pledge by the FDIC to guarantee all deposits, regardless of size, stemmed the outflow. Continental was able to meet its daily liquidity requirements only through loans from the Fed and other large commercial banks. Although this experience is the exception, not the rule, it demonstrates that acquisition of liquidity or the pursuit of growth through liability management is riskier than storing liquidity in the asset portfolio or tailoring growth to traditional deposit flows.

In the 1990s, large corporate customers have been especially vigilant in their decisions about whether to purchase negotiable CDs from banks with high loan losses or weak capital positions, and some money-center banks have had to pay interest costs as much as a full percentage point higher than their stronger competitors. The FDICIA provisions mandate regulators to take prompt corrective action if a bank appears weak and to avoid following the severely criticized "too big to fail" policies of the 1980s. This leads many observers (including customers) to predict that some large banks may, in fact, be forced to close in the 2000s, potentially leaving uninsured deposits unprotected, unlike the Continental case. Thus, savvy corporate treasurers are sure to avoid the negotiable CDs of banks they believe are at risk.[14]

Eurodollar Deposits   Eurodollar deposits (**Eurodeposits**) are time deposits denominated in dollars but held in banks outside the United States, including foreign branches of U.S. banks. Eurodeposits are created in several ways, but the most straightforward is when a domestic customer transfers funds on deposit in the United States to a foreign bank or branch. The motivation is usually to obtain a higher rate of interest, and the depositor faces no currency exchange risk because the deposits remain in dollars. For many years, in fact, Eurodeposits were the only time deposits on which Reg Q ceilings were not binding, because they did not apply to funds held outside the United States.

Eurodeposits become a source of funds to domestic institutions when they borrow from foreign banks or branches, creating a liability reported on the domestic bank's balance sheet as "Due to Foreign Banks or Branches." Eurodeposits may range in maturity from as short as overnight to as long as five years, but most have

---

[14]See Willemse (1986); Furlong (1984); Jeff Bailey and G. Christian Hill. "Continental Illinois Gets Full U.S. Support." *The Wall Street Journal* (May 18, 1984), 3; Larry Light et al. "Taking from Weak Banks and Giving to the Rich." *Business Week* (February 4, 1991), 76–77; and Wall (1993).

maturities of six months or less. They are nonnegotiable, and all funds obtained through Eurodeposits are not currently subject to Fed reserve requirements.[15]

How Eurodollar Deposits Are Created   Figure 20.4 traces the creation of a typical Eurodeposit. If a large corporation such as General Motors (GM) wishes to withdraw funds from its domestic demand deposit account to earn interest, it may notify one of

---

Figure 20.4   ✦   CREATION OF A EURODOLLAR DEPOSIT

A Eurodollar deposit is created as a customer moves an account from a U.S. bank to a dollar-denominated deposit in a foreign branch of the bank. The bank exchanges a deposit account for a "due to" liability to its foreign branch. Required reserves are not affected.

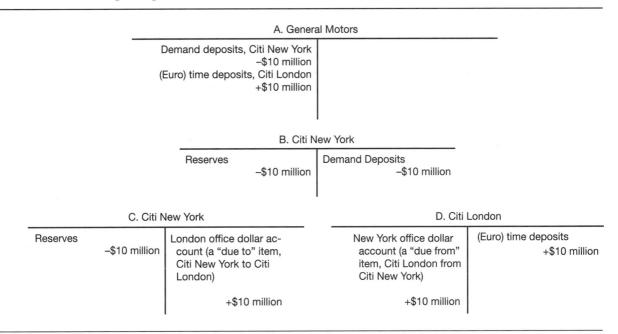

Source: Adapted from Marcia Stigum, *The Money Market*, 3d ed. (Homewood, Ill.; Dow Jones-Irwin, 1990), 201. Reprinted with permission.

Panel B: Rates in 1998 for Selected Fed Fund and Eurodollar Futures

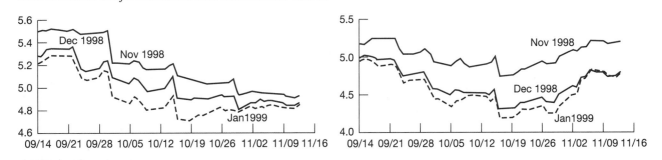

Source: The Federal Reserve Bank of St. Louis Monetary Trends, December 1998, p. 11.

---

[15]As noted in Chapter 5, there are also *negotiable* Eurodollar CDs, for which there is a secondary market centered in London. This market is relatively small, however, and few institutions are able to raise funds by issuing them. Nonnegotiable Eurodeposits, the subject of the current discussion, are much more common sources of funds to U.S. banks.

its New York banks—Citibank, for example. To avoid losing the funds, Citibank can encourage GM to make a Eurodollar deposit at a London branch, where the going rate of interest may be higher than on deposits of similar maturity in the United States (Panels A, B, and D). Citibank's London branch will then deposit the funds received in an account at its parent bank in New York (Panel C). The New York branch now has a "due to" liability on its books, and the London branch has a "due from" asset. By tradition, all transactions are carried out electronically over the **Clearing House Interbank Payments System (CHIPS)**, a privately owned funds transfer system in New York. GM keeps $10 million on deposit with Citibank (Panel A) and earns a competitive rate of return. Citibank not only retains the deposit but gains loanable funds, because there are no reserve requirements on "due to" liabilities.

Citibank could use the same approach to obtain GM's business from a competing bank. If GM had demand deposits in Chemical Bank, for example, Citibank might offer to pay a relatively high rate of return on Eurodollar deposits in its London branch. If GM withdrew its funds from Chemical to hold a Eurodeposit in Citibank's London office, the London branch would again show a "due from" asset in the amount of the deposit, and Citibank New York would show a "due to" liability.

An important point about both examples is that *at no time does a Eurodeposit actually leave the home country*. Funds that start out in the United States end up there as well. Eurodeposits are really nothing more than a series of accounting entries, resulting in the customer's holding a time deposit and the domestic bank's incurring a liability.

Cost of Eurodeposits   The costs of Eurodollar liabilities and alternative sources of funds are very closely related. For example, overnight Eurodollars often (but not always) cost slightly more than Fed funds. A larger difference exists between three-month Eurodollar deposits and domestic CDs with similar maturities. Because most Eurodeposits are held by U.S. investors, a premium is demanded as protection against the lack of deposit insurance and against country risk, or potential loss caused by unanticipated problems in a foreign country. A depository must weigh the additional costs of Eurodollars against the benefits, such as the potential for growth, the absence of reserve requirements, and the fact that no deposit insurance premiums are paid on them. Eurocurrency futures and Fed Fund Futures are traded on major on future exchanges, as well, as shown in Panel B of Figure 20.4.[16]

Repurchase Agreements   Repurchase agreements (repos), explained in earlier chapters, are another tool of liability management. Repos are the "sale" of marketable securities by an institution, with an agreement to repurchase at a specified future date. The seller obtains use of cash for other purposes. Buyers are seeking liquid, short-term investments as an alternative to nonearning demand deposits; they consider the transactions "reverse repos."

The depository institution secures the funds obtained by pledging some of its own investment securities as collateral. As long as securities pledged against repos are U.S. government or government agency securities, repos are not subject to re-

---

[16]It is difficult to assess the riskiness of Eurodeposits versus domestic deposits accurately. The elements of risk previously discussed are given from the viewpoint of an American deposit holder. An Iranian, in contrast, might consider Eurodeposits less risky than dollar-denominated deposits in a bank in the United States. For more discussion of the problems involved in evaluating Eurodollar risk, see Goodfriend (1986).

serve requirements. The cost of issuing repos is ordinarily lower than the rate paid on similar maturities in the Fed funds or negotiable CD markets. Because repos are backed by high-quality securities, default risk is lower. If the investor insists that the institution transfer the collateral elsewhere for safe keeping, the rate paid on the repo may be even lower, because of the increased cost to the depository and lower risk to the investor.

Repo maturities range from overnight to 30 days or longer. Transactions can occur between institutions and individuals, in which case they are called "retail repos," or between financial institutions. Because they involve collateral, they are not considered deposits and are therefore ineligible for deposit insurance. This lowers the cost to the issuing institution.

Mortgage-Backed Bonds[17]   The growth of the repo market in recent years has encouraged depository institutions to envision other ways to use existing assets as collateral to obtain new funds. For mortgage lenders, using mortgages to back new securities is a logical step. They enable an institution to raise funds for new mortgage loans at current rates without having to sell existing mortgages, which may have declined in value. Among the most popular of the securities are **mortgage-backed bonds**, mentioned in Chapter 19. A mortgage-backed bond is the debt obligation of an institution backed by expected cash flows from its general mortgage portfolio. Because mortgages are high-quality collateral, institutions issuing mortgage-backed securities often do so at only a slight premium over the Treasury bond (T-bond) rate. Initially, only fixed-rate mortgages were believed to be suitable collateral. By 1985, however, standardization of adjustable-rate mortgages (ARMs) and increasing familiarity with mortgage-backed securities encouraged issuance of ARM-backed securities. This development is important to mortgage lenders, who can use ARMs to shorten the interest sensitivity of asset portfolios while retaining access to the mortgage-backed bond market as a source of nondeposit funds.

Because of administrative and flotation costs, mortgage-backed bonds are usually issued with minimum face values of $100 million. To make it easier for small depositories to use mortgage-backed securities, methods have been developed by which several firms working together can pool collateral and issue bonds. Pooling has increased the participation of small thrift institutions in this form of liability management.[18]

Deposit Notes and Bank Notes   Two of the newer instruments of liability management appeared in the mid-1980s, when several large depositories began issuing **deposit notes** and **bank notes**. Both these instruments are medium-term sources of funds (maturities ranging from two to five years) and are designed to appeal to investors with particular risk/return preferences. Deposit notes are similar to negotiable CDs, in that an investor receives deposit insurance protection up to $100,000.

---

[17]Information in this section was obtained from *Freddie Mac Reports*, various issues. Their primary risk is that of early prepayment of underlying mortgages if interest rates fall after the bonds are issued.

[18]Another type of mortgage-backed security, the pass-through, is also one on which borrowers' monthly payments on a package of mortgages are passed directly each month to the mortgage-backed security holder. These and CMOs are discussed in more detail in Chapter 19. See Puglisi and McKenzie (1983).

Unlike CDs, however, deposit notes are evaluated by rating agencies and are often accompanied by a brief circular describing the financial condition of the issuing institution. Although they are not negotiable, the existence of a formal rating for the notes makes them attractive to some investors, such as insurance companies, which ordinarily do not (or cannot in some states) own unrated securities. As a result of costs associated with the rating process, deposit notes carry lower interest rates than negotiable CDs issued by the same institution.

Bank notes are similar to deposit notes, in that they carry agency ratings, but they differ in that they are completely uninsured and can be traded in secondary markets. The lack of insurance means that they pay a higher interest rate than deposit notes issued by the same institution. The additional interest cost is offset, however, by the fact that the issuer need not pay deposit insurance premiums on its notes. Bank notes came into the spotlight in 1988 when the FDIC briefly considered extending deposit insurance to them; the proposal was criticized by bankers as being solely motivated by the agency's need to raise new resources. Bank notes, particularly those issued by thrifts, have also been controversial in that some critics fear that unwitting investors may purchase them under the assumption that they are covered by deposit insurance. Issuing institutions counter the criticism by pointing out that the notes are marketed primarily to sophisticated investors investing large sums.[19]

FACTORS INFLUENCING THE USE OF LIABILITY MANAGEMENT

Confidence-sensitive money is any source of funds sensitive to a loss of confidence either in a particular institution or in the banking system in general. Many tools of liability management are confidence-sensitive. Further, even when an institution is not the object of a loss of confidence, major investors in the instruments of liability management are willing to move funds from one institution to another to gain a few basis points. Funds that move quickly in response to yield differences are often called **hot money** or **money at a price**.[20] Institutions relying heavily on either confidence-sensitive or hot money adopt an aggressive strategy; as financial conditions change, they can lose access to those funds. In contrast, managers who prefer to rely on their own resources for immediate liquidity needs and "store" those resources in the asset portfolio are adopting a more conservative stance, as are those institutions that plan their asset growth at the same pace as expected growth in deposits and net worth. Several factors are associated with a depository's choice between these management styles.

Size and Industry Membership   The smaller an institution, the less likely that it will issue large CDs, repurchase agreements, or Eurodollar liabilities, simply because it lacks a large enough capital base or securities portfolio to support those operations. Also, the customers may be individuals or small local businesses lacking the funds to make these investments. Further, access to the Eurodollar markets is diffi-

---

[19]See Harless (1984); "Statement of Robert L. Clarke, Comptroller of the Currency, Before the House Subcommittee on General Oversight and Investigations of the Committee on Banking, Finance, and Urban Affairs," *Quarterly Journal*, Office of the Comptroller of the Currency 8 (September 1989): 32–36; "Conference Report on HR 1278," 1989; Moore (1991); and *FDIC Annual Report* (1991).

[20]See Stigum (1990), Chapter 24.

cult for non-money center banks or for those without foreign branches. Thus, liability management continues to remain in the realm of very large commercial banks and a few savings institutions.

In the past, thrifts using liability management have issued large-denomination CDs through New York dealers, but the volume is small. Recently, thrifts have also increased their use of mortgage-backed bonds. Credit unions, with the common-bond requirement, are greatly restricted in the use of liability management tools. They can use repurchase agreements, Fed funds, or borrowings from federal regulators, and some have done so. But because one of their objectives is to offer relatively low loan rates to members, credit unions' aggressive use of high-cost nonshare sources of funds is not great.

Financial Strength   The firm's financial position affects its access to uninsured liabilities. When an institution issues liabilities beyond the protective umbrella of federal insurance, all fund suppliers assess their exposure to default risk. Increasing depository failure rates have made prospective investors and uninsured depositors more cautious. When an institution's financial performance deteriorates, investors require a larger risk premium, and they may eventually withdraw all funds regardless of the premium the institution is willing to pay. In 1984, the nation's largest thrift institution, American Savings (a subsidiary of Financial Corporation) faced just such a scenario; uninsured depositors withdrew substantial sums when its financial condition worsened. The chief executive officer, architect of American's aggressive liability management strategy, was forced to resign. American eventually became hopelessly insolvent and was the object of a controversial bailout in December 1988. American is one of many such stories in the 1980s.

NONINTEREST COMPETITION AMONG DEPOSITORIES

New deposit instruments and liability management are not the only consequences of historical restrictions on deposit taking. Both Reg Q and the prohibition of interest on demand deposits led to the use of **implicit interest payments**, or services provided to depositors in lieu of explicit interest, as discussed in Chapter 3. Implicit interest payments continue today when managers want to attract funds but do not want to raise explicit rates. Over the years, implicit interest has ranged from pots and pans for new account holders to opening branch offices or drive-through windows to increase convenience. Depositories also offer a wide range of account-related services such as free checking, automatic transfer of funds from savings to checking, preauthorized bill payments, automatic payroll deposits, or preferential treatment on loans.

ECONOMIC EFFICIENCY OF NONINTEREST COMPETITION

An important question for individual institutions and for the financial system as a whole is whether implicit interest payments benefit financial market participants. Most experts conclude that they do not.

The Institution's Point of View   Before the removal of Reg Q, small depositories in particular argued that they could not afford to pay market rates on so-called **core deposits**—transactions accounts, passbook savings, and small consumer CDs.

Research indicates, however, that savings in explicit interest costs under Reg Q did not result in increased profits; rather, they were redirected toward increased operating expenses. Estimates of implicit annual interest rates paid to demand depositors through the provision of services range from less than 1 percent in 1954 to nearly 5 percent in the late 1960s.[21]

It is easy to see how these costs arise. Suppose a bank offers "free" checking to demand deposit customers, who then have no economic incentive to restrict the number of checks they write. To the extent that the institution's resources are tied to check processing rather than to income-producing activities, the cost of providing services to depositors may equal or even exceed what the bank saves by not paying interest on the deposits. Of course, if profits are significantly less variable as a result of implicit rather than explicit interest, institutions may benefit despite higher operating expenses. Evidence indicates, however, that explicit interest costs are unrelated to systematic risk and negatively related to total risk for banks, implying that institutions would not be more risky if they used explicit versus implicit payments.[22]

Some implicit interest payments, such as building additional branches or hiring additional staff, are analogous to fixed costs in industrial firms. Although the analogy is not perfect, it is useful for examining why implicit interest payments may be financially undesirable for a depository. The costs of operating a branch or employing a new staff member are harder to adjust downward with revenue decreases than are explicit interest payments. As students of corporate financial management know, a high level of fixed costs in a firm means a high **degree of operating leverage (DOL)**. The DOL is defined as the percentage change in operating profits resulting from a 1 percent change in total revenues (TR):

$$DOL_{TR} = \frac{\% \, \Delta \text{ Operating Income}}{\% \, \Delta \text{ Revenues}}$$

A degree of operating leverage of 3, for example, means that each 1 percent change in revenues, up or down, is expected to result in a 3 percent change in operating income in the same direction.

DOL is a function of the variable-cost versus fixed-cost structure of a firm at its current level of revenue, calculated as follows[23]:

$$DOL_{TR} = \frac{TR - VC}{TR\text{-}VC\text{-}FC} \qquad [20.1]$$

where TR = total revenues
VC = total variable costs
FC = total fixed costs

The higher the level of fixed costs, the higher the degree of operating leverage. The higher the degree of operating leverage, the greater the variation in operating income as revenue varies. In a depository institution, total revenues vary as the general level of interest rates or the term structure changes. It follows that a higher level of implicit interest payments, which are usually fixed costs, results in greater varia-

[21]White (1976); Taggart (1978); and Dotsey (1983).
[22]This research is examined in Benston (1984).
[23]The derivation and assumptions underlying Equation 20.1 can be found in Brigham (1992), Chapter 11, and in other finance texts.

tion in the operating income of a depository than if the institution paid more in explicit interest, a variable cost.

The Customer's Point of View   The use of implicit rather than explicit interest may not benefit depositors. For instance, an individual may not want a new toaster from a bank, preferring to earn the equivalent amount in cash. Many economists also argue that interest rate controls, which force implicit interest competition, increase loan rates at depositories. Without rate controls, the quantity of deposits should increase, increasing the availability of loanable funds and simultaneously reducing wasteful implicit interest costs. The result should be lower, not higher, lending rates.[24]

There are reasons, however, why some customers prefer implicit to explicit interest. Implicit interest is not taxed, whereas for most recipients, explicit interest is. For instance, the higher the personal tax bracket, the more likely this is to be true; thus, high tax bracket customers simply prefer some services or gifts. This argument suggests that even if interest were paid on demand deposits, some forms of implicit interest would remain.

Implicit Interest Still Offered   Despite being able to offer market rates after Reg Q, with low interest rates in the 1990s banks have continued to offer implicit interest. For example, a bank in Boulder, Colorado, offers costly implicit interest benefits, including hunting rifles, and at times has offered VCRs, and Rolex watches, to customers opening new CDs. Some banks use a combination of explicit interest at the market rate *and* premiums such as jewelry and rare coins. Several banks have offered their premiums through a marketing technique rarely used in depository institutions: coupon offers. Prospective customers receive coupon booklets in the mail; they redeem the coupons when opening a new deposit account, and the free gifts are sent directly to their homes.[25]

Despite this array of creative implicit interest schemes, other institutions compete solely with explicit interest, offering above-market rates to keep depositors from disintermediating. For example, in times of extremely low interest rates, such as the early 1990s, some institutions have offered multiple-year CDs on which yields are guaranteed to increase every three or six months. Similarly with a booming stock market, **linked CDs** were created that offer a guaranteed return of principal (and, of course, FDIC insurance on the first $100,000 of that principal), plus the possibility of appreciation based on the increase in the value of the S&P 500 during the term of the deposit. Institutions offering these CDs protect themselves against the potentially higher costs of these products by hedging in the index options market. The wide variety of competitive strategies illustrated in this section is likely to continue, as there appear to be clienteles for many explicit-implicit interest combinations.[26]

Increased Use of Deposit Service Charges   Another recent development is the imposition of deposit service charges where none existed or the increase in charges at

---

[24]See Friedman (1970) and Keeley (1984) for arguments in support of benefits of explicit interest.

[25]See Zimmerman and Keeley (1986) and Mahoney (1988).

[26]Georgette Jasen. "This Bank Uses Hunting Rifles, Shotguns as It Targets Depositors." *The Wall Street Journal* (February 15, 1989), C1, C10; Zimmerman and Neuberger (1990); William Glasgall. "Souped-up Certificates of Deposit." *Business Week* (August 3, 1992), 55; Cohn and Edleson (1993).

institutions that had previously had them. At many institutions, customers with high balances are given "free" checking and other implicit interest benefits. Customers with lower minimum balance accounts are charged explicitly for each deposit or withdrawal and in some cases for simply using a teller. A study conducted for the House Banking Committee estimated that the average U.S. household faced an increase of 104 percent in the cost of basic banking services from 1979 to 1983—from $91.94 per year to $187.59. A study by economists at the Federal Reserve Board concluded that the overall profitability of personal checking accounts did not increase, however, and that banks were simply charging fees necessary to cover their costs.[27]

Because new pricing systems permit those with high balances to receive free or low-cost banking services, they are consistent with the idea that wealthy customers benefit from the nontaxable implicit interest.

Lifeline Banking   Concern has been raised about the ability of low-income households to afford services formerly offered as a substitute for market interest rates. Many consumer groups have called for **basic** (or **lifeline**) **banking** legislation at the federal level, requiring that depositories offer a minimum level of financial services to households at low or even no cost. "Basic banking" is generally considered to include the right to a checking account with a low minimum balance requirement and a limited number of free checks per month. Data from the Fed suggest that almost 50 percent of financial institutions had no-frills service packages as early as 1988 and that the proportion of households without checking accounts has not increased despite deregulation. Although regulators have opposed making lifeline banking compulsory for banks if it could not be offered at least on a break-even basis, the U.S. government decided that that welfare-related payments would only be transmitted electronically in 1998, and banks were asked to provide lifeline banking accounts for recipients.[28]

Costs as Policing Agent for Depositors   Legislation has also mandated in the 1990s that banks help the government in its money-laundering enforcement efforts. Under the Bank Secrecy Act, banks must report cash transactions, including cash deposits, of $10,000 or more and give collecting information on the customers making this transaction. A "Know Your Customer" proposal by the Fed in November 1998 requires bankers to know their customers using a "top to bottom" approach, which includes the following: (1) establishing the true identity of customers including beneficial owners of accounts; (2) determining the customer's source of funds; (3) determining the customer's normal and expected transactions, (4) monitoring transactions to determine whether they are consistent with the expected customer profile; (5) identifying those transactions that fall outside the expected profile; and (6) investigating and determining whether a transaction is unusual or suspicious and requires the filing of a Suspicious Activity Report (SAR). Although banks on a more informal basis have been asked to have "know your customer" policies, the proposed rules re-

---

[27]Daniel Hertzberg. "Smaller Customers Get Less Service at Banks and Pay More Charges," *The Wall Street Journal*, October 18, 1984, 16; and Glenn B. Canner and Robert D. Kurtz, "Service Charges as a Source of Bank Income and Their Impact on Consumers," Federal Reserve Board Staff Study No. 145, August 1985.

[28]See Canner and Maland (1987); Board of Governors (1988), 157; Scott (1988); and Robert Trigaux. "Right or Wrong, 'Lifeline' Battle Looms for Banks." *American Banker* (February 1, 1990), 1, 8.

quiring more formal standards can be costly. In response to the Federal Reserve Board's proposal, thousands of consumers complained of violations of personal privacy issues. Consequently, the Fed's formal proposal will not be implemented. Banks in addition are also often called upon to find and microfilm checks for accounts involved in lawsuits, including SEC investigations, at their own cost, which can be significant, particularly for small banks.[29]

ACQUISITION OF FUNDS IN A DEREGULATED ENVIRONMENT

The managers of depository institutions are faced with a complex set of decisions when planning how to raise and retain funds. Although no single, comprehensive model is available for a mechanical analysis of these problems, certain issues must be considered systematically. They can be classified into three categories:

1. The broad choice between wholesale and retail funds sources;
2. The balance between deposit and nondeposit liabilities and the mix of deposit sources; and
3. The costs and pricing of accounts and services.

WHOLESALE VERSUS RETAIL FUNDS

The first major decision is whether to seek wholesale or retail funds. **Wholesale funds** are those provided by nonfinancial businesses and other financial institutions; **retail funds** are provided by households. This decision is part of strategic planning, because it determines many operating policies thereafter. Managers must evaluate several points in making the decision; these points are discussed in the following sections.

Availability   Chapter 14 notes that only the household sector is a net supplier of funds and that businesses and governments are net borrowers. Thus, in the financial system as a whole, more retail funds are available than wholesale funds, and few depository institutions can afford to ignore the retail market altogether. Still, in some areas—midtown Manhattan, for example—wholesale funds may be more plentiful. In 1980, Bankers Trust of New York, one of the nation's 10 largest banks, abandoned retail business completely by selling the few branches it operated. The bank already had a solid base of corporate customers, and its prime New York location positioned it well to pursue additional wholesale funds. Continental Illinois embarked on a similar strategy in 1988; more than $600 million in retail accounts were sold to the First National Bank of Chicago. These strategic steps away from retail banking reflect the conclusion that the long-run benefits were greater in the wholesale markets.

The discussion of liability management noted other factors that influence an institution's decision to use nontraditional funds sources: size, industry membership, and financial condition. Because the tools of liability management are largely wholesale, those characteristics also play a role in a depository's strategic choice between wholesale and retail funds. Yet even large banks on solid financial ground do

---

[29]See Carol M. Beaumier, "Industry Awaits New 'Know Your Customer' Rules from the Regulators." *Banking Policy Report* 17 (November 30, 1998), 5–6.

not always depend solely on wholesale funds just because they can get them. Citibank, for example, with its extensive branch network, continues its commitment to retail banking by expanding credit card operations and other consumer services. The choice between wholesale and retail funds affects the entire range of products and services offered.

Funds Volatility   Retail and wholesale funds can both be volatile, but wholesale funds ineligible for deposit insurance are especially rate- and confidence-sensitive, as the cases of Continental Illinois and American Savings indicate. Institutions relying heavily on wholesale funds must be prepared to bid aggressively to keep them when rates increase and to have alternative funds sources in case of emergencies.

In contrast, retail deposits may involve commitments to depositories on the part of the consumer. Households choose institutions based not only on their rates and reputations but also their locations and convenience. Although consumers did not hesitate to switch to other forms of investment in the mid to late 1970s, they returned to depositories quickly when given a reasonable opportunity to do so in 1982. MMDAs gained market share quickly, even though MMDA yields were below money fund rates from 1983 through early 1985. Fed surveys of households' financial preferences continue to substantiate the significance of convenience and physical proximity to consumers when they establish their banking relationships. Once they choose, consumers are also reasonably loyal. For example, one survey reported that more than 40 percent of households with interest-bearing checking accounts said they would not move an account to an equally convenient depository on the basis of interest rate differentials. Another 30 percent said that only a rate differential of at least 2 percent would induce them to move.[30]

Cost   Many managers argue that the cost of retail funds is higher because retail banking requires a branch network and/or a large staff, but the pursuit of wholesale funds is also costly. For small institutions, or for thrifts only recently involved with commercial customers, the cost of locating sources of corporate and institutional money can be substantial. Some depositories have turned to brokers, but they lack loyalty to individual institutions and are willing to move funds to capture small interest rate differentials.

Anticipated Uses of Funds   For many institutions, the decision to pursue particular types of liabilities depends on planned uses of the funds. For instance, it is risky to make 10-year mortgage loans if they are funded by hot money in times of rising rates. Conversely, if funds are needed temporarily to meet a shortfall of required reserves, raising the money through retail CDs would be inappropriate. Further, if the planned use of funds is commercial loans, management may wish to develop a customer base by first obtaining wholesale deposits. If consumer credit is the desired investment, it may be appropriate to seek retail deposits.

---

[30]Mark Flannery has argued that retail deposits can be considered quasi-fixed sources of funds, because the depositor is required to incur both search and setup costs when choosing an individual institution. Still, there is likely to be some threshold yield on alternate investments that will cause the depositor to switch to another institution, even though additional costs will be incurred. See Flannery (1982b). See also Elliehausen and Wolken (1992) on the importance of local deposit relationships to households.

MIX OF FUND SOURCES

Beyond the choice between deposit and nondeposit liabilities, which has been explored in earlier sections, many decisions remain regarding the mix of deposit accounts. In the past, the rule of thumb for choosing the deposit mix was relatively simple: Attract as many core (checking) deposits as possible, because they were relatively cheap, plentiful, and uncomplicated. Competition was limited by Reg Q and restrictions on geographic expansion, and core deposit inflows were based on convenience and location. The environment has changed significantly, however, and now the cost of core deposits and the sensitivity of their costs in a changing interest rate environment must be compared with other sources of funds. For example, when the cost of reserve requirements is considered, an MMDA paying higher explicit interest may actually be less costly than a demand deposit or a NOW account.

Further, the variety of deposit types available to institutions continues to grow. For example, in 1990, the Federal Reserve Board began allowing U.S. banks to accept deposits denominated in foreign currencies, opening the door to a new category of customers involved in international transactions and investments. Several banks have since offered new types of foreign currency-denominated CDs. Institutions must also evaluate the maturity and stability of different deposit categories, and the choice among account alternatives may reflect an institution's strategy for marketing other financial services to depositors as well.

PRICING

Pricing deposit accounts involves four separate but related analyses: the explicit interest rate to be offered, the costs incurred in servicing each account, the division of costs between explicit and implicit interest, and the effect of one deposit account's price on customer acceptance of other accounts and services. After the pricing decision is made, institutions must provide clear explanations to customers. Target levels for different sources of funds are unlikely to be realized unless effective pricing strategies are used to achieve them.

Setting Explicit Interest Rates   Most depository institution managers had little experience in setting rates to attract funds before 1980. The negotiable CD, Fed funds, and Eurodollar markets are national or international in scope, so even managers practicing liability management faced limited discretion in rate setting. Today, managers of all depositories are required to use judgment. One course of action is simply to follow the crowd—to establish interest rates similar to those offered by key competitors, especially ones viewed as market leaders. For many years, some depositories have used this strategy to establish loan rates, and some studies find evidence of smaller institutions following rate changes of very large institutions within metropolitan areas in the mid 1980s. However, in the late 1980s and the 1990s, there is increasing evidence of expanding geographic retail banking markets.[31]

---

[31]See Lawrence J. Radecki. "The Expanding Geographic Reach of Retail Banking Markets." *Federal Reserve Bank of New York Policy Review* 4 (June 1998), 15–34; Elizabeth S. Cooperman, Winson B. Lee, and James P. Lesage. "Geographical Integration and the Retail CD-Pricing Decisions of Large Depository Institutions." *The Review of Economics and Statistics* 73 (August 1991), 546–552; and "Commercial Bank and Thrift Interdependence and Local Market Competition for Retail Certificates of Deposit." *Journal of Financial Services Research* 4 (March 1990), 37–51.

Many institutions appear to take more control over the explicit prices paid for deposits. A study of retail deposit pricing between 1983 and 1985, conducted by researchers at the Board of Governors, finds a number of differences in account pricing patterns among depositories. At that time, thrifts tended to pay higher prices than banks for every category of deposits (although the difference declined markedly by the end of the decade). But within each industry, banks and thrifts seldom followed the crowd all the time. An individual institution would often raise or lower rates relative to its market competitors. Further, as market rates rose or fell, not all institutions adjusted rates equally quickly or in the same magnitude.

Further study substantiates that depository institutions' pricing decisions are more than imitation. Researchers at the New York Fed interviewed bankers in that Federal Reserve District in 1986 and 1987 and found that they took an aggressive approach to pricing consumer deposits. An important factor the bankers considered was the cost of alternative sources of wholesale funds; the rates set by competitors were less influential. Managers were also concerned about the degree to which customers would respond to changes in interest rates, and they gathered data to estimate depositors' sensitivity to pricing decisions.

For example, by collecting data on account balances over time, managers can use statistical techniques such as regression analysis to study the relationship of deposits to many factors, including past interest rates, rates paid by competitors, or rates available on alternative investments. With the increasing accessibility of microcomputers and statistical software, all depositories can use quantitative models to improve deposit pricing, and many do.

Withdrawal penalties for time deposits must be priced as well. A recent study finds that the bank CD-Treasury rate spreads for 100 large commercial banks from June 1990 to May 1997 were negative, averaging 41 basis points, suggesting that depositors accept lower yields on CDs in return for their withdrawal option.[32]

Costs Incurred for Specific Account-Related Services   Fee-based services, whether specifically related to deposits or offered as supplements to traditional depository services, have become so important that Chapter 9 is entirely devoted to them. Deposit account pricing now also involves identifying prices for each type of service formerly included in a deposit-related package. Pricing theorists refer to this development as the **unbundling** of services.

Ideally, prices should be related to the costs incurred by the institution, so cost analysis has begun to attract more attention. The Fed provides a functional cost analysis (FCA) service, through which it calculates the unit costs of key services for institutions providing the necessary data. Some depositories also seek other sources of cost data, such as Sheshunoff. Many have recently instituted cost accounting sys-

---

[32]See Mahoney et al. (1987). The bankers' survey is reported in Davis, Korobow, and Wenninger (1986–87). Quantitative analyses of the interest rate sensitivity of deposits are illustrated by Murphy and Kraas (1984), who used weekly deposit data from a small bank. Two researchers at the Federal Reserve Bank of Atlanta used a similar approach to assess the rate sensitivity of MMDA balances and concluded that longer-term rather than weekly data were more useful. See Wall and Ford (1984). For a study of CD withdrawal options, see James. H. Gilkeson, John A. List, and Craig K. Ruff. "The Impact of the Early Withdrawal Option on Time Deposit Pricing," forthcoming, *Quarterly Review of Economics and Finance*, 1999.

tems and use the data to price products. Trade groups in each industry have been active in assisting small institutions with cost accounting problems.

Besides estimating the cost of providing a service, some institutions estimate the value of that service to customers. If the cost of providing it exceeds the value to the recipient, the service is eliminated. For example, preauthorized bill payment services are offered by some depositories as part of a transactions account package. Through this service, a depository automatically transfers funds from a customer's account to pay regular household expenditures such as insurance and utilities. The value of this service to a customer is unlikely to exceed the sum of the costs of a stamp, an envelope, and the time necessary to write and record a check, probably no more than $0.40 to $0.50 for most persons. If the institution can provide the service and make a profit for less than that, both parties will benefit. If not, the service is not worth its cost.[33]

Estimating the Marginal Cost of a Deposit Account   After determining the interest and servicing costs of each type of deposit account, managers must consider additional costs imposed by regulation. One model widely cited in the academic and practitioner literature estimates the marginal interest and noninterest costs of an additional deposit dollar (MCD) as follows[34]:

$$MCD = \frac{I + S + DI}{(1 - RR)} \qquad [20.2]$$

where

I = current market interest rate on type of deposit;
S = servicing costs of deposits expressed as percentage of each dollar acquired
DI = deposit insurance premium (expressed as percentage of each insured dollar)
RR = Fed reserve requirement on type of deposit

Suppose an institution's managers have decided to pursue a retail banking strategy. They have determined that the current market interest rate on NOW accounts is 6.5 percent and the cost of servicing a basic NOW account is 3.4 percent (including unlimited transactions and the use of a teller window). Also, Fed reserve requirements on transactions accounts are 10 percent, and the deposit insurance premium is 0.254 percent. Using Equation 20.2, the marginal cost of offering a NOW account in this interest rate and regulatory environment is as follows:

$$MCNOW = \frac{.065 + .034 + .00254}{(1 - .10)} = .1128 \text{ or } 11.28\%$$

A similar analysis can be performed for each fund source customarily used by the institution, and a weighted average of these costs can also be estimated (i.e., the sum of each marginal cost × the fraction of funds used as a percentage of total financing). The weighted marginal average cost of deposits and other liabilities is one of the main determinants of required lending rates. Marginal costs are also used in deciding how to price accounts to attract the quantity of desired deposits from target customer segments.

---

[33]See Gardner and Lammers (1988) and Logue (1983).
[34]See Watson (1977) and Watson (1978).

Explicit versus Implicit Pricing   Since some customers may prefer implicit pricing or a combination of explicit and implicit price, two general explicit-implicit pricing strategies have been suggested. One is based on the New England experience with NOW accounts in the 1970s. A **conditionally free account** is, as the name implies, one for which no service charges are imposed under certain conditions—usually, that the depositor keeps a specified minimum balance in the account. If the balance falls below the minimum, a service charge is imposed as a flat fee, a price per service rendered, or both. The customer determines the mix of implicit and explicit interest by the way the account is managed.

An alternative to the conditionally free account is the **interest buydown account**. With this approach, each service associated with an account is priced on a markdown basis from the explicit interest rate. Table 20.4 illustrates such a strategy. Suppose that using data from the previous section, management sets the explicit interest rate on a NOW account at 6.5 percent. Also, suppose that the services listed in Table 20.4 are available to account holders, although the basic NOW account includes only two: unlimited transactions, and the use of a teller window. With the interest buydown pricing strategy, the customer selects the desired additional services in exchange for a lower explicit rate of interest. Should the customers wish to use services not initially "bought," fees can be charged as services are used. In this exam-

---

Table 20.4 ✦ THE INTEREST BUYDOWN PRICING STRATEGY

As institutions emphasize explicit pricing strategies, customers may be offered the opportunity to exchange explicit interest on deposit accounts for "free" services that would otherwise carry an explicit fee.

Service	Cost (%)	Desired by Customer
Unlimited transactions	2.90%	Included
Use of automatic teller machines	0.50	Yes
Use of teller window	0.50	Included
Free travelers checks	0.50	No
Free safe deposit box	0.50	No
Preauthorized bill payments for:		
Mortgage	0.50	Yes
Car	0.50	No
Insurance	0.50	No
Credit life insurance for:		
Mortgage	1.00	Yes
Car	1.00	No
Personal computer linkage with:		
Stock market data	1.50	No
Bond market data	1.50	Yes

Base explicit interest rate: 6.5%
Total cost of "bought" services: 3.5%
Explicit interest rate: 3%

Source: Adapted from Elmer 1985.

ple, the explicit interest is bought down to 3 percent, because the account holder has selected services considered equivalent to a 3.5 percent annual return.[35]

Pricing and Customer Relationships   A final consideration in deposit pricing is the potential effect of one pricing decision on a customer's acceptance of other services or accounts. Many institutions now consider their total relationship with a customer when setting prices on accounts customers view as important in the selection of a primary financial institution. For example, some banks have recognized that higher fee structures for demand deposits alienated many younger customers, who turned to credit unions or thrifts for their transactions account services. Because this customer group also constitutes an important segment of the demand for other financial services, such as consumer loans, that demand also moved to credit unions and thrifts.

Some institutions have revised pricing structures for basic checking account services to reestablish relationships with an important market segment. Some depositories have introduced **tiered pricing systems**, recognizing that wealthier customers may be more rate-sensitive than customers with lower incomes. Tiered systems offer higher explicit rates as a customer's balance increases beyond a threshold level. For example, one rate may be paid on NOW balances less than $500, and successively higher rates may be offered as the account balance exceeds $1,000, $5,000, and so forth. Alternatively, using the example in Table 20.4, a high-balance customer might be given access to free travelers' checks and personal computer linkage to stock market data with no reduction in the base explicit interest rate of 6.5 percent. The institution would set this price assuming the customer might use other income-generating services, such as borrowing money or trust department services.

Other strategies include packaging financial accounts, or cross-selling different financial services. For example, when a customer accepts a core service such as a checking account or a loan, he or she is also offered access to another group of financial services, such as preapproved credit cards or an MMDA. A third tier of value-added services, such as credit card protection, free checks, or combined monthly statements, can also be made available to the new customer. Presumably, the value of the available services will be recognized even if they are never actually used.[36] The challenge for financial institution managers is to evaluate the costs of each service individually (as with unbundled strategies) so that appropriate and profitable terms can be offered when the financial services are packaged and offered to customers.

DISCLOSURE REQUIREMENTS: TRUTH IN SAVINGS

Managers must carefully communicate the results of pricing decisions to customers, declaring the annual percentage rate, as required under FIRREA, which became effective in 1993. The Fed's truth-in-savings rules stipulate that depositories must

---

[35]Further discussion of pricing strategies is provided in Rogowski (1984); Elmer (1985); and Parliment (1985).

[36]For further discussion, see Terrence P. Paré. "Banks Discover the Consumer." *Fortune* (February 12, 1990), 96–104; Cook (1989); "Checking Accounts Build the Base for Retail Banking." *Savings Institutions* 109 (June 1988): 118–119; and "Financial Service Packages Continue to Draw Interest." *Savings Institutions* 108 (December 1987): 142–143.

uniformly publish the fees, service charges, and annual yields associated with each account, to promote intelligent shopping for financial services among consumers. Key provisions include a prohibition against advertising accounts as "free" if they contain any conditions, such as a minimum account balance, that might cost the customer if the conditions were violated. The **annual percentage yield (APY)** on accounts must be disclosed, including the effect of service charges and fees. In its simplest form, the APY on deposits is calculated just like the money market yields in Chapter 14 (basically what the customer gets divided by what he or she invested for the number of times a year this could occur):

$$\text{APY} = [(1 + \text{PMT/PO})^{365/N}] - 1 \qquad [20.3]$$

where PMT is the amount of interest received during a period less service charges;

PO = the amount invested by the customer

N = the number of days over which interest is earned.

Suppose a customer purchases a 91-day, $10,000 share CD on which her credit union offers a stated annual rate of 3 percent. Interest will be paid at the end of the 91 days, with a $2 service charge on the account. At the end of the quarter, the customer will receive (3 percent/4) = .75 percent interest or in dollars $10,000 × .0075 = $75, which net of the $2 service charge will be $73. Calculating the APY, it is

$$\text{APY} = [(1 + \$73/\$10,000)^{365/91}] - 1 = .029603 \text{ or } 2.9603\%.$$

Because of the service charge, the APY is less than the stated 3 percent rate. Generally, the longer the maturity of the deposit and the more complex its features, the greater the required information for consumers.[37]

Pricing Strategies in Practice

As expected in a deregulated environment, depository managers have approached pricing problems in a variety of ways in recent years, as discussed in the following sections.

Use of Conditionally Free Accounts   By 1985, thrifts and banks' use of conditionally free accounts was common, with minimums to avoid service charges ranging from more than $1,000 to more than $3,300. In response to proponents of basic banking and to the incentives offered in FDICIA, both regulators and trade organizations have urged depositories to develop "no-frills" accounts on which fees are minimized. The American Bankers Association reported in 1993 that 95 percent of banks and thrifts offered such accounts. A Federal Reserve Board poll of 81 banks in all 50 states found that 84 percent charged a fixed monthly fee for a package of basic

---

[37]See Brian P. Smith. "Adding Up Truth in Savings." *Savings and Community Banker* 2 (August 1993): 46–48; "Truth in Savings." *Banking Legislation and Policy* (Federal Reserve Bank of Philadelphia) (September/October 1992), 3; Phil Roosevelt. "Banks Race Truth-in-Savings Deadline." *American Banker* (January 7, 1993), 1, 10; Francis A. Grady. "Innocent Errors Create Liability Under the Truth-in-Savings Act." *American Banker* (March 23, 1993), 4, 17.

banking services; the fee averaged $2.58. These basic banking accounts usually limit the number of transactions and pay no explicit interest on deposited funds.[38]

Other Pricing Strategies   Studies by the Federal Reserve Banks of Cleveland and New York found respectively the use of a tiered system for setting explicit interest rates as early as 1983, with tiering more common for CDs and minimum balances being larger for less liquid accounts, and with most banks requiring a minimum balance to earn interest on NOW and MMDAs accounts by 1987. Generally, monthly fees were waived if the account balance exceeded an established level, suggesting that conditional free account mechanisms, such as minimum balance requirements remain an important pricing strategy. Ideally, cost-based pricing strategies should allow customers to pay no more, but no less, than their fair share of the cost of receiving deposit services.[39]

Summary of Factors that Research Finds to Affect Bank/Thrift Rates   With rate deregulation, a number of studies have examined factors that affect bank/thrift CD rates. Studies of CD rates in the later 1980s suggest that better capitalized and larger depository institutions pay lower rates. Studies have also found greater price rigidity, whereby deposit rates remain fixed despite movements in market rates, varies among different types of deposit, with greater rigidity for savings and NOW accounts. Whereas CD rates tend to be priced weekly against T-bills rates and competitor's rates, savings and NOW accounts tend to be more stable. Deposit rates have also been found to be quicker to fall when Treasury yields decreased than when Treasury yields increase, with more stickiness in more concentrated banking markets. Although studies show mixed results, depository institutions with a larger branch network have at times been shown to have lower deposit rates, suggesting a trade-off between implicit rates (in terms of convenience) and explicit rates.[40]

EFFECT OF FEDERAL DEPOSIT INSURANCE

A discussion of deposit taking and liability management in a deregulated world is incomplete without examining the relationship between depository institution management and the federal deposit and share insurance funds. Previous chapters discussed the moral hazard of fixed premium deposit insurance. In an efficient market, funds should flow to the most efficient users of funds. However, with federal deposit insurance, allocational inefficiencies may be created, because depositors may put funds in ʹinsured depository regardless of their performance or risk. With flat

---

[38]See Staten (1989); and Robyn Meredith. "95 Percent of Banks Offer Basic Checking, Study Finds." *American Banker* (August 5, 1993), 8. Supporters of basic banking legislation cited research findings that only 14 percent of banks surveyed by the U.S. Public Interest Research Group offered low-cost accounts. The group of researchers with the most representative sample is unknown, but the Federal Reserve Board could be considered the most objective source. For other discussions of deposit pricing, see Rogowski (1984) and Zimmerman (1985).

[39]See Davis and Korobow (1987); and Watro (1984).

[40]For a summary of these studies, see James H. Gilkeson, John A. List, and Craig K. Ruff. "The Impact of the Early Withdrawal Option on Time Deposit Pricing." *Quarterly Review of Economics and Finance* (1999), forthcoming.

insurance premiums for all depositories regardless of their risk prior to FDICIA,[41] the cost of insurance did not vary according to an institution's risk, creating a severe moral hazard problem. As discussed in Chapter 7, in particular troubled thrifts were able to attract insured deposits to finance growth regardless of their risk because depositors knew that their deposits were insured. In effect, all depository institutions received a risk-free (guaranteed) cost of funds, despite the fact that many had great risk. With the thrift crisis in the 1980s, the FSLIC became bankrupt with insufficient insurance reserves to rescue failing thrifts and pay back insured depositors. Similarly, in the early 1990s, the FDIC was severely undercapitalized.

Fearing a funding crisis at the FDIC large enough to rival the FSLIC bailout, Congress at last insisted in FDICIA that deposit insurance be assessed on a risk-adjusted basis. The act also required premiums be high enough to cover any losses. After several different initial schemes that were somewhat more complex,[42] as of January 1993 the FDIC put in place risk-based capital based on institution's capitalization category (as described in Chapter 8). Premiums per $100 of insured deposits ranged from 23 cents for well-capitalized banks to 31 cents for undercapitalized banks with severe supervisory problems. In January 1996, when the FDIC-BIF fund had achieved reserves of 1.25 percent of insured deposits, premiums were reduced and currently range from 4 cents for sound banks to 27 cents for troubled banks per $100 of insured deposits. Deposit insurance premiums were higher to bring up FDIC-SAIF reserves, as discussed in Chapter 7. They remain in a 23–31 cent range. Many analysts argue that deposit insurance continues to be underpriced, so a moral hazard problem remains.[43]

Credit Union Insurance The National Credit Union Share Insurance Fund (NCUSIF), is operated quite differently from SAIF or BIF. Between its founding in 1970 and 1984, NCUSIF used a premium system similar to that of the FDIC and the FSLIC. As a result of funding inadequacies that became apparent in the early 1980s, however, the Deficit Reduction Act of 1984 changed the way NCUSIF was financed. The 1984 law requires federally insured credit unions to maintain a deposit in NCUSIF equal to 1 percent of their insured shares. Interest earned on NCUSIF investments made with these deposits adds to the fund each year, although

---

[41]Bank Premiums prior to 1989 were $\frac{1}{12}$ of 1 percent (8.3 basis points) per year on average total domestic deposits, payable in advance on a semiannual basis. Rebates were given if reserves exceeded a level between 1.25 percent and 1.4 percent of insured deposits. Thrift premiums were assessed similarly, but special assessments were made in 1985 to mid-1989 to help pay for the escalating thrift crisis. Under FIRREA bank premiums were scheduled to almost double to 15 basis points and thrifts to 23 basis points by early 1991, with a decline in later years. The FDIC was also given the power to raise premiums to a maximum of 32.5 basis points per year if funds seemed imperiled. The FDIC raised BIF premiums for 1991 to 19.5 basis points and in 1992 to 23 basis points. See Chapter 7.

[42]The FDIC's initial scheme was based on bank CAMEL and thrifts MACRO ratings. However, critics objected that many institutions received no premium decreases.

[43]See Galloway, Tina M., Winson B. Lee, and Dianne M. Roden. "Banks' Changing Incentives and Opportunities for Risk Taking." *Journal of Banking and Finance* 21 (April 1997), 509–527; and Kidwell, Peterson, and Blackwell (1997), p. 507. Also see Avery and Kwast (1985), Evanoff (1992); Flood (1992); and Baer and Brewer (1986) for discussions of risk based insured and other sources of market discipline.

NCUSIF's assets may not exceed 1.3 percent of total insured shares in any year. Accumulations in excess of that amount are returned to credit unions. Special assessments are prohibited, although annual premiums can be charged if regulators deem them necessary. As of 1996, the fund was operating with a balance between 1.3 percent of insured shares. No premiums were levied until 1992, when for the first time since 1984, credit unions were charged $\frac{1}{12}$ of 1 percent of insured shares. The premium was necessary to replenish NCUSIF after it handled several large credit union failures in the early 1990s.[44]

Insurance Fund Resources   None of the three funds has, nor is intended to have, resources equal to the total amount of deposits for which insurance coverage is provided. This point is often misunderstood. The best insurance any depositor has (indeed, any creditor of any business firm has) is the quality of the firm's assets, which is, in turn, based on the present value of the assets' expected cash inflows. The creditors of most depositories have no need of the guarantee, because returns on the firm's assets are used to pay interest and to repay principal to fund suppliers. Even if most depositories were closed today, the liquidation of assets would provide cash to pay off liabilities in full. Insurers, furthermore, have lines of credit with the Treasury, assuring them of cash should funds be depleted in an emergency. To ensure public confidence, CEBA of 1987 also included an explicit Congressional guarantee of insured funds.[45]

Coverage Provided

Because of insurance coverage rules and financial resources of consumers and businesses differ, the effect of federal insurance on depositor behavior varies according to type of depositor.

Effect on Consumer Depositors   A commonly held notion of federal insurance coverage is that depositors are insured up to a maximum of $100,000, exclusive of individual retirement accounts (IRAs), at each depository in which they have funds. Additional coverage of up to $100,000 is provided for IRAs at the same institution. As Table 20.5 demonstrates, however, the possibilities for coverage beyond these amounts are considerable. A family of four could have deposit insurance of up to $1.4 million *at each institution* with which it had a relationship. The key is identifying the ownership of different accounts in such a way that no more than $100,000 is claimed by any one legal owner. In this example revocable trust accounts are shown for all family members. Because they are established for another's benefit, they are legally separate accounts owned by the individual and can be established by a simple deposit signature card. Hence, under the currently system, most consumers can

---

[44]Details on NCUSIF's operations are reported regularly in its annual reports and in the annual reports of the NCUA.

[45]See Kane (1985; 1989); Cooperman, Lee, and Wolfe (1992); and Cook and Spellman (1991) The last three studies mention find evidence of rate contagion for insured deposits associated with the decapitalization of the FSLIC in the mid to late 1980s. The research by Kane points out that prior to explicit guarantees, if insurers failed, depositors were uncertain if and when insured deposits would be repaid.

Table 20.5 ✦ Extending Deposit Insurance Coverage

The maximum amount of federal deposit insurance available is generally believed to be $100,000 per individual per institution. The regulations actually allow a higher level of coverage, however, if trust or joint accounts are established. A family of four could receive full deposit insurance coverage on $1,400,000 at one bank, thrift, or CU.

HUSBAND, WIFE, AND TWO CHILDREN: INSURED ACCOUNTS TOTALING $1,400,000	
Individual Accounts	
Husband	$100,000
Wife	100,000
Child 1	100,000
Child 2	100,000
Joint Accounts[a]	
Husband and wife	$100,000
Husband and child 1	100,000
Wife and child 2	100,000
Child 1 and child 2	100,000
Revocable Trust Accounts	
Husband as trustee for wife	$100,000
Husband as trustee for child 1	100,000
Husband as trustee for child 2	100,000
Wife as trustee for husband	100,000
Wife as trustee for child 1	100,000
Wife as trustee for child 2	100,000

[a]Joint account with right of survivorship.

Source: Adapted from "Insured Accounts for Savers," Federal Reserve Bank of Richmond, September 1989.

have full insurance coverage for all their deposits, so depositors have little reason to examine the creditworthiness of institutions.

Effect of Institutional Depositors   Commercial and institutional investors are different. Establishing insured accounts in many different names would usually be legally impossible and, in any case, too costly. Consequently, many corporate and institutional deposits exceed the federally insurable limit. In theory, these large depositors should be prime sources of **market discipline**, which is the possibility that creditors, owners, or both will react negatively to management's decisions and subsequently refuse to entrust funds to the institution. Confronted by market discipline, bank, thrift, or credit union managers facing the loss of confidence-sensitive money should think twice before investing funds in excessively risky loans or securities.

SUMMARY

Deposit and nondeposit liabilities for depository institutions and regulations governing their management are the subjects of this chapter. The phase-out of Reg Q gave institutions new freedom to offer a wide variety of accounts with different maturities and interest rate characteristics. Larger and more aggressive institutions also rely heavily on managed liabilities, including negotiable CDs, Eurodollar deposits, repurchase agreements, mortgage-backed securities, brokered deposits, deposit notes, and bank notes. Even contingent liabilities serve as sources of discretionary funds for some institutions.

The elimination of restrictions on institutions' access to funds has given managers new challenges. Institutions formerly relying on implicit interest payments as the only allowable form of competition now develop pricing strategies, and the choice between explicit and implicit interest affects the volatility of returns. Many firms offer flexible pricing mechanisms that provide more choices to customers and to management. New Fed rules require uniform disclosure of an institution's fee structure and yields on deposits. In conjunction with pricing decisions, management must evaluate wholesale and retail market strategies and choose the mix of funds that firms will seek.

Federal deposit insurance continues to influence management decisions. Insurance reduces the risk borne by depositors and therefore reduces the potential instability of funds to insured institutions. Because insurance premiums have only recently been adjusted to reflect the relative riskiness of an institution, it is too early to know whether the substantial moral hazard, which contributed to many depository failures over the past decade, has been brought under control. Several recommendations for additional reform have been considered, but there is no doubt that some form of deposit insurance will continue to provide a buffer against loss of confidence in the financial system.

Questions

1. Why have banks lost their percentage of deposit financing over time? What have banks done to try to retain deposit customers?

2. What advantages do direct banks or cyberbanks have over other banks? What disadvantages do they have?

3. How has the efficiency of bank deposit processing improved with check imaging systems and electronic check presentment (ECP)? Briefly explain what these systems do.

4. Why has online banking not taken off as much as expected in the late 1990s? Why is the OCC concerned about bank technology risks?

5. Discuss public relations problems that bank have had in connection with public perceptions of the fees and service that banks offer. How can banks improve this image?

6. What factors affect the type of deposits that banks can attract? How does consumer sophistication affect the volatility of bank deposits?

7. Discuss the structure of bank and savings institution deposits using Tables 20.1 and 20.2. Why do you think larger banks (with assets greater than $1 billion) have more uninsured deposits than smaller banks? Why do you think so many short-term versus long-term CDs have been issued?

8. What is liability management? Explain its purposes and the types of funds used for each purpose. Compare and contrast the risks of each liability source with those of traditional deposit sources of funds.

9. How do deposit notes and bank notes compare with negotiable CDs as tools of liability management? How do market perceptions of a bank's riskiness affect its ability to pursue successful liability management strategies?

10. TRX Incorporated is a large corporate customer of The Big World Bank. TRX's cash managers have just contacted the bank to arrange a withdrawal of $50 million from the corporate checking account for reinvestment in interest-bearing marketable securities. Bank management suggests, as an alternative, that the corporation consider a Eurodollar deposit in its branch in Zurich. Illustrate with T-accounts the creation of the Eurodollar deposit and its effect on the assets and liabilities of both the domestic and foreign branches of the bank.

11. Explain how mortgage lenders use mortgage-backed bonds to obtain new funds.

12. What are brokered deposits and what advantages do they offer to financial institutions? What are the risks involved? Do you agree with restrictions placed on issuing brokered deposits under FIRREA of 1989 and FDICIA of 1991? Why or why not?

13. Explain the difference between confidence-sensitive money and hot money. What factors influence a depository institution manager's choice between aggressive and conservative approaches to funds management?

14. What are implicit interest payments? Why have depositories used them, and why do some depositors prefer them even after the removal of interest rate ceilings? How can implicit-interest pricing strategies affect the stability of earnings as interest revenues change?

15. Compare the cost and volatility of retail and wholesale funds. What additional factors affect a depository's decision to specialize in one source of funds or the other?

16. Review bank and thrift advertisements in current newspapers, in periodicals, or on the Internet. What strategies are institutions using to attract retail deposits? What implicit pricing strategies can you identify? How would you measure their potential cost?

17. Do you agree with government mandates that banks provide a policing role for the government under the Bank Secrecy Act and proposed Know Your Customer Rules? Explain why or why not. What additional costs are entailed for banks?

18. Setting deposit account prices is a complex process. What types of analyses are required? Find an example of an innovative pricing strategy used by a depository in your area.

To what type of customer does this strategy seem designed to appeal?

19. What factors determine the marginal cost of a deposit account? Why is knowledge of this marginal cost important to managers?

20. What motivates a depository to offer conditionally free accounts? Are such accounts really "free" to the customer? Why or why not?

21. Do you think risk-based insurance premiums have solved the moral hazard problem? Explain.

22. Could the financial system survive without federal deposit insurance? Why or why not? Would your answer change if you were retired and living on Social Security? If you were on *Forbes* magazine's annual list of the 400 richest Americans? In your opinion, whom should the ideal federal insurance program protect? How much protection should be available? Who should pay the cost? What responsibilities should be placed on depository institution managers under the ideal system?

Problems

1. The Atlantic Bank has agreed to sell the Pacific National Bank $6 million in federal funds for two days at a quoted rate of 8.5 percent. How much must Pacific repay to Atlantic? What is the effective annual yield to Atlantic? (Fed funds yields are illustrated in Chapter 14.)

2. Singapore Suburban Bank is purchasing $300 million in Fed funds at a rate of 7.85 percent. How much must the bank repay in three days? What is the effective annual cost of the transaction?

3. Yosemite Savings sells a jumbo CD to Alta Vista Corporation in a face amount of $1.75 million. The stated annual rate is 8.00 percent, and the maturity is 180 days. How much must Yosemite provide to Alta Vista upon maturity? What is the effective annual cost of the CD? Carry your percentage to three decimal places. (Yields on negotiable CDs are illustrated in Chapter 14.)

4. Suppose, instead, that the maturity of the CD in Problem 3 was 182 days. How much must Yosemite repay, and what is the effective annual cost? Compare your results with those in Problem 3 and explain the similarities and differences.

5. a. Calculate the degree of operating leverage (DOL) for the Euphoria Savings Bank if total revenues are $1.3 billion, variable costs are $850 million, and fixed costs are $350 million. If revenues increase by 15 percent, by how much will operating income increase?

   b. Assume that total revenues increase to $1.5 billion and that fixed costs do not change. Also assume that variable costs increase to $980 million. Recompute the DOL. Why is your answer different from that in part a? What are the implications for management?

6. Phil and Roz Lerner, the management of Euphoria Savings Bank, are analyzing the bank's cost structure. You have been asked to evaluate the effect of implicit interest payments on operating income; approximately 25 percent of fixed costs is traced to implicit interest. The following information is provided:

   Total revenues: $65 million
   Total variable costs: 80 percent of total revenues
   Total fixed costs: $8.0 million

   a. If explicit interest were substituted for implicit interest, what percentage of total revenues would variable costs be? What would total fixed costs be?

   b. Calculate the degree of operating leverage with and without implicit interest payments (i.e., under the current structure *and* under the one described in part a).

   c. If revenues increase by 10 percent, by how much would you expect operating income to change under the current cost structure? under the alternative structure?

   d. If revenues decrease by 10 percent, what would operating income be under the current and alternative cost structures?

   e. What risk/return trade-off is involved with implicit versus explicit interest?

7. a. The manager of Great Smoky Mountains Savings and Loan wishes to estimate the total marginal cost of retail MMDAs. Reserve requirements are 0 percent, and the cost of deposit insurance is 0.23 percent. Competing institutions are paying 8 percent on MMDAs, and the manager estimates that servicing costs are 2.5 percent.

   b. The manager is considering a marketing campaign to attract NOWs that pay only 5.5 percent compared with 8.0 percent on MMDAs. The unlimited transactions feature of NOWs increases reserve requirements to 10 percent and servicing costs to 4 percent. Will the institution enjoy cost reductions if customers switch from MMDAs to NOWs? Explain why or why not.

8. The Big Apple Bank in New York City is estimating the average marginal cost of its retail deposit accounts. Alison and David Cooperman, the finance department, have collected the following data:

	Explicit Effective Interest Rate	Servicing Cost	Insurance Premium	Reserve Requirement	Expected Total Balance (bil.)
Demand Deposits	0%	6.5%	.23%	10%	$1.77
NOWS	5%	4.0%	.23%	10%	1.27
MMDAs	8%	1.5%	.23%	0%	1.92
Passbook Svgs.	4.5%	.5%	.23%	0%	.64
CD°	8.9%	.25%	.23%	0%	1.03

°(<$100,000 per account)

    a. What is the average marginal total cost? (Hint: Weight the total cost of each deposit by its proportion of total deposits.)

    b. From the perspective of cost, should the bank seek additional dollars through the federal funds market or should it attempt to attract more MMDA accounts? Fed funds are customarily purchased with three-day maturities, and the current rate is 7.75 percent. What other factors besides cost should management consider in making this decision?

9. In the following situations, would the depositor have any uninsured deposits? If so, explain how much and why.

    a. Ann Fox has a NOW account with a $10,000 balance and an MMDA with a $45,000 balance. She and her husband Al have two joint accounts, one for $70,000 and the other for $35,000. Ann also has an IRA in which she has accumulated $35,000. All accounts are held at the same bank.

    b. Jeff Cooperman purchased a $90,000 CD at the beginning of the year on which he has earned one year's interest at 12 percent. The interest was reinvested in the account. He also has a joint savings account for $20,000 with his daughter Alison. All accounts are at the same savings bank.

    c. Jeff and Lori Cooperman have two joint accounts for $60,000 each. The accounts are at two different S&Ls. Jeff has also recently opened a $50,000 account for Lori at one of the S&Ls, for which he serves as trustee.

Selected References

Avery, Robert B., Gerald A. Hanweck, and Myron L. Kwast. "An Analysis of Risk-Based Deposit Insurance for Commercial Banks." In *Proceedings of the Conference on Bank Structure and Competition.* Chicago: Federal Reserve Bank of Chicago, 1985, 217–250.

Baer, Herbert, and Elijah Brewer. "Uninsured Deposits as a Source of Market Discipline." *Economic Perspectives* (Federal Reserve Bank of Chicago) 10 (September/October 1986): 23–31.

Benston, George. "Interest on Deposits and the Survival of Chartered Depository Institutions." *Economic Review* (Federal Reserve Bank of Atlanta) 69 (October 1984): 42–56.

Brigham, Eugene F. *Fundamentals of Financial Management,* 6th ed. Fort Worth, Tex.: Dryden Press, 1992

Canner, Glenn B., and Ellen Maland. "Basic Banking." *Federal Reserve Bulletin* 73 (April 1987): 255–269.

Cohn, Jeffrey, and Michael E. Edleson. "Banking on the Market: Equity-Linked CDs." *AAII Journal* 15 (March 1993): 11–15.

Cook, Douglas O. and Lewis J. Spellman. "Federal Financial Guarantees and the Occasional Market Pricing of Default Risk." *Journal of Banking and Finance* 15 (1991), 1113–1130.

Cooperman, Elizabeth S., Winson B. Lee, and Glenn A. Wolfe. "The 1985 Ohio Thrift Crisis, the FSLIC's Solvency, and Rate Contagion for Retail CDs." *Journal of Finance* 47 (July 1992), 914–941.

Davis, Richard G., and Leon Korobow. "The Pricing of Consumer Deposit Products—The Non-Rate Dimensions." *Quarterly Review* (Federal Reserve Bank of New York) 11 (Winter 1986–87): 14–18.

Davis, Richard G., Leon Korobow, and John Wenninger. "Bankers on Pricing Consumer Deposits." *Quarterly Review* (Federal Reserve Bank of New York) 11 (Winter 1986–87): 6–13.

Dotsey, Michael. "An Examination of Implicit Interest Rates on Demand Deposits." *Economic Review* (Federal Reserve Bank of Richmond) 69 (September/October 1983): 3–11.

Dotsey, Michael, and Anatoli Kuprianov. "Reforming Deposit Insurance: Lessons from the Savings and Loan Crisis."

Economic Review (Federal Reserve Bank of Richmond) (March/April 1990): 3–28.

Elliehausen, Gregory E., and John D. Wolken. "Banking Markets and the Use of Financial Services by Households." *Federal Reserve Bulletin* 78 (March 1992): 169–184.

Elmer, Peter J. "Developing Service-Oriented Deposit Accounts." *Bankers Magazine* 168 (March/April 1985): 60–63.

Evanoff, Douglas D. "Preferred Sources of Market Discipline: Depositors vs Subordinated Debt Holders." Federal Reserve Bank of Chicago, Working Paper #92–21, 1992.

Flannery, Mark. "Deposit Insurance Creates a Need for Bank Regulation." *Business Review* (Federal Reserve Bank of Philadelphia) (January/February 1982a): 17–24.

———. "Retail Bank Deposits as Quasi-Fixed Factors of Production." *American Economic Review* 72 (June 1982b): 527–536.

Flood, Mark D. "The Great Deposit Insurance Debate," *Review* (Federal Reserve Bank of St. Louis) 74 (July/August 1992): 51–77.

Friedman, Milton. "Controls on Interest Rates Paid by Banks." *Journal of Money, Credit, and Banking* 2 (February 1970): 15–32.

Furlong, Frederick. "A View on Deposit Insurance Coverage." *Economic Review*, Federal Reserve Bank of San Francisco (Spring 1984): 31–38.

Gardner, Mona J., and Lucille E. Lammers. "Cost Accounting in Large Banks." *Management Accounting* 69 (April 1988): 34–39.

Goodfriend, Marvin. "Eurodollars." In *Instruments of the Money Market*, 6th ed.. Richmond, Va.: Federal Reserve Bank of Richmond, 1986, 53–64.

Goodfriend, Marvin, and William Whelpley. "Federal Funds." In *Instruments of the Money Market*, 6th ed. Richmond, Va.: Federal Reserve Bank of Richmond, 1986, 8–22.

Harless, Caroline T. "Brokered Deposits." *Economic Review* (Federal Reserve Bank of Atlanta) 69 (March 1984): 14–25.

Kane, Edward J. "The Three Faces of Commercial Bank Liability Management." In *The Political Economy of Policy-Making*, ed. M. J. Dooley. Beverly Hills, CA: Sage Publications, 1979.

———. "A Six-Point Program for Deposit Insurance Reform." *Housing Finance Review* 2 (July 1983): 269–278.

———. *The Gathering Crisis in Federal Deposit Insurance.* Cambridge, Mass.: The MIT Press, 1985.

———. *The S&L Insurance Mess: How Did It Happen?* Washington, D.C.: The Urban Institute Press, 1989.

Keeley, Michael C. "Interest-Rate Deregulation." *Weekly Letter* (Federal Reserve Bank of San Francisco), January 13, 1984.

Keeley, Michael C., and Gary C. Zimmerman. "Competition for Money Market Deposit Accounts." *Economic Review* (Federal Reserve Bank of San Francisco) (Spring 1985): 5–27.

Kidwell, David S., Richard L. Peterson, and David W. Blackwell. *Financial Institutions, Markets, and Money*, 6th ed. Fort Worth, Tex.: Dryden Press, 1997.

Logue, James A. "Pricing Strategies for the 1980s." *Magazine of Bank Administration* 59 (September 1983): 28–34.

Mahoney, Patrick I., et al. "Responses to Deregulation: Retail Deposit Pricing from 1983 through 1985." Board of Governors of the Federal Reserve System, Staff Study Number 151, January 1987.

McKinney, George W. "Liability Management: Its Costs and Uses." In *Financial Institutions and Markets in a Changing World*, ed. Donald R. Fraser and Peter S. Rose. Dallas: Business Publications, 1980, 90–104.

Moore, Robert R. "Brokered Deposits: Determinants and Implications for Thrift Distributions." *Financial Industry Studies* (Federal Reserve Bank of Dallas) December 1991, 15–27.

Murphy, Neil B., and Richard H. Kraas. "Measuring the Interest Sensitivity of Money Markets Accounts." *Magazine of Bank Administration* 60 (May 1984): 70–74.

Parliment, Tom. "Not Paying Market Is an Option." *Savings Institutions* 106 (April 1985): S12-S17.

Puglisi, Donald J., and Joseph A. McKenzie. "Capital Market Strategies for Thrift Institutions." *Federal Home Loan Bank Board Journal* 16 (November 1983): 2–8.

———. "Research on Federal Deposit Insurance." In *Proceedings of a Conference on Bank Structure and Competition*. Chicago: Federal Reserve Bank of Chicago, 1983, 196–298.

Rogowski, Robert J. "Pricing the Money Market Deposit and Super-NOW Accounts in 1983." *Journal of Bank Research* 15 (Summer 1984): 72–81.

Scott, Charlotte H. "Low-Income Banking Needs and Services." *Journal of Retail Banking* 10 (Fall 1988): 32–40.

Staten, Michael. "Retail Banker's Review of Laws and Regulations—Winter 1989." *Journal of Retail Banking* 11 (Winter 1989): 62–63.

Stigum, Marcia. *The Money Market*, 3d ed. Homewood, Ill.: Dow Jones-Irwin, 1990.

Taggart, Robert A., Jr. "Effects of Deposit Rate Ceilings: The Evidence from Massachusetts Savings Banks." *Journal of Money, Banking, and Credit* 10 (May 1978): 139–157.

Watson, Ronald D. "Estimating the Cost of Your Bank's Funds." *Business Review* (Federal Reserve Bank of Philadelphia) (May/June 1978): 3–11.

———. "The Marginal Cost of Funds Concept in Banking." *Journal of Bank Research* 8 (Autumn 1977): 136–147.

White, Lawrence J. "Price Regulation and Quality Rivalry in a Profit Maximizing Model: The Case of Bank Branching." *Journal of Money, Credit, and Banking* 8 (February 1976): 97–106.

Willemse, Rob J. M. "Large Certificates of Deposit." In *Instruments of the Money Market*, 6th ed. Richmond, Va.: Federal Reserve Bank of Richmond, 1986, 36–52.

Wood, John H., and Norma L. Wood. *Financial Markets*, Chapter 9. San Diego: Harcourt Brace Jovanovich, 1985.

Zimmerman, Gary C. "Shopping Pays." *Weekly Letter* (Federal Reserve Bank of San Francisco) (November 8, 1985).

Zimmerman, Gary C., and Michael Keeley. "Interest Checking." *Weekly Letter* (Federal Reserve Bank of San Francisco) (November 14, 1986).

Zimmerman, Gary C., and Jonathan A. Neuberger. "Interest Rate Competition." *Weekly Letter* (Federal Reserve Bank of San Francisco) (July 27, 1990).

Chapter 20 Internet Exercises

1. The Financial Services Technology Consortium (FSTC) is a not-for-profit organization whose goal is to enhance the competitiveness of the United States financial services industry. Members of the consortium include banks, financial services providers, research laboratories, universities, technology companies, and government agencies. The FSTC conducts the Bank Internet Payment System Project at http://fstc.org/projects/bips

   There are several classes of commercial transactions necessary for Internet Commerce. One of the more important of these transaction classes, payment systems, enables consumer-oriented activities such as online shopping and bill payment. Payment systems also enable business activities such as invoice payment, cash management, supply chain settlement, and procurement.

   There are various currently available or emerging payment systems designed to provide payment transactions over the Internet. You can find a survey of Internet payments systems in Microsoft Excel^R format at: http://www.fstc.org/projects/bips/vandmatrix.xls. It is the intent of the survey to assist perspective Internet users, merchants, and service providers in understanding the various Internet payment alternatives. The survey is meant as a starting place to learn about these payment systems. To that end, the survey provides links to more information and a matrix, or "at-a-glance comparison," of some of the payment systems. The matrix shows the features of different payment systems all on one page in order to make it easier for the beginner to understand some of their similarities and differences.

2. PM Publishing offers information on daily Eurodollars option analysis at http://www.pmpublishing.com/volatility/ed.html. To test your ideas about options trading, go to http://www.pmpublishing.com/price/index.html. You enter trade inputs, market inputs, contract specifications, and projection increments. You can find an example of contract specifications at: http://www.pmpublishing.com/options/onspecs.html.

3. Basic banking accounts, or lifeline accounts, are required to be offered by any bank, trust company, savings bank, savings and loan association, credit union (share draft accounts), or branch of a foreign banking corporation, the deposits of which are insured by the Federal Deposit Insurance Corporation (FDIC). Information on lifeline accounts can be found at: http://www.banking.state.ny.ns/bba.htm.

The attractive features of these basic banking accounts are as follows:

1. The initial deposit amount required by the banking institution to open the account may not be more than $25;

2. The minimum balance required by the banking institution to maintain the account may not be more than $.01 (one cent);

3. The charge by the banking institution per periodic cycle (28 to 31 days) for the maintenance of the account may not be more than $3;

4. The minimum number of withdrawal transactions that may be made during any periodic cycle at no charge to the customer is eight. A banking institution must allow at least eight withdrawals but can allow more if it should decide to do so. A withdrawal transaction consists of writing a check or getting cash from an automatic teller machine (ATM) operated by your own banking institution. An extra fee may be charged if you use an ATM that is not operated by your banking institution.

Useful Links:

Bank Rate Monitor
http://www.bankrate.com

Compubank
http://www.compubank.com

Netbank
http://www.netbank.com

"The country's banking troubles are one of several factors in an economic slowdown, in which lending has all but halted and much business activity is on hold. . . . An absence of rigorous controls allowed inexperienced bankers to engage in risky practices and private deals, lending to themselves or their affiliates and pouring their reserves into unsound ventures, particularly in property development. . . . The money flowed out, and by the end of last year reserves were dangerously depleted, with bad loans accounting for 25 percent of lending (and the closure) of 16 banks at the end of October . . . the banking system has virtually come to a standstill."

Seth Mydans
"Indonesia Begins the Rescue and Consolidation of Banks," *The New York Times*, January 20, 1998, C2.

Bankok, Thailand (February 1998):

"Problem-plagued Thai banks . . . lie at the heart of the country's economic difficulties. Some have so many bad loans they no longer grant new loans, making it hard even for promising Thai companies to borrow. . . . Late last year, the Government also shuttered 56 of 58 nonbank finance companies, speculative lenders that helped inflate Thailand's stock and real estate bubble in the early 1990s. . . . Purging the system of those crippled banks is a condition of the International Monetary Fund's $17 billion bailout of the country."

Joseph Kahn
"Thailand Nationalizes Three Faltering Private Banks," *New York Times*, February 7, 1998, 1B-3B.

Seoul, South Korea (February 1998):

"Bad loans at South Korean banks nearly quadrupled in 1997, the government said, but analysts worry that those figures understate the problems. Nonperforming loans at the country's 26 banks totaled 10 trillion won ($6.1 billion) at the end of 1997, or 2.7% of all loans . . . That figure includes loans without collateral . . . if substandard loans— loans on which payments are six months overdue, but have collateral—are included, the total number of problem loans rises to 22.6 trillion won, or 6% of all loans."

Namju Cho
"In South Korea, Bad Loans Soar to $6.1 Billion," *The Wall Street Journal*, February 27, 1998, A 11.

"The collapse of financial markets has shrunk the assets of banks an average of 90% since their peak last fall, forcing some banks to default on loans to Western creditors. . . . The real problem is . . . the banks themselves. Shoddy management, risky bets on the ruble, huge investments in government securities and a failure to develop real traditional banking businesses have pushed some to the brink of collapse."

Betsy McKay
"Russia's Banks Planted Seeks of Their Own Problems," *The Wall Street Journal*, August 31, 1998, A10.

Tokyo, Japan:

"The Japanese Government disclosed . . . (that) the nation's banks carry . . . 76.7 trillion yen in bad or questionable loans, or about $580 billion (with) . . . . $87 billion worth of those tarnished loans . . . absolutely unrecoverable. . . . Japan's bank-debt problem exploded after the speculative bubble economy of the 1980s burst and the high value of real estate collapsed. Many loans were backed by real estate."

Sheryl WuDUNN
"Tokyo Tries to Calm Fears on Bad Loans," *The New York Times*, November 13, 1998, C1-C5.

Washington, D.C., United States:

"Banks are exposing themselves to increased levels of risk as 1998 loan underwriting standards declined for the fourth consecutive year, a Federal regulator said today. . . . The annual survey of the (OCC) examiners at the 77 largest banks found easier commercial loan standards at 69% of banks compared with 59% in 1997. . . . Edward Kelley, a Federal Reserve governor, said loans that were appropriate during good times might not be appropriate if the economy soured. 'We have to be careful as this expansion is now seven years old.' (T)here was pronounced easing of standard in syndicated loans, middle market lending and real estate portfolios."

Reuters: "U.S. Cites Lower Bank Loan Standards," *The New York Times*, September 18, 1998, C4

21

ASSET MANAGEMENT: COMMERCIAL, CONSUMER, AND MORTGAGE LENDING

*A*s the preceding quotes suggest, 1998 was a year when banks in many countries faced severe problems from loan losses, which in turn often had a significant effect on that country's economy. In Indonesia, Korea, Japan, Russia, and Thailand, banks and finance companies faced the results of speculative commercial real estate and other risky loans made during the early 1990s that later soured. Their experience was similar to that of thrifts and some banks in the late 1980s in the United States, discussed in Chapter 7. Other factors often listed in the financial press to explain bank failures in Asia and Russia include (1) close, relaxed relationships between banks and industries in bank-oriented financial systems; (2) lax regulation, fraud and bribery by regulators; and (3) cronyism including powerful families who own banks and use them as "private finance houses for their business empires." Poor lending practices were associated with crises in Thailand, Indonesia, Korea, Japan, and Russia.[1]

Bank loan losses exacerbated economic problems within these countries. With banks failing and depositors pulling funds out of the financial system, countries faced severe economic slowdowns. Accordingly, exchange rates fell, and countries experienced significant currency devaluations. The fall in the value of Asian and Russian currencies created other economic problems, including the inability of countries and companies to pay back loans to foreign lenders. This, in turn, affected financial institutions and markets world wide. The Asian crisis created a significant global credit crunch, as lenders were reluctant to invest additional capital in many countries. In addition, large Japanese banks that were severely undercapitalized pulled back on their global lending in 1998.[2] The Asian and Russian crises had some currency contagion effects as well, with a weakening of currencies in several Latin American countries unrelated to their economic conditions. The fall in currency values contributed to financial problems in countries like Brazil, leading to the eventual devaluation of the Brazilian real in January 1999.[3]

Although only some large U.S. financial institutions with international holdings were significantly affected by the Asian and Russian crises, in 1998, regulators were concerned about U.S. commercial bank lending as well. As mentioned in the last quote, an OCC survey

---

[1]See Seth Mydans. "Indonesia Begins the Rescue and Consolidation of Banks." *The New York Times* (January 20, 1998), C2; Joseph Kahn. "Thailand Nationalizes Three Faltering Private Banks." *The New York Times* (February 7, 1998), 13–3B; Namju Cho. "In South Korea, Bad Loans Soar to $6.1 Billion," *The Wall Street Journal* (February 27, 1998), A11; Betsy McKay. "Russia's Banks Planted Seeds of Their Own Problems." *The Wall Street Journal* (August 31, 1998), A10; and Sheryl WuDUNN. "Tokyo Tries to Calm Fears on Bad Loans." *The New York Times* (November 13, 1998), C1-C5.

[2]See David E. Sanger. "Japanese Tell U.S. That Their Banks Are in Big Trouble," *The New York Times* (October 5, 1998), A1; Jathon Sapsford. "Japanese Exodus from Overseas Banking Pick Up Speed and Prestigious Names." *The Wall Street Journal* (November 13, 1998), A15.

[3]See "The Asian Contagion Continues to Spread." *The Wall Street Journal*, (August 24, 1998), pp. A1, A6; and Stan Lehman. "Brazil Stocks, Currency Erode Amid Skepticism." *The Denver Post* (February 6, 1994), 3C.

showed a relaxation of credit standards by large U.S. banks, as the U.S. expansion continued in its seventh year in 1998. Since loan losses often do not appear until several years after loans are made, whether loans at this time represented overly optimistic risk taking has yet to be seen.[4]

In the early 1990s, analysts have predicted a continued long-term decline in bank lending in the United States, with large corporate customers disintermediating to the direct lending markets. However, bank lending rose dramatically in the mid- to late-1990s and continues to be a dominant activity for most U.S. depository institutions.[5] In many other *countries, such as Japan, Germany, Thailand, Indonesia, Russia, and Korea, bank lending continues to be the dominant form of company financing. As indicated by the 1998 Asian and Russian bank crises, poor lending practices can result in bank failures and severe economic problems. This chapter examines bank lending, focusing on U.S. banks. International lending is discussed in Chapter 22 along with other international issues. The first section discusses general trends in types of lending for U.S. commercial banks, followed by sections discussing commercial, consumer, and mortgage lending and loan policies and analysis in greater detail.*

♦ ♦ ♦

TRENDS IN TYPES OF LOANS

As of October 1998, U.S. commercial banks had $3.272 trillion of loans on their balance sheets, amounting to about 63 percent of total assets of $5.213 trillion. As shown in Figure 21.1, of these loans, $.943 trillion or about 29 percent were commercial loans; $1.286 trillion or about 39 percent were real estate loans with about 8 percent of these home equity loans. Consumer loans were $.496 trillion or about 15 percent of total loans. The remaining 17 percent of loans consisted of security loans, other loans and leases, and interbank loans. As pointed out in Chapter 5, commercial banks have moved from commercial lending to consumer and mortgage lending. Many credit unions and savings institutions, where allowed, have diversified as well, but remain on average primarily respectively consumer and home mortgage lenders. The following sections discuss key factors for the three primary types of lending for depository institutions and finance companies: commercial, consumer, and mortgage lending, beginning with brief overviews of trends in each of these areas.

COMMERCIAL LENDING: RECENT TRENDS

Figure 21.2 shows trends in bank credit from 1989 to 1998. The first panel shows a severe drop in bank credit during the recession of the early 1990s. However, credit rose dramatically in the mid-1990s with an economic expansion, reaching a peak in 1995, and rising with occasional dips throughout the rest of the 1990s.

---

[4]See "U.S. Cites Lower Bank Loan Standards." *The New York Times* (September 18, 1998), C4. Also, see A. Sinan Cebenoyan, Elizabeth S. Cooperman, and Charles A. Register. "Ownership Structure, Charter Value, and Risk-Taking Behavior for Thrifts." 28 Spring, *Financial Management*, 1999, pp. 43–60. The authors find evidence of greater risk-taking for manager-owned thrifts in 1986 to 1988 and in 1994 and 1995, suggesting a rise in thrift stockholder preferences for taking on greater risk in the late 1990s.

[5]See *Federal Reserve Bank of St. Louis Monetary Trends* (December 1998), 14.

Figure 21.1   ✦   TYPES OF COMMERCIAL BANK LOANS, OCTOBER 1998

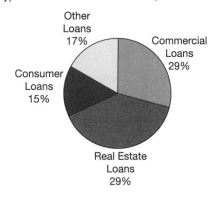

Types of Commercial Bank Loans, October 1998

Other Loans 17%
Commercial Loans 29%
Consumer Loans 15%
Real Estate Loans 29%

Source: Compiled by Authors from *Federal Reserve Bulletin*, January 1999, Table 1.26, A15.

Growth in bank credit securities (such as mortgage backed, credit card receivables, and automobile loan-backed securities), shown in the second panel, rose in 1991 and 1992, fell in the mid-1990s, rising again in 1997 and 1998. Growth in commercial and industrial loans and total loans and leases at commercial banks shown in panel four fell during the recession of the early 1990s to 0 percent growth in the later part of 1991 to 1993. This period is often known as the **credit crunch**, following the implementation of FDICIA and strict regulatory standards, when banks were hesitant to lend.[6] In 1994, as the economic expansion continued, loan growth rose rapidly, peaking at about 13 percent for all loans and 15 percent for commercial loans in 1995. In 1996 to most of 1998, commercial loan growth averaged about 10 percent, with a rise to 12 percent in the later part of 1998, demonstrating a dramatic recovery during the expansion of the mid to late 1990s.

UNIQUE ASPECTS OF BANK LENDING TO MEDIUM-SIZED TO SMALL FIRMS

With the information and technological age from 1970 on, the "special role" of depository institutions in assessing relevant information on large borrowers, information that is readily available to investors, has become less important. The availability of information makes it easier for large corporations to issue bonds and commercial paper in the direct markets, reducing the special role of banks in lending to large

---

[6]See John Wagster. "The Basle Accord of 1988 and the International Credit Crunch of 1989–1992," Working Paper, Wayne State University, October 1997; Kevin L. Kliesen and John A. Tatom. "The Recent Credit Crunch: The Neglected Dimensions." *Federal Reserve Bank of St. Louis Review* (September/October 1992), 13–36. Kliesen and Tatom argue in contrast that the credit crunch of the early 1990s was more likely due to the recession, reflecting lower demand for loans versus on the supply side by banks.

Figure 21.2 ✦ TRENDS IN BANK CREDIT 1989 TO 1998

Bank Credit
Percent change from year ago

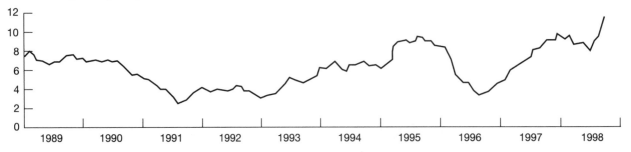

Investment Securities in Bank Credit at Commercial Banks
Percent change from year ago

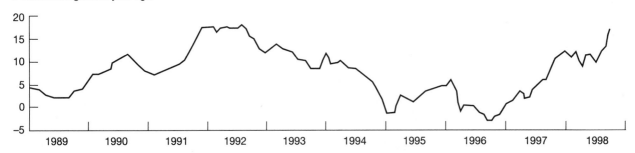

Total Loans and Leases in Bank Credit at Commercial Banks
Percent change from year ago

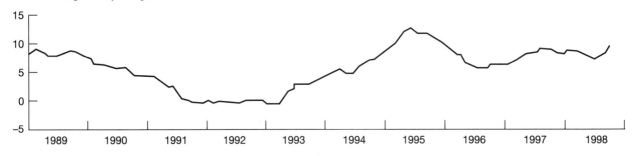

Commercial and Industrial Loans at Commercial Banks
Percent change from year ago

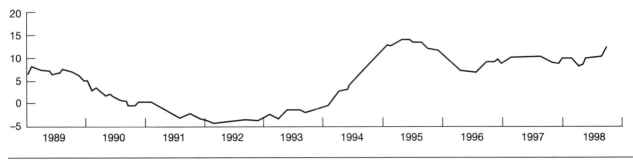

Source: The Federal Reserve Bank of St. Louis Monetary Trends, December 1998, 14.

corporations in the United States. Depository institutions, however, continue to play an important information role for the financing of small to medium-sized firms where information is not readily available.

It is difficult for investors to obtain information on small to medium-sized privately held firms. Hence, there are significant information asymmetries between borrowers and lenders. The cost of monitoring individual borrowers' behavior can also be substantial. Depositories reduce monitoring costs by entering into financial contracts with (lending to) many borrowers on similar contract terms, then using specialized personnel and resources that can be devoted entirely to enforcing the contracts. Depositories can, in the context of a lending relationship exert direct influence on a borrower's financial conduct and decisions. Also, once relevant data on a borrower has been collected and an initial loan application processed, cost economies are associated with the next application from that borrower. Information asymmetry is reduced because the lender knows more about the borrower's ability and intention to pay than at the time of the first application. Cost reductions can be significant for depositories that cultivate a strong clientele of regular borrowers. These depositories can, in turn, pass the cost savings to their depositors and shareholders.

Borrowers, too, benefit from information reusability and reduction of information asymmetry. For example, applying for a loan becomes less arduous as more financial contracts are made with the same lender. Further, research shows that a corporate borrower's shareholders bid up the firm's stock price after the firm announces it is undertaking new bank borrowing. If a commercial bank, with its "inside" knowledge, is willing to give a firm its "seal of approval," the securities markets appear to interpret that fact as reducing their need to monitor that same firm. Hence, from this perspective, despite greater competition from direct markets and nondepository institutions, depositories are indeed still special. With large corporations getting more financing from the direct markets, banks from the 1970s on have increased their lending to small and medium-sized businesses, which costs more in terms of credit analysis and monitoring. By being willing to provide additional liquidity and solving problems when they arise, including being flexible, many banks have been able to differentiate themselves from the impersonality of the direct finance marketplace.[7]

The issue took on added significance in the early 1990s when many would-be borrowers accused banks of creating a "credit crunch" in response to tightening regulation and supervision, and as shown in Figure 21.2, in 1990–1992, bank loan growth was close to zero. Some small and medium-sized business applicants claimed they could not get loans because banks' credit standards had become so unreasonable that no one could qualify. To the extent that a bank's unwillingness to lend served as a signal to other potential investors in a business, some borrowers believed

---

[7]See Jeffrey Marshall. "Rolling the Dice on Asset Management," *U.S. Banker* (March 1994), 33–40; "Roundtable Discussion on Current Issues in Banking." *Bank of America Journal of Applied Corporate Finance*, Vol. 9 (Summer 1996), 24–41; Raghuram G. Rajan. "Why Banks Have a Future: Toward a New Theory of Commercial Banking." *Bank of America Journal of Applied Corporate Finance*, Vol. 9 (Summer 1996), 114–128; Christopher James and Joel Houston. "Evolution or Extinction: Where Are Banks Headed?" *Bank of America Journal of Applied Corporate Finance* 9 (Summer 1996), 8–23. For more discussion of the special nature of depository lending, see Becketti and Morris (1992); Greenbaum, Kanatas and Venezia (1989); James (1987); Berlin (1987); and Fama (1985).

they were being shut out of the credit markets altogether. One Kansas City Fed study showed that bank relationships continue to be "special" for small and medium-sized firms in the United States, implying that if banks cut off funds to this group, few alternative funding sources would arise.

CONSUMER LENDING: RECENT TRENDS

Trends in household credit market debt, which include mainly first and second mortgages, credit-card borrowings and auto loans are show in Figure 21.3. Panel A shows trends in credit market debt relative to personal income. In the 1980s and 1990s this ratio rose, with U.S. household credit market debt nearly 81 percent of personal income by mid-1998. A Federal Reserve Bank of St. Louis report notes that the rise in this ratio is worrisome, because it cannot be explained by a life cycle explanation of a large population of young adults (ages 20–39 years); since baby boomers (born between 1946 and 1965) dominate the demographic picture.

The report suggests that one explanation for the rise in household debt ratios may be the fact that consumers feel wealthy with a higher household net worth (the value of stocks, bonds, houses, insurance policies, and other financial assets less total debt) than in the past, with household net worth rising relative to income from the 1960s to the 1990s.

Other factors contributing to the growth in consumer credit during the 1980s and 1990s include changing societal attitudes toward personal indebtedness; increased willingness of lenders to service consumer credit needs; and rising demand for consumer goods, as items once considered luxuries are now viewed as necessities. Innovations such as student loans, the growth of home equity loans, and the relatively low proportion of households with existing mortgage debt may have also been contributing factors.[8]

The Federal Reserve Bank of St. Louis report expresses concern that this trend may continue, despite the fact that future household income may not rise as much as it has in recent years. The broken line in Panel A shows the difference between the growth of personal income and the average effective rate on new home mortgages as a proxy for the cost of household borrowing. Income growth was greater than the level of the mortgage rate by about 1 percent on average between 1950 and 1979. From 1980 to 1997, however, income growth was on average more than 4 percent less than the effective mortgage rate.[9]

Panel B of Figure 21.3 shows growth rates in consumer credit over the 1980s and 1990s, with large rise in the growth rate during the expansion of the mid-1990s, reaching a peak growth rate of 15 percent in 1995 and a flattening out to a growth rate of about 5 percent in 1997 and 1998.

Growth Rates in Loans and Risk Measures in the 1990s   As shown in Panel C of Figure 21.3, loan growth has been strong over the 1990s, with a low percentage of nonperforming loans. Loan growth has also been broad-based with every major category of loans demonstrating growth. Real estate loans grew at an average rate of 7.9

---

[8]See William R. Emmons. "Is Household Debt Too High?" *The Federal Reserve Bank of St. Louis Monetary Trends* (December 1998), 1.
[9]Ibid.

Figure 21.3   ◆   TRENDS IN CONSUMER LENDING, LOAN GROWTH, AND ASSET QUALITY

PANEL A: PERSONAL INCOME IN U.S. RELATIVE TO CREDIT MARKET DEBT

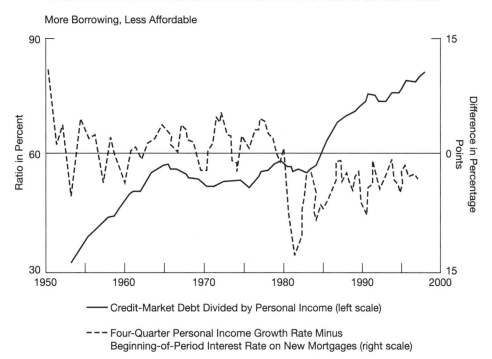

Source: *Federal Reserve Bank of St. Louis Monetary Trends*, December 1998, 1.

PANEL B: GROWTH RATES IN CONSUMER CREDIT

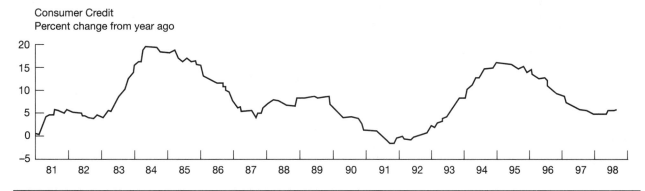

Source: *Federal Reserve Bank of St. Louis Monetary Trends*, December 1998, 7.

Figure 21.3 ✦ TRENDS IN CONSUMER LENDING, LOAN GROWTH, AND ASSET QUALITY *(CONTINUED)*

PANEL C: LOAN GROWTH RELATIVE TO ASSET QUALITY

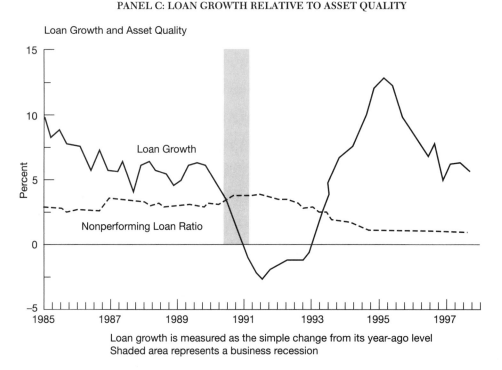

Loan growth is measured as the simple change from its year-ago level
Shaded area represents a business recession

Source: Federal Reserve Bank of St. Louis Monetary Trends, April 1998, 1.

percent from 1993 to 1998; commercial loans at a 8.8 percent rate, and consumer loans at an 8.1 percent rate with a strong economy and healthy bank balance sheets. The ratio of nonperforming loans (loans 90 days or more past due or in nonaccrual status) peaked at 3.91 percent in 1991, but fell over the 1990s to about .95 percent in 1998. Net charge-offs were also very low during most of the 1990s for loans on average. However, the ratio of nonperforming consumer loans to total consumer loans, which declined to 1.01 percent at the end of 1994 rose to 1.46 percent by 1998, along with a rise in the net charge-off rate for consumer loans, mostly related to credit card debt defaults. One of the reasons for the improvement in U.S. bank asset quality has been the diversification of commercial banks into residential mortgage loans, which traditionally have had the lowest default and loss rates for loans. Since the first quarter of 1993, residential mortgage and home equity loans have accounted for 27 percent of the $937 billion rise in bank loans. With declining interest rates and rising household income and bank thrift acquisitions, mortgage lending by banks has increased rapidly. In contrast, credit card loans, which are often among the most risky of bank loans, only accounted for 9.7 percent of the rise in bank loans, with commercial loans accounting for 27.9 percent of the rise.[10]

---

[10]Michelle Clark Neely. "How Long Can Strong Loan Growth Continue?" *The Federal Reserve Bank of St. Louis Monetary Trends* (April 1998), 1.

WHO MAKES CONSUMER AND HOME MORTGAGE LOANS?

Holders of Consumer Credit   Figure 21.4 shows the major suppliers of consumer credit, as of year-end 1997. Commercial banks are the largest holder of consumer credit, with 40 percent of total consumer credit outstanding in 1997. Securitized pools is the second largest supplier, with 25 percent, including pass-through securities for credit cards and automobile loans (CARs) discussed earlier in Chapter 9. The percentage of securitized consumer debt has risen rapidly in the 1990s, with only 15 percent of consumer debt in securitized pools in 1992. Credit card banks, commercial banks, and finance companies are large securitizers of consumer debt. Finance companies and credit unions were the next largest holders of consumer debt with respectively 13 percent and 12 percent, followed by nonfinancial firms (retailers) with 6 percent and savings institutions with 4 percent.

Hence, commercial banks continue to be the largest holder of consumer debt, other than securitized pools, which are continuing to grow dramatically. Credit unions and finance companies continue to be large suppliers of consumer credit. Finance companies such as General Motors Acceptance Corporation (GMAC) are constantly coming up with new innovations to promote the products of their retailer holding company. In 1992, for instance, GM introduced a GM MasterCard used to promote GM products. Customers could earn rebates equal to 5 percent of their charge purchases (up to a specified limit) and then are encouraged to apply those rebates toward the purchase of a new GM car or truck. Thus, policies that financial institutions develop for managing consumer lending have an important effect on their competitive position and financial performance.[11] Studies show more national competition for consumer borrowing and greater attention to interest rates and fees, particularly for credit card loans.

Holders of Mortgage Debt   Figure 21.5 shows the major holders of mortgage debt at the end of the second quarter of 1998. Mortgage debt includes one- to four-family residences, multifamily residences, non-farm residences, and farm mortgages.

Figure 21.4 ✦ SUPPLIERS OF CONSUMER CREDIT, 1997

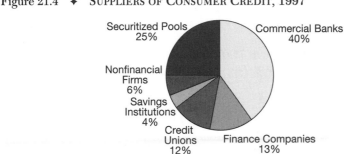

Source: Federal Reserve Bulletin, January 1999, A36.

---

[11]See Aguilar (1990); *Federal Reserve Bulletin*, various issues; and Kathleen Kerwin. "Can GM Sell Cars with a Credit Card?" *Business Week* (September 21, 1992), 78.

Figure 21.5 ◆ HOLDERS OF MORTGAGE DEBT, SECOND QUARTER 1998

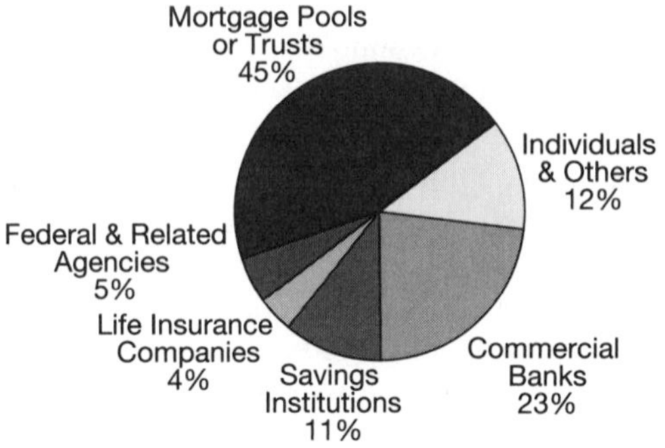

Source: Federal Reserve Bulletin, January 1999, A35. Mortgage Debt Outstanding includes one to four family
residences, multifamily residences, nonfarm residential, and farm mortgages. Mortgage Pools or trusts include
GNMA, FHLMC, FNMA, FHA pools, along with private mortgage pools.

Securitized mortgage pools or trusts are the largest holders, holding 45 percent of
mortgage debt, including mortgages originated by depository institutions. Mortgage
pools and trust are generated by the Government National Mortgage Association
(GNMA), Federal Home Loan Mortgage Association (FHLMC), Federal National
Mortgage Association (FNMA), and the Farm Home Administration (FHA), as well
as private mortgage pools. GNMA, FHLMC, and FNMA hold about 85 percent of
the assets in the mortgage pools and trusts. These agencies also held 5 percent of
mortgages outside of pools. Savings institutions held about 11 percent of mortgage
debt, with individuals and others, including credit unions and pension funds, holding
12 percent, and life insurance companies holding 4 percent. Hence, banks and savings institutions continue to be large holders of mortgage debt and also large suppliers for securitizations. Pensions and life insurance companies also maintain significant mortgage holdings, often purchased from depository institutions.

The following sections discuss the overall credit process including its function,
policies and objectives, and credit analysis, and the pricing and structure for different types of loans.

FUNCTIONS OF THE CREDIT PROCESS: THE CREDIT PROCESS AS PROTECTION AGAINST DEFAULT RISK

Loans have significant risks, including default risk from internal factors within a firm
such as mismanagement, risk of dishonesty in a loan application, and other firm-
related factors. They also have default risk from external factors such as an economic
downturn in a geographic region, the entry of new competitors, or other industry related factors. In addition, loans have interest rate risk if they are longer-term and
fixed rate. Variable rate loans have less interest rate risk, but since borrowers will
have to make higher loan payments if interest rates rise, the default risk of variable
rate loans is higher than fixed rate loans. The structuring of loans to ensure repayment by the borrower is one of the keys to an effective bank lending process. The
credit evaluation process is also crucial.

To protect the bank and maximize the profitability of loans that are made, banks must have a credit process in place. The structure of the credit process is discussed in greater detail in the following sections. It includes a carefully written loan policy; loan request procedures and a process for credit analysis, a process for credit execution and administration, and a credit review process to identify problems early for loans that have been made. The loan process must also conform with a large number of lending regulations, discussed in more detail in a later section.

THE ROLE OF THE CREDIT PROCESS IN BUSINESS DEVELOPMENT

In addition to protecting the bank against nonpayment, the bank credit process includes business development for the bank. This includes loan call programs, advertising, marketing, and developing relationships. Targets must be identified in terms of what areas will be targeted for potential business, what the forecast demand for bank services is, and how employees will be trained regarding all bank products. Loan officers have become more market oriented, gathering business for the bank, including becoming active in community organizations and calling on desirable firms to get their business for the bank. Lenders must also be trained in cross-selling other products, such as cash management products including online banking services, sweep accounts, lockboxes, automatic check deposits and bill paying services, among others. Credit analysts assist the loan officer in obtaining financial statements, credit reports and rating, and in performing financial statement analysis. Bank procedures ensure that credit information is collected and presented in a uniform fashion.

LOAN COMMITTEE REVIEW

Loan officers are given some flexibility depending on their seniority and bank policies in determining whether loans should be granted. For larger loans, loans must be approved by a loan committee consisting of loan officers, often the bank's regulatory compliance officer, and often for smaller banks the chief officers of the bank. The loan officer presents the loan request information and the weaknesses and strengths of the loan. Often loan officers have close relationships with loan customers, so they act as the advocate for their customers at the loan committee meetings. In turn, bank officers and other lending officers grill the loan officer presenting the loan in terms of potential weaknesses or problems that the loan might have. Loan request procedures, as shown for example in Appendix 21.A have a uniform format for ease of presentation, discussed later in the chapter. Before presenting procedures, the following section provides an overview of a bank's overall written loan policies.

BANK WRITTEN LOAN POLICIES

A bank's overall loan policy reflects long-term strategic planning for the overall asset portfolio including setting general guidelines for the size of the loan portfolio, its composition, and the maximum acceptable level of default risk. For example, in a commercial bank, decisions must be made about the proportion of loan funds to be invested in C&I loans and the proportion earmarked for other purposes. These decisions influence the way a depository advertises its services, the customers whose loan applications will be given preference, and many other aspects of lending. Specific industries or markets that the bank wishes to target where lending officers have expertise are also included. Goals for loan volume and loan quality balances with a bank's liquidity, capital, and rate of return objectives are also incorporated, along with systems and controls to reduce credit risk. In addition, standards and procedures are included in terms of loan quality and procedures for documenting and reviewing loans and loan pricing.

COMPLIANCE POLICIES

Loan policies and procedures for complying with lending regulations also need to be put in place. Some of the major consuer lending regulations are as follows:

- ✦ The **Equal Credit Opportunity Act (Reg B)**, whereby the bank is forbidden to discriminate in lending on the basis of race, color, national origin, sex, age, religion, marital status, and/or receipt of public assistance.
- ✦ The **Fair Housing Act**, which forbids discrimination based on any handicap or family status.
- ✦ The **Fair Credit Reporting Act of 1970**, which requires consumer credit reporting agencies to stress accuracy, correct errors promptly, and release individual's consumer histories only for legitimate purposes. Customers also must be told why they are not given loans, and have the right to know of any discrepancies in their credit reports.
- ✦ **Truth in Lending (TIL)**, which requires that a bank must quote its rates as annual percentage rates (APRs).
- ✦ **REG Z**, which sets standards for disclosing the terms and costs of a consumer credit agreement before the borrower becomes obligated, established a period during which a consumer may cancel a transaction and procedures through which a consumer can challenge billing errors on revolving credit agreements. Institutions must comply with both state and federal legislation; if there are any contradictions between the two, federal statutes prevail. There are many mortgage lending regulations as well, including the following:
- ✦ A **Uniform Residential Loan Application (FNMA)** for home purchase of refinancing of home purchase of the applicant's principal dwelling where that dwelling will be used as collateral also must be provided, along with a notice of the right to receive a copy of the appraisal if applicable.
- ✦ The **Real Estate Settlement Procedures Act (RESPA)**, which provides servicing transfer disclosure and a good faith estimate (GFE) within three business days of receipt of a completed application, the provision of a settlement cost brochure for home purchases only, and a **HUD-1 or HUD-A1A Settlement Statement** provided at loan closing that must be prepared and available prior to loan closing.
- ✦ The **Home Mortgage Disclosure Act (HMDA)**, which obligates a bank to obtain HMDA information (race, sex, national origin) for home purchases, home improvement, or refinance applications.
- ✦ The **Community Reinvestment Act (CRA)**, which requires that the bank meet the credit needs of its area, especially low and moderate-income areas.

Examinations for CRA have become increasingly rigorous in recent years. Since July 1990, institutions have been required to disclose the CRA ratings they receive from examiners from outstanding to substantial noncompliance.

Since 1992, lenders have been required to analyze their lending on a detailed geographic basis, correlating the location of borrowers to whom they give loans against demographic data for that location, such as income, percent of minority population, and so on. Although the historical focus of CRA enforcement has been mortgage lending, commercial lending to small businesses is also under scrutiny. Institutions failing to demonstrate community reinvestment can face denial when they seek regulators' permission to branch, merge, or acquire another institution. Recent changes in CRA rules are discussed later in the chapter.[12]

✦ **Loans to Insiders Act (REG O)**, which says that banks are not allowed to give preferential loan terms to insiders. Loans given to insiders are limited and must be submitted to regulators, and require prior board approval.

✦ **Limits on lending to one party as a percentage of total capital**, which means that banks are not allowed to make loans to one individual or firm greater than 15 percent of capital, 25 percent if collateralized by safe securities.

CREDIT EXECUTION POLICIES

Policies also include an overview of the credit execution and administration process in terms of loan committee reviews, collateral and documents required for loans and loan reviews and the follow-up procedures for loans once they have been made. From these policies specific procedures for the credit analysis, credit execution and administration, and credit review process are put in place. Policies also include a **code of ethics and conflict of interest policy** for board of directors and senior management including treatment of confidential information from customers.

LENDER COMPENSATION POLICIES

In addition to policies for the bank's overall lending strategy and regulatory compliance policies, banks also have lender compensation policies that are crucial to the bank's business development process. In the 1990s, compensation policies for lenders became more performance-based. Bonuses were given based on how well lenders performed in bringing in new loans, having low loan losses on the loans that they made, serving current loan customers, and in cross selling other bank products such as working capital management services.

---

[12]New rules came in the wake of a Fed study in 1990 that found minority mortgage applicants to be rejected four times more often than nonminority applicants. Lenders responded that the study failed to control for applicants' credit histories and existing debt, but many institutions subsequently reexamined their loan approval practices to eliminate policies that may have resulted in discrimination, even if inadvertent. See Paulette Thomas. "Mortgage Rejection Rate for Minorities Is Quadruple that of Whites, Study Finds." *The Wall Street Journal* (October 21, 1991), A2; "CRA Policy Released." *Fedwire* (Federal Reserve Bank of Chicago), January 1992; and Garwood and Smith (1993).

In the 1980s banks often had separate departments where lenders simply made loans and credit administrators monitored loans that had been made and resolved loan problems. Loan officers were compensated for the business they brought in and were not penalized for bad loans which other administrators saw too. Consequently, a number of lenders became very aggressive in bringing in risky loans, such as risky commercial real estate loans in the northeast United States. When the commercial real estate loan market crashed in the northeast in the late 1980s, the problems associated with such compensation policies came to roost, with huge loan losses for many banks. New policies penalizing lenders for loan losses encourage more care in making loans. In additions, lenders are often asked to continue their relationships with their loan customers and be involved in the monitoring of the loans that they have made.

LOAN REQUEST PROCEDURES

Appendix 21.1A shows a sample of loan request procedures for loan officers used by Signet Bank in 1990 (now part of Crestar Bank). The loan request procedures are the implementation of the bank's overall lending policy. The procedures make loan presentations uniform and accessible to loan committee members. The procedures include the following:

1. The source of the business
2. The principal contacts for the loan
3. The participation structure (if other banks are participating in the loan)
4. The amount and reason for the loan request
5. Brief history and operations of the firm
6. Optional industry analysis if needed
7. Profile of managers and their experience and expertise
8. Financial statement analysis, including historical and proformas and ratios focusing on the companies ability to repay its debt
9. Collateral/risk analysis, summarizing collateral available and risks involved in the loan, such as barriers for entry in a particular industry
10. Loan review and rating recommendation by the loan officer, which includes whether the loan would be categorized as A, B, C from excellent to average or below ratings, based on the bank's classification of ratings for loans
11. Conclusion and opinion: favorable or unfavorable factors for the loan.

Basically, the loan procedures focus on the risks inherent in the business of the loan applicant, how risks have been mitigated, the use and amount of the loan, the ability of the borrower to repay the loan in terms of cash flow, and secondary sources of repayment including collateral.

This framework of this presentation basically includes what banker's call the **5 C's of Credit**:

1. **Character (the willingness of customer's to pay)**. Often loan officers use their experience to evaluate the character of individuals during a loan interview. Other evidence of character include past credit history, credit ratings of firms, and reputation from customers and suppliers.
2. **Capacity (the ability of a customer to pay in terms of cash flow)**. Capacity can be shown by looking at current and projected cash flow statements of corporate customers to determine if cash flow will be adequate to cover loan

payments. For consumer loans, annual income from tax returns and an employment contract and pay-stubs can be used. For mortgage loans, comparing the borrower's gross monthly income with the monthly loan payment is widely used to assess the burden on the borrower. The payment is sometimes adjusted to include homeowners' insurance and property taxes, although research has shown this **payment-to-income ratio** is not a reliable predictor of default.

3. **Capital (the soundness of a borrower's financial position in terms of equity).** The net worth or equity position of a corporate borrower relative to assets provides information on the cushion that the borrower has to absorb potential losses. For consumer customers, net worth is estimated as personal assets less personal liabilities.

4. **Conditions** (the industry and economic conditions that may affect a firm's ability to repay a loan). Particularly, for corporate customers, external conditions related to the industry and economic environment of the firm are particularly important for the loan officer to analyze. Lenders in the Southeastern United States, for instance, did not consider the effect of a fall in oil prices for firms they lent to in the 1980s, which later plunged otherwise healthy companies in the oil industry into bankruptcy. Similarly, during recessions, mortgage loan delinquencies also tend to rise.

5. **Collateral (secondary sources of repayment**, now often called **asset-based lending).** Collateral and at times personal guarantees against personal assets by a corporate lender are used as a secondary source of payment for the bank, particularly for more risky loans. However, taking possession of the collateral is expensive, so lenders rely for primary payment from cash flow, with the hope of not having to take possession.

With asset-based lending, rules of thumb are often used, such as lending from 40 percent to 60 percent against raw materials and finished goods inventory, which are easier to collect on; 50 percent to 80 percent against accounts receivables depending on the aging schedule and collection experience. Since asset-based lending often incorporates costly monitoring, loan rates are often higher than safer, unsecured loans, often 2 percent to 6 percent above a bank's basic lending rate.

Collateral is generally matched with the use for the loan. For instance a working capital loan to finance seasonal inventory and accounts receivables is often collateralized by those assets, whereas a term loan to purchase equipment is collateralized by the equipment to be purchased. Maintaining accurate records, known as *loan documentation*, is important when examiners are assessing the quality of outstanding loans, especially under FDICIA's tripwire provisions.[13]

One important form of self-protection for lenders for consumer and mortgage loans is to make sure that the value of the property at the time of application exceeds the loan amount by enough to protect the lender in case of default. Also, this provides an incentive for the borrower not to default. Research indicates that the initial **loan-to-value ratio** is positively related to both delinquency and default. The difference between the outstanding loan balance and the value of the property is the borrower's equity in the home. When the loan-to-value ratio is high (the maximum initially allowed by most lenders is 95 percent), the borrower has only a small

---

[13]For a more detailed discussion of the 5 C's of credit and terms used in asset-based lending, see Gill (1983). The Fed's surveys of commercial lending periodically report the percentage of total loans that involve collateral.

personal investment and if the market value of the property falls, the reduction in the borrower's equity may contribute to default even several years after the loan agreement is made. To estimate property values, lenders hire trained real estate appraisers. As noted in a previous chapter, FNMA and FHLMC often require certain loan-to-value ratios before being willing to securitize mortgage loans or mortgage insurance if loan to value ratios do not meet these sitpulations.[14]

QUANTITATIVE CREDIT SCORING MODELS

Many lenders, particularly large lenders, use quantitative credit-scoring models to integrate information from a variety of sources. Data on an applicant are weighted according to predetermined standards, and a score for credit worthiness is calculated. Applicants falling below a predetermined minimum acceptable score are rejected or given more attention in the loan application process before loans can be made.

Example of a Commercial Loan Credit Scoring Model   One of the most popular classification models for commercial loans is **Zeta Analysis**, designed by Edward Altman at New York University. This model uses a multiple discriminant analysis technique to identify important ratios used classify firms likely to fail from those that are not likely to fail. For instance, in an early model, significant ratios included working capital to total assets (WC); retained earnings to total assets (RE); return on assets based on operational earnings (ROA); a firm's market value of equity to book value of debt ratio (Equity); and asset turnover (AT). Given statistically determined weights for each of the ratios, a Zeta or Z-score can be calculated by plugging in a firm's ratios, as follows:

$$Z = 1.2\,WC + 1.4\,RE + 3.3\,ROA + .6\,EQUITY + 1.0\,AT$$

If the score is greater or equal to the cutoff score of about 2.675, the firm is more like the non-failed group, and the loan is less likely to default. Such classification models can be purchased by banks as computer packages or developed in house.[15]

Example of a Consumer Credit Scoring Model

Consumer credit scoring models are attempts to both assess all important factors about an applicant and to simultaneously evaluate all applicants objectively by the

---

[14]In the late 1980s, as thrift industry problems worsened, regulators found may severely undercapitalized thrifts to have wildly inflated appraisal values for loans. Under FIRREA, Congress mandated that the appraisal industry be more strictly regulated including requiring each state to establish criteria for appraiser licensing and certification (attesting to a higher level of competency than mere licensing) and stipulating that only certified appraisers may be employed for certain types of tasks. See "Appraising the Appraiser." *Freddie Mac Reports* (July 1989); and Michael Allen. "Appraisers Culprits in S&L Crisis Are Now Key to S&L Recovery." *The Wall Street Journal* (January 24, 19990), 1, 11.

[15]See Altman (1968; 1981); Saunders (1997). Credit scoring has also been implemented by some banks for home mortgages; see Robert B. Avery, Raphael W. Bostic, Paul S. Calem, and Glenn B. Canner. "Credit Risk, Credit Scoring, and the Performance of Home Mortgages." *Federal Reserve Bulletin* (July 1996), 621–648.

same standards to comply with Reg B. Hence, credit scoring models are often more widely used by consumer lenders.

Table 21.1 provides information on a hypothetical credit scoring system for consumer loans. The first step in developing a model is to determine from past data, borrower characteristics most often associated with bad and good loans, where "bad" is defined as slow-paying, delinquent, or in default. Typical characteristics include how long the applicant has been employed at his or her current job, whether the credit history is good, number of dependents, whether the applicant rents or owns a home, and his or her income and occupation. Points are assigned to new applicants based on these characteristics. For example, a borrower with a higher income would be assigned more points on that characteristic than one with a lower income. In Table 21.1 some characteristics have higher points than others as determined by statistical analysis of historical data, such as by using discriminant analysis. As shown at the bottom of Table 21.1 scores greater than 90 fall closer to the profile of a "good" customer, while scores lower than 50 fall closer to that of a "bad customer." In between 50 and 90 is an overlap range. Consequently, lenders would have to use more judgment for these cases. For most institutions, the costs (including cash losses and the penalties of regulatory displeasure) of accepting a "bad" applicant are higher than the opportunity costs of rejecting a "good" one.[16]

Performance and Limitations of Credit Scoring Models   Research has indicated that the accuracy of classifying loan applicants improves when a combination of statistical credit scoring models and judgmentally determined decision rules are used. The experience of some institutions provides even stronger endorsement for quantitative models. For example, NationsBank uses credit-scoring models for virtually all its consumer loan applications, but allows loan officers to override a score with approval from supervisors. One study showed that the delinquency rate for loans granted on the basis of loan-officer overrides was seven times higher than for loans approved solely on the basis of credit scores. Such findings will lead, undoubtedly, to the refinement of expert systems for consumer lending. One application of the credit scoring concept is behavior scoring, which attempts to predict the behavior of borrowers in the future rather than simply scoring the acceptability of a current loan applicant. Credit scoring and behavior scoring are also being used more frequently to evaluate mortgage applicants, particularly for affordable loan programs that attempt to provide home mortgage loans for lower to moderate income borrowers.[17]

Like all models, credit scoring schemes have limitations. The statistical complications of gray ranges are one problem. Also, models focus only on default risk and may ignore such information as deposit or other service relationships with the customer. They also must be carefully structured to comply with Reg B: Applicant characteristics included in a model must be "demonstrably and statistically sound," as

---

[16]A thorough review of the theory, history, and statistical properties of credit-scoring models can be found in Altman (1981). Another good source is Capon (1982).

[17]See Edmister (1988); Alexander (1989); and Alan Radding. "Credit Scoring's New Frontier." *The Magazine of Bank Management* (September 1992): 57. Interesting anecdotes on how some lenders use scoring models can be found in Robert Guenther. "Credit Card Issuers Ease Their Standards to Get New Accounts." *The Wall Street Journal* (May 22, 1989), A1, A4; and Sanford Rose. "Improving Credit Evaluation." *American Banker* (March 13, 1990), 4.

Table 21.1 ◆ Hypothetical Credit-Scoring System

Credit scoring models are designed to allow lenders to classify credit applicants into "good" or "bad" risks based on past credit history, employment history, and other variables. The table illustrates a typical scoring system.

Applicant Characteristics	Allotted Points	Applicant Characteristics	Allotted Points
Own or rent		Checking or savings account	
Own	41	Neither	0
Rent	0	Either	13
Other finance company		Both	19
Yes	−12	Applicant age	
No	0	30 years or less	6
Bank credit card		30+ to 40 years	11
Yes	29	40+ to 50 years	8
No	0	Older than 50 years	16
Applicant occupation		Years on job	
Professional and officials	27	5 or less	0
Technical and managers	5	5+ to 15	6
Proprietor	−3	More than 15	18
Clerical and sales	12		
Craftsman and nonfarm-laborer	0		
Foreman and operative	26		
Service worker	14		
Farm worker	3		

Source: Adapted from Gilbert A. Churchill, Jr., et al., "The Role of Credit Scoring in the Loan Decision," *The Credit World* 65 (March 1977): 7. *The Credit World* is the official publication of the International Credit Association, headquartered in St. Louis, MO. Reprinted with permission.

EVALUATING CREDIT SCORES

Difficulty arises when an applicant's score does not fall clearly into either group. Lenders must then decide between the opportunity cost of not giving credit to a potentially "good" customer and the risk of loaning to a "bad" one.

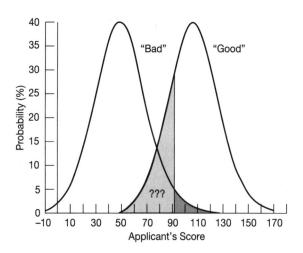

defined by the Fed.[18] But despite these limitations, major consumer lenders, especially retailers, regularly use the models, as do many depositories offering credit cards.

CreditMetrics and Other Portfolio Approaches   In recent years, bank managers have attempted to develop measures of a financial institution's credit risk more from an overall portfolio approach, looking at the total diversification of a bank's loan or total asset portfolio. In 1997, J.P. Morgan with several other large banks released to the public a model for quantifying portfolio risk based on a **Value at Risk (VAR)** approach discussed in Chapter 9. The CreditMetrics approach estimates changes in the market value of a bank's loan portfolio as well as other financial instruments in the event of a credit upgrade or downgrade as well as potential loan defaults. Probabilities based on historical data are calculated for the occurrence of such events. Using these probabilities, the expected change in the value a loans, value at risk, for a given confidence level can be calculated. Correlations between the value at risk for different loans and other financial instruments can be used to derive an aggregate measure of the volatility or value at risk for a bank's entire loan portfolio and other instruments, such as swaps, futures, and forward contracts. This approach is fairly new and is primarily used by very large banks that have borrowers with publicly rated debt. It is important by being one of the first formal models to incorporate the overall risk of a bank's loan portfolio including diversification effects.[19]

COMMERCIAL LENDING: FINANCIAL STATEMENT ANALYSIS

For commercial loans, financial statement analysis by credit analysts and lenders is crucial not only in deciding whether a loan should be granted, but also in determining the proper structure for the loan.

Financial statement analysis includes an analysis of historical trends in financial statements including common size income statements (put as a percentage of revenues), balance sheets (put as percentage of assets), and cash flow statements. In addition, pro forma statements showing whether cash flow is adequate to repay a loan need to be reviewed. Financial ratios are also calculated and compared with trends and peer industry ratios.

Table 21.2 shows the 15 financial ratios considered to be most important in analyzing commercial loans by lenders at the largest 100 banks in the United States These include ratios associated with cash flow, which indicate the ability of the borrower to repay the loan. At the bottom of the table, other basic ratios are listed including measures of overall profitability, revenue generation, cost management, and liquidity.

---

[18]See Smith (1985) and Board of Governors of the Federal Reserve System. "Revisions of Regulation B: Official Staff Commentary" (November 13, 1985). Reg B is frequently amended.

[19]For a more detailed discussion of CreditMetrics, see Marcia Millon Cornett and Anthony Saunders. *Fundamentals of Financial Institutions Management*. Chicago: Irwin McGraw Hill, 1999, pp. 239–243. Also see J.P. Morgan. *Introduction to Credit Metrics*. New York: J.P. Morgan Securities, April 1997.

Table 21.2 ✦ FINANCIAL RATIOS PERCEIVED AS IMPORTANT BY LOAN OFFICERS

Although many financial ratios can be calculated, loan officers believe that some are better than others. One survey showed that a firm's debt/equity ratio was viewed as the most useful ratio, followed by the current ratio.

Ratio	Significance Rating	Primary Measure
Debt/equity	8.71	Debt
Current ratio	8.25	Liquidity
Cash flow/current maturities of long-term debt	8.08	Debt
Fixed charge coverage	7.58	Debt
Net profit margin after tax	7.56	Profitability
Times interest earned	7.50	Debt
Net profit margin before tax	7.43	Profitability
Degree of financial leverage	7.33	Debt
Inventory turnover (days)	7.25	Liquidity
Accounts receivable turnover (days)	7.08	Liquidity
Quick ratio	6.79	Liquidity
Cash flow/total debt	6.71	Debt
Return on assets after tax	6.69	Profitability
Accounts receivable turnover (times)	6.58	Liquidity
Return on equity after tax	6.30	Profitability

Significance:

0–2 Low Importance

7–9 High Importance

Source: Charles Gibson, "Financial Ratios as Perceived by Commercial Loan Officers," *Akron Business & Economic Review*, Vol. 14, No. 2, Summer, 1983, pp. 23–27. Reprinted with permission.

REVIEW IMPORTANT FINANCIAL RATIOS

Overall Profitability:	Return on Equity = Net Income/Equity
	Return on Assets = Net Income/Assets
Cost Efficiency:	Net Profit Margin = Net Income/Revenues
	Operating Profit Margin = Operating Income/Revenues
	Gross Profit Margin = Gross Income/Revenues
Revenue Generation:	Total Asset Turnover = Revenues/Assets
	Fixed Asset Turnover = Revenues/Fixed Assets
	Inventory Turnover = Cost of Goods Sold/Inventory
	Accounts Receivables Turnover = Revenues/Accounts Receivables
Bankruptcy Risk:	Debt to Assets = Total Debt/Total Assets
	Times Interest Earned = Earnings Before Interest and Taxes (EBIT)/Interest Expense
	Fixed Charge Coverage = EBIT & Fixed Charges/(Interest Expense & Fixed Charges)
Liquidity:	Current Ratio = Current Assets/Current Liabilities
	Quick Ratio = (Current Assets − Inventory)/Current Liabilities
	Cash Flow to Total Debt = Operating Cash Flow/Total Debt

Cash Flow to Maturing Long-Term Debt = Operating Cash Flow/Maturing Long-Term Debt (Previous Period)

$$\text{Days Cash to Cash Cycle} = \frac{365}{\text{Accts. Rec. Turnover}} + \frac{365}{\text{Inventory Turnover}} - \frac{365}{\text{Cost Goods Sold/Accounts Payable}}$$

SAMPLE LOAN PRESENTATION

Appendix 21.B shows an example of a short, sample loan presentation for a loan renewal request from the Euphoria Bank of New York City by the Big Apple Real Estate and Storage Company, a real estate and storage company partnership operating in New York City. The loan request is presented by the company's loan officer, Eleanor Winters, at the weekly loan committee meeting of the bank with Phil Lerner, CEO; Roslyn Lerner, President; Albert Singleton, the Regulatory Compliance Officer; and other senior loan officers at the bank including Robert Cooperman, Leendert Van Der Pool, Patty Moran, and Gary Patterson.

Background and Request   Eleanor Winters' report shown in Appendix 21.B includes **background** on the company and its partners and the nature of the **loan request**, along with a repayment analysis based on the proposed loan structure. This loan request from the Big Apple Real Estate and Storage Company of New York City is to renew its current term debt of about $830,000 with the bank, which will be maturing in 1997 on the company's facility in downtown Manhattan.

Repayment Analysis   Based on the proposed loan structure, Patty Moran has prepared a repayment analysis for the loan based on historical figures for the past four years. **Net operating income (NOI)** is calculated by adding back depreciation and amortization and interest expense to net income. The debt service (loan payment) for the amortized mortgage loan has been estimated to be $101,784 including interest and principal. Subtracting the debt service from NOI gives **net cash flow**. Dividing NOI by the debt service gives a debt coverage ratio of greater than 2 for each of the previous four years.

For commercial real estate loans, occupancy rates are also very important. As noted in the repayment analysis, the storage facility for the loan has had a high level of 95 percent occupancy in the summer to a low of 87 percent. Hence, based on the operating expenses of $282,579 in 1996, rental income would have to drop by over 40 percent of $174,666 for the company to fall below a break-even point (i.e., have a loss). Other points made in the repayment analysis are that revenue growth over the past three years has been the result of rate increases and that the average occupancy rates for the storage facility have been relatively stable. In 1995, expenses rose on a one-time basis because of the need to temporarily replace a manager who was hospitalized. Projections for 1997 reflect annualized revenue similar to 1996, with seasonality considerations taken into account.

Secondary and Tertiary Sources of Repayment   Other sources of repayment are presented next. The primary partner is the only guarantor of the loan. The financial statements of the guarantor show sufficient secondary strength to be considered. The tertiary repayment will be the refinance or sale of the subject property. A collateral section is provided with an independent appraisal of the market value of the property.

Financial Analysis Summary   A financial analysis summary is presented based on the attached spreadsheets of the company for the past four years that were CPA reviewed. The spreadsheets include common size and dollar financial statements including income statements, balance sheets, and cash flow statements, along with summary key ratios. The presentation includes the key points from these statements.

Balance Sheet   For the **balance sheet**, after the sale of assets in 1995 and early 1996, assets dropped while net worth rose. Cash balances and liquidity have improved in 1996. It is interesting to note on the balance sheet that net worth was negative in 1992 to 1994, which reflects accumulated depreciation of real estate assets and the amortization of goodwill which reduced assets in those years making liabilities greater than assets. With the sale of assets in later years, net worth became positive in 1995 and 1996. This demonstrates the importance for the credit analyst to understand such factors that affect balance sheet for real estate companies. Otherwise, the negative net worth figures would be particularly alarming.

Income Statement   Highlights for the **income statement** include fluctuating revenue and operating margins over the past five years as the firm grew and sold off assets. Operating profits are expected to return to their normal range of 40 to 50 percent in 1997. Net profits have been strong for the past two years as the result of gains realized from the sale of partnership interests.

Guarantor and Collateral   The final portion of the presentation includes more detailed information on the **guarantor and collateral** as secondary and tertiary sources of repayment. Reviewing the assets of John Jahera, the guarantor of the loan, indicates a quite strong annual cash after debt service for other partnerships. A review of the collateral including a fair market value appraisal of $1.6 million for the property and a valuation of $2.21 million based on a net income valuation approach (using net income divided by a capitalization rate of 12.5 percent). With the $2.21 million valuation ratio, the loan to value ratio would be 38 percent. If a less conservative discount rate of 10 percent is used, the valuation is $2.76 million or a loan to value ratio of 30 percent for the approximately $.830 million loan.

An environmental property audit was performed on the property used as collateral, which did not indicate any potential hazards, although a service station across the street had an unknown disposition.

Risk Analysis and Recommendation   Based on the financial analysis, the loan was rated as a grade 1-C (average risk) based on the bank's ranking system. Risks mentioned included inherent economic and market risk associated with a real estate investment as well as limited information supplied by the chief guarantor. However, the firm had a profitable history, experience, financial strength in the guarantor, and a solid collateral position, so the loan officer recommended approval.

Proposed Loan Structure   Eleanor Winters presented a proposed loan structure that sets the original loan to be renewed for five years at a fixed rate equal to the current five-year Treasury bond + a 2.65 percent premium, plus a loan fee of $\frac{1}{2}$ percent. The collateral for the loan would be the first deed of trust on the company's downtown New York City facility.

After much discussion including some concerns about the collateral for the loan and the financial condition of the guarantor, the loan was unanimously approved by the committee, based on the solid cash flow and the very good current and future prospects for the Big Apple Real Estate Storage Company operating in a brisk real estate market in New York City.

ESTABLISHING LOAN TERMS

Terms of individual loans are particularly important for a lender's financial performance. The dominance of loans in institutions' asset portfolios suggests that keeping loan rates at approximate levels is a prerequisite to earning a target NIM and target ROE. Loan terms include the lending rate, noninterest terms and fees for the loan, the maturity and timing of payments, the loan amount, collateral or other secondary sources of payment, and any restrictive covenants associated with the loan.

The base lending rate for the loan plus a premium to cover expected default risk, administrative costs, and the bank's desired spread to achieve its NIM and ROE targets discussed in the following section.

Base Lending Rates Base lending rates are established at the institutional level and used as benchmarks for determining specific loan rates. Very good customers may be offered a lower rate, and higher-risk customers are charged a higher rate. But the base sets the boundaries within which the loan officer can exercise discretion.[20]

Earlier chapters introduced the relationship between the target ROE and the target NIM. Although interest revenues earned on the loan portfolio are an important influence on the NIM, other assets also must be considered in the base loan-rate calculation. For example, suppose the hypothetical institution shown in Table 21.3 has nonearning assets equal to 10 percent of total assets. Also, suppose that 30 percent of the institution's total assets are invested in securities on which the before-tax average rate of return is 10.5 percent. The remaining 60 percent of total assets are invested in loans. The mix of assets and rates of return, as well as the fact that some assets are nonearning, must be considered in planning for the total spread, Interest Revenues − Interest Expenses (IR − IE), as shown in the following equation:

$$IR - IE = [\Sigma r_i \times A_i] - (c \times TL) \qquad [21.1]$$

where:

r_i = the interest rate earned on asset category i

A_i = total dollar investment in asset category i

c = average interest cost of financial liabilities

TL = total liabilities

Note that the first term equals total interest revenues and the second term equals total interest expense. Equation 21.1 can be used to solve for the base loan rate r_L.

Table 21.3 notes that the average cost of liabilities is 9 percent and that liabilities total $92 million. If the target NIM—a calculation based on total assets—is 3.2 percent, the necessary spread between interest revenues and interest cost of liabilities is $3.2 million. Using Equation 21.1, the target spread is expressed in million as follows:

$$\text{Spread} = [(0\% \times \$10) + (10.5\% \times \$30) + (r_L \times \$60)] - \$8.28$$

Solving for r_L:

$$r_L = \$8.33/\$60 = 13.88\%$$

---

[20]Historically, the base rate at commercial banks was known as the "prime" lending rate. For reasons explained later in the chapter, the terms *base rate* and *prime rate* are no longer always synonymous; rather a bank's base rates reflects its average cost of funds.

Table 21.3 ✦ THE BASE LENDING RATE REQUIRED TO MEET TARGET RATES OF RETURN

A base lending rate is established after considering an institution's target NIM, its target RONW, and its asset mix. The base rate is the starting point from which loan terms for individual borrowers are established.

I. BALANCE SHEET AND PLANNING ASSUMPTIONS

Assets		Liabilities and Net Worth	
Securities	$ 30	Liabilities	$ 92
Loans	60		
Nonearning assets	10	Net worth	8
Total	$100	Total	$100

Return on securities: 10.5%

Return on nonearning assets: 0%   Average cost of liabilities: 9%

Target NIM: 3.2%   Net worth multiplier: 12.5

$t = 34\%$ Target ROE: 18%

Base loan rate: 13.88% (as calculated in text)

II. PRO FORMA INCOME STATEMENT

Interest revenues:

$10.50\% \times \$30 = \$3.150$

$13.88\% \times \$60 = 8.328$

$0.00\% \times \$10 = 0.000$

Total	$11.478

Interest expense:

$9.00\% \times \$92 =$	(8.280)
Spread	$ 3.198

Less net noninterest expenses:

$1.00\% \times \$100 =$	(1.000)
Income before taxes	$ 2.198
Less income taxes (0.34)	(0.747)
Net income	$ 1.451

NIM = $3.2/$100 = 3.2%

ROE = $1.451/$8 = 18%

Because nonearning assets and securities contribute to the target NIM at a lower rate than do loans, interest earned on loans must provide a higher than average return for the institution's financial objectives to be achieved. The pro forma (projected) income statement at the bottom of Table 21.3 illustrates this point. The base rate of 13.88 percent is appropriate only for customers of average cost and average risk; it is a starting point for loan officers in setting loan rates for individual customers. Competitive conditions including loan rates offered by other banks also affect such lending rates.

NONINTEREST TERMS AND CONDITIONS

Commercial lenders use more than the interest rate to determine the effective yield on loans. A term commonly used to describe the evaluation of the total institutional relationship with a loan customer is customer profitability analysis. It involves examining the funds received from and the nonlending services provided to a customer as well as a specific loan application. For example, a customer voluntarily keeping large demand deposit balances is a valuable one, because no explicit interest is paid on these balances. Similarly, customers using the institution's cash management services or those whose pension fund balances are managed by the bank's trust department are also valuable. These factors can affect noninterest loan terms and conditions, the most common of which are compensating balances, commitments and commitment fees, discounting, and collateral.

Compensating balance requirements require that the borrower keep a minimum non-interest earning deposit balance with the institution, which guarantees the lender access to inexpensive funds and liquidity. In turn, the borrower has a higher effective cost of funds equal to interest expense/(loan less the compensating balance). Banks at times allow compensating balances to be kept in low-interest time deposits, which avoids reserve requirements. Many banks offer two pricing schemes, one with compensating balances and one with alternative fees and/or a higher loan rate for customers who prefer to pay separately for loan and deposit services.[21]

Lines of credit and commitments are agreements to extend funds to the borrower over some prearranged time period. Lines of credit is an informal arrangement like a credit card arrangement with loan rates determined at the time of borrowing if funds are available. In contrast, a loan commitment is a formal arrangement with a legal guarantee that funds will be available at a given rate, amount, and maturity. With a commitment, the customer can borrow or "take down" some, all, or none of the authorized funds. The terms of the commitment usually require the borrower to pay a **commitment fee** based on any amount of unused credit over the life of the agreement and to pay interest on funds actually taken down. The fee compensates the lender for the liquidity that must be provided. The most common type of commitment is a revolving commitment, guaranteeing that funds can be borrowed, repaid, and borrowed again over an extended period, often as long as three years. The interest rate may be fixed or pegged to a reference market rate. The lender assumes risk of a potential financial deterioration of the borrower during the period, so the commitment fee will be higher. Some banks include protective clauses to avoid a commitment if the borrower's condition significantly deteriorates. It is not uncommon for commitments to require a compensating balance as well.

Effect of Noninterest Terms on a Lender's Expected Return   Table 21.4 shows an example of the combined effect of interest and noninterest terms on the lender's total return from a loan commitment.[22] The base rate plus the appropriate risk premium is 11.5 percent, with a .25 percent commitment fee on the unused portion of the commitment, an 8 percent compensating balance on the entire commitment and 4 percent compensating balance on the amount actually borrowed. To estimate the bank's effective rate of return, the portion of the line will actually be taken down on average over the commitment period is estimated to be 60 percent of the $2 million commitment during the next 1-year period.

The commitment fee of .25 percent will be paid on $800,000 (the 40 percent of the commitment expected to be unused), and the interest rate of 11.5 percent will be paid on the portion taken down, or $1,200,000. The lender earns total interest

---

[21]See Ulrich (1985); Nadler (1989); Mahoney (1988); and Stigum (1990).
[22]This example draws on a presentation in Brick (1984).

Table 21.4 ✦ Effect of Noninterest Terms on the Lender's Expected Return

The cost to a borrower and the yield to the lender can be significantly affected by noninterest loan terms. The table illustrates how a commitment fee on a line of credit can increase an institution's rate of return.

Stated interest rate	11.5% (base rate plus risk premium)
Commitment fee	0.25% on unused portion of the commitment
Term	1 year
Compensating balances	8% of commitment plus 4% of borrowed funds
Estimated average loan balance	60% of commitment
Maximum line of credit	$2,000,000
Loan Interest and Noninterest Revenues	
Interest [$2,000,000(0.6)(0.115)]	$138,000
Fees [$2,000,000(0.4)(0.0025)]	2,000
Total revenues	$140,000
Net Funds Invested	
Average loan balance	$1,200,000
Portion offset by compensating demand deposit balances	
$2,000,000(0.08)	$ (160,000)
$1,200,000(0.04)	(48,000)
Deduct reserve requirements [10% × ($160,000 + $48,000)]	20,800
Total offsetting funds	(187,200)
Net invested funds	$1,012,800
Total Expected Return	

$$\frac{\text{Interest and Noninterest Revenues}}{\text{Net Invested Funds}} = \frac{\$140,000}{\$1,012,800} = 13.82\%$$

and fee revenues of $140,000. Net funds extended, however, are $187,200 less than $1,200,000 or $1,012,800 because of compensating balances after adjustments for a 10 percent marginal reserve requirement. As shown in Table 21.4, the expected yield is 13.82 percent. The lending institution also incurs implicit costs not included here, such as additional uncertainty about the timing and quantity of funds demanded. No one knows when, or in what quantity, the borrower will actually request the committed funds.

Discounted Loans A lending practice that also increases the return to the lender beyond the stated interest rate is discounting. With discounting the first interest payment is paid at the beginning of the loan period by being deducted before loan funds are made available to the borrower. In effect, the borrower's effect rate is the interest expense based on the entire loan / (the actual amount borrowed less the first interest payment). For instance, if the borrower borrowed $100,000 with a 10 percent annual rate, the actual effective annual rate would be $10,000/$90,000 = 11.11 percent. Thus, discounting increases the lender's yield and the borrower's cost.

Similarly for mortgage loans, lenders customarily charge initial service fees, known as points at the time of the loan origination. A point is 1 percent of the principal of the loan. Points are similar to discounted loans with the point amount deducted upfront from the loan, increasing the effective cost for the borrower and the effective return to the lender. Points were originally established to compensate lenders for not being allowed to charge market rates because of mortgage usury ceilings (ceilings on loan rates) established in many states. Although mortgage usury ceilings were eliminated in most states after DIDMCA, points still influence the pricing of mortgages of all types.[23]

Customer Pricing Using Profitability Analysis

Based on the relationship that a customer has including noninterest terms, banks often set a loan rate for a customer based on the total net income brought in by a relationship. The loan rate including noninterest factors is set based on the total revenues and expenses of a customer, so that total expenses plus a given profit are equal to the total revenues generated from the loan.

Appendix 21.C shows a profitability analysis used to price the loan to the Big Apple Real Estate and Storage Company presented earlier. The loan amount authorized by the bank was $820,487. Subtracting the average demand deposits held by the customer less float and reserve requirements, the amount actually given to the customer equals **$748,514.** With a 9.15 percent annual loan rate on the loan amount of $820,487 plus a $835 fee, the gross income on the loan per year is $75,910 less the cost of $600 the banks speeds for maintenance and setup expenses, resulting in net income of $75,310. Hence, the relationship yield that the bank is getting is $75,310/$748,514 = 10.06 percent, if a 9.15 percent loan rate is charged with a $835 fee.

Based on a profitability index analysis at the bottom of the page, the bank wants to make its marginal cost of funds of 5.25 percent plus a profit spread of 4.35 percent + a 1 percent adjustment for risk equal to a minimum required yield of 10.6 percent. With the 10.06 percent yield based on the preceding pricing analysis, the bank reaches just 94.917 percent of its required yield. To achieve the 10.6 percent, either the fee would have to be raised, additional basis points added to the loan, or an additional compensating balance would need to be required.

QUOTED BASE RATES ON COMMERCIAL LOANS

As shown in the preceding profitability analysis, commercial loan officers often tailor the terms of a loan to fit customers' preferences and the needs of the lending institution. Rates are often set off a bank's marginal cost of funds as noted in the above example. As noted in Chapter 8, for large banks loan rates are also set with a premium added for the risk adjusted return on capital (RAROC) based on the likelihood of losses for that loan. In setting rates, particularly variable rates, however, an index is often used, such as the 5-year Treasury rate in the loan presentation example or the **Prime Rate**.

---

[23]A point is equal to 1 percent of the principal of the loan. Thus, for a 10 year, annual payment mortgage loan of $100,000, 1 point would be equal to (.01) $100,000 = $1,000; 2 points = $2,000, and so on. If the rate on the loan was 6 percent, then the loan payment would be $100,000 divided by the present value of annuity factor (PVIFA) for 10 years, 6 percent, equal to 7.360, resulting in a loan payment of $100,000/7.36 = $13,587. Setting the actual amount given for the loan with 2 points, $98,000 = $13,587 (PVIFA y, 10 years) and solving for the yield using trial by error or a financial calculator, the effective annual yield is about 6.43 percent.

The Prime Rate historically was the rate charged on short-term commercial loans to a bank's best customers. Historically, the prime rate was used to identify the interest rate charged on short-term loans to a bank's most creditworthy customers and was used in the early 1970s often as an economic indicator of business activity. In the later 1970s with financial managers issuing commercial paper, bonds, or Eurobonds in place of taking on bank loans, many large money center banks began to link their prime rates to the commercial paper rate, but later returned to an administered prime rate, with prime rates differing for money market and other regional banks. However, at times banks used the practice of offering below prime rates. This led to some lawsuits by customers who were quoted a bank's prime rate, which was not the bank's lowest rate. For instance, First National Bank of Atlanta was sued by a small business customer.[24]

Use of Cost of Funds as a Base Rate   As a result, institutions have redefined the prime or, perhaps more accurately, have given it a "nondefinition." Morgan Guaranty Trust, for example, announced that the "bank's prime shall mean the rate of interest publicly announced by the bank in New York from time to time as the prime rate." At many institutions base rate replaces the prior usage of the prime rate, with different base rates based on customer preferences, such as LIBOR for large borrowers with access to funds in the international as well as the domestic markets. Other rates announced as prime may actually reflect a bank's average cost of funds with a risk premium added. By using the average versus marginal cost of funds as a base, small borrowers who may be unable to bear the risk associated with highly volatile interest rates benefits, as do lenders who avoid the administrative cost of frequent rate changes and who can maintain higher loan yields for a longer period if rates fall.[25] By using an index such as the Treasury rate, lenders can also help borrowers who want to hedge their interest-rate risk. Interest rate futures are traded on Treasury bill rates, so borrowers would not have to cross-hedge.[26]

---

[24]The customer had borrowed from the bank at a rate 1 percent over prime. But the "prime" was identified in the loan contract as the "rate available to the bank's best commercial customers." When the news media reported that the bank routinely offered large commercial customers loans at rates below prime, the litigant requested that his rate be lowered also. When First Atlanta refused, he sued. In following years, more than 40 lawsuits were filed against other commercial banks, and the definition of the prime has been carefully reevaluated. In March 1984, First Atlanta proposed a settlement to avoid the cost of further litigation. Under the settlement, all plaintiffs were given the opportunity to negotiate loans at preferable rates.

[25]See Koch (1995) for a more detailed discussion of base lending rates, including a discussion of liability cost transfer price systems used at large banks for pricing loans. Research on determinants and use of the prime rate includes Slovin and Sushka (1983); Goldberg (1984); Benston (1984); Thomas F. Brady. "The Role of the Prime Rate in the Pricing of Business Loans by Commercial Banks, 1977–1984," Board of Governors of the Federal Reserve System, Staff Study No. 146, November 1985; Elizabeth Laderman. "The Changing Role of the Prime Rate." *Weekly Letter* (Federal Reserve Bank of San Francisco) (July 13, 1990); Furlong. "Is the Prime Rate Too High?"; and Forbes and Mayne (1989).

[26]Using an index such as the T-bill rate associated with the bank's cost of funds is sometimes called a "synthetic fixed-rate loan." See Brady (1985), 12–13. For a more detailed discussion of loan pricing including pricing for risk, see Saunders (1997) and Sinkey (1998).

RISK PREMIUMS ON LOANS

Determining the risk premium to be added to a loan is a controversial issue. As noted in discussing RAROC pricing in Chapter 8, risk premiums can be added based on the expected losses of the loan. Other strategies for risk premiums include rating loans and using similar risk premiums to those between different grade bonds and Treasury bonds in bond markets. For instance, the rate spread between a Treasury security and a BBB Corporate bond might be 50 basis points, so such a premium would be used for a loan that the bank gives a "Good" BBB rating. Other premiums may be based on rules of thumb, such as 10 basis points for a loan with a very high rating with higher basis points added for higher risk loans, as commonly practiced in the industry. Additional risk premiums might be added for credit, maturity, and collateral risk, as well. Loans were typically underpriced for risk in the 1980s, so the proper pricing of loans for risk has been an important issue in the 1990s. Of course, competitive rates must be considered as well.

OTHER TERMS: COLLATERAL

Collateral is discussed briefly earlier in the chapter. By requiring collateral, a lender can service customers who would be too risky for an unsecured loan. But because lenders do not want to be forced to take possession of the borrower" assets, credit analysis is just as important (if not more so) for a secured loan agreement as for an unsecured one. Small banks are more likely to make collateralized loans than their larger counterparts. Asset-based lending adds several important dimensions to loan analysis:

1. Determining the value of the assets to be pledged as collateral
2. Meeting all legal requirements for securing those assets
3. Monitoring the condition of the collateral during the loan period.

The legal agreement assigning the assets as collateral is called the **security agreement**. The Uniform Commercial Code, a body of law adopted individually by states but containing many common provisions across states, establishes guidelines under which these agreements are drawn. Different types of collateral arrangements include a **floating lien**, which gives the lender recourse to the borrower's entire inventory, even if portions are acquired after the loan is made. In the case of riskier loans, **warehouse receipts** place specific inventory items assigned as collateral under the control of a third part, and the goods are often physically transferred to a bonded public warehouse for safekeeping. **Floor planning**, often used by automobile dealers, allows the borrower to retain possession of the collateral. It is an agreement often used to finance expensive retail items such as major appliances or heavy equipment that can be distinguished by serial number or description.

In the case of accounts receivable financing, the collateral may be either pledged or actually sold to the lender. The latter arrangement is called **factoring** and means the bank assumes default risk and responsibility for collection. Whether pledged or factored, the loan amount should always be less than the face value of the receivables.

RESTRICTIVE COVENANTS

Banks often protect their interests as well by establishing restrictive covenants, such as minimum liquidity or debt ratios or a borrower taking on additional debt. Covenants may require life insurance on a key person in a firm, that the bank be notified if any change in management occurs, that the bank be sent quarterly statements from the firm, as well as many other covenants structured to protect the bank's interests. The loan may state that if covenants are not met the loan will be called.

OTHER CONSIDERATIONS

Type of Loan and Proper Structuring and Maturity

A loan is structured in terms of when payments are made to ensure that loan customers will be able to make these payments. Banks must also be careful to lend the proper amount. Often companies request a loan larger or smaller than they actually need. With too large a loan, a company may have difficulty paying the loan back, and with too small a loan, the company may find itself having liquidity difficulties. By forecasting financial statements including a source or use statement or cash flow statements, the proper amount needed for a loan can be determined, as the missing use that makes total sources equal total uses. Projected monthly cash flow statements also can be used to determine when a loan can be repaid and the proper payment structure.

SPECIAL CONSIDERATIONS FOR DIFFERENT TYPES OF LOANS

Seasonal Working Capital Loans

Seasonal working capital loans are generally repaid with one year once inventory has been sold and accounts receivables have been collected. To determine the approximate loan amount needed for a seasonal working capital loan, quarterly balance sheet statements need to be projected. Performing a sources and uses statement based on the differences between the balance sheet for the peak and low seasons will determine the total uses and sources needed, with the difference between uses and sources as the approximate amount of the loan needed from the bank or another external source.

A rule of thumb method for determining the amount of a working capital loan needed is often calculated as a firm's cash to cash cycle times its daily average cost of goods sold (CGS/365). A firm's cash to cash cycle (CC) is typically calculated as:

$$CC = \text{Days Inventory} + \text{Average Collection Period} - \text{Days Accounts Payable} \qquad [21.2]$$

where:

$$\text{Days Inventory} = 365 / (\text{CGS/Inventory});$$

$$\text{Average Collection Period (ACP)} = 365 / (\text{Credit Sales/Accounts Receivables});$$

$$\text{Days Accounts Payable} = 365 / (\text{CGS / Accounts Payable}).$$

Risks in Credit Cards   Because credit cards carry preestablished lines of credit, consumers may accumulate substantial borrowings before the card issuer knows financial problems have developed. Mass mailing have increased such risks. Although credit cards often offer a 2 percent to 3 percent net return after administrative costs, expected loan losses, and the interest cost of funds, they also entail higher risk. In the early 1990s some banks introduced **secured cards**, which require customers with poor credit risk to leave a security deposit at a bank to become a cardholder, and higher interest rates and fees were charged.

Narrowing Margins on Cards with Competition   With bank and nonbank competition, such as MBNA, AT&T, American Express, General Electric, and General Motors and innovative pricing schemes and promotions, banks have been forced to respond with similar offers, such as lower fees or tiered pricing programs, in which customers with good payment records are offered lower rates. Some issuers, such as MBNA, a large credit card bank in Wilmington, Delaware, have also issued **affinity cards** to members of special interest groups, with which issuing banks share profits on cardholders' purchases or for which a portion of profits are donated to charitable causes, or purchasers are entitled to extra mileage contributing towards free flights from airlines, such as United and Delta. Adding to competitive pressure, customers have become more aggressive in the demands they place on issuers. Suits were filed in 1991, for instance, to limit or even prevent issuers from charging penalties for late payment on credit card accounts. With these pressures, returns on assets in the credit card business have fallen.[30]

Installment Loans   Other types of consumer loans are often made on an installment basis. Annual percentage rates (APRs) must be quoted on these loans, which were targeted particularly by Congress, because of confusion in stated rates. In an installment agreement, the borrower makes equal periodic payments. In addition, many automobile and other consumer loans use the add-on-interest method. The interest on the full amount borrowed must be paid for each year of the loan term, even though the entire balance is not outstanding for the full term. For example, suppose a couple decides to buy a new car priced at $12,000. After making a $2,000 down payment, they approach their CU for a $10,000 loan and are quoted an add-on rate of 9 percent for 4 years. They will repay a total of:

$$\$10,000(.09)(4) + \$10,000 = \$13,600$$

The repayment schedule will be $13,600/48 = $283.33 per month, resulting in a monthly interest rate of 1.3322 percent and an annual percentage rate (APR) of just under 16 percent, based on setting the $10,000 = $283.33 (PVIFA 48 periods). Using a financial calculator or trial by error, the monthly rate is 1.3322 percent × 12 = approximately 16 percent annually. Note with an add-on rate, the effective rate is a little less than double the quoted rate. Reg Z requires lenders to disclose the

---

[30]See "Plastic Profits Go Pop." *Economist* (September 12, 1992), 92; Tim Smart. "Mad As Hell About Late Fees." *Business Week* (February 24, 1992), 32; Bruce W. Morgan. "Credit Card Interest Rates: Perceptions, Politics, and Realities." *Banking Policy Report* 11 (January 20, 1992), 1; "The Nonbanks Muscle In." *Economist* (May 25, 1991), 84, 89; and Leah N. Spiro. "More Cards in the Deck." *Business Week* (December 16, 1991), 100–104; and Michael Auriemma. "Bank-Card Strategies: Weight Your Choices." *Bank Management* (September/October 1994), 23–26.

APR to borrowers. The Fed defines the APR as the periodic rate multiplied by, not compounded by, the number of periods in a year. Thus, the APR is a legal definition of an interest rate and is not the effective annual yield to the lender.[31]

The Rule of 78s as a Prepayment Penalty for Installment Loans　　When a borrower repays an installment loan before the original maturity date, lenders often apply the rule of 78s to calculate the remaining principal balance. This approach, also called the sum-of-digits involves adding together the digits for the number of payments to be made. The 78 in the name is derived from the sum of digits for a 12-month loan:

$$12 + 11 + 10 + 9 + 8 + 7 + 6 + 5 + 4 + 3 + 2 + 1 = 78$$

For the example of a 4-year (48 month) automobile loan, the sum of digits is 1,176 $[(N/2) \times (N+1)]$, where N is the number of payments. According to the rule of 78s, were the borrowers to pay the loan off early, they would be charged for 48/1,176 of their total interest payment owned in the first month, 47/1,176 in the second month, and so on as interest. For instance, if the borrowers repaid the loan after 1 year, after 12 payments of $283.33, they have paid $3,399.96. Under the rule of 78s, they would be charged with (510/1,176) or .4337 of the total interest payment of $3,600 [$10,000 (.09) × 4] = $1,561.22 as interest. The numerator 510 is the sum of 48, 47, 46, and so on, through 37. Subtracting this $1,561.22 of interest from the total payment $3,399.96 − $1,561.22 = $1,838.74 that would be considered as repaid principal. To discharge their obligation, the borrowers would have to pay the credit union $10,000 − $1,838.74 = $8,161.26. The rule of 78s is controversial because it specifies a balance for repayment higher than the balance indicated by an amortization schedule based on an APR of 16 percent. In most states, however, lenders are permitted to use the rule of 78s, although a few states have adopted laws specifically prohibiting it. Lenders argue that it is justified because it helps them recover fixed lending costs, although consumer advocates argue that the rule of 78s is unfair to borrowers.[32]

Home Equity Loans　　The Tax Reform Act of 1986 spurred intense interest in home equity loans, a type of credit with characteristics of both mortgage and non-mortgage consumer lending. The Tax Reform Act phased out the tax deductibility of interest expenses for consumer borrowers with the exception of interest on home mortgage loans and home equity loans (hels). Hels are different from second mortgages, which are additional loans backed by the property on which a first mortgage has been issued, with fixed dollar amounts, specified maturity dates, and a higher interest rate than first mortgages. The amount that homeowners can borrow is limited by the amount of equity they have accumulated in their homes. A hel, in contrast, is a revolving line of credit against which a homeowner can borrow with the maximum amount allowed to borrow using 70 to 85 percent of the equity the borrower has in the home. Because the lender has the security of a junior lien on the borrower's

---

[31]Board of Governors of the Federal Reserve System, "Official Staff Commentary on Regulation Z Truth-in-Lending as Amended April 1, 1990" (June 1990).

[32]Thanks to Jim McNulty for assistance with this discussion. See "The Rule of 78's or What May Happen When You Pay Off a Loan Early." *Federal Reserve Bank of Philadelphia, Department of Consumer Affairs Pamphlet*, 1986.

home in case of default, hels are offered at lower interest rates than credit card or unsecured consumer loans. Interest rates are variable, sometimes changing monthly and often tied to movements in a prime rate or T-bill index. Repayment schedules are more flexible than second mortgages, and the borrower often may draw on unused but approved credit simply by writing a check. In response to consumer organization pressure for stricter regulation of hels, in 1987, the Competitive Equality Banking Act (CEBA) mandated that hels must have lifetime interest rate caps. In 1988, Congress passed the Home Equity Loan Consumer Protection Act. It specifies rigid disclosure rules and restricts the right of creditors to charge loan terms after a hel has been approved. Thus, the flexibility in hel terms was reduced.[33]

SPECIAL CONSIDERATIONS OF MORTGAGE LOANS

ARMS   As mentioned earlier in the chapter there are many special regulations for mortgage loans. Adjustable rate mortgage loans (ARMs) also have special regulations. National banks have only three choices: indexes of long-term mortgage rates, T-bill rates, or Treasury bond rates. Thrifts may use any interest rate series that is widely published, verifiable by the borrower, and not in the direct control of an individual lender. The lender must explain to the borrower exactly how the loan interest rate is related to the index and how it will be adjusted as the index changes. A 15-year history of the index must be provided. Studies show that the one-year Treasury index is more popular, since it tends to vary with lenders average cost of funds index. Federal regulations allow thrifts to offer ARM plans with any frequency of rate adjustments, but national banks may not change the mortgage interest rate more than once every 6 months.

Banks also have limits called **caps** on the size of the periodic rate adjustment. An overall rate cap is required by federal law. Research indicates that some type of interest rate cap is a very influential factor in gaining borrower acceptance of ARMs. Federal regulations prohibit prepayment penalties on ARMs. As mentioned earlier ARMs reduce a lender's interest rate risk, but increase the risk of borrower default when interest rates rise and borrower's have larger interest payments. Convertible ARMs have also been developed whereby borrowers may switch their ARMs to FRMs during a specified period.[34]

---

[33]Information on this section was drawn from several excellent articles, including Thomas A. Durkin. "Home Equity Credit Lines in Perspective." *Finance Facts* (June-July 1987); "Home Equity Lines of Credit Revisited." *Finance Facts* (August 1987); Canner, Fergus, and Luckett (1998); Canner and Fergus (1988); Canner and Luckett (1989); John Meehan. "It's Like Being on the Edge of a Precipice." *Business Week* (July 6, 1992), 56–58; and Steve Rodgers. "CUs Gain Home Equity Market Share." *Credit Union Magazine* (June 1992), 20–24; Eugeni 1993.

[34]See Mills and Gardner (1986); Carroll (1989); and Peck (1990). For more information on convertible ARMs, see Nothaft and Wang (1992); Peek (1990); Josie McElhone. "Convertibles Cruise to New Popularity." *Freddie Mac Reports* (November 1987); and James P. Miller. "Interest-Rate Savings Spawn New Breed of More Flexible Convertible Mortgages." *The Wall Street Journal* (July 2, 1987), 21. Since convertibles provide and attractive option to the borrower, lenders typically levy higher points, charge a higher interest rate, or build in higher spreads over the index than they would with comparable nonconvertibles.

Due on Sale Clauses   Increasingly common for mortgage loans is the due-on-sale clause, in which the lender can require the borrower to repay the outstanding loan balance when the mortgage property is sold. Mortgages without due on sale clauses are assumable by the new homeowner.[35] Due on sale clauses protect the lender by allowing the lender to evaluate the financial position of the new owner before deciding whether to continue the loan and allowing the lender to raise the interest rate if necessary that was on the original loan. The Garn St. Germain Act of 1982 established the ability of lenders to enforce due-on-sale clauses in all mortgage agreements originated thereafter.

Innovative Mortgages   Other innovative mortgages are **graduated payment mortgages (GPM)** where monthly payments are set at a low level in the early years with payments increased according to a known schedule and then stabilizing. **Reverse annuity mortgages (RAMs)** for elderly home owners that face cash shortages allow borrowers to receive cash payments from a depository institution, with the depository institution gradually becoming the owner of the property. At a specified maturity date, or when the homeowner with a RAM moves or dies, the property is sold and the lender receives the repayment with interest from the proceeds. With **growing equity mortgages (GEMs)** initial payments are set at the level that would amortize the mortgage over 30 years, but scheduled increases in payments result in a shorter actual maturity. **Price-level adjusted mortgages (PLAMs)** have an adjustable interest rate tied to an inflation index rather than an interest rate index. Under the PLAM, a borrower pays for actual versus expected inflation and benefits from lower initial interest costs that are not adjusted for expected inflation.

SMALL BUSINESS LOANS

Small lending grew rapidly in the 1990s with many large banks, such as Norwest, Key Bank and others setting up setting up special divisions to help small businesses with loans, working capital management and other needs. These services are often also associated with Community Reinvestment Act lending activities. In addition small and medium-sized firms have become specialists in small business lending.

Banks often become designated as small business lenders, with the ability to make **Small Business Administration (SBA) loans**. To be eligible to apply for a SBA loan, a borrower must first be denied a conventional loan. A borrower can then apply for a SBA loan through a designated lender. The SBA guarantees a portion of the loan, so the lender is protected against default risk, which allows the lender the ability to take on a loan to a small business which can entail considerable risk. The SBA guaranteed portions of SBA guaranteed loans, however, are securitized with yields close to those of government-issued securities.[36]

---

[35]Federal agency policies require that VA and FHA mortgages be assumable; conventional mortgages usually have a due-on-sale clause. Federal regulations carefully define sale for purpose of enforcement of due-on-sale clauses. For a review of the technicalities, see Priess (1983).

[36]See Hempel, Simonson, and Coleman (1994) for more details concerning the securitization and profits from securitization of SBA loans. Congress has debated legislation to attempt to develop greater securitization of other small business loans to increase funds available for small businesses.

The *Federal Reserve Bulletin* periodically publishes a summary of lending to small businesses. In 1996 for a survey of 1,564 commercial banks and 514 saving institutions reporting under CRA requirements made 2,414,805 small business loans, valued at $147 billion to 216,629 small firms. With a very weak secondary market for small business loans, only about 2 percent of small business loans and less than 1 percent of small farm loans were purchases from another institution. Commercial banks and savings institutions with assets of $1 billion or more originated or purchased the majority (60.5 percent) of reported small business loans, but the largest 1 percent of institutions only extended 18.6 percent of the total dollar value of small business loans.[37]

TYPES OF HIGHER RISK LENDING

Leveraged Buyouts   Especially harsh criticisms have been leveled at bank lenders in **leveraged buyouts (LBOs)** particularly in the late 1980s and early 1990s. LBOs are transactions in which a group of investors, often including a firm's managers, buys a firm by using huge amounts of debt capital and relatively little net worth. At year-end 1988, LBO and related loans accounted for over 10 percent of the commercial loan portfolios at 60 of the largest commercial banks.[38] Although few LBOs occurred before the mid-1980s, when the economy was comparatively robust, weakening economic indicators in the late 1980s and early 1990s caused many observers to be concerned that LBO borrowers would not be able to meet their debt obligations in the future, thereby putting their lenders substantially at risk. Although most observers believe that additional regulation against bank and thrift involvement in LBOs is not needed, most also believe that the practice should be confined to lenders with high levels of capital.[39]

Mezzanine Lending   Some commercial banks have approached participation in highly leveraged transactions through the practice of mezzanine lending. Mezzanine loans are longer-term, unsecured loans in which a firm's cash flow is the major source of repayment; in addition, the financial contract contains an option through which the lender can share in the increased value of the business if the venture is particularly successful. The potentially high return on the option is designed to compensate for the relatively high risk of the loan. The option is used in place of a higher interest rate, which might increase the probability of borrower default in the short run. Mezzanine financing often contains layers of investors with senior and junior debt including warrants attached that allow future equity stakes in a firm. Bond financing is privately placed. With mezzanine financing, different layers appeal to different preferences for risk by groups of investors. Venture capital is often involved. Also, bonds issued with payment in kind (pik) similar to a zero coupon bond with interest accumulating increasing the principal payment to be received at maturity. By providing additional financing to growing firms that may not be large enough to issue

---

[37]See Raphael W. Bostic and Glenn B. Canner. "New Information on Lending to Small Businesses and Small Farms: The 1996 CRA Data." *Federal Reserve Bulletin* (January 1998), 1–21.

[38]See Wolfson and McLaughlin (1989), 464.

[39]See Pozdena (1989); Kenneth H. Bacon. "Indebted Firms to Get Relief on Bank Loans." *The Wall Street Journal* (January 22, 1992), A2; Osterberg (1993).

public debt, such as junk bonds, mezzanine financing serves as a good example of financial innovation at work.[40]

LENDING TO HEDGE FUNDS

Previous chapters discuss huge losses for banks in 1998 from loans made to Long-Term Capital Management, L.P, a highly leveraged giant investment fund for wealthy private investors, known as a hedge fund. The potential failure of Long-Term Capital led to a FED-arranged $3.625 billion bailout by 14 banks and securities firms. In response to this bailout, the Federal Reserve Board in 1999 told banks to tighten their standards for lending to hedge funds and to avoid focusing too much on easy profits while ignoring credit risks posed by some funds. The Fed also issued guidelines to regulators for assessing bank lending to hedge funds including self-imposed limits by banks on the amount of their loans to hedge funds and improving their models for credit risks. The OCC also issued guidelines and recommendations for monitoring risk for hedge fund loans, as did a leading group of international bankers in 1999. A number of securities firms including Goldman Sachs, Merrill Lynch, and Morgan Stanley Dean Witter & Co. formed an industry group in 1999 to develop risk standards for financial institutions extending credit in global markets.[41]

LOAN MONITORING AND REVIEW

Despite even the best credit analysis and loan policies, problems occur. Monitoring procedures are designed to identify problems early enough to circumvent a need for legal action later. A comprehensive loan review system also serves to monitor the effectiveness of an institution's loan officers by providing incentives for them to make good decisions initially and then periodically to assess the borrower's subsequent financial position. Recent data suggest that banks have significant investments in loan monitoring and that the investment is positively related to the riskiness of the loan portfolio.[42]

As previously noted, many lending institutions assign a special group of personnel to workouts in an effort to avoid default. Workout specialists know that most of the financial problems of borrowers are traced to mismanagement arising from inadequate training and experience or perhaps even fraud.

Problems are accelerated by the state of the local or national economy or by the condition of a particular industry. Consider, for example, the effect of declining oil prices on energy-related industries throughout the 1980s. Similarly, overbuilding of commercial properties in many of the nation's largest cities posed severe problems for thrifts that invested directly in these properties or lent to the developers. As

---

[40]For more details, see Stacy (1988); and "Roundtable Discussion of Issues in Commercial Banking." *Bank of America Journal of Applied Corporate Finance* 9 (Summer 1996), 24–51.

[41]Matt Murray. "Fed Tells Banks to Tighten Standards for Loans They Extend to Hedge Funds." *The Wall Street Journal* (February 2, 1999), A4.

[42]Gregory F. Udell. "Loan Quality, Commercial Loan Review, and Loan Officer Contracting." Salomon Brothers Center for the Study of Financial Institutions, Working Paper No. 459 (March 1988).

banks increased their commercial real estate lending, some were faced with prospects of problem loans. Unfortunately for lenders, even secured loans provide little protection under those conditions, because the property obtained on default has usually declined in value.[43]

Loan Monitoring, Regulation, and Financial Reporting

Loan monitoring has important ramifications for financial reporting to the public and to regulatory agencies. Loans are often classified as **past due** for 30 to 89 days, **non-performing** if they are past due for 90 or more days, and **nonaccruing** when payments are not received. As explained in Chapter 5, institutions estimate problem loans and report them in the **allowance for possible loan losses** account on their balance sheet. The loan loss allowance account is increased by current estimates of anticipated loan losses (**the provision for loan losses**) and reduced by **actual net loan chargeoffs** (actual loans charged off as losses less any actual loan recoveries). Thus, the allowance account is always an estimate of future loan losses, not a record of past losses.[44]

Estimating future loan losses for planning purposes is of considerable concern to depositories. To estimate losses with a reasonable degree of accuracy, lenders develop procedures to identify when a borrower moves into the "questionable" category. Regulators expect these policies to accomplish their purpose; when they do not disciplinary actions may be taken. Examiners in periodically reviewing a bank's loans will classify problem loans into categories of substandard, doubtful, and loss. Accordingly, regulators may ask bank's to write-down their capital for loans that are likely to be losses and for a percentage of likely losses such as 20 percent for substandard loans and 50 percent for doubtful loans.[45] In the late 1980s and early 1990s, some banks felt regulators were unduly harsh in writing down loan losses. Maryland National Bank in Baltimore for instance was forced to write down a large number of its loans as losses which severely hurt its capital position and led to the bank's sell to the public its profitable credit card and securitization subsidiary, MBNA, and to the bank's ultimate merger with Nationsbank.

Delinquent Loans   Despite careful scrutiny of loan applications, some borrowers inevitably will be unable or unwilling to meet their repayment schedules. When a borrower is seriously delinquent, management of the loan moves from the loan officer to those responsible for collection. In all cases, collection personnel want to avoid legal action, because it consumes resources and time. For example, a savings institution does not really want to foreclose on a mortgage loan; the legal expenses are large, and the institution must sell or maintain the repossessed property. Lenders

---

[43]For some examples of experiences with problem loans, see John Meehan. "America's Bumbling Bankers: Ripe for a New Fiasco." *Business Week* (March 2, 1992), 86–87; Neil Barsky. "Tired of Endless Talk with Big Developers, Banks Try Foreclosure." *The Wall Street Journal* (May 8, 1991), A1, 18; John Meehan. "Suddenly All This Terra Doesn't Feel So Firma." *Business Week* (October 23, 1989, 64.

[44]For more details, see Walter (1991).

[45]See Koch (1994).

will usually work closely with borrowers to set up revised repayment plans, suggest general financial counseling, or provide advice on financial management. Such efforts are often termed **workouts**.

Monitoring collateral can be difficult in some cases. When vehicle loans become delinquent, the lender must move quickly—because the collateral is mobile! As with other aspects of loan management, the more resources committed to the collection effort, the greater the protection against instability in the NIM but also the greater the addition to net noninterest expenses. Close relationships with borrowers helps the bank to discover problems and provide help before they become too overwhelming. Small and medium-sized banks often have an advantage in this respect, and many banks have instituted policies that loan officers must contact and visit their previous customers as a condition for compensation.

OTHER LENDING CONSIDERATIONS

Loan Participations and Syndications

A **loan participation** is an arrangement by two or more lenders to share a loan in some agreed on proportion. A lead institution initiates the loan and usually has all of the contacts with the borrower. Closely related to participations are **loan syndications**, in which several lenders simultaneously lend to a single borrower and all lenders have a direct relationship with the borrower. Participations and syndications are often necessary in large loans because of regulatory limitations placed on the amount a commercial bank may loan to a single borrower as a percentage of the depository's capital. Both types of agreements allow institutions to share the risk.[46]

Loan participations and syndications allow smaller institutions to enlarge their loan portfolios, especially if they lack ready access to a business community large enough to support a direct lending program. Such agreements also permit lenders to diversify geographically. But they can lead to severe problems, especially if the participants do not perform their own credit analysis. Publicity surrounded the heavy losses incurred by Continental Illinois, Chase Manhattan, and other commercial lenders on loan participations with Penn Square Bank of Oklahoma City, which failed in 1982 when most of its loans to energy-related companies went into default. Fed data suggest that fewer than 15 percent of commercial loans result from participation agreements.

Pricing of syndicated loans switched dramatically from fixed upfront pricing for loans to flexible pricing, often at the time of closing in 1998. With this policy, known as "**market flex**," banks are willing to complete loans that might otherwise not have been made; however, the policy places great price uncertainty on corporate borrowers. In 1998, according to research from Loan Pricing Corp., total syndicated loans fell in 1998 by 22 percent to $872 billion from 1997 as the result of global financial

---

[46]For commercial banks with federal charters, these limitations were revised in the Garn-St Germain Act of 1982. A bank may lend to one borrower an unsecured amount not to exceed 15 percent of capital and surplus. If "readily marketable collateral" is pledged as security, the limit rises to 25 percent of capital and surplus. FIRREA imposed the same limitations on savings associations but allowed loans up to $500,000, regardless of the percentage of capital. For more information, see Garcia et al. (1983); Bush and Morrall (1989); Conference Report on H.R. 1278 (1989); and Simons (1993).

turmoil, with many deals restructured using market flex that otherwise would have been pulled. With competition for loans and greater stability in global financial markets, however, banks may have less bargaining power for market flex in future years or corporate borrowers may ask for caps on rate changes. However, with Japanese banks under capital pressure pulling out of global lending markets and continued consolidation of U.S. banks, in late 1998 and 1999, there was less competition for syndicated loans. Banks face competition from other nonbank competitors including Merrill Lynch Asset Management and Eaton Vance Management that held an estimated 40 percent of syndicated loans issued to noninvestment grade companies in 1999. Nonbank competitors also use market-based pricing offering tentative pricing that can later be changed and adjusting for risk by comparing returns from loans with returns on high yield or junk bonds.[47]

LENDER LIABILITY INCLUDING ENVIRONMENTAL LIABILITY

A growing problem for commercial lenders is the threat of a suit by a borrower if the borrower is in financial difficulty. A recent study of lender liability showed that most suits arose because an institution has refused to advance funds or has attempted to take possession of collateral. In addition, lawsuits have appeared in which a lender failed to renew a loan which defendants claim led to their firms' failures. Lenders are also often cited in environmental liability suits if collateral used for loans is associated with environmental hazards. Consequently, lenders perform environmental audits on land or buildings used as collateral, as shown in the loan presentation for the Big Apple Real Estate and Storage Company discussed earlier. Lawsuits are expensive for lenders even if they win cases. Consequently, most experts caution lenders that the best way to prevent lawsuits is to follow institutional monitoring and foreclosure procedures scrupulously, to give ample notice to borrowers if credit is not be extended, and to keep excellent records.

But even careful record keeping may not be enough. Courts have interpreted lending contracts in inconsistent, even contradictory, ways. For example, some lenders have been fined for failing to provide advance notice that a line of credit will not be renewed, whereas others have been sued for "threatening" borrowers by providing just such notice! Some financial economists have concluded that the specter of being held liable for monitoring borrowers' actions may eventually result in credit rationing against borrowers whom lenders believe are most likely to need monitoring. At best, such high-risk borrowers may pay even higher interest rates to compensate lenders for the extra cost of being sued. Although acknowledging that borrowers are entitled to protection from the capricious act of lenders, these experts conclude that lending markets are sufficiently competitive and the permissible construction of financial contracts is sufficiently flexible that borrowers already enjoy adequate protection without having to sue banks. Thus,

---

[47]See Paul Beckett. "Syndication of Loans Sees Big Changes." *The Wall Street Journal* (January 26, 1999), C1. An example of how market flex works is the $400 million loan sought by IXC Communications, an Austin, Texas, long-distance carrier in 1998. Originally, the loan consisted of $200 million revolving credit and a $200 million fixed-term loan at an initial price of 2 percent above LIBOR underwritten by BankAmerica Corp., Credit Suisse First Boston, and Goldman Sachs & Co. When the syndication was completed in late October, the structure changed with a price increase of 2.5 percent over LIBOR.

the lender liability battleground is likely to be a lively one for the rest of this decade.[48]

COMMUNITY REINVESTMENT ACT REVISIONS

The Community Reinvestment Act (CRA) of 1977 introduced earlier requires regulators to encourage depositories to meet the credit needs of their local communities, including low-and moderate-income neighborhoods. The act is enforced primarily through regulators' examinations of credit policies and practices. Examinations have become increasingly rigorous in recent years. Institutions may be required to provide evidence that personnel have met with community leaders to determine credit needs, that they have taken an active role in economic development and that they have responded to past complaints about credit allocation in the community.

In the 1990s both lenders and community leaders criticized the focus of CRA performance evaluations on process and paperwork versus actual results of efforts made by a financial institution to serve its local community. Other criticisms included the failure of CRA ratings to distinguish between banks that performed well and those that performed poorly. Very few institutions received high or low evaluations. In response to these concerns, in July 1993 President Clinton asked supervisory agencies to reform the regulations that implement CRA.

In May 1995, new regulations were presented to make CRA assessments "more performance-based, more objective, and less burdensome for covered institutions.[49] The original regulation had 12 assessment factors. The new regulations substitute three performance measures in terms of **lending**, **investment**, and **service**. The **lending tests** measures lending activity measures lending activity for a variety of loan types including small business and small farm loans. Assessment criteria includes the geographic distribution of lending, the distribution of lending across different types of borrowers, the extent of community development lending, and the use of innovative or flexible lending practices to address the needs of low or moderate income individuals or areas. The **investment test** considers the institution's involvement with qualified investments, such as providing capital for an investment group in the community that invests in low income areas. A qualified investment includes an investment, deposit, or grant that benefits the institution's assessment area or a broader statewide or regional area. The **service test** considers the institution's availability and responsiveness for delivering retail banking services and judges the extent of its community development services and their degree of innovation. Alternative systems for delivering services to low and moderate income areas, for instance are considered, as well as the provision of community development services. Some banks developed traveling loan offices to provide information to low income areas about the bank's lending services and community low-income loan grants. In assessing CRA compliance, evaluations are made in the context of information about the lending institutions and its community competitors

---

[48]For more information, see Benjamin E. Hermalin. "The Negative Effects of Lender Liability." *Weekly Letter* (Federal Reserve Bank of San Francisco) (September 20, 1991); Fischel (1989); Glancz, Freer, and Melton (1989); and Elyse Tanouye. "Investors Burned in Commodities Deals Sue Lenders that Supplied the Money." *The Wall Street Journal* (January 24, 1992), C1, C17.

[49]For a summary of the new CRA regulations, see Raphael W. Bostic and Glenn B. Canner. "New Information on Lending to Small Businesses and Small Farms: The 1996 CRA Data." *Federal Reserve Bulletin* (January 1998), 1–21.

and peers. The capacity and constraints of an institution are considered as well as economic and demographic characteristics of the local service areas and the institution's business strategy. CRA disclosure information for each financial institution is available for purchase through the Federal Financial Institutions Examination Council (FFIEC) in CD-ROM or hard copy form through the FFIEC's web site at http://www.ffiec.gov or by calling the CRA Assistance Line at (202) 872–7584.[50]

SALES OF COMMERCIAL LOANS AND SOME SECURITIZATIONS

Chapters 9 and 19 discuss loan sales and securitization as sources of noninterest revenues and as investment securities for depository institutions. Many large banks have turned away from so-called **portfolio lending**—in which financial contracts are written with the intent that the lender will hold the loan until maturity. This trend has important implications for the future of the banking industry. Although purchasers of loans, including small non-money-center banks, can benefit from the resulting diversification, issues of information reusability and asymmetry become somewhat more complicated. For example, if the original lender has no intention of holding a loan to maturity, will credit analysis be as rigorous as before? Will originating lenders conclude that it is in their best interests to sell weaker credit and to retain only the less risky loans for themselves? If so, are purchasers—especially less sophisticated banks or even thrifts—equipped to evaluate the risk exposure they assume, particularly when the information required to make proper evaluations in one instance may not be reusable in another? Although sales of loans of all types is undoubtedly one of the most important asset/liability management tools today, it brings up a new set of unanswered issues. Because commercial loans are less homogenous than other loans, being tailored and negotiated in terms of size, rate, and maturity, they are not securitized as pools as often as other types of loans.

PROVIDING ONE STOP SHOPPING FOR ALL CORPORATE NEEDS

Many large banks have also changed their traditional lending focus from being simply "product-oriented" institutions to solution-oriented companies, providing expertise and innovative ways to find tailor made solutions that are unique to the particular circumstances of a company. For instance, banks have developed products like mezzanine debt for unrated firms to anchor relationships in the middle market. Many larger banks have also transformed themselves into firms that can offer one-stop shopping for all kinds of financial products from investment services to banking to working capital management. Lending relationships have become more than just lending relationships. Commercial banks have streamlined the loan process, allowing customers to get loans on line. In 1998 online mortgages accounted for about $4.2 billion, less than 1 percent of total mortgage lending, but rapid growth is expected.[51]

---

[50]Ibid.

[51]See "Roundtable Discussion on Current Issues in Banking," *Bank of America Journal of Applied Corporate Finance*, Vol. 9 (Summer 1996), 24–41; "Click for a Mortgage." *The Wall Street Journal* (February 4, 1999), A1; and Carlos Tejada. "Guide to On-Line Mortgages, Refinancing." *The Wall Street Journal* (February 6, 1998), B8. Online sites also give information on the best mortgage rates, such as E-Loan, http://www.eloan.com.

IMPROVEMENT IN CREDIT RISK MANAGEMENT

Banks have attempted to improve their risk management. One aspect of this new focus is the growing use of **risk adjusted return on capital (RAROC)** to measure how much risk the bank is taking and to determine if returns are providing adequate compensation for risk, and if the bank is providing shareholders with value added through its participation in that business. Capital accordingly is allocated to a business in proportion to the risk contribution of that business. For instance, Bank America had a stated policy to have enough capital to support any given activity to cover 99.97 percent of the unexpected losses in that business. RAROC is calculated as the expected yearly income for a loan divided by the amount of supporting economic capital (representing the expected loss on the loan).[52] Alternatively it can be calculated as the expected net income per dollar on an activity (subtracting out interest and noninterest expenses and expected losses) divided by the expected loss rate on the loan including what can not be recaptured through collateral or other sources. For instance, if the expected income per dollar on the loan less its interest costs and administrative fees was 50 basis points or .50 percent and the expected losses for this type of loan was 5 percent for a 99.97 percent confidence level, with 80 percent likely not to be recaptured through collateral, RAROC would be .005/(.05)(.80) = 12.5 percent. Accordingly, loans or other activities with RAROC's lower than a bank's cost of capital would not be acceptable.[53]

Managers at BankAmerica, First Union, and other banks argue, however, that RAROC should not be used alone to select a bank's activities, and activities should not be ranked according to RAROC. Rather, concepts such as Economic Value Added (EVA) should be used in selecting activities that will maximize the firm's value:

$$\text{EVA} = \text{NOPAT} - \text{DOLLAR COST OF CAPITAL FOR OPERATIONS} \quad [21.3]$$

where NOPAT = Earnings Before Interest and Taxes (1 − marginal tax rate), and the DOLLAR COST of CAPITAL = investor supplied capital × the after-tax percent cost of capital. EVA discussed in Chapter 9, is increasingly being used by banks as a performance measure including ensuring that loans are profitable; however, new performance measures are constantly being developed as well.[54]

SUMMARY

Loans are the largest category of assets of depository institutions. Although depository institutions specialize in different types of loans, important elements of successful lending are shared by all depositories. In fact, lending is one of the functions that makes depositories "special" financial institutions in regulators' eyes. Lending policies must incorporate specific objectives for the size, composition, maturity, interest rate characteristics, and default risk of the loan portfolio.

Procedures for evaluating and approving loan appli-

---

[52]See "Roundtable Discussion on Current Issues in Banking." *Bank of America Journal of Applied Corporate Finance*, Vol. 9 (Summer 1996), 24–41; and Cornett and Saunders (1999) for a more detailed discussion RAROC and strategies by different banks for its use.

[53]See Marcia Millon Cornett and Anthony Saunders. *Fundamentals of Financial Institutions Management*, Chicago: Irwin McGraw-Hill 1999 for a more detailed illustration of RARCO, which this example is based on.

[54]See "Roundtable Discussion on Current Issues in Banking." *Bank of America Journal of Applied Corporate Finance*, Vol. 9 (Summer 1996), 24–41; and Eugene F. Brigham, Louis C. Gapenski, and Michael C. Ehrhardt, *Financial Management: Theory and Practice*, 9th ed. Fort Worth, Tex.: Dryden Press, 1999, pp. 47–50.

cations must then be devised to achieve those objectives. A major step is to establish a base lending rate from which individual loan-pricing decision follow. The process of evaluating and approving a loan includes decisions regarding what rate to charge a given customer, how often the rate will change, and whether special terms and conditions should be attached. Finally, procedures must be developed to monitor the loan's performance to avoid borrower default.

Loans to businesses are of particular interest to commercial banks, although thrifts have begun to enter the market in small numbers in recent years. Of special importance in commercial lending is an analysis of the borrower's financial condition. Applicants must be categorized according to the level of default risk to which the institution is exposed. Credit scoring systems have often played a part in this screening. New risk-based pricing techniques including RAROC have also become popular.

After analysis of an applicant's financial condition, specific loan terms must be determined. In the past, the standard pricing practice was to charge the institution's best customers the prime rate and to scale other loan rates upward from there. Today a more two-tiered pricing system has emerged for large and small borrowers. Further decisions involve compensating balances, commitments, discounting, and collateral. The expected yield to the depository will reflect all these decisions. Some institutions choose loan participations or syndication agreements originated by a lead bank instead of, or in addition to, direct lending, and many banks have become loan originators and servicers entering the loan sales market. Environmental liability and Community Reinvestment Act assessments have also become very important considerations for lenders.

Questions

1. In 1998, on average the percentage of bank loans included 29 percent commercial loans; 39 percent real estate loans, and 15 percent consumer loans. Why have bank loans to large corporations fallen, and why has real estate lending risen? How are banks still special to medium-sized and small firms?

2. Why are regulators concerned about increased consumer lending by depository institutions? What factors have contributed to the growth in consumer credit in the United States from the 1970s to the 1990s?

3. Why did loan losses fall for banks in the mid- and later 1990s? What are past due loans, nonperforming loans, and nonaccruing loans? Why do some banks feel that regulators were harsh in forcing banks to write down loan losses in the early 1990s? What was the credit crunch of the early 1990s? What factors contributed to it?

4. Who are the primary suppliers of consumer loans and primary suppliers of mortgage debt? Why do you think the percentage of securitized consumer and mortgage debt has grown so rapidly in the 1990s?

5. Why do banks need an overall lending policy? What does a bank's lending policy include? Explain lenders' role in bringing business in to the bank. How can this role conflict with the lender's credit analysis role? How have lender compensation policies changed to encourage lenders to make "good" loans?

6. Briefly give the major provisions for the Equal Credit Opportunity Act (Reg B), the Fair Housing Act, the Fair Credit Reporting Act, the Truth in Lending Act, Reg Z, the Uniform Residential Loan Application, the Real Estate Settlement Procedures Act, the Home Mortgage Disclosure Act, the Community Reinvestment Act, and the Loans to Insiders Act (Reg O). Why are lenders subject to so many regulations?

7. Why are code of ethics and conflict of interest policies particularly important for financial institutions? Can you give an example of an institution that failed in the last two decades that was related to ethical problems?

8. Briefly list the typical items that are included in a loan request procedure. What are the 5 C's of credit? How many can be measured objectively?

9. Discuss rules of thumb for lending on collateral. Why are loan to collateral value ratios important? Why do collateralized loans typically have higher rates?

10. Explain what a quantitative scoring model is, such as Zeta Analysis or a Consumer Scoring Model. What type of information do corporate and consumer loan scoring models emphasize? Why have they been popular? What are their limitations?

11. What is CreditMetrics? What advantage does this approach have?

12. What is a depository institution's base lending rate? Using equation [21.1] explain how this rate can be solved for. How do competitive conditions also affect loan pricing?

13. What are some noninterest terms and conditions of a loan including compensating balance requirements, loan commitments, and discounts (or points). How do noninterest terms affect loan rates? How are loans priced using profitability analysis?

14. What has been the historical definition of the term prime rate? How has this changed?

15. Why are indexes such as Treasury rates used often by lenders as a base rate?

16. How are risk premiums on loans set? Explain what RAROC is and how it is calculated. How do restrictive covenants help to protect a lender?

17. Briefly define the following types of loans: seasonal working capital loan, term loan, commercial real estate/construction loans, agriculture loans. What special considerations need to be made for each of these respective loans?

18. How do bankruptcy acts affect the risk of consumer loans? How do banks make profits on credit card loans? What are the risks and trends in credit card loans?

19. Discuss how the rates on consumer installment loans are set. How are these rates converted to annual percentage rates (APRs). What is the rule of 78?

20. Explain how home equity loans differ from second mortgages. What provisions does the Home Equity Consumer Protection Act have to protect consumers taking out home equity loans?

21. What rules does a lender have to abide by in setting rates on ARMs? What are due on sales clauses? What is a GPM? RAM? GEM? PLAM?

22. Why has lending to small businesses increased banks? How can a Small Business Administration (SBA) loan be securitized?

23. Explain what leveraged buyout lending, mezzanine lending, and hedge fund lending are. Why are these types of loans risky?

24. What are loan participations and syndications? Who do banks compete against for this type of lending? In the 1990s why did lenders switch to market flex pricing?

25. Why has lender liability including environmental liability become an important issue for banks? How can banks protect against these types of liabilities?

26. Briefly discuss revisions in the Community Reinvestment Act. How do the new provisions respond to previous criticisms of previous CRA procedures?

Recommended Cases: See Darden School Case Catalog:

Case 20: Padgett Blank Book Company, Structuring a Term Loan; **Case 19: Hoosier Hose Company**, restructuring a troubled seasonal loan; and **Case 22: Patriots Hall:** evaluating a proposed commercial mortgage in Richard D. Crawford and William W. Sihler. *Financial Service Organizations: Cases in Strategic Management*, New York: HarperCollins College Publisher, 1994.

Problems

1. Minicase: Loan Application. The Bronco Badges Company has the following projected financial statements 2002 and its current balance sheet for 2001, along with projected financial ratios for 2002.
   a. Fill in the missing items in the sources & uses statement and statement of changes in cash flow. How much does the firm need to borrow in 2002?
   b. Based on the uses (increases in assets in this case for funds in 2002 shown in the Source & Use Statement, how would you structure the loan in terms of short-term notes payable (1 year or less maturity) and long-term debt.
   c. Analyze the projected key ratios compared to last year's ratios and the industry averages. What strengths and weaknesses does Bronco Badges Company have?
   d. As a lender, what types of other information would you like to know about the company or its managers in determining whether to grant the loan or not?
   e. How would you price this loan? What kind of loan structure (maturity, terms, loan covenants, collateral) would you suggest?

Current Balance Sheet 2001 and Projected Balance Sheet for Bronco Badges Co.

Income Statement (mils.)	2002	Balance Sheets	2002	2001	Source	Use
Sales	$3,000	Cash	$500	$450		50
CGS	1,000	Accts. Rec.	1,000	900		100
Gross Profit	2,000	Inventory	1,500	1,350		150
Depreciation	500	Net Fixed Assets	2,000	1,800		200
Operating Costs	500	Accts. Payable	500	450	50	
Operating Profit	1,000	Accruals	500	450	50	
Interest Expense	200	Notes Payable	?	142	?	
Earnings Before Tax	800	Long-term Debt	?	500	?	
Taxes (30%)	240	Common Stock	2,000	2,000		
Net Income	$ 560	Retained Earnings	1,138	958	$180	
Dividend	380			Total	$500	$500
Add to Ret. Erngs.	$ 180					

Statement of Changes in Cash Flow:

			Beg. Cash	$450

Cash Flow from Operating Activities:

Net Income $560
+ Depreciation Expense   500

	Accounting Cash Flow	$1,060

- − Rise in Accounts Receivable   − 100
- − Rise in Inventory   − 150
- + Rise in Accounts Payable   + 50
- + Rise in Accruals   + 50

Net Sources/Uses Oper. Activities   − 150

Cash flow from Operations $910

Cash flow from Investing Activities:

Change in Gross Fixed Assets = Change in Net Fixed Assets + Depreciation

Cash flow from Investing Activities = 200 + $500 = $700

Cash flow from Financing Activities:

- − Dividends Paid   − $380
- + Increase in Notes Payable   ?
- + Increase in Long-term Debt   ?
-

Cash flow from Financing =

Change in Cash = $910 − $700 − ? = $50

Ending Cash Balance = $500

Key Information and Financial Ratios for Bronco Badges

Sales 2001 = $2,700   Sales 2002 = $3,000   Projected growth rate = 11.11%

Total Assets 2001 = $4,500   Total Assets Projected 2002 = $5,000

Projected growth rate assets = $5,000/$4,500 − 1 = 11.11%

Overall Profitability:	*Projected 2002*	*2001*	*Peer Average*
Return on Equity (ROE)	17.8%	21.3%	25%
Return on Assets (ROA)	11.2%	14.0%	15%
Debt to Assets	37.2%	34.2%	40%
Equity Multiplier (Assets/Equity)	1.59 ×	1.52 ×	1.67 ×
Cost Efficiency:			
Net Profit Margin (NPM)	18.67%	23.33%	30%
Operating Profit Margin (OPM)	33.33%	40.00%	45%
Gross Profit Margin (GPM)	66.67%	70.00%	80%
Asset Utilization:			
Total Asset Turnover	.6 ×	.6 ×	.5 ×
Fixed Asset Turnover	1.5 ×	1.5 ×	1.2 ×
Inventory Turnover	.67 ×	.6 ×	.7 ×
Average Collection Period	122 days	122 days	120 days
Bankruptcy Risk:			
Times Interest Earned Ratio	5 ×	6 ×	5 ×
Liquidity Risk:			
Current Ratio	3 ×	3 ×	3.5 ×
Quick Ratio	1.5 ×	1.5 ×	2.0 ×

2. Find the cash to cash cycle for Bronco Badges projected in 2002. Based on the firm's daily average cost of goods sold in 2002, what is the approximate working capital loan needs for the firm in 2002?

3. Using the sample Zeta model example (an old version of the current model that is sold to financial institutions), what is the Zeta score for Bronco Badges in 2002?

4. Based on the lending rate(s) and terms that you decide for any loans to Bronco Badges, what will be the expected interest expense for Bronco Badges in 2002? How will this affect the firm's projected TIE and Net Income for 2002? How many times could the new interest expense be paid from Cash flow from Operations in 2002?

5. The Imperial Ski Bank in Imperial, Colorado is considering a loan application from Dean Taylor, an avid skier, who wants to purchase a video store and needs $50,000. The bank's best loan officer, Stu Rosenstein considers the loan to be of above-average risk, and will add a 2 percent risk and administrative cost premium to the bank's base rate. The bank's total assets are $200 million, interest expense is $14 million, net noninterest expense is $2 million, and the marginal tax rate is 35 percent. The target NIM is 3.8 percent, and the bank's asset structure is as follows:

Securities: $35 million; average yield, 9.45 percent

Loans: $120 million Nonearning Assets: $15 million

   a. Based on the above, using equation [21.1] rate, what is the bank's base lending rate, and what loan rate will Dean be offered?
   b. Prepare a pro forma income statement, assuming that the bank earns, on average, the base rate you calculated in a on its loan portfolio. Calculate the NIM under this assumption.
   c. What ROE is expected if the equity multiplier is 12?
   d. How would the base rate you calculated in a change if the yield on securities fell to 8.5 percent? If the yield on securities rose to 10.5 percent?

6. The Remarkable Bank of Gold Creek in Gold Creek, Colorado has total assets of $140 million, an equity multiplier of 12.5, and net noninterest expense of $1.5 million. Its target NIM is 2.9 percent, and its liability cost averages 8 percent annually. Assets are distributed as follows:

   Securities: $25 million; average yield 8.25 percent

   Mortgages and consumer loans: $110 million

   Nonearning assets: $5 million

   a. Marcelle Arak, president, asks you to calculate the base lending rate Remarkable Bank must earn to achieve its target NIM?
   b. Prepare a pro forma income statement, assuming that First National earns the base rate on its loans. Show that this rate will allow the bank to earn its desired NIM.
   c. What ROE is expected if the marginal tax rate is 35 percent?
   d. Suppose that Remarkable Bank reduces its target NIM to 2 percent, what base rate must be earned to achieve this target?
   e. Suppose the average liability rate rises to 9 percent, what base rate is needed to achieve a 2.5 percent NIM? What is the significance of this for banks with negative funding gaps?

7. Larry Cunningham is negotiating a $4 million line of credit for his ski board business with the Enchanted Bank of Santa Fe, New Mexico. The one-year agreement requires a .20 percent commitment fee, with a 12 percent compensating balance on the entire commitment and an additional 5 percent on funds actually borrowed. The stated rate of interest is 11 percent, and J.C. Bosch, the bank's extraordinary loan officer, estimates that Larry will use on average 85 percent of the line.

   a. Calculate the total expected dollar return and rate of return for the Enchanted Bank, assuming a 10 percent marginal reserve requirement.
   b. What would be the expected dollar return and rate of return for the Enchanted Bank if Larry borrowed on average 70 percent of the line? 90 percent of the line?

8. Suppose Woody Eckerd, the superb loan officer of the Superlative Bank of Santa Fe instead offers Larry Cunningham (in the problem above) the $4 million line of credit with a stated rate of 11.9 percent, a 6 percent compensating balance requirement on the total line, and an additional 4 percent compensating balance on the amount borrowed. If other terms stay the same, does the Superlative Bank expect to earn more or less on the agreement than the Enchanted Bank of Santa Fe?

9. Your bank is willing to offer a $1 million line of credit for one year to help you establish your own consulting firm. The agreement requires a .15 percent commitment fee, a 10 percent compensating balance on the entire commitment, and 4 percent more on funds actually borrowed. The stated rate is 12 percent, and you have told the bank that you probably will not need more than an average of 60 percent of the line.

   a. Calculate the expected dollar return and rate of return for the bank, assuming a 10 percent marginal reserve requirement.
   b. What would be the expected dollar return and rate of return for the bank if you drew down your line by 80 percent. Is the bank better off it you more borrow or less of you line? Explain why.

10. Ann Singleton of Singleton Savings asks you what is the annual yield on a one-year loan if interest is discounted and the stated rate is 10 percent? If it is 13 percent? If it is 9.6 percent?

11. What is the effective annual rate that Gary Patterson is paying for a home mortgage loan for $100,000 with annual loan payments for 15 years and a stated annual rate of 6 percent, if he has points on the loan?

12. Jim Morris is purchasing a new van priced at $24,000 and has saved enough money to make a 20 percent down payment. His credit union will finance the remaining balance at an 11 percent add-on rate for four years (48 months).
    a. Calculate the annual percentage rate.
    b. Would you be better off borrowing from your bank for only 36 months?
13. Rich Foster has decided to purchase a recreational vehicle to have fun with in the mountains. The RV costs $30,000, and Rich is able to make an $8,000 down payment. The bank has quoted an add-on rate of 14 percent, with 60 months to finance the remaining balance.
    a. Based on this information, what is Rich's monthly payments.
    b. If Rich prepays the loan after 15 months, using the rule of 78s, what would Rich have to pay to pay off the loan?
    c. If instead, Rich negotiates a 14 percent, 60 month loan without add-on interest, how much would each monthly payment be? If the rule of 78s does not apply to this new loan, how much principal would remain after 15 months? (Hint: To find the remaining principal without preparing an amortization schedule, compute the present value of the remaining 45 payments). Compare your answers with parts a and b.
    d. If the rule of 78s does apply to the loan in part c, how much would Rich owe after 15 months? Based on your comparisons, does the rule of 78s or the add-on interest provision make a greater difference in Rich's rate of principal repayment?
14. Ajeyo Banerjee is buying a super sports car. After extensive negotiations, he has agreed on a price of $40,000. He plans to make a down payment of $ 10,000 and will finance the remaining balance over a 48-month period. The bank has offered an add-on rate of 6 percent. The car manufacturer's subsidiary, however, is offering four-year loans at an annual percentage rate of $6\frac{3}{4}$ percent. Compare the APRs on the two loans and decide which one Ajeyo should accept.
15. Sylvia Hudgins is planning on buying a condo in Creste Butte, Colorado for $300,000. She plans to borrow $250,000 from the Mountain Beauty Bank at a 6.5 percent interest rate. The bank offers a standard 30-year, fixed rate loan or a quicker 15-year loan with annual loan payments.
    a. Calculate the monthly payments under each loan.
    b. How much total interest will Sylvia pay under each loan?
    c. Assuming Sylvia can comfortably meet either monthly payment, which loan should she choose? Why?

Selected References

Aguilar, Linda. "Still Toe-to-Toe: Banks and Nonbanks at the End of the 80s." *Economic Perspectives* (Federal Reserve Bank of Chicago) 14 (January/February 1990); 12–23.

Alexander, Walter. "What's the Score?" *ABA Banking Journal* 81 (August 1989), 58–63.

Altman, Edward I. "Financial Ratios, Discriminant Analysis, and the Prediction of Corporate Bankruptcy." *Journal of Finance* 23 (September 1968), 589–609.

Altman, Edward I., et al. *Application of Classification Techniques in Business, Banking, and Finance.* Greenwich, Conn.: JAI Press, 1981.

Becketti, Sean and Charles Morris. "Are Bank Loans Still Special?" *Economic Review* (Federal Reserve Bank of Kansas City) 77 (Third Quarter 1992): 71–84.

Benston, George. "Interest on Deposits and Survival of Chartered Depository Institutions." *Economic Review* (Federal Reserve Bank of Atlanta) 69 (October 1984); 42–56.

Berlin, Mitchell. "Loan Commitments: Insurance Contracts in a Risky World," *Business Review* (Federal Reserve Bank of Philadelphia) (May/June 1986): 3–12.

Brady, Thomas F. "Changes in Loan Pricing and Business Lending at Commercial Banks." *Federal Reserve Bulletin* 71 (January 1985): 1–13.

Brick, John R. "Pricing Commercial Loans." *Journal of Commercial Bank Lending* 66 (January 1984); 49–52.

Canner, Glenn B. "Changes in Consumer Holding and Use of Credit Cards." *Journal of Retail Banking* 10 (Spring 1988): 13–24.

Canner, Glenn B., Thomas A. Durkin, and Charles A. Luckett, "Recent Developments in the Home Equity Loan Market," *Journal of Retail Banking* 11 (Summer 1989); 35–47.

Canner, Glenn B., and James T. Fergus. "Home Equity Lines of Credit—How Well Do They Fit the Needs of Consumers and Creditors?" *Journal of Retail Banking* 10 (Summer 1988), 19–23.

Canner, Glenn B., James T. Fergus, and Charles A. Luckett. "Home Equity Lines of Credit." *Federal Reserve Bulletin* 74 (June 1988), 361–373.

Canner, Glenn B. and Charles A. Luckett. "Home Equity Lending." *Federal Reserve Bulletin* 75 (May 1989), 333–344.

———. "Payment of Household Debts." *Federal Reserve Bulletin* 77 (April 1991); 218–229.

———. "Developments in the Pricing of Credit Card Services," *Federal Reserve Bulletin* 78 (September 1992), 652–666.

Canner, Glenn B. and Delores S. Smith. "Expanded HMDA Data on Residential Lending One Year Later." *Federal Reserve Bulletin* 78 (November 1992); 801–824.

Capon, Noel. "Credit Scoring Systems: A Critical Analysis." *Journal of Marketing* 46 (Spring 1982): 82–91.

Carroll, David. "Benchmark Pricing Enhances ARM Design." *Savings Institutions* 110 (February 1989): 69–74.

DeMong, Richard F. and John H. Lindgren, Jr. "Home Equity Lending in 1988: Market Trends and Analysis." *Journal of Retail Banking* 11 (Fall 1989); 23–34.

Edmister, Robert O. "Combining Human Credit Analysis and Numerical Credit Scoring for Business Failure Prediction," *Akron Business and Economic Review* 19 (Fall 1988), 6–14.

Fama, Eugene. "What's Different About Banks?" *Journal of Monetary Economics* 15 (1985), 29–36.

Fischel, Daniel. "The Economics of Lender Liability." *Yale Law Journal* 99 (1989): 131–154.

Forbes, Shawn M. and Lucille S. Mayne. "A Friction Model of the Prime." *Journal of Banking and Finance* 13 (1989); 127–135.

Garwood, Griffith L. and Dolores S. Smith. "The Community Reinvestment Act: Evolution and Current Issues," *Federal Reserve Bulletin* 79 (April 1993); 251–267.

Gill, Edward G. *Commercial Lending Basics.* Reston, Va.: Reston Publishing Co., 1983.

Glancz, Ronald R., Kenneth O. Freer, and Tina W. Melton. "Suing the Lender." *Magazine of Bank Administration* 65 (February 1989): 24–32.

Goldberg, Michael A. "The Sensitivity of the Prime Rate to Money Market Conditions." *Journal of Financial Research* 7 (Winter 1984); 269–280.

Greenbaum, Stuart I., George Kanatas, and Itzhak Venezia. "Equilibrium Loan Pricing Under the Bank-Client Relationship." *Journal of Banking and Finance* 13 (1989): 221–235.

Hempel, George H., Donald G. Simonson, and Alan B. Coleman. *Bank Management: Text and Cases.* New York: John Wiley & Sons, Inc., 1994.

James, Christopher. "Are Bank Loans Special?" *Weekly Letter* (Federal Reserve Bank of San Francisco) (July 24, 1987).

Koch, Timothy W. *Bank Management,* 3d ed. Fort Worth, Tex: Dryden Press, 1995.

Mahoney, Patrick I. "The Recent Behavior of Demand Deposits." *Federal Reserve Bulletin* 74 (April 1988); 195–208.

Mills, Dixie L. and Mona J. Gardner. "Consumer Response to Adjustable Rate Mortgages: Implications of the Evidence from Illinois and Wisconsin." *Journal of Consumer Affairs* (Summer 1986), 77–105.

Nadler, Paul. "Balances and Buggy Whips in Loan Pricing." *Journal of Commercial Bank Lending* 72 (February 1989), 4–9.

Nothaft, Frank E. and George H. K. Wang. "Determinants of ARM Share of National and Regional Lending." *Journal of Real Estate Finance and Economics* 5 (June 1992), 219–234.

Osterberg, William P. "Bank Exposure to Highly Leveraged Transactions." *Economic Commentary* (Federal Reserve Bank of Cleveland) (January 15, 1993).

Peek, Joe. "A Call to ARMS, Adjustable Rate Mortgages in the 1980s." *New England Economic Review* (Federal Reserve Bank of Boston) (March/April 1990); 47–61.

Pozdena, Randall. "Banks and High Leverage Debt." *Weekly Letter* (Federal Reserve Bank of San Francisco), December 8, 1989.

Priess, Beth. "The Garn-St. Germain Act and Due-on-Sale-Clause Enforcement." *Housing Finance Review* 2 (October 1983), 369–377.

Saunders, Anthony. *Financial Institution Management: A Modern Approach.* Chicago: Irwin, 1997.

Sinkey, Joseph F., Jr. *Commercial Bank Financial Management,* 5th edi. Upper Saddle Ridge, N.J.: Prentice Hall, 1998.

Slovin, Myron B. and Marie Elizabeth Sushka. "A Model of the Commercial Bank Loan Rate." *Journal of Finance* 38 (December 1983), 1583–1596.

Smith, Dolores S. "Revision of the Board's Equal Credit Regulation: An Overview." *Federal Reserve Bulletin* 71 (December 1985); 913–923.

Stacy, Ronald L. "Mezzanine Lending: A Primer for Asset-Based Lenders," *Journal of Commercial Bank Lending* 71 (October 1988): 54–66.

Stigum, Marcia. *The Money Market*, 3d ed. Homewood, Illinois: Dow Jones-Irwin, 1990.

Ulrich, Thomas A. "Are Compensating Balance Practices Declining?" *Magazine of Bank Administration* 61 (January 1985); 48–52.

Walter, John R. "Loan Loss Reserves." *Economic Review* (Federal Reserve Bank of Richmond) 77 (July/August 1991): 20–30.

Wolfson, Martin H. and Mary M. McLaughlin. "Recent Developments in the Profitability and Lending Practices of Commercial Banks." *Federal Reserve Bulletin* 75 (July 1989): 461–484.

Chapter 21 Internet Exercise

Chicago Mercantile Exchange

How difficult is it to trade currency futures and options? Although trading itself is relatively simple,consistently making a profit-well, that's a bit harder. If you want to go into the simulation with a better understanding of currency futures and options, look at the CME How to Trade Currency Futures and Options guide on the Internet (http://www.cme.com/market/cfot/howto).

If you just want a quick overview of the basic terms and concepts of currency futures and options trading before you start the simulation, then click on the following simulation site: http://www.cme.com/market/cfot/simulation

The Bank Rate Monitor has a useful discussion, with an example, of credit scoring at http://www.bankrate.com/brm/news/pf/19981204b.asp. In his article "A Credit Score Can Make—or Break—a Would-Be Borrower," Michael D. Larson notes that credit scoring is perhaps the most important technological advance of all for the countless Americans who try to borrow money every day. Some examples of credit scores are given at: http://www.bankrate.com/brm/news/pf/19981204.asp. Named for credit scoring industry leader Fair, Isaac and Co., the FICO score is derived in part from a borrower's past credit history, says David Shellenberger, product manager for the company's credit bureau products. The company's software and services take that history and measure it against a database of habits in the general borrowing population. That, in turn, determines whether the borrower's tendencies match those of borrowers who default on debt, declare bankruptcy or end up in other types of financial trouble.

Useful Links:

Government National Mortgage Association (Ginnie Mae)
http://www.ginniemae.gov/

Federal National Mortgage Association (Fannie Mae)
http://fanniemae.com/

Federal Home Loan Mortgage Corporation (Freddie Mac).
http://www.freddiemac.com/

Sample Loan Underwriting Guidelines

Signet Bank Presented 1990 Michael B. Bronfein Senior Vice Pres. Com. Finance Division

The following is an outline of the form that the credit memo should follow with a few brief comments about the information to be contained in each section.

The following outline provides the standard form to be utilized when preparing a credit memo and the minimum requirements for underwriting issue that must be addressed. The loan officer should use his/her discretion to determine if additional information is necessary. If so, then it should be added.

The credit memo should be titled "Credit Memorandum" with the company's name listed directly below. Next should be the Bank unit and division in which the credit will be housed. And directly under that it should say "Prepared by" with a colon and the account officer's name as well as the date prepared.

Thereafter, the following Roman Numeral structure should be employed:

I. Source of Business: (referral source—new, or existing customer)

II. Principal Contacts: (These are the one or two contacts with which the Bank communicates on a regular basis)

III. Participation Structure: (Optional)

If the credit accommodation is either a bought or sold participation, all of the salient details of the participation should be clearly articulated. This information should include the lead bank, what their role will be in the management of the credit (if it is a bought participation) and all other participants. Additionally, each participants' share should be highlighted as well as the effective yield that the Bank will enjoy on the credit accommodation.

When the requested accommodation is a bought participation, information should be provided about the lead bank and their experience in leading participants. References from other banks who have bought participations from the proposed lead lender should be obtained if Signet does not have prior experience with the lead bank.

In the case of a lead position by Signet, all fees attendant to the transaction, including rate overrides on the participants portion of the loans, should be clearly shown and utilized in the computation of the yield analysis.

Loan closing fees should be amortized over the term of the commitment when calculating yield. The amortization period shall be noted.

Finally, this section should also indicate the voting rights and the operational structure of the participation so that the loan committee has a clear understanding of what rights Signet shall obtain or convey in the course of the loan participation.

IV. Requested Accommodation:

There should be two sub-sections, A and B. Section A should contain the reason for the requested accommodation (i.e., LBO, refinance, equipment acquisitions) and should articulate the structure of the transaction including a general narrative about the rationale for the transaction and structure, as well as complete delineation with regard to all components of the capital structure (i.e., both debt and equity).

Section B should be a Sources and Uses of funds relative to the transaction. This section should clearly demonstrate to the reader that Signet's and any other source of funds provide the financing necessary to accomplish the contemplated transaction.

V. History and Operations:

First, the history of the company should be given including how and when it was formed, general background about the company's products, services, and markets, and how it has evolved over time. Thereafter, there should be a detailed explanation of the company's operations, including the market it serves (geographical customers), the products its sells, and the competitive environment in which it operates. This section should address competitive advantages or disadvantages the company enjoys and how they relate to the overall economic environment in which the company operates.

In general, this section should give the reader a sense of the company's mission, how it relates to the general economic conditions with regard to both its industry and the geographic region in which it operates, and the resultant competitive situation it enjoys.

VI.   Industry Analysis: (Optional)

In cases of large credit requests, unusual credit requests, or credit request in which the Bank/Division has a large concentration, an Industry Analysis should be provided.

Sources of information for the industry analysis could include trade associations, trade journals, the Credit Administration Department's *computer based information services*, recognized industry experts, and lastly the customer. The credibility of the industry analysis to a large extent will be based on the source of the information utilized in providing the analysis and therefore should be as independent as possible.

VII.   Management Performance/Profiles:

This section should contain "practical resumés" of the executive management of the company. It should also contain a section that provides editorial comments about the account officer's assessment of management, their professional accomplishments, and their overall capabilities.

The information needed for this narrative should be one of the primary focuses of the underwriting effort (i.e., assessment of management).

VIII.   Financial Performance:
    A. Historical Financial Performance:

This section should include Historical Financial Performance with subsections; Income Statement, Balance Sheet, and Uniform Cash Flow.

The income statement section should provide a narrative as to the trends that are occurring with insightful analysis as to why the trends are either negative or positive. It should also examine the mix of sales, if applicable, and the complexion of the cost of sales.

Operating expenses should be closely examined for negative trends on a common size basis and explanations therefore should be provided. Any unusual or extraordinary expenses or revenues should be clearly explained. The reader of this section should have a clear indication that the account officer is conversant with the company's earning capabilities or lack thereof as a result of the income statement analysis.

The balance sheet section should contain explanations for all major accounts on the balance sheets and changes thereto. There should also be insightful trend analysis with regard to asset turnover with specific emphasis on accounts receivable, inventory, accounts payable, and accruals.

There should also be an explanation as to the rationale for the existing capital structure and discussion as to whether or not it is appropriate to the company's operating strategy.

Analysis of the uniform cash flow should provide the reader with insight to the sources and uses of cash and the *company's ability to generate sufficient cash flow to sustain its growth and/or repay its debt*.
    B. Future Prospects/Projections:

This section should contain two sub-sections: 1) Future Prospects—a narrative about the future prospects of the company as it relates to its markets, products, competition, management, and general capabilities; and 2) Financial Projections—an analysis of the projected operating results *with reconciliation of the projected operating results to the historical operating results*. In this section, there should be a clear indication of any operating changes that are being contemplated, why they are being contemplated, and the effect on operating results.

The reconciliation between the past and the future is imperative as it relates to the credibility with which the Loan Committee will view the attainability of the company's projected results.

Whenever possible, the "Cash Forecasting" monthly model should be used for projection purposes. The monthly model is preferred for working capital or related transactions; however, where a multi-year commitment is being requested, the "Cash Forecasting" annual model should also be prepared.

It is imperative that the model be used as structured and that no significant format changes be made to the cells within the lotus model. In order for loan administration to allow this model to be utilized, we must be responsible and thereby insure the integrity of the underlying architecture.

IX. Collateral/Risk Analysis:

This section should contain three sub-sections: A, a narrative on the collateral; B, a liquidation analysis (Micro); and C, a general risk analysis (Macro).

A. The first sub-section should contain a narrative about the accounting systems, their integrity, and their competency. It should then list the collateral which is securing the obligation and the nature of that collateral. Information from the Auditor's preliminary audit should be utilized in writing this section and should reconcile with the Collateral Analysis Sheet performed by the auditors.

When the account officer's analysis of the collateral and the attendant advance rates on current asset collateral differs from the auditors then a paragraph should be included to discuss the differences and the loan officer's rationale for his or her position.

This sub-section should provide the reader with significant detail with regard to the nature and quality of the collateral being taken. This section should also include a sources and uses of cash; specifically an availability schedule relative to the current asset availability which is being generated under the loan formula; how much of that availability will be used for closing and the amount of estimated excess availability at the closing date. This analysis should indicate that there is sufficient availability to pay off all existing indebtedness (required to be paid), closing costs, and any past due payables.

B. The second sub-section should be a detailed liquidation analysis (when applicable) of what the writer expects to be the mode of liquidation, the realization of liquidation values on the collateral, and the expenses associated with liquidation. In this section there should also be a schedule of events that would occur in a liquidation scenario.

C. The third sub-section, Risk Analysis, should be a general summation of the risk as viewed by the loan officer. This section should take into account the barriers to entry for this particular industry, the quality of management, the quality of the products and services offered, the "franchise" value of the assets, and other factors that may impact the company's ability to operate in the future.

The conclusion of the section should clearly demonstrate to the loan committee members that the loan is either fully collateralized or that a gap exists. When a gap exists, rationale should be provided for why the bank should entertain such a risk.

X.   Loan Review Recommendation:

In this section, the writer should recommend the loan review rating that is appropriate to the requested accommodation.

XI.   Conclusion:

In this section there should be a summation of all of the salient items that lead the writer to conclude that this is a reasonable risk for the organization to enter into. There should be a *Favorable* column and an *Unfavorable* column and only the most salient points should fall into each category.

Appendix 21.B

FICTIONAL SAMPLE LOAN PRESENTATION

I. Background:

The Big Apple Real Estate & Storage Company was organized in 1980 to acquire, hold, and operate transportation storage facilities in downtown Manhattan. The firm is a general partnership and the guarantor John Jahera owns 60 percent of the partnership. Other partners own respectively 20 percent, 10 percent, and 10 percent shares in the partnership. The partnership owns 100 percent of three other transportation storage facilities. The company has had a loan with the bank since 1992. At that time the company was much larger. Since that time it has scaled down, selling two previous facilities that it owned.

II. Request:

The request is for the renewal of its term debt on its facility in downtown New York which originated in 1992. It should be noted that the mortgage on another facility matures in 1998 which may be a future business opportunity for the Bank.

III. Repayment Analysis:

Primary repayment is from cash flows from property. Based on notes to the firm's CPA-reviewed statements, a summary cash flow of the downtown New York facility on a stand-alone basis is as follows:

(in $'s)	1993	1994	1995	1996
Revenue	$365,298	$396,783	$414,524	$428,161
Operating Expense	266,921	289,486	316,959	282,579
Net Income	$ 78,377	$107,297	$ 97,565	$145,582
+Deprec. & Amortiz.	45,214	44,630	44,871	44,883
+Interest Expense	90,597	89,265	87,231	85,985
(NOPAT) Net Operating Income	214,188	241,192	229,667	276,450
Less: Debt Service°	101,784	101,784	101,784	101,784
Net Cash Flow	112,404	139,408	127,883	174,666
Debt Coverage Ratio	2.10	2.37	2.26	2.72

°Based on proposed loan structure

Historic debt service coverage is more than adequate in the years reviewed. The facility operates between a high level of 95 percent occupancy in the summer to a low of 87. Based on 1996 operating expenses, rental income would have to drop by over 40 percent (or $174,666) to fall below break-even.

Revenue growth over the past three years is attributed solely to rate increases as average occupancy rates have been relatively stable. Expenses jumped somewhat in 1995 in the form of wages due to large one-time expenses for a replacement for a hospitalized manager, while continuing to pay for the hospitalized employee.

A four-month interim Income Statement ending April 30 of 1997 on the downtown New York facility reflects annualized revenue of $408,501, which is on par with 1996 with seasonality taken into account.

Secondary Source:

Secondary repayment will look to the partners. The primary partner is the only guarantor on the loan, and is considered to provide ample secondary strength, so another guarantor is not needed.

Tertiary Source:

Tertiary repayment will be the refinance or sale of the subject property (see Collateral section).

Financial Analysis:

Attached are spreadsheets for the company for years 1992 through 1996. The statements are CPA reviewed. In all of the years examined, the Accountants Review Report notes a G.A.A.P. exception in the firm's accounting practices. The company has been amortizing its non-purchased goodwill because management believes there has been no diminution of value. G.A.A.P. requires amortization of goodwill over the lesser of its estimated useful life or forty years.

Balance Sheet:

✦ Over the past five years the firm's balance sheet has improved considerably, particularly after the sale of assets in 1995 and early 1996. Total Assets dropped from $7.06MM in 1992 to $3.16MM in 1996, while Net Worth rose from ($732M) to $978M.

✦ The firm's leverage position has gradually improved from an upside-down position in 1992 to a Debt/Tangible Net Worth of 4.27 × for year end 1996 with over $1.44MM in cash distributions taken in 1995 and 1996.

✦ The firm's cash balances from $196M for the end of the year 1992 to $847M at the end of the year 1996, substantially improving its Current and Quick ratios which reached 3.9× and 3.65×, respectively, at yearend 1996.

Income Statement:

✦ Revenue and Operating Margins have fluctuated over the past five years as the firm grew and sold off assets.

✦ Operating profits dropped off in 1996 as a result of extra professional expenses incurred with the fore mentioned sales, and are expected to return to their normal range of 40–50 percent. The Partnership has always turned a healthy Operating Profit in the periods reviewed.

✦ Net Profits were particularly strong in the last two years as a result of the gains realized from the sale of the partnership interests. The 1996 property distribution was recorded with the resulting gain reflected in Gain on Sale of Assets.

Guarantor:

John Jahera submitted a Personal Financial Statement. The statement reflects and outside net worth of $2.65 million. Liabilities consist of a minimal amount of revolving credit card debt and mortgage debt of $352,000. Assets are centered around real estate and partnership interests, and a substantial $880,000 in cash and marketable securities. 1996 Federal Tax returns are on extension. John Jahera submitted his 1995 tax return to the Bank, which reflects an aggregated gross income of $1.65 million centered around $.437 million in capital gains and $.892 million in Schedule E S-Corp/Partnership Income. However, a true cash flow picture cannot be ascertained as K-1's on Jahera's 20 S-Corps and Partnerships were not available for analysis, and the majority of capital gain income was from the sale of business property which is not a solid source of recurring income. Nevertheless, based on a relatively minimal $49,000 in annual debt service and the know distributions from the firm, Jahera's annual cash after debt service is estimated to be quite strong—as evidenced by his personal savings.

Collateral:

The Bank has a first mortgage on the downtown New York Transportation Storage Center. The property consists of a 15,600 s/f lot containing a 62,687 s/f building with an 8,000 s/f basement. This building was originally built by Moving Company circa 1925. The building is several stories tall, and the original open warehouse space on each floor has been finished with individual storage spaces. Two large freight elevators are located in the center of the building. There is office space on the first floor where John Jahera conducts business for his various partnerships.

An appraisal was prepared in 1992 for our bank by James Gilkeson of Gilkeson & Sons assigning a fair value of $1.6MM to the property. The valuation was based primarily on an Income approach, utilizing a cap rate of 12.5 percent. Based on FY96 net income capitalized at 12.5 percent, which is considered to be very conservative for current market conditions, the property values at $2.21 million—a respective LTV of 38 percent. At a more updated cap rate of 10 percent, the property values at $2.76 million for an LTV of 30 percent. An updated appraisal is not considered to be necessary by this Officer as there have been no adverse changes in market conditions or physical aspects of the property that would threaten the Bank's collateral position.

A Phase I was performed by Environmental Property Audits, Inc. on 9/11/92, which came up clean. Present and past use of the property did not reveal any potential hazards. It was noted, however, that a service station was located across the street from 1929–1967 for which there were no records or knowledge available regarding its disposition.

Risk Analysis & Recommendation:

There is inherent economic and market risk associated with real estate investment, as well as the fact that personal income information supplied by the Guarantor is somewhat limited. However, these risks are mitigated by a profitable history, the extensive experience and strong liquid strength of the guarantor, and a solid collateral position.

Recommend approval as presented at a Grade of 1-C.

Proposed Loan Structure:

Credit Request: Renewal—Real Estate Loan   Grade: 1-C

Amount: $835,314

Rate/Index: 5-yr. Treasuries + 2.65 percent, fixed° (°currently at 10 percent)

Loan Fees: $\frac{1}{2}$ percent

Renewal of existing real estate debt and continue amortization. Loan matures 9/97.

Requesting a five-year renewal plus number of months remaining until maturity.

Approximately 15-years remaining amortization (original amortization was 20 years).

Collateral: First deed of trust on downtown Manhattan Facility.

BIG APPLE REAL ESTATE & STORAGE

Statement in Thousands $	Review Dec. 31 1993	Review Dec. 31 1994	Review Dec. 31 1995	Review Dec. 31 1996
INDIRECT METHOD—FASB 95 CASH FLOW				
Net Income	159	326	1,188	1,234
Adjustments to reconcile				
Depreciation & Amortization	247	245	179	113
Other adjustments	0	0	0	0
Changes in Assets/Liabilities				
Change in Accounts Receivable	(41)	12	54	13
Change in Inventory	0	0	0	0
Change in Prepaids	(33)	6	58	8
Change in A/P & Accrued Exp.	(39)	179	(57)	(275)
Change in Interest Payable	0	0	0	0
Change in Income Taxes Payable	0	0	0	0
Change in Deferred Taxes	0	0	0	0
Change in Other Assets/Liab.	(94)	(279)	(300)	(21)
Total Adjustments	40	163	(66)	(162)
Net Cash Provided by Operating Activities	199	489	1,122	1,072
Cash Flows from Investing Activities				
Capital Expenditures	(38)	(40)	2,309	1,415
Change in Long Term Investments	0	0	0	0
Net Cash Used-Investing	(38)	(40)	2,309	1,415
Cash Flows from Financing Activities				
Current Portion Long Term Debt	(2)	0	0	0
Change in Short Term Debt	0	0	0	0
Change in Long Term Debt	(95)	(153)	(2,563)	(1,832)
Change in Contributed Capital	123	42	55	0
Oth. Chgs in Retained Earnings	1	(1)	1	(1)
Dividends or Owners Withdrawals	0	0	(838)	(579)
Change in Dividends Payable	0	0	0	0
Net Cash Provided by Financing Activities	27	(112)	(3,345)	(2,412)
Change in Cash & Equivalents	188	337	86	75
Cash & Equivalents-Beginning	233	421	758	844
Cash & Equivalents-Ending	421	758	844	919

BIG APPLE REAL ESTATE & STORAGE

Statement in Thousands $	Review Dec. 31 1992		Review Dec. 31 1993		Review Dec. 31 1994		Review Dec. 31 1995		Review Dec. 31 1996	
	ASSETS	COMMON SIZED								
Cash	196	2.8	362	5.1	668	9.2	774	16.6	847	26.8
Escrow	37	0.5	59	0.8	90	1.2	70	1.5	72	2.3
Trade Accounts Receivable	34	0.5	41	0.5	40	0.6	32	0.7	20	0.6
Other Accounts Receivable	47	0.7	81	1.1	70	1.0	24	0.5	23	0.7
Net Accounts Receivable	81	1.1	122	1.7	110	1.5	56	1.2	43	1.4
Prepaid Expenses	80	1.1	113	1.6	107	1.5	49	1.1	41	1.3
Total Current Assets	394	5.6	656	9.2	976	13.6	949	20.4	1,003	31.8
Land	1,937	27.4	1,937	27.2	1,937	26.8	1,230	26.5	492	15.6
Buildings	5,941	84.2	5,941	83.3	5,945	82.3	3,600	77.4	2,605	82.5
Furniture & Fixtures	107	1.5	91	1.3	95	1.3	59	1.3	49	1.6
Gross Fixed Assets	7,985	113.1	7,969	111.7	7,977	110.5	4,889	105.1	3,146	99.6
Accumulated Depreciation (−)	(1,876)	(26.6)	(2,069)	(29.0)	(2,282)	(31.6)	(1,682)	(36.2)	(1,467)	(46.4)
Net Fixed Assets	6,109	86.6	5,900	82.7	5,695	78.9	3,207	69.0	1,679	53.1
Other Assets	88	1.2	111	1.6	85	1.2	27	0.6	10	0.3
Non-purchased Goodwill°	467	6.6	467	6.5	467	6.5	467	10.0	467	14.8
TOTAL ASSETS	7,058	100.0	7,134	100.0	7,222	100.0	4,650	100.0	3,159	100.0
	LIABILITIES	COMMON SIZED								
Current Portion Capital Leases	2	0.0	0	0.0	0	0.0	0	0.0	0	0.0
Accounts Payable & Accruals	374	5.3	335	4.7	514	7.1	457	9.6	182	5.8
Security Deposits	25	0.4	28	0.4	28	0.4	10	0.2	8	0.3
Prepaid Rental Income	81	1.1	123	1.7	122	1.7	96	2.1	67	2.1
Total Current Liabilities	482	6.8	486	6.8	664	9.2	563	12.1	257	8.1
Mortgage Notes Payable	6,567	93.0	6,472	90.7	6,319	87.5	3,756	80.8	1,924	60.9
Due to Related Parties	724	10.3	519	8.7	314	4.3	0	0.0	0	0.0
Deferred Income	11	0.2	0	0.0	0	0.0	0	0.0	0	0.0
Minority Interest	7	0.1	6	0.1	7	0.1	7	0.2	0	0.0
Other Liabilities	(1)	0.0	0	0.0	0	0.0	0	0.0	0	0.0
Total Liabilities	7,790	110.4	7,583	106.3	7,304	101.1	4,326	93.0	2,181	69.0
Minority Interest	(220)	(3.1)	(97)	(1.4)	(55)	(0.8)	0	0.0	0	0.0
Partners' Equity	(512)	(7.3)	(357)	(4.9)	(27)	(0.4)	324	7.0	978	31.0
Total Net Worth	(732)	(10.4)	(449)	(6.3)	(82)	(1.1)	324	7.0	978	31.0
TOTAL LIABILITIES & NET WORTH	7,058	100.0	7,134	100.0	7,222	100.0	4,650	100.0	3,159	100.0

BIG APPLE REAL ESTATE & STORAGE

Statement in Thousands $	Review Dec. 31 1992		Review Dec. 31 1993		Review Dec. 31 1994		Review Dec. 31 1995		Review Dec. 31 1996	
INCOME STATEMENT COMMON SIZED										
Rent	1,354	77.4	1,524	77.5	1,729	79.7	1,349	72.9	800	78.4
Mgmt. & Consulting Fees	188	10.7	196	10.0	222	10.2	197	10.6	106	10.4
Late Charges & Other	207	11.8	246	12.5	218	10.1	305	16.5	114	11.2
Total Sales	1,749	100.0	1,966	100.0	2,169	100.0	1,851	100.0	1,020	100.0
Gross Profit	1,749	100.0	1,966	100.0	2,169	100.0	1,851	100.0	1,020	100.0
Guaranteed payments to partnrs	120	6.9	129	6.6	135	6.2	135	7.3	135	13.2
Other Operating Expenses	696	39.8	747	38.0	731	33.7	667	36.0	464	45.5
Depreciation & Amortization	285	16.3	247	12.6	245	11.3	179	9.7	113	11.1
Operating Expenses	1,101	63.0	1,123	57.1	1,111	51.2	981	53.0	712	69.8
Operating Profit	648	37.0	843	42.9	1,058	48.8	870	47.0	308	30.2
Gain on Sale of Assets	0	0.0	0	0.0	0	0.0	1,734	93.7	1,133	111.1
Income—Minority Interest	28	1.6	0	0.0	0	0.0	0	0.0	0	0.0
Total Other Income	28	1.6	0	0.0	0	0.0	1,734	93.7	1,133	111.1
Interest Expense	783	44.8	651	33.1	656	30.2	493	26.6	207	20.3
Other Expense	0	0.0	0	0.0	0	0.0	36	1.9	0	0.0
Loss—Minority Interest	0	0.0	33	1.7	76	3.5	887	47.9	0	0.0
Total Other Expenses	783	44.8	684	34.8	732	33.7	1,416	76.5	207	20.3
Profit Before Tax	(107)	(6.1)	159	8.1	326	15.0	1,188	64.2	1,234	121.0
NET INCOME	(107)	(6.1)	159	8.1	326	15.0	1,188	64.2	1,234	121.0
RECON. OF NET WORTH COMMON SIZED										
Beginning Net Worth	(625)	85.4	(732)	163.0	(449)	547.6	(82)	(25.3)	324	33.1
Changes in Retained Earnings:										
Net Income (Loss)	(107)	14.6	159	(35.4)	326	(397.6)	1,188	366.7	1,234	126.2
Cash Dividends	0	0.0	0	0.0	0	0.0	838	258.6	579	59.2
Other Incr(Decr) to RE	0	0.0	1	(0.2)	(1)	1.2	1	0.3	(1)	(0.1)
Total Change in RE	(107)	14.6	160	(35.6)	325	(396.3)	361	108.3	654	66.9
Changes in Other NW										
Other Equity	0	0.0	123	(27.4)	42	(51.2)	55	17.0	0	0.0
Ending Total Net Worth	(732)	100.0	(449)	100.0	(82)	100.0	324	100.0	978	100.0

BIG APPLE REAL ESTATE & STORAGE

Statement in Thousands $	Review Dec. 31 1992	Review Dec. 31 1993	Review Dec. 31 1994	Review Dec. 31 1995	Review Dec. 31 1996
HIGHLIGHTS					
Income Statement:					
Sales	1,749	1,966	2,169	1,851	1,020
Gross Margin	1,749	1,966	2,169	1,851	1,020
Operating Expenses	1,101	1,123	1,111	981	712
NPBT	(107)	159	326	1,188	1,234
NPAT	(107)	159	326	1,188	1,234
Cash Dividends	0	0	0	838	579
Balance Sheet:					
Total Current Assets	394	656	975	949	1,003
Net Fixed Assets	6,109	5,900	5,695	3,207	1,679
Total Assets	7,058	7,134	7,222	4,650	3,159
Short Term Obligations	2	0	0	0	0
Total Current Liabilities	482	486	664	563	257
Long Term Debt	6,567	6,472	6,319	3,756	1,924
Total Liabilities	7,790	7,583	7,304	4,326	2,181
Net Worth	(732)	(449)	(82)	324	978
Ratios:					
Sales Growth		12.41%	10.33%	(14.66%)	(44.89%)
Gross Margin	100.00%	100.00%	100.00%	100.00%	100.00%
Profit Margin	(6.12%)	8.09%	15.03%	64.18%	120.98%
Current Ratio	0.82	1.35	1.47	1.69	3.90
Quick Ratio	0.55	0.95	1.20	1.56	3.65
Working Capital	(88)	170	311	386	746
Age of Receivables	7	8	7	6	7
Days Supply in Inventory	0	0	0	0	0
Age of Payables	0	0	0	0	0
Debt/Tangible Net Worth	(6.50)	(8.28)	(13.30)	(30.25)	4.27
Breakeven Sales—Cash Basis		1,741	1,741	758	(402)
Actual Sales/Breakeven Sales		1.13	1.25	2.44	(2.54)
Cash Flow: Incr (Decr) in Cash					
Cash From Sales		1,959	2,170	1,859	1,032
Cash From Trading		1,920	2,349	1,802	757
Net Cash After Operations		873	1,119	1,557	1,262
Cash After Financing Costs		222	463	226	476
Cash After Debt Amortization		220	463	226	476
Capital Expenditures		(38)	(40)	2,309	1,415
Financing Surplus (Requirement)		159	449	2,593	1,908

BIG APPLE REAL ESTATE & STORAGE

Statement in Thousands $	Review Dec. 31 1992	Review Dec. 31 1993	Review Dec. 31 1994	Review Dec. 31 1995	Review Dec. 31 1996
RATIOS					
Operating Ratios:					
Sales Growth		12.41%	10.33%	(14.66%)	(44.89%)
Pre-Tax Profit Margin	(6.12%)	8.09%	15.03%	64.18%	120.98%
Profit Margin	(6.12%)	8.09%	15.03%	64.18%	120.98%
Return on Assets (ROA)	(1.52%)	2.23%	4.51%	25.55%	39.06%
Return on Equity (ROE)	(8.92%)	17.36%	59.38%	830.77%	241.49%
Asset Turnover	0.25	0.28	0.30	0.40	0.32
Current Position:					
Current Ratio	0.82	1.35	1.47	1.69	3.90
Quick Ratio	0.55	0.95	1.20	1.56	3.65
Working Capital	(88)	170	311	386	746
Working Capital/Assets	(1.25%)	2.38%	4.31%	8.30%	23.62%
Working Capital Turnover	(19.88)	11.56	6.97	4.80	1.37
Receivable Turnover	51.44	47.95	54.23	57.84	51.00
Age of Receivables	7	8	7	6	7
Inventory Turnover					
Days Supply in Inventory	0	0	0	0	0
Payable Turnover					
Age of Payables	0	0	0	0	0
Equity Position:					
Owner Equity/Assets	(10.37%)	(6.29%)	(1.14%)	6.97%	30.96%
Creditor Equity/Assets	110.37%	106.29%	101.14%	93.03%	69.04%
Debt/Tangible Net Worth	(6.50)	(8.28)	(13.30)	(30.25)	4.27
Fixed Assets/Long Term Debt	83.59%	83.13%	85.77%	85.22%	87.27%
Fixed Assets/Tangible Net Worth	(509.51%)	(644.10%)	(1,037.34%)	(2,242.66%)	328.57%
Plant Turnover	0.29	0.33	0.38	0.58	0.61
Other:					
Interest Coverage (NPBT)	0.86	1.24	1.50	3.41	6.96
Prin & Interest Coverage (NPBT)		1.24	1.50	3.41	6.96
Interest Coverage (Operating Cash)		1.34	1.71	3.16	6.10
Prin & Interest Coverage (OC)		1.34	1.71	3.16	6.10
Sustainable Growth Rate	9.09%	(13.96%)	(35.71%)	(68.77%)	(1,183.31%)
Breakeven Sales—Cash Basis		1,741	1,741	758	(402)
Actual Sales/Breakeven Sales		1.13	1.25	2.44	(2.54)
Basic Defense Interval	(20)	41	75	109	338
Bankruptcy Ratio: Z value	0.44	0.58	0.75	1.67	2.36
Z < 1.23 Weak; > 2.90 Strong					

Appendix 21.C

EXAMPLE COMMERCIAL LOAN PRICING FORMULA— DATE JUNE 1997

Customer Name

Period of Analysis: (Historical/Projected?)		Projected		
Today's Prime Rate:	8.50%			
Average Balance THIS LOAN:	$820,487	SOP =	0.65%	$75,075
Average Balance LOAN #2:	$0	SOP =	0.00%	$0
Average Balance LOAN #3:	$0	SOP =	0.00%	$0
Total # Loans:	1			

I. Source and Use of Funds

1. Average loan and/or line balance		$820,487
2. Ledger Demand Deposit Balances (NOT on analysis)	$81,857	
3. Less: Reserve (12% of Ledger)	$9,823	
Float (historic avg. or 15%)	$61	
4. Available Balances		$71,973
5. Savings & NOW Accounts Deposits	$0	
6. Less Reserves (3%)	$0	
7. Available Balances		$0
8. Net Funds Needed	91.23%	$748,514

II. Loan/Line Income/Expense (Relationship Costs)

9. Gross Loan Interest: Relationship a.n.y. =	9.15%	$75,075
10. Account Analysis Profit (applicable to time period of analysis)		$0
11. Fees (applicable to time period of analysis)		$835
12. MMA Margin on balance of:	$0	$0
13. Total Gross Income		$75,910
14. Account Analysis Loss (applicable to time period of analysis)	$____	
15. Time Deposit Costs (based on 5.5% interest paid)	$0	
16. Maintenance and Setup Expenses ($600 per loan above)	$600	
17. Other Costs (T & E, overhead, etc.)	____	
18. Total Loan Costs		$600
19. Net Income		$75,310
20. Relationship Yield		10.06%

III. Profitability Index

21. Marginal Cost of Funds (As set by Sr. Mgmt or ALCO)	5.25%
22. Margin (asset/liability management spread)	4.35%
23. Risk Adjustment (inclusive of allocation for loan loss provision: $-1 < RA < 3$)	1.00%
24. Minimum Required Yield	10.60%
25. Profitability Index (Target > 100%)	94.917%
Additional/(Less) Ledger Demand Balances Required to achieve 100% P.I. =	$56,783
Additional/(Less) Fees Required to achieve 100% P.I. =	$4,033
Additional/(Less) BASIS POINTS needed on THIS LOAN to achieve 100% P.I. =	0.004915

"It seems as if every company and every government in Latin America is borrowing money these days as money managers, mutual funds and commercial banks scramble to buy their bonds or give them loans. The current lending boom rivals, and in some respects surpasses, the lending frenzy of the later 1970s and early 1980s. That boom ended after Mexico defaulted on its debt in 1982 and spawned a region-wide economic crisis with banks writing down billions of dollars of loans. It was the start of Latin America's so-called lost decade. Now less than three years after Mexico's peso crisis rocked the region's financial markets yet again, bankers are saying that this time it's different."

Thomas T. Vogel, Jr. and Stephen E. Frank
"Lending Boom Sweeps Latin America: Some Banks' New Aggressiveness Worries Analysts," *The Wall Street Journal*,
July 9, 1997, A10.

"Because of Brazil's enormous deficits, the collapse of emerging markets has hit the nation particularly hard, draining foreign currency reserves and pushing the economy toward recession. Finance officials in Washington and around the world fear that a collapse of Brazil, because of its size and links to other economies would worsen financial instability throughout the hemisphere. With 160 million people, Brazil represents the world's ninth largest economy and is the financial engine of Latin America."

Diana Jean Schemo
"Brazil's Plan on Deficits Is Still Under Construction," *The New York Times*, October 21, 1998, C4.

"A major credit rating service today downgraded its assessment of Brazil's ability to repay debts, and the value of the Brazilian currency fell nearly 4 percent in a further sign of investor anxiety about Latin America's biggest economy. The developments came as Brazilian officials sought to reassure financial markets that their decision a week ago to let the currency float, the real trade without artificial controls would not be changed. Since then, however, the currency has fallen by nearly a third. Duff & Phelps Credit Rating Service said it saw a one-in three risk that Brazil would default on some of its debts, partly because the devaluation of the real means it costs much more to repay them."

Diana Jean Schemo
"Brazil's Ability to Repay Debt Is Downgraded," *The New York Times*, January 26, 1999, p. C12.

"In the tumultuous days since Jan. 15 [1999], when Brazil's government let go control of the exchange rate, the currency has plummeted—from 1.16 to the dollar Jan. 13 to a low of 2.13 to the dollar Friday. . . . The more optimistic economists in and outside Brazil are calling the plunge an 'overshooting,' implying the real will soon bounce back—similar to what occurred in Mexico in 1994 and Asia more recently when their currencies were set free. But to currency traders—the uncertainty feels like a danger zone—On Monday, the Central Bank . . . raised interest rates to a stifling 39 percent, trying to seduce investors to keep cash in the country. But raising interest rates is risky—it dampens consumer demand and economic growth, and penalizes the government, Brazil's largest debtor. . . . Many corporations with debts in dollars are buying dollars now to pay off the debts early, gambling that the real will fall further."

Katherine Ellison
"Brazil's Frantic Course: 39% Interest Rates Latest Move in Crisis." *The Denver Post*, February 3, 1999, 2A, 17A.

"After weeks of uncertainty about the course Brazil would pursue to stabilize its troubled economy, officials here reached a revised agreement with the International Monetary Fund tonight, pledging to enforce substantially greater budget discipline than originally promised and to keep inflation below 10 percent. . . . The new agreement calls on Brazil to increase the independence of the central bank, to contain debt at a level below 45.6 percent of the gross domestic product, and to produce a primary spending surplus in the range of 3 to 3.5 percent this year—substantially greater than the 2.6 percent surplus the original accord promised. . . . The revised agreement was essential for the I.M.F. to release the second portion of a $41.5 billion standby loan pledged to Brazil in November, when this vast nation . . . . began hemorrhaging dollar reserves as investors lost confidence in the nation's solvency."

Diana Jean Schemo
"Brazil Pledges Curbs on Debt and Budgets," *The New York Times*, February 5, 1999, C1.

"After being shut out of the foreign bond markets for a year, Brazil sold $2 billion in global bonds yesterday, demonstrating that an aggressive mix *of deficit cuts and market reforms has restored confidence in its economy. U.S. and European money managers who until recently were cleansing their portfolios of Brazilian debt, eagerly gobbled up the five-year bonds, prompting managers Morgan Stanley Dean Witter & Co. and Citigroup Inc's Salomon Smith Barney unit to double the issue size. But market watchers caution that Brazil's finances will remain fragile until the government proves it can stay its course over the long term. They note that domestic political pressures could make it tough to keep government spending in check and that events outside Brazil could quickly send investors packing again. Brazil's borrowing costs surged after Russia defaulted on its domestic debt last fall, and jumped again before Brazil bowed to market pressure and allowed its currency to float freely in January."*

Pamela Druckerman
"Brazil Returns to International Bond Market: Money Managers Gobble Up Issue," *The Wall Street Journal*, April 23, 1999, A11.

22

GLOBAL FINANCIAL CRISES & INTERNATIONAL MANAGEMENT ISSUES

*T*he preceding quotes capture the history of the currency crisis that occurred in Brazil in 1998 and 1999. In 1997, lenders in Europe and the U.S. were happy to give Brazil loans to finance its rapid growth, despite concerns about rising Latin American debt and major bank's lending exposure (see Figure 22.1). Brazil, similar to Asian countries in the 1990s, took on dollar-denominated loans to finance operations generating revenues in Brazil's currency, the real, creating positions with significant foreign exchange risk. In effect, if the value of the real fell relative to the dollar, Brazilians with dollar-denomi-

nated debt would be hard pressed to generate revenues in reals high enough to pay off their now more expensive dollar debt payments.

When currency crises occurred for Asian countries, investors became wary about the economic condition of Brazil and other less developed countries. In late August 1998, in response to economic problems in Russia and volatility in Asian markets, international investors dumped emerging market stocks and moved funds into U.S. dollars and Treasury bonds. This resulted in global stock market plunges in Asia, Eastern Europe, and Latin America (see Panel A of Figure 22.2), as well as

Figure 22.1   ✦   GROWTH IN LATIN AMERICAN LENDING IN THE MID-1990S

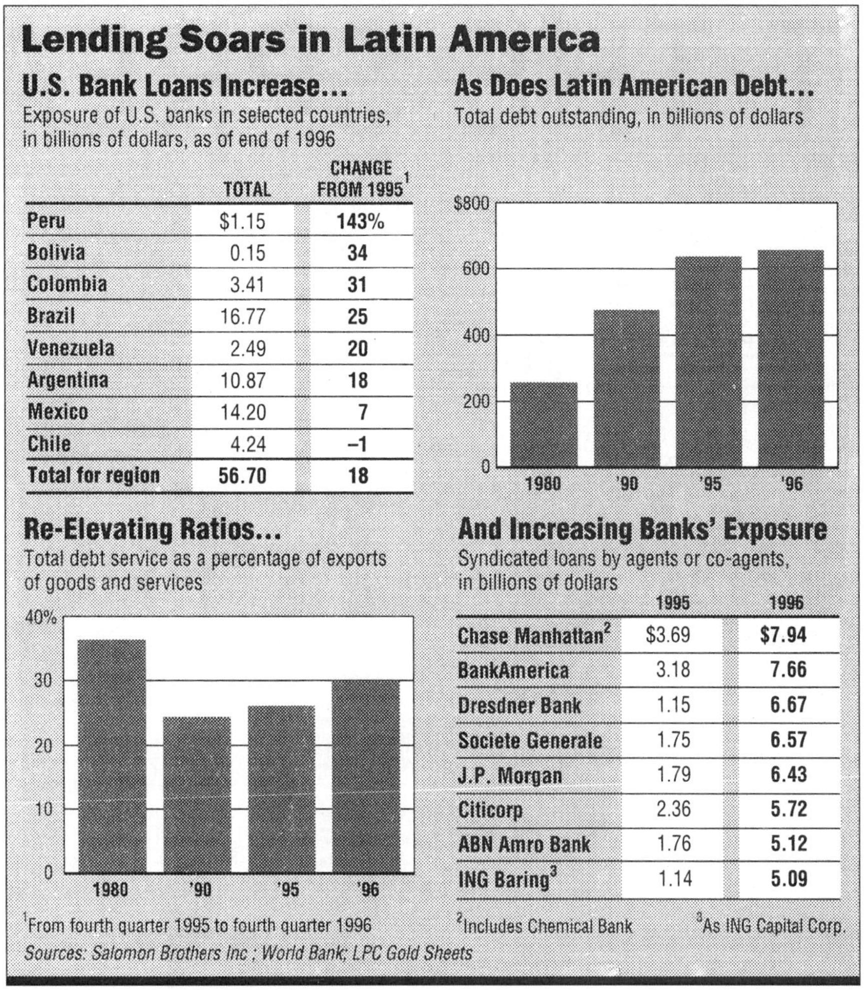

Lending Soars in Latin America

U.S. Bank Loans Increase...

Exposure of U.S. banks in selected countries, in billions of dollars, as of end of 1996

	TOTAL	CHANGE FROM 1995[1]
Peru	$1.15	143%
Bolivia	0.15	34
Colombia	3.41	31
Brazil	16.77	25
Venezuela	2.49	20
Argentina	10.87	18
Mexico	14.20	7
Chile	4.24	−1
Total for region	56.70	18

As Does Latin American Debt...

Total debt outstanding, in billions of dollars

Re-Elevating Ratios...

Total debt service as a percentage of exports of goods and services

And Increasing Banks' Exposure

Syndicated loans by agents or co-agents, in billions of dollars

	1995	1996
Chase Manhattan[2]	$3.69	**$7.94**
BankAmerica	3.18	**7.66**
Dresdner Bank	1.15	**6.67**
Societe Generale	1.75	**6.57**
J.P. Morgan	1.79	**6.43**
Citicorp	2.36	**5.72**
ABN Amro Bank	1.76	**5.12**
ING Baring[3]	1.14	**5.09**

[1]From fourth quarter 1995 to fourth quarter 1996   [2]Includes Chemical Bank   [3]As ING Capital Corp.

Sources: Salomon Brothers Inc ; World Bank; LPC Gold Sheets

Source: Thomas T. Vogel, Jr. and Stephen E. Frank, "Lending Boom Sweeps Latin America: Some Banks' New Aggressiveness Worries Analysts," *The Wall Street Journal*, July 9, 1997, A10.

sharp declines in the value of lesser developed countries' currencies including the real. *To defend the exchange rate for its currency, the Brazilian government's foreign exchange reserves were being depleted, necessi-* *tating international loans from the private sector or the International Monetary Fund (IMF).[1]*

Finance officials in the U.S. and other major countries were particularly concerned about a future debt

---

[1]See Thomas T. Vogel, Jr. and Stephen E. Frank. "Lending Boom Sweeps Latin America: Some Bank's New Aggressiveness Worries Analysts." *The Wall Street Journal* (July 9, 1997), A10; Sara Webb and Michael R. Sesit. "Stock Markets Around Globe Roiled by Russia." *The Wall Street Journal* (August 27, 1998), C1; Marianne Sullivan. "Risk Aversion Will Likely Drive Markets; Shake-Up in Russia Brings New Concern." *The Wall Street Journal* (August 24, 1998), C16.

Figure 22.2 ✦ EFFECT OF SHOCKS IN RUSSIAN MARKET ON STOCK AND CURRENCY MARKETS

PANEL A: EFFECT OF RUSSIA'S DEBT RESTRUCTURING
IN AUGUST 1998 ON GLOBAL MARKETS

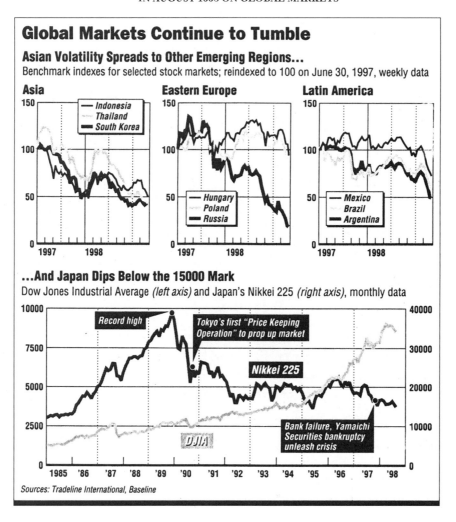

Global Markets Continue to Tumble

Asian Volatility Spreads to Other Emerging Regions...
Benchmark indexes for selected stock markets; reindexed to 100 on June 30, 1997, weekly data

...And Japan Dips Below the 15000 Mark
Dow Jones Industrial Average *(left axis)* and Japan's Nikkei 225 *(right axis)*, monthly data

Sources: Tradeline International, Baseline

Source: Sara Webb, Michael R. Sesit, and Bill Spindle, "Stock Markets Around Globe Roiled by Russia," *The Wall Street Journal,* August 27, 1998, C1.

crisis in Brazil. Despite moral suasion for a private bailout fund by the Group of 7 (central bankers from major countries including the United States, Japan, Britain, Italy, Canada, France and Germany), bankers with significant loan exposures in Latin America that had already experienced large losses were reluctant to take on greater risk (see first column of Panel B of Figure 22.2). Officials were concerned that without an IMF bailout, major banks and other international investors might continue to pull out funds and sink Brazil's economy, as well as other financial sectors. Global stock fund avoided Brazilian shares in the later

Figure 22.2 ✦ **EFFECT OF SHOCKS IN RUSSIAN MARKET ON STOCK AND CURRENCY MARKETS** *(CONTINUED)*

PANEL B: INTERNATIONAL INVESTOR EXPOSURE TO BRAZILIAN AND OTHER LATIN AMERICAN DEBT AT THE END OF 1997 AND 1997–1998

Private Bankers were reluctant to make additional loans to help bail out Brazil. Global stock funds also avoided Brazilian shares in the later months of 1998.

Examining Risk
International claims on Brazil and the rest of Latin America by nationality of reporting banks, in billions of U.S. dollars, as of December 1997

	Brazil	Other Latin America
U.S.	$15.8	$47.6
Germany	10.7	25.9
Spain	4.2	32.4
France	8.6	16.4
U.K.	4.6	16.9
Netherlands	6.0	12.4
Japan	5.0	9.7

	Brazil	Latin America
Global total	$76.29 billion	$283 billion

Source: Bank for International Settlements

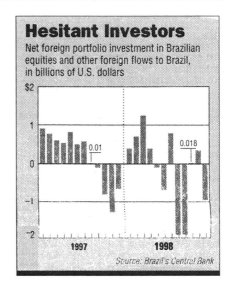

Hesitant Investors
Net foreign portfolio investment in Brazilian equities and other foreign flows to Brazil, in billions of U.S. dollars

Source: Brazil's Central Bank

Sources: Matt Murray and Pamela Druckerman, "Big Banks Cool to Major Role in Brazil Bailout," *The Wall Street Journal*, October 13, 1998, A16; and Pamela Druckerman and Jonathan Friedland, "Global Stock Funds Shun Brazilian Shares," *The Wall Street Journal*, January 22, 1999, A9.

months of 1998, with net foreign portfolio flows to Brazil plunging (see second column, Panel B, Figure 22.2).[2]

As the largest economy in Latin America, Brazil's currency plunge could have a contagious effect on other Latin American currencies, putting these countries at risk. After much consideration, in November 1998 the International Monetary Fund (IMF) conditionally agreed to provide Brazil funds to stem its loss of reserves and help make its large debt payments. The funds would not be provided unless the Brazilian government demonstrated a concrete plan of action to lower its deficit by cutting its spending and implementing policies of economic austerity (see Panel A Figure 22.3). At that time investors were still skeptical about Brazil's political situation, with a fragmented Congress,

---

[2]Michael M. Phillips. "Amid the Brazil Rescue Effort, Private Sector Remains Aloof." *The Wall Street Journal* (November 16, 1998), A29; Matt Murray and Pamela Druckerman. "Big Banks Cool to Major Role in Brazil Bailout." *The Wall Street Journal* (October 13, 1998), A16, A18.

Figure 22.3 ✦ INITIAL TERMS FOR BRAZIL'S RESCUE BY IMF IN NOVEMBER 1998 AND CONDITION OF BRAZIL'S DEBT IN 1999

PANEL A: BAILOUT TERMS UNDER THE IMF'S CONDITIONAL RESCUE AS OF NOVEMBER 16, 1998

Rescuing Brazil

What Brazil Gets...		What Brazil Promised...
IMF	**$18 billion**	■ Government deficit of 3.6% of gross domestic product in 1999 vs. 5.6% in 1998[2]
Soon	$5.25 billion	
By February	$5.25 billion	
Later	$7.5 billion	■ Inflation rate of 2% in 1999
Development banks	**$9 billion**	■ Current-account deficit in 1999 of 3.5% of GDP vs. 4.2% in 1998
World Bank	$4.5 billion	
Inter-American Development Bank[1]	$4.5 billion	■ Maintain exchange-rate regime
Donor countries	**$14.5 billion**	■ State and local government surplus of 0.4% of GDP in 1999 vs. deficit of 0.4% in 1998
U.S.	$5 billion	
Germany, Japan, others	$9.5 billion	
TOTAL:	**$41.5 billion**	■ Raise taxes, reform pension system

[1]Includes $1.1 billion approved in Sept.

[2]2.6% surplus in 1999, excluding debt service payments

Sources: U.S. Treasury, Brazilian Finance Ministry, IMF

Source: Michael M. Phillips and Pamela Druckerman, "Brazil Bailout Spurs Hope for New Momentum," *The Wall Street Journal*, November 16, 1998, A28, A29.

limiting its ability to ratify major fiscal measures that were mandated under the rescue package for Brazil to receive aid. Panel B of Figure 22.3 shows the extent of Brazil's debt and its cost. Brazil's interest rates stood at 39.5 percent at the time of the agreement, and 74 percent its debt was floating rate debt, with 24 percent dollar-linked.[3]

Although the IMF's promise of a conditional loan package helped to calm investors and stem the fall in Brazil's currency, the declaration of a 90-day moratorium by a Brazilian state governor on its state debt in early January 1999 resulted in skittishness in financial markets, and the real's value continued to fall. This made it very costly for the government to continue to use its dwindling foreign reserves to purchase reals for dollars to prop up the real. Consequently, bond rating agencies downgraded Brazil's debt. In response to downgrades, the value of the real plunged. For exam-

---

[3]See Matt Moffett and Peter Fritsch. "Real Politics: Brazil Strives to Steady Its Markets as Election Adds to Uncertainty." *The Wall Street Journal* (September 14, 1998), A1, A10; Michael M. Phillips and Pamela Druckerman. "Brazil Bailout Spurs Hope for New Momentum." *The Wall Street Journal* (November 16, 1998), A28, A29; Diana Jean Schemo. "Brazil's Plan on Deficits Is Still Under Construction." *The New York Times* (October 21, 1998), C4. Measures considered in a three-year austerity package included a tax increase on financial transactions to .3 percent from .2 percent, and extending the Fiscal Stabilization Fund, which sets aside 20 percent of all taxes collected for presidential discretionary spending, which was to have expired by 1999.

Figure 22.3   ✦   INITIAL TERMS FOR BRAZIL'S RESCUE BY IMF IN NOVEMBER 1998
AND CONDITION OF BRAZIL'S DEBT IN 1999 *(CONTINUED)*

PANEL B: IN LATE 1998 AND EARLY 1999, BRAZIL'S HIGH DEBT
AND FALLING CURRENCY VALUE CREATED CONCERN OVER THE
COUNTRY'S ABILITY TO SERVICE ITS DEBT

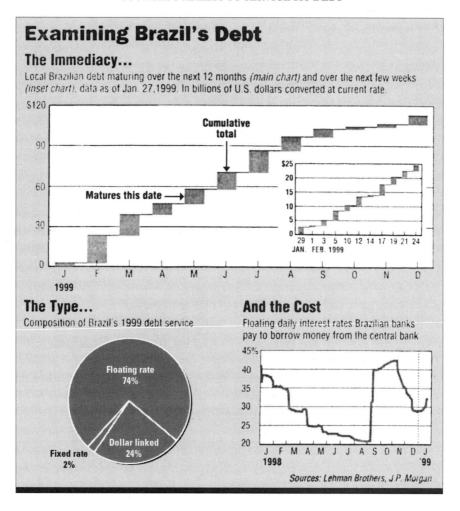

Source: Peter Fritsch and Pamela Druckerman, "Brazil's Falling Currency Stirs Concern Over Its Ability to Keep Up
With Debt." *The Wall Street Journal,* January 28, 1999, A13, A15.

ple, the direct rate of the real to the dollar fell from
.8621 to .4695 or 45.5 percent over the period January
13 to January 30.

Brazil initiated a dramatic change in policy, allowing the devaluation of the real and letting it float
against the dollar. The government, however, continued
to offer very high interest rates of about 39 percent to
attract investors back into reals. Analysts were concerned at this time that a plunging real would impose
severe inflation, which could slow the economy and result in a severe recession (Panel A, Figure 22.4). They
also worried about possible contagion effects on other

Figure 22.4 ✦ BRAZIL'S NEW FLOATING CURRENCY POLICY IN JANUARY 1999
RECEIVES BOTH PRAISE AND CRITICISM

PANEL A: TRENDS IN BRAZIL'S ECONOMY AND CURRENCY IN THE 1990s

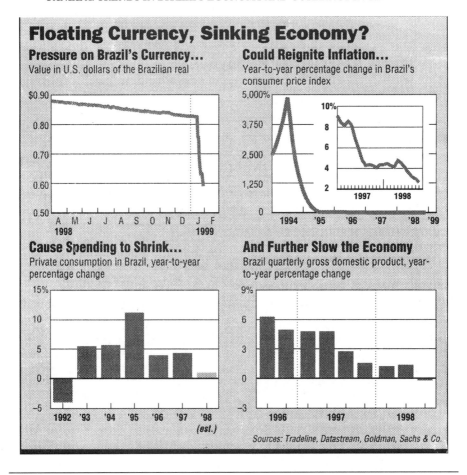

Source: Peter Fritsch and Matt Moffett, "Brazilians Brace Again for Inflation as Devaluation Reaches Shops," *The Wall Street Journal,* January 22, 1999, A8.

Latin American currencies, which showed signs of economic slowdowns and had experienced recent currency exchange rate declines (Panel B of Figure 22.4).[4]

Argentina at this time considered a radical defense for its peso by relying on the U.S. dollar instead as its currency. By having a policy of rigidly fixing its peso

[4]Katherine Ellison. "Brazil's Frantic Course: 39% Interest Rates Latest Move in Crisis." *The Denver Post* (February 3, 1999), 2A, 17A; Peter Fritsch and Michael M. Phillips. "Brazil's Devaluation Reignites Global Fears of Spreading Malaise." *The Wall Street Journal* (January 14, 1999), A1, A8; Diana Jean Schemo. "Brazil's Ability to Repay Debt Is Downgraded." *The New York Times* (January 26, 1999), C12; Diana Jean Schemo. "Jitters Anew in Brazil as Currency Plunges Again." *The New York Times* (January 30, 1999), B1, B2; "Markets in Brazil Tumble on Uncertainty about Aid." *The New York Times* (February 6, 1999), B15; Pamela Druckerman and Jonathan Friedland. "Global Stock Funds Shun Brazilian Shares." *The Wall Street Journal* (January 22, 1999), A9.

Figure 22.4   ✦   Brazil's New Floating Currency Policy in January 1999
Receives Both Praise and Criticism *(continued)*

PANEL B: DOWNWARD TRENDS FOR OTHER LATIN AMERICAN
CURRENCIES IN 1997 & 1998

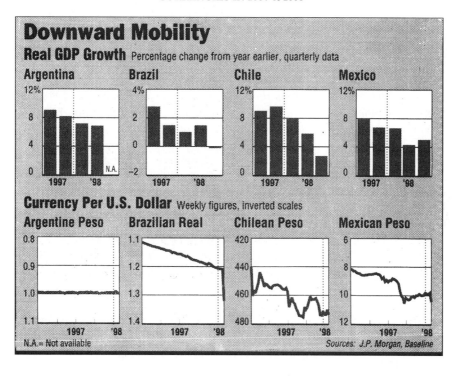

Source: Craig Torres and Thomas Vogel, Jr. "Brazil's Woes Threaten Recession for Region," *The Wall Street Journal,*
January 14, 1999, A14. In 1999, slower Gross Domestic Product (GDP) growth in other Latin American countries
combined with falling currency rates posed the threat of recession for other Latin American countries in response to
Brazil's crisis.

*to the dollar, Argentina realized that it had subjected
itself already to the economic disadvantages of tying its
economy to the United States and the Federal Reserve.*

*Such a pegged rate policy limited Argentina's ability to
use policy measures such as rate cuts to stimulate its
economy.[5]*

[5]Jonathan Friedland, Craig Torres, and Thomas T. Vogel, Jr. "Brazil's Woes Threaten Reces-
sion for Region." *The Wall Street Journal* (January 14, 1999), A14, A16; "Others Risk of
Financial Contagion from Brazil." *The New York Times* (February 11, 1999), C8; E. S.
Browning and Gregory Zuckerman. "U.S. Stocks Beaten, but Not Broken, by Brazil." *The
Wall Street Journal* (January 14, 1999), C1, C21; David Wessel, Craig Torres, and Jose de
Cordoba. "Argentina Considers a Radical Peso Defense: Use Dollars Instead." *The Wall
Street Journal* (January 18, 1999), A1, A8. This article points out that already two-thirds
of the $472 billion of U.S. currency in existence circulates outside its borders, so that if
Argentina made the dollar its sole currency, it might make "surprisingly little difference
to the U.S." Also see Craig Torres. "Argentina Mulls Ways to Switch to Dollar." *The Wall
Street Journal* (January 22, 1999), A8; and Steve H. Hanke. "How to Make the Dollar Argentina's Currency." *The Wall Street Journal* (February 19, 1999), A19.

Despite a continued fall in the real, Brazil eventually managed to stem its currency crisis. In early February of 1999, Brazil replaced its central bank president for the second time in a period of three weeks. Arminio Fraga Neto, Brazil's new central bank president, was the manager of one of the largest investment funds of George Soros (the billionaire investor). He brought confidence to foreign investors and creditors, because he had practical experience and knowledge of how international investors operate. Brazil was able to make a revised agreement with the IMF by promising to reduce its estimated $65 billion public deficit by the end of the year by about $16.4 billion. This step allowed the IMF to release the second portion of the $41.5 billion standby loan that it pledged in November. In response, investor and foreign creditor confidence returned and the real recovered, as did the Bovespa *index for Brazil's stock market, with inflation forecasts about half of the 17 percent originally expected. Brazil's interest rates also fell (Figure 22.5). By late April 1999, as discussed in the final quote introducing this chapter, investors were very reception to a $2 billion Brazilian global bond issue. Brazilian bonds maturing in 2008 traded at a yield of 11.58 percent, about 6.5 percent over a comparable U.S. Treasury note, well below previous Brazilian interest rates. This successful sale served as a benchmark for other Brazilian debt.*[6]

In contrast, to the 1997 and 1998 Asian currency crisis, in which financial institutions did not hedge their foreign exchange risk, many Brazilian financial institutions were well insulated from the devaluation's initial impact by being overhedged. Brazil also had a much lower debt-to-gross national product ratio than Asian countries that experienced currency crises in 1997 and 1998. Latin American economies were not as dependent on foreign trade as other Asian countries, such as Thailand and Japan. Argentina, for instance, only had 8 percent of its economy based on foreign trade.

However, large U.S. banks, including Citigroup, Chase Manhattan, and J. P. Morgan, suffered large stock price declines during the crisis, amidst concerns over trading losses and loan exposure in Latin America. Some large banks trimmed their exposure in Brazilian debt in the final quarter of 1998. Chase Manhattan, for instance, reduced its exposure in Brazil from $4.9 million to $3.8 million; and J. P. Morgan lowered its exposure from more than $4 billion to $2.2 billion. However, Germany's Dresdner Bank and Deutsche Bank and Spain's Banco Bilbao Vizcaya and Groupo Santander, which had very large loan exposures, suffered stock price drops ranging from 7 percent to 14 percent.[7]

As the Brazilian currency crisis demonstrates, with the globalization of financial markets in the past few decades and with increased foreign investing and lending, major financial institutions have become exposed to considerable international risk. This risk includes foreign exchange risk discussed in Chapters 14 and 17; investment and trading risk for security firms that invest or do trading in foreign stocks and bonds; and international default risk for lenders. This chapter provides a brief overview of considerations for international risk management including for the management of international loans, measures of sovereignty risk, and other aspects of international risk management.

✦ ✦ ✦

---

[6]See Peter Fritsch. "Brazil's Central Banker Picks a Private-Sector Team." *The Wall Street Journal* (February 16, 1999), A17, A18; Larry Rohter. "Bank Chief Vows to Curb Brazilian Debt." *The New York Times* (March 11, 1999), C5; Diana Jean Schemo. "Brazil Names A Soros Ally to Head Bank." *The New York Times* (February 3, 1999), C1; and Jonathan Fuerbringer. "Brazil Bounces Back, Offering $1 Billion in Debt for Sale." *The New York Times* (April 20, 1999), C4; Jonathan Fuerbringer. "Brazilians Raise $2 Billion in Sale of Notes." *The New York Times* (April 23, 1999), C17; and Larry Rohter, "There's a Lot of Grit in Brazil." *The New York Times* (April 23, 1999), C1.

[7]Clifford Krauss. "Latin Markets Rebound, but Storm Hasn't Passed." *The New York Times* (January 16, 1999), B4; Robert O'Brien. "Citigroup, Colgate-Palmolive Fall on Concerns about Brazil's Woes." *The Wall Street Journal* (January 14, 1999), C4; and "Brazil's Woes Chill Some Multinationals." *The Wall Street Journal* (January 14, 1999), A8.

Figure 22.5 ✦ Brazil's Economy Regains Self Control

Brazil's currency, the *real*, which plunged in January 1999 when it was allowed to trade freely, recovered in late April, although lower than its level in early January. Interest rates and inflation expectations also fell at this time, and Brazil's stock market index, the Bovespa, improved dramatically.

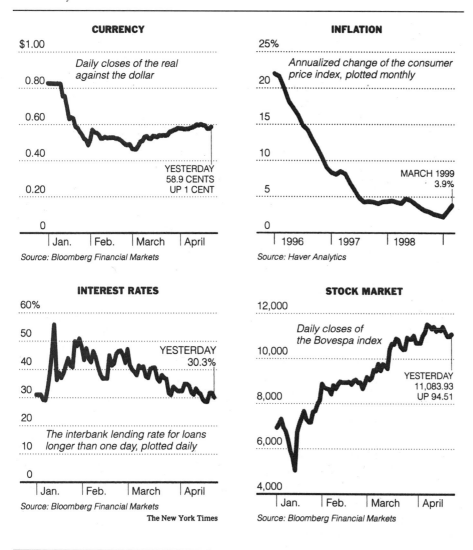

CURRENCY

Daily closes of the real against the dollar

YESTERDAY
58.9 CENTS
UP 1 CENT

Jan. Feb. March April

Source: Bloomberg Financial Markets

INFLATION

Annualized change of the consumer price index, plotted monthly

MARCH 1999
3.9%

1996 1997 1998

Source: Haver Analytics

INTEREST RATES

YESTERDAY
30.3%

The interbank lending rate for loans longer than one day, plotted daily

Jan. Feb. March April

Source: Bloomberg Financial Markets

The New York Times

STOCK MARKET

Daily closes of the Bovespa index

YESTERDAY
11,083.93
UP 94.51

Jan. Feb. March April

Source: Bloomberg Financial Markets

Source: Larry Rohter, "There's a Lot of Grit in Brazil: A Once-Jittery Economy Is Getting Under Self-Control." *The Wall Street Journal*, April 23, 1999, C1.

MANAGEMENT OF INTERNATIONAL LOANS

International lending, a special category of commercial loans, is confined to large commercial banks for several reasons. Gaining access to international markets is difficult and usually requires special facilities. Also, lenders bear added regulatory burdens because of separate provisions applying to international loans. Finally, the additional risk that accompanies international lending acts as a deterrent. Neverthe-less, the volume of international loans, even in the more risky categories, increased dramatically in the early to mid 1980s and again in the mid 1990s.

Banks gain access to international markets in several ways. The simplest is through **loan participations**, in which another bank acts as the lead institution. A bank just beginning to expand beyond the domestic market might choose this route while developing the necessary expertise. Just as in the domestic markets, however, loan participations expose banks to significant risks, so even nonlead banks must pro-ceed carefully and perform conscientious credit analysis.

A more extensive commitment to foreign lending involves a larger investment and greater risk exposure. Banks have been allowed since 1981 to establish **inter-national banking facilities (IBFs)**, which are located in the United States but serve international customers exclusively. Another alternative for originating in-ternational loans is through **Edge Act subsidiaries**, branches of the parent insti-tution serving international customers. Unlike IBFs, Edge Act offices operate as full-service branches and are subject to regulation. International banks also have **shell branches**, which are offices overseas that permit banks to participate in the Eurocurrency markets in terms of Eurodollar liabilities or issuing foreign loans. Such **offshore offices** often operate in places such as the Bahamas where opera-tions can be free of local taxes. In addition, **full service foreign branches** are often used to conduct wholesale banking activities often utilizing deposits that are purchased from a network of international banks, often called the *interbank market*.[8]

Bank holding companies under the **Bank Export Services Act of 1982** are also allowed to invest and participate and lend to **export trading companies**. Such an investment allows banks to engage in the export/import business, including han-dling transportation and shipping documents, field warehousing, and insurance cov-erage. Also, since banks are not allowed to take title to trade items, they can do so in-directly through export/import companies.[9]

Growth and Regulation of International Lending after Problems with LDCs

Loans to borrowers in less-developed countries (LDCs) received special atten-tion in the 1980s as regulators have become painfully aware of a serious level of risk exposure. LDC loans are affected by changes in world economic conditions and the price level of energy products and other products that LDC countries may depend on for foreign exports. The volume of LDC loans for U.S. banks grew rapidly after the mid-1970s, with debt highly concentrated among the largest commercial banks. For example, in 1987, two-thirds of the almost $90 billion in loans to the 15 most heavily indebted nations was held by just nine money-center banks; this amount of indebtedness was 113 percent of the total capital of those banks, putting them sub-stantially at risk. Although the Office of the Comptroller of the Currency reported that risk exposures in the LDC market declined in 1988, significant risks remained.

---

[8]See Hempel, Simonson, and Coleman (1994).
[9]See Maxwell (1992) and Koch (1995).

In 1989, major banks had large LDC loan losses, reducing the industry's profitability. As shown in Figure 22.1, in the mid-1990s, major bank increased their LDC exposure.[10]

Problems and Proposed Solutions in the 1980s   As early as 1981, there were 32 foreign governments in arrears on international payments as early as 1981. In 1982, Mexico and other LDC borrowers announced that they were unable to service their debt agreements. Observers generally attribute this crisis to three factors: overly aggressive lending efforts by U.S. banks, which sought to compensate for declining loan demand at home during the 1981–1982 recession by greatly increasing the volume of foreign lending; rising interest rates, which caused cash-flow problems for borrowing nations attempting to make payments; and poor use of the borrowed funds by debtor countries, resulting in returns on invested capital that were inadequate to service their debts.[11]

Congress responded to the crisis in 1983 by passing the **International Lending Supervision Act (ILSA)** in an attempt to control the magnitude of future problems. The act established special examination procedures for international loan portfolios, granted power to supervisory agencies to set minimum capital guidelines to ensure adequate support in the case of loan losses, and required a special allocation to loan loss reserves by institutions engaged in foreign lending. A final deterrent to excessive international exposure came in the form of a requirement that income from loan origination fees be amortized over the life of the loan rather than recognized as income in the year negotiated, generally diluting the importance of those fees to bank earnings.

Since 1982, the ratio of bank capital to international loans has increased. Federal banking regulators carefully monitor the financial position of foreign government that borrow heavily from U.S. banks, and they have at times issued special directives for reporting interest income and reserves for loans to specific countries deemed highly risky.[12]

LDC Debt in the Late 1980s and 1990s   Despite the hopes of Congress and regulators after the 1983 legislation, concern about LDC loans again escalated in 1987 when Brazil, then the largest debtor nation in the world, announced that it was suspending payment on its loans to foreign banks. Although Brazil's action could hardly be termed good news, it did cause many large banks to develop specific plans for solving their LDC dilemmas. One of the first to act was Citicorp, whose Chairman announced in mid-1987 that the bank was adding $3 billion to its loan loss reserves.

---

[10]These and other statistics on LDC debt are found in Todd (1988); "Statement of Robert J. Herrmann, Senior Deputy Comptroller for Bank Supervision Policy, before the House Subcommittee on International Development, Finance, Trade, and Monetary Policy of the Committee on Banking, Finance, and Urban Affairs." *Quarterly Journal* 8 (September 1989), 47–52; John Meehan, David Woodruff, and Chuck Hawkins. "For Most Banks, There Was Nowhere to Hide." *Business Week* (April 2, 1990), 94–95; and Duca and McLaughlin (1990).

[11]Extensive details on the 1982 crisis and related trends in LDC lending are provided in Young (1985); Fieleke (1983); Terrell (1984); Corrigan (1988); and Truman (1989).

[12]For more details on examination and supervision of international lending, see Martinson and Houpt (1989).

Other large banks followed, and the financial markets interpreted these moves as a necessary fresh breath of realism. Similar large write-offs continued in 1988 and 1989.[13]

Fortunately, as a result of the 1982 and 1987 crises, as well as subsequent actions by Congress, regulators, and the banking industry itself, large money center banks have attempted to limit LDC exposure or hold more diversified LDC debt in the 1990s. In 1990, net long-term private investment flows to developing countries fell to $42 billion. As noted in the previous discussion of the 1998–1999 Brazilian currency crisis, major banks have tried to reduce their exposures when problems within a country become apparent. Recognizing the growing interdependence of world markets, most experts believe that continued foreign investment in LDCs is necessary if both developing and developed nations are to prosper.

Bank managers are engaging in better and more realistic risk assessment of LDC loans. Also, new techniques for managing LDC debt exposure have developed, including **secondary markets for these loans; securitization of international debt as bonds; debt-for-equity swaps**, in which a lender converts a debt contract to an equity investment in the debtor nation; and the **restructuring of existing debt agreements** to ease cash-flow burdens on LDCs.

Particularly noteworthy are 1992 agreements between several large U.S. banks with the largest risk exposures and the government of Argentina and Brazil. The arrangements called for banks to swap nonperforming loans to those governments for long-term bonds, often called **Brady Bonds**, since they were developed under the U.S. Treasury and other international organization's **1989 Brady Plan**. The bonds are collateralized by Argentina's and Brazil's holdings of U.S. Treasury securities. As a result of this agreement, banks that once thought their loans to these countries might bring as little as 35 percent of book value expect to be repaid more than 65 percent of the loans' original value. Since the first Brady bonds hundreds of billion of LDC loans have been converted into bonds under loan swap program. Central banks of countries assist in this securitization process by consolidating and assuming loans made by citizens or businesses in their country with relatively homogeneous terms. By having the bonds collateralized by Treasury securities, the principal payments on the bonds are default free, leaving only the interest payments at risk. This makes Brady bonds desirable; also these bonds have liquidity because they have a secondary market. Salomon Brothers and other investment banks also post benchmark bond prices for different countries. The risk premiums on these bonds provide an indication of a particular country's default risk, and by being able to buy and sell these bonds, financial institutions can have more diversified international loan portfolios.[14]

13See Sarah Bartlett, et. al. "A Stunner from the Citi." Business Week (June 1, 1987) 42–43; and Fissel (1991).

[14]See Saunders (1997) for a detailed description of Brady bonds and their pricing and for a detailed description of a debt for equity swap. Under a debt for equity swap, a country's loans in dollars owned by a major bank are sold at a discount to a major U.S. company that wants to invest in that country. The company can then arrange with that country to swap the dollar debt for funds in that country's currency less a discount to purchase a factory or other real capital investment in that country. The bank is able to get rid of the loan, taking a loss, the country is able to pay off the loan at a double discount relative to what it owed, and the company is able to purchase a real assets investment at a significant discount, reflecting the risk of future expropriation of assets purchased, as well as currency risk for this new investment.

With higher capitalization for international banks, LDC debt problems have been reduced for many U.S. banks, although these problems still exist. In December 1994, Mexico suffered a significant currency crisis for the *peso*, resulting in losses for some banks and necessitating a $50 billion rescue from the United States. This crisis demonstrated how rapidly foreign investors can move funds out of a country, just as funds can be quickly brought in. By 1997, emerging market debt for U.S. and other foreign lenders reached $256 billion. Major banks and securities firms suffered losses or faced potential losses associated with the currency crises in Asia, Russia, and Brazil, and China's moratorium on debt payments in 1998 and 1999.[15] Banks have attempted to come up with better measures of country risk to be aware of foreign debt problems in particular countries and reduce their exposure.

Risk Analysis in International Lending

Along with the usual concerns about the financial stability of a borrower, institutions competing in the international markets face other sources of risk. One of these, exchange rate risk, arises from floating currency exchange rates, as discussed in Chapters 14, along with hedging techniques for this risk in Chapter 17. Others are addressed in this section.

Country Risk   Several related sources of variability are grouped together under the term *country risk*, also known as transfer risk or **sovereign risk**. Country risk includes any political, economic, social, cultural, or legal circumstances in the home country of the borrower that could prevent the timely fulfillment of debt obligations. The uncertainty can arise from many sources, such as social unrest; dependence on one export, which can lead to unrest if prices for that product fall; civil or international wars; economic decline; or a change in political ideology, and is clearly illustrated by the rapid, global economic changes that followed Iraq's unexpected invasion of Kuwait in 1990. A slightly different problem is one that occurs when a country's economic condition weakens and a foreign borrower's government prohibits a currency exchange for repayment of debts (hence the term *transfer risk*). Even cultural attitudes toward indebtedness can affect borrowers' timely repayment of obligations.[16] In short, country risk includes any source of uncertainty specific to international rather than domestic lending.

---

[15]See Phillips (1999). The sources in notes 10 and 11 discuss steps taken by both borrowers and lenders to solve LDC debt problems, as do Lane (1987); Garg (1989); Fissel (1991); and John Meehan. "Now the Third World May Do Banks a World of Good." *Business Week* (June 8, 1992), 94–96. For a detailed discussion of the causes of Mexico's banking system crisis in the 1990s, see Gruben and McComb (1997).

[16]An interesting example of country risk occurred after the price of crude oil fell dramatically in 1986. Many Islamic borrowers with significant indebtedness to U.S. banks invoked the doctrine of *sharia*, which holds that the payment of interest is against the teaching of the Koran. Although they had avoided earlier conflict with the doctrine by encouraging banks to call interest charges "administrative fees," when oil prices fell, some borrowers again began viewing the fees as interest and decided it was against this doctrine to pay charges previously incurred. See Bill Powell. "The Sheiks Rediscover Religion." *Newsweek* (May 12, 1986), 62–63.

As a result of the proliferation of problem foreign loans, regulators have struggled with methods of measuring and predicting country risk. The ILSA requires special procedures for rating the country risk of a bank's international loan portfolio. These ratings are ex post assessments that reflect the repayment record of a borrower once a loan has been granted. Finding reliable signals for ex ante risk is difficult, because it depends on a country's future economic and political stability. Measuring that with any degree of confidence is indeed difficult, yet it is necessary if the institution expects to earn a rate of return sufficient to compensate for the additional risk. The debt moratorium of Russia in the later part of 1998 is a vivid illustration of assessing ex ante lending risk.

Moody's and Standard and Poor's assign Sovereign Ratings for bonds in different countries, which provides information on country risk. As pointed out by Cantor and Packer in a 1995 Federal Reserve Bank of New York study, however, difficulties in assessing sovereign have resulted in disagreements over specific rating assignments by different agencies. For instance, in 1995, Moody's and Standard and Poor's had quite different ratings across below investment grade issues. Consequently, risk premiums on sovereign bonds often have not been priced according to such rankings by financial markets.[17] Other financial magazines, including *Euromoney* and the *Institutional Investor* also provide rankings of country risk based respectively on economic and political factors and surveys of loan officers of multinational banks. Multinational banks have developed their own internal country risk measures. One prominent ratio that is incorporated in risk indexes is a country's **debt service ratio equal to the interest plus amortization on a country's debt divided by its exports**. If this ratio is high, a country will have greater difficulty repaying its debt and has a higher probability of default or rescheduling.[18]

Diversification   Although exchange rate and country risk can increase variability in an institution's earnings, international loans do provide an avenue for diversification. International lending offers access to different geographical regions and economic climates. If expected returns on international loans have low correlations with expected returns on domestic loans, the overall riskiness of the institution's loan portfolio can be reduced. International financial institutions can diversify their international loan portfolios by selling or securitizing loans in countries where they have a large exposure and purchasing loans, Brady bonds, or other government bonds for other countries.

UNDERSTANDING SURPRISES IN COUNTRY AND CURRENCY RISK

Despite great efforts at assessing and measuring a country's risk, in recent years financial institutions have been caught off guard by a sudden unexpected change in a country's economic situation and its currency risk. A recent and very good example of this is the Asian crisis from July 1997 to 1999, which encompassed many countries including Indonesia, Thailand, Malaysia, Korea, and Japan. These countries had

---

[17]See Cantor and Packer (1995).
[18]See Saunders (1997) for a detailed discussion of different risk indexes used by outside evaluators and ratios used in statistical models used internally by financial institutions.

been deemed as very vibrant economies, as late as early 1997. The following section provides a brief recap of some of the explanations for this crisis and what can be learned from it.

A RECAP OF THE ASIAN FINANCIAL CRISIS AND HOW IT SPREAD

Table 22.1 summaries the major events of the Asian Financial Crisis and its spread from 1997 to 1999, as summarized by Michael M. Phillips in *The Wall Street Journal* on April 26, 1999.[19] Major events are discussed in the following subsections.

July and August 1997   The global financial crisis began in July 1997 with the collapse of the Thai currency, the **baht**. With foreign speculators betting that the *baht* would continue to fall, the Thai government's spent foreign currency reserves to defend the *baht*. Such attempts failed, and the government was forced to devalue the *baht* by 20 percent of its value against the dollar in one month. The Thai government called on the IMF for help and received a $17.2 billion rescue package. Currencies in the Philippines, Malaysia, and Indonesia weakened as well, which was often blamed on "rogue speculators," including the billionaire investor George Soros. Indonesia was forced to allow its national currency, the *rupiah*, to fall freely against other currencies. South Korea announced emergency steps to keep its banking system afloat. Banks had serious problems as the result of bad loans to conglomerates, which were closed tied to their banks. A contagious effect occurred in Hong Kong with the stock market falls 17 percent in five days.

November and December 1997   In November, the IMF approved a $42 billion rescue for Indonesia. South Korea drained its foreign-currency reserves trying to protect the value of the *won* and sought $20 billion in assistance from the IMF. Thailand's government resigned, and Japan's fourth-largest brokerage firm, Yamaichi Securities Co., collapsed. Foreign investors began divesting their Russian bonds. Brazil announced a $13 billion deficit-cutting plan to assure investors. In December, South Korea's situation worsened, and its foreign-currency reserves reached dangerously low levels. South Korea faced the threat of not being able to pay $20 billion in short-term debt due by the year's end. The IMF initiated a $58.4 billion international bailout for Korea, and Korea decided to let the *won* float. The IMF and leaders in the United States and Great Britain persuaded large international commercial banks into rolling over credit lines to Korean financial institutions to ensure global stability in exchange for Korean-government guarantees for the debt. This rescheduling covered about $22 billion in debt.

January, March, and May 1998   In January 1998 Indonesia consented to major economic reforms, including combating a system of crony capitalism for large conglomerates controlled by President Suharto's family, in exchange for continuing IMF and international support. In March 1998, the Thai *baht* and Korean won stabilized

---

[19]This summary of the Global Financial Crisis in 1997 to 1999 comes from Michael M. Phillips, "One by One: A Look at How the Global Finance Crisis Began and How It Spread," *The Wall Street Journal* (April 26, 1999), R4, R7.

Table 22.1 ✦ SUMMARY OF MAJOR EVENTS FOR THE GLOBAL FINANCE CRISIS OF 1997 TO 1999

July 1997	Collapse of the Thai Currency, the *baht*. Thailand has a large current-account deficit and budget shortfall. Attempts to defend the *baht* fail and foreign-currency reserves dwindle. The *baht* is devalued, losing 20 percent of its value in one month. Thailand calls for IMF help.
	Currencies of Indonesia and the Phillipines weaken as foreign currency speculators bet against these currencies.
August 1997	The IMF provides a $17.2 billion rescue package for Thailand. Indonesia is forced to let its currency, the *rupiah*, float freely against other currencies. South Korea setups emergency measures to prevent its banking system from collapsing from bad loans. The Hong Kong market falls 17 percent over a five-day period.
November 1997	IMF approves rescue package for Indonesia that eventually totals $42 billion. South Korea drains its foreign currency reserves to protect its currency, the *won*. South Korea requests $20 billion in assistance from the IMF. Thailand's government resigns. Yamaichi, Japan's fourth largest security firm fails.
	Foreign investors desert the Russian bond market. Brazil announces $18 billion deficit cutting plan to maintain investor confidence.
December 1997	IMF puts together $58.4 billion international bailout for Korea. Korea lets the *won* float but keeps high interest rates to attract funds. International financial institutions are convinced to roll over credit lines to Korea's financial institutions in return for Korean-government guarantees of debt. Reschedulings are to cover $22 billion in debt.
January 1998	Indonesia consents to radical economic reforms, including crony capitalism (whereby large conglomerates were controlled by members of the President's family) to gain IMF support.
March 1998	The Thai *baht* and Korean *won* stabilize, and investor confidence returns.
May 1998	Riots plague Indonesia, with 1,200 people killed and parts of Jakarta, the capital in ruins. President Suharto after 32 years in power resigns. Countries in other emerging countries fall under pressure.
August 1998	Speculators bet against the Russian *ruble*, based on steep declines in oil revenues in Russia and problems with its tax collection system. The IMF proposes a $11.2 billion package, but reforms necessary can not be pushed through the *Duma*, Russia's lower house of parliament. Russia devalues its ruble, restructures short-term public debt and sets a moratorium on private-sector payments of foreign debt. The IMF cuts Russia off after $4.8 billion disbursed. The *ruble* continues to fall, and contagion effects occur for Brazil based on its large budget deficit.
September 1998	Investors express risk-aversion for risky debt in response to Russia's turmoil, and fears of a U.S. credit crunch, with risk premiums on debt rising for U.S. corporate debt and emerging market debt. Stock market and currency exchange rates plunge for Brazil and other Latin American countries. Long-Term Capital, a prominent hedge fund with a "complex web" of international investments collapses and is bailed out at the Fed's request by a group of large financial institutions with large stakes in the fund. The Fed lowers interest rates three times in quick succession over the fall. Other nations including Canada, Japan, and European nations adopt policies of monetary ease as well.
October 1998	U.S. Congress provides $18 billion for the IMF in return for minor reforms in the way the IMF operates. Other countries contribute $72 billion. Brazil continues negotiations with the IMF.
November 1998	U.S. joints a $41.5 billion rescue effort for Brazil, fearing contagion in other Latin American countries, and potential losses for major U.S. banks with large Latin American debt holdings. Signs of recovery occur in Thailand and South Korea.
December 1998	A third of the world's economies are in recessions or experience very slow growth. Data reports that Indonesia's economy shrank at an annual rate of 17.4 percent in the third quarter of 1998 and Japan's contracted by 3.5 percent.
January 1999	State governor of Brazil sets off a run on the *real* by declaring a moratorium on the state's debts. With dwindling foreign-currency reserves, Brazil devalues the *real* and allows it to float. Brazil negotiates with the IMF for a second $9 billion installment. The *real* continues to fall.

Table 22.1 ✦ Summary of Major Events for the Global Finance Crisis of 1997 to 1999 *(continued)*

February 1999	G-7 ministers meet to discuss the crisis. Reports show Asian country economies to be on the mend, and the U.S. economy to grow at a very fast 6.1 percent annual rate in the fourth quarter of 1998. Brazil negotiates with the IMF.
March–April 1999	U.S. economy continues to show strength. Signs of recovery in Asia continue. Economic uncertainties exist in Japan, Europe, and some developing countries. Russia and the IMF negotiate a new loan arrangement, allowing Russia to pay funds back directly to the IMF. Brazil arranges a new agreement with the IMF. The *real* stabilizes and interest rates fall. Confidence improves, and Brazil successfully issues $2 billion in bonds underwritten by U.S. investment banks. The G-7 meets and designs reforms to help prevent future crises.

Source: Michael M. Phillips, "One by One: A Look at How the Global Finance Crisis Began—And How It Spread," *The Wall Street Journal*, Special Section on Global Investing, April 26, 1999, R4, R7, along with other news articles during the crisis period.

as investor confidence began to return. In May 1998, riots plagued Indonesia, resulting in the deaths of 1,200 people and leaving parts of Jakarta, Indonesia's capital in ruins. President Suharto resigned after 32 years in power. Currencies in other LDC countries as distant as South Africa found their currency values falling in response.

August to October 1998 In August 1998, Russia faced a crisis with a ballooning deficit, as the result of declining oil revenues and an ineffective tax-collection system. Russia's stock market plunged, and speculators bet heavily on the *ruble* falling. Reforms required for a $11.2 billion IMF package could not be pushed through Russia's lower house of parliament, the *Duma*. Faced with declining foreign-currency reserves in an attempt to stabilize the *ruble*, Russia decided on a devaluation, and announced a 90-day moratorium on private-sector payments of foreign debt and a restructuring of its short-term public debt. The IMF cut Russia off, and investors reacted by divesting the ruble and Russian investments. Investors also soured on Brazil, concerned about the size of its budget deficit and the ability of Brazil to undertake stringent policies to reduce its deficit.

In September, investors pulled back from emerging markets, causing currencies and stock market prices in these markets to fall. Risk premiums for international debt, as well as corporate bonds rose, with LDC debt premiums averaging 17 percentage points in early September versus a previous less than 6 percentage point spread in early 1998. Long-Term Capital Management, LP, a prominent U.S. hedge fund with a "complex web of international investments" almost collapsed as a result of unexpected volatility in emerging markets. At the request of the Fed, a group of large financial institutions lent $3.5 billion to the fund to bail it out. The Fed lowered rates three times over the Fall to avoid a U.S. credit crunch. Other countries including most in Europe, and in Canada and Japan adopt easing monetary policy positions as well.

In October, the G-7 endorsed a U.S. plan to permit the IMF to lend to countries before they face financial difficulties and promised to develop a redesigned global financial system to avoid financial instability. The U.S. Congress agreed to provide $18 billion to the IMF in return for a pledge of minor reforms. Other countries contributed $72 billion. Brazil negotiated with the IMF for funds.

November to December 1998 In November, the U.S. joined in for a $41.5 billion rescue of Brazil. Thailand and South Korea demonstrated signs of recovery. In December, IMF data indicates that Indonesia's economy shrank at an alarming rate of 17.4 percent in the third quarter of 1998, while Japan's contracted by 3.5 percent.

January to April 1999 In January, the Brazilian *real* plunged in response to a state governors refusal to pay his states debt to the federal government. Facing depleted foreign-currency reserves, Brazil devalued its currency and then allowed the *real* to float. Brazil renegotiated its economic program with the IMF. In March and April, economic uncertainty persisted for developing countries. However, the United States showed continued economic strength, and Thailand and South Korea showed signs of improvement. Russia and the IMF engaged in a new loan to allow Russia to pay its debt back to the IMF. Brazil arranged a new agreement with the IMF to reduce its high interest rates and stabilize its currency. Confidence in LDC debt improved. In late April 1998, senior officers from the G-7 nations indicated cautious optimism over the end of the financial panic that had pervaded their previous meeting six months earlier, with indications of improved economic performance in Asia and Brazil, although global growth was slow.[20]

WARNING SIGNS FOR THE ASIAN FINANCIAL CRISIS

In 1997, many investors and financial institutions were shocked and caught off guard by the Asian crisis. Asian counties experienced robust economies in the early to mid 1990s. As pointed out by David Marshall in a *Federal Reserve Bank of Chicago Economic Perspectives* article concerning the crisis:[21]

"The years preceding the crisis were a period of exceptional growth in the East Asian economies. In the months preceding the crisis, no real macroeconomic distortions were observed. The economies of the five crisis countries (Thailand, Malaysia, Indonesia, South Korea, and the Philippines) were characterized by low inflation (less than 10 percent), budgets generally in surplus, and declining government foreign debt (as a fraction of gross domestic prod-

---

[20]This section heavily relies on Phillips, as cited in note 19. Also, see Michael M. Phillips. "G-7 Nations Show Cautious Optimism." *The Wall Street Journal* (April 27, 1999), A2.

[21]See Marshall (1998), p. 14. For other views on what caused the Asian crisis, including too much government control and bad private-sector decisions, see Wolfe (1998) and Stiglitz (1998). Wolfe points out that policies based on the Japanese model of subsidizing favored industries versus market-mediated allocations resulted in excess capacities built up in certain export industries versus market-mediated allocations. He argues that such a favored allocation structure resulted in overcapacity in export industries and a neglect of domestic economies. Stiglitz points out that problems (including misallocations of investment, unhedged short-term borrowing, and very high debt-to-equity ratios) were the result of poor private-sector financial decisions. A buildup of "short-term unhedged" debt made East Asian economies very vulnerable to a "sudden collapse of confidence." Stiglitz notes that governments were to blame in terms of misguided exchange rate and monetary policies that created incentives for greater external financing and the misallocation of resources internally. Governments liberalized certain financial activities, such as lending limits for real estate loans, but failed to put in place a sound regulatory framework at the same time.

uct [GDP]. For example, Indonesia experienced 10.4 percent export growth in the year preceding the crisis, its government budget was in surplus each of the previous four years, and its current account deficit was only 3 percent to 5 percent of GDP. During the 1990s, these governments engaged in responsible credit creation and monetary expansion. Unemployment rates were low and did not provide an incentive for governments to engage in currency depreciation or monetary expansion as a short-term stimulus."

However, he points out that despite the prosperity in these counties, there were signs that indicated vulnerability of these economies to crisis, at least in retrospect. These included a high and growing ratio of short-term debt to short-term assets. Short-term debt to foreign exchange reserves were particularly high in Thailand, Korea, and Indonesia, exceeding 1.0 after 1994. Also, countries had increased their foreign bank lending, with foreign bank lending in the five countries experiencing a rise by 24 percent in 1996, with an additional increase of 10 percent during the first half of 1997. Much of the expanded credit was invested in real estate markets versus in improving a country's productive capacity. In retrospect, other economic factors were unfavorable for the economy of some countries including a fall in demand for semiconductors in 1996 and contractions in monetary policy in the Japan and United States in the spring of 1997.[22]

Darren McDermott in an April 1999 article in *The Wall Street Journal* on warning signals points out that there were other warning signs for investors. These included Thailand's use of massive short-term dollar borrowing for long-term investments with returns that would not come for years that were tied to the Thai *baht*. Hence, in addition to having maturity risk by financing long-term assets with short-term borrowings, Thailand faced great foreign currency risk by financing assets with returns in *bahts* with liabilities that would be paid back in dollars, and not hedging these risks. If the *baht* fell in value relative to the dollar, revenues would not be sufficient to pay back higher costing dollar debts. Furthermore, most of these investments were invested in real estate investments whose values were inflated. Later this property bubble exploded, and real estate prices plunged. Consequently, these foreign loans could not be repaid. Thailand also suffered from an "overextended and poorly regulated banking system," slumping exports, and a currency that was dangerously linked to an appreciating U.S. dollar.[23]

Although a number of analysts predicted problems, such as Robert Zielinski, an international banking analyst who predicted the crises in Japan and Thailand, others did not. Again, some major banks such as Citicorp heeded signals of problems and started pulling back on loans to the property and financial sectors in Asia in 1997, whereas other international lenders did not notice problems and did not pull back. Despite some signals, many analysts that saw problems appearing in Thailand did not predict the extent of problems in other economies, such as Indonesia.

One reason many analysts were unable to realize the extent of East Asian debt problems was because of lack of transparency in accounting and government reports. As McDermott notes, Thai, Indonesian and South Korean companies often hid or misrepresented to stockholders the extent of the huge liabilities that they had taken

---

[22]Marshall (1998).

[23]Darren McDermott. "Warning Signs: What Did Investors Know—And When Should They Have Known It?" *The Wall Street Journal*, Special Section on Global Investing (April 26, 1999), R4, R11.

Market Meltdowns

Key indicators for the countries at the center of the global economic turmoil

Economic Output

Annual percentage change in gross domestic product, adjusted for inflation

	'96	'97	'98	'99
Thailand	6.7%	−0.4%	−8.0%	1.0%
Indonesia	7.8	4.6	−15.3	−3.4
S. Korea	7.1	5.5	−7.0	−1.0
Russia	−5.0	0.7	−5.7	−8.3
Brazil	2.8	3.5	0.5	−1.0

Current Account

Current-account surplus or deficit as a percentage of GDP

	'96	'97	'98	'99
Thailand	−7.9%	−2.0%	11.4%	8.4%
Indonesia	−3.3	−1.8	3.0	2.0
S. Korea	−4.7	−1.8	13.2	8.7
Russia	0.6	−0.1	1.6	6.7
Brazil	−3.0	−4.1	−4.2	−3.6

Inflation

Annual percentage change in consumer prices

	'96	'97	'98	'99
Thailand	4.8%	5.6%	8.0%	2.5%
Indonesia	6.6	11.6	61.1	26.8
S. Korea	4.9	4.4	7.8	3.8
Russia	48.0	15.0	26.0	56.0
Brazil	9.3	7.9	3.9	NA

Foreign Debt

Total external debt as a percentage of nominal GDP for end of each year*

	'95	'96	'97	'98
Indonesia	56.1%	55.4%	62.3%	168.6%
S. Korea	23.2	28.2	34.7	49.8
Thailand	47.0	52.2	63.5	77.1
Brazil	26.3	26.2	27.1	30.9
Russia	30.3	28.4	31.9	55.0

NOTE: Figures for 1999 are projections.   *Projection for 1999 not available.

Foreign Exchange

Change in dollar value of currencies (Jan. 1, 1997 = 100)

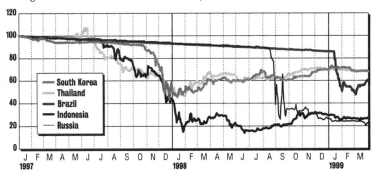

Stock Markets

Stock-market performance (Jan. 1, 1997 = 100)

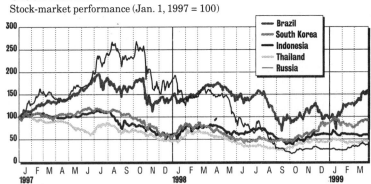

Sources: International Monetary Fund; J.P. Morgan & Co.; Dow Jones Indexes; Baseline; Russian Trade System

Source: Michael M. Phillips, "One by One: A Look at How the Global Finance Crisis Began—and How It Spread," *The Wall Street Journal*, April 26, 1999, R4; and Darren McDermott, Special Section on Global Investing "Warning Signs," *The Wall Street Journal*, April 26, 1999, R4.

on. Similarly, central banks misrepresented the extent of their debt in reporting to the forward-foreign exchange markets. When global investors realized that they had invested in Asian firms that were likely to go under, they panicked and pulled funds out, creating a stampede that could not be stopped. This stampede created difficulties by making other investors unwilling to purchase debt at a discount. Hence, countries were not able to roll over or repay their debts. With investors more wary, the potential for contagion increased, and Russia's isolated debt moratorium in the Fall 1998 resulted in a plunge in Brazil's currency and stock returns. Darren McDermott suggests that "the markets had stopped being reasonable—or at least changed their standards," becoming less tolerant of fixed exchange rates and weak banking systems, making Brazil a target.[24]

Similarly, David Marshall points out that the Asian crisis took the world by surprise. Just before the Asian crisis, bond risk spreads between emerging debt (including the five Asian countries that had difficulties) and U.S. Treasury securities declined. Similarly, agency ratings of sovereign debt gave no indication of an impending crisis.[25]

Figure 22.6 shows the dramatic meltdown that occurred in economic indicators for emerging country debt in 1998. For Indonesia, for instance, economic output fell by −15.3 percent, inflation went up by 61.1 percent, foreign debt to GDP rose to 63.5 percent, and the country's exchange rate and average stock market performance plunged.[26]

FINANCIAL INSTITUTION INVOLVEMENT IN THE CRISES

Financial institutions were deeply involved in each of the five countries suffering crises in Asia. Korean *chaebols* (industrial conglomerates) that failed were tied to banks that provided loans based on relationships versus prospects for repayment. These failures also brought Korean banks down. In Thailand, nonbank finance companies with close relationships to their borrowers also failed as the result of making numerous speculative real estate loans. In Japan scandals and failures occurred for major security firms and banks that involved some hidden bribery on the part of regulators. In Indonesia, cronyism existed in the financial system as well, with loans being made based on relationships to conglomerates owned by President Suharto and his family. Russian bankers did not follow good lending practices, and made very risky loans.

International lenders also in certain instances were not wary of warning signals, such as the large rise in debt for many countries prior to the crises, and were often unaware of the riskiness of the firm's and the country's they lent to. This included an unawareness of the maturity risk and foreign currency risk that debtors were taking on. Emerging countries taking on short-term debt to finance long-term investments, taking on debt in dollars to finance projects tied to their countries currencies, financing with variable rate loans, and pegging their country's currency to the U.S. dollar, were all very risky practices. With any fall in the country's exchange rate, debt payments would become enormous, and revenue streams based on a country's currency

---

[24]Ibid.

[25]Marshall (1998).

[26]Phillips (1999), cited in note 19, and Marshall (1998).

would be insufficient to pay back dollar debt. Although lenders in countries like Brazil avoided some of these risks by hedging against foreign currency risk, other major banks did not.[27]

ATTEMPTS TO TRY TO HELP NATIONS AVERT FINANCIAL CRISES

To avert a global crisis, G-7 nations were much more coordinated in their rate-cutting activities in 1998 and 1999. The European Central Bank cut interest rates by a half percentage points to stimulate growth in the first quarter of 1999, as did Japan. Japan also introduced a fiscal spending policy to stimulate its economy, and began cleaning up its troubled banks. At a meeting in February of 1999, economic officials considered whether to establish formal limits on movements between the yen, dollar, and euro, but facing U.S. opposition, such a limit was not passed. At a meeting in April of 1999, the G-7 made a statement supporting less volatility in currency markets. One major concern was the euro's slide of more than 10 percent of its value in dollars, since its initiation in January. In concern for Russia' economic crisis, Russia had concluded tough negotiations with the IMF over a new loan and economic plan.[28]

In late April 1998, the G-7 Countries also proposed a better lending system to help nations to avert future financial crises. Provisions for this system included allowing the IMF to intervene and providing lending before serious problems arose to avoid future crises. At this time the IMF approved plans to develop a **Contingent Credit Line Facility (CCLF)** to assist countries and help avert financial crises and stave off investor panics. The IMF can use this line to provide billions of dollars in loans to protect against market turmoil, such as that faced by Brazil in late 1998. Countries will be allowed to draw on a pre-approved basis from the IMF if their economies are in fairly good shape and their policies meet various criteria. These criteria include having appropriate debt-management policies, meeting international standards for transparency, having a solid banking sector, and having proper corporate governance procedures, which allow board of directors for companies to be independent of managers. Countries will also have to meet last-minute reviews before drawing funds.

The hope of the IMF is that the fund will provide reassurance to investors and that it will never have to be actually activated. If the credit is tapped, it can be tapped rapidly. To discourage unnecessary borrowing, the interest cost will be set at a rate 3 percentage points above the interest rate prevailing on normal IMF loans (currently 4.75 percent), with a rising surcharge every six-months.[29]

In late April 1999, Secretary of the Treasury, Robert E. Rubin, also outlined a

---

[27]For additional information on the Asian crisis, see Gough (1998). For information on International Bank Failures, their causes and remedies, see Gup (1998). For a discussion of corporate governance problems in Thailand in the late 1990s, see Limpaphayom and Polwitoon (1998).

[28]Michael M. Phillips. "G-7 Nations Show Cautious Optimism." *The Wall Street Journal* (April 27, 1999), A2, A12.

[29]David Pearson. "IMF Backs Plan for Credit Facility to Help Nations Avert Financial Crises." *The Wall Street Journal* (April 26, 1999), A2.

five-point American Plan for warding off a financial crisis including a call for strengthened financial disclosure rules and guidelines to discourage countries from taking excessive risk when they borrow funds. The five areas of reform include:

1. forcing lenders to pay a greater share of the cost of bailing out nations;
2. discouraging most countries from using fixed exchange rates;
3. encouraging nations to rely more on long-term borrowing and less on short-term;
4. disclosing more information about outstanding debt; and
5. protecting the poor and middle class during crises.

The first area of reform reflects criticism of the IMF and U.S. bailouts that did not penalize lenders and borrowers created a moral hazard problem encouraging lenders and borrowers to take on greater risk than otherwise. By making creditors bear the consequences of the risks that they take, market discipline would be allowed to work. The second area of reform reflects concern about rigid exchange-rate regimes associated with each of the recent crises, which resulted in huge IMF loans, as nations tried to defend fixed exchange rates. The third area reflected a need of countries to do a better job of managing debt, including risky practices of taking on short-term debt to avoid the cost of paying more for long-term borrowing. This practice resulted in many countries not being able to make short-term debt payments when their currencies were devalued. Mr. Rubin also suggested that in some cases, rules might be adopted to limit the foreign currency exposure of banks, and that tighter disclosure rules be adopted for countries, banks, securities houses, and hedge funds, including data on how much debt they were carrying.[30]

The Need for Greater Transparency in International Accounting

International panels have also submitted recommendations to the **Organization for Economic Cooperation and Development (OECD)** for foreign companies to improve their accountability and transparency in reporting to their shareholders. A survey of institutional investors in Australia, France, Britain, and the U.S. in 1998 conducted by Wirthlin Worldwide, an opinion research form in McLean, Virginia found three-quarter of investors surveyed had holdings in companies outside their home country. More than 25 per cent of U.S. institutions, 60 percent in France, 52 percent in Australia, and 27 percent in Britain felt transparent global accounting standards was important for them. Corporate governance for foreign companies, including the quality of a company's board and its independence from top management, was also important.[31]

A recent *Wall Street Journal* article on global investing pointed out problems with less rigorous accounting rules in many countries. For instance, two-thirds of the 73 largest banks and companies in East Asia did not disclose problem loans and debts from related parties, such as loans between a parent and its subsidiary—cited by the United Nation's analysis of bookkeeping as a contributing factor to the crises in many countries. Also, about 85 percent of the banks did not properly disclose their net foreign currency gain and losses, and two-thirds did not properly disclose the amounts they had invested

---

[30]David E. Sanger. "Rubin Proposes Modest Limit on Lending Risk." *The New York Times* (April 22, 1999), C4.
[31]Kenneth N. Gilpin. "Shareholders Push for Tighter Rules Abroad." *The New York Times* (April 6, 1998), C2.

in derivatives. Of 34 banks surveyed, two-thirds also did not provide loan-portfolio information indicating which borrowers held the majority of a bank's debt. Nonfinancial companies also often have less accounting transparency in many countries. For instance, Japanese companies have large unrecorded pension obligations Cross-country valuations may become easier, however, if global market regulators approve a new set of international accounting rules recently completed by the International Accounting Standards Committee in London, due to be approved in the spring of 2000.[32]

CULTURAL MANAGEMENT ISSUES

As financial institutions become international with mergers becoming increasingly frequent across countries, managers have to be very sensitive about cultural differences. For instance, Nomura Securities' New York branch and Morgan Stanley's Tokyo branch resulted in a number of cultural challenges over the past few decades. Similarly, American executives hired to invigorate Deutsche Bank's (DB's) investment subsidiary in London, Deutsche Morgan Grenfell (DMG) ran into cultural difficulties when they approached DB to try to remove the head of the old line's investment bank. In contrast, to the New York investment bankers who took on a "me-centered, take-no-prisoners" approach, DB held a long-time view of gradually integrating and building an institution. Consequently, the American executives lost their battle. Ultimately, after sinking hundreds of millions of dollars to build DMG as a global investment bank by hiring Wall Street Investment Bankers to revitalize it, DB decided to refocus on Germany and Europe. Part of this decision was related to the fact that DMG was being torn apart by infighting between hired Wall Street Executives and more conservative British Morgan Grenfell veterans. For instance, the high spending by Americans for big parties did not sit well with the "staid Germans" and "conservative British." High entertainment and other expenses cut into the profits of DMGs.[33] However, DB continued with its investment banking activities in the U.S. by purchasing Bankers Trust in 1998, which owns Alex Brown, a major Baltimore investment bank, with a more conservative culture than the typical Wall Street firm. DB made this acquisition, as one of its major German clients, Daimler-Benz acquired Chrysler, giving it a major presence in the United States.

With globalization, financial institution managers need to be very aware of cultural differences, which often require different approaches to entering new international markets. Only through sensitive cross-cultural awareness can international operations become successful. in building up strong companies in Japan, where other firms often failed.[34]

---

[32]Elizabeth MacDonald. "What Happened? A Number of Problems: Accounting Rules Are Less Than Rigorous in Many Countries. It Makes All the Difference." *The Wall Street Journal*, Special Section on Global Investing (April 26, 1999), R6

[33]Michael R. Sesit and Anita Raghavan. "Kulturshock: Deutsche Bank Hit Many Costly Snags in Its American Foray." *The Wall Street Journal* (May 4, 1998), A1, A10.

[34]See Hayes and Hubbard (1990) and Hayes and Meerschwam (1992). For an excellent book giving anecdotes of cultural problems in negotiations and deal making for U.S. investment bankers, see Smith (1989). Also see Smith and Walter (1997) for in-depth information on international banking issues. For an excellent discussion of the evolution of financial structures for emerging countries and formerly planned economies switching to a capitalistic form, see Sundararajan (1992).

SUMMARY

Major banks can enter the international lending arena through loan participation with other banks, international banking facilities, edge act subsidiaries, offshore offices, full service foreign branches, and by investing and participating in export trading companies. U.S. banks have had a checkered past with loans to borrowers in less-developed countries (LDCs). The volume of LDC loans for major U.S. banks ballooned after the mid-1970s, exposing U.S. banks to great rid relative to their capitalization. In the early 1980s and in 1987, banks suffered large losses on loans to Latin America with moratoriums declared on debt, respectively by Mexico and Brazil. In response to these losses, Congress passed bills to control the magnitude of future problems including the International Lending Supervision Act of 1983. This act established special procedure and capital allocations for international lending. In 1989 Congress passed the Brady Plan, which helped banks to get risk of bad international loans by permitting international loans of a country to be securitized as bonds, collateralized by U.S. Treasury securities. This made international debt markets more liquid. International banks, rating agencies, and other organizations also developed better measures of sovereign risk.

Despite improved capital ratios, foreign currency risk hedging techniques, and diversification by major banks in their international lending portfolios, in the late 1990s, many major banks were caught off-guard by the sudden global currency crises that occurred in Thailand, Indonesia, Korea, and Japan, as well as in Russia. A debt moratorium in Russia in turn had a contagious effect on the value of Brazil's currency. A lack of accounting transparency in terms of the debt that had been taken on by companies and countries contributed to many international banks being caught off-guard. In addition, the advent of technology in the 1990s that permits tremendous movements of capital in and out of countries on a daily basis increases the volatility of foreign currency exchange rates.

The East Asian and Brazilian currency crises were partly the result of poor debt management practices by companies, countries, and financial institutions. These risky practices included financing long-term projects with short-term debt; financing revenues linked to a country's currency with foreign loans tied to the dollar, with the risk exacerbated by the use of foreign exchange rates by many countries that were pegged to the dollar. As a result, companies and countries faced significant maturity and foreign exchange rate risk. Large debt to gross domestic product ratios increased this risk by creating repayment difficulties for countries.

Financial institutions also contributed to the crises by having poor corporate governance structures with close links between banks and corporate borrowers with often fraud and cronyism involved. Similar to the savings and loan crisis in the U.S., many financial institutions over-invested in risk commercial real estate and other risky ventures. A lack of transparency in accounting in different countries, also made it difficult for investors to determine the full extent of companies and countries debt burdens. Finally, although some lenders hedged their foreign currency risk, other international banks did not. This resulted in the potential for tremendous loan losses when foreign exchange rates for countries in which they had a large exposure plunged. Global regulators have recently adopted new policies to try to avert such a large global currency crisis in the future.

Relevant Web Sites:

Detailed chronology of events in Asia maintained by Nouriel Roubini:

http://www.stern.nyu.edu/~nroubini/asia
Chicago Federal Reserve Web Site: www.frbchi.org
Contains economic and financial data, research publications including *Economic Perspectives* and *Chicago Fed Letter*, which often have articles on international financial institution issue, a bank condition and income database, and information on seminars

Recommended Cases Examining International Issues

Harvard Business School (These cases can also be found in Hayes and Meerschwam (1992). These cases provide examples of international challenges of investment banking firms.

Deutsche Bank Group

This case examines Deutsche Bank's strategy in 1990 of integrating its West and East German banking markets, with the reunification of the East and West after 1989.

Nomura Securities (A) and (B)

These cases examine Nomura's strategy, as a Japanese investment bank in building up a presence in U.S. markets.

Morgan Stanley: The Tokyo Branch

This case examines cultural and strategic issues facing Morgan Stanley as it commits resources to its Tokyo Branch to become a leading investment bank in Japan.

CSFB and the International Capital Markets (A and B)

These cases examine difficulties merging First Boston and Credit Suisse and the global environment that the combined firm CSFB faces.

J. P. Morgan's Mexican Bank: Debt-Bond Swap

This case demonstrates the difficulties in creating a complex financial product. It also examines Less Developed Country (LDC) debt and debt to equity swaps as solutions. Calculations must be made for an exchange ratio between a new bond (finding the market value using a discounted cash flow analysis) and Mexican loans trading at a discount in secondary markets.

Darden School (This case can also be found in Crawford and Sihler 1994).

Credit Suisse

This case evaluates the development of a global financial service organization, including its integration with First Boston and strategic issues.

Questions

1. Professors Ji Chen and Hung Gay Fung ask you to briefly discuss the events that led to Brazil's currency crisis. Do you think investors overreacted by pulling funds out of Brazil and converting *reals* to dollars? Why do you think the Russian debt moratorium in the fall of 1998, which was an isolated event, affected Brazil's financial markets?

2. What are different ways that banks can become involved in international lending? Why must a bank generally be a major bank to become involved?

3. What problems did many major U.S. banks have in taking on international loans in the 1980s? What did the International Lending Supervision Act of 1983 do?

4. What did the Brady Plan of 1989 do to improve the liquidity of international loan markets? What alternatives do international banks have of getting rid of their bad loans?

5. What is sovereign or country risk? What are some sources of rating information? Why do you think rating agencies often disagree on appropriate ratings? Did rating agencies predict the East Asian financial crisis?

6. Briefly list the different stages of the East Asian Financial crisis. What steps were taken to alleviate the crisis? Do you think the IMF was justified in providing loans to countries without penalizing those responsible for the crisis?

7. What were some of the causes of the East Asian Financial crisis? How were financial institutions involved?

8. Do you think the Brazilian government was justified in devaluating its currency and letting it float against the U.S. dollar in January 1999? Explain why or why not. How was Brazil's crisis ultimately resolved? How did Brazil's situation differ from the crises of other Asian countries?

9. Joseph Stiglitz (1998) points out in a *Wall Street Journal* article that restoring growth in East Asia requires restoring confidence which includes establishing an effective regulatory system, improving corporate governance, and enhancing transparency. Explain how the lack of these factors may have contributed to the East Asian Crisis in 1997–99.

10. What attempts were made in April of 1999 to prevent future financial crises? Do you think these proposals will work? What other suggestions would you make?

11. During the Brazil crisis in early 1998, Argentina proposed taking on the U.S. dollar as its currency. What would be the advantages and disadvantages of such a proposal? How did pegged currency rates exacerbate the global financial crisis of the late 1990s?

12. Suppose you were a Brazilian company with $100 million debts in dollars on January 12th, with the *real* valued at $.8621, what would be the cost of the debt in *reals*? What would be the cost in *reals* on January 30 when the *real* fell to $.4695? What was the percentage rise in your cost in *reals* between January 12 and January 30?

13. Why do financial institutions with international operations need to be sensitive about cultural differences within different countries?

14. Give an example of some cultural differences in negotiating between managers in the U.S. and another culture, such as Germany or Japan.

References

Cantor, Richard and Frank Packer. "Sovereign Credit Ratings." *Federal Reserve Bank of New York Current Issues in Economics and Finance*, Vol. 1, No. 3 (June 1995), 1–5.

Corrigan, E. Gerald. "A Balanced Approach to the LDC Debt Problem." *Quarterly Review* (Federal Reserve Bank of New York) 13 (Spring 1988), 1–6.

Duca, John V. and Mary M. McLaughlin. "Developments Affecting the Profitability of Commercial Banks." *Federal Reserve Bulletin* 76 (July 1990): 477–499.

Fieleke, Norman S. "International Lending on Trial." *New England Economic Review* (Federal Reserve Bank of Boston) May/June 1983, 5–13.

Fissel, Gary S. "The Anatomy of the LDC Debt Crisis," *FDIC Banking Review* 4 (Spring/Summer 1991), 1–14.

Garg, Ramesh C. "Exploring Solutions to the LDC Debt Crisis." *The Bankers Magazine* 172 (January/February 1989), 46–51.

Gough, Leo. *Asia Meltdown: The End of the Miracle?* Oxford, England: Capstone Publishing Limited, 1998.

Gruben, William and Robert P. McComb. "Liberalization, Privatization, and Crash: Mexico's Banking System in the 1990s," *Federal Reserve Bank of Dallas Economic Review* (First Quarter 1997), 21–30.

Gup, Benton E. *Bank Failures in the Major Trading Countries of the World: Causes and Remedies.* Westport, Conn.: Quorum Books, 1998.

Hayes, Samuel L., III. and Philip M. Hubbard. *Investment Banking: A Tale of Three Cities.* Boston: Harvard Business School Press, 1990.

Hayes, Samuel L., III. and David M. Meerschwam. *Managing Financial Institutions: Cases Within the Financial Services Industry.* New York: Dryden Press, 1992.

Hempel, George H., Donald G. Simonson, and Alan B. Coleman. *Bank Management: Text and Cases*, 4th ed. New York: John Wiley & Sons, Inc., 1994.

Koch, Timothy. *Bank Management*, 3d ed. Fort Worth, Tex.: The Dryden Press, 1995.

Lane, Leroy O. "The Secondary Market in Developing Country Debt: Some Observations and Policy Implications." *Economic Review* (Federal Reserve Bank of Dallas) (July 1987), 1–12.

Limpaphayom, Piman and Sirapat Polwitoon. "The Relationship between Bank Equity Ownership and Firm Behavior: Empirical Evidence from Thailand." Working Paper, University of Rhode Island, 1998.

Marshall, David. "Understanding the Asian Crisis: Systemic Risk as Coordination Failure." *Federal Reserve Bank of Chicago Economic Perspectives* (3rd Quarter, 1998), 13–28.

Martinson, Michael G. and James V. Houpt. "Transfer Risk in U.S. Banks." *Federal Reserve Bulletin* 75 (April 1989), 255–258.

Maxwell, Charles E. *Financial Markets and Institutions: The Global View.* New York: West Publishing Company, 1992.

Phillips, Michael M. "One by One: A Look at How the Global Finance Began—And How It Spread." *The Wall Street Journal*, Special Section on Global Investing (April 26, 1999), R4, R7.

Saunders, Anthony. *Financial Institutions Management: A Modern Perspective.* Chicago: Irwin Publishing Co., 1997.

Smith, Roy C. *The Global Bankers.* New York: Truman Talley Books/Plume, 1989.

Smith, Roy C. and Ingo Walter. *Global Banking.* New York: Oxford University Press, 1997.

Stiglitz, Joseph. "What Caused Asia's Crash? Bad Private-Sector Decisions." *The Wall Street Journal* (February 4, 1998), A22.

Sundararajan, V. "Central Banking Reforms in Formerly Planned Economies," *Finance and Development* (March 1992), 10–13, reprinted in *The International Finance Reader*, 2d ed.. Miami, Fla.: Kolb Publishing Company, 1993, 137–140.

Terrell, Henry S. "Bank Lending to Developing Countries: Recent Developments and Some Considerations for the Future." *Federal Reserve Bulletin* 70 (October 1984): 755–763.

Todd, Walker F. "Developing Country Lending and Current Banking Conditions." *Economic Review* (Federal Reserve Bank of Cleveland) 24 (Quarter 2, 1988), 27–36.

Truman, Edwin M. "U.S. Policy on the Problems of International Debt." *Federal Reserve Bulletin* 75 (November 1989); 727–735.

Wolf, Charles, Jr. "What Caused Asia's Crisis? Too Much Government Control." *The Wall Street Journal* (February 4, 1998), A22.

Young, John E. "Supervision of Bank Foreign Lending." *Economic Review* (Federal Reserve Bank of Kansas City) 70 (May 1985), 31–39.

Chapter 22 Internet Exercises

1. Thomson Financial Bankwatch http://www.bankwatch.com is the world's largest bank rating agency, providing research and analysis on over 1000 financial institutions in more than 94 countries. Thomson Bank Watch provides regularly updated ratings of global banks. For example, in May 1999, the rating and outlook for Brazil was:

Brazil Sovereign Risk Affirmed at B
Rating Outlook Stable

Additional information and links are also provided on topics such as:

- Asia DebtWatch—Timely Reasearch on Hot Topics in Asian Banking

- Latin DebtWatch—Timely Research on Hot Topics in Latin Banking

- See What Thomson Financial Bankwatch Said About the Asian Banking Crisis

- Learn More About our Ratings Characteristics and Methodology

- Global Rating Coverage—A List of All of Banks We Rate—Find the Banks You Need to Know About

2. You can find information on the foreign branches of U.S. banks by using the Federal Financial Institution Examination Council's National Information Center at:

http://www.ffiec.gov/nic/default.htm

From this page under Foreign Institution Search, click on "Foreign Branch of U.S. Bank."

Then enter your criteria and then click on submit. You must select either a specific Foreign Institution, City, or Country. If Country is set to [All], you must provide a Name of City for your query.

For example, you can look up Argentina and find that there are 239 branches of U.S. banks in Argentina, but there are none in Zimbabwe (as of May 1999). You can also enter a bank name, Citibank, for example, and find all of its foreign branches (378 as of May 1999), or branches in particular countries.

3. An extremely useful site on the Asian Financial Crisis is maintained by Nouriel Roubini at the Stern School of Business at New York University.

http://www.stern.nyu.edu/~nroubini/asia/AsiaHomepage.html

Included in the site are basic readings and references on topics such as the causes of the Asian crisis new links, global economic turmoil, recovery and prospects for the world economy, proposed policy solutions to the crisis, the IMF's role and the debate on its refunding, the debate on the international capital flows, alternative views on the reform of the architecture of the international financial system, and hedge funds, derivatives and systemic risk.

Useful Links

International Monetary Fund
http://www.imf.org

The World Bank
http://www.worldbank.org

Bank for International Settlements
http://www.bis.org

Organization for Economic Cooperation and Development
http://www.oecd.org

Appendix

◈ TABLE A-1 ▪ PRESENT VALUE OF $1 DUE AT THE END OF n PERIODS

◈ TABLE A-2 ▪ PRESENT VALUE OF AN ANNUITY OF $1 PER PERIOD FOR n PERIODS

◈ TABLE A-3 ▪ FUTURE VALUE OF $1 AT THE END OF n PERIODS

◈ TABLE A-4 ▪ FUTURE VALUE OF AN ANNUITY OF $1 PER PERIOD FOR n PERIODS

Table A-1 ▪ Present Value of $1 Due at the End of n Periods:

Equation:

$$PVIF_{i,n} = \frac{1}{(1+i)^n}$$

Financial Calculator Keys:

N	I	PV	PMT	FV
n	i		0	1.0

TABLE VALUE

Period	1%	2%	3%	4%	5%	6%	7%	8%	9%	10%	12%	14%	15%	16%	18%	20%	24%	28%	32%	36%
1	.9901	.9804	.9709	.9615	.9524	.9434	.9346	.9259	.9174	.9091	.8929	.8772	.8696	.8621	.8475	.8333	.8065	.7813	.7576	.7353
2	.9803	.9612	.9426	.9246	.9070	.8900	.8734	.8573	.8417	.8264	.7972	.7695	.7561	.7432	.7182	.6944	.6504	.6104	.5739	.5407
3	.9706	.9423	.9151	.8890	.8638	.8396	.8163	.7938	.7722	.7513	.7118	.6750	.6575	.6407	.6086	.5787	.5245	.4768	.4348	.3975
4	.9610	.9238	.8885	.8548	.8227	.7921	.7629	.7350	.7084	.6830	.6355	.5921	.5718	.5523	.5158	.4823	.4230	.3725	.3294	.2923
5	.9515	.9057	.8626	.8219	.7835	.7473	.7130	.6806	.6499	.6209	.5674	.5194	.4972	.4761	.4371	.4019	.3411	.2910	.2495	.2149
6	.9420	.8880	.8375	.7903	.7462	.7050	.6663	.6302	.5963	.5645	.5066	.4556	.4323	.4104	.3704	.3349	.2751	.2274	.1890	.1580
7	.9327	.8706	.8131	.7599	.7107	.6651	.6227	.5835	.5470	.5132	.4523	.3996	.3759	.3538	.3139	.2791	.2218	.1776	.1432	.1162
8	.9235	.8535	.7894	.7307	.6768	.6274	.5820	.5403	.5019	.4665	.4039	.3506	.3269	.3050	.2660	.2326	.1789	.1388	.1085	.0854
9	.9143	.8368	.7664	.7026	.6446	.5919	.5439	.5002	.4604	.4241	.3606	.3075	.2843	.2630	.2255	.1938	.1443	.1084	.0822	.0628
10	.9053	.8203	.7441	.6756	.6139	.5584	.5083	.4632	.4224	.3855	.3220	.2697	.2472	.2267	.1911	.1615	.1164	.0847	.0623	.0462
11	.8963	.8043	.7224	.6496	.5847	.5268	.4751	.4289	.3875	.3505	.2875	.2366	.2149	.1954	.1619	.1346	.0938	.0662	.0472	.0340
12	.8874	.7885	.7014	.6246	.5568	.4970	.4440	.3971	.3555	.3186	.2567	.2076	.1869	.1685	.1372	.1122	.0757	.0517	.0357	.0250
13	.8787	.7730	.6810	.6006	.5303	.4688	.4150	.3677	.3262	.2897	.2292	.1821	.1625	.1452	.1163	.0935	.0610	.0404	.0271	.0184
14	.8700	.7579	.6611	.5775	.5051	.4423	.3878	.3405	.2992	.2633	.2046	.1597	.1413	.1252	.0985	.0779	.0492	.0316	.0205	.0135
15	.8613	.7430	.6419	.5553	.4810	.4173	.3624	.3152	.2745	.2394	.1827	.1401	.1229	.1079	.0835	.0649	.0397	.0247	.0155	.0099
16	.8528	.7284	.6232	.5339	.4581	.3936	.3387	.2919	.2519	.2176	.1631	.1229	.1069	.0930	.0708	.0541	.0320	.0193	.0118	.0073
17	.8444	.7142	.6050	.5134	.4363	.3714	.3166	.2703	.2311	.1978	.1456	.1078	.0929	.0802	.0600	.0451	.0258	.0150	.0089	.0054
18	.8360	.7002	.5874	.4936	.4155	.3503	.2959	.2502	.2120	.1799	.1300	.0946	.0808	.0691	.0508	.0376	.0208	.0118	.0068	.0039
19	.8277	.6864	.5703	.4746	.3957	.3305	.2765	.2317	.1945	.1635	.1161	.0829	.0703	.0596	.0431	.0313	.0168	.0092	.0051	.0029
20	.8195	.6730	.5537	.4564	.3769	.3118	.2584	.2145	.1784	.1486	.1037	.0728	.0611	.0514	.0365	.0261	.0135	.0072	.0039	.0021
21	.8114	.6598	.5375	.4388	.3589	.2942	.2415	.1987	.1637	.1351	.0926	.0638	.0531	.0443	.0309	.0217	.0109	.0056	.0029	.0016
22	.8034	.6468	.5219	.4220	.3418	.2775	.2257	.1839	.1502	.1228	.0826	.0560	.0462	.0382	.0262	.0181	.0088	.0044	.0022	.0012
23	.7954	.6342	.5067	.4057	.3256	.2618	.2109	.1703	.1378	.1117	.0738	.0491	.0402	.0329	.0222	.0151	.0071	.0034	.0017	.0008
24	.7876	.6217	.4919	.3901	.3101	.2470	.1971	.1577	.1264	.1015	.0659	.0431	.0349	.0284	.0188	.0126	.0057	.0027	.0013	.0006
25	.7798	.6095	.4776	.3751	.2953	.2330	.1842	.1460	.1160	.0923	.0588	.0378	.0304	.0245	.0160	.0105	.0046	.0021	.0010	.0005
26	.7720	.5976	.4637	.3607	.2812	.2198	.1722	.1352	.1064	.0839	.0525	.0331	.0264	.0211	.0135	.0087	.0037	.0016	.0007	.0003
27	.7644	.5859	.4502	.3468	.2678	.2074	.1609	.1252	.0976	.0763	.0469	.0291	.0230	.0182	.0115	.0073	.0030	.0013	.0006	.0002
28	.7568	.5744	.4371	.3335	.2551	.1956	.1504	.1159	.0895	.0693	.0419	.0255	.0200	.0157	.0097	.0061	.0024	.0010	.0004	.0002
29	.7493	.5631	.4243	.3207	.2429	.1846	.1406	.1073	.0822	.0630	.0374	.0224	.0174	.0135	.0082	.0051	.0020	.0008	.0003	.0001
30	.7419	.5521	.4120	.3083	.2314	.1741	.1314	.0994	.0754	.0573	.0334	.0196	.0151	.0116	.0070	.0042	.0016	.0006	.0002	.0001
35	.7059	.5000	.3554	.2534	.1813	.1301	.0937	.0676	.0490	.0356	.0189	.0102	.0075	.0055	.0030	.0017	.0005	.0002	.0001	*
40	.6717	.4529	.3066	.2083	.1420	.0972	.0668	.0460	.0318	.0221	.0107	.0053	.0037	.0026	.0013	.0007	.0002	.0001	*	*
45	.6391	.4102	.2644	.1712	.1113	.0727	.0476	.0313	.0207	.0137	.0061	.0027	.0019	.0013	.0006	.0003	.0001	*	*	*
50	.6080	.3715	.2281	.1407	.0872	.0543	.0339	.0213	.0134	.0085	.0035	.0014	.0009	.0006	.0003	.0001	*	*	*	*
55	.5785	.3365	.1968	.1157	.0683	.0406	.0242	.0145	.0087	.0053	.0020	.0007	.0005	.0003	.0001	*	*	*	*	*

*The factor is zero to four decimal places.

Table A-2 ▪ Present Value of an Annuity of $1 per Period for n Periods:

Equation:

$$PVIFA_{i,n} = \sum_{t=1}^{n} \frac{1}{(1+i)^t} = \frac{1 - \frac{1}{(1+i)^n}}{i} = \frac{1}{i} - \frac{1}{i(1+i)^n}$$

Financial Calculator Keys:

n	i		1.0	0
N	I	PV	PMT	FV

TABLE VALUE

Number of Periods	1%	2%	3%	4%	5%	6%	7%	8%	9%	10%	12%	14%	15%	16%	18%	20%	24%	28%	32%
1	0.9901	0.9804	0.9709	0.9615	0.9524	0.9434	0.9346	0.9259	0.9174	0.9091	0.8929	0.8772	0.8696	0.8621	0.8475	0.8333	0.8065	0.7813	0.7576
2	1.9704	1.9416	1.9135	1.8861	1.8594	1.8334	1.8080	1.7833	1.7591	1.7355	1.6901	1.6467	1.6257	1.6052	1.5656	1.5278	1.4568	1.3916	1.3315
3	2.9410	2.8839	2.8286	2.7751	2.7232	2.6730	2.6243	2.5771	2.5313	2.4869	2.4018	2.3216	2.2832	2.2459	2.1743	2.1065	1.9813	1.8684	1.7663
4	3.9020	3.8077	3.7171	3.6299	3.5460	3.4651	3.3872	3.3121	3.2397	3.1699	3.0373	2.9137	2.8550	2.7982	2.6901	2.5887	2.4043	2.2410	2.0957
5	4.8534	4.7135	4.5797	4.4518	4.3295	4.2124	4.1002	3.9927	3.8897	3.7908	3.6048	3.4331	3.3522	3.2743	3.1272	2.9906	2.7454	2.5320	2.3452
6	5.7955	5.6014	5.4172	5.2421	5.0757	4.9173	4.7665	4.6229	4.4859	4.3553	4.1114	3.8887	3.7845	3.6847	3.4976	3.3255	3.0205	2.7594	2.5342
7	6.7282	6.4720	6.2303	6.0021	5.7864	5.5824	5.3893	5.2064	5.0330	4.8684	4.5638	4.2883	4.1604	4.0386	3.8115	3.6046	3.2423	2.9370	2.6775
8	7.6517	7.3255	7.0197	6.7327	6.4632	6.2098	5.9713	5.7466	5.5348	5.3349	4.9676	4.6389	4.4873	4.3436	4.0776	3.8372	3.4212	3.0758	2.7860
9	8.5660	8.1622	7.7861	7.4353	7.1078	6.8017	6.5152	6.2469	5.9952	5.7590	5.3282	4.9464	4.7716	4.6065	4.3030	4.0310	3.5655	3.1842	2.8681
10	9.4713	8.9826	8.5302	8.1109	7.7217	7.3601	7.0236	6.7101	6.4177	6.1446	5.6502	5.2161	5.0188	4.8332	4.4941	4.1925	3.6819	3.2689	2.9304
11	10.3676	9.7868	9.2526	8.7605	8.3064	7.8869	7.4987	7.1390	6.8052	6.4951	5.9377	5.4527	5.2337	5.0286	4.6560	4.3271	3.7757	3.3351	2.9776
12	11.2551	10.5753	9.9540	9.3851	8.8633	8.3838	7.9427	7.5361	7.1607	6.8137	6.1944	5.6603	5.4206	5.1971	4.7932	4.4392	3.8514	3.3868	3.0133
13	12.1337	11.3484	10.6350	9.9856	9.3936	8.8527	8.3577	7.9038	7.4869	7.1034	6.4235	5.8424	5.5831	5.3423	4.9095	4.5327	3.9124	3.4272	3.0404
14	13.0037	12.1062	11.2961	10.5631	9.8986	9.2950	8.7455	8.2442	7.7862	7.3667	6.6282	6.0021	5.7245	5.4675	5.0081	4.6106	3.9616	3.4587	3.0609
15	13.8651	12.8493	11.9379	11.1184	10.3797	9.7122	9.1079	8.5595	8.0607	7.6061	6.8109	6.1422	5.8474	5.5755	5.0916	4.6755	4.0013	3.4834	3.0764
16	14.7179	13.5777	12.5611	11.6523	10.8378	10.1059	9.4466	8.8514	8.3126	7.8237	6.9740	6.2651	5.9542	5.6685	5.1624	4.7296	4.0333	3.5026	3.0882
17	15.5623	14.2919	13.1661	12.1657	11.2741	10.4773	9.7632	9.1216	8.5436	8.0216	7.1196	6.3729	6.0472	5.7487	5.2223	4.7746	4.0591	3.5177	3.0971
18	16.3983	14.9920	13.7535	12.6593	11.6896	10.8276	10.0591	9.3719	8.7556	8.2014	7.2497	6.4674	6.1280	5.8178	5.2732	4.8122	4.0799	3.5294	3.1039
19	17.2260	15.6785	14.3238	13.1339	12.0853	11.1581	10.3356	9.6036	8.9501	8.3649	7.3658	6.5504	6.1982	5.8775	5.3162	4.8435	4.0967	3.5386	3.1090
20	18.0456	16.3514	14.8775	13.5903	12.4622	11.4699	10.5940	9.8181	9.1285	8.5136	7.4694	6.6231	6.2593	5.9288	5.3527	4.8696	4.1103	3.5458	3.1129
21	18.8570	17.0112	15.4150	14.0292	12.8212	11.7641	10.8355	10.0168	9.2922	8.6487	7.5620	6.6870	6.3125	5.9731	5.3837	4.8913	4.1212	3.5514	3.1158
22	19.6604	17.6580	15.9369	14.4511	13.1630	12.0416	11.0612	10.2007	9.4424	8.7715	7.6446	6.7429	6.3587	6.0113	5.4099	4.9094	4.1300	3.5558	3.1180
23	20.4558	18.2922	16.4436	14.8568	13.4886	12.3034	11.2722	10.3711	9.5802	8.8832	7.7184	6.7921	6.3988	6.0442	5.4321	4.9245	4.1371	3.5592	3.1197
24	21.2434	18.9139	16.9355	15.2470	13.7986	12.5504	11.4693	10.5288	9.7066	8.9847	7.7843	6.8351	6.4338	6.0726	5.4509	4.9371	4.1428	3.5619	3.1210
25	22.0232	19.5235	17.4131	15.6221	14.0939	12.7834	11.6536	10.6748	9.8226	9.0770	7.8431	6.8729	6.4641	6.0971	5.4669	4.9476	4.1474	3.5640	3.1220
26	22.7952	20.1210	17.8768	15.9828	14.3752	13.0032	11.8258	10.8100	9.9290	9.1609	7.8957	6.9061	6.4906	6.1182	5.4804	4.9563	4.1511	3.5656	3.1227
27	23.5596	20.7069	18.3270	16.3296	14.6430	13.2105	11.9867	10.9352	10.0266	9.2372	7.9426	6.9352	6.5135	6.1364	5.4919	4.9636	4.1542	3.5669	3.1233
28	24.3164	21.2813	18.7641	16.6631	14.8981	13.4062	12.1371	11.0511	10.1161	9.3066	7.9844	6.9607	6.5335	6.1520	5.5016	4.9697	4.1566	3.5679	3.1237
29	25.0658	21.8444	19.1885	16.9837	15.1411	13.5907	12.2777	11.1584	10.1983	9.3696	8.0218	6.9830	6.5509	6.1656	5.5098	4.9747	4.1585	3.5687	3.1240
30	25.8077	22.3965	19.6004	17.2920	15.3725	13.7648	12.4090	11.2578	10.2737	9.4269	8.0552	7.0027	6.5660	6.1772	5.5168	4.9789	4.1601	3.5693	3.1242
35	29.4086	24.9986	21.4872	18.6646	16.3742	14.4982	12.9477	11.6546	10.5668	9.6442	8.1755	7.0700	6.6166	6.2153	5.5386	4.9915	4.1644	3.5708	3.1248
40	32.8347	27.3555	23.1148	19.7928	17.1591	15.0463	13.3317	11.9246	10.7574	9.7791	8.2438	7.1050	6.6418	6.2335	5.5482	4.9966	4.1659	3.5712	3.1250
45	36.0945	29.4902	24.5187	20.7200	17.7741	15.4558	13.6055	12.1084	10.8812	9.8628	8.2825	7.1232	6.6543	6.2421	5.5523	4.9986	4.1664	3.5714	3.1250
50	39.1961	31.4236	25.7298	21.4822	18.2559	15.7619	13.8007	12.2335	10.9617	9.9148	8.3045	7.1327	6.6605	6.2463	5.5541	4.9995	4.1666	3.5714	3.1250
55	42.1472	33.1748	26.7744	22.1086	18.6335	15.9905	13.9399	12.3186	11.0140	9.9471	8.3170	7.1376	6.6636	6.2482	5.5549	4.9998	4.1666	3.5714	3.1250

Table A-3 ■ Future Value of $1 at the End of n Periods:

Equation:
$FVIF_{i,n} = (1 + i)^n$

Financial Calculator Keys:

n	i	PV	PMT	FV
N	I	PV	PMT	FV
				TABLE VALUE

Period	1%	2%	3%	4%	5%	6%	7%	8%	9%	10%	12%	14%	15%	16%	18%	20%	24%	28%	32%	36%
1	1.0100	1.0200	1.0300	1.0400	1.0500	1.0600	1.0700	1.0800	1.0900	1.1000	1.1200	1.1400	1.1500	1.1600	1.1800	1.2000	1.2400	1.2800	1.3200	1.3600
2	1.0201	1.0404	1.0609	1.0816	1.1025	1.1236	1.1449	1.1664	1.1881	1.2100	1.2544	1.2996	1.3225	1.3456	1.3924	1.4400	1.5376	1.6384	1.7424	1.8496
3	1.0303	1.0612	1.0927	1.1249	1.1576	1.1910	1.1250	1.2597	1.2950	1.3310	1.4049	1.4815	1.5209	1.5609	1.6430	1.7280	1.9066	2.0972	2.3000	2.5155
4	1.0406	1.0824	1.1255	1.1699	1.2155	1.2625	1.3108	1.3605	1.4116	1.4641	1.5735	1.6890	1.7490	1.8106	1.9388	2.0736	2.3642	2.6844	3.0360	3.4210
5	1.0510	1.1041	1.1593	1.2167	1.2763	1.3382	1.4026	1.4693	1.5386	1.6105	1.7623	1.9254	2.0114	2.1003	2.2878	2.4883	2.9316	3.4360	4.0075	4.6526
6	1.0615	1.1262	1.1941	1.2653	1.3401	1.4185	1.5007	1.5869	1.6771	1.7716	1.9738	2.1950	2.3131	2.4364	2.6996	2.9860	3.6352	4.3980	5.2899	6.3275
7	1.0721	1.1487	1.2299	1.3159	1.4071	1.5036	1.6058	1.7138	1.8280	1.9487	2.2107	2.5023	2.6600	2.8262	3.1855	3.5832	4.5077	5.6295	6.9826	8.6054
8	1.0829	1.1717	1.2668	1.3686	1.4775	1.5938	1.7182	1.8509	1.9926	2.1436	2.4760	2.8526	3.0590	3.2784	3.7589	4.2998	5.5895	7.2058	9.2170	11.703
9	1.0937	1.1951	1.3048	1.4233	1.5513	1.6895	1.8385	1.9990	2.1719	2.3579	2.7731	3.2519	3.5179	3.8030	4.4355	5.1598	6.9310	9.2234	12.166	15.917
10	1.1046	1.2190	1.3439	1.4802	1.6289	1.7908	1.9672	2.1589	2.3674	2.5937	3.1058	3.7072	4.0456	4.4114	5.2338	6.1917	8.5944	11.806	16.060	21.647
11	1.1157	1.2434	1.3842	1.5395	1.7103	1.8983	2.1049	2.3316	2.5804	2.8531	3.4785	4.2262	4.6524	5.1173	6.1759	7.4301	10.657	15.112	21.199	29.439
12	1.1268	1.2682	1.4258	1.6010	1.7959	2.0122	2.2522	2.5182	2.8127	3.1384	3.8960	4.8179	5.3503	5.9360	7.2876	8.9161	13.215	19.343	27.983	40.037
13	1.1381	1.2936	1.4685	1.6651	1.8856	2.1329	2.4098	2.7196	3.0658	3.4523	4.3635	5.4924	6.1528	6.8858	8.5994	10.699	16.386	24.759	36.937	54.451
14	1.1495	1.3195	1.5126	1.7317	1.9799	2.2609	2.5785	2.9372	3.3417	3.7975	4.8871	6.2613	7.0757	7.9875	10.147	12.839	20.319	31.691	48.757	74.053
15	1.1610	1.3459	1.5580	1.8009	2.0789	2.3966	2.7590	3.1722	3.6425	4.1772	5.4736	7.1379	8.1371	9.2655	11.974	15.407	25.196	40.565	64.359	100.71
16	1.1726	1.3728	1.6047	1.8730	2.1829	2.5404	2.9522	3.4259	3.9703	4.5950	6.1304	8.1372	9.3576	10.748	14.129	18.488	31.243	51.923	84.954	136.97
17	1.1843	1.4002	1.6528	1.9479	2.2920	2.6928	3.1588	3.7000	4.3276	5.0545	6.8660	9.2765	10.761	12.468	16.672	22.186	38.741	66.461	112.14	186.28
18	1.1961	1.4282	1.7024	2.0258	2.4066	2.8543	3.3799	3.9960	4.7171	5.5599	7.6900	10.575	12.375	14.463	19.673	26.623	48.039	85.071	148.02	253.34
19	1.2081	1.4568	1.7535	2.1068	2.5270	3.0256	3.6165	4.3157	5.1417	6.1159	8.6128	12.056	14.232	16.777	23.214	31.948	59.568	108.89	195.39	344.54
20	1.2202	1.4859	1.8061	2.1911	2.6533	3.2071	3.8697	4.6610	5.6044	6.7275	9.6463	13.743	16.367	19.461	27.393	38.338	73.864	139.38	257.92	468.57
21	1.2324	1.5157	1.8603	2.2788	2.7860	3.3996	4.1406	5.0338	6.1088	7.4002	10.804	15.668	18.822	22.574	32.324	46.005	91.592	178.41	340.45	637.26
22	1.2447	1.5460	1.9161	2.3699	2.9253	3.6035	4.4304	5.4365	6.6586	8.1403	12.100	17.861	21.645	26.186	38.142	55.206	113.57	228.36	449.39	866.67
23	1.2572	1.5769	1.9736	2.4647	3.0715	3.8197	4.7405	5.8715	7.2579	8.9543	13.552	20.362	24.891	30.376	45.008	66.247	140.83	292.30	593.20	1178.7
24	1.2697	1.6084	2.0328	2.5633	3.2251	4.0489	5.0724	6.3412	7.9111	9.8497	15.179	23.212	28.625	35.236	53.109	79.497	174.63	374.14	783.02	1603.0
25	1.2824	1.6406	2.0938	2.6658	3.3864	4.2919	5.4274	6.8485	8.6231	10.835	17.000	26.462	32.919	40.874	62.669	95.396	216.54	478.90	1033.6	2180.1
26	1.2953	1.6734	2.1566	2.7725	3.5557	4.5494	5.8074	7.3964	9.3992	11.918	19.040	30.167	37.857	47.414	73.949	114.48	268.51	613.00	1364.3	2964.9
27	1.3082	1.7069	2.2213	2.8834	3.7335	4.8223	6.2139	7.9881	10.245	13.110	21.325	34.390	43.535	55.000	87.260	137.37	332.95	784.64	1800.9	4032.3
28	1.3213	1.7410	2.2879	2.9987	3.9201	5.1117	6.6488	8.6271	11.167	14.421	23.884	39.204	50.066	63.800	102.97	164.84	412.86	1004.3	2377.2	5483.9
29	1.3345	1.7758	2.3566	3.1187	4.1161	5.4184	7.1143	9.3173	12.172	15.863	26.750	44.693	57.575	74.009	121.50	197.81	511.95	1285.6	3137.9	7458.1
30	1.3478	1.8114	2.4273	3.2434	4.3219	5.7435	7.6123	10.063	13.268	17.449	29.960	50.950	66.212	85.850	143.37	237.38	634.82	1645.5	4142.1	10143.
40	1.4889	2.2080	3.2620	4.8010	7.0400	10.286	14.974	21.725	31.409	45.259	93.051	188.88	267.86	378.72	750.38	1469.8	5455.9	19427.	66521.	*
50	1.6446	2.6916	4.3839	7.1067	11.467	18.420	29.457	46.902	74.358	117.39	289.00	700.23	1083.7	1670.7	3927.4	9100.4	46890.	*	*	*
60	1.8167	3.2810	5.8916	10.520	18.679	32.988	57.946	101.26	176.03	304.48	897.60	2595.9	4384.0	7370.2	20555.	56348.	*	*	*	*

*FVIF > 99,999.

Table A-4 ▪ Future Value of an Annuity of $1 per Period for n Periods:

Equation:

$$FVIFA_{i,n} = \sum_{t=1}^{n} (1 + i)^{n-t} = \frac{(1 + i)^n - 1}{i}$$

Financial Calculator Keys:

n	i	0	1.0	
N	I	PV	PMT	FV
				TABLE VALUE

Number of Periods	1%	2%	3%	4%	5%	6%	7%	8%	9%	10%	12%	14%	15%	16%	18%	20%	24%	28%	32%	36%
1	1.0000	1.0000	1.0000	1.0000	1.0000	1.0000	1.0000	1.0000	1.0000	1.0000	1.0000	1.0000	1.0000	1.0000	1.0000	1.0000	1.0000	1.0000	1.0000	1.0000
2	2.0100	2.0200	2.0300	2.0400	2.0500	2.0600	2.0700	2.0800	2.0900	2.1000	2.1200	2.1400	2.1500	2.1600	2.1800	2.2000	2.2400	2.2800	2.3200	2.3600
3	3.0301	3.0604	3.0909	3.1216	3.1525	3.1836	3.2149	3.2464	3.2781	3.3100	3.3744	3.4396	3.4725	3.5056	3.5724	3.6400	3.7776	3.9184	4.0624	4.2096
4	4.0604	4.1216	4.1836	4.2465	4.3101	4.3746	4.4399	4.5061	4.5731	4.6410	4.7793	4.9211	4.9934	5.0665	5.2154	5.3680	5.6842	6.0156	6.3624	6.7251
5	5.1010	5.2040	5.3091	5.4163	5.5256	5.6371	5.7507	5.8666	5.9847	6.1051	6.3528	6.6101	6.7424	6.8771	7.1542	7.4416	8.0484	8.6999	9.3983	10.146
6	6.1520	6.3081	6.4684	6.6330	6.8019	6.9753	7.1533	7.3359	7.5233	7.7156	8.1152	8.5355	8.7537	8.9775	9.4420	9.9299	10.980	12.136	13.406	14.799
7	7.2135	7.4343	7.6625	7.8983	8.1420	8.3938	8.6540	8.9228	9.2004	9.4872	10.089	10.730	11.067	11.414	12.142	12.916	14.615	16.534	18.696	21.126
8	8.2857	8.5830	8.8923	9.2142	9.5491	9.8975	10.260	10.637	11.028	11.436	12.300	13.233	13.727	14.240	15.327	16.499	19.123	22.163	25.678	29.732
9	9.3685	9.7546	10.159	10.583	11.027	11.491	11.978	12.488	13.021	13.579	14.776	16.085	16.786	17.519	19.086	20.799	24.712	29.369	34.895	41.435
10	10.462	10.950	11.464	12.006	12.578	13.181	13.816	14.487	15.193	15.937	17.549	19.337	20.304	21.321	23.521	25.959	31.643	38.593	47.062	57.352
11	11.567	12.169	12.808	13.486	14.207	14.972	15.784	16.645	17.560	18.531	20.655	23.045	24.349	25.733	28.755	32.150	40.238	50.398	63.122	78.998
12	12.683	13.412	14.192	15.026	15.917	16.870	17.888	18.977	20.141	21.384	24.133	27.271	29.002	30.850	34.931	39.581	50.895	65.510	84.320	108.44
13	13.809	14.680	15.618	16.627	17.713	18.882	20.141	21.495	22.953	24.523	28.029	32.089	34.352	36.786	42.219	48.497	64.110	84.853	112.30	148.47
14	14.947	15.974	17.086	18.292	19.599	21.015	22.550	24.215	26.019	27.975	32.393	37.581	40.505	43.672	50.818	59.196	80.496	109.61	149.24	202.93
15	16.097	17.293	18.599	20.024	21.579	23.276	25.129	27.152	29.361	31.772	37.280	43.842	47.580	51.660	60.965	72.035	100.82	141.30	198.00	276.98
16	17.258	18.639	20.157	21.825	23.657	25.673	27.888	30.324	33.003	35.950	42.753	50.980	55.717	60.925	72.939	87.442	126.01	181.87	262.36	377.69
17	18.430	20.012	21.762	23.698	25.840	28.213	30.840	33.750	36.974	40.545	48.884	59.118	65.075	71.673	87.068	105.93	157.25	233.79	347.31	514.66
18	19.615	21.412	23.414	25.645	28.132	30.906	33.999	37.450	41.301	45.599	55.750	68.394	75.836	84.141	103.74	128.12	195.99	300.25	459.45	700.94
19	20.811	22.841	25.117	27.671	30.539	33.760	37.379	41.446	46.018	51.159	63.440	78.969	88.212	98.603	123.41	154.74	244.03	385.32	607.47	954.28
20	22.019	24.297	26.870	29.778	33.066	36.786	40.995	45.762	51.160	57.275	72.052	91.025	102.44	115.38	146.63	186.69	303.60	494.21	802.86	1298.8
21	23.239	25.783	28.676	31.969	35.719	39.993	44.865	50.423	56.765	64.002	81.699	104.77	118.81	134.84	174.02	225.03	377.46	633.59	1060.8	1767.4
22	24.472	27.299	30.537	34.248	38.505	43.392	49.006	55.457	62.873	71.403	92.503	120.44	137.63	157.41	206.34	271.03	469.06	812.00	1401.2	2404.7
23	25.716	28.845	32.453	36.618	41.430	46.996	53.436	60.893	69.532	79.543	104.60	138.30	159.28	183.60	244.49	326.24	582.63	1040.4	1850.6	3271.3
24	26.973	30.422	34.426	39.083	44.502	50.816	58.177	66.765	76.790	88.497	118.16	158.66	184.17	213.98	289.49	392.48	723.46	1332.7	2443.8	4450.0
25	28.243	32.030	36.459	41.646	47.727	54.865	63.249	73.106	84.701	98.347	133.33	181.87	212.79	249.21	342.60	471.98	898.09	1706.8	3226.8	6053.0
26	29.526	33.671	38.553	44.312	51.113	59.156	68.676	79.954	93.324	109.18	150.33	208.33	245.71	290.09	405.27	567.38	1114.6	2185.7	4260.4	8233.1
27	30.821	35.344	40.710	47.084	54.669	63.706	74.484	87.351	102.72	121.10	169.37	238.50	283.57	337.50	479.22	681.85	1383.1	2798.7	5624.8	11198.0
28	32.129	37.051	42.931	49.968	58.403	68.528	80.698	95.339	112.97	134.21	190.70	272.89	327.10	392.50	566.48	819.22	1716.1	3583.3	7425.7	15230.3
29	33.450	38.792	45.219	52.966	62.323	73.640	87.347	103.97	124.14	148.63	214.58	312.09	377.17	456.30	669.45	984.07	2129.0	4587.7	9802.9	20714.2
30	34.785	40.568	47.575	56.085	66.439	79.058	94.461	113.28	136.31	164.49	241.33	356.79	434.75	530.31	790.95	1181.9	2640.9	5873.2	12941.	28172.3
40	48.886	60.402	75.401	95.026	120.80	154.76	199.64	259.06	337.88	442.59	767.09	1342.0	1779.1	2360.8	4163.2	7343.9	22729.	69377.	*	*
50	64.463	84.579	112.80	152.67	209.35	290.34	406.53	573.77	815.08	1163.9	2400.0	4994.5	7217.7	10436.	21813.	45497.	*	*	*	*
60	81.670	114.05	163.05	237.99	353.58	533.13	813.52	1253.2	1944.8	3034.8	7471.6	18535.	29220.	46058.	*	*	*	*	*	*

*FVIFA > 99,999.

NAME INDEX

ABA Banking Journal, 330n
Abken, Peter J., 469n, 604n, 662n, 711n, 718n, 720n
Abramson, Jill, 74n
Adams, Lynn W., 515n
Aguilar, Linda, 495n, 825n
Aharony, J., 279n
Akella, Srinivas R., 35n, 146n
Akerlof, G.A., 276n
Akhavein, Jalal D., 159, 159n
Alexander, Gordon J., 555n
Alexander, Walter, 833n
Allen, Linda, 35n
Allen, Michael, 832n
Allen, Pat, 152n
Altman, Edward I., 832n, 833n
Ambachtsheer, Keith P., 328n, 469n, 470n, 473, 473n, 474n, 475n, 478n, 479n, 481n, 482n
Ambler, Diane E., 340n
American Banker, 334n
American Council of Life Insurance, 468n, 470n
American Council of Life Insurance Fact Book, 359n
Amihud, Y., 123n
Andrews, Edmund L., 41n
Angrist, Stanley W., 478n, 706n
Apilado, Vincent P., 135n, 140n, 321n, 336n, 339n
Arshadi, Nasser, 411n
Asinov, Lynn, 273n
Atkinson, Bill, 273n
August, James D., 494n
Auriemma, Michael, 326n, 849n
Avery, Robert B., 260n, 806n, 832n

Bacon, Kenneth H., 79n, 85n, 853n
Bae, Sung C., 630n
Baer, Herbert, 806n
Baig, Edward C., 395
Bailey, Jeff, 492n, 539n, 788n
Bailey, Ronald, 556n
Bajtelsmit, Vickie L., 476n
Baldoni, Robert, 711n
Baldwin, Carliss Y., 249, 251, 251n
Baldwin, Robert, 395, 409
Banerjee, Ajeyo, 116n
Banham, Russ, 148n
Bank of America, 859n, 860n
Bank, David, 154n
Bank Management, 338n
Bank Performance Annual, 350n
Banking Legislation and Policy, 79n, 145n
Banking Policy Report, 51n, 54n, 135n, 138n, 160n, 250n, 251n, 254n, 262n, 333n, 335n, 337n, 340n, 506n, 508n, 775n, 849n
Barboza, David, 409n
Barro, Jason R., 124n
Barro, Robert J., 124n, 699n
Barsky, Neil, 855n
Barth, James R., 62n, 122n, 123n, 131n, 146n, 252n, 266n, 267n, 277n

Bartholomew, Philip E., 146n
Bartlett, Sarah, 896n
Bauer, Daniel L., 82n, 130, 130n
Baum, Dan, 147n
Beaumier, Carol, 577, 577n, 796n
Beckett, Paul, 321n, 322n, 332n, 482n, 483n, 857n
Becketti, Sean, 642n, 821n
Beidleman, Carl R., 718n
Belongia, Michael T., 605n
Bennett, Barbara A., 122n, 139n
Benston, George J., 18n, 71n, 132n, 134n, 135n, 140n, 159n, 276n, 321n, 492n, 502n, 844n
Berger, Allen N., 40, 116n, 159, 159n, 288n
Bergman, Dru Johnston, 494n
Berkowitz, Stephen A., 479n
Berlin, Mitchell, 18n, 821n
Berton, Lee, 267n, 288n, 753n
Bianco, Anthony, 407n, 518n
Bicksler, James, 711n
Bierwag, Gerald O., 633n, 639n, 640n, 642n
Birnbaum, Jeffrey H., 147n
Bisignano, Joseph, 638n
Black, 476, 476n
Blackwell, David W., 127n, 756n, 806n
Blalock, Joseph, 594n
Bleakly, Fred R., 539n, 622n, 752n
Bloch, Ernest, 399n, 401n, 407n
Bloom, Steven, 689
Blount, Donald, 250n
Blyn, Martin R., 144n
Board of Governors, 797n
Boardman, William T., 40
Bodie, Zvi, 469n
Bogle, John C., 468n, 477n, 478n
Boitano, Margaret, 447n
Bonte-Friedheim, Robert, 447n
Booth, James R., 659n
Bostic, Raphael W., 260n, 832n, 853n, 858n
Bowers, Barbara, 377n, 378n
Boyd, John H., 140n
Bradley, Michael G., 146n
Brady, Thomas F., 844
Brannigan, Martha, 753n
Bransten, Lisa, 395, 398n
Brewer, Elijah, 35n, 124n, 140n, 160n, 785n, 806n
Brick, John R., 841n
Brigham, Eugene F., 428n, 794n, 860n
Brimelow, Peter, 375n
Britt, Phillip, 149n
Broaddus, Alfred, 49n
Brock, Bronwyn, 62n
Brodsky, William J., 657
Brooks, Rick, 115n
Brown, Keith C., 711n, 718n
Browning, E.S., 891n
Brumbaugh, R. Dan, Jr., 71n, 82n, 130n, 141n, 152n, 252n, 267n, 276n
Bryan, Michael F., 556n
Bryant, Adam, 123n

Buckman, Rebecca, 396n, 397n, 401n, 409n, 429n
Burns, Joseph E., 732n
Burns, Richard M., 146n
Buser, Stephen A., 122n, 289n, 291, 291n
Bush, Vanessa, 4n, 272n, 856n
Business Conditions Digest, 589n
Business Week, 1, 375n, 501n, 502n, 514n
Buynak, Thomas M., 469n
Bygrave, William D., 427n

Cacy, J.A., 734n
Cagle, Julie, 146n
Cahill, Joseph B., 199, 205n, 215n
Caks, John, 633n
Calem, Paul S., 260n, 832n
Callan, Sara, 447n
Calomiris, Charles W., 91, 96, 123n
Campbell, John Y., 605n
Canner, Glenn B., 260n, 796n, 797n, 832n, 851n, 853n, 858n
Canter, Michael S., 721n
Cantor, Richard, 495n, 898n
Caouette, John B., 495n
Capon, 833n
Carey, Mark S., 425n
Cargill, Thomas F., 66n, 69n
Carhill, Mike, 146n
Carlson, John A., 552n
Carner, William J., 142n
Carreker, J.D., 774n
Carrington, Tim, 279n
Carroll, David, 851n
Carron, Andrew S., 66n, 69n
Carson, Teresa, 200n
Carter, David A., 659n, 711n
Carter, Richard B., 146n
Caskey, John P., 22n
Casserley, Dominic, 677n, 689
Cassidy, John, 410n, 416n
Cebenoyan, A. Sinan, 35n, 71n, 77n, 82n, 124n, 130, 130n, 131n, 145n, 160n, 267n, 268n, 274n, 291n, 818n
Chance, Don M., 674n, 703n
Chase, Samuel B., Jr., 140n
Chaudhry, Mukesh K., 658n
Chen, Andrew H., 122n, 289n, 291, 291n, 711n
Chen, Carl R., 124n
Chen, Le In, 642n
Chernow, Ron, 395, 403n, 409, 409n
Chicago Board of Trade, 661n, 677n, 691n, 707n, 718n
Chicago Tribune, 658n
Cho, Namju, 815n, 817n
Chorafas, 677n
Christie, Andrew A., 630n
Christopher, Benjamin B., 705n
Chua, Jess B., 633n
Citicorp, 733n
Clair, Robert T., 129n
Clark, Jeffrey A., 159n
Clements, Jonathan, 152n, 446n, 455n

Cline, Kenneth, 311n, 312n
Coggin, T. Daniel, 479n
Cogley, Timothy, 594n
Cohen, Laurie P., 515n
Cohn, Jeffrey, 795n
Cole, Joseph B., 721n
Cole, Rebel A., 35n, 77n, 146n, 160n, 732n
Coleman, Alan B., 131n, 635n, 748n, 847n, 848n, 852n, 894n
Conference on Report on H.R. 1278, 856n
Conner, 745n
Conover, Michael C., 132n
Cook, Douglas O., 276n, 807n
Cook, J. Michael, 173
Cook, Timothy, 604n
Cooperman, Elizabeth S., 35n, 72n, 77n, 82n, 116n, 124n, 130, 130n, 131n, 146n, 160n, 267n, 268n, 274n, 276n, 291n, 509n, 511n, 799n, 807n, 818n
Cope, Debra, 338n, 339n
Cordell, Lawrence R., 35n, 145n, 146n, 268n
Corman, Linda, 342n, 343n
Cornett, Marcia Millon, 358, 358n, 369n, 380n, 835n, 860n
Cornyn, Anthony G., 140n
Corrigan, E. Gerald, 80n, 84, 139n, 410n, 895n
Corwin, Philip, 155n
Costa, Leilani, 328n
Coulter, David, 311n
Cox, John C., 595n, 602n, 604n
Cox, William N., III, 552n
Crandell, Greg, 273n
Crane, Dwight B., 346n
Crawford, Richard D., 21n, 116n, 249, 263n, 300n, 305n, 309n, 322n, 399n, 416n, 423n, 492n, 493n, 496n, 512n, 514n, 518n, 521n
Crawford, William B., Jr., 658n, 662n, 669n, 718n
Credit Union Magazine, 153n
Crevoor, Susan, 346n
Croushore, Dean, 546n
Culbertson, John M., 601n
Cullison, William E., 546n
Culp, Christopher, 343n, 344n
Cummins, J. David, 469n
CUNA Annual Report, 263n, 331n
Cuneo, 745n
Cyrnak, Anthony W., 142n

Dalio, Raymond, 584
Danielson, Arnold G., 115, 285, 304n, 310, 310n, 311n, 506, 506n, 510n, 520n
Dankner, Harold, 468n
Darby, Michael R., 552n
Davis, Donald, 304n, 307n, 311n
Davis, Richard G., 800n, 805n
Davis, Sean, 398n
de Cordoba, Jose, 891n
De Leon, Albert V., 130n
De Lisser, Eleena, 401n
de Regnacourt, Francis, 147
Demirguc-Kunt, Asli, 131n
Demsetz, Rebecca, 495n
Dennon, A.R., 383
Denver Post, 459n

Deshmukh, Sudhakar D., 31n
Deutsch, Hunting F., 337n, 339n
Deutschman, Alan, 481n
Dewhurst, 476, 476n
DeYoung, Robert, 122n, 130
Diamond, Douglas W., 18n
DiPaolo, Vince, 328n
Dobson, Steven W., 605n
Doherty, Neil A., 721n
Dorgan, Richard J., 494n
Dotsey, Michael, 794n
Drabenstott, Mark, 677n
Dresser, Michael, 154n
Drew, Christopher, 481n
Druckerman, Pamela, 884, 887n, 888n, 890n
Drzik, John P., 346n
Dua, Pami, 604n, 605n
Duca, John V., 895n
Dufey, Gunter, 576n
Duke, Paul, Jr., 4n, 74n
Dunham, Constance, 145n
Durkin, Thomas A., 492n, 851n
Dvorak, Brian, 638n
Dwyer, Gerald P., Jr., 556n

Eaton, Leslie, 140n
Eccles, Robert G., 346n
Echols, Michael E., 605n
Economic Policy Review, 195n
Economist, 849n
Edleson, Michael E., 795n
Edminster, Robert O., 833n
Edmonds, Charles P., 386n
Edwards, Donald G., 720n
Edwards, Franklin R., 34n
Ehrhardt, Michael C., 428n, 860n
Eichenfield, Samuel L., 491
Eickhoff, Gerald, 142n
Eisenbeis, Robert A., 35n, 140n, 146n, 160n
Eiteman, David K., 328n
Elliehausen, Gregory E., 492n, 798n
Elliott, J. Walter, 605n
Elliott, Steven, 621
Ellis, James E., 513n
Ellis, M.E., 399n, 407n
Ellison, Katherine, 883, 890n
Elmer, Peter J., 803n
Elstrom, Peter J.W., 662n
Emmons, William R., 822n
Endlich, Lisa, 410n
English, William B., 325n
Ernst, 76n
Estrella, Arturo, 469n
Esty, Ben, 658n, 715n
Esty, Benjamin C., 35n, 121n, 124n, 146n, 249, 251, 251n, 268n
Eugeni, Francesca, 556n
Euromoney, 285
Evanoff, Douglas D., 159n, 330n, 806n
Evans, Charles, 556n
Ewing, Terzah, 658n, 662n
Ezra, D. Don, 328n, 469n, 470n, 473, 473n, 474n, 475n, 478n, 479n, 481n, 482n
Ezzell, John R., 124n

Fabozzi, Frank J., 479n, 635n, 756n, 759n
Fama, Eugene A., 552n, 821n
FDIC Annual Report, 780n, 781n, 790n
FDIC Statistics on Banking, Year-End 1996, 14n
Feder, Barnaby J., 326n
Federal Credit Union Act, 756
Federal Reserve Bank, 11n, 818
Federal Reserve Bank of Kansas, 142n
Federal Reserve Bulletin, 12n, 180n, 202, 410n, 496, 498n, 773n, 832n
Fein, Melanie L., 138n, 340n
Feinman, Joshua N., 734n
Feldstein, Martin, 552n
Felgran, Steven D., 339n, 340n, 711n
Felsenthal, Edward, 250n
Fenn, George W., 732n
Fergus, James T., 851n
Fields, Joseph A., 146n
Fieleke, Norman S., 682n, 895n
Financial Economists Roundtable, 464n
Finnerty, John D., 47n, 49n
Finney, Louis D., 479n
First Chicago Corporation, 732n
Fischel, Daniel, 858n
Fisher, Irving, 32n
Fisher, Lawrence, 639n
Fissel, Gary S., 896n, 897n
Fite, Gilbert C., 153n
Flannery, Mark J., 276n, 630n, 798n
Fleming, Charles, 148n
Flood, Mark D., 47n, 570n, 806n
Flynn, Julia, 513n
Fogler, Russell H., 630n
Foote, Jennifer, 375n
Forbes, 464n, 479n
Forbes, Shawn M., 844n
Ford, 800n
Ford, William F., 518n
Fortune, 481n
Fortune, Peter, 13n, 336n, 443n, 448n, 451n, 453n, 455n, 457n, 747n
Foust, Dean *et al,* 4n
Frank, Stephen E., 1, 116n, 142n, 882, 885n
Fraser, Katherine, 321n, 325n, 338n
Freddie Mac Reports, 272n, 832n, 851n
Freeman, Douglas, 772
Freer, Kenneth O., 858n
French, Dan W., 464n
Frieder, Larry A., 140n, 154n, 199, 216n, 521n
Friedland, Jonathan, 890n, 891n
Friedman, Benjamin M., 604n, 605n
Friedman, Milton, 795n
Friend, 399n
Frisbee, 331n
Fritsch, Peter, 888n, 890n, 892n
Fromson, Brett Duval, 410
Froot, Kenneth A., 604n
Fuerbringer, Jonathan, 584, 622n, 892n
Furash, Edward E., 320, 345, 346n
Furlong, Frederick T., 290n, 593n, 788n, 844n

Galai, D., 121n
Gallo, John G., 135n, 321n, 336n, 339n
Galloway, Tina M., 267n, 806n

Galuszka, Peter, 508n
Gapenski, Louis C., 428n, 860n
Garabedian, John, 341n
Garcia, Gillian, 66n, 69n, 856n
Gardner, Mona J., 659n, 801n, 851n
Garg, Ramesh C., 897n
Garsson, Robert M., 78n, 300n
Garwood, Griffith L., 829n
Gasparino, Charles, 396n, 455n, 458n
Gasteyer, Phil, 153n
Gavin, William T., 556n
Geisst, Charles, 407n
Gerson, Mark, 321n
Giannone, 124n
Gianton, Eileen, 412n
Gibson, A.H., 549n
Giddy, Ian H., 576n
Gilbert, R. Alton, 48n, 55n, 139n, 738n
Gilkerson, James H., 800n, 805n
Gill, Edward G., 831n
Gillan, Stuart L., 512n, 518n
Gilman, Hank, 510n
Gilpin, Kenneth N., 264n, 907n
Giroux, Gary, 743n
Glancz, Ronald R., 858n
Glasgall, William, 712n
Glick, Reuven, 576n
Glynn, 513n
Goldberg, Lawrence A., 126n, 129n, 130
Goldberg, Michael A., 844n
Golding, E.L., 276n
Gonzales, Henry, 91
Good, Barbara A., 260n, 273n
Goodfriend, Marvin, 734n, 785n, 790n
Goodman, Laurie S., 84
Gordon, Marcy, 116n
Gordon, Mary, 139n
Gorton, Gary, 18n, 34n, 55n, 124n
Gough, Leo, 906n
Grady, Francis A., 804n
Graham, Stanley L., 140n
Greenbaum, Stuart I., 31n, 35n, 146n, 821n
Greenspan, Alan, 139n
Gregory, Deborah W., 642n
Greising, David, 508n, 513n, 662n
Grisdella, Cynthia S., 426n
Gross, William H., 621
Gruben, William, 897n
Gruber, William, 340n
Grupe, Michael R., 494n
Guenther, Robert, 833n
Gup, Benton E., 906n
Gupta, Atul, 146n

Hafer, R.W., 604n
Haggerty, Alfred G., 513n
Hahn, Thomas, 604n
Haler, 556n
Hamdani, Kausar, 735n, 738n
Hampton, Ted, 148n
Hanke, Steve H., 891n
Hann, Leslie Werstein, 378n
Hannan, Timothy H., 34n, 276n
Hansell, Saul, 154n, 521n, 715n
Hanweck, Gerald A., 126n, 129n, 130, 140n, 159n

Hargraves, Monica, 734n
Harless, Caroline T., 790n
Harrington, Scott, 57n, 364n, 373n, 381n
Harris, Marlys, 374n
Harris, Maury, 494n
Harris, Robert S., 140n
Harrison, J. Michael, 475, 476n
Hasan, Iftekhar, 130, 146n
Haskins, Matthew P., 251n, 253n
Haubrich, Joseph G., 18n, 349n
Hawkins, Chuck, 517n, 895n
Hayes, Samuel L., III, 346n, 401n, 403n, 420n, 908n
Headley, Jonathan, 658n, 715n
Heady, Robert, 558n, 775n
Healy, Thomas S., 374n
Hedges, Robert B., Jr., 199, 216n, 521n
Heimann, John, 148n
Hein, Scott E., 604n
Hempel, George H., 131n, 635n, 748n, 847n, 848n, 852n, 894n
Henderson, Glenn V., Jr., 464n
Hendricks, Darryll, 464n
Hermalin, Benjamin E., 124n, 858n
Herman, Tom, 551n, 556n
Herres, Gen. Robert T., 357
Hershey, Robert D., Jr., 130n, 138n
Hertzberg, Daniel, 796n
Hess, Alan C., 637n
Heuson, Andrea J., 605n
Hewitt, R. Shawn, 140n
Hicks, J.R., 594n, 598n, 631n
Higgins, Andrew, 534n, 561n
Hilder, David B., 340n, 375n, 510n, 513n, 517n
Hill, G. Christian, 788n
Hill, Joanne M., 674n, 694n
Hirsch, James S., 152n, 446n, 453n
Hirschhorn, E., 276n
Hirschleifer, Jack, 32n
Hirtle, Beverly, 312n, 469n
Ho, Thomas, 604n
Holland, A. Steven, 552n
Holland, Kelly, 320n
Hollis, Donald R., 772
Holson, Laura M., 492n
Homer, Sidney, 533
Horn, Charles M., 340n
Houpt, James V., 895n
Houston, Joel F., 124n, 821n
Hoyt, Robert E., 659n
Hubbard, Glenn R., 35n, 124n
Hubbard, Philip M., 401n, 403n, 908n
Hube, Karen, 258n
Hudgins, Sylvia, 35n, 77n, 160n
Hughes, Joseph P., 122n, 130
Hull, Jennifer Bingham, 200n
Humphrey, David B., 140n, 159, 159n
Humphrey, Thomas M., 548n, 552n
Hunter, William C., 140n, 159, 159n
Hurtz, Rebecca M., 659n
Hutchinson, Michael M., 711n
Hylton, Richard D., 476n

Ibbotson, Roger G., 146n
Ingersoll, Jonathan E., Jr., 595n, 602n, 604n
Ingrassia, Lawrence, 4n

Ip, Greg, 536n, 630n
Ippolito, Richard A., 476n
Isele, Gerhard, 711n
Israelevich, Philip R., 159n

Jackson, William E., 160n
Jaffe, Charles A., 441, 447n, 459n
Jahera, John S., Jr., 35n, 146n, 386n
Jain, Anshuman, 694n
James, Christopher, 124n, 304n, 322n, 630n, 821n
Jasen, Georgette, 584n, 795n
Jensen, Michael C., 33n, 121n
Jensen, Michael D., 464n
Jenster, Per V., 495n
John, Kose, 121n, 124n
John, Teresa A., 121n, 124n
Johnson, Brian A., 41n
Johnson, Robert W., 502n
Johnson, Verle B., 55n
Jordan, Bradford D., 146n, 332n
Joskow, Paul L., 35n
Journal of American Insurance, 56n
Journal of Financial Services Research, 495n

Kaden, Alan S., 251n, 253n
Kahn, Joseph, 321n, 397n, 509n, 815, 817n
Kalette, Denise, 4n
Kanatas, George, 31n, 821n
Kane, Edward J., 42n, 49n, 62n, 71, 72n, 122n, 252n, 266n, 276n, 278, 278n, 288n, 289n, 291, 291n, 604n, 784n, 807n
Kantor, Charles C., 345, 347n
Kantrow, Yvette, 325n, 334n, 340n, 495n, 513n
Karels, Gordon V., 411n
Kashyap, Anil K., 40, 116n
Katz, Donald, 690n
Kaufman, Daniel J., Jr., 741n
Kaufman, George G., 132n, 134n, 135, 135n, 268n, 279n, 290n, 321n, 637n, 642n
Keefe Bruyette & Woods, Inc., 215n
Keehn, Silas, 139n
Keeley, Michael C., 122n, 139n, 267n, 268n, 795n
Keeton, William R., 139n
Keir, Peter M., 590n
Kelling, Gabriella, 304n, 319, 322n
Kensinger, John W., 512n, 518n
Keran, Michael W., 290n
Kerber, Rose, 2n
Kerwin, Kathleen, 690n, 731n, 825n
Kessel, Reuben A., 598n, 604n
Key, Janet, 513n
Keynes, John M., 540n
Kidwell, David S., 127n, 756n, 806n
Kimball, Ralph C., 304n, 305, 305n, 322n
King, Ralph T., Jr., 262n
King, Resa W., 149n
Kirchoff, Bruce, 130
Kirsch, Clifford E., 756n
Kleege, Stephen, 495n
Klein, Robert W., 373n
Kliesen, Kevin L., 819n
Knight, Robert E., 734n
Kobren, Eric, 441

Koch, Timothy W., 22n, 179n, 348n, 349n, 353n, 521n, 749n, 844n, 847n, 855n, 894n
Koedik, Kees G., 605n
Kohers, Theodor, 146n
Kolari, James W., 336n, 339n
Kolb, Robert W., 386n, 674n, 682n
Komansky, David H., 395, 515n
Kool, Clemens J.M., 605n
Kopcke, Richard W., 357
Koppenhaver, Gary D., 659n, 677n, 705n
Korobow, Leon, 800n, 805n
Kraas, Richard H., 800n
Krauss, Clifford, 892n
Kreps, Daniel J., 346n
Kristof, Kathy, 483n
Kubarych, Roger M., 576n
Kuester, Kathleen A., 288n
Kuritzkes, Andrew, 760n
Kurtz, Robert D., 796n
Kwast, Myron L., 140n, 160n, 806n

Laderman, Elizabeth, 336n, 844n
Laderman, Jeffrey, 453n, 697n
Laing, Jonathan R., 715n
Lakonishok, Josef, 140n, 464n, 479n
Lambert, Wade, 340n
Lamm-Tennant, Joan, 659n
Lammers, Lucille E., 801n
Lane, Leroy O., 897n
Lang, William, 130
Langley, Monica, 128n
Lascelles, David, 80n
LeCompte, Richard L., 146n, 160n
Lee, David R., 741n
Lee, Kevin, 304n, 307n, 311n
Lee, Sang-Bin, 604n
Lee, Wayne, 605n
Lee, Winson B., 72n, 267n, 276n, 509n, 511n, 799n, 806n, 807n
Leggett, Karby, 534n
Lehman, Stan, 817n
Lehrman, Thomas, 321n
Leibowitz, Martin, 637n, 639n
Leonard, David C., 552n
Leonitades, M., 511n
Lesage, James P., 799n
Lev, B., 123n
Lewis, Al, 447n
Liang, J. Nellie, 140n, 276n
Life Insurance Fact Book, 14n
Light, Larry, 479n, 482n, 517n, 788n
Limpaphayom, Piman, 906n
Lindgren, John H., Jr., 495n
Lindley, James T., 633n
Lindsey, Lawrence B., 546n
Lipin, Steven, 116n, 129n, 321n, 492n, 752
Lipman, Frederic D., 426n, 427n, 428n, 429n
List, John A., 800n, 805n
Litan, Robert E., 123n
Litzenberger, Robert, 711n
Livingston, Miles, 642n
Lloyd-Davies, Myron L., 140n
Loeys, Jan G., 711n
Logan, John, 494n
Logue, Dennis E., 469n, 470n, 473n, 475, 475n, 476n, 477n, 478n, 479n, 480n, 481n, 482n, 801n

Loomis, Carol J., 516n
Lopez, Jose A., 293n
Lopez, Leslie, 534n, 561n
Louargand, Marc A., 476n
Louis, Arthur M., 154n
Lowry, Kim E., 329n
Lublin, Joann S., 173n
Lucchetti, Aaron, 409n, 429n
Luckett, Charles A., 494n, 851n
Luckett, Dudley G., 740n
Lutz, Frederick, 594n
Luytjes, Jan E., 720n

Macaulay, Frederick R., 631n
McColl, Hugh, 29
McComb, Robert P., 897n
McCoy, John, 154n, 199, 216n, 285, 319, 521n, 731
McCulloch, Huston J., 605n
McDermott, Darren, 534n, 561n, 903n
MacDonald, Elizabeth, 908n
MacDonald, Gregor D., 35n, 145n, 146n
McDonald, Lee, 386n
McDonley, Anne O'Mara, 677n
McElhone, Josie, 851n
McGeehan, Patrick, 116n, 399n, 411n, 413n, 421n, 514n
McGough, Robert, 152n, 441n, 446n, 449n, 453n
McKay, Betsy, 816, 817n
McKenna, 745n
McKenzie, Joseph A., 77n, 160n, 791n
McKinney, George W., 785n
McLaughlin, Mary M., 853n, 895n
McMorris, Frances A., 481n
McNamara, Michael J., 148n
McNamee, Mike, 300n, 396n
McNulty, James E., 711n, 850n
McTague, Jim, 273n
Mahoney, Patrick I., 795n, 800n, 841n
Maland, Ellen, 797n
Malkiel, Burton, 594n, 604n, 627n, 628n
Maness, Terry S., 605n
Mann, Steven V., 386n
Marcus, A.J., 122n
Markese, John, 455n
Market Perspectives, 697n
Marshall, David, 902, 903n, 905n
Marshall, Jeffrey, 731, 821n
Marshall, John F., 399n, 407n, 711n
Martin, John D., 512n, 518n
Martinson, Michael G., 895n
Mascaro, Angelo, 544n
Massengill, Buddy, 774n
Masulis, Ronald W., 121n, 146n
Mattingly, J. Virgin, Jr., 80n
Mavinga, Ferdinand, 34n
Maxwell, Charles E., 894n
Mayer, Martin, 1, 2, 3, 29, 154n, 155n, 156n, 157
Mayne, Lucille S., 844n
Meadows, Laura, 147n
Meckling, William H., 33n, 121n
Meehan, Dan, 895n
Meehan, John, 851n, 855n

Meerschwam, David M., 346n, 420n, 908n
Mehr, Robert I., 362n
Mehran, Hamid, 35n
Meiselman, David, 594n, 604n
Melton, Tina W., 858n
Meltzer, Allen H., 544n
Mendonca, Lenny, 519n
Mengle, David L., 288n, 745n
Meredith, Robyn, 805n
Merton, R.C., 122n
Mester, Loretta J., 35n, 130, 139n, 146n, 159n, 160n
Meyer, Phillip C., 153n, 250n
Michelbacher, G.F., 379n
Miles, James A., 124n
Miller, Frederic A., 4n
Miller, James P., 851n
Miller, Merton H., 47n, 64, 343n, 344n, 659n
Milligan, John W., 2n
Mills, Dixie L., 851n
Miltko, Ned, 774n
Mingo, John J., 140n
Misra, K., 146n
Modigliani, Franco, 464n, 466, 602n, 605n
Modigliani, Leah, 464n, 466
Moffett, Matt, 888n
Moffett, Michael H., 328n
Mondaschean, Thomas, 120n, 288n
Mondschean, Thomas H., 160n
Monks, Robert A.G., 479n
Monroe, Ann, 642n
Moody, J. Carroll, 153n
Moon, Choon-Geol, 122n, 130
Mooney, Sean, 373n
Moore, 288n
Moore, Robert R., 781n, 790n
Moore, Thomas, 516n
Morais, Richard, 385n
Morgan, Bruce W., 849n
Morrall, Katherine, 4n, 856n
Morris, Charles, 821n
Morris, Kathleen, 508n
Moser, James T., 633n, 699n, 721n
Muckenfuss, 79n
Muering, Kevin, 715n
Mukherjee, Sougata, 502n
Mullineaux, Donald J., 552n
Mullins, Helen M., 35n, 124n
Mundell, Robert, 551n
Munnell, Alice H., 469n
Murphy, Neil B., 800n
Murray, Matt, 128n, 129n, 205n, 250n, 258n, 321n, 854n, 887n
Mutual Fund Fact Book, 14n, 150n, 441n, 443n, 448, 451n, 456n, 470n, 473n
Mydans, Seth, 7n, 815, 817n

Nadler, Paul, 841n
Napoli, Janet A., 662n
Nash, Robert C., 495n
National Credit Union Administration (NCUA), 756
NCUSIF Annual Report, 745n
Neely, Michelle Clark, 824n
Nelson, Charles R., 605n
Nelson, Emily, 173n
Nelson, William R., 325n

Neuberger, Jonathan A., 630n, 795n
Neves, Andrea M.P., 343n, 344n
New York Times, 41n, 262n, 264n, 773, 816
Newman, A. Joseph, Jr., 331n
Nickerson, Cynthia J., 251n
Niehaus, Gregory R., 364n, 381n, 386n
Nixon, Brian, 149n
Norton, Robert E., 407n
Nothaft, Frank E., 851n
Nye, David J., 386n
Nylian, Paul, 250n

O'Brian, J.A., 31n
O'Brien, James M., 288n
O'Brien, Robert, 892n
O'Brien, Timothy, 262n, 264n
O'Connell, Vanessa, 152n, 154n, 401n, 446n
O'D. Moore, Michael, 341n, 342n
Office of Thrift Supervision, 300n
O'Hara, Maureen, 18n, 279n
O'Keefe, John, 129n
Olin, Harold B., 152n
Olson, Ronald, 31n
Olson, Wayne, 495n
Osterberg, William P., 853n
Osterland, Andrew, 508n
Ott, Robert A., Jr., 642n
Outreville, J. Francois, 358, 359n, 373n, 378,
    378n, 379n, 380n, 381n

Packer, Frank, 898n
Pae, Peter, 128n
Page, Daniel E., 146n
Pagelle, Mitchell, 533
Palia, Darius, 35n, 124n
Pantages, Jeffrey B., 386n
Par˜82, Terrence P., 803n
Park, Sangkyun, 276n
Parkinson, Patrick, 677n
Parliment, Tom, 149n, 751n, 753n, 803n
Pasztor, Andy, 411n
Patel, Jayendu, 464n
Patterson, Gregory A., 513n
Pearce, Douglas K., 745n
Pearson, David, 906n
Peck, Joe, 851n
Pennacchi, George, 18n, 55n
Peristiani, Stavros, 276n
Petersen, Melody, 517n
Peterson, 476
Peterson, David R., 278n, 292n
Peterson, Richard L., 127n, 630n, 756n, 806n
Pettigrew, Gene R., 146n
Pettit, Justin M., 346, 347n
Phillips, Michael M., 887n, 888n, 890n, 897n,
    899n, 902n, 906n
Phillips, Susan M., 40, 657, 677n
Plasencia, W., 339n
Polakoff, Murray E., 542n
Pollack, Andrew, 411n
Polwitonn, Sirapat, 906n
Porter, Gary E., 146n
Powell, Bill, 897n
Power, William, 517n
Pozdena, Randall J., 140n, 853n
Pozen, Robert C., 336, 336n, 337n, 339n,
    448n, 453n, 457n, 459n, 464n, 470n

Priess, Beth, 852n
Pringle, John J., 711n
Property/Casualty Insurance Facts 1998,
    362n
Protopadakis, Aris, 552n
Puglisi, Donald J., 791n
Pui-Wing Tam, 401n, 447n, 458n
Pullian, Susan, 147n, 482n

Quarterly Journal, 790n, 895n

Radding, Alan, 833n
Radecki, Lawrence J., 799n
Rader, Jack S., 469n, 470n, 473n, 475, 475n,
    476, 476n, 477n, 478n, 480n, 481n, 482n
Raghavan, Anita, 116n, 129n, 320n, 399n,
    401n, 514n, 908n
Rahman, Shafiqur, 479n
Rajan, Raghuram G., 821n
Ramo, Joshua Cooper, 21n, 22n
Randall, Richard E., 357
Randle, William M., 773, 774n
Register, Charles A., 35n, 77n, 82n, 124n,
    130n, 130n, 131n, 146n, 160n, 267n, 268n,
    274n, 291n, 818n
Reichert, Alan K., 658n
Reilly, Frank K., 637n
Reising, Joseph J., 130n
Rejda, George E., 369n
Rekenthaler, John, 441
Remolona, Eli M., 500, 712n, 720n
Rhee, S. Ghon, 148n, 154n
Rhoades, Stephen, 140n
Rhoads, Christopher, 539n
Richardson, Gary M., 135n, 321n, 336n,
    339n
Richtel, Matt, 426n
Ries, William Campbell, 328n
Ring, Niamh, 336n, 338n
Ritter, Jay R., 146n
Robertson, William R., 322n, 323, 324,
    324n
Robinson, Roland I., 751n
Rocky Mountain News, 250n
Roden, Diane M., 267n, 806n
Rodgers, Steve, 851n
Rogowski, Robert J., 803n, 805n
Rohter, Larry, 892n
Roley, V. Vance, 605n
Roll, Richard, 605n
Romer, P.M., 276n
Roos, N.R., 379n
Roosevelt, Phil, 513n
Rose, Andrew K., 551n
Rose, John, 140n
Rose, Nancy L., 35n
Rose, Peter S., 116n, 120n, 129n
Rose, Robert L., 479n
Rose, Sanford, 833n
Rose, Terry, 386n
Rosen, Kenneth T., 476n
Rosen, Richard, 34n, 124n, 140n
Rosenbaum, Mary S., 735n, 736n
Ross, Stephen A., 173, 332n, 595n, 602n,
    604n
Rudnitsky, Howard, 492n
Ruff, Craig K., 800n, 805n

Saidenberg, Mark R., 35n, 124n
Salem, George, 715n
Samuelson, Paul, 631n
Sandor, Richard L., 721n
Sanger, David E., 817n, 907n
Santoni, G.J., 548n
Sapsford, Jathon, 7n, 817n
Saunders, Anthony, 35n, 115, 124n, 131n,
    140, 140n, 159n, 296n, 343n, 344n, 348n,
    349n, 353n, 358, 358n, 369n, 380n, 399n,
    403n, 421n, 424n, 430n, 610n, 635n, 637n,
    676n, 756n, 832n, 835n, 844n, 860n, 896n,
    898n
Savage, Donald T., 140n
Savage, Terry, 6n
Savings Institutions, 803n
Scalise, Joseph M., 40, 116n
Scarlata, Jodi G., 662n
Schemo, Diana J., 882, 883, 888n, 890, 892
Schiller, Robert J., 605n
Schleifer, Andrei, 464n, 479n
Schmeitzer, John, 513n
Schmitt, Richard B., 267, 731n
Schneeweis, Thomas, 674n
Schoenholtz, Kermit L., 605n
Schrand, Catherine, 145n, 146n
Schroeder, Michael, 46n, 116n, 139n
Schultz, Ellen E., 447n, 482n
Schwadel, Francine, 513n
Schwartz, David M., 513n
Schwartz, Edward D., 674n
Schweitzer, 784n
Scism, Leslie, 147n, 149n, 517n, 518n
Scott, Charlotte H., 797n
Scott, William L., 630n
Sealey, C.W., 34n
Sease, Douglas R., 630n
Securities Industry Association, 403n, 414n,
    416n
Securities Industry Trends, 398n
Seiberg, Janet, 333n
Selden, Richard T., 55n, 493n
Sesit, Michael R., 885n, 908n
Sevick, Matthew, 458, 458n
Seward, 18n
Shapiro, Alan C., 576n
Shapiro, Harvey D., 495n
Sharpe, William F., 464n, 475, 476n, 555n
Shaw, W., 279n
Sherlock, Patricia M., 642n
Sheshunoff Bank & S&L Quarterly, 179,
    252n, 262n, 277n, 310n, 321n, 325n, 650n
Shiller, Robert J., 549n
Shirkhand, Milind M., 721n
Shulka, Ravi, 464n
Shull, Bernard, 36n, 61n, 131n
Siconolfi, Michael, 412n, 513n, 515n, 517n
Sidhu, Rupinder S., 637n
Siegel, David, 288n, 753n
Siegel, Jeremy J., 549n
Siems, Jeffrey W., 659n
Siems, Thomas F., 659n
Sihler, William W., 21n, 116n, 263n, 300n,
    305n, 309n, 322n, 399n, 416n, 423n, 492n,
    493n, 496n, 512n, 514n, 518n, 521n
Silber, William, 47n
Sill, Keith, 658n

Simmons, Katerina, 467
Simon, Ruth, 321n, 411n
Simons, 856n
Simons, Katerina, 145n, 343n, 344n
Simonson, Donald G., 131n, 635n, 748n, 847n, 848n, 852n, 894n
Simpson, Gary W., 146n
Sindelar, Jody L., 146n
Sinkey, Joseph F., Jr., 348n, 495n, 659n, 711n, 844n
Siwolop, Sana, 409n
Slovin, Myron B., 844n
Slowinski, Samuel M., 494n
Smart, Tim, 849n
Smith, Brian P., 804n
Smith, Brian W., 340n
Smith, Bruce D., 144n
Smith, Clifford W., Jr., 18n, 711n
Smith, Dolores S., 829n, 835n
Smith, Donald J., 633n, 711n, 718n
Smith, Geoffrey, 2n, 453n, 508n
Smith, Randall, 396n, 422n, 515n, 573, 630n
Smith, Richard L., 659n
Smith, Roy C., 20-21, 425n, 711n, 908n
Smith, Stephen D., 160n
Smith, Warren L., 601n
Smithson, Charles W., 711n
Snider, Helen K., 123n
SNL Securities, 496n
Sollenberger, Harold M., 31n
Solt, Michael E., 552n
Spahr, Ronald W., 720n
Special Management Bulletin, 145n
Spellman, Lewis J., 276n, 807n
Spencer, Leslie, 375n
Spencer, Roger W., 604n
Spindle, Bill, 116n, 447n, 534n
Spindt, Paul, 677n
Spiro, Leah N., 395, 397n, 410n, 479n, 495n, 849n
Sprong, Kenneth, 745n
Stacy, Ronald L., 854n
Stahl, David, 502n
Staten, Michael, 805n
Stein, Robert W., 379n
Steinberg, Richard M., 468n
Steiner, Robert, 630n
Steiner, Thomas L., 124n
Steinmetz, Greg, 147n, 148n, 513n
Stevens, E.J., 593n, 734n, 735n
Stickney, Clyde P., 320n
Stiglitz, Joseph, 902n
Stigum, Marcia, 407n, 785n, 790n, 841n
Stoll, Hans R., 699n
Stolz, Richard W., 659n
Stone, Courtney C., 548n
Stonehill, Arthur I., 328n
Stover, Roger D., 146n
Strock, Elizabeth, 35n, 124n
Strongin, Steven, 556n, 576n
Strunk, N., 123n
Studer, Margaret, 148n
Stutzer, Michael J., 144n
Sullivan, Marianne, 561n, 885n
Sundarajan, V., 908n
Sushka, Marie E., 844n

Suskind, Ron, 2n
Sutch, Richard, 602n, 605n
Svaldi, Aldo, 775n
Swanson, Eleanor, 249
Swartz, Steve, 514n, 515n
Swary, Itzhak, 140n, 278n, 279n
Sweeney, Richard J., 630n
Sylla, Richard, 533

Tackett, Michael, 481n
Taggart, Robert A., Jr., 794n
Tagliabue, John, 10n
Talley, Karen, 325n
Talley, Samuel H., 140n
Tannenbaum, Ira L., 142n, 145n, 251n, 253n, 254n
Tanouye, Elyse, 858n
Tarhan, Vefa, 735n
Tatom, John A., 605n, 819n
Taub, Stephen, 515n
Tavakoli, Janet M., 722n
Taylor, David, 341n
Taylor, Herbert, 556n
Taylor, Jeffery, 662n
Taylor, Robert E., 74n, 273n
Taylor, William, 80n
Teitelbaum, Richard S., 358n
Tejada, Carlos, 859n
Templin, Neal, 482n
Tepper, Irwin, 115, 140, 140n, 908n
Terrell, Henry S., 895n
Tetenbaum, Robert M., 319, 325n, 327n, 328n, 329n
Thebner, Eric, 337n
Thomas, Paulette, 4n, 74n, 517n, 829n
Thompson, Roger, 481n
Thomson Savings Institution Directory, 252n, 262n
Throop, Adrian, 605n
Timme, Stephen G., 140n, 159, 159n
Timmons, Jeffrey A., 427n
Tipton, 630n
Tobin, James, 551n
Todd, Walker F., 895n
Toevs, Alden, 642n
Topf, Barry, 140n
Torres, Craig, 612n, 891n
Towey, Richard E., 34n
Travlos, Nicholas G., 35n, 124n
Treaster, Joseph B., 55n, 116n, 138n, 149n, 508n, 517n
Treynor, Jack L., 464n
Trigaux, Robert, 797n
Truell, Peter, 2n, 321n, 412n, 539n
Truman, Edwin M., 895n
Trzcinka, Charles, 464n
Tucker, Paula K., 129n
Tufano, Peter, 458, 458n, 658n, 715n
Tufaro, Paul S., 534n, 577n
Tully, Daniel P., 515n
Tuttle, Donald, 605n

Udell, Gregory F., 854n
Ulrich, Thomas A., 841n
Unal, Haluk, 145n, 146n, 288n
Urang, Sally, 556n
Uyemura, Dennis G., 345, 347n

Vames, Steven, 621, 622n
Van Dyke, Daniel T., 556n
Van Horne, James, 47n, 49n, 604n, 605n, 671n
Vanderford, David E., 605n
Vartanian, Thomas P., 251n, 253n
Vaughn, Emmett J., 362n
Venezia, Itzhak, 821n
Venkataraman, Subu, 343n
Verbrugge, James A., 35n, 146n, 276n
Vishny, Robert, 464n, 479n
Vogel, Thomas T., Jr., 882, 885n, 891n
Vojislav, Maksimovic, 146n

Wagster, John, 302n, 819n
Wakeman, Lee M., 711n
Waldman, Steven, 375n
Walker, Barbara, 249
Walker, David A., 153n, 260n, 263n, 300n, 780n
Wall, 800n
Wall, Larry D., 140n, 278n, 292n, 711n, 721n
Wall Street Journal, 41n, 46n, 74n, 76n, 147n, 173n, 250n, 262n, 320, 375n, 398n, 538, 561n, 817n, 832n
Wallace, David J., 775n
Wallace, Nancy E., 124n
Wallace, William H., 546n
Wallich, Henry C., 65n, 590n
Walter, Ingo, 115, 140, 140n, 908n
Walter, John R., 288n, 304n, 319, 322n, 855n
Walz, Daniel T., 604n
Wang, George H.K., 851n
Ward, Robert A., Jr., 694n
Warehouse receipts, loans and, 845
Warga, Arthur D., 630n
Warner, Joan, 706n
Warshawsky, Mark J., 469n, 482n
Wasserman, Craig M., 137n
Waters, Richard, 492n
Watro, 805n
Watson, Ronald D., 751n, 801n
Wayne, Leslie, 139n, 411n
Wayner, Peter, 156n
Webb, Sara, 885n
Weil, Roman, 631n, 639n
Weill, Sanford I., 40, 491
Weiner, Steve, 510n, 513n, 517n
Weiss, Gary, 479n
Wendel, Charles B., 357, 491
Wenninger, John, 800n
Wermiel, Stephen, 128n, 502n
Wessel, David, 551n, 891n
West, Robert Craig, 61n, 66n
Westerfield, Randolph W., 332n
Whalen, Gary, 123n, 140n
Whaley, Robert E., 699n
Whelpley, William, 785n
White, Lawrence J., 62n, 252n, 266n, 267n, 794n
Whitehead, David D., 129n
Whitehouse, Mark, 534n, 561n
Whittaker, J. Gregg, 711n
Whyte, Ann Marie, 124n
Widder, Pat, 712n
Wilke, John R., 250n
Willemse, Rob J.M., 788n

Williams, Elisa, 375n
Williams, Julie L., 772
Williams, Monci Jo, 512n, 513n
Williamson, Oliver, 33n
Williamson, Stephen D., 18n
Wilson, Greg, 519n, 677n, 689
Wingfield, Nick, 395, 398n
Winkler, Matthew, 517n
Winningham, Scott, 734n
Woerheide, Walter J., 35n, 146n, 453n
Wohar, Mark E., 35n, 145n, 146n
Wolf, Charles, Jr., 902n
Wolfe, Glenn A., 72n, 276n, 807n

Wolfson, Martin H., 853n
Wolken, John D., 798n
Wood, John H., 549n, 594n, 604n, 785n
Wood, Norma L., 549n, 785n
Woodruff, David, 895n
Woodstrom, Eric J., 329n
Woolley, Suzanne, 495n
Worthy, Ford S., 174n, 288n
Worzala, Elaine M., 476n
WuDUNN, Sheryl, 816, 817n
Wulfekuhler, Kurt C., 500
Wyatt, Edward, 458n

Yan, Ying, 35n, 124n
Yang, Catherine, 4n
Yawitz, Jess B., 637n, 642n
Young, 76n
Young, John E., 895n

Zaik, Edward, 304n, 319, 322n
Zeckhauser, Richard, 464n
Zimmerman, Gary C., 795n, 805n
Zuckerman, Gregory, 421n, 491, 492n, 536n, 891n
Zuckerman, Sam, 340n

SUBJECT INDEX

ACH. *See* Automated clearinghouse services
Advanta Corporation, 2
Affiliates, ownership structure, 444-446
Agency costs, defined, 33
Agency relationships, between financial institutions and government, 35
Agency securities, 756-758
Agency theory, asset/liability management and, 32-33
Agent, defined, 32-33
Allstate Insurance, 141
Annual Statistics on Banking, 202
Arbitrage. *See also* Index arbitrage
    discussed, 611-612
Asian financial crisis, 6-7. *See also*
    Financial crisis
    attempts to help, 906-908
    financial institution involvement in, 905-906
    recap, 899-902
    warning signs, 902-905
Asset utilization (AU)
    analysis, 203-205
    trends, 191
Asset/liability management. *See also* Financial institutions; Liability management; Liquidity management; Profit
    burden management, 30-31
    defined, 31
    duration and, 637-638
    financial futures and, 678
    in general, 29
    insurance companies, 386-387
    objectives
      normative approach, 32
      positive approach, 32-33
    spread management, 30
      net interest margin (NIM), 30
Assets. *See* Financial assets
Assurbanking model, 376-377
Asymmetric information, in financial contract, 19
AU. *See* Asset utilization
Automated Clearing House System, 332
Automated clearinghouse services (ACH), 21

Baby Boomers
    investment expectations of, 6
    Social Security and, 12-13
Balance sheets. *See also* Financial statements
    finance companies, 496-499
    insurance companies, 364-366
    in loan application, 838
    securities firms, 421
Banc One, 199, 260
Bancassurance model, 341, 376
Bank of America
    merger with Nations Bank, 5, 116, 260
    stock buybacks, 311
Bank holding companies (BHCs). *See also*
    Financial holding companies
    corporate separateness in, 132
    equity capital regulations and, 125-126

franchising and chain banks, 142
in general, 124
geographic diversification benefits, 126-127, 130-131
IBBEA national model, 128-130
MSLHCs and interstate branching, 130
multibank (MBHC), 126-127, 128, 203
multiple (MSLHCs), 130
non banks, 128
for nonbank financial institutions, 141-142
product restrictions loophole, 131
regulation
    corporate separateness, 132-134
    firewalls separating subsidiaries, 134, 135-140
    franchising and chain banks, 142
    holding companies for nonbank financial institutions, 141-142
    product restrictions on affiliates, 131-132
    relaxation of, 134-135
    universal banking, 140
Section 20 subsidiaries, 132-134
superregionals, 128
universal banking forms, 140
Bank Holding Company Act, provisions, 44, 131
Bank Insurance Fund (BIF), 50, 252
Bank for International Settlements, study, 335
Bank of New England, 2
Bank notes, compared to CDs, 791-792
Bankers acceptances, 181
Bankers' banks, operations, 331
Banker's Trust, merger with Alex Brown, 13
Banking Act of 1933. *See* Glass-Stegall Act
Bankruptcy, 502
Bankruptcy Reform Act, 848
Banks. *See also* Commercial banks; Financial institutions; Savings banks
    consumer, 128
    correspondent, 174, 329-331
    deposit structure, 780-782
    dual banking system, 50
    foreign, 140
    investment portfolio, 753-754
    limited service, 71
    non-bank banks, 71, 128
    peer groups for, 203
    superregionals, 128
Barbell strategy, 750
Barnett Supreme Court Decision, 341
Basle Accord, 84
BCCI scandal, 85, 105
Bear market, hedging in, 694
"Bet the Bank" strategies, in thrift crisis, 276
BHCs. *See* Bank holding companies
BIF. *See* Bank Insurance Fund
Bond theorems, discussed, 627-629
Bonds. *See also* Interest rate risk; *specific bond types*
    annual yield calculation, 623-625

duration, 632-633
Euro zone government bond market, 6
mortgage-backed, 791
reinvestment and price risk, 625-627
Brady Bonds, 896
Brady Commission, 699
Branch banking
    interstate, 5
    regulation effecting, 2
Brazil, financial crisis, 884-893
Bridge banks, 279
Brokers. *See also* Stock
    compared to dealers, 17, 18
    discount brokers, 13
    duties of, 13
    full-service brokers, 13
    for thrift deposits, 71-72
Bull market, hedging in, 696
Burden
    calculating, 187-188
    management of, 30-31
    profit and, 185
Business ethics, 84-85

California, Proposition 103, 57
CAMELS
    applications, 119, 299, 300
    defined, 54
Capital. *See also* Cash; Funds; Money
    compared, of thrifts, banks, credit unions, 266-267
    dividend policies, 311-312
    dividend theories, 312-313
    equity, 119, 125-126
    excess, 310-311
    market vs. book value definition
      cushions against losses, 288-289
      in general, 286
      market value calculation difficulties, 286-288
    preferences by agents
      regulators, 291
      stockholders, 289-290
      uninsured debtholders and managers, 290-291
    RAROC (risk-adjusted return on capital), 304-305
    regulatory definitions, 293-295
      minimum capital requirements, 295
      Tier 1/tangible equity, 293-295
      Tier 1/Tier 2 illustration, 295
      Tier 2/supplemental, 293-295
    regulatory issues
      capital allocations, 304-307
      capital and growth management, 302-304
      capital structure approach, 307-309
      capital structure determination, 304
    returned to shareholders
      excess capital in 1990s, 309-310
      stock buybacks, 311
    risk-based assets calculation, 296-297

Capital (cont.)
  shareholder and regulator interests
    capital structure with deposit insurance, 291-292
    changes over time, 293
    regulatory definitions of capital, 293-295
Capital adequacy
  capital requirements issues, 301-302
  for federal credit unions, 300
  for federal thrifts, 299-300
  in general, 298-299
Capital management, 215
Capital ratios, determining, 298
Capital requirements
  adequacy issues, 301-302
  thrifts, 77, 276
Caps, mortgage, 851
Cash. See also Capital; Liquidity; Money
  digital, 155-157
Cash flow, lending on, 847-848
Cash management, corporate, 331-332
Cash-balance plans (CBP), pension plan conversion to, 482-483
CBP. See Cash-balance plans
CEBA. SEE Competitive Equality Banking Act
Centrust Savings, 33
Certificates of deposit (CDs)
  brokered CDs, 181
  Eurodollar CDs, 181
  jumbo CDs, 181
  money market certificate, 63n
  negotiable (jumbo), 787-788
  retail, 181
  time deposits, 181
  "Wild Card" certificates, 63n
Chain banks, BHCs and, 142
Charles Schwab Corporation, 411
Chase Manhattan, 31
Check-clearing services, by correspondent banks, 330-331
Checking accounts, bank services and, 10
Chemical Bank, mergers, 31
CHIPS. See Clearing House Interbank Payments System
Citicorp
  merger with Travelers Group, 5, 6, 40-41
  Y2K bug costs, 22
Classical theory, mutual organizations and, 34
Clearing balances, 737
Clearing House Interbank Payments System (CHIPS), 96, 790
Clearinghouse, 660-661
Clifford, Clark, 85
CMOs
  types of, 758-759
    plain vanilla, 758
    planned amortization class, 758
    stripped mortgage-backed securities, 758-759
Collateral, loans, 845
Commercial banks. See also Banks; Savings banks
  assets, 9-10, 14, 174, 177-180
    annual compound growth rates, 268-269

    compared to thrifts and CUs, 263-265
  financial statements overview, 174-176
  liabilities, 14
    compared to thrifts and CUs, 265-266
  loan sales by, 348-349
  profitability, 272
  regulation, 50-51
  size and industry structure, 260-261
  vault cash, 174
Common bond requirement. See also Credit unions
  for credit unions, 152-153
Common size statements, analysis, 205-211
Community banking, thrift institutions and, 11
Community protection, under IBBEA, 129-130
Community Reinvestment Act (CRA), 828-829
  requirements, 2, 129
  revisions, 858-859
Compensating balance requirements, loans, 841
Competitive Equality Banking Act (CEBA)
  discussed, 72-74
  provisions, 44, 50, 73, 128, 253
Comprehensive consolidated supervision, 106
Concentration bank, defined, 332
Conduit theory, 60
Confidence-sensitive money, 790
Congress, regulatory and deregulatory periods, 4
Consumer Credit Protection Act (1968), 55
Consumer protection legislation, finance companies, 55-56
Contemporaneous reserve accounting (CRA), 736
Contingent liabilities, in risk measurement, 84
Continental Illinois National Bank, collapse, 97
Contract. See Financial contract; Futures contract
Contractual intermediaries
  contractual savings institutions, 12
  described, 12-13
  insurance companies, 12
  pension funds, 12-13
"Convenience and advantage rule," finance companies, 55
Conversion, of mutual firms to thrifts, 145-146
Corporate credit unions (CCUs), 153, 259-260, 321. See also Credit unions
Corporate separateness, 132
Correspondent banks, 174. See also Banks
  check-clearing services, 330-331
  in general, 329-330
Counterparties, interest rate swaps, 711
Country risk. See also International lending; Risk
  analyzed, 897-898
Covenants, loans and, 846
CRA. See Community Reinvestment Act; Contemporaneous reserve accounting

Credit
  5 C's of, 830-831
  quantitative scoring models, consumer, 832-835
Credit card, loans from, 848-849
Credit card companies, 495
Credit derivatives. See also Derivatives
  discussed, 721-722
Credit process. See also Lending; Loans
  bank written loan policies, 827-828
  business development and, 827
  default risk and, 826-827
  loan committee review, 827
Credit risk management. See also Risk management
  improving, 860
Credit Union Annual Report, 202
Credit union service organizations (CUSOs), 153
Credit unions (CUs). See also Not-for-profit organizations
  assets
    annual compound growth rates, 269-270
    compared to thrifts and banks, 263-265
  capital, 266-267, 300
  common bond requirement, 152-153
  corporate, 153
  deposit insurance coverage, 806-807
  described, 11-12
  federal, 118n, 272
    capital requirements, 300
  in general, 249-250
  history, membership requirements and regulations, 255-258
  insurance activities of, 342
  investment portfolio, 755-756
  liabilities, compared to thrifts and banks, 265-266
  National Credit Union Act (1924) regulations, 46
  National Credit Union Administration (NCUA), 51, 255
  profitability, 272-273
  size and industry structure, 263
  support systems for, 259-260
Cross-intermediation, 62
Currency exchange rates. See also Exchange rates; Foreign exchange transactions
  direct/indirect rate, 569
  forward currency market, 570-571
  in general, 564-570
  introduction of Euro, 576-578
  risk and, 568-570
Currency futures. See also Financial futures
  foreign, 678-680
  illustrated, 680-682
CUs. See Credit unions
CUSOs. See Credit union service organizations
Customer costs, 1
Customer needs, managerial objectives and, 34

Day trading, 408-409
Daylight overdrafts, 96
Dealers, compared to brokers, 17, 18

Debt-for-equity swaps, 896
Defined benefit plans, management issues, 473
Degree of operating leverage, 794. *See also* Leverage
Demand, for loanable funds, 540-542
Deposit accounts
  pricing, 799-803, 804-805
    conditionally free, 802, 804-805
    interest buydown, 802-803
    tiered, 803
Deposit insurance. *See* Federal deposit insurance
Deposit management. *See also* Liability management
  factors to consider, 776-779
  in general, 773-775
Deposit notes, compared to CDs, 791-792
Depository Institution Deregulation and Monetary Control Act (1980) (DIDMCA)
  discussed, 66-68, 252
  provisions, 44, 48, 49, 67, 95
Depository institutions. *See also* Financial institutions; Savings institutions
  described, 9-12
  disclosure requirements, 803-804
  federal deposit insurance and, 805-807
  investment portfolio management, types of securities, 748-749
  liquidity restrictions, 730-731, 749-750
  noninterest competition among, 793
  performance comparisons
    asset annual growth rates, 268-269
    income statement comparisons, 273-274
    profitability, 270-273
  regulation
    analysis, 54-55
    commercial banks, 50-51
    summary, 51-54
    thrifts, 51
Depository institutions failure, contagion of, 278-279
Deposits
  bank liabilities and, 180
  core, 181, 793-794
  nontransaction, 181
  "pledged," 177
  of thrifts, banks, and credit unions, compared, 265
  transaction, 180
  uninsured
    hot funds, 181
    purchased funds, 181
    volatile liabilities, 181
Deregulation. *See also* Regulation
  technology and, 4
Derivatives
  characteristics, 5, 20
  credit, 721-722
  in general, 689-690
  insurance, 720-721
  pension funds and, 477-478
DIDMCA. *See* Depository Institution Deregulation and Monetary Control Act

Digital signature authentication (DSA), 155
Direct marketing, 452
Direct writer system, insurance sales, 377
Disclosure requirements, depository institutions, 803-804
Discount rate. *See also* Interest rate
  Fed policy and, 92, 99-100
Disinflation, 546
Disintermediation, described, 62
Diversification
  geographic, 126-127, 130-131
  international lending and, 898
  IRS test, 457
  provided by mutual funds, 19, 446-447
  of thrifts, banks, credit unions, compared, 265
Dividends
  capital management policies and, 311-312
  insurance companies, 364-365
  theories about, 312-313
Douglas Amendment, Bank Holding Company Act, 44
Downstreaming, by bank holding companies, 126
DSA. *See* Digital signature authentication
Dual banking system, 50
Duration
  asset/liability management and, 637-638
  bonds, 632-633
  defined, 631-632
  interest rate risk measurement and, 621-622, 637, 643-644
  interest rate term structure and, 638
  modified, 636-637
  securities, 633
Duration gap, calculating, 644-647
Duration-based futures hedge, 687-688

E-cash, discussed, 156-157
EC. *See* European Community
ECB. *See* European Central Bank
ECU. *See* European Currency Unit
Edge Act, 105
EDI. *See* Electronic data interchange
Efficiency ratios, performance analysis, 215-216
Efficient markets hypothesis, 690-691
Electronic data interchange (EDI), defined, 332
Emergency acquisitions, 70
Employee Retirement Income Security Act (ERISA)
  pension funds and, 468-473
  provisions, 44, 58
EMU. *See* European Monetary Union
Environmental liability, 857-858. *See also* Liability
Equal Credit Opportunity Act (1974), 55, 828
Equity
  of bank stockholders, 181
  compared, of thrifts, banks, credit unions, 266
  leverage and, 117-118
  measurement, 118-120
Equity capital. *See also* Capital
  defined, 119

Equity capital regulations, bank holding companies and, 125-126
ERISA. *See* Employee Retirement Income Security Act
Ethics, investment banking and, 409-412
Euro, introduction of, 576-578
Euro zone government bond market, 6
Eurodollar deposits, using, 788-790
Eurofed, 107
Europe, common currency issues, 5, 6
European Central Bank (ECB), 107
European Community (EC), monetary policy, 107-108
European Currency Unit (ECU), 107
European Monetary Union (EMU), 6, 107
EVA. *See also* Risk management
  risk management program, 345-346
Exchange rates. *See also* Currency exchange rates
  in general, 564-570
  gold standard and, 104
  risk and, 568-570
  theories and forecasting, 534-535, 571-575

Factoring, loans and, 845
Fair Credit Reporting Act, 828
Fair Housing Act, 828
Fannie Mae. *See* Federal National Mortgage Association
FBSEA. *See* Foreign Bank Supervision Enhancement Act
FCA. *See* Financial Corporation of America
FDIC. *See* Federal Deposit Insurance Corporation
FDICIA. *See* Federal Deposit Insurance Corporation Improvement Act
Fed funds purchased (FFP), 177, 181
Fed funds sold, 177
Fed. *See* Federal Reserve System
Federal Accounting Standards Board (FASB), market-value accounting (MVA) practices, 119-120
Federal deposit insurance
  affecting depository institutions, 805-807
  capital structure for, 291-292
  coverage provided, 807-808
  credit union insurance, 806-807
  moral hazard of, 121-123, 290
Federal Deposit Insurance Corporation (FDIC)
  establishment, 46, 50-51
  operation, 252, 299
Federal Deposit Insurance Corporation Improvement Act (1991) (FDICIA), 50
  provisions, 45, 79, 97, 287
  thrift bailouts, 78-81
Federal Financial Institutions Examination Council (FFIEC), 53
Federal Financing Bank, 80
Federal funds purchased, 785-786
Federal funds rate. *See also* Interest rate
  monetary policy and, 99
Federal Home Loan Bank Act (1932), 46, 51
Federal Home Loan Bank Board (FHLBB), 51, 76, 252
Federal Home Loan Bank System (FHLB), provisions, 43

Federal National Mortgage Association (Fannie Mae), 251
Federal Open Market Committee (FOMC), 99
Federal Reserve System (Fed), 50
  assets, 94-95
  banks and branches, 93
  Clearing House Interbank Payments System (CHIPS), 96
  daylight overdrafts, 96
  discount rate and, 92
  history, 92
  international policy
    coordination, 91-94
    gold standard, 104
    monetary policy and, 104-105
    regulation, 105-108
  as lender of last resort, 92, 94, 96-97
  liabilities and capital, 95
  monetary policy
    asset/liability management, 101-103
    goals, 97
    international policy and, 104-105
    money definition, 97-99
    targets, 99
    tools, 99-101
  organization, 92-94
  payments system and, 95-96
  Section 20 standards, 136-137
Federal Savings and Loan Insurance Corporation (FSLIC), 51, 76, 252
Fedwire, 95
Fee income
  corporate cash management and, 331-332
  correspondent banking and, 329-331
  from off-balance sheet activities
    foreign exchange transactions, 348
    in general, 347
    letters of credit, 348
    loan commitments, 348
    note issuance facilities, 348
  in general, 322-323
  National City Bank Corporation strategy, 323-324
  noninterest revenues, 325
Fee-based activities
  banks entry into, 347
  overview
    additional state powers, 333
    Bank for International Settlements study, 335
    bank mutual funds, 335-336
    in general, 325-327
    performance and risk, 334-335
    trust and personal planning, 327-329
FFIEC. *See* Federal Financial Institutions Examination Council
FFP. *See* Fed funds purchased
FHLB. *See* Federal Home Loan Bank System
FHLBB. *See* Federal Home Loan Bank Board
Fidelity Investment Company, operating companies, 151
Fiduciary responsibility, pension funds, 58
Finance companies
  described, 12

income, expenses, profitability, 499-501
industry structure, balance sheet composition, 496-499
overview, 492-493
performance measurement, 502-504
  credit risk, 504
  financial leverage, 504
  liquidity ratios, 503-504
regulation, 501-502
  consumer protection legislation, 55-56
  licensing restrictions, 55
types of
  commercial, 494
  consumer, 493-494
  credit card companies, 495
  diversified, 494-495
  government sponsored enterprises, 495-496
  securitizations, 495
Financial assets. *See also* Reserves; Revenues
  annual growth rates, 268-269
  compared, of thrifts, banks, credit unions, 263-265
  compared to real assets, 7
  off-balance sheet, 296-298
  risk-based, 296-298
  of U.S. commercial banks, 9-10
Financial conglomerates
  development of, 508-511
  financial megaplayers and, 519-520
  General Electric, 513-514
  Merrill Lynch, 514-515
  Prudential, 515-518
  Sears, 512-513
  trends, 511
Financial contract
  asymmetric information and, 19
  between principal and agent, 32-33
  defined, 19
Financial Corporation of America (FCA), 35n, 200, 252
Financial crisis. *See also* Asian financial crisis
  in general, 884-893
Financial firms
  managerial implications, 518-521
  overview, 504-508
Financial futures. *See also* Hedging; Stock index futures
  in asset/liability management, 678
  contracts, 660-661
    number of, 673-675, 695-696
  currency futures, 678-680
  duration-based futures hedge, 687-688
  financial institutions and, 659
  forward vs. futures markets, 680-682
  future prices and market yields, 665-666
  gap management and, macro vs. micro hedges, 675-676
  interest rate futures
    in general, 663
    hedging and, 665
    terms of contracts, 664
  options, defined, 700-701
  risk and
    basis risk, 670-672
    incorrect rate forecasts, 670

Financial futures transactions
  limits on price changes, 663
  margin, 663
Financial holding companies. *See also* Bank holding companies
  discussed, 124
  for mutual insurance companies, 148-149
  for mutual thrifts, 149
  for nonbank financial institutions, 141-142
  service corporations, 152
Financial innovation
  inflation and, 546-548
  origins, 49-50, 61-66
  procedures, 47-49
  timing and context of, 65
Financial institutions. *See also* Depository institutions; Savings institutions
  assets and liabilities of, 14
  changing times for, 3-7
  described
    contractual intermediaries, 12-13
    depository institutions, 9-12
    finance companies, 12
    investment companies, 13
    securities firms, 13-14
    thrift institutions, 11
  economic functions
    in general, 15
    transfer of funds and, 16-18
  economies of scale and scope, 157-160
  equity ownership effects
    conflicts, 121
    managerial stock ownership risk, 123-124
    moral hazard of deposit insurance, 121-123
  financial assets by percentage distribution, 10
  financial futures and, 659
  industry differences in, 14-15
  intermediation
    maturity intermediation and liquidity, 20
    monitoring costs, 19
    portfolio selection costs, 18-19
    risk management costs, 19-20, 22
    search costs, 18
  leverage effects
    equity effects, 120-121
    equity is ownership, 117-118
    equity/net worth measurement, 118-120
  managerial objectives
    customer needs, 34
    evidence from research, 34-35
    ownership structure affecting, 34
  mergers, 520-521
  mergers between, 5, 6, 11
  role and purposes, 3
  societal concerns with change, 22
  technology effects on, 1-2, 6, 20-22
  virtual, 154-157
  vs. nonfinancial firms, 7-9
Financial Institutions Reform, Recovery, and Enforcement Act (FIRREA)
  in general, 74-75

provisions, 45, 50, 75, 250, 287
thrift bailout legislation, 75-78
Financial investment, indirect, 17
Financial liabilities
  compared, of thrifts, banks, credit unions,
    265-266
  discussed, 8-9
Financial services, defined, 504
Financial statements. *See also* Income state-
    ments
  analysis, 835-836
  balance sheets, securities firms, 421
  bank profits, NIM trends, 184-187
  for commercial banks, 174-176
    balance sheet trends, 175-176
  for FDIC-insured banks
    assets, 177-180
    liabilities, stock, equity capital, 180-182
  in general, 173-174
  off-balance-sheet items
    foreign exchange contracts, 197
    interest rate contracts, 197
    letters of credit, 195
    loan commitments, 195-196
    mortgage transferred with recourse,
      197
    when-issued securities, 197
  securities firms, 412-413
Firewalls, 74
  for BHCs, 134, 135-140
FIRREA. *See* Financial Institutions Reform,
    Recovery, and Enforcement Act
First Direct bank, 154-155
First National Bank of Maryland, perfor-
    mance analysis, 216-223
Fisher effect, evaluation of, 548-549, 551-556
Fleet Financial Group, discussed, 2, 5
FNMA. *See* Uniform Residential Loan Ap-
    plication
FOMC. *See* Federal Open Market Commit-
    tee
Foreign Bank Supervision Enhancement Act
    (FBSEA), 105-106
Foreign banks. *See also* International banking
  national treatment for, 107
  regulation of, 80-81
Foreign exchange contracts, 197
Foreign exchange transactions. *See also* Cur-
    rency exchange; Exchange rate
  fee income from, 348
Franchising, BHCs and, 142
Franklin National Bank, 97
FSLIC. *See* Federal Savings and Loan Insur-
    ance Corporation
Full Employment and Balanced Growth Act
    (1978), 97
Fund management, outsourced, 336-337
Funds. *See also* Capital
  mix of sources, 799
  wholesale vs. retail, 797-798
Funds acquisition, in deregulated environ-
    ment, 797
Funds transfer. *See* Transfer of funds
Futures contracts
  defined, 660
  discussed, 659-661
  hedging vs. speculation, 660

G-7. *See* Group of Seven
G-ST G. *See* Garn-St. Germain Depository
    Act
GAAPs. *See* Generally accepted accounting
    practices
Garn-St. Germain Depository Act (G-ST G)
  discussed, 66-68, 69-70
  provisions, 44, 49, 68, 130, 252, 340
General Electric, 513-514
General Motors Acceptance Corporation
    (GMAC), 12
Generally accepted accounting practices
    (GAAPs), application to thrifts, 71,
    267
Geometric average, 595
GICs. *See* Guaranteed investment contracts
Ginnie Mae. *See* Government National
    Mortgage Association
Glass-Stegall Act (1933)
  provisions, 43, 46, 51
  restrictions on banks and insurers, 40, 81,
    96, 333
  Section 16, 132
  Section 20, 132-134
Global marketplace, developing, 661-662
Globalization
  of financial markets, 84
  opportunities in, 5
  regulation and, 105
Globex, 662
GMAC. *See* General Motors Acceptance
    Corporation
Gold, 94
Gold standard, Fed policy and, 104
Government. *See also* Regulation
  regulatory policies of, 41-42
  relationships with financial institutions, 35
Government National Mortgage Association
    (Ginnie Mae), 251
Government securities. *See also* Securities
  investment in, 760
Government sponsored enterprises, 495-496
Great Depression, 45, 96, 104
Group of Seven (G-7), monetary policy and,
    104-105
Guaranteed investment contracts (GICs),
    479

Hedge funds, 321-322
  lending to, 854
Hedge ratio, calculating, 674
Hedges, short vs. long, 666-670
Hedging
  basis risk and, 673
  contracts, 197, 660-661, 664, 673-675,
    695-696
  cross hedge, 673
  duration-based futures hedge, 687-688
  with interest rate futures, 665
  macro vs. micro hedges, 675-676
  with options, 705-708
  options compared to, 709-711
  in stock index futures, 695
  with swaps, 712-716
  in upturn, 696
  vs. speculation, 660
  vs. swaps, 717

HMDA. *See* Home Mortgage Disclosure Act
Holding companies. *See* Bank holding com-
    panies
Home banking services, 154-157
Home Mortgage Disclosure Act (HMDA),
    828
Home Owners' Loan Act, 254
Hot money, 790
Household, as financial intermediary, 3

IBBEA. *See* Riegle-Neal Interstate Banking
    and Branching Efficiency Act
IBFs. *See* International banking facilities
ILSA. *See* International Lending Supervision
    Act
Immunization. *See* Portfolio immunization
Income statements. *See also* Financial state-
    ments; Net operating income
  depository institutions, 273-274
  FDIC-insured banks
    expenses, 182
    net income, 182-184
    revenues, 182
  securities firms, 416-420
Index arbitrage, program trading and, 697-
    698
Index futures. *See also* Financial futures
  discussed, 700
Individual retirement accounts (IRAs), 470
Indonesia, financial crisis, 6
Inflation
  financial innovation and, 546-548
  interest rates and, 545-549
    Fisher effect, 548-549
  loanable funds theory and, 549-551
  theories and forecasting, 534-535
Information, asymmetric, 19
Initial public offering (IPO), registering and
    marketing, 427-430
Insider trading, 61, 408n
Insider Trading Act, 61
Insider Trading and Securities Fraud En-
    forcement Act (1988), 61
Insurance activities
  bank participation in, 339-341
  distribution systems, technology affecting,
    377-378
  liability and regulatory risk in, 342-343
  of thrifts and CUs, 342
Insurance companies. *See also* Life insurance
    companies; Mutual firms; P/L com-
    panies
  asset management considerations, 386-387
  balance sheets, life insurers, 364-366
  capital requirements, risk-based, 380
  expenses
    life insurers, 361-362
    P/L insurers, 362-363
    statutory accounting procedures, 363-
      364
  liquidity risk, 746-747
  mutual form of organization, 34
    conversion to "demutualize," 146-148
    holding companies for, 148-149
  overview of operations, 378-379
  in general, 358-361
  procedures of, 12

Insurance companies (cont.)
  regulation
    asset structure, 58
    in general, 56-57
    licensing and solvency requirements, 57
    product regulation, 58
    rate regulation, 57
  regulatory monitoring, 381
  revenues, 359-360
  social and economic factors affecting, 373-377
  solvency ratings, 381
Insurance derivatives. See also Derivatives
  discussed, 720-721
Interest payments, implicit, 793
Interest rate caps, 718-720
Interest rate collars, 718-720
Interest rate contracts, 197
Interest rate elasticity, estimating, 635-637
Interest rate floors, 718-720
Interest rate futures. See also Discount rate
  in general, 663
  hedging and, 665
  regulatory restrictions and financial reporting, 676-678
  terms of contracts, 664
Interest rate parity theorem, 572-573
Interest rate risk. See also Bonds
  capital standards and, 301
  defined, 622
  effects on common stock, 630
  implications for financial institutions, 629-630
  market value risk, 626-627
  portfolio immunization and, 639-642
  reinvestment risk, 626-627
Interest rate risk management, discussed, 214-215
Interest rate risk measurement
  duration and, 621-622
  duration gap, 643-644
  estimating percentage price changes, 634-635
  price/yield connection, 622
  price/yield relationship, 623-625
Interest rate swaps
  callable, 718
  exotic swaps, 716-717
    commodity, 716
    equity, 716-717
  in general, 711-712
  as hedging tool, 712-716
    important factors, 713-715
    plain vanilla, 712-713
  motivation for, 712
  regulation, 715
  stock price risk issues, 715-716
  swap options and futures, 717-718
  vs. hedging, 717
Interest rate term structure
  duration and, 638
  emerging theories, 603-604
  empirical tests
    liquidity premium evidence, 605
    measuring expectations, 604-605
    segmented markets and preferred habitats, 605-606

financial institutions management and, 606
  in general, 584-585
  identifying
    in general, 585-586
    general level of interest rates, 589-594
    historical overview, 587-588
  interest rate forecasting
    in general, 606-608
    institutional, 608-610
  loan risk premium establishment, 610-611
  role of lenders
    modified expectations theory, 601
    preferred habitat theory, 602-603
    segmented markets theory, 601-602
  unbiased (pure) expectations theory
    assumptions, 594-595
    mathematics, 595-597
    modifications, 597
Interest rates. See also Loanable funds theory
  annual yield calculation
    bank discount yield, 557
    coupon equivalent yield, 557
    effective, 557
    example, 557-560
    in general, 556-557
  disclosing, 803-804
  effect on profitability, 4
  Federal Reserve policy affecting, 100
  forecasting, 543-545, 555-556
  general level, 539
  historical overview, 535-539
  inflation and, 545-549
  theories
    in general, 534-535
    theory and management, 535
Intermediation
  direct financial investment and, 17
  maturity intermediation and liquidity, 20
  monitoring costs, 19
  portfolio selection costs, 18-19
  risk management costs, 19-20, 22
  search costs, 18
Internal Revenue Code, Subchapter M, 457
Internal Revenue Service (IRS)
  diversification test, 457
  Short 3's Test, 457
International accounting, transparency needs, 907-908
International banking. See also Foreign banks; International lending
  currency translations for, 201n
International Banking Act (1978), 105
International banking facilities (IBFs), 105
International lending. See also International banking; Lending
  country risk, 897-898, 898-899
  diversification, 898
  in general, 893-894
  problems with LDCs, 894-897
International Lending Supervision Act (ILSA), 895
Internet, insurance sales, 377-378
Investment. See Financial investment
Investment accounting, rule restrictions, 753
Investment Act of 1933, 457
Investment Advisers Act (1940), 59

Investment bankers, duties, 13
Investment banking. See also Securities
  BHCs and, 141
  culture and ethics, 409-412
  expenses/revenues growth rate, 420-423
  structure and cycles, types of firms, 398-401
Investment companies. See also Mutual funds; Securities firms
  basic groups, 448-449
  described, 13
  money market mutual funds, 13
  mutual funds, 13
  regulation
    federal securities laws, 59
    funds regulations, 59-60
Investment Company Act, provisions, 43, 46, 150
Investment securities. See also Securities
  of banks, 177
Investment strategies, limitations on, 751-752
Investors, time preference for consumption, 540
IPO. See Initial public offering
IRAs. See Individual retirement accounts
IRS. See Internal Revenue Service

Japan, financial crisis, 7
Johnson, Edward C. "Ned," 151
Jumbo deposits, in thrift crisis, 71-72

Ladder of maturities, 749-750
Lagged reserve accounting (LRA), 736
Layoffs, 30, 31
LEAP. See Long-term equity anticipation securities
Lender liability, environmental liability, 857-858
Lending. See also Loans
  asset management and, 817-819
  bank written loan policies, 827-828
  commercial
    financial statement analysis, 835-836
    medium to small firms, 819-822
    quoted base rates, 843-844
    recent trends, 818-819
  compliance policies, 828-829
  consumer
    recent trends, 822-824
    sources, 825-826
  credit execution policies, 829
  5 C's of Credit, 830-831
  to hedge funds, 854
  high-risk
    leveraged buyouts, 853
    mezzanine lending, 853-854
  lender compensation policies, 829-830
  loan participations and syndications, 856-857
  loan request procedures, 830-832
  one-stop shopping, 859
Less developed countries (LDCs)
  financial crisis in, 107
  loans to, 894-897
Letters of credit, 19, 195
  fee income from, 348

Leverage
   of banks and savings institutions, 8, 9, 285-286
   of commercial banks and life insurance companies, 15
   degree of operating leverage, 794
   double leverage by bank holding companies, 126
   effects, equity is ownership, 117-118
   finance companies, 504
Leveraged buyouts, 853
Liability. See also Risk
   to cover reserve deficiencies, 784-786
   environmental, 857-858
   long tail of, 372
   to meet loan demand, 787-788
Liability management. See also Asset/liability management
   described, 743
   factors to consider, 776-779
   factors influencing use of, 792-793
   in general, 773-775
   history, 782-784
Liens, loans and, 845
Life insurance companies. See also Insurance companies
   asset management considerations, 386-387
   assets and liabilities, 14
   performance evaluation, 366-369
   policy types
      term insurance, 382
      trends in preferences for, 382-383
      universal life, 382
      variable life, 382
      whole life, 381-382
   premium determination, 383-385
   social and economic factors affecting, 375-377
   sources of financial information, 369
Lifetime banking, 796-797
LIFFE. See London International Financial Futures Exchange
Lines of credit, loans and, 841
Liquidity. See also Cash
   borrowing for, 744-745
   calculating, 560
   depository institutions, 730-731, 749-750
   discretionary/nondiscretionary factors
      in general, 740
      liquidity estimation, 741-743
   importance of, 730-731
   in loan securitizations, 746
   managing, 743-745
   maturity intermediation and, 20
   risk/return tradeoff
      in general, 733
      reserve management, 735-737
      reserve requirements, 734-735, 740
   in securities portfolio, 745-746
Liquidity management. See also Asset/liability management
   performance analysis and, 211-212
Liquidity premium hypothesis, 598-600
Liquidity risk
   insurance companies, 746-747
   mutual funds, 747

Loan commitments, fee income from, 348
Loan participations and syndications, 856-857
Loan sales, by banks, 348-349
Loanable funds theory. See also Interest rates
   demand for loanable funds, 542-543
   inflation and, 549-551
   interest rate forecasting
      in general, 543, 555-556
      supply and demand changes, 544-545
   supply of loanable funds, 540-542
Loans. See also Credit process; International loans management; Lending; Mortgages; Securitization of loans
   agricultural, 847-848
   bank assets and, 179-180
      commercial, 179
      consumer, 179
      real estate, 179
   collateral for, 845
   commercial
      quoted base rates, 843-844
      sales of, 859
   commercial real estate, 847
   consumer, 848-851
   consumer/home mortgage, 825-826
   covenants for, 846
   credit card, 848-849
   discounted, 842-843
   establishing terms for, 839-840
      noninterest terms and conditions, 840-843
   home equity, 850-851
   installment, 849-850
   monitoring and reporting, 855-856
   monitoring and review, 854-855
   nonperforming, 855-856
   overnight, 785
   provision for loan losses, 185
   risk premiums on, 845
   rule of 78s, 850
   sample loan presentation, 837-838
   seasonal working capital, 846-847
   securitization of, 350-353
   small-business, 852-853
   term, 847
   trends in types of, 818
   workouts for, 856
Lockbox systems, 332
London International Financial Futures Exchange (LIFFE), 661
Long-term equity anticipation securities (LEAP), 706
Losses, capital cushions against, 288-289
LRA. See Lagged reserve accounting

Maastricht Accord, 107
McCarran-Ferguson Act, provisions, 43, 56, 374
McFadden-Pepper Act, provisions, 43, 46
MACRO system, 54
Managed futures, pension funds and, 477
Management. See also Asset/liability management; Mutual fund management; Risk management
   normative approach, 32

objectives
   customer needs, 34
   evidence from research, 34-35
   market for corporate control affecting, 35
   ownership structure affecting, 34
   regulations affecting, 35
   positive approach, 32-33
   stock ownership risk factors, 123-124
Management consulting, in general, 331-332
Manufacturers Hanover, merger with Chemical Bank, 31
Marché a Terme International de France (MATIF), 661
Margin requirements, for securities firms, 60
Market for corporate control, affecting management, 35
Market discipline, 808
Market risk. See also Risk management
   sensitivity to, 54
Market risk amendment (MRA), adoption, 343
Market-value accounting (MVA) practices, 119-120
MATIF. See March'82 a Terme International de France
MCCs. See Mutual capital certificates
Mergers, restructuring and, 30-31
Merrill Lynch, 514-515
Mezzanine lending, 853-854. See also Lending
Milken, Michael, 61, 84-85
MMDAs. See Money Market Deposit Accounts
Modified expectations theory, 601
Modigliani (M-Square) measure, 466
Mondex system, 21, 156
Monetary aggregates, 97
Monetary base, 98
Monetary policy. See also Federal Reserve System
   European coordination of, 107-108
   G-5 and G-7 agreements, 104-105
   international policy and, 104-105
Money. See also Cash
   confidence-sensitive, 790
   definitions, 97-99
   hot, 790
   options and, 701-702
Money market certificate (MMC), 63n
Money Market Deposit Accounts (MMDAs), 69, 180, 265
Money market mutual funds (MMMFs), 62
   described, 13
Money market securities. See also Securities
   annual yields, 560-564
Money multipliers, 98
Money supply
   Federal Reserve System and, 92, 97, 100
   loanable funds and, 541
Monitoring costs, intermediation and, 19
Montgomery Securities, merger with Nations Bank, 13-14
Moral hazard
   with deposit insurance, 121-123, 290
   in thrift crisis, 276
Morningstar ratings, mutual funds, 467-468

Mortgage financing, government-sponsored, 10-11
Mortgage-backed bonds, discussed, 791
Mortgage-backed securities. *See also* Securities
discussed, 756-758
Mortgages. *See also* Loans
adjustable-rate (ARMs), 69, 851
graduated payment (GPM), 852
growing equity (GEM), 852
packaged as securities, 4, 21
price-level adjusted (PLAM), 852
reverse annuity (RAM), 852
transferred with recourse, 197
MRA. *See* Market risk amendment
Mutual capital certificates (MCCs), features, 266
Mutual firms. *See also* Insurance companies
conversion
to "demutualize" insurers, 146-148
to thrifts, 145-146
distribution, 143
dividends and surplus firms, 364
holding companies
for mutual insurance companies, 148-149
for mutual thrifts, 149
mutual funds organizations, 149-152
origin and characteristics, 143-145
ownership and equity, 118
service corporations, 152
Mutual form of organization, among insurance companies, 34
Mutual fund management
bank mutual funds, profitability and performance, 339
in general, 441-442
overview, 443-444
role of banks in, 336-337
Mutual funds
assets and liabilities, 14
bank mutual funds, 335-337
larger bank competition, 337-338
regulatory concerns, 338-339
closed-end, 448
diversification and consolidation, 446-447
diversification provided by, 19
families, 451-453
investment in, 759-760
liquidity risk, 747
load funds, 453
low load, 453
money market mutual funds, 62
Morningstar ratings, 467-468
no load, 453
nonproprietary/proprietary, 134-135, 336
open-end, 448
organizations for, 149-152
ownership of affiliates, 444-446
ownership costs, 453-456
pension funds and, 468
performance and risk measurement, benchmarks, 459-464
private-label, 134-135
procedures of, 13
regulation, 457-459
risk-adjusted performance measures, 464-465

Rule 12b-1, 453
types of, 449-451
value at risk, 465-466
MVA. *See* Market-value accounting

NAIC. *See* National Association of Insurance Commissioners
NASD. *See* National Association of Securities Dealers
National Association of Insurance Commissioners (NAIC), 56
National Association of Securities Dealers (NASD), 60
National Banking Act (1864), 50
National banks. *See also* Commercial banks
regulation, 50
National Credit Union Act (1924), 46
National Credit Union Administration (NCUA), 51
operations, 249, 255
National Currency Act (1863), 48, 50, 131
National Currency and Banking Acts, 42
National Housing Act (1934), 46, 51, 81
National Securities Markets Improvements Act of 1996, 457
National treatment, in European Community, 107
National Westminster Bank, 2
Nations Bank
capital ratios, 298
merger with Bank of America, 5, 116, 260
merger with Montgomery Securities, 13-14
risk-based assets, 297-298
Tier 1/Tier 2 capital, 295
NationsBank v. Variable Annuity Life Ins. Co., 138
NationsBank v. Variable Annuity Life Insurance Company, 341
NCUA. *See* National Credit Union Administration
Negotiable order of withdrawal (NOW) accounts, 63, 180, 265
Net interest margin (NIM)
forecasting, 189-190
profitability and, 174, 184-187
spread and, 30
Net operating income. *See also* Income
calculating, 837
Net profit margin (NPM), 182
analysis, 203-205
trends, 190-191
Net Underwriting Margin (NUM), insurance companies, 366
Net worth, measurement, 118-120
Net worth certificates, 70
NIE. *See* Noninterest expenses
NIM. *See* Net interest margin
Noninterest expenses (NIE), banks, 187-188
Normative theory, for asset/liability management, 32
Norstar Bank of New York, 2
Not-for-profit organizations. *See also* Credit unions
operations, 152-153
ownership and equity, 118
Note issuance facilities, fee income from, 348

NOW. *See* Negotiable order of withdrawal accounts
NPM. *See* Net profit margin
NUM. *See* Net Underwriting Margin

OCC. *See* Office of the Comptroller of the Currency
OECD. *See* Organization for Economic Co-operation and Development
Off-balance-sheet items, 84
Office of the Comptroller of the Currency (OCC), 50
nationwide trust operations, 328-329
Part 5 rule, 137-138
trust risk management, 328-329
Office of Thrift Supervision (OTS)
data available from, 202n
establishment, 51, 252
MACRO system, 54
One savings and loan holding companies (OSLHCs), 71, 141-142, 250, 254
Open market operations, securities, 94
Options. *See also* Financial futures
defined, 700-701
call option, 701
premiums, 701
put option, 701
financial institutions and, 703-705
hedging compared to, 709-711
hedging with, 705-708
regulation, 705
values illustrated, 701-703
Orange County, 411, 477
Organization for Economic Cooperation and Development (OECD), 907
OSLHCs. *See* One savings and loan holding companies
OTS. *See* Office of Thrift Supervision
Ownership structure, affecting managerial objectives, 34

P/L companies. *See also* Insurance companies
asset management considerations, 386-387
performance evaluation
in general, 369-370
underwriting cycles, 372-373
response to Prop. 103, 375
social and economic factors affecting, 373-374
Part 5 rule, 137-138
Paul, David, Centrust Savings and, 33
Paul v. Virginia, 56n
Pawnshops, 22
Payments system, of Federal Reserve, 95-96
PBGC. *See* Pension Benefit Guaranty Corporation
PC banking, 21-22
Pension Benefit Guaranty Corporation (PBGC), 59, 469
Pension fund management. *See also* Mutual fund management
money managers evaluation, 478-479
role of institution affecting, 470-473
Pension funds
conversion to cash-balance plans, 482-483
derivatives and, 477-478

ERISA and, 468-473
  mutual funds and, 468
  operations, 12-13
  optimal allocation, 475-478
  ownership of surplus overfunds, 480-482
  regulation
    investment management, 58
    pension insurance, 58-59
  risk and management, 474
  stakeholders contract, 473-474
Pension smoothing activities, 479-480
  dedicated bond portfolios, 479-480
  guaranteed investment contracts, 479
  portfolio insurance, 480
Performance analysis objectives
  capital management, 215
  First National Bank of Maryland, 216-223
    performance comparison to peers, 218-220
  interest rate risk management, 214-215
  interpretation of numbers, 201-203
  liquidity management, 211-212
  loan management and credit risk, 212-214
  operating efficiency, 215-216
  overview, 203-205
  performance evaluation
    categories, 203
    common size statements analysis, 205-211
    in general, 205
  profitability, 200
  trend analysis, 201, 220
  volatility of earnings, 216
  Wells Fargo Bank, 205-216
PLL. See Provision for loan losses
Portfolio
  agency securities, 756-758
  banks, 753
  credit unions, 755-756
  liquidity in, 745-746
  mortgage-backed securities, 756-758
  mutual funds, 759-760
  thrifts, 754-755
Portfolio immunization
  costs, 648-650
  discussed, 639-642
  financial institutions and, 643
Portfolio management
  buffer portfolio, 750
  depository institutions, 748-750
Portfolio selection costs, intermediation and, 18-19
Positive approach, to asset/liability management, 32-33
Preferred habitat theory, 602-603
Premiums
  gross written, 358
  insurance companies, 359
  life insurance companies, 383-385
  on loans, 845
  options and, 701
Price changes, estimating, 634-635
Price risk, bonds, 625-627
Prime rate, commercial loans and, 843-844
Principal, defined, 32-33
Profit. See also Asset/liability management
  relation to performance, 200

Profitability
  bank mutual funds, 339
  depository institutions, 270-273
Program trading
  index arbitrage, 697-698
  1987 crash and, 699
Proposition 103, 57, 374
Provision for loan losses (PLL), 185
  ROA effect on, 187-189
Prudential Insurance Co., 515-518
Purchased funds, 211-212
Purchasing power parity theorem, 571-572

QTL. See Qualified thrift lender test
Qualified thrift lender test (QTL), 77, 81, 141, 253, 254
Quick and Reilly, 2

RAPs. See Regulatory accounting practices
RAROC. See Risk adjusted return on capital
RAVNA. See Risk-adjusted net value added
Real assets, compared to financial assets, 7
Real estate activities, savings institution participation in, 339
Real estate loans, risk in, 179-180
Real Estate Settlement Procedures Act (RESPA), 828
Receivables, finance companies, 496
Reciprocal compacts, interstate banking, 71
Reed, John, 40
Reg Z, 828
Regulation
  affecting management style, 35
  bank mutual funds, 338-339
  branch banking, 2
  depository institutions
    analysis, 54-55
    commercial banks, 50-51
    foreign banks, 80-81
    summary, 51-54
    examination process, 52-53, 80
    "systemic risk" exception, 80
    thrifts, 51, 71-72, 72-74
  deregulation and, 4
  finance companies, 501-502
    consumer protection legislation, 55-56
    licensing restrictions, 55
  in general, 41-42, 81-82
  historic, 3
  insurance companies
    asset structure, 58
    in general, 56-57
    licensing and solvency requirements, 57
    product regulation, 58
    rate regulation, 57
    solvency, 381
  interest rate swaps, 715
  international, 105-108
  international lending, 894-897
  investment companies
    federal securities laws, 59
    funds regulations, 59-60
  liquidity concerns, 733
  mutual funds, 457-459
  options, 705
  pace of, 2

pension funds
  investment management, 58
  pension insurance, 58-59
  preferences for capital, 291
  regulatory structure changes, 85
  risk measurement and, 83-84
  risk reduction and, 122
  securities firms, in general, 60-61
  "too big to fail (TBTF)" policy, 278
  tripwires, 53-54, 80
Regulation A, 744-745
Regulation D, 735-737
Regulation Q ceilings
  avoidance of, 48, 49
  disintermediation and, 62, 64, 66
Regulation Y, 132
Regulatory accounting practices (RAPs), provisions, 71, 267
Regulatory dialectic
  antithesis, 42, 47-49
  bank holding companies and, 124-131
  continuation, 70-71
  synthesis, 42, 49-50
  thesis, 42-47
Regulatory reform
  in general, 61
  problems requiring regulatory attention, 62-65
  safety and, 66
Regulatory taxes, 47
Repos. See Repurchase agreements
Repricing gap, 186, 214
Repurchase agreements, 790-791
Repurchase agreements (repos), 177, 181
Reserves. See also Financial assets
  calculating requirements for, 738-739
  clearing balances, 737
  contemporaneous reserve accounting (CRA), 736-737
  covering with liabilities, 784-786
  credit unions, 153
  insurance companies, 358
    asset valuation, 365
    dividend reserve, 364
    interest maintenance reserve, 365-366
  lagged reserve accounting, 736
  liquidity requirements and, 734-735, 740
  managing, 735-737
Residuals, 117
Resolution Trust Corporation (RTC), responsibilities, 76-77, 130
RESPA. See Real Estate Settlement Procedures Act
Restructuring, mergers and, 30-31
Retirement plans. See Pension funds
Return on assets (ROA), 185
  loan losses and, 187-189
  NIM forecasts and, 189-190
  performance analysis of, 203-205
  trends, 190-191
Return on equity (ROE), performance analysis of, 203-205
Revenues. See also Financial assets
  bank noninterest revenues, 325
  insurance companies, 359-360

Riegle-Neal Interstate Banking and Branching Efficiency Act (IBBEA)
   national bank model under, 128-130
   provisions, 41, 45, 50, 82, 116, 127
Risk. *See also* Country risk; Liability
   in bank insurance programs, 342-343
   basis risk, 670-672, 673
   capital allocation and, 304-305
   economic, 304-305
   financial futures and, basis risk, 670-672
   with loans, 179-180
   relaxed product restrictions and, 139-140
   stock ownership affecting, 123-124
Risk adjusted return on capital (RAROC),
   304-305, 344n, 860
Risk comparison, in performance analysis, 221
Risk management. *See also* Credit risk man-
      agement; Market risk
   comprehensive
      RiskMetrics model (J.P. Morgan), 344
      value at risk (VAR), 343-344
      VAR limitations, 344-345
   EVA, 345-346
   securities firms, 424-426
   trusts, 328-329
Risk management costs, intermediation and,
   19-20, 22
Risk measurement
   mutual funds, 459-464
   regulation and, 83-84
Risk-adjusted net value added (RAVNA), 474
RiskMetrics model (J.P. Morgan), 344
ROA. *See* Return on assets
"Rocket Scientists," 689-690
ROE. *See* Return on equity
RTC. *See* Resolution Trust Corporation
Rule 12b-1, 453

S&Ls. *See* Savings and loan associations
SAIF. *See* Savings Association Insurance
      Fund
Salomon Brothers, merger with Travelers
      Group, 13
Savings accounts
   negotiable order of withdrawal (NOW)
      accounts, 63, 180
   passbook, 181, 265
Savings Association Insurance Fund (SAIF)
   establishment, 51, 76
   operation, 252
Savings banks. *See also* Commercial banks
   compared to S&Ls, 252-253
   described, 11, 251
Savings institutions. *See also* Depository in-
      stitutions; Financial institutions;
      Thrifts
   contractual, 12
   deposit structure, 780-782
   disclosure requirements, 803-804
   history and regulatory changes
      in general, 251-252
      size and industry structure, 261-262
Savings and loan associations (S&Ls). *See
      also* Depository institutions; Savings
      banks; Thrifts
   assets, annual compound growth rates,
      269-270

   compared to savings banks, 252-253
   described, 11
   multiple-S&L holding companies
      (MSLHCs), 130
   one savings and loan holding companies
      (OSLHCs), 71, 141-142, 250, 254
   regulation affecting, 46
   relaxation of product restrictions, 254
   zombie S&Ls, 71
Savings and loan crisis, 6
   discussed, 274-277
SBA. *See* Small Business Administration
SCs. *See* Service corporations
Search costs, intermediation and, 18
Sears, financial services, 512-513
SEC. *See* Securities and Exchange Commis-
      sion
Securities. *See also* Money market securities;
      Mortgage-backed securities
   buying vs. selling, 743
   duration, 633
   federal securities laws, 59
   government, 760
      open market operations, 94
   held by depository institutions, 748-749
   held by insurance companies, 360-361
   investment securities of banks, 177
   primary, 16
   secondary, 16
   when-issued, 197
Securities Act (1933), 457
   provisions, 43, 46
Securities Acts Amendments (1975), 60
Securities Exchange Act, provisions, 43, 46
Securities and Exchange Commission (SEC),
   59
   Shelf Registration Rule (Rule 415), 407
Securities firms. *See also* Investment compa-
      nies
   described, 13-14
   financial statements, 412-413
      income statement, 416-420
   historic overview, 403-412
   investment bankers, 13
   overview of activities, 412-413
   regulation, in general, 60-61
   revenue sources, 413-420
   risk management, 424-426
Securities industry
   diversification trends, 422-423
   structure and cycles, types of firms, 398-
      401
Securities Investor Protection Act (1970), 60
Securities Investor Protection Corporation
      (SIPC), 60-61
Securities portfolio, managing, 611-612
Securitization, 180
Securitization of loans. *See also* Loans
   discussed, 350-353
   liquidity in, 746
Security agreement, loans, 845
Segmented markets theory, 601-602
Service corporations (SCs), 152
Shares, for credit unions, 153, 265
Sharpe ratio, calculating, 466
Shawmut National Corporation, 2
Shelf Registration Rule (Rule 415), 407

Short 3's Test, 457
SIPC. *See* Securities Investor Protection
      Corporation
Small Business Administration (SBA), 852-
      853
Small Business Job Protection Act (1996),
      145, 470
Smart cards, e-cash and, 155-156
Solvency, insurance companies, 57-58, 381
Solvency ratings, private insurer, 381
Source of strength doctrine, 139
South Korea, financial crisis, 6
Speculation, vs. hedging, 660
Spence Act (1959), 130
Spread, management of, 30
Stock. *See also* Brokers
   held by bank, 181-182
   insurance companies, 366
Stock index futures. *See also* Financial fu-
      tures
   financial institutions and, hedging, 695
   in general, 690
   history and characteristics, 691-694
   theoretical basis, 690-691
Stock market crash of 1987, 72-74, 96, 407-
      408
   program trading and, 699
Stock ownership, FI risk with, 123-124
Stockholders
   conflicts with debtholders, 121
   preferences for capital, 289-290
Strassel, Kimberly A., 155n
Subordinated notes and debentures, 181
Swaps. *See* Interest rate swaps
Swaptions, 717-718
SWS Associates, industry information re-
      ports, 201

Tax equivalent revenues, 182
Tax Reform Act (1984), 146
Taxes
   accounting practices for, 200
   conduit theory, 60
   on credit unions, 118n
   regulatory, 47
   for thrifts and credit unions, 253-254
Technology
   affecting insurer distribution systems, 377-
      378
   effect on financial institutions, 1-2, 6, 20-
      22
   financial innovation and, 48-49
   risks associated with, 22
Thailand, financial crisis, 6, 7
Theory and Practice of Insurance (Outre-
      ville), 358, 378
Third-party funds, 336
Thrift crisis. *See* Savings and loan crisis
Thrifts. *See also* Depository institutions; Sav-
      ings and loan associations
   assets, compared to banks and CUs, 263-
      265
   capital, 266-267
   capital requirements, 77, 276
   community banking and, 11
   conversion to banks, 253-254
   "credit crunch" in, 78

credit unions (CUs), 11-12
electronic, 154
federal, capital requirements, 299-300
insurance activities of, 342
investment portfolio, 754-755
liabilities, compared to banks and CUs, 265-266
market-to-book values trends, 267-268
mutual conversion to, 145-146
profitability, 270-273
regulation, 51, 251
thrift bailout legislation, 75-78
thrift crisis, 71-72, 72-74
savings banks, 11
savings and loan associations (S&Ls), 11
Time preference for consumption, 540
Tort law reform, 375
Transfer of funds, discussed, 16-18
Travelers Group
history, 115-116
merger with Citicorp, 5, 6, 40-41
merger with Salomon Brothers, 13
Trend analysis, 201
Tripwires, regulatory, 53-54, 80
Trust services, fee-based income and, 327-329
Truth in Lending, 828. *See also* Consumer Credit Protection Act

Unbanked, banking for, 22
Unbiased (pure) expectations theory
assumptions, 594-595
criticisms
in general, 597-598
liquidity premium hypothesis, 598-600
mathematics, 595-597
modifications, 597
Underwriting, risk and, 424-426
Underwriting cycles, P/L insurers, 372-373
Uniform Bank Performance Reports, 201
Uniform Residential Loan Application (FNMA), 828
Unit investment companies, 448-449
United States, assets of commercial banks, 9-10
U.S. economy, changes in during deregulation, 4
U.S. Social Security system, 12-13
Usury ceilings
federal preemption of, 67
finance companies, 56

Value at risk (VAR). *See also* Risk
mutual funds, 465-466
for risk management, 343-344, 835
limitations, 344-345
VAR. *See* Value at risk approach

Venture capital firms, public offerings and, 426-427
Vested benefits, pension funds, 58
Virtual financial institutions, discussed, 154-157

Washington Mutual, 262
Wells Fargo
branches, 205
performance analysis, 205-216
balance sheet (1997-98), 206-209
income statements, 208
profitability, 210
risk measures, 213
When-issued securities, 197
"Wild Card" certificates, 63n
Wright, Jim, 84-85

"Y2K" bug, 22
Yield curve. *See* Interest rate term structure

Zions Bancorporation, 40, 138